FIRST PoemS

ORCHARD BOOKS
96 Leonard Street
London EC2A 4RH
Orchard Books Australia
14 Mars Road, Lane Cove, NSW 2066
1 85213 411 9
First published in Great Britain in 1993
Selection © Julia Eccleshare 1993
Illustrations © Selina Young 1993
The right of Julia Eccleshare to be identified as author and of
Selina Young as illustrator of this work has been asserted by them
in accordance with the Copyright, Designs and Patents Act, 1988.
A CIP catalogue record for this book is available from
the British Library
Printed in Singapore

F I R S T
PoemS

Compiled by Julia Eccleshare
Illustrated by Selina Young

ORCHARD BOOKS

F

CONTENTS

THE FOUR FRIENDS

Ernest was an elephant, a great big fellow,
  Leonard was a lion with a six-foot tail,
George was a goat, and his beard was yellow,
  And James was a very small snail.

Leonard had a stall, and a great big strong one,
  Ernest had a manger, and its walls were thick,
George found a pen, but I think it was the wrong one,
  And James sat down on a brick.

Ernest started trumpeting, and cracked his manger,
  Leonard started roaring, and shivered his stall,
James gave the huffle of a snail in danger
  And nobody heard him at all.

Ernest started trumpeting and raised such a rumpus,
    Leonard started roaring and trying to kick,
James went a journey with the goat's new compass
    And he reached the end of his brick.

Ernest was an elephant and very well-intentioned,
    Leonard was a lion with a brave new tail,
George was a goat, as I think I have mentioned,
    But James was only a snail.

A. A. Milne

FANTASTIC FRIENDS

The Incredible Hulk came to tea.
Robin was with him too,
Batman stayed at home that night
Because his bat had flu.

Superman called to say hello
And Spiderman spun us a joke.
Dynamite Sue was supposed to come
But she went up in smoke.

The Invisible Man might have called,
But as I wasn't sure,
I left an empty chair and bun
Beside the kitchen door.

They signed my autograph book.
But I dropped it in the fire.
Now whenever I tell my friends
They say I'm a terrible liar.

But incredible people *do* call round
('Specially when I'm alone)
And if they don't, and I get bored,
I call them on the phone.

Brian Patten

ON SOME OTHER PLANET

On some other planet
near some other star,
there's a music-loving alien
who has a green estate car

On some other planet
on some far distant world,
there's a bright sunny garden
where a cat lies curled.

On some other planet
a trillion miles away,
there are parks and beaches
where young aliens play

On some other planet
in another time zone,
there are intelligent beings
who feel very much alone.

On some other planet
one that we can't see,
there must be one person
who's a duplicate of me.

John Rice

THE OWL AND THE PUSSY CAT

The Owl and the Pussy Cat went to sea
 In a beautiful pea-green boat,
They took some honey, and plenty of money,
 Wrapped up in a five-pound note.
The Owl looked up to the stars above,
 And sang to a small guitar,
"O lovely Pussy! O Pussy, my love,
 What a beautiful Pussy you are,
  You are,
  You are!
What a beautiful Pussy you are!"

Pussy said to the Owl, "You elegant fowl!
 How charmingly sweet you sing!
O let us be married! Too long we have tarried:
 But what shall we do for a ring?"
They sailed away, for a year and a day,
 To the land where the Bong-tree grows
And there in a wood, a Piggy-wig stood
 With a ring at the end of his nose,
  His nose,
  His nose,
With a ring at the end of his nose.

"Dear Pig, are you willing to sell for one shilling
 Your ring?" Said the Piggy, "I will."
So they took it away, and were married next day
 By the Turkey who lives on the hill.
They dined on mince,and slices of quince,
 Which they ate with a runcible spoon;
And hand in hand, on the edge of the sand,
 They danced by the light of the moon,
  The moon,
  The moon,
They danced by the light of the moon.

Edward Lear

I Love My Darling Tractor

I love my darling tractor
I love its merry din,
Its muscles made of iron and steel,
Its red and yellow skin.

I love to watch its wheels go round
However hard the day,
And from its bed inside the shed
It never thinks to stray.

It saves my arm, it saves my leg,
It saves my back from toil,
And it's merry as a skink
      when I give it a drink
Of water and diesel oil.

I love my darling tractor
As you can clearly see,
And so, the jolly farmer said,
Would you if you were me.

Charles Causley

On The Skateboard

Skimming
an asphalt sea
I swerve, I curve, I
sway; I speed to whirring
sound an inch above the
ground; I'm the sailor
and the sail, I'm the
driver and the wheel
I'm the one and only
single engine
human auto
mobile.

Lillian Morrison

THE SKATEBOARD

My Daddy has bought me a skateboard;
He tried it out first at the store.
And that is the reason why
Mommy says Daddy can't walk any more.

Willard Espy

MOTORWAY WITCH

Here comes the witch.
She's not on her broom
But riding a motor bike
Going ZOOM . . . ZOOM . . . !

She's wearing a helmet
Instead of a hat
And there on the pillion
Is sitting her cat.

Please, no overtaking
For I should explain
With her speed-crazy cat
She prefers the fast lane.

She banished her broom
For that was her wish.
It wouldn't . . . ZOOM . . . ZOOM . . .
But only swish . . . swish!

Max Fatchen

ABC OF NAMES

A is Ann, with milk from the cow.

B is Benjamin, making a row.

C is Charlotte, gathering flowers.

D is Dick, one of the mowers.

E is Eliza, feeding a hen.

F is Frank, mending his pen.

G is Georgiana, shooting an arrow.

H is Harry, wheeling a barrow.

I is Isabella, gathering fruit.

J is John, playing the flute.

K is Kate, nursing her dolly.

L is Lawrence, feeding poor Polly.

M is Maria, learning to draw.

ABC OF NAMES

N is Nicholas, with a jackdaw.

P is for Peter, wearing a coat.

R is Rachel, learning to dance.

T is Tommy, reading a book.

V is Victoria, reading she's seen.

X is Xerxes, a boy of great might.

Z is Zachariah, going to bed.

O is Octavus, riding a goat.

Q is for Quintus, armed with a lance.

S is Sarah, talking to Cook.

U is Urban, rolling the green.

W is Walter, flying a kite.

Y is Yvonne, a girl who's been fed.

Anon

15

MARY AND SARAH

Mary likes smooth things,
Things that glide:
Sleek skis swishing down a mountainside.

Sarah likes rough things,
Things that snatch:
Boats with barnacled bottoms, thatch.

Mary likes smooth things,
Things all mellow:
Milk, silk, runny honey, tunes on a cello.

Sarah likes rough things,
Things all troubly:
Crags, snags, bristles, thistles, fields left stubbly.

Mary says – polish,
Sarah says – rust,
Mary says – mayonnaise,
Sarah says – crust.

Sarah says – hedgehogs,
Mary says – seals,
Sarah says – sticklebacks,
Mary says – eels.

Give me, says Mary,
The slide of a stream,
The touch of a petal,
A bowl of ice-cream.

Give me, says Sarah,
The gales of a coast,
The husk of a chestnut,
A plate of burnt toast.

Mary and Sarah –
They'll never agree
Till peaches and coconuts
Grow on one tree.

Richard Edwards

THE KING'S BREAKFAST

The King asked
The Queen, and
The Queen asked
The Dairymaid:
"Could we have some butter for
The Royal slice of bread?"
The Queen asked
The Dairymaid,
The Dairymaid
Said, "Certainly,
I'll go and tell
The cow
Now
Before she goes to bed."

The Dairymaid
She curtsied,
And went and told
The Alderney:
"Don't forget the butter for
The Royal slice of bread."
The Alderney
Said sleepily:
"You'd better tell
His Majesty
That many people nowadays
Like marmalade
Instead."

The Dairymaid
Said, "Fancy!"
And went to
Her Majesty.
She curtsied to the Queen, and
She turned a little red:
"Excuse me,
Your Majesty,
For taking of
The liberty,
But marmalade is tasty, if
It's very
Thickly
Spread."

The Queen said,
"Oh !"
And went to
His Majesty:
"Talking of the butter for
The Royal slice of bread,
Many people
Think that
Marmalade
Is nicer.
Would you like to try a little
Marmalade
Instead?"

The King said,
"Bother !"
And then he said,
"Oh deary me!"
The King sobbed, "Oh, deary me!"
And went back to bed.
"Nobody,"
He whimpered,
"Could call me
A fussy man;
I *only* want
A little bit
Of butter for
My bread!"

The Queen said,
"There, there!"
And went to
The Dairymaid.
The Dairymaid
Said, "There, there!"
And went to the shed.
The cow said,
"There, there!
I didn't really
Mean it;
Here's milk for his porringer
And butter for his bread."

The Queen took
The butter
And brought it to
His Majesty;
The King said,
"Butter, eh?"
And bounced out of bed.
"Nobody," he said,
As he kissed her
Tenderly,
"Nobody," he said,
As he slid down
The banisters,
"Nobody,
My darling,
Could call me
A fussy man –
BUT
I do like a little bit of butter to my bread!"

A. A. Milne

FAIRY STORY

I went into the wood one day
And there I walked and lost my way

When it was so dark I could not see
A little creature came to me

He said if I would sing a song
The time would not be very long

But first I must let him hold my hand tight.
Or else the wood would give me a fright

I sang a song, he let me go
But now I am home again there is nobody I know.

Stevie Smith

LITTLE GIRL

(from an Arabian nursery rhyme)

I will build you a house
If you do not cry
A house, little girl,
As tall as the sky.

I will build you a house
Of golden dates,
The freshest of all
For the steps and gates.

I will furnish the house,
For you and for me
With walnuts and hazels
Fresh from the tree.

I will build you a house
And when it is done
I will roof it with grapes
To keep out the sun.

Rose Fyleman

SOME THINGS DON'T
MAKE ANY SENSE AT ALL

My mom says I'm her sugarplum.
My mom says I'm her lamb.
My mom says I'm completely perfect
Just the way I am.
My mom says I'm a super-special wonderful terrific little guy.
My mom just had another baby.
Why?

Judith Viorst

24

THE BABY OF THE FAMILY

Up on Daddy's shoulders
He is riding high –
The baby of the family,
A pleased, pork pie.
I'm tired and my feet are sore –
It seems all wrong.
He's lucky to be little
But it won't last long.

The baby of the family,
He grabs my toys
And when I grab them back he makes
A big, loud noise.
I mustn't hit him, so I chant
This short, sweet song:
"You're lucky to be little
But it won't last long."

Everybody looks at him
And thinks he's sweet,
Even when he bellows "No!"
And stamps his feet.
He won't be so amusing
When he's tall and strong.
It's lovely being little
But it won't last long.

Wendy Cope

WHEN I WAS THREE

When I was three I had a friend
Who asked me why bananas bend,
I told him why, but now I'm four,
I'm not so sure . . .

Richard Edwards

MY SISTER LAURA

My sister Laura's bigger than me
And lifts me up quite easily.
I can't lift her, I've tried and tried;
She must have something heavy inside.

Spike Milligan

BETTY AT THE PARTY

"When I was at the party,"
  Said Betty, aged just four,
"A little girl fell off her chair
  Right down upon the floor;
And all the other little girls
  Began to laugh, but me –
I didn't laugh a single bit,"
  Said Betty seriously.

"Why not?" her mother asked her,
  Full of delight to find
That Betty – bless her little heart! –
  Had been so sweetly kind.
"Why didn't you laugh, my darling?
  Or don't you like to tell?"
"I didn't laugh," said Betty,
  "'Cause it was me that fell."

Anon

LAUGHING TIME

It was laughing time, and the tall Giraffe
Lifted his head, and began to laugh:

Ha! Ha! Ha! Ha!

And the Chimpanzee on the ginkgo tree
Swung merrily down with a Tee Hee Hee:

Hee! Hee! Hee! Hee!

"It's certainly not against the law!"
Croaked Justice Crow with a loud guffaw:

Haw! Haw! Haw! Haw!

The dancing Bear who could never say "No"
Waltzed up and down on the tip of his toe:

Ho! Ho! Ho! Ho!

The Donkey daintily took his paw,
And around they went: Hee-Haw! Hee-Haw!

Hee-Haw! Hee-Haw!

The Moon had to smile as it started to climb;
All over the world it was laughing time!

Ho! Ho! Ho! Ho! Hee-Haw! Hee-Haw!

Hee! Hee! Hee! Hee! Ha! Ha! Ha! Ha!

William Jay Smith

Five Little Owls

Five little owls in an old elm tree,
Fluffy and puffy as owls could be,
Blinking and winking with big round eyes
At the big round moon that hung in the skies:
As I passed beneath I could hear one say,
"There'll be mouse for supper, there will, today!"
Then all of them hooted, "Tu-whit, tu-whoo
Yes, mouse for supper, hoo hoo, hoo hoo!"

Anon

Ten Little Mice

Ten little mice sat in a barn to spin,
Pussy came by, and popped her head in:
"What are you at, my jolly ten?"
"We're making coats for gentlemen."
"Shall I come in and cut your threads?"
"No, Miss Puss, you'd bite off our heads."

Anon

JIM, WHO RAN AWAY FROM HIS NURSE, AND WAS EATEN BY A LION

There was a boy whose name was Jim;
His friends were very good to him.
They gave him tea, and cakes, and jam,
And slices of delicious ham,
And chocolate with pink inside,
And little tricycles to ride,
And read him stories through and through,
And even took him to the Zoo
But there it was a dreadful fate
Befell him, which I now relate.

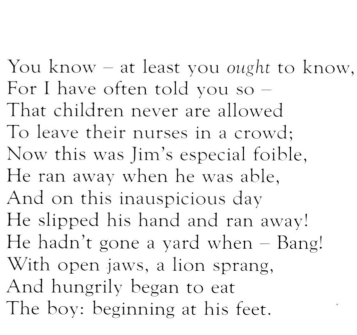

You know – at least you *ought* to know,
For I have often told you so –
That children never are allowed
To leave their nurses in a crowd;
Now this was Jim's especial foible,
He ran away when he was able,
And on this inauspicious day
He slipped his hand and ran away!
He hadn't gone a yard when – Bang!
With open jaws, a lion sprang,
And hungrily began to eat
The boy: beginning at his feet.

Now just imagine how it feels
When first your toes and then your heels,
And then by gradual degrees,
Your shins and ankles, calves and knees,
Are slowly eaten, bit by bit.
No wonder Jim detested it!
No wonder that he shouted "Hi!"
The honest keeper heard his cry,
Though very fat he almost ran
To help the little gentleman.
"Ponto!" he ordered as he came
(For Ponto was the lion's name),
"Ponto!" he cried, with angry frown.
"Let go, Sir! Down, Sir! Put it down!"

The lion made a sudden stop,
He let the dainty morsel drop,
And slunk reluctant to his cage,
Snarling with disappointed rage.
But when he bent him over Jim,
The honest keeper's eyes were dim.
The lion having reached his head,
The miserable boy was dead!

When Nurse informed his parents, they
Were more concerned than I can say:
His mother, as she dried her eyes,
Said, "Well – it gives me no surprise,
He would not do as he was told!"
His Father, who was self-controlled,
Bade all the children round attend
To James's miserable end,
And always keep a-hold of Nurse
For fear of finding something worse.

Hilaire Belloc

THE GREEDY ALLIGATOR

I have a rather greedy pet,
A little alligator;
When he my younger sister met,
He opened wide and ate her.

But soon he learned that he was wrong
To eat the child in question
For he felt bad before too long,
And suffered indigestion.

This story seems to prove to me
That he who rudely gobbles
Will soon regret his gluttony
And get the collywobbles.

Colin West

THE TIGER

A tiger going for a stroll
Met an old man and ate him whole.

The old man shouted, and he thumped.
The tiger's stomach churned and bumped.

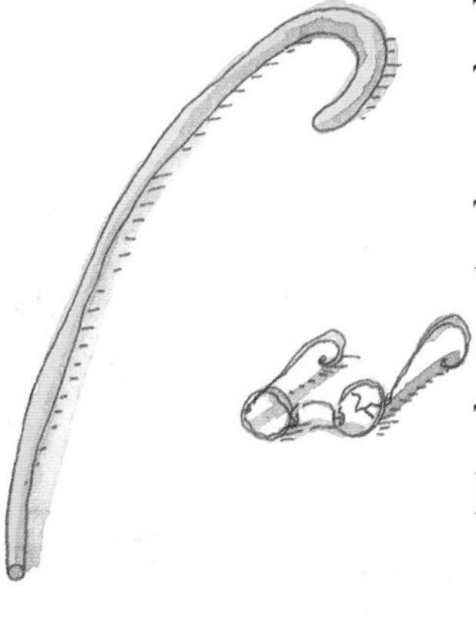

The other tigers said: "Now really
We hear your breakfast much too clearly."

The moral is, he should have chewed.
It does no good to bolt one's food.

Edward Lucie-Smith

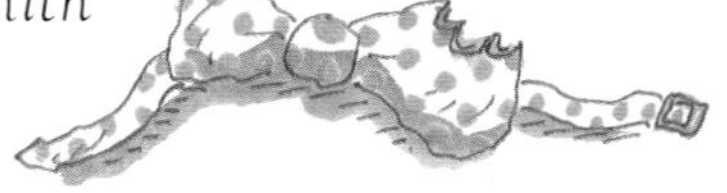

CALL ALLIGATOR LONG-MOUTH

Call alligator long-mouth
call alligator saw-mouth
call alligator pushy-mouth
call alligator scissors-mouth
call alligator raggedy-mouth
call alligator bumpy-bum
call alligator all dem rude word
but better wait

till you cross river.

John Agard

THE PLAINT OF THE CAMEL

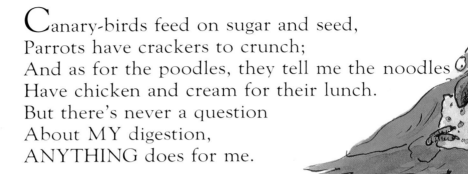

Canary-birds feed on sugar and seed,
Parrots have crackers to crunch;
And as for the poodles, they tell me the noodles
Have chicken and cream for their lunch.
But there's never a question
About MY digestion,
ANYTHING does for me.

Cats, you're aware, can repose in a chair,
Chickens can roost upon rails;
Puppies are able to sleep in a stable,
And oysters can slumber in pails.
But no one supposes
A poor Camel dozes.
ANY PLACE does for me.

Lambs are enclosed where it's never exposed,
Coops are constructed for hens;
Kittens are treated to houses well heated,
And pigs are protected by pens.
But a Camel comes handy
Wherever it's sandy,
ANYWHERE does for me.

People would laugh if you rode a giraffe,
Or mounted the back of an ox;
It's nobody's habit to ride on a rabbit,
Or try to bestraddle a fox.
But as for a Camel, he's
Ridden by families –
ANY LOAD does for me.

A snake is as round as a hole in the ground;
Weasels are wavy and sleek;
And no alligator could ever be straighter
Than lizards that live in a creek.
But a Camel's all lumpy,
And bumpy, and humpy,
ANY SHAPE does for me.

Charles Edward Carryl

THE GUPPY

Whales have calves,
Cats have kittens,
Bears have cubs,
Bats have bittens.
Swans have cygnets,
Seals have puppies,
But guppies just have little guppies.

Ogden Nash

SNAIL

Snail upon the wall,
Have you got at all
Anything to tell
About your shell?

Only this, my child –
When the wind is wild,
Or when the sun is hot,
It's all I've got.

John Drinkwater

M was once a little mouse.
Mousey,
Bousy,
Sousy,
Mousy.
In the housy,
Little mouse!

Edward Lear

A BABY SARDINE

A baby sardine
Saw her first submarine:
She was scared and watched through a peephole.

"Oh come, come, come,"
Said the sardine's mum.
"It's only a tin full of people."

Spike Milligan

YAK

The long-haired Yak has long black hair,
He lets it grow – he doesn't care.
He lets it grow and grow and grow,
He lets it trail along the stair
Does he ever go to the barbershop? NO!
How wild and woolly and devil-may-care
A long-haired Yak with long black hair
Would look when perched in a barber chair!

William Jay Smith

FROG

A frog once went out walking,
In the pleasant summer air,
He happened into a barber's shop
And skipped into the chair.
The barber said in disbelief;
"Your brains are surely bare.
How can you have a haircut
When you haven't any hair?"

Anon

A Frog he Would A-Wooing Go

A frog he would a-wooing go,
 Heigh ho! says Rowley,
A frog he would a-wooing go,
Whether his mother would let him or no.
 With a rowley, powley, gammon and spinach,
 Heigh ho! says Anthony Rowley.

So off he set with his opera hat,
 Heigh ho! says Rowley,
So off he set with his opera hat,
And on the road he met with a rat,
 With a rowley, powley, gammon and spinach,
 Heigh ho! says Anthony Rowley

Pray, Mr Rat, will you go with me?
 Heigh ho! says Rowley,
Pray, Mr Rat, will you go with me,
Kind Mrs Mousey for to see?
 With a rowley, powley, gammon and spinach,
 Heigh ho! says Anthony Rowley.

They came to the door of Mousey's hall,
 Heigh ho! says Rowley,
They gave a loud knock, and they gave a loud call.
 With a rowley, powley, gammon and spinach,
 Heigh ho! says Anthony Rowley.

Pray, Mrs Mouse, are you within?
 Heigh ho! says Rowley,
Oh yes, kind sirs, I'm sitting to spin.
 With a rowley, powley, gammon and spinach,
 Heigh ho! says Anthony Rowley.

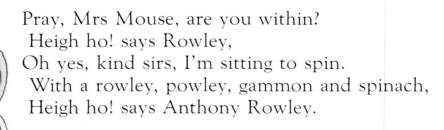

Pray, Mrs Mouse, will you give us some beer?
 Heigh ho! says Rowley,
For Froggy and I are fond of good cheer.
  With a rowley, powley, gammon and spinach,
  Heigh ho! says Anthony Rowley.

Pray, Mr Frog, will you give us a song?
 Heigh ho! says Rowley,
Let it be something that's not very long.
  With a rowley, powley, gammon and spinach,
  Heigh ho! says Anthony Rowley.

Indeed, Mrs Mouse, replied Mr Frog,
 Heigh ho! says Rowley,
A cold has made me as hoarse as a dog.
  With a rowley, powley, gammon and spinach,
  Heigh ho! says Anthony Rowley.

Since you have a cold, Mr Frog, Mousey said,
 Heigh ho! says Rowley,
I'll sing you a song that I have just made.
  With a rowley, powley, gammon and spinach,
  Heigh ho! says Anthony Rowley.

But while they were all a-merry-making,
 Heigh ho! says Rowley,
A cat and her kittens came tumbling in.
  With a rowley, powley, gammon and spinach,
  Heigh ho! says Anthony Rowley.

The cat she seized the rat by the crown,
 Heigh ho! says Rowley,
The kittens they pulled the little mouse down.
 With a rowley, powley, gammon and spinach,
 Heigh ho! says Anthony Rowley.

This put Mr Frog in a terrible fright,
 Heigh ho! says Rowley,
He took up his hat and he wished them good-night.
 With a rowley, powley, gammon and spinach,
 Heigh ho! says Anthony Rowley.

But as Froggy was crossing over a brook,
 Heigh ho! says Rowley,
A lily-white duck came and gobbled him up.
 With a rowley, powley, gammon and spinach,
 Heigh ho! says Anthony Rowley.

So there was an end of one, two, three,
 Heigh ho! says Rowley,
The rat, the mouse, and the little frog-ee.
 With a rowley, powley, gammon and spinach,
 Heigh ho! says Anthony Rowley.

Anon

40

BEAUTIFUL SOUP

Beautiful Soup, so rich and green,
  Waiting in a hot tureen!
Who for such dainties would not stoop?
Soup of the evening, beautiful Soup!
Soup of the evening, beautiful Soup!
 Beau – ootiful Soo – oop!
 Beau – ootiful Soo – oop!
Soo – oop of the e – e – evening,
 Beautiful, beautiful Soup!

Beautiful Soup! Who cares for fish,
  Game, or any other dish?
Who would not give all else for two p
ennyworth only of beautiful Soup?
Pennyworth only of beautiful Soup?
 Beau – ootiful Soo – oop!
 Beau – ootiful Soo – oop!
Soo – op of the e – e – evening,
Beautiful, beauti-FUL SOUP!

Lewis Carroll

PEAS

I always eat peas with honey,
I've done it all my life,
They do taste kind of funny
But it keeps them on the knife.

Anon

IF ALL THE WORLD WERE PAPER

If all the world were paper,
    And all the sea were ink,
And all the trees were bread and cheese,
    What should we do for drink?

Anon

THE FOLK WHO LIVE IN BACKWARD TOWN

The folk who live in Backward Town
Are inside out and upside down.
They wear their hats inside their heads
And go to sleep beneath their beds.
They only eat the apple peeling
And take their walks across the ceiling.

Mary Ann Hoberman

As Wet as a Fish

As wet as a fish – as dry as a bone;
As live as a bird – as dead as a stone;
As plump as a partridge – as poor as a rat;
As strong as a horse – as weak as a cat;
As hard as a flint – as soft as a mole;
As white as a lily – as black as a coal;
As plain as a pike-staff – as rough as a bear;
As tight as a drum – as free as the air;
As heavy as lead – as light as a feather;
As steady as time – uncertain as weather;
As hot as a furnace – as cold as a frog;
As gay as a lark – as sick as a dog;
As slow as a tortoise – as swift as the wind;
As true as the gospel – as false as mankind;
As thin as a herring – as fat as a pig;
As proud as a peacock – as blithe as a grig;
As fierce as a tiger – as mild as a dove;
As stiff as a poker – as limp as a glove;
As blind as a bat – as deaf as a post;
As cool as a cucumber – as warm as a toast;
As flat as a flounder – as round as a ball;
As blunt as a hammer – as sharp as an awl;
As red as a ferret – as safe as the stocks;
As bold as a thief – as sly as a fox;
As straight as an arrow – as bent as a bow;
As yellow as saffron – as black as a sloe;
As brittle as glass – as tough as gristle;
As neat as my nail – as clean as a whistle;
As good as a feast – as bad as a witch;
As light as is day – as dark as is pitch;
As brisk as a bee – as dull as an ass;
As full as a tick – as solid as brass.

Anon

ME AND THE EARTHWORM

Me: Where are you going, Earthworm?
Earthworm: Around the world.

Me: How long will it take?
Earthworm: A long stretch.

Zaro Weil

SQUEEZES

We love to squeeze bananas,
We love to squeeze ripe plums.
And when they are feeling sad
We love to squeeze our mums.

Brian Patten

I'D LIKE TO SQUEEZE

I'd like to squeeze this round world
into a new shape

I'd like to squeeze this round world
like a tube of toothpaste

I'd like to squeeze this round world
fair and square

I'd like to squeeze it and squeeze it
till everybody had an equal share

John Agard

MY SHADOW

I have a little shadow that goes in and out with me,
And what can be the use of him is more than I can see.
He is very, very like me from the heels up to the head;
And I see him jump before me, when I jump into my bed.

The funniest thing about him is the way he likes to grow –
Not at all like proper children, which is always very slow;
For he sometimes shoots up taller like an india-rubber ball,
And he sometimes gets so little that there's none of him at all.

He hasn't got a notion of how children ought to play,
And can only make a fool of me in every sort of way.
He stays so close beside me, he's a coward you can see;
I'd think shame to stick to nursie as that shadow sticks to me!

One morning, very early, before the sun was up,
I rose and found the shining dew on every buttercup;
But my lazy little shadow, like an arrant sleepy-head,
Had stayed at home behind me and was fast asleep in bed.

Robert Louis Stevenson

EVERY TIME I CLIMB A TREE

Every time I climb a tree
Every time I climb a tree
Every time I climb a tree
I scrape a leg
Or skin a knee
And every time I climb a tree
I find some ants
Or dodge a bee
And get the ants
All over me.

And every time I climb a tree
Where have you been?
They say to me
But don't they know that I am free
Every time I climb a tree?
I like it best
To spot a nest
That has an egg
Or maybe three.

And then I skin
The other leg
But every time I climb a tree
I see a lot of things to see
Swallows rooftops and TV
And all the fields and farms there be
Every time I climb a tree.
Though climbing may be good for ants
It isn't awfully good for pants
But still it's pretty good for me
Every time I climb a tree.

David McCord

THE UPS AND DOWNS OF THE ELEVATOR CAR

The elevator car in the elevator shaft,
Complained of the buzzer, complained of the draught.
It said it felt carsick as it rose and fell,
It said it had a headache from the ringing of the bell.

"There is spring in the air," sighed the elevator car.
Said the elevator man, "You are well off where you are."
The car paid no attention but it frowned an ugly frown
when
up   it
going   should
started   be
it   going
And   down.

Down flashed the signal, but *up* went the car.
The elevator man cried, "You are going much too far!"
Said the elevator car, "I'm doing no such thing.
I'm through with buzzers buzzing. I'm looking for the spring !"

Then the elevator man began to shout and call
And all the people came running through the hall.
The elevator man began to call and shout.
"The car won't stop! Let me out! Let me out!"

On went the car past the penthouse door.
On went the car up one flight more.
On went the elevator till it came to the top.
On went the elevator, and it would not stop!

Right through the roof went the man and the car.
And nobody knows where the two of them are!
(Nobody knows but everyone cares,
Wearily, drearily climbing the stairs!)

Now on a summer evening when you see a shooting star
Fly through the air, perhaps it is – that elevator car!

Caroline D. Emerson

49

THE JUMBLIES

They went to sea in a Sieve, they did,
 In a Sieve they went to sea:
In spite of all their friends could say,
On a winter's morn, on a stormy day,
 In a Sieve they went to sea!
And when the Sieve turned round and round,
And every one cried, "You'll all be drowned!"
They called aloud, "Our Sieve ain't big,
But we don't care a button! we don't care a fig!
 In a Sieve we'll go to sea!"
 Far and few, far and few,
  Are the lands where the Jumblies live;
  Their heads are green, and their hands are blue
  And they went to sea in a Sieve.

They sailed away in a Sieve, they did,
 In a Sieve they sailed so fast,
With only a beautiful pea-green veil
Tied with a riband by way of a sail,
 To a small tobacco-pipe mast;
And every one said, who saw them go,
"Oh won't they be soon upset, you know!
For the sky is dark, and the voyage is long,
And happen what may, it's extremely wrong
 In a Sieve to sail so fast!"
 Far and few, far and few,
  Are the lands where the Jumblies live;
 Their heads are green, and their hands are blue,
  And they went to sea in a Sieve.

The water it soon came in, it did,
 The water it soon came in;
So to keep them dry, they wrapped their feet
In a pinky paper all folded neat,
 And they fastened it down with a pin
And they passed the night in a crockery-jar,
And each of them said, "How wise we are!
Though the sky be dark, and the voyage be long,
Yet we never can think we were rash or wrong,
 While round in our Sieve we spin!"
 Far and few, far and few,
  Are the lands where the Jumblies live;
 Their heads are green, and their hands are blue,
  And they went to sea in a Sieve.

And all night long they sailed away;
 And when the sun went down,
They whistled and warbled a moony song
To the echoing sound of a coppery gong,
 In the shade of the mountains brown.
"O Timballo! How happy we are,
When we live in a sieve and a crockery-jar,
And all night long in the moonlight pale,
We sail away with a pea-green sail,
 In the shade of the mountains brown!"
 Far and few, far and few,
 Are the lands where the Jumblies live;
 Their heads are green, and their hands are blue,
 And they went to sea in a Sieve.

waterproof pinky pins
paper

Crockery Jar.

↖ Sieve

They sailed to the Western Sea, they did,
 To a land all covered with trees,
And they bought an Owl, and a useful Cart,
And a pound of Rice, and a Cranberry Tart,
 And a hive of silvery Bees.
And they bought a Pig, and some green Jack-daws
And a lovely Monkey with lollipop paws,
And forty bottles of Ring-Bo-Ree,
 And no end of Stilton Cheese.
 Far and few, far and few,
 Are the lands where the Jumblies live;
 Their heads are green, and their hands are blue,
 And they went to sea in a Sieve.

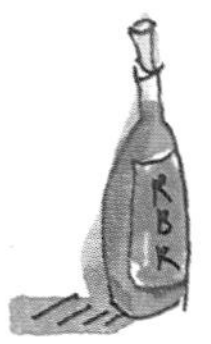

And in twenty years they all came back;
 In twenty years or more,
And every one said, "How tall they've grown!
For they've been to the Lakes, and the Torrible Zone,
 And the hills of the Chankly Bore";
And they drank their health, and gave them a feast
Of dumplings made of beautiful yeast;
And every one said, "If we only live,
We too will go to sea in a Sieve, –
 To the hills of the Chankly Bore!"
 Far and few, far and few,
  Are the lands where the Jumblies live;
  Their heads are green, and their hands are blue,
   And they went to sea in a Sieve.

Edward Lear

Until I Saw the Sea

Until I saw the sea
I did not know
that wind
could wrinkle water so.

I never knew
that sun
could splinter a whole sea of blue.

Nor
did I know before,
a sea breathes in and out
upon a shore.

Lilian Moore

Listen

Shhhhhhhhhhhhhhhhhhhhhhhhhhhh!
Sit still, very still
And listen.
Listen to wings
Lighter than eyelashes
Stroking the air.
Know what the thin breeze
Whispers on high
To the coconut trees.
Listen and hear.

Telcine Turner

BALLOON

```
       a s
     big as
   ball as round
  as sun . . . I tug
 and pull you when
 you run and when
   wind blows I
    say polite
        ly
        H
        O
        L
        D
        M
        E
        T
         I
         G
         H
          T
          L
          Y.
```

Colleen Thibaudeau

SUMMER

When it's hot
I take my shoes off,
I take my shirt off,
I take my pants off,
I take my underwear off,
I take my whole body off,
and throw it
in the river.

Frank Asch

MUD

I like mud.
  I like it on my clothes.
I like it on my fingers.
  I like it in my toes.

Dirt's pretty ordinary
  And dust's a dud.
For a really good mess-up
  I like mud.

John Smith

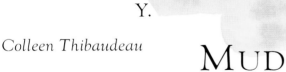

BUSY DAY

Pop in
pop out
pop over the road
pop out for a walk
pop in for a talk
pop down to the shop
can't stop
got to pop

got to pop ?

pop where?
pop what?

well
I've got to
pop round
pop up
pop in to town
pop out and see
pop in for tea
pop down to the shop
can't stop
got to pop

got to pop?

pop where?
pop what?

well
I've got to
pop in
pop out
pop over the road
pop out for a walk
pop in for a talk . . .

Michael Rosen

THE SNOWMAN

Mother, while you were at the shops
and I was snoozing in my chair
I heard a tap at the window
saw a snowman standing there

He looked so cold and miserable
I almost could have cried
so I put the kettle on
and invited him inside

I made him a cup of cocoa
to warm the cockles of his nose
then he snuggled in front of the fire
for a cosy little doze

He lay there warm and smiling
softly counting sheep
I eavesdropped for a little while
then I too fell asleep

Seems he awoke and tiptoed out
exactly when I'm not too sure
it's a wonder you didn't see him
as you came in through the door

(Oh, and by the way,
the kitten's made a puddle on the floor)

Roger McGough

SOMEONE

Someone came knocking
At my wee, small door;
Someone came knocking,
I'm sure – sure – sure;
I listened, I opened,
I looked to left and right,
But nought there was a-stirring
In the still dark night;
Only the busy beetle
Tap-tapping in the wall,
Only from the forest
The screech-owl's call,
Only the cricket whistling
While the dewdrops fall,
So I know not who came knocking,
At all, at all, at all.

Walter de la Mare

WHO'S IN ?

"The door is shut fast
   And everybody's out.
But people don't know
   What they're talking about!
Say the fly on the wall,
And the flame on the coals,
And the dog on his rug.
And the mice in their holes,
And the kitten curled up,
And the spiders that spin –
"What, everyone out?
Why, everyone's in!"

Elizabeth Fleming

THE LAND OF NOD

From breakfast on through all the day
At home among my friends I stay;
But every night I go abroad
Afar into the Land of Nod.

All by myself I have to go,
With none to tell me what to do –
All alone beside the streams
And up the mountain-sides of dreams.

The strangest things are there for me,
Both things to eat and things to see,
And many frightening sights abroad
Till morning in the Land of Nod.

Try as I like to find the way,
I never can get back by day,
Nor can remember plain and clear
The curious music that I hear.

Robert Louis Stevenson

NIGHT COMES

Night comes
leaking
out of the sky.

Stars come
peeking.

Moon comes
sneaking
silvery-sly.

Who is
shaking,
shivery,
quaking?

Who is afraid
of the night?

Not I.

Beatrice Schenk de Regniers

SWEET DREAMS

I wonder as into bed I creep
What it feels like to fall asleep.
I've told myself stories, I've counted sheep
But I'm always asleep when I fall asleep.
Tonight my eyes I will open keep,
And I'll stay awake till I fall asleep,
Then I'll know what it feels like to fall asleep,
Asleep,
Asleeep,
Asleeeep . . .

Ogden Nash

MOONING

What shall we do? O what can we do?
The Man in the Moon has lost his shoe –

We'll search all night on the rubbish-dump
For a star-spangled sneaker or a moon-bright pump.

What shall we do? O what can we do?
Now he's gone and lost his trousers too.

We'll search all night and hope to find
Something that will warm his bare behind.

It's a bit strange and it's a bit sad
But the Man in the Moon has gone quite mad.

He is flinging away all his clothes
And where they'll end up nobody knows.

So don't look at the sky. don't look, it's rude –
The Man in the Moon is completely nude!

Brian Patten

MRS MOON

Mrs Moon
sitting up in the sky
Little Old Lady
rock-a-bye
with a ball of fading light
and silvery needles
knitting the night.

Roger McGough

THE HORSEMAN

I heard a horseman
Ride over the hill;
The moon shone clear,
The night was still;
His helm was silver,
And pale was he,
And the horse he rode
Was of ivory.

Walter de la Mare

Index of Authors and Titles

ACKNOWLEDGEMENTS

The compiler and publishers wish to thank all the poets, agents, publishers and other copyright holders who kindly granted us permission to use the poems in this anthology.

"The Four Friends" and "The King's Breakfast" by A.A. Milne from *When We Were Very Young* published by Methuen Children's Books, reprinted by permission of Reed International Books. "Billy Dreamer's Fantastic Friends" © Brian Patten, reprinted by permission of the author. "On Some Other Planet" © John Rice, reprinted by permission of the author. "I Love my Darling Tractor" from *Early In The Morning* by Charles Causley, reprinted by permission of David Higham Associates. "On the Skateboard" from *The Sidewalk Racer And Other Poems Of Sports And Motion* by Lillian Morrison, © 1965, 1967, 1968, 1977 Lillian Morrison, reprinted by permission of Marian Reiner for the author. "Motorway Witch" by Max Fatchen, reprinted by permission of John Johnson Ltd. "Mary and Sarah" from *A Mouse In My Roof* by Richard Edwards, published by Orchard Books, reprinted by permission of the author. "Fairy Story" from *The Collected Poems Of Stevie Smith* published by Penguin Books, reprinted by permission of James MacGibbon, Executor of the Estate of Stevie Smith. "Little Girl" by Rose Fyleman, reprinted by permission of The Society of Authors as the literary representative of the Estate of Rose Fyleman. "Some Things Don't Make any Sense at All" from *If I Were In Charge Of The World And Other Worries* published by Atheneum, an imprint of the Macmillan Publishing company, © 1981 Judith Viorst, reprinted by permission of Lescher and Lescher and Ashton Scholastic. "The Baby of the Family" by Wendy Cope from *Casting A Spell* published by Orchard Books, reprinted by permission of the author. "Laughing Time" and "Yak" from *Laughing Time: Collected Nonsense* by William Jay Smith, © 1990 William Jay Smith, reprinted by permission of Farrar, Straus and Giroux, Inc. "Jim Who Ran Away From his Nurse and Was Eaten by a Lion" by Hilaire Belloc, reprinted by permission of Peters Fraser and Dunlop Group Ltd. "The Greedy Alligator" by Colin West, reprinted by permission of the author. "The Tiger" by Edward Lucie-Smith from *Beasts With Bad Manners*, reprinted by permission of Rogers, Coleridge and White Ltd. "Don't Call Alligator Long Mouth till you Cross the River" from *Say It Again Granny* published by The Bodley Head, © 1986 John Agard, printed by permission of John Agard c/o Caroline Sheldon Literary Agency. "The Guppy" from *I Wouldn't Have Missed It* by Ogden Nash, reprinted by permission of André Deutsch Ltd. "Snail" by John Drinkwater, reprinted by permission of Samuel French Ltd on behalf of the Estate of the late John Drinkwater. "The Baby Sardine" by Spike Milligan, reprinted by permission of the author and Norma Farnes. "The Folk Who Live in Backward Town" by Mary Ann Hoberman from *Hello And Good-bye* published by Little Brown and Company, reprinted by permission of Gina Maccoby Literary Agency, copyright © 1959, copyright renewed 1987 by Mary Ann Hoberman. "Me and the Earthworm" from *Mud Moon And Me* published by Orchard Books, © 1989 Zaro Weil, reprinted by permission of the author. "Squeezes" from *Gargling With Jelly* published by Viking Kestrel, © 1985 Brian Patten, reprinted by permission of Penguin Books. "I'd Like to Squeeze" from *You'll Love This Stuff* published by Cambridge University Press 1986, reprinted by permission of John Agard c/o Caroline Sheldon Literary Agency. "Every Time I Climb a Tree" from *My Bidery's Spidery Garden* by David McCord, reprinted by permission of Harrap Publishing Group Ltd. "Until I Saw the Sea" from *I Feel The Same Way* by Lilian Moore, © 1967 Lilian Moore, reprinted by permission of Marian Reiner for the author. "Balloon" by Colleen Thibaudeau reprinted by permission of the author. "Summer" from *Country Pie* by Frank Asch, © 1979 Frank Asch, reprinted by permission of Greenwillow Books, a division of William Morrow and Company, Inc. "Busy Day" from *You Tell Me* by Michael Rosen and Roger McGough published by Kestrel Books, © 1979 Michael Rosen, reprinted by permission of Penguin Books Ltd. "The Snowman" and "Mrs Moon" from *Sky In The Pie* by Roger McGough, reprinted by permission of the Peters Fraser and Dunlop Group Ltd. "Someone" and "The Horseman" by Walter de la Mare, reprinted by permission of the Literary Trustees of Walter de la Mare and The Society of Authors as their representative. "Night Comes" from *A Bunch Of Poems And Verses* by Beatrice Schenk de Regniers, © 1977 Beatrice Schenk de Regniers, reprinted by permission of Marian Reiner for the author. "Sweet Dreams" by Ogden Nash from *The New Nutcracker Suite And Other Innocent Verses* published by Little, Brown and Company, © 1962 Ogden Nash, reprinted by permission of Curtis Brown Ltd. "Mooning" by Brian Patten from *Thawing Frozen Frogs* published by Viking Kestrel, © 1990 Brian Patten, reprinted by permission of Penguin Books Ltd.

Every effort has been made to trace all the copyright holders and the publishers apologise if any inadvertent omission has been made.

Ernst-Detlef Schulze • Erwin Beck • Klaus Müller-Hohenstein

Plant Ecology

Ernst-Detlef Schulze • Erwin Beck • Klaus Müller-Hohenstein

Plant Ecology

With 506 Figures, most of them in colour, and 101 Tables

Professor Dr. Ernst-Detlef Schulze
Max-Planck-Institute for Biogeochemistry
P.O. Box 10 01 64
07701 Jena
Germany

Professor Dr. Erwin Beck
Department of Plant Physiology
University of Bayreuth
95440 Bayreuth
Germany

Professor Dr. Klaus Müller-Hohenstein
Department of Biogeography
University of Bayreuth
95440 Bayreuth
Germany

Translated by:

Gudrun Lawlor, FIL
Dr. Kirsten Lawlor
Dr. David Lawlor
9 Burywick
Harpenden
Hertfordshire
AL5 2AQ
UK

Original title:
Ernst-Detlef Schulze/Erwin Beck/Klaus Müller-Hohenstein, Pflanzenökologie
Copyright © 2002 Spektrum Akademischer Verlag GmbH, Heidelberg

ISBN 3-540-20833-X Springer-Verlag Berlin Heidelberg New York

Library of Congress Control Number: 2004107209

Springer is a part of Springer Science+Business Media
springeronline.com

© Springer Berlin · Heidelberg 2005
Printed in Germany

Editor: Dr. Dieter Czeschlik, Heidelberg
Desk editor: Dr. Andrea Schlitzberger, Heidelberg
Production: Karl-Heinz Winter, Heidelberg
Cover design: design & production GmbH, Heidelberg, Germany
Cover illustration: Claus Diercks, Willy Giltmann, Hamburg, Germany
Typesetting: K & V Fotosatz GmbH, Beerfelden
31/3150   5 4 3 2 1 0 – Printed on acid-free paper

Preface

Content: This textbook starts at the level of the cell and molecular aspects of plant responses to the environment, which is never stress free. Building on this molecular ecophysiology, the organisation and regulation of metabolism of whole plants will be described from an autecological perspective. In the following parts, this book deals with the interactions with other organisms at the level of the ecosystem. Finally, geographical and long-term conditions for the expansion and dynamics of plant populations and species on earth are discussed. The book closes with the element cycles on earth and thus stresses the influence of man on original, so-called natural ecosystems.

As the book covers several different conceptual levels, many aspects and facts will be illuminated from very different viewpoints: the cell, the plant, the ecosystem, the zones of distribution and earth as a whole. Thus, the authors have tried to fully consider the enormous width and complexity of plant ecology.

The reader: The textbook is aimed at advanced students and their teachers. Knowledge in various disciplines of natural sciences is expected, from molecular biology to the earth sciences. The authors have tried to recommend textbooks and articles from the relevant literature in each chapter. This "further reading" is intended to deepen the relevant knowledge and to help develop an understanding in relation to neighbouring fields. Additionally, basic knowledge is revisited in concise box-type texts. Conceptual knowledge is abstracted and strengthened in extensive summaries at the end of each section.

Thanks: Writing this textbook has been a pleasure, but has also cost the authors much of the one commodity which they lack most: time. A great deal of what could and should have been done was left by the wayside. We therefore ask all those whom we did not give enough of our time to make allowances, in particular our associates and last, but not least, our families. Without the support and help of many colleagues, friends and coworkers, it would not have been possible to finish this book in time so that it does not contain chapters which are outdated before publication. Particular thanks are given to Mrs Barbara Lühker, without whose thorough editorial work this book probably would have never been completed. For the critical reading of individual chapters, for advice and pointers to the literature, the authors would like to thank many colleagues, in particular: A. Arneth (Jena), K. Beierkuhnlein (Bayreuth), C. M. P. Blum (Utrecht), H. Bohnert (Urbana), U. Deil (Freiburg), W. H. O. Ernst (Amsterdam), S. Fettig (Bayreuth), E. Gloor (Jena), G. Guggenberger (Halle), F. Haakh (Stuttgart), U. Heber (Würzburg), H. W. Heldt (Göttingen), J. Kaplan (Jena), O. Kolle (Jena), U. Küper (Bayreuth), O. L. Lange (Würzburg), W. Larcher (Innsbruck), C. Neßhöfer and G. Orlich (Bayreuth), C. Ploetz (Wuppertal), M. Popp (Vienna), R. Voeseneck (Utrecht), R. Scheibe (Osnabrück), W. Schulze (Tübingen), E. Steudle (Bayreuth), C. Wirth (Jena) and W. Zech and P. Ziegler (Bayreuth).

Special thanks are also extended to Springer-Verlag for having translated the original German book published by Spektrum Akademischer Verlag. Both publishers obliged most of the requests by the authors in a constructive manner and respected the individuality of the authors, even though they had to consider the homogeneity of the final product.

The authors hope for a good reception of *Plant Ecology* by interested readers and welcome constructive criticism in the knowledge that the writing of a textbook about plant ecology in its entirety is an almost insurmountable task.

E.-Detlef Schulze, Erwin Beck and
Klaus Müller-Hohenstein
Bayreuth and Jena, October 2004

Contents

Introduction

The term **"ecology"** was defined by Ernst Haeckel in 1906 in his book, *Principles of General Morphology of Organisms*, as follows: "Ecology is the science of relations of the organism to the surrounding environment which includes, in its broadest sense, all 'conditions for existence'. These conditions may be organic or inorganic; both are of the greatest importance for the form of organisms, because they force the organism to adapt."

Haeckel included in the science of ecology the areas physiology, morphology and chorology (the science of the distribution of organisms) to understand the "conditions for existence" and "adaptation". In this book, we try to comply with Haeckel's understanding of plant ecology and to include the breadth of ecology as it was demanded by Haeckel. **Adaptation** to the environment starts at the molecular and cellular level where environmental conditions are detected and the responses to changes in the environment are accomplished. Starting from these physiological mechanisms, the morphological characteristics of organisms/plants become important at the level of the whole plant. Cellular metabolic reactions and structural (morphological and anatomical) organisation are the biological "tools" with which organisms make use of certain environmental conditions, avoid them or "adapt" to them. The combination of physiological and morphological "adaptation" is particularly important for plants, as they are fixed in their habitat and the conditions for life are determined by the variety and numbers of the organisms of the ecosystem and not by the individual plant alone. These environmental conditions and the interaction of a plant with the environment determine "fitness", i.e. the possibility for growth and reproduction in a spatial and temporal dimension, thus resulting in an association with Haeckel's "chorology". Haeckel's understanding of ecology was broader than our present botanical usage. The present book views ecology in as broad a context as Haeckel did, ranging from molecular stress physiology via ecology of whole organisms and the ecosystem to the temporal and spatial differentiation of vegetation.

Figure 1 shows the relations between (cellular) **stress** or **ecophysiology, whole plant physiology** and **synecology** (i.e. the ecology of vegetation cover) and **ecosystem science** where other organisms, not only plants, are increasingly considered. The interrelations between stress physiology, whole plant physiology and synecology are very close and obvious. In contrast, the path from stress physiology to ecosystems runs via whole plant ecology and synecology because morphology, i.e. the structure of plants, and the responses of populations are not primarily metabolic. **Applied ecology** includes all disciplines related to human activities. These include not only **agriculture** and **forestry**, but also **global change**. Agriculture and forestry contain also physiological aspects of high-yielding and pest-free varieties of crops and the biological interactions between crop plants and other organisms,

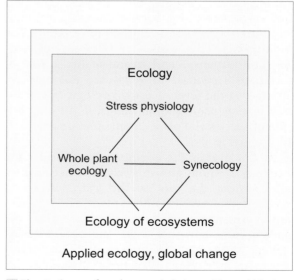

Fig. 1. Areas of ecology and their position within botany, ecosystem studies and in applied ecology

e.g. for pollination. Research on global change also includes the assessment of possible management systems for earth with respect to their effects on climate and maintaining biodiversity. Research on global change leads to model predictions on future effects of human activities.

In this book, an attempt is made, for the first time, to bring together and clearly organise the large subdisciplines of plant ecology. We start from the molecular **stress** and **ecophysiology** of plants in the broadest analysis yet attempted. **Chapter 1** lays down the molecular basis for ecological "adaptations" to all essential environmental factors. This ranges from climatic factors via salt stress in the soil to environmental pollutants. The **stress theory** considers the basic possibilities of stress responses resulting from **strains** and leading to **resistance**; finally, these provide the basis for understanding adaptive radiation of genotypes, and the processes leading to the evolution of new species. Plants not only react to stress in the sense of a response, the so-called **feed-back** reponse. There are also preparatory adaptations to changing environmental conditions, the so-called **feed-forward** reactions, setting off before an organism is stressed (e.g. pre-winter frost hardening). In both cases, signal chains are activated, leading to changes in the physiological/cell biological performance of plants, enabling them to continue to exist under new conditions. The response to one stress factor often protects the organism also from damage by other stresses (**"cross-protection"**). This results in responses to a variety of stresses resulting from a changing environment where not one single factor (e.g. heat or drought), but multiple stress types are acting in combination. The basic principles of avoidance (as a sort of feed-forward response) and tolerance (as a sort of feed-back response) to stress are not only restricted to the level of ecophysiology, but occur also in responses of whole plants, in the distribution of species and plant communities, particularly at extreme sites.

At the level of the organism, we consider the plant as a whole and the relations between its organs from the root to the leaf, flower and seed. At the level of **whole plant ecology** new, not (primary) metabolic characteristics are added: although these are genetically determined, they may be modified within limits. These include **plant structures** including size and the **life cycle** (phenology, life span, strategies for reproduction and distribution). Because

of these strategies, certain species are able to avoid extreme conditions and use or change their habitat. Annual plants form the largest proportion of plant species in dry areas. However, their active life is limited to favourable conditions after rain, even if this only occurs sporadically, perhaps only every few years or even decades. In contrast, perennial species have mechanisms that regulate the water relations and enable survival in unfavourable climatic periods. These include, for example, special leaf and root anatomy that allows the species to survive with intact shoot systems or to change their site conditions. **Hydraulic lift**, for example, enables roots to transport water from deep soil layers to the upper horizons and thus moisten the upper soil layers. In temperate climates, the accumulation of carbon in the soil changes site fertility. The scope for "adaptations" by whole plants is very broad, as are the responses of cells to stress. They range from leaf structure and leaf movement, via the formation of variably dimensioned vessels in the stem, to differentiation of the roots. In **Chapter 2**, the use of resources by whole plants is discussed. This includes the plant–water relations, the heat and nutrient balances and the carbon relations.

Cellular metabolism and structural characteristics are not only the basis for the spatial and temporal patterns of plant species, dealt within synecology (**Chap. 4**), but also the basis for **element cycles** in ecosystems, which are characterised by the diversity of species and forms of organisation. These include indirect interactions between individual plants and other plant species. Here applies the wisdom that: "Even the most pious cannot live in peace if it does not please the nasty neighbour". **Competition** exists in the effective use of resources on limited space. If the resources become scarce, **"efficiency"** means a better use of limiting resources at the cost of the neighbour. This, of course, does not always imply saving resources or using them most economically. Indeed, it may be more useful to use more resources than required, if this brings advantages in competition with the neighbours. Growth also plays an important role in ecosystems, and the "ecological equilibrium" of an ecosystem probably does not exist in "nature" as it is. Metabolic cycles in ecosystems are not as closed as previously assumed. This means that the actual status as it may be observed as a momentary picture of a system is in the long term very dynamic. Not all processes of a system move

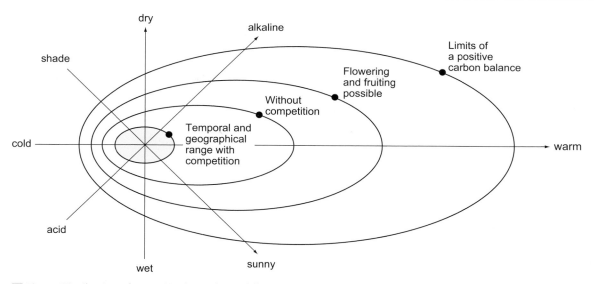

Fig. 2. Distribution of a species depends on different environmental factors. The actual distribution area is significantly smaller than the potential areas of distribution which are reached without competition at the extreme limits of flowering or at the boundaries of a positive material balance. In the example shown, temperature is the dominant factor, but this may differ in other cases. According to the species, the limits of distribution change

linearly in one direction. There are strengthening and weakening processes with a consequential complex, non-linear temporal behaviour. The scientific basis of ecosystems is, for the first time, presented in **Chapter 3** of this volume. General conclusions are drawn about how individual organisms interact within the diversity of vegetation. This leads to the question about the degree to which vegetation is more than the sum of its individual plants. Many characteristics of vegetation result from material fluxes which dictate the performance of individual plants. For example, the "aero-dynamic roughness" of the surface of vegetation determines coupling to the meteorological conditions in the atmosphere and thus determines the survival of plant individuals or a species in the vegetation. It is only by large numbers of individuals of the same species which, through distribution of seeds or other ways of propagation, determine the habitat in relation to a dynamic diversity of other species.

Synecology is the next higher level of plant ecology, extending to populations based on the strategies of propagation and distribution. Synecology does not consider the fate of a single individual, but the dynamic spatial and temporal behaviour of populations, including population growth, homoeostasis and decline. Only in exceptional cases does a single species form a vegetation. Generally, natural vegetation includes a diversity of species which make complementary

use of the available resources. In synecology, the broad spectrum of responses at the cellular and whole plant level is replaced by the enormous diversity of species (350,000 species of vascular plants) which determine in different proportions the composition of the vegetation cover of the earth. In **Chapter 4**, the historical and spatial dimensions of species distributions and their biological interactions are discussed.

Combining the ecology of ecosystems with the field of synecology enables us to understand also the distribution of species. Both the potential and actual **areas** (Fig. 2) are determined by several parameters. For example, considering only the carbon balances, a plant species could grow on a much larger area than the region in which it actually reproduces. However, even this region is limited by different types of competition with other species, so that the area eventually occupied is even further restricted. Agricultural crop plants (maize, beans, wheat, potato, soya and many others) are an interesting example of evolution in a geographically limited area (the so-called genetic centres of origin), but these species are now distributed worldwide after domestication and management by humans.

The science of geobotany relates to global aspects in plant ecology, which are included in the term **global change**, where the direct and indirect influences of man through land use, changes in land use and the subsequent changes in climate are becoming increasingly felt. The pivotal question in **Chapter 5** is: "How are conditions for human existence affected by the reactions of the vegetation cover of the earth?" In this book, plant ecology is broadened to include the effects of plant life on global element cycles. At present, the primary focus is on the "management" of the global carbon cycle by humans. It is obvious that in future questions concerning global management of water and nutrient cycles will have to be considered as being just as important. Here, ecology is no longer "pure" science and will play an important and even vital role in providing information for politicians on questions concerning humanity as a whole. Research into global change is developing very fast at present, similarly to the development of molecular plant ecophysiology.

Based on these considerations, the book deals with the main areas of plant ecology in the following chapters:

- Stress physiology
- Whole plant physiology
- Ecology of ecosystems
- Synecology
- Global aspects of plant ecology

Chapter 1

Stress Physiology

The cold tropics: The author of this chapter has been working for more than 20 years on plant stress in high tropical mountains. The photograph, taken in the morning of a day during the rainy season (in July) at about 4700 m on Mt. Kenya, shows that man and plants can suffer from cold, even right on the equator. Several species of flowering plants can grow even at this altitude in moist sites

Environment as Stress Factor: Stress Physiology of Plants

Plants are bound to places. They, therefore, have to be considerably more adaptable to stressful environments and must acquire greater tolerance to multiple stresses than animals and humans. This is shown very clearly by the limitations in the distribution of particular types of vegetation, for example, the tree line on mountains. Extremely high light intensities, mechanical stress by wind, frequent periods of frost, and a winter period of many months have left their marks on these spruces and pines at about 3000 m altitude on Mt. Hood in Oregon (USA). Photo E. Beck

Recommended Literature

- Aarts MGM, Fiers MWEJ (2003) What drives plant stress genes? Trends Plant Sci 8:99–102
- Bohnert HJ, Nelson DL, Jensen RG (1995) Adaptations to environmental stress. Plant Cell 7:1099–1111
- Couzin J (2002) Breakthrough of the year. Small RNAs make big splash. Science 298: 2296–2297
- http://www.ambion.com/hottopics/rnai RNA interference
- http://www.nature.com/nature/fow/ 000316.html RNA interference
- Larcher W (ed) (2003) Physiological plant ecology, 4th edn (chapter: Plants under stress). Springer, Berlin Heidelberg New York, pp 345–450
- Robertson D (2004) VIGS vectors for gene silencing: many targets, many tools. Annu Rev Plant Biol 55:495–519
- Stokes T (2003) DNA-RNA-protein gang together in silence. Trends Plant Sci 8:53–55
- Taiz L, Zeiger E (eds) (2002) Plant physiology, 3rd edn (chapter: Stress physiology). Sinauer Associates, Sunderland, MA
- Waterhouse PM, Wang M-B, Finnegan EJ (2001) Role of short RNAs in gene silencing. Trends Plant Sci 6:297–301

1.1.1

Abiotic and Biotic Environments Cause Stress

The environment affects an organism in many ways, at any time. To understand the reactions of a particular organism in a certain situation, individual external influences, so-called **environmental factors**, are usually considered separately, if at all possible. Environmental factors can be of abiotic and biotic nature. **Biotic environmental factors**, resulting from interactions with other organisms, are, for example, infection or mechanical damage by herbivory or trampling, as well as effects of symbiosis or parasitism. **Abiotic environmental factors** include temperature, humidity, light intensity, the supply of water and minerals, and CO_2; these are the parameters and resources that determine the growth of a plant. Many other influences, which are only rarely beneficial to the plant (wind as distributor of pollen and seeds), or not at all beneficial or are even damaging (ionising rays or pollutants), are also classified as abiotic factors. The effect of each abiotic factor depends on its quantity. With optimal quantity or intensity, as may be provided in a greenhouse, the plant grows "optimally" and thus achieves its

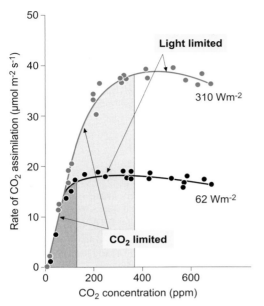

Fig. 1.1.1. Limitation of photosynthesis by CO_2 and light. The rate of photosynthesis of a sorghum leaf (*Sorghum sudanense*) is shown at different light intensities and CO_2 concentrations in air. (After Fitter and Hay 1987)

If the dosage is inappropriate, stress is caused, as is obvious with the effects of the following factors: **light** (weak light, strong light), **temperature** (cold, heat), **water** (drought, flooding), **nutrients** (lack of ions, over-fertilisation, salt stress), **carbon dioxide** and **oxygen** (photosynthesis, respiration/photorespiration, oxidative stress, anaerobiosis; Fig. 1.1.3). Optimal intensities and concentrations of these may also differ not only for individual organisms, but also for particular organs of the same organism.

Environmental noxae are stress factors which trigger stress reactions when applied in any concentration or intensity: UV-B, ozone, ionising radiation, xenobiotics, heavy metals and aluminium. In this context, electrical and strong magnetic fields can also be considered as stress factors.

Endogenous stress may also occur, for example, by separating an organ from its water supply, as is the case during ripening of seeds and the desiccation of embryo and endosperm.

"physiological normal type", maximising its physiologically achievable performance.

Plants almost never find the optimal quantities or intensities of all essential abiotic factors (Fig. 1.1.1). Thus the "physiological normal type" is rather the exception and deviation from the rule. It is very important to realise that growth is only one of many reactions of a plant to its environment. Flowering and fruiting determine the plant's success in reproduction and propagation and might equally be used as a measure of the plant's reaction to the environment. The value of the factors might, in this case, change but the principal behaviour would be similar.

Deviations from the physiological normal type are regarded as reactions to suboptimal or damaging quantities or intensities of environmental factors, i.e. situations for which we use the term **stress**. Thus stress and reactions caused by it (**stress reactions**) can be used as a measure of the strength of the stress on a scale of intensity, ranging from deficiency to excessive supply. Environmental factors deviating from the optimal intensity or quantity for the plant are called **stress factors**. The optimal quantity can, in fact, be zero, e.g. with xenobiotics. Stress factors which could potentially influence the plant are listed in Fig. 1.1.2.

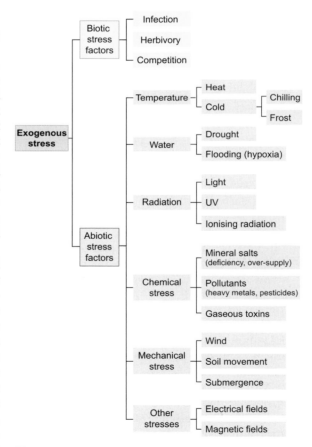

Fig. 1.1.2. Biotic and abiotic environmental factors creating stress for plants

Symptoms of deficiency

Stunted growth, small pale leaves,
stiff habitus, root/shoot ratio large,
lodging resistance high, premature
ripening.
Limited reproductive production.
Reduced resistance to drought,
increased susceptibility to fungal infections.

Symptoms of excess fertilisation

Luxuriant, large deep green leaves,
soft growth, root/shoot ratio small,
lodging resistance low (often lodges),
maturation delayed.
Limited reproductive production.
Reduced resistance to drought,
increased susceptibility to fungal
infections.

Winter wheat: N requirements in spring

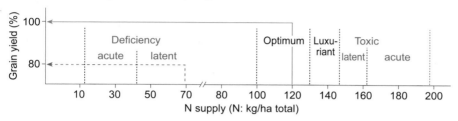

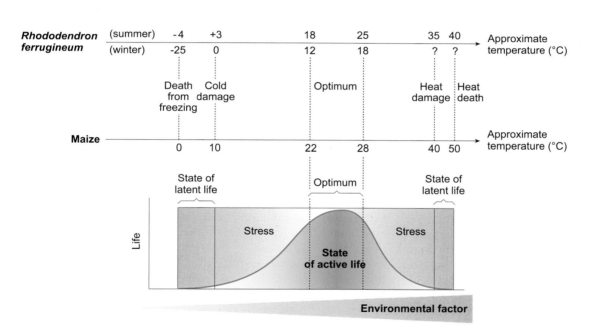

Fig. 1.1.3. Life processes of an organism described as a function of an (abiotic) environmental factor. The **relative growth rate**, **R**, may be used as a measure of life processes:

$$R = \frac{\Delta biomass}{\Delta t} \times \frac{1}{biomass}$$

Usually, an organism is subjected to several stress factors, e.g. lack of water and heat, or a "secondary" stress factor follows a "primary" one: When the plant lacks water and closes its stomata, internal CO_2 deficiency occurs when the plant is illuminated, and as a further consequence oxidative stress ensues. Combination of several stress factors is the normal case and is referred to as **multiple stress**.

1.1.2

Specific and Unspecific Reactions to Stress

An organism that is stressed, for example, by elevated temperature, not only increases its metabolic rate, but other reactions occur which are usually not observed in the unstressed organism, or take place only to a very small degree. An example of this is the formation of "heat shock proteins" (see Chap. 1.3.4.2). The modification of the basic metabolism could be interpreted as an **unspecific** reaction, whilst the production of heat shock proteins would be considered a **specific stress reaction** of the organism. The differentiation of these two components of a stress reaction is based on the findings of Hans Selye (1973), a Canadian general practitioner, who, in the 1970s, summarised the various complexes of stress reactions of human beings as follows: "Everything which endangers life causes stress reactions and adaptive reactions. Both types of reactions are partly specific and partly unspecific." Contrary to plants there is, in humans, also a strong psychic-humoral stress component. The concept of both components of the stress reaction is complicated by the fact that even the specific reactions often lack specificity: The above-mentioned heat shock proteins also assist the folding of proteins during synthesis and after denaturing (see Chap. 1.3.4.2), not only by high-temperature stress, but also under other stresses. They are produced in high amounts, for example, under stress by xenobiotics (e.g. heavy metals). This does not exclude that there are in addition more specific responses by which an organism differentiates between stress by heat and by heavy metals (see Chap. 1.7.5).

There is yet another facet to the question of specificity of stress reactions which is described by the term **cross-protection**. Previous drought stress or salt stress (osmotic stress) is known to harden plants against temperature stress, and particularly cold stress (Fig. 1.1.4). Is this an unspecific stress response? The apparent lack of specificity of the adaptation is explained, on the one hand by considering the physiological effects of salt and drought stress on cells and, on the other, the effects of frost. All three factors lead to a partial dehydration of cells (in an ivy leaf at –7 °C, ca. 90% of the total leaf water is frozen, forming ice, and thus is no longer available as free water; see Fig. 1.3.25). This causes problems with the stability of biomembranes in particular, as the lipid bilayers are stabilised by so-called hydrophobic interactions, which are disturbed if the availability of water, or the ion concentration at the surface of membranes, is drastically changed (see also Chap. 1.3.5.2). If too much water is removed from the aqueous environment of the biomembranes (by evaporation or freezing), the concentration of solutes increases, e.g. in the cytosol or the chloroplast stroma. Increase in the ion concentrations in turn changes the charges at the surface of membranes, and as a consequence the membrane potentials. This usually leads to destabilisation of membrane structure. High charge densities, however, not only result from water deficiency, but also from excessive salt concentration. A general reaction to stress is the synthesis of hydrophilic low molecular protectants, so-called compatible solutes (sugars, sugar alcohols and cyclitols, amino acids and betaines, see Chaps. 1.5.2.6 and 1.6.2.3), which replace water at the membrane surfaces and dislodge the ionic compounds upon loss of cellular water. Production of compatible solutes requires, of course, synthesis of respective enzymes, triggered by stress. Synthesis of these enzymes is often preceded by signals transmitted by certain phytohormones – particularly abscisic acid (ABA) or the stress hormone jasmonate, but also ethylene, may transiently change their concentration. One ex-

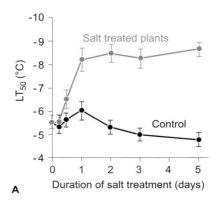

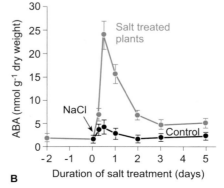

Fig. 1.1.4. Frost hardening through salt treatment. Cuttings of potato plants (*Solanum commersonii* Dun Pl 458317) were grown in Murashige-Skoog medium to which NaCl was added (100 mM final concentration). A Frost hardiness of plants and B ABA content of plants. (After Ryu et al. 1995)

ample of such cross-protection is induction of frost hardening in wild potatoes by salt stress (Fig. 1.1.4). Potato plants treated with NaCl are able to tolerate lower temperatures than untreated controls. A transient increase in ABA concentration mediates this hardening reaction.

1.1.3

Stress Concepts

Based on physical principles, Levitt (1980) published a theoretical understanding of stress reactions that is applicable to all groups of organisms, as illustrated by an abstract experiment. It is known as the **physical stress concept** (Fig. 1.1.5). A body is deformed if it is stretched by a force (**stress**); this deformation is at first reversible ("**elastic**"), but upon intensifying the force it becomes irreversibly ("**plastic**") deformed and finally breaks. The change in the body caused by the force is called **strain**. The force required to produce a unit of change is the **elastic modulus, M**. In this sense, elasticity does not mean expansion in the sense of maximum elastic deformation. The modulus of elasticity M corresponds in principle to ε, the elastic modulus of a cell wall, which is a measure of the cell wall's flexibility (see, e.g., Fig. 1.5.2)

$$M = \frac{\text{force}}{\text{deformation}} = \frac{\text{stress}}{\text{strain}} \qquad (1.1\,a)$$

According to this relation, M is also a measure of the resistance of the system to an externally applied force on the system.

In biological systems, stress is not commonly a single physical force affecting the organism, but a load from many individual environmental factors. Primarily, metabolic processes are changed or deformed. The concept by Levitt convincingly explains the relation of stress and strain, but it can be applied to biological systems only to a limited extent, as the following, biologically important parameters are lacking:

- **Time factor:** In a physical system, the amount of stress equals the strength of stress; in a biological system, the amount of stress is the **product of the intensity of stress and duration of stress.** For example, if one cools the tropical ornamental *Saintpaulia ionantha* (African violet) for a short time (6 h) to 5 °C

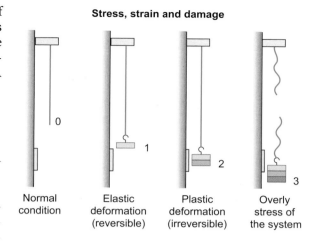

Stress, strain and damage

| Normal condition | Elastic deformation (reversible) | Plastic deformation (irreversible) | Overly stress of the system |

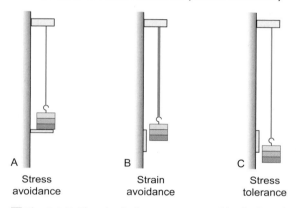

Three types of strain resistance (stress resistance)

| A Stress avoidance | B Strain avoidance | C Stress tolerance |

Fig. 1.1.5. The physical stress concept of Levitt (1980)

and then returns it to the original temperature, some of the metabolic reactions may change their rates in accordance with their activation energy (Q_{10}), but the increase or decrease in metabolite pools is not changed so dramatically that the plant is damaged. However, if the plant is left for a longer period (48 h) at 5 °C, metabolic chaos results, as individual metabolite pools empty whilst others grow disproportionally. The plant is damaged, in other words: **Elastic strain has passed into plastic strain** (Fig. 1.1.6).

- **Repair:** Plastic change or deformation is not completely irreversible. In most cases, the organism is able to repair the damage, if it is not too severe. One example is DNA repair after damage by UV irradiation. **Plastic strain can change to elastic strain** (see Box 1.2.4). Because of the open life form of plants, "repairs" can also be accomplished through premature senescence or shedding of damaged

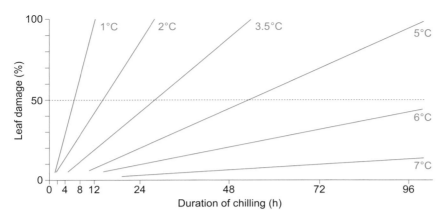

Fig. 1.1.6. Chilling damage to the African violet (*Saintpaulia ionantha*). Below the threshold temperature of +8 °C leaves suffer chilling damage, recognisable by the incidence of necroses. Strength of stress can be estimated as the product of cold stress (above the freezing point) multiplied by the duration of exposure; it is proportional to the extent of damage. (After Larcher and Bodner 1980)

organs, for example, of leaves damaged by radiation or drought.

- **Adaptation:** Under stress conditions organisms are able to adapt to more stressful living conditions by changing their elastic modulus and thus their resistance to stress. Such adaptations occur in stress reactions which are not part of the "normal" metabolic changes, for example, the induction of CAM by salt stress or drought (see Chap. 1.5.3.1).

Adaptation may be achieved in two different ways, by **avoidance** of the stress or strain, as in CAM plants, which can close their stomata during the hot and dry daytime because of

their ability to fix CO_2 during the night, or by developing an **intrinsic tolerance**, for example, by water storage and by increasing (numerically decreasing) the water potential of the plant.

- **Seasonally recurring stress** requires timely hardening of the plants, for example, development of frost resistance in the case of perennials (see Chap. 1.3.6.7). It might be assumed that such plants, once they have become frost-resistant, would maintain this capacity. However, frost hardening involves not only metabolic changes, but also alterations of the cellular ultrastructure. Frost-hardened plants

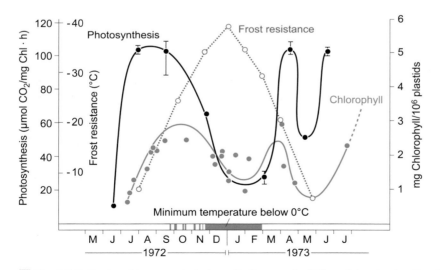

Fig. 1.1.7. Frost resistance and photosynthetic capacity (CO_2 uptake at saturating light and 1% CO_2 concentration) of one generation of spruce needles measured under identical conditions over the course of a year. Note that the annual fluctuation of photosynthesis shows the same dynamics as the chlorophyll content of the chloroplasts. Needles were taken from a 50-year-old spruce tree in the Botanical Garden in Munich. (After Senser and Beck 1979)

are significantly less efficient (measured in terms of their productivity) than in the frost-sensitive state. Upon decrease of the stress they therefore undergo a dehardening process, in which they regain their former efficiency (Fig. 1.1.7). They thus adapt to their particular environmental conditions within the limits of their genetic disposition.

- Normally, plants react to stresses with a change of their metabolism (strain) which may be interpreted as an **alarm signal**. If this strain is tolerated, **hardening** occurs. If the strain exceeds the range of tolerance, the organism is injured and, if the damage overstrains the plant's capability of repair, it will not survive.

- **Multiple stress and multiple stress responses**: Let us continue with the above example of frost hardening and dehardening. When subjected to subfreezing temperature, a large portion of the water in the plant freezes, also in frost-hardened tissue, and crystallised water is not available to the plant. Nevertheless, during bright winter days, leaves, for example, needles of conifers, are exposed to very high radiation intensities. The photosynthetic apparatus is energised, as the absorption of solar radiation does not depend on temperature, but this energy cannot be used because of frost dehydration of the tissue and the low temperatures. Various other possibilities of energy dissipation, for example, photorespiration or photosynthetic oxygen reduction (Mehler reaction), are, for the same reason, not functional (see Chap. 1.2.1.3). An increased energy dissipation via radicals would result in so-called oxidative stress, which can easily be observed by the destruction of pigments. Frost hardening thus not only requires development of tolerance to freeze-desiccation of the cells, but also of protective measures against the damaging effects of oxidative stress, and of strategies to avoid the formation of radicals. **Multiple stress requires a multiple stress response** and thus frost hardening and dehardening are not simple reactions, but concerted reaction complexes (often termed syndromes) where avoidance strategies and the development of tolerance are combined and usually cannot be clearly differentiated from one another.

Larcher (1987) developed a new concept of stress based on the concepts of Levitt and Selye, but incorporating the additional points mentioned above. Starting with the stress induced, a beneficial stress (**eustress** after Selye) and a detrimental stress (**distress**) are differentiated. In the reaction coordinate "time", this component is also included and shows that hardening is reversible and that increased stress or multiple stress can also overstrain even a hardened organism and damage it lethally. However, these additional modes of reaction are difficult to include in a two-dimensional diagram.

In Fig. 1.1.8, a three-dimensional model is shown where stress, strain (deformation) and time are shown as the three coordinates.

1.1.4
Perception of Stress and Creation of Signals

How is stress, as a multifactorial complex, detected and how is the signal triggering the stress reaction produced? It is known that pathogens produce degradation products of their own cell walls or of the cell walls of the host plant, termed elicitors, which trigger a response, mostly synthesis of so-called phytoalexins (see Chaps. 1.3.5.1 and 1.10.2). But how does abiotic stress – cold, heat, mechanical stress, osmotic stress, lack of oxygen – become a signal? How specific are such signals? Can hardening occur even without stress?

Little is known about the perception of abiotic stress at the molecular level. An example is the perception of osmotic stress in the unicellular green alga *Dunaliella salina*. This alga does not produce a firm cell wall but it is able to adapt its osmotic potential to that of the medium (0.1–5.5 M NaCl in the medium) and so avoids dramatic changes in volume. Adaptation to the osmotic potential of the medium is accomplished exclusively through the metabolite glycerol, one of the compatible solutes which in a medium saturated with NaCl accumulates up to 60% of the cell weight. Upon hyperosmotic shock the cell shrinks transiently, but is able to regain its original volume within 30–120 min through glycerol production. The mechanism by which glycerol accumulates in cells without leaching into the medium is not known. De novo synthesis of new proteins is apparently not involved. Furthermore, stressor specificity is

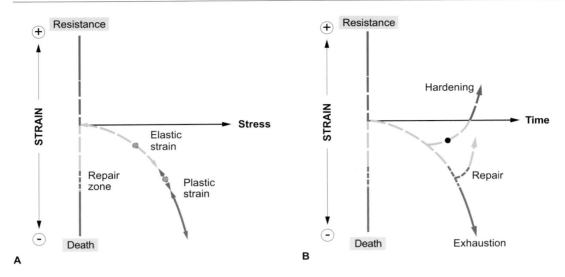

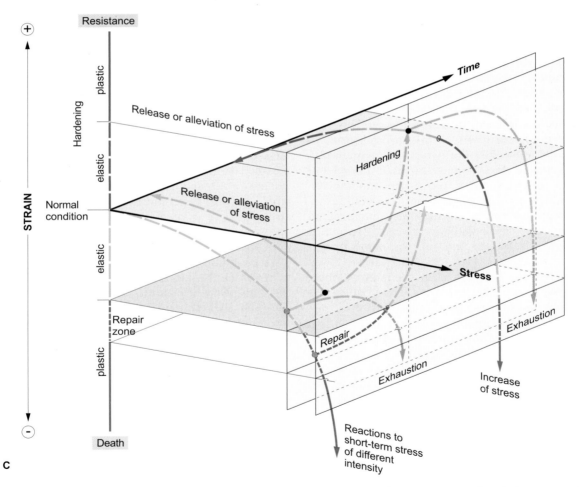

Fig. 1.1.8. The stress concept according to Beck and Lüttge. A Relationship between stress and strain in a system that is not capable of hardening (e.g. chilling of the African violet, cf. Fig. 1.1.6). The stress factor time is not considered. B Relationship between strain and duration of stress in a system capable of repair and hardening. C Relationship of strain and stress allowing also for time as a factor that increases or alleviates stress. The system under consideration is capable of hardening (e.g. frost hardening of spruce needles in autumn). For clarification, two panels are inserted into the three-dimensional coordinate system in the transition zone between elastic and plastic strain. (After Beck and Lüttge 1990)

low, as other osmotica, e.g. polyols, if producing hyperosmotic stress, likewise trigger glycerol accumulation. It is assumed that the transient shrinking process itself produces the signal (see Fig. 1.3.18). Consequently, there are two possibilities for the creation of signals: a sensor located in the plasma membrane (see Chap. 1.2.2.1) or, arising from the contraction of volume, exceeding a threshold concentration of a metabolite in the cytosol. There is more support for the first possibility. A transient, short-term stiffening of the membrane appears to be important, which results in a closer packing of the lipid molecules in the bilayer (a volume contraction must, after all, also lead to a decrease in the surface of the plasma membrane, see Fig. 1.3.18). The high sterol content of the plasma membrane appears to be important in this respect for signal creation (sterols form 35–45% of the total lipids of the cell!). If cells are stressed in the presence of an inhibitor of steroid biosynthesis ("tridemorph"), the sterol content of the membrane is dramatically decreased. At the same time, the ability of the cell to regain its volume by glycerol accumulation after a hyperosmotic shock is lost. The effect of the inhibitor can be completely reversed if an artificial sterol (cholesterol hemisuccinate) is applied to the cells via the medium. It is assumed in the model shown in Fig. 1.1.9 that

sterols interact in such a way with an osmosensor protein located in the membrane that the protein is activated by membrane stiffening. Perception of cold is probably also via cold-triggered stiffening of the membrane (Sung et al. 2003).

With respect to regularly recurring stresses, as for example frost in winter, "feed-forward" signals could be suggested, which might trigger the hardening process without the perception of a stress. It has been shown that shortening of day length induces frost hardening in pine. Temperatures around freezing point are also effective (even under a long-day light period). In the end, both signals lead to the same frost hardening, but the process induced by short days takes considerably longer (0.4 °C/day) than that triggered by cold (0.9 °C/day; Hansen and Beck 2002). A transient increase in viscosity of biomembranes appears to act as a cellular signal as in Dunaliella (see also Vigh et al. 1993). In nature, both factors perform synergetically, but the decreasing day length in autumn is probably always the first triggering signal. It has been proven that the phytochrome and cryptochrome systems both take part in the triggering of frost hardening (and dehardening). However, little is known about signal transduction in the cell (cf. Chap. 1.3.6.1).

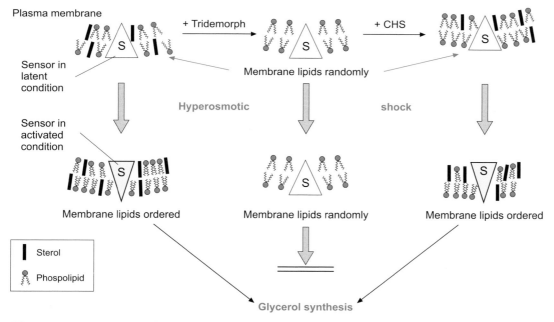

Fig. 1.1.9. Hypothetical model of the osmosensor of the cell wall-free alga *Dunaliela salina*. Tridemorph is an inhibitor of sterol biosynthesis, cholesterol hemisuccinate (CHS) is an exogenous sterol that can be incorporated into the plasma membrane of *D. salina*. (After Zelazny et al. 1995)

Most of the strains imposed on a plant by its environment are spontaneously rather than regularly recurring. A feed-forward signal causing stress avoidance therefore appears to be fairly exceptional. Most of the adaptation reactions are triggered by actual stress and thus correspond more to the feed-back mode (see also Chap. 2.2). Our knowledge about the signal transduction in the cell is still rather patchy (see Chap. 1.5.2.4). Signal transduction and effects of signals constitute a broad field of research in molecular ecophysiology.

1.1.5

How to Measure Stress on Plants?

Stress as such, of course, cannot be measured as it is only effective in the interaction between environmental factors and organisms. However, the strain, as caused by the action of stress on an organism, can be measured. Switching protein synthesis from the normal protein metabolism to the formation of heat shock proteins is a measurable parameter for particular strains (see Chap. 1.3.4.2) which might be well bearable or only just bearable. However, ecologists working in the field do not usually have access to a laboratory for molecular biological research. Therefore, it must suffice to quantify the strain by a measure of survival, i.e. the degree of damage incurred. Several, usually unspecific quantitative assays have been developed. In addition, non-invasive techniques can be employed to measure specific strains, e.g. on photosynthesis via chlorophyll fluorescence (Lichtenthaler and Miehé 1997). This is particularly practicable if the parameter in question is the "weak point" of the entire reaction complex. Unspecific methods usually allow only the determination of the limits of tolerance, e.g. the so-called LD50, i.e. at which dosage 50% of the cells are killed. The LD50 value, however, does not provide information about the degree of alterations within the range of tolerance. Box 1.1.1 shows the most frequently employed methods for quantification of damage after stress treatment.

A completely different strategy for strain detection is the molecular analysis of stress-induced gene expression or suppression of expression. DNA, representing genes from the organisms of interest, preferentially from those whose genome has been sequenced, can be spotted on

so-called chips or microchips. Then the plant is subjected to a stressful treatment and the mRNA is isolated and labelled by coupling to a dye. This sample is then hybridised with the DNA on the chip. Binding of the colour-coded RNA shows which genes have undergone strong expression (and produced much RNA). If the position of the individual genes on the chip is known, stress-induced gene expression can be assessed.

1.1.6

Production of Stress-Tolerant Plants by Genetic Engineering?

Recommended Literature

- Holmberg N, Bülow L (1998) Improving stress tolerance in plants by gene transfer. Trends Plant Sci 3:61–66
- Pilon-Smits EAH, Ebskamp MJM, Paul MJ, Jeuken MJW, Weisbeek PJ, Smeekens SCM (1995) Improved performance of transgenic fructan-accumulating tobacco under drought stress. Plant Physiol 107:125–130
- Tarczynski MC, Jensen R, Bohnert HJ (1993) Stress protection of transgenic tobacco by production of the osmolyte mannitol. Science 259:508–510

The concept of producing stress-tolerant plants by genetic engineering contradicts the idea in Chapter 1.1.3 that strain and strain tolerance are not single reactions but reaction complexes, so-called syndromes. It is therefore not possible, even by targeted alterations of one characteristic, to change a stress-sensitive plant into a tolerant one. However, it is possible, if the most sensitive component of the stress syndrome is known, to reduce the total sensitivity and to improve the resistance. Aims of this strategy are, for example, production and accumulation of compatible solutes to protect membranes, decrease in the viscosity of biomembranes by fatty acid desaturation to increase the cold tolerance, or the increase in desiccation tolerance by gene transfer for so-called LEA proteins (late embryogenesis abundant proteins), which protect the embryo from drying out during seed maturation. Currently, not all crop plants are useful targets for stable genetic transformation. This ap-

Box 1.1.1   Quantification of damage to plant tissues

1. **Counting necrotic areas after stress application.** Plant tissue, for example, pieces of a leaf, are exposed to a defined stress and then placed for 2 days on moist filter paper. Damage is shown by the formation of necroses (brown, often soggy areas).

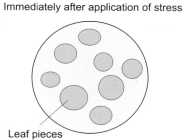

Immediately after application of stress

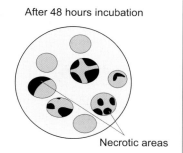

After 48 hours incubation

Leaf pieces

Necrotic areas

Petri dish with moist filter paper, 5-8 °C

2. **Absorption and accumulation of neutral red in the vacuole of undamaged cells.** Only living cells can accumulate neutral red in the vacuole; this is generally accompanied by a change in colour of the indicator, because the vacuolar pH is slightly acidic.

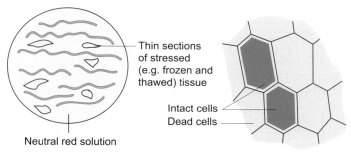

Thin sections of stressed (e.g. frozen and thawed) tissue

Intact cells
Dead cells

Neutral red solution

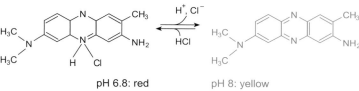

pH 6.8: red   pH 8: yellow

3. **Plasmolysis of undamaged cells.** Only intact cells can undergo plasmolysis. This reaction is tested after stressing the tissue.

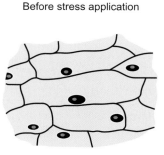

Before stress application

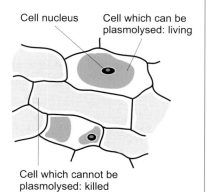

Cell nucleus   Cell which can be plasmolysed: living

Cell sap (vacuole) stained with anthocyanin

Cell which cannot be plasmolysed: killed

Box 1.1.1   Quantification of damage to plant tissues (continued)

4. **Measurement of electrical conductivity: loss of ions from damaged cells into distilled water.** Damage to plant tissues leads initially to loss of selective permeability of the cell membranes. In consequence, solutes leak from the cells. When pieces of tissue (e.g. leaf discs) are floated on distilled water, low molecular weight compounds diffuse into the medium. They include many ions so that the conductivity of the water increases. This can be measured conductiometrically. Conductivity is expressed in μSiemens.

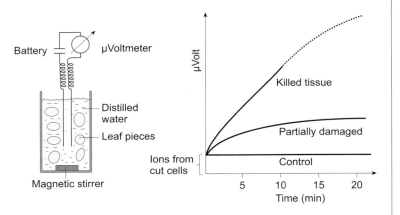

5. **Measurement of chlorophyll fluorescence in photosynthesis.** Photosynthetic electron transport may be measured by means of the chlorophyll fluorescence from photosystem II (red colour). With modern imaging systems, the impact of stress on photosynthesis may be seen immediately as a fluorescence quenching. In the example shown, a foxglove (*Digitalis*) plant was treated by applying the herbicide Diuron (DCMU) to the roots. The increase in fluorescence quenching can be seen within 3.5 days (after Lichtenthaler and Miehé 1997).

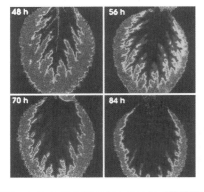

plies particularly to genetically complicated cereals like wheat and to Chenopodiaceae (e.g. sugar beet), where regeneration of plants from transformed cells is the major problem (see also Chap. 1.1.7). Considering the actual progress in molecular gene technology, transformation of the more difficult species will be achieved in the foreseeable future. However, the conditions un-

Table 1.1.1. Increased drought and salt resistance in rice plants by introduction of the HVA 1 gene (LEA protein) of barley (*nd* not determined) (Xu et al. 1996)

Transgenic line and wild type, respectively	Amount of HVA1 protein in soluble protein (%) in		Growth				Surviving plants (%)
	Leaves	Roots	Under drought stress		Under salt stress		
			Height of plants (cm)	Fresh weight of roots (g)	Height of plants (cm)	Fresh weight of roots (g)	
Wild type	0	0	22±1.4	0.9±0.1	19±1.1	1.2±0.1	0
30	0.5	0.3	29±1.1	1.4±0.1	23±0.9	1.9±0.1	60
36	1.5	1.0	37±1.8	2.1±0.1	29±0.8	nd	80
41	1.0	0.7	33±1.8	2.3±0.3	26±0.8	2.6±0.1	80

der which these transformed plants will then be capable of making use of their increased stress tolerance (which undoubtedly has been proven in some cases) to increase yields can only be determined experimentally. Table 1.1.1 shows the effect of transforming rice with LEA protein from barley (*Hordeum vulgare*, "HVA1"). In this case, growth (fresh weight production) and the capacity for survival under drought and salt stress were significantly increased. Whether this advantage is sufficient to achieve increased grain yields can only be shown in field experiments.

1.1.7

Gene Silencing

Recommended Literature

- Kooter JM, Matzke MA, Meyer P (1999) Listening to the silent genes: transgene silencing, gene regulation and pathogen control. Trends Plant Sci 4:340–347
- Meyer P, Saedler H (1996) Homology-dependent gene silencing in plants. Annu Rev Plant Physiol Plant Mol Biol 47:23–48

In several cases, the transferred genes were not expressed, although the transformation of the receiver plant had been successful. This failure occurred frequently when the genes were introduced by the biolistic technique, i.e. by shooting DNA-coated particles with a so-called particle gun into the cells. Transformation with *Agrobacterium tumefaciens* with the Ti-plasmid as vector was also susceptible to that effect. Meanwhile, this phenomenon has been identified as part of a regulatory mechanism termed "**gene silencing**". Obviously, there is a connection between the incidence of gene silencing and the number of copies of the heterologous gene. Multicopy genes are silenced more frequently than single copy ones. Gene silencing has been recognised as an important mechanism for the regulation of the development of an organism. Expression of many genes, the products of which are not required or even deleterious at a given developmental phase, must be suppressed and the multifaceted complex of gene silencing comprises several biochemical mechanisms. On a high hierarchical level the formation of transcriptionally silent, highly condensed heterochromatin

prevents gene transcription. The same gene can be well expressed or completely shut off, depending on whether it lies in the easily accessible regions of euchromatin or in the compacted heterochromatin (Bender 2004). Formation of heterochromatin requires prior methylation of the cytosine by a specific DNA-methyltransferase (Stokes 2001). Methylation is preferentially targeted to repeated sequences which could explain the above-mentioned silencing of multicopy genes. The question arises which component targets the methylation of DNA. Evidence is accumulating that an aberrant RNA aligns with homologous sequences of the DNA and thereby marks the regions for cytosine methylation. Silencing of DNA regions by the formation of heterochromatin is known as **epigenetic changes** or effects. Whether the so-called **position effects**, resulting from the positioning of the transgene in the neighbourhood to heterochromatin also results from cytosine methylation, is not quite clear. If so, extension of the methylation to the promoter of the transgene must be concluded. Whereas epigenetic gene silencing is triggered by an RNA–DNA interaction, the so-called **post-translational gene silencing** (**PTGS**) results from an RNA–RNA interaction. For this type of silencing, homologous RNA molecules act as catalysts forming regions of double-stranded RNA (dsRNA) with the messenger RNA. Regions of dsRNA are cleaved by a "dicer-ribonuclease" (Schauer et al. 2002) into small (about 25 nt long) fragments which target homologous mRNA into a multiprotein **RNA-induced silencing complex** (**RISC**). Several types of small RNAs have been identified and their nomenclature (siRNA, small interfering or inhibitory RNA; miRNA, microRNA; stRNA, small temporal RNA) is still somewhat confusing. Interestingly, the small RNA fragments can pass plasmodesmata and travel into neighbouring cells where they likewise trigger RNA destruction. Such PTGS is not confined to transgenes, but often occurs between corresponding sequences of transgenes and endogenous genes, and in this case has been termed "**cosuppression**". This suggests that the small RNAs or their precursors could help to coordinate development at the whole-plant level in a non-cell-autonomous manner and that PTGS is a molecular mechanism that can be used to control gene expression by selective destruction of specific endogenous or viral RNA species. In virus-infected plants, the process is triggered by the cytosolic accumulation of double-stranded replicative forms of viral RNA (Wood 2002). It not only leads to degradation of cognate mRNAs in the invaded cell, but also to the spread of a systemic silencing signal, conferring virus resistance (**RNA-mediated resistance**) to distant tissues. However, as everywhere in evolution, counter-defence strategies have been developed by viruses which produce PTGS suppressors. In molecular engineering, the use of small inhibitory RNAs for gene silencing and creation of loss of function transformants, the so-called RNA-interference technique (**RNAi**), has gained enormous importance.

Based on the general considerations of stress and strain outlined in this chapter, the effects of various abiotic and biotic environmental factors will be discussed in some detail. Stress and strain will be explained, subject to available knowledge, down to the molecular level; in some areas, but not in all, this part could also be termed "molecular ecophysiology" of plants.

Summary

1. All organisms are limited in their development by the environment. These limitations and impacts can be abiotic or biotic. Effects of abiotic factors such as light, temperature or water on an organism usually follow an optimum characteristic. Deviation from the optimal intensity or concentration creates stress and the environmental factors become stressors. There is no optimum for the biotic factors. The stronger the effect (e.g. infection, competition or herbivory), the stronger the stress. Usually, an organism is subjected to several stressors at the same time.
2. If subjected to stress, an organism reacts with a stress reaction (so-called strain) whose intensity corresponds to the strength of the stress. Strain reactions are, with regard to the stress factor, specific as well as unspecific and are reactions which would not occur, or to a small extent only, without the imposed stress. Unspecific stress reactions lead to hardening also against other stressors. Depending on the strength of stress and the strain reaction, the term eustress is used in the case of hardening and distress in the case of damage.
3. Organisms are capable of altering their stress tolerance by adaptation and, to a certain extent, can repair damage. Stress and strain, repair and adaptation, are summarised in so-called stress concepts explaining the reaction patterns deviating from the "normal performance", the strain reactions.
4. Whilst stress reactions are usually relatively easily recognised, the perception of stress by an organism is not yet fully understood. The question, which molecular signal a stressor creates in an organism can be answered only in a few cases. Feed-forward hardening is typical of regularly recurring stress situations, for example, frost hardening of plants in regions subjected to cold winters. However, usually adaptation is triggered by the stress itself. Adaptations lead to an increased stress tolerance or to a more effective stress avoidance.
5. Stress can be demonstrated experimentally by the intensity of strain reactions. These are mostly unspecific and only the degree of damage is quantifiable. Usually, an actual "weakest point" in sensitivity to stress cannot be defined.
6. Strain usually consists of several reactions, so it is principally difficult to produce stress-tolerant plants with gene technology. Obvious "weakest points" in the plant's defence against stress may, however, be improved by genetic engineering, for example, drought resistance of cereals by transformation with genes encoding for membrane-protecting proteins or for biosynthesis of low molecular weight solutes (compatible solutes). Such transformation often does not lead to success, as heterologous genes, particularly if introduced in multiple copies, are not be expressed because of the mechanisms of gene silencing.

References

Bender J (2004) DNA methylation and epigenetics. Annu Rev Plant Biol 55:41–68

Finnegan EJ, Genger RK, Peacock WJ, Dennis ES (1998) DNA-methylation in plants. Annu Rev Plant Physiol Plant Mol Biol 49:223–248

Fitter AH, Hay RKM (1987) Environmental physiology of plants. Academic Press, London, p 8

Hansen J, Beck E (2002) Kälte und Pflanze: Updating classical views. Schriften des Vereins zur Verbreitung naturwissenschaftlicher Kenntnisse 137(140):337–381

Larcher W (1987) Stress bei Pflanzen. Naturwissenschaften 74:158–167

Larcher W, Bodner M (1980) Dosisletalität-Nomogramm zur Charakterisierung der Erkältungsempfindlichkeit tropischer Pflanzen. Angew Bot 54:273–278

Levitt J (1980) Responses of plants to environmental stresses, vol I. Academic Press, London

Lichtenthaler HR, Miehé JA (1997) Fluorescence imaging as a diagnostic tool for plant stress. Trends Plant Sci 2:316–320

Ryu SB, Costa A, Xin Z, Li PH (1995) Induction of cold hardiness by salt stress involves synthesis of cold- and abscisic acid-responsive proteins in potato (*Solanum commersonii* Dun). Plant Cell Physiol 36:1245–1251

Schauer ES, Jacobsen SE, Meinke DW, Ray A (2002) DICER-LIKE1: blind men and elephants in *Arabidopsis* development. Trends Plant Sci 7:487–491

Selye H (1973) The evolution of the stress concept. Am Sci 61:693–699

Senser M, Beck F (1979) Kälteresistenz der Fichte. Ber Dtsch Bot Ges 92:243–259

Stokes T (2001) Methylation of a different kind. Trends Plant Sci 6:503

Sung D-Y, Kaplan F, Lee K-J, Guz CL (2003) Acquired tolerance to temperature extremes. Trends Plant Sci 8:179–187

Vigh L, Los DA, Horvath I, Murata N (1993) The primary signal in the biological perception of temperature: Pd-catalyzed hydrogenation of membrane lipids stimulated the expression of the desA gene in synechocystis PCC6803. Proc Natl Acad Sci USA 90:9090–9094

Wood NT (2002) Unravelling the molecular basis of viral suppression of PTGS. Trends Plant Sci 7:384–385

Xu D, Duan X, Wang B, Hong B, Ho T-HD, Wu R (1996) Expression of a late embryogenesis abundant protein gene, HVA1, from barley confers tolerance to water deficit and salt stress in transgenic rice. Plant Physiol 110:249–257

Zelazny AM, Shaish A, Pick U (1995) Plasma membrane sterols are essential for sensing osmotic changes in the halotolerant alga *Dunaliella*. Plant Physiol 109:1395–1403

1.2

Light

Light stress is not always a consequence of too much light; competition for light in the shade of a tree canopy is likewise stressful and can lead to complex morphological and physiological changes. One characteristic of shade leaves is a large leaf area but a low leaf weight. This feature increases the light-harvesting area, and also shades competing neighbouring plants. The genus *Cecropia* is particularly successful in adapting to light conditions in forming enourmous leaves. *Cecropia* trees also live in symbiosis with the ants that colonise the hollow stems. The ants chase damaging insects and provide the host with nitrogen and phosphate, nutrients which are limiting factors in tropical forests. La Carbonnera Reserve near Merida, Venezuela. Photo E.-D. Schulze

Recommended Literature

- Dekker JP, Boekema EJ (2004) Supramolecular organization of thylakoid membrane proteins in green plants. Biochim Biophys Acta (Bioenergetics) in press
- Huner NPA, Öquist G, Sarhan F (1998) Energy balance and acclimation to light and cold. Trends Plant Sci 3:224–230
- Long SR, Humphries S (1994) Photoinhibition of photosynthesis in nature. Annu Rev Plant Physiol Plant Mol Biol 45:633–662
- Lüttge U (1997) Physiological ecology of tropical plants. Springer, Berlin Heidelberg New York
- Pessarakli M (1997) Handbook of photosynthesis. Marcel Dekker, New York
- Wada M, Suetsugu N (2004) Plant organelle positioning. Curr Op Plant Biol 7:626–631

Sunlight, by far the dominating energy source for all life on earth, varies from place to place, time of day to time of day, and season to season, in intensity and also in spectral composition (UV light will be discussed in a separate chapter). As primary producers, plants need to adapt to different light environments. Too little light means a negative energy balance, i.e. gain from photosynthesis does not cover energy require-

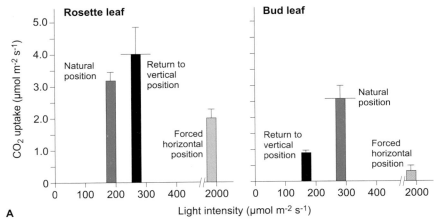

Fig. 1.2.1. Demonstration of photoinhibition in *Lobelia rhynchopetalum* of high mountains in East Africa [Sanetti Plateau (3900 m), Ethiopia]. A Net photosynthetic rate of a leaf from the rosette and from the bud in natural positions, when held horizontally (excess radiation) and after their return to the natural position. Whilst the rosette leaves are only marginally affected by the high light intensity and even have a higher rate when returned to the normal position, the photosynthetic rate of the outer leaves of the leaf bud is inhibited by more than 90% by the excess light and returning them to the normal position results in only a small recovery. B Structure of the terminal leaf rosette of *L. rhynchopetalum*. Photo E. Beck

ments. Excess light enters the chloroplast, is absorbed, but the energy is not used by assimilation, fluorescence or dissipated as heat, and so may lead to severe oxidative stress.

Adaptation to each light environment is present at all levels from the molecular to the morphological and may be permanent, e.g. formation of sun or shade leaves, or dynamic as observed in the movement of chloroplasts or leaves.

1.2.1

Visible Light

1.2.1.1
Morphological and Structural Adaptation

Lack of light is the main stressor for vegetation on the forest floor. At the edge of the forest, stems or shoots of plants of the forest floor bend so that the leaf area is able to absorb as much light as possible. This can be easily observed with bracken (*Pteridium*) that is often

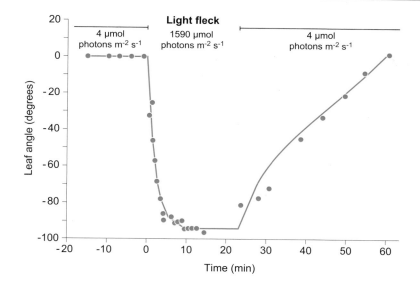

Fig. 1.2.2. Avoidance of light stress by changing the leaf angle. In the shade plant *Oxalis oregana*, the lowering of leaflets upon exposure to a light fleck, and then return to the normal day position after the light fleck moves away, are shown. (After Björkman and Powles 1981)

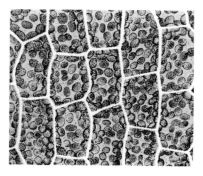
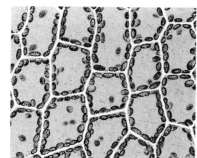

Fig. 1.2.3. Minimisation of light stress by chloroplast movement. Surface view of leaf cells of the moss *Funaria hygrometrica*. A Position of the chloroplast on the horizontal cell surface in weak light. B Position on the side walls of cells under high light. (Nultsch 1996)

found at the edges of clearings in a forest. Lianas and epiphytes are light parasites avoiding the scarcity of light within the stand by using trees as support, and thus capturing resources which are then available for the development of their own leaves and flowers in the canopy of the supporting plant.

It is different for **surplus of light**: leaves often avoid excessive radiation by adopting a parallel position to the incident light (see also Chap. 2.1, Fig. 2.1.14). The hanging leaves of *Eucalyptus* are well known, forming the "shade-less forests" in Australia. The vertical position of leaves has been shown to be an important avoidance strategy for tropical plants in high tropical mountains (Fig. 1.2.1).

The position of the leaves of many plants changes during the day, affecting the angle of the incoming light and thus the intensity of incoming radiation. Such leaves often have pulvini (particularly Leguminosae), which enable plants to change the position of their leaves or pin-

nules (see also Fig. 2.1.14). The reaction of the North American wood sorrel to a short-term light stress of strong intensity caused by a sun ray ("light fleck") is shown in Fig. 1.2.2. The sensor for the light intensity is possibly a pigment absorbing blue light.

Avoidance of light stress in shade plants can also be observed at the cellular level. In many algae and mosses, but also in some cormophytes, chloroplasts move to the lesser irradiated, vertical surfaces of the cell and turn their front side towards the incoming light. In weak light they are found in positions with their larger surface exposed to the incident light (Fig. 1.2.3).

Besides such short-term adaptations (reaction time within minutes), the development of leaves is also affected by the light environment, with the formation of sun and shade leaves (Fig. 1.2.4 and Table 1.2.1).

Sun leaves are usually small, but thick, because they possess a well-developed mesophyll, frequently with several layers of palisade cells.

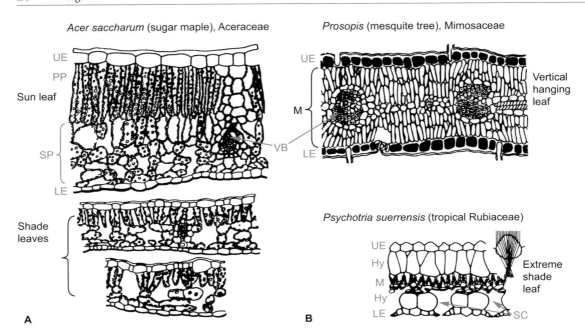

Acer saccharum (sugar maple), Aceraceae   Prosopis (mesquite tree), Mimosaceae

Psychotria suerrensis (tropical Rubiaceae)

A   B

Fig. 1.2.4. Anatomical adaptation of leaves to the light environment. A The anatomical structure of leaves from light and shade positions in the crown of sugar maple is shown. The weaker the light intensity, the less developed is the photosynthetic parenchyma. B The mesquite tree has hanging leaves of equifacial anatomical structure which only absorb diffuse solar light when the sun is at its highest. The vacuoles of the thick-walled epidermal cells are filled with protective pigments. *Psychotria*, a relative of coffee, grows in deep shade in tropical rain forests in very low light. Lens-shaped cells in the upper epidermis are very characteristic and could gather light for the weakly developed mesophyll. *UE* Upper epidermis; *LE* lower epidermis; *PP* palisade parenchyma; *SP* spongy parenchyma; *M* mesophyll; *Hy* hypodermis; *VB* vascular bundle; *SC* substomatal cavity. (After Larcher 1994)

Table 1.2.1. Comparison of characteristics of sun and shade leaves of beech (*Fagus sylvatica*) and ivy (*Hedera helix*), and the range of adaptation of various characters. (Larcher 1994)

Characteristic		*Fagus sylvatica*		*Hedera helix*	
		Sun	Shade	Sun	Shade
Leaf surface	[cm^2]	28.8	48.9		
Thickness of leaf	[μm]	185	93	409	221
Density of stomata	[dm$^2 \cdot$g^{-1} TS]			0.97	2.6
Stomatal conductance	[N$\cdot$mm^{-2}]	214	144		
Number of chloroplasts					
per surface of leaf	[N$\cdot 10^9 \cdot$dm^{-2}]			5.09	2.45
per volume of leaf	[N$\cdot 10^9 \cdot$cm^{-3}]			1.24	1.11
Chlorophyll concentration (a+b)					
Chl/leaf	[mg]	1.6	1.9		
Chl/surface	[mg$\cdot$dm^{-2}]			8.7	5.5
Chlorophyll a/b		3.9	3.9	3.3	2.8
RuBP-carboxylase activity	[μmol CO$_2 \cdot$dm^{-2} h^{-1}]			398	202
Net photosynthesis	[mg CO$_2 \cdot$dm^{-2} h^{-1}]	3.5	1.3	22.3	9.4
Light compensation point	[W$\cdot$m^{-2}]	2.5	1		
Light saturation	[W$\cdot$m^{-2}]	8.5	44		
of net photosynthesis	[μmol$\cdot$m^{-2} s^{-1}]			600	250
Dark respiration	[mg$\cdot$dm^{-2} h^{-1}]	0.5	0.16		

Leaves with predominantly vertical orientation are usually equifacial, i.e. palisade cells are found on both sides. **Shade leaves**, on the other hand, are large and tender with a rather weakly developed mesophyll and may possess additional facilities to trap light, e.g. with the epidermis or hypodermal cells acting like lenses (*Psychotria*, Fig. 1.2.4 B). Further differentiation of the epidermis, e.g. by production of dense hairs that reflect incident light, in contrast reduces the light intensity on chloroplasts (see also Chap. 2.1, Fig. 2.1.12). Protective pigments, called chymochromes, in epidermal cells are particularly effective against short-wave radiation. A typical example of that is the so-called juvenile anthocyanin, which protects not yet fully green leaves against the destructive effects of high light intensities (see Fig. 1.2.15).

1.2.1.2
Ultrastructural Adaptation

Adaptation at the subcellular level is, of course, also observed in chloroplasts (Fig. 1.2.5). Chloroplasts of sun leaves possess only small thylakoid grana and only a few individual stromal thylakoids, but plastids of shade leaves possess very large grana and many stromal thylakoids. The importance of the size of the grana and distribution of thylakoids becomes obvious when considering the molecular structure of thylakoid membranes (Box 1.2.1).

As photosystem II (PS II) has a larger antenna apparatus than photosystem I (PS I), over half of chlorophyll-a, almost all chlorophyll-b and most of the xanthophylls are associated with PS II. The largest part of a cross section of a photosystem consists of antenna. Thus a **shade chloroplast** possesses, because of the large proportion of appressed regions (contact areas of thylakoids), a very large proportion of antennae and very few reaction centres relative to the number of chloroplasts. **Chloroplasts of sun leaves**, in contrast, contain very small antennae, but many reaction centres. This can be interpreted as adaptation, as both combinations allow optimal utilisation of the incident light. Such differences are not only found in shade and sun leaves, but also within a single leaf. Chloroplasts on the upper side of the leaf, usually in better light, correspond to the sun type whilst those on the lower side correspond to the shade type. If a leaf is fixed with the upper side down, the thylakoid structures change accordingly.

The dimensions of the antenna complexes may change as well as the proportion of antennae to reaction centres. The so-called major antenna of PS II, **LHC II (light-harvesting chlorophyll protein)**, is subdivided into a smaller, inner complex, termed the **core antenna**, and into a larger, outer circle, the **peripheral or mobile antenna**. Excessive energy pressure on PS II leads to **"photoinhibition"**, a transient destruction of the D1 protein of the affected reaction centre (see Fig. 1.2.8). Permanent photoinhibition leads also to greater damage, resulting in destruction of the thylakoid. When the energy pressure on the reaction centre is high, a large phosphorylation potential is produced; protein kinases are activated which phosphorylate threonine residues in the mobile antenna proteins. The negative charges accumulated as a consequence of the added phosphate groups dissociate

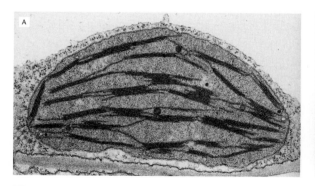
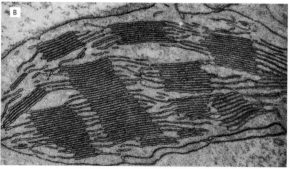

Fig. 1.2.5. Adaptation of chloroplast ultrastructure to the light environment. A Chloroplast from a sun leaf of tobacco. The small granal stacks are typical of chloroplasts from "high-light leaves" (Hall and Rao 1994). B Transverse section of a chloroplast from a shade leaf of antirrhinum (*Antirrhinum majus*) showing substantial thylakoid stacking. (Strasburger 1983)

Box 1.2.1   Ultrastructure of thylakoid membranes

Photosystem I and ATP-synthase occur predominantly in the non-appressed regions of the thylakoid and in those parts of the thylakoid system that have direct contact with the chloroplast stroma; in contrast, photosystem II is predominantly found in the appressed regions or the partition regions and also in the stacks (*blue*). The cytochrome-b$_6$/f complex is distributed in both regions of the thylakoid systems. The reason for this uneven distribution ("lateral heterogeneity") is not completely clear. As a rule, a chloroplast contains substantially more PS II than PS I. The ratio of PS II to PS I is variable not just between different plants but even within the same plant, and can also change, in the short term, in a single chloroplast (Fig. 1.2.6, from Anderson and Andersson 1988).

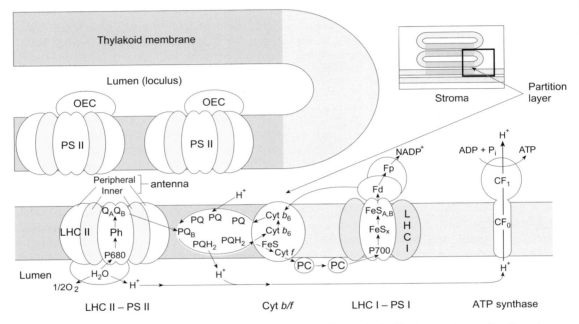

OEC Oxygen-evolving complex; *LHC II* light-harvesting chlorophyll protein II; *PQ* plastoquinone; Q_A, Q_B quinones bound to PS II; *Ph* pheophytin; P_{680}, P_{700} chlorophyll dimers of the reaction centres of PS II and PS I; *FeS* Rieske protein; *FeSx*, *FeS$_{A,B}$*: iron-sulfur proteins in PS I; *Fd* ferredoxin; *Fp* flavoprotein; CF_o integral membrane proton channel of ATP-synthase; CF_1 coupling factor of ATP-synthase.

the phosphorylated external antennae from PS II. This, in turn, reduces their light-absorbing cross section (Fig. 1.2.6). The accumulation of negative charges is also thought to cause a "loosening" of the appressed regions, enabling the lateral movement of protein complexes. There are indications that mobile antennae partially associate with PS I and thus guarantee a more uniform excitation of PS II and PS I and avoid over-reduction of PS I. With decreasing light intensity, protein phosphatases are thought to cause dephosphorylation of LHC II and, subsequently, the mobile antennae return to PS II. This shift of mobile antennae triggered by the over-excitation of PS II, resulting in a higher efficiency of the total electron transport, was described in the early phases of photosynthetic research as state transitions or state I ⇒ state II transition without, however, the molecular mechanisms being understood.

1.2.1.3
Physiological Adaptation

Besides the morphological and structural adaptations of plants to the dominant light environment, physiological-biochemical mechanisms of

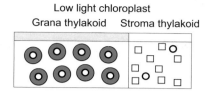

Fig. 1.2.6. Dynamics of the photosynthetic membranes in response to light climate and temperature. (After Anderson and Andersson 1988)

Long-term acclimation

High light chloroplast
Grana thylakoid   Stroma thylakoid

Low light chloroplast
Grana thylakoid   Stroma thylakoid

Short-term regulation

Excess light in PS II
Dissociation of peripheral
LHC II from PS II

Heat shock (T > 30°C)
Separation of LHC II and PS II;
migration of PS II

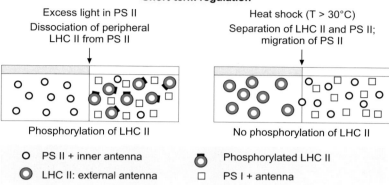

Phosphorylation of LHC II

No phosphorylation of LHC II

○ PS II + inner antenna   ◐ Phosphorylated LHC II

◉ LHC II: external antenna   □ PS I + antenna

adaptation are known. These mechanisms are able to react even faster than the structural adaptations and thus always take place, regardless of whether structural or morphological changes occur or not.

Starting from the photosynthetic reductive pentose phosphate cycle (Calvin cycle), 2 mol NADPH is required for the assimilation of 1 mol CO_2, corresponding to 4 mol electron and 8 mol light quanta. The cycle also consumes 3 mol ATP. As four electrons produce about 2.7 molecules of ATP, the real requirements for photons or quanta are a little higher. Lowest measured values are 9.4 quanta per mol assimilated CO_2. Light must be the limiting factor to achieve such measured values, i.e. measurements must be in the linear range of the light response curve (see Fig. 1.1.1).

If it is CO_2 supply or activities of the photosynthetic enzymes (e.g. because of cold) rather than light intensity that limit CO_2 assimilation, then more light energy is absorbed than is required. However, what happens to the excess light energy? This energy must be safely dissipated. The plant has several ways of doing this:

- The **glycolate pathway** associated with photorespiration (Box 1.2.2). If the CO_2 supply limits photosynthesis, photorespiration is able to keep the Calvin cycle running by making phosphoglycerate available and thus maintain-

ing a certain consumption of reducing and energy equivalents.

- The **reduction of nitrite and sulphate** also consumes electrons and ATP. However, it plays a relatively minor role in photosynthetic electron flow.

- **Oxygen** may also be **reduced photosynthetically** (see Chap. 1.3.5 concerning reactive oxygen species). This is called the Mehler reaction. Chloroplasts require NADPH to detoxify the reduced oxygen.

If sufficient electrons are able to flow from water to one of the acceptors, they do not accumulate in one of the components of the electron transport chain. If the rate of consumption falls below the rate of production of reducing power and energy equivalents, other mechanisms of energy dissipation (as yet unexplained) are activated.

- **Non-photochemical energy quenching (NPQ)** and **photoinhibition**.
Plotting the rate of photosynthesis in relation to increasing light, the initial slope of the curve is linear before the rate becomes constant as photosynthesis is saturated (Fig. 1.2.7). The difference between extrapolation of the initial straight line and the rates measured at higher light intensities shows the incident light energy which cannot be used photosynthetically. The higher this value, the more "closed" the reaction centres, i.e. they

Box 1.2.2   **Schematic of the photosynthetic reactions determining gas exchange in a leaf**

Even when the stomata are closed, CO_2 is produced via photorespiration from the oxidative photosynthetic carbon cycle, and the CO_2 is re-assimilated by the reductive photosynthetic carbon cycle. Consequently, under these conditions, at least part of the absorbed light energy is used. **A** Formal scheme, **B** schematic of gas exchange (after Tolbert 1994).

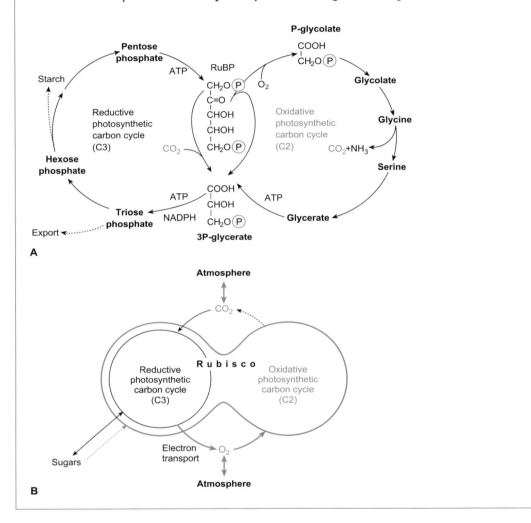

are unable to reoxidise by passing on the excited electrons because of the lack of acceptors: the excited reaction centres cannot become photochemically active. A small proportion of the excitation energy will be dissipated as fluorescence with an emission maximum at 685 nm (see Box 1.2.3, Fig. 1). At room temperature this fluorescence is derived exclusively from PS II; excited PS I fluoresces only at −70 °C or at even lower temperatures. Even though the proportion of fluorescent light emitted from the excited PS II is very low, it nevertheless can provide much information about the status of the photosynthetic electron transport chain and the CO_2 assimilation (Schreiber et al. 1994). The most important parameters measured in this way are the dynamics and the proportion of the absorbed light energy used and the proportion of accumulated electrons (over-excitation) dissipated as heat (thermal dissipation; non-photochemical fluorescence quenching: Box 1.2.3). Change

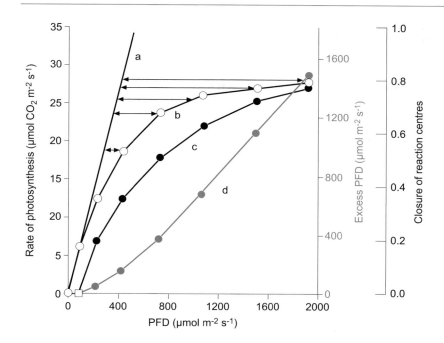

Fig. 1.2.7. Interpretation of a light response curve. *Curve a* Linear increase of the photosynthetic rate in weak light. *Curve b* Photosynthetic rate. *Curve c* Calculated closure of reaction centres of PS II with excess light. *Curve d* Excess light energy (corresponds to the *horizontal arrows* between *a* and *b*). PFD Photon flux density. (After Schäfer and Björkman 1989)

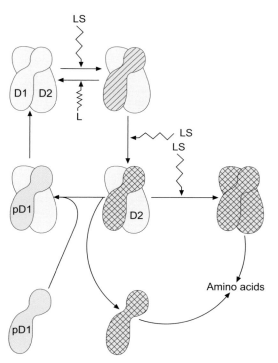

Fig. 1.2.8. Model of the sequence of reactions during damage and repair of the reaction centres of photosystem II. Light stress (*LS*) leads to transient or irreversible damage to the D1 protein (*hatched* or *cross-hatched*, respectively). Irreversible damage triggers cleavage and the subsequent degradation of the D1 protein (presumably to amino acids). A precursor (*pD1*) forms a new reaction centre with the persistent D2 protein which associates again with the antenna protein. In particularly high light stress the D2 protein is also attacked (*cross-hatched*). In the plant cell, the D1 protein has a high turnover rate; the D1 protein is coded in the chloroplast genome. *L* Light. (Schäfer and Schmid 1993)

in these proportions, the so-called rate constants, in favour of thermal energy dissipation is an efficient short-term de-energising reaction which operates during over-excitation of PS II.

Upon long-term exposure to high light, or during particularly strong light stress and during irradiation with UV-B light, this mechanism is not sufficient protection, however. In this case, the core protein, D1, of the PS II reaction centre is degraded, probably with the help of active oxygen species (Fig. 1.2.8) at a specific site and thus the photosystem is deactivated. This process is called **photoinhibition** (of photosynthesis) and is being investigated in many laboratories. It is assumed that

Box 1.2.3   Chlorophyll a fluorescence as an indicator of excitation and redox states

On illumination the chlorophyll molecule can be excited to both states, singlet 2 (absorption of blue light) and singlet 1 (absorption of red light) (Fig. 1). Singlet 2 is too short-lived to induce a photochemical reaction. The singlet 2 state can change to singlet 1 or to the ground state by dissipating energy as heat. Singlet 1 is produced by absorption of a quantum of red light and is sufficiently long-lived to donate an electron to an acceptor and thereby to initiate a photochemical process. Emission of fluorescence is also related to singlet 1. By losing energy as heat, singlet 1 transfers to the ground state but may also, to a lesser extent, convert to the triplet state. Production of the triplet state is dangerous because this excited chlorophyll molecule can

react with the normal triplet oxygen, producing singlet oxygen which is a particularly strong oxidising molecule.

If a pre-darkened leaf is illuminated, the absorbed light energy can be used in three ways: by emission of heat (which is the major part), by "photochemistry" and by emission of fluorescence photons. Photochemistry and fluorescence change in opposite ways and in particular proportions, i.e. the distribution (the so-called rate constants) of energy flux to heat and [photochemistry + fluorescence] is constant within the leaf. Maximum fluorescence results when there are no photochemical processes, i.e. when there is no acceptor for the excited electrons in PS II.

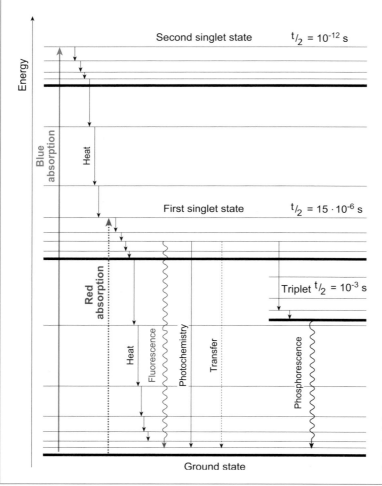

Fig. 1. Different excited states of chlorophyll a caused by light absorption and energy conversion into heat, fluorescence, photochemical work, state 1–state 2 transfer and phosphorescence. (After Heldt 1999)

Box 1.2.3   (continued)

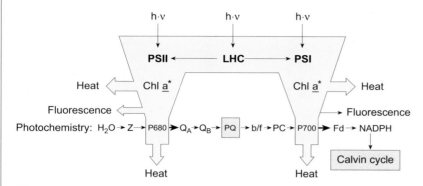

Fig. 2. Use and dissipation of light energy in the photosynthetic apparatus. Light energy absorbed by the photosynthetic apparatus is mainly lost as heat. A small proportion (<10%) is emitted as fluorescence. A variable proportion can be used for photochemical work. With strong illumination the external antenna of PS II can dissociate and, at least in part, associate with PS I. Thereby PS II absorbs less and PS I more light energy. This type of balancing is called "state 1–state 2 transition". The rate constants (thickness of the *arrows*) can be changed by over-energetisation. (After Schreiber et al. 1994)

The photosystem is then closed. The more photosystems that are "open", the more oxidised acceptor is available, the smaller is the fluorescence. From the rate constants of fluorescence, i.e. its intensity, it is possible to determine the rate (efficiency) of the actual photosynthetic process. It is interesting that with a long period of excitation during which electrons are not transferred completely to $NADP^+$ and further to CO_2 or another reducible substrate, a strong decrease in the maximum fluorescence occurs. This reduction of fluorescence with closed reaction centres shows the redistribution of the rate constants in favour of heat emission (thermal dissipation). This is called "non-photochemical quenching" (Figs. 2 and 3).

A number of parameters can be derived from the analysis of chlorophyll fluorescence (Fig. 3). The maximum fluorescence upon illumination of a pre-darkened leaf: F_m. The reduced maximum fluorescence after a saturating light flash: F_m'. The minimal fluorescence of the antenna pigments of a pre-darkened leaf in which photosynthesis does not occur: F_0; in an illuminated leaf, this is generally slightly reduced; it is then called F_0'. The difference between F_m and F_0 is the theoretical maximal useful energy available for photochemistry: $F_v = F_m - F_0$. The actual fluorescence F, which is between F_0' and F_m', shows the portion of energy which is not used for photochemistry, although in theory this could be used. The maximum quantum efficiency of PS II (Φ_{II}) is shown through the relation of F_v and F_m $\Phi_{II} = F_v/F_m$. The effective quantum efficiency is $\Phi' = (F_m' - F)/F_m'$. The fluorescence quenching by photochemistry ("non-photochemical quenching"): $q_p = 1 - (F_m' - F_0')/F_v$ is a measure of increased thermal dissipation.

Box 1.2.3   (continued)

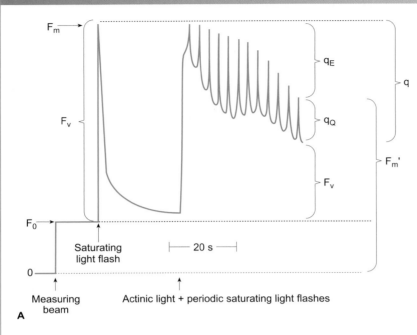

F$_0$: Fluorescence from the antenna

F$_m$: maximum fluorescence of a predarkened leaf

F$_m$': maximum fluorescence of an illuminated leaf (saturating light flash)

F$_v$: variable fluorescence during illumination with actinic light

q$_Q$: (new q$_p$) photochemical quenching

q$_E$: (new q$_{NP}$ or q$_N$) non-photochemical quenching at great ΔpH (increase in the rate constant for thermal dissipation)

q: total quenching under continuous light

A

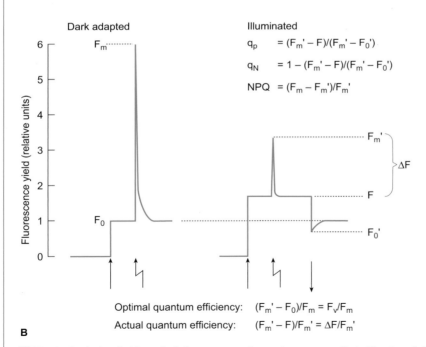

Dark adapted

Illuminated

$$q_p = (F_m' - F)/(F_m' - F_0')$$

$$q_N = 1 - (F_m' - F)/(F_m' - F_0')$$

$$NPQ = (F_m - F_m')/F_m'$$

Optimal quantum efficiency: $(F_m' - F_0)/F_m = F_v/F_m$

Actual quantum efficiency: $(F_m' - F)/F_m' = \Delta F/F_m'$

B

Fig. 3. Analysis of chlorophyll fluorescence from photosystem II. A Kinetics of fluorescence and explanation of the parameters (after Walker 1992). B Nomenclature used for characteristic fluorescence parameters, definition of quenching coefficients and calculation of the quantum efficiency of photosystem II. (After Schreiber et al. 1994)

De-epoxidase   **Epoxidase**

Thylakoid lumen   Stroma
pH 5.0   pH 7.5-8.0

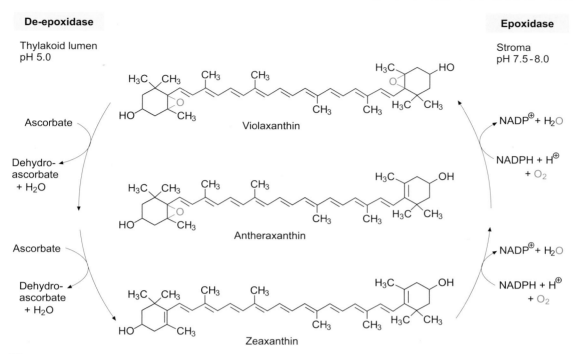

Ascorbate

Dehydro-
ascorbate
+ H₂O

Ascorbate

Dehydro-
ascorbate
+ H₂O

NADP⊕+ H₂O

NADPH + H⊕
+ O₂

NADP⊕+ H₂O

NADPH + H⊕
+ O₂

Fig. 1.2.9. The xanthophyll cycle in chloroplasts. In high light violaxanthin is converted into zeaxanthin by the de-epoxidase; in darkness re-oxidation is catalysed by the epoxidase. (Heldt 1999)

defence against light stress developed during evolution in the form of the extremely easily degradable D1 protein. A special metabolic cycle for the replacement of the damaged D1 protein via an undamaged D1 precursor, followed by processing of the preprotein, is associated with this repair cycle (Fig. 1.2.8). Photoinhibition is reversible, as the D1 protein has a very fast turnover (it is exchanged after 10^6–10^7 excitation cycles). **Photodestruction** occurs if the capacity for replacement of D1 is overstretched, leading to loss of photosynthetic capacity.

Photoinhibition of PSI has also been described (Sononike 1996a, Jiao et al. 2004). It is particularly strong for algae and higher plants during cold. The primary damage probably occurs at the acceptor side of PS I, upon which the B protein (which corresponds to the D1 of PS II) is degraded. This photoinhibition is, surprisingly, also observed during weak light and is also attributed to reactive oxygen species (Sonoike 1996b). It is thought that PS I is more robust, with photoinhibition or damage only occurring under extreme conditions.

- **Dissipation of excitation energy in the xanthophyll cycle.** Non-photochemical energy quenching requires a large proton gradient across the thylakoid membranes and thus an acid pH in the lumen of thylakoids. An acid environment of the thylakoid membrane activates an enzyme in the membrane, **violaxanthin de-epoxidase** (maximum activity at pH 5, Fig. 1.2.9).

In dark or low light the pH value of the lumen increases and another enzyme, **zeaxanthin-epoxidase**, is activated. Both reactions result in a light-dependent reaction cycle involving the xanthophylls violaxanthin, antheraxanthin (as an intermediary compound) and zeaxanthin (Fig. 1.2.9).

These xanthophylls are in the antenna complexes of PS II and probably also in PS I. Although the physiological importance of the xanthophyll cycle may be different in various species, there is no doubt that this cycle plays an important role in quenching excess photosynthetic energy.

- In the short term, in excess light, violaxanthin is converted into zeaxanthin, which de-energises the triplet excitation state of the chlorophyll which can form easily from excess energy. Zeaxanthin is probably able to react also with the first singlet state of chlorophyll and take up its energy. However, this has not yet been proven conclusively. Excitation energy

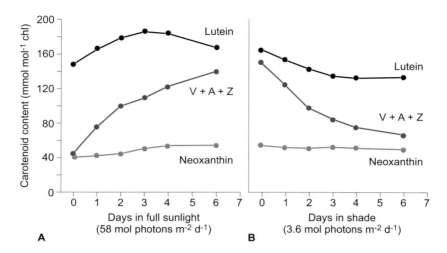

Fig. 1.2.10. Dynamic changes in the xanthophyll pools of young leaves of cotton in strong and weak light. The *left-hand diagram* shows the effects of transferring plants from shade into full sun light; the *right-hand diagram* the transfer from sunlight into shade. Note that the pools of lutin and also neoxanthin change relatively little in comparison with the total pool of violaxanthin, antheraxanthin and zeaxanthin. (Björkman and Demming-Adams 1994)

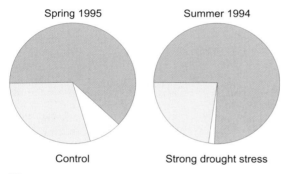

Fig. 1.2.11. Use of absorbed light energy in leaves of the Pacific madrone (*Arbutus menziesii*) in full sunlight. *Blue* Dissipation as heat; *white* photosynthetic CO_2 assimilation; *light blue* all additional uses including photorespiration and the Mehler reaction. (After Osmond et al. 1997)

transferred to zeaxanthin is released as heat; it is still an open question whether the formation of zeaxanthin from violaxanthin is the cause of the changes in membrane leading to NPQ, or whether the changes run in parallel. The physiological importance of the xanthophyll cycle is also shown in the selective and reversible accumulation of the three xanthophylls involved in the photosynthetic membranes during longer exposure to excess light (Fig. 1.2.10).

If one considers all physiological reactions for adaptation to, and avoidance of, excess light, and all the possibilities for repair in PS II, it is not surprising that many reactions and mechanisms are more or less attuned to each other. However, not all plants have all these possibilities available to the same extent; there are plants in which, for example, the xanthophyll cycle

does not play an important role because these pigments only occur in very small concentrations and do not accumulate even after longer stress. That the removal of excessive energy can become a problem is shown by the various paths for the de-activation of absorbed light energy in the chloroplast (Fig. 1.2.11).

During drought stress (closed stomata and therefore secondary light stress through lack of CO_2), only a very small proportion of the light energy is used for photosynthesis and almost all available energy must be disposed of safely. It is obvious that one single mechanism is not sufficient for this.

Another argument for the use of many mechanisms for adaptation is the large variation in light intensities to which plants are subjected; e.g. with changing cloud cover or with light flecks on forest floors, light intensity can vary by a factor of 10^3 within seconds and plants must be able to cope with this stress (see Fig. 1.2.2 and Chap. 2.4, Fig. 2.4.9).

Summary

1. Light is the indispensable precondition for all plant life. Plants adapt to light intensities at all levels of organisation, from the molecular to the morphological, as light environments vary on earth not only in regions, but also in time. Continuously changing light conditions, or extremely low or high light intensities, together with other stressors, for example, lack of water, heat or cold, are particularly challenging to plants. Plants in those environ-

ments display very dynamic, adaptive behaviour.

2. The stressor "weak light" means lack of energy. Plants have adapted to this situation by developing different life forms (lianas, epiphytes as light parasites) and by adjusting the positions of their leaves (positive phototrophic reaction). A weakly developed mesophyll, but very large stacks of thylakoids in chloroplasts, are features of the anatomical and ultrastructural design of shade leaves. Shade leaves are characterised at the molecular level by a relatively low density of PS II reaction centres, but a correspondingly large area of antenna complexes.

3. Stress through high light intensity damages plants acutely because of over-excitation and formation of chemical radicals. These radicals easily react with oxygen to form reactive oxygen species (ROS). ROS destroy membranes, including proteins and other components (e.g. chlorophyll). Plants possess detoxification systems for ROS (see Chap. 1.3.5.3).

4. Because of the very substantial damage arising from over-excitation, there are many different mechanisms for avoidance and adaptation. Adaptation at the morphological level is explained in Chapter 2 "Autoecology". Many plants deal with high light energy by reactions which alter the position of the leaf. These positions may be permanent or dynamic. Sun leaves have a highly developed mesophyll, often with several layers of palisade cells. Chloroplasts are able to position themselves on the sides of the cell according to the light intensity, moving from the position with the stronger to the weaker radiation, and vice versa. The thylakoid system of sun leaves is not well developed, but consists of many photosynthetic reaction centres and a smaller antenna area (particularly the LHC II is more weakly developed). Dissociation of peripheral antenna from PS II, and a partial association with PS I, is often observed, resulting in a better balanced electron flow.

5. At the biochemical level strong light produces a change in the rate constant of energy flow in favour of heat (non-photochemical quenching). If this mechanism does not suffice, the absorbed light energy is disposed of via zeaxanthin, which is produced in the xanthophyll cycle from violaxanthin. At the same time, particularly because of closed stomata in heat or drought, light energy is dissipated with the help of photorespiration. This process produces CO_2 which is then photosynthetically assimilated.

6. If energetisation still exceeds the capacity of these quenching systems, D1, one of the core proteins of PS II, is degraded. The resulting inhibition of photosynthesis is reversible as long as the capacity of the specific repair system, the "D1 cycle", is sufficient. This reversible inhibition is called photoinhibition. If strain on the D1 cycle is persistent, "photodestruction" occurs with strong bleaching of the chloroplast.

7. Light energy can also be absorbed by pigments in the epidermis, as well as by the photosynthetic apparatus. Light can be reflected by the surface of the epidermis. A hairy tomentum can increase the proportion of reflected light.

1.2.2

UV Radiation

Recommended Literature

- Gyula P, Schäfer E, Nagy F (2003) Light perception and signalling in higher plants. Curr Opinion Plant Biol 6:446–452
- Jansen MAK, Gaba V, Greenberg BM (1998) Higher plants and UV-B radiation: balancing damage, repair and acclimation. Trends Plant Sci 3:131–135
- Short FT, Neckles HA (1999) The effects of global climate change on seagrasses. Aquatic Botany 63:169–196
- Stratmann J (2003) Ultraviolet-B radiation co-opts defense signaling pathways. Trends Plant Sci 8:526–533

Ultraviolet radiation coming from the sun is divided into three ranges: The long wave **UV-A** (315–400 nm), the biologically effective **UV-B** (280–315 nm) and the even shorter wavelength and therefore particularly energy-rich **UV-C** (100–280 nm). The atmospheric ozone layer absorbs very little UV-A, a considerable amount of UV-B and all the UV-C. Therefore, the population of the world is currently very concerned about the **ozone hole**, i.e. the decrease in stratospheric ozone concentration particularly in the polar and subpolar regions (Fig. 1.2.12).

It should, however, be realised that, because of the sun's position above the equator, solar radiation crosses the atmosphere in regions of high geographical latitude at an angle and thus

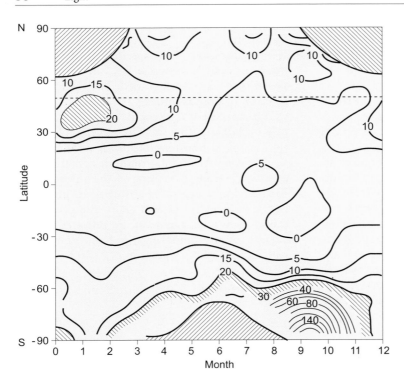

Fig. 1.2.12. UV-B radiation and the "ozone hole". The trends in daily UV dose (in DNA destruction units) in % for a 10-year period in different geographical latitudes and throughout the year are shown. (Zellner 1996)

encounters a considerably "thicker" ozone layer than at the equator, where it takes the shortest path through the atmosphere. The UV radiation is thus relatively high in the tropics and relatively low in polar regions. The higher intensity of UV radiation with increasing elevation above sea level is also known. This is caused by an attenuation of the tropospheric ozone layer as well as by a decrease in the intensity of haze.

UV radiation may damage cells and so is dangerous to organisms (Table 1.2.2); its intensity is therefore often not given as the flux of quanta, but in units expressing the damaging effects, e.g. as **DNA thymine dimerisation** or erythema formation (reddening of skin, sunburn). There is consensus that plants may suffer UV damage; thus the debate is how much UV radiation is tolerated by plants, or the extent to which damage can be repaired. Scientists vary considerably in their opinions. The phytoplankton of cooler seas appears to be particularly susceptible and significant reduction in their mass has been repeatedly shown, despite the shallow depth to which UV light penetrates into a body of water (Fig. 1.2.13). The effect of increased UV-B radiation on the growth and yield of food plants has been extensively studied. Significant differences in sensitivity of various cultivars, e.g. of soya bean or maize, have been shown. Decreased yields

Table 1.2.2. Physiological effects of increased UV-B radiation

DNA damage	Dimerisation of thymine; breakage of strands
Biomembranes	Lipid peroxidation
Photosynthetic apparatus	Inactivation of PS II; acceleration of the turnover of D1 (and D2?); damage to thylakoid membranes; bleaching of pigments; decrease in the activity of photosynthetic enzymes (particularly Rubisco); inactivation of photosynthetic genes
Phytohormones UV avoidance:	Photooxidation of auxin
Secondary metabolism	Activation of the UV-B/blue light receptors; activation of expression of the key genes of phenylpropane metabolism and accumulation of flavonoids; accumulation of alkaloids, waxes and polyamines
Radical scavengers	Increased capacity of the antioxidative system (ascorbate peroxidase, SOD, glutathione reductase, and others)

have been statistically established occasionally, but the reductions were relatively small (usually < 10%). For sensitive species, the onset of flowering was delayed. However, by harvest, this delay was usually balanced out. For a long-day plant (*Hyoscyamus niger*, henbane), UV even stopped the induction of flowering.

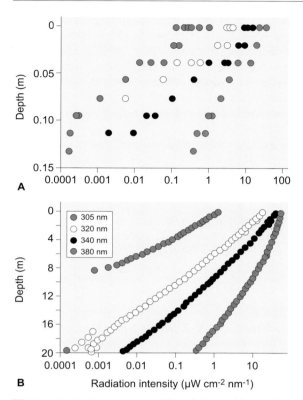

Fig. 1.2.13. Decrease in UV radiation with depth of water. A In the humin-rich Lake Neusiedler (Austria) and B in the northern Adriatic. Both measurements were made on a cloud-free August day. The intensity of UV radiation at a depth of 5 cm in Lake Neusiedler corresponds approximately to a depth of 5 m in the Adriatic. (Herndl 1996)

1.2.2.1
UV-B Damage and Its Repair

Recommended Literature

- McCullough AK, Dodson ML, Lloyd RS (1999) Initiation of base excision repair: glycosylase mechanisms and structures. Annu Rev Biochem 68:255–285

Morphological-anatomical symptoms of a UV-B stress that is still tolerated are swollen but shorter internodes, smaller leaves with the edges usually rolled in at the top surface, and increased growth of lateral buds (Ballaré et al. 1996). Leaves tend to be succulent, have a particularly thick, usually pigmented epidermis and low density of stomata. Tolerated UV stress often results in accumulation of vitamin C and soluble sugars in fruits, thus increasing the quality of foods.

The damage caused to organisms by UV radiation is undisputed, but there is considerable discussion about if – and to what extent – damage is caused by this radiation in the open field (Searles et al. 2001). Contradictory results could have methodological causes, e.g. the relative proportions of UV-B and PAR or the use of plant species differing in sensitivity. The main reason for different scientific statements is the type and dosage of UV radiation. Often, because of the experimental limitations, the increased UV radiation is applied as a pulse, with unnaturally high intensity, to compensate for the short duration of exposition. The same stressful radiation may be applied using long-term, slightly increased amounts of radiation, but completely different physiological reactions (strain) result. With the UV stress applied in short pulses, the damage, and its possible repair, are the dominant effects, whilst continuous but low-intensity stress leads to hardening and avoidance (e.g. by protective pigments). Table 1.2.2 shows the various physiological reactions of plants to UV-B stress. The effects of UV-B on DNA have been particularly well studied, namely the dimerisation of thymine, where cyclobutyl pyrimidine dimers or 4,6-thymine dimers are formed.

Higher doses of UV lead to breakage of single or double strands of DNA and finally to loss of DNA. Naked DNA of mitochondria and probably also of the chloroplasts is particularly sensitive. UV radiation of yeast cells caused a 10% loss of nuclear DNA, but at the same time a 50–60% loss of mitochondrial DNA.

There are several mechanisms to repair such damage, of which two are mentioned here: photolyase, and base excision and recombination reactions. DNA of mitochondria can also be repaired if the damage is not too severe. Repair usually takes only a few hours. Strong UV stress, however, leads directly to irreparable chromosome breakage and deletions; this is the basis for sterilisation of rooms and instruments with intense UV light.

In addition to the damage to DNA, photooxidation of UV-absorbing pigments is known: Yellowing and complete bleaching of leaves of house plants after abrupt transfer to the open air are frequent phenomena. Here, the protective effect of photosynthetic pigments which absorb short-wave radiation like proteins can be seen. Photodestruction of thylakoid pigments leads to a significant reduction of the Rubisco content.

1.2.2.2
UV Detection

In plants and animals UV radiation triggers protective reactions which means that these organisms must possess photoreceptor systems for detecting this radiation. It is known that plants have a sensor for UV-B and two further sensors (cryptochrome or phototropin 1 and 2) for UV-A/blue light, which cooperate with the phytochrome system, i.e. they determine the sensitivity of the plant for visible and UV light (Ballaré 1999; Fig. 1.2.14).

Signal transduction chains from the UV-A/blue light and UV-B receptors possibly react only with the signal from phytochrome A, i.e. from that phytochrome form which accumulates in seeds and controls germination, for example. In addition to the morphogenetic effects mentioned above, the effects of UV radiation on me-

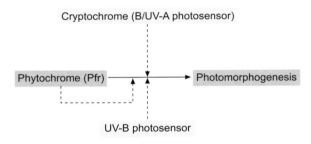

Fig. 1.2.14. Model of the interaction between phytochrome and the blue/UV-light receptor. Activation of the blue/UV-light sensor regulates the sensitivity of the photoresponse to activate phytochrome (Pfr). Pfr itself can autocatalytically increase the efficiency of the phytochrome system. (Mohr 1996, see also Elliott et al. 2004)

tabolism, particularly on **secondary metabolism**, have also been studied in detail. Products of **phenylpropane metabolism** exhibit strong absorbance of short-wave irradiation and are thus able to function as effective UV filters. Also, the anthocyanins (Fig. 1.2.15), mentioned above, are protective pigments because they absorb visible as well as UV light.

The key enzyme of the phenylpropane metabolism (Box 1.2.4, Fig. 2) is chalcone synthase (CHS), whose formation is strongly induced by UV-B as well as UV-A/blue light. Both wavebands of light achieve their effects via the Ca^{2+}-dependent signal transduction pathways. Upon UV stress, calcium is released from cellular stores. However, the transduction pathways differ in their degrees of dependence on calcium.

1.2.2.3
Avoidance of UV-B Stress and Development of UV-B Resistance

Research with pine needles and beech leaves has shown that, in addition to the various flavonoids formed constitutively and independently of UV, there are other related compounds in the epidermis. For example, after UV-B radiation, the concentration of 3″, 6″-DCA and 3″,6″-DCI (= 3″,6″-di-*para*-coumaroylastragalin and 3″,6″-di-*para*-coumaroylquercetin) for pines, as well as 2″,2″-di-*para*-coumaroylkaempferol-3*a*-D-arabinoside for beech had risen five-fold (Table 1.2.3; Figs. 1.2.16 and 1.2.17).

Compounds which can be induced by UV are exclusively located in the epidermis, while those

Fig. 1.2.15. Anthocyanins in the young leaves of the tropical Sapotacee *Inhambanella henriquesii* in the coastal forests of Kenya. The anthocyanin is contained in the vacuoles of the leaf epidermis and protects the leaves, which are not yet fully green, from radiation damage. The close-up (*right*) clearly shows the mixture of colours between the red anthocyanins and the chlorophyll. (Photo E. Beck)

Box 1.2.4   Plant phenols

A large number of the phenolic compounds formed by plants are synthesised by the so-called shikimate pathway named after the characteristic intermediate shikimic acid. The second aromatic ring of the C_{15}-derived phenylpropane derivatives (flavonoids) results from the condensation of three acetyl residues from malonyl-CoA (Fig. 1).

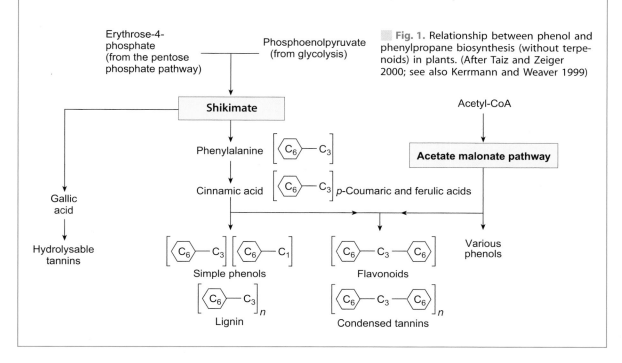

Fig. 1. Relationship between phenol and phenylpropane biosynthesis (without terpenoids) in plants. (After Taiz and Zeiger 2000; see also Kerrmann and Weaver 1999)

Table 1.2.3. Calculated concentrations and shielding effects of UV-B-absorbing pigments in the epidermis of needles of pine seedlings. The volume of the epidermis (ca. 104 µl/g fresh weight) was calculated from the needle surface und the mean thickness of the epidermis. The absorption at 300 nm, and the corresponding value of transmission, were calculated using the Lambert-Beer law. (After Schnitzler et al. 1996)

	Control needles			UV-irradiated needles		
	Concentration (mM)	Total absorption at 300 nm (%)	Transmission at 300 nm (%)	Concentration (mM)	Total absorption at 300 nm (%)	Transmission at 300 nm (%)
Cell wall-bound pigments						
p-Coumaric acid	13.4	7.9	30.8	13.0	6.1	31.8
Ferulic acid	1.6	1.2	83.9	1.9	1.1	81.5
Astragalin	16.7	10.7	20.1	19.1	9.8	15.9
Lignin	6.5	1.2	83.6	6.5	0.9	83.5
Sum	–	21.0	4.3	–	17.9	3.45
Soluble pigments (vacuole)						
Diacylated flavonoids	35.4	79.0	0.0007	46.1	82.1	0.00002
All pigments	–	100.0	0.00003	–	100.0	0.0000009

that are formed constitutively are distributed throughout the mesophyll. The non-conjugated (p-coumaric acid) phenylpropanes are localised in the epidermal cell wall, while the conjugates are mainly sequestered into the vacuoles of these cells (Fig. 1.2.17). The anthocyanin accumulation induced during leaf flushing by tropical trees (see Fig. 1.2.15) takes place in the vacuoles of the epidermal cells.

Plant phenols (continued)

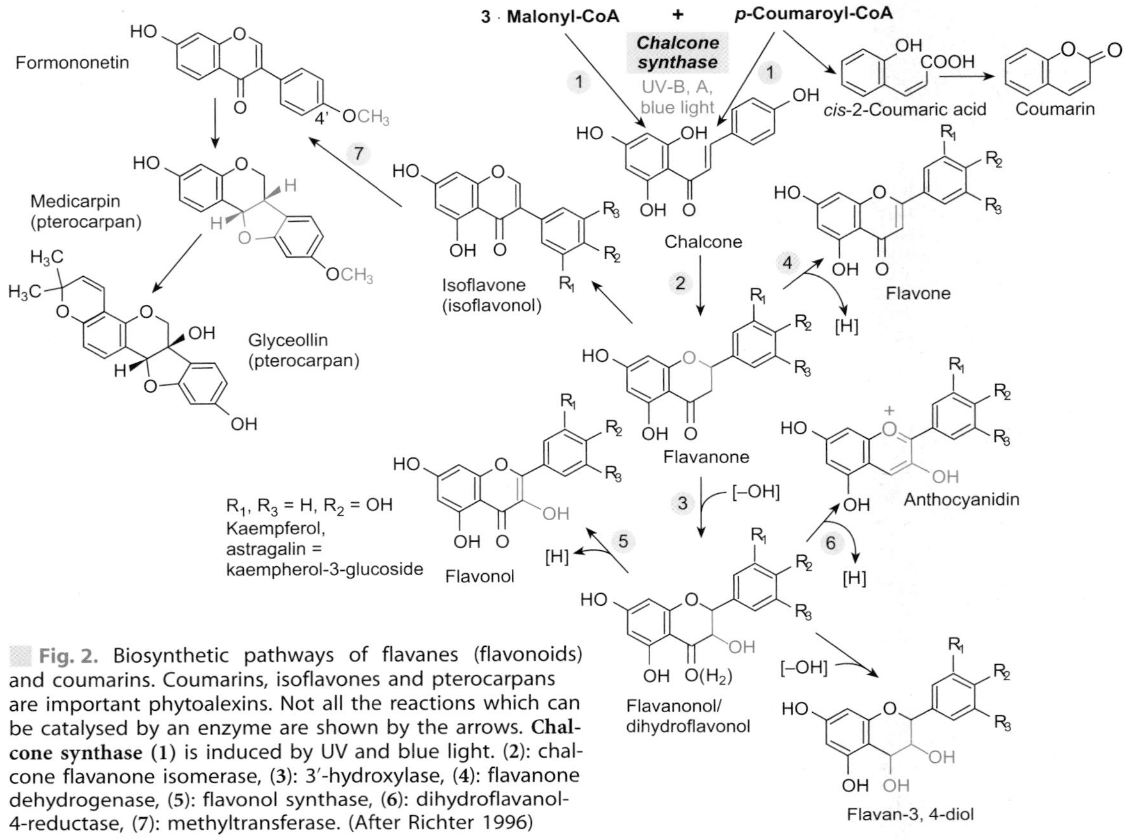

Fig. 2. Biosynthetic pathways of flavanes (flavonoids) and coumarins. Coumarins, isoflavones and pterocarpans are important phytoalexins. Not all the reactions which can be catalysed by an enzyme are shown by the arrows. **Chalcone synthase (1)** is induced by UV and blue light. (2): chalcone flavanone isomerase, (3): 3'-hydroxylase, (4): flavanone dehydrogenase, (5): flavonol synthase, (6): dihydroflavanol-4-reductase, (7): methyltransferase. (After Richter 1996)

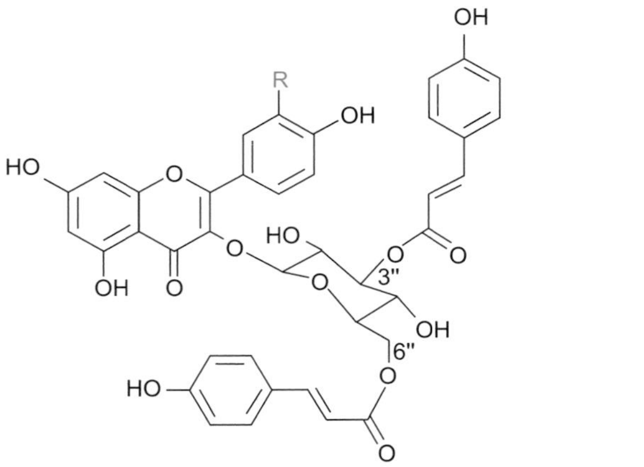

3",6"-di-p-cumaroylastragalin (DCA; R=H) and 3",6"-di-p-cumaroylisoquercitrin (DCI; R=OH)

Fig. 1.2.16. 3'',6''-Di-p-coumaroylastragalin (R=H) and 3'',6''-di-p-coumaroylisoquercitrin (R=OH) as examples of diacylated flavonoids (see Table 1.2.3)

However, the particularly effective UV absorbers *p*-coumaric acid and astragalin are deposited in the cell wall. It is estimated that the outer cell walls of the epidermis allow about 4% of the UV-B to pass through. Diacylated flavonoids, dissolved in the cell, are able to filter out the residual UV-B radiation because of their greater absorbing capacity.

It is likely that plants with low or even no capability of synthesising such protective pigments are UV-sensitive. Other types of protective pigments, belonging to the class of mycosporines, are found in phytoplankton and other marine algae; they are not degraded in the nutritional chain and provide organisms of the next trophic level with a certain degree of UV protection.

In addition to flavanoid metabolism, other enzymes producing or activating radical acceptors are formed: Glutathione reductase, ascorbate- and glutathione-peroxidase.

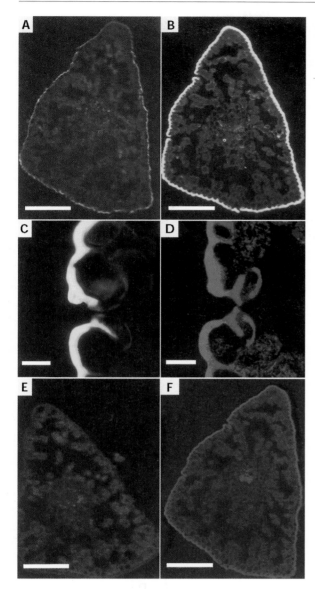

Fig. 1.2.17. Histochemical evidence for UV-absorbing substances in the epidermis of pine needles. A–C Fluorescence (excited by light of 450–490 nm wavelength, determined at $\lambda > 520$ nm); A control, B and C after treatment with a reagent which intensifies flavonoid fluorescence. D–F Observation with a confocal laser microscope (which shows the cells and their contents more clearly). E control, D and F after staining as above. A, B, E, F Transverse section of a needle, C, D stomata. (After Schnitzler et al. 1996)

Summary

1. The ultraviolet spectrum is divided according to the energy content of the radiation (wavelength); UV-C (100–280 nm), UV-B (260–315 nm) and UV-A (315–400 nm). The shorter the wavelength of the UV radiation, the stronger is its destructive effect, but the more it is absorbed by atmospheric ozone. UV-C is completely absorbed when passing through the atmosphere; UV-A does not damage most organisms. The biologically effective UV light is UV-B.

2. Strong UV-B radiation damages plants, particularly DNA (breakage of strands and deletions) of nuclei, chloroplasts and mitochondria, and also damages the photosynthetic apparatus (bleaching of photosynthetic pigments, destruction of photosynthetic enzymes). The strength of UV radiation required to produce such damage probably does not occur in nature or only in extreme cases. Organisms have very efficient repair systems, particularly for damaged DNA.

3. Tolerable UV-B radiation is morphologically effective: thickening and shortening of internodes, reduced growth in area but increased thickness of leaves, increased growth of side shoots.

4. At the biochemical level, UV leads to increased phenylpropane metabolism and the formation of UV-absorbing protective pigments in the epidermis, and to increased detoxification systems for ROS.

5. Plants possess a UV-B receptor and at least two UV-A/blue light receptors (cryptochromes). These receptors cooperate with the phytochrome system.

References

Anderson JM, Andersson B (1988) The dynamic photosynthetic membrane and regulation of solar energy conversion. Trends Biochem Sci 13: 351–355

Ballaré CL (1999) Keeping up with the neighbours: phytochrome sensing and other signalling mechanisms. Trends Plant Sci 4:97–102

Ballaré CL, Scopel AL, Stapleton AE, Yanovsky MJ (1996) Solar ultraviolet-B radiation affects seedling emergence, DNA-integrity, plant morphology, growth rate, and attractiveness to herbivore insects in *Datura ferox*. Plant Physiol 112:161–170

Björkman O, Demmig-Adams B (1994) Regulation of photosynthetic light energy capture, conversion, and dissipation in leaves of higher plants. Ecological studies 100. Springer, Berlin Heidelberg New York, pp 17–47

Björkman O, Powles SB (1981) Leaf movement in the shade species *Oxalis oregana*. I. Response to light level and light quality. Carnegie Inst Wash Yearb 80:59–62

Elliott RC, Platten JD, Watson JC, Reid JB (2004) Phytochrome regulation of pea phototropin. J Plant Physiol 161:265–270

Hall DO, Rao KK (1994) Photosynthesis. Cambridge University Press, Cambridge

Heldt HW (1999) Pflanzenbiochemie. Spektrum Akademischer, Heidelberg

Herndl GH (1996) Ultraviolett-Strahlung und Bakterioplankton. Biol Unserer Zeit 26:234–239

Jiao S, Emmanuel H, Guikema JA (2004) High light stress inducing photoinhibition and protein degradation of photosystem I in *Brassica rapa*. Plant Science 167:733–741

Kerrmann KM, Weaver LM (1999) The shikimate pathway. Annu Rev Plant Physiol Plant Mol Biol 50:473–504

Larcher W (1994) Ökophysiologie der Pflanzen. UTB, Eugen Ulmer, Stuttgart

Mohr H (1996) Sind Landpflanzen durch erhöhte UV-Strahlung besonders gefährdet? Biol Unserer Zeit 26:240–244

Nultsch W (1996) Allgemeine Botanik. Thieme, Stuttgart

Osmond B, Badger M, Maxwell K, Björkman O, Leegood R (1997) Too many photons: photorespiration, photoinhibition and photooxidation. Trends Plant Sci 2:119–120

Richter G (1996) Biochemie der Pflanzen. Thieme, Stuttgart

Schäfer C, Björkman O (1989) Relationship between efficiency of photosynthetic energy conversion and chlorophyll quenching in upland cotton (*Gossypium hirsutum* L.). Planta 178:367–376

Schäfer C, Schmid V (1993) Pflanzen im Lichtstress. Biol Unserer Zeit 23:55–62

Schnitzler JP, Jungblut TP, Heller W, Köfferlein M, Hutzler P, Heinzmann U, Schmelzer E, Ernst D, Langebartels C, Sandermann H Jr (1996) Tissue localization of UV-B-screening pigments and of chalcone synthase mRNA in needles of Scots Pine seedlings. New Phytol 132:247–258

Schreiber U, Bilger W, Neubauer C (1994) Chlorophyll fluorescence as a nonintrusive indicator for rapid assessment on in vivo photosynthesis. Ecological studies 100. Springer, Berlin Heidelberg New York, pp 17–47

Searles PS, Flint SD, Caldwell MM (2001) A meta-analysis of plant field studies simulating stratospheric ozone depletion. Oecologia 127:1–10

Sonoike K (1996a) Photoinhibition of photosystem I: 1st physiological significance in the chilling sensitivity of plants. Plant Cell Physiol 37:239–247

Sonoike K (1996b) Degradation of psaB gene product the reaction center subunit of photosystem I, is caused during photoinhibition of photosystem I: possible involvement of active oxygen species. Plant Sci 115:157–164

Strasburger F (1983) Lehrbuch der Botanik. Fischer, Stuttgart

Taiz L, Zeiger E (2000) Physiologie der Pflanzen. Spektrum Akademischer, Heidelberg

Tolbert NE (1994) Role of photosynthesis and photorespiration in regulating atmospheric CO_2 and O_2. In: Tolbert NE, Preiss J (eds) Regulation of atmospheric CO_2 and O_2 by photosynthetic carbon metabolism. Oxford University Press, Oxford, pp 8–33

Walker D (1992) Energy plant and man. Packard, Brighton

Zellner R (1996) Stratosphärischer Ozonabbau: Ausmaß, Ursachen und Folgen. Biol Unserer Zeit 26:209–214

1.3

Temperature

Winter flowering: The shrivelled petals of the witch hazel (*Hamamelis virginiana*) clearly show the effects of water loss from the cells caused by frost. As a consequence of the low average temperatures, the flowers of the North American or Japanese (*H. mollis*) witch hazel persist for many months. Witch hazel does not tolerate extreme cold and dryness, but is well adapted to the moderate winters of central Europe, where it is much prized as an ornamental shrub. Its green leaves in summer are like those of hazel. Photo K. Liedl, Munich

Recommended Literature

- Allen DJ, Ort DR (2001) Impacts of chilling temperatures on photosynthesis in warm-climate plants. Trends Plant Sci 6:36–42
- Apel K, Hirt H (2004) Reactive oxygen species: metabolism, oxidative stress, and signal transduction. Annu Rev Plant Biol 55:373–399
- Hoffmann WA, Orthen B, Nascimento PKV (2003) Comparative fire ecology of tropical savanna and forest trees. Functional Ecology 17:720–726
- Körner Ch (1999) Climatic stress. In: Alpine plant life. Springer, Berlin Heidelberg New York, chap 8
- Larcher W (2003) Physiological plant ecology, 4th edn (chapter: Plants under stress). Springer, Berlin Heidelberg New York, pp 345–450
- Taiz L, Zeiger E (2002) (eds) Plant physiology, 3rd edn (chapter: Stress physiology). Sinauer Associates, Sunderland, MA, USA
- Thomashow MF (2001) So what's new in the field of plant cold acclimation? Lots! Plant Physiol 125:91–95
- Xin Z, Browse J (2000) Cold comfort farm: the acclimation of plants to freezing temperatures. Plant Cell Environ 23:891–907

1.3.1

Temperature Ranges and Temperatures Limiting Life

For many organisms temperature limits for active life can be determined, as well as those beyond which life is no longer possible. Before an organism reaches lethal temperatures of heat or cold, it usually falls into a "rigid" or "stiff" condition in which the active processes of life only occur at minimal, hardly measurable rates without lethal damage. This is termed the "condition of latent life". The stages of cold death, cold rigidity, range of active life, heat rigidity and heat death are designated as the **cardinal points of temperature tolerance**. These differ in their totality from species to species (see Fig. 1.1.3), whereby different cardinal points can be exhibited even among the individual tissues and organs of a single plant. Active life is quite generally dependent on the temperature range of liquid water. Hydrated plant tissues thus have cardinal points which are closer together than those of dry plant tissues (e.g. seeds or plants resistant to drying out – poikilohydric plants). Tables 1.3.1 and 1.3.2 show some examples. Limiting temperatures, however, are not decisive for the growth and development of a plant, but

Table 1.3.1. Maximum temperature resistance of microorganisms and poikilohydric plants in the turgescent state and in the rigid states caused by drought. (Larcher 2003)

Plant group	Cold damage[a] at °C		Heat damage[b] at °C	
	Moist	Dry	Moist	Dry
Bacteria				
Archaebacteria			100–110	
Cyanobacteria and other photo-authotropic bacteria			55–75	
Saprophytic bacteria			60–70	
Thermophilic bacteria			Up to 95	
Fungal fruiting bodies				
Bacterial spores		LN$_2$[c]	80–120	Up to 160
Fungi				
Plant pathogenic fungi			45–65 (70)	
Saprophytic fungi	0 to below –10		40–60 (80)	75–100
Fungal fruiting body	–5 to –10 (–30)			
Fungal spores		LN$_2$	50–60 (100)	Above 100
Algae				
Marine algae				
Tropical seas	+14 to +5 (–2)		32–35 (40)	
Temperate seas				
Eulitoral	–2 to –8		25–30	
Tidal zones	–8 to –40		30–35	
Polar seas	–10 to –60		(15)20–28	
Fresh water algae	–5 to –20 (–30)		35–45 (50)	
Airborne algae	–10 to –30	LN$_2$	40–50	
Eukaryotic thermal algae	+20 to +15		40–50	
Lichens				
Polar regions, high mountains, deserts	–80	LN$_2$		
Temperate climate zones	–50	LN$_2$	33–45	70–100
Mosses				
Humid tropics	–1 to –7			
Temperate zone				
Humid locations	–5 to 15		40–45	
Ground mosses in forests	–15 to –25		40–50	80–95
Epiphytic and epipetric mosses	–15 to –35	LN$_2$		100–110
Polar regions	–50 to –80	LN$_2$		
Poikilohydric ferns	–20	LN$_2$	47–50	60–100
Seed plants				
Ramonda myconi	–9	LN$_2$	48	56
Myrothamnus flabellifolia		LN$_2$		80

[a] After at least 2 h of exposure to cold
[b] After 30 min of heat treatment
[c] Temperature of liquid nitrogen (–196 °C)

rather the temperature range of active life is. Plants are much more similar in this respect than they are with regard to their limiting temperatures. Day temperatures (air temperatures) of between 15 and 25 °C and night temperatures of about 10 K lower are, on average, optimal for plant growth. Organisms inhabiting extreme locations, such as snow and ice algae (*Haematococcus pluvialis*, and various Diatomeae) with a life range of between +5 and –5 °C or cyanobacteria and bacteria living in geysers or in the black smokers of the deep sea with optimal temperatures of between +80 and above 100 °C, are exceptions.

Types of organisms constitutively adapted to cold are called **psychrophiles** and those requiring high temperatures are called **thermophiles** (or extreme thermophiles), but most organisms are **mesophiles**.

Not all life processes of a plant have the same optimal temperatures. The temperature requirements of these processes must be adapted to the

Table 1.3.2. Temperature resistance of the leaves of cormophytes from various climate zones. The data quoted correspond to the limiting temperatures causing 50% damage (TL$_{50}$ in °C) after at least 2 h of exposure to cold or after 30 min of heat treatment. (After Larcher 2003)

Plant group	Cold damage in hardened state	Heat damage during vegetative period
Tropics		
Trees	+5 to −2	45–50
High mountain plants	−5 to −15 (−20)	about 45
Subtropics		
Evergreen woody plants	−8 to −12	50–60
Palms	−5 to −14	55–60
Succulents	−5 to −10 (−15)	58-67
C4 grasses	−1 to −5 (−8)	60–64
Winter annual desert grasses	−6 to −10	50–55
Temperate zones		
Evergreen woody plants of mild winter coastal areas	−7 to −15 (−25)	46–50 (55)
Dwarf shrubs of Atlantic heathlands	−20 to −25	45–50
Summer green trees and shrubs	(−25 to −35)[a]	about 50
Herbaceous plants		
Sunny sites	−10 to −20 (−30)	47–52
Shady sites	−10 to −20 (−30)	40–45
Halophytes	−10 to −20	
Water plants	−5 to −12	38–44
Homeohydric ferns	−10 to −40	46–48
Winter cold areas		
Evergreen conifers	−40 to −90	44–50
Boreal deciduous trees	(to LN$_2$)*	42–45
Arctic-alpine dwarf shrubs	−30 to −70	48–54

[a] Vegetative buds

conditions under which the individual steps of development take place. This can be illustrated by the example of germination in contrast to growth and development. Seeds which germinate in the autumn or winter (such as those of winter cereals) do so at temperatures that are considerably lower than those relevant for germination in the spring or summer. Independently of the temperature range in which germination is possible, the rate of germination itself shows the typical temperature dependence of biological processes (Q$_{10}$ between 1.5 and 2.5; see Chap. 1.3.2). Such germination behaviour can be modified by inhibitory mechanisms (e.g. the requirement for a prolonged exposure of imbibed seeds to cold – **stratification** – or the fire-dependent opening of seeds in **pyrophytes**), which prevent premature germination at unfavourable times.

Frost represents a long-term stress situation in contrast to, for example, fire, and can last for hours, days and even months. Frost acts not only as a temperature stress, but primarily as a drought stress due to the freezing of tissue water. Plants undergo a process of hardening during the advent of the colder season or in the presence of permanent frost during their juve-

nile development. This enables them to withstand even the sometimes extremely severe frosts which occur in nature (air temperatures as low as −70 °C have been recorded in Siberia).

Temperature stress does not occur only in extreme locations, and plants can be subjected to large ranges of temperature even during the course of a "normal" day (see Chap. 2.1, section on radiation climate). Temperatures of above +50 °C occur frequently at the immediate surface of the soil during extended periods of solar irradiation, particularly if there is no plant growth and the soil is dark and thus reflects little of the incident sunlight. However, air temperature decreases rapidly with the distance from the soil surface, and the temperature gradient within the soil itself is even steeper (see Figs. 4.3.2 and 2.1.6). Whereas an air temperature of +40 °C was measured about 10 cm above soil exhibiting a surface temperature of +50 °C, the soil temperature at a depth of 10 cm was below 25 °C (see Fig. 2.1.6). Temperature gradients within the soil and within the surface-near air layer also occur on clear nights, whereby their direction is reversed and their amplitude is of a lesser magnitude. Cooling of surfaces to tempera-

Fig. 1.3.1. Influence of the microclimate on the growth of *Lobelia rhynchopetalum* in the Ethiopian Highlands. A Night ground frosts (hoar frost on the leaves) stimulate the plant to form "night buds" (cf. Chap. 1.3.6.7). B The leaf crowns of the specimens which have already developed a trunk are subjected to a considerably milder microclimate, i.e. they are exposed to significantly smaller temperature fluctuations. The rate of growth therefore increases the further the leaf rosette is removed from the soil on the growing trunk (C). (After Fetene et al. 1998; photos E. Beck)

tures below that of the air is caused by radiation from all horizontal and sloping areas. This type of heat radiation also occurs during the daytime; the heat gain via absorption of the sun's rays is then, however, considerably greater than the heat lost through radiation. Young plants situated directly on the soil surface are understandably subjected to greater temperature stress than plants which have formed a stem, and they therefore grow only slowly. As soon as a stem is formed and leaves have grown away from the severe microclimate near the soil surface, the plant's rate of growth increases considerably (Fig. 1.3.1).

1.3.2

The Temperature Dependence of Biochemical Processes, Q_{10} and Activation Energy

Recommended Literature

- Nelson DL, Cox MM (2005) Lehninger Principles of Biochemistry, 4th edn. Freeman, New York

The rate of reaction of uncatalysed reactions, as well as of enzymatic reactions, depends on temperature.

The measure for the temperature dependency is the so-called Q_{10} (quotient of the rates of reaction at two temperatures differing by 10 K):

$$Q_{10} = \frac{v_{T+10}}{v_T}$$

If the rate constants k_{T1} and k_{T2} are inserted instead of the rate of reaction v, the activation energy E_a can be calculated with the following equation:

$$\ln \frac{k_{T_1}}{k_{T_2}} = \frac{E_a}{R} \left(\frac{1}{T_1} - \frac{1}{T_2} \right)$$

The Q_{10} is a readily illustrative measure of the activation energy of a reaction. For enzymatic reactions it is between 1.4 and 2.5, for biophysical processes between 1.03 and 1.3.

An increase in temperature leads to a speeding up, and a decrease in temperature to a slowing down of biological processes.

1.3.3

Temperature and the Stability/ Functionality of Biomembranes

1.3.3.1
Influence of Temperature on the Lipid Composition of Biomembranes

In addition to its influence on the rate of metabolism, temperature affects the stability and accordingly also the chemical structure of biomembranes. Active life is absolutely dependent on functional biomembranes. The lipids of these extremely complex structures must be present in a viscous-fluid state for the proteins and protein complexes anchored within them to fulfil their function. The melting point and viscosity of the lipids depend on the length of the component fatty acids and the degree of their unsaturation. The longer the chain length of the fatty acids and the lower the number of double bonds, the higher the melting point is (Box 1.3.1).

Box 1.3.1   Chemical structures and melting points of the fatty acids most commonly found in plant biomembranes

Carbon skeleton	Structure	Common name	Melting point (°C)
16:0	$CH_3(CH_2)_{14}COOH$	Palmitic acid	63.1
18:0	$CH_3(CH_2)_{16}COOH$	Stearic acid	69.6
20:0	$CH_3(CH_2)_{18}COOH$	Arachidic acid	76.5
16:1 (Δ^9)	$CH_3(CH_2)_5CH=CH(CH_2)_7COOH$	Palmitoleic acid	−0.5
18:1 (Δ^9)	$CH_3(CH_2)_7CH=CH(CH_2)_7COOH$	Oleic acid	13.4
18:2 ($\Delta^{9,12}$)	$CH_3(CH_2)_4CH(=CHCH_2)_7COOH$	α-Linoleic acid	−5.0
18:3 ($\Delta^{9,12,15}$)	$CH_3CH_2CH=CHCH_2CH=CHCH_2CH=CH(CH_2)_7COOH$	α-Linolenic acid	−11
20:4 ($\Delta^{5,8,11,14}$)	$CH_3(CH_2)_4CH=CHCH_2CH=CHCH_2CH=CHCH_2CH=CH(CH_2)_3COOH$	Arachidonic acid	−49.5

Table 1.3.3. The effect of growth temperature on the lipid composition of the biomembranes of the cyanobacterium *Synecchocystis*. Increasing growth temperature results in a lesser degree of desaturation of the fatty acids. The chemical structures of the individual fatty acid species are shown in Box 1.3.1. *X* denotes a phospho-component ("phospholipid"). (Murata et al. 1993; Gombos et al. 1996)

Cultivation temperature (°C)	Fatty acid species					
	16:0 / 16:0 / X	18:1 / 16:0 / X	18:2 / 16:0 / X	18:3γ / 16:0 / X	18:3α / 16:0 / X	18:4 / 16:0 / X
	Total fatty acid species (%)					
22	2	4	16	42	16	16
34	16	16	24	34	0	0

Table 1.3.4. Changes in the composition of the lipids of a defined biomembrane (chloroplast envelope membrane of spruce needles) during the course of frost hardening ("winter") or dehardening ("summer"). (Senser and Beck 1992)

Lipid	Fatty acids (%) 16:0+18:0 (+18:1^{tr})	Fatty acids (%) 16:3+18:1+18:2+ 18:3+18:4+18:2- hydroxy+20:3
Phospholipids		
Summer	55.4	41.2
Winter	25.6	66.0
Galactolipids		
Summer	33.4	64.4
Winter	9.4	84.8

Organisms are able to adapt the viscosity of their biomembranes to temperature to a certain extent by exchanging certain types of fatty acids for others. This enables metabolism to proceed in an orderly manner upon temperature changes. For example, more saturated fatty acids are incorporated into the membranes upon an increase in temperature (Table 1.3.3).

Changes in lipid composition also take place during frost hardening and dehardening, which can be related to the maintenance of optimal viscosity and functionality of the biomembranes. Here, the viscosity is decreased by increasing the degree of unsaturation of the membrane lipids (Table 1.3.4).

1.3.4

Heat (Hyperthermy)

Recommended Literature

- Scharf K-D, Höhfeld I, Nover L (1998) Heat stress response and heat stress transcription factors. J Bioscience 23:313–329
- Sun W, Van Montagu M, Verbruggen N (2002) Small heat shock proteins and stress tolerance in plants. BBA 1577:1–9

Heat should be understood here as the upper temperature range in which active life is possible. In this range strain increases with increasing temperature, and there is a direct correlation between the stressor and strain. In addition to this obvious relationship, however, biphasic relations, i.e. discontinuity between stressor and strain, have also been observed. Figure 1.3.2 shows such a stress response for poplar leaves in the month of September. Similar observations have been made for privet and for bindweed. In all three cases, the damage within two different temperature ranges was only observed in late summer, possibly an indication of the transition into the frost-hardening phase. During this stage, there are evidently two temperature ranges in which metabolic flows and metabolic pools are relatively well balanced and therefore no damage occurs. However, this phenomenon must still be studied in more detail.

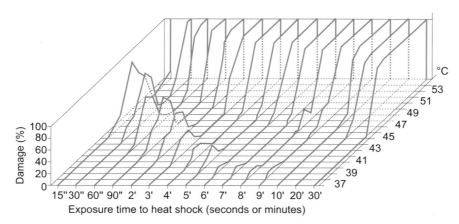

Fig. 1.3.2. Course of heat damage in poplar leaves (*Populus deltoidis* x *simonii*) in dependence on the amount of heat (stress duration×exposure time) during September. The heat treatment corresponded to, in principle, the cold treatments described in Box 1.3.6. Damage was quantified by determining the frequency of necroses (compare Box 1.1.1). (After Kappen and Zeitler 1977)

Heat (Hyperthermy) 51

1.3.4.1
Heat: Metabolism and Growth

Temperature above the optimal range not only accelerates, but also redirects metabolic processes and leads to changes in metabolite pools and to growth anomalies. This can be seen by the example of the heat-sensitive potato cultivar 'Up-to-Date' and the heat-tolerant cultivar 'Norchip' (Box 1.3.2). The potato plant comes from the medium-altitude mountain areas of the South American Andes and requires a relatively cool climate. Potato can tolerate neither very warm weather nor frost. Not only the enzyme activities and metabolite pools of the potato are altered under heat stress, but also morphogenesis, particularly the way in which the distribution of biomass between the green shoot and the tubers results in a change of sink strengths.

Although only growth and tuber formation and some parameters of carbohydrate metabolism were measured in this experiment, the complete redirection of the physiology of these plants becomes evident. One explanation may be the different Q_{10} values of the affected reactions which lead to changes in the steady states of the reactions. However, the redirection may also be a consequence of the heat shock reaction of the plants.

1.3.4.2
Heat Shock

Recommended Literature

- Nover L, Scharf KD (1997) Heat stress proteins and transcription factors. Cell Mol Life Sci 53:80–103
- Nover L, Scharf KD, Gagliardi D, Vergne P, Czarnecka-Verner E, Gurley WB (1996) The Hsf world: classification and properties of plant heat stress transcription factors. Cell Stress Chaperones 1:215–223
- Vierling E (1991) The roles of heat shock proteins in plants. Annu Rev Plant Physiol Plant Mol Biol 42:579–620

Heat shock is a short- or longer-term increase of temperature within the range of temperature which can still be tolerated.

Table 1.3.5 shows various reactions of normal metabolic functions (the so-called **housekeeping reactions**) in leaf tissue to a heat shock treatment lasting for 5 min. Instead of a short – but sharp – heat pulse, less heat can be applied for a longer time, i.e. the product of $+\Delta T \times t$ is the stress dosage.

The example of the potato plant mentioned earlier (Box 1.3.2) demonstrates that changes already take place at temperatures of around $+30\,^\circ C$. These changes result to a large extent,

Table 1.3.5. The effect of a 5-min heat pulse at the specified temperatures on various housekeeping functions of leaves of *Tradescantia fluminensis*. (Nover and Höhfeld 1996)

Tissue type	Change	Temperature range (°C) in which the change was observed
		37 39 41 43 45 47 49 51 53 55 57 59 61 63 65
Epidermis	1. Anthocyanin loss from the vacuole	59–63
	2. Loss of plasmolysis	55–57
	3. Loss of plasma streaming	57–61
	4. Increase in viscosity	43–45
Parenchyma	5. Loss of photosynthesis	45–49
	6. Loss of chloroplast phototaxis	43–45
	7. Loss of chlorophyll fluorescence	43–47
All tissues	8. Uncoupling of oxidative phosphorylation	51–55
	9. Loss of electrolytes	51–55
	10. Loss of respiration	59–63

Box 1.3.2

The effect of heat stress on the growth, tuber formation, carbohydrate level and enzyme activities of a heat-tolerant potato (*Solanum tuberosum*) variety ("Norchip") and a heat-sensitive variety ("Up-to-Date") (Lafta and Lorenzen 1995)

Both varieties were grown initially at 19/17 °C day/night temperatures and a daily 14-h light period. In experiment 1 the heat stress was applied at the onset of tuber formation (Tables 1 and 2) and in experiment 2 (Table 3) after the induction of the tubers. The heat stress consisted of raising the temperature from 19/17 °C to 31/29 °C in experiment 1 and to 29/27 °C in experiment 2. The duration of exposure to the heat treatment is given in the tables

Table 1. Biomass production and growth of the potato plants after a 4-week heat stress. 19/17 °C: control; 31/29 °C: growth at increased day/night temperatures. The variety "Norchip" is considered to be heat-tolerant, "Up-to-Date" is a temperature-sensitive variety. (Lafta and Lorenzen 1995)

Cultivar	Temp. (°C)	Shoot (g/plant)	Tuber (g/plant)	Total weight (g/plant)	Plant height (cm)
"Norchip"	19/17	244±6	134±3	378±4	35±1
	31/29	253±4	5±3	258±4	45±2
"Up-to-Date"	19/17	197±17	131±14	328±13	42±1
	31/29	96±2	0.6±0.6	96±3	57±0.5

Table 2. The influence of temperature on the carbohydrate level in the fully developed leaves of the heat-tolerant and -sensitive potato plants. The carbohydrate pools are filled by photosynthesis at the end of the day; at the end of the night they have been depleted. (Lafta and Lorenzen 1995)

Cultivar	Temp. (°C)	Carbohydrate	3 Days after temperature increase		8 Days after temperature increase	
			End of day	End of night	End of day	End of night
Norchip	19/17	Glucose	3.3±0.2	2.8±0.1	5.2±0.9	3.8±0.3
	31/29	(mg g⁻¹ dry wt.)	5.3±1.1	2.5±0.0	6.2±0.9	3.0±0.1
Up-to-Date	19/17		3.0±0.1	2.9±0.3	3.5±0.0	2.9±0.2
	31/29		4.2±0.2	2.6±0.2	6.2±0.6	3.1±0.7
Norchip	19/17	Sucrose	10.6±0.1	6.4±0.8	10.1±1.0	3.4±0.2
	31/29	(mg g⁻¹ dry wt.)	13.1±1.4	3.8±1.0	17.6±0.9	4.8±0.6
Up-to-Date	19/17		9.8±0.3	5.2±0.8	12.5±0.8	4.6±0.3
	31/29		12.9±1.3	3.6±0.3	17.0±1.2	4.5±0.9
Norchip	19/17	Starch	294±2	195±9	290±9	180±12
	31/29	(mg g⁻¹ dry wt.)	202±14	92±9	129±2	72±3
Up-to-Date	19/17		222±32	117±19	242±14	126±12
	31/29		168±16	64±1	99±12	50±6

however, solely due to an acceleration of the normal housekeeping reactions.

The so-called **heat shock reaction** of the cell is quite a different matter. For plants with a temperature optimum between 15 and 25 °C, this reaction takes place at temperatures above +35 °C and consists of:

- the slowing down of housekeeping reactions, particularly of the expression of the housekeeping genes;
- an almost exclusive synthesis of so-called **heat shock proteins** (HSPs);
- cessation of the production of the HSPs after 6–8 h; and
- a gradual resumption of the expression of the **housekeeping genes**.

Box 1.3.2   (continued)

Table 3. Enzyme activities in the potato tuber tissue after 2 weeks of exposure to the day/night conditions quoted in column 2. The increased temperature treatment began 10 days after the initiation of tuber formation. (Lafta and Lorenzen 1995)

Cultivar	Temp. (°C)	Sucrose synthase (mg starch g^{-1} h^{-1})	AGPase (µmol g^{-1} min^{-1})	UGPase (µmol g^{-1} min^{-1})	Sucrose-P-synthase (mg sucrose g^{-1} h^{-1})	
					V_{max}	V_{lim}
Norchip	19/17	33.4±11.9	1.2±0.11	40.2±5.1		
	29/27	13.7±3.8	0.93±0.05	39.9±5.2	21±1[a]	6±0.9[a]
					15.2±1.5[a]	5±0.5[a]
Up-to-Date	19/17	15.0±4.2	1.17±0.12	27.8±3.1		
	29/27	4.2±2.3	0.84±0.08	24.4±3.1		

[a] In these cases potatoes grown under the 31/29 °C treatment were used; there was no statistical difference between the two cultivars. V_{max}: in the enzyme assay the substrates UDP glucose and fructose-6-P were saturating; V_{lim}: the concentrations of both substrates were reduced to about one-third, i.e. they were limiting in relation to the amount of enzyme used. Sucrose-synthase: sucrose + UDP ↔ UDP glucose + fructose; sucrose-phosphate-synthase: UDP glucose + fructose-6-P ↔ sucrose-6-P + UDP; AGPase = ADP glucose pyrophosphorylase: glucose-1-P + ATP ↔ ADP-glucose + PP$_i$; ADP glucose → → starch; UDPase = UDP glucose pyrophosphorylase: glucose-1-P + UTP ↔ UDP-glucose + PP$_i$; UDP glucose → → sucrose

From the selection of data presented in Tables 1, 2 and 3 the following can be derived:

1. Biomass production (growth) is inhibited at temperatures above the optimum. This inhibition was significantly less in the heat-tolerant than in the heat-sensitive variety.
2. Tuber formation was almost completely suppressed in both varieties.
3. Heat-stressed plants exhibited greater growth length than the controls.
4. The total levels of carbohydrate in the leaves of the heat-stressed plants were drastically reduced, primarily due to the starch contents. The comparatively low levels of soluble carbohydrates were not (glucose) or only slightly (sucrose) affected.
5. The sucrose-phosphate synthase activity (SPS) in the leaves was significantly increased at elevated temperature, whereby there was no difference in the responses of the two cultivars.
6. In the rudimentary tubers of the high-temperature plants the activities of both the enzymes involved in starch metabolism sucrose synthase (active phloem unloading: sucrose + UTP ↔ UDP glucose + fructose + P$_i$) and ADP glucose-pyrophosphorylase (supplies the substrate for starch synthase: glucose-1P + ATP ↔ ADP glucose + PP$_i$) were clearly decreased, while UDP glucose-pyrophosphorylase (sucrose synthesis) showed no noticeable differences in activity. SPS activity of the tubers was also reduced in the high-temperature plants. Thus neither starch nor sucrose synthesis takes place in these plants: the tubers have no sink strength.

The total redirection of protein synthesis in favour of HSPs occurs, in principle, only a few K above the optimal temperature of the organism. In other words: Many organisms already live near the upper temperature limit at which the stress reaction occurs, i.e. where activation of the heat shock genes starts. For example, E. coli has a optimum temperature of 37 °C versus 42 °C for the heat shock reaction; baking yeast: 23/ 37 °C; human beings: 37/42–45 °C; Euglena: 25/ 37 °C; tomato: 25/37 °C.

At present ten families of HSPs are known, which are ordered according to their molecular weight (Box 1.3.3). They occur in all compartments of cells.

Most HSPs are constitutively expressed proteins, so-called **molecular chaperones** ("governesses"), and are present under "normal" condi-

Box 1.3.3 — Overview of the heat shock protein families (After Nover and Höhfeld 1996)

HSP family / Group of organisms	Cellular localisation			Comments
	Cytoplasm/nucleus	ER/Golgi	Mitochondria (m)/ chloroplasts (c)	
HSP100 family (Ec-ClpA/B)				ATP-binding proteins with chaperone activity which are part of a protease complex in bacteria; in mammalian cells HSP110 is in the nucleolus
Mammals	**HSP110**	?	?	
Plants	ClpB, HSP101	?	ClpCc	
Yeast	**HSP104**	?	**ClpB (HSP78)**	
HSP90 family (Ec-HtpG)				ATP-binding, autophosphorylating proteins; interact with Ca-calmodulin; cytoplasmic representatives form complexes with steroid hormone receptors, protein kinases and HSP70
Mammals	**HSP90 α, β**	GRP94	–	
Plants	**HSP80**	GRP94	HSP90c	
Yeast	**HSP90**, HSC90	–	–	
HSP70 family (Ec-DnaK, Ec-Hsc66)				ATP-binding autophosphorylating proteins; bind to denatured/ unfolded proteins; part of a chaperone machinery together with representatives of the HSP40 and HSP23 families
Mammals	**HSP70, A, B** HSC72, p73	GRP78 (BIP)	HSC70m	
Plants	**HSP70**, HSC70	GRP78	HSC70c **HSP68m**	
Yeast	**SSA 1–4**, SSB1,2 **MSI3**, SSE1/2	KAR2	SSC1m	
HSP40 family (Ec-DnaJ, Ec-CbpA)				Always closely associated with representatives of the HSP70 family; responsible for recognition of unfolded protein substrates by HSP70; ANJ1 with farnesyl side chains integrated into the glyoxysome membrane
Mammals	**HDJ-1, HDJ-2**	?	?	
Plants	**ANJ1**	+	?	
Yeast	YdJ1, SIS1	SEC63	**SCJ1**, Mdj1	
HSP60 family (Ec-GroEL)				ATP-binding, oligomeric protein complexes; interact with representatives of the HSP10 family; essential role in protein folding; various TCP1-type proteins in the cytoplasm form complexes of ~ 900 kDa which interact with actin and tubulin systems
Mammals	TCP1	–	**Cpn60m**	
Plants	TCP1	–	HSP60c	
Yeast	TCP1 α, β BIN2/3 ANC2	–	**HSP60m** HSP60m	
HSP10 family (Ec-GroES)				Heptameric complexes which work together with the HSP60 complexes; presence of corresponding subunits for TCP1 complex is still not clear
Mammals	?	–	Cpn10m	
Plants	?	–	Cpn10m Cpn12c	
Yeast	?	–	Cpn10m	
HSP23 family (Ec-GrpE)				Little studied subunits of the HSP70 chaperone machinery; binds to SSC1 in yeast mitochondria; essential for protein import into mitochondria; nucleotide exchange factor
Mammals	?	?	?	
Plants	?	?	?	
Yeast	?	?	Mge1p	

Box 1.3.3 (continued)

HSP family / Group of organisms	Cellular localisation			Comments
	Cytoplasm/nucleus	ER/Golgi	Mitochondria (m)/ chloroplasts (c)	
HSP20 family (Ec-lbp A/B)				
Mammals	**HSP 25/27,** **α,β-Crystallin**	?	?	More variable in number and sequence than other HSP families; sequence relationship to eye lens proteins (α,β-crystallin); frequently forms oligomeric aggregates of 200–500 kDa; protective function for mRNA in plants
Plants	**HSPs 15–18**	**HSP22**	**HSP 21/22c**	
Yeast	**HSP26**	–	–	
HSP8,5 family (Ec not present)				
Mammals	Ubiquitin	–	–	Small protein which is considered to act as a marker for protein breakdown via isopeptide links with Lys side chains (substrate for proteosome complexes)
Plants	Ubiquitin	–	–	
Yeast	Ubiquitin	–	–	
Immunophilins (Ec-cyclophilin/-FKBP)				
Mammals	FKBP 12, 25 CYP 18, 22, 40 **HSP56**	FKBP 13 CYP 22	?	Proteins with prolyl-*cis,trans* isomerase activity with ubiquitous distribution; activity is inhibited by immunosuppressants (cyclosporin A, FK 506)
Plants	**CYP**	–	CYP, FKBP	
Yeast	**CYP 1, 2**	**FKBP 13**	CYP 20	

The multiprotein families are summarised on the basis of sequence homologies and functional similarities. The representatives that are induced by heat stress are shown in **boldface type**. The family name is followed by the designation of the proteins which have been identified in *Escherichia coli* (Ec). Designations which deviate from the standard nomenclature for heat stress proteins (e.g. HSP70) often originate from the identification of the corresponding gene defects in microorganisms

tions only in very small amounts. During stress, the housekeeping genes are "switched off" and subsequently only HSPs are produced.

Every stress that leads to a denaturing of proteins and to the formation of "false" proteins, i.e. which attacks at the level of proteins (heavy metals, insertion of amino acid analogues into proteins, inhibitors of protein biosynthesis, alcohol), triggers heat shock reactions, which are thus a general and not a specific stress reaction. Heat shock reactions are currently one of the best-investigated reactions to stress and confer a number of highly interesting insights into cell physiological aspects at the molecular level. These are, in particular:

- the switching off of the expression of the housekeeping genes;

- the reaction of existing proteins to heat shock;
- the switching on of the heat shock genes: what is the molecular signal and how does the switch function?
- the function of the HSPs;
- the function of the HSPs in the unstressed cell;
- the return of the cell to "normal" life after the heat shock and the switching off of the heat shock response.

These aspects are discussed in the following sections. At times it will be necessary to consider results from microorganisms and animals, when research in plants has not yet progressed far enough in itself.

How is the Expression of Housekeeping Genes Switched Off During Heat Shock?

After its synthesis, mRNA is normally packed with small nuclear ribonucleoproteins (snRNPs), which together with small nuclear RNA molecules (snRNAs) form the spliceosome. This excises the introns from the pre-mRNA, and thus plays an essential part in mRNA processing. This splicing reaction does not occur after heat stress, so that no functional mRNA of the housekeeping genes is formed. The processing of ribosomal precursors in the nucleolus also ceases at the same time, i.e. no new ribosomes are formed.

Translation is also interrupted: Heat stress leads to the inactivation of initiation factors. In biochemical terms this happens via the dephosphorylation of an initiation factor (the eukaryotic IF-4Fa) which binds to the 5' cap [7mG(5') ppp(5')nucleotide] of the mature mRNA and thus contributes to the formation of the initiation complex. Protein synthesis, which is still ongoing, ceases after a few minutes, as the still-active polysomes can no longer bind to new mRNA molecules and thus dissociate into their subunits.

Heat shock genes do not possess introns; they need not be spliced and thus form functional mRNA (or functional mRNPs) even when the splicing reaction is inhibited. This can then form functional ribosomes and polysomes with the dissociated ribosomal subunits. The formation of the HSmRNA-ribosome complex evidently does not require the formation of an initiation complex with "capped" mRNA.

Most of the no longer active housekeeping mRNA is conserved and deposited in so-called **heat shock granules**, where it is associated with two heat shock proteins, an HSP70 and an HSP17. These granules are held in the immediate vicinity of the cell nucleus by the cytoskeleton.

How Does Heat Shock Affect Proteins?

Heat causes denaturation of proteins. Denaturation means partial or total unfolding of the tertiary structure and the dissociation of subunits, in short the production of non-functional polypeptides. Partial unfolding can explain how hydrophobic side chains are no longer "shielded" within the protein (hydrophobic interactions), but are exposed. As a consequence, several proteins associate via hydrophobic interactions: they aggregate and form insoluble complexes, which can only be removed by proteolysis. Heat shock thus causes a disturbance of the protein homeostasis of the cell via denaturation; the "internal equilibrium" of the cell is disrupted.

Switching On Heat Shock Genes: What Is the Molecular Signal and How Does the Switch Function?

The promoters of the heat shock (HS) genes are of prime importance for switching on the expression of these genes. These promoters exhibit conserved motifs, so-called **heat shock elements** (HSEs), which display a mirror sequence in the two complementary strands (a so-called **palindrome**):

- 5'.... AGAA n n TTCTAGAA n n TTCT ....3'
- 3'.... TCTT m m AAGATCTT m m AAGA ....5'
  ... n and m are variable and not fixed.

Heterologous insertion of these HSEs into other promoters makes these promoters responsive to heat stress.

The simplest type of HS promoter contains a TATA box for association with the transcription apparatus about 30 base pairs upstream of the start of transcription, and one to several HSEs a further 20–30 base pairs upstream. Such promoters could be of great importance in biotechnology: They enable genes to be switched on in a specific manner.

Which Factors Activate Heat Shock Promoters By Reaction with Heat Shock Elements (cis-Responsive Elements)?

These are proteins which interact with the DNA of HS elements, the so-called **HS-transcription factors** (HSFs). These proteins exhibit similar sequencing motifs associated with particular functions in all eukaryotes. Their expression is activated by heat. They are divided into families according to their size. Any one plant will contain HSFs from different families.

Ubiquitous functional motifs of heat shock factors are (Fig. 1.3.3):

- a DNA binding domain of about 100 amino acids near the N-terminus which binds to the *cis* elements (HS elements);
- an adjacent region in the C-terminal direction with repetitive hydrophobic heptapeptides which is important for the association of several monomer HSFs via hydrophobic interactions (the so-called oligomerisation domains: HR 1, HR 2 and sometimes also HR 3). Only

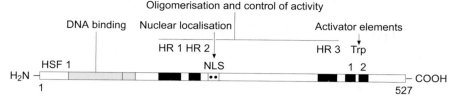

Fig. 1.3.3. Structure of a heat shock (transcription) factor from tomato. *H₂N-* N-terminus; *DNA-binding* binding domain on the HSE; *HR 1,2,3* regions for oligomerisation via hydrophobic interactions; *NLS* nuclear localisation sequence; *Trp* central tryptophan of the activator element. (After Nover and Höhfeld 1996)

the oligomerised HSF (trimer) is active, i.e. binds to DNA and HSPs;

- a cluster of alkaline amino acids C-terminal to HR 1, 2: the signal peptide for import into the nucleus (NLS: nucleus localisation signal);
- peptide motifs with a central tryptophan (Trp) as activator element which can interact with the transcription apparatus and thereby activate it. In larger HSFs the activator region contains a further hydrophobic heptade.

A Heat Shock Factor Must First Be Activated

Monomeric HSFs are inactive, i.e. they cannot bind to a heat shock element. The pool of HSFs is probably kept small in the normal state of the cell because of binding to the free HSPs (HSP70 and probably also HSP90). After dissociation from the HSP70/90 (and perhaps due to heat),

the HSF changes its form so that it is able to form trimers. The trimer formed in the cytoplasm must now be imported into the nucleus to bind to the heat shock element of the promoter. The activator region becomes active because of binding to the HSE, and transcription can start.

What is the "actual signal" in the reaction chain leading to the activation of HSFs? The prerequisite for the activation of the HSFs is the dissociation of the HSF-HSP70/90 complex. Such dissociation would, of course, be favoured by a decrease in the free pools of HSP70/90. But how can the free pool of these HSPs decrease as a result of heat shock? These proteins bind as a consequence of the heat shock to other, denatured, proteins. It may be readily assumed that heat-denatured housekeeping proteins bind the free HSP70.

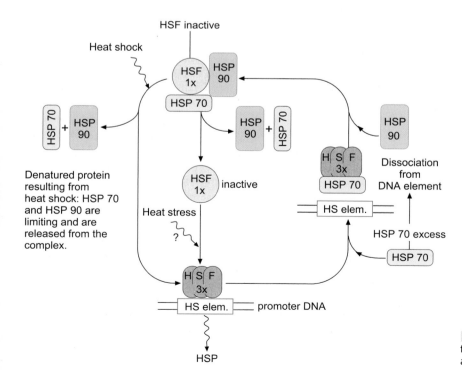

Fig. 1.3.4. The heat shock factor (HSF) cycle. (After Nover and Höhfeld 1996)

Box 1.3.4   Do HSPs have functions in non-stressed cells?

Most heat shock proteins (HSPs) are produced in small quantities even in non-stressed cells. This is the basis for the genesis of the signal for the activation of the HSF described in the text by the lowering of the homeostatic HSP level due to binding to denatured or partially denatured housekeeping proteins. It can be asked whether the HSPs also have other functions in cellular processes. The answer comes from protein biochemistry: Nascent polypeptides already tend to fold while still attached to the ribosome during their synthesis. The structural elements of the α-helix and the β-folded sheets arise more or less spontaneously in this way via H-bonds, van der Waals forces and hydrophobic interactions between the adjoining amino acid residues. Further folding, and in particular the formation of domains, requires, however, a fully synthesised polypeptide. This is because the active form of a protein is not always that possessing the lowest energy, but is rather a metastable form which is more flexible. Two phenomena must thus be counteracted: the formation of a basically incorrect domain during the synthesis of the polypeptide and (inappropriate) folding into the lowest energy state.

First, the nascent protein must be protected. A chaperone of the HSP70/DnaK family therefore associates with the growing polypeptide during its synthesis and prevents misfolding under ATP consumption (see Fig. 1.3.5). In order to fold correctly, the complete protein is transferred to HSP60/GroEL-ES (TCP-1). These chaperones form two rings, in the central cavity of which the folding proceeds; this once again requires the consumption of ATP.

The cell thus requires an effective system of molecular chaperones to ensure the correct folding of its proteins. These chaperones present in the non-stressed cells are considered to be related to the HSPs and have been termed HSCs, i.e. heat shock cognates, by some authors.

A second important function of chaperones relates to **topogenesis**: Most of the proteins of a cell are synthesised in the cytosol. Many of them, however, are part of the protein complement of organelles, i.e. the proteins must first find their way into the correct organelle. This takes place with the help of additional sequences, so-called signal peptides, which are mostly N-terminal sequences but can also be localised within polypeptides or at the C-terminus. The organelles possess receptors for the relevant signal peptides, which bind to the protein to be imported and are mostly also involved in the transport of the protein across the membrane. The signal peptides are usually removed upon import into a specific organelle or incorporation into a specific membrane, a process termed protein maturation. A complicated pathway can be dependent on several signal sequences, e.g. the incorporation of a protein into the thylakoid membrane requires the sequential removal of four such signal peptides.

In order to pass through a biomembrane a polypeptide (pre-protein) must unfold, i.e. it must be stretched out as linearly as possible. It must thus depart from its energetically favourable tertiary structure, for which chaperones are once again required. The movement through the membrane is furthermore favoured in that the polypeptide assumes a different configuration on the inner side; for this HSCs are also necessary. When it has arrived at its destination, the protein must be brought into its functional form and in some cases be incorporated into the membrane; these processes also require HSCs. Since the function of the HSP/HSCs is usually coupled with energy consumption, it is not surprising that up to 100 ATP molecules must be used up to ensure that a newly synthesised protein arrives at its final destination. The large number of HSP/HSCs in an organism (Hartl et al. 1994) is quite understandable when one assumes that these polypeptides are also specific for particular organelles and are correspondingly widely distributed.

This process may be illustrated as the HSF cycle (Fig. 1.3.4), which provides a fine example of a self-regulating system.

The question as to why HSPs bind to denatured proteins goes far beyond the aspect of "heat shock" itself and points to the function of constitutively expressed heat shock or stress proteins (Box 1.3.4).

What Is the Function of Heat Shock Proteins in the Cell Stressed by Heat?

Heat shock proteins have at least three different functions in relation to the stresses which denature proteins:

- chaperone function,
- conservation of housekeeping mRNA in HS granules,
- catalysing proteolysis of irreversibly denatured, aggregated proteins.

Heat Shock Proteins as Chaperones

The system of the HSP70 chaperones is that having been best investigated. It consists of at least three HSPs – HSP70, HSP40 and HSP23; in the bacterial system they are called DnaK, DnaJ and GrpE. The mechanism of chaperone operation is best understood for prokaryotes and the prokaryote system will therefore be explained here as a model (Fig. 1.3.5).

HSP70 (DnaK) has an N-terminal ATP- or ADP-binding domain and a C-terminal domain for interaction with proteins. HSP40 (DnaJ) binds to the partially unfolded protein ("U" in Fig. 1.3.5) via a cysteine-rich C-terminal zinc finger domain. After hydrolysis of the bound ATP ($\rightarrow$ ADP-DnaK), the ADP-DnaK binds to the N-terminal J domain of DnaJ-U. Denatured proteins (probably in the form of HSP40 complexes) stimulate the ATPase activity of HSP70/DnaK. A ternary complex is formed, in which the partially unfolded protein U is bound to both HSPs. The ternary complex interacts with

HSP23 (GrpE: nucleotide exchange factor), which leads to the dissociation of ADP from the complex and the weakening of the interaction of U with HSP70/DnaK. The complex dissociates completely upon renewed binding of ATP to HSP/70/DnaK, and U is now able to fold back into its native state or to enter into the cycle again if it possesses other denatured components. How many and how often HSP70 molecules react with U is not known. The energy required to completely fold a medium-sized protein corresponds to around 100 ATP.

HS Granules

Since it is non-functional upon heat stress, housekeeping mRNA would be predestined for rapid degradation by RNAses. The return to normal cell metabolism, however, requires large amounts of housekeeping mRNA, and it is therefore advantageous to conserve this mRNA during the heat stress response. Association of released mRNA with HSPs protects the housekeeping mRNA from degradation. This association leads to the formation of heat stress granules of 40 nm in size with a molecular mass of about 500 kDa, which are held in the vicinity of the nucleus by the cytoskeleton and contain mainly proteins of the HSP70 and HSP20 types. The HS granules dissociate again after the heat stress response subsides, whereby it is not clear how this dissociation is triggered.

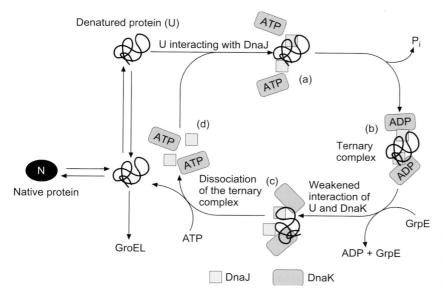

Denatured protein (U)

U interacting with DnaJ

ATP

(a)

ATP

P_i

(b) ADP

Ternary complex

ADP

(d)

ATP

ATP

N
Native protein

Dissociation of the ternary complex

(c)

Weakened interaction of U and DnaK

GrpE

ATP

ADP + GrpE

GroEL

DnaJ

DnaK

Fig. 1.3.5. Model of the HSP cycle using the bacterial DnaK, DnaJ, GrpE and GroEL system as an example. Explanations in the text. (After Hartl et al. 1994; see also Georgopoulos 1992; Nover and Höhfeld 1996)

Catalysis of Proteolysis of Irreversibly Denatured and Aggregated Proteins

Some proteins cannot be rescued after a heat pulse: They are irreversibly denatured, i.e. incorrectly folded, and have already formed aggregates with each other to some extent. Incorrectly or irreversibly denatured proteins must be removed from the cell rapidly and efficiently; this also costs energy. First, these proteins must be recognised and marked. This takes place upon cleavage of the N-terminal methionine by the protein **ubiquitin**, which exhibits enhanced expression in stressed cells. The expression of the helper enzymes of the ubiquitin conjugation reaction pathway, which are required for marking, is also enhanced. The protein marked repeatedly by ubiquitin is now broken down in **26S proteasomes** under consumption of ATP. The manner in which the HSPs are involved in the proteolytic degradation of "protein rubbish" has not yet been convincingly elucidated. Mutants which cannot form HSP70/DnaK also have a defect in ATP-dependent, rapid protein degradation.

How Does the Cell Return to "Normal Life" After Heat Shock, i.e. How Is the Heat Stress Response Switched Off?

If the depletion of the free pool of HSP70 is the signal for triggering the heat shock response, the growth of this pool, e.g. after the removal of defective protein, should lead to normal protein synthesis again. A higher concentration of free HSP70 leads to inactivation of the heat protection factors, and this would also stop the synthesis of HSPs or at least reduce it to the normal level. At the same time, the transiently immobilised, but conserved housekeeping functions, which also include the processing of the large precursor rRNPs accumulated in the nucleolus, could be activated again. Many of the questions as to the switching on of the housekeeping functions are not understood at present. This applies particularly to the other stressors which disturb protein homoeostasis, such as in heavy metal stress, etc.

As mentioned earlier, long-term exposure of plants to temperatures 10 K above the optimum suffices to induce heat stress reactions. This means that plants already live close to the verge of this reaction. There is a relatively great danger that overheating during the day can progress to the point where this complete rearrangement of metabolism can occur. Figure 2.1.15 shows that irradiated leaves can rapidly reach such temperatures. Avoidance mechanisms to reduce overheating are therefore of great importance.

1.3.4.3
Avoidance of Heat Stress

Avoidance mechanisms may be morphological (see also Chap. 2.1): Slit leaves heat up less than do undivided leaves, and hairy leaves reflect more radiation than do those without hair. The position of the leaf, and thus the extent of direct (solar) radiation it absorbs, also plays an important role. Transpiration cooling is an important physiological avoidance mechanism which can result in considerable lowering of leaf temperatures (see Fig. 2.1.15). The combination of heat and drought is problematic for plants in this regard, in which transpiration is substantially limited (see Chap. 2.2).

1.3.4.4
Hardening

In addition to heat avoidance, there is, naturally, also heat tolerance acquired through hardening. The changes in membrane lipids which take place during the course of the year have already been mentioned (Chap. 1.3.3.1). It is not known to what extent heat shock proteins (HSPs) play a role in hardening. The mechanism of the heat shock response would suggest that a certain degree of hardening occurs within the period of the accumulation of HSPs – hours or days, at most. It is difficult to envisage long-term hardening occurring via HSPs.

Hardening based on damage repair was shown by Larcher (1987) for fir needles (Fig. 1.3.6). In this example, recuperation from the initial heat stress takes 5–6 days, i.e. it took this much time to effect repair and to switch from heat stress reactions to normal housekeeping photosynthesis. It can be assumed that a higher level of HSPs was still present at the time of the second heat stress. On the other hand, there are also so-called **chemical chaperones** which can increase the heat resistance of cells and shift the triggering of the HS response toward higher temperatures. These are the compatible solutes, such as glycerol, proline and betaine, which stabilise the native folding of mature proteins. It is not known to what extent such effects play a role in heat stress hardening.

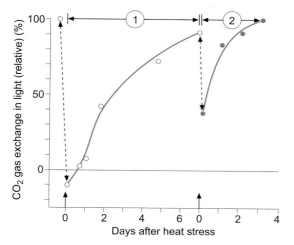

Fig. 1.3.6. Hardening of fir needles after a heat stress treatment. Damage and hardening were measured by the photosynthetic activity of the needles. *1* Recovery phase after the initial heat stress treatment; *2* after the second heat stress treatment (44 °C, 30 min). The extent of damage and the length of the recovery phase (repair) are clearly less after the second stress treatment than they were upon the first heat pulse. (Larcher 1987)

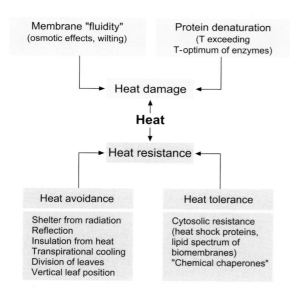

Fig. 1.3.7. The effects of heat on plants and the ways in which they react to the heat stress

The aspects of heat damage, heat avoidance and heat tolerance described above are summarised in Fig. 1.3.7.

1.3.5

Cold

Recommended Literature

- Bigras FJ, Colombo SJ (2001) Conifer cold hardiness. Kluwer, Dordrecht
- Guy CL (1990) Cold acclimation and freezing stress tolerance: role of protein metabolism. Annu Rev Plant Physiol Plant Mol Biol 41:187–223
- Hughes MA, Dunn MA (1996) The molecular biology of plant acclimation to low temperature. J Exp Bot 47:291–305
- Li PH, Chen THH (1997) Plant cold hardiness. In: Molecular biology, biochemistry and physiology. Plenum Press, New York
- Sakai A, Larcher W (1987) Frost survival of plants: responses and adaptation to freezing stress. In: Ecological studies, vol 62. Springer, Berlin Heidelberg New York
- Thomashow MF (1999) Plant cold acclimation: freezing tolerance genes and regulatory mechanisms. Annu Rev Plant Physiol Plant Mol Biol 50:571–600

On about two-thirds of the land mass of the earth the annual minimum temperatures fall to below 0 °C, on half of the land mass to −10 °C. Thus it is not surprising that cold is the best studied of any abiotic stressor for plants and animals, and it is of enormous economic importance.

In comparison with the stressor heat, where the primary reaction affects membranes and metabolic and protein homeostasis, the environmental factor cold additionally causes stress by desiccation of tissues with accompanying ice formation at temperatures below the freezing point (freeze-desiccation). Distinction is therefore made between cold stress above the freezing point, so-called **chilling**, and stress by frost, i.e. at temperatures below the freezing point, which always includes a temperature component and a desiccation component caused by ice formation (Fig. 1.3.8).

The phenomena of chilling (see Allen and Ort 2001), rather than those of freezing, are thus analogous to heat stress. In heat stress the physiological strain occurs through the (dissimilar) speeding up of metabolic processes culminating in the specific heat stress response. While metabolic processes also get out of equilibrium during cold stress due to the different activation en-

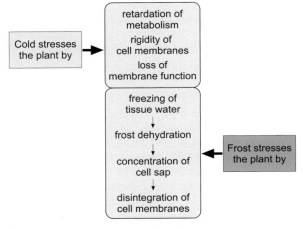

Fig. 1.3.8. Stress from cold and frost

ergies of individual reactions, the strain is altogether less because all of the reactions are slowed down. A rapid cold stress response like that of heat shock in the form of heat shock proteins is therefore not to be expected, even though the term "cold shock proteins" is used at times in the literature. These are not proteins with chaperone functions, but rather proteins whose names indicate their various functions: antifreeze proteins, cold acclimation proteins or proteins of the group of "dehydrins".

A problem specific to cold stress is the increase in viscosity of the membranes. An organism which cannot react rapidly due to low temperatures and possibly also due to severe tissue desiccation is much more prone to secondary

---

Box 1.3.5   Measurement of cold and frost damage

In order to determine damage due to cold or frost or to determine the limits of resistance, a standardised stress treatment is required. In contrast to the case with heat shock, a comparatively slow change in temperature is preferred when analysing the effects of cold, in order to allow for the slower rate of biochemical reactions at lower temperatures.

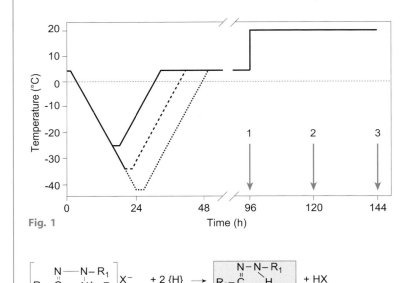

Fig. 1

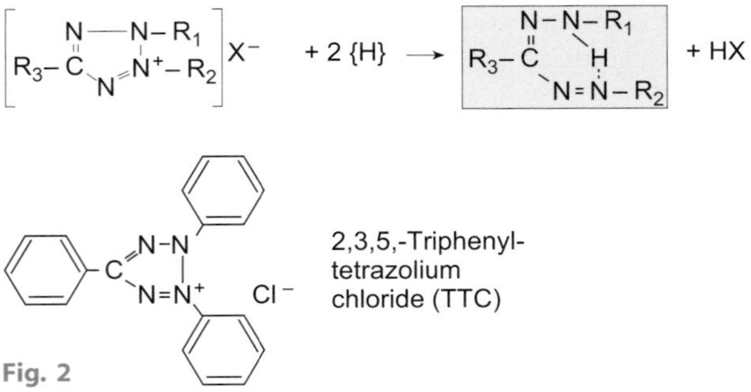

Fig. 2

2,3,5,-Triphenyl-tetrazolium chloride (TTC)

Fig. 1. shows the temperature course during the entire test. First, the sample is slowly cooled (1–2 K/h). It is then exposed to a defined final temperature for 2 h before being slowly warmed (1–2 K/h) again. The sample is then held at +5 °C for 48 h to enable any incurred damage to develop. It is then placed in a solution of TTC. Dehydrogenases now reduce the tetrazolium to coloured formazan (Fig. 2, formazan is shown in blue). After 24 h this is extracted (for ca. 12 h) and quantified photometrically.

In addition to this test, the vitality tests presented in Box 1.1.1 can also be used.

stressors. Particularly interesting in this regard is the stress combination of cold and high light energy, which leads to considerable damage in non-hardened plant organs, especially in the photosynthetic apparatus (see Chap. 1.2.1.3). Frost hardening and frost dehardening are, therefore, classical topics for the study of adaptation reactions. The response of plants to cold takes the form of both specific adaptations and general stress reactions (strain). The latter relate to changes in membranes, as well as to strengthening of systems for the detoxification of radicals and reactive oxygen species (see Fig. 1.3.32).

Because of the slower rate of metabolism in the cold, experiments to measure cold tolerance and cold damage must be very carefully designed. Plants must not be cooled too rapidly, nor should they be warmed up too quickly at the end of the experiment. Box 1.3.5 shows an appropriate procedure.

1.3.5.1
Stress by Cold Above the Freezing Point (Chilling): Cold Damage Is Predominantly Membrane Damage

Damage due to temperatures which are low, but above the freezing point, occurs practically only in tropical and subtropical plants which are ge-

netically adapted to a temperature range of between +5 and about 50 °C (see Table 1.3.1). Palms, mangroves, coffee plants and some tropical herbs known to us as houseplants, such as *Peperomia* and the African violet (*Saintpaulia ionantha*), have been studied particularly intensively. As is the case for temperature stress in general, the individual organs of a plant show different sensitivities. A good example is the coffee plant (*Coffea arabica*, Fig. 1.3.9). It is typical of chilling that the old leaves (as well as the cambium in the root) are most sensitive to cold, not the young leaves. Individual metabolic processes also exhibit different sensitivities. Among the most sensitive are membrane-bound processes, such as ion homeostasis and photosynthesis. Certain stages in the development of a plant are also particularly cold sensitive, namely germination and fruit ripening. In general, those stages are most sensitive in which the system for the detoxification of radicals and aggressive oxygen species is not yet, or no longer, very efficient. Pollen ripening is, at any rate, the most sensitive stage.

The actual amount of chilling stress is, as far as is known, the product of intensity and the duration of the stress, i.e. a 4-h period of cooling to +1 °C results in approximately the same degree of damage as lowering the temperature to 3.5 °C over a 20-h period (Chap. 1.1.3, Fig. 1.1.6). At the subcellular level, chilling damage

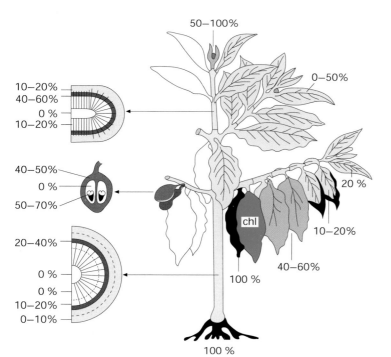

Fig. 1.3.9. Differences in sensitivity to cold in organs of the coffee tree. Percentual damage after 3 days of continual cooling to +1 °C. *Black* Complete damage; *chl* chlorotic. (Larcher 2003)

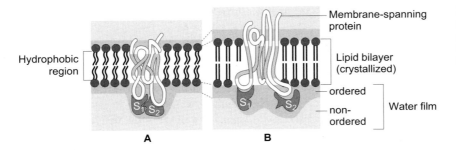

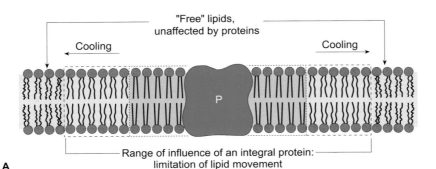

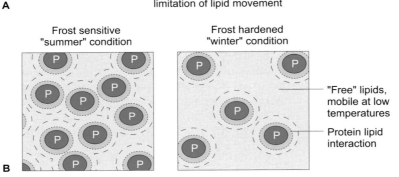

Fig. 1.3.10. Model of a bio-membrane in cross section, in a fluid (active A) and in a rigid (inactive B) state. S_1, S_2 substrates. (After Wolfe 1978)

Fig. 1.3.11. A Schematic representation of the interactions between proteins and lipids in thylakoid membranes during cooling. B Influence of frost hardening on the processes taking place during cooling of the thylakoid membranes of *Pinus sylvestris*. (After Vogg et al. 1998)

occurs through metabolic imbalances and membrane "stiffening".

How does cold inactivate membranes? The classical conception is that when cells which are not cold resistant are cooled, the biomembrane lipids change from the fluid aggregation state to the crystalline, inflexible state. This is accompanied by a thickening of the biomembrane and a deformation (inactivation) of integral membrane proteins (**thermotrophic phase transition**). This explanation is plausible, but is certainly over-simplified (Fig. 1.3.10).

It is much more likely that a zone of lipid molecules with limited mobility surrounds the proteins spanning the membrane. This zone expands during cooling; at dense protein packing, i.e. at high membrane protein content, such zones can aggregate and form larger areas with high viscosity (Fig. 1.3.11).

In such regions membranes appear to be no longer "tight", making it difficult to form and maintain concentration gradients. Furthermore, ion pumps are inactivated by cold, which also results in a progressive breakdown of compartmentation. This applies particularly to the proton gradients which are required for the supply of ATP in the cell. It is still unresolved as to whether the water loss which is often observed from damaged cells is merely a consequence of the loss of solutes from the cell (passive flux) or whether aquaporins play a role (see Box 1.5.2).

The sensitivity with which particular membranes react to cold appears to depend on the type of plant involved. In some cases the plasma membrane has been identified as the site of primary damage (e.g. for *Eucalyptus* cell cultures), in other cases the tonoplast is probably particularly cold sensitive (e.g. in spruce).

In contrast to the annual cycle of frost hardening and dehardening, there is almost no acclimation to chilling. No appreciable shifts to lower LD50 values could be observed with either mangroves or palms. However, there are genotypes with different cold sensitivities within the same plant species. The less cold-sensitive genotypes are usually found in the subtropics (10 to 23 °N and S of the equator), and the more sensitive ones in the tropics (10 °N and S of the equator). Molecular mechanisms effecting hardening in the more resistant genotypes are usually based above all on a higher degree of unsaturation of the membrane lipids.

It is of particular interest in this connection to modify the membrane lipids of important crop plants to confer greater cold tolerance. One way of achieving this is to lower the proportion of saturated fatty acids (see Box 1.3.6 and Table 1.3.4) in favour of unsaturated fatty acids. In principle, this concerns the group of the glycerol lipids which can be either phosphatides or glycolipids. Initial genetic engineering attempts to increase the amount of unsaturated fatty acids

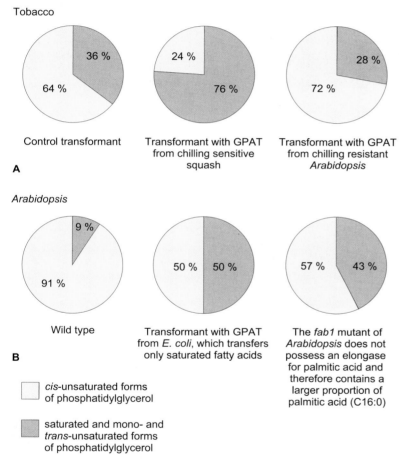

Tobacco

Control transformant

Transformant with GPAT from chilling sensitive squash

Transformant with GPAT from chilling resistant *Arabidopsis*

A

Arabidopsis

Wild type

Transformant with GPAT from *E. coli*, which transfers only saturated fatty acids

The *fab1* mutant of *Arabidopsis* does not possess an elongase for palmitic acid and therefore contains a larger proportion of palmitic acid (C16:0)

B

☐ *cis*-unsaturated forms of phosphatidylglycerol

▨ saturated and mono- and *trans*-unsaturated forms of phosphatidylglycerol

Fig. 1.3.12. Changing chilling sensitivity by altering the degree of unsaturation of the fatty acids in phosphatidylglycerol. Chilling-resistant and -sensitive plants are available for gene transfer. It is important that chloroplastic glycerol-3P-acyltransferase (GPAT) from chilling-resistant plants (*Arabidopsis*) uses almost exclusively 18:1-ACP as substrate, whereas the enzyme from chilling-sensitive plants (e.g. cucurbits) can transfer fatty acids from both 18:1-ACP and from 16:0-ACP (see Box 1.3.6). When glycerol-3P-acyltransferase from cucurbits is overexpressed in tobacco (A), a transgenic plant is produced with a large proportion (76%) of saturated fatty acids in phosphatidylglycerol: If, in contrast, the enzyme from *Arabidopsis* (B) is used, the percentage of unsaturated fatty acids in this lipid increases. In *Arabidopsis* the wild type exhibits hardly any saturated fatty acids in phosphatidylglycerol, so that the proportion of unsaturated fatty acids cannot be increased any further; but the opposite experiment – to increase the proportion of saturated fatty acids – is feasible by means of gene technology. What influence does the altered proportion of unsaturated fatty acids have on sensitivity to low temperatures? Increasing the proportion of *cis*-unsaturated fatty acids increases chilling tolerance, both of photosynthesis and with regard to macroscopically visible damage after exposure to cold. Conversely, the resistance decreased when the proportion of saturated fatty acids was increased. (After Nishida and Murata 1996)

Box 1.3.6   Lipid biosynthesis in plants (After Frentzen and Heinz 1983, see also Ohlrogge and Browse 1995)

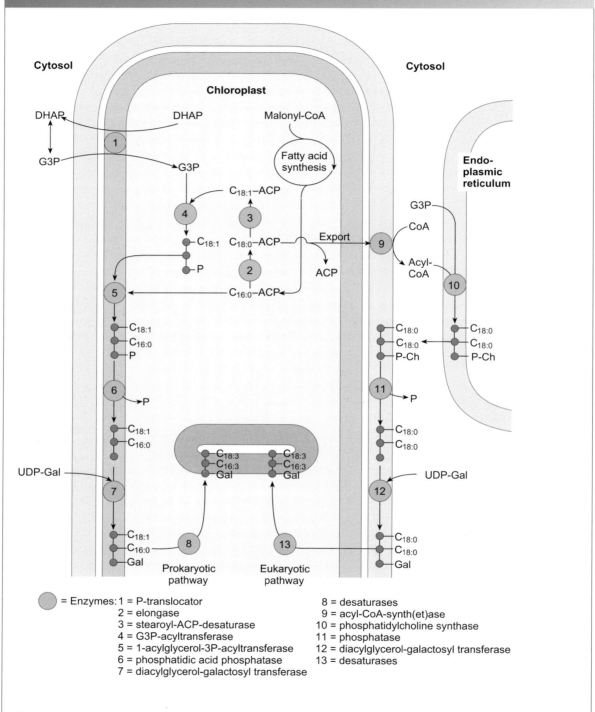

= Enzymes: 1 = P-translocator
2 = elongase
3 = stearoyl-ACP-desaturase
4 = G3P-acyltransferase
5 = 1-acylglycerol-3P-acyltransferase
6 = phosphatidic acid phosphatase
7 = diacylglycerol-galactosyl transferase

8 = desaturases
9 = acyl-CoA-synth(et)ase
10 = phosphatidylcholine synthase
11 = phosphatase
12 = diacylglycerol-galactosyl transferase
13 = desaturases

Desaturases are important for the development of chilling resistance in plants: acyl-ACP desaturase (3), acyl-lipid desaturases (13) [including prokaryotic acyl lipid desaturase (8)], glycerol-3P-acyltransferase (4) and possibly also the 1-acylglycerol-3-P-acyltransferase (5), which can only use fatty acids as substrates which are esterified or occur as thioesters (ACP).

have indeed resulted in increased cold resistance (Fig. 1.3.12).

1.3.5.2
Imbalances in Metabolism Caused by Cold

There have been extensive investigations on damage caused by imbalances of metabolism which has been slowed due to low temperatures. Such imbalances usually result primarily from the different Q_{10} values for the biophysical and biochemical processes involved.

Metabolic Imbalances

Diurnal fluctuations of enzyme activities and their metabolite pools of plants favouring warm conditions are particularly sensitive to cold. If such plants are kept in permanently weak light under otherwise normal surrounding conditions, an endogenous metabolic rhythm of so-called free **circadian** (i.e. periodicity of about 24 h) **oscillations** becomes evident. Two key cytosolic enzymes, **sucrose phosphate synthase** (SPS) and **nitrate reductase**, show this phenomenon. In correspondence with photosynthetic processes, their activities are higher during the light period and lower during the night, with a free periodicity of about 26 h. If the photosynthetic production of triosephosphate in the chloroplast and its further metabolism to sucrose in the cytosol are not synchronised, imbalances naturally result. One reason for this is that phosphate released in the cytosol during sucrose synthesis must be returned to the chloroplast from which it was withdrawn due to its having been bound to triose during the export of carbohydrate into the cytosol. In the example shown in Fig. 1.3.13 the free oscillations of SPS during a 12 h lowering of the temperature from 26 to 4 °C were disturbed to the extent that an exactly phase-reversed oscillation resulted upon a return to normal temperatures, in which minimal activity was exhibited during the light period and maximum activity during the dark period. A corresponding shift in rhythm also occurred with nitrase reductase. However, not all endogenous rhythms of warmth-loving plants are affected by chilling. For example, the endogenous oscillations of stomatal movement in avocado leaves maintained their original frequency even upon cooling, despite photosynthesis itself being strongly inhibited (Allen and Ort 2001).

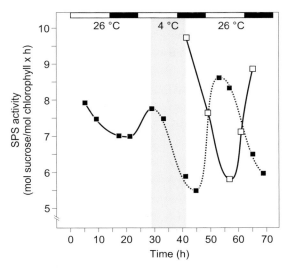

Fig. 1.3.13. Shift in endogenous metabolic rhythm caused by chilling. Tomato plants were grown at normal temperature (26 °C) in continuous weak light and the endogenous oscillation of SPS activity was observed (■). The oscillation period was about 26 h ("circadian"). The rhythm of the previously applied light–dark phases is shown in the *bar* at the top of the diagram. In a second experiment, plants having been treated in the same way were cooled to 4 °C between 29 and 41 h; this resulted in a reversal of the endogenous oscillation of SPS (□) because the rhythm was delayed. (Jones et al. 1998)

Chilling is also very important when it occurs together with high light intensity (Fig. 1.3.14). In such a stress combination the thylakoid system is usually overloaded, as the photosynthetic carbohydrate metabolism cannot keep up with the light reactions because of the low temperatures. As a consequence, photosystem II (PS II) in particular is inhibited, so-called **photoinhibition** due to light inactivation of the sensitive D1 protein (see Chap. 1.2.1.3). To regenerate complete photosynthetic capacity, the damaged D1 protein must be replaced. According to current knowledge, the five steps shown in Fig. 1.2.8 are required: removal of the inactivated D1 protein; synthesis of new pre-D1; insertion of pre-D1 into PS II; processing of the pre-D1; and reconstitution of the entire core of PS II.

The degree of unsaturation of the thylakoid lipids affects particularly the insertion and the processing of pre-D1. It is therefore assumed that the chilling tolerance of plants with a higher degree of unsaturation is based on a more efficient exchange of damaged for intact D1 proteins.

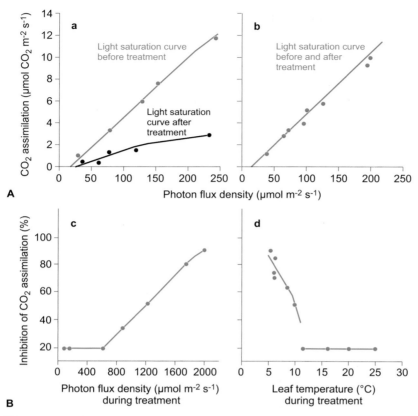

Fig. 1.3.14. The impact of a combination of stresses: The effect of chilling and light on photosynthesis. A Runner bean leaves (runner beans are tropical plants and thus chilling sensitive) were kept for 6 h at 6 °C under intense illumination (*a* 2000 µmol photons m^{-2} s^{-1}) and the light saturation curves for CO_2 assimilation were measured before and after the treatment. The stressed leaves showed a drastic inhibition of photosynthesis, even 1 h after treatment. When the leaves were exposed to only weak light (*b* 70 µmol photons m^{-2} s^{-1}) during the chilling, no inhibition was observed. However, light saturation curves were only measured up to about 250 µmol photons m^{-2} s^{-1}. B In this experiment, the bean leaves were exposed to different light intensities during a 3-h chilling period (5.5 °C). Above about 500 µmol photons m^{-2} s^{-1} photosynthesis begins to become inhibited (*c*). If the light intensity is held constant at 2000 µmol photons m^{-2} s^{-1} and the temperature is varied, the inhibition decreases as expected with rising temperature and does not occur at all at above about 10 °C (*d*). (After Powles et al. 1983) see also Powles 1984)

1.3.5.3
Metabolic Imbalances Often Lead to Oxidative Stress

It is nowadays thought that photosystems are mainly damaged by so-called oxidative stress. The stressors are termed **ROS** – reactive O_2 species. These not only consist of oxygen as such, but also include the products of the reactions of activated oxygen with metabolites and structural components of the cell, e.g. biomembranes (Box 1.3.7). In an undamaged cell living without particular stress, these ROS form at only very slow rates which present no problem for the endogenous detoxification and repair systems. Such reactive molecules, however, are produced in much larger amounts upon metabolic imbal-

ances, under stress or in senescing cells, and can cause damage before they are detoxified. In the following, some situations and reactions are described in which ROS are formed:

Oxygen in the air possesses two unpaired electrons and thus occurs in the rather unreactive triplet state. Oxygen in this state is not able to react with molecules in the singlet state, but can react with others in the triplet state. An example is the reaction with chlorophyll, which has passed from the first singlet state into the first triplet state due to the loss of excitation energy. This chlorophyll is able to transfer its remaining energy to the O_2 molecule (exciton transfer), which is thus subjected to spin reversal and becomes extremely reactive **singlet oxygen** ($^1O_2$). $^1O_2$ has a pair of very labile electron

Box 1.3.7   Oxygen-activating reactions

1. Photodynamic reactions

$P^* + {}^3O_2 \rightarrow P + {}^1O_2$; singlet oxygen ${}^1O_2 + RH \rightarrow ROOH$; if RH is, for example, an unsaturated fatty acid, a fatty acid hydroperoxide is produced. ROOH can be reduced via electron donation (Fe^{2+}, Cu^{1+}) and so form alkoxyradicals:

$$ROOH + Fe^{2+} \rightarrow RO^\bullet + OH^- + Fe^{3+};$$
$$RO^\bullet + RH \rightarrow R^\bullet + ROH$$

this can be the start of a chain reaction

2. Reductive oxygen activation

In the presence of reducing agents with an ε value < -160 mV, oxygen can accept an elec-

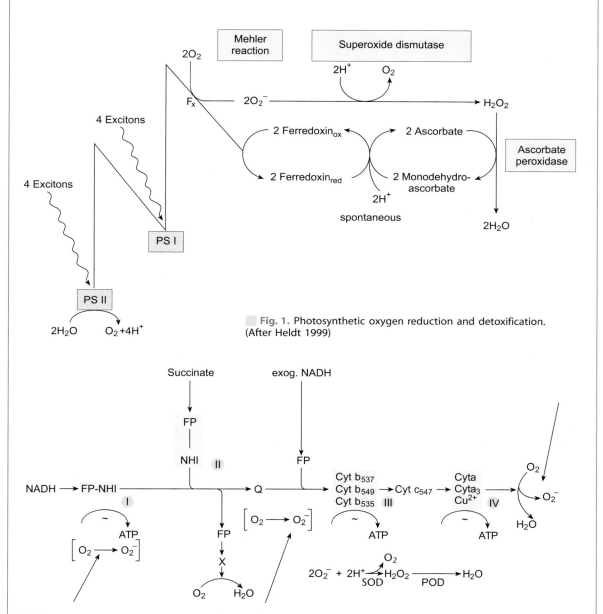

Fig. 1. Photosynthetic oxygen reduction and detoxification. (After Heldt 1999)

Fig. 2. Oxygen activation in the mitochondrial respiratory chain. *FP* Flavoprotein; *NHI* non-haeme-iron; *POD* cytochrome-c-peroxidase; *I, II, III, IV* protein complexes of the respiratory chain; *SOD* superoxide dismutase. (After Elstner 1996)

Box 1.3.7   **(continued)**

tron and become superoxide or an oxygen radical:

$$^3O_2 + e^- \rightarrow {}^3O_2^-$$

Superoxide can originate in photosynthesis (electron transfer to O_2 instead of to NADP), in the respiratory chain (from iron-sulfur proteins or from hydroquinone, during the stepwise reduction of oxygen by cytochrome a/a_3), as well as in reactions with monooxygenases.

Superoxide dissimilates spontaneously (10^4 times faster with SOD, however);

$$2O_2^- \rightarrow H_2O_2 + O_2$$

H_2O_2 can be reduced monovalently, e.g. by Fe^{2+}: **Haber-Weiss reaction, Fenton chemistry**:

$$H_2O_2 + Fe^{2+} \rightarrow OH^- + OH^\cdot + Fe^{3+}$$

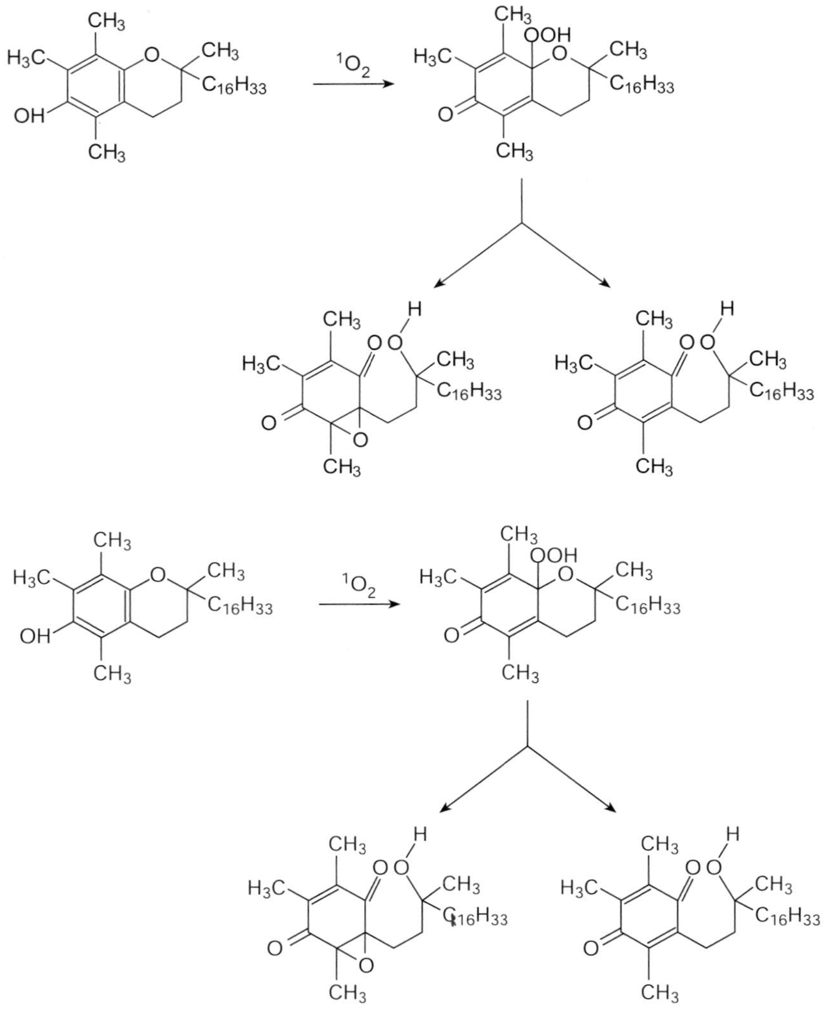

Fig. 3. Detoxification of singlet oxygen by tocopherol. (After Neely et al. 1988)

pairs which react with many organic substances, particularly readily with unsaturated compounds under formation of hydroperoxides.

Oxygen can also be activated by reduction. This happens, for example, in photosynthesis (see Box 1.3.7, Fig. 1) when no other electron acceptor is available for reduction by Fd, or when reduction is catalysed by the total herbicide methyl viologen (Paraquat). Oxygen can also be reduced by the respiratory chain (see Box 1.3.7, Fig. 2), via sulfur-iron proteins, via hydroquinone or via damaged endooxidases which have effected only partial electron transfer to O_2. The superoxide or oxygen radical anion is formed, which dismutates spontaneously to hydrogen peroxide and oxygen, a reaction which takes place 10,000-fold more rapidly in the presence of superoxide dismutase.

Hydrogen peroxide can be reduced monovalently [e.g. via the oxygen radical ion and iron-(III) ions], whereby the **Haber-Weiss reaction** gives rise to the even more reactive **OH radical**, which immediately causes oxidative damage in its immediate environment.

In the case of chilling, the rate of metabolic NADPH consumption (re-oxidation of NADPH to NADP) is less than the rate of NADP reduction due to the low temperature, i.e. NADPH accumulates and the NADP pool becomes "over-reduced". The photosynthetic electrons are then transferred by linear electron transport to oxygen (**Mehler reaction**) and superoxide is thus formed. This and ROS formed in this connection oxidise methionine and histidine residues of the D1 protein and thus cause its inactivation.

As shown in the above, ROS are not only formed at low temperatures, but also under the influence of other stressors, such as light. The establishment of a multifaceted **anti-oxidative system** is thus a general stress reaction, not a specific one. This anti-oxidative system consists of a number of enzymes and their substrates, the so-called radical scavengers.

The Anti-oxidative System Detoxifies Reactive Oxygen

Plants have recourse to several biochemical mechanisms to detoxify ROS (Box 1.3.7, Fig. 3):

1. Quenchers and Scavengers
   The group of quenchers and scavengers consists of small molecules which react with ROS in often non-enzymatic reactions and thus de-

toxify them. These are protective compounds localised in the membranes such as tocopherol and many carotenoids, but they also include water-soluble compounds such as ascorbic acid and phenol derivates – particularly flavonoids and coumarins. They react with $^1O_2$ as well as with the OH radical and thus intercept the most toxic ROS (thus the terms quencher, scavenger). The OH radical, which is very effective in its own vicinity, reacts particularly well with flavonoids. It is thus not surprising that the key enzymes of flavonoid biosynthesis, phenylalanine-ammonium lyase and chalcone synthase, are formed to a particularly great extent in frost-hardy plant organs during frost hardening or during stress by chilling coupled with high light intensities (see Chap. 1.2; Box 1.2.5). Flavonoids are also formed in response to infections and wounding, and are then called **phytoalexins**. They thus have a multiple role in stress defence.

2. Enzymatic ROS Detoxification
   ROS are enzymatically detoxified in the compartments in which they are most frequently formed, i.e. in the chloroplasts, mitochondria and peroxisomes, during the course of which water is usually produced. Corresponding enzymes have also been observed in the cytosol (Box 1.3.7, Fig. 3).

The water-soluble, detoxifying enzyme system consists of superoxide dismutase (SOD), a peroxidase – usually ascorbate peroxidase, (mono)-dehydroascorbate reductase and the NAD(P)H-dependent glutathione reductase, and is known as the **ascorbate-glutathione cycle** (Box 1.3.7, Fig. 3). The enzyme activities present in the individual compartments can be very high, so that the system works very efficiently. During frost hardening the individual enzymes of this detoxification pathway are additionally activated or more strongly expressed.

1.3.5.4
Repair Systems Mend Damage to Biomembranes, Nucleic Acids and Proteins

A number of repair mechanisms are known which remove peroxidised fatty acids and their resultant products (hydroxyoctadecadaic acids, so-called HODEs) from membranes (most membrane lipids remain quite generally for only a very short time in the membrane), detoxify them and replace them with intact fatty acids. Such repair mechanisms also exist for damaged nucleic acids (see Box 1.2.4). Damaged proteins are repaired by means of the chaperone system or are degraded after marking with ubiquitin.

1.3.6

Frost

Stress caused by low temperatures is greatly increased in the case of frost due to freeze-desiccation. Secondary strains such as high light intensity play, of course, an additional important role at temperatures below 0 °C. Frost also occurs in tropical climates, namely in tropical high mountains. As the temperature in these regions only falls below the freezing point for a matter of hours, freezing avoidance mechanisms are very important. In contrast to chilling, frost is characterised by seasonal hardening (acquisition of frost resistance or frost tolerance) and dehardening. These processes involve many physiologically important aspects. Particularly topical are the many so-called cold-related proteins (CORs) which have been discovered recently. These constitute an important starting point for introducing frost hardening into cold-sensitive crop plants, in addition to the genetic engineering of biomembrane frost hardening described in Chapter 1.1.6. It should be mentioned in this regard that 70% of the annual harvest losses in the USA was caused by cold and drought in the 1980s, while insects, weeds and pathogens together were responsible for only about 10%. Late frosts caused damage of more than US$ 1 billion during 1981–1985 in southern Florida (Yelenosky 1985).

1.3.6.1
Freezing Temperatures and Biomembranes

The manner in which chilling affects membrane fluidity applies in principle to frost as well, but to a more severe extent. Measurements of fluidity by means of electron spin resonance or fluorescence polarisation show primarily the stiffening effect which a high protein/lipid ratio has on the fluidity of biomembranes at low temperatures. Particularly protein-rich biomembranes, such as those of the thylakoids, reduce the protein/lipid ratio during frost hardening. In addi-

tion, a desaturation of the fatty acids in the membrane lipids is often observed. More details in this regard will be given in Chapter 1.3.6.9.

It is important to realise that the freeze-desiccation of frost-hardened tissues is inevitably accompanied by a more or less pronounced shrinkage of the protoplast.

As the biomembrane cannot expand or shrink like a balloon would [the intrinsic elastic flexibility of a biomembrane should not exceed 2–3% (Wolfe and Steponkus 1983)], shrinking processes are often associated with a removal of lipids from the membrane and expansion processes with the insertion of lipids. During reversible freeze-desiccation, this material must be deposited in such a way as to be immediately available upon thawing (Fig. 1.3.15).

A quite similar problem occurs during plasmolysis. Steponkus et al. (1983) showed with isolated protoplasts from rye mesophyll cells that damage to frost-sensitive cells occurs during thawing, because the amount of material available for re-incorporation is no longer sufficient for the "areal growth" of the plasma membrane. The resulting lysis of the cells was called "expansion-induced lysis". Protoplasts of frost-hardy winter rye leaves did not show this phenomenon. They do not deposit the material removed from the membrane during contraction within the cell, but deposit it at the external side of the membrane where it is not accessible to lipases. The different behaviour of the lipids depends on the degree of their unsaturation: Frost-sensitive plasma membranes of protoplasts can be artificially "hardened" if they are treated with a surplus of unsaturated lipids (in the experiments phosphatidylcholine with one- or two-fold unsaturated fatty acids was used) and a partial exchange of the membrane lipids takes place. Even though protoplasts are an excellent in vitro system for the study of many processes, they can only provide answers to some partial aspects of frost hardening in biomembranes.

In considering the freezing of cellular water, it is very important to regard the involvement of the cell wall in stabilising the protoplast. The freezing of cell water has often been compared to plasmolysis – a very different process. During freezing, the cellular fluid must crystallise in the intercellular spaces, as otherwise biomembranes bordering the ice crystals would disintegrate, because the hydrophobic interactions of the lipids which stabilise the membranes require the presence of liquid water. This also means that no ice

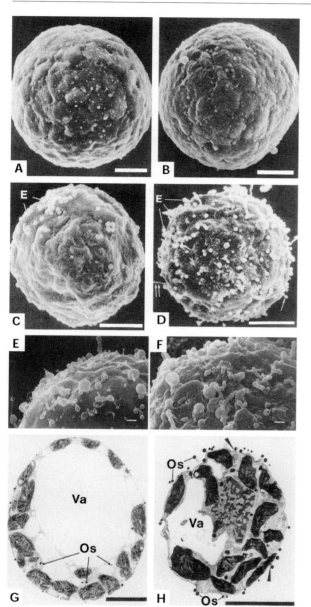

Fig. 1.3.15. Behaviour of isolated protoplasts from rye leaves in isotonic and hypertonic solutions. Protoplasts were isolated from leaves of frost-sensitive (A, B) and frost-hardened (C, D) rye plants and incubated in isotonic medium (A, C, G) and in a medium with a concentration double that of the isotonic medium (B, D, H). The outer surface of the non-hardened protoplasts remained almost smooth on shrinking (B), i.e. lipids excluded from the membrane were displaced to the interior of the protoplast. Protoplasts from frost-hardened cells deposited their excluded lipids in extrusions of various shapes (E) on the outside of the plasma membrane when they shrank, where they cannot be degraded by endogenous lipases (D). The transmission electron micrographs (G, H) also show the shrinking (compare the size of the vacuoles in G and H) and the lipid extrusions (*arrow*) which are strongly contrasted by osmium staining (Os). The *bar* corresponds in each case to 5 μm. E An enlarged section of a protoplast from frost-hardened leaves in hypertonic medium. F The surface of a protoplast from non-hardened leaves in hypertonic medium, after fusion of the protoplast with liposomes consisting of dilinoleoylphosphatidylcholine. Protoplasts which deposit lipids internally on shrinking burst upon swelling in isotonic medium, because the lipids are degraded by phospholipases. Lipids which are deposited externally can be reintegrated into the membrane upon swelling of the protoplast. The *bar* corresponds to 1 μm. (After Steponkus et al. 1983, 1988)

may be formed between the plasma membrane and the cell wall. This space, which in the case of plasmolysis is filled with the plasmolyticum, would have to fill with air during the extracellular freezing of cellular liquid if the protoplast were to withdraw from the cell wall. The air would have to enter through the pores of the cell wall. These pores are very small (about 4 nm diameter in the primary wall), and they are filled with water due to the high matrix potential of the cell wall. It would require a suction of more than 80 MPa to suck air through the cell wall pores (Zhu and Beck 1991). Such high suction has never been observed in living cells, however. The protoplast is therefore not normally able to detach itself from the cell wall during the exogenous freezing of the cellular liquid of the protoplast, and the entire cell must collapse upon the dehydration resulting from freezing (Fig. 1.3.16).

Cells which are not particularly rigid, e.g. those of the mesophyll, indeed wrinkle and fold under these conditions (**freezing cytorrhysis**). Since the cell wall itself cannot shrink, the plasma membrane must not reduce its surface significantly. The problem as to the extra- or intracellular deposition of membrane material de-

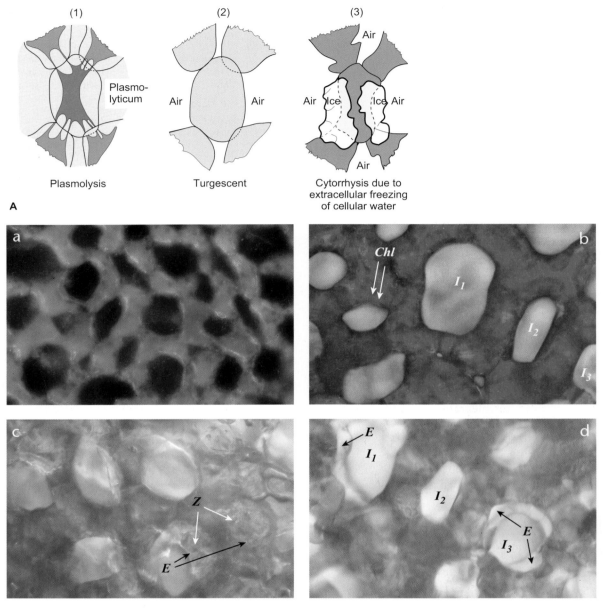

Fig. 1.3.16. A Plasmolysis and freezing of mesophyll cells from a leaf of *Pachysandra terminalis*. During plasmolysis (*1*), the plasmolyticum intrudes into the space between the cell wall and the protoplast, and the cell wall is relaxed. During freezing (*3*) the protoplast remains attached to the cell wall despite the export of cell fluids into the intercellular spaces, because the cell wall is air-tight in the swollen state. The cell wall dents or buckles, depending on the extent of the freeze-desiccation. Since crystallisation takes place extracellularly, no ice is formed between the cell wall and the protoplast. B: *a–d* Spongy parenchyma of a leaf of *Pachysandra terminalis*. *a* Surface view of the spongy parenchyma following removal of the lower epidermis; chloroplasts can be clearly seen in the cells. *b* Spongy parenchyma after taking up neutral red through the leaf stalk. *Chl* Chloroplasts. *d* The same section of the spongy parenchyma at $-12\,^{\circ}$C (I_1–I_3 indicate the same intercellular spaces). Deposition of colourless ice (*E*) can be clearly recognised within the intercellular spaces. *c* Spongy parenchyma was stained with neutral red and then killed before cooling to $-12\,^{\circ}$C. The ice crystals are not restricted to the intercellular spaces, and they contain drops of coloured cell sap (*Z*). Note also the change in the neutral red colour resulting from acidification as a consequence of killing the tissue. (Photos J.J. Zhu)

scribed above is thus of hardly any consequence in this regard. Freezing plasmolysis does not occur even in rigid cells which are tightly integrated into a tissue if the cells are to survive the freezing (see Chap. 1.3.6.3).

1.3.6.2
Intra- and Extracellular Formation of Ice

Amphiphilic lipids (lipids with a hydrophobic and a hydrophilic pole) only unite to form micelles and membrane surfaces if they are in a sufficiently hydrophilic medium, i.e. stabilised by a structured water film. If this structured water film is removed, the stabilising effect of the hydrophobic interactions is lost and the lipids aggregate in droplets: This is called the lipid hexagonal II phase (Fig. 1.3.17). An example of lipids in this hexagonal II phase is the lipid droplets (plastoglobuli) in senescing chloroplasts. Intracellular ice formation probably starts at biomembranes, because of the structured water film associated with them. This ice formation, however, would remove the membrane-stabilising component and consequently the membrane would disintegrate. Earlier research described this as the perforation of biomembranes by ice crystals, because it is the hexagonal, pointed forms of the ice crystals that form at temperatures above $-100\,°C$ which cause the dehydration. Extremely rapid cooling (cooling rates of $> 1000\,°C/min$) down to the temperature of liquid nitrogen, so-called **vitrification** (which can only be carried out with very small sample volumes of a few mm^3), leads to solidification of the cell liquid into amorphous ice, which does not have the destructive effect just described. However, there is a danger of recrystallisation of the amorphous ice into hexagonal, damaging crystal forms upon the slow thawing of the samples. Vitrification is an artificial, special case which does not take place in nature because of the very rapid cooling rates required. However, it is important for the preservation of bacterial cultures, for example.

Whether the crystallisation takes place inside or outside the cell depends on several factors. One of these is the rate of cooling: The faster the tissue cools, the greater is the danger of intracellular ice formation (Fig. 1.3.18). This is not damaging in the case of vitrification, due to the very abrupt and sudden deep-freezing of the entire tissue. Another factor which determines where ice is deposited is the state of the plasma membrane: Frost-hardened membranes allow water (more exactly: the liquid of the cell) to exit into the apoplast more easily than do frost-sensitive membranes.

The mechanism of this efflux of water has not yet been explained. It is often assumed that ion pumps (especially H^+-ATPases) are inactivated in the cold, and that ions and other dissolved materials diffuse out of the cell into the water film surrounding the intercellular spaces and are followed by water. The liquid accumulating in the intercellular spaces now requires a trigger for crystallisation. Such a nucleation stimulus can originate from the xylem if the formation of ice first starts there (Gross et al. 1988) or if it rapidly spreads from a nearby nucleation centre. On the other hand, certain surface structures of the cell walls or of microorganisms which are found predominantly in the substomatal respiratory cavity can also trigger the nucleation.

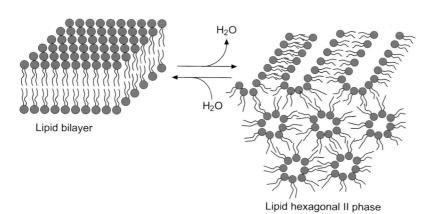

Lipid bilayer

H_2O

H_2O

Lipid hexagonal II phase

Fig. 1.3.17. Disintegration and reconstruction of a phospholipid bilayer by water removal (e.g. freeze-dehydration) and rehydration. Phospholipids form lipid drops or threads in the hexagonal II phase. (After Crowe et al. 1983)

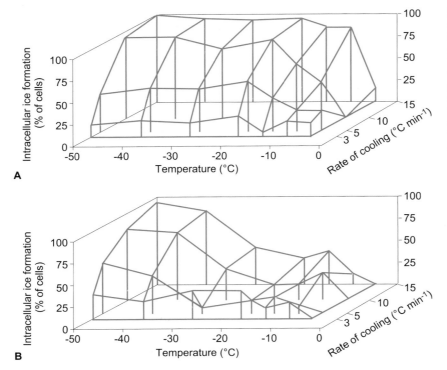

A

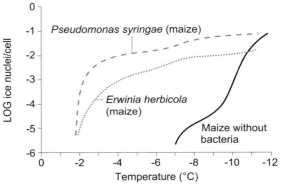

Fig. 1.3.18. Formation of intercellular ice in protoplasts of frost-sensitive (A) and frost-hardened (B) rye leaves as a function of the rate of cooling and the minimum temperature (*abscissa*). Protoplasts from frost-sensitive leaves do not permit the exclusion of cellular liquids during cooling, so that ice forms intracellularly. Consequently, the cells are lethally damaged. (After Dowgert and Steponkus 1983)

B

1.3.6.3
Heterogeneous Nucleation; the Example of INA Bacteria

The molecular details of the surface structures of plant cell walls which are active in nucleation, i.e. which trigger the formation of crystals at relatively low frost temperatures, are not yet known. However, it is known that such a phenomenon does exist. Examples are winter cereals and leaves of other winter-hardy plants, e.g. speedwell (*Veronica* spp.) and some species of box trees. Extracts of the internal surfaces (intercellular spaces) of these plants contain proteins which are formed during frost hardening. It is very probable that these proteins trigger the early nucleation, but this has not yet been shown definitely. The principle of nucleation initiation has been investigated thoroughly for a number of microorganisms which live on plant surfaces and trigger the crystallisation of water there (so-called heterogeneous nucleation). These microorganisms are called INA bacteria (*ice nucleation active bacteria*). The more effective their surface structures are in ordering the water clusters into a matrix-like arrangement, the more efficient they are as catalysts for crystallisation, and the lower is the degree of supercooling required for crystallisation (Fig. 1.3.19 and Table 1.3.6).

Fig. 1.3.19. The effect of INA bacteria on ice formation in maize leaves. Upon incubation with *Pseudomonas syringae* at –4 °C, 0.01 ice crystals per bacterial cell were determined, i.e. one ice crystal per 100 bacteria. (After Lindow 1982)

In these cases, the nucleation activity can be related at least in part to certain proteins, the so-called ice nucleating proteins (INPs). The amino acid sequence for one INP from *Pseudomonas syringae* is known: a particular octapeptide repeats itself 122 times in this polypeptide. Deletion mutants show that a 68-fold repetition of the motif is sufficient to trigger nucleation. If the periodicity of the octapeptide is changed, the nucleating activity is lost immediately

Table 1.3.6. Ice nucleation activity of bacterial cultures. Thirty drops (each 0.01 ml) of test material were placed on a controlled surface and the temperature was slowly lowered from room temperature to $-25\,°C$. The temperature at which the first ice crystals formed (T_1) and the temperature at which 90% of the drops were frozen (T_{90}) were recorded. (Maki et al. 1974)

Bacterial species	(Ice) nucleation temperature (°C)	
	T_1	T_{90}
Pseudomonas syringae C9	−2.9	−3.5
Pseudomonas syringae	−3.2	−3.9
Pseudomonas aeruginosa	−7.5	−17.8
Staphylococcus epidermidis	−6.9	−19.5
Escherichia coli	−8.3	−17.1
Enterobacter aerogenes	−9.6	−17.0
Proteus mirabilis	−8.0	−19.4
Proteus vulgaris	−7.8	−17.0
Bacillus subtilis	−10.6	−18.0
Bacillus cereus	−6.9	−17.0
Pure culture medium	−9.2	−17.0

(Green and Warren 1985). No relationship between the periodicity and the dimension of the distance between the water molecules in the hexagonal ice crystal could be shown. Such proteins could force a *quasi* crystalline fixation of the water molecules which would minimise the supercooling required to "quieten" the water clusters (see Box 1.3.8).

INA bacteria often cause great economic damage when they settle on plants which are able to tolerate moderate cold, but not ice formation, such as maize, strawberries and citrus fruits. In the presence of *Pseudomonas syringae*, an ice crystal is formed per 100 bacteria already at $-4\,°C$. The natural occurrence of such bacteria on plants varies with the season (Fig. 1.3.20), among other things.

INA bacteria are used in meteorology (after killing by γ-radiation) for the production of artificial snow and to induce cloud formation above dry areas. They have also been used for the protection of cereal seed against seed beetles: Bacterial powder eaten by the beetles reduced the

---

Box 1.3.8   Ice nucleators

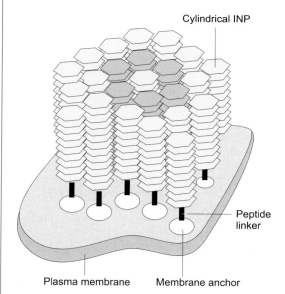

Cylindrical INP

Peptide linker

Plasma membrane   Membrane anchor

Nucleation temperature (°C)	Estimated molecular mass (kDa)	Number of INPs required for nucleation
-12 to -13	150	1
-3	870	60
-2	19800	132
-1	83700	558

The schematic diagram shows an INP superstructure ("ice nucleator") on a bacterial membrane. It is assumed that the membrane lipid phosphatidylinositol is the anchor of the individual INPs in the membrane (after Hew and Yang 1992, see also Burke and Lindow 1990). The table shows the correlation between the size of an ice nucleator and the reduction in supercooling temperature. (After Hew and Yang 1992, see also Burke and Lindow 1990).

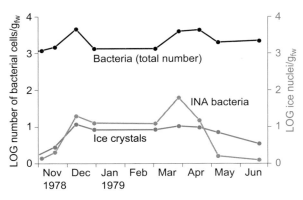

Fig. 1.3.20. Seasonal dependence of the number of all bacteria (total number) and INA bacteria, as well as the formation of ice nuclei at –9 °C, on avocado leaves. (After Lindow 1982)

Table 1.3.7. The effect of INA antagonists on the formation of ice nuclei upon frost

Bacterial culture	Damage Change in leaf colour after 1 week
Control (*Pseudomonas syringae*)	95%
Mutant A 510	12%
Mutant A 509	18%
Mutant A 507	27%
Mutant A 506	33%
Mutant A 508	51%

Pear leaves were inoculated with the respective bacterial culture 3 weeks prior to frost, to give the bacteria time to establish themselves. Frost damage was quantified by assessing necrosis. (After Lindow 1982)

ability of the insects to supercool to such an extent that they were killed by internal ice formation upon a frost shock of –10 °C, a temperature which is completely harmless to the seed (Fields 1993). In agriculture, however, attempts are being made to dilute out the INA bacterial infestation of crop plants by replacement with antagonists. These are obtained by plating out wash solutions from leaves and cooling them to –5 or –9 °C. Antagonists of the INA bacteria should be present wherever there is no ice formation. These organisms are mostly natural mutants of the original bacterial strains (Fig. 1.3.21 and Table 1.3.7).

Successful production of antagonists has also been achieved by altering the octapeptide periodicity of the INPs. However, the release of these transformed bacteria into the environment has not been permitted (Wilson and Lindow 1993), partially because of fears that they would interact with meteorological processes, particularly with cloud formation. Plants able to tolerate extracellular freezing appear to profit from an early triggering of nucleation, however, as this minimises the very unstable state of supercooling.

1.3.6.4
How Much Water Freezes in Frost-Hardy Tissues?

Liquid water can be distinguished from frozen water by nuclear magnetic resonance (NMR) spectroscopy. If the total water content of, for example, a leaf is known and the residual liquid water content is determined at different frost temperatures, so-called freezing curves are obtained which display the percentage of frozen water at each frost temperature (Fig. 1.3.22).

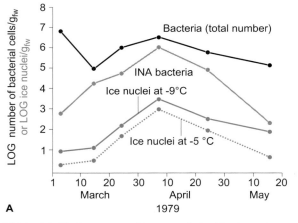

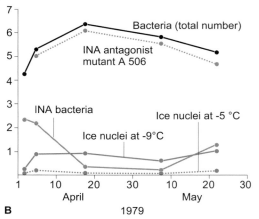

Fig. 1.3.21. Formation of ice crystals by INA bacteria on pear leaves (A) and displacement of the INA bacteria by mutants which are ineffective in nucleation (B). (After Lindow 1982)

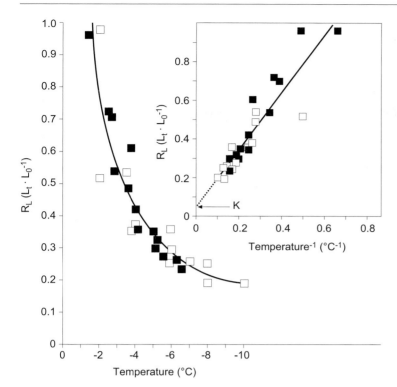

Fig. 1.3.22. Freezing curve of frost-hardened ivy (*Hedera helix*). The *curve* shows the proportion of liquid water (R_L) of the total water content (L_0) in dependence on the frost temperature (t). Ideally, a rectangular hyperbola is obtained which can be depicted as a simple linear reciprocal relationship (*insert*). The point at which the line cuts the ordinate (K=4.9%) indicates the proportion of the water which can theoretically not freeze. ■ R_L calculated from $P_{(t)}/V_{(t)}$ and $\Psi_{\text{leaf(t)}}$. □ R_L measured. (After Hansen and Beck 1988)

The lower the temperature, the more water is present in the form of ice, i.e. the water must be excreted from the cells into the apoplast. The curve can be mathematically transformed to obtain a straight line which cuts the ordinate at the so-called K-value. This specifies the proportion of the water which cannot freeze due to binding to macromolecules. This value is in the order of a few percent of the total water content.

The proportion of frozen tissue water also depends, of course, on the original concentration of the cellular liquid. It may be assumed in a first approximation that there is a physicochemical balance in a frozen leaf between the unfrozen, residual solution of the cells and the extracellular ice. This is because the vapour pressure of water is reduced over both ice and a solution, and the water potential is thus correspondingly larger (numerically more negative: see Box 1.3.9):

$$\Psi \text{ ice} = \Psi \text{ cell} = \Psi \text{ tissue} \approx \Psi \text{ leaf}$$

The water potential of a cell consists of the osmotic potential π, the matrix potential τ and the pressure potential ("wall pressure", P). Water potential, osmotic potential and matrix potential have negative signs, whereas the pressure potential, the wall (+ tissue) pressure, has a positive sign.

$$(-)\Psi \text{ tissue} = (-)\pi + (-)\tau + P$$

At moderate frost and only little freeze-desiccation, τ is still 0, but P already approaches 0. At the turgor-loss point (P=0) the following applies:

$$(-)\Psi \text{ tissue} = (-)\pi = (-)\Psi \text{ ice}$$

and dehydration stops. In this case, the degree of dehydration is determined solely by the concentration of the cellular liquid. There is a steady-state water potential between cell compartments; otherwise the intracellular water fluxes would change the volumes of the compartments. If this relation applies, and this is usually so in the case of mild frosts, an **ideal equilibrium freezing** takes place (Fig. 1.3.22).

If more water remains in the liquid state than would be expected upon ideal equilibrium freezing, a **non-ideal equilibrium freezing** occurs. This is usually observed at moderate frosts of below –8 °C, at which rates of water loss of about 90% frequently occur. In such a case $(-)\tau$ and/or P must contribute to the water potential of the frozen plant organ. During severe freeze-desiccation, the cell wall is strongly invaginated and thus develops a suction instead of the pressure which it usually exerts: P becomes negative

Box 1.3.9   Freezing of water and aqueous solutions

In liquid water, clusters of water molecules are in temperature-dependent motion (**Brownian molecular motion**). For crystallisation to take place, this movement must be minimised as far as possible. If factors which trigger crystallisation can be avoided, it is possible to cool pure water to −39 °C, whereupon it suddenly freezes. At this temperature larger clusters are formed as a consequence of the limited mobility of the water molecules, so-called critical embryos of about 190 H_2O molecules, which then initiate crystallisation. As the nucleation in this case originates from water itself, it is called **homogeneous nucleation**. The cooling energy expended for this crystallisation is released as heat of crystallisation. This spontaneous development of heat can be measured as a **freezing exotherm** and thus serves to monitor the freezing process (Fig. 1).

The melting process during thawing also requires energy, which is called the heat of fusion and can be recognised by a delay in warming during the course of the thawing process.

If nucleation is initiated in other ways, e.g. by seeding with ice crystals, supercooling does not need to take place to such a great degree. Depending on the type of initiation, crystallisation can already take place upon supercooling to only a few degrees. This is called **heterogeneous nucleation**, and is again dependent on the production of critical embryos, i.e. the reduction of Brownian molecular motion. Particular hydrophilic surface structures can force the water cluster into a type of lattice structure which facilitates crystallisation. An only small degree of supercooling is then required to initiate nucleation.

The vapour pressure (P) of water over ice is less than that over supercooled liquid water (see Table), and the water potential Ψ of ice is accordingly more strongly negative ("larger") than that of supercooled water at the same temperature. Put another way: More energy must be expended to remove a water molecule from crystalline ice than to remove it from liquid water.

$$P_{ice} < P_{supercooled\ water}$$

$$\Psi_{ice(T)} = \frac{R \times T(K)}{\overline{V}} \times \ln\frac{P_{ice(T)}}{P_{water(T)}}$$

$\overline{V}$ = mole volume of ice

$$\Psi_{ice} = \frac{RT}{V_W} \ln\frac{P_{ice}}{P_{water}}$$

The dependence shown by the black triangle is calculated from the following equation:

$$\Psi_{ice} = \frac{\Delta H_f}{V_W 273} t$$

The values of the dots showing the dependence were determined psychrometrically. For the theoretical basis of the equations, see Hansen and Beck (1988).

As the vapour pressure of water above ice (as well as above water) is directly dependent

Table. Partial pressure of water vapour (mbar) above ice and above supercooled water in relation to temperature

(°C)	0	1	2	3	4	5	6	7	8	9
Ice										
−30	0.38	0.34	0.31	0.27	0.25	0.22	0.20	0.18	0.16	0.14
−20	1.0	0.94	0.85	0.77	0.70	0.64	0.57	0.52	0.47	0.42
−10	2.6	2.4	2.2	2.0	1.8	1.7	1.5	1.4	1.2	1.1
0	6.1	5.6	5.2	4.8	4.4	4.0	3.7	3.4	3.1	2.8
Water										
−30	0.51	0.46	0.42	0.38	0.35	0.31	0.28	0.26	0.23	0.21
−20	1.3	1.2	1.1	1.0	0.88	0.81	0.74	0.67	0.61	0.51
−10	2.9	2.6	2.4	2.3	2.1	1.9	1.8	1.6	1.5	1.4
0	6.1	5.7	5.3	4.9	4.5	4.2	3.9	3.6	3.3	3.1

Box 1.3.9   (continued)

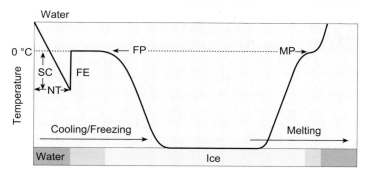

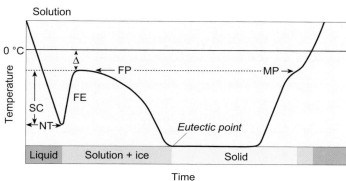

Fig. 1. Temporal sequence of freezing and melting of water and an aqueous solution. *FP* Freezing point; *FE* freezing exotherm; *MP* melting point; *SC* supercooling; *NT* nucleation temperature; *D* lowering of the freezing point of the solution. (After Sakai and Larcher 1987)

Fig. 2. Temperature dependence of the water potential of ice. The *dotted line* is calculated from the equation

on the temperature, the water potential of ice is also linearly dependent on the temperature (Fig. 2).

The vapour pressure of water over aqueous solutions is also lowered. The extent of the reduction depends on the concentration of the solution, more precisely on the mole fraction (M) of the water in the solution (**Raoult's law**):

$$P = P_0 \times M_{water}$$

$$M_{water} = \frac{mol_{solvent}}{mol_{solvent} + mol_{solute}}$$

[mole fraction]

In the same way, it follows that the free energy of the water in a solution depends on its mole fraction:

$$G_{water} = G_{0water} + RT \ln M_{water}$$

and

$$\Delta G = RT \ln M_{water}$$

It follows from this that the water potential of solutions Ψ_π, or following the modern nomenclature π, is more negative than that of pure water:

Box 1.3.9   (continued)

$$\pi = \frac{RT}{V_{water}} \ln(1 - M_{solute})$$

since M_{solute} is generally small, then

$$\ln(1 - M_{solute}) \approx -M_{solute};$$

substituting the equation for the mole fraction of the solute into the equation

$$M_{solute} = \frac{mol_{solute}}{mol_{solute} + mol_{water}},$$

gives

$$\pi \approx -\frac{n_s RT}{\overline{V}_{water}(n_s + n_{water})};$$

in a dilute solution

$$\overline{V}_{water}(n_s + n_{water}) \approx \overline{V}_{water} n_{water} = V_{water}$$

and

$$\frac{n_s}{V_{water}} = Cs \text{ [concentration]}$$

$$\pi = -RT \times C_s$$

It follows, furthermore, that the freezing point/melting point is lower than that of pure water and that it, too, depends on the mole fraction or concentration of the dissolved substances (s):

$$\Delta_{Tm} = 1.86 \times n_s$$
$$n_s = mol_{solute} \text{ in 1 kg water (molality)}$$

The molal constant for the lowering of the freezing point of water is $1.86\,°C$. The more concentrated the solution is, the greater is the lowering of the freezing point.*

In ideal solutions pure water freezes first, whereupon the remaining solution becomes concentrated. At a particular temperature, the **eutectic point**, the remaining solution then also freezes. In colloidal solutions such as are present in a cell, a small proportion of the water which is firmly bound to the macromolecules remains liquid even at very low temperatures, e.g. in liquid nitrogen. This proportion of the water can be determined by means of a diagram, in which the proportion of liquid water at various frost temperatures is plotted against the reciprocal of the temperature, and is given at the point at which the line crosses the ordinate (cf. Fig. 1.3.22). This residual water, in which enzymes are dissolved, is a problem in frozen food. At freezer temperatures these enzymes naturally function only very slowly, but hydrolytic enzymes in particular are quite stable and are usually not destroyed during freezing. Only few degradation products are to be reckoned with when frozen foods are used immediately after thawing. However, if the thawed material is later refrozen, the hydrolases (e.g. proteases) will have been provided with favourable conditions for their activity and the frozen products can suffer from a loss of quality.

_____

* This applies strictly only to dilute, i.e. ideal solutions. In concentrated solutions, interactions occur between the dissolved particles, which result in an apparent reduction of the concentration. The factor a, by which the concentration appears to decrease, is termed the activity factor.

(negative turgor) and strengthens the osmotic potential. A matrix potential develops similarly during strong dehydration. All three potentials now act together:

$$(-)\varPsi \text{ tissue} = (-)\pi + (-)\tau + (-)P = (-)\varPsi \text{ ice}$$

This occurs even at only moderate frost in the ground-covering plant *Pachysandra terminalis* (Fig. 1.3.23).

Significantly less water freezes in this case than would be expected from the prevailing osmotic relations, and the effect of the negative pressure potential becomes particularly evident. However, the influence of the matrix potential may also become apparent during such strong dehydration. At the extent of the freeze-desiccation shown, 12% more liquid water (32% residual water compared with 20% at $-7\,°C$) signifies considerably less strain on the cells.

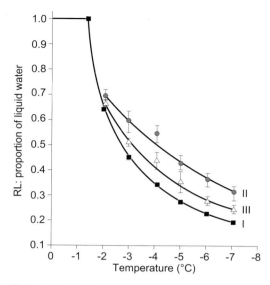

Table 1.3.8. Reduction of the freezing point by anti-freeze proteins as measured by thermal hysteresis

Organism	Tissue	Reduction in freezing point (°C)
Bony fish	Muscle	0.7–1.5
Insects	Digestive tract, muscle	3–6
Bacteria		0.3–0.35
Fungi	Fruiting body	0.3–0.35
Mosses	Whole plant	0.3–0.68
Horsetail or Dutch rush (*Equisetum hyemale*)	Rhizome	0.2
Ferns	Shoot	0.25
Winter wheat	Leaves	0.2
Carrot	Tuber	0.4
Carrot	Shoot	0.15
Poplar	Twig	0.22

Fig. 1.3.23. Freezing curves for *Pachysandra terminalis*. *Pachysandra* leaves show non-ideal equilibrium freezing: the residual amount of unfrozen water measured in the tissue at various frost temperatures (*curve II*) is significantly greater than that calculated from the concentration of the cellular solutions (*curve I*). In this case, the cell wall as well as the cell sap must therefore develop a "negative pressure potential" corresponding to suction. This is the result of the close contact between the plasma membrane (protoplast) and cell wall. The share of the matrix potential in the suction can be determined by killing the tissue prior to the freeze-desiccation (*curve III*). The more severe the frost is, the greater is the proportion of the total potential due to the matrix potential. (After Zhu and Beck 1991)

1.3.6.5
Antifreeze Proteins

A further possibility to impede ice formation and thus to decrease cell desiccation is constituted by special proteins which are excreted from the protoplast into the apoplast and influence the formation of ice there. These have been termed antifreeze proteins (AFPs) or thermal hysteresis proteins (THPs). Antifreeze proteins have long been known in fish and insects (De-Vries and Cheng 1992; Duman et al. 1992), where they apparently prevent or alleviate the freezing of body fluids. In these animals they do appear to significantly reduce the freezing point in a non-colligative (non-physicochemical) manner.

An effect of these proteins is illustrated in the test carried out to detect their presence: The growth of an ice crystal and the formation of new ice crystals in a very diluted AFP solution can be observed under the microscope during cooling. It is thereby observed that the tempera-ture required for nucleation is significantly lower, and an existing ice crystal grows much more slowly during cooling than in pure water; the melting point, however, is not affected. This results in hysteresis during freezing and thawing, and is the reason why these proteins are also called THPs (Table 1.3.8).

Antifreeze proteins are a mixture of small to medium-sized proteins which can be extracted from the tissue of frost-hardy leaves, but not of frost-sensitive leaves (Urrutia et al. 1992). They are divided into several groups: Antifreeze proteins and antifreeze glycoproteins are both subdivided into further groups based on the tertiary structures of the two major types of protein. There are clear conceptions as to how these proteins function at the molecular level, although this is not yet true of plant AFPs.

The already classical antifreeze glycoproteins of cold-water fish are built around the repeating tripeptide -[Ala-Ala-Thr]-, where the threonine bears a sugar residue.

The AFP of the winter flounder is also characterised by such repetitive sequences, namely of an undecapeptide. The 11 amino acid units consist mainly of alanine with rhythmically interspaced polar amino acids (Thr, Asp and Asn). These are ordered in such a way that their polar residues are all on one side of the helix (Fig. 1.3.24), so that the protein has a hydrophilic and a hydrophobic side. The hydrophilic face of these proteins is thought to attach to the main growing surface of the ice crystal, and the hydrophobic side of the protein, which is now turned to the outside, makes it difficult for further water clusters to associate with the ice

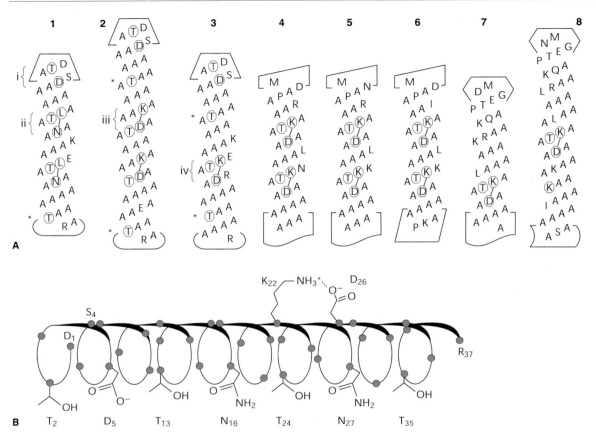

Fig. 1.3.24. Antifreeze proteins (AFPs) of fish. A Various alanine-rich α-helical AFPs. *1* Winter flounder; *2* yellow tail flounder; *3* plaice; *4–8* different AFPs from sculpin. The N- and C-terminal caps, which stabilise the α-helical structures, are shown by structure symbols. Ice- (water-) binding motifs (*i–iv*) are shown by *circles*. B Side view of the AFP B of the winter flounder, in which the unilateral orientation of the hydrophilic groups can be clearly recognised. K22 and D26 form a salt bridge (amino acids are specified in *single letter code*). (After Sicheri and Yang 1995)

crystal. The matrix for this attachment is set by the ice crystal, while the manner in which the attachment takes place is determined by the protein. Since α-helical polypeptides are dipoles, the AFP preferentially attaches to the prism surfaces of the ice crystal in an antiparallel manner. Due to the blocking of its normal growth surfaces, the ice crystal now grows less rapidly and extends mainly in the direction of the c-axis. This leads to the formation of small, needle-like crystals (Antikainen et al. 1996; Fig. 1.3.25).

It is quite evident that the effect of AFPs in delaying freezing depends on the concentration of the proteins. Since they must be bound to the surface of the ice to achieve their effect, they can be said to be used up. This also explains why AFPs do not provide a general protection against freezing. AFPs reduce the formation of ice in the organism, but they cannot suppress it completely. The partially frozen state of the tis-

sue liquid arrived at in this manner is certainly more stable during supercooling than the completely liquid state, which tends to freeze abruptly. It is quite plausible that many small ice crystals which are inhibited in their growth and cloaked in proteins are less damaging to the organism than is a large crystal. The protein cloak of the ice crystal is possibly the deciding factor in frost protection by AFPs. A further effect of AFPs could be to prevent recrystallisation of ice concomitant with the formation of larger ice crystals during the thawing process (Carpenter and Hansen 1992). This is of particular importance with regard to ice crystals in the body fluids of cold-water fish and insects, where the formation of larger ice crystals would lead to circulatory damage. The combination of INPs and AFPs could constitute an effective method of regulating the formation of ice crystals in tissues (Griffith et al. 1993; Worland and Block

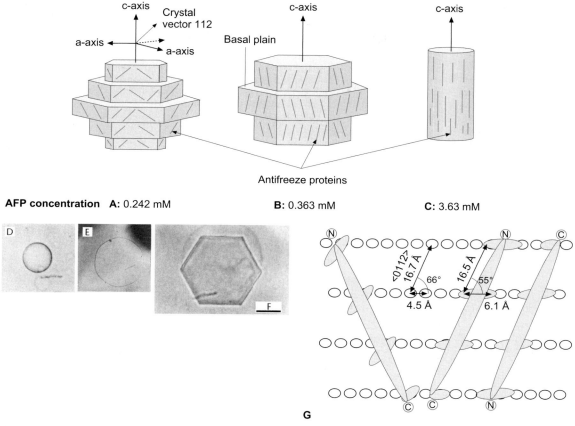

AFP concentration   A: 0.242 mM   B: 0.363 mM   C: 3.63 mM

Fig. 1.3.25. The effect of antifreeze proteins (AFPs) on the formation of ice crystals. A–C Schematic drawings of crystals in the presence of increasing concentrations of winter flounder AFP. In the most dilute solution, there is not yet any interaction between the individual protein molecules, which orient themselves mainly according to the ice crystal vectors. In the more concentrated solutions, the protein molecules interact and bind in an antiparallel manner to the prism surfaces. E, F Micrographs of ice crystals which have formed in the presence of protein extracts from the apoplast of unhardened (E) and frost-hardened rye leaves (F). Length of the *bar*: 25 µm. For comparison an ice crystal in pure water is shown in D. G Molecular model of the binding of the winter flounder protein (*grey*) to an ice crystal (*circles* denote water molecules). The four ice-binding motifs correspond to the distance between the water molecules in the ice crystal. (A–C after Yang et al. 1988; D–F after Griffith et al. 1992; G after Sicheri and Yang 1995)

1999). Attempts to transform potato plants with the AFP of flounder genetically engineered to optimise codon usage yielded plants with significantly increased cold tolerance (Wallis et al. 1997).

1.3.6.6
Protection of Biomembranes and Freezing Tolerance

Soluble material accumulates in the residual liquid of the cell to an enormous extent during extracellular freezing. In addition to the danger of membrane disintegration as a consequence of water withdrawal (see above), severe stress is incurred by the concentration of ions at membrane

surfaces. High ionic charge at the membrane surface changes the membrane potential, and can thus also lead to membrane disintegration or at least to the dissociation of peripheral proteins.

The Degree of Frost Hardiness Depends on the Extent and Quality of Membrane Protection

Relatively high concentrations of soluble, low molecular weight, so-called cryoprotective substances can be found in frost-tolerant plants [polyols, sucrose and its galactosides raffinose and stachyose, poorly degradable carbohydrates such as hammamelitol (Fig. 1.3.26), amino acids, polyamines and many more]. These compounds "dilute" the ionic charge at the membrane surface and, at the same time, stabilise the bilayer struc-

Fig. 1.3.26. Frost protection in the eastern Alpine *Primula clusiana* Tausch (A). Hamamelose = 2-hydroxymethyl-D-ribitol (B), and its galactoside clusianose (C), accumulate irreversibly in the overwintering leaves during the cold season (D). These old leaves die subsequent to the formation of new leaves in the following vegetation period without the branched chain sugar derivatives, which are present in high amounts, having been removed for further use. The accumulation of hamamelose can also be induced by cooling the plant in summer. (Photo E. Beck)

ture in being weakly polar (as is water). The main effect of cryoprotective substances is thus to protect membranes. Their effect in lowering the freezing point first comes into play during freeze-desiccation of the cells. For example, the sap expressed by pressure from frost-hardy spruce needles is only 1.5 osmolar, corresponding to a reduction of the freezing point by 2.8 K. This is physiologically insignificant, as a greater degree of supercooling is required to trigger crystallisation. The cell liquid becomes more concentrated during freeze-desiccation, however, and would be ten-fold more concentrated at a residual volume of 10%. The colligative (physicochemical) properties of the cryoprotective substances would then, of course, be of considerable importance. In the example of spruce needles, this would result in the lowering of the freezing point by 28.5 K, which would prevent the freezing of the residual liquid water.

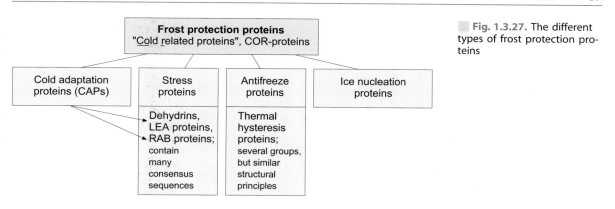

Fig. 1.3.27. The different types of frost protection proteins

Freezing Protection Proteins

So-called cold protection proteins (CORs) or cold adaptation proteins (CAPs), which can play an essential role in the development of frost hardiness, are of particular contemporary interest. Many such proteins and corresponding genes, which become expressed upon cold treatment, have been described since the late 1980s (Fig. 1.3.27). Among them are antifreeze proteins and isoforms of housekeeping enzymes with a lower temperature optimum such as, e.g., lactate dehydrogenase (in animals) or PEP carboxykinase (Sáez-Vásquez et al. 1995), as well as enzymes for the biosynthesis of cryoprotectants.

Membrane-protective proteins also belong to this group, proteins which interact with the surfaces of membranes and stabilise these during freeze-desiccation. They are similar to the so-called dehydrins, extremely hydrophilic protective proteins which are formed during drought stress or during regulated desiccation, e.g. during seed ripening. They usually have a molecular mass of between 15 and 50 kDa (see Chap. 1.5.2.5), but very large (~200 kDa) CORs have also been described recently. These proteins are rich in glycine, are boiling- and acid-stable and possess a high proportion of random-coil secondary structure. On a molar basis they are about 20,000–40,000 times more effective than sucrose in conserving membranes. These proteins are described in detail in Chapter 1.5 on drought stress. There are some indications that cold protection proteins can be membrane-specific; e.g. a 7-kDa protein has been found which specifically protects chloroplast thylakoids (Hincha and Schmitt 1992). Even though heat shock proteins have been linked with cold tolerance, the CORs and CAPs are not related to them in any way either in structure or function. Like antifreeze proteins, most CORs and CAPs

are amphiphilic but, in contrast to the AFPs, they attach with their hydrophobic side to the structures they are protecting, e.g. membrane surfaces. Their hydrophilic side faces the cytosol. This attachment results in the displacement of lower molecular weight solutes such as ions from the membrane surface. As is the case with dehydrins, it is possible to induce the synthesis of CAPs by treatment with abscisic acid (ABA, see Chap. 1.5.2.3) in place of cold treatment. Treatment of citrus plants with ABA and other growth regulators was successful in conferring cold tolerance, but had a number of negative side effects such as disadvantageous biomass distribution and premature fruit shedding. Thus spraying with such chemicals cannot be recommended as a general method for artificially improving the frost-hardiness of threatened crops (Yelenosky et al. 1987).

1.3.6.7
Avoidance of Freezing

Supercooling

The avoidance of the formation of ice crystals at freezing temperatures leads to **supercooling**. The supercooled state of plant tissues can usually be maintained for only some hours, in which case it can, for example, help plants to cope with the nightly radiation frosts which occur regularly in high mountain regions of the tropics. Supercooling has been observed to persist at length only in tissues possessing very rigid cell walls. Leathery leaves, for example, can remain unfrozen at temperatures of –12 °C, and the buds of trees and the wood of certain species (e.g. of the North American *Cornus stolonifera*) are able to supercool at –30 to –50 °C for long periods (Ashworth 1993). Supercooling has the advan-

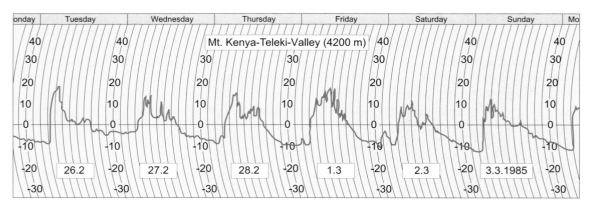

Fig. 1.3.28. Temperature courses (close to the ground) in tropical high mountains during the dry period: Hedberg (1964) characterized this recurrent-frost climate as summer every day, winter every night. Night frosts occur even during the rainy season, although the temperature then seldom drops to below −5 °C

tage over freezing tolerance in that the hydration of the cells is maintained and no dehydration stress occurs. Metabolic reactions are extremely slow at the low temperatures of supercooling to be sure, but during freeze-desiccation they cease completely. Supercooling also brings the risk of **intracellular ice formation** upon sudden nucleation, however (see Fig. 1.3.18), which then leads irrevocably to the death of the cell. This may be triggered by movement due to wind or animals in open spaces, for example. In general, those plants possessing nucleation barriers are not tolerant of freezing. Supercooling as a strategy may be regarded as a form of stress avoidance (avoidance of freezing).

Transient Avoidance of Freezing in Plants of Tropical High Mountain Regions

Typical of high mountain areas in the tropics is the so-called recurrent-frost climate: this is a special version of the daily fluctuation type of climate characteristic of the tropics, in which several hours of frost usually occur during the course of the night (Fig. 1.3.28).

Even though these frosts occur regularly, they do not last long and are only moderate (temperatures below −15 °C are very rare and occur at most in hollows), and the indigenous flowering plants have developed special facilities to provide temporary avoidance of freezing.

This is particularly evident in the tropical alpine giant rosette plants of the genera *Senecio*, *Lobelia* and *Espeletia*. These seemingly archaic plants (Fig. 1.3.29) bear a single large rosette of leaves of up to over 1 m in diameter and consisting of usually more than 100 large leaves at the end of the above- or below-ground stem.

There are no marked quiescent periods during the course of the year and, therefore, young leaves are continuously formed and older leaves also die continuously. At least the first half of the development of the leaf takes place in a conical leaf bud in the centre of the leaf rosette, from which the leaves emerge after greening and carry out the rest of their longitudinal growth in the rosette. The principle means by which these plants avoid freezing are **supercooling** and **delayed cooling** (Beck 1994).

Supercooling has been shown above all for the South American *Espelitias*, the cell sap of which does not freeze even at −8 °C. Temperatures lower than this almost never occur in areas colonised by these plants, which are lethally damaged if ice formation is artificially induced. Delayed cooling can be achieved by insulation and via heat buffers. **Cloaking** of the above-ground stems of these plants confers permanent heat insulation through the dead, partly rotted leaves, which delay cooling but do not prevent the stem temperature from rising to 15–20 °C during the day under intense solar radiation (Fig. 1.3.29). A stem temperature in the range of between 0 and 20 °C is important, as a large share of the water required by the leaf rosette is supplied by the living pith tissue and does not stem from the weakly developed xylem with its extremely narrow vessel lumens. Water transport via living cells depends to a large degree on temperature.

The so-called **night buds** of the giant rosettes provide thermal insulation in accordance with the prevailing temperature (Fig. 1.3.30): When the temperature falls at night the rosette leaves bend in towards the top and thus form a closed

Fig. 1.3.29. Rosette plants of the genera *Senecio* (A–C) and *Espeletia* (D) from the alpine tropics. Neither the East African *Senecio keniodendron* (endemic to Mt. Kenya) nor *Espeletia corymbosa* from the Andes lose their dead leaves, but retain them as an insulating cloak around the stem. The effect of this insulating layer is indicated in the schematic diagram (C) which illustrates the inner structure of the plant. The massive pith serves as a water reservoir, as the xylem itself is only relatively weakly developed. The Espelitias are called "Freilejones" (fat monks) on account of the appearance of the cloak of dead leaves. (Photos E. Beck)

Fig. 1.3.30. Protection against freezing by adaptive insulation in *Senecio keniensis* (endemic to Mt. Kenya). Rosettes open during the day (A) and close when it becomes cold, forming a so-called night bud (B). The insulative effect (C) applies to only the young leaves in the interior of the rosette. While the outer leaves are frozen stiff, the inner ones remain at above the freezing point. The leaves of the giant rosette plants (D) frequently exhibit a "polystyrene foam" structure which increases the insulative effect (*Lobelia keniensis*). (Photos E. Beck)

shell around the still-growing buds and young leaves still in the bud cone (Fig. 1.3.30 B). This night bud consists of many layers of leaves and thus provides considerable insulation. Although the outer leaves are frozen stiff in the morning, the temperature inside does not fall below the freezing point (Fig. 1.3.30 C). Upon warming in the morning, the rosette opens within a few minutes and is then immediately ready for photosynthesis.

Water is a very effective heat buffer on account of its high specific heat and its even higher latent heat of crystallisation (Fig. 1.3.31). The inflorescence of *Lobelia telekii* contains several

Fig. 1.3.31. Water or aqueous solution as a thermal buffer. A, B *Lobelia telekii* in the rosette stage and during flowering, respectively. The rosette clearly shows the structure of a "giant rosette". The young leaves develop in the centre of the rosette and, closely appressed, form a cone-shaped leaf bud. The infloresence is up to 3 m in height (B) and contains 3 l of watery pith fluid according to Kroog et al. (1979). From the specific heat of water (4.2 J/g×K) and the heat of its crystallisation (331 J/g), a thermal buffering capacity of 1005 kJ can be calculated. At −6 °C only 2% of the liquid in the pith was frozen, according to which only 1.8% of the total heat buffering capacity was used. C The numerous leaves (>150) of the rosette of *Lobelia deckenii* (Mt. Kilimanjaro) form cisterns in which rain as well as gutated liquids accumulate. A rosette contains more than 2 l of such liquid. This liquid is pushed up during the formation of the night buds and surrounds the leaf bud as an additional heat buffer. (Photos E. Beck)

litres of water in its pith cavity with an enormous heat capacity: At an exterior temperature of −6 °C only about 2% of this liquid was frozen and only 1.8% of the heat storage capacity was made use of. The cistern-like bases of the rosette leaves also collect litres of water, which is only partially frozen after cold nights and thus constitutes a considerable heat reservoir (Fig. 1.3.31C). Investigations have shown that all of the leaves of a giant rosette (except, seemingly, the leaves of the genus *Espeletia*), including those still in the bud, can tolerate freezing. What is, then, the value of the avoidance of freezing? Daily de- and rehydration processes evidently put a great strain on tissues: Outer rosette leaves that more or less freeze every night age relatively quickly. Tips of leaves which are exposed to the sunlight in their frozen state yellow after only a few days. It therefore appears to be ad-

vantageous for tissues to avoid freezing stress even when they are frost-hardy.

1.3.6.8
Seasonal Tolerance to Freezing

Phases of frost hardening and dehardening alternate with the seasons in native "lowland" plants. Signals for hardening or dehardening are the day length and temperature. In nature both factors work together; in experiments they also act individually. Short day length and a slow decrease in temperature to a low, but not yet damaging, value induce rapid hardening (~−1 K/day). The phytochrome system participates in the signalling that leads to the effect of day length: far-red light stimulates hardening, red light dehardening. Since resistance to freezing is a process that affects the whole plant, hardening and dehardening are extremely complex processes which are currently being intensively studied at the level of cell biology. Some well-investigated individual processes, such as the formation of cryoprotective substances including proteins, have already been mentioned. A particularly important process is the adaptation of biomembranes to heat and cold. According to present knowledge, frost hardening is not possible during the main growth period because the cell wall is probably not able to cope with the strain of water loss during freeze-desiccation.

Molecular Biology of Frost Hardening

Even though *Arabidopsis thaliana* can develop at most only moderate frost resistance, research using this plant has yielded important insights into frost hardiness due to the complete sequencing of the *Arabidopsis* genome and the relative ease of carrying out mutant studies (Thomashow 1999). The constitutive "frost hardiness" of this plant has been shown to be genetically independent of its ability to harden to frost. Constitutive frost hardiness is understood as the degree of frost hardiness which can be measured with plants grown at room temperature. Constitutive as well as induced frost hardiness constitute a syndrome, i.e. they involve the concerted action of many genes (more than 100 genes have been reported: Xin and Browse 2000). The most important features which occasion frost hardiness have been treated in detail in earlier chapters. The existence of the syndrome "frost hardiness" or "frost hardening" suggested a search for "master genes" which regulate the frost-hardening process. Such master genes were found at the level of transcription factors and transcription activators (Fig. 1.3.32), e.g. the activators of the CBF group (CRT-Repeat Binding Factor) that bind to the promoter element AAGAC which occurs in many COR genes. CBF1 has also been described as DREB1B (Drought Regulated Element Binding factor 1B; see Chap. 1.5: stress due to drought), which again illustrates the phenomenon of cross-protection. The induction of some COR genes by abscisic acid (ABA) via the transcription activator "bZip" (alkaline leucine zipper) can be understood in the same context. Figure 1.3.32 shows how such master genes can activate several other genes at the transcription level, and how the regulatory effects of several master genes can overlap. The identification of a master gene begs the retrogressive question as to how this master gene is activated. An increase in cal-

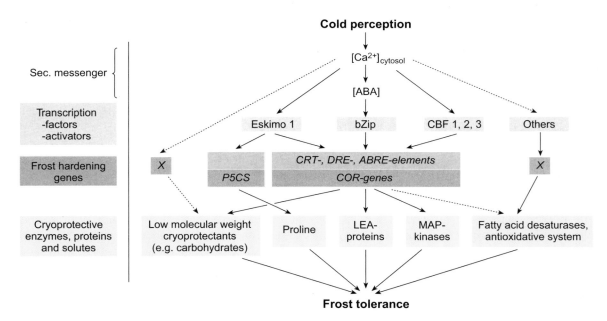

Fig. 1.3.32. Molecular biology of the induction of frost hardening. Overview of the established (*continuous arrows*) and presumed (*dotted arrows*) signal transduction pathways in *Arabidopsis thaliana* which lead from the perception of the cold signal (molecular basis unknown) to the development of frost hardiness (maximum degree of resistance is to −12 °C). *ABA* Abscisic acid; *bZIP* alkaline leucine zipper; *CBF* CRT-repeat binding factor; *DRE* drought-regulated element; *ABRE* ABA-responsive element; *P5CS* gene for Δ-1-pyrroline-5-carboxylate synthetase (cf. Box 1.5.5). (After Xin and Browse 2000)

cium concentration in the cytosol appears to be a decisive trigger in this regard (Tahtiharju et al. 1997). At any rate, such an increase is observed immediately after the onset of a frost hardening program and precedes gene activation. It is not yet known how the increase in the cytoplasmic calcium concentration is triggered. It is supposed, however, that the membrane stiffening due to cold is involved in the stress perception (Vigh et al. 1993; see also the section on stress perception in Chap. 1.1).

1.3.6.9
Frost Hardening Decreases Efficiency

The "strategy" of winter-green plants such as conifers for coping with frost is to promote the extracellular freezing of tissue water. Photosynthesis ceases when the formation of ice takes place due to the severe dehydration and low temperatures. About 30% of the chlorophyll-binding antenna proteins of the chloroplasts of Scots pine are degraded during the course of frost hardening (pines appear somewhat yellow-green in winter). This can be seen as a protection of the photosynthetic membranes against light stress during sharp frosts (Hansen 2000). It results in a considerable restriction of photosynthetic function in the non-frozen state, however. Experiments in this regard on the CO_2 assimilation of pine needles have shown an about 80% reduction in potential photosynthetic capacity (see Chap. 1.1.3, Fig. 1.1.7). This limitation of photosynthesis does not necessarily have negative consequences, however, as respiration is also considerably restricted at lower temperatures (Hansen and Beck 1994).

1.3.6.10
Secondary Stress: Frost Drought

Plants cannot take up water from frozen soil, and thus are in danger of suffering drought damage during permanent frost. Since the activity of roots depends on temperature, the uptake of water and nutrient salts deteriorates even at temperatures of a few degrees above the freezing point (Chap. 2.3). Plants of warmer regions already have similar difficulties at temperatures of about 5–10 °C: In various citrus species cold-induced drought damage is already evident at +5 °C.

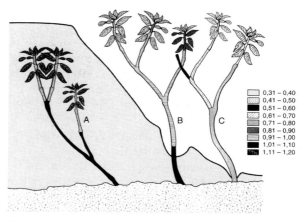

Fig. 1.3.33. Frost drought. Water contents (in g H_2O/g dry wt.) in leaves and shoots of the Alpine rose (*Rhododendron ferrugineum*) in winter. A Continually covered with snow; B only the stem basis covered by snow; C on frozen ground without any snow cover during the entire winter (measurement in March). (After Larcher 2003)

Frost drought occurs particularly at sites bearing little snow, when the soil is deeply frozen and the sun's rays induce transpiration while an effective water delivery from the frozen stem and soil is impossible (Fig. 1.3.33). This is accompanied by increased danger of embolism in the xylem and in the cells as well. During prolonged frost drought, the volume of the cells, e.g. in conifer needles, shrinks to a fraction of the volume in the turgescent state. According to Larcher (2001), the tree line is determined by the duration and the severity of soil frost and by the extent of snow cover. Snow cover provides protection against desiccation and extremely low temperatures during severe frosts.

Snow cover also causes considerable strain, however: The pressures incurred lead to snow and ice breakage, light incidence is reduced (under a 20-cm-thick snow cover the residual light is 1–15% of that in the open) and gas exchange is impeded. The situation under prepared ski runs is particularly critical: Reductions of biomass production by 20–30% and in extreme cases by up to 70% have been observed (Cernusca 1984).

Table 1.3.9. Plants and cold: an overview

Temperature range (°C)	Plant response	Survival strategy	Example	Description
+8 to 0	Sensitive	None; unable to adapt	African violet	"Chilling-sensitive"
+8 to 0	Tolerant	None; unable to adapt	Tomato, potato	"Chilling-tolerant"
0 to –12, possibly lower	Tolerant	Lipid desaturation, cryo-protective substances	Spruce, pine, ivy in summer state	Frost-tolerant, but not tolerant to freezing
0 to –70, possibly lower	Tolerant	Lipid saturation, cryoprotective substances, lipid enrichment	Spruce, pine, ivy in winter state	Tolerant to frost and freezing

1.3.7

Concluding Comments

The expositions having been made in the section on "cold" show that the stressor low temperatures gives rise to a whole battery of strain reactions. The rather ambiguous term "syndrome" is often used in the literature to designate the multilayered changes which are thereby brought about, e.g. the frost-hardening syndrome. Table 1.3.9 summarises the various aspects of the cold syndrome of plants.

Summary

1.

General

1. Every organism in nature is subject to limiting temperatures which define the temperature range in which active life is possible; these can in some cases significantly exceed or be lower than the limits of the temperature range of liquid water. Living beings (microorganisms) which have a temperature optimum of above 100 °C are able to exist only under high pressure, in the deep oceans. All living organisms evidence so-called cardinal points of temperature compatibility: Cold death, cold rigidity, the range of active life, heat rigidity and heat death. Living organisms which are adapted to low temperatures are said to be psychrophilic, those requiring high temperatures are thermophilic to extremely thermophilic, while most organisms are mesophilic. Not all parts of a plant have the same temperature compatibility; this also applies to the different stages of their development.

2. Plants are able to adapt to conditions other than their "normal" temperature conditions, within certain limits. This requires that the lipid composition of the biomembranes be modified, so that the membranes are able to maintain the liquid-viscous state at all temperatures which may occur. If the temperature conditions significantly approach the limits of active life, high or low molecular mass protective substances ("chemical chaperones") are additionally formed. Plants are also able to adapt in this way to large temperature fluctuations occurring during the course of a day.

2.

Heat

1. The typical strain triggered by heat is the production of heat shock proteins and the switching off of housekeeping genes. These reactions already start at only a few degrees above the optimal temperature of an organism; this means that plants live close to their heat stress limits. Heat avoidance mechanisms are, therefore, of great importance. A small leaf area, appropriate phyllotaxis, a strong indument and transpirational cooling all work against the overheating of leaves.

2. The heat shock response is one of the best-understood stress reactions at the molecular level. Proteins denatured by heat associate with heat shock proteins (HSPs, chaperones). Certain HSPs are normally present in association with heat shock transcription factors (HSFs). The HSFs are released and activated (trimer formation) as a result of the reaction with denatured proteins. The active HSF then reacts with corresponding palindromic sequences in the promoter region of the heat

shock genes, the so-called heat shock elements. This leads to the expression of these genes and to the production of HSPs. The HSPs "re-nature" heat-damaged proteins or mark them for proteolytic degradation. Their concentration then increases in the cell and they thus bind free HSFs again, which leads to the switching off of the production of further HSPs.

3. The way in which housekeeping genes are switched off is also at least basically understood at the molecular level. Heat prevents the association of the subunits of the spliceosome and thus the processing of mRNA. The unspliced mRNA of the housekeeping genes is stored in conjunction with HSPs in heat shock granules. Translation is also switched off by inactivation of an initiation factor. Heat shock proteins evidently do not require this initiation factor and their mRNA does not contain introns, so that it does not need to be spliced.

3.

Cold

1. With respect to the stressor cold, a distinction is made between damage arising at temperatures above the freezing point (damage through chilling in subtropical and tropical plants) and damage occurring upon frost and the subsequent formation of ice in the plant. Ice formation results in freeze-desiccation of tissues and cells, and frost damage is often damage due to dehydration. The freezing of water within the cell (intracellular ice formation) is always lethal (the exception is the artificial "vitrification" employed to conserve organisms).

2. Cold damage is primarily damage to membranes. This applies to chilling as well as to frost. If the proportion of high melting point lipids or the protein/lipid ratio is too high, large membrane domains are immobilised and their functions are lost when the temperature is lowered. Membrane damage is also caused by severe freeze-desiccation and the resulting accumulation of charged solutes (e.g. salt ions) at membrane surfaces.

3. Tropical and subtropical crop plants usually cannot harden to cold, or only to a very small extent. Metabolic imbalances and disturbances of cellular metabolism occur due to the different temperature tolerances of various metabolic reactions, even at temperatures not yet low enough to account for membrane damage. The inactivation of ion pumps, particularly of those associated with the energy supply or the homeostasis of membrane potentials, is the major cause of the damage referred to as being due to membrane "leakiness".

4. Energisation of the photosynthetic apparatus when photosynthetic metabolism is disturbed leads to the formation of reactive oxygen species (ROS) which cause further damage, particularly through the formation of radicals in the biomembranes. This then exceeds the capacity of the plant's well-developed detoxication system to intercept the ROS and the reactive products which they subsequently form. The photoinhibition observed during the over-energisation of photosystem II, particularly in connection with chilling, is mainly triggered by ROS. ROS are not formed only in the context of photosynthesis, but also during dysfunction of the respiratory chain and in other reactions in which molecular oxygen participates. ROS detoxification systems occur, on the one hand, in membranes, e.g. as evidenced by tocopherol and xanthophylls in the photosynthetic membranes. In the cytosol or in the stroma of the chloroplasts, ascorbate and glutathione are the main compounds involved in the detoxification of ROS, but flavonoids also play a role.

5. Frost causes stress not only because of the low temperatures involved, but additionally due to (freeze-)desiccation. Therefore, the exact cause of the incurred damage cannot always be determined unequivocally. Freezing of tissue and cell water must always occur outside the cells in the intercellular spaces. Water must thus exit from the cells into the intercellular spaces prior to freezing. Cold inactivation of pumps in the plasma membrane could be a reason for this phenomenon. Ice formation in the intercellular spaces requires a nucleation trigger. Bacteria are often found on the epidermal surface of the plant, but also in the substomatal intercellular spaces, which act as nucleation triggers.

6. Bacteria which are active in nucleation, the so-called INA bacteria, possess "nucleators" consisting of aggregates of INPs (ice-nucleating proteins), whose molecular construction favours the fixation of water clusters into ice matrix-like structures and thus reduces the supercooling required for crystallisation. Nucleation-active proteins have also been ex-

tracted from the intercellular spaces of plant tissues, but their molecular effect has not yet been clarified. Ice formation, which takes place at relatively mild freezing temperatures, reduces the danger of the sudden intercellular freezing of cell water which takes place when supercooling has progressed too far. On the other hand, there are many plants that are frost-tolerant but not tolerant to freezing. Avoidance of nucleation is the only means of surviving frost for these plants (which include many crop plants).

7. The desiccation of cells stemming from the freezing of cellular water is enormous even upon moderate frost. As a rule, more than 80% of tissue water is already frozen at temperatures of about $-10\,°C$. Freezing ceases when the water potential of the (extracellular) ice, which depends on the (freezing) temperature, equals the water potential of the cell. This is called "equilibrium freezing", whereby ideal and non-ideal equilibrium freezing are distinguished. In ideal equilibrium freezing, the water potential of the freeze-desiccated cell is determined solely by its osmotic potential. In non-ideal equilibrium freezing, a negative wall pressure (suction) which arises during the desiccation of the cell augments the water potential of the cell, so that more water remains in the liquid state than would be expected from the osmotic potential. The plasma membrane must always remain in contact with the cell wall in an intact cell during freeze-desiccation, as the matrix potential of the cell wall prevents the penetration of air from the intercellular spaces. Shrinkage of the cell volume caused by freeze-desiccation therefore leads to (reversible) deformation of the whole cell and even to wrinkling of the cell wall (freezing cytorrhysis).

8. Extreme freeze-desiccation leads to the breakdown of biomembranes, as the ordering of hydrophobic interactions between membrane lipids requires the presence of liquid water. Membrane breakdown is further stimulated by high concentrations of charged solutes, which can drastically alter the membrane potential.

9. The degree of frost hardening depends not only on the composition of the lipids (and the protein/lipid ratio) of the biomembranes, but also on the effectiveness of so-called cryoprotectants. These are low molecular weight solutes such as many carbohydrates, which take over the membrane-stabilising role of water molecules during freeze-desiccation, and at the same time prevent the accumulation of ions at the membrane surfaces. In addition to low molecular weight cryoprotectants, frost-hardy plants also synthesise proteins which protect membranes and other proteins. These are, for example, proteins from the family of the dehydrins, which associate protectively with membranes during dehydration. The formation of such proteins is a good example of cross-protection, i.e. of a multiple protective system, the formation of which is triggered by one particular stressor but then also hardens the plant against other stressors (e.g. frost, drought and high salt concentrations). The synthesis of such proteins may also be induced by the plant hormone abscisic acid.

10. The phenomenon of cross-protection suggests the existence of a molecular "master switch". Indeed, in addition to the presence of plant hormones, there appears to be a higher hierarchical level of genes, the products of which activate a whole series of further genes. The products of these lower-level genes contribute to stress management either directly or indirectly (e.g. via the synthesis of low molecular weight osmolytes – here cryoprotective solutes). Such a system is called a "regulon". Finding such master-switch genes would be of particular interest with regard to increasing the stress tolerance of plants by genetic transformation. It seems more feasible at present, however, to transform plants by introducing several genes from the lower hierarchical level into a crop plant (Holmberg and Bülow 1998). Candidate genes for transforming plants with a master switch would be, for example, those encoding transcription activators such as DREB 1A, B, C and others (see Chap. 1.6: "proline"). These genes are high up in the cascade hierarchy for drought tolerance (Sarhan and Danyluk 1998).

11. So-called antifreeze proteins are well known in the animal kingdom, and have recently also been found in plants. They impede crystallisation of water and hinder the growth of ice crystals, thus delaying freezing, but not thawing. They are, therefore, also called THPs (thermal hysteresis proteins). The molecular structures and mechanisms of action of some of these proteins are known. They attach to ice crystals and turn their hydrophobic side towards the aqueous medium, thus making it difficult

for other water molecules to associate with the ice. The formation of many, small ice crystals instead of fewer large ones is the consequence.

12. Perennial plants from moderate and higher latitudes exhibit the phenomenon of seasonal frost hardening and dehardening. Frost hardening is accompanied at the molecular level by desaturation of membrane lipids, reduction of the protein/lipid ratios in biomembranes, and the synthesis of cryoprotective and ROS-detoxifying compounds and possibly also of proteins which promote or hinder ice nucleation. Plants have only a low photosynthetic capacity in the frost-hardened state. This is predominantly due to the degradation of the photosystems in the thylakoid membranes, but it also significantly reduces the danger of over-energisation in the frozen state. Arctic and tropical high mountain plants are permanently frost-hardy. The latter have developed various mechanisms to avoid freezing in accordance with the daily-frost climate, such as insulation and heat storage which can be of a permanent (cloaking of the stem) or transient (night buds) nature. Such mechanisms only work, however, because the nightly frost periods last, at most, for only a few hours before the tropical sun raises the temperature above the freezing point again.

13. Frost drought comprises a stress situation for the entire plant, for which there is no avoidance response except leaf shedding and also no specific tolerance. Frost drought results from the transpiration of above-ground plant parts when water cannot be taken up from the frozen soil. Frost-hardened plant organs can survive this situation only as long as the mechanisms for damage avoidance are not overtaxed.

References

Allen DJ, Ort DR (2001) Impacts of chilling temperatures on photosynthesis in warm-climate plants. Trends Plant Sci 6:36–42

Antikainen M, Griffith M, Zhang J, Hon W-C, Yang DCS, Pihakashi-Maunsbach K (1996) Immunolocalization of antifreeze proteins in winter rye leaves, crowns, and roots by tissue printing. Plant Physiol 110:845–857

Ashworth EN (1993) Deep supercooling in woody plant tissues. In: Li PH, Christersson L (eds) Advances in plant cold hardiness. CRC Press, Boca Raton, pp 203–213

Beck E (1994) Cold tolerance in tropical alpine plants. In: Rundel PW, Smith AP, Meinzer FC (eds) Tropical alpine environments. Plant form and function. Cambridge University Press, Cambridge, pp 77–110

Burke MJ, Lindow SE (1990) Surface properties and size of the nucleation site in ice nucleation active bacteria: theoretical considerations. Cryobiology 27:80–84

Carpenter JF, Hansen TN (1992) Antifreeze protein modulates cell survival during cryopreservation: mediation through influence on ice crystal growth. Proc Natl Acad Sci USA 89:8953–8957

Cernusca A (1984) Beurteilung der Schipistenplanierung in Tirol aus ökologischer Sicht. Verh Ges Ökol 12:137–148

Crowe JH, Crowe LM, Mouradian R (1983) Stabilization of biological membranes at low water activities. Cryobiology 20:346–356

DeVries AL, Cheng CHC (1992) The rule of antifreeze glycopeptides and peptides in the survival of cold water fishes. In: Somero GN, Osmond CB, Bolis CL (eds) Water and life. Springer, Berlin Heidelberg New York, pp 301–315

Dowgert ME, Steponkus PL (1983) Effect of cold acclimation on intracellular ice formation in isolated protoplasts. Plant Physiol 72:978–988

Duman JG, Wu DW, Yeung KL, Wolf EE (1992) Hemolymph proteins involved in the cold tolerance of terrestrial arthropods: antifreeze and ice nucleator proteins. In: Somero GN, Osmond CB, Bolis CL (eds) Water and life. Springer, Berlin Heidelberg New York, pp 282–300

Elstner EF (1996) Die Sauerstoffaktivierung als Basis pflanzlicher Stressreaktion. In: Brunold C, Rüegsegger A, Brändle R (Hrsg) Stress bei Pflanzen. UTB Paul Haupt, Bern, pp 347–363

Fetene M, Gashaw M, Nauke P, Beck E (1998) Microclimate and ecophysiological significance of the tree-like life-form of *Lobelia rhynchopefalum* in a tropical alpine environment. Oecologia 113:332–340

Fields PG (1993) Reduction of cold tolerance of stored-product insects by ice-nucleating-active bacteria. Environ Entomol 22:470–476

Frentzen M, Heinz E (1983) Membranlipid-Biosynthese in Chloroplasten. Biol Unserer Zeit 13:178–187

Georgopoulos C (1992) The emergence of the chaperone machines. Trends Biochem Sci 17:295–299

Gombos Z, Wada H, Varkonyi Z, Los DA, Murata N (1996) Characterization of the Fad12 mutant of synechocystis that is defective in delta 12 acyllipid desaturase activity. Biochim Biophys Acta 1299:117–123

Green RL, Warren GJ (1985) Physical and functional repetition in a bacterial ice nucleation gene. Nature 317:645–648

Griffith M, Ala P, Yang DSC, Hon W-C, Moffatt B (1992) Antifreeze protein produced endogenously in winter rye leaves. Plant Physiol 100:593–596

Griffith M, Marentes E, Ala P, Yang DSC (1993) The role of ice-binding proteins in frost tolerance of winter rye. In: Li PH, Christersson L (eds) Advances in plant cold hardiness. CRC Press, Boca Raton, pp 177–186

Gross DC, Proebsting EL Jr, Maccrindle-Zimmerman H (1988) Development, distribution, and characteristics of intrinsic, nonbacterial ice nuclei in *Prunus* wood. Plant Physiol 88:915–922

Hansen J (2000) Überleben in der Kälte – wie Pflanzen sich vor Froststress schützen. Biol Unserer Zeit 30:24–34

Hansen J, Beck E (1988) Evidence for ideal and non-ideal equilibrium freezing of leaf water in frost hardy ivy (*Hedera helix*) and winter barley (*Hordeum vulgare*). Bot Acta 101:76–82

Hansen J, Beck E (1994) Seasonal changes in the utilization and turnover of assimilation products in 8-year-old Scots pine (*Pinus sylvestris* L.) trees. Trees 8:172–182

Hartl F-U, Hlodan R, Langer T (1994) Molecular chaperones in protein folding: the art of avoiding sticky situations. Trends Biochem Sci 19:20–25

Hedberg O (1964) Features of afro-alpine plant ecology. Acta Phytogeogr Suecica 48:1–144

Heldt HW (1999) Pflanzenbiochemie. Spektrum, Heidelberg

Hew CL, Yang DCS (1992) Protein interaction with ice. Eur J Biochem 203:33–42

Hincha DK, Schmitt JM (1992) Freeze-thaw injury and cryoprotection of thylakoid membranes. In: Somero GN, Osmond CR, Bolis CL (eds) Water and life. Springer, Berlin Heidelberg New York, pp 316–337

Holmberg N, Bülow L (1998) Improved stress tolerance in plants by heterologous gene transfer: Recent achievements and future prospects. Trends Plant Sci 3:61–66

Jones TL, Tucker DE, Ort DR (1998) Chilling delays circadian pattern of sucrose phosphate synthase and nitrate reductase activity in tomato. Plant Physiol 118:149–158

Kappen L, Zeitler A (1977) Seasonal changes between one- and two-phasic response of plant leaves to heat stress. Oecologia 31:45–53

Kroog JO, Zachariassen KE, Larsen B, Smidsrod O (1979) Thermal buffering in afro-alpine plants due to nucleating agent-induced water freezing. Nature 282:300–301

Lafta AM, Lorenzen JH (1995) Effect of high temperature on plant growth and carbohydrate metabolism in potato. Plant Physiol 109:637–643

Larcher W (1987) Stress bei Pflanzen. Naturwissenschaften 74:158–167

Larcher W (2001) Ökophysiologie der Pflanzen, 6 Aufl. UTB, Eugen Ulmer, Stuttgart

Larcher W (2003) Physiological plant ecology, 4th edn (chapter: Plants under stress). Springer, Berlin Heidelberg New York, pp 345–450

Lindow SE (1982) Population dynamics of epiphytic ice nucleation active bacteria on first sensitive plants and frost control by means of antagonistic bacteria. In: Li PH, Sakai A (eds) Plant cold hardiness. Academic Press, New York, pp 395–416

Maki LR, Galyan ME, Chien ME, Caldwell DR (1974) Ice nucleation induced by Pseudomonas syringae. Appl Microbiol 28:456–459

Murata N, Wada H, Gombos Z, Nishida I (1993) The molecular mechanism of the low-temperature tolerance of plants studied by gene technology of membrane lipids. In: Jackson MB, Black CR (eds) Interacting stresses on plants in a changing climate. NATO ASI Series 16. Springer, Berlin Heidelberg New York, pp 715–723

Neely WC, Martin JM, Barker SA (1988) Products and relative reaction rates of the oxidation of tocopherols with singlet molecular oxygen. Photochem Photobiol 48:423–428

Nishida I, Murata N (1996) Chilling sensitivity in plants and cyanobacteria. Annu Rev Plant Physiol Plant Mol Biol 47:541–568

Nover L, Höhfeld I (1996) Hohe Temperaturen. In: Brunold C, Rüegsegger A, Brändle R (Hrsg) Stress bei Pflanzen. Paul Haupt, Bern, pp 49–70

Ohlrogge JB, Browse J (1995) Lipid biosynthesis. Plant Cell 7:957–970

Powles SB (1984) Photoinhibition of photosynthesis induced by visible light. Annu Rev Plant Physiol 35:15–44

Powles SB, Berry JS, Björkman O (1983) Interaction between light and chilling temperature on the inhibition of photosynthesis in chilling-sensitive plants. Plant Cell Environ 6:117–123

Sáez-Vásquez J, Raynal M, Delseny M (1995) A rapeseed cold-inducible transcript encodes a phosphoenolpyruvate carboxykinase. Plant Physiol 109:611–618

Sakai A, Larcher W (1987) Frost survival of plants: responses and adaptation to freezing stress. Ecol Studies 62

Sarhan F, Danyluk J (1998) Engineering cold-tolerant crops – throwing the master switch. Trends Plant Sci 3:289–290

Senser M, Beck E (1982) Frost resistance in spruce [Picea abies (L.) Karst]: IV. The lipid composition of frost resistant and frost sensitive spruce chloroplasts. Z Pflanzenphysiol 105:241–253

Sicheri F, Yang DCS (1995) Ice-binding structure and mechanism of antifreeze protein from winter flounder. Nature 375:427–431

Steponkus PL, Dowgert MF, Gordon-Kamm W (1983) Destabilization of the plasma membrane of isolated plant protoplasts during a freeze-thaw cycle: the influence of cold acclimation. Cryobiology 20:448–465

Steponkus PL, Uemura M, Balsamo RA, Arvinte T, Lynch DV (1988) Transformation of the cryobehavior of rye protoplasts by modification of the plasma membrane lipid composition. Proc Natl Acad Sci USA 85:9026–9030

Tahtiharju S, Sangwan V, Monroy AF, Dhinsda RS, Borg M (1997) The induction of kin genes in cold-acclimating Arabidopsis thaliana. Evidence of a role of calcium. Planta 203:442–447

Thomashow MF (1999) Plant cold tolerance: freezing tolerance genes and regulatory mechanisms. Annu Rev Plant Physiol Plant Mol Biol 50:571–599

Urrutia ME, Duman JG, Knight CA (1992) Plant thermal hysteresis proteins. Biochim Biophys Acta 1121:199–206

Vigh L, Los DA, Horvath I, Murata N (1993) The primary signal in the biological perception of temperature: Pd-catalyzed hydrogenation of membrane lipids stimulated the expression of the desA gene in synechocystis PCC6803. Proc Natl Acad Sci USA 90:9090–9094

Vogg G, Heim R, Gotschy B, Beck E, Hansen J (1998) Frost hardening and photosynthetic performance of Scots pine (Pinus sylvestris L.). II. Seasonal changes in the fluidity of thylakoid membranes. Planta 204:201–206

Wallis JG, Wang H, Guerra DJ (1997) Expression of a synthetic antifreeze protein in potato reduces electrolyte release at freezing temperatures. Plant Mol Biol 35:323–330

Wilson M, Lindow SE (1993) Release of recombinant microorganisms. Annu Rev Microbiol 47:913–944

Wolfe J (1978) Chilling injury in plants – the role of membrane lipid fluidity. Plant Cell Environ 1:241–247

Wolfe J, Steponkus PL (1983) Mechanical properties of the plasma membrane of isolated plant protoplasts. Plant Physiol 71:276–285

Worland MR, Block W (1999) Ice-nucleating bacteria from the guts of two sub-antarctic beetles Hydromedion sparsutum and Perimylops antarcticus (Perimylopidae). Cryobiology 38:60–67

Yang DSC, Sax M, Chakrabarty A, Hew CL (1988) Crystal structure of an antifreeze polypeptide and its mechanistic implications. Nature 333:232–237

Yelenosky G, Mauk CS, Bausher MG, Kushad MM (1987) Chemical bioregulation of growth and cold hardiness in citrus. In: Li PH (eds) Plant cold hardiness, vol 5. Liss, New York, pp 299–321

Yelenosky G (1985) Cold hardiness in citrus. Hort Rev 7:201–237

Zhu JJ, Beck E (1991) Water relations of Pachysandra leaves during freezing and thawing: evidence for a negative pressure potential alleviating freeze-dehydration stress. Plant Physiol 97:1146–1153

Xin Z, Browse J (2000) Cold comfort farm: the acclimation of plants to freezing temperatures. Plant Cell Environ 23:893–907

1.4

Oxygen Deficiency (Anaerobiosis and Hypoxia)

Nelumbo nucifera, the lotus flower, is a typical swamp plant in the monsoon climate of northern Australia. The rhizomes grow in the oxygen-deficient mud and are supplied with oxygen via an aerenchyma. The flow of air in the aerenchyma is driven by thermo-osmosis. Because of crocodiles, researchers in this area should exercise caution. Kapalgam Northern Territories. Photo E.-D. Schulze

Recommended Literature

- Blom CWPM, Voesenek LACJ (1996) Flooding: the survival strategies of plants. Trends Ecol Evol 11:290–295
- Chang C, Bleeker AB (2004) Ethylene Biology. More than a Gas. Plant Physiol 136:2895–2899 (and subsequent articles in this issue)
- Drew MC (1997) Oxygen deficiency and root metabolism: injury and acclimation under hypoxia and anoxia. Annu Rev Plant Physiol Plant Mol Biol 48:223–250

Common soils consist of **four components**: soil particles, water, air and organisms including plant roots (Fig. 1.4.1). Freely draining soils can only retain water in pores with diameters smaller than 10–60 µm. Even at water saturation up to the field capacity (see Chap. 2.2) the air-filled pore volume is 10–30% of the total soil volume. However, in partially or permanently waterlogged soils, there are almost no air-filled pores, as the air dissolves in the water.

Gas exchange in well-aerated soils is mainly through diffusion in the continuum of the air-filled pores, but is accelerated by a number of active processes in the soil and thus becomes a relatively fast process. For example, if oxygen is consumed by the respiratory activity of microorganisms and plant roots, oxygen from the atmosphere flows quickly into the soil following the concentration gradient. As a result, the partial pressure of O_2 in the soil air, at least in pore-rich soils, remains in the range of 15–20%. Similarly, CO_2 that accumulates in the soil pores quickly leaks out from the soil. The situation is completely different when gas exchange is via the water-filled pores of waterlogged soils. **Fick's first law of diffusion** describes the amount of gas diffusing per unit of time, i.e. the net gas flux, as depending on the diffusion coefficient D, on the size of the exchange area, and on the concentration gradient. At the same temperature, the diffusion coefficient of oxygen in water is about 10,000 times (exactly 11,300 times) smaller than in air. Oxygen has also a very low solubility in water (0.03 ml O_2 l^{-1} H_2O). Thus, gas exchange in waterlogged soils is very slow and oxygen becomes one of the limiting factors for growth and the development of plants. Oxygen supply to roots is enhanced by a temperature gradient as well as by water flow in the soil. For roots, the critical oxygen concentration is generally 5–10%, although some plants are able to grow at lower O_2 concentrations, e.g. cotton grass (*Eriophorum angustifolium*) roots grow at 2–4% O_2 (Armstrong and Gaynard 1976). The apparent tolerance of these plants is easily explained by the large intracellular channels extending from the

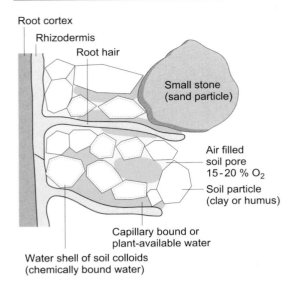

Fig. 1.4.1. Four-component system: Root/soil organism, soil particle, soil water (solution), soil air

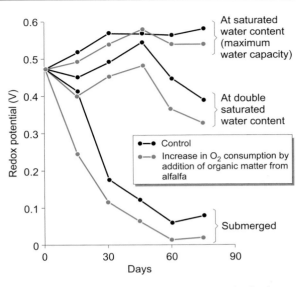

Fig. 1.4.2. Development of redox potential of a loamy clay soil as influenced by the water content and the amount of organic matter. (After Amberger 1988)

shoot and leaves into the roots maintaining a sufficiently high oxygen concentration in the root tissue. A similar **aeration tissue** (termed **aerenchyma**) is found in deep-water rice, the roots of which are able to grow at 0.8% oxygen (Armstrong and Webb 1985). In such cases, a corky exodermis is often produced, forming a gas-tight outer cell layer of the root that renders the escape of gases from the interior of the root into the soil very difficult. If such a diffusion barrier tissue is missing, oxygen leaks out of the aerenchyma to the surrounding soil, where the heavy metal ions in the immediate proximity of roots are oxidised forming "rusty spots and root channels" in pseudogley and are, thus, "detoxified" for soil organisms.

Regarding the relationship between oxygen concentration and metabolism, a situation, where biochemical reactions are not limited by partial oxygen pressure, is called **normoxia**. If mitochondrial ATP synthesis is affected, but not completely inhibited by low O_2, it operates under **hypoxia**. In the absence of oxygen (**anoxia**), oxidative phosphorylation in the mitochondria is negligible, compared with ATP synthesis by glycolysis and fermentation.

Long-term waterlogged soils have a negative redox potential because of the low oxygen partial pressure (see Box 1.7.1), i.e. they exhibit reducing properties. Oxygen entering such soils (e.g. through root or earth worm channels) is readily consumed by soil organisms.

The redox potential of soils decreases dramatically already after a few days of flooding (Fig. 1.4.2) and microaerophilic and anaerobic microorganisms start to grow. They mainly live on the organic matter of the soil as energy source, but require ions as electron acceptors that can be reduced. If nitrate is used as electron acceptor, giving rise to nitrite, N_2O and finally N_2 (denitrification), the process is termed nitrate respiration and, accordingly, in sulfate respiration sulfide is formed from SO_4^{2-} (see Chap. 3.3.3). Similarly, three-valent iron and four-valent manganese can be reduced to two-valent ions. In addition, CO_2 may be used as electron acceptor, resulting in the production of methane. Table 1.4.1 shows the sequence of redox reactions occurring in the soil when the redox potential decreases. Such reactions often consume protons, i.e. result in an alkalinisation of the soil.

However, reduced heavy metal ions are toxic. Thus, the growth of roots is not only inhibited by the lack of oxygen, but also by toxic ions in the vicinity of roots (Fig. 1.4.3). This applies particularly to the very sensitive symbiosis of plant roots with mycorrhizal fungi: Plants growing on waterlogged soils are very sensitive to pathogens and rarely form mycorrhizae; therefore, their capability of nutrient acquisition and growth is usually very limited (Table 1.4.2).

Two-thirds of the earth's land mass is flooded, at least occasionally (e.g. the monsoon regions of Southeast Asia or the areas at the lower

Table 1.4.1. Sequence of soil-bound redox reactions. The redox potential provides important information about the reactions in the soil, as these reactions take place in the sequence listed [i.e. sulfate is not reduced if iron(III) ions are still present]. (After Marschner 1986)

Redox reaction		Redox potential E (mV) at pH 7
Start of nitrate reduction (denitrification)	$NO_3^- \rightarrow NO_2^-$	450–550
Start of manganese reduction	$MnO_2 + 4H^+ + 2e^- \rightarrow Mn^{2+} + 2H_2O$	350–450
Absence of free oxygen	$O_2 + 4H^+ + 4e^- \rightarrow 2H_2O$	350
Absence of nitrate	$(\rightarrow N_2O \rightarrow N_2)$	250
Start of Fe^{2+} formation	$Fe(OH)_3 + 3H^+ + 1e^- \rightarrow Fe^{2+} + 3H_2O$	150
Fe^{3+} completely consumed		120
Start of sulfate reduction	$SO_4^{2-} + 10H^+ + 8e^- \rightarrow H_2S + 4H_2O$	−50
Sulfate completely consumed		−180
Methane formation	$CO_2 + 8H^+ + 8e^- \rightarrow CH_4 + 2H_2O$	<−180

Table 1.4.2. Effect of flooding on biomass production, and on nutrient content of leaves, of two flooding-sensitive and one flooding-tolerant representatives of the genus *Rumex*. (After Laan et al. 1989a, b)

Species/conditions for growth	Dry weight of shoot (g)	Nutrient content of leaves (mol per g dry weight)				
		Nitrogen	Phosphorus	Sodium	Calcium	Magnesium
R. thyrsiflorus						
Dry site	15.2±1.4	1878±45	143±10	1238±37	323±11	435±22
Flooded	7.2±1.4	1006±64	44±2	355±15	190±2	218±3
R. crispus						
Dry site	13.6±1.4	1372±54	90±5	857±39	532±27	311±7
Flooded	12.7±2.5	702±35	58±10	347±23	315±13	160±8
R. maritimus						
Dry site	24.8±2.6	1018±91	59±2	478±11	615±19	401±4
Flooded	25.4±3.9	1052±52	59±2	272±10	761±40	398±11

Data are average values of five identical experiments ±SD

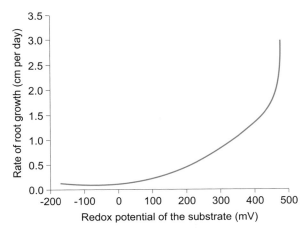

Fig. 1.4.3. Dependence of root growth of the grass *Spartina patens* on the redox potential of the soil. (After DeLaune et al. 1993)

reaches of the large Siberian rivers). Many higher plants, therefore, have developed mechanisms to survive hypoxia, the major stress factor. The frequency of flooding, and the tolerance of certain species, can be extrapolated from the zonation of the riparian vegetation.

Physiologically, **primary** and **secondary hypoxia** or anaerobiosis should be differentiated. In primary hypoxia, germination of a plant already takes place in an oxygen-deficient environment, which does not change during the whole lifetime of the plant. This applies, for example, to obligate marsh plants (Chap. 1.4.1.1). Secondary hypoxia occurs when plants normally growing in well-aerated soils are temporarily flooded.

1.4.1

Energy Metabolism of Plants Under Oxygen Deficiency

The daily oxygen demands of soils during the growth period of plants are in the range of 10–20 l/m², depending on the density of the roots and the activity of soil microbes. The minimum

Box 1.4.1	Energy metabolism of heterotrophic organs in normoxia and hypoxia

Energy charge of cells is usually determined by the degree of phosphorylation of the adenylate system (adenylate energy charge, AEC, often called EC).

The following formula is applied:

$$(A)EC = \frac{[ATP] + 0.5[ADP]}{[ATP] + [ADP] + [AMP]}$$

By definition, maximum EC equals 1. Since ADP possesses only one energy-rich phosphate bond, its concentration has to be multiplied by the factor 0.5. A cell supplied with sufficient oxygen has an AEC between 0.8 and 0.95. Under anaerobic conditions the energy charge may drop to 0.2 (see Fig. 1.4.4). Acute ATP deficiency leads to the breakdown of compartmentation as the energy-driven ion pumps are no longer sufficiently energised.

oxygen partial pressure in the soil for the growth of flooding-sensitive plants is at 2–3% (about 5 kPa). Inhibition of growth under hypoxic conditions is a multifactorial phenomenon, which is basically caused by the very low efficiency of the energy metabolism. During inhibition of mitochondrial respiration, many heterotrophic organisms and plant tissues are able to switch to fermentative metabolism. This type of metabolism, however, requires increased throughput of energy carriers such as glucose. Under these conditions, reserve material is quickly consumed and poisonous or stressful end products, such as ethanol or lactic acid, accumulate. Despite stimulation of glycolysis and fermentation by the so-called **Pasteur effect**, the **energy charge** of cells remains low so that during extended periods of hypoxia, or even short-term anaerobiosis, values of below 0.5 result (see Box 1.4.1). These values are too low for anabolic metabolism, i.e. for growth. Inhibition of phloem transport and phloem unloading is another consequence of the low-energy charge of the plant tissues. Thus cells are depleted not only because of the faster turnover of storage material, but also because of the shortage of stock. **Helophytes** (swamp plants) avoid the problems caused by hypoxia by the development of an **aerenchyma**.

1.4.1.1
Primary Hypoxia: Germination Under Hypoxic Conditions

Dry cereal seeds contain carbohydrates, mainly starch; to germinate they require catabolising enzymes: α- and β-amylase, amylopectin-de-

branching enzymes and α-glucosidases (maltase, diastase). Neither wheat nor barley seeds are able to germinate under anaerobic conditions, but rice can (Fig. 1.4.4). In the rice grain, starch debranching enzymes and α-glucosidases are present as inactive precursors, which are activated during germination, even without oxygen. Upon germination in the absence of oxygen, α- and β-amylases are synthesised de novo (Guglielminetti et al. 1995). This happens during the first 2 days of germination when the soluble carbohydrates already present serve as the energy source. After this, starch-catabolising enzymes become active and starch is hydrolytically degraded and the degradation products become available for further metabolism, predominantly as glucose-6-P and fructose-6-P.

1.4.1.2
Changes in Metabolism Caused by Hypoxia

Energy Metabolism Under Hypoxia and Anoxia In addition to the energy deficit caused by hypoxia and anaerobiosis, toxic metabolic products accumulate, e.g. ethanol (see Box 1.4.1). Higher concentrations of this poisonous compound destroy the selective permeability of membranes and prevent formation of proton gradients and in turn the gain of energy. On the other hand, ethanol easily permeates through biomembranes and cell walls and thus only rarely reaches damaging concentrations of 50–100 nM in the cell. Acetaldehyde, the biochemical precursor of ethanol, is much more poisonous than ethanol, but is usually immediately reduced. It only accumulates when alcohol dehydrogenase is inhibited or

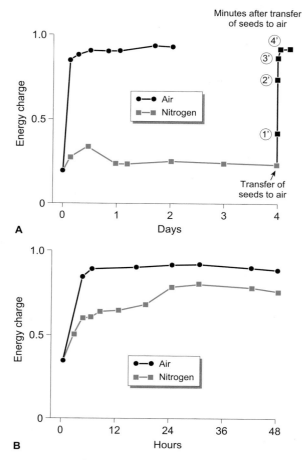

Fig. 1.4.4. The energy charge of lettuce seeds (A) or rice grains (B) during germination in air or under nitrogen. (After Pradet et al. 1985)

amino acids [asparagine, arginine, γ-amino butyric acid (GABA)]. Synthesis of GABA from glutamate releases CO_2 and consumes protons, and is a reliable marker for metabolism under hypoxia:

$$^-OOC - CH_2 - CH_2 - CHNH_2 - COO^- + H^+$$
$$\rightarrow \ ^-OOC - CH_2 - CH_2 - CH_2NH_2 + CO_2$$

1.4.1.3
"Anaerobic Polypeptides"

Fine root systems and root meristems are particularly sensitive to oxygen deficiency. In species not tolerant to flooding, those parts of the root system used for water and ion uptake die off at oxygen partial pressures below 0.5–5 kPa and the plant becomes drought stressed, even if standing in water. Drought stress is indicated by an increased production of ABA that is distributed via the xylem sap, and leads to stomatal closure. As a consequence, the rate of photosynthesis decreases as well as growth and the plants finally become stunted while their leaves show strong **epinasty** (downward bending of the leaves and petioles because of increased growth of the upper side). Such phenomena are often observed in indoor plants which are watered too much, where hypoxia in the water-saturated soil leads to death of the root system and withering of the shoot.

In flooding-tolerant plants hypoxia triggers a change in gene expression. Synthesis of normal housekeeping proteins (see Chap. 1.3.4.2) attenuates and synthesis of about 20 or more so-called **anaerobic polypeptides** (ANPs) or **anaerobic stress proteins** (ASPs) is induced (Fig. 1.4.5). These are predominantly fermentative enzymes: **Alcohol dehydrogenase**, pyruvate decarboxylase, lactate dehydrogenase, glyceraldehydephosphate dehydrogenase, aldolase, glucose-6-P-isomerase, alanine aminotransferase and enolase have been identified. The promoters of the ANPs contain a consensus sequence, the so-called **anaerobic response element** (ARE; Christopher and Good 1996).

The trigger and signal chain leading to the induction of ANPs are still unknown. The formation of ANPs is suppressed above O_2 concentrations of 2–5%. In anoxia-tolerant plants mainly ethanol is formed due to the kind of ANPs which promote glycolysis and fermenta-

switched off by mutation or genetic modification. Acidification of the cytosol by lactic acid is another metabolically detrimental effect of hypoxia. When oxygen deficiency sets in, **lactate dehydrogenase** (LDH) is the first enzyme to be activated and the pH in the cytosol decreases as lactic acid forms and accumulates. As the pH optimum of LDH is in the neutral range, it inhibits itself upon acidification of the cytosol. **Pyruvate decarboxylase** is less susceptible to acidity and therefore takes over, producing acetaldehyde and, together with alcohol dehydrogenase, ethanol.

Biochemical Adaptation to Oxygen Deficiency
Besides anatomical-morphological strain reactions to the shortage of oxygen (as explained later), biochemical adaptation can take place: In addition to lactate, rice seedlings and sweet flag (*Acorus calamus*) rhizomes mainly produce basic

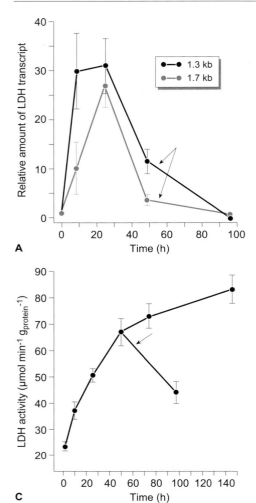

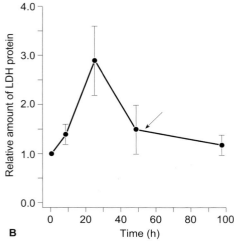

Fig. 1.4.5. Induction of lactate dehydrogenase (LDH)-ANP in maize roots under hypoxic conditions. The LDH is quickly broken down in maize roots (half-life 4 h), especially if the roots are kept in nitrogen before the enzyme is extracted (half-life <2 h). Immediately after the change of the aerobic for an anaerobic atmosphere, synthesis of LDH mRNA started (A). The expression of two separately regulated LDH genes (1.3 and 1.7 kDa) became apparent after 8 and 24 h, respectively. After 20 h of anaerobiosis the maximum amount of LDH transcript was measured. Thereafter, despite prolonged anaerobiosis, the amount of mRNA quickly dropped. After transfer into air the transcript disappeared completely. The synthesis of the LDH-ANP protein followed generally the kinetics of the mRNA (B), due to the short half-life of the protein. Under aerobic conditions (*arrow*) the amount of protein declined only slowly. Despite the reduction of the LDH protein, the activity of the enzyme increased to 3.5 times its original value (C) during the entire anaerobic treatment. Upon transfer of the roots into air the activity of the LDH also dropped drastically (*arrow*). (After Christopher and Good 1996)

tion and the energy charge of the tissue is kept high, thus maintaining gross metabolic activities.

Longer phases of anoxia (e.g. during winter) may be bridged in rhizomes and roots by periods of suspended metabolism, called **anaerobic retreat**. In spring, elongation growth starts again, but how this happens is still unknown.

Differences between anoxia-tolerant and anoxia-sensitive plants are gradual: There are neither absolutely tolerant nor absolutely intolerant species. Membrane lipids appear to play a crucial role: It appears to be important how fast membrane lipids are damaged and can subse-

quently be replaced. In intolerant species membrane lipids are damaged readily, while those of the tolerant species are more persistent (Fig. 1.4.6). Oxygen-dependent desaturation of lipids appears to be inhibited. In anoxia-sensitive plants, a higher proportion of saturated membrane lipids was found, in contrast to tolerant species where a higher degree of desaturation can be maintained for a longer period. Membranes of mitochondria and of the endoplasmic reticulum are particularly endangered. In pea seeds, mitochondria are destroyed after only 3–4 days of anoxia, whereas biomembranes of tolerant species remain functional for a long period.

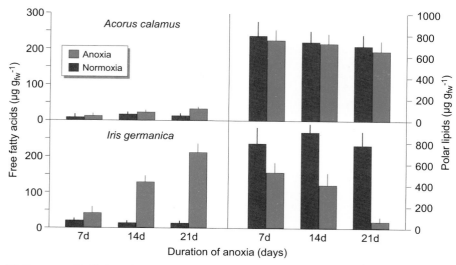

Fig. 1.4.6. Lipid degradation in rhizome tissue of iris which is sensitive to anoxia, and sweet flag (*Acorus*) which is insensitive. (After Jackson and Black 1993)

1.4.2

Anatomical-Morphological Changes Caused by Hypoxia

1.4.2.1
Elongation of Internodes

As with other stresses, there are also obvious avoidance reactions induced by hypoxia and anaerobiosis. Submerged plants usually produce strikingly long internodes. By such elongation growth, the apical parts of the shoots quickly reach the surface of the water and thus escape the hypoxic environment. This reaction has been particularly well studied in deep-water rice, where the submerged shoots elongate up to 25 cm/day.

A marked increase in the intercellular ethylene concentration is regarded as the phytohormonal signal which stimulates elongation growth. However, the real initial signal is the low oxygen partial pressure in the submerged internode, leading to increased expression of the ACC-oxidase gene (ACC: <u>a</u>mino<u>c</u>yclopropane <u>c</u>arboxylic acid) and finally to increased ethylene synthesis (Box 1.4.2). The ACC produced by the hypoxic roots is transported by the xylem stream into the better aerated shoot since the ACC-oxidase requires molecular oxygen as substrate. The increased ethylene partial pressure triggers the decrease in the endogenous ABA level and thus in turn increases the effectiveness of the elongation hormone gibberellic acid. Thus, at least four phytohormones participate in the elongation growth of shoots and petioles triggered by hypoxia: ethylene, ABA, auxin and gibberellin.

Expansins are cell wall proteins with a molecular mass of 24.5 kDa (Box 1.4.3). In the shoots of deep-water rice, two such proteins occur in the intercalary meristem and in the adjacent extension zone (but not in the differentiation zone) mainly around the vascular bundles and in the tissue lining the inner epidermis, i.e. towards the pith channel (Cho and Kende 1997 a, b).

Submerged internodes accumulate considerably more expansins than those in air, and substantially expand their elongation zone. The molecular mechanism of expansins is still not well understood; it is assumed that they loosen the hydrogen bridges between the hemicellulose $[(1 \rightarrow 3),(1 \rightarrow 4)\text{-}\beta\text{-}D\text{-glucans})]$ and the paracrystalline segments of the cellulose microfibrils and thus increase the extensibility of the cell wall. Although this effect suggests a catalytic mechanism, expansins do not show any hydrolase activity.

Auxin also plays a role in shoot expansion: It stimulates acidification of the cell wall, probably by activating the ATP-dependent proton pumps in the plasma membrane. The effect of expansins can be mimicked by acidification of the cell wall. When rice grains were germinated under aerobic and anaerobic conditions, respectively, a

Box 1.4.2 — Ethylene biosynthesis from S-adenosylmethionine (AdoMet) and formation of the precursor

In addition to the biochemical pathways, the scheme shows internal and external factors that influence the synthesis or accumulation of ethylene. (After Taiz and Zeiger 2000)

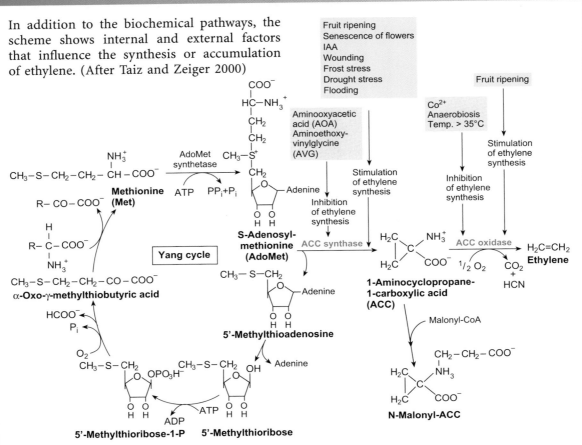

fast breakdown of auxin took place in air, but not under anaerobiosis (Mapelli and Bertani 1993; Mekhedov and Kende 1996). Persistence of auxin contributes to a prolonged elongation growth of the shoot.

1.4.2.2
Formation of Aerenchyma

Under hypoxic conditions ethylene formation is increased, and it accumulates in and around roots and submerged shoots because of its low solubility in water. Concentrations of 0.1–0.5 ppm are sufficient to induce formation of intercellular space-rich tissues by **programmed cell death (PCD)** or **apoptosis**. PCD does not take place in differentiated older cells, rather an aerenchyma is initiated already at the end of the

elongation zone of the organ. Formation of aerenchyma is lytic, e.g. in maize, *Luronium*, and *Nymphoides*, but usually schizogenous in petioles, e.g. of *Caltha*, *Rumex*, or *Filipendula*. Formation of aerenchyma is not restricted to helophytes and submerged plants; even terrestrial plants, such as maize and sunflower, may develop aerenchyma in roots and the basal part of the shoot. In many helophytes (such as rice and arrowhead), the formation of aerenchyma is genetically fixed (constitutive), and the induction of PCD is not dependent on oxygen deficiency or ethylene accumulation. Aerenchyma formation caused by hypoxia commonly results in irregular air spaces, whereas those constitutively developed show regular patterns of air channels. Aerenchyma allows air circulation in tissues, additionally supported by pressure ventilation (misleadingly often termed "thermo-osmosis",

Box 1.4.3   Expansin(s) and internode extension in deep-water rice

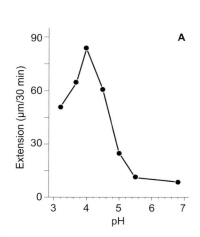

A shows the dependence of the extensibility of isolated cell walls on the pH. Cell wall preparations were incubated in media of different pH and subsequently subjected to tension; the stretching rate is shown. This technology was also used in the experiments presented in B–D. In B, the extensibility of different sections of the internode upon acid-induced growth (B1) and after addition of a protein extracted from cell walls ("expansin" preparation) (B2) is shown. *IM* Intercalary meristem; *EZ* elongation zone; *DZ* differentiation zone. C shows the effect of submergence on the elongation growth of the internode (C1) and the acid-induced extension of shoots which have grown aerobically and submerged (C2); the *insert* shows the plot of the recordings. D shows the influence of submergence on the length of the elongation zone. Shoots grown submerged have a considerably longer elongation zone than those grown in air. (After Cho and Kende 1997 a, b).

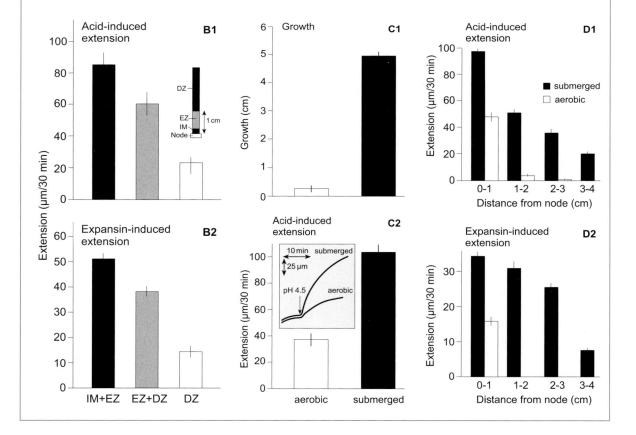

Box 1.4.4   Thermo-osmosis

Table. Position of thermo-osmotically active layers and their average pore diameter. (After Grosse 1997)

Plant species	Tissue	Pore diameter (nm)
Nuphar lutea (yellow water lily)	Young leaf	700–1200
	Old leaf	>15 000
Nelumbo nucifera (lotus)	(Air) leaf	30
Nymphoides peltatum (fringed water lily)	Young leaf	29
Alnus glutinosa (alder)	Cork cambium	14–113
	Cambium	>>100

Convectional air flow in intercellular spaces improves the gas exchange of plant tissues. This **thermo-osmosis**, in combination with aerenchyma formation, is often put forward as a mechanism to improve gas flow in tissues of helophytes, mangroves and plants of river basins. Thermo-osmosis includes several phenomena which are not dependent on biological activity but are of a purely physical nature. Easiest to understand is the efflux of gas from the tissue caused by evaporation of water from those cell surfaces bordering intercellular spaces; the more water evaporates, the greater is the partial pressure of the intercellular water vapour, but the volume of that gas efflux is very small. Gas fluxes arising from differences in temperature, e.g. between the leaves floating on the water surface and the rhizomes in the anoxic bottom of the pond, are more effective, as is also gas exchange caused by the differences in molecular mass of the gases involved. Such gas fluxes are called thermo-osmosis, as they require gas-filled pores or cavities, the dimensions of which are smaller than the mean free path of the gas molecules in Brownian motion (ca. 100 nm at atmospheric pressure and 20 °C). Therefore, not only plant tissues, but also ceramic filters or other porous materials with pore diameters of similar size to the intercellular spaces of plant material are used as **thermo-osmotic active layers** in studies (Table).

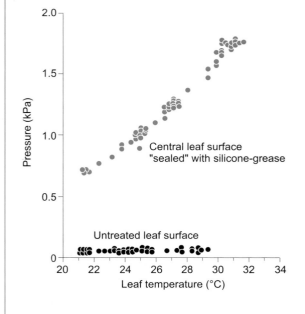

Fig. 1. The relationship between thermo-osmotically created pressure ("lacunar pressure") and temperature in a petiole of a young leaf of *Nelumbo nucifera*. An untreated leaf with open stomata was compared with a leaf in which the central portion of the surface (where the lacuna joins the petiole) was sealed with silicone. (After Dacey 1987)

Box 1.4.4   (continued)

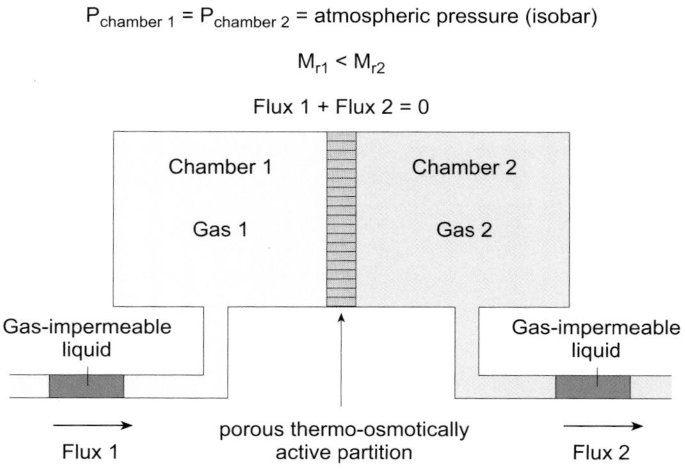

$P_{chamber\ 1} = P_{chamber\ 2}$ = atmospheric pressure (isobar)

$M_{r1} < M_{r2}$

Flux 1 + Flux 2 = 0

Chamber 1		Chamber 2
Gas 1		Gas 2

Gas-impermeable liquid

Gas-impermeable liquid

→ Flux 1

porous thermo-osmotically active partition

→ Flux 2

Fig. 2. Model of the isothermic formation of a thermo-osmotic gas flow in a porous layer. Gas flux originates from a concentration gradient of the gas on both surfaces of the porous layer. This gradient originates from the resistance to gas permeation of the thermo-osmotic layer whose pores are smaller than the mean free path length of the moving gas molecules. Gas 1, due to its smaller molecular mass, permeates through the layer easier than gas 2; therefore, there is a net gas flow from chamber 1 to chamber 2. The flow can be measured with the shift of liquid in the tubes. (After Schiwinsky et al. 1996)

Gas fluxes by thermo-osmosis are explained on the basis of two principles: A pressure difference because of a temperature gradient (when diffusion is limited, Fig. 1) and at the same pressure and temperature if the gases have different molecular masses (according to Graham's law, the relation of counter-fluxes of two gases through a thermo-osmotically active surface is inversely proportional to the square root of their molecular masses). Pressure always builds up if the mean free path of the gas molecules is longer than the available actual space and the gas molecules collide with the walls of the pores (Fig. 2). The major gas fluxes in a plant are those of nitrogen and oxygen; however, exchange of CO_2 and O_2, the molecular masses of which are substantially different (42 vs. 32), is physiologically more important.

The upper part of a lotus leaf consists of a very dense palisade parenchyma whose intercellular spaces are sufficiently narrow to create a thermo-osmotic pressure, whereas the diameters of the intercellular channels in the petiole and rhizome are much too wide to create such a pressure. It is assumed that the gas pressure produced especially in the young leaves pushes air predominantly into the rhizomes from which it is released into the atmosphere via the lacunae of the old leaves. Gas flow occurs also within an individual leaf from the margin to the centre where the intercellular lacunae are located. Depending on

the pressure in the interior of the aerenchyma, this leaks out of the leaf or enters the petioles and subsequently the rhizomes. Likewise, respiratory CO_2 produced in the rhizomes can escape from the plant via the lacunar systems of the rhizomes and the leaves.

The extent of gas fluxes may be considerable. In leaves of *Nuphar luteum* the thermo-osmotically produced pressure of 0.2 kPa (see Fig. 1) creates a gas flow of 50 ml min^{-1} through the lacunar system of the petioles (Dacey 1981; see also Armstrong 1990 and Kohl et al. 1996).

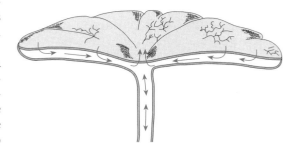

Fig. 3. Thermo-osmotic gas fluxes in an illuminated leaf of *Nelumbo nucifera*. Thermo-osmosis leads to a pressure resulting in an air flow towards the centre of the leaf. Much of that air exits from the leaf in its adaxial centre where the lacunae enter the petiole. Part of the gas can also flow into the rhizomes, following the pressure gradient. Conversely, air from the rhizome may also enter the atmosphere via the lacuna system of the petiole. (After Dacey 1987)

Box 1.4.5   **The ethylene receptor**

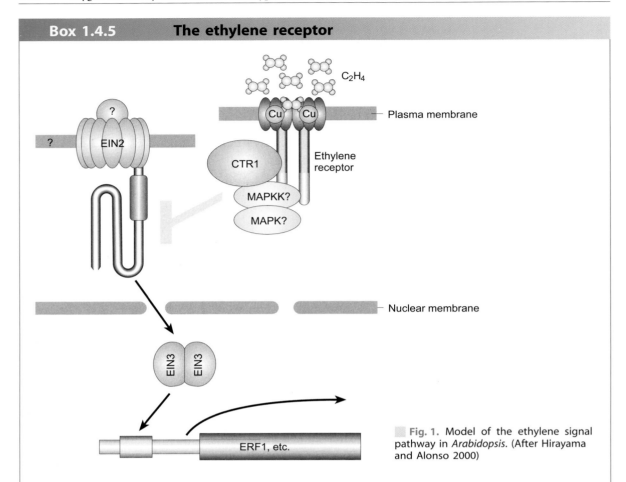

Fig. 1. Model of the ethylene signal pathway in *Arabidopsis*. (After Hirayama and Alonso 2000)

The ethylene receptors of *Arabidopsis thaliana* (Fig. 1) are relatively well understood. Ethylene induces in dark-grown *Arabidopsis* seedlings the so-called triple response consisting of an increased apical hook of the cotyledons, thickening of the hypocotyl instead of extension growth, and loss of gravitropical sensitivity. With the triple response mutants differing in reaction to ethylene may be found. Such mutants are divided into three groups: ethylene-insensitive mutants (*etr*, *ein*), constitutive ethylene-response mutants (*eto*, *ctr*) and tissue-specific ethylene-response mutants (*his*, *eir*). There are also "response to antagonist" (*ran*) mutants showing the ethylene response in the presence of the ethylene antagonist *trans*-cyclooctene. It has been shown, with the help of the *ran* mutants, that the ethylene receptor requires copper ions for the binding of ethylene. Probably they change their coordination number upon reaction with ethylene.

The structure of the ethylene receptor ETR1 is known. The active receptor is a homodimer that is probably located in the plasma membrane. ETR1 (as ETR2 and EIN4) belongs to the group of two-component histidine kinases (phospho-relay signal transducers, Fig. 2). These consist of a sensor (histidine kinase) and a response regulator. The histidine kinase contains an N-terminal signal input domain and a C-terminal kinase domain with a conserved histidine residue. The response regulator contains an N-terminal receiver domain with a conserved aspartate residue and a C-terminal signal output domain. The figure shows the well-analysed osmolarity sensor of *E. coli* as a simple example of the two-component histidine-kinase receptors. In this case, high osmolarity leads to auto-phosphorylation of the histidine residue of the sensor and to a transfer of phosphate to the aspartate residue of the receiver domain OmpR. The phosphorylation state of the (*E.*

Box 1.4.5   (continued)

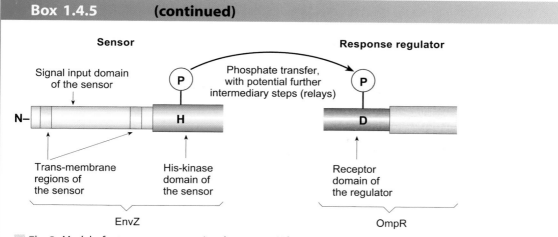

Fig. 2. Model of a two-component signal receptor. (After Urao et al. 2000)

coli) signal output domain changes its DNA-binding activity and thereby gene expression. In ETRI, for the internal transfer of the phosphate residue, a relay amino acid residue is positioned between the sensor and the regulatory domain and the phosphorylated regulatory domain does not react directly with the DNA in the nucleus, but with another protein, the CTR1 (constitutive triple response). CTR1 could react directly or indirectly via a cascade of MAP-kinases with another cell internal sensor (e.g. for divalent cations), the EIN2 protein, which is also membrane-bound. EIN2 would activate effector proteins (e.g. EIN3), which would then bind, after passing the nuclear membrane, to the promoter region of the ethylene response genes. Understanding the transduction of the ethylene signal is difficult because of the fact that the CRT must be inactivated for the ethylene response to occur. This means that binding of ethylene to the receptor inactivates the receptor and, in turn also CTR, so the inhibition of EIN is released and the signal chain becomes activated. For PCD triggered by ethylene, individual steps are not yet fully clear.

see Box 1.4.4). If light and CO_2 are available, submerged plants are able to produce oxygen photosynthetically, thus counteracting hypoxia.

Primary roots of terrestrial plants usually cannot tolerate hypoxia and die. Hypoxia-resistant plants (e.g. maize, ash, willow, *Forsythia*, *Rumex palustris*) are able within a few days to produce adventitious roots with a well-developed aerenchyma from basal shoot parts or the lower nodes (Fig. 1.4.7). These roots do not penetrate as deeply into the soil as the primary root system into a well-aerated substrate.

The individual cell layers of young adventitious roots are differently supplied with oxygen. The exodermis is the only cell layer which is usually oxygen-free; cell walls of this layer are often suberinised, thus preventing diffusion of oxygen from the interior of the root to the external medium. Formation of aerenchyma not only guarantees the aeration of tissues, but also re-duces the number of oxygen-consuming cells in that tissue.

Lytic aerenchyma formation (i.e. from disintegration of cells; Drew et al. 2000) occurs selectively in the cortex of adventitious roots, starting in those parts of the tissue that are least supplied with oxygen. Lysis of cells often requires not more than 24 h. Ethylene induces this process more or less independently of normoxia or hypoxia, but hypoxia stimulates ethylene synthesis in root tips. Increased concentrations of CO_2 and ethylene itself also stimulate ethylene synthesis. Inhibition of ethylene synthesis, on the other hand, suppresses formation of aerenchyma. The genus *Rumex* comprises hypoxia-sensitive (*R. acesota, acetosella*) as well as hypoxia-tolerant species (*R. palustris*). In the flooding-tolerant *R. palustris* ethylene production is relatively low and almost the same under aerobic and anaerobic conditions. The internal ethyl-

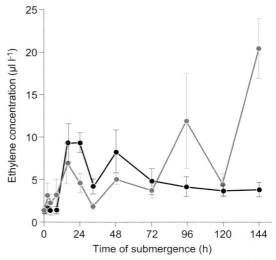

Fig. 1.4.8. The internal ethylene concentration in the tissues of two *Rumex* species of different flooding tolerance during extended waterlogging; *Rumex palustris* (•) is flooding-tolerant while *Rumex acetosella* is (•) flooding-sensitive. Decrease in the internal ethylene concentration results from inhibition of ethylene synthesis during the daily light period. (After Banga et al. 1996)

Fig. 1.4.7. The formation of adventitious roots in the flooding-tolerant *Rumex palustris* upon flooding of the root bed. The newly formed roots appear white as a consequence of the air-filled spaces in the aerenchyma and are thus clearly distinguished from roots grown under aerobic conditions which senesce under prolonged hypoxia. (After Laan et al. 1989 a, b, 1991)

ene concentration even slightly decreases upon long-term submergence. In the flooding-intolerant sorrel, however, internal ethylene concentration increases with the duration of submergence (Fig. 1.4.8). A constant, low concentration of ethylene increases elongation growth, while a long-term increasing ethylene concentration, as in *R. acetosella*, causes premature senescence of the whole organ.

In addition to the above-mentioned elongation of internodes or senescence of individual cells (PCD) and whole organs (senescence), ethylene also induces ripening of fruits. Therefore, research has since long focused on the transduction of the signal emitted from ethylene. The first element of such a signal chain is the receptor and the ethylene receptor was the first receptor of a phytohormone to be elucidated; it be-

longs to the group of so-called two-component sensors (Box 1.4.5).

By combining various experimental setups and by using specific biochemical effectors, further insight could be gained into the mechanism of aerenchyma formation by PCD in the cortical tissue of maize roots (Fig. 1.4.9).

It has been shown that ethylene as a signal induces the protein kinase signal transduction pathway via a G-protein, Ca^{2+} and inositol-P, which leads to synthesis of lytic enzymes, e.g. cellulase and hemicellulase (Saab and Sachs 1996). Calcium activates endonucleases, so that the cell death is caused by a controlled breakdown of nucleic acid (by an endonuclease, activated by caspases) and not through breakdown of cell membranes, as after cell damage. Formation of aerenchyma is promoted by further effectors: For example, mechanical resistance of a heavy soil stimulates ethylene synthesis by the growing root and scarcity of minerals increases the sensitivity of the plant tissue to ethylene. Figure 1.4.10 shows a model of the biochemical processes that take place in the formation of aerenchyma.

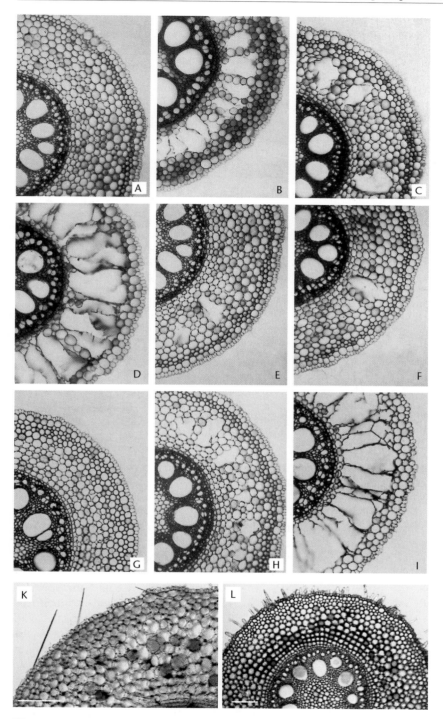

Fig. 1.4.9. Analysis of aerenchyma formation in a maize root. Ocadaic acid blocks protein phosphatases; GTP-γ-S activates G proteins; K252a inhibits protein kinases; neomycin inhibits inositol phosphate metabolism; EGTA complexes Ca^{2+}; disintegrating cells are coloured purple by neutral red and Evans blue accumulates in dying cells. (After He et al. 1996; Drew et al. 2000). A Normoxic; B hypoxic; C normoxic+ocadaic acid; D hypoxic+ocadaic acid; E hypoxic+neomycin; F hypoxic+K252a; G hypoxic+EGTA; H normoxic+GTP-γ-S; I hypoxic+GTP-γ-S; K hypoxic+neutral red; L hypoxic+Evans blue

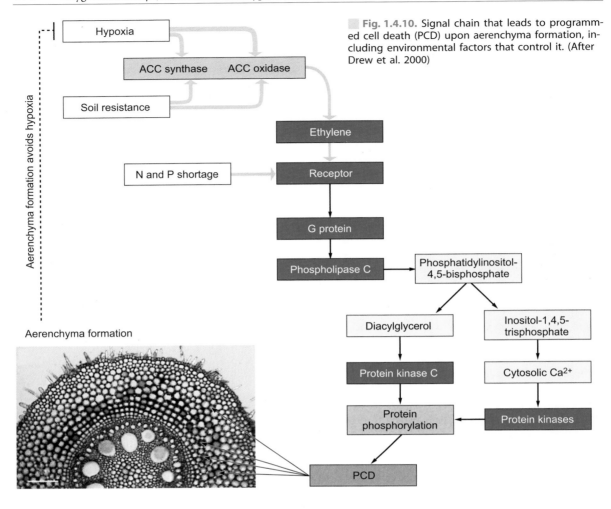

Fig. 1.4.10. Signal chain that leads to programmed cell death (PCD) upon aerenchyma formation, including environmental factors that control it. (After Drew et al. 2000)

1.4.3

Post-anoxic Stress

Tissues tolerating hypoxic stress are often damaged by subsequent aeration. This post-anoxic stress usually results from ROS (see Chap. 1.3.5.3). Cells in which metabolism is adapted to hypoxic or anaerobic conditions have a relatively negative redox potential, i.e. high electron pressure from a high $NADH/NAD^+$ ratio. In the presence of O_2 this leads to oxygen reduction and to the formation of ROS. During the hypoxic phase, activities of enzymes detoxifying ROS are decreased and the pools of scavenger metabolites are reduced so that the tissue is not capable of coping with increased oxidative stress. However, some plants are known to tolerate post-anoxic stress as, e.g., the yellow iris, where the enzyme superoxide dismutase is part of the ANP.

Summary

1. Lack of oxygen occurs after extended periods of soil flooding because the diffusion of oxygen in water is about 10,000 times slower than in air. The critical oxygen content required for growth of roots is about 5–10%. Helophytes (swamp-inhabiting plants) and submerged plants are able to live in partly hypoxic environments by supplying their roots and rhizomes with oxygen through an intercellular aeration system (aerenchyma). Gas flow in the interior of the plant is substantially accelerated by thermo-osmosis.

2. Normoxia, hypoxia and anoxia describe the conditions of sufficient, insufficient and deficient oxygen supply to organisms. Hypoxia and anoxia produce negative redox potentials of the soils, under which conditions oxidised heavy metal ions become reduced and in this form are poisonous. As a consequence of bio-

logical activity, the pH of the soil shifts into the alkaline range. Mycorrhizae are particularly sensitive to such changes in the soil.

3. Low oxygen partial pressure in particular affects the energy metabolism of plant organs. Switching from the aerobic respiratory metabolism to fermentation is uneconomic and creates problems in cell biology, but enables the plant to survive for a limited time. Roots and rhizomes of certain plants are capable of surviving longer periods of anoxia or hypoxia in a metabolically quiescent state which is called anaerobic retreat.

4. Upon switching to fermentative metabolism, so-called anaerobic polypeptides (ANPs) are formed and, at the same time, synthesis of many housekeeping proteins is reduced. Insofar as they have been identified, ANPs are predominantly enzymes of fermentative metabolism. Promoters of their genes contain a specific anaerobic response element (ARE).

5. Constitutive tolerance of anoxia is usually based on avoidance of anoxia. In addition to the already mentioned formation of aerenchyma, elongation of internodes and of petioles is frequently observed. By elongation growth, apical parts of plants quickly extend into an environment with a better oxygen supply. Lack of oxygen activates the expression of the ACC-oxidase gene, the product of which is a pacemaker in ethylene synthesis. Increased ethylene partial pressure triggers the lowering of the ABA concentration, resulting in an increased efficacy of gibberellin and auxin as elongation hormones. Certain cell wall proteins, so-called expansins, play a vital role in the elongation reaction, as they are able to loosen the bonds between individual cell wall polymers. Hypoxia leads to increased formation and accumulation of such expansins.

6. In addition to the elongation of the internodes, ethylene induces, under hypoxic conditions, also the formation of aerenchyma via programmed cell death (PCD). Aerenchyma formation triggered by hypoxia and mediated by ethylene is partially understood at the molecular level. G-proteins and intracellular calcium play important roles as signal transmitters in this process. The ethylene signal receptor is principally understood at the molecular level. It belongs to the so-called two-component signal receptors. Genetically fixed aerenchyma formation of helophytes is independent of ethylene.

7. Damage often occurs during re-aeration of plant organs which have adapted to hypoxia, as the ROS-detoxifying system is decreased under anoxic and hypoxic conditions. This phenomenon is called "post-anoxic stress".

References

Amberger A (1988) Pflanzenernährung. UTB Ulmer, Stuttgart, p 41

Armstrong JAW (1990) Light enhanced convective through-flow increases oxygenation in rhizomes and rhizosphere of *Phragmites australis* (Cav.) Trin ex Steud. New Phytol 114:121–128

Armstrong W, Gaynard TJ (1976) The critical oxygen pressure for respiration in intact plants. Physiol Plant 37:200–206

Armstrong W, Webb T (1985) A critical oxygen pressure for root extension in rice. J Exp Bot 36:1573–1582

Banga M, Slaa EJ, Blom CWPM, Voesenek LACJ (1996) Ethylene biosynthesis and accumulation under drained and submerged conditions – a comparative study of two *Rumex* species. Plant Physiol 112:229–237

Cho HT, Kende H (1997a) Expansins and internodal growth of deepwater rice. Plant Physiol 113:1145–1151

Cho HT, Kende H (1997b) Expansins in deepwater rice internodes. Plant Physiol 113:1137–1143

Christopher ME, Good AG (1996) Characterization of hypoxically inducible lactate dehydrogenase in maize. Plant Physiol 112:1015–1022

Dacey JWH (1981) Pressurized ventilation in the yellow waterlily. Ecology 62:1137–1147

Dacey JWH (1987) Knudsen-transitional flow and gas pressurization in leaves of Nelumbo. Plant Physiol 85:199–203

DeLaune RD, Pezeshki SR, Patrick WH Jr (1993) Response of coastal vegetation to flooding and salinity: a case study in the rapidly subsiding Mississippi River deltaic plain, USA. In: Jackson MB, Black CR (eds) Interacting stresses on plants in a changing climate. NATO ASI Series I 16. Springer, Berlin Heidelberg New York, pp 211–229

Drew MC, He Ch-J, Morgan PW (2000) Programmed cell death and aerenchyma formation in roots. Trends Plant Sci 5:123–127

Grosse W (1997) Gas transport in trees. In: Rennenberg H, Eschrich W, Ziegler H (eds) Trees – contribution to modern tree physiology. Backhuys, Leiden, pp 57–74

Guglielminetti L, Perata P, Alpi A (1995) Effect of anoxia on carbohydrate metabolism in rice seedlings. Plant Physiol 108:735–741

He Ch-J, Morgan PW, Drew MC (1996) Transduction of an ethylene signal is required for cell death and lysis in the root cortex of maize during aerenchyma formation induced by hypoxia. Plant Physiol 112:463–472

Hirayama T, Alonso JM (2000) Ethylene captures a metal! Metal ions are involved in ethylene perception and signal transduction. Plant Cell Physiol 41:548–555

Jackson MB, Black CR (1993) Interaction of stresses on plants in a changing climate. NATO ASI Series I 16. Springer, Berlin Heidelberg New York, pp 243–266

Kohl J-G, Henze R, Kühl H (1996) Evaluation of the ventilation resistance to convective gas-flow in the rhizomes of natural reed beds of *Phragmites australis* (Cav.) Trin ex. Steud. Aquat Bot 54:199–210

Laan P, Clement JMAM, Blom CWPM (1991) Growth and development of *Rumex* roots as affected by hypoxic and anoxic conditions. Plant Soil 136:145–151

Laan P, Smolders A, Blom CWPM, Armstrong W (1989a) The relative roles of internal aeration, radial oxygen losses, iron exclusion and nutrient balance in flood-tolerance of *Rumex* species. Acta Bot Neerl 38:131–145

Laan P, Berrevoets MJ, Lythe S, Armstrong W, Blom CWPM (1989b) Root morphology and aerenchyma formation as indicators for the flood-tolerance of *Rumex* species. J Ecol 77:693–703

Mapelli S, Bertani A (1993) Endogenous phytohormones and germination of rice under anoxia: indoleacetic acid and abscisic acid. NATO ASI Series I 16. Springer, Berlin Heidelberg New York, pp 353–363

Marschner H (1986) Mineral nutrition of higher plants. Academic Press, London, 674 pp

Mekhedov SL, Kende H (1996) Submergence enhances expression of a gene encoding 1-amino-cyclopropane-1-carboxylate oxidase in deepwater rice. Plant Cell Physiol 37:531–537

Pradet A, Mocquot B, Raymond P, Morisset Ch, Aspart L, Delseny M (1985) Energy metabolism and synthesis of nucleic acids and protein under anoxic stress. In: Key JL, Kosuge T (eds) Cellular and molecular biology of plant stress. Liss, New York, pp 227–245

Saab IN, Sachs MM (1996) A flooding-induced xyloglucan-endo-transglycosylase homolog in maize is responsive to ethylene and associated with aerenchyma. Plant Physiol 112:385–391

Schiwinsky K, Grosse W, Woermann D (1996) Convective gas flow in plant aeration and Graham's law of diffusion. Z Naturforsch 51c:681–690

Taiz L, Zeiger E (2000) Physiologie der Pflanzen. Spektrum, Heidelberg, 773 pp

Urao I, Yamaguchi-Shinozaki K, Shinozaki K (2000) Two-component systems in plant signal transduction. Trends Plant Sci 5:67–74

1.5

Water Deficiency (Drought)

Poikilohydric lichens are "world champions" in tolerating drought stress, which usually is accompanied by heat or cold and high light intensities. Despite the extremely harsh habitat, every square millimetre of this gneiss boulder in the Austrian Alps is occupied by more or less colourful crustose lichens. The community is dominated by the yellowish green *Rhizocarpon* cf. *geographicum*. Photograph E. Beck.

Recommended Literature

- Blatt MR (2000) Cellular signaling and volume control in stomatal movements of plants. Annu Rev Cell Dev Biol 16:221–242
- Close TJ, Bray EA (1993) Plant responses to cellular dehydration during environmental stress. Current topics in plant physiology 10. American Society of Plant Physiology, Rockville
- Errington JR, Debenedetti PG (2001) Relationship between structural order and the anomalies of liquid water. Nature 409:318–321
- Hoekstra FA, Golovina EA, Buitink J (2001) Mechanisms of plant desiccation tolerance. Trends Plant Sci 6:431–438
- Ingram J, Bartels O (1996) The molecular basis of dehydration tolerance in plants. Annu Rev Plant Physiol Plant Mol Biol 47:377–403
- Maurel C (1997) Aquaporins and water permeability of plant membranes. Annu Rev Plant Physiol Plant Mol Biol 48:399–430
- Zhu J-K (2002) Salt and Drought Stress Signal Transduction in Plants. Annu Rev Plant Biol 53:247–273

Life requires water in the liquid state and is, thus, based on the physicochemical properties of the **water molecule** causing the so-called **anomalies** (Box 1.5.1). These properties result from the dipole nature of the molecule $H^{\delta+}-O^{\delta-}-H^{\delta+}$; the dipoles produce H-bonds between the individual molecules and thus guarantee a high degree of cohesion with, at the same time, low viscosity. The results are variable or flickering (mobile) clusters or aggregates, which continuously exchange individual molecules. Despite the low molecular mass of the water molecule, water is, therefore, in the liquid rather than the gaseous state at temperatures between 0 and 100 °C and standard air pressure. Also based on the dipole nature of water is its adhesion to polar surfaces, for example, cell walls, and its capillary action based on the high surface tension. Adhesion, capillary action, together with cohesion and low viscosity, are decisive factors for the transport of water from roots to leaves (cohesion theory of water conductance). Another consequence of the dipole nature of the water molecule is its suitability as solvent for polar and polarisable compounds. In addition, water develops a structuring force in amphiphilic systems (hydrophilic–hydrophobic) giving rise to lipid micelles and contributing to the tertiary structures of proteins. These so-called hydrophobic interactions are based on the strength of the interaction between the hydrophilic domains of the molecules with each other and with the water clusters, as well as on the hydrophobic domains between one another. The term **hydrophobic in-**

Box 1.5.1   The physico-chemical properties (anomalies) of water

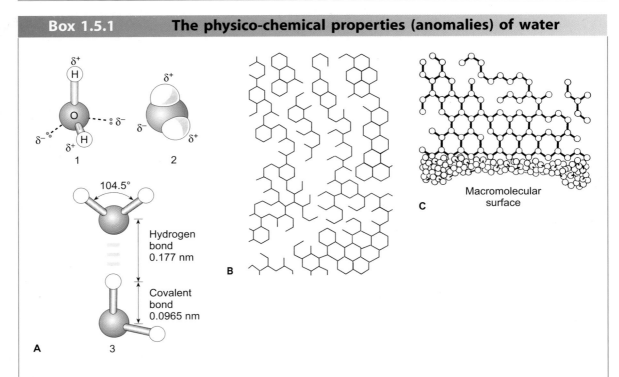

Due to their dipole nature, water molecules [Fig. A (1), (2)] associate via hydrogen bonds to a three-dimensional lattice (clusters; B, from Larcher 1994), which is in permanent molecular rearrangement. The physico-chemical anomalies of water can be explained as a consequence of this cluster formation.

Water forces amphiphilic molecules into particular associative structures, e.g. biomembranes (C, from Larcher 1994). These, in turn, interact with the water molecules, forming an ordered water layer which at some distance from the membrane surface again takes on the nature of flickering (mobile) clusters.

Compound	Molecular weight	Melting point (°C)	Boiling point (°C)
H_2O	$[18]_x$	0	100
H_2S	34	−86	−61

Further biologically important physical properties of water are listed below.

Specific heat capacity	$1\ cal\ g^{-1} = 4.2\ J\ g^{-1}$
Latent heat of crystallisation	$333.6\ J\ g^{-1}$
Latent heat of evaporation	$2441\ J\ g^{-1}$
Surface tension (at 15 °C)	$73.5\ g\ sec^{-1}$

teraction is slightly misleading, as there are also interactions between the water molecules and the hydrophobic domains of the amphiphilic molecules, which are, however, weaker than the interactions of the hydrophobic domains with one another. Water is a very effective heat buffer for organisms, because of its relatively high heat of crystallisation (freezing avoidance) and very high heat of evaporation (transpiration cooling). As its radiation absorption is beyond the borders of the visible spectrum, water does not absorb visible light and thus does not interfere with photosynthesis or processes regulated by blue or red light.

Water Potential

The thermodynamic state of water is described by the water potential, ψ, which is, figuratively speaking, a measure of the energy required to remove water molecules from any water-containing system. As the (chemical) potential of pure water is taken as a reference system, and under the actual conditions is defined as zero, ψ is a measure of a difference in the chemical potentials. Commonly, the water potential of a system is expressed in the dimension of pressure and not of energy: If the chemical potential of water is related to the molar volume, the dimension "pressure" results. Other details and the derivation of the definition of water potential are given in Chapter 2.2, Eq. (2.2.7) (see also Chap. 1.3).

The water potential of a cell is made up of several components:

$$(-)\psi = (-)\pi + (-)\tau + P,$$

where π is the **osmotic potential** (negative sign) of the equilibrated cellular solutions in a steady state [see Chap. 2.2, Eq. (2.2.6)], τ the **matrix potential** (negative sign) and P the **pressure potential** (cell wall and tissue pressure, positive sign). The pressure of the wall (plus tissue) is numerically equal to the **turgor pressure** (the pressure of the protoplast on the cell wall) and has the opposite, positive, sign in the water potential equation. In a hydrated cell, τ cannot be measured. It becomes apparent only after the cell has been desiccated to such an extent that only the water bound to cellular and subcellular structures remains. To remove that portion of cellular water requires either extreme low (negative) water potentials or extreme high pressures (see Chap. 1.3.6.4).

Intercellular and Intracellular Water Flow, Aquaporins

A water potential difference between two systems (e.g. two cells) corresponds to a voltage in an electrical circuit and causes the flux of water in the direction of the system with the more negative potential, provided that the pathway is conductive to water (**hydraulic conductivity**). The flux of water may be in the apoplast, i.e. through and along the cell walls (**apoplastic path**) or also through the protoplasts (**symplastic path**; see Chap. 2.2, Fig. 2.2.8). The importance of the symplastic path for water transport has been greatly underestimated, but the discovery of **aquaporins** (Box 1.5.2) has gained more attention. Aquaporins are specific proteins, with a molecular mass of 15–30 kDa, which form water channels through cellular membranes (Johannson et al. 2000). Usually, oligomers accumulate to complexes. The density of such aquaporin aggregates in a membrane determines its hydraulic conductivity, which is in the range 2×10^{-8} to 10^{-5} m s^{-1} MPa^{-1}. Water flow through these channels is characterised by the high permeability of the membrane ($P_f \approx 700$ μm s^{-1}) and a low activation energy of the transport ($E_a = 8$–12 kJ mol^{-1}). Additional to this pathway is the so-called **lipid pathway**, namely the diffusion of water molecules through the lipid bilayer of the biomembrane, which is characterised by a low permeability and a high activation energy ($P_f \approx 10$ μm s^{-1}; $E_a = 48$–64 kJ mol^{-1}). Water transport by these two pathways can be differentiated by the kinetic data, and by blocking the aquaporins with heavy metals, for example, Hg^{2+}, as most of the aquaporins contain cysteine in the helices spanning the membrane.

Usually, the permeability for water of the tonoplast is considerably higher than that of the plasma membrane. As the water relations of the cell are dominated by the vacuole, the high water permeability of the tonoplast guarantees fast equilibration of the intracellular water potentials upon changes in the cell's water status. In *Arabidopsis* aquaporin clusters, so-called **plasmalemmasomes** (Robinson et al. 1996) have been described. They are thought to establish a direct connection between the plasmalemma and the tonoplast. Other membrane transport proteins, e.g. ion channels, also contribute to water transport, as they form hydrated pores. Depending on the structure of these pores, each transported molecule or ion carries up to 25 water molecules over the membrane. The effectiveness of an aquaporin, however, is about 20 times higher.

1.5.1

Water Balance of Drought-Stressed Cells

Upon drought plants lose water to the atmosphere: if water uptake cannot keep pace with water loss, transpiration is mainly fed from the vacuoles. It flows via the plasmalemma into the apoplast from where it evaporates into the intercellular spaces. Because of the decrease in volume caused by water loss, the osmotic potential in the protoplast is increased (i.e. becomes numerically more negative). At the same time, the turgor pressure as well as the cell wall pressure decrease. At the so-called turgor-loss point the cell wall is completely relaxed and both pressures are zero. Consequently, the water potential of the cell is then equal to its osmotic potential. In this state plants show substantial wilting. With further loss of water, wilting increases, as the cell walls are not only relaxed, but in responding to the intracellular suction bend in-

Box 1.5.2   Aquaporins

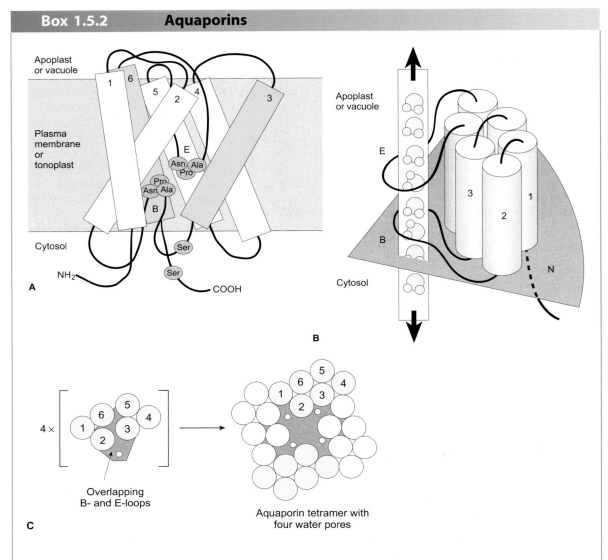

A shows the hourglass model of an aquaporin monomer. The labelled amino acids in the centre form the constriction of the hourglass, while the membrane-spanning helices, *1*, *2*, *3*, and their counterparts, *4*, *5*, *6*, form the "con-tainer". The loops *B* and *E* form the actual water pore (B). The two halves of the hour-glass are homologous, but inverted in their ori-entation in the membrane: Helix 1 corresponds to helix 4, helix 2 to 5 and helix 3 to 6. Aqua-

wards giving rise to cell cytorrhysis (Chap. 1.3.6.1), if their rigidity is low enough to allow folding. As described for the case of freezing de-hydration, this happens because the water-im-bibed cell wall (Fig. 1.5.1) does not allow any air to penetrate. Suction develops and correspond-ingly a negative pressure potential (−1 to −2 MPa) increases the water potential of the cell. As a consequence, more water is retained in the cell than would correspond to the osmotic po-tential alone. Despite the increase in the water potential of the cells by a negative pressure po-tential, during prolonged drought, cells can lose so much of their water that dehydration damage arises, breaking down the bilayer structure of the membranes whereupon the osmotic system of the cell collapses.

Box 1.5.2   Aquaporins (continued)

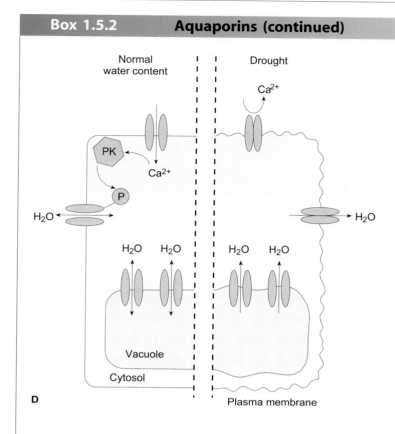

porins form complexes (C). A model with four monomers is shown (CHIP 28 from erythrocytes), which also represents the most common form of water pores in plants. The model applies to the aquaporins of the plasma membrane (PIPs) and of the tonoplast (TIPs). The efficiency of some aquaporins can be controlled by protein phosphorylation and dephosphorylation (D). The model shows the state under sufficient water supply (*left*) and under drought (*right*). An as yet unidentified osmoregulator holds the cytosolic Ca^{2+} concentration high and a protein kinase keeps the aquaporin phosphorylated, which keeps the pore open. Protein phosphorylation takes place at the serine residues labelled in A. Under drought stress the cytosolic Ca^{2+} concentration decreases, the aquaporin becomes dephosphorylated and the pore closes. In this way, water loss is reduced. It is presumed that selective regulation of the protein phosphorylation keeps the pores in the tonoplast open, so that the water potential of the cytosol is little affected by water loss from the cell (A and D after Kjellbom 1999; B after Schäffner 1998; C after Jung et al. 1994).

Water Storage

Water storage tissues, for example, of succulents, have special cellular water relations. Cell walls of succulents are very flexible (but not extendable) and thus convey a high water storage capacity (**hydraulic capacity**) to the cells. Upon water loss, the cell walls of these living tissues fold like a concertina, or the cells as a whole collapse cytorrhytically, and this reduces the cell volume. The flexibility (elasticity) of the cell wall, with which they react to pressure changes, must not be mistaken for expansion or contraction. It is a passive change in the shape of the cells depending on the **elasticity modulus** ε of the cell wall:

$$\varepsilon = \frac{dP}{dV/V} \ [MPa]$$

where dP is the change in turgor and dV/V the relative change in volume.

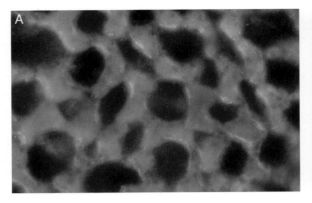

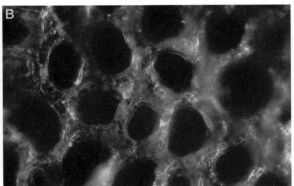

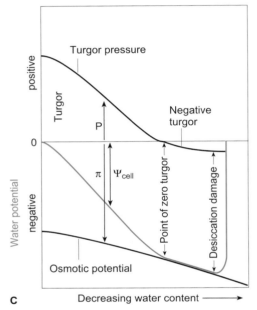

Fig. 1.5.1 Desiccation of plant cells upon exposure to air. A Spongy parenchyma of *Pachysandra terminalis* in turgid state. B The same tissue after 2 h exposure to air. The collapse of the cells, whose volume has shrunk by more than 50%, is clearly visible. C Water relations of a cell in the course of desiccation. After loss of turgor the protoplast remains attached to the cell wall, due to the matrix potential of the latter, and a negative wall pressure (tension) develops. A, B, photos by J.J. Zhu, C after Larcher (1994), modified

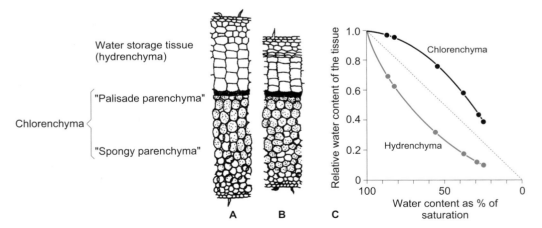

Fig. 1.5.2. Water storage in leaves of peperomia (*Peperomia trichocarpa*). A, B Cross sections of water-saturated leaves (A) and the leaves after drying (B). The hydrenchyma shrinks much more than the chlorenchyma. This phenomenon is shown quantitatively in C: at a total water content of 50% saturation, the portion of water in the hydrenchyma has dropped to 25%, whilst the water content of the chlorenchyma is still 75%. (After Larcher 1994)

For soft plant tissues, $\varepsilon \leq 5$ MPa, so larger changes in volume create only small changes in turgor (P). For leaves of sclerophyllous trees, ε is between 30 and 50 MPa, and they have only limited ability to change their shape upon water loss. Thus, softer tissues are able to shrink substantially, whilst harder tissues cannot. Water storage tissue (**hydrenchyma**) possesses cells with a particularly low elasticity module, i.e. they can easily take up and release lots of water. Leaves with marked water storage tissue, usually surrounded by the chlorenchyma (e.g. *Peperomia*), therefore change their cross section in accordance to their state of water. Because of the different elasticity modules, only the water storage tissue, but not the chlorenchyma, shrinks (Fig. 1.5.2).

Many water storage tissues consist of dead cells, for example, the *velamen radicum* of the air roots of orchids, where water uptake and storage depend mainly on capillary forces.

1.5.2

Cellular Reactions to Drought Stress

At the cell level, water deficit is not only a result of drought, but also of salt stress and of frost. The loss of up to 90% of the cell water is a necessary process during seed and fruit ripening and thus is a regular component of a plant's development. Plants have, therefore, developed biochemical mechanisms to cope with drought stress. Our understanding of the molecular processes triggered by drought and of the adaptation to water shortage is, however, still patchy. There is no doubt that each cell has more than one mechanism for reacting to drought; there is, so to say, a multiple safety net. However, not all changes in cell biology occurring upon drought stress are specific to that situation. Some strains are primarily targeted to other stressors, e.g. metabolic changes triggered by cold or pathogen attack can also be effective to cope with dehydration stress. In addition to specific stress-directed reactions, desiccation interferes with the normal housekeeping machinery of the cell. This holds in particular for **poikilohydric plants** (see Chap. 2.2.1.1) where photosynthesis is reduced in order to minimise the danger of photooxidation. In the resurrection plant *Craterostigma plantaginea* expression of genes of the photosynthetic machinery is attenuated, probably concomitantly with the induction of genes whose products – proteins and metabolites

– increase drought resistance of cells directly or indirectly. A key role in coping with **dehydration stress** is attributed to the phytohormone **abscisic acid** (ABA; see Fig. 1.5.3 and Box 1.5.3), which triggers fast reactions as well as long-term adaptation. Complying with the above-mentioned complexity of stress-induced cellular reactions, ABA-independent reactions are also well known. Current knowledge shows cellular responses to drought to be no less complicated than the responses to heat stress.

1.5.2.1

Perception of Dehydration Stress

Water loss may cause the following changes:
- shrinkage of the protoplast,
- concentration of cellular solutions,
- decrease or loss of turgor,
- changes in the water potential gradient across membranes,
- in the worst cases, disintegration of biomembranes and denaturing of proteins.

Which of these phenomena play a role as cellular signals in plants has not yet been determined. Probably it is the change in the water potential or pressure gradient across membranes. **Osmosensors** are known from *E. coli* and yeast. Their functions were shown in complementation studies with mutants deficient in osmotic adaptation (Wurgler-Murphy and Saito 1997; see also Box 1.4.5). One of the transmembrane osmosensors of yeast, Sho1p, forms a protein of four closely packed membrane-spanning peptides with a peripheral C-terminal domain that is responsible for triggering signal transduction. If the osmotic gradient across the plasma membrane is increased, Sho1p activates a four-step MAP kinase cascade, leading finally to the production and accumulation of glycerol, which is an osmoprotectant of yeast. Successful complementation of the osmosensor-deficient mutant of yeast with a corresponding gene of *Arabidopsis* (*ATHK1*; Shinozaki and Yamaguchi-Shinozaki 1997) leads to the assumption that similar systems of drought perception are also effective in plants. Due to the multiplicity of stress responses of plants, it must be concluded that plant cells have several receptor systems which might render tissue specificity (Bonetta and McCourt 1998). Receptors for ABA should be differentiated from direct osmosensors, as

Box 1.5.3   Biosynthesis, metabolism and inactivation of ABA

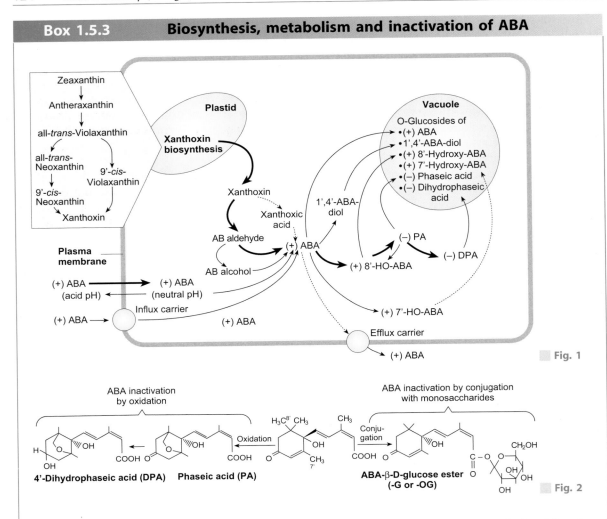

Fig. 1

Fig. 2

As far as is currently known, ABA is a derivative of chloroplastic xanthophylls. These are not synthesised via the mevalonate pathway, but originate from the chloroplastic DOXP pathway (1-desoxy-D-xylulose-5-phosphate pathway; Lichtenthaler 1999). Key enzymes of ABA biosynthesis are zeaxanthin epoxidase (ZEP), encoded for by the gene *ABA2*, and 9-*cis*-epoxycarotenoid dioxygenase (NCE), encoded for by the gene *VP14*. NCE can cleave the xanthophylls: all-*trans*-violaxanthin, all-*trans*-neoxanthin, 9′-*cis*-neoxanthin (Cutler and Krochko 1999).

Figure 1 shows the metabolism of (+)-ABA at the cellular level. The first steps of ABA biosynthesis, until cleavage of the 9′-epoxycarotenoids by the dioxygenase, occur in the plastids. The cleavage product xanthoxin after export from the plastid (by an unknown mechanism) is metabolised in the cytoplasm to (+)-ABA. The *bold arrows* show the main route and *fine*

arrows the shunt via ABA-alcohol, whilst the pathway via xanthoxic acid is still disputed (*dotted line*). The fast import of ABA from the apoplasm into the cell is induced by the neutral pH of the cytoplasm (after Cowan 2000).

The main pathway of ABA degradation as shown in Fig. 2 starts with the hydroxylation of the 8′-carbon, followed by a cyclisation to phaseic acid which is converted by a reductase to dihydrophaseic acid. The three degradation products are physiologically inactive. Hydroxylation of the 7′-carbon is also known, but similar to the direct reduction of the ABA keto group to 1′,4′-ABA diol is quantitatively insignificant. The formation of conjugates of ABA and its derivatives, in particular with glucose, is physiologically relevant, as these compounds are water-soluble and are exported from the cytoplasm into the vacuole (after Taiz and Zeiger 2000).

ABA is already a stress signal at the cellular or subcellular level. The biochemical structure of ABA sensors has not yet been elucidated.

1.5.2.2
ABA-Mediated Stress Response

Mild drought stress leads to a ten-fold increase in the endogenous ABA concentration (Fig. 1.5.3). This applies to higher, as well as to lower, plants. Mutants lacking the ability to synthesise ABA are not viable, as they wilt even with the slightest drought stress. However, they may be kept alive by adding ABA[1]. The receptor for the dehydration signal leading to ABA synthesis and accumulation is unknown.

Even though the biochemistry of **ABA sensing** is not yet known, it is clear that there are ABA receptors on the outside of the cell membrane and inside the protoplast (Bray 1997). The receptors may be activated or inactivated by interaction with an effector protein. Prenylation (farnesylation) of that protein leads to its binding to the receptor and to its inactivation. In this way, the sensitivity of the cell for ABA may be adjusted (Bonetta and McCourt 1998). However, ABA is not the only signal molecule that is recognised by the ABA receptors. The derivative (+)-8′-methylene-ABA is more efficient, probably because this compound persists longer than ABA, i.e. is metabolised more slowly. The cyclic ADP-ribose (cADP-Rib) and nicotinic acid-adeninedinucleotide phosphate have been identified as **secondary intracellular messengers** of the ABA signal (Quatrano et al. 1997). They probably react to the ABA signal and affect intracellular calcium

stores, triggering increase in free cytosolic Ca^{2+}. This acts as a further secondary messenger, starting one or more phosphorylation cascades which directly or indirectly lead to metabolic responses (strain reactions) to drought stress.

Processes induced by ABA are either fast reactions, as seen in stomatal closure, or slow reactions connected to the expression of ABA-responsive genes.

Reaction of Stomates to ABA

The ABA signal is detected at the outer face of the plasma membrane of guard cells, causing a fast decrease in the turgor and closure of the stomates (Schroeder et al. 2001).

The compartment that is effective in the control of ABA-triggered reactions is thus the apoplast of the guard cells. ABA, as a **signal originating in the roots**, reaches the leaves via the xylem stream and, by **ion trapping**, is quickly absorbed by the protoplast. Usually, the apoplast is more acidic than the cytosol, whose pH is around 7. Thus ABA, as an acid, is protonated to a higher extent in the apoplast (pH 5–5.5) than in the cytoplasm. The protonated, i.e. undissociated, acid easily diffuses through the plasma membrane into the cytosol where it is trapped after dissociation. The apoplastic concentration of ABA, which is that concentration perceived by the outer face of the plasma membrane, is, therefore, low. It has been recently shown that stressful situations, such as low water availability in the soil, lead to an alkalisation of the xylem sap by up to one pH unit (Wilkinson 1999). This decreases the efficacy of the cytosolic ion trap and shifts the pH-dependent equilibrium between the intra- and extracellular ABA concentrations in favour of the apoplast

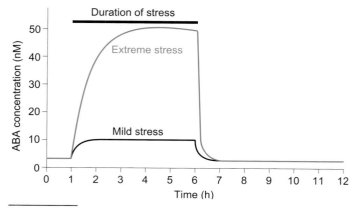

Fig. 1.5.3. Computer simulation of ABA export from the guard cell protoplasts into the surrounding apoplasts following alkalisation of the latter upon drought stress. The simulation of the distribution of ABA is based on the ion trap principle. Following rehydration, the original pH relations are restored and ABA diffuses back into the cytoplasm. The duration of the applied stress is shown by the *black bar* at the top of the figure. (Hartung 1996)

[1] Fungi also synthesise ABA, probably directly from mevalonic acid (Walton and Li 1995)

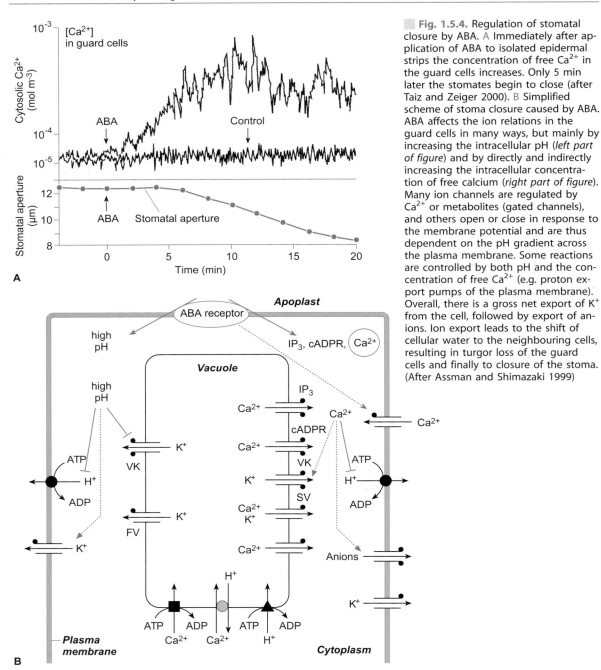

Fig. 1.5.4. Regulation of stomatal closure by ABA. A Immediately after application of ABA to isolated epidermal strips the concentration of free Ca^{2+} in the guard cells increases. Only 5 min later the stomates begin to close (after Taiz and Zeiger 2000). B Simplified scheme of stoma closure caused by ABA. ABA affects the ion relations in the guard cells in many ways, but mainly by increasing the intracellular pH (*left part of figure*) and by directly and indirectly increasing the intracellular concentration of free calcium (*right part of figure*). Many ion channels are regulated by Ca^{2+} or metabolites (gated channels), and others open or close in response to the membrane potential and are thus dependent on the pH gradient across the plasma membrane. Some reactions are controlled by both pH and the concentration of free Ca^{2+} (e.g. proton export pumps of the plasma membrane). Overall, there is a gross net export of K$^+$ from the cell, followed by export of anions. Ion export leads to the shift of cellular water to the neighbouring cells, resulting in turgor loss of the guard cells and finally to closure of the stoma. (After Assman and Shimazaki 1999)

and, in turn, increases the strength of the ABA signal (Fig. 1.5.3).

Moreover, the ABA concentration in the xylem fluid increases under that kind of stress. Neither the structure of the ABA receptor nor the biochemistry of its reaction with ABA is known. Knowledge of the ABA signal cascade starts with an increase in the cytosolic calcium concentration by import of Ca^{2+} from the apoplast and by release from intracellular reservoirs. In addition, the cytosolic pH also increases. Because of this and the increased calcium level, proton-exporting pumps and potassium-importing channels are inactivated and potassium-exporting channels are activated. Ca^{2+} also activates anion channels (chloride or malate) in the plasma membrane. Flow of such anions from the vacuole into the cytoplasm has been shown, but the transport mechanism and the nature of the activator of the channels are still debated. For many of these channels, a guard cell-specific control is assumed. Thus, there is a direct and a calcium-dependent signal transduction pathway (Fig. 1.5.4) and both have the same effect, i.e. a concerted reaction of ion channels resulting in an export of potassium and anions (e.g. chloride and malate) from the guard cell protoplast. As a consequence of the decreasing osmotic potential of the guard cells and the corresponding increase in the water potential of the neighbouring cells, water moves from the guard cells to the neighbouring cells. Because of the concomitant decrease in the turgor in the guard cells, the stomata close. As mentioned above, the sensitivity of the plasma membrane towards ABA can change in the course of the day; this could be due to salts or other phytohormones transported in the xylem sap.

Besides the reaction to ABA, guard cells also react to other signals, e.g. CO_2 concentration or light (see also Chap. 2.2, Fig. 2.2.17). Increased concentrations of CO_2 reduce stomatal conductivity (Morison 1998) while light acts as a signal for the opening of stomata. It has been shown that it is mainly the blue light portion of the daylight that triggers ion influx and stoma opening (Zeiger and Zhu 1998).

Regulation of Gene Expression by ABA

The control of gene expression mediated by ABA aims at two different groups of gene products: **functional** and **regulatory proteins**. The latter may be components of regulation cascades leading to the synthesis of functional proteins (enzymes or protective proteins; Fig. 1.5.5).

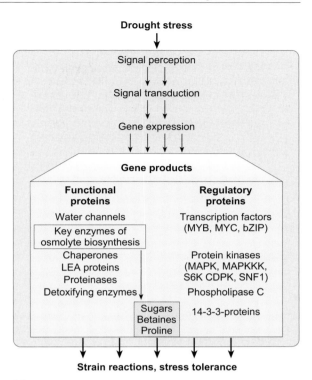

Fig. 1.5.5. The response of plant cells to stress caused by desiccation. (After Shinozaki and Yamaguchi-Shinozaki 1997)

The regulation of gene expression at the transcription level requires the interaction of *cis*-acting elements in the promoters with corresponding transcription factors, usually DNA-binding proteins. The *cis*-elements are fairly well known, but knowledge of transcription factors is still patchy. The **ABA responsive *cis*-element** is a highly conserved motif, the so-called ABRE (ABA-responsive element), which consists of the base sequence PurPyr**ACGTGG**PyrPur (Pur, Pyr: purine base, pyrimidine base). The central piece of this element is the sequence CACGT(G,C), the so-called **G-box**, which is typical of promoters of many stress- and light-responsive genes.

Changing of only two of the conserved bases in ABRE reduces the responsiveness of this *cis*-acting element enormously. The transcription factors binding to ABRE are the G-box-binding proteins, which belong to the so-called **basic leucine zipper** (so-called bZIP proteins), containing several basic amino acids after the zipper motif. How ABA activates the bZIP protein so that it binds to the ABRE is not yet known.

Natural genes usually contain several ABREs (Fig. 1.5.6 A). Thus, those promoters that contain a single ABRE react only weakly to ABA. They

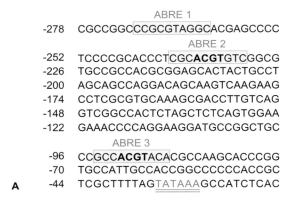

                    ABRE 1
    -278   CGCCGGCCCGCGTAGGCACGAGCCCC
                    ABRE 2
    -252   TCCCCGCACCCTCGCACGTGTCGGCG
    -226   TGCCGCCACGCGGAGCACTACTGCCT
    -200   AGCAGCCAGGACAGCAAGTCAAGAAG
    -174   CCTCGCGTGCAAAGCGACCTTGTCAG
    -148   GTCGGCCACTCTAGCTCTCAGTGGAA
    -122   GAAACCCCAGGAAGGATGCCGGCTGC
                    ABRE 3
    -96   CCGCCACGTACACGCCAAGCACCCGG
    -70   TGCCATTGCCACCGGCCCCCCACCGC
A   -44   TCGCTTTTAGTATAAAGCCATCTCAC

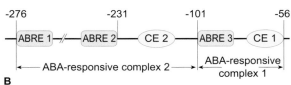

Fig. 1.5.6. The HVA22 promoter from barley (*Hordeum vulgare*) contains several ABA-responsive elements (ABREs) and further *cis*-active elements (CEs). A The complete HVA22 promoter with the ABREs 1–3 and the TATA box. B ABREs and CEs form a complex that determines signal specificity. (After Shen and Ho 1995)

require a second promoter element for strong reactions. The dehydration protective protein of barley is called the coupling element (CE3), with a base sequence similar to that of ABRE (Pur-ACGCGTGTC) and can even be experimentally replaced by it, without affecting gene expression. Both elements bind the same ABA-responsive bZip-factor TRAB1 (Hobo et al. 1999). This factor also binds to other **non-G-box-ABRE**s.

The specificity of the gene response to ABA requires further DNA-binding proteins. In the *rab17* gene of maize, nine promoter elements have been identified, which bind to such proteins. Five of these elements are ABREs, four contain other motifs. Six of these *cis*-elements induce the strong expression of the *rab 17* gene in the course of embryo maturation in the ripening seed, three are responsible for expression of the gene specifically in leaves (Busk et al. 1997). The principle of combining two or several promoter elements ("bipartite promoter"), for example, a general ABA-responsive element with one element mediating signal and site specificity, is widespread (Fig. 1.5.6 B; Shen and Ho 1995).

It is assumed that certain DNA-binding proteins, such as the VPI, represent a new class of nucleus-specific factors, so-called **DNA chaper-**ones, which modify the structure of DNA in a way which is not sequence-specific and thus enables the binding of other regulatory factors.

Not all ABA-responsive genes possess a G-box containing ABRE. They are activated by products of other genes, the synthesis of which is induced by ABA (Fig. 1.5.7). The gene *Rd22*, expressed in drought-stressed *Arabidopsis* plants, probably coding for a protective protein, reacts to ABA but does not possess an ABA-responsive element in its promoter. This promoter possesses motifs known to bind frequently occurring transcription factors, e.g. homologues of the human gene activators MYC and MYB (Hiroshi et al. 1997). The bZIP proteins mentioned above belong also to that group of transcription factors. In this case, they react with motifs similar to the G-box in the promoter. This mode of ABA-mediated induction of genes whose promoters do not contain an ABRE is apparent in drought but has been shown also for salt and cold stress and, of course, after application of ABA.

1.5.2.3
ABA-Independent Gene Activation by Drought

Besides gene expression mediated by ABA, there are several examples in which drought alone or together with salt or cold stress lead to activation of a promoter without participation of ABA. The best-investigated gene of this type is *Rd29A*, which is activated in all vegetative tissues of *Arabidopsis* upon desiccation and probably codes for a thiolprotease. Such ABA-independent genes contain also a consensus sequence in the promoter (TACC-GACAT), the so-called **d**ehydration **r**esponsive **e**lement (DRE) or C-repeat (Yamaguchi-Shinozaki and Shinozaki 1994). It is assumed from the frequent occurrence of this motif that specific DNA-binding proteins (DRE-binding proteins) exist. It could be shown that the *Rd29A* promoter contains a DRE as well as an ABRE. However, the ABRE is only activated during prolonged drought stress. The DRE was also found in promoters of genes activated by cold, the so-called COR genes (cold response), but then was ultimately controlled by ABA via a further cascade.

Figure 1.5.7 presents an overview of the pathways leading to gene expression induced by drought.

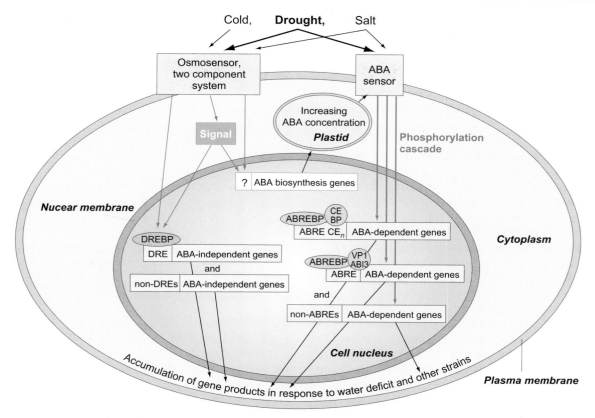

Fig. 1.5.7. Multiple pathways which lead to induction of gene expression upon stress by desiccation. *DRE* Dehydration responsive element; *DREBP* DRE-binding protein; *ABRE* abscisic acid binding element; *ABREBP* ABRE-binding protein; *CE* coupling element; *CEBP* protein binding to CE; *VP1/ABI3* sequentially akin proteins which regulate a MYB-related transcription factor. (After Bray 1997)

1.5.2.4
Signal Transduction

There is very little information on transduction cascades, from the various drought signals to the promoters of genes. It is well established that Ca^{2+} and inositol 1,4,5-trisphosphate, liberated from the membrane lipid phosphatidylinositol by phospholipase C, act as secondary messengers, giving rise to protein phosphorylation and dephosphorylation at the next lower level of the signal transduction cascade. In some cases, the participation of MAP kinases (mitogen-activated protein kinases) has been shown (Neill and Burnett 1999). It should also be noted that there are internal receptors for ABA in the cell (see Sect. 1.5.2.2) and that an interaction of various signals, a so-called signal cross talk with signals like gibberellins, requires further biochemical mechanisms (Shinozaki and Yamaguchi-Shinozaki 1997).

1.5.2.5
Function of Proteins Induced by Dehydration Stress

As mentioned above, water deficit induces proteins, some of which increase the stress tolerance of cells more or less directly (functional proteins), and others which are part of a signal transduction chain (regulatory proteins; see Fig. 1.5.5), leading finally to the synthesis of functional proteins.

Functional proteins are mainly aquaporins, or enzymes which catalyse the biosynthesis of **osmolytes** (compatible solutes, e.g. various carbohydrates, amino acids and betaines), also proteases for the degradation of damaged proteins (ubiquitin, thiolproteases) and ROS-detoxifying enzymes[2], such as catalase, SOD, ascorbate peroxi-

---

[2] During drought, stomata close (see Chap. 2.2, Fig. 2.2.19), resulting in CO_2 shortage if the light intensity is high. This leads to the formation of ROS and radicals.

dase, glutathione-S-transferase, etc. Overexpression of these genes or of gene constructs, in which the corresponding proteins are directed by specific signal peptides into sensitive cell compartments, leads to increased drought tolerance and to a stabilisation of metabolic processes, such as photosynthesis (this will be discussed in greater detail in Chap. 1.6.2, salinity stress).

A special group of protective proteins are **dehydrins, LEA** or **Rab proteins**, which occur in all plants (Campbell and Close 1997); apparently, they do not possess any enzymatic activity, but are very effective in protecting the cellular membranes and proteins with quaternary structures (Close 1996). Unfortunately, the nomenclature of these protective proteins is not yet conclusive[3].

These protective proteins occur regularly during desiccation of the embryo and the endosperm when seeds ripen. Discovered in 1981, they were therefore called **late embryogenesis abundant (LEA) proteins**. They belong to the group of drought-induced proteins, the promoters of which contain one or several ABREs, and thus can be directly induced by ABA. Therefore, they have also been termed **Rab (responsive to ABA) proteins**. Most of them occur not only during seed ripening, but form and accumulate also during dry periods and upon osmotic stress in all plant organs. Being of particular importance for poikilohydric plants, they are also known as **dehydrins**. According to their structural characteristics (consensus sequences) and the high proportion of certain, usually hydrophilic, amino acids, LEA proteins were classified into 18 families, representatives of four of which are widely distributed.

Most of the known LEA proteins have not yet been isolated as proteins but are only known as genes or as mRNAs, which become prominent during drought. They are all nuclear coded and occur mainly in the cytoplasm, but also in the nucleus. Most strikingly, they cannot be denatured by boiling or acid treatment, probably because they do not have a globular structure, but rather form **random coils** or **amphiphilic α-helices**. Such helices carry on one lateral side hydrophobic, on the other side, hydrophilic functional groups (Fig. 1.5.8). Random coil proteins contain significantly more water than helical proteins. The size of the LEA proteins, however, is very variable, ranging from 15 to almost 200 kDa.

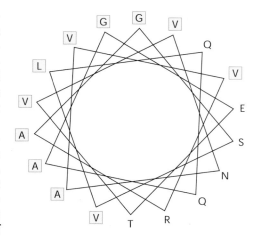

Fig. 1.5.8. Representation of a LEA protein as a helical wheel. Hydrophobic amino acid residues are highlighted by *boxes*, thus illustrating the amphiphilic character of the helix. Amino acids are represented by the *single letter code*. (After Curry and Walker-Simmons 1993)

Individual families of these proteins will not be discussed here in detail, only dehydrins as prominent representatives shall be described, as there are about 80 currently known types belonging to the LEA-D11 family. Of this family, a further 200 or so species are known from partial gene sequences or cDNAs. In some plant species, they are constitutively expressed, but always accumulate under dehydration, forming then between 0.1 and 5% of the total soluble protein or of the total mRNA. These proteins contain between 82 and 575 amino acids, and are modularly structured with many repeats. The 15 amino acids comprising **K(rich)segment** (EKKGIMDKIKEKLPG, the antigenic component of dehydrins) is highly conserved in cyanobacteria, lower and higher plants, and often occurs in several copies. There is also the **S(rich)segment** containing up to seven serine residues which can be phosphorylated. The **Y(rich)segment** (T/VDEYGNP) is commonly at the N-terminus of many dehydrins in one or several copies. These modules are interconnected by less conserved segments, the so-called **Φ-segments**. The amino acids cysteine and tryptophan are completely missing, which could explain the stability of these proteins against denaturing treatment and chemicals. The YSK_2 dehydrin from maize seeds is given as an example of the modular structure of dehydrins (Box 1.5.4).

Many dehydrins contain a bipartite nuclear localisation sequence, suggesting a protective role of these proteins in the cell nucleus. They

---

[3] One of these proteins is also known under the name of osmotin (see Chap. 1.6.2.3).

Box 1.5.4   Typical structure of dehydrins

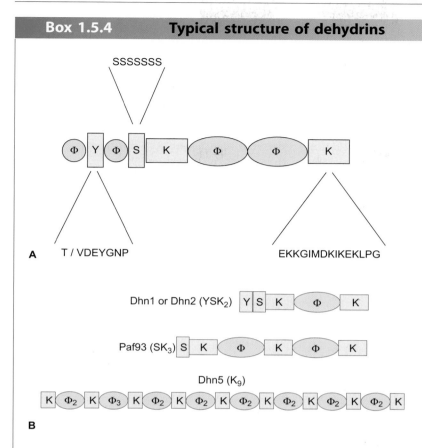

A   T / VDEYGNP   EKKGIMDKIKEKLPG

B

The YSK$_2$-dehydrin from maize seeds shows the typical structure of a dehydrin with Y- and K-consensus sequences (A). The number of serine residues in the S-segment is variable. Φ indicates less conserved sequences, which may be repetitive in individual dehydrins (after Close 1997). B shows dehydrins from barley with different combinations of the conserved motifs: YSK$_2$, SK$_3$, and K$_9$ (after Campbell and Close 1997).

can accumulate in "protein bodies", but also can stabilise cellular membranes by preventing the disintegration of the bilayer into lipid droplets (hexagonal structure of lipids; see Fig. 1.3.16) upon attenuation of the stabilising water film. The hydrophobic stretches of the amphiphilic α-helices interact with the surface of the membranes, whilst the hydrophilic parts are oriented towards the cytoplasm (see Fig. 1.3.24). Preventing the formation of globular lipid structures, they have been called "reversible chaperones". Protection of membranes with dehydrins hinders the accumulation of low-molecular ions at the membrane surface upon withdrawal of cellular water which would result in a change of the membrane potential of that membrane. Dehydrins are very suitable for genetic transforma-

Table 1.5.1. Growth of rice plants, transformed with the *HVA1* gene from barley under drought stress. The plants were exposed to several cycles, each consisting of 5 days of drought and 2 days of recovery. Leaf growth was measured before, and 3 days after, the onset of drought. Leaf growth rates of the two youngest leaves were measured. The height of the plants was measured after four stress cycles and an additional 2 days of recovery (Xu et al. 1996)

Line	Leaf growth rate (%)	Height of plant (cm)	Root fresh weight (g)
Wild type	69	22 ± 1.4	0.9 ± 0.1
Line 30	90	29 ± 1.1	1.4 ± 0.1
Line 36	129	37 ± 1.8	2.1 ± 0.1
Line 41	113	33 ± 1.8	2.3 ± 0.3

tion in drought-sensitive plants. For example, the *HVA1* gene from barley (*Hordeum vulgare*) was successfully transferred to rice; transgenic rice plants were considerably more tolerant to drought and salt (Table 1.5.1; Xu et al. 1996).

1.5.2.6
Accumulation of Osmolytes (Compatible Solutes) During Drought

In addition to desiccation-induced synthesis and accumulation of dehydrins, protection of cells and tissue by low molecular (mass) solutes is also very important. Formation of enzymes which catalyse the synthesis of such protective substances (**compatible solutes**) is also directly or indirectly induced by ABA (see Fig. 1.5.5). The protective action of compatible solutes on stressed cells is attributed to two effects:

1. Increase in the osmotic potential counteracts the osmotic dehydration of the cells. Compatible solutes, therefore, are also called **osmolytes**. They can achieve considerable concentrations, often 5–10% of the dry weight. Upon extreme water loss, e.g. during the drying of poikilohydric plants, solutions of sugars such as sucrose adopt a glassy almost solid state, which effectively prevents the disintegration of biomembranes into lipid droplets (the so-called hexagonal-II phase, see Fig. 1.3.16). However, only solutions of such carbohydrates which do not readily crystallise can achieve this state.

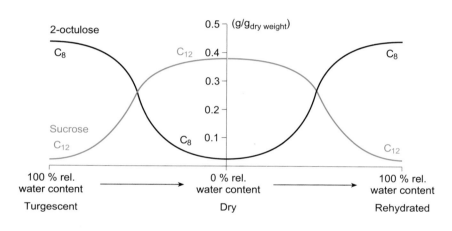

Fig. 1.5.9. Changes in the proportions of soluble carbohydrates in correspondence with the water relations of the resurrection plant *Craterostigma plantaginea*. In the fully hydrated state, leaves mainly contain the C_8 sugar octulose, which upon desiccation is almost quantitatively converted to sucrose, a compatible solute. This reaction is reversible. (After Bartels et al. 1993)

Table 1.5.2. Accumulation of metabolic products in organs of terrestrial plants under drought stress and their physiological effects

Type of compound	Compounds	Function upon drought	Cross-protection
Ions	Potassium	Osmotic balance, acquisition of macronutrients, sodium exclusion and export	Salt
Proteins	LEA/dehydrins, osmotin, SOD/catalases	Membrane and protein protection, pathogen-related proteins, detoxification of radicals	Frost, defense against pathogens
Amino acids	Proline, ectoin	Osmotic balance, membrane and protein protection	Frost
Sugars	Sucrose, fructans	Osmotic balance, membrane and protein protection, storage of carbohydrates	Frost
Polyols	Acyclic (e.g. mannitol), cyclic (e.g. pinitol)	Osmotic balance, membrane protection, storage of carbohydrates, radical scavengers	Frost, salt
Polyamines	Spermine, spermidine	Ion balance, protection of chromatin	Anaerobiosis
Quaternary amines	Glycinebetaine, β-alaninebetaine	Membrane protection	Frost, salt
Tertiary sulfonium compounds	Dimethyl sulfoniopropionate	Membrane protection	Frost, salt
Pigments and carotenoids	Carotenoids, anthocyanins and betalains	Protection against excess light and photoinhibition	

2. Because of their increased concentration and high water solubility, compatible solutes compete with other dissolved materials, particularly with ions of high charge density, displacing them from the surfaces of biomembranes and proteins. Owing to their hydrophilic characteristics, they are able to become a constituent part of the structured portion of the water film on the membrane surface. Carbohydrates which provide only relatively weak protection may become reversibly converted into more effective ones, such as sucrose during drought stress (Fig. 1.5.9).

Besides carbohydrates and their derivatives (sugar alcohols, cyclitols) in drought stress, quaternary ammonium bases (so-called betaines) and tertiary sulfonic acids (Fig. 1.5.10), amino acids (mostly proline, Box 1.5.5) and polyamines may accumulate as protective osmolytes (Fig. 1.5.11). In Table 1.5.2 such osmolytes are listed and characterised.

Besides dehydrins, enzymes which catalyse the biosynthesis of compatible solutes are also suitable targets for genetic transformation, in order to produce crop plants that are less sensitive to drought stress (Fig. 1.5.12).

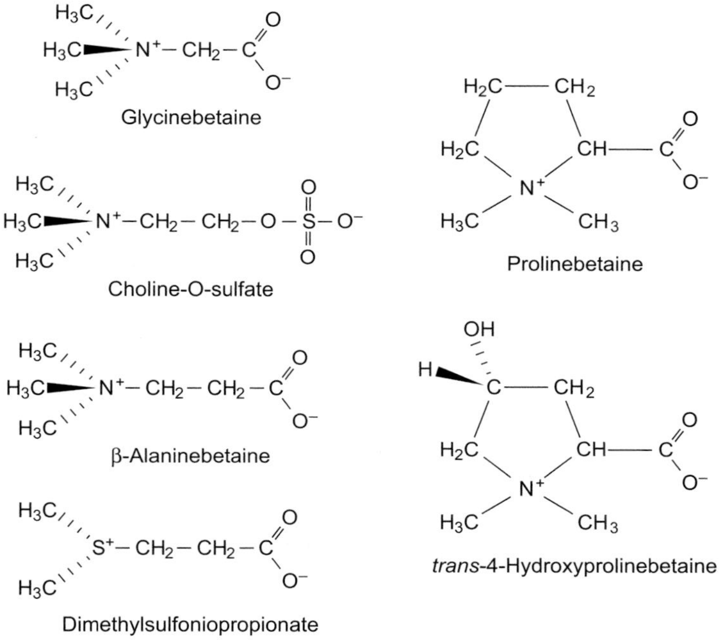

Fig. 1.5.10. Some quaternary amino compounds and tertiary sulfonium compounds which have been identified as compatible solutes in plants. The amphiphilic group $(CH_3)_3–N^+...O^-$ renders these compounds their membrane-protective capacity. (Hanson 1993)

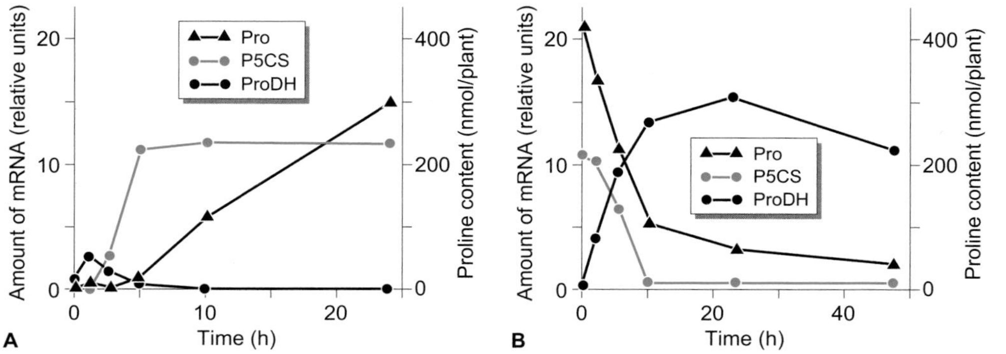

Fig. 1.5.11. Time course of accumulation and decrease in proline (Pro), the mRNAs for Δ^1-pyrroline-5-carboxylate synthase (P5CS), and for proline dehydrogenase (proline oxidase, ProDH) in *Arabidopsis* during the development of drought (A), and 10 h after rehydration (B). (After Yoshiba et al. 1997)

Box 1.5.5   Proline metabolism

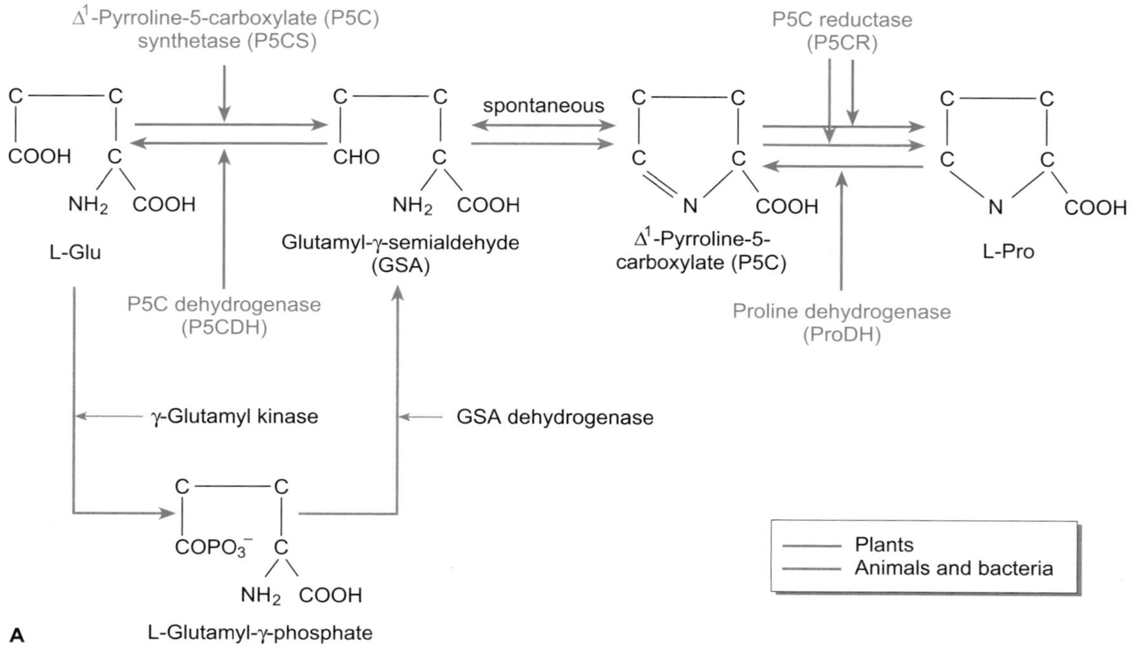

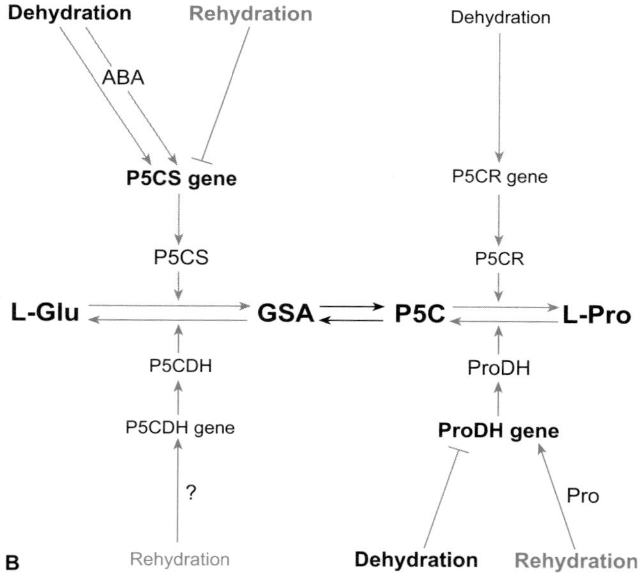

A

B

A shows a comparison of biosynthesis and metabolism of L-proline in plants and in bacteria. In green plants, the main precursor of proline is L-glutamic acid. However, when subjected to osmotic stress and N limitation, ornithine can be the precursor. The initial enzyme in proline metabolism is proline dehydrogenase, often also called proline oxidase (after Yoshiba et al. 1997).

B shows the regulation of proline synthesis under drought stress and subsequent rehydration. In the unstressed plant, proline synthesis and degradation are in balance and the cellular proline concentration is very low. The rise in the proline level occurs by activation of the gene for Δ^1-pyrroline-5-carboxylate synthetase and concomitant inhibition of expression of the proline dehydrogenase (proline oxidase) gene. Activation of P5CS gene expression takes place dependently as well as independently of ABA. In the well-watered status, expression of this gene is extremely low. Upon rehydration proline dehydrogenase is activated by the high concentration of proline that accumulated during the period of drought. In contrast, the second gene involved in proline synthesis, the P5CR gene, is neither significantly influenced by drought nor by ABA (after Yoshiba et al. 1997).

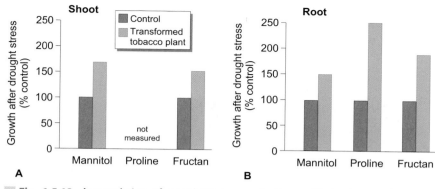

Fig. 1.5.12. Accumulation of osmolytes in genetically modified tobacco plants under drought stress. The gene for mannitol-1-phosphate dehydrogenase (from *E. coli*) or P5CS (from *Vigna aconitifolia*) or levan-sucrase (from *Bacillus subtilis*) was transferred into tobacco using *Agrobacterium tumefaciens*. All three metabolites accumulate in the transformed plants in comparison to the controls, and there was a significant increase in growth of the transgenic plants compared with the controls under drought, and in the case of P5CS also upon salt stress. (After Bray 1997)

1.5.3

CAM (Crassulacean Acid Metabolism)

Recommended Literature

- Cushman JC, Bohnert HJ (1999) Crassulacean acid metabolism: molecular genetics. Annu Rev Plant Physiol Plant Mol Biol 50:305–332
- Griffith H (1989) Carbon dioxide concentrating mechanisms and the evolution of CAM in vascular epiphytes. In: Lüttge U (ed) Vascular plants as epiphytes. Evolution and ecophysiology. Ecological studies 76. Springer, Berlin Heidelberg New York
- Lüttge U (1993) The role of crassulacean acid metabolism (CAM) in the adaptation of plants to salinity. New Phytol 125:59–71

A particular type of metabolic response to drought is the so-called **crassulacean acid metabolism (CAM)**, which is also addressed in Chapter 2.4.1.2 (Fig. 2.4.3). Plants growing in dry and hot regions (where transpiration often greatly exceeds water loss) with this type of metabolism avoid "dying of thirst" and "dying of hunger" (due to limitation of photosynthetic CO_2 uptake by closed stomata) by opening their stomata only at night, when the humidity deficit of air due to low temperatures is fairly small. In this case, CO_2 is taken up in the dark and, catalysed by **PEP carboxylase**, bound to phosphenolpyruvate (PEP). The resulting oxaloacetic acid is converted into malic acid by **NAD-dependent malate dehydrogenase** in the cytosol. Malic acid

is then stored in large amounts in the vacuoles (acidification up to pH 3), which can easily be tasted! During the day, malate is released from the vacuole (de-acidification) and converted, in the chloroplast, by the **NADP-dependent malic enzyme** into CO_2, reduction equivalents (NADPH) and pyruvate. CO_2 is assimilated in the reductive photosynthetic carbon cycle (Calvin cycle). Pyruvate may be metabolised in different ways: direct respiration (in the mitochondria) as well as phosphorylation to PEP by **pyruvate P_i dikinase** in the chloroplast are discussed. Phosphoenolpyruvate may leave the chloroplast via a specific **PEP translocator** and contribute to glycolytic or gluconeogenetic carbon flow. The product of photosynthesis, starch, is stored in the chloroplast and used for PEP formation during the night.

As CAM plants are able to fix only as much CO_2 by PEP carboxylation as PEP is supplied, those only relying on the CAM cycle would not be able to grow. In the extreme, CAM is thus a mechanism for survival but does not allow growth. With sporadic precipitation, and in the early morning hours and perhaps also in late afternoon, stomata usually open or are at least not fully closed, so that direct net photosynthesis and growth are possible. Gas exchange, content of malic acid and starch, as elements of photosynthesis, are shown for the course of a day in Fig. 1.5.13.

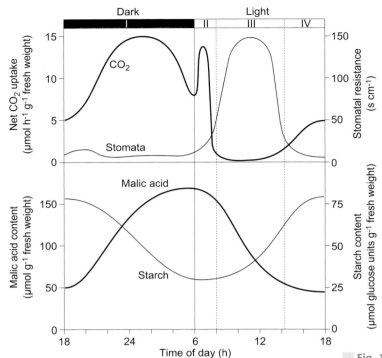

A

Phase	I		II	III	IV
Net CO₂ fixation	From the atmosphere			(From respiration)	
Malic acid accumulation	Vacuolar influx			Vacuolar efflux	
Storage glucan	Glycolysis			Gluconeogenesis	
PEPC	Active			Inactive	
PEPC kinase	Active			Inactive	
Rubisco	Inactive			Active	
ME/PEPCK	Inactive			Active	
Stomata	Open			Closed	
Photoperiod	**Dark**			**Light**	

B

Fig. 1.5.13. Typical gas-exchange curve (CO_2 uptake rate and stomatal resistance = stomatal conductance^{-1}) of a CAM plant. The changes in concentration of the typical metabolites starch and malate are also presented. Gas exchange shows the phases *I* nocturnal CO_2 fixation; *II* dawn with the start of CO_2 fixation by Rubisco; *III* assimilation of the internally released CO_2 by Rubisco with stomates closed; *IV* stomates begin to open after the internal CO_2 has been depleted and daytime temperatures are dropping. In B, the time courses of the different reactions are shown in different shades of *blue*. A from Lüttge et al. (1994); B from Cushman and Bohnert (1999)

1.5.3.1
Flexibility of CAM

CAM plants are superior to other photosynthetic types in their **water use efficiency (WUE)**, but their photosynthetic rates and growth rates are much lower (Table 1.5.3).

During long periods of drought, stomata remain continuously closed, even at night; fixation and assimilation of CO_2 are limited to carbon dioxide generated internally in the plant tissue by respiratory processes. This state is called **CAM idling** (Fig. 1.5.14). The photosynthetic assimilation of internal CO_2 provides some protection from photooxidation. However, the low in-ternal CO_2 content, at the usually extremely high radiation, is not sufficient to allow a substantial flow of electrons and full relief of the photosystems. Consequently, radicals are formed and oxidative stress occurs. Therefore, CAM idling is of only limited use, as it can only be sustained for a relatively short time, and because even with closed stomata water is lost by cuticular transpiration.

Many bromeliads show diurnal CAM metabolism, even though their stomata are not – or are only partially – closed during the day when they perform "normal" C3 photosynthesis. This is called **CAM cycling**. An extreme example of CAM cycling occurs in the usually submerged

Table 1.5.3. Water use efficiency, photosynthesis and biomass production of C3, C4 and CAM plants. (After Lüttge et al. 1994)

Type of photosynthesis	C3	C4	CAM
Water use efficiency (g water/g C)	450–950	250–350	18–100 (nighttime); 150–600 (daytime)
Maximum rate of net photosynthesis ($\mu mol\ CO_2\ m^{-2}\ s^{-1}$)	9–25	25–50	0.6–8
Growth (g biomass $m^{-2}\ day^{-1}$)	50–200	400–500	1.5–1.8

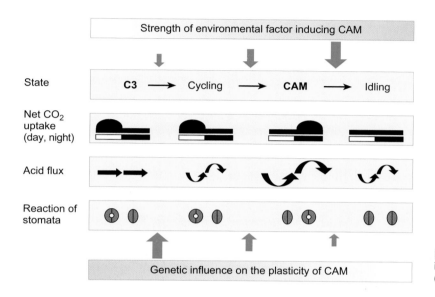

Fig. 1.5.14. Plasticity of CAM in facultative CAM plants. (After Cushman and Bohnert 1999)

water plant *Isoëtes* (*howellii*). The epidermis of this plant has, of course, no stomates and the plant does not experience water stress (Keely 1998); the reason for the CO_2 fixation during the night is assumed to be lack of CO_2 in the usually acidic waters where *Isoëtis* grows.

Many CAM plants, particularly those from the families of Crassulaceae and Aizoaceae, are C3 plants with a facultative, i.e. inducible, CAM. Perennial facultative CAM plants are able to switch between the two modes of photosynthesis many times during their life: C3 photosynthesis – CAM – CAM idling – C3 photosynthesis, ...

Drought or high salinity, and in some cases also day length (short day in *Kalanchoë*, *Aloe* and *Opuntia*), can also induce CAM. In some species, dependence of CAM induction on the age of the individual plant has been described: This holds for agaves or cacti, whose saplings cannot produce vacuoles that are large enough for the storage of sufficient malic acid, as do the adult individuals (Fig. 1.5.15).

CAM induction need not occur in all photosynthesising organs of a plant. The succulent stem of *Frerea indica* (an asclepiad) performs

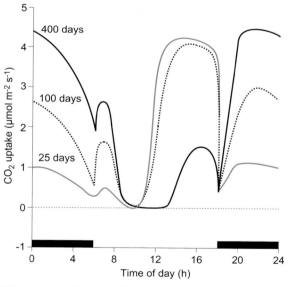

Fig. 1.5.15. Daily net CO_2 uptake by seedlings and plantlets of *Agave deserti* in its first 13 months. The seedlings were 25 days old and 14 mm in height; at 100 days their average height was 31 mm, and 400-day-old plantlets were 63 mm in height. The four phases of diurnal CO_2 uptake typical of CAM plants were only clearly visible after 1 year of growth, despite the fact that the young plants are capable of CO_2 fixation at night. (After Nobel 1988; Larcher 1994)

CAM, whilst the green leaves at least in rainy periods photosynthesise by the C3 mode; in tropical *Clusia* species, with opposite leaves at a node, one leaf may perform C3 photosynthesis, whilst the opposite leaf uses CAM (Lüttge 1987). This ecophysiological plasticity allows the C3-CAM intermediates optimal adaptation of their photosynthetic capacity to the prevailing conditions, making effective use of the humid season or of sporadic precipitation.

Whether a facultative CAM plant, or a part of the plant, follows C3 photosynthesis or CAM photosynthesis can be realised using the δ^{13}C **value**. Carbon dioxide in the air consists of 98.89% of the ^{12}C isotope and 1.11% of ^{13}C. The content of the radioactive isotope ^{14}C is, compared with those values, negligible (10^{-10}%). Rubisco consumes CO_2 as substrate and discriminates more strongly between ^{12}C and ^{13}C than does PEP carboxylase (PEPC), which uses HCO_3^- instead of CO_2. Carbon assimilated only by Rubisco thus contains less ^{13}C than that fixed first by PEPC. The **change of** ^{13}C in the biomass, therefore, allows the realisation of the mode of CO_2. The ratio of ^{13}C:^{12}C is determined by mass spectrometry and calculated with the following formula:

$$\delta^{13}C[\text{‰}] = \left(\frac{^{13}C/^{12}C \text{ of sample}}{^{13}C/^{12}C \text{ of standard}} - 1 \right) \times 1000$$

The standard is a defined limestone.

δ^{13}C values of C3 plants are around −28‰, those of C4 plants at −14‰, and for CAM plants with predominantly nocturnal CO_2 fixation between −10 and −20‰, and for daytime CO_2 fixation between −25 and −34‰.

1.5.3.2
CAM Causes Problems in Biochemical Regulation

Various instructive reaction schemes were developed to show the biochemistry of CAM (see Lüttge et al. 1994; Heldt 1997) and therefore need not be presented here.

The understanding of CAM as PEPC-mediated dark fixation of carbon dioxide, more exactly of HCO_3^-, the transient storage in the form of malic acid in the vacuole and the release by the malic enzyme for the final assimilation by Rubisco, assumes a complicated network of regulatory characteristics and processes.

Two of these metabolic processes will be discussed in more detail, namely the storage of malic acid in the vacuole and the competition for CO_2 between PEPC and Rubisco.

Storage of Malic Acid in Vacuoles

The tonoplast is the membrane that solves the problem of regulating transitory malic acid storage in the vacuole: During dark fixation of carbon dioxide, malic acid must be imported against the concentration gradient into the vacuole (and be retained there), but, during daytime, flow (probably even controlled) in the opposite direction must be enabled. The import of malic acid is well understood, but export still poses certain unsolved questions. A pH value of 7 (to perhaps 8) is assumed in the cytosol; at those values malic acid is dissociated as the pH value of both carboxyl groups is in the acidic range (C1: at pH 3.1; C4: at pH 5.1). Import of divalent malate ions into the vacuole would soon come to an end and can only be maintained if the negative charges are balanced by positive charges. This is achieved through the **proton-ATPase of the tonoplast (V-ATPase)**, which is supplied with energy from glycolysis together with a **pyrophosphate-dependent proton pump**. Uptake of the divalent malate ion into the vacuole takes place via **dicarboxylate channels** which transport malate as well as fumarate. Because of the acidification of the vacuole (to pH 3.5–3.0) malate becomes increasingly protonated and finally only malic acid is present. This is also important for osmotic reasons, because three osmotically active solutes ($2 \times H^+$ and malate) unify. Little is known about the efflux of malic acid from the vacuole. The undissociated acid could permeate the tonoplast via the "lipid path" (see Sect. 1.5.1). Some results also suggest a carrier in the tonoplast which catalyses a malate/2H$^+$ symport. However, why this carrier is not active during dark fixation has not yet been elucidated. It is interesting that a decrease in temperature during the night is an absolute requirement for acidification: During warm nights, there is no accumulation of malic acid in vacuoles (Lüttge et al. 1996).

The CAM-PEP Carboxylase as Pacemaker Enzyme

PEPC is a cytosolic enzyme which binds bicarbonate to PEP in an irreversible reaction:

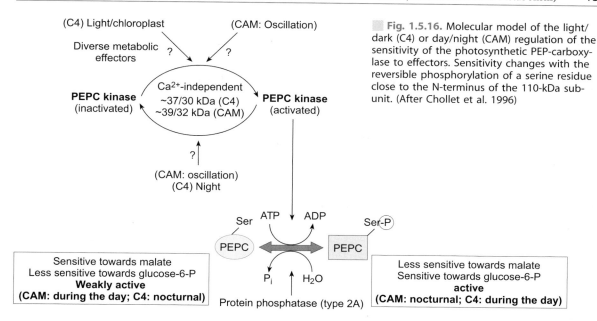

$$PEP + HCO_3^- + Mg^{2+} \rightarrow oxaloacetate + P_i + Mg^{2+}$$

In the reaction, the energy-rich phosphate group of PEP is transferred to the bicarbonate ion forming carboxyphosphate as an intermediate.

The final product of the reaction, oxaloacetate, is an unstable β-keto acid and is reduced by NAD malate dehydrogenase to the stable malate. The NADH originates from glycolysis.

Since PEPC does not react with CO_2 but with HCO_3^-, the carboxylation of PEP is insensitive to O_2, in contrast to the carboxylation of RuBP by Rubisco.

PEPC is an extensively analysed plant enzyme because of its function as the pacemaker enzyme of CAM. Differences in the reported kinetic parameters (Michaelis constant, v_{max}) are not because of the different sources of the enzyme but are due, most of all, to differences in the isolated protein; often a protein was isolated which had been partially truncated by proteolysis. Furthermore, the enzyme also reversibly forms dimers or tetramers, which originally was regarded as allosteric regulation of the mechanism. The activity of the enzyme is allosterically influenced by effectors. Glucose-6-phosphate and triosephosphate stimulate activity, whilst malate and aspartate have a strong inhibitory effect, particularly at a slightly alkaline (cytosolic) pH. The regulation of the CAM-PEPC has been shown to take place via the reversible phosphorylation of

a serine residue of the 110-kDa subunit (e.g. Ser 8 for millet, Ser 15 for maize) near the N-terminus. Phosphorylation at this single site renders the enzyme insensitive to malate; even in the presence of this allosteric inhibitor it remains in the active form, in particular as it now reacts more sensitively to the positive effectors mentioned above. The phosphorylation of CAM-PEPC occurs through a strongly regulated **protein kinase**, dephosphorylation (and inactivation) by a **protein phosphatase** of the type 2A. This phosphatase does not show any fluctuations in activity, in contrast to the kinase. The activity of the protein kinase is controlled diurnally, which, in contrast to the C4-PEPC, does not react to a change from dark to light (Fig. 1.5.16).

The question why CAM-PEPC does not compete during the day for CO_2 released by malic enzyme (in the chloroplast) can be answered by the consideration that the dephosphorylated enzyme is inhibited by malate. In addition to the post-translational regulation of activity by phosphorylation and dephosphorylation, there is another regulation through gene expression, which was observed during the induction of CAM in C3/CAM intermediates. The genome of *Mesembryanthemum crystallinum*, for example, contains two genes for PEPC, *Ppc1* and *Ppc2*. Regulation of expression is induced by drought, ABA and high salinity, where certain transcription factors recognise AT-rich regions in the promoter.

The problems of transitory malic acid storage in the vacuole and the diurnal oscillations of CAM-PEPC activity have been discussed here in more detail, but CAM also shows other peculiarities which are only partly understood, e.g. the question of what happens to the pyruvate formed during the release of CO_2 in the chloroplast. Some scientists assume it is used in regeneration of PEP catalysed by pyruvate P_i dikinase, analogous to the C4 pathway of photosynthesis, whilst others believe that respiration in the mitochondria is more probable. A further unsolved question is the opening of the stomates during the dark period, as stomata usually close in the dark (blue light is the effective component of the white light for the opening of stomata, see Fig. 2.2.15).

1.5.4

Anatomical and Morphological Adaptation to Drought

Besides physiological adaptations to drought, there are several anatomical and morphological responses of plants to this stressor: enlargement of root systems, improvement of hydraulic conductance and water transport systems, reduction of transpiring surfaces, increase in the stomatal density, production of a hairy tomentum, apoptosis of assimilation organs (shedding of leaves at the beginning of dry periods), and many more (see Chap. 2.2). All these changes are, of course, based on physiological processes; these and their regulatory mechanisms are still, to a large extent, poorly understood.

Summary

1. Life requires liquid water and is thus based on its particular physico-chemical properties which result from the dipole nature of the water molecule (the so-called anomalies of water).
2. The water potential, ψ, is a measure of the thermodynamic state of water in any system and is given in the dimension of pressure. The components are the osmotic potential of the cellular liquids, π, the water potential of the solid cell components (e.g. the cell wall), the so-called matrix potential, τ, and the pressure potential, i.e. the pressure of the cell wall on the protoplast which is numerically equal to the turgor pressure, i.e. the pressure of the protoplast on the cell wall.

$$(-)\psi = (-)\pi + (-)\tau + P$$

3. A water potential gradient between two systems (e.g. plant–air or plant–soil) causes water flow from the system with the lower (numerically less negative) water potential to that with the higher (numerically more negative) water potential. This is the reason for water loss from plants to the atmosphere. As a consequence of large water loss the protoplasts of the plant cells shrink concomitantly with a decrease of the wall pressure (which completely disappears at the turgor loss point or may even convert to a suction) and the plant wilts. During prolonged drought, so much water may be lost by transpiration that cellular membranes disintegrate, as can happen upon the loss of water by freezing dehydration.
4. The capacity of the "lipid path", i.e. the permeation of water through the lipid bilayer of the biomembrane, is not sufficiently high for a fast equilibration of water potential gradients in a cell. In these membranes, special integral proteins, so-called aquaporins, give rise to the high permeability of most biomembranes for water. The highest hydraulic conductivity of cellular membranes is usually with the tonoplast.
5. Desiccation is a natural phenomenon in the life cycle of a plant, for example, during seed ripening. Therefore, plants must have the capability to react in a manifold way to this stress. One reaction sequence is triggered by the phytohormone abscisic acid (ABA), but at least one other is ABA-independent. In these reaction cascades, transcription factors are synthesised, which upon interaction with other promoters switch on several genes: these genes may code for further regulatory factors or for proteins which contribute either directly (e.g. protective proteins) or indirectly (compatible solutes) to the maintenance of cell viability. The desiccation sensor or osmosensor of plants is not yet known; from yeast and bacteria such proteins are known however.
6. ABA synthesis is not via the mevalonate pathway, as previously assumed, but results from

degradation of the xanthophyll zeaxanthin. Biosynthesis of zeaxanthin, in turn, is synthesised in the recently discovered DOXP pathway (1-deoxy-D-xylulose-5-phosphate pathway).

7. Receptors for ABA are on the outer surface of the plasma membrane, as well as in the interior of the cell. Though their molecular structure is not yet known, modes of changing their effectiveness have been elucidated. In addition, details are known about secondary intracellular messengers (e.g. cyclic ADP ribose). Calcium, inositol-trisphosphate, protein kinases and protein phosphatases further take part in signal transduction. Reactions induced by ABA are either fast reactions such as the regulation of the stomates or slow reactions resulting from the expression of ABA-sensitive genes.

8. In stomatal movement, the apoplastic ABA signal is perceived by a receptor in the plasma membrane and the increase in the intracellular concentration of free calcium is one of the early steps in signal transduction. This activates anion channels, through which anions (malate, chloride) leave the cell, changing the membrane potential and triggering K^+ efflux. More than 90% of the ions exported from cells must first be released from the vacuole into the cytosol. The corresponding channels are also regulated by cytosolic free Ca^{2+}. Because of ion export from the guard cells and the concomitant release of water, turgor declines and the stomates close. In addition to their reaction to ABA, guard cells also react to other signals, e.g. blue light or the internal CO_2 concentration.

9. Cellular reactions to drought result from ABA-induced as well as from ABA-independent gene expression. The promoters of ABA-responsive genes contain the ABRE motif. This motif, in turn, contains the so-called G-box as "core motif", that is typical of promoters of many stress- and light-responsive genes. In order to bind the corresponding transcription factor, the promoter requires either several ABREs and/or binding enhancing elements. Further elements are required for organ-specific expression. Such functionally diversified promoters are called "bipartite promoters".

10. ABA-independent reactions to drought result from gene expression triggered by desiccation, high salinity or even cold. Promoters of such genes contain the so-called DRE element, to which specific transcription factors bind. There are also promoters which possess both elements, the DRE and the ABRE motif. As far as is known, the latter becomes effective only during prolonged drought or cold. Under these conditions the promoter changes to an ABA-responsive one.

11. The final gene products are proteins, which immediately or by their products improve the stress tolerance of cells: aquaporins, proteases, ROS-detoxifying enzymes, and enzymes which catalyse the synthesis of compatible solutes. A special group of protective proteins are the LEA or Rab proteins, which are attributed to the family of dehydrins. They are not catalytically active, but are very efficient in protecting membranes and protein complexes. Dehydrins are usually medium-sized proteins which either form amphiphilic helices or only random coils. Usually, they have a modular (segmented) structure and are resistant to boiling and denaturing by acids as they do not contain cysteine or tryptophan. In some cases, detailed understanding of the protective effect of these proteins has been achieved. Dehydrins and compatible solutes are the major components of membrane stabilisation in poikilohydric plants.

12. Dehydrins have proven useful for the transformation of drought-sensitive plants (crop plants). The same applies to enzymes which catalyse the synthesis of compatible solutes.

13. CAM is a special physiological adaptation of plants in hot and dry regions. Their stomata remain closed during the hot day and open only at night. CO_2 originating from bicarbonate is bound to PEP by phosphoenolpyruvate carboxylase (PEPC). The resulting chemically unstable oxaloacetate is stabilized by reduction to L-malate (malate dehydrogenase). Malic acid accumulates in the vacuole as an ATP-dependent proton pump shuffles protons into that organelle. During daytime, malic acid is released from the vacuole and after entering the chloroplast is decarboxylated by malic enzyme. The CO_2 is fixed by Rubisco and the pyruvate formed from the original PEP is either phosphorylated with pyruvate-P-dikinase to PEP or broken down in respiratory metabolism. Loading and unloading malic acid into and from the vacuole create particular biochemical problems

which are partly solved by using different pathways. Another problem is the reversible inhibition of PEPC during daytime to allow the CO_2 to be assimilated by Rubisco: A CAM plant-specific PEPC has been demonstrated which in its dephosphorylated form (daytime) is inhibited by malate, whereas the activity of the phosphorylated enzyme (nighttime) is not affected.

14. CAM plants have a much higher water use efficiency (WUE) than plants photosynthesising by the C3 or the C4 mechanism, but their growth is considerably slower than that of other homoiohydric plants.

15. Many CAM plants are able to switch from CAM to C3 photosynthesis if the environmental conditions are favourable (facultative CAM plants). Such change may be seasonal or diurnal, e.g. C3 photosynthesis may be performed for a short time in the early morning or late in the afternoon, when the stomata are not yet fully closed as for the rest of the day. During prolonged periods of drought, stomata remain closed even at night and photosynthesis is restricted to internally produced CO_2. Under these conditions growth is not possible (CAM idling). Crassulacean acid metabolism with completely or partly open stomates during the daytime is called "CAM cycling".

16. From the stable carbon isotope ratio (the so-called δ^{13} value), it is possible to detect whether a plant has photosynthesised by the C3, C4 or CAM mode: C3: −28‰, C4: −14‰, CAM: −10 to −20‰.

References

Assman SM, Shimazaki K-I (1999) The multisensory guard cell. Stomatal responses to blue light and abscisic acid. Plant Physiol 119: 809–815

Bartels D, Alexander R, Schneider K, Elster R, Velasco R, Alamillo J, Bianchi U, Nelson D, Salamini F (1993) Desiccation-related gene products analyzed in a resurrection plant and in barley embryos. In: Close TJ, Bray EA (eds) Plant responses to cellular dehydration during environmental stress. The American Society of Plant Physiologists, Rockville, Maryland, pp 119–127

Bonetta D, McCourt P (1998) Genetic analysis of ABA signal transduction pathways. Trends Plant Sci 3:231–235

Busk PK, Jensen AB, Pages M (1997) Regulatory elements in vivo in the promoter of the abscisic responsive gene rab17 from maize. Plant J 11:1285–1295

Campbell SA, Close TJ (1997) Dehydrins: genes, proteins, and association with phenotypic traits. New Phytol 137: 61–74

Chollet R, Vidal J, O'Leary MH (1996) Phosphoenolpyruvate carboxylase: a ubiquitous, highly regulated enzyme in plants. Annu Rev Plant Physiol Plant Mol Biol 47:273–298

Close TJ (1996) Dehydrins: emergence of a biochemical role of a family of plant dehydration proteins. Physiol Plant 97:795–803

Close TJ (1997) Dehydrins: a commonality in the response of plants to dehydration and low temperature. Physiol Plant 100:291–296

Cowan AK (2000) Is abscisic aldehyde really the immediate precursor to stress-induced ABA. Trends Plant Sci 5:191–192

Curry J, Walker-Simmons MK (1993) Sequence analysis of wheat cDNAs for abscisic acid-responsive genes expressed in dehydrated wheat seedlings and the Cyanobacterium, Anabaena. In: Close TJ, Bray EA (eds) Plant responses to cellular dehydration during environmental stress. The American Society of Plant Physiologists, Rockville, Maryland, pp 128–136

Cushman JC, Bohnert HJ (1999) Crassulacean acid metabolism: molecular genetics. Annu Rev Plant Physiol Plant Mol Biol 50:305–332

Cutler AJ, Krochko JE (1999) Formation and breakdown of ABA. Trends Plant Sci 4:472–478

Hanson AD (1993) Accumulation of quaternary ammonium and tertiary sulfonium compounds. In: Close TJ, Bray EA (eds) Plant responses to cellular dehydration during environmental stress. The American Society of Plant Physiologists, Rockville, Maryland, pp 30–36

Hartung W (1996) Trockenheit. In: Brundold Ch, Rüegsegger A, Brändle R (Hrsg) Stress bei Pflanzen. UTB, P Haupt, Berlin, pp 119–131

Heldt H-W (1997) Plant Biochemistry & Molecular Biology. Oxford Univ Press, Oxford New York Tokyo, 597 pp

Hiroshi A, Yamaguchi-Shinozaki K, Takeshi U, Toshisuke I, Daijiro H, Shinozaki K (1997) Role of Arabidopsis MYC and MYB homologs in drought- and abscisic acid-regulated gene expression. Plant Cell 9:1859–1868

Hobo T, Asada M, Kowyama Y, Hattori T (1999) ACGT-containing abscisic acid response element (ABRE) and coupling element 3 (CE3) are functionally equivalent. Plant J 19:679–689

Johansson I, Karlsson M, Johanson U, Larsson C, Kjellbom P (2000) The role of aquaporins in cellular and whole plant water balance. Biochem Biophys Acta 1465:324–342

Jung JS, Preston GM, Smith BL, Guggino WB, Agre P (1994) Molecular structure of the water channel through aquaporin CHIP. J Biol Chem 269:14648–14654

Keeley JE (1998) CAM photosynthesis in submerged aquatic plants. Bot Rev 64:121–175

Kjellbom P, Larsson Ch, Johansson I, Karlsson M, Johanson U (1999) Aquaporins and water homeostasis in plants. Trends Plant Sci 4:308–314

Larcher W (1994) Ökophysiologie der Pflanzen. UTB Eugen Ulmer, Stuttgart, 394 pp

Larcher W (2001) Ökophysiologie der Pflanzen. UTB Eugen Ulmer, Stuttgart

Lichtenthaler HK (1999) The 1-deoxy-D-xylulose-5 phosphate pathway of isoprenoid biosynthesis in plants. Annu Rev Plant Physiol Plant Mol Biol 50:47–63

Lüttge U (1987) Carbon dioxide and water demand: crassulacean acid metabolism (CAM), a versatile ecological adaptation exemplifying the need for integration in ecophysiological work. New Phytol 106:593–629

Lüttge U, Grams TEE, Hechler B, Blasius B, Beck F (1996) Frequency resonances of the circadian rhythm of CAM under external temperature rhythms of varied period length in continuous light. Bot Acta 109:422–426

Lüttge U, Kluge M, Bauer G (1994) Botanik. VCH, Weinheim, 600 pp

Morison JIL (1998) Stomatal response to increased CO_2 concentration. J Exp Bot 49: 443–452

Neill SJ, Burnett EC (1999) Regulation of gene expression during water deficit stress. Plant Growth Regul 29:23–33

Nobel PS (1988) Environmental biology of agaves and cacti. Cambridge University Press, Cambridge

Quatrano RS, Bartels D, Ho T-HD, Pages M (1997) New insights into ABA-mediated processes. Plant Cell 9:470–475

Robinson DG, Sieher H, Kammerloher W, Schäffner AR (1996) PIP1 aquaporins are concentrated in plasmalemmasomes of *Arabidopsis thaliana* mesophyll. Plant Physiol 111:645–649

Schäffner AR (1998) Aquaporin function, structure, and expression: are there more surprises to surface in water relations? Planta 204:131–139

Schroeder JI, Kwak JM, Allen GJ (2001) Guard cell abscisic acid signalling and engineering drought hardiness in plants. Nature 410: 327–330

Shen Q, Ho T-HD (1995) Functional dissection of an abscisic acid (ABA)-inducible gene reveals two independent ABA-responsive complexes each containing a G-box and a novel *cis*-acting element. Plant Cell 7:295–307

Shinozaki K, Yamaguchi-Shinozaki K (1997) Gene expression and signal transduction in water stress response. Plant Physiol 115:327–334

Taiz L, Zeiger E (2000) Physiologie der Pflanzen. Spektrum, Heidelberg, 773 pp

Walton DC, Li Y (1995) Abscisic acid biosynthesis and metabolism. In: Davies PJ (eds) Plant hormones: physiology, biochemistry and molecular biology. Kluwer, Dordrecht

Wilkinson S (1999) pH as a stress signal. Plant Growth Regul 29:87–99

Wurgler-Murphy SM, Saito H (1997) Two-component signal transducers and MAPK cascades. Trends Biochem Sci 22:172–176

Xu D, Duan X, Wang B, Hong B, Ho T-HD, Wu R (1996) Expression of a late embryogenesis abundant protein gene, HVA1, from barley confers tolerance to water deficit and salt stress in transgenic rice. Plant Physiol 110: 249–257

Yamaguchi-Shinozaki K, Shinozaki K (1994) A novel *cis*-acting element in an *Arabidopsis* gene is involved in responsiveness to drought, low-temperature, or high-salt stress. Plant Cell 6:251–264

Yoshiba Y, Kiyosue T, Nakashima K, Yamaguchi-Shinozaki K, Shinozaki K (1997) Regulation of levels of proline as an osmolyte in plants under water stress. Plant Cell Physiol 38:1095–1102

Zeiger E, Zhu J (1998) Role of zeaxanthin in blue light photoreception and the modulation of light-CO_2 interactions in guard cells. J Exp Bot 49: 433–442

1.6

Salt Stress (Osmotic Stress)

Salt lakes are almost uninhabitable for plants because of the enormous osmotic potential of the substrate, which is often also very alkaline due to the high soda ($NaCO_3$) content. Nevertheless, plant life can be found in such habitats. The white expanses in the picture of Lake Magadi in southern Kenya are not snow, but salt incrustations. The banks of sediment in the lake are overgrown with thick layers of algae. The shoreline also supports, in part, a vegetation of halotolerant bushes. Photo E. Beck

Recommended Literature

- Blumwald E (2000) Sodium transport and salt tolerance in plants. Curr Opin Cell Biol 12:431–434
- Hasegawa PM, Bressan R, Pardo JM (2000) The dawn of plant salt tolerance genetics. Trends Plant Sci 5:317–319
- Larcher W (2003) Ecophysiology of plants, 3rd edn. Springer-Telos
- Marschner H (1995) Mineral nutrition of higher plants, 2nd edn. Academic Press, chap 16.6
- Osmond CB, Björkman O, Anderson DJ (1980) Physiological processes in plant ecology: towards a synthesis with *Atriplex*. Ecological Studies 36. Springer, Berlin Heidelberg New York
- Zhu J-K (2002) Salt and drought stress signal transduction in plants. Annu Rev Plant Biol 53:247–274

That stress occurs when certain environmental factors exceed or are below the useful or tolerable range of intensities becomes particularly obvious with nutrients. The concentrations at which nutrients occur or exert their effect often differ greatly from element to element and from plant to plant (see also Chap. 2.3). This is partic-

ularly apparent for ions which are not obligate nutrients, such as sodium. This ion – in contrast to the case with animal metabolism – plays no essential role in the metabolism of plants, but it often occurs at high concentrations as sodium chloride where plants grow. Salts found in nature (mainly NaCl and $CaSO_4$) may occur at concentrations which are either toxic, tolerated or even required as an osmoticum, and plants are accordingly referred to as **glycophytes** (non-salt plants) or **halophytes** (salt plants). In the following, stress caused by high **NaCl concentrations** will be the main topic of discussion.

The electrical conductivity (EC_e) of salts in liquid solutions is used for the standardisation of salt contents and is expressed in [Siemens (S)/m] or [mS/cm]:

$$1\,S = \frac{1}{Ohm}\,[Mho]$$

1 S/m corresponds to –0.36 MPa and the dimension Mho is the reciprocal of Ohm, the measure of electrical resistance.

The conductivity of seawater corresponds to 4.4 S/m; that of water used for irrigation must be lower than 0.2 S/m. Soils with a conductivity of >0.4 S/m are termed saline soils. The salt concentration of seawater (3%: 480 mM Na^+, 50 mM Mg^{2+} and 560 mM Cl^-) corresponds to

Table 1.6.1. Salt tolerance of important agricultural plants grown under a range of high salt concentrations. EC_e is a measure of salinity and is the electrical conductivity of the water extracted from the saturated soil solution. (After Marschner 1986)

Plant type	Maximum tolerance (EC_e in mMho/cm)	Reduction of harvest per EC_e unit above the tolerance value (%)
Barley	8.0	5.0
Sugar beet	7.0	5.9
Wheat	6.0	7.1
Soybean	5.0	20.0
Tomato	2.5	9.9
Maize	1.7	12.9
Green bean	1.0	19.0

Table 1.6.2. Yields of salt-tolerant barley plants from the gene and seed banks of the USA upon cultivation on Californian sand dunes and irrigation with seawater supplemented with phosphate and nitrogen fertilisers. (After Lüttge et al. 1994)

Barley variety	Yield (t/ha)
Standard variety on saline soil (average)	0.83
Var. XXI, 1st experiment	1.08
Var. XXI, 2nd experiment	1.50
World average on non-saline soil	2.00

an osmotic potential of –2.7 MPa. Table 1.6.1 shows the salt tolerance of various crop plants.

Irrigation water in dry areas contains between 0.1 and 1 kg mineral salts per cubic metre. While this is significantly below the damage threshold (–0.15 MPa), it can still lead to soil salinity and to the loss of useful agricultural land in a few years due to the intense evaporation.

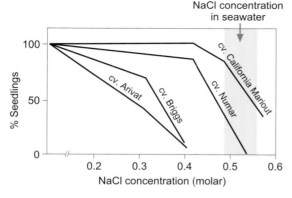

Fig. 1.6.1 Salt tolerance of various barley varieties, measured by the development of young plants on salt-containing substrates. (After Lüttge et al. 1994)

It follows from the theory that life arose in the sea that salt tolerance must have been an original characteristic of living systems; sensitivity to salt should then be seen as a loss of this original characteristic. "Regaining" salt tolerance of important crop plants is accordingly one of the most important aims of plant breeding. An example is the improvement of salt tolerance in barley (Fig. 1.6.1 and Table 1.6.2), which has per se the highest salt tolerance of all cereals (see Table 1.6.1).

1.6.1

Physiological Effects of Salt Stress (NaCl)

- Barkla BJ, Pantoja O (1996) Physiology of ion transport across the tonoplast of higher plants. Annu Rev Plant Physiol Plant Mol Biol 47:159–184

1.6.1.1
Effects on the Ion Metabolism of the Cell ("Primary Effects")

Sodium and chloride ions are regarded as being biologically aggressive osmolytes on account of their small ionic diameters and high surface charge densities and their consequent strong tendency to attract water. High concentrations of these ions in the apoplast accordingly lead to imbalances in water and ion relations. **Stress caused by salinity** is thus both **dehydration stress** and **ionic stress**. The latter rapidly leads to destruction of biomembranes, because ion imbalances result not only in altered concentration relations, but also in changes of membrane potential. Homeostatic ion concentrations, i.e. cytosolic concentrations maintained at equilibrium in glycophytes not subject to salinity stress, are in the ranges of 100–200 mM K^+, 1–10 mM Na^+ and Cl^- and 0.1–0.2 mM Ca^{2+} (Fig. 1.6.2; Niu et al. 1995).

These ion concentrations are kept constant in plant cells in the main by electrophoretic flows, i.e. passive flows which are coupled to H^+-ATPases and H^+-pyrophosphatases in the plasma membrane and the tonoplast (in contrast to animal and yeast cells, plant cells do not possess Na^+/K^+-ATPase pumps). In addition, import and

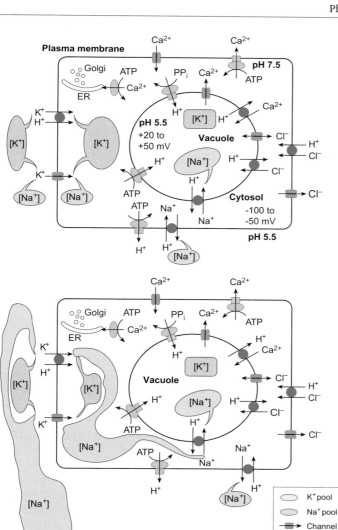

Fig. 1.6.2. Ion relations in plant cells in the non-stressed (A) and strongly salt-stressed (B) states, as well as subsequent to adaptation to high salt concentrations (C). The schematic overview incorporates all hitherto described types of transport systems that have been associated with ion homeostasis under salt stress. (After Niu et al. 1995)

Table 1.6.3. Transport systems potentially involved in ion homeostasis in the plasma membrane and the tonoplast. (After Hasegawa et al. 2000 b)

Substrate	Subcellular localisation	Direction	Source of energy or counter ion
Pumps			
H^+	Plasma membrane	Apoplast	ATP
H^+	Tonoplast	Vacuole	ATP
H^+	Tonoplast	Vacuole	PPi
Ca^{2+}	Plasma membrane	Apoplast	ATP
Ca^{2+}	Tonoplast	Vacuole	ATP
Channels			
K^+ (Na^{2+})	Plasma membrane	Cytosol	Membrane potential
K^+ (Na^{2+})	Plasma membrane	Cytosol	H^+ (symport)
K^+	Plasma membrane	Cytosol	$H^{+,}$ Na^+ (symport)
Ca^{2+}	Plasma membrane	Cytosol	Membrane potential
Ca^{2+}	Tonoplast	Cytosol	Membrane potential
Cl^- (anion)	Plasma membrane	Apoplast	Membrane potential
Cl^- (anion)	Tonoplast	Vacuole	Membrane potential
Carriers			
Na^+	Plasma membrane	Apoplast	H^+ (antiport)
Na^+	Tonoplast	Vacuole	H^+ (antiport)
Ca^{2+}	Tonoplast	Vacuole	H^+ (antiport)
Cl^- (anion)	Plasma membrane	Cytosol	H^+ (symport)
Cl^- (anion)	Tonoplast	Vacuole	H^+ (antiport)

export channels for K^+ and anions which are regulated by the membrane potential (so-called gated channels) have been described, as well as a Ca^{2+}-ATPase for Ca^{2+}. The activity of these pumps and channels results in a membrane potential of 0.2 V at the plasmalemma (the cytosolic side is negatively charged) and a tonoplast potential of between 0 and +20 mV, with the cytosolic side again being negatively charged. When the volumes of the participating apoplast, cytosol and vacuole compartments are taken into account, the membrane potentials give rise to pH gradients, whereby the normal pH value for the cytosol is always 7 and that of the apoplast and the vacuole is 1–2 units more acidic. An overview of the transport systems at present known to participate in the ion homeostasis of higher plants is given in Table 1.6.3.

High salinity places this homeostasis under considerable stress, because particularly Na^+, but also Ca^{2+}, enter passively into the cell along the concentration gradient and form large pools there. The accumulation of positive charges in the cytosol breaks down the natural barrier of the membrane potential for Cl^- and, consequently, leads to a massive influx of this anion through the anion channels.

In particular the potassium relations of the cell are threatened by high sodium concentrations. On the one hand, K^+ and Na^+ compete for the not particularly selective, but very efficient,

K^+ uptake systems. These are channels and K^+/Na^+-symporters: low affinity cation transporters, or LCTs. At high apoplastic Na^+ concentrations the potassium uptake by the cell is accordingly strongly reduced, and the cytosolic potassium pool shrinks (Fig. 1.6.2 B).

On the other hand, the flooding of the cytosol with Na^+ results in increased activity of proton pumps, especially of the plasma membrane ATPases but also of the tonoplastic Na^+/H^+ antiport system, and thus in an increase in ATP consumption.

The situation becomes further aggravated in that increased proton transport also results in changes in the intracellular pH relations. External application of NaCl at seawater concentrations results in an alkalisation of the cytosol of barley roots of between 0.5 and 1 pH unit. This alkalisation detrimentally affects the activity of various cytosolic enzymes, particularly of those of catabolic energy metabolism (Katsuhara et al. 1997).

Uptake of Na^+ into the vacuole, which effects salt removal from the cytosol, requires a Na^+/H^+ antiporter (sodium-H^+ exchange) which has been found in barley roots and beet in addition to the above-mentioned H^+-transporting system. This antiporter couples the increased proton charge of the vacuole with sodium uptake. The synthesis of this transport system can be induced by salinity stress (Fig. 1.6.2 C). The sodium and chloride concentrations in the vacuoles of salt-stressed tobacco cell cultures were eight-fold greater than those in the cytosol (Binzel et al. 1988). A consequence of this is a further alkalisation – now of the vacuole – due to the proton-sodium antiport.

Flooding of the cell with Na^+ leads finally to an increased uptake of calcium by the cell and release of Ca^{2+} from cellular compartments, and thus to an increase in the size of the cytosolic Ca^{2+} pool. Since the cytosolic pool of free Ca^{2+} has signal function, the augmentation of this pool triggers regulatory processes in the cell, which can in the main be interpreted as constituting repair or adaptation reactions. The increase in the cytosolic Ca^{2+} concentration could take place due to water potential-induced calcium uptake similar to that occurring in the stomata (see also Chap. 1.5.2.4), or upon the opening of Ca^{2+} channels in the ER or tonoplast in connection with the inositol-triphosphate system.

1.6.1.2
Secondary Damage Caused by Severe Salt Stress

Salt stress, which makes excessive demands on the cell's ability to maintain homeostasis and thus leads to increased salt concentrations in the cell, results in functional disturbances. On the one hand, processes requiring balanced water relations, such as cell elongation, react particularly sensitively. Since a great deal of energy is consumed by the strain reactions and a considerable proportion of produced photosynthate is used in the production of compatible osmolytes, **cell division growth** is also detrimentally affected due to lack of building blocks and energy.

In salt-sensitive plants, e.g. maize and beans, even relatively low internal salt concentrations result in considerable reductions in growth (see Table 1.6.1). Indeed, the constitutive types of glycophytes and halophytes introduced at the beginning of this chapter can be relatively easily identified and even further subdivided on the basis of the sensitivity of growth to salt. Most of our highly efficient crop plants are unfortunately glycophytes which exhibit significantly reduced yields at even only relatively low salt concentrations.

In addition to growth processes, **photosynthesis**, particularly that of C3 plants, is detrimen-

tally affected by elevated intracellular salt contents. Even though enzyme activities may be influenced by salt, the salt concentrations which build up in the chloroplast are usually too low to result in significant inhibition of the Calvin cycle. On the other hand, photosynthetic electron transport is impaired at even relatively low salt concentrations, whereby the nature of the detrimental effect has not yet been clarified. It is known that enhanced ROS formation takes place in the chloroplasts of plants under salt stress upon illumination (see Chap. 1.3.5). These ROS lead to damage of the photosystems, to chlorophyll degradation and, finally, to necrotic death of cells and tissues. Typical **salinity damage** symptoms become apparent (see Fig. 2.3.7 G), above all necroses at the edges of leaves and in the youngest generation of needles of conifer needles. It is interesting that the inhibition of photosynthetic CO_2 assimilation is not primarily due to an effect of salt on the opening of the stomata. The stomata remain functional even at high salinity. It must thereby be borne in mind that the damage having been caused results from NaCl taken up by the roots, in contrast to the direct effects of salt in salt sprays and splashings (e.g. at road edges) which damage old and young tissues in the same manner.

1.6.2
The Adaptive Response of the Plant Cell to Salt Stress

An osmotic stressor such as salt causes strain in plant cells, which can be interpreted as adaptation to the new osmotic conditions. Adaptation means new synthesis of proteins to alleviate the stress. In the case of osmotic stress, this alleviation comprises:

- reactions to regain ion homeostasis,
- reactions to adapt to the osmotic potential,
- synthesis of specifically acting, protective proteins.

1.6.2.1
Intracellular Signals

The adaptation commences with the perception of the osmotic stress. This has already been discussed for *Dunaliella* (see Chap. 1.1.4). Since lit-

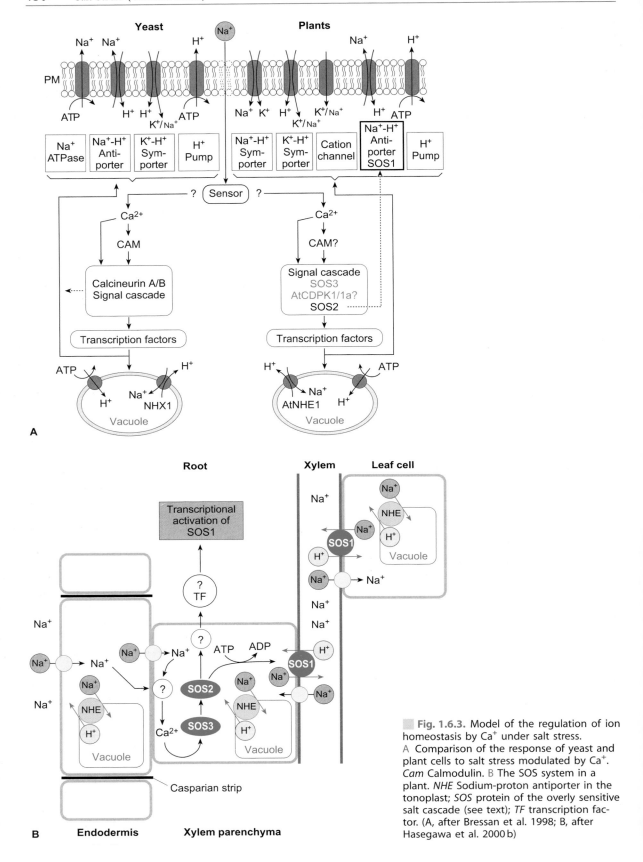

Fig. 1.6.3. Model of the regulation of ion homeostasis by Ca[+] under salt stress. A Comparison of the response of yeast and plant cells to salt stress modulated by Ca[+]. *Cam* Calmodulin. B The SOS system in a plant. *NHE* Sodium-proton antiporter in the tonoplast; *SOS* protein of the overly sensitive salt cascade (see text); *TF* transcription factor. (A, after Bressan et al. 1998; B, after Hasegawa et al. 2000b)

tle is known about osmosensors, particularly as they apply to salt stress, the next step – the genesis of the signal – will now be considered. Genes and proteins have recently been identified which point to a biochemical connection between the osmotic adaptation of the plant and an increase in the cytosolic Ca^{2+} level. Yeast has served in this regard as a model, for which it has been known for some time that there is an interaction between Ca^{2+}, the subunit B of the calcium-binding protein calcineurin and salt tolerance. In this organism the protein phosphatase calcineurin activates on the one hand transcription factors, which lead to increased expression of a plasma membrane Na^+-ATPase and a tonoplastic Na^+/H^+ antiporter. On the other hand, active calcineurin modulates a not very selective K^+/H^+ symporter in such a way that it becomes both more effective and more strongly selective for K^+ (Fig. 1.6.3 A). A gene family has been correspondingly discovered in *Arabidopsis*, a mutation in which makes plants particularly sensitive to Na^+ and also to Li^+ ("salt overly sensitive": SOS). The functions of three SOS proteins have now been elucidated: SOS1 is a Na^+-H^+ antiporter in the plasma membrane, SOS2 is a serine-threonine protein kinase which activates SOS1, and SOS3 is a calcium-binding protein with an EF-hand domain typical of such proteins, which – after being activated – itself activates SOS2 (Fig. 1.6.3 B; Hasegawa et al. 2000). In addition to the direct activation of SOS1, the SOS cascade also positively influences the activation of transcription factors and leads to increased expression of the antiporter.

Corresponding to the ways in which plant cells respond to drought, there are several parallel calcium-dependent regulatory systems which apply to NaCl stress as well. These are only understood in part, however, e.g. a protein kinase (calcium-dependent protein kinase, CDPK) involved in the expression of a LEA protein or non-stress-specific MAP kinases. It is known that certain phytohormones also act as signals.

A strongly elevated abscisic acid (ABA) level has often been determined in salt-stressed plants (Fig. 1.6.4). An enhanced formation of ethylene has also been observed, whereas the cytokinin content usually decreases.

Since salinity has an ionic as well as a dehydration component (due to the binding of water to ions) and ABA plays an important role as a phytohormonal signal during drought (see Fig. 1.5.8), it cannot be excluded that the in-

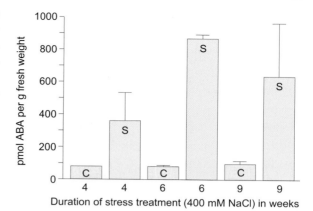

Fig. 1.6.4. Reaction of the endogenous ABA levels in leaves of *Mesembryanthemum crystallinum* to salt stress. The concentrations of the osmolytes proline, pinitol and ononitol, as well as the amounts of the CAM form of PEP carboxylase and the protective protein osmotin, increased along with the level of ABA. *C* Control (without salt); *S* 400 mM NaCl in the nutrient solution. (After Thomas and Bohnert 1993)

creased ABA level is – according to the type of plant and the conditions – related to the dehydration syndrome rather than to salt toxicity (Fig. 1.6.5).

Nevertheless, a physiological relation between an increase in the ABA level and adaptation to salt stress does exist, as shown in an experiment in which the autonomous osmotic adaptation of tobacco cultures to salt was compared with an accelerated adaptation resulting from exogenous ABA supply.

As is the case with drought stress, numerous specific proteins can be shown to be expressed upon salt stress (see Chap. 1.5.2.2); the induction paths can be ABA-dependent or ABA-independent (Jin et al. 2000). However, it is again not clear with regard to these strain reactions whether the induction is due to drought or to ion effects.

In addition to the ABA level, the level of jasmonates in the plant responds to salinity. However, the behaviour of this group of hormones is very different to that of ABA. While the concentration of ABA increases only transiently upon salt shock (transferring plants from a salt-free medium to one with an elevated NaCl content) and then falls off again (Fig. 1.6.6), the concurrent increase in jasmonate is maintained over a longer period. Jasmonate accumulates about 20-fold upon longer-term salinity stress, whereas the ABA level increases only about 4-fold. Each of the hormones, if applied externally, induces

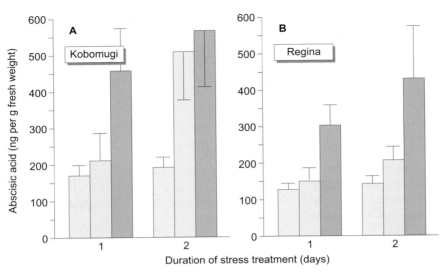

Fig. 1.6.5. The reaction of the ABA level in the leaves of two wheat varieties subjected to salt stress and to combined salt and drought stress. Control (*grey*), salt stress (200 mM, *light blue*), salt and drought (200 mM salt and 21% poly-ethyleneglycol, *blue*). (After Nagy and Galiba 1995)

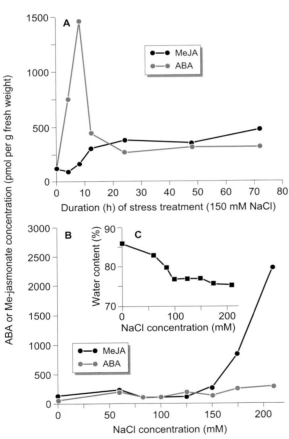

Fig. 1.6.6. Endogenous concentrations of ABA and methyl jasmonate in roots of rice plants subjected to different forms of salt stress. A "Salt shock": Transfer of seedlings from a salt-free medium to a salt-containing medium (150 mM). B ABA and methyl jasmonate contents of rice seedlings after 2 days of treatment with different salt concentrations. C Water content of the shoots after 2 days of exposure to salt stress of different intensities. (After Moons et al. 1997)

the expression of specific genes with only limited overlap. Together they tend to act antagonistically, however, with regard to gene expression (Moons et al. 1997).

1.6.2.2
Adaptation Reactions to Restore Ion Homeostasis

Glycophytes and halophytes basically make use of the same mechanisms to deal with salinity stress. Halophytes are able to adapt faster and to tolerate extreme salinity, whereas glycophytes adapt stepwise to develop tolerance to a moderate degree of salinity. In both constitutive types salt tolerance requires the expression of certain, similar genes. However, the transition from extremely salt-sensitive plants to extremely salt-tolerant plants is not clear cut, and differentiation between the two types is difficult because of the plant's ability to adapt.

Considering the many examples of salt-stressed glycophytes and halophytes having been investigated, it becomes clear that adaptation serves to regain ion homeostasis and the original membrane potentials and pH values. The better the plant is able to achieve this, the better it becomes tolerant of osmotic stress. However, regaining ion homeostasis does not signify a "return" to the original ion concentrations. Rather, the plant attempts to achieve homeostasis with the entire ionic load, including the NaCl that has been taken up (see Fig. 1.6.2 C). Depletion of the aggressive NaCl ions in the cytoplasm during adaptation requires considerable energy, which cannot be supplied with the normal provision of the cellular transport systems. Therefore, more of those proteins are synthesised which contribute either directly or indirectly to the removal of NaCl from the cytoplasm. Both the apoplast and the vacuole can be compartments for the "final" deposition.

Relief of the cytosol by removal of the Na^+ ions from the cytoplasm and their transport into the vacuole and the apoplast is effected mainly by means of Na^+/H^+ antiporters, both in the plasmalemma (e.g. in *Atriplex nummularia*; Hassidim et al. 1990; see also Chap. 1.6.2.1) and in the tonoplast (NHE, Fig. 1.6.3 B), e.g. in *Beta vulgaris* (Barkla and Blumwald 1991). These antiporters are induced by elevated cytosolic Na^+ (NaCl) concentrations and require high proton concentrations in the external medium and in the vacuole, i.e. effective H^+ pumps. These pumps are synthesised to a greater extent upon salt stress. If ion homeostasis is established, the increased expression of, e.g., the plasma membrane H^+-ATPase decreases once more. Adapted cells no longer exhibit enhanced pump activity. Figure 1.6.2 C shows the result of salt adaptation with regard to the distribution of ions. The Na^+ concentration in the cytosol has returned to the original value (Fig. 1.6.2 A), while that in the vacuole has increased many-fold. The original membrane potential and pH value have nevertheless been reestablished. Over-expression of a vacuolar Na^+/H^+ antiporter gene in *Arabidopsis* increased salt tolerance considerably (Apse et al. 1999). The K^+ status is the weak point in the cellular ion budget subsequent to an adaptation process, irrespective of ion homeostasis. The reduced growth of halophytes and glycophytes under salt stress is possibly related to the problematical provision of the cell with K^+ (see Box 1.6.1).

The effectiveness of salt elimination into the apoplast is supported, in many halophytes, by salt glands (Fig. 1.6.7), which lead to the deposition of NaCl onto the surface of the leaf, where it then crystallises. This applies particularly to some mangrove species, but also to desert plants (e.g. the genus *Reaumuria* and other Chenopodiaceae).

Other halophytes can enhance the sequestration of salt in the vacuole by developing large salt-storing mesophyll cells (**salt succulence**, Fig. 1.6.8 A) or by loading large **bladder hairs** with NaCl (Fig. 1.6.8 B). Both these excretion mechanisms are also termed **recretion**. Leaves which have accumulated high concentrations of salt are shed.

1.6.2.3
Adaptation of Osmotic Potential

Plants must possess a higher osmotic potential than their medium if they are to take up water and nutrients from a saline milieu, i.e. they must increase their own osmotic potential. It is thus inevitable that changes in their internal concentration relations must take place, something which necessitates further adaptive action. In addition to maintaining ion homeostasis, in-

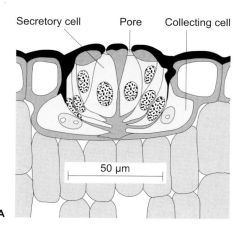

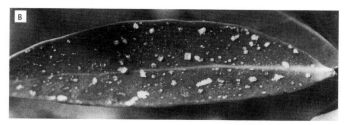

Fig. 1.6.7. Salt elimination ("recretion") via the apoplast. A Salt gland in the leaf of sea lavender (*Limonium vulgare*). B Leaf of the mangrove plant *Avicennia germinans* (*Verbenaceae*) showing salt crystals excreted via the salt glands. (Lüttge et al. 1994)

| Box 1.6.1 | Ion relations of salt-sensitive and salt-tolerant glycophytes under salt stress (after Speer and Kaiser 1991) |

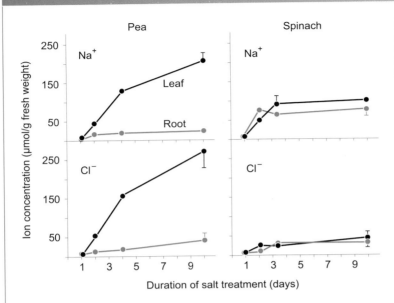

Figure. Salt content of the leaves and roots of pea and spinach plants during the course of growth on nutrient solution containing 100 mM salt for 10 days

Seedlings of pea (salt-sensitive) and spinach (salt-resistant, Chenopodiace) were transferred to nutrient solution and exposed to 100 mM NaCl. The ion concentrations of the roots and leaves (see Fig.), as well as the intercellular distribution of the ions, were monitored (see Table).

In both plants the salt concentration in the roots remains distinctly lower than the salt concentration externally applied, whereas the leaves of the salt-sensitive pea plant accumulate salt to a concentration 2.5-fold higher than that applied. In the relatively salt-resistant spinach, Na^+ accumulates in the roots and leaves up to the applied concentration, while Cl^-, as is the case with pea shoots, accumulates to only 50% of the concentration present in the medium.

It can be assumed that the ion concentrations in the cytosol are similar to those in the chloroplast, mitochondria and other organelles. Together with data from the figure, the following picture of adaptation becomes apparent:

The total ion load in the cytosol has remained the same or has even been reduced somewhat (spinach), while that in the vacuole has increased slightly. In contrast, the ion concentration has increased two- to four-fold in the apoplast, where it constitutes the least physiological inconvenience. However, the concentration relations of the individual ions have clearly been altered: The proportion of NaCl has increased drastically – with the exception of the cytoplasm – mainly to the detriment of K^+ and NO_3^-. This of course induces nutritional problems. These changes are considerably greater for pea than for spinach.

creasing the osmotic potential is the most immediate requirement for adaptation.

Halophytes make use of the available salt for this purpose (Fig. 1.6.9 A). The salt must be retained within the cell, and thus not eliminated. Figure 1.6.9 B shows that most of the salt is compartmented in the vacuole[1]. Only one fifth of the Na^+ concentration and one quarter of the Cl^- concentration present in the vacuole is found in the cytoplasm and its other organelles. Since, however, osmotic equilibrium must prevail within the symplast (protoplast), the cytosol must

---

[1] Of course, the capacity of the vacuole to store NaCl is limited. Long-term utilisation of the full capacity leads to rapid senescence of the tissue and to shedding of the leaves.

Box 1.6.1   (continued)

Table. Intracellular ion distribution and budgets in pea and spinach leaves grown without salt and after 10 days of adaptation to treatment with 100 mM NaCl. Only the most important ions are shown

Ion	Control/salt (C/S)	Pea [ion concentration (mM) in mesophyll]			Spinach [ion concentration (mM) in mesophyll]		
		Vacuole	Cytosol	Apoplast	Vacuole	Cytosol	Apoplast
K^+	C	104±23	53±5	13±4	260±31	147±25	10±4
	S	42±12	29±17	14±4	172±33	78±18	18±4
Na^+	C	3±1	19±4	1.5±1	0.5±0.1	26±16	1±1
	S	114±7	60±19	50±16	109±15	43±15	6±1
Mg^{2+}	C	12±3	6±2	4±2	37±6	17±6	2±1
	S	6.5±1	4±3	2±1	29±5	15±7	3±1
Cl^-	C	4±1	5±3	6±2	1±1	6±5	4±1
	S	245±34	60±35	89±67	50±5	9±4	14±6
NO_3^-	C	33±15	6±2	2.1±1.1	29±13	10±6	5±1
	S	0	1±1	0	19±8	4±1	6.6±5
$\Sigma_{cations}$	C	131	84	22.5	334.5	207	15
	S	169	97	68	339	151	30
Σ_{anions}	C	289	55	20	73	88	13
	S	292	77	96	106	53	26

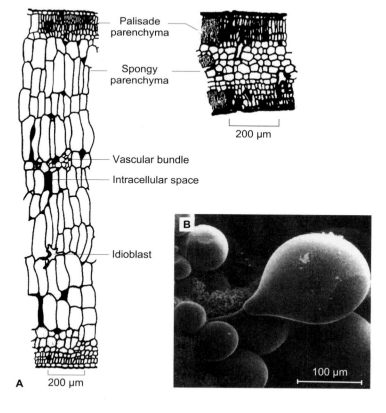

Palisade parenchyma

Spongy parenchyma

200 µm

Vascular bundle

Intracellular space

Idioblast

B

100 µm

A   200 µm

Fig. 1.6.8. Sequestration of salt in the vacuole. A Salt succulence in mangrove plants: development of salt-storage tissue from the spongy mesophyll of the leaves. *Right* Young leaf with still small, isodiametrical spongy parenchyma cells. *Left* Cross section of a fully grown leaf with large, elongated spongy parenchyma cells, in the vacuoles of which salt is deposited. The stone cell-like idioblast serves to stiffen the tissue. B "Bladder hairs" of the halophyte *Atriplex hymenelytra* (Chenopodiaceae). The salt is sequestered in the large vacuoles of the numerous bladder hairs and is thereby removed from the mesophyll. (A, after Larcher 1994; B, from Lüttge et al. 1994)

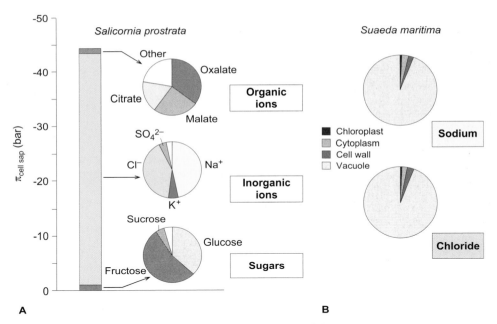

Fig. 1.6.9. A Osmotic potential of the cell sap of leaves of the halophyte *Salicornia prostrata* (Chenopodiaceae) with the components specified in the segments of the pie charts. B Intracellular distribution of the salt ions present in the leaves of the halophyte *Suaeda maritima* (Chenopodiaceae). (Larcher 1994)

have the same osmolarity as the vacuole. This is achieved in that the cell enriches the cytoplasm with compatible organic osmolytes. The adjustment of the osmotic potential of the cytoplasm by means of low molecular weight organic compounds is not as costly as it might appear at first sight. The volume of this compartment (with all its constituent organelles) is usually less than 10% of the volume of the vacuole, so that the required osmolarity is effected with a relatively small amount of solutes. The chemical nature of the organic osmolytes is discussed in the following section.

Compatible Solutes, Osmolytes
Salt adaptation is the classical field of osmolyte research, which has already been briefly considered in relation to dehydration stress (Chap. 1.5.2.2) and will be discussed in more detail here.

Stress osmolytes have two coupled functions:

1. Increasing the osmotic potential ("osmolyte") and thus the retention of water in the cytoplasm;
2. Multiple protective functions:
   - to maintain the integrity of membranes and proteins (dilution and displacement of aggressive ions from the surfaces),
   - to scavenge ROS, which are in general formed to an increased extent under stress, including salt stress.

Several groups of low molecular weight organic compounds, which belong to the carbohydrates and amino compounds, fulfil these functions (see Chap. 1.5.2.6, Fig. 1.5.11). In the following, the various osmolytes are discussed individually:

1. glycerol
2. polyols
3. proline
4. QACs and TSCs

1. Glycerol
The simplest osmolyte is **glycerol**. The green alga *Dunaliella*, which does not have a cell wall (see Chap. 1.1.4), adjusts to salt stress in the cytoplasm by rapid synthesis of glycerol. In this instance it is a predominantly osmotic phenomenon, as a cell without a cell wall is, of course, particularly endangered by changes in the osmotic potential of the medium. *Dunaliella* also responds with glycerol synthesis if the osmotic stress is artificially generated by polyols (Zelazny et al. 1995).

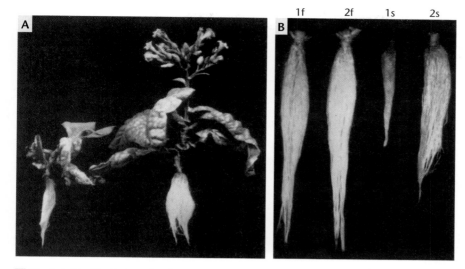

Fig. 1.6.10. Alleviation of salinity stress by constitutive expression of mannitol-1-phosphate dehydrogenase in transformed tobacco. The transformed plants synthesise and accumulate the osmolyte mannitol. A Control plants (*left*) and transformed plants (*right*) after 30 days of growth in nutrient solution containing 250 mM NaCl. B Roots of control (*1*) and transformed (*2*) plants in salt-free (*f*) and salt-containing (*s*) nutrient solution after 30 days of growth. (Tarczynski et al. 1993)

2. Polyols

The second important subgroup of carbohydrates is composed of **polyols** (sugar derivatives). Their numerous hydroxyl groups bestow these compounds with hydrophilic properties, i.e. properties which closely approximate those of water clusters. Many algae of brackish water synthesise polyols rapidly and effectively as reduced derivates of monosaccharides in response to osmotic stress; they possess the corresponding dehydrogenases.

The **manna** of the Bible could well have been a polyol produced by desert plants (Crum 1993). Since the synthesis of these sugar alcohols requires only a single enzyme – a dehydrogenase which reduces the corresponding sugar – the sugar alcohols can easily be made use of to artificially enhance salt tolerance. Figure 1.6.10 shows the effect of the constitutive expression of mannitol in tobacco plants transformed with mannose dehydrogenase under the control of the S35 promotor. The mannitol accumulates, because wild-type tobacco plants do not produce the polyol and cannot further metabolise it when it is synthesised. Despite the carbohydrate expenditure required to produce this osmolyte, the transgenic tobacco plant does not grow notably more poorly than does the wild type in the absence of salt stress, but it does grow considerably better when stressed with salt.

Open-chain polyols occur in many plants, but they are more frequently found in glycophytes (e.g. in many Rosaceae) than in halophytes.

In addition to their osmotic effect, glycerol and open-chain sugar alcohols also provide protection against ROS when they accumulate (see Chap. 1.3.5). The reduction of monosaccharides (glyceraldehyde-3-phosphate and mannose- or fructose-6-phosphate) to their corresponding sugar alcohols requires reduction equivalents, i.e. electrons, which could also be transferred to oxygen under appropriate circumstances and would then contribute to the formation of ROS. Glycerol is a far more favourable osmolyte than a hexose in terms of the carbohydrate-to-hydrogen consumption rate. Transgenic organisms producing glycerol as an osmolyte thus show better growth than those making use of equiosmolar concentrations of higher sugar alcohols (Shen et al. 1999).

Cyclic sugar alcohols, so-called **inositols** or **cyclitols**, are very often accumulated as osmolytes in halophytes. They have the cell biological advantage over open-chain polyols in turning over slowly, i.e. they are withheld from rapid metabolism under deficiency situations (e.g. when photosynthesis is severely restricted because of stomatal closure) and are thus retained to function osmotically. Their biosynthesis originates from glucose-6-phosphate, and the great

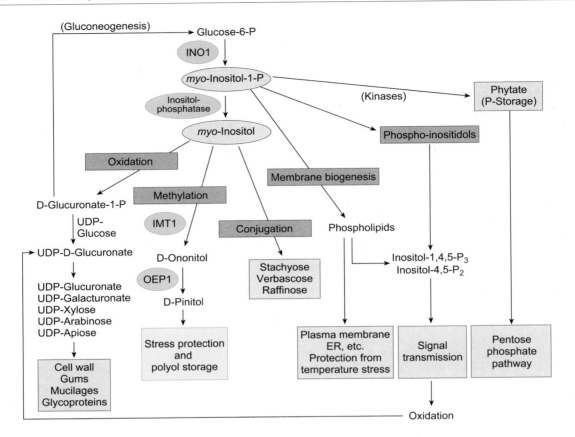

A

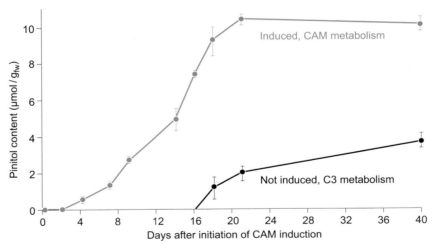

B

Fig. 1.6.11. A The physiological functions of *myo*-inositol and its derivates in plant cells (after Bohnert et al. 1995). B Pinitol accumulation during the induction of CAM in *Mesembryanthemum crystallinum* by irrigation with 400 mM NaCl solution. On day 21 the share of D-pinitol of the soluble carbohydrate fraction was 71% in the salt-treated plants and only 5% in the control plants. The experiment shows that a slight amount of pinitol synthesis also takes place in plants not subjected to salinity stress. (After Paul and Cockburn 1989)

Table 1.6.4. Contents of osmolytes in leaves of 6-week-old transgenic tobacco plants after 2 weeks of drought. The plants had been transformed with the gene for inositol methyltransferase from *Mesembryanthemum crystallinum*. (After Sheveleva et al. 1997)

Osmolyte	Leaf 11		Leaf 7	
	Day (µmol/g FW)	Night (% of value during the day)	Day (µmol/g FW)	Night (% of value during the day)
Proline	4.2	39	1.6	17
Glucose	7.0	7	5.7	25
Fructose	7.6	5	15.7	27
Sucrose	8.4	19	6.8	12
K$^+$	352	79	236	72
Na$^+$	24	113	11.1	96
Cl$^-$	200	91	129	88
myo-Inositol	6.4	137	3.8	88
Ononitol	34.6	89	25.8	77

variety of these cyclitols is synthesised by means of relatively few biochemical reactions (Box 1.6.2). As is shown in Fig. 1.6.11, inositol metabolism is linked with many cellular functions. The metabolically centrally placed *myo*-inositol is not accumulated as an osmolyte, but its metabolically inactive methyl derivatives are. Well known in this regard are mangroves, which accumulate above all bornesitol, pinitol and quebrachitol in their leaves (Popp and Smirnoff 1995).

In the facultative CAM plant *Mesembryanthemum crystallinum*, the gene for inositol methyltransferase is activated primarily by salinity and cold. Salinity additionally induces the transition from C3 to CAM metabolism. In this process the expression of inositol methyltransferase is induced in the leaves, and the synthesis of the key enzyme for inositol biosynthesis – inositol-1-phosphate synthase – is intensified coordinately (Nelson et al. 1998). D-Ononitol and D-pinitol thus accumulate in *Mesembryanthemum* during salt stress (and drought) (Fig. 1.6.11 B). The synthesis of the latter compound requires a further epimerase (OEP1), which transforms D-ononitol into D-pinitol (Box 1.6.2). At the same time, the osmolyte proline accumulates ten-fold. The induction of CAM and the accumulation of proline are both independent of ABA.

The induction of CAM and the production of osmolytes are not, however, obligately coupled in *Mesembryanthemum*: In young plants, which do not yet possess sufficiently large cells (vacuoles to store malic acid), CAM cannot be induced, or only to a small extent. Full CAM induction is only possible in plants older than 5 weeks. Younger plants are, however, able to activate specific protective measures under salt stress (polyol accumulation, regulation of ion homeostasis, facilitated water uptake).

Considering the many ways in which cyclitols are incorporated into cell metabolism, it is difficult to ascribe a particular protective function to them. Whereas concentrations of metabolically active sugars (and also of proline) vary markedly between day and night, the concentrations of the cyclitols (and of the ionic osmolytes) remains largely constant during the day-night cycle (Table 1.6.4). This demonstrates, on the one hand, the sluggish metabolism of the methylated cyclitols, but this is also understandable in a cell biology context, as the osmotic stress is not subjected to day–night cycles either. The cyclitols are most probably also ROS scavengers (Smirnoff and Cumbes 1989).

3. Proline

In addition to methylated cyclitols, the amino acid L-proline (Box 1.6.3) accumulates during salt stress in a similarly ABA-independent manner. Proline is regarded as a general stress metabolite and accumulates at up to enormous concentrations in a great variety of stress situations, particularly also in relation to water deficiency. Proline is produced by microorganisms and green plants in different ways (see Box 1.5.5). *E. coli* synthesises proline from glutamate via glutamate-γ-semialdehyde and Δ^1-pyrroline-5-carboxylate. In eukaryotes, proline may also be formed from ornithine by δ-transamination. Upon osmotic stress, however, the activity of Δ^1-pyrroline-5-carboxylate synthetase (P5CS) increases, so that the

Box 1.6.2   Metabolism of *myo*-inositol

myo-Inositol is shown with its natural isomers; the formation of further inositols by methylation is indicated by *blue arrows* (methyltransferases, e.g. inositol methyltrans- ferase 1, IMT1) and that by epimerisation is shown by *grey arrows* (e.g. ononitol epimerase 1, OEP1). The *grey boxes* show the site of epimerisation. (After Kindl 1994)

prokaryote pathway then dominates in all organisms (Delauney et al. 1993).

The endogenous proline level in tobacco (a glycophyte)[2] was drastically increased by the over-expression of Δ^1-pyrroline-5-carboxylate synthetase (P5CS; Fig. 1.6.12). Both the wild type and plants transformed with the plasmid pBI121 lacking the P5CS gene served as controls in these experiments. As shown in Fig. 1.6.12 A, B, proline synthesis was controlled by the availability of both water and – obviously – nitrogen. The proline level rose distinctly in the P5CS transformants upon water stress; however, the observed concentration of 6 mg Pro/g FW (~0.6%) was still far below that usually exhibited by salt plants. The osmotic potential thus did not differ from that of the wild-type. The osmotic potential of the wild-type and of the control transformant increased under salt stress (Fig. 1.6.12 A), but not that of the plant transformed with P5CS. This is because the P5CS transformant has a distinctly better developed root system[3]. In this case the stress-alleviating effect (Fig. 1.6.12 C–F) could indeed be traced to the accumulation of an osmolyte, namely proline, while in most wild plants other osmolytes accumulate in addition to proline (see Box 1.6.3).

4. QACs and TSCs

The last group of low molecular mass osmolytes to be discussed are the quaternary ammonium compounds (QACs) and tertiary sulfonium com-

---

[2] The fact that transgenic tobacco is used in so many experiments is not due to molecular geneticists being smokers, but is based on the ease with which tobacco can be genetically transformed!

[3] The reason for the better root growth is not known.

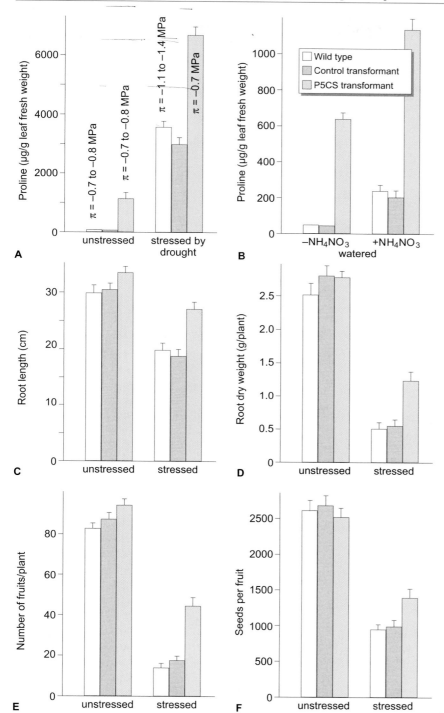

Fig. 1.6.12. Proline as an osmolyte. Tobacco plants were transformed by over-expression of Δ^1-pyrroline-5-carboxylate synthetase and thereby made less sensitive to osmotic stress. A Increase in the proline level in the leaves. B Dependence of the over-production of proline on the nitrogen supply to the tobacco plants. C–F Morphometric data for the wild-type and the transformants upon cultivation without stress and under salinity stress (500 mM NaCl). (After Kavi Kishor et al. 1995)

Box 1.6.3   How does proline function, and why is this particular amino acid suitable for stress amelioration?

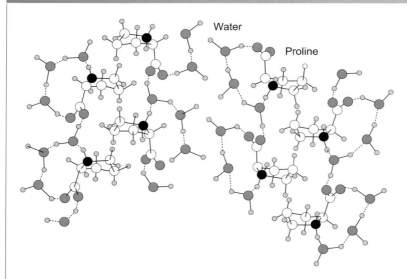

Fig. 1. Molecular model of an aqueous solution of proline. Both the water and the proline molecules form clusters. (After Schobert and Tschesche 1978)

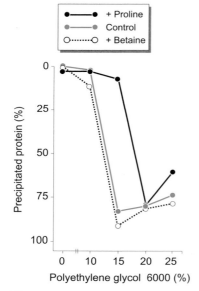

Fig. 2. Reduced precipitability of proteins due to water removal by polyethylene glycol in the presence of proline. (After Schobert and Tschesche 1978)

hydrophobic interactions between the rings. The amphiphilic Pro-multimers attach themselves readily to poorly soluble proteins, with the hydrophobic side to the protein surface and the hydrophilic side facing outwards, thus increasing the hydrophilic surface of the proteins. Pro accordingly works against the unfolding and denaturation of proteins which result from water removal, e.g. during salting-out by ammonium sulfate or precipitation with ethanol or polyethylene glycol (Fig. 2). It is interesting that another group of osmolytes, the betaines, does not work at all in this manner. It appears that there is something akin to a specificity for osmolytes, as if the individual classes of osmolytes have particular target structures and target molecules in the cell. This would also explain the parallel appearance of several different osmolytes in a single organism. Unfortunately, our knowledge in this regard is still extremely incomplete. Rice seedlings produce a large number of compatible solutes under salt stress, including many carbohydrates. It was thereby observed that Pro does not, e.g., protect against secondary oxidative stress (measured as chlorophyll bleaching), whereas trehalose effectively reduces this stress, as does also, e.g., mannitol and perhaps also cyclitols. Pro has no protective effect in these plants, at least not at low concentrations.

Proline (Pro) is a special amino acid which, due to its chemical structure, shows unusual properties in aqueous solution. It has the highest solubility of all the proteinogenic amino acids, but at higher concentrations it forms clusters which aggregate via hydrogen bonds between the hydrophilic side chains (Fig. 1). These clusters are strengthened by

Biosynthesis pathway	Enzymes

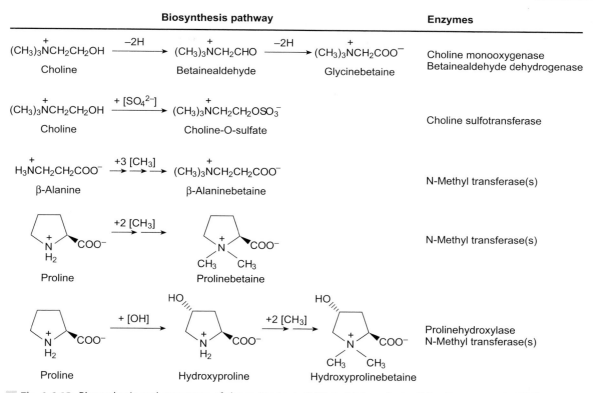

Fig. 1.6.13. Biosynthesis and structures of the zwitterionic QACs in higher plants. (After Hanson et al. 1994)

pounds (TSCs). These compounds are regularly found at high concentrations (>5 μmol/g dry weight; Rhodes and Hanson 1993) in halotolerant representatives of the Chenopodiaceae, the Poaceae and the Asteraceae, as well as in some halophilic genera of the Convolvulaceae and the Plumbaginaceae. They occur in heavy metal-tolerant species, too, and are by no means restricted to plants alone; bacteria, cyanobacteria and animals are also capable of producing these substances. A selection of these osmolytes has already been briefly referred to (see Chap. 1.5.2.6, Fig. 1.5.11).

The biosynthetic pathways leading to these compounds are now known (Fig. 1.6.13), and the corresponding genes have largely been cloned. **Glycine betaine**, the simplest representative of this family of substances, is not formed – as one might assume – by the methylation of glycine, but rather by the oxidation of choline by means of a ferredoxin-dependent monooxygenase. *β*-Alanine betaine, proline betaine and hydroxyproline betaine are, however, indeed formed by the transfer of a methyl group from *S*-adenosyl methionine. These osmolytes are zwitterionic, i.e. they have a cationic as well as an anionic centre.

It has been shown in the example of the salt-tolerant Plumbaginaceae that individual plants can synthesise and accumulate various species of these zwitterionic osmolytes. All accumulate **choline sulfate** and – with the exception of the mangrove *Aegialitis* – at least one betaine, some species even several. Since the mangrove plant *Aegialitis* actively secretes salt, it is probably less dependent on osmolytes and therefore produces only choline sulfate. For most representatives of the family, the stress consists of salinity and drought, and is sometimes compounded by oxygen deficiency due to the presence of salt crusts. Although there is no direct relationship between stressor combinations resulting from particular habitats and preferentially accumulated osmolytes, there appears to be a vague coincidence of choline sulfate and its derivative glycine betaine with drought stress, and of alanine betaine with salt stress (Hanson et al. 1994).

In addition to its osmotic function, choline sulfate undoubtedly also plays a role in the disposal of sulfate, which is important at marine sites. This is because sulfate cannot be excreted via the epidermal salt glands.

Table 1.6.5 A. Composition of the sap of maize leaves of the glycine betaine-producing line *Bet1/Bet1* and the *bet1/bet1* line lacking glycine betaine. The plants were grown on a defined soil mixture and watered with an inorganic nutrient solution. The salt treatment took place 3 weeks after sowing by means of a gradual adaptation from 42.5 to 127.5 mM NaCl during the course of 4 weeks. (After Saneoka et al. 1995)

Conditions of growth	Genotype	Organic solutes (mM)			Ions (mM)					
		Betaine	Amino acids	Sugars	K^+	Na^+	Ca^{2+}	Mg^{2+}	Cl^-	NO_3^-
NaCl-free	*bet1/bet1*	0.2	17.0	156.9	97	0.2	11.2	13.5	48.3	54.7
	Bet1/Bet1	3.2	21.0	149.5	102	0.2	11.4	14.0	43.9	46.8
With NaCl	*bet1/bet1*	0.2	22.4	88.1	112	13.3	13.0	13.0	194	32.7
	Bet1/Bet1	10.9	23.4	110.9	120	13.6	14.4	14.4	231	24.0

Table 1.6.5 B. Growth rates of the lines *bet1/bet1* and *Bet1/Bet1* under salt-free and saline conditions. Plants were grown as specified in Table 1.6.5 A; the salt treatment commenced 30 days after sowing. (After Saneoka et al. 1995)

Growth conditions	Genotype	Leaf growth rate (cm²/day) after salt application			
		Days 5–10	Days 10–15	Days 15–20	Days 20–25
NaCl-free	*bet1/bet1*	289	268	233	175
	Bet1/Bet1	260	260	224	184
With NaCl	*bet1/bet1*	207	168	82	84
	Bet1/Bet1	218	190	121	121

Since glycine betaine has long been thought to be an efficient osmolyte, efforts have been made to develop lines of crop plants which produce large amounts of this compound upon salt stress by classical breeding. This has been achieved with maize: The sister lines *Bet1/Bet1* are glycine betaine producers, the homozygotic *bet1/bet1* are glycine betaine-deficient.

Table 1.6.5 A shows the enhanced glycine betaine accumulation of the *Bet1/Bet1* maize, particularly in relation to salt stress; the contents of Na^+ and particularly Cl^- are also distinctly higher on salt. The decrease in the concentration of carbohydrates in the expressed sap of the leaves (which is much higher than that of glycine betaine) correlates with the increase in the glycine betaine concentration. Presumably some of the carbohydrate carbon was used for the synthesis of the physiologically superior osmolyte glycine betaine.

Salt inhibits growth, but in this regard *Bet1/Bet1* is seen to suffer considerably less (i.e. it exhibits better leaf growth) than does *bet1/bet1* under salt stress (Table 1.6.5 B). The less impaired growth correlates with an at least partial maintenance of cell turgor under salt stress (0.06 MPa in *bet1/bet1* and 0.2 MPa in *Bet1/Bet1*; Saneoka et al. 1995).

Glycine betaine accumulates particularly in young tissues, where it competes with NaCl and somewhat reduces the content of the salt. There is, however, no indication that glycine betaine is transported within the plant. It evidently is stored at the site at which it is produced from choline (Nakamura et al. 1996).

Because glycine betaine ameliorates stress and plants are evidently unable to metabolise this compound and thus accumulate it, attempts have long since been made to transform crop plants lacking glycine betaine with the key gene encoding choline monooxygenase (CMO), which is required for glycine betaine synthesis. This is difficult in that this enzyme contains a Rieske-[2Fe-2S]-centre. Since glycine betaine synthesis takes place in the chloroplast, it must also be taken into consideration that the recombinant protein (CMO) would have to be transported into the chloroplasts. Such a transformation has recently been successful with tobacco (Nuccio et al. 1998). Accumulation of glycine betaine was, however, only weakly pronounced, because tobacco produces choline – the starting compound for glycine betaine synthesis – only in very small amounts (McNeil et al. 1999).

What Is the Special Protective Effect of QACs?
Transformation of the cyanobacterium *Synechococcus* with an *E. coli* glycine betaine synthesis cassette consisting of choline monooxygenase, betaine aldehyde dehydrogenase, a choline

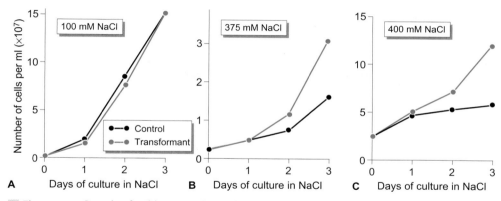

Fig. 1.6.14. Growth of wild-type and transformed *Synechococcus* cells under salinity stress. The cells were grown in choline-containing medium which was supplemented with NaCl at the indicated concentrations after 2 days (time 0 in the graph). The transformants contained the glycine betaine cassette. The glycine betaine concentration in the cells stressed with the higher NaCl concentrations was about 15 times higher than in the unstressed cells. (After Nomura et al. 1995)

Table 1.6.6. Effect of salinity on the photosynthetic electron transport of glycine betaine-accumulating *Synechococcus* cells (transformants) and non-accumulating *Synechococcus* (control) cells. $DADH_2$ reduced 2,3,5,6-tetramethylphenylenedia-mine; *MV* methyl viologen; *PBQ* phenyl-1,4-benzoquinone. The reaction of photosystem I consumes (reduces) O_2 and that of photosystem II produces O_2. (After Nomura et al. 1995)

Reaction	O_2 production or uptake (µmol/mg Chl×h)			
	Synechococcus control cells		*Synechococcus* transformants	
	−NaCl	+200 mM NaCl	−NaCl	+200 mM NaCl
$H_2O \rightarrow CO_2$	57	40	52	39
PS I ($DADH_2 \rightarrow MV$)	−152	−96	−217	−177
PS II ($H_2O \rightarrow PBQ$)	71	60	78	77

transport protein and a regulatory protein led to glycine betaine accumulation in the transformants, in particular under high salt stress. These cells grew significantly better under salt stress than did control cells, although their growth was distinctly slower than at low salt stress (Fig. 1.6.14).

The reason for the improved growth is that the photosynthetic electron transport is less impaired by salt in the glycine betaine-containing cells (Table 1.6.6). Glycine betaine is synthesised in the chloroplast and performs its protective function principally in this organelle, where it appears to stabilise mainly the protein complexes of the photosynthetic membrane (Papageorgiou and Murata 1995). In this it differs markedly from the osmolyte glycerol, which has no stabilising effect on the protein complexes. Betaines are so-called **chaotropic compounds**, i.e. zwitterions, which counteract effects caused by ionic forces. They develop their maximum protective effect specifically at those sites where

complexes or subunits of proteins threaten to dissociate as a result of salt stress.

DMSP (3-Dimethyl Sulfoniopropionate)

Less is known about TSCs than about QACs. The best-known osmolyte of this group is dimethyl sulfoniopropionate (DMPS), which has been found mainly in algae, but it has also been recently found in certain grasses and Compositae[4]. The starting material for the synthesis of DMSP is the amino acid methionine, which is metabolised to DMSP in marine algae and terrestrial plants according to different pathways. Since the starting compound and the end product are the same in each case, the pathways differ in principle only in the sequence of the individual steps involved (removal of the amino group, addition of a methyl group, decarboxyla-

[4] DMSP is the biogenetic precursor of the atmospheric trace gas dimethyl sulfide, which is released above all by algae.

tion). The various groups of land plants do synthesise DMSP in different ways, however, whereby they all require betaine aldehyde dehydrogenase for the last enzymatic step.

1.6.2.4
Induction of Protective Proteins by Salt Stress

The previous sections have made it clear that salt stress triggers numerous cellular reactions which are all interrelated and complement each other synergistically.

These reactions also include the synthesis of more or less specific protective proteins (Fig. 1.6.15). These may be, on the one hand, osmolyte-producing enzymes or, on the other, proteins from the LEA group (see Chap. 1.5.2.5) which ameliorate the dehydration stress triggered by high salt impact. In addition to these rather specifically acting proteins, another group of polypeptides is formed and accumulated during salinity stress whose function in relation to the stressor salt is not evident. This group includes both proteins which are also often formed during pathogen attacks and proteins of the cell wall and extracellular matrix.

The great variety of proteins which are synthesised and in some cases also strongly accumulated due to the effect of salt makes it difficult to assign the proteins to particular stress responses. The fact that LEA proteins are typical dehydration protection proteins (see Chap. 1.5.2.5) of course does not mean that they specifically ameliorate only the dehydration stress component of salinity.

One explanation for the occurrence of proteins which are not specific for salt stress in organisms subjected to salinity stems from the signal compounds leading to the strain resulting from salinity (see Chap. 1.6.2.1). Salt stress leads to an increase in the levels of ABA and jasmonate in the cell. ABA mediates the linkage of the responses of the cell to salt stress and drought. This stress response is carried over into the responses to stress caused by wounding or pathogen attack via the jasmonates (see Chaps. 1.10.1 and 1.10.2). However, a NaCl-dependent gene expression has been observed which can be assigned to neither ABA, nor jasmonate, nor the ethylene which is occasionally detected in connection with salt stress. This corresponds to the circumstances during drought stress which were described earlier (see Chap. 1.5.2.3).

Osmotins

Osmotins are proteins which accumulate in cells under salt stress and may constitute, e.g. in tobacco cell cultures, up to 12% of the total protein content. To the extent to which their expression is induced via ABA, they can also be synthesised and accumulated under drought conditions (Singh et al. 1989). If their expression is regulated via the jasmonate signal, they are also found upon pathogen attack. Although they were discovered during investigation of the cellular reaction to salt stress and were accordingly termed osmotins, these proteins are not specific for salt stress. Nowadays, they are rather classified as pathogen-related proteins (see Chap. 1.10.2) and referred to as osmotin-like proteins (OLPs), which are products of a multigene family.

Osmotins are relatively small proteins (M_r between 24 and 50 kDa) which are conspicuous in terms of their alkaline isoelectric point (Table 1.6.7). They have a net positive charge at the pH values of the cell, i.e. they are cations. As such, they are probably able to interact efficiently with most anionic membrane proteins (Kononowicz et al. 1993). They possess a large number of disulfide bridges, but no free SH groups (Zhu et al. 1995).

Several osmotins have been found in each of the plants that have been subjected to detailed study; they differ not so much in their molecular mass as in their isoelectric points and other protein characteristics. For tobacco, the best-studied species, a pre-protein has been discovered in addition to the mature protein, from which it could be concluded that mature osmo-

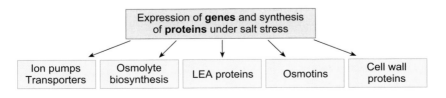

Fig. 1.6.15. The various groups of proteins induced by salinity stress

Table 1.6.7. Characterisation of osmotin and some related proteins ("OLPS"). a: known from the cDNA; b: probably targeted to the vacuole. (From various publications, above all Singh et al. 1989)

Type/constitutive type/ protein designation	Molecular mass (M$_r$) kDa	Isoelectric point	Expression	Characteristics
Atripex nummularia/halophyte				
pA8	23.8	8.3	Constitutive and ABA-controlled	a
pA9	23.8	6.9	NaCl-inducible, ABA-independent	a
Tobacco/glycophyte				
Pre-osmotin	28.5		ABA-, jasmonate-, and NaCl-inducible	Signal peptide present, soluble, protease-sensitive, probably ubiquitous in the cell
Osmotin I	26.0	7.8		
Osmotin II		8.2		Vacuolar inclusion bodies, protease resistant
Potato (*S. comersonii*)/glycophyte				
pA13	26.7	6.7	ABA-, cold-, NaCl-, wounding-, and infection-inducible	a, b
pA35	26.7	5.7	ABA-, cold-, NaCl-, wounding-, and infection-inducible	a, b
pA81	27.5	8.0	ABA-, cold-, NaCl-, wounding-, and infection-, inducible	a, b
Tomato/glycophyte				
Osmotin 24	24.0		Constitutive, ABA-controlled	
Osmotin 26	26.0		NaCl-inducible	
Thaumatococcus daniellii/glycophyte				
Thaumatin I and II	22.1	12.0		Weight for weight 3000 times sweeter than sucrose
Maize/glycophyte				
α-Amylase/trypsin inhibitor	22.1		Inducible by infection and wounding	

tins occur in specific compartments. However, the sequence which is considered to represent a signal peptide gives no indication as to the compartment to which the protein is targeted.

In tobacco cells, osmotin is found in a soluble form (osmotin I) and an insoluble form (osmotin II), the latter in the form of inclusion bodies in the vacuole. Because both forms react with the same antibody, it is presumed that osmotin II is an aggregation product of osmotin I (Singh et al. 1989).

It is striking that there is a high degree of homology between the amino acid sequences of the osmotins and of proteins involved in defence against plant pathogens (the so-called PR proteins: see Chap. 1.10.12) or of proteins that can be induced by wounding (e.g. the inhibitor of animal α-amylase and of the trypsin of maize and other cereals). Although these proteins do not interact with antibodies against osmotins, much speaks for including them in the family of the osmotins (therefore the term OLPs, see above). It is particularly noteworthy that they

are similar to **thaumatin**, a related protein from the East African plant *Thaumatococcus daniellii* (Marantacae) which tastes 100,000 times sweeter than sucrose on a molar basis. This protein has an extremely alkaline isoelectric point (IEP) on account of its particularly high content of basic amino acids. The secondary structure of thaumatin is known (de Vos et al. 1985), and it is thought that osmotins have a similar hydrophobic barrel structure of antiparallel pleated sheets with projecting hydrophilic loops. An interaction with biomembranes might be initiated via these loops (see below). At any rate, however, no other osmotins have any taste.

Expression of Osmotins

An increase in endogenous ABA concentration or an application of ABA stimulates adaptation to salinity and promotes the expression of osmotins. In most cases, however, it becomes apparent that osmotin synthesis is not exclusively, but only partly under the control of ABA, and that salt and ABA contribute synergistically to

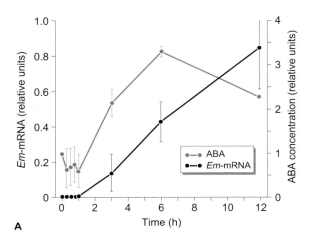

A

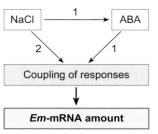

Fig. 1.6.17. Model of the interaction between NaCl and ABA in the induction of Em expression in suspension culture cells of rice. Salt can effect induction of the LEA gene Em via ABA (route 1) or directly, i.e. independently of ABA (route 2). Both routes converge on a common intermediate where they interact and lead to enhanced expression of the mRNA. (Bostock and Quatrano 1992)

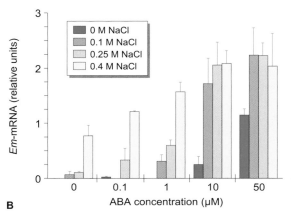

B

Fig. 1.6.16. A Kinetics of ABA accumulation and Em transcript enrichment after treatment of rice suspension culture cells with 400 mM NaCl. The ABA content at time 0 was 0.79±0.27 nmol/g dry weight. B Interaction between externally applied ABA and NaCl in the induction of Em expression in suspension culture cells of rice. The cell cultures were simultaneously inoculated with ABA and NaCl and harvested after 24 h. Em is one of the LEA proteins of rice. (After Bostock and Quatrano 1992)

the expression of osmotin mRNA (Grillo et al. 1995).

Salt is therefore required for the maximum expression of osmotin genes, and the accumulation of osmotins upon salt stress, too, requires a high osmotic potential. Osmotin synthesis evidently does not take place only under the transcriptional control of ABA and salt, but is also under the translational or post-translational control of both or one of these factors (La Rosa et al. 1992). The result is an increase in sensitivity towards ABA due to NaCl (see also Fig. 1.6.16).

Gene fusion products of the osmotin promoter and a reporter gene (GUS) have been used to study the spatial and temporal expression patterns of osmotins in the plant as well as the sensitivity of the promoter to the various types of stress. The region of the promotor which is responsive to ABA, ethylene, viral infections, salt, drought, UV, wounding, and fungal infections is quite large (~1100 base pairs); the minimum region required for the ABA effect is considerably smaller (the so-called fragment A of base pairs −248 to −108; Liu et al. 1995). The expression of the osmotin gene can be clearly separated from the accumulation of the protein itself. The latter can only be detected upon salt stress or fungal infection.

Corresponding to its stimulation by ABA, the osmotin gene is expressed in all situations in which drought results in an elevated ABA level: During the ripening of pollen grains, during the drying of seed pods, during the senescence of flowers, and in senescing leaves. An accumulation of osmotin does not take place in these cases, however. Osmotin does accumulate though during salt stress, particularly in the elongation zone of the root, in old leaves, in the xylem parenchyma of the shoot, and in the epidermis (Kononowicz et al. 1993).

Salt induces the expression of other protective proteins in addition to osmotins; best known are the **LEA proteins** and how these work. The expression of these proteins is partly dependent on ABA (see Chap. 1.5.2.2), but exhibits – as is the case with osmotin – at least one additional inducer, namely salt (see Figs. 1.6.16 and 1.6.17).

Induction by salt may be mediated via the "stress hormone" jasmonate in certain cases. Jasmonates induce the expression of many proteins with protective effects, amongst them os-

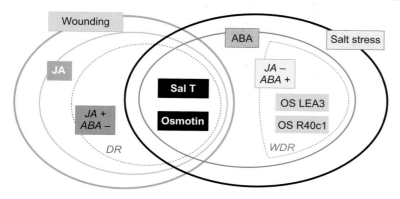

Fig. 1.6.18. Model of the effects of jasmonate and ABA on the expression of genes which are induced by salt stress. *ABA, JA* Gene expression influenced by ABA or JA or both; *JA+/ABA–* and *JA–/ABA+* antagonistic effects of JA and ABA. *Overlap* Synergistic effects; *WDR* water deficit response; *DR* defence response. *Sal T*, osmotin, *OS LEA3* and *OS R40c1*: genes. (After Moons et al. 1997)

motins and PR proteins. The expression of some of these (osmotins) is induced by both jasmonate and ABA. In this case, various stressors each probably preferentially trigger one of the two signal pathways to a particular extent. Special attention is thereby paid to the interaction of salt stress and stress due to infection or wounding, because it has become apparent that the response to one of these stressors causes a **"systemically induced resistance"** (immunity) to the other stressors. The next section will explain what this cross protection is due to.

The Function of Osmotins
In contrast to the LEA proteins (see Chap. 1.5.2.5), the function of osmotins in salt stress is unclear. If the conception of an unspecific function as a consequence of the induction pathway is not acceptable (it would be uneconomical in light of the sometimes enormous accumulation of osmotins), the cell biological role of the osmotins must be deduced from their relationship to PR proteins.

Transformation of potato plants with the osmotin gene from tobacco under the control of the strong (CaMV)35S promoter leads to osmotin accumulation and increased resistance to *Phytophthora infestans* (potato blight).

Osmotin inhibits the growth and spore germination of a number of pathogenic fungi such as *Phytophthora, Botrytis* and *Helminthosporium* in a manner which is nevertheless species-specific. It depolarises the cell membrane potential of the fungal hyphae by eliminating the pH gradient. This could be brought about by a two-fold mechanism: Thaumatin (see above) exhibits a tertiary structure fixed by eight disulfide bridges, of which the N-terminal domain has similarities to receptor-binding proteins. This highly conserved domain, which is also present

in osmotin, could bind to certain regions of the fungal membrane and integrate its hydrophobic "barrel" of antiparallel β-pleated sheets into this membrane. This "barrel" would then produce a pore (a hole) in the membrane.

PR proteins and chitinases bind preferentially to actin and thus accumulate at the sites at which fungal hyphae penetrate into the cell, where the cytoskeleton is also amassed. The defence enzymes and the poration mechanism put the intruding fungal hyphae under particularly strong attack.

Can this situation be connected with osmotic stress? Pathogen attack destroys the host cell directly or during the course of the hypersensitive reaction (see Chap. 1.10.2), and the enzymes and substrates released damage the neighbouring cells, beginning with the plasma membrane. The breakdown of the selective permeability of this membrane leads to osmotic stress, whereby the toxins of the pathogen intensify the effect. This damage can be recognised macroscopically by the wilting of the infested plant parts and organs.

Fungal attack and osmotic stress are thus causally linked. Both induce not only the expression of the *OSM* gene, but also the accumulation of osmotin. Osmotic stress exerts itself mainly via ABA, pathogenic stress via jasmonate.

Osmotin and LEA proteins, as well as PR proteins, are expressed and accumulated via both pathways, and probably also by means of a third, ABA- and jasmonate-independent route (Fig. 1.6.18). Since osmotins are metabolically very inert, as indicated by the vacuolar inclusion bodies, it is understandable that the component of salt resistance contributed by osmotin is maintained for a long time after a salinity stress. Similarly, pathogen resistance (latent) is also maintained because of the supply of osmotin in the cell. Osmotins thus represent a very interest-

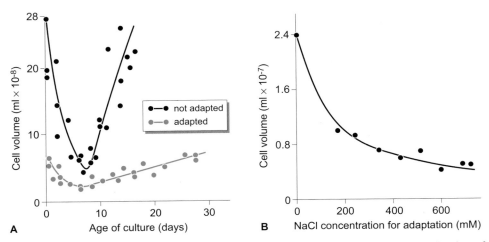

Fig. 1.6.19. Cell growth under salinity stress. A Cell volume during the course of a cell culture from the inoculum until into the stationary phase. The adapted tobacco cells grew at 428 mM NaCl in the medium. B Dependence of the cell size in the stationary phase on the salt content of the medium. (After Iraki et al. 1989a)

Table 1.6.8. Excretion of cell wall material from tobacco suspension culture cells in the stationary phase. The medium of the non-adapted cells contained no NaCl, that of the NaCl-adapted cells contained 428 mM salt. Drought stress was achieved with 30% polyethylene glycol. Uronic acid is a measure of pectin. (After Iraki et al. 1989b)

Cell type	(mg/25 ml cell culture)			
	Extracellular material (total)	Carbohydrate (total)	Uronic acid	Protein
Not adapted	26.0	18.4	7.2	0.4
Adapted to NaCl	28.0	24.1	1.1	2.8
Adapted to PEG	1.0	0.8	0.1	0.1

ing possibility for the molecular genetic transfer of pathogen and salt resistance on account of their longevity.

The Effects of Salt Stress on Cell Wall Proteins

Salt stress also leads to reactions in the cell wall. The structural proteins in this compartment are proline- and hydroxyproline-rich proteins (so-called extensins), and glycine- and arabinogalac-tan-rich proteins which are fixed in the cell wall by cross-linkage with one another or with poly-saccharides (Showalter 1993). Since salinity-stressed cells are considerably smaller than non-stressed cells (Fig. 1.6.19), it was thought that changes in cell wall proteins could also take place under these conditions. Cells growing un-der osmotic stress often have considerably high-er turgor than cells without salinity stress. Although their cell walls have the same thick-ness as those of non-stressed cells, they appear to have considerably less tensile strength (Iraki et al. 1989a). This was explained in terms of the walls of the cells adapted to salt containing

much less cellulose and extensin than do those of the non-adapted cells. On the other hand, suspension culture cells adapted to salt excrete significantly more and above all more protein-rich cell wall material into the medium than do non-stressed cells (Table 1.6.8). These data show that salt stress inhibits cell wall metabolism, especially the dynamics of its polysaccharide metabolism (Iraki et al. 1989b).

The synthesis of cell wall-specific proteins is also influenced by stressors other than salt. Cer-tain extensins are formed in greater amounts upon wounding or fungal infection. They be-come interconnected with one another or with hemicelluloses and pectin ("formation of papil-lae") under the influence of H_2O_2, an elicitor or high concentrations of GSH, and are thus inso-lubly deposited within the cell wall.

Salt stress evidently leads to increased synthe-sis of cell wall material, but not to its cross-link-ing, for which the so-called oxidative burst is re-quired (Lamb and Dixon 1997). The polymers so formed are thus increasingly excreted into the medium, especially since cell wall synthesis is inhibited (see above). Another protein secreted into the medium upon salt stress has been identified as chitinase, which is deposited in small pools in both the cell wall and the vacuole in non-stressed cells. Such chitinases are synthesised in increased amounts and secreted during a pathogen attack. The connection between osmotic stress and pathogenic stress can also be seen here.

1.6.3

Avoidance of Salt Stress

Plants growing in salty surroundings (e.g. along sea coasts) often exhibit the phenomenon of salt exclusion, which is interesting in the context of avoiding salt stress. In mangroves, e.g. *Rhizophoria* or *Sonneratia*, the solution in the xylem vessels is very dilute, constituting 0–1% NaCl compared with 3% salt in the environmental medium. Here, the principle of selective Na^+ exclusion (no or only very low affinity of the cation transporter for Na^+) appears to be very effectively realised. Ion barriers may occur in the rhizodermis or also further into the root. If such

barriers do not exist, salt is taken up by the plant and distributed via the xylem stream. Both Na^+ and Cl^- are phloem-mobile and are thus usually transported from the leaves back to the shoot and then deposited in the parenchyma there (this happens when the older leaves are not the final site of deposition and are shed after being loaded with salt, as, e.g., in cereals; Colmer et al. 1995). A salt gradient is then formed from the base of the stem to the tip, and from the older to the younger leaves. The meristems, which are not yet connected to the vascular system and in which transport (including that of salts) takes place from cell to cell, are spared the burden of the salt load.

To conclude the chapter on stressor salt, the various aspects that have been discussed are summarised in Fig. 1.6.20.

Summary

1. In contrast to the case with animals, salt (NaCl) plays no or only a subordinate role in the metabolism of plants. Only true salt plants require salt to flourish optimally. A distinction is made between plants which are

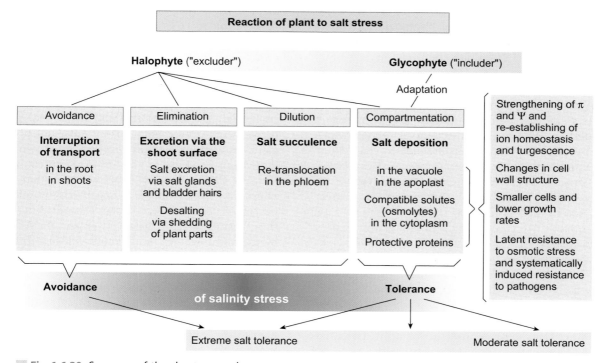

Fig. 1.6.20. Summary of the chapter on salt stress

not tolerant of salt (glycophytes) and those which are (halophytes).

2. Because of the small diameters of Na^+ and Cl^- ions and the consequent high charge density at their surfaces, both of these components of salt are considered to be aggressive osmolytes. In addition to the so-called salinity stress resulting directly from these ionic properties, the high charge densities of the salt ions also result in the binding and effective withdrawal of water (dehydration stress).

3. The most important membrane potentials in a functional plant cell are those of the plasmalemma (about 200 mV) and the tonoplast (up to 20 mV). The cytosolic side of the membranes is always the electronegative side. These potentials derive from the activity of ion pumps and channels, and result from the intracellular pools of cations and anions which the pumps and channels maintain in equilibrium. These equilibria (ion homeostasis) are dynamic, and their maintenance is aided by the action of proton-ATPases. This ensures that the pH values of the vacuole (about 5), of the cytoplasm (about 7) and of the apoplast (about 5) remain fairly constant. Non-stressed plant cells contain only very small cytoplasmic and vacuolar pools of Na^+ and Cl^-.

4. Salt stress leads to an influx of Na^+ and Cl^- and to augmentation of cytoplasmic Ca^{2+} pools. Na^+ and K^+ thereby compete for transport systems, with the result that not only the intracellular Na^+ pools increase in size, but also that the K^+ pool sizes shrink. The attempt by the cell to re-establish the original membrane potentials by increased pumping activity (particularly that of the H^+ pumps) results in the pH of the cytosol being shifted by up to 1 pH unit, which leads to changes in enzyme activities. The elevated calcium level triggers regulatory processes (activation of genes), which may be interpreted as adaptation to high salinity.

5. Growth by cell division and elongation is particularly affected, as are photosynthetic electron transport (with secondary damage due to ROS) and cell water relations. In particular young tissues often become necrotic.

6. Adaptive responses of plant cells to salinity stress include measures to re-establish ion homeostasis, to adjust the osmotic potential and to synthesise protective proteins.

7. How osmotic stress is perceived is still poorly understood (see Chap. 1.1.4). A signal cascade which reacts to the elevated Ca^{2+} level (SOS system) activates a Na^+-H^+ antiporter in the plasma membrane. Another signal chain, which is also calcium-dependent, leads to synthesis of LEA proteins and of protein kinases. Further signals result from augmentation of the intracellular concentrations of ABA and jasmonate, which induces the expression of numerous proteins.

8. Among the proteins which are newly synthesised or are synthesised in increasing amounts are those which serve to re-establish an ion homeostasis which exhibits changes in some of the pool sizes while maintaining the original membrane potentials and pH gradients, i.e. Na^+-H^+ antiporters in both the plasma membrane and the tonoplast membrane. Since these antiporters also require high proton concentrations, the synthesis of H^+-ATPases is also intensified. The salt tolerance of *Arabidopsis* was considerably increased by over-expression of one of the vacuolar Na^+-H^+ antiporters.

9. Halophytes are able to eliminate salt from the cytosol by excreting it from the apoplast onto the leaf surface or by forming large vacuoles in the mesophyll ("salt succulence") or in "bladder hairs". These excretion mechanisms are termed "recretion".

10. In addition to re-establishing ion homeostasis, increasing the osmotic potential of the cell is an important part of adaptation to salt stress. Halophytes are able to use salt as an osmoticum in the vacuole, whereas glycophytes, which do not (and cannot) produce such high osmotic potentials, usually augment their osmotic potential by means of organic osmolytes. Halophytes, too, must produce such compatible solutes to osmotically stabilise the cytosol, as they, too, must maintain a low salt concentration in this compartment. In addition to their osmotic function, organic osmolytes stabilise and protect biomembranes and additionally also often act as scavengers for ROS.

11. The most important osmolyte groups with respect to salinity are open-chain and cyclic polyols (sugar alcohols and cyclitols), which are only slowly metabolised and therefore guarantee long-term protection. The slow metabolism of the cyclitols is due to methylation (of *myo*-inositol). Sugar alcohols and

cyclitols are well suited for the transformation of crop plants to increase salt tolerance. Other important osmolytes are the amino acid proline, quaternary ammonium compounds (QACs, e.g. betaine) and tertiary sulfonic acid compounds (TSCs, e.g. 3-dimethyl sulfoniopropionate). They protect above all protein complexes against dissociation caused by salt.

12. In addition to LEA proteins and the proteins which catalyse the biosynthesis of osmolytes, protective proteins are synthesised and accumulated upon salinity stress. It is doubtful as to whether the functions they perform are really specific for salt stress. Amongst these protective proteins are osmotins and osmotin-like proteins, which are now regarded as belonging rather to the pathogen-related proteins, since their synthesis is also induced by pathogens. Osmotins have a strikingly alkaline isoelectric point; they are thus positively charged at the pH values of the cell and can accordingly readily interact with negatively charged membrane proteins. It is assumed, on the basis of their molecular structure, that they penetrate into the plasma membrane of the pathogen and form pores there, which make it easier for the host to combat the pathogen. Their function in relation to salinity stress is less clear. Osmotins, as well as the LEA proteins, are induced by ABA, jasmonate and ethylene and by the stressors which effect the accumulation of these phytohormones. They thus constitute a component of a system that cross-protects against all sorts of possible stressors. Because they are also deposited in vacuolar inclusion bodies, they are thought to provide long-term protection.

13. In addition to the production of the above-mentioned proteins, salt stress also influences cell wall metabolism. The cell walls of salinity-stressed cells contain less cellulose and fewer cell wall proteins (extensins). Salt stress evidently impairs the cross-linking of the extensins to one another and to the carbohydrates of the cell wall.

14. Avoidance of salinity stress: Plants of saline environments, e.g. mangroves, have developed a very effective mechanism for selective cation uptake. They evidently possess potassium transporters with no or only very little affinity for sodium, and are thus able to exclude Na^+ from their tissues. Other halophytes with a less selective K^+ uptake system make use of the fact that Na^+ and Cl^- are phloem-mobile ions which are able to circulate within the plant. They accumulate salt at the base of the stem, while the growing parts of the plant are kept largely salt free.

References

Apse MP, Aharon CS, Snedden WA, Blumwald E (1999) Salt tolerance conferred by overexpression of a vacuolar Na^+/H^+-antiport in *Arabidopsis*. Science 285:1256–1258

Barkla BJ, Blumwald E (1991) Identification of a 170-kDa protein associated with the vacuolar Na^+/H^+-antiport of *Beta vulgaris*. Proc Natl Acad Sci USA 88:11177–11181

Binzel ML, Hess FD, Bressan RA, Hasegawa PM (1988) Intracellular compartmentation of ions in salt-adapted tobacco cells. Plant Physiol 86:607–614

Bohnert HJ, Nelson DE, Jensen RG (1995) Adaptations to environmental stress. Plant Cell 7:1099–1111

Bostock RM, Quatrano RS (1992) Regulation of Em gene expression in rice. Plant Physiol 98:1256–1263

Bressan RA, Hasegawa PM, Pardo JM (1998) Plants use calcium to resolve salt stress. Trends Plant Sci 3:411–412

Colmer TD, Epstein E, Dvorak J (1995) Differential solute regulation in leaf blades of various ages in salt-sensitive wheat and salt-tolerant wheat x *Lophopyrum elongatum* (Host) Love, A. amphiploid. Plant Physiol 108:1715–1724

Crum CP (1993) A lichenologists view of lichen Manna. Contrib Univ Mich Herbarium 19:293–306

de Vos AM, Hatada M, Van del Wel H, Krabbendam H, Peerdeman AF, Kim S-H (1985) Three-dimensional structure of thaumatin I, an intensely sweet protein. Proc Natl Acad Sci USA 82:1496–1509

Delauney AJ, Hu C-AA, Kavi Kishor PB, Verma DPS (1993) Cloning of ornithine δ-aminotransferase cDNA from *Vigna aconitifolia* by trans-complementation in *Escherichia coli* and regulation of proline biosynthesis. J Biol Chem 268:18673–18678

Crillo S, Leone A, Xu Y, Tucci M, Francione R, Hasegawa PM, Monti L, Bressan RA (1995) Control of osmotin gene expression by ABA and osmotic stress in vegetative tissues of wild-type and ABA-deficient mutants of tomato. Physiol Plant 93:498–504

Hanson AD, Rathinasabapathi B, Rivoal J, Burnet M, Dillon MO, Gage DA (1994) Osmoprotective compounds in the Plumbaginaceae: a natural experiment in metabolic engineering of stress tolerance. Proc Natl Acad Sci USA 91:306–310

Hasegawa PM, Bressan RA, Pardo JM (2000a) The dawn of plant salt tolerance genetics. Trends Plant Sci 5:317–319

Hasegawa PM, Bressan RA, Zhu J-K, Bohnert HJ (2000b) Plant cellular and molecular responses to high salinity. Annu Rev Plant Physiol Plant Mol Biol 51:463–499

Hassidim M, Braun Y, Lerner HR, Reinhold L (1990) Na^+/H^+- and K^+/H^+-antiport in root membrane vesicles isolated from the halophyte *Atriplex* and the glycophyte cotton. Plant Physiol 94:795–801

Iraki NM, Bressan RA, Hasegawa PM, Carpita NC (1989a) Alteration of the physical and chemical structure of the primary cell wall of growth-limited plant cells adapted to osmotic stress. Plant Physiol 91:39–47

Iraki NM, Bressan RA, Carpita NC (1989b) Extracellular polysaccharides and proteins of tobacco cell cultures and changes in composition associated with growth-limiting adaptation to water and saline stress. Plant Physiol 91:54–61

Jin S, Chen CCS, Plant AL (2000) Regulation by ABA of osmotic stress-induced changes in protein synthesis in tomato root. Plant Cell Environ 23:51–60

Katsuhara M, Yazaki Y, Sakano K, Kawasaki T (1997) Intracellular pH and proton-transport in barley root cells under salt stress: in vivo ^{31}P-NMR study. Plant Cell Physiol 38:155–160

Kavi Kishor PB, Hong Z, Miao G-H, Hu C-AA, Verma DPS (1995) Overexpression of Δ^1-pyrroline-5-carboxylate-synthetase increases proline production and confers osmotolerance in transgenic plants. Plant Physiol 108:1387–1394

Kindl H (1994) Biochemie der Pflanzen. Springer, Berlin Heidelberg New York, 290 pp

Kononowicz AK, Ragothama KG, Casas AM, Reuveni M, Watad A-EA, Liu D, Bressan RA, Hasegawa PM (1993) Osmotin: regulation of gene expression and function. In: Close TJ, Bray EA (eds) Plant responses to cellular dehydration during environmental stress. Am Soc Plant Physiol, Rockville. Curr Topics Plant Physiol 10:144–158

La Rosa PC, Chen Z, Nelson DE, Singh NK, Hasegawa PM, Bressan RA (1992) Osmotin gene expression is posttranscriptionally regulated. Plant Physiol 100:409–415

Lamb C, Dixon RA (1997) The oxidative burst in plant disease resistance. Annu Rev Plant Physiol Plant Mol Biol 48:251–275

Larcher W (1994) Ökophysiologie der Pflanzen. UTB Eugen Ulmer, Stuttgart, 394 pp

Liu D, Narasimhan ML, Xu Y, Raghothama KG, Hasegawa PM, Bressan RA (1995) Fine structure and function of the osmotin promoter. Plant Mol Biol 29:1015–1026

Lüttge U, Kluge M, Bauer G (1994) Botanik. VCH, Weinheim, 600 pp

Marschner H (1986) Mineral nutrition of higher plants. Academic Press, London, 527 pp

McNeil SD, Nuccio ML, Hanson AD (1999) Betaines and related osmoprotectants. Targets for metabolic engineering of stress resistance. Plant Physiol 120:945–949

Moons A, Prinsen E, Bauw G, Van Montagu M (1997) Antagonistic effects of abscisic acid and jasmonates on salt stress-inducible transcripts in rice roots. Plant Cell 9:2243–2259

Nagy Z, Galiba G (1995) Drought and salt tolerance are not necessarily linked: a study on wheat varieties differing in drought tolerance under consecutive water and salinity stress. J Plant Physiol 145:168–174

Nakamura T, Ishitani M, Harinasut P, Nomura M, Takabe T (1996) Distribution of glycinebetaine in old and young leaf blades of salt-stressed barley plants. Plant Cell Physiol 37:873–877

Nelson DE, Rammesmayer G, Bohnert HJ (1998) Regulation of cell-specific inositol metabolism and transport in plant salinity tolerance. Plant Cell 10: 753–764

Niu XM, Bressan RA, Hasegawa PM, Pardo JM (1995) Ion homeostasis in NaCl stress environments. Plant Physiol 109:735–742

Nomura M, Ishitani M, Takahe T, Rai AK, Takabe T (1995) Synechococcus sp. PCC7942 transformed with Escherichia coli het genes produces glycine betaine from choline and acquires resistance to salt stress. Plant Physiol 107:703–708

Nuccio ML, Russell BL, Nolte KD, Rathinasabapathi B, Gage DA, Hanson AD (1998) The endogenous choline supply limits glycine betaine synthesis in transgenic tobacco expressing choline monooxygenase. Plant J 16:487–496

Papageorgiou GC, Murata N (1995) The unusually strong stabilizing effects of glycine betaine on the structure and function of the oxygen-evolving photosystem II complex. Photos Synth Res 44:243–252

Paul MJ, Cockburn W (1989) Pinitol, a compatible solute in Mesembryanthemum crystallinum L. J Exp Bot 40:1093–1098

Popp M, Smirnoff N (1995) Polyol accumulation and metabolism during water deficit. In: Smirnoff N (eds) Environment and plant metabolism: flexibility and acclimation. BIOS Scientific Publ, Oxford, pp 199–215

Rhodes D, Hanson AD (1993) Quaternary ammonium and tertiary sulfonium compounds in higher plants. Annu Rev Plant Physiol Plant Mol Biol 44:357–384

Saneoka H, Nagasaka C, Hahn DT, Yang W-J, Premachandra GS, Joly R, Rhodes D (1995) Salt tolerance of glycinebetaine-deficient and -containing maize lines. Plant Physiol 107:631–638

Schobert B, Tschesche H (1978) Unusual solution properties of proline and its interaction with proteins. Biochim Biophys Acta 541:270–277

Shen B, Hohmann S, Jensen RG, Bohnert HJ (1999) Roles of sugar alcohols in osmotic stress adaptation. Replacement of glycerol by mannitol and sorbitol in yeast. Plant Physiol 121:45–52

Sheveleva E, Chmara W, Bohnert HJ, Jensen RG (1997) Increased salt and drought tolerance by D-ononitol production in transgenic Nicotiana tabacum L. Plant Physiol 115:1211–1219

Showalter AM (1993) Structure and function of plant cell wall proteins. Plant Cell 5:9–23

Singh NK, Nelson DE, Kuhn D, Hasegawa PM, Bressan RA (1989) Molecular cloning of osmotin and regulation of its expression by ABA and adaptation to low water potential. Plant Physiol 90:1096–1101

Smirnoff N, Cumbes QJ (1989) Hydroxyl radical scavenging activity of compatible solutes. Phytochemistry 28:1057–1060

Speer M, Kaiser WM (1991) Ion relations of symplastic and apoplastic space in leaves from Spinacia oleracea L. and Pisum sativum L. under salinity. Plant Physiol 97:990–997

Tarczynski MC, Jensen R, Bohnert HJ (1993) Stress protection of transgenic tobacco by production of the osmolyte mannitol. Science 259:508–510

Thomas JC, Bohnert HJ (1993) Salt stress perception and plant growth regulators in the halophyte Mesembryanthemum crystallinum. Plant Physiol 103:1299–1304

Zelazny AM, Shaish A, Pick U (1995) Plasma membrane sterols are essential for sensing osmotic changes in the halotolerant alga Dunaliella. Plant Physiol 109:1395–1403

Zhu B, Chen THH, Li PH (1995) Expression of three osmotin-like protein genes in response to osmotic stress and fungal infection in potato. Plant Mol Biol 28:17–26

1.7

Heavy Metals

Lower plants, algae, and especially fungi, are superior to higher plants in coping with heavy metals. In general metals are deposited on surfaces. A particular type of crust formation is the so-called desert varnish that is formed by biological activity. Rock inhabiting algae and fungi solubilise iron and manganese ions from the rocks and deposit them on the surface. The advantage of the crustaceous life form on rocks (mostly dolomite) is a higher CO_2 concentration, and a prolonged water availability after dewfall: Rocks absorb dew by capillary action. This moisture is sufficient for net CO_2 assimilation by endolithic lichens. Cliff drawings, close to Avdat, Negev, showing a rider on an ostrich hunt; ostriches were extinct in the Negev a long time ago.

Recommended Literature

- Abadia J, Lopéz-Millán A-F, Rombolà A, Abadia A (2002) Organic acids and Fe deficiency: a review. Plant Soil 241:75–86
- Cobbett C, Goldsbrough P (2002) Phytochelatins and metallothioneins: roles in heavy metal detoxification and homeostasis. Annu Rev Plant Biol 53:159–182
- Marschner H (1995) Mineral nutrition of higher plants, 2nd edn. Academic Press, San Diego, pp 313–434
- Salt DE, Smith RD, Raskin I (1998) Phytoremediation. Annu Rev Plant Physiol Plant Mol Biol 49:643–668
- Schmidt W (2003) Iron solutions: acquisition strategies and signaling pathways in plants. Trends Plant Sci 8:188–193
- Stephan UW (2002) Intra- and intercellular iron trafficking and subcellular compartmentation within roots. Plant Soil 241:19–25
- Vara Prasad MN, de Oliveira Freitas MH (2003) Metal hyperaccumulation in plants – Biodiversity prospecting for phytoremediation technology. http://www.ejbiotechnology.inf/content/vol6/issue3/

Heavy metals are metallic elements with a density ≥ 5 g/cm^3, namely the elements Ag, As, Au, Bi, Cd, Co, Cu, Cr, Fe, Hg, Mn, Mo, Ni, No, Pb, Pt, Sb, Sn, Ti, Tl, U, V, Zn, and Zr. In addition to their high specific weight, most of them can occur in more than one coordination number, i.e. they can become oxidised or reduced. They often occur as metallic components of enzymes which transfer electrons, for example:

- Fe in heme (e.g. in cytochromes) and in S-Fe proteins (e.g. in aconitase),
- Mn in photosynthetic water oxidase, in many dehydrogenases and in superoxide dismutase (SOD),
- Cu in cytochrome oxidase, in plastocyanin, in catalases and in other oxidases,
- Zn is often a component of dehydrogenases, certain species of SOD, of carboanhydrase and of nucleic acid binding proteins (zinc finger),
- Mo occurs in enzymes of N metabolism (e.g. in nitrogenase and nitrate reductase),
- Co in cobalamine (coenzyme B$_{12}$ which is a derivative of vitamin B$_{12}$).

This listing is, of course, not exhaustive; nevertheless, it shows the requirement of plants for (some) heavy metals. Related to multiplicity of valences is also the tendency of heavy metals to form chelates, which are important for uptake by plants but also for sequestration in the plant.

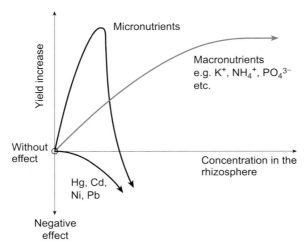

Fig. 1.7.1. Influence of ion availability in the rhizosphere on yield. (After Wallnöfer and Engelhardt 1984)

Some heavy metals are **micronutrients** (Fe, Mn, Zn, Cu, Ni, Mo, Co), others are potent **cell toxins**: Hg, Pb, Cd, Cr and As. However, also micronutrients may become toxic if they accumulate in the organelles of plant cells to higher concentrations. For heavy metals the concentration ranges of deficiency, optimal supply and toxicity are very close together (Fig. 1.7.1 and Table 1.7.1).

While the thresholds of symptoms of heavy metal deficiency are more or less independent of the plant species and within a relatively narrow concentration range, toxicity of heavy metals shows a broad concentration range (Table 1.7.1): Many plants are able to diminish uptake, detoxify or sequester (the so-called **hyperaccumulators**) heavy metal ions and thus avoid metabolic problems. Certain plants growing on soils with a surplus of heavy metals are called **metallophytes**. For example, *Silene vulgaris* is able to tolerate cadmium, cobalt, copper, lead, manganese, nickel and zinc in the substrate, *Festuca ovina, Agrostis tenuis* and *Minuartia verna* have ecotypes with similar metal resistance as *Silene vulgaris, Viola calaminaria* grows on soils rich in zinc and the fern *Pteris vittata* accumulates arsenic.

1.7.1
Availability of Heavy Metals

The heavy metal content of soils is usually sufficient for the nutrition of plants, it rather may be too high due to human activities. The total content of heavy metals of a soil is not crucial for the plant (e.g. Fe ca. 10,000 to 50,000 mg/kg, Mn up to 3000 mg/kg, Zn up to 300 mg/kg, Cu up to ca. 50 mg/kg), rather the availability of heavy metal ions is the determining factor. Availability, however, is a question of the solubility of heavy metals as ions or complexes, of the pH and the redox potential of the soil, and of the activity of plant roots and their association with mycorrhizal fungi. Unfavourable constellations of these factors may, at a similar total content, cause heavy metal deficiency or toxicity.

1.7.2
Heavy Metal Deficiency – Example Iron

1.7.2.1
Uptake of Heavy Metals

The effects of heavy metal deficiency on plants will be discussed for iron as an example. Except for poorly aerated mineral soils (gleys and pseudogleys), iron usually occurs in its oxidised, i.e. trivalent, form: goethite (a-FeOOH), haematite (a-Fe$_2$O$_3$) and as a lattice element in many minerals. Ferric oxides become insoluble in an alkaline environment and thus **iron deficiency** occurs in alkaline, well-aerated soils. In plants iron deficiency causes **chlorosis** particularly in the intercostal fields of leaves. This phenomenon intensifies at a high supply of phosphate and HCO$_3^-$, as insoluble ferric phosphates, hydroxides and (bi)carbonates are formed.

The plant root only takes up the ferrous ion. In the soil, however, the ferric ion is usually

Table 1.7.1. Assessment of the microelement concentrations (mg/kg dry matter) in fully developed leaves of agronomical crop plants (Amberger 1988)

Micronutrient	Deficiency	Adequate supply	Toxicity
Mn	< 20	20–250	> 500
Fe	< 50	50–250	(> 500)
Zn	< 20	20–150	> 400
Cu	< 40	5–20	> 40
B (monocots)	< 2	2–5	> 20
B (dicots)	< 15	15–100	> 200

Table 1.7.2. Critical toxicity of manganese ions in shoots of various higher plants. The "critical value" is that concentration at which the plant produces 10% less than its normal biomass (Marschner 1986)

Crop	Mn content (mg/g dry weight)
Maize	200
Soybean	600
Cotton	750
Sweet potato	1380
Sunflower	5300

present and, therefore, iron must be reduced in order to enter the plant (Fig. 1.7.2 A). This is accomplished by the enzyme **chelate reductase**.

Dicots and monocots (except grasses) are capable of increasing their capacity to reduce Fe^{3+} and thus take up iron more efficiently in iron-deficient situations. Chelate reductase is bound to the plasma membrane of the rhizodermis and the surface of this membrane is increased several-fold by formation of cell wall labyrinths of the so-called rhizodermal transfer cells (Fig. 1.7.3).

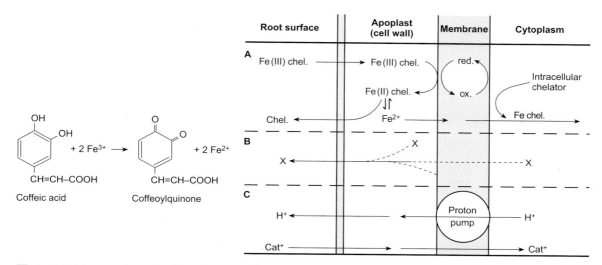

Fig. 1.7.2. Increased uptake of iron by iron "efficient" dicotyledonous plants, upon iron deficiency. A Increase in the reductive capacity. B Exudation of phenolic compounds. C Increase in proton excretion. *Chel* Chelator; *Cat*⁺ cation; *X*, e.g. caffeic acid. (After Marschner 1986)

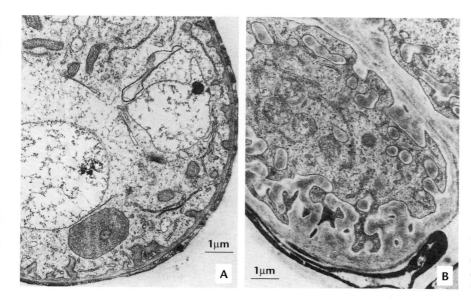

Fig. 1.7.3. Root cells with wall labyrinth (transfer cells). A Cross section through a root hair with weakly developed wall labyrinth. B Papillate rhizodermal cell (transfer cell) with amply developed labyrinth. (After Kramer et al. 1980)

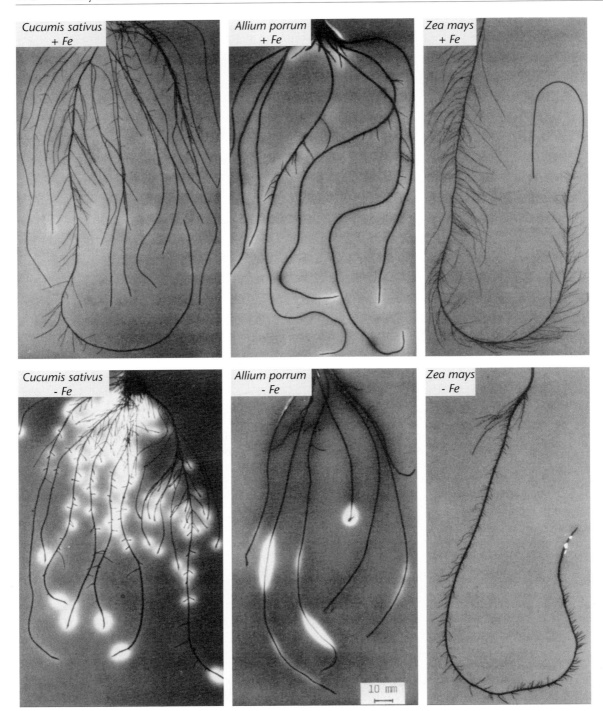

Fig. 1.7.4. Demonstration of proton excretion induced by iron deficiency in roots of different plant species. Roots of intact plants (pre-cultured in ca. 0.1 µM FeEDTA) were placed for 2 h in agar medium containing the pH indicator bromo-cresol (violet at pH 6.0); *yellow regions* (in the pictures *white*) show acidification of the agar medium to pH 4.5 and even below. (After Römheld and Kramer 1983)

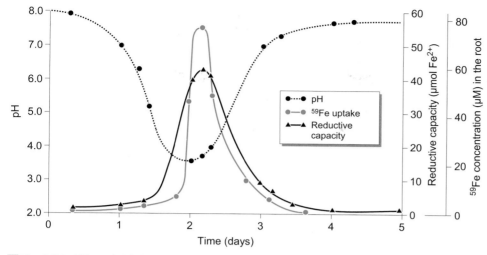

Fig. 1.7.5. Effect of Fe(III) supply on the pH of the medium and on the reductive capacity and uptake of iron, by sunflower, an iron-"efficient" plant. Such a plant, when placed in an Fe(III) solution of neutral pH, becomes iron-deficient within a short time. After only 1 day the plant commences to excrete protons and reducing compounds: the pH of the solution drops and the reduction capacity of the roots increases. With an increased iron(II) uptake the deficiency symptoms disappear and the root system returns to its normal state. The pH of the solution shifts towards the neutral point and the cycle starts again. Iron-"efficient plants" are mainly dicots, whilst many monocots, mostly grasses and cereals, cannot perform such a cycle. (After Amberger 1988)

At the same time, the root exudes large amounts of substances which chelate trivalent iron and thus dissolve ferric ions from the soil-borne stock. Citric and malic acid are common **chelators** exuded from plant roots. Fulvic and humic acids, which originate in the soil, are also chelators for iron ions. In addition, in some cases, phenolic compounds, e.g. caffeic acid, can be involved in formation of soluble complexes, in their chemical transformation and in the reduction of the metal ion (see Fig. 1.7.2 B). Upon iron deficiency, root cells form large amounts of such phenolic compounds. Much improvement of low iron availability is achieved by an increase in the rate of proton extrusion by the H^+-ATPase of the plasma membrane which lowers the pH in the rhizosphere and increases the solubility of ferric ions (Figs. 1.7.2 C, 1.7.4 and 1.7.5). All these phenomena, which increase under iron deficiency, are most probably an outcome of the enormous increase in the surface area of the rhizodermal transfer cells. Likewise the rate of root–hair formation from rhizodermal cells increases, which also enhances the absorbing surface area of the roots.

At the outer surface of the plasma membrane, Fe^{3+} ions are released from the chelates and are reduced by a ferric chelate reductase to Fe^{2+} which is taken up by an Fe(II) transporter (Fig. 1.7.2 A). In order to protect the intracellular environment against the reactive species of iron (see below), iron ions are handled again as chelates, e.g. with nicotinamide. From such chelates iron is then incorporated into the target compounds. As soon as the iron supply of the plant normalises and the deficiency symptoms have disappeared, the rate of root growth returns to normal without the special amenities for iron uptake being formed. This status is maintained until iron deficiency comes up again. Cu deficiency also induces plasma membrane Fe-reductase activity (Cohen et al. 1997).

All these processes have been investigated in laboratory experiments with roots lacking any mycorrhizal symbiosis. In nature, however, roots of most plant species are associated with mycorrhizal fungi which can explore smaller soil pores than fine roots and considerably contribute to the supply of the plant with macro- and micronutrients.

Grasses possess a particular chemical mechanism for heavy metal uptake: The roots exude so-called **phytosiderophores** (Greek: *sideros* = iron, *pherein* = carry) into the soil. These compounds are complicated non-proteinogenic amino acids (Fig. 1.7.6 A), which solubilise iron from sparingly soluble complexes, and convert it to water-soluble Fe(III)–siderophore complexes from which it is available to plants. Fungi and bacteria also produce siderophores. The latter bind Fe(III) as hydroxamates, whilst plant side-

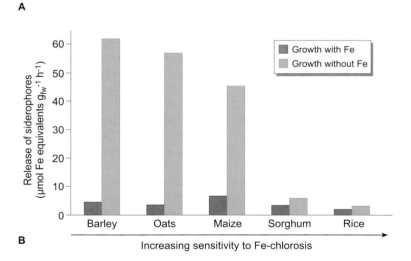

Fig. 1.7.6. A Chemical structures of microbial siderophores (*1* and *2*) and phytosiderophores (chelators) from higher plants (*3–6*). *1* Ferrichrome (cyclohexapeptide derivative of hydroxamates); *2* ferrienterobactin (cyclotris(*N*-2,3-dihydroxybenzoyl-L-serine) derivative of catechols); *3* nicotinamide; *4* muginic acid; *5* avenic acid A; *6* avenic acid B. After Schlee (1992). B Release of siderophores by various cereals upon sufficient Fe supply and Fe shortage. (After Mengel 1991)

rophores bind the ferric ion to the carboxy groups. A transporter mediating the uptake of Fe(III)–siderophore complexes has been recently demonstrated in maize. Cleavage of the siderophore complex, by ligand exchange or some other mechanism, occurs within the cell. Formation and exudation of siderophores are dramatically stimulated by iron deficiency (Fig. 1.7.6 B).

The siderophore-mediated uptake of heavy metals has been termed "strategy II" in contrast to the uptake by chelate reductase and the ferrous transporter which is known as "strategy I".

In poorly aerated soils with a negative redox potential, iron usually occurs in its ferrous, easily soluble form. At identical pH, the solubility of Fe(II) oxide/hydroxide is by several orders of

Box 1.7.1   Redox potential of soil

The redox potential of soil results from the ratio of the oxidised to the reduced forms of metals:

$$E = E_O + \frac{RT}{nF} \ln \frac{a_{ox}}{a_{red}} \ [V]$$

$$E = E_O + \frac{0.059}{n} \log \frac{a_{ox}}{a_{red}}$$

where n denotes the number of electrons exchanged between the oxidised and the reduced form, a_{ox} is the activity of the oxidised form, and a_{red} is the activity of the reduced form.

Well-aerated soils have redox potentials of up to +0.8 V and poorly aerated soils within the level of ground water or peat soils of up to –0.35 V.

The **reductive potential** of the soil is characterised by the **pe** value. The pe value (analogous to pH) is the negative log of the "concentration of electrons (n)" in the soil:

e.g. pe = 2   [e] = 10^{-2} M
      pe = –1 [e] = 10^1 M

The conversion factor between E and pe is: pe = E (V) × 16.9

The pe values of a paddy rice field are between +4 (surface) and –3 (middle layer).

magnitude greater than that of the corresponding Fe(III) salts. At a soil redox potential of pe = 1 the solubility of iron ions is 10^{-5} M, but under aerobic conditions, at pe = 2–4, it is 10^{-16} M (for explanation of the pe value, see Box 1.7.1). In soils with a pe < 1, iron deficiency usually does not occur in plants. A soil redox potential of ca. +150 mV is required for the reduction of Fe(III) to Fe(II).

1.7.2.2
Physiological Consequences of Iron Shortage

Chlorosis caused by iron shortage shows that the biosynthesis of porphyrines is particularly sensitive to iron deficiency. This not only applies to iron as the central atom of heme, but also to the Mg-protoporphyrin-IX-monomethylester cyclase which forms the isopentanone ring of chlorophyll using oxygen from air. Such a monooxygenase requires a cytochrome P450 as cofactor which contains an iron ion. Thus an impact on chlorophyll synthesis by iron deficiency is conceivable. In addition, many ROS-scavenging enzymes (see Chaps. 1.3.5 and 1.6.2.2), e.g. peroxidases, contain heme and iron shortage limits their synthesis. This leads to an incomplete detoxification of ROS which, in turn, oxidise chlorophyll in a photodynamic, i.e. light-dependent, reaction. A lower rate of chlorophyll biosynthesis, concomitant with an increased rate of oxidative chlorophyll destruction, results in the phenomenon of **Fe chlorosis**. Lower chlorophyll

Table 1.7.3. Effects of iron shortage in tobacco plants: iron limitation is particularly noticeable by reduced chlorophyll synthesis, which leads to chlorosis (bleaching) especially in the intercostal spaces (Marschner 1986)

Availability of iron(III) ions	Pigment concentration (mg/g fresh weight)		Protein content (mg/g fresh weight)	
	Chlorophyll a+b	Carotenoids	Chloroplast	Cytoplasm
Sufficient	0.98	0.45	8.6	12.8
Mild shortage	0.34	0.33	5.0	11.9

concentrations require smaller amounts of chlorophyll-binding proteins. It is therefore not surprising that chloroplasts of iron-deficient plants have significantly less contents of pigments and proteins than those of plants sufficiently supplied with iron (Table 1.7.3).

Physiological iron deficiency may also occur at a good supply of iron ions. At high internal phosphate concentrations, Fe(III) ions are sequestered as phytoferritin in the chloroplasts and are no longer metabolically available.

Phytoferritin is a hollow spheric protein that can store up to 5000 Fe(III) ions as alkaline iron phosphates $[FeO(OH)]_8[FeO(H_2PO_4)]$ (Casiday and Frey 2000).

The physiologically active form of iron is the Fe(II) ion, as a constituent of various complexes, e.g. in the heme or iron-sulfur proteins; only this form is able to transfer charges.

Many metabolic processes are more or less directly dependent on iron ions but discussion of an impact of iron deficiency on all of them is beyond the scope of this presentation. The reader is referred to textbooks on plant biochemistry, e.g. Buchanan, Gruissem, Jones: *Molecular Biology of Plants* (American Society of Plant Physiologists, 2000, Rockville, MD). Iron is a relatively atoxic heavy metal, required in larger amounts than other heavy metals in cell metabolism (see Table 1.7.1). However, the uncomplexed Fe^{2+} ion is toxic, as it catalyses Fenton reactions (see Box 1.3.8), which always result in the formation of ROS. Therefore, deposition of iron as ferritin, upon over-supply of iron, is important as a detoxifying process.

1.7.3

Stress by Heavy Metal Toxicity

Even metabolically essential heavy metal ions, e.g. Cu^{2+}, Mn^{2+} or Zn^{2+}, become toxic at concentrations exceeding the range of trace elements. Heavy metals such as Ag, Au, Cd and Pb which are not natural constituents of cells are toxic even at very low concentrations. However, heavy metal-tolerant plants are able to detoxify also such heavy metals which do not normally occur in a plant. Both phenomena will be discussed in the following section.

1.7.3.1
Copper

Copper belongs to those heavy metals which are essential for organisms, but required in only very small amounts (see Table 1.7.1). In the soil, Cu occurs almost exclusively as Cu(II), usually adsorbed to iron- and manganese-containing minerals, to soil colloids and as chelate with organic compounds. Copper ions are scarcely mobile in the soil, and because of the strong binding to soil particles copper concentrations in soil solutions are extremely low (ca. 0.01 mg/l). Even in such solutions copper occurs usually as a complex with organic low molecular weight compounds.

The copper content of untreated soils is in the range of 20–50 mg/kg soil, but in vineyards and hop fields, as well as citrus and coffee plantations, the concentration is considerably higher (>300 mg/kg soil) because of spraying with Cu-containing fungicides and fertilisation with sewage sludge and manure.

Because of the strong adsorption to soil particles, these high concentrations initially remain in the topsoil but ploughing displaces the copper-rich soil into the root region and thus may lead to copper intoxication of the crop (see Section "Copper Toxicity").

Copper uptake is in part similar to the uptake of iron, and as suggested by a pronounced ion antagonism, plants probably use metal-specific as well as general carriers for copper, iron, manganese and zinc. High affinity Cu uptake is specifically regulated by COPT genes. Amino acids and metallothioneins may be the relevant and often tissue- and age-specific transport metabolites to which Cu ions are bound.

Copper in Plant Metabolism
Relatively high Cu contents are found in carrots, potatoes, buckwheat, and in other soil-borne storage organs, less in above-ground plant organs. Buckwheat is also known as a copper-accumulating species. Obviously, mobility of Cu in plants is fine-tuned by a variety of Cu chaperones delivering Cu to the subcellular sites of demand.

Copper is well known as a component of electron-transporting proteins in photosynthesis (plastocyanin), in the respiratory chain (cytochrome oxidase) and in creating functional ethylene receptors (see Chap. 1.4). In plastocyanin, copper only mediates electron transfer whereas, in the cytochrome oxidase, copper takes part in electron transfer and, in cooperation with iron, in the binding of O_2. Oxidases, e.g. ascorbate and amino acid oxidases, peroxidases and phenol oxidases, often contain Cu. Copper proteins, like the above-mentioned cytochrome oxidase, frequently contain a second heavy metal: e.g. the copper-zinc-SOD where both heavy metals are linked by a histidine residue.

Copper Deficiency
Copper-deficient soils are characterised by a low sorptive capacity, such as well-aerated sand, heath (Podsols) and boggy soils. However, because of the higher plants' extremely low requirement for Cu (see Table 1.7.1), copper deficiency occurs mostly on boggy soils. Most of the typical symptoms of copper deficiency could only be recognised in pot culture experiments. Copper deficiency results in a reduced significa-

tion of the cell walls and a clammed sclerenchyma formation. This could be explained by the low contents or activities of phenol oxidases and peroxidases involved in lignin synthesis.

Copper Toxicity

In contrast to copper deficiency, Cu toxicity is widespread, less because of natural cuprous soils but more because of human activities: Rubbish tips, sewage deposits and agricultural areas with recurrent application of copper-containing chemicals, e.g. vineyards and orchards. Toxic copper concentrations give rise to many macroscopically and biochemically recognisable symptoms, which, however, develop after quite different time-spans. Similar to iron deficiency, copper toxicity causes chlorosis, as the Cu ion can readily replace the Fe ion in protein complexes and thus inactivate their enzymatic activities. In addition, Cu acts as a Fenton reagent and catalyses the formation of ROS and their reaction products which primarily attack the unsaturated fatty acids of membrane lipids and thus damage the cell membranes (see Chap. 1.3.3).

Such damage affects transmembrane ion transport, and in particular disturbs the intracellular K^+ relations which in turn control turgidity of the cell. This results in an inhibition of cell division. One of the fastest effects of toxic copper concentrations is the inhibition of the elongation growth of lateral and subsidiary roots. Instead of a well-structured root system, short, hairy, brown laterals are produced – a phenomenon which may be used to quantify copper damage. Such damage can be evaluated using an **EC system** (effect concentration: EC_{10} refers to an inhibition of the observed parameter by 10%, EC_{50} indicates 50% inhibition). However, EC and lethal concentration (LC) are not identical. EC measures the current inhibition, LC the irreversible damage. Concentrations which show no recognisable effects are called **NOEC** (no observable effect concentration).

At the cellular and subcellular level, increased Cu concentrations cause two major effects: removal of functional ions or central atoms from an enzyme, e.g. the replacement of Fe ions in cytochrome, or interference with the Ca^{2+} signalling system of the cell, on the one hand, and formation of cuprous sulfides in cysteine-containing enzymes, an example of which is the inhibition of nitrate reductase.

Substitution of an original metal ion by another excessively supplied heavy metal ion suggests a certain specificity which is probably defined in the protein. For example, ribulose bisphosphate carboxylase is much more affected by Mn^{2+} and Ni^{2+} than by Cu^{2+} or Zn^{2+}. On the other hand, Zn^{2+} replaces Mn^{2+} very effectively from the photosynthetic water oxidase. However, these are results of in vitro studies, showing possible reactions, but do not necessarily occur in planta: plants exhibit different ways to intercept heavy metals before their interaction with enzymes. The efficiency of such intercepting mechanisms, amongst other factors, may evoke different sensitivities of various plant species to copper and other heavy metals. It is assumed that the concentration ranges of heavy metal toxicity are shifted in metallophytes to higher concentration by such interception processes.

1.7.3.2
Cadmium

Cadmium is very toxic for any kind of organism. As far as is known, Cd is not a constituent of any metabolically important compound, i.e. there is – in contrast to copper and iron – no useful concentration of this ion in plants. Therefore, Cd is a true xenobiotic. Nevertheless, some plants may contain larger amounts of Cd (up to 100 mg/kg dry weight). Depending on their Cd content, plants are addressed as Cd accumulators or Cd avoiders.

Cd^{2+} accumulates in sewage sludge, waste water and river sediments from where it is taken up by plant roots. Cd can also be taken up from dust on the leaves. Cd^{2+} is readily distributed in the plant via the xylem stream, and then accumulates in all organs of the plant.

Plants are not defenceless towards Cd^{2+} supply by the substrate, as is shown in a comparison of Cd supply and Cd accumulation in leaves of various crop plants (Table 1.7.4). Beans belong to the excluders, but lettuce accumulates Cd. Thus plants show different sensitivities towards Cd (Table 1.7.5).

Toxicity of Cadmium

In soils, Cd rarely occurs as the only heavy metal pollutant as it is most frequently accompanied by Zn. Many toxic effects, therefore, result from multiple stresses by heavy metals or from ion replacement: In vitro substitution of Zn by Cd in the enzyme carbonic anhydrase leads to rapid inactivation (Table 1.7.6). The toxicity of

Table 1.7.4. Cadmium content of plants (mg Cd per kg dry weight) in relation to the cadmium content of the soil (Wallnöfer and Engelhardt 1984)

Plant	Organ	Cd content of the soil (mg Cd per kg soil)			
		1.4 (control)	4	10	30
Green cabbage	Leaves (old)	0.7	9.0	18	36
	Leaves (young)	0.4	2.3	5.6	21
	Shoot	0.5	3.1	4.5	9.6
	Root	0.7	2.3	6.7	8.3
Lettuce	Leaves (old)	1.2	9.6	26	44
	Leaves (young)	0.9	3.8	8.1	18
	Root	0.9	4.2	11	21
Red radish	Leaves	0.9	11	21	49
	Tuber	0.4	3.1	7.4	13
	Root	0.8	5.3	11	34
Leek	Leaves	0.6	3.5	16	28
	Stem	0.5	3.4	3.7	17
	Root	0.7	4.1	9.3	24
Bean	Leaves	0.2	0.4	0.5	0.9
	Seeds	0.2	0.2	0.2	0.2
	Shoot	0.5	0.6	0.9	1.6
	Root	0.9	2.8	8.2	14

Table 1.7.5. Toxicity of Cd for crop plants, measured as Cd content of the leaves that causes 10% reduction of the harvest (Wallnöfer and Engelhardt 1984)

Plant	Cd content of leaves (mg Cd per kg dry weight)
Bean	0.7
Leek	3.0
Green cabbage	>30
Radish	40
Lettuce	>40

Table 1.7.6. Loss of carbonic anhydrase enzyme activity (in vitro) after substitution of the original Zn ion in the purified enzyme by another heavy metal ion. The activity of the Zn enzyme is set at 100% (Ernst 1996)

Heavy metal	Activity
Zn	100
Co	55.9
Ni	4.9
Cd	4.2
Mn	3.9
Cu	1.2
Hg	0.05

Cd results from the strength of its links with cysteine residues in proteins.

A generally observed effect of xenobiotic heavy metals is the inhibition of photosynthesis caused by closure of stomata. This phenomenon is particularly pronounced with Cd (Fig. 1.7.7).

Inactivation of metabolically important enzymes results in a stimulation of catabolic reactions comparable to what is known as "wound respiration" (Table 1.7.7). At the subcellular level, swelling of mitochondria, vacuolization, i.e. demixing of the plasma, and deposition of Cd-containing granules have been described.

At the whole plant level, strong stress by Cd in addition to the reduced growth produces yellow streaked leaves (Table 1.7.5).

1.7.4

Reaction of Plants to Excessive Supply of Heavy Metals

At the same EC level sensitive as well as tolerant plants to stress by heavy metal generally show similar reactions when exposed to this kind of stress.

The first reaction complex may be considered an avoidance strategy, aiming at immobilisation of the heavy metals outside the protoplasts of root cells in order to prevent physiological effectivity. Complexing Cu^{2+} ions by root exudates in the soil, but also in the cell wall, on the one hand reduces the supply to the protoplast but, on the other, requires continuous root growth. Depending on the composition of the cell wall and the types and amounts of the exudates, the

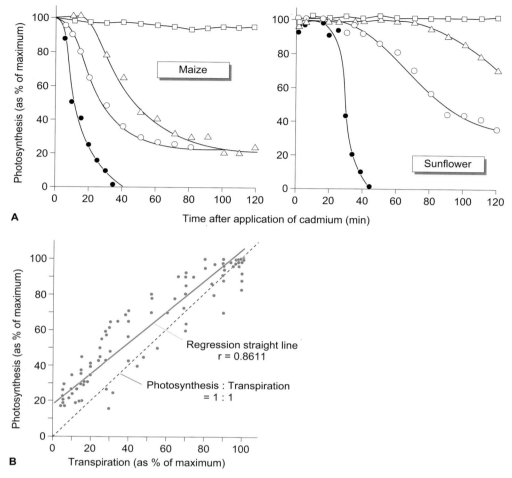

Fig. 1.7.7. Inhibition by cadmium of photosynthesis and transpiration of maize and sunflower. A Time kinetics of the influence of various Cd^{2+} concentrations on the rates of photosynthesis. □=control (27 mM KCl); △=4.5 mM $CdCl_2$; ○=9 mM $CdCl_2$; ●=18 mM $CdCl_2$. B Relationship between the inhibition of photosynthesis and transpiration by cadmium. The regression line shows a quasi-linear relationship between the two processes. As the regression line does not cross at zero, transpiration, i.e. stomatal conductance, must be inhibited to a greater extent than photosynthesis. This suggests that inhibition of photosynthesis by cadmium principally occurs through closure of stomates. The data points have been produced with both plant species. (After Bazzaz et al. 1974)

Table 1.7.7. Respiration and enzyme activity of leaves from soybean seedlings after 10 days growth at various concentrations of cadmium chloride. The measured activity is normalised to 1 g fresh weight. Respiration as well as activity of catabolic enzymes show a clear "injury effect" (Lee et al. 1976)

Activity	Cd^{2+} concentration (µM)			
	0 (Control)	0.45	0.9	1.35
Respiration (µl $O_2 \times g^{-1} \times h^{-1}$)	480	539	784	737
Malate dehydrogenase (µmol $NADH \times g^{-1} \times h^{-1}$)	230	250	400	390
RNase (µmol nucleotide $\times g^{-1} \times h^{-1}$)	3.0	10.1	6.4	9.8
DNase (µmol nucleotide $\times g^{-1} \times h^{-1}$)	1.2	3.6	3.6	4.8
Acid phosphatase (µmol phosphate $\times g^{-1} \times h^{-1}$)	190	260	400	410
Peroxidase (µmol $H_2O_2 \times g^{-1} \times h^{-1}$)	880	840	3440	4450

capacity of ion exclusion differs from species to species but less so with respect to the type of the heavy metal.

The second reaction complex is less well known. Competition of heavy metals for uptake has already been mentioned; that between copper and iron would also mean that copper uptake by the carrier is reductive. Apparently, Cu^{2+} can partially displace Ca^{2+} in biomembranes and thus changes the transport properties of the membrane. As far as is known adaptation to stress by excess copper reduces the K^+ efflux from cells. In the cytosol (reaction complex 3) Cu^{2+} is incorporated into the target enzymes or bound to polypeptides, oligopeptides or amino acids for transport into the vacuole and the xylem, respectively.

1.7.4.1
Polypeptides Induced by Heavy Metals

Two types of cysteine-rich peptides are effective in the sequestration of heavy metals in the vacuole: The larger **metallothioneins** (Fig. 1.7.8) and the smaller **phytochelatins** (Box 1.7.2). The role of both types will be discussed with respect to detoxification of elevated concentrations of heavy metals, because both types of polypeptides are synthesised in most plants in correspondence to the severity of heavy metal stress. However, their role in cell biology is still not completely understood.

Metallothioneins
Metallothioneins were originally discovered in microorganisms, animals and fungi, particularly in yeasts, and have recently been demonstrated also in plants; a Cu-binding metallothionein with a molecular mass of 8.5 kDa, the formation

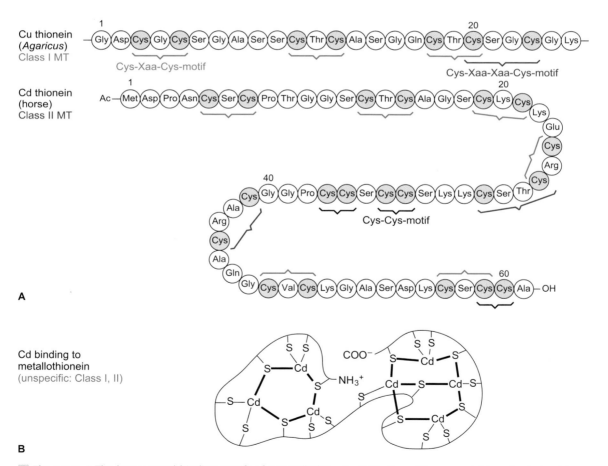

Fig. 1.7.8. A The heavy metal binding motifs of a metallothionein. B Binding of heavy metal ions (cadmium) to a metallothionein. (After Schlee 1992)

Box 1.7.2   Phytochelatins

Phytochelatins are derivatives of the tripeptide γ-Glu-Cys-Gly. This tripeptide is not a protein building block as the "peptide bond" is not between the carboxyl group next to the α-amino group (of Glu) and the amino group of Cys, but between the γ-carboxyl group of Glu, in other words, "at the wrong end of Glu". Phytochelatins are built along the following principle:

$$(\gamma\text{-glutamyl-cysteine})_n\text{-glutathione}$$
$$\equiv (\gamma\text{-glutamyl-cysteine})_{n+1}\text{-glycine}$$

Biosynthesis of these molecules is by dipeptide transfer from glutathione and not en route of a normal polypeptide. The corresponding enzyme is the phytochelatin synthase (γ-glutamyl-cysteine dipeptide transpeptidase) a protein of M_r 4×25 kDa$=\sim96$ kDa:

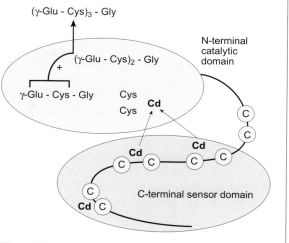

Model of the phytochelatin synthase

$$2 \text{ glutathione} \rightarrow (\gamma\text{-glutamyl-cysteine})_2-\text{glycine} + \text{glycine}$$
$$(\gamma\text{-glutamyl-cysteine})_2-\text{glycine} + \text{glutathione} \rightarrow (\gamma\text{-glutamyl-cysteine})_3-\text{glycine} + \text{glycine}$$

and so forth.

Current understanding is that the Cys-rich C-terminal domain is a sensor for heavy metals; the cysteines bind the metal ions and concentrate them at the catalytically active N-terminal domain which thereby is activated (see Figure, after Cobbett 1999).

---

of which is specifically induced by a high supply of copper ions, was found in the roots of the cuprophyte *Silene cucubalus*. This is one of the few instances where heavy metal specificity appears to exist.

Metallothioneins are polypeptides of about 60 amino acids, whose chain is kinked in many places, and whose N- and C-termini are particularly rich in cysteine residues. It is remarkable that they do not contain aromatic amino acids and that the cysteines always appear in the sequence Cys-Xaa-Cys. This motif suggests the formation of metal sulfide clusters (Fig. 1.7.8 B).

The two cysteine-rich domains are separated by a cysteine-free central part, the so-called spacer, which comprises about 40 amino acid residues as seen primarily in mammalians (Klaassen et al. 1999) and in the metallothionein A from *Pisum sativum*. Such metallothioneins, referred to as class I type, have been found – at least as genes – in pea, maize, barley, wheat and *Mimulus*.

Metallothioneins of the class II type are characterised by slightly different cysteine motifs; in addition to -Cys-Xaa-Cys-, they contain the motifs -Cys-Cys- and -Cys-Xaa-Xaa-Cys- (see Fig. 1.7.8 A) as found in fungi, invertebrate animals and plants (soybean, *Ricinus* and *Arabidopsis*; Cobbett and Goldsbrough 2002).

As the genes of these metallothioneins are known (MT genes) analysis of their function can be performed, and the regulatory characteristics of their promoters can be studied using molecular biological methods. The promoters contain at least partly *cis* elements that bind transcription factors responsive to metals, but also ABA-responsive elements. In that respect they correspond to animal representatives whose expression is also regulated by heavy metal stress and internal factors. The spacer apparently gives structure to the cysteine-rich termini. Metallothionein knockout mutants show an increased sensitivity to stress by heavy metals.

This applies also to yeasts, where CUP1₀ cells are hypersensitive to copper stress, in contrast to the wild type. In "normal", i.e. heavy metal sensitive plants, metallothioneins are produced from single copy genes, but the genome of metallophytes contains multiple copies of MT genes. For yeasts, which produce metallothioneins correspondingly to the number of copies of MT genes, a connection between the content of metallothioneins and resistance to heavy metal stress has been shown. Plant MTs are classified into four types according to the arrangement of Cys residues. Type MT1 is expressed more in roots than in leaves, type MT2 primarily in leaves. The expression of MT1 and MT2b is mainly in the phloem and seems to play a major role in Cu homeostasis. MT2a and MT3 are mainly expressed in leaf mesophyll and strongly induced by Cu^{2+} in young leaves, root tips and ripening fleshy fruits. The occurrence of type MT4 seems to be restricted to developing seeds (Guo et al. 2003).

For plants, even though an increased transcription of MT genes has been observed under stress by heavy metals, it is not clear whether the corresponding proteins are formed in amounts sufficient for detoxification. In that context, other interpretations have been put forward:

• a storage function of metallothioneins, as one protein molecule is able to bind several heavy metal ions (see Fig. 1.7.8);
• a role as transporters for the sequestration of heavy metals into the vacuole (see Chap. 1.9.1.1).

Considering induction of metallothionein expression, as well as binding of heavy metal ions as "sulfides", it appears that metallothioneins are not very substrate-specific. The binding constants for Zn^{2+}, Cd^{2+} and Cu^{2+} are not dramatically different, even though Cu^{2+} is usually slightly stronger bound than the others. From that finding a type of cross-protection could be concluded, or, for tolerant species, a type of "cross-tolerance".

Phytochelatins

The second type of metal-binding peptides, the phytochelatins (sometimes also called metallothioneins class III), differs from metallothioneins in as much as they are not primary gene products, but are produced by enzymatic peptide transfer from tripeptides. Their molecular

masses range from 2–10 kDa. Phytochelatins were discovered in cell cultures of *Datura innoxia* and *Rauvolfia serpentina* as well as in cultures of yeast; recently, they have also been found in cell cultures of tomato, tobacco and other species, usually upon stress by Cd and Cu. Also mosses, ferns and fungi are capable of producing phytochelatins (Grill et al. 1987).

Phytochelatins are derivatives of the tripeptide glutathione with the general formula (γ-Glu-Cys)$_n$-Gly where n ranges between 2 and 11 (Box 1.7.2).

In phytochelatins of grasses glycine is replaced by serine, and in some members of the Fabaceae by β-alanine (**homophytochelatins**).

Phytochelatin is synthesised by phytochelatin synthase (a dipeptidyltransferase), which is constitutively expressed but is activated by heavy metals with high affinity to SH groups. Mercury, Cd, Cu, and Pb are particularly effective in that respect, while Fe, Mn, Mo, Cr, U and V have no effect on PC synthase expression.

Occurrence of metallothioneins and phytochelatins is not mutually exclusive. Upon heavy metal stress synthesis of both types of polypeptides is intensified. Metallophytes, however, produce significantly less phytochelatins than heavy metal-sensitive plants (Fig. 1.7.9).

This is the reason that heavy metal tolerance of metallophytes cannot be traced back to direct detoxification by phytochelatins. They probably play an important role in the sequestration of heavy metals to the vacuole (see Chap. 1.9.1.1);

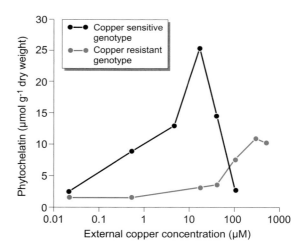

Fig. 1.7.9. Phytochelatin synthesis as related to the copper concentration in the root medium of copper-sensitive and -resistant genotypes of *Silene vulgaris*. (After Ernst 1996)

there, polymers of heavy metal phosphates can be formed, such as polymeric zinc phosphate in *Deschampsia* or *Lemna*.

More or less specific heavy metal binding proteins are usually interpreted as detoxifying elements. However, this would mean that the heavy metal–protein complexes or clusters would accumulate during the lifetime of a plant. This is not the case, although a correlation between the concentration of the heavy metal and that of the thioneins has been shown. However, the concentrations of the thioneins are much too low for such a function (less than 0.1% of dry weight). Rather than for direct detoxification heavy metal binding polypeptides may serve to maintain a heavy metal homeostasis of the tissue. Such a storage function could transiently contribute to a detoxification mechanism (Tomsett and Thurman 1988, but see also Cobbett and Goldsbrough 2002).

Heavy Metal Ion Pumps

Special consideration should be given to the discovery of **heavy metal ion pumps** in the plasma membranes of microorganisms, animals (including man), fungi and of the model plants *Arabidopsis thaliana* (AXA2p; Harper 1997), *Arabidopsis halleri* (Becker et al. 2004) and *Thlaspi caerulescens* (Assunção et al. 2003). Heavy metal pumps in plants belong to different types.

These enzymes are ATP-dependent pumps with a structure similar to that of K^+/Na^+-ATPases of the plasma membrane which remove heavy metals from the protoplast. Best investigated are the so-called copper ATPases (Solioz and Vulpe 1996). Two of these pumps have been described: CopA accomplishes the import of copper as the Cu^{1+} ion upon copper shortage. CopB functions in export, also of univalent copper. Defects in these copper ATPases lead to diseases in humans (e.g. Menke syndrome). These copper ATPases have certain structural features which are partly unique and partly similar to those of other metal

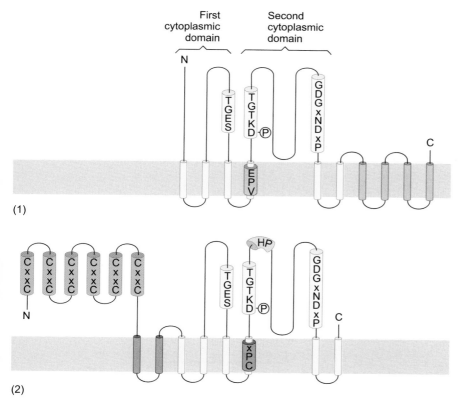

Fig. 1.7.10. Comparison of a Na^+/K^+-ATPase (1) with a heavy metal ATPase (2). The transmembrane helices and the conserved structural motifs of all P-type ATPases are in *light blue*. *TGES* Phosphatase domain; *DKTGT* aspartate kinase domain; *GDGxNDxP* ATP-binding domain. The sequences of such ion pumps that do not transport heavy metals are shown in *blue-grey*. The helices and sequences that only occur in heavy metal ion pumps are *grey*. The repetitive heavy metal binding domains are *in blue*. (Solioz and Vulpe 1996)

ion transporting ATPases (Fig. 1.7.10). The partial structures must fit into the transport cycle. All metal-transporting ATPases have in common an aspartate (D) in a very conserved sequence, TGTKD, which is phosphorylated by ATP. The phosphorylating domain is also conserved and is located in the sequence DKTGT. Dephosphorylation of the aspartylphosphates by a domain with phosphatase activity (TGES) forces a conformational change resulting in the transport of one to two metal ions across the plasma membrane. In addition to the structural elements of a Na^+/K^+-ATPase, the heavy metal ATPases possess an N-terminal extension, consisting of a series of Cys-Xaa-Xaa-Cys elements. In humans there are six repeats, in yeast only two. Further characteristic traits of copper ATPases are a conserved intramembrane motif: CPC, CPH or CPS 9 (so-called CPX motif), a His-Pro dipeptide and a smaller number of integral membrane peptides. The proline residue appears to be an essential part of a Ca^{2+}-binding domain, forming the channel or the transport domain. By the heavy metal binding domain the CPX-ATPases attain a

- certain degree of specificity for heavy metals,
- storage function for cytoplasmic heavy metals (CopA of *Pseudomonas syringae*, e.g. forms a CPX-ATPase, which stoichiometrically binds 11 copper ions).

It is to be assumed that the CPX-ATPases, as enzymes of the plasmalemma, play a major role in achieving homeostasis of essential heavy metals. However, this has not yet been shown in physiological experiments. Up- and downregulation of Zn transporters (ZIP family) seems to be responsible for zinc homeostasis in plants.

1.7.4.2
Cellular Response to Heavy Metal Stress: the Example of Cd

It was unclear for a long time whether thioneins or phytochelatins are produced as cellular response to Cd stress. The first Cd-binding polypeptides were found in Schizosaccharomyces and called "cadystins" because of the numerous cysteine residues in these compounds. Meanwhile these Cd-binding proteins have been identified as phytochelatins. In addition to the phytochelatins, Cd excretion by an ATP-driven $Cd^{2+}/2H^+$ exchange plays a role in Cd tolerance (Fig. 1.7.11).

As in the case of Cu^{2+}, binding of Cd^{2+} to phytochelatins does not serve as a long-term detoxification mechanism, but as short-term storage and probably plays a major role in intracellular Cd^{2+} transport. Mainly phytochelatins of

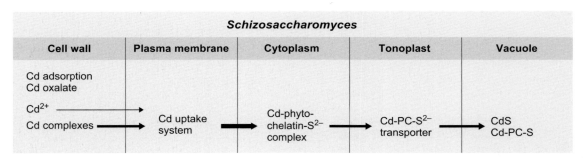

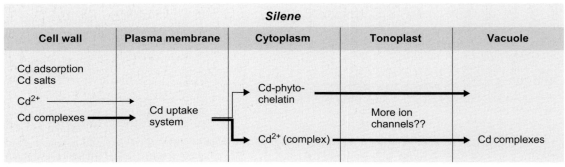

Fig. 1.7.11. Model of cellular and molecular detoxification mechanisms for cadmium in yeast and higher plants. (After Ernst 1996)

the $(\gamma\text{-Glu-Cys})_3$-type and $(\gamma\text{-Glu-Cys})_4$-Gly have been observed.

1.7.5

Heavy Metal Tolerance

Metallophytes, e.g. cuprophytes, use several strategies to counter the excess of heavy metals. However, they are not forearmed to cope with any concentration of these toxic ions, only the threshold at which damage occurs is higher. In principle, it is not possible to define a particular mechanism by which a plant achieves heavy metal resistance. Rather there is a gradual transition from metal-sensitive to metal-resistant plants, as the cellular responses to that stress are qualitatively similar and only differ quantitatively (Table 1.7.8). Simultaneous stresses from several heavy metals may readily overstretch the capacity even of strongly resistant plants. Such multiple supply often corresponds to real conditions, e.g. on ore outcrops, slag heaps from mines and in sewage sludge. Particularly in the latter, there are in addition to high copper and iron concentrations relatively high concentrations of cadmium or mercury, heavy metals that, in contrast to Cu, Mn and Fe, are true xenobiotics. How do plants cope with an excess supply of such ions?

1.7.6

Heavy Metal Extraction and Soil Decontamination by Plants (Phytomining, Phytoremediation)

Metal tolerance, and in particular heavy metal tolerance, of some plants offers two economically interesting possibilities: **Heavy metal extraction (phytomining)** and **soil decontamination** with the help of so-called **metal accumulating plants (phytoremediation)**. Plants can exploit substrates the mining of which is technically difficult and therefore unprofitable. Plants may also be used for the extraction of toxic materials, particularly heavy metals, organic pollutants and radionuclides from contaminated soils (soil remediation). For the latter possibility, five different procedures are used (Fig. 1.7.12):

- **phytoextraction:** toxin-accumulating plants extract the pollutant from the soil and accumulate it in the organs to be harvested,
- **rhizofiltration:** plant roots adsorb or take up toxins (particularly heavy metals) from water and sewage,
- **phytodegradation:** Plants and associated microorganisms decompose the pollutant (organic noxes),
- **phytostabilisation:** by synthesising complexes that bind the pollutant or by precipitation plants can decrease the bioavailability of the toxins,
- **phytovolatilisation:** plants detoxify the soil by production of volatile compounds (e.g. selenium).

Table 1.7.8. Heavy metal hyperaccumulating plants. Hyperaccumulating plants are able to accumulate heavy metals from 100 times to 10,000 times (e.g. *Haumaniastrum* for Co) the content of non-accumulating plants. The value of physiological tolerance of most heavy metals is at approx. 0.1% of plant dry matter. Exceptional values are for Zn (up to 1%), for Cd (0.01%) and gold (0.00001%). Surprisingly, some lichens, e.g. *Lecanora vinetorum*, also hyperaccumulate heavy metals (Brooks et al. 1998)

Element	Number of known hyperaccumulators	Examples (species)	Concentration (mg per g dry weight)	Biomass production (t per ha and year)
Ni	300	*Berkheya coddii*	17	18
Co	26	*Haumaniastrum robertii*	10.2	4
Cu	24	*Haumaniastrum katangense*	0.83	5
Se	19	*Astragalus pattersoni*	6	5
Zn	16	*Thlaspi calaminare*	10	4
Mn	11	*Macadamia neurophylla*	55	30
Ta	1	*Iberis intermedia*	0.3	8
Cd	1	*Thlaspi caerulescens*	3	4

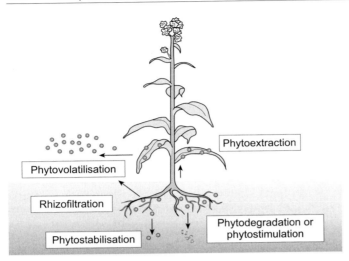

Fig. 1.7.12. The various strategies of phytoremediation. (After Pilon-Smits and Pilon 2000)

1.7.6.1
Phytoremediation

Plants which are able to extract large amounts of heavy metals from soil by accumulating them in an ample biomass even in a short vegetation period are particularly suited for **phytoremediation**. This technique is based on the work of the German botanist, Baumann, who in 1885 discovered accumulation of Zn in the mountain pansy (*Viola lutea* ssp. *calaminaria*), also called the calamine violet, and in an alpine penny-cress (*Thlaspi caerulescens*; Assunção et al. 2003). Two strategies of phytoremediation have been successfully employed: Continuous phytoextraction with hyperaccumulators and chelate-mediated extraction.

For the continuous removal of pollutants **hyperaccumulators** are preferred. Effective hyperaccumulation is obtained with many heavy metals, independent of whether they are metabolically active, or true xenobiotics, such as Cd. Hyperaccumulators may gain a kind of protection against biotic stress such as fungal infection as the pathogen is usually less resistant to intoxication by heavy metals; on the other hand, such protection is physiologically expensive, as it requires biochemical bulwarks mechanisms, e.g. synthesis of metallothioneins and phytochelatins, sequestration mechanisms to the vacuole or cell wall, excretion by salt glands and hydathodes, conversion of toxic amino acids, such as selenocysteine to the volatile methylselenocysteine, or repair after damage.

For **chelate-mediated extraction of pollutants**, annual plants with a high biomass production are particularly useful, e.g. large grasses, as long as the metal contamination of the soil is low or moderate. These plants that do not belong to the hyperaccumulators are allowed to develop to their full size on the contaminated soil. Heavy metal extraction is then initiated by solubilisation by applying artificial chelators such as EDTA to the soil.

An interesting possibility for **detoxification of mercury** has been described by Meagher (2000). Elemental mercury and mercury ions are released from gold mining, from industrial waste and upon burning of fossil energy carriers and medical wastes. Sulfate-reducing bacteria produce from such mercury-containing waste the extremely poisonous methylmercury ion $(MeHg)^+$, which accumulates in the food chain, and also in aquatic sediments. Gram-negative bacteria possess two enzymes which reduce methylmercury to elemental mercury, which is volatile and much less poisonous (about hundred times) than mercury ions. Organomercury lyase converts methylmercury to Hg^{2+} which by an NADPH-dependent mercurate reductase is reduced to mercury. *Arabidopsis* but also bigger plants, such as tobacco or *Liriodendron*, were transformed with the gene of one of these enzymes and crossed with a partner plant, into which the other gene had been transferred. The plants of the F_1 generation were considerably more resistant to mercury salts in the substrate, from which elemental mercury was evaporated. Transfer and expression of these genes also in aquatic plants are most desirable aims for the decontamination of the wastewaters especially from gold mines. However, phytovolatilisation is not a solution, but a dilution of the problem, comparable with the construction of high chimneys in central Europe in the 1960s and 1970s to get rid of industrial sulfur dioxide locally, which was then transported predominantly to northern Europe.

Summary

1. About 25% of the heavy metals (Fe, Mn, Cu, Zn, Mo, Co) belong to micronutrients in plant nutrition; the majority of the heavy metals do not have a metabolic function in plants. Nevertheless, they are naturally present in all plants, but often in very low concentrations. They can be classified as xenobiotic heavy metals. Some of the micronutrients occur in several oxidation states and are therefore components of systems that transfer electrons (e.g. Fe in cytochromes). Free heavy metal ions in the reduced form (e.g. Fe^{2+}, Cu^+, Mn^{2+}) can easily react with oxygen and are therefore toxic Fenton reagents. Mobility of heavy metal ions in the soil and availability to plants depend on the redox potential and pH of the soil. Heavy metal deficiency occurs very rarely, in contrast to metal toxicity which is usually due to human activities. Plants which are capable of accumulating larger amounts of particular heavy metals in their tissues are termed metallophytes.

2. Upon heavy metal shortage, plants increase their capacity for uptake by producing a larger root surface (root hairs, labyrinth in the rhizodermis/transfer cells) and by enhancing secretion of chelators and protons (by plasma membrane H^+-ATPases) into the substrate, thus increasing the dissolved proportion of heavy metal ions. Because uptake of heavy metal ions frequently requires prior reduction (e.g. $Fe^{3+} \rightarrow Fe^{2+}$), the capacity of the plasmalemma chelate reductase is also increased. Grasses excrete so-called phytosiderophores instead of the chelators into their substrate. Phytosiderophores are non-proteinogenic amino acids which transfer heavy metal ions from insoluble into water-soluble complexes.

3. Heavy metal toxicity also occurs with plant micronutrients if the optimal concentrations are exceeded; of chemically reactive xenobiotic heavy metals already very low concentrations are toxic. Uptake of the latter is via the uptake system for micro- or macronutrients such as Ca. Heavy metal toxicity as well as deficiency result in chloroses which, however, are of different origin in the two cases. Chlorosis from toxicity results from bleaching of the photosynthetic pigments by ROS (heavy metals act as Fenton reagents). Chlorosis from shortage is caused by failing chlorophyll synthesis because of a lack of cofactors (e.g. cytochrome P450). Because heavy metal ions are also part of ROS-scavenging systems, chlorosis from shortage might also be the consequence of a less efficient anti-oxidative system. Apart from oxidative stress caused by heavy metals, they also very effectively replace functional ions from biochemically important complexes and form sulfides with the free sulfhydryl groups of proteins and therefore are toxic, even at very low concentrations. The mobility of heavy metal ions differs in the plant (Cu^{2+} is almost immobile, Fe^{2+} and Cd^{2+} are very mobile).

4. Sensitive and tolerant plants react in a similar way to heavy metal stress. On the one hand, enhanced exudation from the root cells traps heavy metal ions as insoluble complexes in the soil or in the cell wall and, on the other, the concentration of the cytosolic heavy metals is decreased by binding to specific oligo- and polypeptides.

5. Heavy metal binding polypeptides are metallothioneins and phytochelatins. Synthesis of both groups of peptides is enhanced under heavy metal stress. They are rich in cysteine residues by which several up to many heavy metal ions per polypeptide can be fixed. Metallothioneins are gene-encoded proteins with certain repetitive cysteine-containing motifs. The promoters of the MT genes contain elements for metal-responsive transcription factors and frequently also ABA-responsive elements. Metallothioneins are rather unspecific for heavy metals. They are considered as heavy metal storage proteins rather than as means for detoxification. In contrast to thioneins, phytochelatins are not oligo- or polypeptides arising from gene expression. They are synthesised by dipeptide transfer from glutathione. Their general structure is (γ-Glu-Cys)$_n$-Gly, where n ranges from 1 to 11. Glycine can be replaced by serine or β-alanine. They are synthesised by phytochelatin synthase, whose synthesis in turn is induced by the highly toxic heavy metal ions. Phytochela-

tins probably serve to sequester heavy metals to the vacuole and thus, though not representing direct detoxifying compounds, are involved in the relief of heavy metal stress. In the vacuole of some metallophytes polymeric heavy metal phosphates have been demonstrated. Recently, heavy metal pumps have been found in microorganisms, animals and yeast and in *Arabidopsis* as well. These enzymes are ATP-dependent pumps similar to the Na^+/K^+-ATPases, but with a cysteine-rich N-terminal extension.

6. Stress by heavy metals evokes multiple responses of plants, which are scarcely element-specific. Differences in tolerance between metallophytes and heavy metal sensitive plants are gradual. Protein denaturing by heavy metal ions can induce heat shock reactions (accumulation of chaperones).

7. Metallophytes can be used for phytomining and for phytoremediation. Phytomining is essentially a question of profitability and is only economically effective for rare heavy metals (Co, Ta, Ni, U). Heavy metal remediation of soils may be carried out by continuous extraction of the toxic compounds with perennial hyperaccumulators or by chelate-mediated removal of materials, using moderately heavy metal tolerant, annual plants with ample biomass production. These grow on the contaminated soils until maturity when the heavy metals are brought into solution by application of chelators. After the uptake of the metal the plants usually rapidly die and are then disposed of.

References

Amberger A (1988) Pflanzenernährung. UTB Ulmer, Stuttgart, 264 pp

Assunção AGL, Schat H, Aarts MGM (2003) *Thlaspi caerulescens*, an attractive model species to study heavy metal hyperaccumulation in plants. New Phytol 159:351–360

Bazzaz FA, Rolfe GL, Carlson RW (1974) Effect of Cd on photosynthesis and transpiration of excised leaves of corn and sunflower. Physiol Plant 32:373–376

Becker M, Talke IN, Krall L, Krämer U (2004) Cross-species microarray transcript profiling reveals high constitutive expression of metal homeostasis genes in shoots of the zinc hyperaccumulator *Arabidopsis halleri*. Plant J 27:251–268

Brooks RR, Chambers MF, Nicks LJ, Robinson BH (1998) Phytomining. Trends Biochem Sci 3:359–362

Casiday R, Frey R (2000) Iron use and storage in the body: ferritin and molecular representations: http://wunmr.wustl edu/Edu Dev/Lab Tutorials/ferritin.htm

Cobbett CS (1999) A family of phytochelatin synthase genes from plant, fungal and animal species. Trends Plant Sci 4:335–337

Cobbett C, Goldsbrough P (2002) Phytochelatins and metallothioneins: role in heavy metal detoxification and homeostasis. Annu Rev Plant Biol 53:159–182

Cohen CK, Norvell WA, Kochian LV (1997) Induction of the root cell plasma membrane ferric reductase (an exclusive role for Fe and Cu). Plant Physiol 114:1061–1069

Ernst WHO (1996) Schwermetalle. In: Brunhold C, Rüegsegger A, Brändle R (Hrsg) Stress bei Pflanzen. UTB, Bern, pp 191–219

Grill E, Winnacker EL, Zenk MH (1987) Phytochelatins, a class of heavy-metal-binding peptides from plants, are functionally analogous to metallothioneins. Proc Natl Acad Sci USA 84:439–443

Guo WJ, Bundithya W, Goldsbrough PB (2003) Characterization of the *Arabidopsis* metallothionein gene family: tissue-specific expression and induction during senescence and in response to copper. New Phytol 159:369–381

Klaassen CD, Liu J, Choudhuri S (1999) Metallothionein: an intracellular protein to protect against cadmium toxicity. Annu Rev Pharmacol Toxicol 39:267–299

Kramer D, Römheld V, Landsberg E, Marschner H (1980) Induction of transfer-cell formation by iron deficiency in the root epidermis of *Helianthus annus* L. Planta 147:335–339

Lee KC, Cunningham BA, Paulsen GM, Liang GH, Moore RB (1976) Effect of cadmium on respiration rate and activities of several enzymes in soybean seedlings. Physiol Plant 36:4–6

Marschner H (1986) Mineral nutrition of higher plants. Academic Press, London, 527 pp

Meagher RB (2000) Engineered phytoremediation of mercury pollution in soil and water using bacterial genes. In: Terry N, Banuelos G (eds) Phytoremediation of contaminated soil and water. CRC Press, Boca Raton, pp 201–221

Mengel K (1991) Ernährung und Stoffwechsel der Pflanze. G Fischer, Jena, 466 pp

Pilon-Smits E, Pilon M (2000) Breeding mercury-breathing plants for environmental cleanup. Trends Plant Sci 5:235–236

Römheld V, Kramer D (1983) Relationship between proton efflux of rhizodermal transfer cells induced by iron deficiency. Z Pflanzenphysiol 113:73–83

Schlee D (1992) Ökologische Biochemie. G Fischer, Jena, 587 pp

Solioz M, Vulpe C (1996) CPx-type ATPases: a class of P-type ATPases that pump heavy metals. Trends Biochem Sci 21:237–241

Tomsett AB, Thurman DA (1988) Molecular-biology of metal tolerances of plants. Plant Cell Environ 11:383–394

Wallnöfer PR, Engelhardt G (1984) Schadstoffe, die aus dem Boden aufgenommen werden. In: Hock B, Elstner E (Hrsg) Pflanzentoxikologie, Band I. Wissenschaftsverlag, Mannheim

1.8

Aluminium

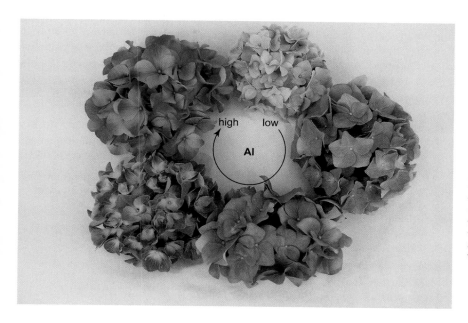

Aluminium ions form complexes with water-soluble vacuolar pigments. Gardeners use this to great effect in the ornamental plant *Hydrangea* sp., which at different Al^{3+} concentrations changes the colour of its flowers from white through red to deep blue. The colours in *Hydrangea* are the result of aluminium complexes with the anthocyanin delphinidin-3-glucoside and with chlorogenic acid (caffeoylquinic acid). The aluminium concentration in the flowers shown are (from red to blue) 51, 106, 640, 804, and 3959 mg Al^{3+}/kg dry weight. After Ma et al. (2001)

Recommended Literature

- Barceló J, Poschenrieder C (2002) Fast root growth responses, root exudates, and internal detoxification as clues to the mechanisms of aluminium toxicity and resistance: a review. Environm Experimental Bot 48:75–92
- Delhaize E, Ryan PR (1995) Aluminum toxicity and tolerance in plants. Plant Physiol 107: 315–321
- Kochian LV (1995) Cellular mechanisms of aluminum toxicity and resistance in plants. Annu Rev Plant Physiol Plant Mol Biol 46: 237–260
- Kochian LV, Hoekenga OA, Piñeros MA (2004) How do crop plants tolerate acid soils? Mechanisms of aluminum tolerance and phosphorous efficiency. Annu Rev Plant Biol 55:459-493
- Macdonald TL, Martin RB (1988) Aluminum ion in biological systems. Trends Biochem Sci 13:15–19

Aluminium toxicity is a worldwide problem affecting growth of crop plants and yields on acid soils (see also Chap. 3.5.1 on forest damage): Al is the most frequent metal element in the earth's crust. In acid soils, i.e. at pH < 5.5, the phytotoxic Al^{3+} ion becomes soluble to an extent which inhibits root growth and, as secondary effects, decreases uptake of nutrients and water and thus growth of the plant. In only slightly acidic or neutral soils aluminium forms insoluble oxides or silicates. More than 30% of the (potential) agricultural land has a pH of < 5.5 with aluminium toxicity being a serious problem. The widespread acidic red soils, called oxisols, of the tropics and subtropics are particularly affected. Aluminium toxicity also occurs in temperate climates because of acid rain or mist.

However, there is growing awareness that on acid soils several factors in addition to Al toxicity may limit plant growth, such as high concentrations of iron and manganese ions or deficiency in several essential mineral elements, in particular of phosphorus.

According to present knowledge, aluminium is not a trace element required for the nutrition of plants. Though not belonging to the heavy metals, it is considered a toxin because of its negative effects on plant growth. Nevertheless – as with most xenobiotics – inheritable resistance to Al ions in the root zone occurs, and possibly even tolerance of aluminium ions in the cell. Research into Al toxicity and resistance mechanisms has been made possible by breeding of almost isogenic lines, e.g. of wheat, which differ only in their sensitivity to Al. Because of the multiplicity of secondary effects of Al toxicity, the interpretation of the physiological effects of Al ions is still very controversial. However, methods of analysis have become more sophisticated and hence interpretation is clearing up.

1.8.1

Forms of Aluminium Available to Plants

There are three classes of aluminium ions available to plants: The **mononuclear** forms of Al^{3+}, **polynuclear aluminium**, and **complexed aluminium** (Macdonald and Martin 1988). The latter occurs usually in complexes with low molecular weight compounds, but, particularly at neutral pH, macromolecules are also able to bind Al ions.

In acidic solutions (pH < 5.0), mononuclear Al^{3+} occurs as the hexahydrate, $Al(H_2O)_6^{3+}$, conventionally called the Al^{3+} ion (Fig. 1.8.1). With increasing pH this hexahydrate is progressively deprotonated producing $Al(OH)^{2+}$, then $Al(OH)_2^+$, and, finally, at neutral conditions, the insoluble $Al(OH)_3$, also called gibbsite, is formed. In an alkaline milieu, the aluminate ion $[Al(OH)_4^-]$ is produced, which is again soluble, but as an anion has different sites of attack than the cation Al^{3+}.

At higher aluminium concentrations, particularly at neutral conditions, polynuclear forms occur, most frequently the triskaidea-aluminium $[AlO_4Al_{12}(OH)_{24}(H_2O)_7]^{7+}$, the so-called Al_{13}. All positively charged forms are phytotoxic, including Al_{13}. Mononuclear aluminium easily forms complexes with oxygen donor ligands, e.g. carboxyl groups, phosphates (inorganic P_i and polyphosphates) and sulfate.

1.8.2

Aluminium Toxicity

1.8.2.1
Aluminium Uptake

The kinetics of Al^{3+} uptake in wheat roots is biphasic, an initial fast and a subsequent slow phase. The fast phase results from the uptake into the cell wall and in the mucilage (the so-called mucigel) around the root tip. The slow phase represents the uptake into the symplast. Al^{3+} deposited in the cell wall, which either forms precipitates or is adsorbed, can be desorbed and solubilised with citrate. Three hours of exposure of wheat roots to citrate released between 50 and 75% of their Al^{3+} content, whereas in *Arabidopsis* roots only a quarter of the absorbed Al^{3+} could be extracted from the cell wall (Table 1.8.1). Aluminium-resistant cultivars absorb Al^{3+} more slowly and in much smaller quantities than sensitive species. This applies to uptake into the apoplast as well as into the symplast.

Al^{3+} enters the symplast either via cation carriers or by adsorption and endocytosis. In addition, in the acidic apoplast (pH ≈ 4.5), aluminium citrate complexes are uncharged and can slowly permeate the plasma membrane.

Since the radius of the Mg^{2+} ion is similar to that of the Al^{3+} ion (Table 1.8.2), it is assumed

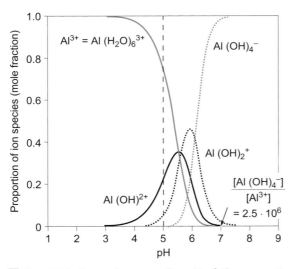

Fig. 1.8.1. Dependence on the pH of the proportion (mole fraction) of soluble, mononuclear aluminium ion species in aqueous solution. At higher concentrations "Al_{13}" = $[AlO_4Al_{12}(OH)_{24}(H_2O)_7]^{7+}$, the triskaidea-aluminium is formed. (After Macdonald and Martin 1988)

Table 1.8.1. Cell-wall-bound Al^{3+}: roots of wild-type and an aluminium-resistant mutant of *Arabidopsis* were incubated for 0 and 3 h, respectively, in 25 µM $AlCl_3$ solution and subsequently washed for 5 min with either Al-free nutrient solution or (Al-free) nutrient solution containing citrate. The amount of Al^{3+} remaining in the roots was then measured. Somewhat more than 25% of the Al^{3+} absorbed by the roots could be extracted from the cell wall by forming a complex with citrate (Larsen 1998)

Plant	Extraction with water		Extraction with 0.5 mM citrate (pH 4.4)	
Treatment	0 h	3 h	0 h	3 h
		Remaining Al^{3+} [nmol/mg dry weight]		
Wild type	0.2±0.1	42.3±3.4	0.2±0.1	29.3±0.8
Mutant alr-104	0.3±0.1	28.6±1.6	0.4±0.2	31.7±0.9

Table 1.8.2. Toxicity of soluble aluminium ions can be ascribed to the similarity of their ionic radii with those of essential nutrient elements (arrows). Effective ion radii (in Å) are shown in relation to the coordination number (Macdonald and Martin 1988)

Ion	Coordination number					
	4	5	6	7	8	9
Be^{2+}	0.27		0.45			
Al^{3+}	0.39	0.48	0.54			
Ga^{3+}	0.47	0.55	0.62			
Fe^{3+}	0.49	0.58	0.65			
Mg^{2+}	0.57	0.66	0.72		0.89	
Zn^{2+}	0.60	0.68	0.74		0.90	
Gd^{3+}			0.94	1.00	1.05	1.11
Ca^{2+}			1.00	1.06	1.12	1.18

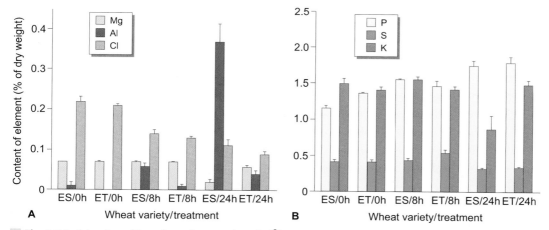

Fig. 1.8.2. Extrusion of ions from the root tips of Al^{3+}-sensitive and -tolerant wheat varieties by incubation of seedlings in 100 µM Al^{3+} solution for 0, 8 and 24 h. A Mg^{2+}, Al and Cl^- content of dried root tips. B P, S and K^+ content. *ES* Homozygous, sensitive line, *ET* homozygous, tolerant line. (After Delhaize et al. 1993a)

that the latter penetrates through Mg^{2+} channels, which can be seen by the concomitant reduction of Mg^{2+} uptake or by a decreased Mg^{2+} content (Fig. 1.8.2). Because of the similar ionic radius, the Al^{3+} ion might also use the siderophore uptake system for Fe^{3+}, which is well developed in grass roots.

Finally, it cannot be excluded that positively charged Al ions adsorb at the external side of the plasma membrane and reach the cytosol via endocytosis. Al^{3+} does not interact with K^+ channels and, considering the usually high K^+/Al^{3+} ratio, has therefore almost no influence on the membrane potential.

1.8.2.2
Phenomena of Aluminium Toxicity

In plants Al^{3+} is not very mobile and, therefore, usually remains in the root, which is therefore the organ where Al toxicity has its biggest impact and where toxic symptoms and resistance mechanisms have primarily been investigated.

The visible effect is a drastic inhibition of the elongation growth of the main and lateral roots, occurring within 1–2 h of exposure. Upon moderate stress elongation growth is resumed later on, but at a significantly lower rate. Therefore, sensitivity to Al^{3+} is highest in the elongation zone (Fig. 1.8.3); Al^{3+} accumulates in that zone and callose forms in response to the stress. In Al-resistant plants these phenomena are less pronounced.

Al^{3+} also inhibits cell division, but with a delay of hours with respect to cell elongation, and therefore inhibition of DNA synthesis cannot be the primary reason for the inhibition of root growth. On the other hand, inhibition of cell division activity is the reason for a long-term inhibition of root growth.

1.8.2.3
Symplastic Aluminium Toxicity

It was previously assumed that Al^{3+} binds to the weakly alkaline phosphate groups of DNA and thus inhibits cell division. However, this interpretation appears more and more unlikely. Likewise the earlier assumption that Al^{3+} predominantly affects the root cap could not be proven. It is

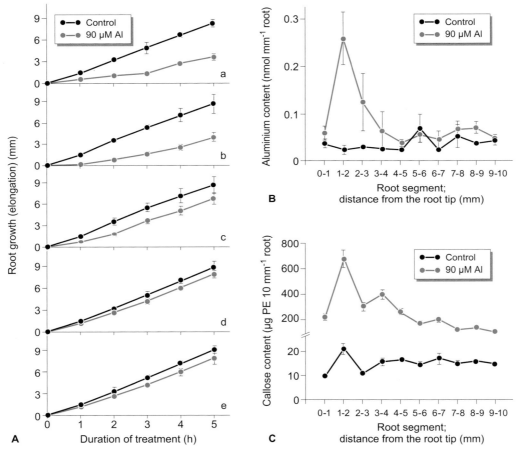

Fig. 1.8.3. A Effect of Al^{3+} ions (90 µM) on the elongation growth of individual 1-mm-long sections of an intact maize root. These sections could be selectively exposed to the 90-µM aluminium solution. *a* 0–1 mm; *b* 1–2 mm; *c* 2–3 mm; *d* 3–4 mm; *e* 4–5 mm. The standard deviation refers to five replicates. B Aluminium content of the individual segments of the apex of a maize root after 1-h exposure to 90 µM Al^{3+}. C Aluminium stress causes deposition of the polyglucan callose [determined with aniline blue, in so-called Pachyman equivalents (PE)] in those zones where aluminium affects root growth. (After Sivagura and Horst 1998)

Box 1.8.1   Role of phospholipase C (PLC) in the intracellular signal network

PLC liberates inositol-1,4,5-trisphosphate (InsP$_3$) from the membrane lipid inositol-diacylglycerol. InsP$_3$ controls the cytosolic level of Ca^{2+} which acts as second messenger. The other component of the PLC reaction, diacylglycerol, autocatalytically activates PLC. InsP$_3$ is the target of Al^{3+} which in this way interferes with the Ca^{2+} metabolism of the cell.

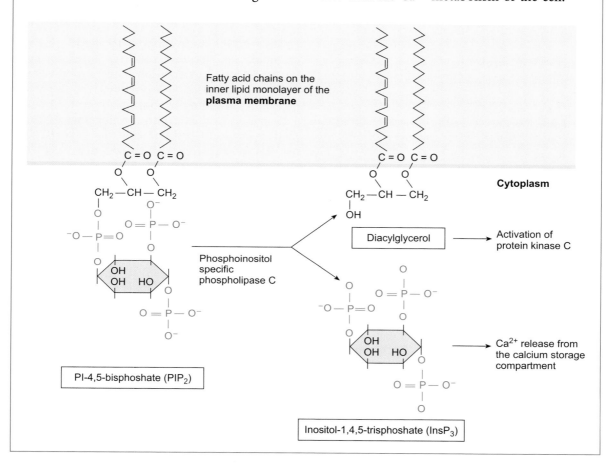

now thought to interact with the phosphorylated proteins of the cell nucleus. In dicotyledons, Al(OH)$^{2+}$ and Al(OH)$_2^+$ have a stronger toxic effect than Al^{3+}, in grasses (monocotyledons) Al^{3+} is more toxic. However, the soluble complexes with sulfate, fluoride and with organic acids (chelates) as well as insoluble salts such as Al(OH)$_3$ or AlPO$_4$ are not toxic. Because of the similarity of the radii of their ions (Table 1.8.2), Al^{3+} interferes predominantly with the Mg^{2+} and Fe^{3+} metabolism. Increase in Mg^{2+} ion concentration thus counteracts aluminium toxicity. Inhibition of Ca^{2+}-dependent reactions was also observed, but this is not yet understood at the molecular level.

The molar fraction of positively charged Al ions depends on the pH of the solution (see Fig. 1.8.1). While an acid pH is common in the apoplast, the cytosol is usually neutral to weakly alkaline (pH >7). In this pH range almost the total aluminium occurs as aluminate and the concentrations of Al^{3+} and its derivatives are in the nanomolar to picomolar range. In addition, several chelating agents in the cytosol are able to decrease the concentration of Al^{3+}.

Despite the low concentrations of cytosolic Al^{3+}, malfunctions occur, e.g. of reactions which are controlled by Mg^{2+}. The Al^{3+} ion replaces Mg^{2+} from the ATP–Mg complex, as the Al–ATP

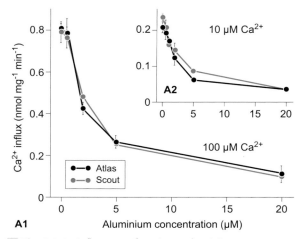

Fig. 1.8.4. Influence of various aluminium concentrations on the voltage-dependent ($E_{membrane} = -100$ mV) Ca^{2+} uptake by plasma membrane vesicles, isolated from roots of Al-sensitive (Scout 66) and -resistant (Atlas 66) wheat cultivars. A1 Inhibition of Ca^{2+} uptake at a concentration of 100 μM Ca^{2+} in the solution. A2 Inhibition of Ca^{2+} uptake at a concentration of 10 μM Ca^{2+} in the solution. (After Huang et al. 1996)

complex binds 1000 times stronger to hexokinase than does the Mg–ATP complex. In addition, Al^{3+} inhibits Ca^{2+} uptake into the cell by inactivating the voltage-gated Ca^{2+} channel, even though it does not interact with the membrane potential (Fig. 1.8.4). Interference with calcium is also obvious from the derangement of the intracellular signal transduction (Buchanan et al. 2000).

Al^{3+} prevents the signal-induced increase in inositol-1,4,5-trisphosphate ($InsP_3$) and the subsequent release of Ca^{2+}: Either Al^{3+} binds to the Mg^{2+}-binding site of the G-protein or it reacts directly with phospholipase C; direct binding of Al^{3+} to $InsP_3$ is, however, not likely (Jones and Kochian 1995) any more than a reaction with calmodulin and an interference with its function in the control of Ca^{2+} metabolism.

Because of the inhibition of root growth, with concomitant thickening of the root tips, it is to be expected that Al^{3+} also reacts with the cytoskeleton, the **microtubules** and **actin filaments**. Biochemical studies have shown that Al^{3+} inhibits the Mg^{2+}-dependent association of the tubulin molecules with the microtubule and the Ca^{2+}-dependent dissociation. As microtubules have a dynamic structure with a growing (+) and a decreasing (–) pole, the interaction of Al^{3+} with microtubules leads to a fixation of the cytoskeleton. In microtubule association, Mg^{2+} binds to the GTP and GDP receptor sites. The

association constant of Al^{3+} with this site is 3×10^7 higher than that of Mg^{2+} and an Al^{3+} activity of 40 nM replaces Mg^{2+} at millimolar concentrations!

When maize roots were treated with 50 μM Al^{3+}, microtubules of the outer cortex cells showed fixation in the transverse direction and stabilisation after 1 h simultaneously with the onset of growth inhibition. Al^{3+} requires about 30 min to migrate through the outer three cortex layers.

Three to 6 h after application of Al^{3+}, the microtubules of the inner cortex layer changed their transverse orientation to a random distribution, giving rise to isodiametric cell growth and thus thickening of root tips.

Because of radial expansion, together with the fixation of the cytoskeleton in the external cortex layers, fractures and lesions occur and the outer cell layers peel off. The reorientation of microtubules in the inner cortex is most likely a secondary effect as indicated by the delayed incidence. Microfilaments also show a response to Al^{3+}, but not as strong as that of microtubules (Fig. 1.8.5). Microfilaments of the outer cortical layer reorient from random texture towards a longitudinal direction, whilst the random texture of the inner microfilaments is fixed.

1.8.3
Al^{3+} Resistance

The relative resistance of isogenic lines of plants towards Al^{3+} is usually based on several properties, the genes for which are found in one to several loci. Al resistance is almost always dominant, Al sensitivity on the other hand recessive, and in crossings the F_1 generation is therefore usually Al-resistant.

Resistance may be based on avoidance or tolerance. Avoidance means exclusion of Al^{3+} (Pellet et al. 1997), tolerance chelate formation. Exclusion, too, is mostly achieved via (external) chelates.

1.8.3.1
Al^{3+} Exclusion

Exclusion of the Al^{3+} ion is usually achieved by excretion of chelating acids such as citric, malic or oxalic acid from the root tip (Fig. 1.8.6). By

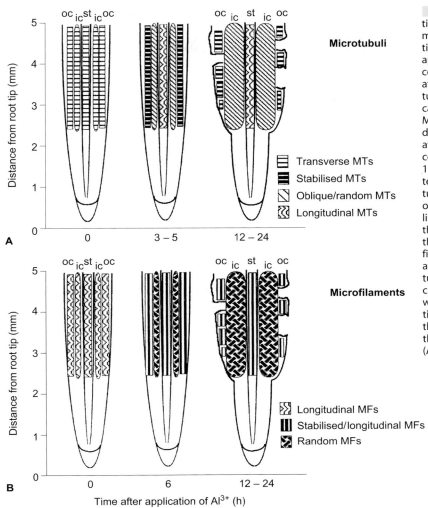

Microtubuli

▤	Transverse MTs
▦	Stabilised MTs
◧	Oblique/random MTs
▩	Longitudinal MTs

Microfilaments

▨	Longitudinal MFs
▥	Stabilised/longitudinal MFs
▨	Random MFs

Time after application of Al³⁺ (h)

Fig. 1.8.5. Changes in orientation of A microtubules (MT) and B microfilaments (MF) in the elongation zone of a maize root following application of aluminium (Al³⁺ concentration = 50 μM). A One hour after application of Al³⁺, the microtubules in the outer cortex (*oc*) became fixed in transverse direction. Microtubules with oblique to random texture were produced 3 h after Al³⁺ application in the inner cortical layer (*ic* inner cortex), and 1 h later in the stele (*st*). This alteration in the orientation of microtubules may lead to an expansion of cells of the ic and thus to swelling of the root. After 12 h, cells of the oc are deformed and lesions in the outer cell layers result. B Microfilaments become stabilised 3 h after Al³⁺ application; random texture and increased clustering of microfilaments in the ic and stele were seen 6 h after Al³⁺ application. Fixation and reorientation of the microfilaments occurred later than that of the microtubules. (After Blancaflor et al. 1998)

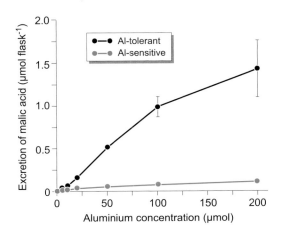

Fig. 1.8.6. Excretion of malic acid by seedling of Al-sensitive and -resistant wheat varieties. Six-day-old seedlings were exposed for 24 h to different concentrations of an Al³⁺ salt solution. (After Delhaize et al. 1993b)

binding to these acids, the Al³⁺ ion is no longer available to the uptake system.

Malate excretion is a specific reaction to Al³⁺, as it is not triggered by other trivalent cations (La³⁺, Sc³⁺), and also not by Al₁₃. Citric acid chelates strongest, succinic acid weakest (Fig. 1.8.7).

Under aluminium stress, Al³⁺-sensitive cultivars excrete malic acid, too, but much less than tolerant cultivars (see Table 1.8.3). Scavenging of Al³⁺ by excretion of malic acid by Al-sensitive cultivars could be boosted by the addition of malic acid to the nutrient solution (Fig. 1.8.8).

Resistance of wheat is mainly due to excretion of malic acid, whilst maize reacts to Al³⁺ stress by excreting citric acid (Kollmeier et al. 2001). Al³⁺-sensitive and -resistant cultivars of these crops likewise differ mainly in the amount of secreted acid. It is not the acidification of the rhizosphere

Table 1.8.3. Excretion of organic acids by Al-tolerant and -sensitive wheat seedlings after 24-h exposure to Al (5 seedlings each in 20 ml nutrient solution, containing 50 µM Al^{3+}). (After Delhaize et al. 1993b)

Organic acid	Excreted acid (nmol seedling^{-1} h^{-1})			
	Sensitive –Al	sensitive +Al	Tolerant –Al	Tolerant +Al
Malic acid	0.08 ± 0.08	0.33 ± 0.00	< 0.08	3.57 ± 0.08
Succinic acid	0.08 ± 0.08	0.08 ± 0.08	0.08 ± 0.08	0.58 ± 0.08
Citric acid	0.17 ± 0.08	0.08 ± 0.08	0.08 ± 0.00	0.17 ± 0.00

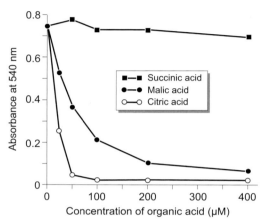

Fig. 1.8.7. Chelation of Al^{3+} by organic acids. Citric, malic and succinic acids were incubated for 1 h with a nutrient solution containing 50 µM Al^{3+}, 3.2 mM Na acetate buffer (pH 4.2) and 250 µM haematoxylin. The formation of Al–haematoxylin complexes was measured by absorption at 540 nm. The reduction of absorption in the presence of organic acids shows that organic acids chelate part of the aluminium which is then no longer available for the formation of a complex with haematoxylin. (After Delhaize et al. 1993b)

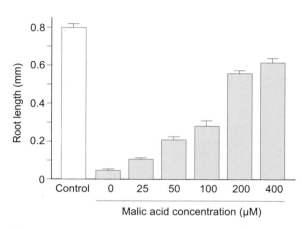

Fig. 1.8.8. Alleviation of the toxic effect of Al^{3+} by malic acid. Al-sensitive seedlings were grown in a nutrient solution containing 50 µM Al^{3+} and various concentrations of malic acid. Control seedlings were grown without aluminium and without malic acid. (After Delhaize 1993b)

that finally effects aluminium tolerance, but the complexing of the Al^{3+} ion. Similarly, some Al^{3+}-insensitive species secrete phosphate by their roots, leading to the formation of insoluble $AlPO_4$.

Rapid, Al^{3+}-triggered excretion of chelating acids leads to the question how aluminium ions are perceived. Excretion of malic or citric acid can be blocked by inhibitors of anion channels. This, and the fact that malate is a common metabolite of the cytosol, suggest that the primary effect of Al^{3+} is the opening or activation of a malate-transporting channel. But how Al^{3+} gates this channel is still unsolved.

1.8.3.2
Significance of the Apoplast for Al^{3+} Resistance

Cell walls, particularly pectin-rich primary cell walls, carry many negative charges which are usually compensated by bivalent ions (Mg^{2+}, Ca^{2+}). It is assumed that Al^{3+} replaces such bivalent ions from their binding sites, and that the cell wall thus acts as an **aluminium trap**. Such binding sites would quickly saturate with Al^{3+} ions, but upon continuous root growth new ion-binding sites originate so that protection of the protoplast by the cell wall does not seem unrealistic. However, so far differences in cell walls of sensitive and resistant cultivars have not been shown.

1.8.3.3
Al^{3+} Exclusion by Alkalinisation of the Rhizosphere

Even slight changes in pH alter the composition pattern of the aluminium ions (see Fig. 1.8.1). It

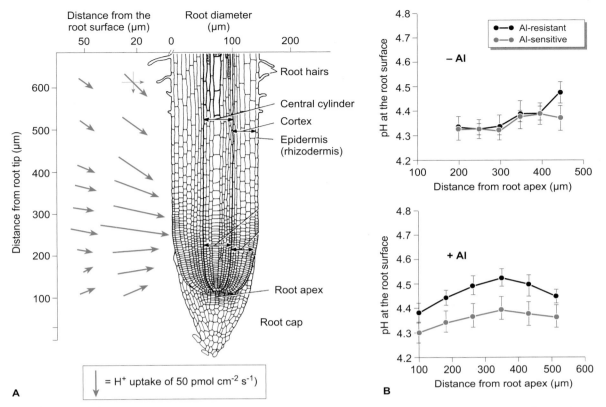

Fig. 1.8.9. A Diagram of the proton uptake by the tip of an *Arabidopsis* root. The length of the *arrow* indicates the extent of the proton influx. B Influence of aluminium ions on the pH in the rhizoplane ("root surface") of the Al-sensitive wild-type and the Al-resistant mutant alr-104. (After Degenhardt et al. 1998)

was therefore assumed that aluminium resistance, based on exclusion, could also be achieved by alkalinisation of the rhizosphere. Such a mechanism has been recently shown with Al-resistant *Arabidopsis* plantlets, using a pH microelectrode. This alkalinisation is achieved by proton uptake through the root tip leading to a small increase in alkalinity (ca. 0.1 pH units) of the medium at the root surface. Measurements of root growth confirm the significance of the seemingly small pH difference (Fig. 1.8.9). However, such an effect could also result from a reduced H^+ release from the root. This would then mean that Al^{3+} inhibits the proton pump of the root cell plasma membrane. The slight inhibition of root growth by Al^{3+} at pH 4.5 compared with that at pH 4.4 could also be due to a decrease in the mole fraction of Al^{3+} in favour of $Al(OH)^{2+}$ (see Fig. 1.8.1).

1.8.4

Al^{3+} Tolerance

Aluminium tolerance is imputed to species or cultivars that tolerate an increased intracellular aluminium concentration. Examples are old leaves of tea which accumulate up to 30 g Al per kg dry mass, or hydrangea, whose bracts (sepals) turn blue with the addition of a little Al^{3+} to the irrigation water and whose leaves accumulate up to 3 g Al per kg dry weight (Ma et al. 1997, see also figure introducing Chap. 1.8).

Corresponding to the high content of soluble Al^{3+} in acid soils of the tropics substantial concentrations of Al ions (up to 1 g/kg) occur in wild plants (*Melastoma*, *Vaccinium*) of rain forests. The Al tolerance of these plants could result from an effective sequestration (excretion by the plasma membrane or deposition in the vacuole) or from intracellular detoxification by chelating agents or Al-binding proteins. Buckwheat is an example of an Al-tolerant plant (the

Table 1.8.4. Concentrations of aluminium and oxalic acid in leaves, roots and in the cell sap of buckwheat. Plants were grown in nutrient solution (pH 4.5), which was exchanged every second day by a nutrient solution containing 0.5 mM $CaCl_2$ and 0 or 50 µM Al. Plants were harvested after 10 days of treatment (after Ma et al. 1998)

Plant organ	Al (mmol/kg fresh weight)	Water content (%)	Cell sap		
			Al (mM)	Al (%)[a]	Oxalic acid (mM)
Leaves					
+Al	2.01	87.5	2.03	88.4	51.08
−Al	0.02	87.4	0.01	–	46.79
Roots					
+Al	3.45	94.7	2.09	57.3	8.80

[a] Percent of total aluminium. Rest deposited in cell wall.

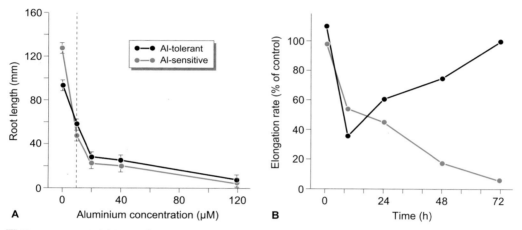

Fig. 1.8.10. A Inhibition of root growth of a sensitive and tolerant bean variety grown for 3 days in an Al^{3+}-containing nutrient solution. B Dependence of inhibition on the Al^{3+} concentration is the same in both cultivars. However, the tolerant variety recovers quickly from moderate stress (10 µM Al^{3+}), whereas root growth of the sensitive variety remains inhibited. (After Cumming et al. 1992)

cultivar *Jianxi* accumulates up to 0.5 g Al/kg leaf dry weight) which sequesters Al^{3+} from the cytosol into the vacuole where it forms complexes with oxalate (Al^{3+}/oxalate = 1:3; Table 1.8.4). In addition, Al-stressed, buckwheat roots excrete considerable amounts of oxalic acid, which complexes Al ions immediately in the rhizosphere. Exogenous Al oxalate (1:3 and 1:2) does not inhibit root growth, and thus is not toxic. Apparently, such complexes are so stable that under physiological conditions Al is not released.

In hydrangea the counter ion is citrate instead of oxalate. The corresponding complex contains aluminium and citrate at a ratio of 1:1 and accumulates in the vacuole. In contrast, in tea leaves, the bulk of Al ions seems to be bound to tannins.

The assumption that Al tolerance is inducible arises from experiments in which the initially inhibited root growth recovered completely after

a few days (Fig. 1.8.10), indicating induction and achievement of Al tolerance.

Upon stress by Al, resistant wheat cultivars produced two additional proteins (51 kDa) in the plasmalemma fraction, which occurred only in the root tips and disappeared again when the stress was alleviated. Formation of these proteins was induced most effectively by Al^{3+}, to a lesser extent also by Cd^{2+} and Ni^{2+}, but not by Cu^{2+}, Zn^{2+} or Mn^{2+}. In the corresponding Al-sensitive cultivar only traces of these proteins were found under Al stress. One of these proteins could be a metallothionein. Another protein could be related to the production of "defence mucilage" by the outer root cap cells. Strong mucilage formation was observed upon incubation of root tips in solutions of Al salts. After excretion of the mucigel, root growth (of peas) recovered so fast that it was assumed that the mucilage had adsorbed the aluminium ions and thus detoxified them (Hawes et al. 2000).

These examples show that Al stress may induce a more or less specific protein response, while the physiological role of such proteins still remains to be explained.

Summary

1. Aluminium is the most frequent metallic element in the earth's crust, where it appears in many, usually insoluble compounds and complexes. Three classes of aluminium ions available to plants are distinguished: Mononuclear Al^{3+}, polynuclear Al and complexed Al. At an acid pH (<5) the mononuclear $Al(H_2O)^{7+}$ occurs, at neutral pH and at higher Al concentrations polynuclear forms develop, in particular the soluble $[Al_{13}]^{3+}$. All soluble Al ions are phytotoxic.

2. Aluminium is quickly taken up by adsorption to the cell wall and in the mucigel of the root tip. From there it enters into the cytosol via cation carriers (probably through a Mg^{2+} channel). Endocytotic uptake from the apoplast and, in grasses, uptake by the siderophore system are also discussed. Al^{3+} is almost immobile in the plant; aluminium damage occurs, therefore, predominantly in the roots.

3. Inhibition of root elongation growth by Al^{3+} is particularly striking; upon long-term stress, cell division is also affected. Because of similar ionic radii, Al^{3+} particularly affects Mg^{2+} (e.g. replacing Mg in the Mg–ATP complex) and Fe^{3+} metabolisms, and interferes with the regulation of the cytosolic level of free Ca^{2+}. By these effects and by the inhibition of signal transduction via an increase in inositol-trisphosphate, aluminium causes major changes in the regulation of cellular reactions. In addition, Al^{3+} leads to a reorientation and fixation of the cytoskeleton, resulting in anomalous growth in thickness of root tips and the incidence of numerous lesions.

4. (Relative) aluminium resistance may be based on avoidance or tolerance. Exclusion of aluminium ions (stress avoidance) is usually achieved by excretion of chelating acids (e.g. malic acid) which form aluminium complexes outside the root or the protoplast, thus rendering aluminium ions unavailable for uptake systems. Excretion of such chelators appears to be species-specific and is a typical reaction

to Al^{3+}, but not to other trivalent cations. A pectin-rich cell wall, carrying numerous negatively charged carboxyl groups, may act as aluminium trap, normally displacing the cross-linking cations Mg^{2+} and Ca^{2+}. Al^{3+} in the rhizosphere may also be immobilised or made unavailable for plants by alkalinisation (via proton uptake or reduced proton release).

5. Aluminium-tolerant species are able to accumulate Al^{3+} in high concentrations. The most important mechanisms for this are export into the apoplast or sequestration into the vacuole. At the sites of deposition the aluminium ions must be complexed (e.g. by Al oxalate or with tannins) or fixed to Al-binding proteins to become inactivated.

References

Blancaflor EB, Jones DL, Gilroy S (1998) Alterations in the cytoskeleton accompany aluminum-induced growth inhibition and morphological changes in primary roots of maize. Plant Physiol 118:159–172

Buchanan BB, Gruissem W, Jones RL (2000) Biochemistry and molecular biology of plants. American Society of Plant Physiologists, Rockville, MD, pp 952–963

Cumming JR, Buckelew-Cumming A, Taylor GJ (1992) Patterns of root respiration associated with the induction of aluminum tolerance in Phaseolus vulgaris L. J Exp Bot 43:1075–1081

Degenhardt J, Larsen PB, Howell SH, Kochian LV (1998) Aluminum resistance in the Arabidopsis mutant alr-104 is caused by an aluminum-induced increase in rhizosphere pH. Plant Physiol 117:19–27

Delhaize E, Craig S, Beaton CD, Bennet RJ, Jagadish VC, Randall PJ (1993a) Aluminum tolerance in wheat (Triticum aestivum L.). Plant Physiol 103:685–693

Delhaize EM, Ryan PR, Randall PJ (1993b) Aluminum tolerance in wheat (Triticum aestivum L.). Plant Physiol 103:695–702

Hawes MC, Gunawardena U, Miyasaka S, Zhao XW (2000) The role of root border cells in plant defense. Trends Plant Sci 5:128–133

Huang JW, Pellet DM, Papernik LA, Kochian LV (1996) Aluminum interactions with voltage-dependent calcium transport in plasma membrane vesicles isolated from roots of aluminum-sensitive and -resistant wheat cultivars. Plant Physiol 110:561–569

Jones DL, Kochian LV (1995) Aluminum inhibition of the 1,4,5-trisphosphate signal transduction pathway in wheat roots: a role in aluminum toxicity? Plant Cell 7:1913–1922

Kollmeier M, Dietrich P, Bauer CS, Horst W, Hedrich R (2001) Aluminium activates a citrate-permeable anion channel in the aluminium-sensitive zone of maize root apex. A comparison between aluminium-sensitive and an aluminium-resistant cultivar. Plant Physiol 126:397–410

Larsen PB, Degenhardt J, Tai C-Y, Stenzler LM, Howell SH, Kochian LV (1998) Aluminum-resistant Arabidopsis mutants that exhibit altered patterns of aluminum accumulation and organic acid release from roots. Plant Physiol 117:9–18

Ma JF, Hiradate S, Nomoto K, Iwashita T, Matsumoto H (1997) Internal detoxification mechanism of Al in *Hydrangea*. Identification of Al form in leaves. Plant Physiol 113:1033–1039

Ma JF, Hiradate S, Matsumoto H (1998) High aluminium resistance in buckwheat. II. Oxalic acid detoxifies aluminium internally. Plant Physiol 117:753–759

Ma JF, Ryan PR, Delhaize E (2001) Aluminium tolerance in plants and complexing role of organic acids. Trends Plant Sci 6:273–278

Macdonald TL, Martin RB (1988) Aluminum ion in biological systems. Trends Biochem Sci 13:15–19

Pellet DM, Papernik LA, Jones DL, Darrah PR, Grunes DL, Kochian LV (1997) Involvement of multiple aluminium exclusion mechanisms in aluminium resistance in wheat. Plant Soil 192:63–68

Sivagura M, Horst WJ (1998) The distal part of the transition zone is the most aluminum-sensitive apical root zone of maize. Plant Physiol 116:155–163

1.9

Xenobiotics

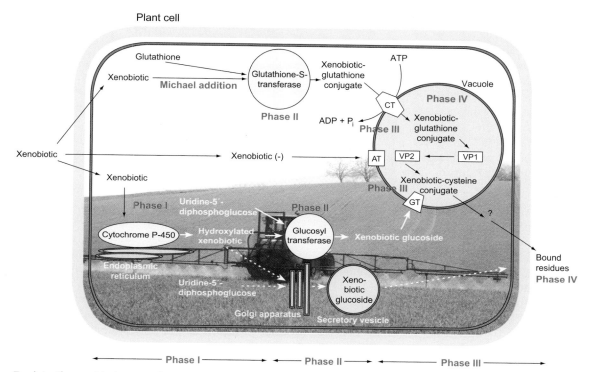

To detoxify xenobiotics organisms use reactions from their normal metabolism. With a clever combination of such reactions, foreign compounds can be detoxified and then deposited in the vacuole or in the cell wall in a form which is not harmful. Such detoxification passes through a sequence of four phases: Biochemical "opening" of the mostly lipophilic xenobiotic, formation of conjugates, sequestration of the conjugate into the vacuole or the secretory vesicle, and finally deposition in the vacuole or the cell wall via chemical modification of the conjugate (see also Fig. 1.9.5). After Coleman et al. (1997)

Recommended Literature

- Darrall NM (1989) The effect of air pollutants on physiological processes in plants. Plant Cell Environ 12:1–30
- Edwards R, Dixon DP, Walbot V (2000) Plant glutathione-S-transferases: enzymes with multiple functions in sickness and in health. Trends Plant Sci 5:193–198
- Grossmann K (2000) Mode of action of auxin herbicides: a new ending to a long, drawn out story. Trends Plant Sci 5:506–508
- Larcher W (2003) Physiological plant ecology, 4th edn. Springer Telos, 450 pp
- Marrs K (1996) The function and regulation of glutathione-S-transferases in plants. Annu Rev Plant Physiol Plant Mol Biol 47:127–158
- Morgan PB, Bernacchi CJ, Ort DR, Long SP (2004) An in vivo analysis of the effect of season-long open-air elevation of ozone to anticipated 2050 levels on photosynthesis in soybean. Plant Physiol 135:2348–2357
- Roberts T (ed) (2000) Metabolism of agrochemicals in plants. John Wiley, 300 pp

Box 1.9.1 Safeners and herbicides

Safeners are non-lethal xeno-biotics which protect herbi-cide-sensitive (crop) plants from the effects of herbicides. If a plant is pre-treated with a safener, it can be sprayed with the herbicide and the "pro-tected" plant will remain un-damaged. In this way the se-lectivity of a herbicide can be indirectly increased. Safeners elicit a xenobiotic protective response, usually induction of glutathione-S-transferases (see Fig. 1.9.3). With the aid of these enzymes the herbicide is made "harmless". There are different classes of herbicide for which safen-ers have been developed. Two of these are

Herbicide group chloroacetamides:

Dichloroacetamide $HCCl_2-C\langle{}^O_{NH_2}$

"Metolachlor"   2-Chloro-N-acetamide

Herbicide group thiolcarbamates:

$-S-\underset{\underset{O}{\|}}{C}-N\langle$

e.g. Ethyl-N,N-di-n-propylthiolcarbamate $C_2H_5-S-\underset{\underset{O}{\|}}{C}-N(CH_2-CH_2-CH_3)_2$

shown. The corresponding safeners are, e.g., flurazole and dichlorimide.

- Sandermann H Jr (1994) Higher plant meta-bolism of xenobiotics: the "green liver" con-cept. Pharmacogenetics 4:225–241
- Sandermann H (2004) Molecular ecotoxicol-ogy of plants. Trends Plant Sci 9:406–413
- Sandermann H Jr, Wellburn AR, Heath RL (eds) (1997) Forest decline and ozone. Ecolog-ical Studies 127. Springer, Berlin Heidelberg New York, 400 pp

Xenobiotics are chemicals (or, more generally, a chemical mix) which are not normal compo-nents of the organism which is exposed to it. However, xenobiotics are biologically active and may cause, dependent on toxicity and the amount taken up, defence reactions, damage or even death of an organism. With respect to plants, xenobiotics are, in addition to the pre-viously discussed toxic heavy metals and alumi-nium, mainly pesticides and waste products, which enter soil, water and air – even in coun-tries where waste management and control is well developed. Except for fertilisers, **herbicides** have the greatest share of the agrochemical mar-ket amongst all pesticides (insecticides, acari-cides, nematicides, fungicides, rodenticides, her-bicides) used for plant protection. Herbicides target plant metabolism and are well researched regarding their reactions in plants and in the soil.

A particular problem of the pesticides is the **selectivity**. Herbicides are supposed to kill off weeds, but crops must be spared. Crops are commonly not able to detoxify herbicides (an exception is maize which detoxifies Atrazine) and therefore a modern trend is towards two-component systems: Herbicide and herbicide safener (antidotes or "immune chemicals", Box 1.9.1), with the latter activating the defence system of the crop so that it can cope with the herbicide. More difficult is the situation if the pesticide targets processes that are similar in the organisms to be protected and the pest (e.g. the use of fungicides in orchards). In many cases, the different sensitivity of the organisms or dif-ferent time slots of a targeted process (e.g. mito-sis in host and parasite) can be used to achieve some selectivity. Scab, mildew and grey mould (*Botrytis*) develop on mature leaves and fruits, so that toxins inhibiting mitosis, e.g. the fungi-cide "Benomyl" (a benzimidazole derivative) (Box 1.9.2 A), when not applied too early, only affect the parasite and thus render sufficient se-lectivity. Often the pests and the crop differ naturally in the mode of pesticide uptake or it is possible to formulate ("package") the chemicals in such a way that differential uptake is achieved. Differences in the structure or the chemistry of the plant surface of weeds and crops, as well as in their morphological charac-

Box 1.9.2 Herbicides

Some of the most important herbicides and their main effects (Fig. A).

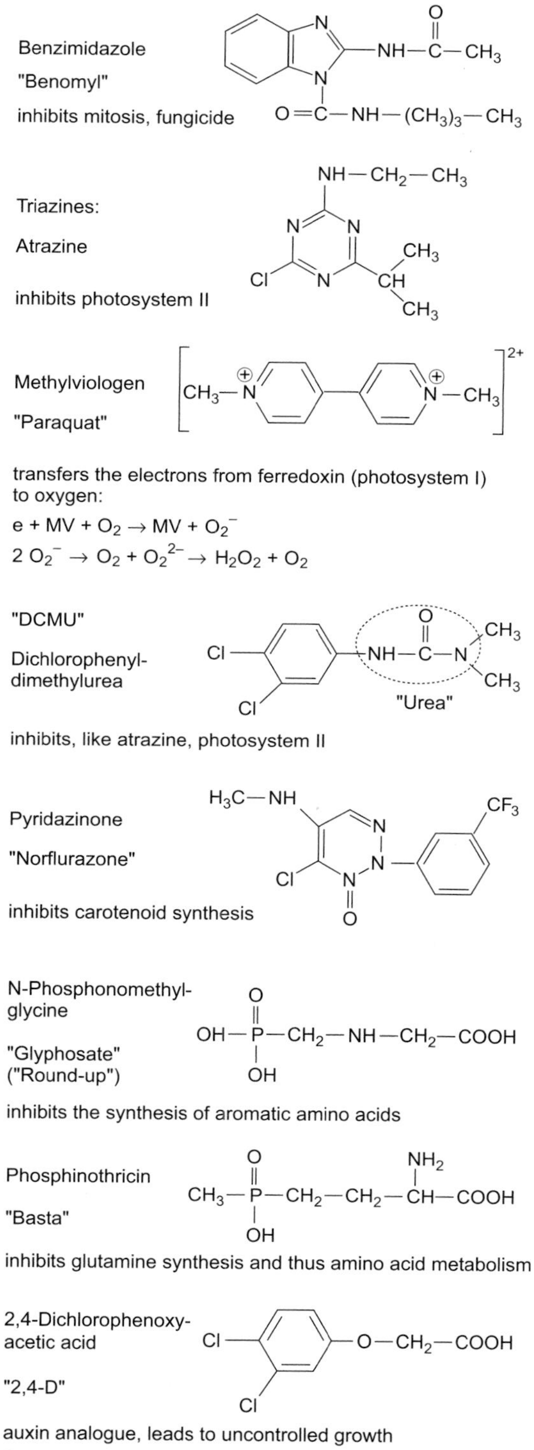

Benzimidazole
"Benomyl"
inhibits mitosis, fungicide
Triazines:
Atrazine
inhibits photosystem II
Methylviologen
"Paraquat"
transfers the electrons from ferredoxin (photosystem I) to oxygen:
e + MV + O2 → MV + O2⁻
2 O2⁻ → O2 + O2²⁻ → H2O2 + O2
"DCMU"
Dichlorophenyl-dimethylurea
"Urea"
inhibits, like atrazine, photosystem II
Pyridazinone
"Norflurazone"
inhibits carotenoid synthesis
N-Phosphonomethyl-glycine
"Glyphosate"
("Round-up")
inhibits the synthesis of aromatic amino acids
Phosphinothricin
"Basta"
inhibits glutamine synthesis and thus amino acid metabolism
2,4-Dichlorophenoxy-acetic acid
"2,4-D"
auxin analogue, leads to uncontrolled growth

A

Measurement of herbicide effects

Simple visual and analytical tests are differentiated. As in the assay of frost resistance (Box 1.3.6), a few days are usually required before damage has developed to a stage which allows quantification of yellowing or necroses (Box 1.1.1, Figs. 1–4). Analytical tests are more sensitive; for a first screening for herbicidal effects, algae are most suited, as the herbicide is in close proximity to the cells. In further rounds of screening the individual specific stress reactions can be examined, e.g. induction of PAL as the starting point for the formation of phytoalexins, or the release of ethylene from methionine (Fig. B). A relatively simple method of measuring damage is provided by chlorophyll fluorescence (cf. Box 1.1.1, Fig. 5).

Sequence of events
Indicators
Xenobiotic
Stress
Ethylene, PAL, antioxidants
Oxidative cell degradation
Ethane, malondialdehyde
Cell death
Expiration of gas exchange

B

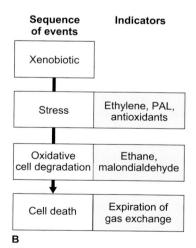

Fig. B. Time course of poisoning by a xenobiotic and useful diagnostic parameters. *PAL,* increase in activity of phenylalanine ammonium lyase. (After Kuhnert 1996)

ters (e.g. leaf-form and orientation in the space), are important in this respect, resulting in differences in uptake.

In crop production, **toxicity** of xenobiotics and of their metabolites for humans and animals as well as the development of resistance of the pest to the pesticide are very important. Resistances develop very quickly if the non-resistant population is completely eradicated. Resistance inheritance is usually recessive. The population quickly looses the dominant targeted gene, if only homozygous recessive organisms propagate.

In the following, the effects of non-metallic xenobiotics on plants and in particular the reactions of plants to these compounds are exemplarily presented. Such reactions may be used for phytoremediation to clean and detoxify air, soil and water, an idea leading to the concept of the "green liver" (Sandermann 1994) in the sense that plants, in analogy to the livers of animals, are able to withdraw toxins (e.g. formaldehyde) from our environment and metabolise them to harmless substances.

The spectrum of xenobiotics is inexhaustible, but in contrast there are only few cellular mechanisms for detoxification. Most xenobiotics are lipophilic, and so diffuse easily into cells. They are also able to accumulate in biomembranes, decreasing their effectiveness and concomitantly the possibility of their metabolism.

1.9.1

Herbicides

Herbicides are the most used pesticides worldwide, constituting 49% of the agrochemical market; they accounted for 68% of total US pesticide sales at approximately US$ 6 billion.

Herbicides inhibit germination and growth of weeds but their use is only profitable if losses in yield were to exceed 5–10%. In general, a distinction is made between herbicides applied **before sowing** (pre-emergent herbicides) and those applied **after sowing** (post-emergent herbicides). Pre-emergent herbicides are applied directly to the soil, thus being also known as **soil herbicides**; they are designed to interfere with germination or to kill the seedlings. Post-emergent herbicides are sprayed on the standing crop (sometimes sprayed from aeroplanes). They interfere with photosynthesis or growth, and are therefore also called **leaf herbicides**.

1.9.1.1
Modes of Herbicide Action

By inhibiting specific physiological reactions herbicides should kill (Box 1.9.2A) unwanted plants. In the extreme case, when all plants are unwanted, so-called total herbicides are used, which are mostly **inhibitors of the photosynthetic light reactions**. Many **total herbicides** have a very specific effect, e.g. inhibition of plastoquinone reduction by blocking its binding site on photosystem II, e.g. by s-Triazine (s stands for symmetric Triazine), such as Atrazine or by urea derivatives, e.g. DCMU, or by production of ROS in photosystem I (e.g. by methylviologen = Paraquat).

Inhibitors of carotene biosynthesis, such as Norflurazon which inhibits phytoen-desaturase, also increase oxidative stress and thus stop the formation of shading and protective pigments.

Also **N metabolism** is a possible target. The chemical structure of Glyphosate resembles that of phosphoenol pyruvate and therefore this herbicide is bound very effectively by the enoylpyruvyl-phosphoshikimate synthase instead of the natural substrate, thus abandoning the synthesis of the aromatic amino acid. Similarly, "Basta" (=phosphinotricin) inhibits synthesis of glutamine which is the starting metabolite for amino acid synthesis in plants.

The herbicides listed above affect photosynthesis, carotenoid and amino acid biosynthesis, but other metabolic activities are also targets of herbicide design to achieve better selectivity and efficiency, e.g. mitochondrial respiration, lipid biosynthesis, nucleic acid synthesis, turnover of the cytoskeleton, phytohormone metabolism and steps in seed germination (pre-emergent herbicides). One of the most frequently used herbicides is 2,4-D, whose molecule is similar to that of the growth hormone auxin, wherefore it is able to disrupt its action.

Even if the principal effects of herbicides are known, e.g. the inhibition of a certain metabolic reaction, in many cases the molecular mechanisms still remain unknown, as the protein structures involved are themselves not known in sufficient detail. Of 2,4-D, e.g., the receptor (probably at the plasma membrane) is still not known. Many herbicides, particularly those affecting photosynthesis and respiration, produce oxygen- and other radicals, lipid peroxides and other particularly reactive substances, of which only the most basic chemistry is known. Fig-

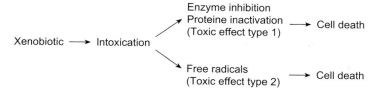

Fig. 1.9.1. Modes of action of total herbicides. In type 1 the toxic effect results from direct interaction of the xenobiotic with a "target" system whose inhibition causes the damage (e.g. inhibition of glutamine synthetase by the phosphinotricin "Basta", see Boxes 1.9.2 and 1.9.3). In type 2 mode of action, targets are also hit, but the damage is caused by the reaction of the plant (e.g. by the ROS response of the herbicide "Paraquat"). Likewise, inhibition of the synthesis of protective compounds (e.g. carotenoids by the herbicide "Norflurazon") leads to a type 2 toxic effect. (After Kuhnert 1996)

ure 1.9.1 shows an overview of the ways in which herbicides act.

A general principle seems to be that toxicity of a herbicide increases with its electrophilicity, as this determines its ability to react with nucleophilic biological macromolecules such as proteins and nucleic acids. Weakly polarised electrophilic agents react with weak nucleophiles of the cell, and strongly polarised ones with strong nucleophiles.

1.9.1.2
The Four Steps of Xenobiotics Detoxification by Plants

Detoxification of xenobiotics usually requires a reaction sequence which can be separated into four distinct steps (phases). Many pesticides and other xenobiotics are lipophilic compounds which are difficult to attack in the aqueous milieu of the plant cell.

1. **Phase 1** or **step I** of the **detoxification process** is therefore the introduction of a hydrophilic group. Oxidation, reduction or hydrolysis is the usual reaction to increase the compound's water solubility and to start detoxification. Aromatic rings are preferentially oxidised by monooxygenases (mixed function oxygenases; Fig. 1.9.2 A), which contain a cytochrome P450 and require molecular oxygen and a second electron donor. By oxidation electrophilic groups are introduced or created in the molecules which leads to an activation, i.e. increases their toxicity. Seemingly, the system of oxidases, monooxygenases and hydrolases exhibits little substrate specificity, but this is not the case: In *Arabidopsis thaliana* more than 60 genes coding for monooxygenases have been identified! The apparent non-speci-

ficity can be explained by the great number of relatively substrate-specific enzymes.

2. In **phase II** the now more hydrophilic compounds are conjugated, i.e. bound to other hydrophilic molecules. Conjugation is either by glycosylation of the newly formed functional groups or by formation of a thioether ("Michael-addition"; Fig. 1.9.2 B) with glutathione and its homologues (Fig. 1.9.2 C). Glycosylation is catalysed by glucosyl transferases with uridine diphosphate-glucose as the substrate, whereas thioethers are produced by the so-called glutathione-S-transferases (GSTs). The latter group of enzymes can use many natural and artificial compounds as substrates. Amongst these are many herbicides (Atrazine, 2,4-D, Metolachlor), but also typical plant pigments (anthocyanins), growth substances (auxin) or defence substances (salicylic acid; Marrs 1996).

As with the glycosyl transferases the apparent non-specificity of GSTs results from the concomitant presence of a larger number of very specific enzymes. Thus the selectivity of many herbicides is based on the occurrence of certain, substrate-specific GSTs in crop plants and the lack of such (iso-)enzymes in weeds. Also, the effects of "safeners" (antidotes) may be achieved via the induction of a specific GST. However, specificity of conjugation of xenobiotics depends on the specificity of GSTs for natural substrates, e.g. tannins and flavonoids (pigments) or auxins. Usually, safeners effect the induction of such transferases. Infections may also lead to the induction of GSTs. As well as GSTs other transferases are also able to increase the water solubility of xenobiotics by conjugation (Table 1.9.1).

3. In **phase III** the conjugated product is sequestered, either in the vacuole or in the cell wall,

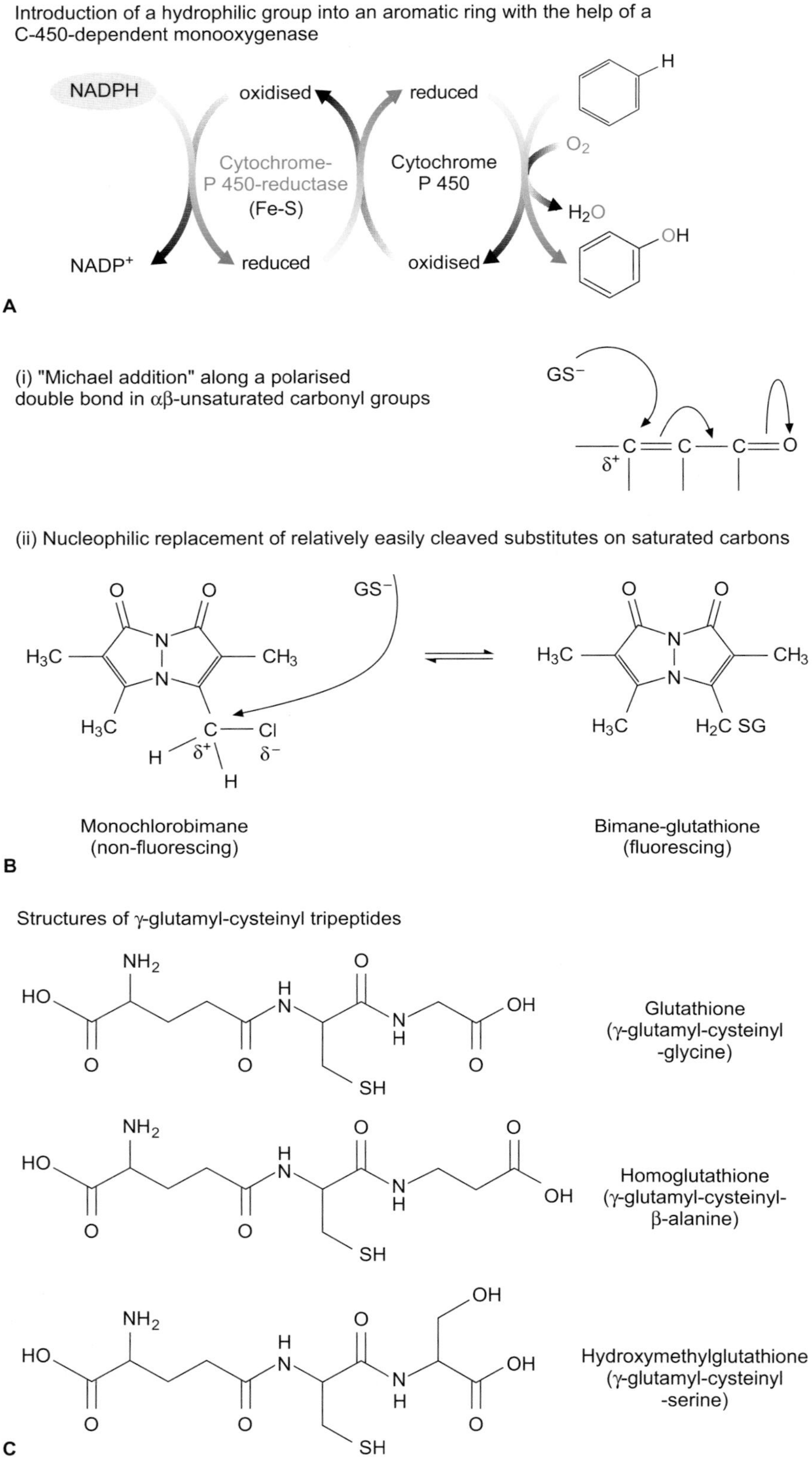
Introduction of a hydrophilic group into an aromatic ring with the help of a C-450-dependent monooxygenase
NADPH
oxidised
reduced
Cytochrome-P 450-reductase (Fe-S)
Cytochrome P 450
O2
H2O
H
OH
NADP+
reduced
oxidised
A
(i) "Michael addition" along a polarised double bond in αβ-unsaturated carbonyl groups
GS−
δ+
(ii) Nucleophilic replacement of relatively easily cleaved substitutes on saturated carbons
GS−
H3C
CH3
H2C SG
Monochlorobimane (non-fluorescing)
Bimane-glutathione (fluorescing)
B
Structures of γ-glutamyl-cysteinyl tripeptides
Glutathione (γ-glutamyl-cysteinyl -glycine)
Homoglutathione (γ-glutamyl-cysteinyl-β-alanine)
Hydroxymethylglutathione (γ-glutamyl-cysteinyl -serine)
C

Fig. 1.9.2. Biochemistry of detoxification of xenobiotics (A from Lehninger et al. 1994; B, C from Coleman et al. 1997)

Table 1.9.1. Classes of plant enzymes that metabolise xenobiotics and their natural substrates. After Sandermann (1994)

Enzyme class	Xenobiotic substrate	Natural substrate
Cytochrome P450	4-Chloro-*N*-methylalanine	Cinnamic acid, pterocarpanes
Glutathione-S-transferase	Fluorodifen, alachlor, atrazine	Cinnamic acid
Carboxylesterases	Diethylhexylphthalate	Lipids, acetylcholine
O-Glucosyltransferases	Chlorinated phenols	Flavonoids, coniferylalcohol
O-Malonyltransferases	*β*-D-Glucosides from pentachlorophenol and from 4-hydroxy-2,5-dichlorophenoxyacetic acid	*β*-D-Glucosides from flavonoids and isoflavonoids
N-Glucosyltransferases	Chlorinated anilines, metribuzin	Nicotinic acid
N-Malonyltransferases	Chlorinated anilines	1-Aminocyclopropylcarboxylic acid, D-amino acids, anthranilic acid

again by enzymes of the natural secondary metabolism. Key enzymes are the so-called glutathione pumps. Sequestering is required because the GS conjugates can inhibit glutathione-S-transferases as well as glutathione reductases; and, in some cases, they themselves are potent toxins and must, therefore, be removed.

Glutathione Pumps (GS-X Pumps)

GS-X pumps transport the GS conjugates into the vacuole and are, thus, transport proteins of the tonoplast (Rea et al. 1998). They belong to the so-called ABC superfamily, a group of transporters which play an important role in animal, fungal and plant tissues, particularly in connection with secondary metabolism. These proteins have a "Walker" Box A and a "Walker" Box B, which are separated by a characteristic C-motif, hence the term ABC transporter. So far, more than 130 representatives of the superfamily are known, which translocate sugars, peptides, alkaloids, phenolic compounds and inorganic and organic ions.

This superfamily has two large subfamilies, multidrug resistance proteins (MDRs) and multidrug resistance associated proteins (MPRs), the latter being typical of plants. Their assembly is relatively uniform, even if the sequence homologies are, in part, below 40%. It is a large protein with several modular domains, namely one to two membrane-spanning domains (TMDs), two domains forming a nucleotide binding fold (NBF) and the regulatory unit R (Fig. 1.9.3).

These transporters are directly activated by MgATP, resulting in an "active" transport that is not dependent on a H$^+$ gradient (H$^+$-ATPase independent). Even though the mechanism is not fully explained, it is assumed that an intermedi-

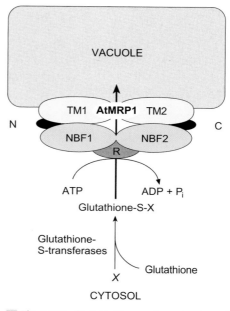

Fig. 1.9.3. Composition and mechanism of a plant ABC transporter from the multidrug resistance associated protein (MRP) family. After the compound X is conjugated with glutathione by a glutathione-S-transferase, it can be transported by the MRP into the vacuole. *N*, N-terminus; *C*, C-terminus; *TM* (*1,2*) trans-membrane domains; *NBF* (*1,2*) nucleotide binding pockets; *R* putative regulatory domain. (After Rea et al. 1997)

ary acyl phosphate (perhaps with glutathione) is formed, indicated by the very strong inhibition by vanadate (formation of an acyl vanadate instead of the acyl phosphate). Remarkably, these transporters translocate glutathione conjugates, as well as GSSG (oxidised glutathione), but not reduced glutathione (GSH). So far, three such transporters which differ in substrate specificities have been described from *Arabidopsis thaliana* (AtMRP).

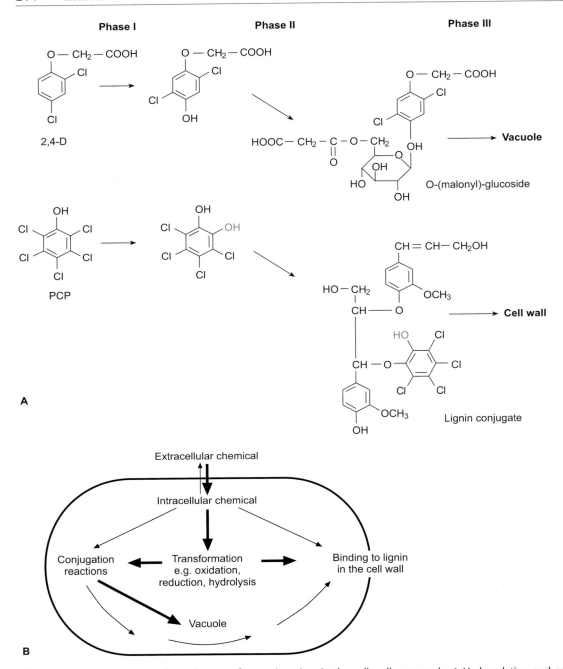

Fig. 1.9.4. Sequestration of xenobiotics, after conjugation, in the cell wall or vacuole. A Hydroxylation and conjugation of 2,4-dichlorophenoxyacetic acid and pentachlorophenol. B Map of reactions which result in the sequestration of xenobiotics after uptake into the cell. (Sandermann 1994)

Natural Substrates of GS-X Pumps

Of course, organisms did not develop GST-GS-X pumps for xenobiotics. Their natural substrates are nucleophilic substances of secondary metabolism: anthocyanins (flavonoids), auxin, salicylic acid, cinnamic acid, hydroxy fatty acids and degradation products of DNA. The Michaelis constant of AtMRP 1 and 2 for cyanidin-3-glucoside-GS conjugate (an anthocyanin) is ca. 50 µM and V_{max} is ≈ 5 nmol/mg protein per minute, for example. Similar kinetic data were reported for glucosyl conjugates, e.g. of degradation products of chlorophyll.

4. In **phase IV** the conjugates are immobilised in the vacuole. Conjugates with glutathione are often further metabolised in the vacuole in order to avoid their diffusion back into the cytoplasm. Thus, for example, a carboxypeptidase (exopeptidase) may cleave the glycine residue from glutathione. A vacuolar dipeptidase is able to remove the amino terminal glutamic acid, with the consequent formation of cysteine conjugates. The final fate of these cysteine conjugates is unclear. One possibility would be that they leave the vacuole again via the Golgi system and become irreversibly incorporated into the cell wall as "bound residues" (Fig. 1.9.4).

1.9.1.3
Immunochemicals

Some xenobiotics, e.g. 2,6-dichloroisonicotinic acid and its methyl ester, not only induce the three to four step detoxification system, but also PR proteins (pathogenesis related proteins), e.g. chitinases and β-glucanases (see Chap. 1.10.2.1), serving to combat pathogens (although their mode of action is frequently not known). Such xenobiotics are called **immunochemicals**. They are often formed to such a low extent that detection in cell extracts is hardly possible. When screening for a potential immunogenic effect of a xenobiotic a trick is generally used: Instead of the protein, the activation of the gene encoding for it is examined: Since several of these genes are known, activity of their promoter as induced by a potential immunochemical can be investigated. Fusion of the promoter with a reporter gene – e.g. the GUS-(glucuronidase-)gene of E. coli – provides a DNA probe. This probe can then be introduced, via the Agrobacterium system or the particle gun, into the genome of the test plant. After spraying a plant with the potential inducer, induction of the PR promoter by the herbicide can be seen as a stained product from the action of the glucuronidase.

The development of crop plants which respond to immunochemicals is considered as better than development of more herbicides (Box 1.9.3), because immunochemicals do not kill the weed, but rather increase the resistance of the crop. Thus, protective treatment with fungicides and insecticides could be strongly reduced. Treatment with a chemical would, however, still be required, but would induce the nat-

ural defence of the plant in the battle against detrimental organisms.

1.9.2
Gaseous Air Pollutants

The most important gaseous pollutants damaging plants are sulfur dioxide, ozone, nitrogen oxides (NO_x), peroxyacetyl nitrate (PAN), ethylene, and various other substances which are adsorbed on dust particles (Table 1.9.2).

Particularly noxious are the reductive smog (London type) which contains mostly SO_2, and the oxidative, photochemical smog (Los Angeles type), which is characterised by PAN. The large number of air pollutants cannot be covered here, but it is clear that sulfur dioxide results mainly from burning of S-containing fossil fuels and from smelting of metal sulfide ores. The main component of photochemical, oxidative smogs, PAN, is produced in a complicated chain reaction from nitrogen oxides and unsaturated hydrocarbons during incomplete burning of motor fuels.

Increasing use of oil and gas as domestic fuels and desulfurisation of industrial emissions have reduced the SO_2 concentration in industrial and heavily polluted areas to less than 10% of that in the immediate post-war years (Fig. 1.9.5). However, concentrations of nitric oxides rose or stagnated in many countries, despite the use of catalytic converters in cars. In addition to industrial and car exhaust gases many other gaseous pollutants accumulate in houses, e.g. formaldehyde (see below).

Of course, such gases are not only problematic to humans, but when present at higher concentrations may also damage plants. Forest decline in recent years (Fig. 1.9.6; see also Chap.

Table 1.9.2. Airborne substances, toxic to plants. From Elstner (1984)

Oxidative smog	NO_2, PAN, O_3 (Los Angeles type)
Reductive smog	SO_2 (London type)
Acids	HF, H_2SO_3, H_2SO_4, HCl
Dusts	Most importantly cement dust and blown soil particles
Phytoeffectors	Ethylene, airborne herbicides and plant protective agents
Allelopathic effectors	(e.g. terpenoids)

Box 1.9.3   Production of herbicide-resistant crop plants

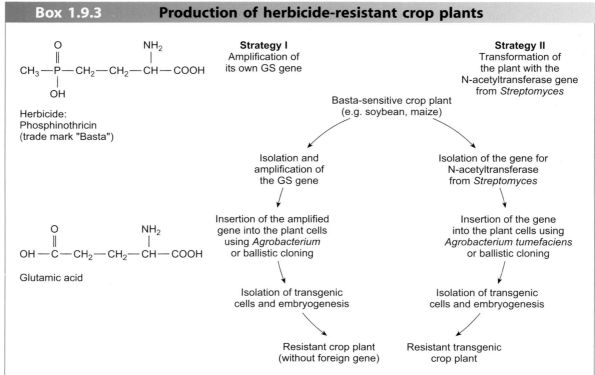

Due to its similarity with glutamic acid, phosphinotricin ("Basta") inhibits glutamine synthetase. It is inactivated by N-acetylation.

Strategies for the creation of Basta-resistant crops

In principle, there are two strategies to introduce Basta resistance into a plant:

1. Increasing the expression of the plant's own gene that the herbicide targets, i.e. the gene for glutamine synthetase. Thus plants remain undamaged or only slightly damaged at Basta concentrations that kill wild-type plants (strategy I).
2. Introduction of a Basta-inactivating foreign gene, i.e. the gene for N-acetyltransferase from *Streptomyces* (strategy II).

In the first case a non-transgenic plant is produced, whereas in the second the plant is transgenic.

3.5.1 and Fig. 2.3.7 F) has been mainly attributed to such atmospheric pollutants.

In the past, trees in the areas of smelting works and power stations fuelled by lignite were damaged lethally by the high SO_2 concentrations (e.g. in the Erzgebirge of Germany). Current regulations on air pollution have resulted in a decrease in the concentrations of these pollutant below the threshold of damage (Fig. 1.9.5). However, this raises the question: "What is the damaging concentration?" In principle, the impact of stress depends on the product of time and concentration of a noxious substance; however, in practice, this applies only conditionally. For almost all gaseous pollutants exists a range of concentration (below the so-called threshold) where the pollutant does no damage, and may even be useful. Not everything emitted from the exhaust of a motor vehicle is, from the perspective of the plant, a damaging gaseous pollutant – CO_2 and nitric oxides, and to a certain extent even SO_2, can contribute to the mineral nutrition of plants. In making such a general statement, the different sensitivities of the individual plant species must be considered (Table 1.9.3), which in turn depend on the developmental stage of the plant.

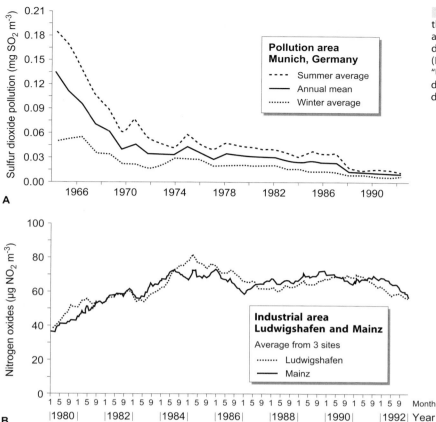

Fig. 1.9.5. Development of the annual, summer, and winter average concentrations of sulfur dioxide (A) and nitrogen dioxide (B) in the past 20 years. (From "Umweltbereich Luft", Folienserie des Fonds der Chemischen Industrie, 1995, Frankfurt)

Fig. 1.9.6. Typical symptoms of the "new forest decline". A Extreme crown attenuation in spruce. The trees carry leaves of only the most recent years (2–3 years). B Yellowing of the current years needles probably resulted from acute magnesium deficiency ("advanced apical yellowing"). Soils are depleted of cations, in particular magnesium, as a consequence of acid deposition ("acid rain"). (Hock and Elstner 1984)

Table 1.9.3. Different sensitivities of plants to SO_2 in the air. Source: VDI-Richtlinie 2310 "Maximale Immissionswerte für SO_2 zum Schutz der Vegetation"

Very sensitive plants	Sensitive plants	Less sensitive plants
Deciduous woody plants		
Walnut (*Juglans regia*)	Lime (*Tilia* sp.)	Plane (*Platanus* sp.), oak (*Quercus* sp.)
Red current (*Ribes rubum*)	Beech (*Fagus silvatica*)	Poplar (*Populus* sp.), Sycamore (*Acer* sp.)
Gooseberry (*Ribes uva-crispa*)	Hornbeam (*Carpinus betulus*)	Alder (*Alnus* sp.), Lilac (*Syringa vulgaris*)
	Apple (*Malus domestica*)	Willow (*Salix* sp.), Robinia (*Robinia pseudoacacia*)
	Hazelnut (*Corylus avellana*)	Birch (*Betula* sp.), cherry and plum (*Prunus* sp.)
		Grape vine (*Vitis vinifera*)
		Rhododendron (*Rhododendron* sp.)
Coniferous trees		
Fir (*Abies* sp.)	Scots pine (*Pinus sylvestris*)	Austrian pine (*Pinus nigra austriaca*)
Spruce (*Picea* sp.)	Weymouth pine (*Pinus strobus*)	Western red cedar (*Thuja* sp.), yew (*Taxus baccata*)
Douglas fir (*Pseudotsuga menziesii*)	Larch (*Larix* sp.)	Juniper (*Juniperus* sp.)
		Cypress (*Chamaecyparis* sp.)
Agronomically and horticulturally important plants		
Clover (*Trifolium* sp.)	Barley (*Hordeum vulgare*)	Potato (*Solanum tuberosum*)
Alfalfa (*Medicago sativa*)	Oats (*Avena sativa*)	Tomato (*Lycopersicon esculentum*)
Lupin (*Lupinus* sp.)	Rye (*Secale cereale*)	Maize (*Zea mays*), sugar beet (*Beta vulgaris* ssp.)
Common vetch (*Vicia sativa*)	Wheat (*Triticum aestivum*)	Cabbage (*Brassica oleracea* ssp.)
Broad bean (*Vicia faba*)	Lettuce (*Lactuca sativa*)	Carrot (*Daucus carota*)
Spinach (*Spinacia oleracea*)	Beans (*Phaseolus* sp.)	Strawberry (*Fragaria chiloensis*)
Pea (*Pisum sativum*)	Rape (*Brassica napus*)	Leek (*Allium* sp.)
Ornamental plants		
Begonia (*Begonia* sp.)	Dahlia (*Dahlia variabilis*)	Rose (*Rosa* sp.), Gladiolus (*Gladiolus* sp.)
Sweet pea (*Lathyrus odorata*)	Geranium (*Pelargonium zonale*)	Tulip (*Tulipa gesneriana*), iris (*Iris* sp.)
	Petunia (*Petunia hybrida*)	Daffodil (*Narcissus pseudonarcissus*)
	Carnation (*Dianthus caryophyllus*)	Marguerite (*Chrysanthemum leucanthemum*)
	Fuchsia (*Fuchsia hybrida*)	Heather (*Calluna vulgaris*)

Table 1.9.4. Summary of the stomatal responses to airborne pollutants. (After Darrall 1989)

	Category of response		
Pollutant (ppb)	Low Open or no change	Medium Open, closed or no change	High Closed
SO_2	<100	100–950	>1865
O_3		≤200	>200
NO_2	≤100	≤1000	≥2000
NO		≤1000	>1000
HF	≤0.6		≥14

Only above an appropriate threshold is there usually a range of concentration in which an impact correlates with the product of concentration and exposure time [e.g. for SO_2 short-term (28 h) fumigation with 21 ppm, for long-term exposition (7–50 days) 0.04–0.2 ppm]. At higher concentrations the exposure time is less important, as the concentration alone is responsible for the damage.

In general and for practical reasons, a distinction is made between short-term stress (2–5 h) and chronic stress (7 days, 50–200 days: Fig. 1.9.7). Of course combinations of stresses must be considered in the context of air pollutants, e.g. if gaseous pollutants increase stomata conductance (Table 1.9.4), the danger of desiccation increases substantially. On the other hand, drought stress, and closing of stomates triggered by it, protects against diffusion of gaseous pollutants into a plant.

Many gaseous pollutants are able to enter the leaves by two routes: physically (by diffusion; Fig. 1.9.8 and Table 1.9.5) and/or chemically, e.g. by damaging the cuticle.

Sulfur dioxide, ozone and formaldehyde will be discussed in the following as examples of pollutants that damage plants.

1.9.2.1
Sulfur Dioxide

SO_2 mainly enters the atmosphere because of human activities and also, to a lesser extent, by natural processes (Box 1.9.4). In the atmosphere SO_2 may be converted, e.g. to sulfurous acid (bisulfite) or sulfuric acid. This chapter will discuss mainly the pollutant SO_2.

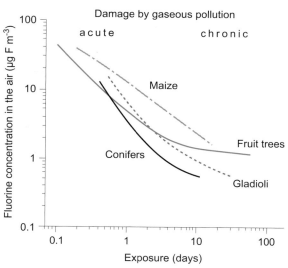

Fig. 1.9.7. Acute and chronic damage to various plants by fluorine as airborne pollutant. In hours to days the plant reacts with a type of "stress-quantity law" (intensity×duration of exposure). Acute damage is evident by the loss of chlorophyll with subsequent necroses; chronic damage expresses itself through slower growth, alterations in the structure of the wood, and reduction in fertility after a transient flush in fertility. (After Larcher 1994)

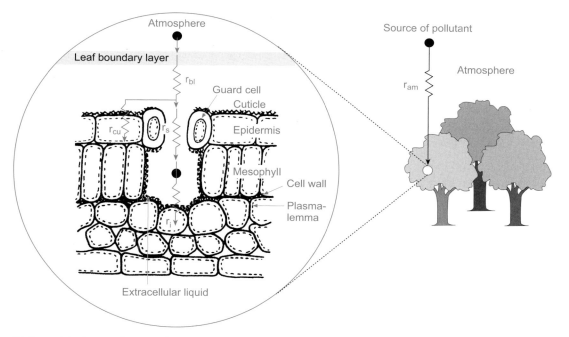

Fig. 1.9.8. Route of entry of gaseous airborne pollutants into leaves. The entry into leaves requires that pollutants overcome various resistances (r). In the air the rates of transport depend mainly on exogenous factors: Wind, the roughness of the terrain (vegetation), temperature and humidity are major determinants of the rate of dispersal and the fluxes. These factors together are considered to be the "atmospheric resistance" (r_{am}). Further resistance results from the boundary layer on the leaf surface (r_{bl}), from the narrow aperture of the stomates (r_s), and structure and tightness of the cuticle (r_{cu}) and the wall of the mesophyll cells (r_i). Differentiation of these individual resistances is meaningful as their efficacy depends on the nature of the pollutant. In addition, the individual pollutant can influence the opening of the stomates or reduce the density of the cuticle. (Modified after Fuhrer 1996)

Table 1.9.5. Typical range of values for the relative diffusivities of gaseous pollutants (Wesley 1989) and the diffusion resistance (r_c) of leaves to specific gases (Taylor et al. 1988)

Air pollutant (P)	Relative diffusivities [a] (D_{H_2O}/D_P)	Leaf diffusion resistance (s cm^{-1})
Ozone, O_3	1.6	1.4–5
Nitrogen monoxide, NO	1.3	1–10
Nitrogen dioxide, NO_2	1.6	0.1–0.8
Nitric acid, HNO_3	1.9	0.2–2
Ammonia, NH_3	1.0	1.7–5
Peroxyacetylnitrate (PAN)	2.6	1.7–10
Sulfur dioxide, SO_2	1.9	0.03–0.5
Hydrogen sulfide, H_2S	1.4	0.25–0.5

[a] Calculated as the square root of the molar mass ratio M_P/M_{H_2O}

Table 1.9.6. Cuticular and stomatal conductances in a *Citrus* leaf for various gases (including the boundary layer resistance; from Lange et al. 1989)

Gas	Cuticular conductance (cm s^{-1})	Stomatal conductance (cm s^{-1})
SO_2	2.01×10^{-5}	0.12
O_2	3.05×10^{-5}	0.18
CO_2	5.4×10^{-6}	0.14
H_2O	1.09×10^{-7}	0.22

centrations of SO_2 lead to turgor loss of the auxiliary cells and to opening of the stomata, high concentrations to closure of stomata. NO_2 permeates easily and quickly through biomembranes whilst hydrogen sulfite or sulfite ions hardly pass through undamaged membranes.

SO₂ Uptake into the Plant

Even though the stomatal conductivity for sulfur dioxide is almost the same as for CO_2, SO_2 is able to penetrate the cuticle (with stomata closed) better than oxygen and about 20 times faster than CO_2 (Table 1.9.6). Low external con-

Metabolism of SO₂ in the Plant

SO_2 is a reducing as well as an oxidising agent because of its mid-range redox potential. It reacts easily with many biomolecules (see Box 1.9.4) and thus inhibits many enzymes; it is even mutagenic, as it forms dihydrosulfonates

---

Box 1.9.4   The air pollutant SO₂

A few interesting facts:
Sulfur dioxide is produced naturally (20 million t/year) and by human activity (150 million t/year). Naturally, sulfur dioxide is produced upon degradation of terrestrial and marine biomass and through volcanic activity.

Clean air contains approx. 1 µg SO_2/m^3 = 0.3 ppb (1 ppm = 2.67 mg SO_2/m^3), highly contaminated air contains up to 1500 µg SO_2/m^3.

In air, SO_2 gives rise to sulfurous acid:

$$SO_2 + H_2O \leftrightarrow HSO_3^- + H^+$$

and OH radicals oxidise this to sulfuric acid:

$$SO_2 + OH^\bullet \leftrightarrow SO_3 + H_2O$$

$$SO_3 + H_2O \leftrightarrow H_2SO_4$$

Carbonyls $\longrightarrow$ Hydroxysulfonic acids

Unsaturated fatty acids $\longrightarrow$ Sulfonic acids

Pyrimidines $\longrightarrow$ Dihydrosulfonates

Disulfides $\longrightarrow$ cleavage of the $-S-S-$ bridge $\longrightarrow$ Thiosulfate

Oxygen radical $O_2^{\bullet-} \longrightarrow HSO_3^{\bullet-} + H_2O_2$

For plants the strong reducing agent HSO_3^- is about 20 times more poisonous than SO_4^{2-}.

Sulfurous acid or SO_2 reacts with almost all biomolecules and this is how the sulfonate acids originate.

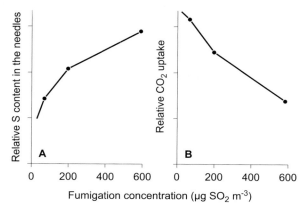

Fig. 1.9.9. Accumulation of sulfur (A) and inhibition of photosynthesis (B) in young spruce trees after 3 months of fumigation with the SO_2 concentrations shown on the abscissa. (After Larcher 1994)

with pyrimidine bases. It can also interfere directly with the plant's CO_2 metabolism by binding, e.g. to ribulosebisphosphate in the RuBP-Rubisco complex, and thus contribute to the well-known inhibition of photosynthesis (Fig. 1.9.9). Inhibition of photosynthesis by SO_2 is not based on a single reaction, but a reaction complex or a syndrome (Darrall 1989). Particularly striking is the bleaching of green tissues caused by SO_2: originally this was interpreted as an effect of acidity inferred by sulfurous acid, but this probably only applies very rarely, because the required concentration of acid and the required low intracellular pH are usually not reached. Only in a very acidic milieu is the magnesium ion removed from the porphyrin ring of chlorophyll producing the brown pheophytin. It is more likely that SO_2 damage results from oxidation of the unsaturated fatty acids of membrane lipids or from SO_2 addition to unsaturated membrane constituents, thus affecting the chlorophyll–protein complexes to such an extent that chlorophyll is released, or is at least easily available for chemical reactions. In the oxidation of linolenic or linoleic acid, for example, fatty acid hydroperoxides are formed ("LOOH", L = lipid) which trigger a chain reaction producing radicals upon reaction with sulfurous acid:

$$HSO_3^- + LOOH \rightarrow HSO_3^\bullet (\text{bisulfite radical})$$
$$+ LO^\bullet (\text{fatty acid radical}) + OH^- \quad (1.9.1)$$

$$LO^\bullet + HSO_3^- + H^+ \rightarrow HSO_3^\bullet + LOH \quad (1.9.2)$$

$$LO^\bullet \rightarrow \text{reactive aldehyde} \quad (1.9.3)$$

e.g. hexenal, nonenal as well as ethane (a parameter for monitoring the reaction).

$LO^\bullet$ also oxidises chlorophyll ("bleaching"), aided by the formation of sulfuric acid during the decay of the hydrogen sulfite radical:

$$2HSO_3^\bullet + H_2O \rightarrow SO_4^{2-} + HSO_3^- + 3H^+ \quad (1.9.4)$$

as well as by further formation of radicals:

$$HSO_3^\bullet + O_2 + H_2O \rightarrow SO_4^{2-} + O_2^{\bullet-} + 3H^+ \quad (1.9.5)$$

$$O_2^{\bullet-} + H^+ \rightarrow HO_2^\bullet (\text{hydroperoxyl radical}) \quad (1.9.6)$$

and the formation of the peroxide ion (hydrogen peroxide):

$$2O_2^{\bullet-} + 2H^+ \rightarrow H_2O_2 + O_2 \quad (1.9.7)$$

The last reaction is catalysed by the enzyme superoxide dismutase.

In almost all areas with high pollution lower chlorophyll contents are measured, particularly in trees. However, this should not be explained exclusively by chlorophyll oxidation but can often result from magnesium deficiency as a consequence of the acidification of soils by "acid rain" (see Chaps. 2.3 and 3.5.1).

The destruction of membranes does not only pertain to photosynthetic membranes, but may, in principle, be assumed for all cellular membranes. This is indicated by the damage caused to plants by SO_2 concentrations at which no visible symptoms occur.

Part of the SO_2 taken up by the plant is photosynthetically assimilated (reduced) and may thus contribute to the sulfur nutrition. According to the ion trap principle, SO_2 and HSO_3^- accumulate in the alkaline stroma of the chloroplast (Table 1.9.7); however, it must first be oxidised to a sulfate.

Table 1.9.7. Intracellular distribution of HSO_3^- in the individual cell organelles, following the ion trap principle and the proportions of the volumes. (After Pfanz et al. 1987)

Organelle	Chloroplast	Cytosol	Vacuole
pH	8.0	approx. 7.0	approx. 5.0
Percentage distribution of HSO_3^-	96	3	1

The oxidising agent is photosynthetically reduced oxygen, the oxygen anion radical. The reaction occurs via the hydrogen sulfite radical:

$$O_2^{\bullet -} + HSO_3^- + 2H^+ \rightarrow HSO_3^{\bullet} + H_2O_2 \quad (1.9.8)$$

$$2HSO_3^{\bullet} + H_2O \leftrightarrow SO_4^{2-} + HSO_3^- + 3H^+ \quad (1.9.9)$$

$$SO_4^{2-} + 8e^- + 8H^+ \rightarrow S^{2-} + 4H_2O \quad (1.9.10)$$

After its activation with ATP (to adenosine phosphosulfate, APS) sulfate is reduced to S^{2-} by the well-known assimilatory sulfate reduction pathway. The sulfide ion (S^{2-}) is incorporated into the amino acid cysteine via serine. With protons it may alternatively produce H_2S which is released in considerable amounts into the atmosphere. However, this does not generally exceed 10% of the SO_2 taken up (Rennenberg 1984). Whereas reduction of SO_2 consumes protons, oxidation to sulfate produces sulfuric acid as well as sulfurous acid. If the strain remains below the threshold of damage, these acids may be buffered intracellularly (Lange et al. 1989). Whether proton transport from SO_2-stressed leaves via sulfate into the roots and finally into the soil can take place needs further clarification. Stress by sulfate to assimilatory organs is not only caused by uptake and conversion of SO_2. Research on the sulfur relations of spruce (Köstner et al. 1998) showed that uptake of sulfur from the soil may exceed gaseous sulfur uptake by a factor of 4 to 5.

SO₂ Resistance

Beside the different capacity of plants to assimilate SO_2 there is no specific resistance against this pollutant, as it has many effects. Known differences in the sensitivity of various plants and their developmental stages are usually not based on SO_2-specific interactions or reactions, but on general characteristics of individual plant types, e.g. the higher resistance of C4 plants is based on the fact that SO_2 inhibits PEP-carboxylase less than Rubisco. Other favourable characteristics are frequent renewal of leaves and a greater capacity for buffering or adsorption.

Lichens are an example for a very broad spectrum of SO_2 sensitivity (Box 1.9.5), because they do not possess stomata and are, therefore, more directly and evenly subjected to pollutants in air than higher plants. Because of the close symbiotic interactions between algae and fungi, lichens are particularly delicate and easily disturbed, and they are not able to drop stressed tissues like shedding leaves.

Figure 1.9.10 summarises possible mechanisms for avoidance and tolerance which are used by lichens to cope with air pollution, particularly by SO_2. However, the role of the typical compounds of lichens, the lichenous acids, in this process is not quite clear. Possibly these acids adsorb some of the gaseous noxes (Box 1.9.6).

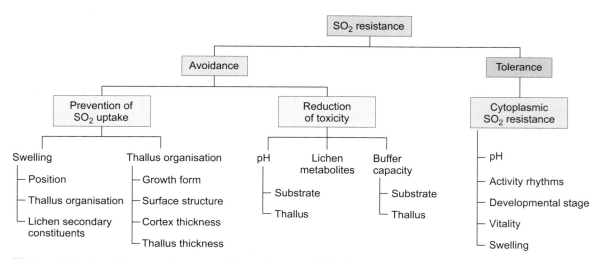

Fig. 1.9.10. The different mechanisms of SO_2 resistance exhibited by lichens; in this case tolerance encompasses also repair. (Türk et al. 1974)

Box 1.9.5 Biomonitoring of air pollutants using lichens

Table 1. Lichen occupation and communities on trees (bark as an organic substrate) and walls, and the influence of SO$_2$ stress (after Larcher 1994)

Average SO$_2$ concentration (μg m^{-3})	Epiphytic lichens		Epipetric lichens	
	Eutrophic bark	Non-eutrophic substrate	Alkaline substrate	Acid substrate
>125	Lecanora conizaeoides Lecanora expallens	Lecanora conizaeoides Lepraria incana	Lecanoraion dispersae	Conizaedion
ca. 70	Buellia canescens Physcia adscendens	Hypogymnia physodes Lecidea scalaris		
ca. 60	Buellia canescens Xanthoria parietina Physcia orbicularis Ramalina farinacea	Hypogymnia physodes Evernia prunastri	Xanthorion	Conizaeoidion Acarospora fuscata
ca. 50	Pertusaria albescens Physiconia pulverulenta Xanthoria polycarpa Lecania cyrtella	Parmelia caperata Graphis elegans Pseudovenia furfuracea		
ca. 40	Physcia aipolia Ramalina fastigiata Candelaria concolor	Parmelia carperata Usnea subfloridana Pertusaria hemisphaerica	Xanthorion (increasing diversity)	Cladonia spp.
<30	Ramalina calicaris Caloplaca aurantiaca	Lobaria pulmonaria Usnea florida Teloschistes flavicans	Up to 20 species of Xanthoria	Increasing diversity, no Lecanora conizaeoides

The high sensitivity of many species of lichens to atmospheric pollutants is often used to monitor long-term air pollution, particularly in towns. The presence of lichens can be mapped on areas to be studied, but several precautions must be observed if there is to be value in the results for prediction. For example, only lichen thalli which occupy bark should be used (because basic rocks provide different strengths of buffering capacity); then only those that grow at a particular height and on the side with optimal growth should be counted and their appearance should be rated. In addition, in any one area a number of trees (10–50) should be examined in order to obtain statistically significant data. Of course, only known species of lichens can be used and it is often recommended that only lichen communities should be analysed (Table 1). Even if these include species which are particularly sensitive to air pollutants (e.g. *Xanthoria parietina*, *Grimmia pulvinata* and *Parmelia saxatilis* for SO$_2$), other pollutants must be taken into consideration. Frequently, in urban areas, dusts containing heavy metals attack lichens more strongly than gaseous pollutants. If these data, particularly the cover abundance, have been recorded, area classification into lichen deserts, struggling zone

and clean air zone can be accomplished using Table 2. For many cities in Europe, such lichen maps already exist. Nevertheless, for long-term biomonitoring, they must be revised from time to time. Short-term biomonitoring can be done with standardised lichen exposure panels. For this the widely distributed and fast growing foliose lichen *Hypogymnia physodes* is used. It is picked with sufficient bark as substrate and is exposed on the panel in ten replicates. These panels are then exposed in the study areas and the state of the thalli is recorded from time to time.

Table 2. Lichen growth in situ as a parameter of lichen zonation (after Seitz 1972)

Cover abundance	Lichen zone
No growth or crustose lichens, maximum 0.5% cover	Lichen desert
Growth only of crustose lichens, foliose lichens absent	Inner struggle zone
Foliose and fruticose lichens 1–25% cover abundance (if >25% cover then partially dying)	Middle struggle zone
Foliose and fruticose lichens 25–50% cover abundance (if 50% then partially clearly dying)	Outer struggle zone
Foliose and fruticose lichens >50% cover abundance, no damage	Clean air zone

Box 1.9.6   Plant secondary metabolism induced by ozone

Erythrose-4-phosphate + Phosphoenolpyruvate

↓

Shikimate pathway

↓

$CH_2-CH-COOH$ with NH_2

Phenylalanine

↓ PAL/4CL

Cinnamoyl-CoA

PAL Phenylalanine ammonium lyase; *STS* stilbene synthase; *CHS* chalcone synthase; *CHI* chalcone isomerase; *PMT* pinosylvine-3-*O*-methyl transferase; *F3'H* flavonoid-3'-hydroxylase; *FHT* flavanone-3-hydroxylase; *DFR* dihydro-flavanol-4-reductase; *LAR* leuco-anthocyanidine-4-reductase; *CCR* cinnamoyl-CoA-reductase; *CAD* cinnamoyl alcohol dehydrogenase. (After Langebartels et al. 1997)

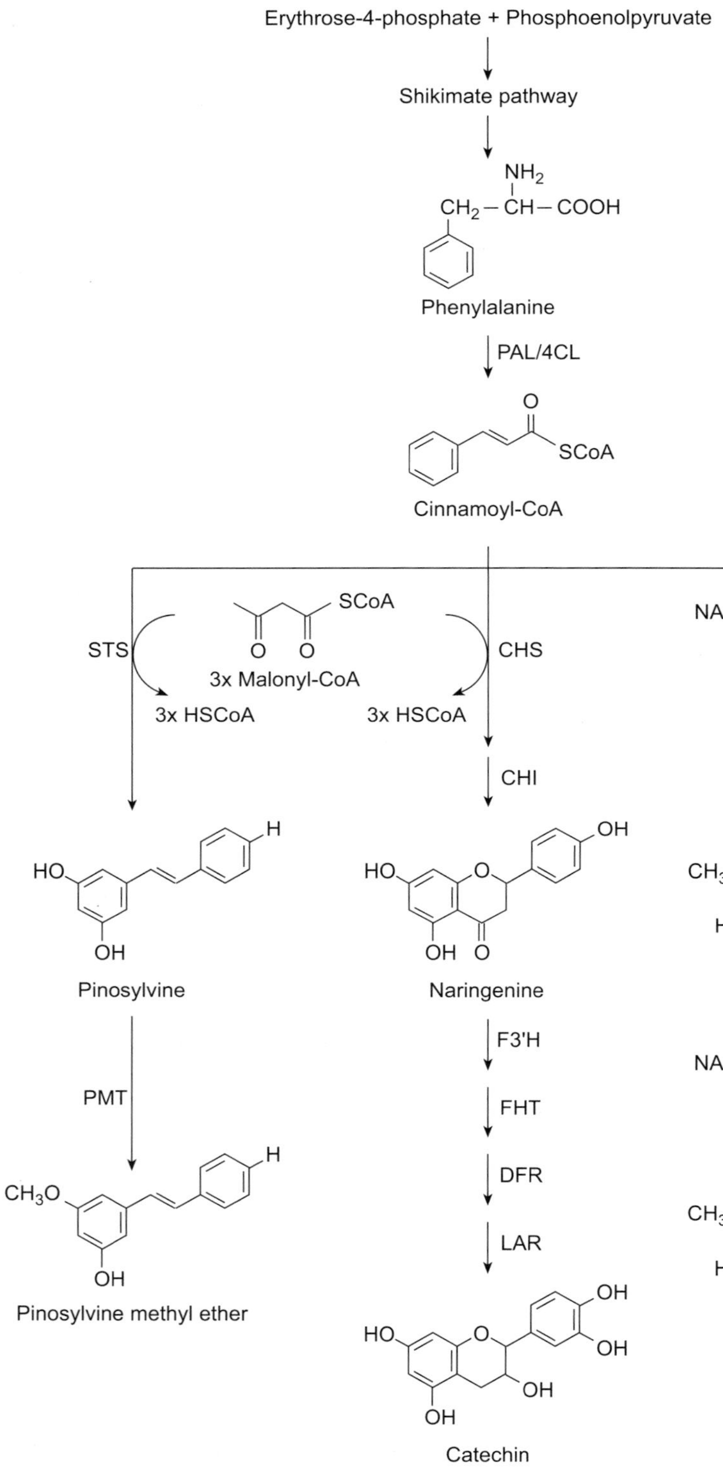

STS ← 3x Malonyl-CoA → 3x HSCoA

CHS → 3x HSCoA

CCR ← NADPH/H⁺ → NADP⁺

Pinosylvine

Naringenine

Coniferyl aldehyde

↓ PMT

Pinosylvine methyl ether

↓ F3'H
↓ FHT
↓ DFR
↓ LAR

Catechin

↓ CAD ← NADPH/H⁺ → NADP⁺

Coniferyl alcohol

↓

Lignin

1.9.2.2
Ozone

High ozone concentrations occur in the stratosphere and troposphere (Fig. 1.9.11). Ozone is continuously produced in the stratosphere [Eqs. (1.9.11) and (1.9.12)] and degraded again [Eqs. (1.9.13) and (1.9.14)].

$$O_2 + h\upsilon \ (\lambda \ 250 \, nm) \rightarrow 2O \qquad (1.9.11)$$

$$O + O_2 + M \rightarrow O_3 + M \qquad (1.9.12)$$

M is a neutral hit-partner taking up the energy of the $O{=}O_2$ bond, e.g. N_2, O_2.

$$Y + O_3 \rightarrow YO + O_2 \qquad (1.9.13)$$

$$O + YO \rightarrow Y + O_2 \qquad (1.9.14)$$

Y represents free radicals, e.g. OH, NO, Cl and Br, which are released by photolysis from stable compounds such as water, CFCH or N_2O. In the area of the ozone hole, degradation exceeds formation of ozone (catalysed by Cl^-, Br^- and NO_3 ions). Outside the ozone hole, formation and degradation are balanced. The maximum concentration of ozone in the stratospheric layer is up to 600 $\mu g/m^3$.

In the lower troposphere (the atmosphere at ground level), ozone is formed at high solar radiation in oxidative smog from oxygen and nitric oxide. The ozone concentration in the lower troposphere follows an annual cycle and a diurnal cycle (Fig. 1.9.12). The highest ozone concentrations are reached at high air temperatures and high solar radiation.

Different countries have defined different ozone stresses (concentration × period of exposure) as toxic thresholds: California 400 $\mu g/m^3$ for 1 h, Federal Republic of Germany 180 $\mu g/m^3$ for 2 h, Switzerland 120 $\mu g/m^3$ for 1 h. On sunny days values up to 200–280 $\mu g/m^3$ can be reached in central Europe (summer smog). Normal average values are 20–60 nl/l. In previous times spas advertised their ozone-containing air and ozone-rich forests, which were considered ideal for recreation in summer. Today, ozone is a toxic trace gas which, in areas with clean air, is held responsible for forest decline. Explanation for the relatively high ozone content in clean air of mountain regions is difficult. It is assumed that monoterpenes, emitted mainly by fir and spruce trees but also by broad-leaved plants during exposure to high radiation, catalyse formation of ozone (Fehsenfeld et al. 1992).

Ozone is, according to its molecular structure

$$^{(-)}O = O^{(+)} = O \qquad (1.9.15)$$

a very strong oxidant with a redox potential of +2.1 V. It reacts easily with unsaturated compounds forming ozonides, peroxides and hydroperoxides. It also oxidises thiols to sulfonic acid or disulfides.

As with other stresses, the critical question also applies to ozone: How much ozone can a plant tolerate? It is easy to subject plants to a high dosage of ozone and to obtain typical damage symptoms (Fig. 1.9.13). In the ample literature on the connection between ozone concentration and forest decline, different thresholds of damage by O_3 are reported depending on the mode of ozone application. One standard is the average concentration of central Europe which is 40 nl/l (40 ppb). Since there is practically no ozone-free natural air, ozone stress is expressed as the concentration above **AOT40** (accumulated exposure of ozone above the threshold of **40 nl/l**). It could also be expressed directly as concentration. The total dosage is given as **SUMO** (sum of all hourly mean O_3 concentrations).

In the experiment shown in Fig. 1.9.13 beeches were fumigated from April to October with twice the natural ozone concentrations. The

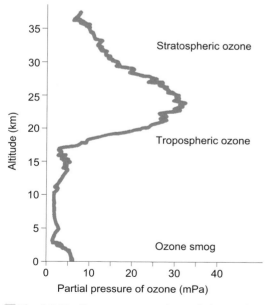

Fig. 1.9.11. Ozone concentrations of the earth's atmosphere. (Häder 1996)

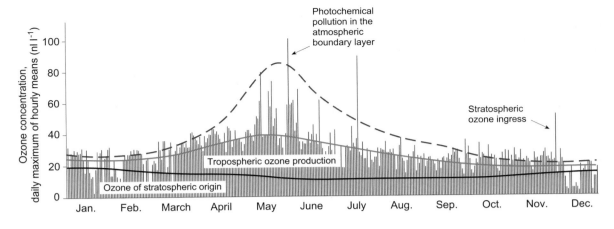

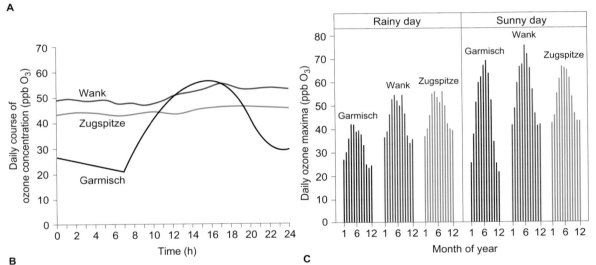

A

B

C

Fig. 1.9.12. Changes in tropospheric ozone concentration in the course of the day and of the year. A Proportion of various tropospheric ozone sources in a rural setting. The *bars* indicate the hourly mean maximum of a day. Tropospheric ozone production increases during the year with its own dynamics and contributes to stratospheric ozone which, however, changes little during the year. Individual peaks can arise from tropospheric pollution events as well as from stratospheric breakthroughs. B Daily changes in ozone concentration measured between 15 and 30 March from 1977 to 1980 at Garmisch (740 m), Mount Wank (1780 m), and Mount Zugspitze (2962 m). The peaks of ozone concentration during the day and in the early evening are probably correlated with the rush hour traffic in the city of Garmisch. High above the valley of Garmisch such changes do not appear. The monthly daily maxima of ozone concentrations in these high places are, however, significantly greater than those in the valley (C). Gaseous terpenes, produced mainly by coniferous trees, function as catalysts in ozone formation, as can be seen in both the yearly changes and the dependence on solar radiation. *RSD* Relative sunshine duration. All figures after Stockwell et al. (1997)

photograph was taken by mid-August. Brown spots are visible, some of which have developed into necroses. In Fig. 1.9.14 the development of ozone damage is quantified.

The picture of typically yellow-banded spruce needles was taken in June of the year following fumigation with 80 nl/l ozone from April to October every day for 24 h, and then grown on in the field. Symptoms occurred a year later, but led then to rapid senescence and to premature loss of needles. Generally, plants do not show any damage symptoms at the ozone concentrations of normal air if they are not exposed to other, additional stress factors. However, upon increased O_3 stress damage occurs very quickly. These findings show that the product of O_3 concentration and time of exposition cannot be used as a measure of ozone stress, as an underlying accumulation of processes exist that leads to a later "memory effect".

As with other pollutants, ozone tolerance of different plant species varies considerably (Ta-

Fig. 1.9.13. Ozone damage caused by controlled fumigation in beech (A), spruce (B) and pine (C). For explanation, see text. (Sandermann et al. 1997)

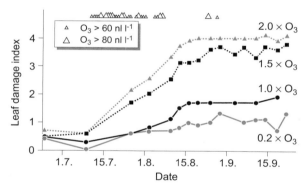

Fig. 1.9.14. Development of visible damage in leaves of 3-year-old beech trees after fumigation with different concentrations of ozone during one growing season. The treatment in the chamber started in April, when the buds opened, and ended in September with leaf fall. Days on which the ambient ozone concentration was above 60 or 80 ppb are indicated by *symbols* at the top of the graph. The symptoms of damage, small brown lesions, are shown in Fig. 1.9.13. The graph shows a rating of the intensity of the lesions. At 0.2 and 1× the natural ozone concentration there was hardly any visible damage. (After Langebartels et al. 1997)

Table 1.9.8. Sensitivity of various cultivated plants to ozone

Sensitivity (fumigation with O_2)		
Sensitive (0.1 ppm)	Relatively sensitive (0.2 ppm)	Relatively resistant (0.35 ppm)
Spinach	Onion	Beet
Radish	Wheat	Carrot
Bean	Maize	Strawberry
Potato	Chrysanthemum	Zinnia
Tomato	Begonia	

lack of nutrients, water shortage, high UV-B dosage) and/or biotic stresses (e.g. pathogen attack; Fig. 1.9.15), even if they do not show any direct damage.

Physiological Effects of Ozone Stress

Ozone only enters the leaf through the stomates, as the cuticle is practically impermeable for this molecule. If stomates are closed, e.g. because of drought, damage by ozone of processes taking place in the mesophyll, such as photosynthesis, is small. On the other hand, long-term exposure to ozone reduces stomatal resistance so that drought stress intensifies (Fig. 1.9.16). However, in well-watered plants with open stomates an increased stomatal resistance was observed, i.e. a reduction of conductivity, and CO_2 uptake was reduced. The change in the response can be explained by ozone damage to the guard cells and

ble 1.9.8). Amongst forest trees, spruce appears as very tolerant, larch and birch more sensitive. However, this interpretation depends on the design of the experiment and on the measured parameters (Matyssek et al. 1977).

Ozone damage has been extensively studied in relation to the new type of forest decline and for crops. After treatment with O_3 plants may become predisposed to subsequent abiotic (e.g.

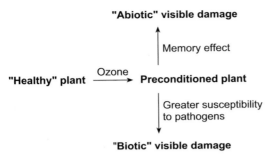

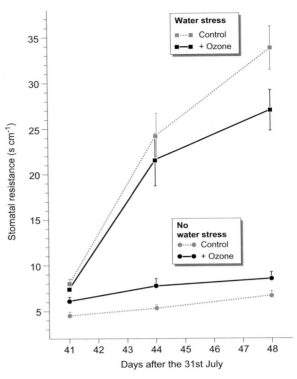

Fig. 1.9.15. Induction of visible ozone damage in conifers. The relatively low ozone concentration (e.g. twice natural background) stimulates the abiotic pathway, which includes the "memory effect" of a previous ozone stress, as described in the text. The biotic pathway includes reactions that also occur upon pathogen attack. This, however, does not occur in an organised mode, i.e. there is no coordinated regulation of gene expression in time and space. From this, decreased resistance (however, in individual cases sometime also increased resistance) to pathogens and other environmental stresses result. (After Langebartels et al. 1997)

Fig. 1.9.16. Effect of interaction of ozone and drought stress on the stomates (expressed as stomatal resistance) of beech leaves. The drought-induced rise in stomatal resistance is decreased by ozone, i.e. the stomates are open. Water loss, and therefore the effect of drought, is enhanced. Ozone treatment was started on day 31 and water supply was stopped on day 39. (After Pearson and Mansfield 1993)

their auxiliary cells. Because of the high reactivity of ozone, a steep concentration gradient occurs across the epidermis as O_3 is consumed by oxidation reactions already in the outer cell layer. Model calculations show that the internal ozone concentration in the leaf is almost zero at slightly elevated external ozone concentrations (Laisk et al. 1989). In contrast to oxygen, ozone is hydrophilic and thus reacts mainly with water-soluble or at least hydrated molecules, e.g. with SH-groups of proteins on the outer surfaces of the plasma membrane. Direct and rapid inhibition by ozone was shown by Heath and Taylor (1997) for a K^+-responsive ATPase of the plasma membrane and a Ca^{2+} transporter. This might explain the changed stomatal responses (see Figs. 1.5.5 and 1.6.2).

The steepness of the concentration gradient of ozone across the epidermis, and the stomatal conductivity for O_3 are factors determining the ozone sensitivity of plants. Spruces have a very low O_3 conductivity and a particularly steep gradient, and are thus relatively insensitive towards ozone. For pines and deciduous trees, it is the other way round.

Influence of Ozone on Primary and Secondary Metabolism

O_3 is a polar molecule and therefore probably does not permeate through the plasma membrane, but produces radicals and signals there and in the cell wall. Increased ozone stress causes several reactions, starting with the destruction of chlorophyll and xanthophyll by radicals. It thus affects photosynthesis, changing allocation of assimilates and causing loss of compartmentation (oxidation of unsaturated membrane lipids). Ozone also reacts with soluble proteins, e.g. Rubisco: Quantity and activity of this enzyme were reduced by 50% in 1-year-old pine needles (*Pinus halepensis*) under O_3 stress. At average light intensities, this did not cause a reduction in the rate of photosynthesis, as Rubisco is usually well in excess. However, in full sun, it became the limiting factor (see Chap. 1.2). This effect is, however, not only attributable to a destruction of Rubisco, but results also from a change in gene expression, because under O_3 stress more PEP-carboxylase is formed (Fontaine et al. 1999).

In the more resistant spruce, moderate O_3 treatment (one to two times ambient O_3 concentration) only causes a predisposition to such

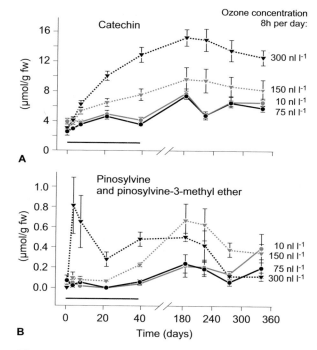

Fig. 1.9.17. Induction of secondary metabolism by ozone stress. One-year-old Scots pine (*Pinus sylvestris*) plants were exposed for 40 days to various ozone concentrations (8 h daily) and afterwards grown under natural conditions until autumn of the following year. A The flavane catechin (see Box 1.9.6), an antioxidant secondary metabolite, accumulated after the termination of ozone treatment and remained high during the following year. The concentration required to induce flavane accumulation was above the naturally occurring concentration but less than double the natural concentration. B Stilbenes are inducible phytoalexins (see Chap. 1.10.2.1) in sap wood and needles, but are constitutive in the heart wood. Their accumulation depends on the time and ozone concentration; incorporation into the cell wall caused a reduction in the soluble stilbene. The memory effect can clearly be seen in the case of stilbenes. (After Langebartels et al. 1997)

symptoms, which are expressed upon Mg or N deficiency.

In contrast to inhibition of primary metabolism, ozone causes a fast activation of secondary metabolism, particularly of the phenylpropane metabolism (Box 1.2.6). At severe stress when damage becomes visible the antioxidative ascorbate/glutathione system is likewise stimulated. Activation of secondary metabolism always precedes the occurrence of visible damage. This also applies to the apoplastic ascorbate peroxidase, pointing to an apoplastic detoxification system for ozone (and other oxidants).

Activity of some enzymes of flavonoid and stilbene metabolism is increased after O_3 treatment. These are possibly the rate-limiting en-zymes, because phenolics, particularly stilbenes and flavanes, accumulate as a result of the increased enzyme activities (Fig. 1.9.17). Both are powerful radical scavengers which polymerise after formation of radicals and whose polymers associate with the cell wall.

The concentration of biogenic amines (see Box 1.5.6), e.g. tyramine and its conjugates (peptides), with cinnamic acid is also increased. They are particularly potent radical scavengers, almost as effective as the ascorbate system.

At higher doses of O_3 these defence systems are not sufficiently strong, as is shown by increased ethylene formation and premature senescence and shedding of the leaves. Expression of several typical senescence-associated genes was shown in *Arabidopsis* plants after fumigation with ozone, including aminocyclopropane-1-carboxylic acid synthase which is responsible for the production of ethylene (Miller et al. 1999; see also Box 1.4.3). Critical O_3 stress as indicated by the onset of measurable damage and leading to premature senescence is one and a half to two times ambient ozone for beech during the complete vegetative period.

Ozone and Pathogen-Related Proteins

In addition to enzymes of phenylpropane, glutathione and ascorbate metabolism, and the processes of senescence, the activities of which are stimulated by O_3, further enzymes are known which are not only induced by ozone, but also by pathogen attacks (Table 1.9.9). They belong to the group of **PR proteins** (pathogenesis-related proteins), e.g. hydrolases which can break down fungal cell walls and usually are expressed in context with a hypersensitive reaction (see Chap. 1.10.2.1). Expression of some of the ozone-related proteins is also induced by elicitors, i.e. by soluble fragments of plant or fungal cell walls.

An example for the latter is coniferyl alcohol dehydrogenase which is one of the major enzymes in the biosynthesis of lignin. Upon stress by ozone, enhanced lignin formation was observed that is probably similar to **stress lignin** which is also typical of pressure wood and has a different chemical composition to normal lignin.

In total there are specific as well as unspecific biochemical stress responses to ozone which are, of course, related to the oxidising effects of O_3. They may damage the plant or even protect it (cross protection). In many conifers, particularly the ozone-tolerant species, ozone stress

Table 1.9.9. Overview of the induced genes or stimulation of enzyme activity upon ozone stress. (Langebartels et al. 1997)

Enzyme	Tree type	Site of action
Cinnamoyl alcohol dehydrogenase	Spruce, pine	Transcription, enzyme activity
Alcohol dehydrogenase	Spruce	Transcription
Stilbene synthase	Pine	Enzyme activity, transcription
Phenylalanine ammonium lyase	Pine	Enzyme activity
Chalcone synthase	Pine	Enzyme activity
3-Hydroxymethyl-glutaryl-CoA synthase	Pine	Transcription
Extensin	Pine	Transcription
	Spruce	Transcription
	Beech	Enzyme activity
β-1,3-Glucanase	Beech	Enzyme activity
	Spruce	Translation, enzyme activity
Chitinase	Beech	Enzyme activity
	Pine	Translation
Pathogenesis-related proteins 1a, b, c	Spruce	Transcription
Ozone-dependent activities	Spruce	Translation
	Pine	Transcription

first produces a predisposition which either protects the plant (ca. 50% of the investigated cases) or weakens it, especially when secondary stresses come along, e.g. acid fog, drought, attacks by bark beetles or pathogenic fungi (see Fig. 1.9.15).

Considering high ozone concentrations an an unnatural stress situation, it cannot be expected that in the course of evolution plants have evolved a "structured defence" system. The plant therefore responds to the multiplicity of impacts by ozone with a complex of more general defence reactions which usually are less specific to the incurred damage.

1.9.2.3
Formaldehyde

Formaldehyde emanates from all kinds of furniture made from chipboard. Glues used in carpets are also often a cause of formaldehyde in dwellings. The permissible indoor concentration of 0.12 mg/m^3 (=0.1 µl/l=0.1 ppm) is frequently considerably exceeded. Particularly high concentrations are usually measured in caravans, where not only the furniture, but also the living area is made of chipboard or lined with it.

Since Calvin's research in the late 1940s and early 1950s, it is known that formaldehyde is not an intermediary product of photosynthesis, contrary to earlier hypotheses. Nevertheless, the earlier ideas still contain some truth, because

formaldehyde is assimilated by plants in light, being converted to sugar, and other biomolecules, e.g. amino acids. Several **formaldehyde dehydrogenases** have been described. The detoxifying effect of indoor plants on the air in rooms has often been mentioned, without providing ideas on the involved biological mechanisms. Detoxification of air by plants is not only accomplished by enzymatic biochemical reaction, but also by adsorption on the surface of plants and on soil; in addition air pollutants enter the plant tissue via the stomates and, depending on the toxicity of the compound, may cause more or less harm.

The spider plant (*Chlorophytum comosum*) is able to reduce the concentration of formaldehyde in room air from 4–7 µl formaldehyde/l (40–70 times the admissible maximum value) to 0.2 µl/l (=double the admissible concentration)[1] within 5 h. Other plants, e.g. tobacco, are also able to achieve this (Giese et al. 1994).

Spider plants did not show any damage symptoms at 10 µl/l air (=100 times the admissible maximum value) and are more resistant to the pollutant than tobacco which produced strong local necroses; at ten times the admissible concentration tobacco plants developed insignificant symptoms. However, inhibition of growth occurs already at considerably lower concentrations.

---

[1] Adsorption effects of the surface of the soil are considerable, as a decrease to 3 µl/l was achieved already by unplanted pots.

After 24-h fumigation of *Chlorophytum* with air and ^{14}C-formaldehyde, most of the radioactivity taken up in the plant was in the soluble fraction with about one fifth incorporated in structural substances (lignin). In the soluble fraction ^{14}C-labelled sugars dominated, but the amino acid serine was also strongly labelled, indicating incorporation by serine hydroxymethyl transferase. Phospholipids (phosphatidyl serine) likewise contained significant amounts of [14]C.

Enzymatic studies revealed two formaldehyde dehydrogenases. One of these, the more active, was glutathione dependent[2]. Formaldehyde is probably oxidised to formic acid which is then assimilated via C1 metabolism. Detoxification activity was 12.8 μg formaldehyde/h×g FW and the apparent K_m value was 30 μM. If these values are extrapolated, a *Chlorophytum* plant would be able, within 6 h, to detoxify a room of 100 m^3 containing twice the admissible maximum value of formaldehyde. However, the reaction of stomates to increasing amounts of formaldehyde in the air has not yet been properly examined. Formaldehyde detoxification is a further example of phytoremediation, supporting the concept of the "green liver" (Sandermann 1994).

Summary

Xenobiotics are foreign substances (with respect to an organism) which have biological activity and, depending on the toxicity and amount taken up, trigger defence reactions, cause damage or even death of the organism. Apart from **toxins** which are unintentionally or unavoidably released into the **environment**, as, for example, air pollutants (also heavy metals and aluminium are occasionally called xenobiotics), xenobiotics are mainly pesticides which on purpose are released in large amounts into the environment. Herbicides are the most important pesticides.

1. **Herbicides** are supposed to have a targeted effect, whereby either individual enzymes or reaction complexes (e.g. photosystem II) are blocked or cell biological damage results from the formation of radicals (total herbicides).

2. Only in very few cases are crop plants able to specifically detoxify particular herbicides. However, with certain substances (herbicide safeners, antidotes or immunochemicals), the endogenous detoxifying potential is stimulated and they become desensitised to the corresponding herbicide. This can also be achieved by genetic engineering.

3. The spectrum of xenobiotics is immense. In contrast, there are relatively few biochemical mechanisms by which plants can detoxify them. In a plant cell detoxification occurs in four steps: Most of the pesticides are lipophilic; detoxification therefore requires prior conversion to a hydrophilic derivative. After uptake into the cell, a hydrophilic group is introduced. This is usually done by monooxygenases or oxidases. The hydrophilic group is then used to form conjugates. Glycosyl transferases or glutathione-S-transferases catalyse the "conjugation" with sugars (usually glucose) and glutathione, respectively. In the third step, the conjugates are sequestered into the vacuole or to the apoplast by glutathione pumps (GS-X pumps). These belong to the family of so-called ABC transporters. Plant ABC transporters are mainly members of the subfamily of multidrug resistance associated proteins (MRPs). Natural substrates of these GS-X pumps are water-soluble secondary plant constituents, deposited in the vacuole, such as flavonoid glycosides, phytohormone conjugates, but also degradation products of DNA and chlorophyll. In the fourth and final step, the sequestered conjugates are modified to detain them in the vacuole, or after translocation by the Golgi covalently incorporate them into the cell wall.

4. In addition to detoxification, pesticides may induce the synthesis of defence proteins, the so-called pathogenesis-related proteins, and thus increase plant resistance to pathogen attack (cross protection). In modern agrochemistry, such xenobiotics are applied under the term **immunochemicals**.

5. **Gaseous xenobiotics** (air pollutants) affect plants by oxidation (oxidising smog, ozone), reduction (reductive SO_2 smog), acidification ("acid rain", hydrofluoric acid), or in other ways (e.g. denaturation of proteins by formaldehyde, or by a phytohormonal effect, e.g. ethylene). Below the damage threshold SO_2 and NO_x may even act as sources of sulfur or nitrogen (sulfate or nitrate) for plant nutri-

---

[2] The GSH-dependent formaldehyde dehydrogenase shows sequential similarities with alcohol dehydrogenase. It is assumed that the latter developed phylogenetically from the former, as formaldehyde probably is one of the components of the early atmosphere of the earth (Fliegmann and Sandermann 1997).

tion. In this case the oxidant is usually photosynthetically reduced oxygen ($O_2^{\bullet-}$).

6. Above the threshold of damage the "law of stress quantity" applies, i.e. the strain or damage corresponds to the product of stress intensity and duration of exposure. Differentiation between a short-time stress peak and chronic, i.e. long-term, stress is also useful.

7. Air pollutants are taken up by plant tissues through stomates or directly through the cuticle and epidermis. Both paths undergo pollutant-specific modification: Opening of stomates may be increased or reduced by air pollutants; and the cuticle may become more permeable due to damage (etching), e.g. by hydrofluoric acid.

8. **Sulfur dioxide** has a mid-range redox potential and therefore affects a wide range of reactions in plant cells. The well-known inhibition of photosynthesis is not an outcome of a single reaction, but results from a reaction complex. The visible phenomenon is bleaching of chlorophyll-containing plant parts, which is due to the oxidation of unsaturated membrane lipids rather than to the acidity of SO_2 or sulfurous acid. Damage of chlorophyll-binding proteins results in the release of chlorophyll which is then accessible to photooxidation. If the damage continues, necroses form and leaves or needles die.

9. Bleaching of leaves ("yellow tips") may also indicate magnesium deficiency. Acid deposition ("acid rain") causes increased leaching of cations, in particular of magnesium, from the soil into the groundwater and as a consequence a shortage of these cations in the plant tissue.

10. Because of the large range of biological reactions in which sulfur dioxide can become involved plants have not developed any specific resistance against this pollutant. Different sensitivities of individual plant species are based on individual features, e.g. increased capabilities of buffering or adsorption.

11. Lichens are particularly sensitive to SO_2 and other gaseous noxes, because their thalli do not possess stomates and because of the susceptibility of their inherent symbiotic interactions. They are thus very suitable for long-term monitoring of air pollution.

12. **Ozone** is continuously formed in the stratosphere, but is also found in the lower troposphere in oxidative smog, where it is pro-

duced in the reaction of nitric oxides with oxygen but also in forests by reaction of gaseous terpenes with oxygen upon intense irradiation. Therefore, the ozone content of the troposphere varies during the day and with the seasons. Naturally occurring ozone concentrations do not cause any visible damage to plants.

13. Ozone is taken up into the plant through stomates, as the cuticle is impermeable to it.

14. Ozone is a strong oxidant and thus reacts predominantly with SH-containing proteins and with oxidisable structural elements of the cell. It is consumed already in the outer cell layers of plant tissues, e.g. of leaves, where only traces of ozone reach the mesophyll. Potassium and calcium transporters in the guard cells and their auxiliary cells are inactivated by ozone, which explains the reduced reaction of stomates to drought. Ozone damage is therefore often coupled with damage caused by drought. Ozone is a polar molecule and since it hardly permeates biomembranes, membrane-bound components are mainly damaged. At higher concentrations pigments contained in the membrane system of plastids are destroyed by oxidation.

15. Fumigation with ozone leads to rapid activation of secondary metabolism by enzyme induction, as well as by activation of certain enzymes. Good examples are phenylpropane, flavonoid and ascorbate metabolism.

16. The so-called memory effect of ozone can be shown by the increased content of secondary metabolites also in such plant parts which develop after the termination of the stressful treatment. Because of the memory effect the "law of stress quantity" does not apply to ozone damage. As many of these secondary plant constituents are radical scavengers, their accumulation provides chemical protection.

17. In addition to enzymes of secondary metabolism, ozone also induces the formation of so-called pathogenesis-related proteins.

18. Formaldehyde is released particularly from modern furnishings (chipboard furniture, carpet floors). Many plants are able to assimilate formaldehyde and thereby detoxify it. Formaldehyde dehydrogenase is the key enzyme of formaldehyde assimilation; after oxidation to formiate it enters the plant's C1 metabolism. Depending on the plant species,

further metabolism usually leads to carbohydrates or amino acids.

19. The spider plant (*Chlorophytum comosum*) and tobacco are particularly efficient assimilators of formaldehyde. These plants are able to reduce the concentration of formaldehyde in the air of a room from values many times above the admissible concentration to admissible values within a few hours.

20. Formaldehyde detoxification is a further example of phytoremediation, thus providing a good example of the concept of the "green liver".

References

Coleman JOD, Blake-Kalff MMA, Davies TGE (1997) Detoxification of xenobiotics by plants: chemical modification and vacuolar compartmentation. Trends Plant Sci 2:144–151

Darrall NM (1989) The effect of air pollutants on physiological processes in plants. Plant Cell Environ 12:1–30

Elstner EF (1984) Schadstoffe, die über die Luft zugeführt werden. In: Hock B, Elstner ET (eds) Pflanzentoxikologie. BI Wissenschaftsverlag, Mannheim, pp 67–94

Fehsenfeld F, Calvert J, Fall R, Goldan P, Guenther AB, Hewitt CN, Lamb B, Shaw L, Trainer M, Wetsberg H, Zimmerman P (1992) Emission of volatile organic compounds from vegetation and the implications for atmospheric chemistry. Global Biogeochem Cycles 6:389–430

Fliegmann J, Sandermann H Jr (1997) Maize glutathione-dependent formaldehyde dehydrogenase cDNA: a novel plant gene of detoxification. Plant Mol Biol 34:843–854

Fontaine V, Pelloux J, Podor M, Afif D, Gerant D, Crieu P, Dizengremel P (1999) Carbon fixation in *Pinus halepensis* submitted to ozone. Opposite response of ribulose-1,5-bisphosphate carboxylase/oxygenase and phosphoenolpyruvate carboxylase. Physiol Plant 105:187–192

Fuhrer J (1996) Gasförmige Luftschadstoffe. In: Brunold C, Rüegsegger A, Brändle R (eds) Stress bei Pflanzen. UTB Haupt, Bern, pp 221–246

Giese M, Bauer-Doranth U, Langebartels C, Sandermann H Jr (1994) Detoxification of formaldehyde by the spider plant (*Chlorophytum comosum* L.) and by soybean (*Glycine max* L.) cell-suspension cultures. Plant Physiol 104:1301–1309

Häder D-P (1996) UV-Belastung und Ozonproblematik. Biologie Unserer Zeit 26:206–208

Heath RI, Taylor GE Jr (1997) Physiological process and plant response to ozone exposure. Ecological Studies 127. Springer, Berlin Heidelberg New York, pp 317–368

Hock B, Elstner EF (1984) Pflanzentoxikologie. BI Wissenschaftsverlag, Mannheim, 346 pp

Köstner B, Schupp R, Schulze E-D, Rennenberg H (1998) Organic and inorganic sulfur transport in the xylem sap and the sulfur budget of *Picea abies* trees. Tree Physiol 48:1–9

Kuhnert KJ (1996) Xenobiotika. In: Brunold C, Rüegsegger A, Brändle R (eds) Stress bei Pflanzen. UTB Haupt, Bern, pp 247–261

Laisk A, Kull O, Moldau H (1989) Ozone concentration in leaf intercellular air space is close to zero. Plant Physiol 90:1163–1167

Lange OL, Heber U, Schulze E-D, Ziegler H (1989) Atmospheric pollutants and plant metabolism. Ecological Studies 77. Springer, Berlin Heidelberg New York, pp 238–273

Langebartels C, Ernst D, Heller W, Lütz C, Payer H-D, Sandermann H Jr (1997) Ozone responses of trees: results from controlled chamber exposures at the GSF phytotron. Ecological Studies 127. Springer, Berlin Heidelberg New York, pp 163–200

Larcher W (1994) Ökophysiologie der Pflanzen. UTB Eugen Ulmer, Stuttgart, 394 pp

Lehninger AL, Nelson DL, Cox MM (1994) Prinzipien der Biochemie (Tschesche H ed). Spektrum Akademischer Verlag, Heidelberg, 1223 pp

Marrs K (1996) The function and regulation of glutathione-S-transferases in plants. Annu Rev Plant Physiol Plant Mol Biol 47:127–158

Matyssek R, Havranek WM, Wieser G, Innes JL (1997) Ozone and the forests in Austria and Switzerland. Ecological Studies 127. Springer, Berlin Heidelberg New York, pp 95–134

Miller JD, Arteca RN, Pell EJ (1999) Senescence-associated gene expression during ozone-induced leaf senescence in *Arabidopsis*. Plant Physiol 120:1015–1023

Pearson M, Mansfield TA (1993) Interacting effects of ozone and water stress on the stomatal resistance of Beech (*Fagus sylvatica* L.). New Phytol 123:351–358

Pfanz H, Martinoia E, Lange OL, Heher U (1987) Flux of SO_2 into leaf cells and cellular acidification by SO_2. Plant Physiol 85:928–933

Rea PA, Lu Y-P, Li Z-S (1997) Detoxification of xenobiotics revisited. Trends Plant Sci 2:290–291

Rea PA, Li Z-S, Lu Y-P, Drozdowicz YM (1998) From vacuolar GS-X pumps to multispecific ABC transporters. Annu Rev Plant Physiol Plant Mol Biol 49:727–760

Rennenberg H (1984) The fate of excess sulfur in higher plants. Annu Rev Plant Physiol 35:121–153

Sandermann H, Wellburn AR, Heath RL (1997) Appendix. Ecological Studies 127. Springer, Berlin Heidelberg New York, 397 pp

Sandermann H Jr (1994) Higher plant metabolism of xenobiotics: The "green liver" concept. Pharmacogenetics 4:225–241

Schlee D (1992) Ökologische Biochemie. G Fischer, Jena Stuttgart, 587 pp

Seitz W (1972) Flechtenwuchs und Luftverunreinigung im Großraum Saarbrücken. Ber Deutsch Bot Ges 85:239–247

Stockwell WR, Kramm G, Scheel H-E, Mohnen VA, Seiler W (1997) Ozone formation, destruction and exposure in Europe and the United States. Ecological Studies 127. Springer, Berlin Heidelberg New York, pp 1–38

Taylor GE Jr, Hanson PJ, Baldocchi DD (1988) Pollutant deposition to individual leaves and plant canopies: sites of regulation and relationship to injury. In: Heck WW, Taylor OC, Tingey DT (eds) Assessment of crop loss from air pollution. Elsevier Appl Science, London, pp 227–257

Türk R, Wirth V, Lange OL (1974) CO_2-Gaswechsel-Untersuchungen zur SO_2-Resistenz von Flechten. Oecologia 15:33–64

Wesely ML (1989) Parameterization of surface resistances to gaseous dry deposition in regional-scale numerical models. Atmos Environ 23:1293–1304

1.10

Biotic Stress: Herbivory, Infection, Allelopathy

A leaf of the broad-leaved dock (*Rumex obtusifolius*) that has been perforated by leaf beetles (*Chrysomelidae*) and their larvae. Further clutches of eggs are on the leaf lamina. In the right margin of the picture, two spots with red edges, which show the accumulation of anthocyanin, indicate a hypersensitive reaction. This is probably due to an additional pathogen attack. Picture E. Beck

Recommended Literature

- Baldwin IT (2001) Update on *Nicotiana attenuata*: an ecologically motivated analysis of plant-herbivore interactions in native tobacco. Plant Physiol 127:1449–1458
- Dudareva N, Pichersky E, Gershenzon J (2004) Biochemistry of plant volatiles. Plant Physiol 135:1893–1902
- Kessler A, Baldwin IT (2002) Plant responses to insect herbivory. The emerging molecular analysis. Annu Rev Plant Biol 53:275–298
- Memelink J, Verpoorte R, Kijne JW (2001) ORCAnization of jasmonate-responsive gene expression in alkaloid metabolism. Trends Plant Sci 6:212–219

1.10.1

Herbivory

Herbivory is predominantly selective, as long as there is no extreme lack of fodder – almost as if animals had distributed the menu amongst themselves! However, there are many plants that are practically never touched or only attacked by very special herbivores, so-called **poisonous plants**. These plants are protected by **secondary plant metabolites**, which are constitutively formed (so-called anticipators) and accumulated in the vacuoles or cell walls during the life of the plant. Examples are alkaloids (more than 6000 known compounds), terpenoids (more than 5000 substances), steroids (e.g. saponin, bitter-

Box 1.10.1   Biological activities of secondary plant constituents on herbivorous animals

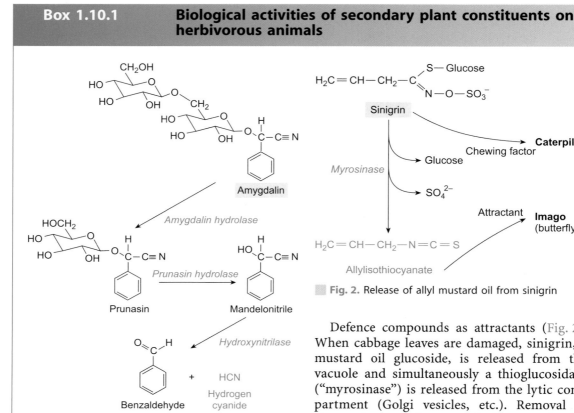

Fig. 1. Release of hydrogen cyanide from amygdalin

Fig. 2. Release of allyl mustard oil from sinigrin

Secondary plant metabolites as potential toxins: Release of hydrogen cyanide from seeds of many Rosaceae. Amygdalin occurs in many seeds (embryos) of stone- and pome-fruit plants. On imbibition of the seeds or after wounding, the glucosidases amygdalin hydrolase and prunasin hydrolase become active, followed by the hydroxynitrilases, which finally lead to the release of hydrogen cyanide (Fig. 1).

Defence compounds as attractants (Fig. 2). When cabbage leaves are damaged, sinigrin, a mustard oil glucoside, is released from the vacuole and simultaneously a thioglucosidase ("myrosinase") is released from the lytic compartment (Golgi vesicles, etc.). Removal of glucose by myrosinase results in a reactive intermediate, which, on hydrolysis of the sulfate residue, is converted into volatile allyl isothiocyanate (allyl mustard oil). This compound, which has a pungent flavour to humans, is extremely toxic to many insects. For the large cabbage white butterfly (*Pieris brassicae*), the allyl mustard oil is, however, an attractant which stimulates the female butterfly to oviposition. For the caterpillars, which hatch from the eggs, sinigrin and its derivatives are feeding stimulants (after Heß 1999).

ing agents, heart-active glycosides), phenolic compounds (e.g. tannins), cyanogenic compounds and mustard oil glycosides (which are hydrolysed upon damage of the cells releasing HCN or mustard oils), and many more.

However, these defence compounds do not provide complete protection, particularly regarding phytophagous insects. Even many vertebrates are able to detoxify such compounds, for example, by converting cyanide ions from cyanogenic glycosides into the non-poisonous thio-cyanate by the liver enzyme rhodanese. Some phytophagous insects detoxify the cyanide ion by binding it with β-cyanoalanine synthase to serine or cysteine. Other phytophages take up such toxins with their food, for example, the butterflies of the genus *Zygaena* accumulate the cyanogenic glycosides linamarin and lotaustralin from the birds-foot trefoil (*Lotus corniculatus*) and protect themselves against their enemies by releasing hydrogen cyanide. Hymenopteran and dipteran insects, on the other hand, when parasitising these phytophages, are able to detoxify HCN with rhodanese. During the course of evolution, phytophagous insects not only adapted to the chemical defence of plants, they also evolved mechanisms to use volatile plant defence compounds as signals to find food. The mustard oils produced by various cabbage species (*Brassica* spp.) prevent many species of insects from feeding on cabbage leaves, but they also serve as a signal for the female butterflies of the genus *Pieris* (cabbage white butterfly) to oviposition. The larvae of these butterflies are specialised for cabbages and have thus found their food niche by overcoming the deterrent effect of mustard oils.

The broad field of interaction between herbivores and their host plants and their chemical defences is inexhaustible and can only be briefly discussed with a few examples within the frame of this book.

In addition to the above-mentioned constitutive defence by plant toxins, there is also an **induced defence reaction** probably for all (higher) plants against herbivores. If a plant is mechanically wounded by feeding or being trodden on, tissues are damaged including – in most cases – the long-distance transport pathways, xylem and phloem. As a consequence, a cascade of hydraulic, electric and biochemical reactions is induced which finally leads to induction of gene expression. Wounding, for instance, induces gene expression which results in closure of the wound by formation of a callus. It also induces the synthesis of defence proteins like **proteinase in**hibitors (PIN), proteins directed against the activity of insect proteinases. The responses are induced **locally** (at the site of wounding) as well as **systemically** (at sites not wounded, demanding spreading of signal(s) throughout the plant). The signal transduction chain from wounding to the new expression of genes has been studied intensively, but is still far from being completely understood.

1.10.1.1
Signal Transduction Chain

When the xylem of a transpiring plant is wounded, the strength of the suction in the xylem is changed as air enters the xylem at the damaged site. A decrease in the strength of tension results in a "positive" pressure wave. Step increases in pressure experimentally applied to tomato leaves (Fig. 1.10.1) or roots (Fig. 1.10.2) lead to:

- a depolarisation wave across the plant (Figs. 1.10.1 and 1.10.2), which has established an electrical potential difference between root (soil) and tip;
- a transient stimulation of petiole growth (Fig. 1.10.1).

The depolarisation propagates slowly in the apical direction, the extent corresponding to the intensity of the pressure wave.

The hydraulic pressure wave signals to the unwounded part of the plant that wounding (of the xylem) has occurred. These signals are changed into electrical signals probably by mechano-sensitive ion pumps or ion channels appearing somewhat later than the hydraulic signals. The strength of the signal decreases with increasing distance from the wounded site. Hydraulic and electric signals are one of the earliest components of the signal transduction chain inducing systemic reactions, but their connection to the biochemical events is not yet resolved.

As a systemic response in leaf 4 after wounding of leaf 1 (Fig. 1.10.1), an increase in the mRNA of proteinase inhibitors (*Pin1* and *Pin2*) and of calmodulin, which plays an important role in the Ca^{2+}-mediated signal transduction chain, was found. On the other hand, total protein synthesis was decreased in the non-wounded leaf indicated by the dissociation of (cytoplasmic) polysomes.

The induced expression of the proteinase inhibitors has been used to find further components of the signal transduction chain. In tomato, an 18 amino acid oligopeptide, called systemin, was detected after wounding. It is able to induce proteinase inhibitors when supplied to young tomato plants via the petiole. Systemin was found to be translocated in the phloem and was suspected to be the signal for the induction of **systemic defence reactions** (hence its name). It is proteolytically cleaved from a 200 amino acid precursor protein, called prosystemin, when leaves are damaged. Systemin leads to an alkalinization of the medium, when applied to a cell suspension culture of tomato (Fig. 1.10.4), and to the activation of a MAP kinase. The effect of systemin is transmitted by its binding to a plasma membrane bound receptor. This 160 kDa protein has an extracellular receptor domain and a cytoplasmic kinase domain characteristic

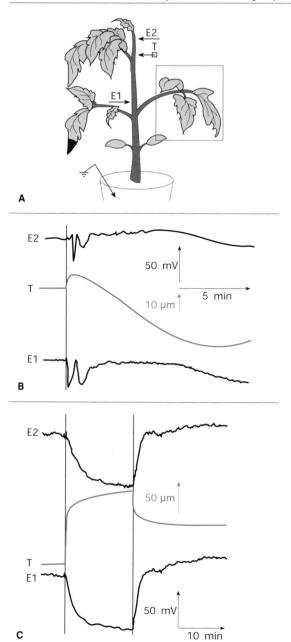

Fig. 1.10.1 Wound reactions of tomato plants. A Test plant with the experimental setup. The pot of the plant is contained in a temperature-controlled water bath in which a reference electrode is placed. *E1* and *E2* indicate the positions of the measuring electrodes. *T* is a position sensing transducer that allows automatic measurements of elongation. In the first experiment, the oldest leaf (leaf 1) below E1 was damaged with a lighted match (*blackened area*) for 3 s. In the second experiment, leaf 2 was placed in the chamber of a pressure bomb (*blue line*) and subjected to a pressure of 0.3 Mpa for 15 min. B Changes in the total electrical potential of the plant and the length of the petiole of leaf 4 (*T*) after damaging the tip of leaf 1. Two waves of depolarisation pass through the plant after wounding for 3 s. Immediately after wounding, the petiole of leaf 4 extends by ca. 10 μm but then contracts by at least 50 μm in the next few minutes. This contraction relaxes again during the next 30 min. C Correlation of pressure-induced changes in electrical potential and the change in petiole length. Leaf 2 (see A) was subjected for 15 min (between the two vertical lines) to a pressure of 3 bar (0.3 MPa) in a pressure chamber. Changes in electrical potential and petiole length proceed in the opposite direction compared to the wounding experiment. (Stanković and Davies 1998)

for proteins involved in the transduction of external signals.

Another component in the jigsaw puzzle of the signal transduction chain after tissue damage is the small, but significant, transient rise of free fatty acids in the tissue, mainly resulting from the release of linoleic acid (C18:2) and linolenic acid (C18:3; Fig. 1.10.3). The rise precedes the induction of *Pin1* and *Pin 2* expression. It is assumed that the release of free fatty acids is based on the transient activation of a lipase, which cleaves predominantly glycolipids from chloroplastic membranes. Whether the MAP kinase, activated by systemin, is involved in the activation of the lipase has not been established. There are indications that abscisic acid (ABA) could be a further signal in the transduction chain.

The release of linoleic and linolenic acids from biomembranes may also be induced in a different way, either by direct mechanical damage to the membrane, or by high temperature or UV radiation, and by so-called **elicitors** – degradation products (oligosaccharides) of cell wall

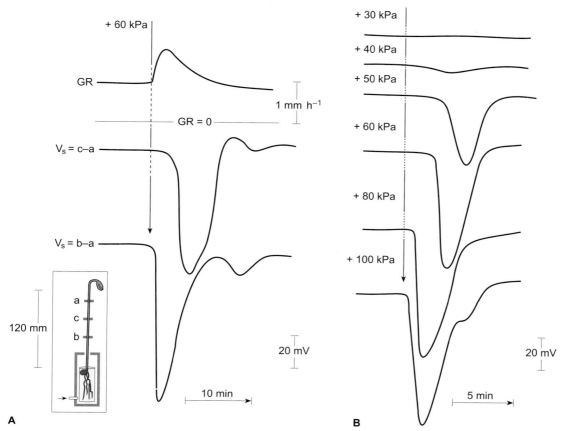

Fig. 1.10.2. Production of an electrical signal as a consequence of an increase in pressure in pea epicotyls. A *Below left*, experimental setup. Dark-grown, etiolated pea seedlings were used. The roots and the basal 10 mm of the epicotyl were incubated in tap water in a small tube and enclosed in a root pressure chamber. At the time point indicated in the diagram by the *vertical arrow*, the pressure in the chamber was increased by 60 kPa. The propagation of the depolarisation signal of the surface potential from *b* to *c* is shown in the dynamics *b-a* and *c-a*; in *c-a* a small hyperpolarisation can be seen before the potential returns to its original level. The growth rate (*GR*) increases immediately after the increase in pressure, showing that the pressure wave reached the tip of the shoot in only a few seconds. *a, b, c* Positions of the surface electrodes; *Vs* surface potentials, *GR* growth rate. B Effect of increasing pressure on the extent and the lag phase of the depolarisation (voltage change) at point c. Below a threshold value of 30 kPa there is no change in potential. Above a pressure of 60 kPa, the extent of the depolarisation hardly alters any longer; however, the response at higher pressures is significantly faster than at lower pressures, which indicates a relatively slow propagation of the potential wave from the base to the apex. (Stahlberg and Cosgrove 1997)

carbohydrates formed during pathogen attack, for example, by a fungus (see Chap. 1.10.2).

This induction, however, which is not via systemin, is effective only locally, i.e. directly at the site of damage. In contrast, induction via systemin is systemic because this peptide can be distributed throughout the plant via the phloem (Fig. 1.10.5). In the signal chain from the first bite into the xylem, via the release of the polyunsaturated fatty acids (PUFA) to the synthesis of the proteinase inhibitors *Pin 1* and *Pin 2*, the immediate inducer for the proteinase inhibitors still requires mentioning. This inducer, **jasmonate**, is synthesised in several steps from the

three-fold unsaturated linolenic acid released by the activity of the lipase. The first reaction is catalysed by **lipoxygenase (LOX)**, which not only initiates the synthesis of jasmonate, but is also responsible for the formation of radicals and reactive derivatives from the PUFAs.

Lipoxygenase produces hydroperoxides from PUFAs, which then react further in multiple enzyme-catalysed and non-enzymatic steps (Box 1.10.2). The sequence of reactions leading to the synthesis of jasmonic acid starts with the formation of an allene epoxide, which is then converted to the cyclic 12-oxophytodienoic acid (12-OPDA). From 12-OPDA three acetate resi-

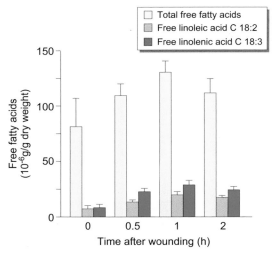

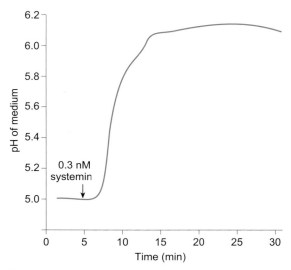

Fig. 1.10.3. Release of fatty acids in tomato leaves after mechanical damage. Only 30 min after a small mechanical damage, the concentrations of free fatty acids rise, compared to an untreated control (time 0). About 85% of the rise is due to the release of linoleic (C18:2) and linolenic (C18:3) acids. Free linolenic acid is the starting point for the synthesis of jasmonate. (After Conconi et al. 1996)

Fig. 1.10.4. Increase in pH of the medium of a cell suspension of wild tomato (*Lycopersicon peruvianum*) after addition of systemin. (Meindl et al. 1998)

dues are removed by β-oxidation, leading to the (+)-7-*iso*-jasmonate, which can be quickly transformed into the stable (−)-jasmonate. This can be conjugated in many ways, for example, by esterification, glycosylation and amidation. These conjugates as well as the derivatives of jasmonate, shown in Fig. 1.10.6, exhibit biological activity which is species-specific in some cases.

Jasmonate is ubiquitous in the plant kingdom, prevailing in young, i.e. meristematic, tissues. The methyl ester of jasmonate is volatile and has been identified as the fragrant constituent of the essential oil from jasmin flowers (hence the term). Free jasmonic acid was first isolated in large quantities from the culture filtrate of fungal cultures.

1.10.1.2
Proteins Induced by Jasmonate (JIPs)

As with many phytohormones, **jasmonate** exhibits pleiotropic effects. It is regarded as a typical stress hormone and, in this context, as a hormone triggering senescence (leaf yellowing). Correspondingly, it acts synergistically with ABA and ethylene (see Chap. 1.6.2).

According to its pleiotropic effects, jasmonate induces the expression of several very different proteins and enzymes which are called **jasmonate-induced proteins (JIPs)**. Table 1.10.1 gives a survey of the most important JIPs. For many of them, however, the biological functions have not yet been elucidated.

Table 1.10.1. Reactions which are induced by stress and/or during developmental phases in which jasmonate is involved. *ABA* Abscisic acid; *ACC* aminocyclopropanecarboxylate oxidase; *Et* ethylene; *JA* jasmonic acid; *JIPs* jasmonate-induced proteins; *S* systemin; *SA* salicylic acid. (After Wasternack and Parthier 1997)

Process	Signal(s)	Protein(s)/reaction	Gene sequence known
Wounding	S, JA, ABA, Et	Proteinase inhibitors	Yes
Pathogen attack	JA, SA	Thionins, "pathogenesis-related proteins"	Yes
Elicitor (fungal) application	JA, Et	Phytoalexin-producing enzymes	Yes
Contact	JA	Tendril movement	No
Drought stress	ABA, JA	Dehydrins, JIPs	Yes
Osmotic stress	ABA, JA	JIPs	Yes
Salt stress	ABA, JA, Et	Osmotin	Yes
Nitrogen storage	JA	N-storage proteins in vegetative tissues	Yes
Fruit ripening	JA, Et	ACC oxidase	No
Senescence	JA, Et	Lipoxygenase, JIPs	Yes
Stabilisation of the cell wall	JA	Hydroxyproline- and glycine-rich proteins	Yes

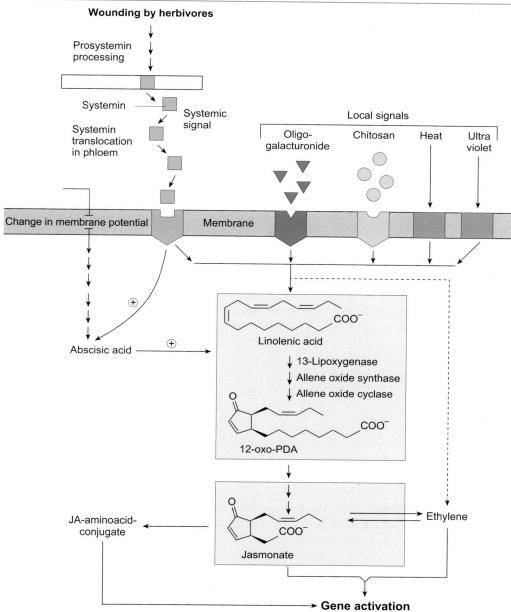

Fig. 1.10.5. Induction of systemic defence. After wounding, the signal peptide systemin is released from the precursor protein prosystemin. Systemin is distributed throughout the whole plant via the phloem. After interaction of systemin with its receptor and/or by influence of other exogenous factors, linolenic acid is released from the plasma membrane. Linolenic acid is the starting point of the so-called octadecanoid pathway, which finally leads to the synthesis of jasmonate. The phytohormone ABA may modulate the activity of this pathway. Jasmonate in turn induces the expression of defence genes, often in combined action with ethylene. (After Wasternack and Parthier 1997)

Box 1.10.2   **Metabolism (detoxification) of alkyl hydroperoxides in plants using the example of α-linolenic acid**

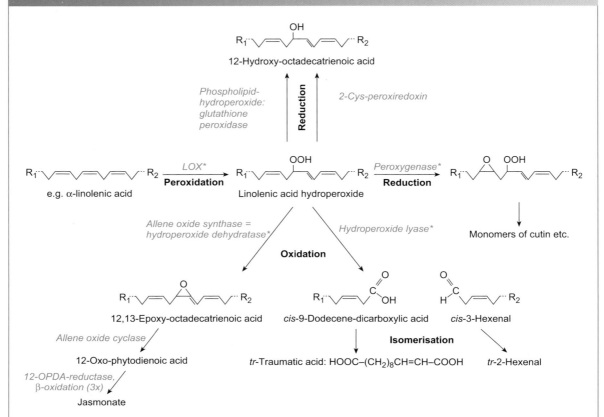

The formation of jasmonate is a response to stress: As soon as a biomembrane is damaged or deformed linolenic acid is released from phospholipids. Lipoxygenase is constitutively present and active, so that the chain of reactions starting from linolenic acid hydroperoxide is initiated immediately. As indicated in the figure, jasmonate is only one of the many possible products, depending on whether the linolenic acid hydroperoxide is metabolised by a dehydratase, lyase, peroxygenase or peroxidase (as, e.g., 2-cys-peroxiredoxin).

Of special quantitative importance are allene oxide synthase and hydroperoxide lyase reactions. The former reaction finally leads to jasmonate. In the lyase reaction, linolenic acid hydroperoxide (or also the 12,13-epoxyoctadecatrienoic acid) is cleaved, resulting in the production of reactive, unsaturated aldehydes: Hexenal and nonenal that in turn can be reduced to their respective alcohols hexanol and nonenol. The strong smell of freshly cut

grass (not that of hay) is largely due to these compounds.

The unsaturated aldehydes themselves (e.g. 2-*trans*-hexenal) have strong bactericide, fungicide and insecticide effects, and so are potent defence compounds. In the hydroperoxide lyase reaction, *cis*-9-dodecenedicarboxylic acid (*cis*-9-oxo-dodecadienic acid) is formed in addition to *cis*-3-hexenal. Both compounds are transformed to the corresponding *trans* compounds with shifting of the double bond (leading to 12-oxododec-10-eneic acid, known as traumatin, and *trans*-2-hexenal). Traumatin, like jasmonate, has a phytohormonal effect. It functions as a wound hormone that stimulates cell division in the cells adjacent to the damaged site (together with other hormones) and so induces callus formation around the wound (after Creelman and Mullet 1997; Baier and Dietz 1999; Feussner et al. 2001).

* reactions that can also occur non-enzymatically, then, however, not stereospecifically.

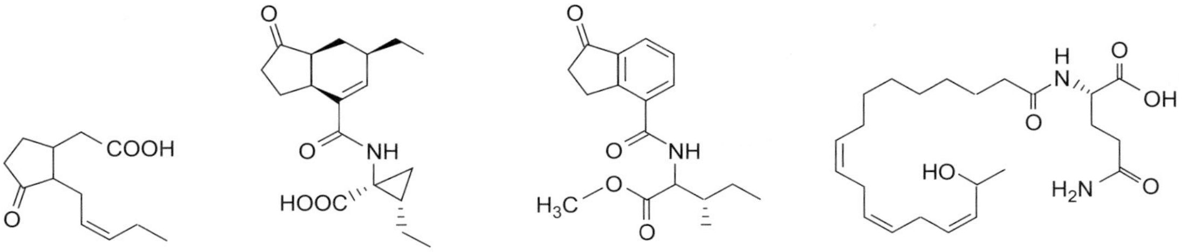

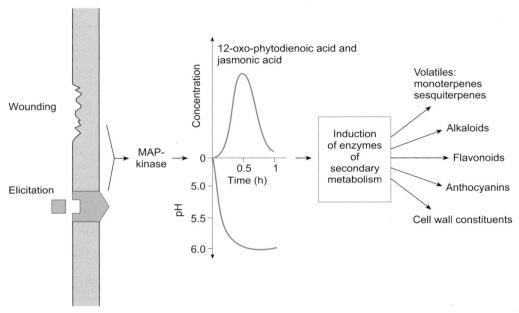

Jasmonic acid   Coronatine   Indanone-isoleucine methyl ester   Volicitine

Fig. 1.10.6. Structure of jasmonic acid and jasmonic acid like compounds or derivatives. In certain plants, these induce the same effects as jasmonate. (After Mitchell-Olds et al. 1998)

Fig. 1.10.7. Induction of secondary plant metabolites by jasmonic acid. Wounding and elicitation lead to an increase in the external pH, to a transient rise in 12-OPDA and jasmonate within the cells, and to the expression of genes encoding enzymes involved in secondary metabolism. Volatile compounds act as signals (e.g. for insects), alkaloids and phytoalexins are defence compounds and the flavonoids protect against light and UV radiation. Re-enforcement of the cell wall by cross-linking also prevents pathogen attack. (After Wasternack and Parthier 1997)

In addition to the induction of *Pin* genes, jasmonate induces particularly the expression of genes whose products serve in some way or the other in defence against stress: PR proteins (pathogenesis-related proteins), phytoalexin-synthesising enzymes, dehydrins and osmotin, as well as genes which are also induced by ABA or ethylene. A possible signal transduction chain leading to these products is shown in Fig. 1.10.7. As can be seen, the concentration of jasmonate (and 12-OPDA) rises only transiently; defence, however, is permanent as a result of the induced synthesis of biologically active proteins. Since these proteins (enzymes) are now also synthe-sised in plant parts which are not wounded or even not existent at the time of wounding, the systemic reaction (with respect to pathogen attack) is also called **immunisation** of plants.

The biochemistry of activation of a jasmonate-responsive promoter of JIPs is still relatively unknown. Promoters of *Pin 2* and *LOX 1* are best analysed. A palindromic element (TGACG) was found in the promoter of *LOX 1* which is essential for inducibility by jasmonate. This sequence is known as the *cis* element of transcription factors possessing a bZIP element (see Chap. 1.5.2.2; Rouster et al. 1997).

Table 1.10.2. Influence of the type of leaf damage on the pattern of enzymes involved in protection against damage (after Stout et al. 1994)

Type of damage	Protein pattern			
	Polyphenol oxidase	Peroxidase	Lipoxygenase	Protease-inhibitor
Caterpillar feeding	+	−	+	+[a]
Feeding by leaf miners	−	+[b]	−	−
Tapping by mites	−	+	+	−
Submerged in soap solution	−	+	+	−
Mechanical damage	+	−	−	+

[a] Statistically significant in two of three replicates.
[b] Significant effect in one of three replicates.

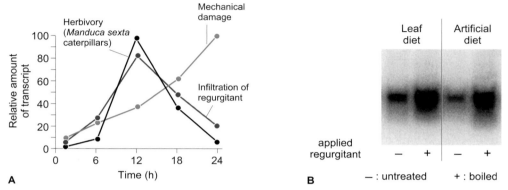

Fig. 1.10.8. A Different rates of accumulation of mRNA of *Pin 2* in potato leaves mechanically damaged or fed on by caterpillars, or supplied with regurgitant of the caterpillars via the petiole. B Proof that the inducer for the *Pin 2* transcription originates from the regurgitant of the caterpillar and not from the damaged leaves: the regurgitant of two differently fed caterpillars were applied to potato leaves, which were then analysed for the induction of *Pin2* mRNA. Caterpillars were fed on potato leaves (*left*) or on a pulp of filter paper soaked in a 1% sucrose solution (*right*). Both diets led to the same induction of *Pin2* mRNA. Shown are the Northern blots probed with a *Pin 2*-specific probe (after Korth and Dixon 1997). The chemical compounds in the regurgitant of *Manduca sexta* that cause this specific response have been identified. They are conjugates of fatty acids (e.g. linolenic acid, linoleic acid, oleic acid, palmitic acid) of membrane lipids with various amino acids. (Baldwin 2001)

Plants distinguish between purely mechanical wounding and wounding by phytophagous insects: Depending on the type of damage, typical patterns of enzymes involved in the defence response are induced (Table 1.10.2). The effects of a caterpillar (*Manduca sexta*) feeding on potato leaves have been extensively studied. Around the damaged site, mRNA of *Pin 2* and 3-hydroxy-3-methyl-glutaryl-CoA-reductase (HMGR) accumulate, as after mechanical wounding, but the accumulation is much faster and, as could be shown, in principle, not dependent on the stimulus by mechanical damage. If diluted regurgitant of the caterpillar is applied to the petioles of potato leaves, the transcripts of *Pin 2* and the *HMGR* gene accumulate in a similar way as after true herbivory. With purely mechanical wounding a similar concentration of mRNAs is achieved, however, only several hours later (Fig. 1.10.8). The regurgitant of the caterpillars stimulates the expression of *Pin 2*, even after they were feeding on a mixture of filter paper and sucrose, but no leaves. It must, therefore, be concluded that the stimulating agent is produced by the caterpillar and not taken up in the food (Fig. 1.10.8 B). In the caterpillar of *Manduca sexta* feeding on potato leaves, this stimulating agent is a conjugate of fatty acids and amino acids.

There must be substances in the regurgitant of insects which act as elicitors and induce transcription. The chemical nature of these "elicitors" is not yet known in many cases. Freezing and thawing the mandible juice and heating to 100 °C increase the inducing efficiency enormously. It is therefore concluded that the elicitor is not an enzyme. Obviously, different insects have different elicitors, as can be realised by the specific protein patterns induced by the different insects (Table 1.10.2).

1.10.1.3
Secondary Metabolism Induced by Jasmonate

Proteins often induced by jasmonate are Pin 2 and HMGR. The effect of Pin 2 as proteinase inhibitor has been mentioned above, but what is the significance of HMGR? It is a pace-maker enzyme of terpenoid biosynthesis. It has been shown that a few hours after insect feeding, volatile terpenoids are newly synthesised and released in large amounts.

The release of terpenoid compounds is modulated in a diurnal cycle, as their synthesis is connected to the photosynthetic metabolism of the chloroplast. Under strong illumination and high temperatures, higher plants divert a considerable amount of freshly assimilated carbon to terpenoid metabolism and secrete, as volatile compounds, isoprene and other low molecular weight terpenoids in considerable quantities during the day (Sharkey 1996). Damage, particularly insect damage, appears to considerably stimulate the sequestration of newly assimilated carbon into these compounds. In addition,

HMGR, the pace-maker enzyme of their biosynthesis, is induced by the wounding (slowly) and by feeding (quickly). This explains the increased secretion of terpenoids after feeding and wounding during the day. Terpenoids are also stored in glandular hairs, and it is therefore possible that they are released during the night, following damage.

In many plants, in addition to terpenoids, secondary plant metabolites are formed under the influence of jasmonate also by other biosynthetic pathways, for example, the alkaloid nicotine in tobacco species, which is highly toxic not only for warm-blooded animals, but also for many invertebrates. Such secondary metabolites can be substantial sinks for carbon and nitrogen.

Beside the secondary metabolites mentioned above, other volatile compounds are released after wounding or feeding; they are formed during peroxidation of linolenic acid liberated from membrane lipids (Fig. 1.10.9). During mechanical damage, various hexenals and their reaction products, hexenols, are formed which produce the typical smell of freshly cut grass (see Box 1.10.2). Damage by insect feeding, on the other hand, produces only hexenyl acetate, which was not found upon mechanical damage.

Shortly after feeding ended, the rapid formation of these compounds ceases. This is of eco-

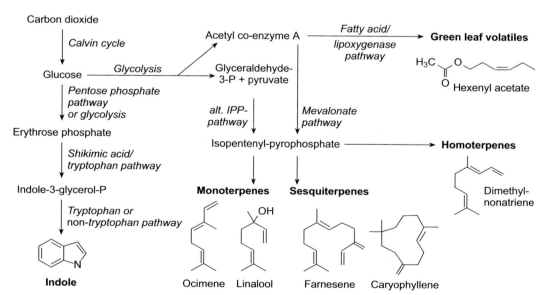

Fig. 1.10.9. Biosynthetic pathways of secondary plant metabolites leading to volatile compounds. Indole can be synthesised via two mechanisms: either as an intermediate during tryptophan synthesis or by a tryptophan-independent path (Frey et al. 1997). Terpenoids may be synthesised via the alt-IPP path [the alternative desoxy-xylulose-5-phosphate (DOXP) pathway] by which isopentenyl pyrophosphate is synthesised in the chloroplast. For further information on the lipoxygenase pathway, see Box 1.10.2. (After Paré and Tumlinson 1999)

nomical importance with regard to the production of secondary plant metabolites, because more carbohydrates (and nitrogen) are then available for growth. In an interesting experiment, the cost-benefit relation of jasmonate-induced defence was analysed (Baldwin 1998). Seed production of the annual *Nicotiana attenuata* was measured after some plants had been treated with methyl jasmonate to induce the defence reactions while others were left untreated. Both "populations" were then exposed to different intensities of herbivory by the natural spectrum of herbivores and phytophagous insects. Under herbivory pressure the (previously) induced plants produced significantly more seeds than the non-induced "unprotected" control plants. With little or no herbivory, however, the non-induced plants were superior. In nature, herbivory is the normal case, and therefore species capable of jasmonate-induced defence are favoured by selection.

Jasmonate plays the role of transmitter not only in the signal cascade after wounding, but also after infestation by pathogens. The reaction to both stimuli may be very different, not only regarding the metabolic end products: If the signal cascade is triggered by a fungal elicitor and if arachidonic acid instead of, or in addition to, linolenic acid is released, a different isozyme of the HMGR is induced, compared to the reaction in which jasmonate is the elicitor ("*hmg1*" vs. "*hmg2*"). The biological sense behind this differentiation is still unknown.

A jasmonate-independent signal pathway was identified, beside the jasmonate-dependent transduction of the wound signal (Titarenko et al. 1997). However, the jasmonate-independent signal pathway does not lead to a systemic induction, but only to a local induction of defensive genes as in the previously discussed systemin-independent signal pathway. This path is shown in Fig. 1.10.5 by the broken arrow.

It is interesting that the isoprenoids which are released function as **kairomones**[1] and particularly attract parasitoids, which then parasitise phytophages. Ichneumon wasps are especially attracted by the volatile terpenoids (Paré and Tumlinson 1999; Kessler and Baldwin 2001). Isoprenoids thus serve as signals with very high specificity regarding the host plant of the phy-

tophage, but the signal does not give much information about the type of phytophage. This is understandable, as the signal originates from the plant and not from the phytophage. It might be a kind of co-evolution that the inducible signals are produced almost exclusively during the day, when parasitoids are active. Induction of HMGR can thus be interpreted as an active defence strategy of plants against herbivory.

1.10.2
Pathogen Attack and Defence

Recommended Literature

- Durrant WE, Dong X (2004) Systemic acquired resistance. Annu Rev Phytopathol 42:185–209
- Hammond-Kosack K, Jones JDG (2000) Responses to plant pathogens. In: Buchanan BB, Gruissem W, Jones RL (eds) Biochemistry and molecular biology of plants. American Society of Plant Physiologists, Rockville, MD, pp 1102–1156
- Heil M, Baldwin IT (2002) Fitness costs of induced resistance: emerging experimental support for a slippery concept. Trends Plant Sci 7:61–67

In addition to phytophagous insects, plants may also suffer from infestation by pathogens like viruses, bacteria and fungi. **Pathogens** often cause considerable damage to the high-yielding cultivars of our crop plants and therefore their interaction with the host plant has been the topic of extensive research in the scientific area of **phytopathology**. Within the scope of this book, the reaction spectrum of plants to pathogen attacks can only be described in a cursory fashion.

We distinguish between **compatible** and **incompatible interactions**. In compatible interactions host and pathogen "get along with each other", i.e. infestation is strong, the pathogen is virulent and the plant is susceptible. In incompatible interactions, the infested plant can cope with the attack of pathogens by establishing defence reactions, i.e. it is resistant and the pathogens are called avirulent. In compatible interactions, pathogens are able to circumvent, inactivate or tolerate the plant defences. Generally, however, the resistance of plants to the broad

---

[1] Kairomones are (usually) volatile signal compounds, which are useful for the detecting organism: attractants, repellents (escape), stimulants, warning signals.

spectrum of potential, more or less omnipresent pathogens, is very high.

Fungi and bacteria proliferate and expand within the extracellular space of the plant, therefore cell walls are one of the preformed barriers these pathogens have to overcome. Often cell walls are very difficult to penetrate because of coating with or insertion of cutin, or because of lignification.

1.10.2.1
Infection by Fungi

A fungal infection starts from a spore adhering to the cuticle by an adhesion pad on the surface of a plant. A germ tube develops from the spore and an **appressorium** is formed (see Fig. 1.10.12). Within this appressorium a high pressure is built up exerting a mechanical force and with the additional help of cutinases, cellulases and pectinases the fungus enzymatically disrupts cuticle and cell wall, without damaging the plant plasma membrane. Primary hyphae expand in the extracellular space and haustoria are formed. Haustoria are nutrient-absorbing cells which invade plant cells by infolding the plant plasma membrane. The plant cell therefore remains intact, but their nutrients are consumed

serving to support growth of the fungus. Other fungi start infection of a plant similarly as described, but instead of forming haustoria they invade the plant cell with secondary hyphae destroying the plant's plasma membrane. The plant cells die and the fungi live from the contents of dead plant cells.

Without appropriate plant defence, fungi overgrow the plant tissue and their virulence is often increased by formation of exo- or zoospores.

1.10.2.2
Induced Defence

Resistant plants are able to prevent proliferation and expansion of pathogens. They do so by induction of defence responses which include (see Fig. 1.10.10)

- stiffening of their cell walls by synthesis of callose, a β-1,3-glucan, synthesis of hydroxy-proline-rich glycoproteins, which cross-link cell wall components, and increased lignification (see Fig. 1.10.12, formation of a papilla),
- synthesis of so-called **PR proteins** (pathogenesis-related proteins), some of which are chitinases and glucanases which hydrolyse fungal and bacterial cell walls, others have anti-oxidative capacities,

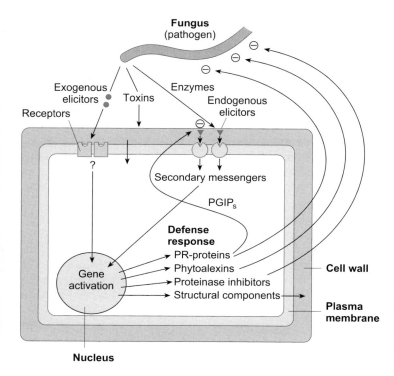

Fig. 1.10.10. Model of the interaction between pathogen and host in the hypersensitive reaction. The fungus releases cell wall lysing enzymes and elicitors from its hyphae, and in some cases also toxins. Via a signal cascade, the fungal elicitors, and the elicitors produced by hydrolysis of the plant cell wall, induce the expression of genes in the nucleus, which are involved in the synthesis of defensive enzymes that either directly attack the fungus (for instance PR proteins) or produce defensive compounds (phytoalexins and enzyme inhibitors). The polygalacturonase inhibitor (PGIP) highlighted in the model prevents degradation of oligogalacturonides, products of the action of a fungal polygalacturonase, which act as elicitors and thus increase the defence reaction. While the defence reactions are induced in cells surrounding the infection site during the hypersensitive response, the infected cell itself is "sacrificed" by programmed cell death. (After Heß 1999)

Box 1.10.3   Salicylic acid

Salicylic acid can be produced via several biosynthetic pathways, either via cinnamic acid coenzyme A thioester or via cinnamic acid glucose ester. Free benzoic acid is probably only a by-product. The storage form of salicylic acid is the glucoside salicin. *C4H* Cinnamate-4-hydroxylase; *PAL* phenylalanine ammonia lyase; *GTase* glucosyl-transferase (after Chong et al. 2001).

- synthesis of **phytoalexins** (Greek *alekein* = "to fend off"), a diverse group of low molecular weight secondary metabolites, predominantly compounds of the classes isoprenoids, flavonoids and stilbenes, which exert an antibiotic effect against a broad spectrum of fungi and bacteria.

The defence responses are induced in cells surrounding the infested cell. One mediator of the induction of PR proteins is salicylic acid[2] (see Box 1.10.3 and Table 1.10.1). In resistant plants, the infested cell itself often dies by programmed cell death, the final result of the so-called **hypersensitive response (HR)**. During an HR, reactive oxygen species ("ROS", see Chap. 1.3.5.3) are produced, leading to an **oxidative burst** (Lamb and Dixon 1997). ROS are toxic for the pathogen

and the host and, therefore, synthesis of antioxidants in cells around the infection site is plausible.

Why are the defence responses induced during incompatible but not during compatible interactions? In an incompatible interaction, signals are transmitted between pathogen and host, which trigger the defence responses. The basis of this "signal transmittance" is a certain genetic background of both partners. Plants contain **R genes (resistance genes)**, while pathogens contain **avr genes (avirulence genes)** or vir genes (virulence genes). For an interaction to be incompatible, host and pathogen must have corresponding R and avr genes (Hammond-Kosack and Jones 2000; Staskawicz 2001). The products of R genes are often integral plasma membrane proteins which function as receptors. Binding of a proper elicitor to the receptor then induces – via a signal transduction chain (similar as during herbivory) – the defence responses. The products of avr genes may be the elicitors per se or, in most cases, avr genes encode proteins which are involved in the synthesis of elicitors.

Upon a fungal infestation, elicitors are often degradation products of cell walls, either of plant or fungal origin. They are very specific oligosac-

[2] Acetylsalicylic acid, aspirin, is the most produced medicine worldwide. It is better tolerated by humans than free salicylic acid, the actual agent. This substance from the bark of the willow tree (*Salix*) was used in ancient times in western Europe and by North American Indians to relieve pain and fever. In plants, it increases resistance against pathogens, and is also used as a spray to prevent mildew. Many amateur gardeners water their plants from time-to-time with aspirin solutions.

Fig. 1.10.11. Systemic acquired resistance of cucumber plants to the Anthracnose fungus *Colletotrichum lagenarium*. One cotyledon of the *plant on the left* was infected with spores of the fungus. Obviously, it is suffering severely from necrosis. The *plant on the right* was left untreated. One week later, 20 drops of a spore suspension were placed on a main leaf of both plants. The leaf of the plant on the left remained fully healthy as it had become resistant. The leaf of the plant on the right, which experienced no "immunisation", exhibited necrotic areas at the positions of every drop of spore suspension. (Conrath and Kauss 2000)

charides. In one case, this elicitor is produced by the combined action of a fungal polygalacturonase (hydrolysing pectin of the plant cell wall) and a polygalacturonase inhibitor protein (PGIP), which is synthesised by the plant after infection, leading to oligogalacturonides of the appropriate length to function as elicitor (see Fig. 1.10.10). This is probably the result of a co-evolution between a former virulent fungus and a susceptible plant cultivar. Elicitors may also be secreted glycoproteins which bind to plant receptors. Regarding bacteria, avr-gene products are proteins which often are transferred into the plant's cytoplasm interacting with intracellular receptor proteins which "guard" the defence response. In the presence of a corresponding avr-gene product, the defence responses are induced.

The difference between resistant and susceptible plants is not that susceptible plants were unable to produce PR proteins or phytoalexins, but that their production is not triggered or not triggered in time because a proper signal (from the pathogen) or a proper receptor (in the plant) is missing.

1.10.2.3
Systemic Acquired Resistance

The hypersensitive response often includes the establishment of a systemic acquired resistance (SAR) against pathogens. SAR is reminiscent of the systemic defence against phytophagous insects. It means that the defence response (mainly synthesis of PR proteins) is induced in non-in-

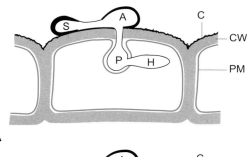

A

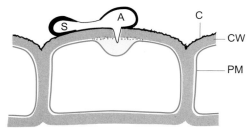

B

Fig. 1.10.12. Compatible (A) and incompatible (B) interactions during infestation by a fungus. A A germinating spore (S) develops a germ tube from which an appressorium (A) is formed. Within the appressorium a high pressure is built up and by secretion of cell wall lysing enzymes a primary hypha (P) is growing through the cuticle (C) and cell wall (CW). Later secondary hyphae (H) enter the cell by destroying the plasma membrane (PM). B Defence against a fungal infestation in a (systemically) resistant plant. The fungus is unable to penetrate the outer wall of the epidermal cell, as a papillose wall thickening develops under the appressorium. This papilla is also "impregnated" with a strong layer of lignin. (After Conrath and Kauss 2000)

fested plant organs remote from the infection site (Fig. 1.10.11). When pathogens later try to infect these plant organs they fail because of the defence mechanisms already preformed (Fig. 1.10.12). As during the local defence response, salicylic acid is part of the signal transduction chain leading to the expression of PR proteins in the non-infested tissue. Interestingly, the SAR is directed against a broad spectrum of pathogens, not only against the pathogen of the primary infection.

Establishment of a SAR requires a mobile signal probably moving in the phloem. Salicylic acid has been found to be translocated in the phloem, but despite this fact and though it is necessary for the induction of PR-protein synthesis in the remote site, it does not seem to be the mobile signal responsible for SAR induction. This still remains elusive.

1.10.3

Allelopathy

Many interactions between plants and herbivores and plants and pathogens are known. Less well known is that plants affect the growth of other plants. Such a phenomenon, **allelopathy** (Greek *allelos*, "another"; *pathos*, "suffering"), cannot always be unequivocally demonstrated, and was often said to be responsible for reduced plant growth without good evidence for such an interpretation.

The classical example for allelopathy is the inhibitory effect on germination by leaves of the walnut trees (*Juglans regia*, *J. nigra*). The inhibition is caused by juglone (1-hydroxynaphthalene), which is formed from 5-glucosyl-1,4,5-trihydroxynaphthalene under the influence of bacteria. Another classical example is the inhibition of grasses in the garigue of southern California, in the presence of the shrubs *Salvia leucophylla* and *Artemisia californica*. They produce a broad spectrum of possibly toxic, volatile terpenoids which impair growth of grasses. However, recently, doubts have been expressed about this interpretation; it is now thought that rabbits shelter under the bushes and graze the grasses causing their low biomass production. In most cases known, compounds which act allelopathically are phenolics which are metabolised by soil microorganisms and are thus "activated".

A good example of intraspecific allelopathy is shown by several representatives of the genus *Kalanchoë*, where root exudates from the mother plant inhibit growth of the daughter plants which are formed at the edge of the leaf (Fig. 1.10.13). The main components of the root exudate (in decreasing amounts) are gallic acid, caffeic acid, *p*-hydroxybenzoic acid, protocatechuic acid and *p*-coumaric acid, again all phenolic substances (Bär et al. 2000).

It is not yet known how these phenolic compounds affect growth of competitors; inhibition of germination often plays an important role.

Summary

1. Poisonous plant compounds, which are constitutively formed and are usually products of secondary metabolism, protect plants from **herbivory**, however, never completely. Some phytophagous insects take up such compounds while feeding on plants and accumulate them to protect themselves from their enemies. During the course of evolution, however, counteractions developed again. Volatile secondary plant metabolites often act as messengers which either frighten off or entice.

2. In addition to the constitutively expressed defence system of plants, reactions are also induced after **wounding** or infestation by pathogens. These reactions are triggered by pressure waves in the case of wounding, and by elicitors in the case of pathogen infestation.

3. If a plant is wounded, the vascular bundles are almost always affected. If air enters into the xylem, which is under negative pressure, a positive pressure wave is triggered across the whole plant. A depolarisation wave, decreasing with increasing distance from the damaged site, follows the change of pressure. The depolarisation wave activates intracellular signal chains, initially the formation of systemin from prosystemin, followed by activation of a lipase which releases linolenic acid from biomembranes. The free linolenic acid undergoes many metabolic reactions, initiated by lipoxygenase. One of the products is jasmonate, a stress hormone, but traumatin, a wound stress hormone, which activates cell division in the damaged tissue, may also be produced.

4. Jasmonate, like many phytohormones, has pleiotropic effects; it induces the expression of various genes, which, insofar as they are known, encode proteins serving to counteract stress. These genes are active even in those

Fig. 1.10.13. Intraspecific allelopathy in Kalanchoë (*Kalanchoë daigremontiana*). A Same age daughter plantlets were placed in a sand soil at regular intervals from the mother plant. After 150 days the height of the daughter plants clearly shows the inhibitory effect of the mother plant on their growth. B Quantification shows that the inhibition of the young plants depends on the distance from the mother plant. (After Bär et al. 2000)

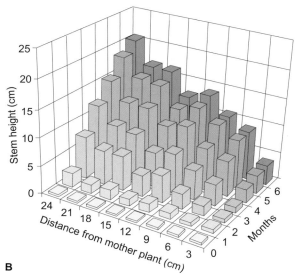

parts of the plant that have not been exposed to stress or develop after the stress. Because of this systemic reaction, this phenomenon is also called "immunisation".

5. Plants distinguish in their reaction between simple mechanical wounding and damage because of herbivory. In damage caused by herbivory, the regurgitant of phytophagous insects or their larvae is very important. This digestive fluid contains fatty acids conjugated to amino acids as elicitors. Synthesis of proteinase inhibitors, as well as synthesis of volatile signal compounds of the group of terpenes, is predominantly induced. Additionally, non-volatile defensive substances are formed after induction by jasmonate, e.g. the alkaloid nicotine, which is toxic for many insects and warm-blooded animals.

6. In addition to the transduction of the wound signal by jasmonates, there is also a jasmonate-independent path which activates the defence reactions.

7. Compatible and incompatible reactions are distinguished in **pathogen attacks**. In compatible reactions, there is a strong infestation, whilst the incompatible reactions indicate resistance. Resistance may be constitutive, directly acquired or acquired by "immunisation", the so-called systemic acquired resistance. Salicylic acid derived from phenolic metabolism is the signal substance inducing the defence system in infected or in non-infected plant parts.

8. The most frequently occurring form of an incompatible reaction is the "hypersensitive response": In addition to the synthesis of PR proteins (pathogenesis-related proteins, mainly lytic enzymes) and low molecular weight antibiotically active phytoalexins, the hypersensitive response comprises the programmed cell death of the infected cell, thereby depriving the pathogen from its resources. The hypersensitive reaction can be recognised by small, well-defined lesions.

9. Hypersensitive reactions are triggered by so-called elicitors, which may be derived from the pathogen, but also from the plant cell wall attacked by the pathogen. They bind specifically to the receptors which are encoded by R(esistance) genes. The specificity of elicitors is based on the avr genes (avirulence genes) of the pathogen.

10. Inhibition of growth and development of plants by neighbouring plants is called **allelopathy**, if it is based on excretion of incompatible chemical substances and not on simple competition. Classical examples are inhibition of germination and growth caused by rotting leaves of walnut trees, and the inhibition of growth of grasses by volatile compounds from Lamiaceae and Asteraceae.

Intraspecific allelopathy is demonstrated by *Kalanchoe daigremontiana*, where the mother plant inhibits growth of plantlets developing at the edges of its leaves by secretion of a broad spectrum of phenolic compounds from the roots.

References

Baier M, Dietz K-J (1999) Alkyl hydroperoxide reductases: the way out of the oxidative breakdown of lipids in chloroplasts. Trends Plant Sci 4:166–168

Baldwin IT (1998) Jasmonate-induced responses are costly but benefit plants under attack in native populations. Proc Natl Acad Sci USA 95:8113–8118

Bär W, Pfeifer P, Dettner K (2000) Biochemische Interaktionen zwischen Kalanchoe-Pflanzen. Biol Unserer Zeit 30:228–234

Chong J, Pierrel M-A, Atanassova R, Werck-Reichhart D, Fritig B, Saindrenan P (2001) Free and conjugated benzoic acid in tobacco plants and cell cultures. Induced accumulation upon elicitation of defense responses and role as salicylic acid precursors. Plant Physiol 125:318–328

Conconi A, Miquel M, Browse JA, Ryan CA (1996) Intracellular levels of free linolenic and linoleic acids increase in tomato leaves in response to wounding. Plant Physiol 111:797–803

Conrath U, Kauss H (2000) Systemisch erworbene Resistenz – Das „Immunsystem" der Pflanze. Biologie unserer Zeit 30:202–208

Creelman RA, Mullet JE (1997) Biosynthesis and action of jasmonates in plants. Annu Rev Plant Physiol Plant Mol Biol 48:355–381

Feussner I, Kühn H, Wasternack C (2001) Lipoxygenase-dependent degradation of storage lipids. Trends Plant Sci 6:268–273

Frey M, Chomet P, Glawischnig E, Stetter C, Grun S, Winklmair A, Eisenreich W, Bacher A, Meeley RB, Briggs SP, Simcox K, Gierl A (1997) Analysis of a chemical plant defense mechanism in grasses. Science 227:696–699

Heß D (1999) Pflanzenphysiologie: molekulare und biochemische Grundlagen von Stoffwechsel und Entwicklung der Pflanzen. UTB Ulmer Stuttgart, 608 pp

Kessler A, Baldwin IT (2001) Defensive function of herbivore-induced plant volatile emissions in nature. Science 291:2141–2144

Korth KL, Dixon RA (1997) Evidence for chewing insect-specific molecular events distinct from a general wound response in leaves. Plant Physiol 115:1299–1305

Lamb C, Dixon RA (1997) The oxidative burst in plant disease resistance. Annu Rev Plant Physiol Plant Mol Biol 48:251–276

Meindl T, Boller T, Felix G (1998) The plant wound hormone systemin binds with the N-terminal part to its receptor but needs the C-terminal part to activate it. Plant Cell 10:1561–1570

Mitchell-Olds T, Gershenzon J, Baldwin IT, Boland W (1998) Chemical ecology in the molecular era. Trends Plant Sci 3:362–365

Paré PW, Tumlinson JH (1999) Plant volatiles as a defense against insect herbivores. Plant Physiol 121:325–331

Rouster J, Leah R, Mundy J, Cameron-Mills V (1997) Identification of a methyl-jasmonate responsive region in the promoter of a lipoxygenase gene expressed in barley grain. Plant J 11:513–523

Sharkey TD (1996) Emission of low molecular mass hydrocarbons from plants. Trends Plant Sci 3:78–82

Stahlberg R, Cosgrove DJ (1997) The propagation of slow wave potentials in pea epicotyls. Plant Physiol 113:209–217

Stanković B, Davies E (1998) The wound response in tomato involves rapid growth and electrical responses, systemically up-regulated transcription of proteinase inhibitor and calmodulin and down-regulated translation. Plant Cell Physiol 39:268–274

Staskawicz BJ (2001) Genetics of plant-pathogen interactions specifying plant disease resistance. Plant Physiol 125:73–76

Stout MJ, Workman J, Duffey SS (1994) Differential induction of tomato foliar proteins by arthropod herbivores. J Chem Ecol 20:2575–2594

Titarenko E, Rojo E, León J, Sánchez-Serrano JJ (1997) Jasmonic acid-dependent and -independent signaling pathways control wound-induced gene activation in *Arabidopsis thaliana*. Plant Physiol 115: 817–826

Wasternack C, Parthier B (1997) Jasmonate-signalled plant gene expression. Trends Plant Sci 2:302–307

Chapter 2

Autecology: Whole Plant Ecology

Cocos nucifera, the coconut palm, a pan-tropical tree with nuts that are capable of floating, has long been used by man for a wide variety of purposes. The trunk is useful as timber for building, the leaves for roof material, the fluid endosperm is vitamin-rich coconut milk, and the hard endosperm is fat-containing copra, whilst the air-containing mesocarp is coconut fibre. Worldwide the production of copra is 4–5 million tonnes. Coconuts may form the pioneer tree vegetation along tropical coasts, especially on coral atolls where it is saline and periodically arid with high incident radiation. A "desert" area at the Atlantic coast, Punta Cahuita, Costa Rica. Photograph E.-D. Schulze

Autecology considers conditions and responses of individual plant species within their habitat. During the course of evolution, plants have occupied every terrestrial habitat with conditions ranging from tropical climates to eternal ice, from moors to deserts, and extremely saline habitats to those where one or other of the ions required for nutrition limits growth. These different environmental conditions require various **adaptations** of plants, but this does not necessarily imply that the individual plant itself adapts to specific conditions. It is much more the case that in a population mutations occur which are possibly not even visible externally and which are not disadvantageous under the prevailing conditions of competition and stress by the habitat. If conditions change, for example, the climate, or supply of nutrients or greater competition, then individual plants with certain advantageous traits are able to compete better and have a better chance of survival to enlarge the area which they occupy. This process is called **pre-adaptation**. Traits that are "advantageous" for certain habitats develop before the actual change of growth conditions and are the precondition for the settlement of new habitats (see Chaps. 4.1 and 4.2).

The subject of autecology is the result of these processes, i.e. to discover which characteristics make it possible for individual plants to flourish under certain conditions. The number of possible responses to the environment is wide and ranges from biochemical through cellular to morphological changes. Plants occur in a wide variety of forms, from giant trees which are hundreds of years old in boreal or tropical forests with a life cycle from germination to formation of seeds in centuries, to annual species of arid regions which form seed in a few days. Thus the characteristics with which a plant responds to the environment are its structure and its life span, as well as its physiological responses to stress. Thus autecology becomes **whole plant ecology**, considering the reactions at the level of individual organs (e.g. height of shoot, size of leaf, depth of root) or relationships between organs (e.g. distribution of resources between shoot and root, regulation of the coordination of shoot and root). Ecology of individual plants provides the connection between stress physiology and environmental conditions.

Whole plant ecology can be divided in various ways; here we consider the classical approach of "balance" or relations. At a particular site the individual plant needs to regulate various components and balance them, particularly:

- Thermal balance: certain extreme temperatures must not be exceeded;
- Water balance: active life requires that cells maintain a high water content;
- Nutrient balance: growth is possible only with the supply of essential nutrient elements;
- Carbon balance: life requires energy to supply existing organs and resources for further growth and reproduction.

2.1

Thermal Balance of Plants

Formation of ice on the branches of beech. Formation of ice crystals is due to freezing of super-cooled water from clouds onto the surface of the vegetation. The "ice beard" grows against the direction of the wind (hoar frost) and can reach such a volume that the crown of the tree may break (ice damage). In contrast to this, rime is composed of ice crystals which are formed from vapour. Solling IBP Beech-area B1. Photograph E.-D. Schulze

Recommended Literature

The most comprehensive book on whole plant ecology was by Lange, Nobel, Osmond and Ziegler in the Encyclopaedia of Plant Physiology, Part Physiological Plant Ecology, vols. 12 A–D (Springer, 1982). Despite being published 20 years ago it is still a landmark in providing understanding of whole plant ecology. The textbook by W. Larcher *Ecophysiology of Plants* (Springer 4th ed. 2003) and Lambers and Chapin: *Plant Physiological Ecology* (Springer, 1998) are recommended for further reading.

The thermal relations of plants deal with the balance of radiation energy. Only slightly more than 1% of the incident solar energy is used for photosynthetic metabolism. The remainder of the energy (about 700–1000 W m^{-2} at full sun light near the ground) has to be released again because the plant is fixed at the site and absorbs short-wave radiation dependent on its **albedo** (reflectivity). The energy balance can only be regulated by release of heat to the surrounding air (**sensible heat**) or by evaporation of water (**latent heat**). The flow of heat into the soil is too slow to regulate the thermal balance in a leaf or plant organ, with rapidly changing incident radiation. The **temperature of organs** (particularly of leaves and flowers) or the **temperature of surfaces** (stems, flowers) results from the energy balance. The temperature must be kept within certain physiological limits, to avoid damage, and energy balance must be regulated by the plant in such a way that damaging temperatures do not occur, even for short periods. Moreover, the temperature should rather be within the range of the physiological optimum of metabolic processes, which could be above or below the general temperature of the habitat. Plants are able to influence their organ temperatures over a wide range. For example, in the inflorescences of the Araceae, temperatures of ca. 17 K greater than the ambient air are produced via cyanide-resistant electron transport in respiration in order to entice pollinators. In arid climates leaf temperatures may be ca. 17 K below the ambient temperature because of evaporation, thus avoiding heat damage. The temperature of the plant thus is a result of the energy balance and is connected within a certain range to edaphic and climatic conditions.

In the following, the atmosphere and air layers near the ground will be considered as part of the habitat followed by the analysis of the energy balance of a leaf and its effects on plant responses. Ecophysiological responses of plants at extreme temperatures were discussed in Chapter 1.3.

Box 2.1.1   Atmospheric composition

Chemical composition of the lower atmosphere

78% N_2, 21% O_2, 0.6–4% H_2O, 0.03% CO_2, noble and trace gases of natural and anthropogenic origin.

Water vapour pressure: The maximum amount of water vapour that can be held by the atmosphere is termed saturation pressure (e_o), and which depends on temperature and pressure. The pressure of the atmosphere without water vapour, P_a, is derived from the measured pressure of the atmosphere, P, and the actual vapour pressure, e ($P_a = P - e$). At a constant air pressure the vapour pressure rises exponentially with a linear increase in temperature. For exact data on the composition of air, see List (1971).

Note: humid air is lighter than dry air, determined by the relationship between the molecular weights of H_2O and N_2, which is 0.62 (18/36). Hence, humid air in the lower atmosphere rises until it condenses on cooling, and forms fog or clouds. For the same reason, condensation forms on the ceilings of humid rooms or on the lids of Petri dishes.

The atmosphere is only rarely saturated with water vapour. The actual vapour pressure of the atmosphere (e) is generally lower than the saturation value (e_o). There are a number of terms that are used to describe the humidity of air (Fig. 2.1.1):

- **absolute vapour pressure:** $c_w = (2.17/T)\,e$, unit: $g\ m^{-3}$ (Note: volume of air is temperature and pressure dependent);
- **relative humidity:** $H = e/e_o$, unit % (Note: at constant vapour pressure this is dependent on T);
- **water vapour saturation deficit of the atmosphere:** $D_a = (e_o-e)/p_a$, unit $Pa\ Pa^{-1}$ (often shortened to VPD: vapour pressure deficit). Note: the value is independent of temperature and pressure;
- **water vapour saturation deficit between leaf and atmosphere:** $D_l = (e_{oL}-e)/p_a$, where e_{oL} is the vapour pressure deficit at leaf temperature and e the actual vapour pressure in the atmosphere; this term is important as it is the driving force for transpiration in plants (used to be abbreviated as WD: water vapour deficit);
- **dew point temperature** °C: T_d for $e=e_o$ (temperature, t, below which condensation temperature is reached and therefore condensation follows);
- **wet bulb temperature T_w:** This unit is used to measure the actual vapour pressure (psychrometer)

$$e = e_{o(Tw)} - \gamma(T_a - T_w)$$

where γ, the psychrometric constant, is 66.1 $Pa\ K^{-1}$ for a ventilated thermometer at 100 kPa air pressure and 20 °C.

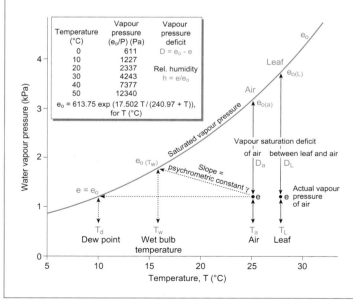

Fig. 2.1.1. Dependence of saturated vapour pressure, e_o, on temperature, T, and the graphical explanation of the various terms needed to define vapour pressure. T_a Air temperature; T_L leaf temperature; T_w wet bulb temperature; T_d dew point temperature; γ the psychrometric constant; e actual vapour pressure of the atmosphere; D_a saturation deficit of air; $e_{o(a)}$ saturation vapour pressure at leaf temperature, where e_o is calculated from $e_o = 613.75\ \exp(17.502\ T/(240.97+T))$, with T in °C

2.1.1

The Atmosphere as Habitat

The thermal balance of plants is closely connected to the chemical composition of and the physical transport processes in the atmosphere, which are part of the discipline of meteorology (textbooks: Lutgens and Tarbuck 2000; Wallace and Hobbs 1977). Variations in solar energy balance are responsible for the climatic conditions in the boundary layer near the ground, compared to the free atmosphere. Gregor Kraus (1911) was the first scientist to describe this phenomenon quantitatively on limestone sites near Würzburg, Germany, and thus founded a new discipline of micrometeorology (textbook: Jones 1994).

Water vapour, CO_2 and O_2 are the most important gases for the plant, independent of several other trace gases (ozone, nitric oxide, ammonia, methane and others) which influence the plant (see Chap. 1.9). Here, we discuss the energy balance in the context of water vapour and CO_2 in the atmosphere. Both gases are important for the existence and growth of plants.

Through the formation of clouds, **water vapour** influences

- absorption and reflection in the atmosphere and thus the solar radiation reaching the earth's surface;
- evaporation from the earth's surface as being dependent on the saturation deficit and on the plant cover;
- density of the atmosphere and the transport processes in it (formation of clouds) via the temperature dependence of saturation, which is the basis for precipitation.

Carbon dioxide influences
- the thermal balance of the lower atmosphere by absorption and radiation of long-wave radiation;
- photosynthesis, as it is the substrate for the process.

The interaction between the optical characteristics of the atmosphere and its constituent gases is explained in Fig. 2.1.2 A (Mitchell 1989; IPCC 1996). The solar radiation entering the earth's atmosphere occurs in the short-wave range at about 6000 K with maximum radiation at about 0.6 μm wavelength (visible light). Mean radiant energy at the upper limit of the atmosphere is 1370 W m^{-2} (**solar constant**, measured in the

stratosphere). Because the earth is not flat, but a sphere, the mean radiation flux during the day, averaged over the illuminated hemisphere, is about 340 W m^{-2} (WBGU 1997). This radiation is balanced by the long-wave radiation (**thermal radiation**, I_1), which by itself is a balance between thermal radiation of the atmosphere and thermal radiation from the stratosphere which operates at a temperature of 255 K. Long-wave radiation follows the **Stefan-Boltzman** law:

$$I_1 = \sigma T^4, \tag{2.1.2}$$

where $\sigma = 5.67 \times 10^{-8}$ (W m^{-2} K^{-4}), the Stefan-Boltzman constant, and T the temperature in Kelvin. Without an atmosphere, there would be no re-radiation from the atmosphere and thus the average temperature on earth would be $-18\,°C$.

Atmospheric gases, particularly water vapour and CO_2, have the effect that part of the incoming solar radiation in the short-wave and near-IR range is absorbed and reflected (Fig. 2.1.2 B). In the atmosphere the short-wave solar radiation (UV radiation) is absorbed particularly by ozone. H_2O and CO_2 absorb in the near-IR, thus limiting the incoming radiation to a narrow **radiation window** with a maximum in the visible range. The incoming energy is balanced by emission of long-wave IR from the earth's surface; this is limited by water vapour and CO_2. There is only a narrow **emission window** between 8 and 14 μm wavelength in which the earth's surface absorbs or emits heat.

Reflection and absorption processes are additive in determining the **energy balance** of the earth (Fig. 2.1.2 C; Mitchell 1989). Short-wave radiation is absorbed in the molecules of the atmosphere and clouds and reflected. Some of the short-wave radiation is reflected from the earth's surface, dependent on the type of vegetation cover.

The thermal balance is determined by the sum of processes of reflection and absorption (Table 2.1.1). A distinction is made between the **radiation balance** and the **energy balance**. The radiation balance comprises the sum of short- and long-wave radiation fluxes and their reflection whilst the energy balance of radiation is the sum of all thermal fluxes and incorporates thermal transport, latent heat of evaporation and the fluxes of heat into the soil. The radiation balance is normally not at equilibrium (i.e. it differs from zero), but the energy balance must be zero as the sum of all processes.

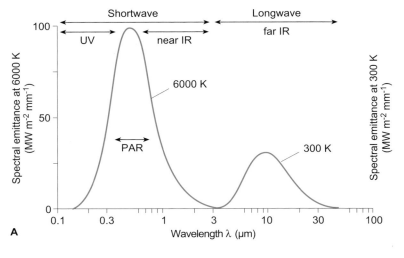

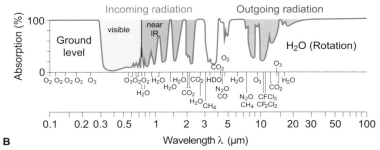

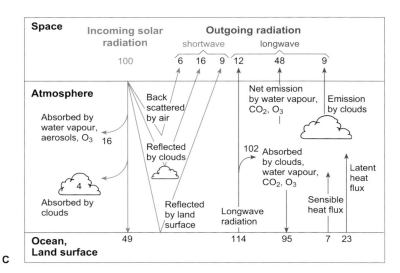

Fig. 2.1.2. Energy distribution and the incident radiation balance of the earth. A Spectral distribution of short wavelength incident solar radiation and the long wavelength heat radiation of the earth. B The spectral absorption of incident radiation by gases in the atmosphere. Note that ozone absorbs short wavelength radiation and CO_2 absorbs in the long wavelength range. In addition CO, N_2O and fluorochlorocarbons absorb incident radiation. C The transformation of incident radiation to heat radiation in the atmosphere. The percentages given are for the average global solar incident radiation of 342 W m^{-2}. (After Mitchell 1989; WBGU 1997)

Table 2.1.1. Energy balance[a] of the earth

Atmospheric radiation balance		Turnover (W m^{-2})	Relative contribution (%)
Incident solar radiation (short-wave)	I_{sA}	+342	100
– reflection (short-wave)	$\rho_{sA}I_{sA}$	–106	–31
– of radiation	(–75 = 22%)		
– of aerosols and clouds	(–31 = 9%)		
– of the soil			
(= net radiation)			
– heat radiation	$\varepsilon_{1A}\,I_{1A}$	–236	–69
– of gases in the atmosphere	(–164 = 48%)		
– of clouds	(–31 = 9%)		
– of the soil to space	(–41 = 12%)		
Atmospheric radiation balance in the upper atmosphere	Q_{nA}	0	0
Radiation balance at the ground surface			
Incident solar radiation (short-wave)	I_{sA}	+342 100	
– reflection (short-wave)	$\rho_{sA}I_{sA}$	–106	–31
– of aerosols and clouds	(–75 = 22%)		
– of soil	(–31 = 9%)		
– absorption in the atmosphere		–68	–20
Short-wave radiation input to the ground surface		+168	+49
Long-wave radiation			
– heat loss by the ground surface	$\varepsilon_{1B}I_{1B}$	–390	–114
– heat re-radiation by clouds	$\varepsilon_{1A}I_{1A}$	+325	+95
Radiation balance of the ground surface	Q_{nB}	+103	+30
Energy losses of soils			
– conductance of sensible heat into the soil	H	–24	–7
– energy loss by vaporisation	λE	–79	–23
Energy balance of soil		0	0

[a] The energy conversion with reflection, absorption and long wavelength emission occurs in the atmosphere and at the ground surface. The solar constant (1370 W m^{-2}) is the amount of energy that arrives at a surface above the atmosphere vertical to the incident radiation from the sun. In contrast, the solar energy arriving at the earth's surface (342 W m^{-2}) is the average amount of energy falling on the half of the earth facing the sun. The parameters are equivalent to the transport equations given in the text

Generally, the net **radiation balance** of the earth (R_n; n = net) may be expressed in the following equation:

Radiation balance of the upper atmosphere (R_{nA})

$$R_{nA} = I_{sA} - \rho_{sA}I_{sA} - \varepsilon_{1A}I_{1A} \qquad (2.1.2)$$

radiation balance = incoming solar radiation – reflection – long-wave outgoing radiation

R_{nA} is the balance of radiation fluxes at the upper boundary of the atmosphere, I_{sA} the short-wave incoming solar radiation at the upper boundary of the atmosphere, ρ_{sA} the ability of the atmosphere (clouds, gases) and soil to reflect incoming solar radiation, ε_{sA} is the ability of the atmosphere to emit long-wave radiation and I_{1A} the long-wave emission of the atmosphere (clouds, gases) and soil.

The radiation balance near the soil may be expressed analogously. The radiation balance at the earth's ground surface (R_{nG}) is the sum of short-wave incoming and outgoing solar radiation.

$$R_{nG} = I_{sG} - \rho_{sA}I_{sG} + I_{1A} - \varepsilon_{1G}I_{1G} \qquad (2.1.3)$$

radiation balance = incoming short-wave radiation – reflection + incoming long-wave radiation – long-wave emission

The incoming short-wave radiation I_{sG} is called solar radiation. $I_{sG} - \rho_{sA}I_{sG}$ denotes the short-wave radiation balance measured by a radiometer with a glass dome and $I_{1A} - \varepsilon_{1G}I_{1G}$ is the long-wave radiation balance measured by a radiometer with selenium glass. The radiation balance is measured with a radiometer with a polyethylene dome which transmits IR radiation.

In contrast to the radiation balance, the energy balance includes further thermal fluxes and thus the balance is in equilibrium.

$$\Phi_{nG} = R_{nG} - H - \lambda E - B - S - M = 0 \quad (2.1.4)$$

energy balance = radiation balance – sensible heat flux – latent heat flux – soil heat flux – storage – metabolism = 0

Φ_{nG} is the net energy flux at the soil surface and R_{nG} the radiation balance near the soil. The sensible heat flux, H, is proportional to the specific heat capacity of air ($c_p = 1012$ J kg^{-1} K^{-1}) and the temperature difference between soil and atmosphere ΔT. ρ is the density of air: 1.1884 kg m^{-3} at 20 °C and 1000 hPa air pressure. H is dependent on the coupling of the exchange from surface to atmosphere. This coupling is expressed by the boundary resistance, r_b:

$$H = (\rho c_p \Delta T)/r_b \quad (2.1.5)$$

In Eq. (2.1.4) λE is the **latent heat flux**, whereby λ expresses the energy required for evaporation of water (2.454 MJ kg^{-1} at 20 °C) and E the evaporation (kg m^{-2}).

Long-wave radiation follows the Stefan-Boltzman law in all cases [see Eq. (2.1.1)].

The annual incoming short-wave solar radiation (solar radiation, Fig. 2.1.3) is unevenly distributed over the earth's surface. Because there are fewer clouds over dry areas of the earth, net radiation is lowest and decreases in polar regions to about 40% and in the tropics to 70% of the radiation in dry areas. The global distribution of radiation reflects the global temperature and in particular low temperatures and **frosts**.

Only 12% of the outgoing radiation from the earth's surface reaches the universe directly and without change by interaction with gases or clouds in the atmosphere (see Fig. 2.1.2). The effect of trace gases on climate is based on their effect on the outgoing radiation from the earth. This effect is often called the **greenhouse effect**. As window glass is more permeable to short-wave radiation than to long-wave radiation, short-wave radiation passes through the window glass without resistance and is absorbed by the surfaces of the room. Long-wave radiation is emitted at the temperature of the room, but cannot pass the glass. It is thus "trapped" in the room – as a consequence, the temperature in the greenhouse increases as energy enters, but does not exit. Trace gases in the earth's atmosphere are analogous to the window pane, with water vapour, CO_2, methane and other trace gases (comparable to the quality of the glass) absorbing long-wave radiation and this influences the temperature of the atmosphere and thus a very large increase in these gases **influences the climate** (Stott et al. 2001). This outgoing window through which long-wave energy is emitted is made even smaller by ozone and anthropogenic **chlorofluorocarbons** (CFCs). These trace gases absorb exactly in the long-wave length and so are in the maximum range of outgoing radiation and are thus significantly more effective than trace gases such as CO_2, methane and nitrous oxide gas (N_2O), which only decrease the outgoing radiation at the edge of the absorption spectrum (i.e. make the atmosphere more impermeable for long-wave heat radiation; via the "greenhouse effect").

The course of **changes in temperature** and CO_2 **concentration** during the last ice ages is surprisingly similar (Fig. 2.1.4) pointing to a causal connection. The earth, during its history, has always been subjected to considerable oscillation in temperature and CO_2, as shown in Fig. 2.1.4 A. However, organisms usually had to cope with lower temperatures than those of the present day. Most plant species developed before the climatic changes in the Tertiary, and yet were able to survive these changes. Figure 2.1.4 B shows the changes in the CO_2 concentration in the last 1000 years. From the course of the curves over this period it becomes clear that early tree felling by humans in central Europe (first to third period of deforestation: 800–1300, see Chap. 4.1) did not change the CO_2 concentration of the atmosphere because the release of CO_2 occurred in a predominantly undisturbed environment which assimilated the CO_2 again. CO_2 concentration has only increased since the eighteenth century, initially slowly but exponentially since the middle of the twentieth century. Pre-industrial CO_2 concentrations are assumed to be 280 ppm. Currently, the increase is 1.5 ppm/year. The CO_2 concentration and the temperatures have reached values never before reached in the recent history of earth. Global effects are discussed in Chapter 5.

The significance of increased trace gas concentrations for the climate can be seen for an event in the earth's history (Norris and Röhl 1999). The boundary between Palaeocene and Eocene

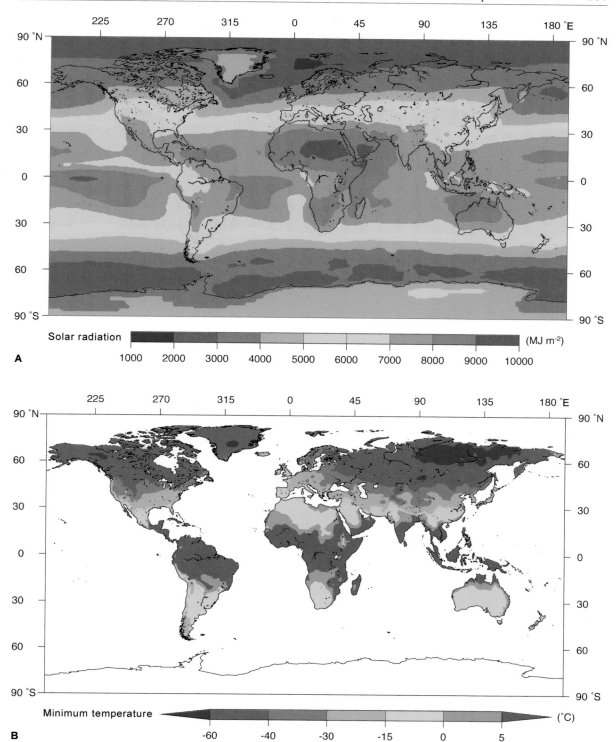

Fig. 2.1.3. A Global distribution of solar radiation (short wavelength incident radiation of the sun at the earth's surface); B global distribution of frosts (drawn by J. Kaplan; A, after http://daac.gsfc.nasa/CAMPAIGN_DOCS/FTP_SITE/INST_DIS/readmew/sre rad.html; Bishop and Rossow 1991)

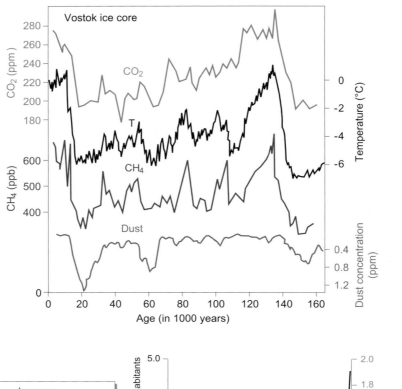

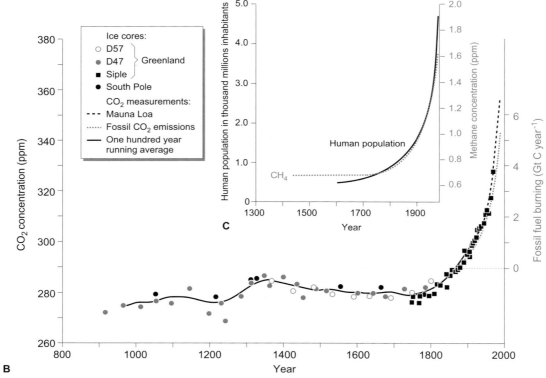

Fig. 2.1.4. A Changes in temperature and CO_2, methane and dust concentration in the last 160,000 years. B CO_2 concentration over the last 1000 years and the consumption of fossil fuels since 1850. The CO_2 concentration was determined from ice cores. Direct measurements of CO_2 concentration have been made on Mount Mauna Loa in Hawaii since 1960. C Change in methane concentration in the atmosphere since 1400 and the increase in the world population since approximately 1600 (WBGU 1997)

(55 million years ago) is characterised by a transient increase of 5–7 K in the mean global temperature. It has been shown that this increase in temperature was triggered by a landslide on the continental shelf of the Atlantic releasing 1000–2000 Gt carbon as methane from **methane hydrate**. This release is similar to the current release of CO_2 from fossil fuels (6 Gt/year×100 years corresponds to 600 Gt). This event in the earth's history may be used as a model to evaluate the consequences of the present human activity.

It cannot be concluded from the parallel course of CO_2 and temperature curves that CO_2 alone causes the climate change (see, e.g., Veizer et al. 2000). There are various factors which increase the **trend of climatic change** or decrease it. These are in particular (Mitchell 1989; IPCC 1996):

- Position of the earth relative to the sun (Milankovitch effect),
- Changes in outgoing radiation from vegetation and snow whilst cooling,
- Changes in absorption of glaciers with increasing dust cover,
- Repeated release of methane hydrates from ocean sediments,
- Complex interactions of various trace gases from aerosols, which may have an increasing as well as decreasing effect (IPCC 1996).

2.1.2

Climate of Air Near the Ground

2.1.2.1
Daily Changes of Temperature Near the Ground

The **climate of the air near the ground** is regulated by the same processes as the climate in the atmosphere. However, bigger extremes occur due to the exchange of energy and are modified by the type of soil and the vegetation (Fig. 2.1.5). This is shown clearly by the **course of temperatures during one day** (Walter 1960; Gates 1965). We shall first consider an area without vegetation, vertical to the incoming radiation source, and then modifications resulting from different inclinations, exposure and, most of all, vegetation cover.

Midnight
The long-wave radiation balance with high outgoing radiation and low incoming radiation substantially cools the earth's surface; the negative radiation balance is partially compensated by heat conduction from the soil, and by the low heat exchange (convection) with the air layers near the soil surface. Formation of dew and hoar frost may compensate this effect due to heat released in condensation and freezing. On a cloud-free night, temperatures may fall more than 10 K below the temperature of the atmo-

---

Box 2.1.2	Summary: The earth's temperature

- The **temperature** of the earth is an equilibrium between short wavelength incident radiation and long wavelength emissions.
- The **incident** radiation reaching the earth's surface is in a narrow "incident radiation window" in the visible light range. The incident radiation is reduced as the cloud cover increases (low clouds with higher reflective properties) and with the amount of aerosols in the atmosphere. Aerosols can be of natural as well as anthropogenic origin.
- **Emissions** result from a relatively narrow "emission window", in which water vapour has the lowest emission minimum. The emission window is getting increasingly

narrower because of the increase in natural as well as anthropogenic trace gases, especially chlorofluorocarbons, ozone, methane, nitrogen dioxide and CO_2. The earth's temperature rose due to a release of trace gases between the Palaeozonic and Eozene periods.
- The **temperature of the earth** results from a balance between the energy flows. It is difficult to predict the temperature and climate, as the slightest imbalance in opposing heat flows has considerable effects on the temperature, as long wavelength radiation emission is proportional to the fourth power of the temperature (Stefan-Boltzman law).

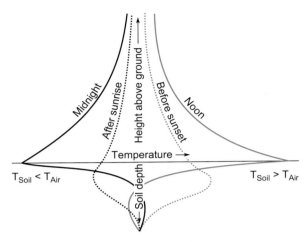

Fig. 2.1.5. Above- and below-ground diurnal temperature profile. (After Gates 1965)

sphere 2 m above ground. In the soil, the temperature increases with increasing depth, reaching a maximum which depends on the heat gain of the previous day and at greater depth corresponds to the mean temperature of the season.

Sunrise
Incoming solar radiation compensates for long-wave outgoing radiation of the soil. Because of the net heat loss to the atmosphere at night and the heat transfer to the soil, soil temperatures during the morning initially decrease with depth before they rise to the mean temperature of the season.

Midday
Temperatures may rise to 20 K above the atmospheric temperature as measured 2 m above ground, dependent on incoming radiation. Heat transfer is via convection (heating of the atmosphere) and heat conductance into the soil, where the temperature decreases with depth and still shows a minimum dependent on the previous night, before reaching the mean temperature of the season at greater depth.

Sunset
Surface temperature decreases with the incoming radiation, but the temperature within the soil still rises, due to the heat wave reaching the soil because of the heat flow during midday.

2.1.2.2
Modification of Environmental Radiation and Temperature by Abiotic Factors

Daily variation of temperature at the soil surface and average annual temperatures are affected by the soil conditions and its exposure (see also Chap. 4.3).

- **Heat conductivity and heat storage in soil:** Dry soils have a very low heat conductivity and warm substantially at the surface during the day due to incoming short-wave solar energy, and cool greatly during the night, as the incoming radiation is balanced by the outgoing long-wave radiation from the soil. Also in dry soils heat exchange is limited to a small volume. On limestone near Würzburg in the Federal Republic of Germany, maximum surface temperatures of 60 °C have been measured (Krause 1911). In contrast, moist soils have a high heat conductivity and heat capacity and thus a lower daily amplitude of temperature. Because of the higher evaporation on moist soils, their annual average temperatures are lower than those of dry soils.
- **Optical characteristics of surfaces:** Absorption of incoming radiation is increased on black surfaces of rock or humus; reflection is increased on white mineral soils and with snow cover. With black organic cover soil surface temperatures of more than 50 °C can be reached even in alpine climates. On organic soil exposed to the sun, the temperature tolerance of seedlings is often exceeded (e.g. beech seedlings "fall over").
- **Exposure and slopes:** In the northern hemisphere, northern slopes receive less radiation than southern slopes, i.e. they do not warm up at midday so much (Fig. 2.1.6 A). Southern slopes receive radiation maxima according to the latitude of the site. Slopes cool less during the night than the bottom of the valley, because cold air is heavier than warm air and flows downhill into the valley. The radiation balance between a slope and the atmosphere is also more favourable during the night than the lowlands, as radiation input from neighbouring slopes positively influences the radiation balance. This is the reason that vines at their northern growth limit are planted on south-facing slopes. The climatic differences between north- and south-facing slopes in the northern and southern temperate climates

Fig. 2.1.6. A Influence of the orientation of a slope on the potential incident radiation (excluding clouds) at 55° latitude (after Jones 1994). B Sub-alpine vegetation (2500–3000 m NN) in the northernly Fergana mountain range (41°N in Sari Chilek, Kirgistan) with a natural differentiation of the vegetation on the north- and south-facing slopes: *Picea schrenkiana* of the northern slope, meadows on the south slope. The shrub vegetation (*Rosa, Lonicera, Berberis*) of the valley are a consequence of the increased snow and soil moisture. (Photo E.-D. Schulze)

may be as large so as to cause differences in the vegetation (Fig. 2.1.6 B).

- **Depth and moisture of soil:** Temperatures within the soil are much more stable than at the surface, i.e. they do not vary as much. Depending on their moisture content, which determines the heat capacity, there is a clear temporal shift in changes in soil temperatures compared to air temperatures, with soils cooler than the air during spring and early summer and warmer in autumn and early winter.

2.1.2.3
Modification of Radiation and Temperature by Biotic Factors

Radiation climate and temperature at the soil surface are particularly affected by vegetation cover:

- **Reflection:** The composition of the vegetation determines its reflection characteristics. The reflection coefficient varies between 30%, e.g. for

birch forests, and 15% for conifers. The low reflection of conifer forests affects the climate at the limit of boreal forests; more radiant energy is absorbed, and thus more energy kept as heat in the stand, than on forest-free areas. The occurrence of evergreen conifers may, thus, cause a shift in the conifer tree limit to the north; the effect is compensated by the shading of roots by the evergreen canopy, which delays thawing in spring and thus shortens the growing season.

- **Radiation absorption:** The largest part of the incoming radiation is absorbed in the canopy, independent of the height of vegetation (Fig. 2.1.7 A). The radiation balance depends on the leaf area and leaf orientation. The leaf area is quantified by the **leaf area index** (LAI), defined as the sum of the projected leaf surface per soil area. With the idealised assumption of a statistically random distribution of leaves in the canopy, the decrease of radiation (extinction) follows the Lambert-Beer law of absorption:

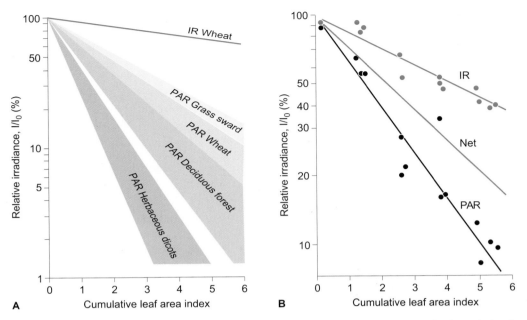

Fig. 2.1.7. A Reduction of photosynthetically active radiation (PAR) with increasing leaf area index for dicotyledonous shrubby plants (horizontal leaf position, extinction coefficient k=0.7), deciduous forests, wheat field and grass meadows (vertical leaf position, extinction coefficient k=<0.5; after Larcher 1994). B Relative reduction of the light intensity of infrared light (IR), net radiation balance (net) and the photosynthetically active radiation (PAR: 400–700 nm) with the leaf area index. (Jones 1994)

$$I = I_0 e^{-kLAI}, \qquad (2.1.6)$$

where I is the radiation flux at a defined site in the vegetation, I_0 is the incoming radiation above the canopy, LAI is the leaf area index above the measuring point, and k is the extinction coefficient [and corresponds thus to the absorption $(1-\varepsilon)$ in the radiation balance, Eq. (2.1.2)], k varies between 0.5 for vertical leaves (e.g. grasses) and 0.7 for horizontal leaves (e.g. clover). Several species (particularly legumes) are able to move their leaves and thus the LAI is actively and variably regulated (see also Fig. 2.1.13). The "clumped" distribution of needles in conifers results in decreased absorption of light with depth in the canopy, and thus to an increased LAI (see Fig. 2.1.8).

The **extinction** of the visible, short-wave light in the canopy (which depends on the LAI) is faster than extinction of the long-wave energy flux (Fig. 2.1.7 B; Jones 1994). Thus long wave radiation (heat) penetrates deeper into the vegetation than the photosynthetically active photon flux. Vegetation is only able to increase the leaf area until all visible light is absorbed, i.e. the maximum LAI is deter-

mined by the incoming radiation (available light) and the angle of the leaf. However, even with complete absorption of visible light, still a part of the IR radiation reaches the soil.

- **Climate within the vegetation:** With changes of radiation in the canopy (Fig. 2.1.8; Monteith 1973) not only the temperature, but all other meteorological factors change, particularly the saturation deficit and the turbulence. Because of mixing in the atmosphere within the canopy, temperature extremes are less than on a vegetation-free soil surface, during the day as well as at night. The gradient in the stand depends on the roughness of its surface. In coniferous forests absorption of light is less steep (related to the height of the canopy) than in cereal crops. Consequently, wind penetrates deeper into the canopy of conifers; temperatures and vapour pressures are more uniform during the day in a coniferous forest than in a cereal field. Because of the difference in coupling to the atmosphere, only in the cereal canopy is there a significant decrease in CO_2 concentration. During the night the gradients of temperature, humidity and CO_2 are reversed. Differences depend mainly on the roughness of the surface and thus on coupling to the atmosphere (see

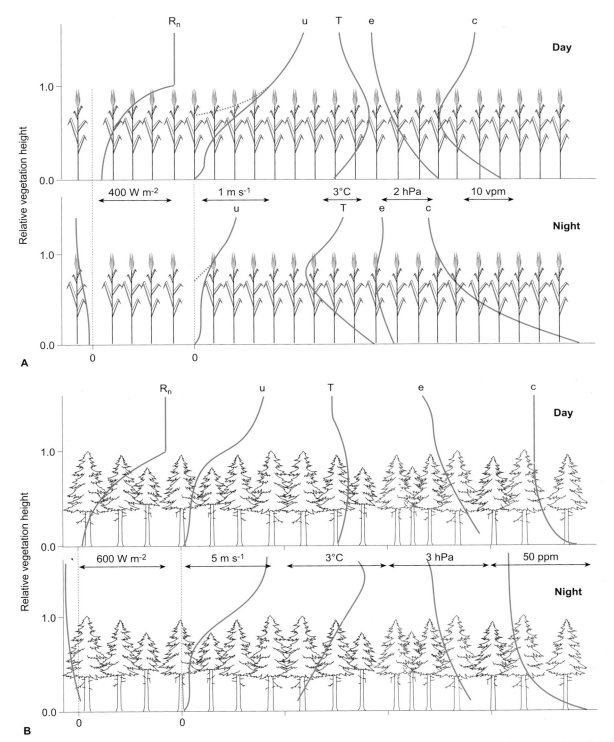

Fig. 2.1.8. Energy transformation changes the meteorological parameters during the day and night in (A) a wheat field and (B) a coniferous forest. R_n Radiation balance; u wind speed; T air temperature; e vapour pressure; c CO_2 concentration. During the day, absorbed radiation leads to a rise in temperature and an increase in vapour pressure. The CO_2 concentration is minimal at the height of the assimilating layer of leaves. The wind speed is reduced. During the night, there is a net loss of energy. This leads to the minimum temperature at leaf height. The CO_2 concentration is maximal at the soil surface. Due to the lower surface roughness, the gradient in wheat fields is more marked than in a forest. From the rise in the profile, the energy and mass balance can be calculated (wheat: after Monteith 1973; spruce: compiled by C. Rebmann)

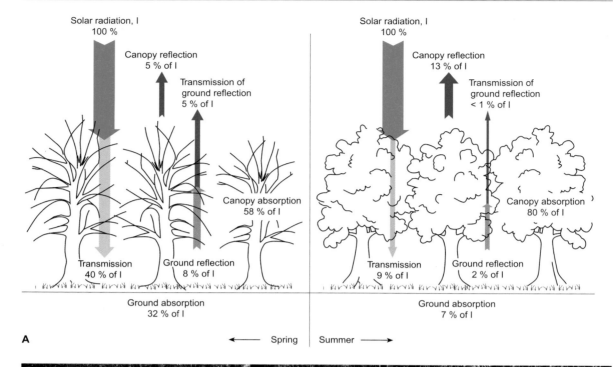

A   ←— Spring | Summer —→

Fig. 2.1.9. A Radiation balance of a beech forest in spring and summer. About 40% of the incident radiation reaches the forest floor in spring. About one-third of the incident radiation is absorbed by the litter layer; this leads to a marked rise in temperature in the litter layer and thereby activating the spring geophytes. In summer the leaf canopy absorbs about 80% of the incident radiation and less than 10% reaches the forest floor. Thus the litter layer remains cool and damp (after Schulze 1982). **B** Picture showing the spring geophytes in a deciduous forest, with *Anemone nemorosa*. Picture taken close to Schweinfurt, Lower Franconia, Germany. (Photo E.-D. Schulze)

Box 2.1.3   Summary: Climate close to the ground

- **Close to the ground conditions** are different to those measured 2 m above the earth's surface, the meteorological climate (–10 to +20 °C).
- The climate in the vegetation canopy is different to that at ground level (turbulence, radiation balance).

- Vegetation, through the **leaf area index** (LAI) regulates the amount of incident radiation it absorbs dependent on the available visible light [LA1 = f(Q)], leaf position and, in exceptional cases, on leaf movement (*Oxalis*, Leguminosae).
- LAI changes with season and determines the type of **vegetation on the forest floor**.

Chap. 2.2.4.1). In the shadow within a forest the daily fluctuations in soil temperature are thus less marked. On a cloud-free summer day the difference in temperature between an open area and inside a forest corresponds to the decrease in temperature resulting from a difference in altitude of 1000 m (see Chap. 4.3).

- **Leaf shedding:** In deciduous temperate forests there is substantial change in the surfaces receiving light energy over the year (Fig. 2.1.9 A). Before the emergence of leaves, 40% of radiation reaches the ground, with the outgoing radiation during the night being decreased because of the canopy of branches. Thus the organic layer on the ground warms up very quickly and the **spring geophytes** (Fig. 2.1.9 B; *Anemone, Corydalis, Primula* and others) develop faster than the leaves of the trees. With the emergence of leaves, 90% of the energy is intercepted in the canopy. Thus the floor of the forest remains relatively cool. The light received is not sufficient for herbaceous plants with horizontal leaves. Shade-tolerant grasses which can use diffuse indirect light, or species able to **move leaves** (*Oxalis*, see also Chap. 1.2.1), develop. Many plants in the herbaceous layer of forests rely on sun flecks resulting from gaps in the canopy (Pearcy and Pfitsch 1994). In evergreen coniferous forests the short seasonal "window", in which the sun's rays reach the floor of the deciduous forests, is missing. In evergreen forests geophytes have little opportunity to grow. Shade in the forest also delays melting of snow on the floor, and thus the beginning of the growing season, with negative effects on the water balance (see Chap. 1.3.6.10, freezing drought). Slow warming of the floor in coniferous forests may offset the positive effects on the energy balance in the canopy (high absorption of radiation); in Siberia deciduous larch forms the boreal forest limit.

2.1.3

Energy Balance of Leaves

The **energy balance of a leaf** is discussed here as an example, as it represents any organ or surface of a plant. The thermodynamic laws applicable to a leaf are basically the same as described for the atmosphere. However, additional parameters need to be considered for a leaf, namely exchange resulting from reflection of short- and long-wave light at the upper and lower side of the leaf and outgoing re-radiation from the soil to the leaf (Fig. 2.1.10; Jones 1994).

In as far as I_s represents the radiation flux to a surface at right angles to the incoming radiation and I_L the net radiation flux to a surface oriented in any direction, then

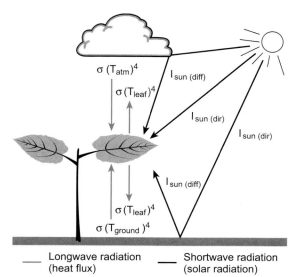

_____ Longwave radiation   _____ Shortwave radiation
(heat flux)   (solar radiation)

Fig. 2.1.10. Radiation balance of a leaf. I_s Radiation from the sun as direct and diffuse radiation; $\sigma(T_{atm})^4$ heat radiation of the atmosphere; $\sigma(T_l)^4$ heat radiation of the upper surface of the leaf; $\sigma(T_B)^4$ heat radiation from the soil (from Jones 1994)

$$I_L = \sin\beta I_s, \qquad (2.1.7)$$

where β the angle between solar ray and object (i.e. the equation describes the energy gain on slopes, see also Fig. 2.1.6). Neglecting possible outgoing heat and storage, the following equation describes the energy gain of a leaf from absorption of short-wave radiation or from IR radiation out from the upper and lower surfaces, from the sensible and latent heat transport, and from metabolism:

$$\Phi_{nleaf} = I_L + \rho_{sB}I_L a_L + \sigma(T_{atm})^4 + \sigma(T_{leaf})^4$$
$$- 2\sigma(T_{leaf})^4 - H - \lambda E - M = 0 \quad (2.1.8)$$

Energy balance = short- and long-wave absorption – heat loss – sensible and latent heat transport – metabolism = 0

Symbols and indices are explained in Eqs. (2.1.1)–(2.1.3). The **sensible heat flux** for a leaf is:

$$H = \frac{c_p(T_{leaf} - T_{atm})}{r_b} \qquad (2.1.9)$$

whereby the **boundary layer resistance, r_b,** is proportional to the length of the leaf (l) and inversely proportional to wind speed (u):

$$r_b = \sqrt{\frac{l}{u}}. \qquad (2.1.10)$$

Neglecting the boundary layer of the leaf, the **latent heat flux** is proportional to the vapour pressure deficit between leaf and atmosphere (D_L) and to the **stomatal conductance** (g_s):

$$\lambda E = D_L g_s, \qquad (2.1.11)$$

and g_s is dependent on D_L. So far, this relation may only be shown as a physiologically regulated, empirical function:

$$g_s = f(D_L) = \frac{1}{1 + \frac{D_L}{D_{L\,1/2}}} \qquad (2.1.12)$$

where $D_{L\,1/2}$ corresponds to the vapour pressure deficit at which the stomata are half closed; g_s is measured in ventilated cuvettes. The conductivity of a non-ventilated leaf depends on the boundary layer [Eq. (2.1.8)] and is lower than g_s.

The equations for the leaf energy balance show that **leaf temperature**, although measurable, cannot be directly calculated (perhaps it may be interpolated as part of the energy balance), as temperature depends both on the laws of physics relating to the energy balance as well as a physiological reaction. Plants have many possibilities of regulating leaf temperature to avoid extremes and to keep it in the optimal range for physiological activity (see Chap. 1.3.2). These possibilities are:

- Short-term (modulated) responses: change of leaf position, and regulation of stomata, and thus cooling by transpiration;
- Modified responses: changes in leaf size (e.g. slitting of banana leaves with high irradiation) and LAI;
- Evolutionary (genotypic) responses: changes in the reflective characteristics of the leaf, e.g. hairs and pigment composition.

2.1.4

Adaptation to Temperature Extremes

The **limit of resistance** of plants and the maximum and minimum temperatures measured in their organs under natural conditions are generally very different (see Chap. 1.3.1). This distance from normal conditions to the limit of resistance is required, as temperatures in the organs depend on the incident radiation and may fluctuate very quickly. Threshold values for changes in metabolism (see Chap. 1.3.4) and the resistance limits should not be exceeded, even for a short time. Seedlings and organs close to the soil are particularly vulnerable to extreme temperatures. The sequence of life forms according to Raunkiaer (trees, shrubs, herbaceous plants, annuals and geophytes), with dominance of trees in the tropical regions and herbaceous plants in the temperate and cold regions of the earth, can nevertheless not be interpreted as adaptation to temperature. There are many different conditions promoting or suppressing growth of trees. The coldest place on earth (–70 °C: Oimikon, eastern Siberia) is dominated by extensive forests of Siberian larch, and also in hot climates trees grow if water is available (e.g. palm trees in an oasis). The tree limit in alpine and boreal regions is caused by other factors (growing season, frost drought, anaerobic conditions in the moors of the tundra, fire). In well-drained sites in Siberia (Chertskii) forests extend almost up to the Arctic Ocean.

There are very few examples of the limitation of **habit for plants** by temperature. One example for the distribution limits is beech (*Fagus sylvatica*). At the eastern borders it is the resistance of buds to the winter cold. The northern and western limits are caused by late frosts, whilst the southern limit is due to drought. Obviously the adaptation to – or avoidance of – extremely low temperatures is not as easy as avoidance of high temperatures, but "death from cold" may often not be differentiated from "death from drought" under field conditions (see Chap. 1.5 and Chap. 2.2).

There are many possible ways for adaptation, but more for adaptation to high temperatures than to low. In the following some examples are given which are representative for many other species and situations.

2.1.4.1
Adaptation to High Temperatures

High temperatures combined with drought lead to many adaptations at the level of the leaf, spanning from molecular reactions (Chap. 1.3.4) to morphological changes:

- **Changes of leaf surface** (wax, hair): the genus *Encelia* comprises several species characterised by variable density of epidermal hair (Fig. 2.1.11; Jones 1994). These hairs reflect the incoming energy to different degrees (Ehleringer 1980).
- **Change in leaf size** (Fig. 2.1.12): with high solar radiation smaller leaves (microphylly) are usually formed. In response to radiation stress the same plant may produce small sun leaves and large shade leaves (Smith 1978). A famous exception to this rule is *Welwitschia mirabilis* of the Namib Desert, which forms very large leaves that may be up to 3 m long and 1 m wide, despite the high incoming radiation. Here, the leaf temperature is regulated by convection and long-wave radiation from the cooler soil (Schulze et al. 1980).
- **Changes in leaf angle** (Fig. 2.1.13): for some plant species, particularly in the Leguminosae, the movement of the leaf plays an important role, by either moving the leaf blade towards the sun to obtain maximum photon flux, or away from the incoming radiation to minimise absorption. Classical examples are the

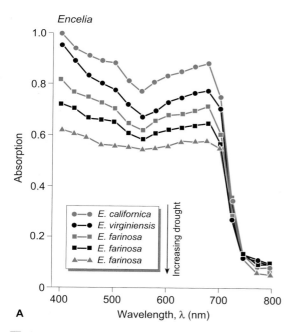

Fig. 2.1.11. A Effect of leaf hairs on radiation absorption of plants of five species of genus *Encelia*. With increasing amount of hairs on the surface, leaves absorb less and less radiation in the visible range. Whilst green *Encelia californica* occurs in coastal regions or where there is a good water supply, *E. farinosa* with white leaves grows on dry slopes and in the Sonora Desert (after Ehleringer, 1980). **B** *Encelia farinosa* in the Sonora Desert, south Nevada. (Photo E.-D. Schulze)

Fig. 2.1.12. Leaf morphology of plants growing in the Namib Desert: A pinnate leaves: *Acacia detinens*, Mimosaceae; B with small leaves: *Boscia foetida*, Capparaceae; C with large leaves: *Welwitschia mirabilis*, Welwitschiaceae; D photosynthetically active shoots: *Acanthosicyos horrida*, Curcurbitaceae. (Photo E.-D. Schulze)

cow pea (*Vigna unguiculata*) and the forage plant *Macroptilium purpureum*. They turn their leaves to the sun or away from it depending on water supply. In extreme cases they turn their leaves so that the plant does not create a shadow (Shakel and Hall 1979). This leaf movement changes the leaf temperature and thus the vapour pressure gradient between leaf and surrounding atmosphere. This in turn affects transpiration [Eq. (2.1.11)] and thus the water relations of the plant (see Chap. 2.2). However, even without leaf movement, the leaf angle is an important factor in the energy balance of vegetation. The hanging leaves of *Eucalyptus* are well known and the reason why eucalypt forests create hardly any shadow.

- **Changes of transpiration** (Fig. 2.1.14; Larcher 1994). *Citrullus colocynthis* is a type of pumpkin which grows near the ground in desert regions of North Africa (Lange 1959). The intact leaf transpires heavily and may have a temperature of about 40 °C when the surrounding temperature of the air layer near the ground is about 53 °C. This is the greatest

transpirational cooling which has been measured in the field. If the leaf is cut off, and thus prevented from transpiring, its temperature rises to more than 60 °C and thus exceeds the upper limit for temperature tolerance which is around 46 °C.

- **Shading:** In a free-standing tree, branches and leaves protect the stem from direct radiation. This applies particularly to subtropical dry regions, where, for example, in *Acacia*, the broad canopy shades the **base of the stem** (Fig. 2.1.15). Alternatively, there is also **antenna growth** where shoots extend as far as possible from the hot air layer near the ground. However, in this case, the hypocotyl requires protection from radiation. Even in a temperate forest, in gaps within the forest or at the edges of the forests (particularly if the forest is economically used), high temperatures may occur around stems causing damage (sun burn on beech). In contrast to the positive effects of having leaves or needles, shading may also be of disadvantage in boreal and alpine climates (see also Fig. 2.1.9).

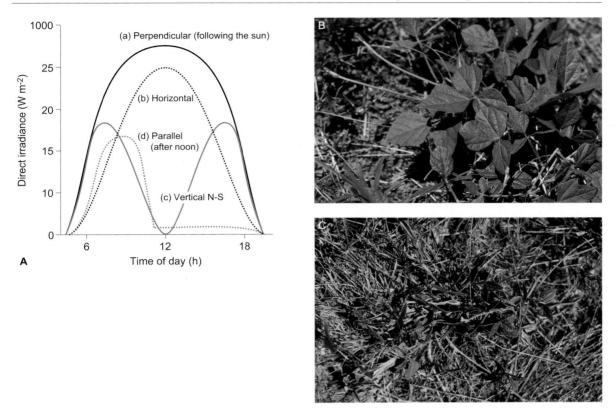

Fig. 2.1.13. A Daily movement of a leaf with changes in the incident radiation (calculated for 50 °N): *a* vertical to the incident radiation and tracking the sun during the day (e.g. beans), *b* horizontal position (e.g. clover), *c* constant vertical position to the south or to the north (e.g. *Lactuca seriola*), *d* parallel to the incident radiation in the later afternoon (*Vigna unguiculata*: from Jones 1994; Vigna: from Shakel and Hall 1979). B *Macroptilium purpureum* (Leguminosae), a cultivar of Australian pastures, in time of good water availability with leaves that follow the sun. C During drought with leaves that are parallel to the sun and have no shadow. Experimental farm Narryen, Queensland, Australia. (Photo E.-D. Schulze)

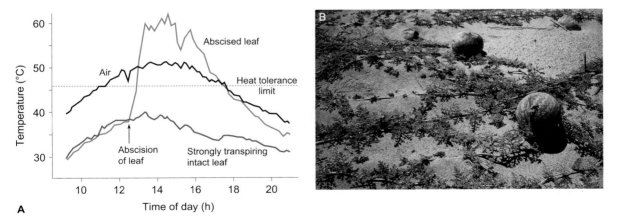

Fig. 2.1.14. A Changes over 24 h in leaf temperature of *Citrullus colocynthis* in North Africa (Lange 1959). In natural conditions a strongly transpiring leaf has a temperature about 12 K below that of air temperature. Cut the leaf off, and the temperature rises 10 K above air temperature due to the loss of the cooling effect of transpiration. The limit of heat tolerance for *Citrullus* is about 46 °C, so the cooling effect of transpiration prevents death by overheating. B Wild *Citrullus colocynthis*, Omaruru, Namibia. It can be clearly seen that the edges of the feathery leaves roll up at midday and also positions themselves facing the sun and so minimise the incident radiation absorbed, i.e. they have no shadow. (Photo E.-D. Schulze)

Fig. 2.1.15. Shading of the trunk by the umbrella-like crown of *Acacia reficiens*. The protection of the base of the trunk is a common phenomenon in subtropical savannahs. Light sensitive, shrubby dicotyledonous plants colonise the shade surrounding the trunk, whereas the shrub-free area is colonised by C4 grasses with vertical leaves. (Photo: E.-D. Schulze)

2.1.4.2
Adaptation to Low Temperatures

There are few mechanisms to protect plants against lower temperatures and radiative cooling and thus against cooling below ambient. Therefore, molecular adaptations are particularly important (see Chap. 1.3.5):

- **Rosette plants** in Alpine climates use the warming of the soil below the rosette and the more favourable conditions on slopes. Similarly, cushion plants and so-called thorny cushions provide their own internal climates, temperature and humidity, because they minimise the surface area, and thus outgoing radiation, due to their spherical form. Branches emerging from the surface experience less favourable conditions and thus stop growth [explanation in Chap. 2.2.4 with Eq. (2.2.25)].

This leads often to thorny, short shoots at the surface.

- **Leaf inclination:** The angle of the leaf (or the angle of the bud) determines the long-wave radiation balance, particularly during the night.
- **Bud scales** are a morphological adaptation for changing the radiation balance. They raise the surface from which energy is re-radiated, away from the bud meristem and thus protect it, because of their low heat and water vapour conductances, not only against cold, but also against drying out (see Chap. 1.5). In addition the bud is round and not a flat surface, thus minimizing the surface of main heat loss to the atmosphere.
- **Heat storage:** In tropical alpine regions, the length of night frosts is limited and the days are warm. Species of *Lobelia* have a large storage of free water and this provides sufficient heat capacity so that the growing point does not freeze (see Chap. 1.3.6.7).

2.1.4.3
Summary of Plant Reactions to Temperature

- Plants exploit many possible ways to avoid heat stress (leaf position, size, surface area, transpiration, insulation).
- Plants have limited ways of avoiding cold stress (position of leaf, insulation, heat storage and heat conductance).
- Structural modifications and regulation of stomata are usually sufficient to keep the temperature of the plant within the physiologically acceptable range and away from damaging temperatures by latent heat loss.

Box 2.1.4   Summary: Leaf temperature

The following factors are important in regulation of leaf temperature:

- **Leaf position** (direction of organs as energy-absorbing and energy-emitting surfaces) and leaf area index (shading);
- **Size of organs** (avoidance of laminar boundary layer and regulation of the sensible heat flux);
- **Insulation** (bud scales, bark);

- **Evaporation** (regulation of the latent heat flux);
- **Heat dissipation** and storage of heat have in particular climatic conditions an additional function (afro-alpine rosette plants, cacti);
- Warming by increased **respiration** is important only under particular conditions (flower spathes of Araceae), but may generally be neglected.

- There are very few documented examples of limitation of plant geographical distribution based only on temperature. The critical period is mostly germination.
- Although global vegetative models use, to a large extent, temperature as the factor determining plant distribution, other factors (salt stress, drought and fire, length of vegetative periods, imbalance between temperature in the soil and in the atmosphere, drought because of freezing) limit distribution to a much larger extent than just temperature.

References

Bishop JKB, Rossow WB (1991) Spatial and temporal variability of global surface solar irradiance. J Geophys Res 96:16839–16858

Ehleringer JR (1980) Leaf morphology and reflectance in relation to water and temperature stress. In: Turner NC, Kramer PJ (eds) Adaptations of plants to water and high temperature stress. Wiley, New York, pp 295–308

Gates DM (1965) Energy exchange in the biosphere. Harper and Row, New York, pp 151

IPCC – Intergovernmental Panel on Climate Change (1996) Climate change 1995: the science of climate change. Cambridge University Press, Cambridge New York, 572 pp

Jones HG (1994) Plants and microclimate; a quantitative approach to environmental plant physiology. Cambridge University Press, Cambridge, 428 pp

Kraus G (1911) Boden und Klima auf kleinstem Raum; Versuch einer exakten Behandlung des Standortes auf dem Wellenkalk. Gustav Fischer, Jena, 184 pp

Lange OL (1959) Untersuchungen über den Wärmehaushalt und Hitzeresistenz mauretanischer Wüsten- und Savannenpflanzen. Flora 147:595–651

Larcher W (2003) Ecophysiology of plants. 4th ed. Springer Berlin Heidelberg New York, 433pp

List RJ (1971) Smithsonian meteorological tables. Smithsonian Institution Press, Washington, DC, 527 pp

Lutgens FK, Tarbuck EJ (2000) The atmosphere: An introduction to meteorology. 8th ed. Prentice Hall. Upper Saddle River, NJ, 484 pp

Mitchell JFB (1989) The greenhouse effect and climate change. Rev Geophys 27:115–139

Monteith JL (1973) Principles of environmental physics. Edward Arnold, London, 441 pp

Norris DR, Rohl U (1999) Carbon cycling and chronology of climate warming during the Palaeocene/Eocene transition. Nature 401:775–778

Pearcy RW, Pfitsch WA (1994) The consequences of sunflecks for photosynthesis and growth of forest understory plants. Ecological Studies 100. Springer, Berlin Heidelberg New York, pp 343–360

Schulze E-D (1982) Plant life forms and their carbon, water and nutrient relations. Encycl Plant Physiol 128:616–676

Schulze E-D, Eller BM, Thomas DA, Willert DJ von, Brinckmann E (1980) Leaf temperatures and energy balance of *Welwitschia mirabilis* in its natural habitat. Oecologia 44:258–262

Shakel KA, Hall AE (1979) Reversible leaflet movements in relation to drought adaptation in cowpea, *Vigna unguiculata* (L.) Walp. Aust J Plant Physiol 6:265–276

Smith WK (1978) Temperatures in desert plants: another perspective on the ability of leaf size. Science 201:614–616

Stott PA, Tett SFB, Jones GS (2001) External control of 20th century temperature by natural and anthropogenic forcings. Science 290:2133–2137

Veizer J, Gooderis Y, Francois LM (2000) Evidence for decoupling of atmospheric CO_2 and global climate during the phanerocoic. Nature 408:689–701

Wallace JM, Hobbs PV (1977) Atmospheric science: An introductory survey. Academic Press, San Diego, 467 pp

Walter H (1960) Grundlagen der Pflanzenverbreitung. Teil I Standortlehre. Ulmer, Stuttgart, 566 pp

WBGU (1997) World in transition. Ways towards sustainable management of freshwater resources. Springer, Berlin Heidelberg New York, 392 pp

2.2

Water Relations of Plants

"Funnel" oases near El Qued, Algeria, northern Sahara: About 10 m of sand is removed in bags on donkeys. The limestone crust of an additional 10 m is broken and removed to reach a layer of loose material in which fresh water is found at a depth of about 4–6 m. On the sandy material typical oasis plants (date palms, pomegranates) and vegetables are grown; water is supplied by wells. The funnel is protected from refilling with sand by a series of concentric circles of dry leaves of date palms which are placed on the perimeter. These trap sand that is blown inwards from the desert. The outer ring is visible on the photograph. The oasis has a total diameter of approx. 1 km. Thus, the donkey moved about 7 million m^3 per garden. Despite the rings of date leaves, permanent removal of sand that is blown in by wind is still necessary (Photo E.-D. Schulze)

Recommended Literature

The classical textbook on water relations of plants is by Slatyer (1967). Lange et al. (1982) devoted one volume of the *Encyclopaedia of Plant Physiology* to "water". Noble (1991) treats the physical-chemical basis of water transport. Kramer and Boyer (1995) is a comprehensive treatment of the water relations of plants and soils.

2.2.1

Water as an Environmental Factor

2.2.1.1
Water Consumption and Plant Production: Comparison of Plant Types with Differing Water Economy

Life on earth developed in water and despite evolution over many millions of years, today as then, all living processes with their underlying biochemical reactions are only possible in the aqueous milieu (see also Chap. 1.5). Most land plants in their active state do not tolerate any drying out. This is illustrated by the **water content**: In the active state the protoplasm of most leaves and fruits contains 0.85–0.90 g H_2O g^{-1} FW (fresh weight). The water content of wood decreases to about 0.50 g H_2O g^{-1} FW because of the high percentage of dead water-conducting tissue in the xylem. Lowest values are reached in ripe seeds: 0.05–0.15 g H_2O g^{-1} FW.

Land plants must keep the water content of cells close to or fully saturated in relatively dry air, and still maintain exchange of CO_2 with the air in order to photosynthesise. Life outside water brings benefits as well as dangers for plants for the following reasons:

The **diffusion coefficient of CO_2** in air is about 0.14×10^{-4} m^2 s^{-1} and decreases in water to 0.16×10^{-8} m^2 s^{-1}. Thus, CO_2 diffuses in air 10,000 times faster than in water (Sestak et al. 1971). However, it must be considered that the CO_2 concentration in the Lower Devonian, the period of first settlement of plants on land, was significantly higher (ca. 4000 ppm) than today (ca. 370 ppm).

During the evolution of plants, no membrane was "invented" which is permeable to CO_2 but remains impermeable to H_2O vapour. Even in the future, there will not be a type of "GoreTex" for CO_2 because the molecular weight of CO_2 is larger than that of H_2O (44/18). Of course, it was the availability of CO_2 in the atmosphere that provided the incentive for plants to adapt

Table 2.2.1. Water use and resources acquisition (CO_2 in plants and O_2 in animals) at 20 °C and 50% relative humidity and taking into account the diffusability of gases which depends on their molecular weight. A human with a body temperature of 36.6 °C acts as an example for the animal kingdom

	Plants		Human	
	CO_2	H_2O	CO_2	H_2O
Concentration (ppm)				
– in the atmosphere	350	12000	210000	12000
– in the mesophyll or in breathed air	250	24000	160000	62000
Gradient	100	12000	50000	50000
Relationship between H_2O/CO_2 or H_2O/O_2	192		13	

from life in water (algae) to life on land. However, in order to use this advantage, mechanisms had to be developed to regulate the water relations of land plants.

Water relations are more important for land plants than for animals because of the **chemical constitution of air**: as **plants** photosynthesise, a CO_2 gradient of the magnitude of 100 ppm (Table 2.2.1) develops between the atmosphere and the mesophyll. At the same time, there is a gradient of water vapour of about 12,000 ppm between the water-saturated mesophyll cell walls and the ambient air. CO_2 diffuses 1.6 times slower than H_2O vapour; the rate is related to the square root of the molecular weights (CO_2 44, H_2O 18 and $\sqrt{44/18} = 1.6$). Thus a mole of CO_2 taken up loses the plant almost 200 mol H_2O ($12,000 \times 1.6/100 = 192$) and so the **water consumption** of plants is very high, relative to the photosynthetic gain.

For **mammals** (warm-blooded with a body temperature of 37 °C) it is quite different: With 210,000 ppm O_2 in the atmosphere and 160,000 ppm O_2 in the breath the O_2 gradient is 50,000 ppm and the air breathed out is water-saturated. Thus there is under the same conditions for humans as well as for plants a water vapour gradient to the atmosphere of 50,000 ppm. However, a warm-blooded animal loses only about 1 mol H_2O per mole of O_2 taken up. The water loss related to O_2 uptake for cold-blooded animals is even lower (about 0.2), i.e. water use related to O_2 gain is comparatively low.

As the loss of water from plants is so rapid, it is usually not cost-effective to have **water storage** (see also Chap. 1.5.1). A sunflower leaf loses in a day about ten times its own weight of water and a forest tree loses about 100–1000 l water, more than is available in the stem of a 25-m-high spruce. This means that the costs of providing organs for water from storage sufficient

to safeguard the supply in arid regions over days or months would be unprofitably large. There are some species of cacti, euphorbias and mesembryanthemums which live transiently on water stored in cell vacuoles (e.g. *Oppophyllum* or *Prenia*); but their biomass production is very low. Even the baobab tree (*Adansonia digitata*) is hardly able to use the water stored in the stem (Schulze et al. 1998b), as the wooden structure is so rigid that it is not able to shrink: The function of the thickened stems of baobab trees is probably to store carbohydrates and amino acids. For 25-m-high spruce trees the available water storage in the stem is only sufficient to maintain transpiration in the humid morning hours for about 2 h (Schulze et al. 1985).

During the evolution of plants, two strategies of water use developed in plants (Fig. 2.2.1):

1. **Desiccation tolerant, poikilohydric** (variable water content) organisms respond similarly to purely physical systems which absorb water and swell to an extent depending on the humidity in the air. When dry plants are exposed to moisture from rain, dew, or high humidity, they become fully active. They dry out with decreasing humidity and lack of water and become dormant during that time. In this cycle of adjustment, there is an optimum water status. If the organism (e.g. a lichen) is too wet, diffusion of CO_2 from the atmosphere is restricted and the rate of photosynthesis decreases with high water contents (see Fig. 2.4.13). Metabolism is restricted to the period when only the tissue and not the intercellular spaces is water-saturated. The most important representatives of this type of water use are algae, lichens and mosses (Fig. 2.2.1A). They are not differentiated into organs for absorption or structures that prevent loss of water. Amongst flowering plants,

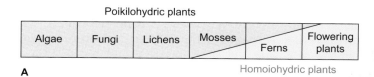

Poikilohydric plants					
Algae	Fungi	Lichens	Mosses	Ferns	Flowering plants

A   Homoiohydric plants

Fig. 2.2.1. A Schematic presentation of the occurrence of desiccation-tolerant (poikilohydric) and non-desiccation-tolerant (homoiohydric) plant types. B Lichen growth dominated by *Teloschistes* sp. with almost no higher plants in the coastal region of the fog desert of Namibia

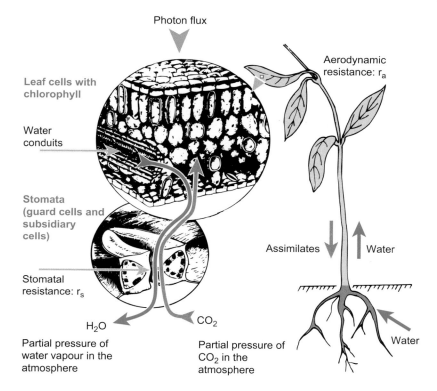

Photon flux

Leaf cells with chlorophyll

Water conduits

Aerodynamic resistance: r_a

Stomata (guard cells and subsidiary cells)

Stomatal resistance: r_s

Assimilates   Water

H_2O CO_2

Partial pressure of water vapour in the atmosphere

Partial pressure of CO_2 in the atmosphere

Water

Fig. 2.2.2. The flow of water and assimilates in cormophytes. Vascular plants are specialised by organs for CO_2, water and nutrient uptake. These are connected via the stem which conducts the water and assimilate flows. In the stem water and assimilates are transported by mass flow, in the leaf there is a phase transition from liquid water to water vapour. At the same time, CO_2 is assimilated into soluble organic substances. Diffusion between the inside of the leaf and the atmosphere is controlled by the stomata. (Evenari et al. 1982; WBGU 1998)

there are also a few species which may be capable of desiccation, e.g. *Myronthamnus flabelliformis* from the Namib Desert (Ziegler and Vieweg 1970; Bewley and Krockho 1982). These species, however, differ from the lower plants in that they may dry out, but are not activated by dew and high humidity as their cuticle prevents water uptake via the shoot. In these species activation is solely by water uptake through roots.

2. **Non-desiccation tolerant, homoiohydric plants** (high water content). These cormophytes are able to maintain living tissue in the state of a high water content independent of dry conditions in the surrounding atmosphere. There is a division of labour between organs (Fig. 2.2.2) which are specialised in uptake of water (roots), transport of water (xylem in the trunk or stem), and organs from which water evaporates simultaneously with absorption and assimilation of CO_2 (leaves, phyllodes, phylloclades). Homoiohydric plants have large vacuoles in their cells, functioning, amongst other things, as buffers for the cellular water supply and thus stabilise the cell and plant water balance (Chap. 1.5). The leaf surface is covered with a cuticle, practically impermeable to CO_2 and H_2O. The

leaf is connected to the free atmosphere only by stomata whose aperture can be regulated. By forming cuticles and stomata, the plant's ability to absorb water vapour from the air in above-ground organs is lost, as is the ability to desiccate and to be rehydrated. However, one developmental stage of intensive dehydration of cells remains also in these homoiohydric plants – the seed.

The expansion of plants into terrestrial habitats, even under extreme edaphic and climatic conditions, was only possible because of the division of labour between organs and by stabilising the cellular water relations through the formation of vacuoles. However, because of their cuticle, higher plants have lost the ability to utilise dew and water vapour from air at high humidity. Where such conditions exist, e.g. in the fog desert of the Namib (no precipitation except dew), higher plants are inferior to lower plants (Fig. 2.2.1 B).

In the following, we will deal predominantly with homoiohydric plants, as they form the largest part of the terrestrial flora and possess control mechanisms beyond stress physiological adaptations. Chapter 1.5 considered the biochemical basis for the plant's response to lack of water.

2.2.1.2
Availability of Water on Earth

The hydrological balance of different parts of the earth's surface provides the overall conditions for plant growth (Ward and Robinson 1990). Disregarding changes of water storage in the soil, the water balance consists of precipitation (P), evaporation (E) and river discharge (F), which is fed by surface runoff and seepage.

$$P - E - F = 0 \qquad (2.2.1)$$

The global distribution of precipitation is determined by the position of the sun and the global circulation of air masses; the result is high precipitation in the tropics, a minimum of precipitation around the tropics and increased precipitation in the temperate latitudes, also determined by distance from the oceans (**oceanity**) and the size of the continents (**continentality**). The gulf stream also provides favourable conditions for the eastern part of the Americas, as well as for Europe. In the higher latitudes of the Arctic and Antarctic precipitation decreases again.

Surface evaporation (E_G), where there is sufficient moisture, depends primarily on the available energy (I_G) at the ground surface (Philip 1957).

$$\lambda E_G = \varepsilon I_G / (\varepsilon + 1) \qquad (2.2.2)$$

where λ is the latent heat of evaporation of water (2.454 J kg^{-1} at 20 °C) and ε the change in amount of water vapour relative to the heat content in water vapour saturated air at air temperature (1.27 at 10 °C). With drying of the ground surface an additional boundary layer resistance must be considered (see Chap. 2.2.7). If the ground surface is covered by plants, free evaporation only occurs after precipitation, when the so-called **intercepted water** (the

---

Box 2.2.1	Summary: Water use and productivity of plants with different types of water economy

- The **chemical composition of the atmosphere** is the reason that animals living on land have more favourable water use during oxygen exchange in respiration than do plants during CO_2 exchange in photosynthesis.
- **Water storage** to support transpiration is uneconomic in the longer term. Therefore, water storage is part of the survival strategies of only a few specialists.

- **Desiccation tolerant and non-tolerant plants** represent different strategies to cope with dry atmospheres, with poikilohydric plants gaining competitive advantage in conditions where dew fall is frequent. (There are many lichens in the Namib Desert but few in the Sahara.)

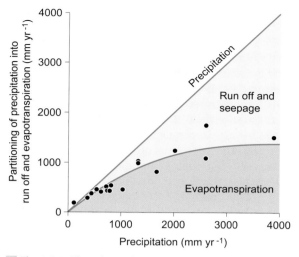

Fig. 2.2.3. The relationship between run-off and evaporation of precipitation (after Schulze and Heinmann 1998). Evaporation reaches a maximum that depends on the incident radiation. Thus the proportion of water that runs off or penetrates into the soil increases with increasing rainfall

amount of precipitation captured in the canopy and not reaching the ground) evaporates. In spring, before plant cover is achieved, arable fields lose water as if it was an open wet surface until the top soil layer dries off. The rate of evaporation decreases as the crop grows (Greenwood et al. 1992). **Transpiration** describes the amount of evaporation lost from the plant, and it is thus subject to physiological control. However, evaporation from the ground also occurs in a closed stand, dependent on the leaf area index (Schulze et al. 1995). The sum of free evaporation and transpiration is called **evapotranspiration**. The global distribution of evapotranspiration shows a maximum in the tropical regions and roughly follows the distribution of precipitation. However, evapotranspiration is additionally influenced by available solar radiation and

mean wind speed (see Chap. 2.2.7). Evapotranspiration decreases with decreasing available solar energy in the higher latitudes (north and south). In humid climates about 30% of the precipitation evaporates and 70% is lost in **surface runoff** and **seepage**.

From the water balance and the temperature, **climate zones** were defined by Köppen (1923), who, however, oriented his climate types also in relation to vegetation maps (e.g. those of Grisebach 1872).

Considering the dependence of evapotranspiration on precipitation, Fig. 2.2.3 shows that evapotranspiration does not increase without limits, but follows a saturation curve, with **discharge** making up a larger proportion of the total precipitation as precipitation increases. Even under extremely low precipitation vegetation does not consume the total amount of precipitation, as in arid climates precipitation occurs as heavy rainstorms, with massive runoff. This water is thus not available for plants at the site of rainfall, but may merely serve plant growth somewhere downhill or reach the ocean.

2.2.1.3
Transport of Water Between Soil and Atmosphere

In soils and plants, water is not freely available but bound to molecules or surfaces to a greater or lesser extent. The following distinctions are made:

- **Constituent water:** this water is formed into organic molecules as H^+ or OH^-.
- **Hydration water:** the layer of water molecules that is arranged as dipoles around ions is called hydration water. The strength of the binding increases with the charge and de-

---

Box 2.2.2   Summary: Water availability

- Precipitation, evaporation and run off determine **the water balance.**
- Water loss includes **evaporation**, which is determined by the chemico-physical conditions in the atmosphere and **transpiration** from plants, which is regulated by physiological processes. Evaporation and transpiration are combined in the term **evapotranspiration.**

- Evaporation from the earth's surface depends primarily on available radiation.
- Global temperature distribution and hydrological balance determine **climatic regions** and thus the distribution of vegetation on earth.

creases with radius of the hydrated ion. Thus Na^+ has a larger hydration shell than K^+ (Lüttge 1973). There are hydration shells for all polar groups in organic molecules. Five to 10% of the total water in a leaf is thereby not freely available.

- **Capillary water:** in cell walls, as well as in the fine pores, water is subject to capillary forces. The rise of the water column in a capillary (h, measured in m) is, as a first approximation, inversely proportional to the radius (r) of the capillary, because the water mass and the gravitational force effecting it ($\pi h \rho g$) must be balanced against the cohesive force produced by the surface tension ($2\pi r \sigma_w$). Neglecting the contact angle a (cos $a = 1$), the following applies (Nobel 1991, p. 55)

$$\pi h \rho g = 2\pi r \sigma_w \qquad (2.2.3)$$

where h is the height in m to which the water column rises, ρ is the density of water (998 kg m^{-3} at 20 °C), g the acceleration of the earth (9.8 m s^{-2}), r is the radius of the capillary (m), and σ_w the surface tension of water (0.0728 N m^{-1} at 20 °C).

Thus the pressure in a capillary, the so-called **capillary force** is:

$$P = h \rho g = 2\sigma/r \, (Nm^{-2}) \qquad (2.2.4)$$

and the height of the meniscus is calculated as:

$$h = 2\sigma_w/(r\rho g); \, h = \left(1.5 \times 10^{-5}/r\right) \qquad (2.2.5)$$

In a clean (lipid-free) glass capillary 3 μm in diameter (1.5 μm radius), water rises to 10 m. In a xylem vessel of 30 μm, typical for tracheids of conifers, water rises by capillarity by only 1 m and in the 300 μm trachea of deciduous trees the water rises only 0.1 m via capillarity. This means that the capillary force is not sufficient to lift water into the canopy of trees and thus does not provide the lifting power required for flow of water (see Chap. 2.2.2).

- **Storage water:** this water is osmotically bound, e.g. in the vacuole (see also Chap. 1.5). The osmotic value (Π, measured as MPa) depends on the number of particles per mole (n), the concentration (c_n), the gas constant R (8.3144 Pa m^3 mol^{-1} K^{-1}) and the temperature (T in K):

$$\Pi = nc_n TR = 2.27 \, c_n \qquad (2.2.6)$$

Π of a 1 molar solution of an undissociated solute at 0 °C is 2.27 MPa and at 20 °C 2.43 MPa.

The osmotic value is generally expressed as pressure, in MPa, based on an experiment which also demonstrates the phenomenon of osmosis: A closed chamber is divided into two compartments by a semipermeable membrane which allows passage of water molecules but it is impermeable for ions. One compartment of the chamber is filled with distilled water, the other with a salt solution. To balance the difference in concentration of both solutions only free water is able to flow into the chamber with the salt solution, so building up a hydrostatic pressure there (i.e. the level of water rises in comparison to the free water in the neighbouring part of the chamber). The height of the water column corresponds to the osmotic value, which is therefore called the **osmotic pressure.**

The flow of liquid between soil, plant and atmosphere is based on several forces. In order to describe the flow between the very heterogeneous compartments of the environment it is necessary to quantify the availability of water uniformly. This is possible by the definition of a common force for water transport, the **water potential**, Ψ (see also Chap. 1.5):

$$\Psi = (\mu_w - \mu_o)/V_w = \left(V_w/V_w^o\right)\Pi \qquad (2.2.7)$$

where μ_w is the chemical potential in the system (J mol^{-1}) and μ_o is the chemical potential of a reference system, i.e. of pure liquid water at a given temperature and at normal pressure (atmospheric pressure). By dividing the difference in the chemical potentials ($\mu_w - \mu_o$) by the molar volume of liquid water (V_w) the water potential is defined in units of pressure. Thus, the water potential describes the driving force for water movement in a practical way because pressures can be easily measured. V_w is slightly dependent on temperature and pressure, but this is normally neglected. V_w^o expresses the molar volume of pure water.

In the gaseous phase the water potential is proportional to the relative humidity:

$$\Psi = RT \ln\left(e/e_o\right)/V_w \qquad (2.2.8)$$

where e/e_o expresses the vapour pressure of bound water (e.g. in solution or solid material) relative to that of free water, and thus corresponds to the relative humidity. The right side of Eq. (2.2.5) is also called **water activity**, describing, e.g., the degree of swelling of colloids and thus characterises the conditions for life of microorganisms or poikilohydric plants. As the chemical potential of bound water, μ_w, is lower than that of free water, μ_o (energy has to be added to change, e.g. bound water in a salt solution into the state of free water), the water potential has a negative sign. Water movement occurs from sites with high potential to sites with low potential.

Water potential describes

- the state of water of plants or particles, and
- the driving force for the movement of water.

Using water potential it is possible to describe water in single-phase systems (e.g. in a plant) as well as in phase transitions (e.g. evaporation of a leaf; see Chap. 1.5, Fig. 1.5.1). In a cell with good water supply, the osmotic pressure is compensated by the counter pressure of the cell wall, the turgor pressure, P_c, the water potential is zero. With decreasing water content the turgor pressure sinks, the osmotic pressure rises because of the increasing concentration of the residual solution in the cell and the difference, $\Pi-P$, corresponds to the water potential, Ψ, which becomes increasingly more negative. Thus, in a tissue, water flows, e.g., from the cell wall into this cell. If desiccation of the cell continues and water potential becomes equal to the osmotic pressure ($\Pi = -\Psi$), then plasmolysis starts.

The water balance of the cell is given by the equation:

$$\Psi = P_c - \Pi - \tau + \rho gh \qquad (2.2.9)$$

where τ represents the binding force in the membrane-free matrix of the cell wall (the so-called **matrix potential**, see Chap. 2.2.2.1 and Chap. 1.5) and ρgh the water pressure, with ρ the density of water, g the gravitational force ($9.807\ \mathrm{m\ s^{-2}}$ at $45°$ latitude) and h the height of the meniscus [m; see Eq. (2.2.4)].

Equation (2.2.9) shows that water potential is dependent on osmotic pressure, the chemical binding of water, and surface properties and on gravity, particularly important for tall trees. The matrix potential is an analogous value to Π, but in this case the value is dependent on surface forces and not on the number of particles in the solution. In the literature, the osmotic pressure is often also called osmotic potential and the

numerical value is given as a negative number. It is basically only a different formulation of the same process. We use the term osmotic pressure because it creates a positive pressure.

If the water potential between plant, soil and air is balanced, there is no evaporation. In nature this state occurs particularly in the early morning, before dawn. Therefore, the **early morning water potential**, $\Psi_{predawn}$, in a plant is used to characterise the water conditions of the soil in the zone from which the roots gain their water. With transpiration, a gradient in water potential develops between soil and atmosphere, which may be up to 100 MPa.

In the continuum of water transport between soil and atmosphere, water follows the potential gradient (from high to lower potential, i.e. to increasingly more negative values), whereby the flow rate is limited by resistances which are dependent on the characteristics of the soil and the types of tissue. In addition there is a phase transition in the leaf from the liquid to the vapour phase, with the rate of diffusion in the vapour phase determined by the water vapour pressure of the atmosphere (e/e_o). In the **soil-plant-atmosphere continuum** (SPAC), the highest water potential gradient is between the surfaces of the cell walls in the mesophyll of leaves where water evaporates and the external air, because the hydraulic resistance is highest there.

2.2.2

Water Transport in the Plant

2.2.2.1
Water Uptake

Precipitation seeps through the soil profile into the groundwater. Only the water stored in pores is retained in the soil. Amount and rate of water movement in the soil are dependent on the type of soil, the size of pores and the water saturation. The **field capacity** describes the content of water which is retained against gravity, i.e. it is the amount of water that does not drip out of a flower pot after watering. However, this water is only partially available for plants, because a proportion is firmly bound as hydration water or capillary water. The amount of bound water depends on the **matrix potential** (Ψ_m) of the soil [see Eq. (2.2.9)] and, neglecting the influence of the angle at the wall of the capillary, is deter-

Box 2.2.3   Summary: Water as an environmental factor

- Water in soils and tissues is not freely available, but bound by chemical, capillary and osmotic forces (**matrix and osmotic components of water potential**).
- **Water potential** describes the state of water in homogeneous and heterogeneous systems. It is a measure of the energy which must be expended to convert bound water to the state of free water. Water flows from a compartment with higher to one of lower water potential.

- Cells regulate their water status by altering the **osmotic potential** (see Chap. 1.5.2.6) and thus maintain positive **turgor**.
- In plants, the greatest change in potential occurs between the mesophyll and atmosphere (**stomatal conductance**, see Chap. 2.2.3) and the most important regulation of plant water status occurs there, regulating water loss.

---

mined by the surface tension of water ($\sigma = 7.28 \times 10^{-3}$ N m^{-1}) and the radius of the soil capillaries [m; see Eq. (2.2.4)],

$$\Psi_m = -2\sigma/r; \quad \tau = 2\sigma/r \qquad (2.2.10)$$

with the unit N/m^2 = Pa.

In pores of 5 nm, which occur in the cell walls of higher plants, the matrix potential reaches 3.0 MPa and decreases in vessels with a radius of 500 μm (xylem vessels of ring-porous woods) to only 30 Pa (Table 2.2.2).

Figure 2.2.4 A (Slatyer 1967; Larcher 1994) shows the relation between the water potential and the water content of sandy and loamy soils. Certain threshold values were defined for the characterisation of soils:

Table 2.2.2. The relationship between water potential and relative humidity calculated using Eq. (2.2.5). The relationship is measurable, if, in a closed vessel, air is allowed to equilibrate with solutions of different osmotic potentials and the relative humidity is measured (in this case – $\Psi = \pi$). The values show what relative humidity must be reached in order to support a particular living process. For example, moulds can already establish themselves if the relative humidity in their environment is >70%

Relative humidity (%)	Water potential (MPa)	Condition in soil or plant
100	0	Field capacity of soil
99	−1.35	Approaching permanent wilting point in soil
98	−2.72	Strong water stress in a plant
90	−14.1	Lowest measured Ψ in a desert plants
80	−30.1	Activation of photosynthesis in lichens
70	−48.1	Activation of respiration in moulds
50	−93.3	Ambient air in an office

- **Hygroscopically bound water** is defined as that water that is bound by forces > 5 MPa;
- The **permanent wilting point** is defined as the water status when water is bound by 1.5 MPa. This is the water potential at which a sunflower plant is no longer able to replace the water lost through transpiration from the water in the soil and thus wilts. Depending on the adaptation of plants to dry habitats the permanent wilting point may be at values between 0.7 and 3 MPa;
- **Field capacity** is defined as water bound at 0.05 MPa. At this point water can no longer be retained by soil particles against gravity and therefore drains out of the soil.

The **amount of water in the soil that is available for plants** corresponds to the water content between field capacity and wilting point. Loam and clay soils differ not only in the amount of available water (for loam with 0.2 g g^{-1} almost ten times higher than in sandy soils), but also in the amount of water which is not available for plants in dry soils; this has consequences for the availability of water to plants with decreasing precipitation (Fig. 2.2.4 B). In areas with high precipitation, sandy soils are drier habitats than clay soils, because sandy soils retain less water. With less precipitation the limit at which water can no longer be taken up by the plant, because of the capillary and matrix forces are reached sooner in clay soils than in sandy soils. In arid regions sandy soils are therefore "moister" for plants than clay soils. This is modified in nature by the frequency of precipitation.

The **transport of water** in the soil to the root occurs along the potential gradient, whereby the rate of flux in the soil is determined by the hy-

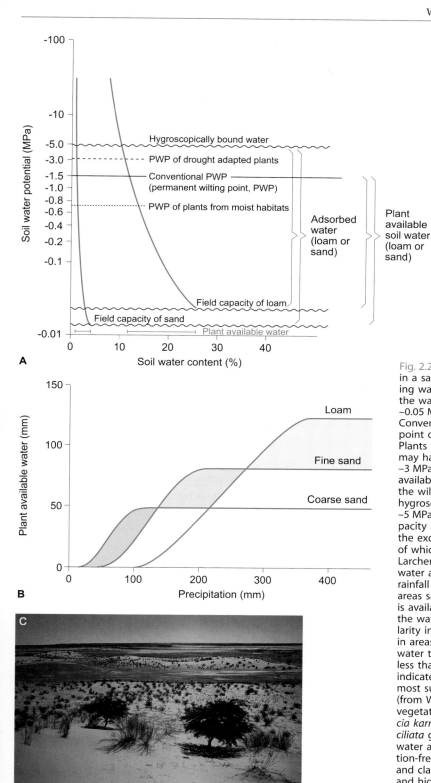

A The change in water potential in a sandy and a loamy soil with increasing water content. Depending on texture the water potential at field capacity is −0.05 MPa (sand) and −0.015 MPa (loam). Convention sets the permanent wilting point of agricultural systems at −1.5 MPa. Plants that live in wet or dry conditions may have wilting points at −0.7 MPa and −3 MPa, respectively, but the additional available water resulting from a shift in the wilting point is small. The limit of hygroscopically bound water is set as −5 MPa. The difference between field capacity and hygroscopically bound water is the exchangeable water, only a proportion of which is available for the plant (from Larcher 1976). **B** Change in the amount of water available to a plant with increasing rainfall on a loam and sandy soil. In arid areas sandy soils contain more water that is available to a plant than a loam soil as the water is not so strongly held by capillarity in sand as it is on loam. In contrast, in areas of high rainfall, the amount of water that can be stored by a sandy soil is less than a loamy soil. The shaded areas indicate the rainfall conditions that are most suitable for plants for that soil type (from Walter 1960). **C** The distribution of vegetation in the Namib Desert with *Acacia karroo*, *Aristida sabulicola* and *Acacia ciliata* growing on the sand dunes (high water availability and low salt) and vegetation-free areas on the plain, where loam and clay soils have low water availability and higher salt concentration. Asab, Namibia. (Photo E.-D. Schulze)

draulic conductivity, which depends on the water content of the soil. In dry soils the limiting factor is the conductivity of the unsaturated soil where water moves in the vapour phase. In contrast, in saturated moist soils, the limiting step for water uptake is the conductivity of roots (the latter is usually the case in temperate climate zones). Depending on texture and saturation of the soil, roots must grow towards the water or "wait" until the water flows from the soil to the root. This determines the surface area of roots required to provide leaves with water.

Water transport in soils is differentiated into saturated (water content above field capacity) and unsaturated states (water content below field capacity). According to Darcy's law (1856), based on studies of water pressure in the wells of Dijon, the rate of flux (v) in saturated soils is proportional to the hydraulic gradient (dh/dx: change in height per change in the length of the flow path, which corresponds to the potential gradient) and the **saturated conductivity** of the soil (k_s),

$$v = -k_s(dh/dx) \qquad (2.2.11)$$

where k_s depends on the particle size. In stony soils k_s is > 0.001 m s^{-1}, in sandy soils $> 10^{-5}$ m s^{-1}, in silty soils $< 10^{-7}$ m s^{-1} and in clayey soils $< 10^{-9}$ m s^{-1}.

In unsaturated soils, the rate of flux is much smaller than in saturated soils; it depends on the **unsaturated conductivity**, k_Θ, which decreases with soil water content, Θ, and is determined by the potential gradient, $\Delta\Psi$, over the distance, x.

$$v = k_\Theta(\Delta\Psi/\Delta x) \qquad (2.2.12)$$

This equation is analogous to Eq. (2.2.11), but for unsaturated soils the water potential is the driving force. The values for k_Θ in silty soils is between 10^{-13} (saturated soils) and 10^{-17} cm s^{-1} Pa^{-1} in the range of the wilting point. Soils are not homogeneous, but structured in horizons and differentiated within the horizons in more or less dense aggregates. Thus the hydraulic conductivity of soil crumbs in close proximity may decrease over a very short distance with the soil water content (Horn 1994). Also, within a soil profile, water is available to very different degrees.

It is not surprising that plants develop many different forms of **root systems**, considering the heterogeneity of water status and flow in soils and the modifications which depend on soil texture. Grasses develop a particularly dense adventitious root system near the soil surface. Dicotyledons, in contrast, form a less extensive root system, but penetrate the ground much deeper with their very large primary root. In horizons where nutrients and water are easier available they are also able to form secondary roots.

The soil layer from which a plant gains its transpiration water may be determined with stable isotopes of hydrogen, D = **deuterium**, and oxygen, ^{18}O. The isotope relation of H/D (the δD value) and of ^{16}O/^{18}O (the δ^{18}O value) increases with the temperature of precipitation (**hydraulic water line**; Dawson 1993), i.e. winter rains have a different isotopic signal than summer rains. In addition, the heavier isotope accumulates at the soil surface, as water molecules with the heavier isotope evaporate slower than molecules with the lighter isotope. Measuring the isotope rates in xylem water and in soil water provides information on the horizons from which certain species get their water.

It is, of course, easier to establish the origin of transpiration water with reference to the soil depth in regions with seasonal rainfall at different temperatures. An example is given in Fig. 2.2.5 A for the Colorado Desert in the southwestern USA (Ehlinger 1994). Summer and winter rains show very different δD values and groundwater is even more depleted of deuterium than winter rain. Various plant species use water sources from different depths. In this subtropical "warm" desert (Fig. 2.2.5 B), annuals and succulents use summer rains, which reach the Sonora Desert as sporadic subtropical fronts (Note: in Mediterranean winter rain regions annuals use mainly winter rains). In contrast to the summer annuals, deeper rooting perennials (usually evergreen herbaceous plants and shrubs) utilise the water of winter rains or groundwater. In between these two contrasting types there is a group of moderately deep-rooting perennial plants which use the water as it percolates through the soil profile. At times between these periods of oversupply of water there are longer dry periods where these plants lose their leaves, i.e. they are deciduous. In the ecological literature, a distinction is made between **arido-active** plants which keep their photosynthetically active leaves during the dry period, and **arido-passive** plants which either shed their leaves or minimise metabolism. Figure 2.2.5 shows that there are many

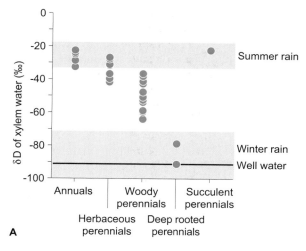

Fig. 2.2.5. A Deuterium isotopic ratio in water from xylem of different types of plants growing in the Sonora Desert, compared with the deuterium ratio in summer and winter rainfall, as well as in ground water (after Ehleringer et al. 1994a,b). The δD value is calculated from D/H of the sample in comparison with a standard $[(D/H)_{sample}/(D/H)_{standard}-1]\times 1000$, where water from deep oceans is used as the standard (SMOW = standard mean ocean water). In the case of the Sonoran Desert, annuals use the summer rain water almost exclusively, which has a high δD value dependent on the temperature. In contrast, deep-rooted perennials almost exclusively use water from winter rainfall with a low δD value due to the lower temperatures. The δD value of water from the xylem of plants shows from which soil level they obtain the water. B Vegetation in the Sonoran Desert close to Oatmans, South Nevada, with summer annual plants *Pectis paposa* (Asteridae, C4 plants), perennial woody plants, *Ambrosia dumosa* (Asteridae, C3 plant) and perennial deep-rooted *Larrea tridentata* (Zygophyllaceae). (Photo E.-D. Schulze)

transitions which make such a classification (as appears so often in the older ecological literature) unsuitable. The differentiation of species according to their source of water not only applies to the Colorado Desert, but also to other dry regions, e.g. the temperate semi-deserts in Argentina (Schulze et al. 1996c).

Water uptake from the soil into a plant occurs at a zone behind the apex of root tips where root hairs develop and the root cortex is not yet suberised (Steudle 1994). In addition, water is taken up at meristematic regions of the side roots. Above the meristematic region, roots are differentiated (Fig. 2.2.6) into an epidermis, in many species a suberised layer called the exodermis, followed by the root cortex, the heavily suberised endodermis (Casparian bands) and the central

cylinder (stele) with the xylem vessels and the phloem. Within the root cylinder, water follows (as a first approximation) the water potential gradients from the soil to the xylem, but it may follow several pathways (Fig. 2.2.6 B). In the region of the root cortex: (a) water may flow in the cell wall (**apoplast**), (b) move from cell to cell via the plasmodesmata (**symplast**), or (c) across the cells (**transcellular path**). At the endodermis (and probably also at the exodermis) water must be moved through the cell. Unsuberised transmission cells exist in this region. **Water transport in the root** may be explained by a model with a series of parallel resistances connected at regular intervals by serial resistors. The hydraulic conductivity in each cell layer is the conductivity of a non-cylindrical tissue (Lp_z).

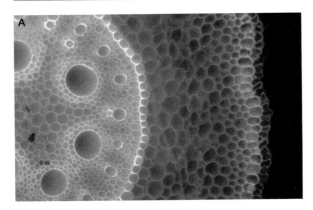

A

Fig. 2.2.6. A Cross section through a maize root in which the lignin and lipids in the exodermis and endodermis are stained with berberin sulfate. B Schematic cross section of a root showing routes of water and nutrient transport. The suberised Casparian bands appear as black dots in this cross section, showing their position in the cell wall. Blue arrows mark clearly different paths that water can take. (After Steudle 1994)

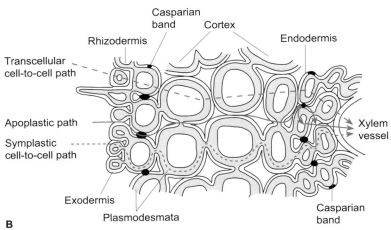

B

$$\text{Lp}_z = \gamma_c \frac{\text{Lp}_c}{2} + \gamma_{cw} \frac{\text{Lp}_{cw}}{\Delta x} \frac{\Delta x}{d} \qquad (2.2.13)$$

where Lp_z is the conductivity of a cell in m s^{-1} MPa^{-1}. Lp_c describes the conductivity of cell membranes, where the factor 2 considers the fact that two membranes per cell must be crossed. Lp_{cw} is the conductivity of the cell wall, γ_c and γ_{cw} the amount of cytosol and cell wall at the cross section in the direction of the flux ($\gamma_{cw} + \gamma_c = 1$), Δx the width of a cell layer and d is the thickness of the tissue. This shows that the relevant fluxes may be differently distributed according to the structure of the root cortex. The distribution of pore size in the cell wall and the size of the hydrated ions determine the conductivity. Pores in the intermicella space are about 1 nm; the space between the cellulose fibrils is about 10 nm. In comparison, a water molecule is about 0.3 nm, Na ions with their hydrated shell reach 0.5–0.7 nm, K ions 0.4–0.5 nm and a glucose molecule is about 0.75 nm (Lüttge 1973). Even though the cross section available for apoplastic transport is much smaller than

that for cellular components, measurements of the components have shown that the apoplastic transport dominates when the flux is hydraulic (transpiration suction) and does not follow the osmotic gradient. If the apoplastic transport path is effectively interrupted (strong suberisation of roots), the cellular component dominates (Michael et al. 1997). The flow of water through the cell membrane in the cellular transport path is actively regulated by **aquaporins** (proteins, which transport water through the otherwise hydrophobic cell membrane: water channels; Tyerman et al. 1999; see Chap. 1.5.2). In strongly differentiated regions of roots and less differentiated regions, water may be taken up in parallel; water flow is also possible in the suberised regions of the root, namely in places where side roots are formed, in the edge between the main and the side root meristematic tissues are retained. The root is thus not a uniform surface vis-à-vis the soil, but a very differentiated region of uptake, called by Steudle and Peterson (1998) a **compound membrane**. Water uptake supports the water status of the plant (Ψ_{shoot}) which, however, depends not only on water uptake – the input –, but also on transpiration – the output –; both are separately regulated but tuned to each other by hormonal and pressure signals.

It has been known for more than 60 years that the **hydraulic resistance** of the root, and thus the water uptake, is variable. In contrast to the shoot and its regulation of water loss via stomata (see Chap. 2.2.3), the regulation of the water uptake is also via the hydraulic architecture of the roots and, because of technical limitations, this is much less studied than the hydraulic architecture of the shoot. Also, processes in the root are not obvious. Regulation appears as a purely physical adaptation to water uptake as well as by metabolic regulation.

The differentiation in root anatomy is, from an ecological point of view, an adaptation of plants to the conditions of water flow between soil and root and the associated flow of nutrients. The process of **water uptake** normally does not limit the supply of water to the plant in moist soils. The water potential in the shoot is, of course, also determined by the transpiration and may fall below a critical value for metabolic processes in the leaf even at wet sites. In moist soils the water potential in the xylem sinks with the amount of water that is transported through the system (Fig. 2.2.7, curve A). In dry soils, corresponding to the low flux and the very low conductivity in the unsaturated soil, a dry zone may develop around the surface of the root, i.e. further supply from the soil may, in this case, be the limiting factor for the flow of water (Michael et al. 1999). This state would be visible in the leaf by a strong reduction of water potential in the xylem without an associated increase in the flux through the vessels (Fig. 2.2.7, curve B). A corresponding turgor loss is expected to occur in the root tip under such conditions, leading to the production of the stress hormone ABA (see Chap. 1.5.2.2). Conversely, there are situations where changes in water transport occur without changes in water potential (Fig. 1.1.7, curve C). This observation is described by the transport model in Fig. 2.2.6. Here, the water potential gradient between soil and xylem reaches a magnitude which allows a flux via additional surfaces, i.e. other roots or root regions which were not participating in water uptake because the potential gradient was too low.

The sites for water uptake also harbour a danger, in as far as the plant is not able to totally seal itself against the soil. The unprotected

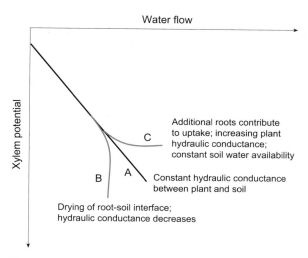

Fig. 2.2.7. Schematic diagram of the change in xylem water potential with the increased water flow, when: (A) the hydraulic conductance is constant, (B) the hydraulic conductance falls when the interface between root and soil dries out, and (C) additional roots contribute to the transport as the soil dries

regions include particularly the meristematic regions of root tips and the axial meristems of side roots. The transmission cells in the endodermis and exodermis are also able to transport water in both directions, i.e. roots are not only able to take up water from the soil, but may lose water to the soil. This is in fact an important ecological process and occurs particularly at times of low transpiration. It is termed **hydraulic lift**, where water is taken up from wet soil in deep horizons, lifted by a water potential gradient to the upper soil horizon, where it is released into the dry soil. Water release of plants to the soil was first observed in dry climates (Richards and Caldwell 1987), but it is also important in temperate climates. For *Acer saccharum* it was observed (Dawson 1993) that the isotopic composition of soil water in the region of the canopy does not correspond to the rain water, but to the much deeper ground water (Fig. 2.2.8). The further the distance from the root regions of the tree, the more similar is the isotopic composition of the xylem water of the herbaceous vegetation to that of the precipitated water. Obviously, during the night, larger amounts of water are transported by tree roots from the moist soil in the proximity of the water table into the dryer upper layer of soil. The isotopic label of the water of the top soil changes correspondingly. The water is utilised during the day not only by the tree, but also by the vegetation

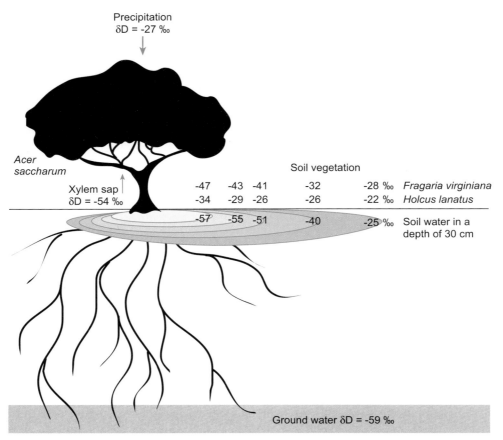

Precipitation
δD = -27 ‰

Acer saccharum

Xylem sap
δD = -54 ‰

Soil vegetation

-47	-43	-41	-32	-28 ‰	*Fragaria virginiana*
-34	-29	-26	-26	-22 ‰	*Holcus lanatus*
-57	-55	-51	-40	-25 ‰	Soil water in a depth of 30 cm

Ground water δD = -59 ‰

Fig. 2.2.8. Isotopic relationship of deuterium (δD) at different soil depths and in plants as a marker of the source of the water. The δD value is calculated from the D/H ratios of the sample in comparison with a standard [(D/H)$_{sample}$/(D/H)$_{standard}$–1)×1000], where water from deep oceans is used as the standard (SMOW = standard mean ocean water). The δD value in vegetation is between the high value in rainfall and a significantly lower δD value in the ground water. The lower δD value in the xylem water shows that *Acer saccharum* derives its water from the ground water. The soil water (0–30 cm deep) shows a gradient in δD value from the low value near the trunk to a high δD value away from the trunk. The water with the lowest δD value can only have come from ground water that is transported by the roots and is released into the soil, during the so-called hydraulic lift. The vegetation reacts differently to the water availability depending on how deep roots penetrate. Where *Fragaria virginiana* is able to use the "lifted" water, roots of *Holcus lanatus* do not go that deep. (After Dawson 1993)

covering the ground in the shade of this tree (water parasitism). In this example, one-third to two-thirds of the water in the xylem of this ground flora stems from the hydraulic lift. This example may explain the often luxurious vegetation of herbaceous species in the shadow of trees in semi-arid regions.

The reverse process, **inverse hydraulic lift** (Schulze et al. 1998a; Burgess et al. 2001), is ecologically just as important as the hydraulic lift. In arid regions the lower soil layers are very rarely moistened as precipitation is only sufficient to wet the upper soil layers to field capacity. The "wave of water" produced in the soil by rain fall only penetrates a few meters, e.g. in sandy soil the water is retained in the upper ho-

rizons. Lower soil layers remain permanently dry unless there is groundwater. Nevertheless, roots are able to penetrate such dry soil to considerable depths (Fig. 2.2.9; Canadell et al. 1996). Plants in deserts and savannahs attain maximum **root depths** of more than 50 m. The absolute record of observed root depth is 68 m in the Kalahari, where the groundwater is more than 100 m deep covered by dry sand to which roots are able to penetrate. Roots up to 100 m deep have not yet been found because wells have only been plated by a wall to 70 m. Penetration of roots into such deep, dry soil layers is only possible by transport of water from the moist top soil, i.e. the root must maintain the rhizosphere in the vicinity of the root moisture in order to sur-

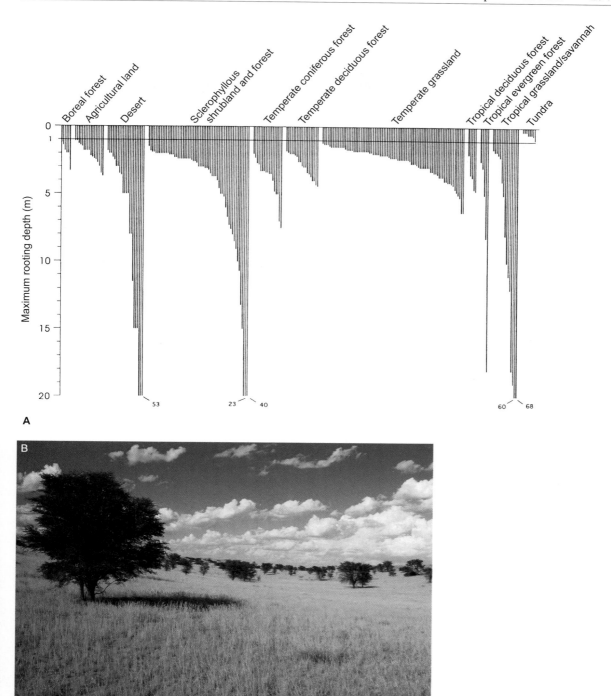

Fig. 2.2.9. A Maximum observed root depth of different types of vegetation. Each line represents a single measurement of a particular plant species. The numbers show the maximum depths that are beyond the y scale (from Canadell et al. 1996). The deepest known root depth was measured in the Kalahari Desert from *Acacia erioloba* when bore holes were sunk. **B** *Acacia erioloba* savannah with perennial C4 grasses *Aristida* and *Stipagrostis* (see Schulz et al. 1996a). Kalahari Desert north of Uppington, South Africa. (Photo E.-D. Schulze)

vive and grow in such an environment. Without additional transport of water, the root tip, which is not protected by a cuticle, would desiccate in the dry soil. Inverse water transport was demonstrated with water labelled with deuterium, which was transported by plants from the watered horizon near the surface into the lower dry layers of soil (Schulze et al. 1998a). Hydraulic conductivity is very important for the effectiveness of such processes, and this depends on the anatomy (see above) as well as on the nature and magnitude of the participating forces. Both processes contribute to a water redistribution in soils.

2.2.2.2
Water Transport in the Xylem

Water transport in the xylem follows the water potential gradient between root and leaf; the conductivity of the xylem is relatively high. The question of the physical conditions in a capillary with negative pressure of more than 10 MPa has been a topic of research for many years. Böhm (1893) was probably the first to postulate that the cohesion between water molecules is sufficient to achieve a continuous water column in the xylem vessels under tension (cohesion theory). With the measurement of negative pressures of more than 1 MPa in xylem vessels (Wei et al. 1999) and the observation that the tension changes with the flux through the xylem vessels, the cohesion theory has also been proven experimentally.

The **rate of flux** (flux density) in a xylem vessel, J_x, is described by the Hagen-Poiseuille law for laminar flows, and depends on the radius, r, of the xylem vessel, the viscosity of the liquid ($\eta = 10^{-3}$ Pa s for water) and the hydrostatic gradient, dP/dx:

$$J_x = (r^2/8\eta)(dP/dx)(m\ s^{-1}) \qquad (2.2.14)$$

The volume flow is in the direction of the decreasing hydrostatic gradient. The flow must be sufficiently slow so that the conditions of laminar flow (in contrast to turbulent flow) are maintained, to avoid rupture of the water columns. This applies at the flow rates occurring in the xylem, as the pore radii (pits) in cell walls are significantly smaller than those in typical xylem vessels (cell wall: d = 5 nm; xylem vessel: r = 10–500 µm). Thus the potential gradient required to transport a certain volume flow (e.g. 1 mm s^{-1}) across the cell wall is very high, about 3×10^5 MPa m^{-1}, according to Eq. (2.2.14) (Nobel 1991). This shows that a particularly large decrease in pressure is to be expected at the evaporation surfaces in the mesophyll and that the enormous forces required to move the water through the cell wall lead to a relatively slow movement of water in the xylem (see Table 2.2.3).

In plants, the volume flux, I_x, in the xylem under a pressure gradient is determined by the area of the cross section per vessel, and the number of xylem vessels, n, per organ:

$$I_x = \frac{\pi r^4}{8\eta}\frac{\Delta P}{\Delta x}n = Lp_x\Delta P \qquad (2.2.15)$$

where I_x is measured in $(m^4\ Pa)/(s\ Pa\ m) = (m^3\ s^{-1})$ and Lp_x corresponds to the hydraulic conductivity in the xylem ($m^4\ s^{-1}\ Pa^{-1}$). The axial hydraulic conductivity is related to a 1 m length of xylem and thus has different dimensions to Lp of the membrane.

According to Eq. (2.2.15), a plant has many possible ways to change the flux in the xylem and thus the water potential gradient (Gartner 1995):

- **Radius of vessels:** The radius varies between 500 µm in lianas, ca. 100 µm in ring-porous woody plants (e.g. oak), and 10–40 µm in the tracheids of conifers; a larger radius allows a

Table 2.2.3. Specific conductance, maximum speed of sap flow through the xylem, vessel radius and length, and maximum capillarity of vessels from different types of plants. (Zimmermann 1983; Carlquist 1991; Nobel 1991)

Plant type	Specific conductance for water (m s^{-1} MPa^{-1})	Maximum rate (m h^{-1})	Vessel diameter (µm)	Vessel length (m)	Capillarity (kPa)
Conifers	5–10×10^4	1–2	10–40	0.002–0.005	29–7
Diffuse porous angiosperms	5–50×10^4	1–6	5–150	1–2	58–1.0
Ring porous angiosperms	50–300×10^4	4–44	10–600	10	29–0.5
Herbaceous plants	30–60×10^4	10–60	10–500	1–2	29–0.6
Lianas	300–500×10^4	150	600	ca. 10	0.5

considerably higher volume flux. However, there is the basic danger that the cohesive force, which determines the continuity of the water column, is exceeded. However, this is not sufficient for **cavitation**. Apparently, cavitation is caused by "air seeding", which is the entry of small air bubbles via the pitted cells in the wall (Tyree 1997; Steudle 2000, 2001). During the breakage of the water column, the flux in the vessel is interrupted, i.e. it no longer participates in the water transport. In wood, pits close this vessel off and the water transport is laterally redirected (Grace 1993). Under normal conditions, such a vessel may be filled with water again (Sperry et al. 1987; Gartner 1995), but it may also occur that the xylem of complete organs (leaves or branches) cavitate and that these parts of the plant dry out. As the volume flow is determined by meteorological conditions in the atmosphere and by stomatal aperture, the water potential gradient in the xylem is a consequence and not a cause of the volume flow. Nevertheless, stomatal conductivity in plants is tuned to the hydraulic conductivity of the stem (see, e.g., Hubbard et al. 2001). Particular hydraulic conditions occur in **grasses**, where nodes provide special barriers (Martre et al. 2001).

With a constant volume flow, the gradient of water potential decreases with increasing radius of the vessels. This means that the advantage of wide vessels for rapid transport of large amounts of water is counteracted by the increased risk of **cavitation** (Tyree and Sperry 1989). The forces of cohesion, maintaining a continuous column of water in the xylem, decrease with increasing radius of the xylem vessels [Eq. (2.2.14)] from about 1500 Pa in tracheids of conifers ($r = 10$ μm) to about 60 Pa in tracheids of ring-porous woods ($r = 500$ μm; see Table 2.2.3), but other processes participate in cavitation (see above: **air seeding**). The process of interruption of the water column is often also called **embolism**. The term embolism could imply that the space created is a vacuum, but this is not the case. The space is filled with water vapour and hence the term cavitation is much more appropriate.

- **Number of conducting elements**: The number of conducting elements is regulated in woody plants by the annual increase of new elements as well as by the transition of old elements from sapwood to heartwood (Fukuda 1997). The conducting sapwood area is thus very

variable and depends on the size of the conduction elements as well as on conditions in the habitat. Thus ring-porous woody plants have only a few actively conducting annual rings, whilst in conifers the conducting elements remain active for decades.

- **Differentiation of the shoot**: Generally, the diameter of vessels is smaller in peripheral organs, particularly in the petiole. Thus the decrease in potential in the xylem of the stem is small and increases with the water transport into the leaf. Thus the risk of cavitation is located into the peripheral organs (Zimmermann 1983).

Despite the manifold possibilities of regulation, there are basic differences in water transport between different groups of species (Table 2.2.3).

In a tropical **liana** the soil water taken up by the root reaches the transpiring leaf in less than 1 h. This applies also to **ring-porous woody plants** and dicotyledenous **herbaceous plants**. In contrast, it takes 2–3 months for the water taken up by the roots to reach the tip of a 100-m-high *Sequoia gigantea*, because of the low rate of flux in **conifer wood** composed of tracheids.

At constant **hydraulic conductivity**, the water potential in the leaf changes linearly with transpiration. This can be used to demonstrate structural differences in the stem between species (Fig. 2.2.10 A; Schulze and Chapin 1987). Plants with lower conductivity have lower rates of transpiration and more negative water potentials. In contrast, plants with high conductivity also have rapid rates of transpiration; however, the water potential does not decrease to the same extent. In these species, the risk of cavitation is particularly great leading to a substantial change in conductivity when the soil dries out (Fig. 2.2.10 B; Schulze and Hall 1982). In these cases, the water transport in moist soils takes place via vessels with large lumen and in dry soils water transport is restricted to vessels with narrow lumen. Regulation of water flux via structural characteristics of the shoot is thus possible and dependent, to some degree, on the conditions under which a species grows.

Risk of **cavitation** occurring with the increased size of xylem vessels, and thus the increased mass flow, is shown in Fig. 2.2.11 A for *Ceratonia siliqua* (Lo Gullo and Salleo 1991). With the increasing water potential gradient apparently cavitation occurs first in vessels with a large lumen, whilst the water column in vessels

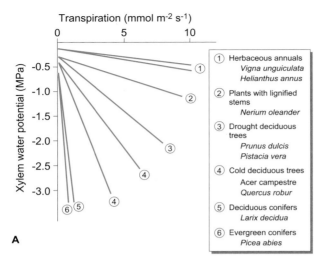

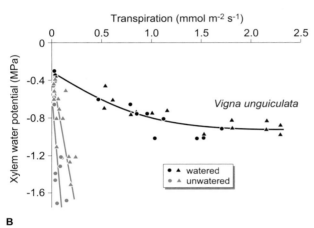

Fig. 2.2.10. Relationship between the water potential in the xylem and the transpiration rate for A different plant functional types (Schulze and Chapin 1987) and B the crop plant *Vigna unguiculata* in drying soil (Schulze and Hall 1982). The increasing transpiration rate causes a lowering of the water potential. The slope of the graph is a measure of the hydraulic conductance of the plant–soil system. Circles and triangles show the two groups of plants measured (see also Fig. 2.2.7)

with a small lumen remains intact, even at high water tension. Obviously, the structure of the conducting tissue is a limiting factor, and thus determines the risk of cavitation at high transport rates of water into the shoot (Grace 1993). However, the plant is not unprotected in face of this danger. With increasing drought water transport in soil and root changes, but stomata will restrict also the water flow (see Chap. 2.2.3) and the relation of leaf area to xylem conducting area is eventually decreased by shedding of leaves. The importance of leaf area in regulating the water flow in stems has been demonstrated for *Artemisia tridentata*, a shrub of the prairies of North America (Kolb and Sperry 1999) shows the close relationship between leaf area and early morning water potential as a measure of the water supply from the soil. The decreased leaf area with soil drying limits transpiration to such an extent that the critical flux rate, at

which cavitation of vessels would be expected, is not reached. Fertilisation increases the risk of early cavitation more than watering because it results in wider vessels (Ewers et al. 2000).

Obviously, species "adapted" to a habitat have generally developed mechanisms to avoid lethal stress situations. Other species would not flourish in these habitats or would restrict their growth and reproductive phase to a short period in which this critical situation does not occur. For example, the Mediterranean *Bromus* species are a successful invasive species in North American prairies and Australian semi-deserts where the vegetative growth is restricted to the period with sufficient water supply, but they gain this water at the cost of the water supply to indigenous perennial dwarf shrubs, particularly *Artemisia tridentata* and *Atriplex* species (West and Young 2000; see Chap. 3.1).

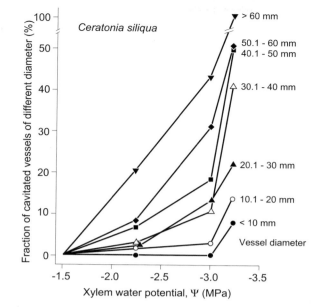

Fig. 2.2.11. Dependence of cavitation in xylem vessels of different size on the water potential in the xylem as the soil dried over several days. At a water potential of approximately –3.3 MPa all large vessels of *Ceratonia siliqua* (>60 μm), but only 10% of the small vessels (<10 μm), are cavitated

Another pointer to the limiting role of the **xylem structure** for water transport is given by the measurement of water flow in the xylem of pines of different ages in the continental climate of central Siberia (Fig. 2.2.12; Zimmermann et al. 2000). In pines, the xylem flow increases linearly with the sapwood area. The greatest sapwood area is achieved at the age of 60 years. At this age the growth of trees is relatively high and the formation of heartwood has not yet started. For very old pines the sapwood area decreases and thus the flow of water. Sapwood area results from growth of annual tree rings and hardwood formation.

2.2.2.3
Water Transport in the Phloem

The importance of water transport in the xylem and the danger of cavitation for the functioning of the whole plant are fully appreciated only when considering also the flow of material in the phloem (**phloem transport**). In vascular bundles of plants, almost all neighbouring cells transport larger amounts of water in the opposite direction, in the xylem from root to shoot, in the phloem from shoot to root. Water transport occurs

- in the xylem along a water potential gradient
- in the phloem along an osmotic pressure gradient (pressure gradient hypothesis; Fig. 2.2.13).

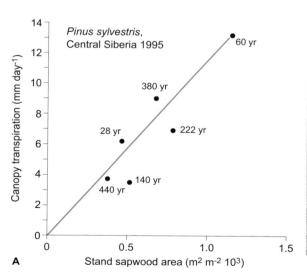

Fig. 2.2.12. A Relationship between canopy transpiration of the stand and the sapwood area of the stand. The rate of water flow rises linearly with the sapwood area: Note that it is not the youngest nor the oldest and largest trees which have the highest transpiration rates, but the 60-year-old pole stand. The small area of sapwood in the oldest stand is caused mainly by the low tree density in older stands (after Zimmermann et al. 2000). B *Pinus sylvestris* woods on Pleistocene sand dunes in central Siberia, 60 °N on the west bank of the Jennesey. Here, cohorts of even-age trees establish after fire (see Wirth et al. 1999). The vegetation of the forest floor is *Cladonia* sp. (Photo E.-D. Schulze)

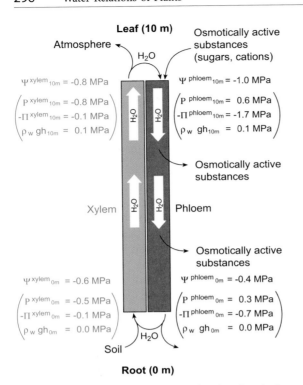

Leaf (10 m)

Atmosphere ←

Osmotically active substances (sugars, cations)

H_2O

$\Psi^{xylem}_{10m} = -0.8$ MPa

$\begin{pmatrix} P^{xylem}_{10m} = -0.8 \text{ MPa} \\ -\Pi^{xylem}_{10m} = -0.1 \text{ MPa} \\ \rho_w gh_{10m} = 0.1 \text{ MPa} \end{pmatrix}$

$\Psi^{phloem}_{10m} = -1.0$ MPa

$\begin{pmatrix} P^{phloem}_{10m} = 0.6 \text{ MPa} \\ -\Pi^{phloem}_{10m} = -1.7 \text{ MPa} \\ \rho_w gh_{10m} = 0.1 \text{ MPa} \end{pmatrix}$

→ Osmotically active substances

Xylem   Phloem

→ Osmotically active substances

$\Psi^{xylem}_{0m} = -0.6$ MPa

$\begin{pmatrix} P^{xylem}_{0m} = -0.5 \text{ MPa} \\ -\Pi^{xylem}_{0m} = -0.1 \text{ MPa} \\ \rho_w gh_{0m} = 0.0 \text{ MPa} \end{pmatrix}$

$\Psi^{phloem}_{0m} = -0.4$ MPa

$\begin{pmatrix} P^{phloem}_{0m} = 0.3 \text{ MPa} \\ -\Pi^{phloem}_{0m} = -0.7 \text{ MPa} \\ \rho_w gh_{0m} = 0.0 \text{ MPa} \end{pmatrix}$

H_2O

Soil

Root (0 m)

Fig. 2.2.13. The internal water cycle of a plant is due to the gradient of water potential, Ψ, which develops as a result of transpiration. In the phloem, the mass flow gradient is a result of the turgor (P), caused by loading and unloading of osmolytes (sugars and cations) in the phloem, and hence the osmotic pressure (Π) changes. In trees there is the additional hydrostatic pressure ($\rho_w gh$) to be taken into account, where ρ_w is the density of water, g is gravity, and H is tree height

Different gradients are maintained as follows: In moist soils the water potential of roots is similar to that of the soil ($\Psi_{root} = 0$). With the uptake of cations the osmotic pressure increases to about 0.1 MPa. Water transport starts because of the decrease of water potential in the leaf ($\Psi_{leaf} = -1.5$ MPa) as a consequence of evaporation and is dependent on the vapour pressure of the external air (e) and the net radiation (R_n). In the leaf, a smaller part of this water mass is redirected into the phloem where, because of the additional loading of the sieve cells with cations and sugars, an osmotic value of 2.0 MPa at a water potential of –1.5 MPa, and a turgor pressure of 0.5 MPa develops. This turgor pushes the phloem water from the leaf to the root. As the tissues along the sieve tubes remove sugar, the hydrostatic pressure decreases with decreasing osmotic value. This pressure-dependent transport occurs contrary to the longitudinal gradient of water potential between shoot and root. In

the root the phloem water partially re-enters the xylem. This internal circulation of water occurs even if the plant grows under extremely moist, i.e. the water potential gradient = 0 (Tanner and Beevers 1990), and under very dry conditions. This transport would only be interrupted if the complete xylem were not functioning due to cavitation during drying. In this case the survival of the plant would no longer be possible. Consequently,

- all species with large xylem vessels also make small xylem vessels so that re-direction of water flows is possible should cavitation occur;
- special closing structures (pits) ensure that the damage is limited, i.e. that cavitation does not continue in the stem.

In the case of drying out, not only the water potential changes but also the osmotic pressure so that the pressure gradient in the phloem is maintained (Schulze 1993).

2.2.3
Regulation of Stomata

Evaporation of water from plants (**transpiration**) takes place at the surfaces of cell walls lining the intercellular spaces, from where the water vapour, as a consequence of the vapour pressure gradient, reaches the external air by diffusion via the stomata. **Stomata** are the regulatory valves limiting diffusion. These valves are regulated by processes in the leaf, as well as by processes in the roots, and by conditions in the environment (see Fig. 2.2.1).

Guard cells of stomata are structured in pairs which only grow together at the ends (Fig. 2.2.14; Meidner and Mansfield 1968). The middle part, which is not fused, forms an aperture. This opens to a varying extent because the expansion of the cell with increasing turgor is radially restricted due to the orientation of the micelles in the cell wall. Thus the cell volume changes mainly by longitudinal expansion, and, together with the counter pressure of the surrounding epidermal cells, both cells form an opening of different widths (aperture). The **number of stomata** per unit epidermal area and the size of the aperture are, to a large degree, species and site specific (Meidner and Mansfield 1968). Thus the number of stomata (mm^{-2} leaf

Box 2.2.4   Summary: Water transport

- **Availability of water** depends on the soil texture. This determines the amount of bound water and conductance of water in the soil.
- Plants exploit water with the formation of **roots of very different anatomy** and morphology.
- Water flux in roots depends on external conditions, as well as on root structure both in the symplast and the apoplast. **Water uptake** is not constrained to the root tips, it can also occur in areas of lateral roots where there is meristematic tissue.
- Limited **water transport** in the soil can lead to deficits in the rhizosphere. Roots can transfer water to the soil if part of the root system is in soil horizons with higher water potential; this leads to the phenomenon of **hydraulic and inverse hydraulic lift** which re-distribute water in the profile.
- With **water transport** in the xylem, the flow of water increases with increasing size of vessels but at the same time the risk of cavitation increases.
- Water transport and the risk of **cavitation** are determined by alterations in xylem radius, the number of vessels involved in

transport and the differentiation of vessel size in the shoot.
- **Conductance of the xylem** is smallest in conifers, and increases progressively in diffuse and ring porous woods, herbaceous plants and lianas.
- The maximum longitudinal water flow is limited by cavitation in vessels and is primarily dependent on the cross-sectional area of the stem occupied by functional **xylem area** (=cumulative cross-sectional area of xylem to stem cross section).
- Xylem transport occurs along a **water potential gradient** and is dependent on the vapour pressure deficit of the air.
- **Phloem transport** occurs along a gradient of osmotic pressure which depends on the loading and unloading of sugars.
- **Circulation of water within the plant** between phloem and xylem is important for plant survival, i.e. it is maintained even under unfavourable environmental conditions. Regulation depends on xylem flux, and is achieved by stomatal closure, leaf abscission and partial senescence (crown drying in oak). Regulation of phloem transport occurs through the osmotic pressure.

---

area) varies between 30 (*Triticum, Larix*) to more than 5000 (*Impatiens*). The **size of stomata** varies between 77×42 μm (*Phyllitis, Tradescantia*) to 25×18 μm (e.g. *Tilia*). The opening mechanism is based on a physiologically regulated change of turgor, where K^+ ions from the neighbouring cells (the so-called subsidiary cells) and the cell wall are taken up. This ion uptake occurs in exchange with H^+ ions, where the protons are released from malate, and this acid metabolism is connected with the degradation of starch. The movement of the stomatal aperture is unsymmetrical, i.e. closing occurs much faster (1–10 min) than opening (30–60 min; Lange et al. 1971).

Measurement of the **apertures of stomata** is possible with a microscope (Kappen et al. 1994), even though for many plant species the aperture is covered by protrusions of the cuticle or by waxy scales. In the field, these investigations are very difficult because of disturbance of the leaf and of the climatic conditions around it. There-

fore, rather than carrying out direct observations, analogous to Ohm's law a resistance (R_L) or a conductance (g_L) are calculated from the transpiration stream (E_L) and the gradient in the vapour pressure between leaf and air (D_L) when the subscript L refers to the leaf as a whole:

$$g_L = \frac{E_L}{D_L} = \frac{1}{R_L} \qquad (2.2.16)$$

with the dimension (mol m^{-2} s^{-1}), conductivity has the same dimension as transpiration. At 15 °C, conductivity of 1 mol m^{-2} s^{-1} corresponds to a conductivity of 4.24 m s^{-1} (3.83 m s^{-1} at 45 °C). This scheme neglects cuticular transpiration, which is very low for most plants. In general conductivity is used as the standard, as it changes in proportion to the flux:

$$E_L = D_L \times g_L \qquad (2.2.17)$$

Stomatal aperture is **regulated** directly by environmental conditions related to climatic fac-

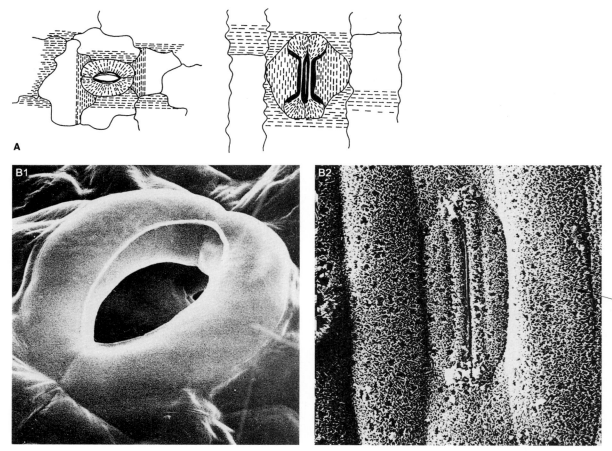

Fig. 2.2.14. A Schematic structure of the cell wall of guard cells of dicotyledonous (*left*) and monocotyledonous plants (*right*). Micelles in the cell wall (*hatched lines*) are arranged so that the expansion of the cell with increasing turgor can only take place perpendicular to their orientation (from Meidner and Mansfield 1968). B Scanning electron micrograph of a guard cell of grape vine (B1) and of wheat (B2; Troughton and Donaldson 1972)

tors (so-called **feed-forward regulation**) and indirectly by processes in the mesophyll (so-called **feed-back regulation**). Feed-back regulation is determined by water status and the carbohydrate balance. Figure 2.2.15 illustrates the different reactions, which are often independent, and which play a role in the regulation of stomata.

2.2.3.1
Non-reversible Response of Stomata to Factors Within the Plant

Non-reversible responses are those connected to the development of leaves, and are only changed by the development of new leaves or shedding of old ones.

Photosynthetic Capacity

Maximum opening of stomata correlates with the capacity for photosynthesis of leaves and is determined by the nitrogen supply and the specific leaf area (leaf area/leaf weight) which depends on species. The responses of stomata which are related to photosynthetic activity apply to all forms of plants, but these are characterised by different specific leaf areas (Reich et al. 1997). From the relation between conductance and leaf nitrogen concentration, global maps of maximum stomatal conductance are produced from which also maximum rates of CO_2 assimilation may be derived (see Fig. 2.4.6 C). Such maps are important means of verifying coupled global climate models, in which the influence of vegetation is considered. Maximum conductivity is shown, as sufficient knowledge is available about the responses of stomatas

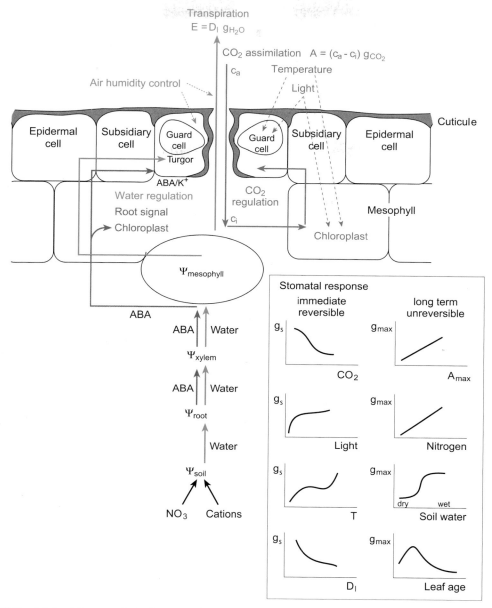

Fig. 2.2.15. Diagram of the factors and control systems which determine conductance of stomata. *ABA* Abscisic acid; *Ψ* water potential; *E* transpiration; *D_l* water vapour pressure deficit between leaf and air; *c_a* atmospheric CO_2 concentration; *c_i* CO_2 concentration in the mesophyll; *g_s* variable stomatal conductance; *g_{H_2O}* stomatal conductance for H_2O; *g_{CO_2}* stomatal conductance for CO_2; *g_{max}* maximum stomatal aperture, a measure of long-term irreversible responses to stress. Box 2.2.5, important responses of stomata to environmental conditions and those in the plant

to environmental factors and these may thus be calculated in a model. It has not been possible to calculate the capacity of plants for stomatal opening, which has only been established empirically; it is functionally correlated with the specific leaf area and the nitrogen content of leaves, pointing to the important role of photosynthesis and CO_2 in the regulation of stomatal behaviour.

Water Status

The availability of water in the soil is globally the most important environmental factor limiting stomatal conductance. During soil drying abscisic acid (ABA) is formed in the root tips (see also Chap. 1.5.2.2), and this is the basis for the regulation of stomatal conductance. ABA reaches the leaf via the water stream in the xylem and closes the potassium channels which

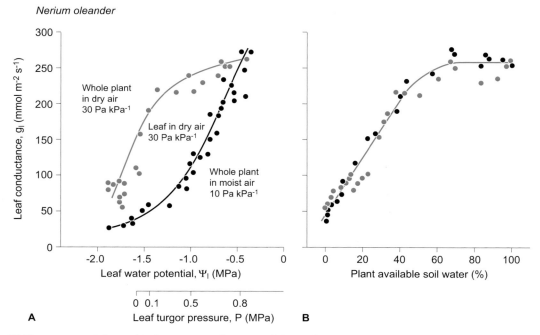

Fig. 2.2.16. A Relationship between conductance of the leaf and water potential in the xylem in *Nerium oleander* with increasing soil drying. The gradient of water vapour pressure between the leaf, on which the stomatal conductance was measured, and of the air around the leaf was constant (10 Pa kPa⁻¹) but the plant itself was either in moist (*black symbols*) or dry (*blue symbols*) air. The stomata close (decreasing conductance) as the soil dries, but the humidity of the air around the whole plant alters the leaf water potential almost 1 MPa in dry compared with moist air, although the measured leaf was under constant conditions. B Leaf conductance in the same experiment, but related to soil water content (after Schulze 1986). This experiment shows that the stomata do not respond to xylem water potential but to soil water content

regulate the turgor pressure of guard cells. This is called a **root signal**, as part of the **root-shoot communication** occurring in dry soils via the production of ABA (Schröder et al. 2001). Stomata close with increasing ABA concentration in the xylem stream. This reaction is modulated by the high pH in chloroplasts, which are a strong sink for ABA. Apparently, the pH value in the cell wall determines whether ABA is immobilised in the mesophyll and metabolised, or whether it reaches the epidermis. Here also a steady state is achieved, determined by the breakdown of ABA in light and by the transport of ABA in the phloem. With ample water supply, and good nutrition, roots produce another plant hormone, cytokinin, which opens stomata, in contrast to ABA (see also Chap. 1.5, Stress physiology).

It has often been observed that stomata close with decreasing **water potential** in the leaf.

However, this correlation does not describe the basic mechanism, as the leaf water potential depends on the rate of transpiration, as well as on the state of water in the soil and the supply of water (Fig. 2.2.16). Stomatal conductance increases with the availability of water in the soil and decreases when the soil dries out (Fig. 2.2.16 A; Schulze 1994). Parallel to transpiration and water supply, the leaf water potential changes as well. Thus, the effects of the influence of water availability in the soil are masked (Fig. 2.2.16 B). The effect of the root signal can be verified by compensating the matrix potential of the drying soil by a hydrostatic pressure applied to the soil. Thus the effect of soil drying may be observed on fully turgid plants. In this case stomatal closure is also dependent on the **soil water content** (Schulze 1994). However, this does not mean that stomata do not also react to the turgor in the leaf (see below).

2.2.3.2
Reversible Responses of Stomata to Factors Within Leaves

Carbon Dioxide
Stomata react to the gradient of CO_2 concentration between the external air and the intercellular spaces of leaves. In a classical experiment, Raschke (1972) was able to open stomata by decreasing CO_2 concentration in the external air and then close them by increasing it.

Water Status of the Epidermis
With decreasing turgor in the epidermis the aperture of stomata decreases (Nonami et al. 1990). In contrast to the reaction of the leaf to changes in root water potential this is a cellular imbalance in the epidermal turgor as dependent on transpiration (Schulze 1993).

2.2.3.3
Reversible Responses to Climatic Factors

Light
Stomata open with increasing light intensity. They are activated by a blue light receptor (Zeiger et al. 1987). Thus stomatal conductance in the morning increases earlier than photosynthesis, which is only activated when the sun has risen further and with a larger proportion of red light. Therefore, stomata open wide and do not limit the flow of CO_2 during the early morning when the humidity is high.

Temperature
At low temperatures (freezing point) stomata are closed and open as temperature increases. This opening is exponential at temperatures above $40\,^\circ C$, so leaf temperature decreases below that of the air because of the strong transpirational cooling (Raschke 1979).

Humidity
Stomata close with increasing vapour pressure deficit between leaf and air, and this can also be observed on isolated epidermis (Lange et al. 1971); where closing is faster than opening (Fig. 2.2.17 A). This response can be so strong that transpiration decreases despite an increasing water vapour gradient between leaf and air (Fig. 2.2.17 B; Schulze et al. 1972). It is still unclear how stomata "measure" humidity. Research on *Tradescantia* suggests that stomata react to local water deficits in the epidermis caused by transpiration from the stomata themselves and not from water loss of the epidermis (Nonami et al. 1990) and this depends on the time constants of water flows.

In high trees the reaction to local deficits probably plays an important role in the regulation of stomata during the course of the day. In the canopy of a forest, turbulence of air movement occurs with fast exchanges of air packages with different humidity (see Chap. 2.2.7). This correlates with fast changes in the xylem flow. Neighbouring trees, exposed to the same air masses, show synchronous changes in xylem flow (Hollinger et al. 1994). Stomatal closure is induced (Köstner et al. 1992) by short-term change in transpiration and the associated change of the water state of the epidermis. As closure is faster in dry air than is opening in moist air, a continuous decrease in stomatal conductance is the consequence. Under ambient

---

Box 2.2.5   Summary: Stomatal regulation

- **Stomata** are the most important valves by which plants can regulate transpiration in an otherwise physically determined process. Stomatal aperture is referred to as "conductance" in analogy to Ohms law.
- Stomata respond to the physiological activity of leaves measured as **photosynthesis**. Stomata determine the maximum conductance which is related to the specific leaf area for different types of plants.

- Stomata respond to **root** signals, during drought (abscisic acid, ABA) and also under favourable conditions of water and nutrition (cytokinin, CK).
- Stomata respond to conditions within the leaf, particularly CO_2 within the mesophyll, which in turn depends on photosynthesis and on the **water status** of the epidermis.
- Stomata respond to environmental factors, particularly **light**, **temperature** and **atmospheric humidity**.

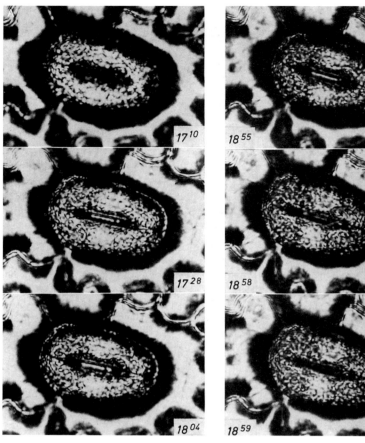

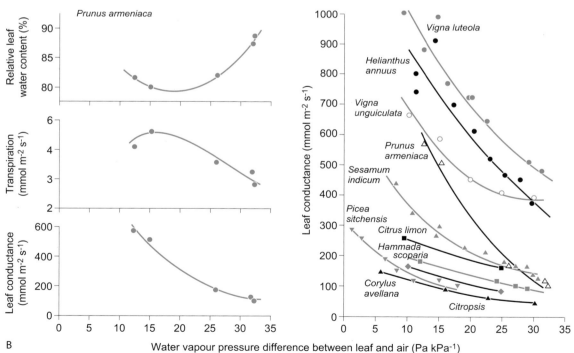

Fig. 2.2.17. A Stomata in isolated epidermis of *Polypodium vulgare*. The lower surface of the epidermis was in contact with water. Only a small air bubble simulated the substomatal air space. On the upper surface dry or moist air was blown over the stomata with a capillary. The experiment started with closed stomata in dry air. Changing to moist air induced slow stomatal opening in 54 min. With constant moist conditions the stomata stayed open but with application with dry air closed within 4 min (Lange et al. 1971). **B** Response of leaf conductance, transpiration and water content of a leaf of *Prunus armeniaca* to dry air. Stomata closed, transpiration decreased and leaf water content increased. **C** Responses of different types of plant to dry air. (Schulze and Hall 1982)

conditions, this observation shows clearly that the water status affects stomata in many more ways than can be seen from experiments in the laboratory.

2.2.4

Transpiration of Leaves and Canopies

2.2.4.1
Coupling of Water and Heat Balance

Transpiration of leaves and vegetation surfaces is only partially regulated by stomata (Schulze et al. 1996b). Stomata are the most important site where individual plants limit the flow of water physiologically but there are other structural possibilities by which plants influence transpiration. These are in particular:

- roughness of the surface of the vegetation;
- leaf area; and
- inclination of leaves.

Because of the physical laws of evaporation, transpiration is primarily dependent on climatic factors, particularly on the available radiation energy and the saturation deficit of air. At a given water supply, transpiration and not stomatal conductance ultimately determines survival of plants. Transpiration is, at the level of whole plants in their natural environments, governed by **turbulence**, the effects of which are hard to assess ecologically. Those interested in mathematics should read the works of Raupach and Finnigan (1988) with the remarkable title "Single-layer models of evaporation from plant canopies are incorrect but useful, whereas, multi-layer models are correct but useless". Here we restrict our considerations to the "large leaf model" which assumes that the total surface of a plant behaves as a single leaf, even if sub-divided. The so-called **Pennman-Monteith equation** (Monteith 1965; the derivation of the equation is also explained by Jones 1994) describes **evaporation as energy turnover** (λE, W m^{-2}; see Chap. 2.1). Evaporation depends on net radiation, R_n, and the water vapour gradient between leaf and air, D (Pa), as well as the conductance of the canopy for water vapour, G_w (mm s^{-1}), and for sensible heat, G_H (mm s^{-1}):

$$\lambda E = \frac{sR_n + \rho c_p G_H D}{s + \gamma(1 + G_H/G_w)} \quad (2.2.18)$$

latent heat flux = (radiation + sensible heat flux)/ (relation of conductance of sensible and latent heat).

The coefficient s (Pa K^{-1}) describes the change in saturation vapour pressure D with temperature, ρ is the density of air (1.204 kg m^{-3}), c_p the specific heat capacity of air (1012 J kg^{-1} J^{-1}) and γ (Pa K^{-1}) the psychrometric constant (66.1 Pa k^{-1}; see Chap. 2.1.1).

The equation combines the turn-over of **latent** (λE) and **sensible heat** ($= \rho c_p G_H D$) with radiation, because, ultimately, the turnover of water from the plant depends on the energy that is available. Under the conditions of simultaneous transport of heat and water vapour, i.e. completely turbulent transport conditions in the boundary layer, G_a and G_s are resistors in series and thus are replaceable by the frequently used terms **boundary layer conductance** (G_a, where a represents the atmosphere) and the **surface conductance** of the canopy (G_s, the **surface conductance**). For $G_H/G_w = (1 + G_a/G_s)$, Eq. (2.2.18) is expressed in the more frequently used form

$$\lambda E = \frac{sR_n + \rho c_p G_a D}{s + \gamma(1 + G_a/G_s)} \quad (2.2.19)$$

It should be noted that G_s is not equal to the stomatal conductance g_s, as the surface of the vegetation also contains the evaporation from the soil (Fig. 2.2.18; Schulze et al. 1994). G_a is composed of the immediate boundary layer of the leaf and the boundary layer of the vegetation, which is the zone in which the horizontal wind speed is influenced by the vegetation (see Fig. 2.1.9).

If the flow is not described as a function of conductance but as a function of the resistance (R), then $R_s = 1/G_s$

$$R_s = \frac{1}{G_s} = \frac{\rho c_p D}{\gamma \lambda E} + \frac{1}{\gamma G_a}\left[\frac{sR_n}{\lambda E} - (s + \gamma)\right] \quad (2.2.20)$$

Equations (2.2.18)–(2.2.20) show:

- Saving water leads to increased heat flux, dependent on the temperature difference between the exchanging surface and the air and thus to increased leaf temperature and also to greater vapour pressure deficit between the leaf and its environment (see Chap. 2.2.1).

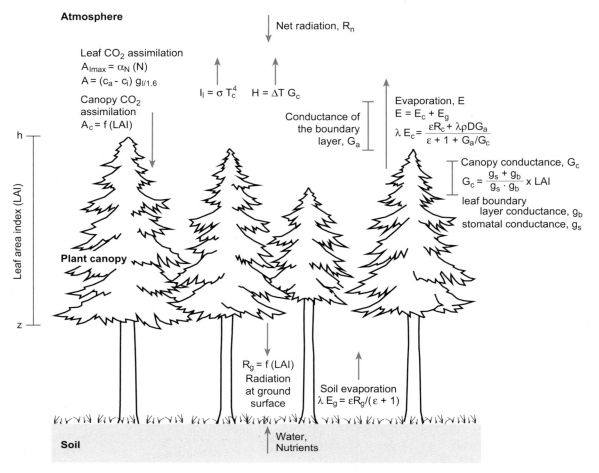

Fig. 2.2.18. Representation of water and CO_2 fluxes in a plant stand. The determining abiotic factors are net radiation, and the water and nutrient supply from the soil. The radiation intensity (and the leaf angle) determines the leaf area index (LAI). Carbon dioxide assimilation is determined by the capacity of the leaf (CO_2 gradient: $c_a - c_i$), stomatal conductance, g_s, nitrogen nutrition and the LAI. In a dense plant stand most of the incident radiation is intercepted before reaching the soil surface. Evaporation takes place against the CO_2 influx. Evaporation consists of water loss from soil (E_g) in equilibrium with radiation at the forest floor and transpiration from the canopy (E_c). Both evaporative fluxes are limited by a number of conductances: soil and plant water loss are dependent on the surface roughness of the whole stand (G_a). G_a describes the turbulence above the canopy where wind speed decreases by contact with the vegetation (2–5 m above the vegetation). The canopy conductance (G_c) is determined by the conductance in the boundary layer around the leaf g_b and the stomatal conductance g_s, with the total conductance dependent on LAI. The surface conductance G_s is the sum of G_a and G_c. Not all of the energy is used as latent heat of evaporation and the energy balance is achieved by alterations in surface temperature (T_c) and the emission of long-wave, infrared radiation dependent on it, and on the sensible heat flux (H) (see Chap. 2.1) ε corresponds to s in Eq. (2.2.18). (After Schulze et al. 1995)

This compensates the effect of stomatal closure on transpiration.

- The plant may change its form or growth. If the conductance of the boundary layer G_a is very large, there is a tight coupling with the temperature of the environment, for example, in trees. Water consumption then depends on the conductance of the surface G_s. In contrast, G_a may become very small, e.g. in a meadow, with a consequent increase in surface temperature because turbulent exchange with the surrounding air layers is limited. In this case, water loss is less dependent on G_s than on radiation and plants could, under certain conditions, maintain open stomata and assimilate CO_2 with little water loss. Differences shown in Fig. 2.1.9 (Chap. 2.1.2.3) between a crop of cereals and a forest are mainly a consequence of the differences in G_a.

- It should be noted that the term $[1/\gamma G_a \ [(sR_n/\lambda E) - (s + \gamma)]]$ is not taken into account in ventilated cuvettes in physiological experiments,

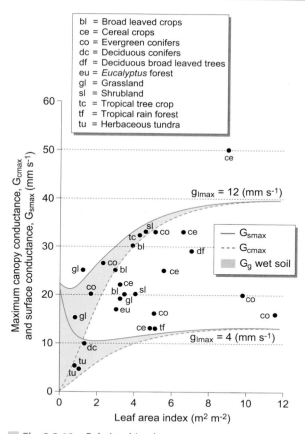

Fig. 2.2.19. Relationship between maximum canopy conductance (G_c = vegetation) and surface conductance (G_s = soil and vegetation) and their relation to leaf area index. The *continuous line* shows the conductance of the surface, the *hatched line* conductance of the vegetation, the *zone between the lines* shows the conductance of moist soil, G_g. (After Kelliher et al. 1995)

as G_a becomes very large in this case. Such experiments provide information on stomata, but not about transpiration which occurs under field conditions.

- The significance of evaporation from the soil surface becomes obvious if the maximum conductance of the canopy, as the component of the surface conductance that is regulated by the plant, is plotted against the leaf area index (LAI; Fig. 2.2.19). Canopy and surface conductances are affected by the maximum stomatal conductance, i.e. dependent on the coupling with the atmosphere, different rates of water turnover are reached. Canopy conductance increases with LAI and becomes saturated at LAI = 5. In contrast, surface conductance behaves somewhat differently. With decreasing LAI, free evaporation from the soil surface becomes important. With LAI = 2 con-

ductance of the soil is as large as that from plants, as long as the soil surface is wet. For LAI < 1 surface conductance increases again, i.e. sparse vegetation cover protects the soil from loss of water, but the component regulated by the plant is very small. In this case "water saving" by plants does not affect the water loss from the site, because the water balance is determined by evaporation from the soil (Greenwood et al. 1992). In Fig. 2.2.19 data from measured plant stands are included. It becomes obvious that the maximum stomatal conductance of the plant cover of the earth is between 4 and 12 mm s^{-1}. Whilst herbaceous vegetation is characterised by a high LAI and high canopy conductance, forests and shrubs have a low LAI and low conductance. The reason for this difference is the coupling of the vegetative types to the atmosphere. The high conductance does not mean that herbaceous vegetation transpires more than forest stands.

2.2.4.2
"Imposed" and "Equilibrium" Evaporation

Two limiting cases are distinguished with regards to the relative significance of stomatal conductance versus the conductance of the boundary layer (Jarvis and McNaughton 1986):

1. Therefore,

$$G_a \gg G_s : \lambda E \to (\rho c_p / \gamma) D G_s \qquad (2.2.21)$$

In this case, transpiration depends on the saturation deficit of air and on stomatal opening. This would be the case in the rough canopy of a forest. For constant stomatal width, transpiration is "forced or imposed" by the saturation deficit of the air. This is called **imposed evaporation** (E_{imp}).

2. Thus,

$$G_a \ll G_s : \lambda E \to (s/(s+\gamma)) R_n \qquad (2.2.22)$$

In this case, transpiration is in equilibrium with the available net incoming radiation, and is thus independent of stomatal conductance, an example is an even lawn. Stomata may be opened wide, but the vegetation loses little water, even if the free atmosphere is dry. This may be observed in long lasting dew, for ex-

Box 2.2.6   Summary: Measurement of transpiration of leaves, of single plants and plant canopies

Measurement in leaves (see Sestak et al. 1971; Pearcy et al. 1991):

- **Porometer:** this is a vessel onto which a leaf is pressed or into which a leaf is sealed. The changes in air humidity and CO_2 concentration are measured and from this a flux is calculated. **Advantage:** simple to use. **Disadvantage:** the response of the plant, i.e. the change in stomatal conductance and not the transpiration rate is actually measured under artificial conditions.

- **Cuvettes:** these are controlled chambers in which all or part of a leaf is enclosed. The temperature and the humidity can be controlled so that it is possible to determine the plant's responses to specific conditions. **Advantage:** experiments are possible in the field. **Disadvantage:** complicated machinery. The measured transpiration rate does not correspond to the transpiration rate under undisturbed conditions.

Measurement on single plants (see Pearcy et al. 1991):

- **Xylem flux:** the water in the xylem is heated at a point and the distribution of temperature in the stem is measured. There are different approaches, either the temperature dissipation is held constant and the current is regulated (Cermak method) or the energy input is held constant and the change in temperature is measured (Granier method). **Advantage:** it allows measurement of the natural rate of transpiration of the plant. **Disadvantage:** the method is best suited for trees, small shoots are difficult to measure: extrapolation to the whole vegetation surface is difficult.

Measurements of canopies (see Aubinet et al. 2000):

- **Eddy correlation method:**
  Turbulence over the surface of vegetation is determined from the vertical profile of wind speed. The size of the air parcels that enter or leave the vegetation is then determined by combining wind profiles with measurements of temperature and humidity. From knowledge of the chemical composition of the air packages (concentration of gases, e.g. CO_2) the water and CO_2 fluxes may be assessed over a large area of vegetation (1–4 km^2). **Advantage:** integrated measurement of fluxes for whole ecosystems. **Disadvantage:** can only be used under particular topographical conditions (small slope, homogeneous canopy and unstable layers).

Measurements at landscape scales (see Lloyd et al. 2001):

- **CBL-balancing** (CBL=convective boundary layer): The lower layer of the atmosphere may be used as a cuvette, i.e. during the day changes in concentration in gases in this zone may be measured from an aeroplane and knowledge of the flux balances with the environment and the troposphere can be obtained at landscape scale from 50–100 km^2. **Advantage:** quantification of flux balances from varied landscapes. **Disadvantages:** technically and meteorologically demanding and limited to particular meteorological conditions.

ample, in the shadow of woods. It is called **equilibrium evaporation** (E_{eq}). In this case, the transport of water vapour from the boundary layer away from the plant is not taking place and evaporation will saturate the non-turbulent air space immediately. Water vapour transport to the atmosphere is only possible if the temperature of the surface rises as a consequence of radiation.

Under natural conditions both limiting cases occur but usually a mixture of transpiration imposed by saturation deficit and in equilibrium with radiation occurs.

$$\lambda E = \Omega \lambda E_{eq} + (1 - \Omega)\lambda E_{imp}, \qquad (2.2.23)$$

where Ω is the **decoupling factor** which quantifies the connection of the vegetation to the at-

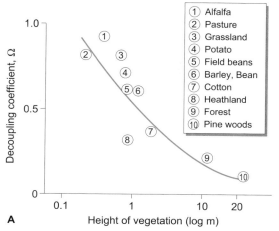

Fig. 2.2.20. A Dependence of the uncoupling factor Ω on the height of the vegetation as a measure of the roughness of the surface (after Kelliher et al. 1995). B In boreal forest the ratio of latent to sensible heat flux is affected by the form of tree canopy. *Picea obovata* x *excelsa* (narrow crown) is more densely covered with needles and therefore warms more than *Picea excelsa* (broad crown) or *Betula pubescens*. The thick ground vegetation with *Vaccinium myrtillus* does not have a very rough surface and thus warms more strongly. Gutulia, central Norway (Photo E.-D. Schulze). C Canopy of a *Eucalyptus marginata* stand with an average height of 100 m in south-western Australia. *Eucalyptus marginata* reaches a height of 140 m. In contrast to boreal forests, the leaf surface is almost uniformly distributed in the canopy, although *Eucalyptus* forms leaf bundles at the ends of braches. Picture taken from the "Glocester tree" near Pemperton. (Photo E.-D. Schulze)

Legend for A:
1. Alfalfa
2. Pasture
3. Grassland
4. Potato
5. Field beans
6. Barley, Bean
7. Cotton
8. Heathland
9. Forest
10. Pine woods

mosphere, λE_{eq} is the equilibrium evaporation and λE_{imp} the imposed evaporation [see Eqs. (2.2.21) and (2.2.22)].

$$\Omega = 1/\left(1 + (\gamma/s + \gamma)\left(R_s/R_a\right)\right) \qquad (2.2.24)$$

at $10\,^{\circ}C$, $(\gamma/s + \gamma) = 0.44$.

The sensitivity with which transpiration reacts to changes of stomata, $(dE/E)/(dG_s/G_s)$, is directly determined by Ω:

$$(dE/E)/\left(dG_s/G_s\right) = (1 - \Omega) \qquad (2.2.25)$$

The above-mentioned relations are very important in the regulation of water loss from plant

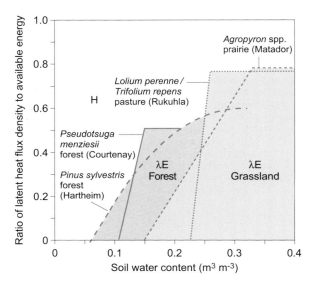

Fig. 2.2.21. Relation between energy exchange of different types of vegetation and soil water content (after Kelliher et al. 1993). The figure shows that the tree vegetation with deeper penetrating roots only limits transpiration at low water contents in the upper soil, in contrast to grasslands. Forest vegetation *Pinus sylvestris* at Hartheim, Germany; *Pseudotsuga menziessi* in Kourtenay, USA. *Agropyron* grassland in Matador, USA; *Lolium/Trifolium* grassland: Rukuhla, New Zealand

canopies. Under certain conditions the characteristics of the vegetation are more important than stomatal regulation. A branch standing out from a "wind swept" canopy of a forest near the coast experiences different evaporative conditions to other leaves protected by the canopy.

The **decoupling factor Ω** decreases with increasing height of vegetation (Fig. 2.2.20). However, this does not explain how and to what extent transpiration takes place, because, at constant Ω, transpiration is dependent on radiation and saturation deficit.

For many types of vegetation the **maximum rate of transpiration** decreases with the height of vegetation (i.e. the stomatal component increasingly regulates the water loss in the stand as well; Kelliher et al. 1993). The faster evaporation for low vegetation is not caused by the regulation of stomata, but because the relative amount of evaporation from the soil increases and becomes more important. In the canopy of the forest it is also possible for individual trees or species to influence, within certain limits, coupling to the atmosphere. This is, for example, the case in very dense canopies of boreal spruces and pines which form, considered as the surface of the forest, a very rough canopy (G_a is very large), but individual trees carry a very dense branch and needle cover (clumped distribution of leaf area; G_a very small). Thus, in the region near the stem, equilibrium evaporation dominates and a differential temperature climate may be formed in the canopy.

Box 2.2.7	Summary: Transpiration of plant canopies

- Factors controlling **transpiration** are net radiation, water vapour deficit in the air, aerodynamics of the boundary layer above the canopy and stomata. The relative influence of these factors depends on the structure of the vegetation cover, especially the roughness of the surface. This is largely dependent on the types of plants that are growing (trees, shrubs and grasses).
- Plants regulate water losses primarily through their **form**. At the same time, the form of a plant is dependent on its environment. Most noteworthy features are the height to which the plants grow and the number of leaves.
- At low **LAI** the proportion of water evaporated from the soil surface increases so that a "water saving" through the abscission of leaves does not lead, necessarily, to a reduction in the amount of water lost by the ecosystem.
- For vegetation with smooth surfaces the transpiration rate is primarily dependent on the net radiation (**steady-state evaporation**) and is mostly independent of the stomata.
- In vegetation with rough surfaces the transpiration rate is primarily dependent on the saturation deficit of air. In this case control of transpiration can occur through stomata. The **uncoupling factor** describes the relative effects of the stomata on the total transpiration of the plant and soil system.
- Plants have a further method of controlling their water balance, by having different root structures (**rooting depth**).

The response of stomata to humidity was observed to be independent of the forms of different herbaceous and woody species, e.g. in low rosette plants and trees. According to Eq. (2.2.20), and (2.2.24), this response is ecologically mainly important for trees, where an effective limitation of transpiration by closure of stomata during the course of the day has been observed (e.g. for *Nothofagus fusca* in New Zealand; Köstner et al. 1992).

Considering water relations of plants from the view of the atmosphere "clouds" the fact that plants have a further, important structural way of regulating their water relations, that is a regulation by **rooting depth.** The available amount of water is an important component in the water balance and differs greatly for different types of plants. Figure 2.2.21 gives an example of the behaviour of different grasslands with drying soils showing the proportion of evaporation which is determined by latent and sensible heat flows. It becomes obvious that agronomically used grassland with good water status turns over 80% of the available energy as latent energy (transpiration) but limits transpiration very early (in this case because of drought). In the prairie with good water supply, a similarly high turnover of latent energy occurs, but this vegetation starts to regulate water loss earlier and maintains a favourable water balance for longer. In contrast, conifer stands have a significantly lower turnover of latent energy, even if much water is available in the soil; they limit transpiration significantly later than grasslands, mainly because of their deeper roots.

References

Aubinet M, Grelle A, Ibrom A, Rannik U, Moncrieff J, Foken T, Kowalski AS, Martin P, Berbigier P, Bernhofer C, Clement R, Elbers I, Cranier A, Gruenwald T, Morgenstern K, Pilegaard K, Rebmann C, Snijders W, Valentini R, Vesala T (2000) Estimates of the annual net carbon and water exchange of European forests: The EUROFLUX methodology. Adv Ecol Res 30:113–175

Bewley JD, Krochko JE (1982) Desiccation tolerance. Encycl Plant Physiol NS 12B:325–378

Böhm J (1893) Capillarität und Saftsteigen. Ber Dtsch Bot Ges 11:203–212

Burgess SSO, Adams MA, Turner NC, White DA, Ong CK (2001) Tree roots: conduits for deep recharge of soil water. Oecologia 126:158–165

Canadell J, Jackson RB, Ehleringer JR, Mooney HA, Sala OE, Schulze E-D (1996) Maximum rooting depth of vegetation types at the global scale. Oecologia 108:583–595

Carlquist S (1991) Anatomy of vine and liana stems: a review and synthesis. In: Putz FE, Mooney HA (eds) The biology of vines. Cambridge University Press, Cambridge, pp 53–71

Darcy H (1856) Las Fontains Publiques de La Villa Dijon. Dalmont, Paris

Dawson TE (1993) Water sources as determined from xylem-water isotopic corn position: perspectives on plant competition, distribution, and water relations. In: Ehleringer JR, Hall AE, Farquhar GD (eds) Stable isotopes and plant carbon-water relations. Academic Press, San Diego, pp 465–498

Ehleringer JR (1994a) Variation in gas exchange characteristics among desert plants. In: Schulze E-D, Caldwell MM (eds) Ecophysiology of photosynthesis. Ecological Studies 100. Springer, Berlin Heidelberg New York, pp 361–392

Ehleringer JR (1994b) Carbon and water relations in desert plants: an isotopic perspective. In: Ehleringer JR, Hall AE, Farquar GD (eds) Stable isotopes and plant carbon-water relations. Academic Press, San Diego, pp 155–172

Evenari M, Shanan L, Tadmor N (1982) The Negev; the challenge of a desert. Harvard University Press, Cambridge, 437 pp

Ewers BE, Oren R, Spery JS (2000) Influence of nutrients versus water supply on hydraulic architecture and water balance in *Pinus taeda*. Plant Cell Environ 23:1055–1066

Fukuda H (1997) Tracheary element differentiation. Plant Cell 9:1147–1156

Gartner BL (1995) Plant stems: physiology and functional morphology. Academic Press, San Diego, 439 pp

Grace J (1993) Consequences of xylem cavitation for plant water deficits. In: Smith JAC, Griffiths H (eds) Water deficits. Bios Scientific Publishers, Oxford, pp 109–128

Greenwood EAN, Turner NC, Schulze E-D, Waton GD, Venn NR (1992) Groundwater management through increased water use by lupine crops. J Hydrol 134:1–11

Griesebach A (1872) Die Vegetation der Erde nach ihrer klimatischen Anordnung. Wilhelm Engelmann, Leipzig, 709 pp

Hollinger DY, Kelliher FM, Schulze E-D, Köstner BM (1994) Coupling of tree transpiration to atmospheric turbulence. Nature 371:60–62

Horn R (1994) The effect of aggregation of soils on water, gas and heat transport. In: Schulze E-D (eds) Flux control in biological systems. Academic Press, San Diego, pp 335–361

Hubbard RM, Ryan MG, Stiller V, Sperry JS (2001) Stomatal conductance and photosynthesis vary linearly with plant hydraulic conductance in ponderosa pine. Plant Cell Environ 24:113–122

Jarvis PG, McNaughton KG (1986) Stomatal control of transpiration: scaling from leaf to region. Adv Ecol Res 15:1–15

Jones HG (1994) Plant and microclimate; a quantitative approach to environmental plant physiology. Cambridge University Press, Cambridge, 428 pp

Kappen L, Schulz G, Vanselow R (1994) Direct observations of stomatal movements. Ecological Studies 100. Springer, Berlin Heidelberg New York, pp 231–246

Kelliher FM, Leuning R, Schulze E-D (1993) Evaporation and canopy characteristics of coniferous forests and grasslands. Agric For Met 62:53–73

Kelliher FM, Lenning H, Raupach M, Schulze E-D (1995) Maximum conductance for evaporation of global vegetation types. Agric For Met 73:1–16

Kolb KL, Sperry JS (1999) Transport constraints on water use by the Great Basin shrub *Artemisia tridentata*. Plant Cell Environ 22:925–935

Köppen W (1923) Die Klimate der Erde. Walter de Gruyter, Berlin, 369 pp

Köstner BMM, Schulze E-D, Kelliher FM, Hollinger DY, Byers JN, Hunt JE, McSeveny TM, Meserth R, Weir PL (1992) Transpiration and canopy conductance in a pristine broad-leaf forest of *Nothofagus*: an analysis of xylem sap flow and eddy correlation measurements. Oecologia 92:236–241

Kramer PJ, Boyer JS (1995) Water relations of plants and soils. Academic Press, London, 495 pp

Lange OL, Lösch R, Schulze E-D, Kappen L (1971) Responses of stomata to changes in humidity. Planta 100:76–86

Lange OL, Nobel PS, Osmond CB, Ziegler H (1982) Physiological plant ecology II: water relations and carbon assimilation. Encyclopaedia of plant physiology, vol 12B. Springer, Berlin Heidelberg New York, 747 pp

Larcher W (1976) Ökophysiologie der Pflanzen. UTB 232, Ulmer, Stuttgart, 399 pp

Larcher W (1994) Ökophysiologie der Pflanzen. UTB, Ulmer, Stuttgart, 394 pp

Lloyd J, Francey RJ, Sogachev A, Byers JN, Mollicone D, Raupach MR, Kelliher FM, Rebmann C, Arneth A, Valentini R, Wong SC, Schulze E-D (2001) Vertical profiles, boundary layer budgets and regional flux estimates for CO_2, its $^{13}C/^{12}C$ ratio, and for water vapour above a forest/bog mosaic in central Siberia. Global Biogeochem Cycles 15:267–284

Lo Gullo MA, Salleo S (1991) Three different methods for measuring xylem cavitation and embolism: a comparison. Ann Bot 67:417–424

Lüttge U (1973) Stofftransport der Pflanzen. Heidelberger Taschenbücher 125. Springer, Berlin Heidelberg New York, 280 pp

Martre P, Cochart H, Durand JL (2001) Hydraulic architecture and water flow in growing grass tillers (*Festuca arundinacea* Schreb.). Plant Cell Environ 24:65–76

Meidner H, Mansfield TA (1968) Physiology of stomata. McGraw-Hill, London, 179 pp

Michael W, Schultz A, Meshcheryakov AB, Ehwald R (1997) Apoplasmatic and protoplasmatic water transport through the parenchyma of a potato storage organ. Plant Physiol 115:1089–1099

Michael W, Cholodova VP, Ehwald R (1999) Gas and liquids in intercellular spaces of maize roots. Ann Bot 84:665–673

Monteith JL (1965) Evaporation and environment. Symp Soc Exp Biol 19:205–234

Nobel PS (1991) Physicochemical and environmental plant physiology. Academic Press, San Diego, 635 pp

Nonami H, Schulze E-D, Ziegler H (1990) Mechanisms of stomatal movement in response to air humidity, irradiance and xylem water potential. Planta 183:57–64

Pearcy RW, Ehleringer J, Mooney HA, Rundel PW (1991) Plant physiological ecology: field methods and instrumentation. Chapman and Hall, London, 457 pp

Philip JR (1957) Evaporation, and moisture and heat fields in the soil. J Meteorol 14:354–366

Raschke K (1972) Saturation kinetics of the velocity of stomatal closing response to CO_2. Plant Physiol 49:229–234

Raschke K (1979) Movements of stomata. In: Haupt W, Feinleib RE (eds) Physiology of movements. Springer, Berlin Heidelberg New York, pp 383–440

Raupach MR, Finnigan JJ (1988) Single-layer models of evaporation from plant canopies are incorrect but useful, whereas multilayer models are correct but useless. Aust J Plant Physiol 15:705–716

Reich PB, Walters MB, Eldsworth DS (1997) From tropics to tundra: global convergence in plant functioning. Proc Natl Acad Sci USA 94:13730–13734

Richards JH, Caldwell MM (1987) Hydraulic lift: substantial nocturnal water transport between soil layers by *Artemisia tridentata* roots. Oecologia 73:486–489

Schröder JI, Kwak JM, Allen GJ (2001) Guard cell abscisic acid signalling and engineering drought hardiness in plants. Nature 410:327–330

Schulze E-D (1986) Carbon dioxide and water vapor exchange in response to drought in the atmosphere and in the soil. Annu Rev Plant Physiol 37:247–274

Schulze E-D (1993) Soil water deficits and atmospheric humidity as environmental signals. In: Smith JAC, Griffiths H (eds) Water deficits. Bios Scientific Publishers, Oxford, pp 129–145

Schulze E-D (1994) The regulation of plant transpiration: interactions of feedforward, feedback, and futile cycles. In: Schulze E-D (eds) Flux control in biological systems. Academic Press, San Diego, pp 203–236

Schulze E-D, Chapin FS III (1987) Plant specialization to environments of different resource availability. Ecological Studies 61. Springer, Berlin Heidelberg New York, pp 120–148

Schulze E-D, Hall AE (1982) Stomatal response, water loss and CO_2 assimilation rates of plants in contrasting environments. Encycl Plant Physiol 12B:181–230

Schulze E-D, Heinmann M (1998) Carbon and water exchange of terrestrial systems. In: Galloway J, Mellilo J (eds) Asian change in the context of global climate change. Cambridge University Press, Cambridge. IGBP Publ Ser 3:145–161

Schulze E-D, Lange OL, Buschbom U, Kappen L, Evenari M (1972) Stomatal responses to changes in humidity in plants growing in the desert. Planta 108:259–270

Schulze E-D, Cermak J, Matyssek R, Penka M, Zimmermann R, Vasicek, Gries W, Kucera J (l985) Canopy transpiration and water fluxes in the xylem of the trunk of Larix and Picea trees – a comparison of xylem flow, pyrometer and cuvette measurements. Oecologia 66:475–483

Schulze E-D, Kelliher FM, Körner C, Lloyd J, Leuning R (1994) Relationships among maximum stomatal conductance, carbon assimilation rate, and plant nitrogen nutrition: a global ecology scaling exercise. Annu Rev Ecol Syst 25:629–660

Schulze E-D, Leuning R, Kelliher FM (1995) Environmental regulation of surface conductance for evaporation from vegetation. Vegetatio 121:79–87

Schulze E-D, Ellis R, Schulze W, Trimborn P, Ziegler H (1996a) Diversity, metabolic types and $\delta^{13}C$ carbon isotope ratios in the grass flora of Namibia in relation to growth form, precipitation and habitat conditions. Oecologia 106:352–36

Schulze E-D, Kelliher FM, Körner C, Lloyd J, Hollinger DY, Vygodskaya NN (1996b) The role of vegetation in controlling carbon dioxide and water exchange between land surface and the atmosphere. In: Walker B, Steffen W (eds) Global change and terrestrial ecosystems. IGBP Book Series 2. Cambridge University Press, Cambridge, pp 77–92

Schulze E-D, Mooney HA, Sala OE, Jobbagy E, Buchmann N, Bauer G, Canadell J, Jackson RB, Loreti J, Oesterheld M, Ehleringer JR (1996c) Rooting depth, water availability, and vegetation cover along an aridity gradient in Patagonia. Oecologia 108:503–511

Schulze E-D, Caldwell MM, Canadell J, Mooney HA, Jackson RB, Parson D, Scholes R, Sala O, Trimborn P (1998a) Downward flux of water through roots (i.e. inverse hydraulic lift) in dry Kalahari sands. Oecologia 115:460–462

Schulze E-D, Williams RJ, Farquhar GD, Schulze W, Langridge J, Miller JM, Walker BK (1998b) Carbon and nitrogen isotope discrimination and nitrogen nutrition of trees along a rainfall gradient in northern Australia. Aust J Plant Physiol 25:413–425

Sestak Z, Catsky J, Jarvis PG (1971) Plant photosynthetic production. Manual of methods. Dr W Junk NV Publishers, Den Haag, 818 pp

Slatyer RO (1967) Plant-water relationships. Academic Press, London, 366 pp

Sperry JS (1995) Limitations on stem water transport and their consequences. In: Gartner BL (eds) Plant stems: physiology and functional morphology. Academic Press, San Diego, pp 105–124

Sperry JS, Holbrook NM, Zimmermann MH, Tyree MT (1987) Spring filling of xylem vessels in wild grapewine. Plant Physiol 83:414–417

Steudle E (1994) The regulation of plant water at the cell, tissue, and organ level: role of active processes and of compartmentation. In: Schulze E-D (eds) Flux control in biological systems. Academic Press, San Diego, pp 237–302

Steudle E (2000) Water uptake by roots: effects of water deficits. J Exp Bot 1531–1542

Steudle E (2001) The cohesion-tension mechanism and the acquisition of water by plant roots. Annu Rev Plant Physiol Plant Mol Biol 847–875

Steudle E, Peterson CA (1998) How does water get through roots? J Exp Bot 49:775–788

Tanner W, Beevers H (1990) Does transpiration have essential function in long-distance ion transport in plants? Plant Cell Environ 13:745–750

Troughton J, Donaldson LA (1972) Probing plant structures. Chapman and Hall, London, 85 pp

Tyerman SD, Bohnert HJ, Maurel C, Steudle E, Smith JA (1999) Plant aquaporins: their molecular biology, biophysics and significance for plant water relations. J Exp Bot 50:1055–1072

Tyree MT (1997) The cohesion-tension theory of sap ascent. Current controversies. J Exp Bot 48:1753–1765

Tyree MT, Sperry JS (1989) Vulnerability of xylem to cavitation and embolism. Annu Rev Plant Physiol Plant Mol Biol 40:19–38

Walter H (1960) Grundlagen der Pflanzenverbreitung. Teil I: Standortlehre. Eugen Ulmer, Stuttgart, 566 pp

Ward RC, Robinson M (1990) Principles of hydrology. McGraw Hill, Berkshire, 365 pp

WBGU (1998) World in transition: ways towards sustainable management of freshwater resources. Springer, Berlin Heidelberg New York, 392 pp

Wei C, Steudle E, Tyree MT (1999) Water ascent in plants: do ongoing controversies have a sound basis? Plant Sci 4:372–373

West NE, Young JA (2000) Intermountain valleys and lower mountain slopes. In: Barbour MG, Billings WD (eds) North American terrestrial vegetation. Cambridge University Press, Cambridge, pp 255–284

Wirth C, Schulze E-D, Schulze W, von Stürzner-Karbe D, Ziegler W, Milukova I, Sogachev A, Varlagin A, Panfyorov M, Grigoriev S, Kusnetzova W, Siry M, Hardes G, Zimmermann R, Vygodskaya NN (1999) Aboveground biomass and structure of pristine Siberian Scots pine forests as controlled by competition and fire. Oecologia 121:66–80

Zeiger E, Lino M, Shimazaki KI, Ogawa T (1987) The blue light response of stomata: mechanisms and function. In: Zeiger E, Farquhar GD, Cowan IR (eds) Stomatal function. Stanford University Press, Stanford, pp 209–228

Ziegler H, Vieweg GH (1970) Poikilohydre Spermatophyta. In: Walter H, Kreeb K (eds) Die Hydratation und Hydratur des Protoplasmas der Pflanzen und ihre ökophysiologische Bedeutung. Springer, Berlin Heidelberg New York, pp 95–108

Zimmermann MH (1983) Xylem structure and the ascent of sap. Springer, Berlin Heidelberg New York, 325 pp

Zimmermann R, Schulze E-D, Wirth C, Schulze EF, McDonald KC, Vygodskaya NN, Ziegler W (2000) Canopy transpiration in a chronosequence of central Siberian pine forests. Global Change Biol 6:25–37

2.3

Nutrient Relations of Plants

Magnesium deficiency in spruce. With insufficient Mg available in the soil the young needles obtain their Mg by retranslocation from the old needles via the phloem, and so the old needles become golden yellow at the time of bud break of new growth in spring. This process is exacerbated by an excess of nitrogen, especially when nitrogen is absorbed into the above-ground biomass directly from the atmosphere, bypassing the roots and hence not being regulated. The above-ground N uptake occurs from gases (NO_x, NH_3) via the stomata, or as ions (NH_4^+, NO_3^-) via the young bark or needles. The exacerbation of Mg deficiency by nitrogen input is because N has a much larger influence on growth than does Mg. However, the amount of Mg required for growth is larger than the Mg availability, and therefore an excess of N results in Mg deficiency. This phenomenon became well known in the 1980s as the "mountain yellowing" syndrome of forest decline. Fichtelgebirge, Upper Warmensteinach, Germany. Photo E.-D. Schulze

Recommended Literature

The classical textbook on plant nutrition is by Epstein (1972). The most comprehensive book on this topic was written by Marschner (1995) and for soil science refer to Brady and Weil (1999).

2.3.1

Availability of Soil Nutrients and Ion Uptake

2.3.1.1
Plant Nutrients

Plants require for their metabolism and growth many elements or their ions which are primarily taken up from the soil. These materials are released into the soil either by weathering from the original rocks, and are then freely available, or from organic substances which are decomposed and "mineralised" (i.e. the elements are released from the dead organic material) and are thus available to plants.

Plants take up required nutrients selectively and usually in the form of ions, from the liquid phase in the soil (soil solution). Proof that plants contain inorganic elements is shown by incineration.

After burning the organic material, non-combustable minerals remain in the **ash**, but C, H, N and O can only be identified as gases. For most plants the ash content is 3–8% of dry weight; in halophytic plants the ash content rises to 20% and in lichens may reach 30% due to mineral depositions on the hyphae. The concentration of individual elements in plants spans about six orders of magnitude (Table 2.3.1).

Macro-elements and **trace elements** are essential for the life of plants. Transitions between macro and trace elements are gradual. Macro-elements participate directly in the metabolism (N, S, P) or indirectly support metabolism (K), and there are transitions to trace elements (Ca, Mg). Trace elements are also termed micro-nutrients and are often heavy metals which are directly required for enzyme reactions (Chap. 1.7). **Facultative elements** are only required in some plant groups (Si for grasses). Iodine and vanadium are not mentioned here, as they are only essential for lower plants (Marschner 1995).

Concentration and consumption of nutrient elements are often expressed in units of mass (gram). However, physiological turnover and physicochemical effects of these elements are usually not measured as mass, but by the number of required molecules; therefore, mole is a better unit than gram.

The following chapter deals with the essential macro nutrients. Heavy metals as trace elements were considered in Chapter 1.7. NaCl is not essential for plants (only under certain conditions does it stimulate growth), and was considered under salt stress in Chapter 1.6.

2.3.1.2
Availability of Nutrients in Soil

Nutrients are available in the soil in different forms (Scheffer/Schachtschabel 1998).

Primary Minerals
Minerals, for example, quartz, feldspar and mica, are created during the formation of rocks by crystallisation from the molten magma (intrusive and igneous rocks) or by re-crystallisation under conditions of high pressures and temperatures (metamorphic rocks) in the upper crust of the earth. Depending on the chemical composition of the magma (acid to alkaline), and the temperature and pressure in the molten material, rocks of different mineral composition are formed (Fig. 2.3.1 C). The largest proportion of primary minerals in the earth's crust is represented by **silicates**, made of silicium-oxygen tetrahedra and with many different crystal structures. Different forms of silicates are distinguished (see Table 2.3.1). In many silicates some of the Si^{4+} ions are replaced by Al^{3+}. Silicates build Si–Si chains similar to C. Thus silicates are to a variable degree negatively charged, allowing positively charged ions (cations) such as K^+, Na^+ and Ca^{2+} to neutralise the charge and become inserted into the crystal structure. Weathering, particularly by hydrolysis, releases these cations from the mineral matrix and they then become available to plants. With the exchange of base cations against H^+ the crystal structure loses its geometry and falls apart.

Weathering of silicates depends on various factors, the degree of reduction of their crystal structure, replacement of Si by Al, the actual cation content and the proportion of elements (Fe) that may be oxidised yielding a series of increasing stability to weathering (olivine → augite → tourmaline → feldspar → quartz).

The composition of primary minerals determines the weathering of rocks, and thus the

Table 2.3.1. Typical concentration of nutrients in plant tissues. (Marschner 1995)

	Element	Average concentration ($\mu mol\ g^{-1}$)
Macroelements	N	1 000
	K	250
	Ca	125
	Mg	80
	P	60
	S	30
Trace elements	Cl	3
	B	2
	Fe	2
	Mn	1
	Zn	0.3
	Cu	0.1
	Mo	0.001
Facultative elements	Si	11 000
	Na	200
	Co	0.1

A

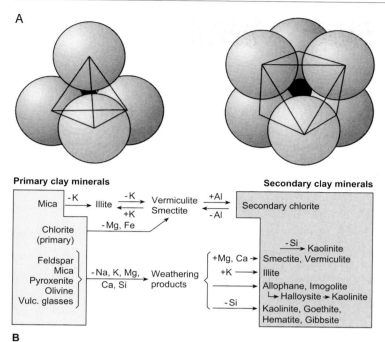

Fig. 2.3.1. A Spatial structure of a Si-tetrahedron (*left*) and an Al-octahedron (*right*). B The conversion of primary minerals into secondary clay minerals. C Composition of important rocks with respect to their base and Si content. (Scheffer-Schachtschabel 1998)

Primary clay minerals   **Secondary clay minerals**

B

C

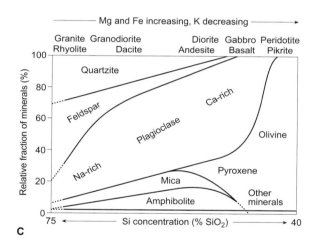

availability of alkaline compounds. Basalt, for example, is much more alkaline than granite, i.e. contains more potassium, calcium and magnesium.

Secondary Minerals

From the primary intrusive and igneous rocks as well as from metamorphic rocks (e.g. slate), secondary sediments are formed during the course of weathering and erosion, and are deposited and solidified. Depending on the original rock and its "weathering history", **sedimentary rocks** have different cation contents. Clay-rich soils possess a greater capacity for exchange of cations than sandy soils, not only be-

cause of their much larger surface area for ion exchange, but also because of the greater number of covalent bonds. Secondary minerals include those in sedimentary rocks; for example, in limestone, there are aluminium oxide, iron oxide, manganese (hydr)oxide. Clay minerals are particularly important components of soils which are formed as new products of the Si-Al minerals during the course of weathering from silicates. According to the climatic conditions when the clay minerals were formed, these could be layer lattices in which the cations are imbedded more or less tightly between the layers of Si-tetrahedra and Al-octahedra. These cations can be reversibly exchanged against H^+ without

Box 2.3.1   The mineral composition of rocks

Rocks

Rocks are mixtures of different minerals, and are classified according to their chemical composition and how they were formed. Distinction is made between magmatite formed from the cooling of molten magma in the earth's crust (intrusive rock) or on the earth's surface (igneous rocks) and sedimentary rocks originating from deposition of weathered loose material or chemical degradation products by sedimentation and subsequently hardened, and metamorphic rocks formed by the partial re-melting and recrystallisation of magmatite and sedimentary rocks.

Primary Silicates

The basic building blocks of the silicates are Si-tetrahedra and Al-octahedra (Fig. 2.3.1A). The original minerals are found in the igneous and intrusive rocks which are distinguished primarily by their Si and cation contents (Fig. 2.3.1C).

Clay Minerals

Weathering produces clay minerals either directly from mica and chlorite or they are newly formed from individual degradation products of silicate weathering. In this case Si-tetrahedra and Al-octahedra are released. They bind to secondary phyllosilicates formed by alternate layers of Si-tetrahedra and Al-octahedra which are linked by covalent bonds (Fig. 2.3.1B). Clay minerals are differentiated by the structure of the layers and the cations which lie between the layers (Fig. 2.3.1C).

- Two-layered minerals
  1 Si-tetrahedral + 1 Al-octahedral layer: kaolinite, serpentinite, no cations in the intermediate layers.
- Three-layered minerals
  1 Si-tetrahedral + 1 Al-octahedral + 1 Si-tetrahedral layer: illite, chlorite, vermiculite, montmorillonite: cations occur in the inter-

mediate layers, and these cations can be reversibly exchanged against hydrogen ions.

The clay minerals allophane and imogolite are exceptions which occur exclusively in soils derived from volcanic activity. They are spherical or tubular and in acid soils can adsorb anions, e.g. phosphate, so tightly that they are no longer available to plants (phosphate fixation).

Oxides and Hydroxides

In parallel to the breakdown of the Si-tetrahedra during silicate weathering, oxidation of metals also occurs, particularly that of Fe^{2+} to Fe^{3+} or Fe-hydroxide, which is linked to changes in solubility and spatial structure. Such oxidation of metals contributes considerably to the breakdown of the primary crystal structure. The most important oxides and hydroxides are those of Fe, Mn and Al: dependent on climatic conditions, these form different types of secondary minerals which are often responsible for the characteristic colours of soils. Tropical soils are often bright red as a consequence of hematite (a-Fe_2O_3), whilst the yellow-brown colour of many soils of the temperate zone is caused by goethite (a-FeOOH).

Sedimentary Rocks

Sedimentary rocks are the consequence of transport and the following compaction of the products of primary rocks. They differ mainly in Si and Ca content. A distinction is drawn between rocks and loose sediments, which are characterised by decreasing Si content:

- Rocks: sandstone (70% Si), greywacke (67% Si), slate (59% Si), limestone (8% Si);
- Loose sediments: drifting sands (97% Si), loess (72% Si), marl (64% Si).

Box 2.3.1   The mineral composition of rocks (continued)

Table. Tetrahedra structures of primary silicates

Nesosilicates SiO_4^{4-}	4 free charges/tetrahedron	Tetrahedra are cation saturated	Olivine $(Mg, Fe)_2[SiO_4]$
Sorosilicates $Si_2O_7^{6-}$	3 free charges/tetrahedron	Few tetrahedra covalently bound	Diopsite $(Ca, Mg)[Si_2O_3]$
Inosilicates SiO_3^{2-}	2 free charges/tetrahedron	Tetrahedra form a chain	Augite $(Ca, Mg, Fe, Al, Na)[SiO_3]_n$
Cyclosilicates $[Si_2O_6]^{1.5-}$	1.5 free charges/tetrahedron	Tetrahedral chains form ribbons	Hornblende amphibole $(Na, K, Ca, Mg, Fe, Al)(OH_4)[Al_{2-4}Si_{14-12}O_{44}]$ Tourmaline $NaMg_3Al_6[(OH)_{1+3} \cdot (BO)_3 \cdot [Si_6O_{18}]$
Phyllosilicates $Si_2O_5^{2-}$	1 free charge/tetrahedron	Tetrahedra form layers	Muscovite $(KAl_2)(OH_2)[Si_3AlO_{10}]$ Biotite $K(Mg, Fe, Mn)_3(OH, F)_2[AlSi_3O_{10}]$
Tectosilicates SiO_2	No free charges 1 free charge with Al replacing SiO_2		quartz SiO_2 Feldspar orthoclase $K[AlSi_3O_8]$ Anorthite $Ca[Al_2Si_2O_8]$

destruction of the Si-crystal structure. The so-called **cation exchange capacity** (CEC) is large in clay minerals which swell (e.g. montmorillonite, 70–130 mval/100 g) and small in non-swelling clay minerals (e.g. kaolinite, 3–15 mval/100 g).

The chemical composition of the original rock or of the deposited sediments (e.g. loess soils) determines, ultimately, the availability of water and nutrients (**fertility of soil**) and thus the type of vegetation. Plant cover may increase the CEC of soils by a factor of 10 (1–3 mol equivalents kg^{-1}) by converting organic matter and increasing the retention capacity of organic residues which are difficult to degrade (humus), but even then the chemical composition of the original rock determines the form of humus and thus the availability of nutrients in the soil: Raw, acidic humus and alkaline humus only have potential CECs of 2 and 3 mol equivalents kg^{-1} respectively (Mitscherlich 1975). This means that the availability of cations in the soil, and thus of nutrients, affects ecosystem processes right up to the carbon metabolism.

As soils developed from abiotic and biotic processes, it is not surprising that the soil map of the earth reflects, in principle, the distribution of different types of vegetation on earth (Fig. 2.3.3).

2.3.1.3
General Aspects of Plant Nutrient Balance

Nutrient Supply and Cellular Ion Transport
In mineral soils, chemically characterised by the content of alkaline cations (**base saturation:** e.g. K, Mg and Ca) and physically determined by the texture (**particle size distribution**), roots also act as ion **exchangers**. Whilst cations in the soil are in equilibrium between the exchanger (clay minerals, oxides, humus) and the free soil solution, roots cause chemical imbalances because of their active transport processes, and ability to take up cations against the concentration gradient. This process may also occur selectively for certain cations. In exchange against cations from the soil, the root releases H^+ and HCO_3^- and organic acids to the soil, which are derived from the carbon cycle. A consequence of the uptake of alkaline cations in exchange with protons is an acidification of soils (Ulrich 1987). In the case of vegetation that is not managed or harvested by man, these minerals are returned in the dead biomass to the soil as litter. In agriculture, cations are removed from the soil by harvesting, grazing or use of litter and the chemical conditions in the soil change (**acidification of soil water, podsolisation**) if the depletion exceeds the re-supply by weathering. Deposition into the soil of strong acids from the atmo-

Box 2.3.2   Ion-exchange capacity of soils

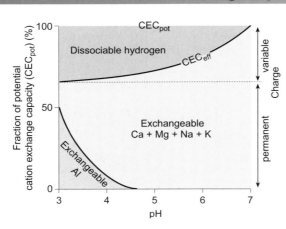

Fig. 2.3.2. Dependence of the effective cation-exchange capacity (CEC_{eff}) pH on a soil with 20–30% clay content and 2–3% humic content. The potential cation-exchange capacity (CEC_{pot}) includes, in addition to the basic cations, the dissociable protons (from Scheffer-Schachtschabel 1998)

Soils

Soils are the product of weathering and transportation of the original materials of the earth's continental land surface by physical and chemical processes and biological agents. They are mixed to different extents with the dead organic matter, the humus.

Cation-Exchange Capacity (CEC)

The CEC is an important measure of the cation availability in soil, giving the number (in moles) of cations which can be adsorbed by a defined quantity of soil (mval/100 g or $mmol_{equiv}$/kg). The magnitude of the CEC depends on the number of available exchange sites of clay minerals, humus and (hydr)oxides. The carboxyl, carbonyl and enol groups can only absorb cations when deprotonated (variable charge) and this depends on the pH. In contrast, a proportion of the exchange sites in the crystal structure of clay minerals occurs by replacement of Si^{4+} by cations of lower valency (e.g. Al) which is independent of soil pH (permanent charge). Distinction is drawn between the **potential CEC** which includes all exchangeable cations (protons, Al and basic cations, measured at pH 8, for example) and the **effective CEC** which is the exchangeable basic cations and Al at soil pH (Fig. 2.3.2). In addition to the CEC, the anion-exchange capacity (AEC) is important.

According to their clay and humus contents, soils are distinguished by their potential CEC (mmol cation equivalents kg^{-1}):

- arable fields: marshland (370), pelosol (220), black earth (180), para brown earth (170),
- forest: brown earth (600), pseudogley (184), podsol (40).

---

sphere due to air pollution (SO_4^{2-}, NO_3^-) has a similar effect as harvesting of plant material. Fertilisation and liming of soils balance the loss of cations caused by harvesting or leaching.

Uptake of cations and anions into the plant occurs via the same mechanisms (transporters, ion channels, see Box 2.3.3). There is a specific interaction between cations and anions; in the presence of Cl^-, for example, the uptake of K^+ decreases (see Marschner 1995).

Ion Uptake by Roots

Roots take up ions primarily at the root tip. In addition they may be taken up or lost via leaves and shoots; this plays an important role in the uptake of air pollutants (Harrison et al. 2000). Along the root tip the uptake of nutrients is not distributed equally (Fig. 2.3.4), as transport depends on ion radius and chemical composition, and occurs either in the cell wall, the **apoplast**, or in the cytosol, the **symplast** (see Chap. 2.2.2). Transport of Ca, Al and heavy metals is mostly through the apoplast, whilst transport of P, K, N and Mg occurs mostly in the symplast. Water transport occurs over a wider area of the root than the active ion transport, but decreases when secondary root cortex is developed. It also decreases towards the root tip because of the

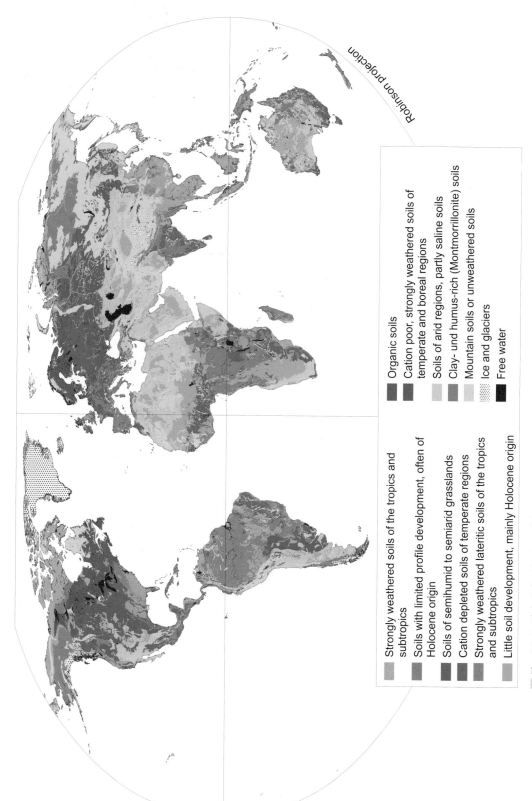

Robinson projection

Strongly weathered soils of the tropics and subtropics

Soils with limited profile development, often of Holocene origin

Soils of semihumid to semiarid grasslands

Cation depleted soils of temperate regions

Strongly weathered lateritic soils of the tropics and subtropics

Little soil development, mainly Holocene origin

Organic soils

Cation poor, strongly weathered soils of temperate and boreal regions

Soils of arid regions, partly saline soils

Clay- und humus-rich (Montmorrillonite) soils

Mountain soils or unweathered soils

Ice and glaciers

Free water

Fig. 2.3.3. Global distribution of the most important soil types. (Compiled by G. Guggenberger)

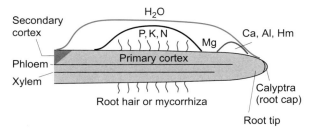

Fig. 2.3.4. Schematic representation of the uptake of nutrients along a root tip. *Hm* Heavy metal

denser cell packing and the thinner cell wall. Phloem reaches further into the root tip, i.e. it is differentiated earlier than xylem.

Ion Transport and Distribution

Plants require and consume nutrients for (see also Chap. 1.7):

- growth (e.g. Mg, Ca in the cell wall)
- catalysis (e.g. Fe in ferredoxin)
- transport of electrons (heavy metals)
- passive accumulation (heavy metals)
- storage and reserve (e.g. N, P).

Nutrient transport in plants and their distribution to sites of uptake, storage and consumption occurs via xylem and phloem (see Chap. 2.2.2.3), with very different amounts transported in both pathways so the concentration in them differs (Table 2.3.2). It is obvious that in

Table 2.3.2. Concentration of substances in the xylem and phloem of *Nicotiana glauca* (Schurr and Schulze 1995). The concentrations do not say anything about the amount transported. The flow in the phloem is slower than that in the xylem. Organic acids were not measured

	Phloem ($\mu g\ ml^{-1}$)	Xylem ($\mu g\ ml^{-1}$)
pH	7.8–8.0	5.6–5.9
Sucrose	170–196	1.1–1.2
Amino substances	10808	283
Potassium	3673	204
Phosphorus	435	68
Chlorine	486	64
Sulfur	139	43
Magnesium	104	34
Sodium	116	46
Calcium	83	189
Ammonium	45	10
Zinc	16	2
Iron	9	0.6
Copper	1	0.1
Manganese	0.9	0.2
Nitrate	<1	70

the phloem not only large amounts of sucrose but also amino acids are transported, and that this transport is connected with that of several cations (particularly K^+; Herdel et al. 2001).

Figure 2.3.5 shows the multiple interactions between **nutrient uptake** and various organs of plants, using the example of nitrate and its turnover (Marschner 1995). Clearly, transport and retention of a nutrient do not occur independently of other nutrients and are almost always

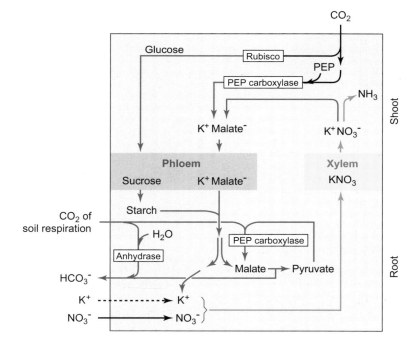

Fig. 2.3.5. Cycling of potassium and the uptake of nitrate in the xylem and phloem. In the phloem K is the counter-ion for transport of malate and sugars. In the root K is released from the phloem and transported into the xylem, where it is the counter-ion for nitrate. Nitrate uptake occurs both by co-transportation with potassium from soil solution, and by an exchange with HCO_3^-. (After Marschner 1995)

Box 2.3.3   Ion uptake (see Marschner 1995)

The following processes lead to the uptake of ions by plants:

- **diffusion:** anion gradient leads to passive transport (example: A1),
- **uniport:** H^+ gradient leads to passive transport via ion channels (K),
- **symport:** H^+ is transported back with anions (Cl, SO_4^{2-}),
- **antiport:** H^+ efflux causes a cation influx (K^+, Ca^{2+}, NH_4^+).

In a plant cell, ion exchange occurs not only on the outer membrane surface, but also at the membranes of plastids and vacuoles. Thus chloroplasts have a characteristically large Mg concentration and mitochondria a large Ca concentration. The vacuole serves as an ion-exchange reservoir. The pH of the cytosol is stabilised by the continuous exchange of cations and/or anions (pH stabilisation mechanism, pH stat). In this, K^+ has a particular part to play in the exchange and regulation of H^+ and thus regulates cellular proton concentration and proton gradients (see also Chap. 1.6.2).

Ion uptake occurs generally through ion channels; these are proteins that span the lipid layers and have an internal passage through which ions can be selectively transported. The selectivity is largely due to the radius of the ion (i.e. K ions pass also through a Ca channel) and amino acids lining the pore that forms the channel. As this is an active, metabolically controlled process, ion uptake is

- **oxygen-dependent;**
- **inhibited by mercury,** if the ion channels are lined with S-containing amino acids;
- **temperature-dependent:** rising exponentially, with an optimum generally at $30\,^{\circ}C$;
- **suited to the external concentration,** i.e. there are ion uptake systems that are most efficient at high or low external ion concentration transporters with a small efficiency for substrate ions can also have a function as sensors (W. Schulze et al. 2000);
- **competition in the presence of other ions:** e.g. the uptake of magnesium falls in the presence of K^+ or Ca^{2+}.

coupled to the transport of organic substances. The initiation of nitrate uptake starts with CO_2 assimilation in the leaf by the enzyme phosphoenolpyruvate-(PEP)-carboxylase, which carboxylates pyruvate to malate. This anion is transported with K^+ via the phloem to the root and there it is decarboxylated to pyruvate and HCO_3^-. This bicarbonate anion is excreted and exchanged with nitrate. Uptake of K^+ occurs simultaneously. Nitrate is transported, together with K^+ as cation, via the xylem into the shoot. With the reduction of nitrate, K^+ is released again and balances the malate transport in the phloem. Simultaneously with K^+ uptake the phloem is also loaded with sucrose (Marschner 1995). Independent of this cycle of potassium, malate may also be formed in the root from starch or via assimilation of CO_2 by PEP-carboxylase. Anhydrases also form HCO_3^- which is used to take up nitrate by antiport (Moroney et al. 2001). As the plant requires more N than K, the soil is also made more alkaline by the nitrate uptake through the exchange with HCO_3^-.

With respect to the **use of nutrients** the following distinctions are made:

- elements transformed in metabolism. They change the level of reduction. N and S belong to this group
- elements which cannot be metabolised but support metabolism. These are:
- freely moving cations (K, Ca, Mg) and anions (PO_4^-) which store energy by polymerisation
- heavy metals with catalytic functions which are bound firmly to proteins and act chemically because of changes in their oxidation state (Fe, Mn, Cu and others).

Analysis of the nutrient balance of the plant shows that a large part of nutrients is continuously exchanged in the plant, i.e. circulated between root and shoot. This applies particularly for individual organs with only a limited **span of life.** Root tips and leaves are periodically or continuously formed anew, utilised transiently and afterwards shed. Obviously, leaves are fixed-term "machines". Old leaves are shed, a response to decreasing physiological activity. At the same time formation and shedding of leaves are mechanisms for adaptation of the whole plant to changing environmental conditions (particularly light). Leaf shedding often serves other functions, e.g. detoxification following excessive salt uptake.

The expanding leaf is first a sink for carbohydrates and nutrients, but trace elements are required for the activation of enzymes earlier than macro nutrients. Organic substances are required for the structure of the leaf. In the young state leaves are thus a carbohydrate sink (see Chap. 2.4.3.6), i.e. "**sink leaves**" import carbohydrates for their growth. The leaf becomes a "**source leaf**" only after the development of about a third of the leaf area, exporting carbohydrates for maintenance or growth at other sites. Even before full development of the leaf's area, its capacity for photosynthesis decreases and finally it becomes unproductive. This process of **leaf ageing** is modified by environmental conditions including nutrition. In contrast to ageing, **senescence** is a genetically regulated process of the fully differentiated cell (Guarente and Kenyon 2000; Thomas et al. 2000). Ageing and senescence finally lead to shedding of leaves, however, before this part of the invested resources of nutrients is remobilised and transported back into the plant. Thus the leaf is a "throughput system" for nutrients, highly adaptable to environmental conditions and the internal requirements of the plant for nutrients. The turnover rate of nutrients in plants may change suddenly depending on the ontogeny of the whole plant, particularly during the change from vegetative to reproductive growth.

2.3.1.4
Nutrient Deficiency and Excess

Nutrient deficiency and excess lead to **plant diseases**, recognisable by typical changes in colour of needles or leaves, and these are important indicators for the diagnosis of nutrient-dependent effects. They are:

- colour changes (browning and yellowing = chlorosis);
- progression of damage on the individual leaf (e.g. dryness starting from the tip);
- progression along the branch (damage starts in old organs);

- presence of pests, as lack of nutrients may be the cause or consequence of biotic stress [e.g. by honey fungus (*Armillaria* spp.) attack];
- nutrient analyses are required to confirm the findings;
- tolerance towards deficiency and excess, and development of symptoms, vary with genotype and are species-specific.

Figure 2.3.6 shows some important nutrient-dependent plant diseases of spruce needles and oak leaves as examples. Regarding SO_2^- and ozone damage, see also Chapter 1.9. The development of symptoms by nutrient deficiency or excess is more marked in evergreen than in deciduous species:

- **nitrogen deficiency**: evenly distributed chlorosis on the whole tree and for all needle ages; small needles, compressed sprouting, growth inhibition. Usually not limited to individual trees. On moor and heathland soils. Possibilities of misidentification: honey fungus (*Armillaria* spp.), but here individual trees or younger needles are turning yellow.
- **manganese deficiency**: light yellow chlorosis of younger needles, starting in the lower canopy, particularly on limestone. Mn is not phloem-mobile, i.e. requirements for growth are only by root uptake, the influx in xylem water. Therefore, with increasing age, symptoms disappear.
- **iron deficiency**: whitish-yellow chlorosis of the youngest needles. Considerable deficiency causing needle tips to brown and die on limestone. Similar to Mn deficiency.
- **potassium deficiency**: pale yellow to violet brown (reddish) colouration starting from needle tips, but at first predominantly on older needles, which are shed prematurely and lead to light canopies. K is phloem-mobile and is thus first re-transported to the youngest organs. K deficiency increases sensitivity to frost. Misidentification: Mg deficiency, but in this case the colouration is more intensely yellow, rarely red.
- **magnesium deficiency**: light yellow to golden yellow chlorosis, starting in older needles from the tip. Shaded branches and the underside of needles are less decolourised. Mg is phloem-mobile and therefore remobilised from old to young needles. Occurs on silicate soils.
- **air pollution (SO₂) damage**: gold-brown to reddish-brown colouration, starting from the

Fig. 2.3.6. Typical nutrient deficiency and damage due to over-availability of nutrients. A Nitrogen deficiency, B manganese deficiency, C iron deficiency, D potassium deficiency, E magnesium deficiency, F SO₂ damage, G NaCl damage, H mild phosphate deficiency, I severe phosphate deficiency. (Hartmann et al. 1988)

Box 2.3.4	**Summary: plant nutrients**

- **Macronutrients** are C, O, H, N, S, P, K, Mg, Ca, Fe;
- **availability** of nutrients is variable and dependent on the original rocks (this determines the texture and the chemical composition), climate (which controls weathering), vegetation (which selectively removes or returns certain elements), and the management of nutrient supply;

- nutrient **uptake** by plants occurs mainly via the roots. Uptake may also occur via shoots (leaves and bark), which is important for aerial pollutants (see Chap. 2.3.2.2);
- dependent on the availability of nutrients or biotic pests, specific **deficiency diseases** may occur, that are recognised by specific symptoms in leaves.

needle tip. Necrotic flecks or bands in the middle part of the needle. Buds often die off. Misidentification: damage from road salt, herbicides (see Chap. 1.9).

- **Road salt damage:** needles of the previous year's growth dark copper-brown in spring, falling in early summer. Buds often fall. Damage along the edge of roads. Misidentification: frost-drought (but here needles light red-brown) or sulfur dioxide.
- **phosphorous deficiency:** starting with dark, blue-green colour (increased formation of chlorophyll), later violet red to copper brown, yellow colouration (anthocyanin), in parts spotty, starting from the edge of the leaf. Misidentification: K deficiency, drought, salt, but then without the violet-red colour.

2.3.2

Nitrogen Nutrition

2.3.2.1
Nitrogen in Plant Metabolism

Nitrogen is the nutrient required in the largest quantity, after carbohydrates, but the huge amount of N_2 in the earth's atmosphere is not directly available to plants.

Plants require nitrogen for:

- amino acids (free amino acids, proteins)
- nucleic acid (DNA)
- heterocyclic and azo-compounds (e.g. pyrrole ring).

The gas N_2 is very inert and thus not directly usable. Nitrogen can only be used in its reduced or oxidised form (NH_4^+ or NO_3^-) or in the organ-

ic form ($-NH_2$). Industrially reduced nitrogen for fertilisers is synthesised by the Haber-Bosch process from N_2 and H_2 at high temperatures and high pressures. In nature the transformation of gaseous N_2 into nitrogen available for plants occurs either in the atmosphere through lightning ($10–40$ mol N m^{-2} year^{-1}) or in the soil by nitrogen-fixing bacteria.

The process of N_2 **fixation** occurs catalytically under anaerobic conditions in root nodules of legumes, for example, or in free-living cyanobacteria (blue green algae; see Marschner 1995). In the primary succession from open soil to a vegetation with a closed nitrogen cycle, there is a stage in where N_2-fixing organisms dominate (see Chap. 3; Fig. 3.2.9). Because of the high-energy requirement for N_2 reduction (and the requirement for P associated with it), these organisms are unable to compete in the later stages of succession, where more nitrogen is available in the oxidised and reduced forms (Read 1993). The nitrogen cycle and the conversion of organic nitrogen to reduced nitrogen are discussed in Chapter 3.3.3. Here we concentrate on N uptake and the turnover in plants.

2.3.2.2
Nitrogen Uptake and Nutrition

Plants gain nitrogen
- from litter and soil solution as
  - amino acids
  - ammonium cation
  - nitrate anion
- from the atmosphere as
  - NH_3, NO or NO_2 gas
  - ammonium cation
  - nitrate anion.

Box 2.3.5   Interactions between nitrogen and carbon metabolism

N and C metabolism are closely intertwined. It starts with photosystem I (PSI) when a surplus of electrons to ferrodoxin not only reduces NADP to NADPH, which is used for CO_2 assimilation, but is also used for nitrate and sulfate reduction (Fig. 2.3.7A). This is important in the N and S cycles (see Chap. 2.3.2.2 and 2.3.3.2).

The main processes involved in the interaction between N and C cycles are (Fig. 2.3.7B):

- production of carbohydrates for root maintenance and growth;
- production of C skeletons for N assimilation;

- influence of N-nutrition on protein metabolism;
- influence of nitrate on the phytohormone balance (especially cytokinin);
- feedback coupling of protein availability and phytohormones on photosynthesis (30% of the N content of a leaf is in the CO_2-fixing enzyme Rubisco; see Chap. 2.3.2.3) and growth (principally of leaves);
- regulation of C-allocation by metabolites of the C cycle and nitrate;
- development is limited by self-shading.

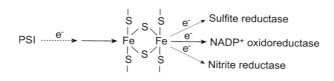

A   Ferredoxin

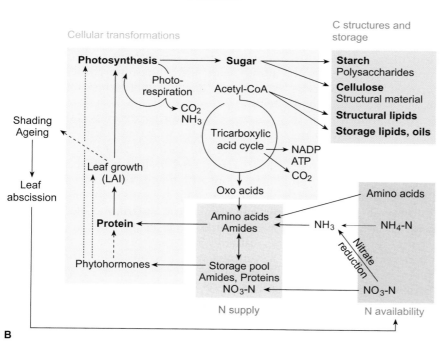

B

Fig. 2.3.7. A Coupling of electron transport from photosystem I (PSI) to sulfite, nitrite, and NADP reduction via ferredoxin. **B** Diagram of the coupling of C and N metabolism in a plant. For a detailed description, see text. (After Marschner 1995)

Amino Acid Uptake and Nutrition

Amino acids are available from N_2 fixation by nitrogen-fixing bacteria, via the direct degradation of litter or from the soil solution (Wallenda et al. 2000). It is known from laboratory experiments that roots are able to take up a broad spectrum of amino acids.

Nutrition with amino acids is very important, particularly in boreal forests, where ammonium- and nitrite-fixing bacteria in the soil are probably not active because of the acute N deficiency (Persson et al. 2000). In these conditions amino acid uptake via mycorrhiza supplies the plant with almost all of its nitrogen requirements. These organisms are able to excrete a protease and thereby break down proteins and use the resulting amino acids directly from the litter (Näsholm et al. 1998; Wallenda 2000). It has been shown (Nordin et al. 2001) that the uptake of amino acids also takes place in the presence of ammonium and nitrate ions and may reach the same level as on poor sites; only the relative contribution to the N requirement is lower, as additional ammonium and nitrate are available and utilised at N-rich sites. At N-deficient sites, plants are adapted to different forms of N nutrition (Schulze et al. 1994; Michelsen et al. 1996).

Ammonium Uptake and Nutrition

Ammonium is taken up directly in the area of the root hair or via mycorrhiza. NH_4^+ would be toxic as an ion, because its ionic radius and strength are very similar to that of K^+, so it could enter the cell instead of K^+, leading to interference with the pH regulation of the cell membrane. Therefore, NH_4^+ taken up by the root is not stored but converted immediately into amino acids via the GOGAT (glutamine–oxoglutamate–amino–transferase) enzyme system. In this process, NH_4^+ is bound to a-ketoglutarate using $NADPH+H^+$. The primary amino acids glutamine and glutamate are formed, which donate the NH_2 group to other organic molecules by transamination and thereby regenerate a-ketoglutarate. GOGAT is the enzyme system which also traps free NH_4^+ ions in all other plant organs.

Ammonium uptake (Fig. 2.3.8; Marschner 1995) occurs generally as antiport to protons released in the assimilation of NH_4^+ to $-NH_2$. The protons are excreted via the root; uptake of ammonium thus leads to acidification of the soil. For NH_4^+ assimilation in the root, organic molecules are required to provide the C-skeletons;

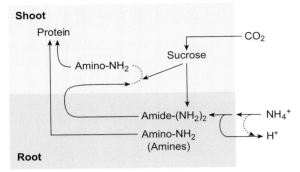

Fig. 2.3.8. Exchange and transport processes in the uptake of ammonium. Protons are released to neutralise ionic charges when NH_4^+ is taken up, i.e. the soil pH decreases (see Fig. 2.3.9 B). Ammonium is immediately assimilated into amino acids in the roots; for this C skeletons have to be transported from the shoot to the root. Ammonium-fed seedlings are deficient in soluble carbohydrates, as the C skeletons are used for assimilation of NH_4^+ in the roots and are thus not available for growth. Detoxification of ammonium leads to a surplus of amino acids, which are not used for protein synthesis, as the assimilates in the roots are required for the assimilation of ammonium ions. (After Marschner 1995)

they are derived from sucrose produced in the leaf and transported, via the phloem, into the root. Because free amino acids act as an osmoticum and could interfere with the metabolism, amino acids and amides are transported via the xylem into the leaf and incorporated into proteins.

Ammonium nutrition is important particularly in acidic soils where nitrification is inhibited and particular cation deficiencies (e.g. Mg, K) may be triggered or increased because of ionic interactions of Mg and NH_4^+.

Nitrate Uptake and Nutrition

Nitrate is taken up by the same area of the root as cations. Some mycorrhiza species also take up nitrate. It is not possible to use nitrate directly in the metabolism, it must first be reduced to $-NH_2$. Nitrate uptake (Fig. 2.3.9; Marschner 1995) occurs either together with cations or in exchange with OH^-. As the requirement for N is larger than that for alkaline cations, the symport with cations is not unlimited. In this case nitrate uptake takes place in exchange with HCO_3^- leading to increased soil pH. Conversely, with nitrate deficiency in the soil, nitrate is missing as anion in the uptake of cations resulting in the uptake of Cl^- and SO_4^{2-} and leading to disturbances in the later metabolism.

Box 2.3.6   Summary: ammonium nutrition

Ammonium nutrition has the following physiological, structural and ecological consequences:

- Supplying only ammonium ions leads to **carbohydrate deficiency**, as C skeletons are largely required for the assimilation and detoxification of ammonium in the root;
- Ammonium nutrition leads to **cation** deficiency (especially Mg deficiency), as the uptake of ammonium results in competitive inhibition of the uptake of other cations;
- In ammonium nutrition Cl^- and SO_4^{2-} are the available ions in the soil which are also taken up by symport, acting as counterions to balance charges. Cl^- can become toxic. SO_4^{2-} can react with other essential cations, especially Ca^{2+}, leading to the formation of the insoluble calcium sulfate and therefore enhancing cation deficiency;
- In the case of ammonium, an excess of **free amino acids** (diamines, e.g. putrescine) occurs. The formation of storage proteins would result in smaller ratio of N to C and therefore an increase in the C deficiency. Formation of amino acids leads to changes in leaf structure; they have a higher water content (as a result of the osmotic effects of amino acids) and lower dry weight per area, making the leaves more susceptible to environmental stress (e.g. temperature and pests and diseases);
- Higher concentration of amino acids leads to a greater **susceptibility of the plant to plant diseases** and pests. Especially damaging are pests that "suck" phloem sap (aphids);
- In the soil (or nutrient solution), feeding ammonium leads to a **reduction in pH**. Ammonium is stored in the soil as an exchangeable ion. This leads to the release of basic cations and heavy metals that are toxic to plant roots (see Chaps. 1.7 and 1.8). Cations are washed out of the soil horizon. Initially, when plants are placed in an ammonium-rich environment, there is an improvement in cation availability (Kreutzer and Göttlein 1991). The high binding affinity of ammonium is used in soil science to determine the cation-exchange capacity (CEC, determination of the exchangeable basic cations by washing with NH_4Cl);
- Ammonium nutrition can, with high cell pH, lead to the release of NH_3 into the atmosphere, as almost half the ammonium at pH 7.2 (cytosolic pH) is already dissociated, i.e. in neutral conditions, half is already present as NH_3. Ammonia (NH_3) is poisonous to cells.

Physiologically, nitrate is not toxic and thus may be stored in the root or shoot. Nitrate storage in the leaf has a regulatory (signal) effect on C allocation (shoot–root growth) of plants (Scheible et al. 1997; Klein et al. 2000). Large nitrate concentration in the leaf stimulates shoot growth and inhibits root growth by regulating the sugar transport to the root whereas in the soil it stimulates root growth.

Generally, nitrate transport is via the xylem into the storage parenchyma of the stem, or into the leaf where nitrate is initially stored together with cations in the vacuole. This increases the osmotic concentration and the water content of leaves (e.g. with "crunchy" nitrate-fertilised vegetables). If required, nitrate may be transported back from the vacuole into the cytosol. This occurs in exchange with organic acids formed via PEP-carboxylase in the leaf. For some plant species, oxalic acid is transported in exchange for nitrate into the vacuole. With a large Ca supply this leads, in the vacuole, to the formation of Ca oxalate which is difficult to dissolve (rhaphides, giving the typical taste of rhubarb and banana peel). Nitrate is reduced to nitrite in the cytosol. In the chloroplast, nitrite is reduced to NH_4^+, which is immediately assimilated by the GOGAT system. The turnover rate of nitrite reductase is faster than that of nitrate reductase, as nitrite is toxic to the cell. Some of the cations taken up with nitrate are transported back into the phloem, particularly K^+ is relocated into the root, accompanied by associated organic acids. These acids are decarboxylated in the root (e.g. malate) and thus support nitrate uptake.

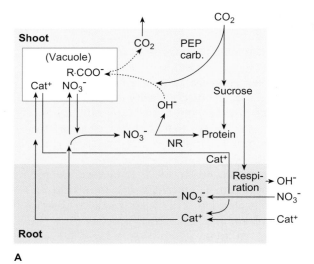

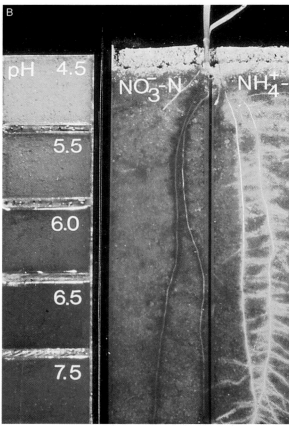

Fig. 2.3.9. A Exchange and transport processes involved in the uptake of nitrate. To balance the charges, OH⁻ ions are released into the soil, i.e. the soil pH rises. Nitrate can be stored in the vacuole until reduction (Marschner 1995). B Changes in soil pH after nitrate or ammonium uptake. Roots of plants were divided between two compartments: in one the N source was nitrate and in the other ammonium. The *yellow colouration* shows the fall in pH in the proximity of the root during ammonium uptake. The *red colour* shows nitrate uptake and the corresponding pH rise. (Photo E. George)

Ammonium Nitrate Nutrition

It becomes clear, from the specific effects of ammonium and nitrate uptake, particularly with respect to the cation uptake, that the uptake of **ammonium nitrate** is most favourable for nutrition. Nutrition with ammonium nitrate

- maintains the **balance of anions and cations** in the plant and in the soil
- **decouples the uptake of cations and anions** from the N nutrition (the N requirement is larger than the requirement for cations)
- **maintains the C/N balance.** The relation of nitrate and free amino acids (in the case of ammonium nutrition) to starch is a sensitive indicator of the state of nutrition in the leaf (Fig. 2.3.10 B). Large nitrate and amino acid concentrations are always connected and indicate too much fertilisation, whilst substantial starch concentrations always correlate with small nitrate and amino acid concentrations and thus indicate N deficiency. Maximum growth rates are achieved under conditions where the nitrate and starch concentration safeguards the supply for growth during the night, as growth and thus the N and C requirement continue during the night, but N and C assimilation requires light.

Nitrogen Input from the Atmosphere

Nitrogen-containing **air pollutants** are taken up as gas (NH_3, NO, NO_2) by the plant via the stomata. NH_3 is more soluble than NO, which in turn is more soluble than NO_2. In the leaf all gases are immediately assimilated to amino acids. Not only gases, but also ions dissolved in rainwater and fog reach the inside of the bark via the medullary rays (Klemm 1989). Dust particles containing Mn on the cortex and cuticle of needles may oxidise gaseous NH_3 and SO_2 to ammonium sulfate in a surface reaction and thus increase N deposits. Uptake of nitrogen from the atmosphere contributes significantly to the N balance for growth in the canopy of trees (20–40% of the N requirements; Harrison et al. 2000).

There is a basic difference between the N uptake via the shoot or the root. Uptake of nitrogen via the root is metabolically regulated, i.e.

Box 2.3.7	Summary: nitrate supply

Nitrate nutrition has the following physiological and ecological effects:

- **Increase in pH in the soil near roots** (Fig. 2.3.9). Nitrate is very mobile and is almost not bound in the soil, so that it is easily leached out and takes with it a corresponding number of basic cations. These are replaced with H^+ on the ion-exchange surfaces and thus, **in the long-term, nitrate leaching leads to soil acidification** (clover and lupins in agriculture). In acidic soils, Al^{3+} (and other heavy metals) can act as cations, and these are also leached into the groundwater; this is not only damaging for the roots but adversely affects the quality of the ground water. Especially in soils with high microbial nitrification and low nitrate uptake rates (e.g. cultivation of spruce on Ca-rich soils), this has a significant effect on the nutrient balance of the ecosystem;
- Occurrence of an equilibrium between cation and anion uptake **without the accumulation of Cl^- or SO_4^{2-}**;
- **Increasing the leaf water content** during storage in the vacuole and formation of Ca-oxalate-rhaphides;
- **Better quantum yields** due to the use of excess electrons from PSI (photosystem I) for nitrate reduction;
- **Re-routing of carbohydrate flows** in the plant. Nitrate is not just a substrate supplying N, but has additional specific "signal effects" in shoot-root communication and allocation of carbohydrates (Scheible et al. 1997). A higher nitrate concentration in the leaf stimulates shoot growth and inhibits root growth by controlling sugar transport into the roots. High nitrate concentrations in the soil stimulate root growth;
- Nitrate has a specific **"signal-effect in germination"**. This is marked in ruderal plants where the presence of nitrate in the soil solution enhances germination;
- **Decoupling of N uptake and N usage**, as nitrate is stored in the vacuole. In contrast to ammonium, nitrate does not damage membranes. Decoupling of uptake and use is significant for growth, for example, in annual plants (cereals) where availability of nitrate is large at the beginning of the growth period and decreases with growth. The consumption of nitrate from the internal store supports seeds maturation. However, even very large nitrate concentrations are not sufficient to maintain long-term growth. A nitrate concentration of 15 mg g^{-1} in leaf cells of *Raphanus sativus* is sufficient to maintain a high growth rate for only 1 day. Then the growth rate drops exponentially. Depending on growth rate, the nitrate pool is used up in 4–10 days (Fig. 2.3.10 A).

the plant takes up nitrogen according to its requirements (or until enough is stored). In contrast to this, the plant has no "defence" mechanisms against uptake of NO_x, NH_3, or NH_4^+ via the shoot. In addition, uptake via the shoot occurs in exchange with cations (K, Mg), i.e. is coupled with a loss of cations. Nitrogen nutrition from air pollutants thus may lead to an imbalance in cations, particularly if cation uptake is limited.

2.3.2.3
Nitrogen Requirements for Growth

Nitrogen nutrition is not only important for plants growing under natural conditions, but also for crops. Here requirements and responses of woody plants are different to those of herbaceous plants; not only the growth form, but also the season determines the requirements for N.

Nitrogen Supply and Growth
Growth is linearly dependent on N supply over a wide range. With ample N this response becomes saturated, but many other environmental factors determine at which nitrogen supply satu-

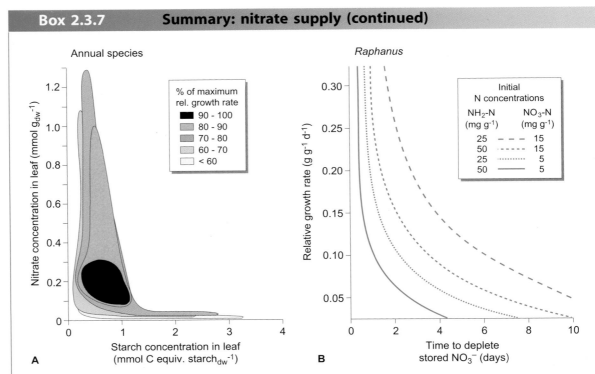

Box 2.3.7   Summary: nitrate supply (continued)

Fig. 2.3.10. A Relative growth rate (RGR, shown as isohypses) in relation to the nitrate and the starch concentration in the leaf. Highest growth rates are in the lower concentrations of the two substances. Starch accumulation is thus an indicator of N deficiency, nitrate accumulation an indicator of C deficiency. B Consumption of nitrate reserves of plants grown with different nutrient conditions, following a sudden decrease in the N availability. Even in plants well supplied with nutrients and with a large nitrate concentration, the supply of nitrate from within the plants lasts only a few days due to their high growth rate. (After Stitt and Schulze 1994)

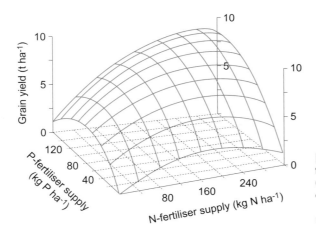

Fig. 2.3.11. Change in the grain yield of maize with different N and P fertilisation. At a high P availability (140 kg P ha^{-1}), 300 kg N ha^{-1} can lead to a high yield. If only 40 kg P ha^{-1} are available then adding only 160 kg N ha^{-1} leads to loss of yield. (Schopfer and Brennicke 1999)

ration is reached (Fig. 2.3.11). With "optimal" supply of other nutrient elements, saturation occurs for agricultural crops at about 200 kg N ha^{-1} a^{-1}. Higher rates of fertilisation yield a small increase of grain, with the benefits of a marginally greater yield determined by the prices of cereals and fertiliser. At the same time, high rates of fertiliser affect the environment by nitrate leaching to ground water. In contrast to the high capacity for N utilisation of crops, consumption by trees is much smaller. If mineralisation exceeds N deposition of about 100 kg N

$ha^{-1} a^{-1}$, beeches and spruce are no longer able to use the available N. This is mainly because the N requirement for production of wood is much less than that for non-lignified tissues. Less than 10% of the nitrogen taken up is used for growth of a tree trunk (Nadelhoffer et al. 1999). This does not take into consideration that 90% of the nitrogen taken up and invested in leaf and branch growth creates the preconditions for the growth of wood by building up the photosynthetic apparatus. However, the biomass of leaves in the canopy may not be increased indefinitely. Maximum leaf area index (LAI) is dependent on the light supply and on structural characteristics such as leaf inclination and leaf clustering (see Chap. 2.1.2.3).

Utilisation of Ammonium and Nitrate

Herbaceous species are better equipped to utilise nitrate than woody species, for many reasons. Herbaceous species usually have smaller dry weights and greater water content per leaf area (Schulze et al. 1994) and are better able to store nitrates because of their larger vacuoles. Because of greater N concentration in the mesophyll (and thus concentration of the CO_2-reducing enzyme Rubisco), herbaceous plants usually have faster rates of photosynthesis and thus an increased capacity for nitrate reduction than woody plants (see Fig. 2.3.7 in Box 2.3.5). A further basic difference is the association of roots of herbaceous plants with VA (vesicular arbuscular) **mycorrhiza** and ectomycorrhiza in woody plants. VAM are able to utilise mineralised P and ectomycorrhiza (Smith and Read 1997) are able to gain amino acids from litter; thus they bypass mineralisation (Wallenda et al. 1999). Ectomycorrhiza are also able to take up ammonium in acid soils, as they precipitate the Al with phosphate. There are also mycorrhiza which reduce nitrate (Wallenda et al. 1999). The distinction, whether plants utilise nitrate, ammonium or amino acids, is partly possible via stable isotopes (Hobbie et al. 2000). The N requirement for growth (C/N relation) of fungi is higher than the N requirement of trees, as the cell wall of fungi consists of chitin (50 mg N g^{-1} dry matter for fungi and 1 mg N g^{-1} dry matter for wood). However, there are exceptions: Ash uses large amounts of nitrate but does not possess any mycorrhiza. In trees the nitrate is reduced in mycorrhiza or roots, so that nitrate can no longer be detected in the xylem water.

Stress Tolerance with Nitrogen Deficiency

In ecology a theory has developed that species with a high material turnover are stress-sensitive and those with a low turnover are stress-tolerant (Orians and Solbrig 1977; see Fig. 2.4.5). This could, however, not be shown for N supply and its interaction with growth (Fichtner and Schulze 1992). Species adapted to high N supply, e.g. *Galeopsis tetrahit* (common hemp-nettle, Labiatae on eutrophicated sites), reduce growth with reduced supply as do species adapted to N-poor sites, e.g. *Teesdalia nudicaulis* (shepherd's cress, Cruciferae, on sandy lawns). The important difference between the two species is that *Teesdalia* flowers at low N supply, but not *Galeopsis* (see also Chap. 2.4.5).

2.3.2.4
Nitrogen Storage

In all natural systems nitrogen is a limiting nutrient. It is therefore to be expected that storage of the nitrogen takes place in different organs and at different times. Nitrogen is stored in various forms:

- as **organic nitrogen** in the vacuole, only in the form of nitrate and together with cations. This storage bridges the changing requirements during the day-night rhythm of growth as well as changing seasonal nitrogen supply.
- as **organically bound nitrogen**. Stored in the form of amino acids, lipids and proteins. Most of these substances have further functions, i.e. storage is a by-product of metabolism, and of imbalance in production and consumption of certain materials.
- as **amino acids**. They serve as storage and transport form for N. Amino acids have an osmotic function and therefore particularly those with several -NH_2 or -NH groups are stored [glutamine (2N/4C), asparagine (2N/4C), arginine (4N/6C), allantoin (4N/4C)]. Storage is short-term to seasonal and occurs in the phloem–xylem cycle or in the vacuoles of the storage parenchyma of stems. Some of the amino acids not only have a storage function, but also protect against frost and salt in winter (proline, Chaps. 1.3.6 and 1.6.2.3). The storage amino acids play an important ecological role in sprouting and growth of young leaves in spring. About 60% of the N content of a beech leaf originates from storage in the

Box 2.3.8   Insectivorous plants

"Carnivorous" or **insectivorous** plant species are found in areas which are particularly deficient in nutrients. They have adapted by changing their leaves in various ways to organs which act as traps and are suitable for trapping insects and at the same time excrete proteases and chitinases that digest them (Fig. 2.3.12 A). They are differentiated into:

- spring traps (e.g. *Dionaea*);
- pitfall traps (e.g. *Nepenthes*);
- sticky traps (e.g. *Drosera*);
- suction traps (e.g. *Utricularia*).

These types have evolved in very different taxonomic groups (Fig. 2.3.12 B). Often the same trap types occur in geographically and taxonomically distinct regions (pitfall traps in *Nepenthes*: Indonesian islands; *Sarracenia*: eastern USA, *Darlingtonia*: western USA; *Cephalotus*: SW Australia).

The effectiveness of insect capture can be measured using stable ^{15}N isotopes, as insects have a higher ^{15}N value, depending on their trophic level, than soil N (Table 2.3.3; Schulze et al. 1991; W. Schulze et al. 1997).

Roridula gorgonias (South Africa) is a special case as it does not excrete proteases. The sticky leaves catch insects, but they are harvested by bugs (Hemiptera) which are adapted to life on the sticky trap and move slowly and carefully. The excrement of the bugs is used by the *Roridula* as N source (Ellis and Midgley 1996).

Nepenthes takes nitrogen from the trapped insects in the form of ammonium which is absorbed via glands (W. Schulze et al. 1997) where amino acids are formed before transport to the bundle sheath. There polypeptides are formed (a N concentration mechanism), and then loaded into the phloem. In young *Nepenthes* shoots 100% of the N content originates from trapped insects. In Venus flytraps (*Dionaea*) survival depends on the seedlings being able to trap insects (W. Schulze et al. 2001). Only after a significant catch can the larger spring traps develop that are suited to catch larger insects; only the rosette is capable of flowering.

Table 2.3.3. The contribution of insects N to the N nutrition of insectivorous plants. (W. Schulze et al. 2001)

Trap type	Genus	Growth form	Proportion of insect in plant N (%)
Sticky trap	*Drosera*	Rosette	20 (e.g. *D. erythrorhiza*, Western Australia)
		Climber	53 (e.g. *D. macrantha*, Western Australia)
		Upright, low	48 (e.g. *D. stolonifera*, Western Australia)
		Upright, high	54, (e.g. *D. gigantea*, Western Australia)
	Roridula	Shrub	70
Pitfall trap	*Cephalotus*	Rosette	26
	Nepenthes	Climber	62 (100% in buds)
	Darlingtonia	Rhizome	76
	Heliamphora	Rhizome	79
	Brocchinia	Erect rosette	59
Spring trap	*Dionaea*	Rosette	80

stem. In the xylem of spruce, amino acid concentrations are greater than 100 mmol/l (Kummetz 1996) during the emergence of new needles.

- as **polypeptides and proteins**. They are formed when the osmotic activity of amino acids may interfere with metabolism, for example, during the loading of phloem the number of molecules must be decreased and N must be concentrated

in a few molecules (Schulze et al. 1999). Important storage proteins, e.g. prolamine, glutelin, and albumin, accumulate in seeds but these proteins are also some of the proteins required in metabolism and have additional storage and protective functions. The CO_2-reducing enzyme Rubisco (ribulose-bis-phosphate-carboxylase/oxygenase) forms about 30% of the N content of a leaf. Only a proportion of this pro-

Box 2.3.8   Insectivorous plants (continued)

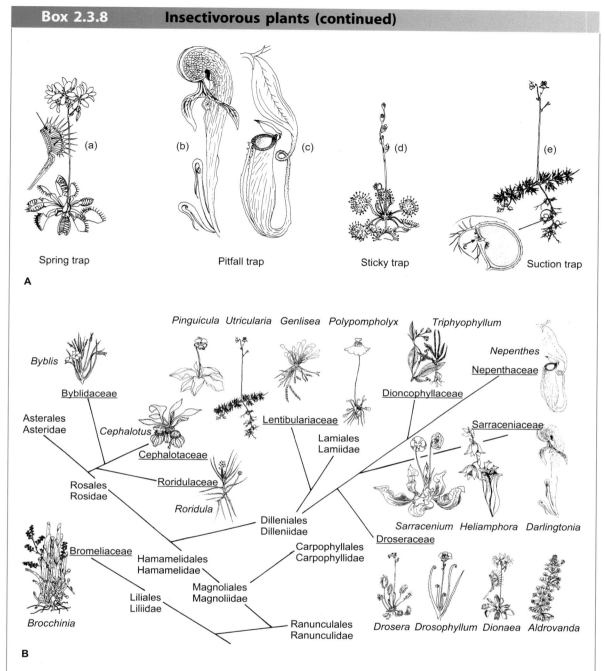

Fig. 2.3.12. A Different forms of leaf used to capture insects. Spring traps: *Dionaea muscipula*, pit-fall trap: *Darlingtonia californica* and *Nepenthes* spp., sticky traps: *Drosera* spp., suction traps: *Utricularia* spp. **B** Distribution of insectivorous plants in angiosperms. (From W. Schulze 1991)

tein is normally active, the excess serving to safeguard the photosynthetic apparatus at high photon flux, or a proportion may be degraded during N deficiency and used for growth (Stitt and Schulze 1994). Before leaves are shed, part of this nitrogen is degraded and the amino acids re-translocated back to the plant. This re-mobilisation of nitrogen from leaves comprises about 20% of the leaf N (Chapin and Kedrovski 1983; Koch et al. 1988).

• as **glucosides**. These plant poisons serve as protection against herbivory and may be transported to sites of growth or metabolised, serving as N storage.

2.3.2.5
Signs of N Deficiency and N Excess

N deficiency and N excess are shown by the following characteristics:

• **N deficiency**: Yellowing, reduction of growth of shoots and leaves, high dry weight/leaf area, starch accumulation, premature ageing and shedding of leaves. Note: Yellowing of leaves is not very specific and is often also caused by deficiency of other nutrients and degradation of chlorophyll. The nitrogen cation imbalance determines deficiency and excess.
• **N excess**: High chlorophyll contents, high water content, low dry weight/area (shade leaf type), nitrate and amino acid storage, long internodes.

Because of the rapid and substantial alterations in N supply with changing conditions in time and location it is very time- and resource-consuming to quantify the N supply. In contrast to nitrate, which is not bound to a soil exchanger and can thus be measured in soil solution, quantifying the exchangeable ammonium in litter is difficult. Ellenberg (1986) suggested, in order to characterise the supply of nitrogen at a particular site, that it would be possible to derive the supply from different sources from the species distribution, i.e. each species is classified by a relative scale, with a range of 1–5 to 1–9 of the so-called **indicator values** (Box 2.3.9). Conversely, it is possible to draw conclusions about the occurrence of a species from the supply of resources. However, this is only possible within the original areas where the plant occurred, as the interaction with other species changes the occurrence and thus the indicator value of a particular species (see Chap. 4).

Box 2.3.9   Indicator plants

Indicator plants are defined as follows (see also Chap. 4.3.3.4):

• About 2000 vascular plants in central Europe occur with varying frequency in different habitats and are classified into particular classes and locations. This classification is also applied to mosses and lichens;
• The classification is based on three climatic factors (light, temperature, continentality) and four soil factors (N availability, soil pH, soil water content and salinity). A classification of species in relation to P-supply is being developed;
• Class values are the so-called indicator values and should allow a general characterisation of a site, without additional analysis in a laboratory;
• The classes rise from 1 (small) to 9 (large);
• Indicator values are not a measured value only, but based on expert knowledge. They are extrapolated from the normal behaviour of a species in its natural environment, i.e. they do not characterise the physiological requirements but the ecological niches that they occupy. Thus they apply only in areas where the initial floristic analysis was performed.

As **nitrogen indicator** they serve in the following way:

• N1: species that only occur in nitrogen-poor environments, e.g. *Trifolium arvense*, *Erophila verna*, *Calluna vulgaris*;
• N2 and N3 species which occur more often in N-poor than on N-rich locations e.g. *Medicago sativa*, *Equisetum arvense*;
• N4 and N5 types of species, occurring in moderate to rich locations but only infrequently on N-poor locations, e.g. *Ribes nigrum*, *Primula vulgaris*;
• N6 and N7 species only flourish on N-rich locations, e.g. *Chenopodium album*;
• N8 species are special N indicators, e.g. *Mercurialis annua*, *Urtica urens*, *Epilobium angustifolium*, *Ballota nigra*;
• N9 species occurring in extremely high N-rich locations, e.g. *Chenopodium bonus-henricus*, *Lamium album*, *Sambucus nigra*.

Box 2.3.10   Summary: nitrogen

The nitrogen economy can be summarised as follows:

- **Nitrogen** is second only to carbon in importance for plant life. Under natural conditions, most plants are subject to nitrogen deficiency;
- **N uptake** occurs from the soil or from the air as ammonium, nitrate, amino acids, or as gaseous NH_3 or NO_x. A number of specialised plants can, together with symbiotic microorganisms, form nodules; these microorganisms assimilate N_2 from the air and change it into ammonia;
- **Ammonia and ammonium** ions are toxic for cells and are rapidly assimilated into amino acids. Ammonium uptake leads to acidification of the soil, C imbalance and cation deficiency.

- The uptake of **nitrate** is coupled with cation uptake in most cases. This leads to increasing pH (alkanisation) in the soil; where nitrate is in excess there is long-term acidification of the soil due to cation leaching, as nitrate cannot be stored in the soil;
- **Indicator plants** allow an assessment of the average N availability of sites;
- **Nitrogen deficiency** leads to specialised adaptations of plants to capture mainly insects and use them as N sources. Nitrogen deficiency can be beneficial in environments which are cation deficient, as the requirement for cations is reduced. With poor N availability there are no signs of cation deficiency syndrome (e.g. in boreal forests).

2.3.3

Sulfur Nutrition

2.3.3.1
Sulfur in Plant Metabolism

Sulfur is a macro-nutrient element which can be metabolised and is available:

- in oxidised form as
  - SO_4^{2-} **ion**: sulfolipid (ester binding of SO_4 to a sugar lipid); occurs in all membranes
  - **-S-S or -S-O group**, occurs in species-specific secondary metabolites, e.g. alliin in *Allium*, isothiocyanate R-N-C-S in Brassicaceae. These substances serve as S storage and protection against herbivory.
- in reduced form as **-SH groups**
  - in **amino acids** (cysteine, cystine, methionine)
  - as **co-enzyme** (acetyl-S-enzyme protein: acetyl-CoA)
  - as non-peptide unit making a functional protein (**prosthetic group**): ferredoxin, thiamine, biotin
  - in **proteins to form the tertiary structure**
  - in **cellular redox systems for regulation of pH** ($R1-SH+R2-SH \rightarrow R1-S-S-R2+H_2$), particularly with participation of glutathione

  - in proteins to **bind heavy metals** (heavy metal resistance; see Chap. 1.7). In particular, cysteine participates in many ion channels and is thus sensitive to heavy metal binding
  - glutathione cycle to **detoxify radicals**.

Sulfur Metabolism

Sulfate is activated by ATP (Fig. 2.3.13) and adenosine phosphatesulfate (APS) is formed. This substance is transformed, either by formation of phosphoadenine-phosphosulfate (PAPS) into the sulfate ester metabolism to give, for example, sulfolipids, or serves as a substrate for sulfur reduction, with the reduced sulfur deposited as thiol groups in C-skeletons (usually an amino acid, e.g. glutathione) synthesised via a sulfotransferase. The S-reduction occurs in the chloroplast, where ferredoxin transfers the electrons to oxidised sulfur. The SH-group is transferred to acetylserine which is split into acetate and cysteine. Cysteine is the starting point for the formation of all organic molecules with an SH-group, and thus makes plants sensitive to heavy metals (see also Chap. 1.9).

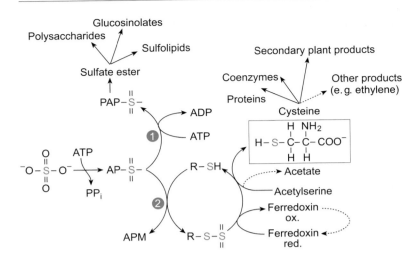

Fig. 2.3.13. Schematic representation of the assimilation of sulfur into various plant metabolites. *ATP* Adenosine triphosphate; *PAPS* phosphoadenine-phosphosulfate; *APS* adenosine phosphosulfate; *APM* adenosine phosphomalate; *1* sulfate esterase; *2* sulfate reductase. (After Marschner 1995)

2.3.3.2
Sulfur Uptake and Plant Requirements

Sulfur is **taken up** as SO_4^{2-} anion in symport with cations. Sulfate is the most important additional anion, next to nitrate, in plant nutrition. Reduction of the sulfate anion to -SH occurs in the chloroplast, via sulfite utilising the electron flow from PS I (see Fig. 2.3.7). With calcium, sulfate forms salts (gypsum) which are difficult to dissolve so it cannot be stored in its inorganic form in the vacuole, but sulfate is bound to organic molecules.

Generally, the requirement for N also regulates the demand for S, as the N/S ratio of proteins is approximately constant (10:1). Only in some plant families does the S requirement increase due to secondary metabolism. This applies particularly to Cruciferae, where mustard oil (glucosinolates) provides protection against herbivory, but also serves as S deposition. Rape belongs to those plants able to grow well with very high S-supply. As a part of the mustard oil is volatile, these plants are also able to remove S via stomata. The S-requirement is also large in Leguminosae, particularly because of the S-containing storage proteins in seeds.

Sulfur is not only taken up via the roots but also via the shoot. This applies particularly to SO_2, which enters the intercellular spaces together with CO_2 (the chemistry of SO_2 turnover is explained in Chapter 1.9.2.1). SO_2 is soluble in the cell wall with formation of the toxic sulfite anion which follows the pH gradient reaching the chloroplast where it is assimilated. In general, SO_2 is oxidised to SO_4^{2-} by heavy metals in

the cuticle and in the cell wall, particularly by Mn which is assimilated in the mesophyll in the same way as sulfate is taken up by the roots. Part of the sulfate reacts in the cell wall with Ca and forms gypsum. Photosynthesis of damaged and undamaged spruce needles is not dependent on their S content, even at very large S contents (Lange et al. 1989). Obviously, the toxic sulfite formed from SO_2 is immediately reduced and sequestered in amino acids. In addition, the mass balance shows that most of the sulfur in a needle does not originate from SO_2, but from the uptake of **sulfate** from the soil solution (Köstner et al. 1998): 97% of S in the xylem was transported in the form of sulfate taken up by roots (Table 2.3.4). Only 15% of the S available in a tree originates from above-ground uptake. This demonstrates that the **forest damage** observed in the 1980s was not classical damage from smoke-SO_2, but indirectly caused by sulfate input and acidification of soils (Schulze et al. 1989; Ulrich 1995). Sulfate stress in the canopy, by uptake from the soil, is about a third greater

Table 2.3.4. Transport of S in the xylem of trees and from the atmosphere in healthy and damaged spruce forests (Köstner et al. 1998); given in mmol m^{-2} soil year^{-1}

	Healthy stand	Damaged stand
Transport in xylem		
Sulfate	25.9	34.7
Glutathione	0.52	0.47
Cysteine	0.14	0.14
Methionine	0.3	0.3
Uptake of SO_2	7.4	7.6
Total S load for the canopy	34.26	43.21

> ## Box 2.3.11   Summary: sulfur balance
>
> - **Sulfur** is required in the plant in the oxidised form (sulfate ester) as well as in the reduced form (-SH-groups of amino acids);
> - **Sulfate reduction** occurs in chloroplasts;
>
> - Even with high anthropogenic S-input, uptake occurs predominantly in the form of sulfate via the roots;
> - Requirement for S is very different for various plant species. Cruciferae have particularly high requirements.

---

in damaged than in undamaged stands (concerning damage to forests, see Chaps. 1.9.2 and 3.5.1).

2.3.3.3
Indicators of Sulfur Deficiency and Excess

- **Deficiency:** symptoms are similar to S deficiency (chlorosis), accumulation of non-S-containing amino acids (arginine, aspartate), inhibition of protein synthesis.
- **excess:** high SO_2 stress leads to the well-known pollution (smog) damage. Lichens are particularly sensitive. The damage is caused by the formation of sulfite and accumulation in the chloroplast. The threshold for SO_2 damage is 5 $\mu g \, m^{-3}$ as average concentration in the air.

2.3.4

Phosphate Nutrition

2.3.4.1
Phosphorus in Plant Metabolism

Phosphorus is the central element in the **energy metabolism** of all living organisms; in this process, storage and transfer of chemical energy by formation and degradation of polyphosphate esters with adenosine take place. Phosphorus is not reduced, in contrast to nitrogen and sulfur, but remains in the highest oxidation state and is esterified in this form. It is taken up as $H_2PO_4^-$. In the cell phosphorus is available in this form (P_i) and binds as PO_4^{3+} to carbohydrates forming simple phosphate esters (C-O-P, e.g. in sugar phosphate) or forming energy-rich pyrophosphate (P–P bonds) or diester bridges between carbohydrate groups (C-P-C).

Structural functions: P participates in the formation of

- RNA as a bridge between the ribose-N bases
- phospholipids of membranes.

Metabolic functions:

- **energy storage and transfer** by polyphosphate esters with adenosine. Di- and triesters are the actual energy storage in the cell (adenosine monophosphate, AMP; adenosine diphosphate, ADP; adenosine triphosphate, ATP)
- **energising of binding sites** for metabolic turnover. Sugar phosphates (e.g. fructose-1,6-diphosphate) play a decisive role in the regulation of sugar metabolism and triosephosphates are an important transport metabolite between chloroplast and cytosol (Stitt 1994).

2.3.4.2
Phosphate Uptake and Plant Requirements

In many habitats, phosphate is a limiting factor for plants because of its low solubility in alkaline conditions (Ca phosphates, apatite) and acidic conditions (Al phosphates, goethite). In the sea, phosphorus accumulates in the trophic levels. Sea birds bring this phosphorus to land: Bird excrement (guano) as the primary source for P fertiliser (for discussion of import nutrients from the sea to islands, see Erskine et al. 1998). Phosphate does not dissolve easily in soils and leaching hardly occurs, in contrast to nitrate which dissolves easily. Root hairs provide good contact with soil particles and the phosphate is dissolved because root hairs secrete protons and organic acids. Mycorrhiza play an important role in dissolving phosphate from minerals and are additionally very important in primary phosphate uptake. After the uptake of phosphoric acid this is directly bound to organic molecules and thus "protected" from transport back into

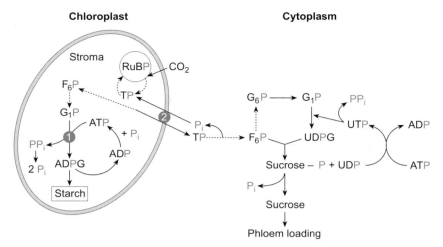

Fig. 2.3.14. The involvement of phosphate in the synthesis of starch and sucrose, and regulation of metabolism by phosphate: ADP-glucose-pyrophosphorylase regulates starch synthesis: inhibition by P_i and stimulation by PGA (*1*). Phosphate translocation regulates the export of photosynthetically produced substrates from the chloroplast: stimulation by P_i and TP (triosephosphate) (*2*). F_6P Fructose-6-phosphate; G_6P glucose-6-phosphate. (After Marschner 1995)

Box 2.3.12	Summary: phosphate balance

- Phosphate serves as the carrier of chemical energy in the plant;
- Phosphate is not reduced in plants, but used in polyphosphate esters.

---

the soil solution. Despite this, transport in the xylem is as P_i.

P_i occurs in the cell as substrate, as well as product, in all activations and enzyme reactions with ATP and ADP and simultaneously regulates many enzyme reactions. Because of this important physiological activity, the concentration of P_i in the cytosol is regulated in a very narrow range, 4–6 mmol l^{-1}, the vacuole serves as storage site. The relative concentration of P_i in the cytosol and chloroplasts regulates (together with the concentration of sucrose in the cytosol) the formation of starch in the chloroplast (Fig. 2.3.14).

Phosphate is stored in plants in the form of polyphosphates or as sugar esters; in **phytate** up to six phosphate molecules may be deposited on one sugar (myoinositol). This form of storage is very important in seeds.

2.3.4.3
Indicators of Phosphorus Deficiency and Excess

- **Deficiency:** interference in reproductive processes (delay in flowering), reduced longitudinal growth, dwarfing, smaller leaves because

of reduced cell growth, increased root growth, dark green colouration of leaves and reddish colouring of needles with chlorosis and premature ageing.
- **excess:** does not occur naturally because phosphate is not easily dissolved and may be regulated by polyphosphate formation.

2.3.5
Nutrition with Alkaline Cations

The alkaline cations potassium, magnesium and calcium are essential macro nutrients which are not metabolised, but are essential to provide the correct environment for particular reactions, to regulate pH and in regulation of cellular water relations.

2.3.5.1
Magnesium

Function
Similar to other alkaline cations, magnesium is not metabolised and it is therefore difficult to determine its actual function.

Structural function of Mg:

- in the structure of chlorophyll (central atom of four pyrrole rings)
- in the cross-connections of cellulose fibrils in the cell wall

Metabolic functions of Mg:

- stabilising enzymes, predominantly during the turnover of phosphates (nitrogenase, ATPase, phosphorylase, and others). In these processes Mg binds to phosphate and, because of allosteric interactions, binding between substrate and phosphate becomes possible
- stabilising energy-rich bonds, e.g. phytate as phosphate storage
- Mg regulates the proton gradient in the stroma of chloroplasts in ATP synthesis and thus determines the pH in the chloroplast (pH 7.6 in the dark and 8 with illumination)
- osmoregulation and pH regulation in the cell, as antagonist to Ca and K.

Uptake and Requirement

In the soil magnesium is bound to the substrate predominantly as an exchangeable cation. Mg is a component of primary and secondary minerals (serpentine) from which it is released by weathering. The uptake of magnesium is particularly antagonistically influenced by ammonium. The most important antagonist for Mg is Ca, but also NH_4^+, K, Mn and even H^+ influence the uptake of Mg.

In the plant magnesium is transported in the xylem and phloem and the ion is stored in chloroplasts. Remobilisation from ageing leaves occurs.

Deficiency and Excess

With Mg deficiency and excess the following symptoms occur:

- **Mg deficiency:** yellowing of older leaves, yellow tips and early shedding of needles, chlorosis because of inadequate chlorophyll synthesis, starch accumulation because of the effect on phosphate metabolism, water relations affected because of poor osmoregulation, dwarf growth.
- **Mg excess:** on Mg-rich substrates (serpentine) because of interactions with other nutrients. Water stress may lead to increased concentrations of Mg.

2.3.5.2
Calcium

Function
Structural function of Ca:

- stabilising cell wall together with Mg
 Metabolic functions of Ca:
- Ca^{2+} is toxic and only transported in the cytosol as bound proteins
- interaction with phytohormones (IAA) in elongation of cells (calmodulin)
- interactions with ABA
- activator of membrane-bound enzymes (amylase) and ATPases of ion channels
- osmoregulation (shrinking)
- Ca functions in the mitochondria, in contrast to Mg which regulates the proton gradient predominantly in chloroplasts.

Uptake and Requirement
Ca occurs in the soil solution as Ca^{2+}; a distinction must be made for "Ca-rich" and "Ca-poor" soils. Calcium-rich soils are predominantly found on limestone. The pH of these soils with almost unlimited $CaCO_3$ is stabilised by the dissolution of $CaCO_3$ at about pH 7. In Ca-poor soils, $CaCO_3$ is quickly consumed because it dissolves easily and is not stable against weathering, so that the dissolved Ca^{2+} is only bound to the ion exchangers of the soil after the dissolution of the carbonate. The pH of Ca-poor soils is usually around pH 5, but may sink on acidic rocks (shales containing pyrite) to 3.5. Below a pH of 5.5 the chemistry of the soil is increasingly determined by aluminium. Ca uptake at the root is antagonistically influenced by other cations, particularly Al. If Al instead of Ca is incorporated into the cell wall, elongation growth is inhibited.

Ca uptake occurs in symport with anions, particularly nitrate, and in acidic soils with sulfate and occurs predominantly at the root tip, where the endodermis is not yet formed, as transport into the xylem via the cell wall is possible there. Ca is transported in the xylem, but is absent from the phloem where, because of the high pH, Ca would react with phosphate forming insoluble apatite. Thus Ca is transported in the phloem only in bound form (Ca protein binding, e.g. calmodulin). Ca is stored in cell walls and vacuoles together with malate, where Ca-oxalate, Ca-sulfate or Ca-carbonate may be formed by precipitation. High Ca concentrations also occur in the endoplasmic reticulum.

Box 2.3.13   Mg deficiency in combination with forest die-back

Mg deficiency was found to be particularly prominent in combination with **forest die-back**, the so-called "mountain yellowing", diagnosed as magnesium deficiency (Zech and Popp 1983). Lange et al. (1989) showed in a simple and impressive experiment that mountain yellowing was not caused by air-borne pollutants (SO₂, ozone; Fig. 2.3.15): On spruce twigs with yellowed needles buds were left either intact or they were removed so that no further growth could occur. On twigs on the opposite side of the same branch it was observed later that only the needles on twigs with buds yellowed. In contrast needles on the shoots without buds were green. The experiment showed that magnesium availability from the xylem was sufficient to fulfil the requirement of a non-growing shoot but was inadequate to supply growing shoots. From this

the question arose as to what factors control growth. Oren and Schulze (1989) were able to show that there is an interaction with the N supply, the unregulated uptake of nitrogen having a particular growth effect on the canopy. Uptake leads not only to dis-equilibrium between N supply and cation uptake, but also has the effect of causing cation loss during the uptake of ammonium ions (Klemm 1989). The low supply of magnesium which trees take up from the soil is further reduced by an antagonism to ammonium, the main nitrogen form in sulfate-contaminated soils (Kaupenjohann et al. 1989). The high ammonium concentration of the soil solution leads to an exchange of ammonium against Al^{3+} on the clay particles, and to Al contamination of the soil water, which may lead to root damage (Ulrich 1995).

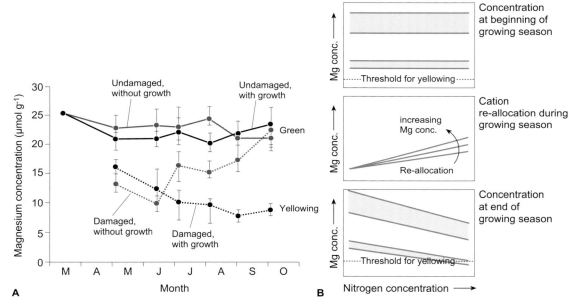

Fig. 2.3.15. A The yearly change (*x*-axis) in magnesium concentration of spruce twigs, that prior to treatment had Mg deficiency symptoms, compared with healthy green twigs. In the damaged and undamaged twigs, buds were either removed and thus growth was halted, or buds were maintained unchanged. Damaged side shoots without buds showed an increase in the Mg concentration during the year and were green at the end of the growing season. This experiment was decisive in showing that yellowing of spruce on silicate soils was not a direct consequence of SO₂ but of the interaction between growth and Mg supply. The Mg deficiency is also clearly visible on the spruce canopy on the title page to Chapter 2.3. Changes in magnesium concentration with N concentration in twigs of spruce before emergence (*top picture*), translocation of Mg from old to new needles (*centre picture*), and after emergence of young needles (*bottom picture*). The change is shown in twigs with high and low Mg supply. Only high N availability and low Mg supply crosses the threshold that leads to yellowing. (After Oren and Schulze 1989)

Box 2.3.14   Indicator plants for soil conditions (for lime and silica indicating plants, see Chap. 4.2.3)

The **reaction number** is a qualitative indicator of soil pH:

- R1+R2: strong acid indicators, never occur on slightly acidic to alkaline soils, e.g. *Scleranthus annuus, Rumex acetosella, Spergula vernalis*;
- R3+R4: acid indicators, mainly on acidic soils, but also occupy soils of neutral pH, e.g. *Raphanus raphanistrum, Stachys arvense, Anthemis arvense*;

- R5+R6: moderate acid indicators, seldom occur on strongly acidic or on neutral to alkaline soils, e.g. *Sinapis arvensis, Veronica persica, Fumaria officinalis*;
- R7+R8: weak acidic to weak basic indicators, never occur on strongly acid soils, e.g. *Aconitum napellus, Arctium lappa, Corydalis cava*;
- R9: base and lime indicators, only occur on chalky soils, e.g. *Delphinium consolida, Adonis aestivalis*.

Ca reaches the leaf in the xylem stream, but may only be transported out via the phloem if bound to proteins, resulting in an excess of Ca in the leaf and accumulation over time. This becomes obvious from the Ca content of leaves which rises with age and is particularly striking in conifers with needles of different age (Oren et al. 1988).

The function of Ca as stabiliser of the primary wall, by binding to pectin, becomes important in elongation growth which essentially depends on the presence of Ca. However, Ca has further functions in growth ranging from the formation of callose to the secretion of the calyptra and the regulation of geotropism. By forming bridges between phosphate and carboxyl groups of phospholipids, Ca maintains the membrane structure.

Deficiency and Excess

Ca deficiency and excess lead to the following reactions:

- **Ca deficiency**: disturbed growth by inhibition of cell division, desiccation of tips and buds, death of root tips and chlorosis of needle tips. Ca deficiency is possible during ripening of fruits and in organs which grow fast but transpire little (bulbs, tubers, tap roots, etc.), as Ca is not transported in the phloem. In fruits, Ca deficiency leads to increased susceptibility to fungal attack.
- **Ca excess**: occurrence of Ca-oxalate, Ca-sulfate and Ca-carbonate. Grasses generally require less Ca than dicotyledons. Low Ca requirements and adverse reactions to high Ca supply also occur in "calcifuge" plants which

are not able to maintain compartmentation of large amounts of Ca (see Chap. 3.5.3).

2.3.5.3
Potassium

Function

Potassium is the most required nutrient in plants (2–5% dry weight) after nitrogen.

Structural functions (no direct involvement in chemical reactions):

- pH regulation
- enzyme activation by changing the conformation of proteins (ATPase)
- influencing protein synthesis (translation, synthesis of RuBP-carboxylase)
- osmoregulation and elongation growth of cells, interacting with IAA and GA
- tropism and movement (stomata regulation)
- phloem transport.

These metabolic functions of potassium cannot be replaced by Na (the most important cation in animals) and NaCl leads to salt stress in plants (Chap. 1.6); however, the osmotic function of K may be replaced by Na, Mg and Ca. The K concentration is high in the cytosol and low in the apoplast (except in movements and tropism: osmotically regulated movement, e.g. of stomata). Transport through the membrane is via K channels.

Besides the general physiological importance of potassium in enzyme activation and protein synthesis it is particularly important in the following processes:

Box 2.3.15   Mistletoes as nutrient parasites

Mistletoes are heterotrophic phloem parasites (leaves without chlorophyll) as well as autotrophic xylem parasites (with green leaves). Xylem parasites have been known for their medicinal use since Hippocrates' time, and not just since Asterix and Getafix. Their alkaloids and lectins (carbohydrate-binding proteins) have major pharmaceutical relevance in the treatment of tumours (Luther and Becker 1987).

Mistletoes are of botanical interest (Calder and Bernhardt 1983) as they have a high potassium concentration in their leaves (40 mg g^{-1}). In hyperparasitic plants (mistletoe growing on mistletoe) an additional accumulation of K and other cations may occur (157 mg g^{-1} Na in arid locations; Ehleringer and Schulze 1985) because the mistletoe takes up the xylem water with the cations which accumulate in the shoot, as there is no connection and re-circulation to the host's phloem. This accumulation of salt can lead to leaf damage and abscission.

In mistletoe it is particularly significant that despite the high, almost toxic, ion concentrations they maintain higher transpiration rates than the host (Ehleringer et al. 1985). Thus, mistletoes are not only significant sinks for cations but they are also water parasites. Under field conditions it is particularly interesting that even at high ion concentration and even under arid conditions mistletoes do not control transpiration but apparently metabolise the ABA entering them in the xylem water. The controlling factor is their nitrogen requirement. Schulze et al. (1984) showed that N requirement is the limiting factor for mistletoes and a high water requirement is needed to provide the N as mistletoes are characterised by substantial seed production. If mistletoe grows on a N_2-fixing plant, then transpiration rate is often not so large as on host plants that do not fix N_2 (Marshall et al. 1994). As trees predominantly transport amino acids in the xylem, their mistletoes gain additional carbon skeletons, i.e. they are not only cation, nitrogen, and water parasites, but also C parasites; 15% of the carbon for an "autotrophic" mistletoe originates from the host (Marshall et al. 1994). Photosynthesis is generally lower in the mistletoe than the host plant.

An unusual botanical feature of Australian mistletoes (Fig. 2.3.16) is that their leaves mimic the shape and form of the host so closely that it is difficult to explain except by horizontal gene transfer (Calder and Bernhardt 1983).

Fig. 2.3.16. Leaf mimicry of Australian mistletoe (see Calder and Bernhardt 1983). *Acacia cambagei* with *Amyema maidenii*. (Photo E.-D. Schulze)

Table 2.3.5. Characteristic features of mistletoe. After Ehleringer and Schulze 1985 (1); Marshall et al. 1994 (2)

	Mistletoe	Host	Source
K concentration (mg g^{-1})	28	11	(1)
P concentration (mg g^{-1})	2	1	(1)
N concentration (mg g^{-1})	28	25	(1)
	10	11	(2)
Transpiration (mmol m^{-2} s^{-1})	4	2	(2)
CO$_2$ assimilation (µmol m^{-2} s^{-1})	4	5	(2)

> ## Box 2.3.16   Summary: cations
>
> Cation nutrition is summarised as follows:
>
> - Basic cations are not metabolised, but they are important in a number of enzymatic reactions and in some cases form the reaction centres of enzymes (Mg in chlorophyll);
> - Requirement for K is higher than for Ca and Mg;
>
> - K regulates osmotic concentrations and pH of the cell;
> - Mg is involved in chlorophyll functions and in the transfer of phosphate from ATP to organic molecules;
> - Ca acts as an osmotic dehydrating ion and as a signal in cell metabolism (calmodulin).

- **regulation of photosynthesis** (photophosphorylation) and drought resistance. K regulates the osmotic potential during drought and maintains growth with decreasing water potential (Fisher and Turner 1978). The effect of K on osmoregulation also explains its importance in frost resistance.
- **regulation of movements**: The function of stomata (see Chap. 2.2.3) is based on oxygen requiring respiratory metabolism, with starch degraded to malate which is then transported into vacuoles and increases their ion content. Simultaneously, malate is decarboxylated in the mitochondria and the ATP produced is available for proton efflux. The HCO_3^- formed is used again in the degradation of starch. The proton efflux results in an influx of K from the apoplast via the antiport. Some of the protons are regained because of the influx of Cl^-. Potassium and chloride are transported into the vacuole, where they balance the ratio of anions/cations to malate. Thus the osmotic potential in the vacuole increases, with a consequential influx of water – and the stomata open. The effect of the stress hormone abscisic acid (ABA) in the regulation of stomata is to close the K channels (Schulze 1994) and thus to stop the movement of K^+.

In this reaction ABA has a signal effect on Ca channels, thus increasing the cytosolic Ca concentration which again affects the K and anion channels of the plasmalemma. K uptake is inhibited and thus stomata are not able to open (Schroeter et al. 2001). Closure of stomata is affected by malate and an efflux of K. A corresponding mechanism affects other movements, e.g. of leaves of *Mimosa pudica* and *Dionae muscipula* on touching, and the orientation of legumes to the sun.

- **phloem transport**: potassium is the most important cation regulating the pH in the phloem and sucrose loading.
- **regulation of fruit and tuber (potato) ripening** occurs because of the effect of K on the cation/anion balance and on sugar/starch metabolism.

Uptake and Requirement

Potassium occurs predominantly in silicate rocks and becomes reversibly bound to exchangers in the soil, particularly to clay minerals. Because of its ionic radius potassium fits optimally into the intermediate layers of clayey minerals and is therefore preferentially accumulated there (specific adsorption). In some soils, accumulation of K^+ in clay minerals which are able to swell results in contraction of these clays which thus "fix" K^+ so strongly that it is no longer available for plants. The ionic radius and physical characteristics of K^+ are similar to ammonium, so that these two ions are easily interchangeable. Excess of ammonium leads to exchange of K (and other anions) and if these cations are leached this stimulates acidification of soils. K and ammonium are both used to determine the cation concentration of the exchanger.

Deficiency and Excess

With K deficiency and excess the following symptoms occur:

- **K deficiency**: reduced growth and increased remobilisation from ageing organs, disturbed water relations (drying of tips), wilting appearance particularly at the edge of older leaves, yellowing and early shedding of needles.
- **K excess**: with K excess (e.g. on granite containing muscovite), Ca and Mg uptake are competitively influenced, thus increasing Mg deficiency at these sites.

References

Brady NC, Weil RR (1999) The nature and properties of soils, 12th edn. Prentice Hall, Upper Saddle River, New Jersey, 881 pp

Calder M, Bernhardt P (1983) The biology of mistletoes. Academic Press, Sydney, 348 pp

Chapin FS III, Kedrovski RA (1983) Seasonal changes in nitrogen and phosphorous fractions and autumn retranslocation in evergreen and deciduous taiga trees. Ecology 64:376–391

Ehleringer JR, Schulze E-D (1985) Mineral concentrations in an autoparasitic *Phoradendron californicum* growing on a parasitic *P. californicum* and its host, *Cercidium floridum*. Am J Bot 72:568–571

Ehleringer JR, Schulze E-D, Ziegler H, Lange OL, Farquhar GD, Cowan IR (1985) Xylem tapping mistletoes: primarily water or nutrient parasites? Science 227:1479–1481

Ellenberg H (1986) Vegetation Mitteleuropas mit den Alpen. Eugen Ulmer Verlag, Stuttgart, 943 pp

Ellis AG, Midgley JJ (1996) A new plant-animal mutualism involving a plant with sticky leaves and a resident hemipteran insect. Oecologia 106:478–481

Epstein E (1972) Mineral nutrition of plants: principles and perspectives. Wiley, New York, 412 pp

Erskine PD, Bergstrom DM, Schmidt S, Stewart GR, Tweedie CE, Shaw JD (1998) Subarctic Macquarie Island – a model ecosystem for studying animal-derived nitrogen sources using ^{15}N natural abundance. Oecologia 117:187–193

Fichtner K, Schulze E-D (1992) The effect of nitrogen nutrition on growth and biomass partitioning of annuals originating from habitats of different nitrogen availability. Oecologia 92:236–241

Fisher RA, Turner NC (1978) Plant productivity in arid and semiarid zones. Annu Rev Plant Physiol 29:277–317

Guarente L, Kenyon C (2000) Genetic pathways that regulate ageing in model organisms. Nature 408:255–262

Harrison AF, Schulze E-D, Gebauer G, Bruckner B (2000) Canopy uptake and utilization of atmospheric pollutant nitrogen. In: Schulze E-D (ed) Carbon and nitrogen cycling in European forest ecosystems. Ecological Studies 142. Springer, Berlin Heidelberg New York, pp 171–188

Hartmann G, Nienhaus F, Butin H (1988) Farbatlas Waldschaden; Diagnose von Baumkrankheiten. Eugen Ulmer Verlag, Stuttgart, 256 pp

Herdel K, Schmidt P, Feil R, Mohr A, Schurr U (2001) Dynamics of concentrations and nutrient fluxes in the xylem of *Rhizinus communis* – diurnal course, impact of nutrient availability and nutrient uptake. Plant Cell Environ 24:41–52

Hobbie EA, Macko SA, Williams M (2000) Correlation betuween foliar δ^{15}N and nitrogen concentrations may indicate plant-mycorrhizal interactions. Oecologia 122:273–283

Kaupenjohann M, Zech W, Hantschel B, Horn R (1989) Mineral nutrition of forest trees: a regional survey. Ecological Studies 77. Springer, Berlin Heidelberg New York, pp 282–296

Klein D, Morcuende R, Stitt M, Krapp A (2000) Regulation of nitrite reductase expression in leaves by nitrate and nitrogen metabolism is completely overriden when sugars fall below a critical level. Plant Cell Environ 8:863–872

Klemm O (1989) Leaching and uptake of ions through above ground Norway spruce tree parts. Ecological Studies 77. Springer, Berlin Heidelberg New York, pp 210–237

Koch LW, Schulze E-D, Percival F, Mooney HA, Chu C (1988) The nitrogen balance of *Paphanus sativus* × *raphanistrum* plants. Growth, nitrogen redistribution and photosynthesis under NO_3-deprivation. Plant Cell Environ 11:755–767

Köstner B, Schupp R, Schulze E-D, Rennenberg H (1998) Organic and inorganic sulfur transport in the xylem sap and the sulfur budget of *Picea abies* trees. Tree Physiol 18:1–9

Kreutzer K, Göttlein A (1991) Ökosystemforschung Högelwald; Beiträge zur Auswirkung von sauerer Beregnung und Kalkung in einem Fichtenbestand. Beihefte zum Forstwissenschaftlichen Zentralblatt 39:1–261

Kummetz E (1996) Die Wurzelentwicklung der Fichte (*Picea abies* (L.) Karst.): Untersuchungen zum C- und N-Haushalt unterschiedlich alter Bestände. Staatsexamensarbeit, Bayreuth

Lange OL, Heber U, Schulze E-D, Ziegler H (1989) Atmospheric pollutants and plant metabolism. Ecological Studies 77. Springer, Berlin Heidelberg New York, pp 238–269

Lange OL, Weikert RM, Wedler M, Gebel J, Heber U (1989) Photosynthese und Nährstoffversorgung von Fichten aus einem Waldschadensgebiet auf basenarmem Untergrund. Allg Forstzeitschr 3:54

Luther P, Becker H (1987) Die Mistel; Botanik, Lectine, medizinische Anwendung. Springer, Berlin Heidelberg New York, 188 pp

Marschall JD, Ehleringer JR, Schulze E-D, Farquhar GD (1994) Carbon isotope composition, gas exchange and heterotrophy in Australian mistletoes. Funct Ecol 8:465–487

Marschner H (1995) Mineral nutrition of higher plants. Academic Press, London, 889 pp

Michelsen AM, Schmidt IK, Jonasson S, Quarmby C, Sleep D (1996) Leaf ^{15}N abundance of subarctic plants provides field evidence that ericoid, ectomycorrhizal and non- and arbuscular mycorrhizal species access different sources of nitrogen. Oecologia 105:53–56

Mitscherlich G (1975) Waldwachstum und Umwelt, Bd. 3. Sauerlanders, Frankfurt, 352 pp

Moroney JV, Bartlett SG, Samuelsson G (2001) Carbonic anhydrase in plants and algae. Plant Cell Environ 24:141–154

Nadelhoffer KJ, Emmett BA, Gunderson P, Kjönaas OJ, Koopmans CJ, Schleppi P, Tietema A, Wright RF (1999) Nitrogen deposition makes minor contribution to carbon sequestration in temperate forests. Nature 398:145–147

Näsholm T, Ekblad A, Nordin A, Giesler R, Högberg M, Högberg P (1998) Boreal forest plants take up organic nitrogen. Nature 392:914–916

Nordin A, Högberg P, Näsholm T (2001) Soil N from and plant N uptake along a boreal forest productivity gradient. Oecologia 129:125–132

Oren R, Schulze E-D (1989) Nutritional disharmony and forest decline: a conceptual model. Ecological Studies 77. Springer, Berlin Heidelberg New York, pp 425–443

Oren R, Werk KS, Schulze ED, Meyer J, Schneider BU, Schraml P (1988) Performance of two *Picea abies* (L.) Karst. stands at different stages of decline. VI. Nutrient concentrations. Oecologia 77:25–37

Orians GH, Solbrig OT (1977) A cost-income model of leaves and roofs with special reference to arid and semi-arid areas. Am Nat 111:677–690

Persson T, Rudebeck A, Jussy JH, Colin-Belgrand M, Priemé A, Dambrine E, Karlsson PS, Sjöberg RM (2000) Soil nitrogen turnover – mineralisation, nitrification and denitrification in European forest soils. Ecological Studies 142. Springer, Berlin Heidelberg New York, pp 297–331

Read DJ (1993) Plant-microbe mutualism and community structure. Ecological Studies 99. Springer, Berlin Heidelberg New York, pp 181–210

Scheffer/Schachtschabel (1998) Lehrbuch der Bodenkunde, Ferdinand Enke Verlag, Stuttgart, 284 pp

Scheible WR, Gonzáles-Fontes A, Lauerer M, Müller-Röber B, Caboche M, Stitt M (1997) Nitrate acts as a signal to induce organic acid metabolism and repress starch metabolism in tobacco. Plant Cell Environ 9:783–798

Scheible WR, Lauerer M, Schulze E-D, Caboche M, Stitt M (1997) Accumulation of nitrate in the shoot acts as signal to regulate shoot-root allocation in tobacco. Plant J 11:671–691

Schopfer P, Brennicke A (1999) Pflanzenphysiologie. Springer, Berlin Heidelberg New York, 695 pp

Schroeter JI, Kwak JM, Allen GJ (2001) Guard cell abscisic acid signalling and engineering drought hardiness in plants. Nature 410:327–330

Schulze E-D (1994) The regulation of plant transpiration: interactions of feedforward, feedback, and futile cycles. In: Schulze E-D (ed) Flux control in biological systems. Academic Press, San Diego, pp 203–236

Schulze E-D, Turner NC, Glatzel G (1984) Carbon, water, and nutrient relations of two mistletoes and their hosts: a hypothesis. Plant Cell Environ 7:293–299

Schulze E-D, Lange OL, Oren R (1989) Forest decline and air pollution: a study of spruce on acid soils. Ecological Studies 77. Springer, Berlin Heidelberg New York, 475 pp

Schulze E-D, Gebauer G, Schulze W, Pate JS (1991) The utilization of nitrogen from insect capture by different growth forms of Drosera from southwest Australia. Oecologia 87:240–246

Schulze E-D, Kelliher FM, Körner C, Lloyd J, Leuning R (1994) Relationships among maximum stomatal conductance, ecosystem surface conductance, carbon assimilation and plant nitrogen nutrition: a global ecology scaling exercise. Anti Rev Ecol Syst 25:629–660

Schulze W (1991) Versuche mit insektenfangenden Pflanzen. Biol Unserer Zeit 21:307–312

Schulze W, Schulze E-D, Pate JS, Gillison AN (1997) The nitrogen supply from soils and insects during growth of pitcher plants Nepenthes mirabilis, Cephalotus follicularis and Darlingtonia californica. Oecologia 112: 464–471

Schulze W, Frommer WB, Ward JM (1999) Transporters for ammonium, amino acids and peptides are expressed in pitchers of the carnivorous plant Nepenthes. Plant J 17:637–646

Schulze W, Weise A, Frommer WB, Ward JM (2000) Function of the cytosolic N-terminus of sucrose transporter AtSUT2 in substrate affinity. FEBS Lett 485:189–194

Schulze W, Schulze E-D, Schulze I, Oren R (2001) Quantification of insect nitrogen utilization by the Venus fly trap Dionaea muscipula catching prey with highly variable isotope signatures. Exp Bot 1041–1049

Schurr U, Schulze E-D (1995) The concentrations of xylem sap constituents in root exudate, and in sap from intact, transpiring castor bean plants (Ricinus communis). Plant Cell Environ 18:409–420

Smith SE, Read DJ (1997) Mycorrhizal symbiosis. Academic Press, San Diego, 605 pp

Stitt M (1994) Flux control at the level of the pathway: studies with mutants and transgenic plants having decreased activity of enzymes involved in photosynthetic partitioning. In: Schulze E-D (ed) Flux control in biological systems. Academic Press, San Diego, pp 13–36

Stitt M, Schulze E-D (1994) Plant growth, storage, and resource allocation: from flux control in a metabolic chain to the whole plant level. In: Schulze E-D (ed) Flux control in biological systems. Academic Press, San Diego, pp 57–118

Thomas H, Thomas HM, Ougham H (2000) Annuality, perenniality and cell death. J Exp Bot 51:1781–1788

Ulrich B (1987) Stability, elasticity, and resilience of terrestrial ecosystems with respect to matter balance. Ecological Studies 61. Springer, Berlin Heidelberg New York, pp 11–49

Ulrich B (1995) The history and possible causes of forest decline in central Europe, with particular attention to the German situation. Envir Rev 3:262–276

Wallenda T, Stober C, Högbom L, Schinkel H, George E, Högberg P, Read DJ (2000) Nitrogen up-take processes in roots and mycorrhizas. Ecological Studies 142. Springer, Berlin Heidelberg New York, pp 122–143

Zech W, Popp E (1983) Magnesiummangel, einer der Gründe für das Fichten- und Tannensterben in NO-Bayern. Forstwiss Zentralbl 102:50–55

Carbon Relations

Nothofagus fusca in a temperate deciduous forest of New Zealand. Beech forests of New Zealand occur mainly on the South Island and form approximately 36 m high mixed stands of the "red beech" *Nothofagus fusca* and the "silver beech" *Nothofagus menziesii*. The stands grow with about 2000 mm rainfall and average yearly temperature of 9.4 °C, and are often very dense >1000 trunks per ha and 67 m² ha⁻¹ basal area, attaining a biomass of >300 t ha. The distribution of trees per hectare is characterised by about 20 very large trees, 300–400 years old, with a diameter at breast height of >5 m. Leaf area index reaches 7. Measurements of the carbon balance of this ecosystem of natural beech forests showed, for the first time, that in an undisturbed primeval forest there is no steady-state carbon balance. The forests are carbon sinks, i.e. they accumulate carbon over thousands of years in the humus layer (Hollinger et al. 1994). Photo E.-D. Schulze

Photosynthesis is not only the basis for growth of individual plants, but also the most important process providing energy in ecosystems. Considered from an ecological point of view, the biochemical process of CO_2 fixation is only a part of the carbon balance. The balance of photosynthesis and respiration and the response of the net process to climatic and edaphic factors is decisive for understanding growth of individual plants as well as for the ecosystem carbon cycle. In addition, it is essential to consider the way by which plants, through their structure and phenology, regulate their carbon balance and thus keep their position during competition with other species. Therefore, the carbon relations involve the broad spectrum from the biochemical reactions of CO_2 reduction to competition in a plant stand.

The following chapter considers the carbon relations of individual plants and of different types of plants. Chapter 3.3.2 considers C turnover in ecosystems. In Chapter 4.3 the phenomenon of competition and in Chapter 5.2 the effects of climate change for the global carbon balance are discussed.

2.4.1

Net Photosynthesis: Physiological and Physical Basis

2.4.1.1
Photosynthesis as a Diffusion Process

Net photosynthesis, also called **CO_2 assimilation** (A), is the difference between biochemical CO_2

fixation (P) and respiration (R_L), which takes place in the leaf simultaneously:

$$A = P - R_L \qquad (2.4.1)$$

Respiration consists of a number of partial processes:

- **respiration in mitochondria of heterotrophic cells (R_{het})**, which do not possess chloroplasts, but are indispensable for the function of the leaf (conducting tissues, epidermis);
- **respiration in mitochondria of photosynthetically active cells (R_{mit})** which depends on ATP concentration in the cytosol and thus on photosynthesis;
- **light-induced respiration (photorespiration, R_{phot})**.

$$R_L = R_{het} + R_{mit} + R_{phot} \qquad (2.4.2)$$

Because it is difficult to quantify these partial processes in an illuminated leaf, net photosynthesis is used in ecology as the standard for assessments of the plant carbon balance (Fig. 2.4.1) and it is usually measured as the net CO_2 exchange. Only the net exchange can be measured in the field. Basically, it should also be possible to measure the O_2 exchange. However, this is much more difficult because of the higher background concentration of O_2 in the atmosphere. However, measurement of O_2 becomes much more important globally (see Chap. 5).

CO_2 assimilation is a **diffusion process**, i.e. CO_2 from the atmosphere diffuses into the leaf as the CO_2 concentration in the intercellular spaces of the mesophyll is smaller than in the external air. The following equation applies to the transport via stomata:

$$A = (C_a - C_i)g_s \qquad (2.4.3)$$

where C_a is the CO_2 concentration in the atmosphere, C_i the CO_2 concentration in the mesophyll and g_s the **stomatal conductance**. It is the same conductance which regulates the water vapour flux (see Chap. 2.2.3), but the conductance of stomata for CO_2 is lower by a factor of 1.6, corresponding to the higher molecular weight of CO_2 as compared with H_2O ($g_{CO_2}/g_{H_2O} = 1.605$; Jarvis 1971).

It would appear reasonable to also express the movement of CO_2 between C_i and the chloroplast as a diffusion process. However, as already noted, respiratory processes occur in the leaf [Eq. (2.4.1)], and also the transport of CO_2 in the cell wall occurs not only in the dissolved form, but also partially as HCO_3^-. Because of the respiratory processes taking place in different tissues, a CO_2 concentration, the **compensation point** (Γ), is reached with decreasing CO_2 concentration, where CO_2 assimilation and respiration are balanced. Therefore, the following analogue equation applies:

$$A = (C_i - \Gamma)g_m \qquad (2.4.4)$$

where g_m is the conductance of the mesophyll and represents all leaf-internal transport processes. If the CO_2 concentration in the atmosphere is decreased experimentally below the compensation point, increased or decreased CO_2 release may occur, depending on the experimental conditions. Under such conditions the photosystems may be irreversibly damaged (Schäfer 1994; see also Chap. 1.2.1).

The response of CO_2 assimilation to the CO_2 concentration in the atmosphere describes the physiological state of photosynthesis in the leaf and is called a response curve (Fig. 2.4.2) with three important ranges:

- a linear range above the compensation point: In this range CO_2 assimilation is limited by the **activation of RuBP-carboxylase** by the substrate CO_2 (Farquhar and von Caemmerer 1982; Lange et al. 1987). The increase ($\Delta A/\Delta c$) describes the efficiency of RuBP-carboxylase. According to Eq. (2.44), $g_m = A/(C_1 - \Gamma)$;
- a saturation range at high CO_2 concentration: With increasing supply of CO_2, RuBP-carb-

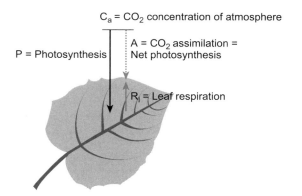

Fig. 2.4.1. Schematic presentation of CO_2 fluxes of a leaf. The flux of CO_2 into a leaf corresponds to the rate of photosynthesis minus respiration occurring at the same time. The net influx is known as net photosynthesis or CO_2 assimilation

$C_a = CO_2$ concentration of atmosphere

$A = CO_2$ assimilation = Net photosynthesis

P = Photosynthesis

R_l = Leaf respiration

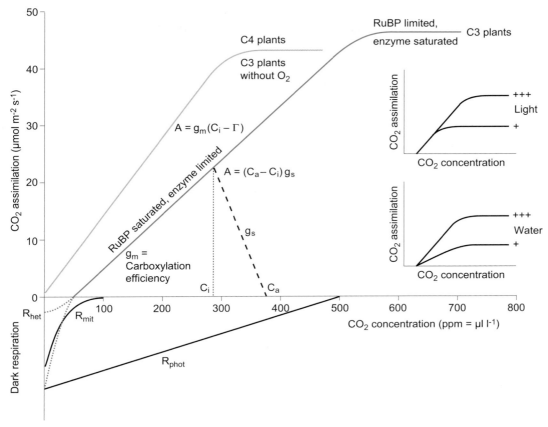

Fig. 2.4.2. Diagram of the dependence of CO_2 gas exchange on the CO_2 concentration in the air. The *y*-axis shows positive values as CO_2 assimilation and the negative values as respiration. The linear part of the curve shows enzyme limitation, the flat part shows saturation because of substrate limitation. The *inserts* show that change in light only affects the saturated region, whereas drought operates via enzyme limitation. For explanation, see text

oxylase is fully activated, but CO_2 assimilation is limited by the **supply of the substrate ribulose-1,5-bis-P (RuBP)**, to which the carbon of CO_2 is bound. In this range the turnover rate of RuBP-carboxylase is saturated and it cannot use the supplied CO_2. Because of the limited capacity of the Calvin cycle, CO_2 assimilation finally reaches a maximum rate at which it is CO_2 saturated;

- the range below the compensation point: In CO_2-free air with 20% O_2 the **oxygenase function of RuBP-carboxylase/oxygenase** is fully activated, i.e. light-induced respiration (R_{phot}) reaches its highest value. At the same time, dependent on ATP consumption in the cytosol, mitochondrial dark respiration (R_{mit}) is activated. R_{mit} decreases with increasing rates of photosynthesis as ATP is also formed in photosynthesis and is probably reduced under conditions of assimilation above the compensation point (Loreto et al. 2001). With de-

creasing CO_2, the R_{mit} approaches asymptotically the rate of respiration of chlorophyll-free heterotrophic leaf cells (R_{het}). Light-induced respiration (R_{phot}) decreases dependent on the CO_2/O_2 ratio and is very low at CO_2 saturation.

Whilst these processes of photosynthesis and respiration occur in an intact leaf, CO_2 supply to the mesophyll is limited by the diffusion resistance of stomata. Analogous to a current/voltage diagram, CO_2 concentration decreases down the diffusion path from ambient air to the intercellular spaces of the mesophyll (see Fig. 2.4.2). Starting from the ambient CO_2 concentration, the CO_2 influx into the mesophyll increases with decreasing concentration in the intercellular spaces (C_i). Plotting C_a against C_i results in a straight line corresponding to the increase in stomatal conductance. According to Eq. (2.4.3), $g_s = A/(C_a - C_i)$. Thus stomata regulate the CO_2

flux, so that the concentration of CO_2 in the mesophyll is lower than in the ambient air (C_a), and lies between Γ and C_a. On average, $C_i/C_a = 0.7-0.8$.

The response of photosynthesis to CO_2 concentration may also be expressed as a function of consumption (Raschke 1979). Stomatal conductance (**function of supply**) and efficiency of carboxylase (**function of consumption**) decrease the CO_2 concentration in the mesophyll.

$$A = (C_a - C_i)g_s = (C_i - \Gamma)g_m \qquad (2.4.5)$$

Therefore

$$(C_i - C_a)/(C_i - \Gamma) = g_m/g_s \qquad (2.4.6)$$

The CO_2 gradient across the stomata (from the atmosphere to the intercellular spaces), Δc, is proportional to the ratio of A to g_s:

$$\Delta c = C_a - C_i = A/g_s \qquad (2.4.7)$$

Stomatal closure means reduced conductance of g_s, leading to a decrease in the **supply function** of Fig. 2.4.2, and at constant photosynthetic capacity (**consumption function**) to a decrease in C_i. Removing the epidermis experimentally would bypass the influence of stomata, and enable CO_2 assimilation to be measured at C_a and thus determine the RuBP-carboxylase activity. In this case, the measured rate (A_{Ca}) would reach the RuBP limiting range (Farquhar and von Caemmerer 1982).

A decrease in light intensity has its primary effect on the chloroplast which results in decreased CO_2 assimilation and to a decrease in the saturated rate of photosynthesis at the same CO_2 concentration, despite constant carboxylase activity. There need not necessarily be an effect on C_i. In contrast, water stress or N deficiency causes reduced efficiency of carboxylase, i.e. at constant stomatal conductance C_i increases. CO_2 assimilation (consumption function) increases more slowly and reaches saturation earlier than in plants with sufficient water supply or N nutrition.

Efficiency of CO_2 fixation may be evaluated by the number of CO_2 molecules diffusing through the stomata and exchanging oxygen with the cell water and diffusing back into the atmosphere, as they are not assimilated by photosynthesis. Of 1000 CO_2 molecules entering the leaf only one is reduced, the others diffuse out to the atmosphere (Lloyd et al. 1996). This process can be shown by the [18]O **content in CO_2**. At the evaporating surfaces in the mesophyll cells [18]O is enriched in the cell wall water (Roden and Ehleringer 1999). This $H_2{}^{18}O$ exchanges oxygen with the oxygen of CO_2, as a consequence of gaseous CO_2 dissolving in the cell wall water and then reacting with the dissociated [18]OH^- ions to give $HC^{18}OO^-$. In this process O atoms are "exchanged" so that the CO_2 diffusing from the leaf back to the atmosphere contains a new [18]O atom as a label showing the significance of the physical process of diffusion in CO_2 uptake: It is possible to increase CO_2 assimilation by increased CO_2 concentration, but large amounts of CO_2 apparently diffuse back into the atmosphere without being used for photosynthesis by the plant because Rubisco is limiting. In this context, turnover of CO_2 by anhydrase plays an additional important role (Gillon and Yakir 2001).

2.4.1.2
C3, C4 and CAM Metabolism

During evolution in the plant kingdom, certain species developed which overcame these physical limitations of CO_2 uptake under conditions of H_2O loss. A distinction is made in photosynthesis between the **light reactions** of photosystems I and II, which supply energy (ATP) and reduction equivalents (NADP) and **dark reactions** of CO_2 assimilation. With regard to these photosystems, land plants evolved from green algae and the photosystems are not very different, but there are considerable differences in the way CO_2 is fixed (see Chap. 1.2). The following distinctions are made:

C3 Plants
CO_2 assimilation occurs by RuBP-carboxylase, with phosphoglyceric acid (PGA), a three-carbon molecule, the first product detected experimentally. C3 plants also undergo a oxygenase reaction (see Chap. 1.2) in which O_2 forms phosphoglycolate with RuBP; during turnover of the pathway of light-induced (photo)respiration, several amino acids (glutamate, glycine, serine, alanine) are metabolised and CO_2, as well as NH_3, are released (ammonia is generally reassimilated). Coupling of the oxygenase reaction to amino acid metabolism involves losses in the C balance, but for the N balance it is a very important metabolic pathway. This photosynthetic

type is found in about 95% of all plant species. They are adapted to average temperatures (20–30 °C), and include trees and shrubs as well as herbaceous plants and grasses of temperate, boreal and humid tropical regions.

C4 Plants

CO_2 fixation in these plants occurs by a PEP-carboxylase (see Fig. 2.4.3) which binds CO_2 to phosphoenol pyruvate and a C4 organic acid malate or aspartate is formed via oxaloacetate. These organic acids are transported into the mesophyll cells surrounding the bundle sheath. The organic acids are decarboxylated and the CO_2 released is assimilated as in the C3 metabolic pathway. The advantage of this pathway for CO_2 fixation is that PEP-carboxylase has a higher affinity for CO_2 than RuBP-carboxylase; it has no oxygenase function, and additionally also uses HCO_3^- (Chap. 1.5.3.1). Thus the plant is able to refix the respiratory CO_2 which is produced by the light-induced respiration, and dark respiration from mitochondria of the vascular bundles. The compensation point for C4 plants is thus almost zero. In addition, several malate-forming mesophyll cells per bundle sheath cell form organic acids (Fig. 2.4.3 A). Therefore, after decarboxylation, there is an increased CO_2 concentration of about 1000 ppm in the bundle sheath which is in the saturation range of C3 photosynthesis. Thus C4 metabolism is a mechanism to concentrate CO_2. Based on the type of organic acids formed, the structure of the bundle sheath, and the location of chloroplasts in the bundle sheath, different C4 metabolic types are differentiated (Hattersley 1992). C4 plants form about 1–2% of the plant species occurring in tropical arid regions with temperatures above 30 °C during the day. The crop plants *Sorghum* and maize are C4 plants. Because of their efficient photosynthetic pathway, C4 plants can grow particularly rapidly with favourable temperature, water and nutrient supply. The highest rates of assimilation of an ecosystem were measured on *Echinochloa polystachya* meadows in tropical swamps (Morison et al. 2000). Some **algae** have a corresponding CO_2 concentration mechanism, using HCO_3^- (Raven 1994).

From anatomical and physiological characteristics, different forms of C4 metabolism are described as follows (see Fig. 2.4.3):

- anatomically: species with or without **Kranz structure** (K = Kranz; n–K + non-Kranz species); the term "Kranz" structure was coined by Volkens (1887) in his famous flora of the Egyptian desert
- physiologically:
  - according to the transport metabolite: **malate** (MS) or **pyruvate** (PS) species;
  - according to the enzyme system: **malate enzyme** (ME) or **PEP carboxykinase** (PCK) type;
  - according to the proton acceptor: $NADP^+$- or NAD^+-dependent malate reduction (in the chloroplast or cytosol, respectively).

The anatomy and site of malate reduction determine whether CO_2 diffuses back out of the bundle sheath. The NADP-ME-type achieves the highest rate of photosynthesis (Hattersley 1992; Schulze et al. 1996). The variety of expression of C4 metabolism points to a polyphyletic evolution, even within grasses (Clayton 1981).

CAM (Crassulacean Acid Metabolism) Plants (see Chap. 1.5.3)

The famous German poet Goethe (1749–1832), who also wrote many articles on natural sciences, cultivated the Crassulacean plant *Kalanchoe pinnata* (previously called *Bryophyllum calycinum*) because this plant grew well even in dry conditions in houses. However, it was the Englishman Heyne who grew *Bryophyllum* as suggested by Goethe, and who discovered in 1815 the acid metabolism in these plants by eating them in the morning and evening. The leaves tasted sour in the morning and sweet in the evening. The acid metabolism is similar to C4 metabolism. The formation of malate is not spatially divided between mesophyll and bundle sheath, but acid formation is temporally restricted to the night and then it is decarboxylated during the day (Lüttge et al. 1988). Storage of the acids formed via PEP-carboxylase occurs in the vacuole, and thus limits the C balance and also the assimilate production. This metabolic pathway is expressed in succulents (plants with high water content/dry weight or high water content/volume) of desert regions of the earth, and in epiphytes of tropical vegetation (see Fig. 2.4.4). The CAM pathway enables plants to avoid transpiration losses as CO_2 assimilation takes place during the night, when irradiation is absent and humidity is high. Thus, the PEP-carboxylase of most CAM plants is adapted to low

---

The term 'Kranz' is used in English, meaning wreath.

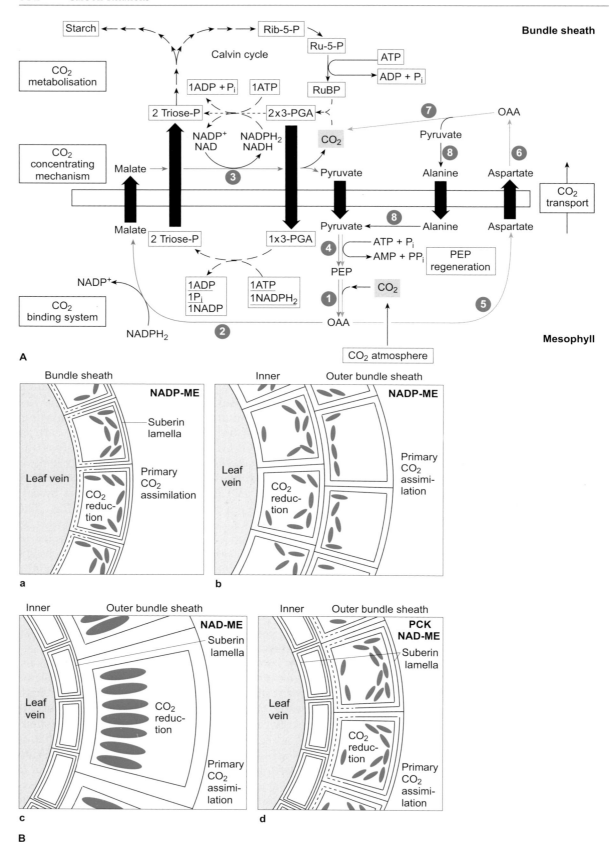

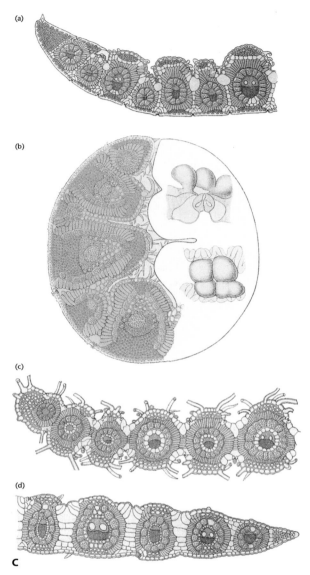

(a)

(b)

(c)

(d)

C

Fig. 2.4.3. A CO_2 assimilation in C4 plants with malate- and aspartate-forming types in the mesophyll and decarboxylation in the bundle sheaths. The distinction between malate- and aspartate-forming types is made according to the organic acid which is initially formed and then transported between the mesophyll and the bundle sheath. Also a distinction is made between NADP and NAD forms of C4 metabolism according to the site at which decarboxylation takes place. In the NADP type CO_2 is released in the chloroplasts, whereas in contrast in the NAD type decarboxylation occurs in the cytosol of the bundle sheath cells. *Rib-5P* Ribose-5-phosphate; *Ru-5P* ribulose-5-phosphate; *RuBP* ribulose-1,5-bisphosphate; *3-PGA* 3-phosphoglyceric acid; *ATP* adenosine triphosphate; *ADP* adenosine diphosphate; *AMP* adenosine monophosphate; *PEP* phosphoenol pyruvate; *OAA* oxalacetate. Enzymes indicated: *1* PEP-carboxylase; *2* NADP+-dependent malate dehydrogenase; *3* malic enzyme; *4* pyruvate-phosphate-dikinase; *5, 6* oxalacetate-aspartate-transaminase; *7* oxalacetate decarboxylating enzyme; *8* pyruvate-alanine-transaminase (from Strasburger 1999). B Schematic of bundle sheath in **a** typical NADP-ME species (ME=malic enzyme), in which the chloroplasts are oriented on the outer side of the bundle sheath cells, **b** the genus *Aristida*, which is characterised by two bundle sheath cells and chloroplasts which are positioned on the wall between the bundle sheaths, **c** typical NAD-ME species with large chloroplasts on the mesophyll cell walls close to the vascular bundle and formation of a suberin lamella between the outer and inner bundle sheaths, and **d** typical PCK species with the formation of a suberin lamella as in the NAD species, but with orientation of the chloroplasts close to the mesophyll cells (after Hattersley 1992). C Leaves with C4 metabolism are obvious from the "Kranz" form of the bundle sheath cells. **a** *Andropogon*: NADP species, **b** *Aristida*: NADP species, **c** *Danthonia forskalii*: NAD-ME species, **d** *Eragrostis*: PCK species. Flora of the Egyptian–Arabian desert (Volkens 1887). Volkens coined the phrase "Kranz" type for the assimilatory cells. The relation between CO_2-assimilating cells and photosynthetically active Kranz cells is clearly seen (3:1) as the anatomical basis of the CO_2-concentrating mechanisms in C4 plants

temperatures which occur, for example, in cool coastal deserts, in Chile, Namibia, and Baja California. However, C3 metabolism of CAM plants takes place at high temperatures during the day. Rates of C fixation are limited by the capacity of the vacuole to store malate.

It becomes obvious from the geographic and taxonomic distribution of C4 and CAM species that these are relatively recent developments in evolution, taking place simultaneously in various parts of the earth, in different, unrelated plant species and as a response to changing climatic conditions (Fig. 2.4.4).

2.4.1.3
Photosynthesis Models and Calculation of $^{13}C/^{12}C$ Rates (contribution by A. Arneth)

The processes taking place during CO_2 fixation in leaves of C3 plants were described mathematically by Farquhar et al. (1980). This **photosynthesis model** is based on biochemical processes and the interactions of three metabolic pathways:

- photosynthetic C reduction;
- photorespiratory oxidation;
- gain in chemical energy (reduction equivalents, ATP) by photosynthesis.

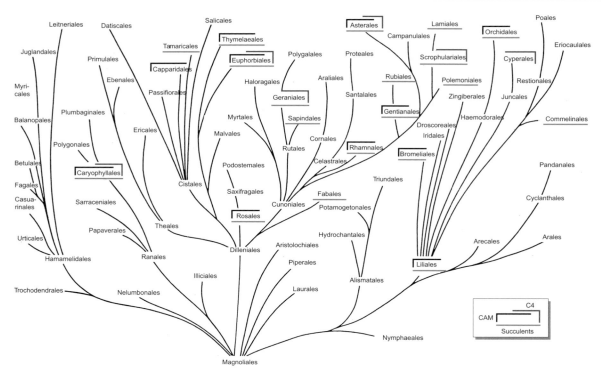

Fig. 2.4.4. The phylogenetic tree of higher plants at the category of Orders showing the distribution of succulents with C3 metabolism and of CAM and C4 plants. It can be seen that certain leaf types are in one taxonomic "guild", whereas in some orders all three types occur. (Evans 1972)

The model is based on the kinetics of carboxylation, specifically on the carboxylase-oxygenase reactions of Rubisco in the chloroplast. The model also combines Rubisco kinetics with the stoichiometry of electron transport and the requirement for NADPH. In the following only some of the most important points are summarised. The derivation of the model is explained in Farquhar et al. (1980), Farquhar and von Caemmerer (1982) and Farquhar and Lloyd (1993).

The rate of CO_2 assimilation may be described as the minimum of two dependent processes, Rubisco limitation (A_v) or RuBP regeneration (A_j), which in turn is limited by the electron transport.

$$A = \min\{A_j, A_v\} \qquad (2.4.8)$$

1.
Rubisco-Limited or RuBP-Saturated Rate A_v

Because of photosynthetic C reduction and photorespiration, the rate of CO_2 assimilation in the stroma of the chloroplast may be described as:

$$A_v = V_c(1 - 0.5V_o/V_c) - R_{mit} \qquad (2.4.9)$$

where V_c is the rate of RuBP carboxylation, V_o the rate of RuBP oxygenation and R_{mit} the rate of mitochondrial respiration in light. This equation takes into account that photorespiratory oxidation loses 0.5 mol CO_2 per mol oxygenation and thus the rate of net C fixation is decreased. V_c and V_o may be described mathematically by the maximum rates of the enzyme system (V_{cmax}, V_{omax}), which are limited by the presence of O_2 or CO_2, respectively, as follows:

$$V_c = V_{cmax}pC_c/[pC_c + K_c(1 + pO/K_o)] \qquad (2.4.10\,a)$$

and

$$V_o = V_{omax}pO/[pO + K_o(1 + pC_c/K_c)] \qquad (2.4.10\,b)$$

where K_c and K_o are the Michaelis-Menten constants for the **carboxylation and oxygenation**, respectively, and pO and pC_c are the partial pressures of oxygen and CO_2 in the chloroplast, respectively.

The ratio of the activities (φ) of the oxygenation and carboxylation of Rubisco is:

$$\varphi = V_o/V_c = V_{omax}K_c pO/(V_{omax}K_o pC_c) \quad (2.4.11)$$

and this is reduced at $R_d = 0$ to:

$$\varphi = 2\Gamma^*/pC_c \quad (2.4.12)$$

where Γ^* is the photosynthetic compensation point in the absence of mitochondrial respiration and R_d the dark respiration.

These general biochemical equations may be used to calculate the **Rubisco limiting rate of CO$_2$ assimilation**, A_v, as follows:

$$A_v = V_c(1 - \Gamma^*/pC_c) - R_d \quad (2.4.13\,a)$$

$$A_v = V_{cmax}[(pC_c - \Gamma^*)/$$
$$(pC_c + K_c(1 + pO/K_o))] - R_d \quad (2.4.13\,b)$$

K_c, K_o and Γ^* are temperature-dependent values (Harley et al. 1986; Kirschbaum and Farquhar 1984; von Caemmerer et al. 1994). At 20 °C the numerical value of $K_c = 30.2$ Pa (CO$_2$), $K_o = 25.6$ kPa (O$_2$) and $\Gamma^* = 3.46$ Pa. V_{cmax} is not only dependent on temperature, but also on the type of plant, the state of nutrition and the light conditions.

2.
RuBP Regeneration Dependent and Electron Transport Limiting Rate A$_j$

A continuous rate of CO$_2$ reduction or oxygenation activity requires continuous and equal rate of RuBP supply. RuBP is regenerated via the pentose phosphate cycle or the photorespiratory C-oxidation cycle. Both processes consume ATP and NADPH and there is a very complex stoichiometry, i.e. PGA (phosphoglycerate) production, the rate of NADPH and ATP consumption, and the number of electrons required to produce the redox equivalents and ATP. This is in turn dependent on the linear rate of electron transport through PS I and PS II as well as on cyclic electron transport. The sum of these processes is:

$$J' = J/(4.5 + 10.5\Gamma^*/pC_c) \quad (2.4.14)$$

where J' is the maximum carboxylation rate maintaining the potential rate of electron transport and J is the potential rate of linear electron transport. It follows that **the Rubisco limiting rate of CO$_2$ assimilation, A$_j$,** is:

$$A_j = J/4(pC_c - \Gamma^*)/(pC_c + 2\Gamma^*) - R_d \quad (2.4.15)$$

where J is the rate of electron transport. J increases hyperbolically with light (Q):

$$J = (Q + J_{max} - SQRT\{(Q + J_{max})^2 - 4\theta QJ_{max}\})/(2\theta) \quad (2.4.16)$$

where θ describes the curvature of the hyperbolic function. V_{cmax} depends, as with J_{max}, on temperature and other growth conditions. In practice the temperature dependence of V_{cmax} and J_{max} is experimentally determined from a regression of the dependence of photosynthesis on conductance, measured experimentally under the climatic conditions of interest.

3.
Supply of CO$_2$ Through Stomata

The relationships described above may only be applied if the supply of CO$_2$ to the chloroplast (C_c) is known. The CO$_2$ supply in the leaf is a **diffusion process**, limited by stomatal conductance (g). Equation (2.4.8) may also be expressed as **diffusion-limited CO$_2$ assimilation, A**

$$A = g(pC_a - pC_c)/P \quad (2.4.17)$$

where pC_a is the CO$_2$ partial pressure in the air which surrounds the leaf and P is the air pressure. It should be noted that the CO$_2$ concentration at the leaf surface also depends on the boundary layer conditions (Chap. 2.2.4).

The calculation of photosynthesis from the model requires simultaneous solution of Eqs. (2.4.8) and (2.4.17). Unfortunately, there is no biochemically based model for stomatal responses corresponding to carboxylation. To solve Eqs. (2.4.8) and (2.4.17) a set of equations is produced which determines the reaction of stomata empirically and this is coupled to the photosynthesis model. In this model g is a function of air humidity, temperature, light, soil water, atmospheric CO$_2$ and other growth factors, insofar as they influence stomata (Jarvis 1976; Leuning 1995; Lloyd et al. 1995b; Arneth et al. 2002).

Although the original equations by Farquhar et al. (1980) were based solely on cellular processes, this model may also be applied to whole leaves, whole plants and whole ecosystems

(Lloyd et al. 1995a; Leuning et al. 1998; Arneth et al. 1999; de Pury and Farquhar 1999). Depending on the question, the successful use of the model requires not only information on V_{max} and J_{max}, but also knowledge about the state of nutrition and water supply from the soil.

4.
$^{13}C/^{12}C$ Discrimination

The photosynthesis model developed by Farquhar et al. (1980) may also be used to model discrimination against ^{13}C in photosynthesis. The most important processes contributing to discrimination against ^{13}C compared to ^{12}C in leaves are the different rates of diffusion of $^{12}CO_2$ and $^{13}CO_2$ and the fractionation related to the carboxylation by Rubisco. According to Farquhar et al. (1989) the **carbon isotope rate (R_p)** is determined by:

$$R_p = {}^{13}A/{}^{12}A \qquad (2.4.18)$$

where ^{13}A and ^{12}A are the rates of assimilation of $^{13}CO_2$ and $^{12}CO_2$. According to the definition the isotopic effect of carboxylation $(1+b)$ is

$$R_i/R_p = 1 + b \qquad (2.4.19)$$

where R_i is the isotope ratio of the intercellular CO_2 and b is the net fractionation during carboxylation which is primarily determined by Rubisco (27‰) in the case of C3 plants (for C4 plants see below).

R_i may be calculated from Eq. (2.4.17), as the kinetic isotope effect for diffusion corresponds to the ratio of the diffusivities of $^{12}CO_2$ and $^{13}CO_2$ in air:

$$^{13}A = g(R_a pC_a - R_i pC_c)/[(1 + a)P]$$

where, corresponding to Eq. (2.4.19), $1+a = g/^{13}A$ and a describe the fractionation by diffusion in air (4.4‰).

These equations may be combined and expressed as:

$$a = 1 + \Delta = \frac{R_a}{R_p} = (1 + a)\frac{pC_a - pC_c}{pC_a} + (1 + b)\frac{pC_c}{pC_a}$$

and

$$\Delta = a\frac{pC_a - pC_c}{pC_a} + b\frac{pC_a}{pC_c} = a + (b-a)\frac{pC_c}{pC_a} \qquad (2.4.20)$$

The above equations for the **discrimination coefficient Δ** only apply to C3 plants. Discrimination in C4 plants is much more complicated because of the higher affinity of PEP-carboxylase for CO_2 and also the transformation of CO_2 into HCO_3^- needs to be considered. In the equilibrium there is more ^{13}C in HCO_3^-. Even though the effective discrimination of PEP-carboxylase is about –5.7‰, a certain proportion of the CO_2 (φ) is lost by back diffusion and the permeability of bundle sheath cells. This contributes to the discrimination by Rubisco in bundle sheath cells. The total effect of **discrimination in C4 plants** is as follows:

$$\Delta = a + (b4 + b\varphi - a)pC_c/pC_a \qquad (2.4.21)$$

The numeric value of $(b4 + b\varphi)$ is smaller than that of b. This value may be positive, zero or negative, depending on the permeability, φ. In C4 plants, Δ may therefore depend positively, be independent, or depend negatively on pC_c/pC_a.

The equations shown here may be used to interpret measured $^{13}C/^{12}C$ ratios in plant materials, with respect to the effects of particular climatic and growth conditions. For example, from the measurements of $^{13}C/^{12}C$ in plant dry matter a time-integrated value of pC_c/pC_a may be calculated [Eq. (2.4.20a,b)]. Alternatively, pC_c/pC_a may be calculated from the climatic conditions, the capacity of photosynthesis and electron transport [Eqs. (2.4.8) to (2.4.18)]. By comparing the calculated and measured values in annual rings of wood the long-term effect of increased CO_2 concentration on stomatal conductance may be deduced (Arneth et al. 2002).

Box 2.4.1	Summary: Photosynthesis

- **Net photosynthesis** is the balance between the rate of CO_2 fixation in the chloroplasts and the simultaneous respiration occurring in the leaf (light-induced respiration) and mitochondrial respiration of both photosynthetic and non-photosynthetic cells.
- **CO_2 concentration within the mesophyll, C_i,** indicates the balance between CO_2-requiring processes and the supply of CO_2 via the stomata. The ratio C_i/C_a depends on the plant type and growth conditions and lies between 0.7 and 0.8. C_i is a sensitive indicator of both changes in stomatal conductance, as well as of changes in the physiological capacity of the enzymes involved.
- For the purposes of carbon balance **CO_2 assimilation** can be described as a **diffusion process:**
- Plants have different ways of fixing CO_2:
  - **C3 plants** (95% of plant species) form a C3 compound (PGA) as the first product of CO_2 assimilation. The CO_2-compensation point in these species is determined by the photorespiration. The temperature optimum lies between 20 and 30 °C.
  - **C4 plants** (ca. 2% of plant species) form organic acids, with four-carbon skeletons, from the reaction of CO_2 with PEP catalysed by PEP-carboxylase. The C4 acids are decarboxylated in the bundle sheath. The CO_2 released is then reduced by the C3 pathway. The advantage of the C4 pathway is in the very large concentration of CO_2 (1000 ppm) in the bundle sheath cells and also in refixation of respired CO_2. C4 plants can maintain smaller stomatal aperture at the same rate of photosynthesis as C3 plants. C4 plants are adapted to the arid sub-tropics with temperatures above 30 °C. Maize is a cultivated C4 plant.
  - **CAM plants** (ca. 3% of plant species) resemble C4 plants biochemically; however, CO_2 fixation and assimilation are not separated spatially as in C4 plants but are separated temporarily into CO_2 uptake at night, when acids are formed and stored in the vacuole, and CO_2 release and assimilation during the day in mesophyll cells. Nocturnal CO_2 uptake results in a very low water use. CAM plants are generally adapted to low night temperatures and high day temperatures. Their assimilate production is limited by the capacity of vacuoles to store acids.
  - **Mathematical models** have been developed to describe the processes of photosynthesis on the basis of the biochemistry of RuBP-carboxylase enzyme activity and RuBP regeneration. Combined with measurements of isotope discrimination between ^{13}C and ^{12}C they can reconstruct the climatic conditions in the habitat during growth.

2.4.2

Specific Leaf Area, Nitrogen Content and Photosynthetic Capacity

2.4.2.1
Specific Leaf Area

Specific leaf area characterises the relation of projected leaf area to leaf weight ($m^2 \, kg^{-1}$) and it is a sensitive indicator of several ecological processes and adaptations. The specific leaf area of organs for assimilation differs by a factor of 5. Annual crop plants reach $23.6 \, m^2 \, kg^{-1}$ leaf area in contrast to $4.1 \, m^2 \, kg^{-1}$ in evergreen conifers. These differences are:

- determined by **evolution**, i.e. in competition with other species; during the course of evolution plants developed ever greater leaf areas per unit of invested dry mass, thus increasing light capture, and supplied these thin leaves with optimal amounts of N (high N concentrations);
- **adaptively** determined, i.e. the habitat, particularly the water and nitrogen supply together with changes in light conditions, result in modifications to the specific leaf area.

The specific leaf area has several ecologically important consequences and effects:

- **elasticity** of leaves and their ability to endure drought and other stress situation; this is not to say that ecological factors determine the structure of the leaf or whether species with certain leaf structures occupy a specific site,

- packaging density (**concentrations**) of nutrients, particularly nitrogen (38.4 mg N g^{-1} in crop plants and 11 mg N g^{-1} in conifers);
- relation of assimilating cells to transpiring surface (**A/E relation**).

In general, species with high specific leaf area show a higher metabolic activity than species with lower specific leaf area. Therefore, there is differentiation of vegetation on the earth: Species with high specific leaf areas are opportunists (ruderal plants), settling in new sites and those with a large supply of resources. In contrast, plants with small specific leaf area occupy less favourable sites. Both groups occupy their respective site, not because they would not grow on other more or less favourable sites (exceptions are stress-tolerant species: e.g. obligate halophytes), but because they are generally "pushed out" from sites outside their niche by competition. Other mechanisms, e.g. shade tolerance and germination, result in plants which reproduce less effectively (see Chap. 4.3).

Orians and Solbrig (1977) formalised this observation in a **cost-benefit analysis** of the adaptation of plant to a gradient of increasing drought (Fig. 2.4.5). The model starts with the assumption that all species are able to live at a well-watered site. Species which assimilate large quantities of CO_2 are less stress tolerant, i.e.

they have a large leaf area per dry weight and are thus sensitive to being dried out. In those plants, CO_2 assimilation decreases with very little soil drying. In contrast, species with low rates of CO_2 assimilation usually possess leaves with a smaller leaf area per dry weight and are thus able to endure drought stress to a greater degree. However, under optimal conditions, these species do not achieve such large rates of CO_2 assimilation as the less stress-tolerant species, but are still able to assimilate CO_2 when stress-intolerant species can no longer photosynthesise.

Obviously, **specific leaf area** is an important parameter in response to favourable and unfavourable conditions, as well as a constitutive characteristic of species (herbaceous annuals in comparison to conifers), which plays a large role in determining the rate of CO_2 assimilation. The relation between specific leaf area (m^2 kg^{-1}) and nutrient (nitrogen) concentration in the leaf is linear (Fig. 2.4.6 A; Schulze et al. 1994). Simultaneously, there is a close relationship between CO_2 assimilation and N concentration (Fig. 2.4.6 B) where, corresponding to the model of Orians and Solbrig (1977), species with large maximum rate of CO_2 assimilation react more sensitively towards N deficiency than species with less photosynthetic capacity. Obviously, the investment to overcome N deficiency (high dry weight per leaf area) reduces physiological efficiency.

2.4.2.2
Maximum Rates of CO_2 Assimilation

Loss of water, as well as uptake of CO_2, occurs via stomata and thus there is a physical connection between the stomatal conductance and the rate of photosynthesis (see Chap. 2.2.3). It is therefore not surprising that **maximum CO_2 assimilation** of a vegetative cover (A_{max}) is linearly correlated with the maximum conductance of the surface for transport of water vapour (Fig. 2.4.6 C). This function is important for global models of carbon budgets because it allows an estimate of the maximum turnover of CO_2 and water vapour. There is no corresponding correlation between E_{max} (maximum transpiration) and A_{max} (maximum assimilation), because transpiration depends on very variable meteorological conditions (water vapour saturation deficit, irradiation; see Chap. 2.2.4), whilst

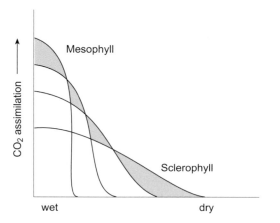

Fig. 2.4.5. The dependence of CO_2 assimilation on soil water content for different functional plant types that are sensitive or resistant to drying. Sensitive types have a much higher rate of CO_2 assimilation than resistant types when water is abundant. Sensitive types reduce CO_2 exchange early as the soil dries, so that under this condition resistant types dominate. (After Orians and Solbrig 1977)

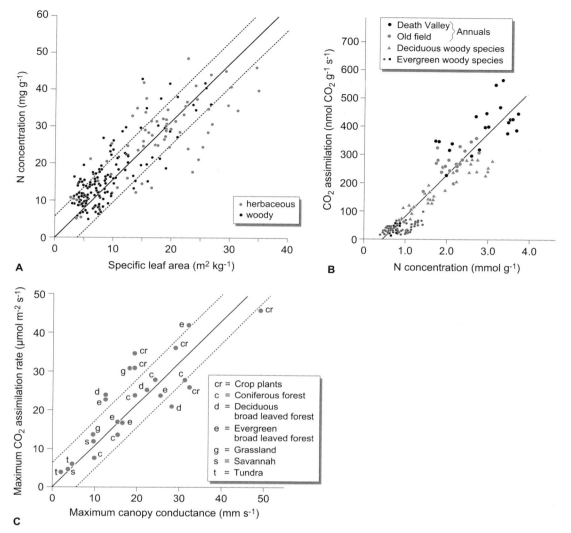

Fig. 2.4.6. A Correlation of N concentration (mg g^{-1}) in a leaf with specific leaf area (m^2 kg^{-1}) for herbaceous and woody species from all climatic regions of the earth (Schulze et al. 1994). B Relations between maximum rate of CO$_2$ assimilation and N concentration in the leaf (Field and Mooney 1986). C Relation between maximum CO$_2$ assimilation (A$_{max}$) and maximum conductance of a leaf surface. Data represent, in this case, measurements of single experimental plots in different vegetation zones of the globe. Lowest values occur in the tundra, highest values in a wheat field. The second highest value is in a tree plantation of *Hevea brasiliensis*. (Schulze et al. 1994)

the maximum rate of photosynthesis is determined by the CO$_2$ concentration in the atmosphere, which is relatively constant in the short term. Maximum rates of CO$_2$ assimilation are very different for different types of vegetation. Ultimately, such a classification is artificial, because there are many intermediates regarding nitrogen concentration and rates of assimilation of the leaf, even within one type of vegetation. Considering the known dependence of CO$_2$ assimilation on climatic and environmental factors, it is possible to estimate the actual rate of CO$_2$ assimilation using maximum rates of CO$_2$ assimilation.

The close relationship between leaf morphology, nutrient supply and physiological activity shows a broad continuum. Nevertheless, for large ranges, it may be generally stated that species with structures to protect assimilatory organs against site-specific stresses are successful in extreme sites and that are poor in resources. As a consequence, metabolic activity decreases (measured at rate per leaf area). Ultimately, the economic principle of **diminishing returns** applies to the occupation of extreme sites.

From the relation between leaf morphology, nutrition and CO$_2$ assimilation, independent of

A

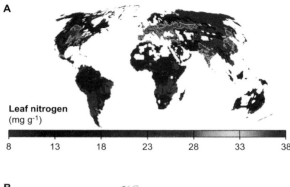

Leaf nitrogen
(mg g⁻¹)

8   13   18   23   28   33   38

B

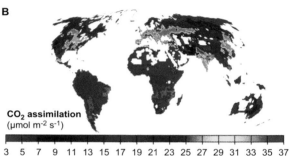

CO₂ assimilation
(μmol m⁻² s⁻¹)

3 5 7 9 11 13 15 17 19 21 23 25 27 29 31 33 35 37

Fig. 2.4.7. A Global distribution of N nutrition measured as leaf N concentration and B global distribution of maximum CO_2 assimilation. The maps are based on correlations given in Fig. 2.4.6 and the global distribution of vegetation types. The original parameter on which the maps are based is the specific leaf area; from this the N concentration is calculated as the basis for calculating A_{max}

the type of plant and measurement conditions at the site, photosynthetic capacity may be plotted globally, as only the specific leaf area and the N supply are required values (Fig. 2.4.7). In contrast to other values, such as stomatal conductance or C assimilation, these two values are easily determined. Agriculturally used areas of the earth, in North America, Europe, India and East Asia, are striking by their high N concentration. Other parts of the continents are characterised by N deficiency. Thus the photosynthetic capacity on earth correlates with potentially maximum rates in agricultural areas and low rates in other regions.

The physiological differentiation between C3, C4 and CAM plants becomes less important in the global perspective of CO_2 assimilation. In addition, Gifford (1974) demonstrated that the differences between C3 and C4 photosynthesis, which are very marked in the chloroplast, disappear progressively if the whole plant or the complete stand is considered. However, despite this reservation, the physiology of the C3 and C4 pathway is very important, considered from a historic perspective of the development of the earth as well as for the present day when considering the geographic distribution of species (Ehleringer and Cerling 2001; see Chap. 2.4.4).

| **Box 2.4.2** | **Summary: Interactions between specific leaf area, nitrogen supply and photosynthesis** |

- The **specific leaf area** is an important measure of the photosynthetic activity of a leaf. In the course of evolution, plants developed leaves with an increasingly large area per unit of dry matter, enabling greater light interception. However, this is tightly related to increased transpiration and thus demanded the adaptation of the whole organism in terms of transport tissues and roots (see Chap. 2.4.4). There is a continuum of leaf forms ranging from herbaceous dicotyledons with high specific leaf area at one extreme to conifer needles or the phyllodes of Australian *Acacia* species with low specific leaf area at the other.

- In leaves the **nitrogen concentration** correlates with the specific leaf area and the rate of net photosynthesis, allowing CO_2 assimilation on a global scale to be modelled based on specific leaf area and N concentration.

- In many cases, greater **physiological activity** is correlated with smaller tolerance to stress, with stress-tolerant species having limited physiological activity. Specific leaf area, N concentration and maximum CO_2 assimilation rate determine very largely the distribution of particular leaf forms and plant species on earth.

2.4.3

Response of Photosynthesis to Environmental Factors

Different conditions determine to what extent A_{max} may actually be used as **mean rate of CO_2 assimilation**. These factors are:

- **climatic factors:** primarily available light which varies by two orders of magnitude (0.5 mol photons m^{-2} day^{-1} on the soil of a tropical forest and 50 mol photons m^{-2} day^{-1} in a tropical grassland), and temperature and humidity;
- **edaphic factors:** primarily nutrition and availability of water (without transpiration there is no assimilation);
- **time-dependent factors:** particularly the duration of the growing season and the age of the leaf.

Climatic factors affect the short-term, usually reversible, responses as well as long-term, nonreversible changes, whilst edaphic factors are only long term and irreversible. The following considers how CO_2 assimilation depends on these conditions. Initially, change is considered with all other conditions remaining optimal and constant. In the natural environment there are, of course, different interactions between the conditions and these will be discussed later.

2.4.3.1
Light Environment

Photosynthesis increases with increasing irradiation. This is shown in Fig. 2.4.8 A, where CO_2 assimilation is a positive value and respiration negative. With increasing irradiation, dark respiration of mitochondria decreases and light-induced respiration increases. As light increases, a compensation point is reached at which CO_2 exchange is zero and above which net CO_2 uptake takes place eventually becoming saturated with increasing light. The immediate, short-term response of photosynthesis to the changing light is generally reversible.

In contrast to these short-term and reversible responses to radiation is adaptation involving structural modifications to the leaf (Chap. 1.2.1.1). **Sun and shade leaves** represent the extreme responses to light; however, there are many intermediate stages. Leaves of shade plants

adapted to low light conditions usually have a large leaf area per leaf weight and a lower compensation point than those species adapted to high light intensities (Fig. 2.4.8 B). A shade leaf is damaged in strong light, shed and replaced by a new leaf adapted to the new light conditions. This may be observed in house plants, when they are put in the open air in spring. Some, but not all, plants are able to adapt to light conditions (Fig. 2.4.8 C,D). For obligate shade plants light dependence of photosynthesis does not change, even if the plant is grown at a sunny site. Specific adaptation to light may also be observed between different populations of a species. In Fig. 2.4.8 C,D clones of *Solidago* which originate from sunny and shady sites are shown. Increased photosynthesis with full light utilisation only occurs in the "sun clone".

There are two ecologically important situations in which adaptation to light is required: At extremely shady sites where **sun flecks** only allow a short time to assimilate CO_2 and in dry areas of the earth where plants close their stomata because of lack of water. Plants at shady sites (e.g. in the herbaceous layer of a forest) receive during the day, and also with the season, often very high light intensities for short periods of time, so-called sun flecks (Fig. 2.4.9; Pearcy and Pfitsch 1994). Photosynthesis of these plants responds to these sun flecks with higher rates than would be expected from the light response curve, as the acceptor for CO_2 is not limiting whilst the carboxylase may be fully activated. In addition, the pools of ATP and NADP formed during the sun fleck may be still utilised for CO_2 fixation after the light has faded so that dark fixation of CO_2 continues at low light intensity. As a result, a short light fleck causes a longer period of CO_2 uptake. Using stable isotopes ($\delta^{13}C$) it was shown that about 50% of the dry matter production of these plants was assimilated in the extremely short periods of sun flecks.

In dry areas of the earth plants have about 50 mol photons m^{-2} day^{-1} to process without sufficient water to open the stomata. Thus a situation arises in the leaf in which PS I and PS II are not able to release electrons to NADPH because no CO_2 enters the stomata and thus CO_2, the substrate for reduction, is inadequate. The CO_2 concentration in the mesophyll is around the compensation point. The consequences of such a "bombardment" with photons are (see Chap. 1.2):

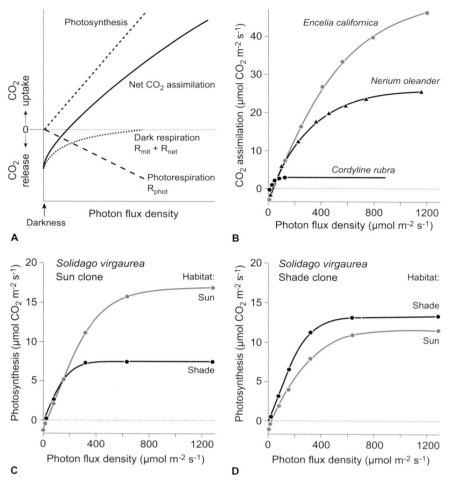

Fig. 2.4.8. A Dependence of CO_2 gas exchange on the light intensity, measured as quantum flux (µmol photons m^{-2} s^{-1}). The y-axis corresponds to a positive value of CO_2 assimilation and a negative value for respiration. The figure shows the processes which occur in the region below light saturation (after Larcher 1994). B Dependence of CO_2 gas exchange on quantum fluxes of species differently adapted to shade. C Change in light-dependent photosynthesis with adaptation to the light climate in *Solidago virgaurea*. Clones that were pre-adapted to full light adapt their rate to the location (i.e. shade) compared with D clones that are adapted to the shaded location and do not change the rate of CO_2 assimilation. (Björkman 1981)

- increased **fluorescence** (Björkman and Demmig-Adams 1994);
- increased **release of heat** (Björkman and Demmig-Adams 1994); or
- damage in PS II at the D1 protein (**photoinhibition**) with subsequent yellowing (Schäfer 1994).

2.4.3.2
Temperature

Starting from temperatures below 0 °C where photosynthesis as well as respiration are at a complete standstill, respiration of leaf cells is generally activated earlier than photosynthesis with increasing temperatures. At low temperatures a range exists at which only respiration is measurable. Photosynthesis starts around –5 °C (Fig. 2.4.10 A), reaches an optimum and decreases at high temperatures. In contrast, respiration increases exponentially over a wide range of temperatures and is only inhibited at very high temperatures. Net photosynthesis as the balance between these two processes shows an optimum shifted to slightly lower temperatures than the physiological process of photosynthesis. The interaction between respiration and photosynthesis is particularly obvious considering the common effect of light and temperature: At low

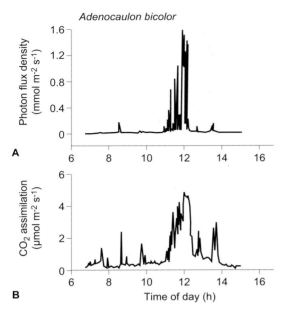

A

B

Time of day (h)

Fig. 2.4.9. A Change with time of a light fleck in a shaded habitat and B delay in CO_2 fixation in *Adenocaulon bicolor*. The period of CO_2 uptake is longer than the duration of the light fleck, i.e. reduction equivalents are stored and, after the light fleck has passed, these are used in dark reactions for CO_2 reduction. (Pearcy and Pfitsch 1994)

light intensities the temperature optimum is shifted to lower temperatures (Fig. 2.4.10 B) with the consequence that plants are able to operate at low light intensity during the cool hours of the morning as well as in the optimum range of their potential net photosynthesis during midday, at high temperatures and full light.

The **temperature optimum** of net photosynthesis is not at all constant, for example, it changes with season (Lange et al. 1975 a). Similarly, the size of plant leaves is "adapted" to the radiation conditions so that the temperature (see Chap. 2.1) remains in the physiologically optimum range.

Even though plants operate most of the day in the photosynthetically optimum range there are two critical ranges of temperature in photosynthesis (see also Chap. 1.3):

- Low temperature is not a factor damaging photosynthesis, but frost together with high light intensities leads to photoinhibition. This effect was first observed in Alpine sites, which is not surprising as the CO_2 concentration decreases with increasing height and thus increases the imbalance between light flux and

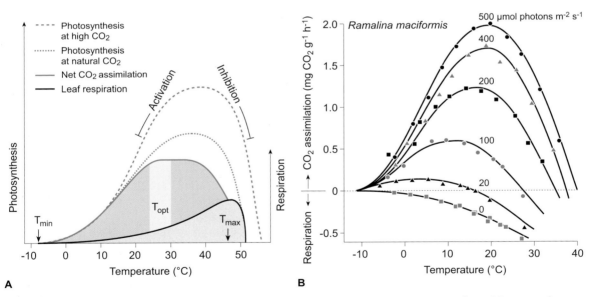

A

B

Fig. 2.4.10. A Schematic presentation of the dependence of photosynthesis, respiration and net CO_2 gas exchange on temperature. Activation of photosynthesis leads to an exponential increase in CO_2 uptake. Increasing temperature also increasingly inhibits photosynthesis. Interaction between activation and inhibition leads to an apparent optimum of CO_2 uptake that finally leads to a lower CO_2 uptake at high temperatures. The rate of net assimilation at increased temperature is balanced in part by the exponential rise in respiration. The temperature optimum for respiration is higher than that of photosynthesis (after Larcher 1994). B Interaction between light and temperature on photosynthesis (positive value on the *y*-axis) and respiration (negative value on the *y*-axis) leads to a decrease in the optimal temperature range at lower light intensities, i.e. for the lichen *Ramalina maciformis* cool mornings with low light are as much "optimum" as are high temperatures at full light. (Lange et al. 1977)

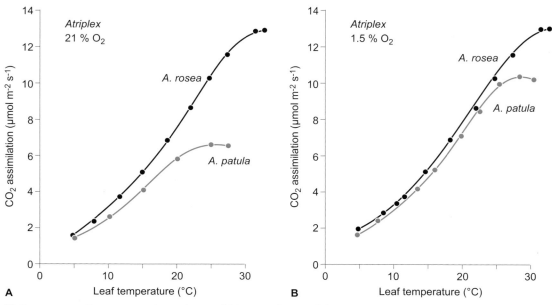

Fig. 2.4.11. A Temperature dependence of CO_2 assimilation of the C4 plant *Atriplex rosea* and the C3 plant *Atriplex patula* showing clearly differences in maximum rate of CO_2 uptake and in the temperature optimum. B The same experimental conditions as in A but 1.5% O_2 and not 21% O_2 in the surrounding air. CO_2 uptake of C3 plants changes so that it is like the C4 plants. Investigation at low partial pressure of O_2 demonstrates experimentally the existence and importance of light-induced respiration on CO_2 assimilation. (Björkman 1971)

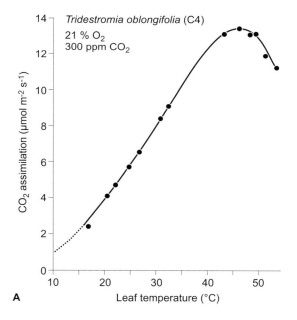

Fig. 2.4.12. A Temperature dependence of CO_2 assimilation of *Tidestromia oblongifolia*, Amacarnthaceae, in Death Valley, California. This plant reaches a maximum rate of CO_2 assimilation at 48 °C. B *Tidestromia oblongifolia* grows in Death Valley as a summer annual in erosion gullies in which rainwater gathers and then percolates into the soil. (Photo E.-D. Schulze)

C fixation. After several frosts net photosynthesis decreases and then recovers slowly, but does not reach the values as during the summer.

- High temperatures affect opening of stomata and result in a disproportional increase in transpiration (Lange 1959); thus a leaf is more likely to dry out completely than to be damaged by heat.

C4 plants have a higher temperature optimum of photosynthesis than C3 plants, because the PEP-carboxylase of C4 plants has its optimum at high temperatures and is thus able to reassimilate respiratory CO_2. This effect may also be achieved by exposing C3 plants to an atmosphere with little O_2 and thus reduce the oxygenase function of RuBP-carboxylase (Fig. 2.4.11). The highest temperatures at which higher plants reach optimum rates of photosynthesis were observed on *Tidestromia oblongifolia* at 46 °C in Death Valley, California (Fig. 2.4.12).

2.4.3.3
Humidity

Net photosynthesis decreases with **stomatal closure** induced by low humidity; however, it has often been observed that CO_2 assimilation does not decrease in proportion to stomatal conductance. It is difficult to explain this, because direct effects of humidity on photosynthesis have also been described (Mott and Parkhurst 1991). Obviously, stomata do not close synchronously, so that some areas between the veins still have open stomata whilst others are closed. Thus, there is a higher CO_2 influx to some small areas, but a lower influx into other areas of the leaf; consequently, the calculated average CO_2 concentration in the mesophyll remains constant, even though the total conductance of the leaf is decreased. The temperature distribution (Jones 1999) shows that a leaf is not a homogeneous area and so the heterogeneity, so-called **patchiness of the leaf**, contributes to a partial decoupling of the flux of CO_2 and water vapour for the whole leaf (Mott et al. 1993).

2.4.3.4
Nutrition

CO_2 assimilation and stomatal conductance change in proportion to the **nutrition** of the leaf. This not only applies to changes in N nutrition (see Chap. 2.4.5), but also to phosphorus (P). C4 plants, despite a generally lower N concentration, have a potentially higher rate of assimilation than C3 plants, as in C4 plants RuBP-carboxylase is concentrated in the bundle sheath. Under natural conditions the higher photosynthetic capacity is not used, but rather a lower stomatal conductance is reached resulting in lower evaporation but similar assimilation as in C3 plants. Therefore, saving water appears more important than maximising photosynthesis. This leads to a decrease of RuBP-carboxylase and of the N concentration compared with C3 plants (see Penning de Vries and Djitèye 1982) with consequences for assimilate production and for distribution of plants exhibiting the two types of photosynthesis (see Chap. 2.4.4).

2.4.3.5
Water

The response of CO_2 assimilation to water stress is easier to study on plants without an epidermis, such as **lichens**, as here stomatal effects do not occur. When dry lichens are moistened, only respiration becomes measurable at a water content (per dry weight) of 20% (Fig. 2.4.13). With increasing water content respiration and photosynthesis increase. The maximum CO_2 assimilation is reached at a water content of 80%. The equilibrium humidity for activation of gas exchange thus corresponds to an air humidity of 80% and a water potential of –30 MPa. This water potential is much lower than ever measured for higher plants (–11 MPa; Kappen et al. 1972).

Obviously, photosynthesis starts at a range which is normally not reached in intact leaves. However, photosynthesis responds to changes in **turgor** (Kaiser 1982). As the changes in cell volume and thus in turgor depend on the rigidity of the cell wall ($\varepsilon = \Delta P/\Delta V$), plants with a large leaf area per dry weight, the so-called mesophytes, are more sensitive towards drying out of the soil than plants with smaller leaf area per dry weight (so-called sclerophytes; Fig. 2.4.5).

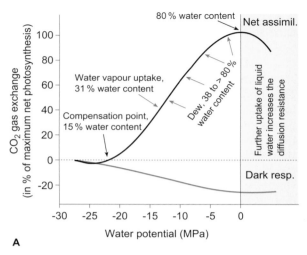

Fig. 2.4.13. A Dependence of CO_2 gas exchange (NP: net photosynthesis) on net water potential of the thallus of the lichen *Ramalina maciformis* in the Negev Desert (temperature 15 °C, saturating light). On the *y*-axis are the positive values of CO_2 assimilation and the negative values of respiration. For an ecologically relevant conditions, the water content of the thallus is presented in percent of its dry weight. The *black arrows* indicate the maximum water contents (given as percent of the dry weight of the thallus), which were measured after dew fall or with increased air humidity in the field (Lange 1965). At low water potential initially respiration is activated followed by photosynthesis. This leads to a water compensation point for CO_2 assimilation that is considerably lower than the water potential so far measured in leaves of higher plants. Note: There are types of plants that have even lower water compensation points: An extreme plant is *Dendrographa minor* (California) with activation of photosynthesis at –38 MPa. *Dendrographa* attains 50% of its net photosynthesis at –18 MPa (Lange 1988). There are also types that are not able to photosynthesise at low water potential. Thus cyanolichens (with cyanobacteria as symbionts rather than green algae) require fluid water (in contrast to water vapour) in order to activate photosynthesis. High water content (right of vertical line, which occurs after rain) increases the diffusion resistance to CO_2 in many lichens to an extent that CO_2 assimilation decreases and in extreme circumstances reaches the compensation point. B *Ramalina maciformis* on flint in Avdat, Negev, Israel. (Photo E.-D. Schulze)

Under field conditions changes in the photosynthetic activity (this comprises not only photosynthesis) are best correlated with the **pre-dawn water potential** ($\Psi_{predawn}$) which indicates the water status of the soil. Photosynthesis decreases with $\Psi_{predawn}$ as the soil dries, closely related to a simultaneous increase in the xylem sap of abscisic acid formed in the roots (see Chap. 1.5.2 and Chap. 2.2).

2.4.3.6
Age of Leaves and Growing Season

During the course of their development from emergence to shedding, leaves undergo an ontogenetic change in activity (see also Chap. 2.3.3). Three phases are distinguished: leaves which are still developing and have formed less than about 30% of the leaf area are carbohydrate sinks. They are often called **sink leaves** as they consume more carbohydrates than they produce photosynthetically. In the next stage, fully grown leaves are **source leaves**, which produce an excess of carbohydrates and export these, via the phloem, for the consumption at other sites. In the **ageing phase**, leaves yellow and there is degradation of structures, providing an additional source of carbohydrates and amino acids for the rest of the plant. Photosynthesis need not necessarily change synchronously with the carbon export, and may reach its highest rates before the leaf is even fully expanded, i.e. the leaf starts to age with its expansion. In many herbaceous plants, new leaves are permanently formed and shed. They age according to a genetic programme of senescence (see also Fig. 2.3.6).

Some examples explain the processes during leaf development:

- **herbaceous species:** in herbaceous species, maximum rate of CO_2 assimilation is reached before complete leaf expansion (Fig. 2.4.14) and decreases continuously after complete expansion of the leaf until the leaf is shed. In the meantime the next leaf is developed, which reaches higher rates, but ages according to the same pattern (Woodward 1976).

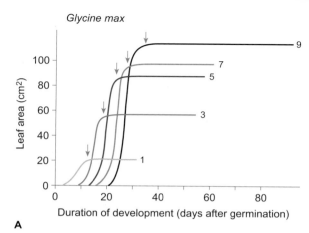

A

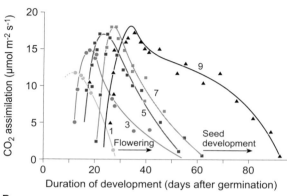

B

Fig. 2.4.14. A Development of leaf area and B associated changes in photosynthesis in leaves of different age *Glycine max*. The figure shows that the leaf starts to age before it has fully developed its leaf area. (Woodward 1976)

- **deciduous trees: beeches in Solling.** Sun leaves of beech emerge very quickly in May and reach maximum activity in mid-June (Fig. 2.4.15). As early as the beginning of August ageing starts, with decreasing rates of CO_2 assimilation, and leaves are shed at the beginning of October. On the same tree, development of shade leaves is significantly slower. Maximum CO_2 assimilation is only reached in August. Ageing then occurs much faster and leaf shedding is only slightly delayed compared to that of sun leaves.
- **coniferous trees: spruce in Solling.** Development of evergreen needles of spruce is very different (Fig. 2.14.16). Needles emerge later than leaves of beech, maximum rates decrease only slightly in autumn and the activity of needles remains constant in the following year. Ageing starts only after 3–5 years.

2.4.3.7
Optimisation of CO_2 Assimilation Relative to Water Use

CO_2 assimilation is obviously a variable process and may fluctuate considerably, depending on climate and soil as well as differences between species. As long as the climatic conditions at the site are favourable for growth the process is primarily determined by soil fertility. As soon as conditions become more extreme, colder as well as drier, there are several options in the plant kingdom for coping when these conditions exist. This is shown by an example from the Negev Desert (Fig. 2.4.17; Schulze and Hall 1982): At the same site lichens, CAM, C3 and C4 plants flourish next to each other. During the course of the day, they behave differently regarding their CO_2 assimilation, transpiration and stomatal conductance. Lichens do not regulate water relations and therefore their CO_2 assimilation is restricted to a few hours in the morning after the falling of dew. Their material production is minimal but despite this lichens belong to the most successful organisms in this desert. They settle on each stone and form extensive crusts on the loess soil. The CAM plant *Opuntia* occurs in the Negev as an introduced plant, but *Caraluma negvensis* is an autochthonous CAM plant which behaves similarly (Lange et al. 1975b). CAM plants assimilate during the night and also under good conditions during the day. Transpiration is substantially lower at night than for other species during the day. Despite the favourable relation of assimilation to transpiration, CAM plants in the Negev are rather rare, probably because of climatic conditions in the late Holocene. C3 and C4 plants respond similarly. Both attain similar rates of photosynthesis on dry soils; the rate decreases with soil drying. In summer both species have a **daily course of two peaks** in CO_2 uptake, with a **"midday depression"** caused by dry air. It is to be expected that the transpiration of C3 plants is slightly higher than that of C4 plants related to the significantly lower stomatal conductance of C4 plants. The potential advantage of a high assimilation capacity is not used by C4 plants in nature, but rather is used to avoid water stress. Despite this, C4 plants do not settle in extremely dry sites in the Negev, but in the more favourable valley floors which also have higher salt levels. This does not mean that C3 plants suffer maximum water stress at the dry sites. They regulate their water

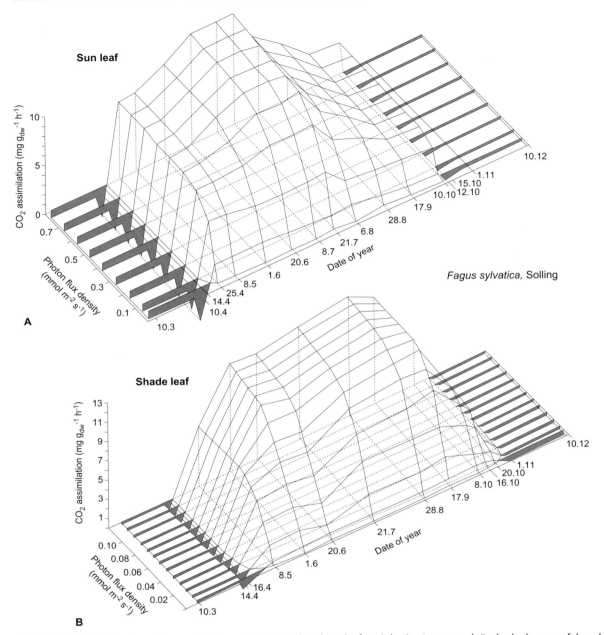

Fig. 2.4.15. Light dependence of CO_2 assimilation related to leaf weight in A sun and B shade leaves of beech, throughout the year. Only in spring do buds show respiration, which however rises sharply with bud break. With leaf emergence CO_2 is assimilated. Also, in autumn, only respiration is measured in buds. Sun leaves develop faster, but age faster than shade leaves. In sun leaves full development takes almost 2 months (until mid-June), they are fully active for only 1 month and start to yellow in August. (Schulze 1970)

relations and physiological activity by leaf shedding, so that at the end of the dry period the water conditions of a dry slope are more favourable than for C4 plants in the valley floors (Kappen et al. 1976).

With such a range of reactions the question remains whether there is a basic principle for

the regulation of physiological activity. As the coupling of CO_2 assimilation to the atmosphere occurs via stomata and as a consequence water is lost, regulation balancing both processes might be feasible. It is striking that maximum photosynthetic rates are only rarely attained at most sites. Most of the time plants operate, in

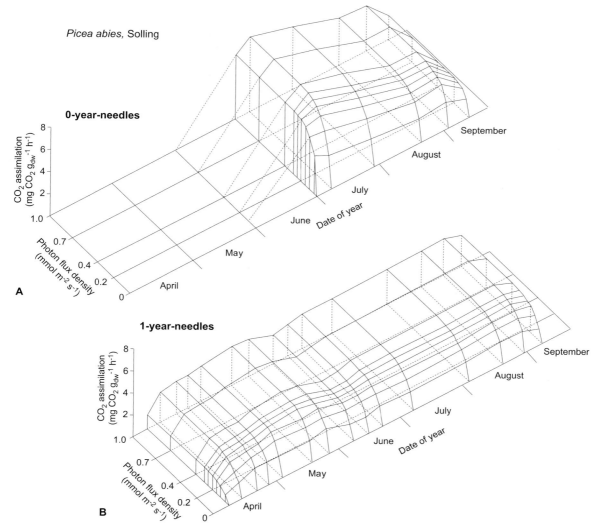

Fig. 2.4.16. Light dependence of CO_2 assimilation based on leaf weight in A current year and B 1-year-old spruce needles throughout the year. Young needles develop later in the year than leaves of beech (see Fig. 2.4.15). Development requires about 5 weeks before they reach the highest rates of CO_2 assimilation. With the reinforcement of the cell wall which continues until the autumn of the current year the rate of CO_2 uptake per dry weight decreases. In contrast the rate of CO_2 assimilation in the 1-year-old needles is lower than in current year's needles, but is constant for about 5 months. Ageing occurs after 3–5 years. (Fuchs et al. 1977)

temperate woodlands as well as in desert regions, at an **average rate of assimilation** that is about 50% of the maximum rate, and this also applies to stomatal conductance. In temperate climates the actual rate of CO_2 assimilation is reduced by light, in arid climates by light and air humidity.

Photosynthesis depends on the physiological activity of Rubisco and the CO_2 concentrations in mesophyll and atmosphere but is also regulated by stomata and energy balance. It is basically not possible to write a simple equation for

the relation between climate and assimilation, as the Penmann-Monteith equation does for the dependence of evaporation on stomatal changes ($\delta E/\delta g$; see Chap. 2.2). It is not possible to express the dependence of assimilation on C_i and the dependence of transpiration (E) on the vapour pressure deficit of air and by solving the energy balance, as the CO_2 flux (in contrast to E) not only depends on external factors, but also on the leaf's internal physiological regulators. Cowan and Farquhar (1977) simplified the problem by assuming that photosynthetic activity re-

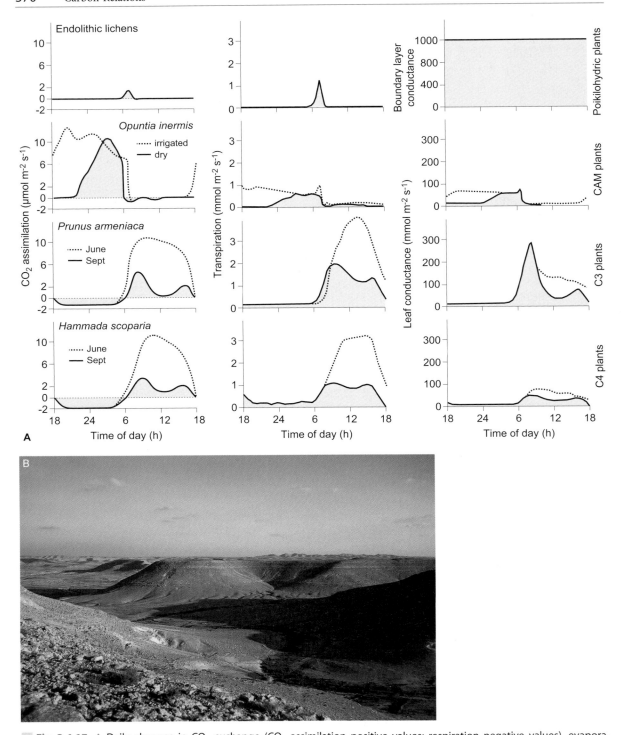

Fig. 2.4.17. A Daily changes in CO_2 exchange (CO_2 assimilation positive values; respiration negative values), evaporation and leaf conductance in various plant types in the Negev Desert: endolithic lichens, CAM plants: *Opuntia inermis*; C3 plants: *Prunus armeniaca*; C4 plants: *Hammada scoparia* (Schulze 1982). **B** The Negev Desert: slopes occupied by dwarf bushes (*Artemisia, Zygophyllum, Reaumuria*), stones are covered with endolithic lichens, in the stone's shade *Caraluma negevensis*, a CAM succulent, may be found. In the valley remains of terracing from Nabatean farmers, currently used by Bedouins for wheat growing, otherwise covered by the C4 plant *Hammada scoparia*. (Photo E.-D. Schulze)

mains constant. They came to the conclusion that there should be a balance between the response of assimilation ($\delta A/\delta g$) and transpiration ($\delta E/\delta g$) resulting from the change in stomata. Neglecting the energy balance and possible changes of photosynthetic capacity they conclude that **"optimal" regulation** occurs when

$$(\delta A/\delta E) = \lambda \qquad (2.4.22)$$

where λ is a species-specific parameter which is constant, at least over the course of a day.

The limits of this interpretation are at the next higher organisational level, the vegetation. What use is it to an individual plant to behave optimally, when the saved water remains in the soil and either seeps further into the soil profile or evaporates from the crust or is used by its neighbours? In "non-cooperative behaviour" of neighbours (i.e. with excessive use of resources by neighbours) the individual which is acting optimally might lose, because the "neighbourly squanderer" has used almost all the water, if the saved resource is required to maintain life of the "optimiser" during drought conditions. This is exactly what is observed under arid conditions as diversity of species and structures: The equalisation of **opportunistic (non-optimised)** and **conservative (optimised) behaviour** in assimilation and use of water. Opportunistic behaviour is usually coupled to the ability of vegetation to complete development quickly (annuals), whilst conservative behaviour is coupled with slow development of vegetation and storage of resources over several growing seasons (**perennials**); an example of this type of behaviour is discussed in Chapter 3.2.5.3: Invasion of *Bromus* into the *Artemisia* steppe of North America. However, here, as so often in nature, there are many transitions which do not fall within such simple classifications.

2.4.3.8
Geological and Recent Distribution of C3, C4 and CAM Plants

Based on the physiological characteristics of C3 and C4 plants there is differentiation of these two photosynthetic types in the earth's vegetation. Because of their high-temperature optima for photosynthesis and the ability to use high light intensities, C4 plants, particularly perennials, are more prevalent than C3 plants in subtropical **savannahs and grasslands with summer rains** (Fig. 2.4.18 A). In contrast, the main distribution area of C3 grasses (often annuals) is in the winter cold steppes (Fig. 2.4.18 B). As the dependence on temperature and light is affected by CO_2 concentration in the atmosphere, the balance in the distribution of the two physiological types is not fixed.

The distribution of CAM plants in comparison to C4 plants is botanically very interesting, but is of rather secondary importance regarding the C cycle of the earth. Succulents are mainly distributed in **coastal deserts with cool nights** (South Africa with Namibia, Chile, Baja California, Tenerife; Fig. 2.4.18 C). The PEP-carboxylase of these coastal succulents is adapted to low night temperatures. Independent of this, CAM plants can also be found in warm, humid, moist rain forests. These include epiphytic orchids and some tree species of the genus *Clusia* (Clusiaceae; Lüttge 1999). The PEP-carboxylase of these genera is adapted, like C4 plants, to high temperatures, showing that the distribution pattern of CAM succulents with their major distribution in cold coastal deserts does not depend on the temperature response of PEP-carboxylase but is probably caused by competition, i.e. succulents grow too slowly in order to compete in the tropics and in the tropical grasslands the humidity at night is too low, so that stomata open during the night would also lose too much water.

Ehleringer et al. (1997) showed, based on the CO_2, light and temperature dependence of photosynthesis during the night, that C3 plants are competitively superior to C4 plants at increasing CO_2 concentrations and as climates become warmer (Fig. 2.4.19 A, B). At the time of the biggest freeze in the **glacial period**, the atmospheric CO_2 concentration was at about 200 ppm; in this CO_2 climate C4 plants were superior to C3 plants even at temperatures of 10 °C during the growing season. It is assumed that with increasing CO_2 concentrations C4 plants will be out-competed and have to move into climates with higher temperatures. For current temperature and CO_2 distributions on earth, C3 plants dominate at latitudes greater than 45° north and south (Fig. 2.4.19 B).

This observation is strengthened by the N requirement, which is higher for C3 than for C4 plants (Fig. 2.4.19 D). Under drier conditions, the N concentration in leaves is high due to the activation of nitrification in the soil after rain. Also, growth of plants is limited by drought and N concentration thus increases. In addition,

Fig. 2.4.18. A View of a tropical grassland in Namibia at about 200 mm rainfall of summer rains, i.e. water is available at high temperatures. Thus perennial C4 grasses and single succulents of the order Euphorbia are typical. **B** View of a continental steppe in Khazacstan. Note: Water is available after snowmelt at low temperature followed by summer drought. The vegetation is characterised by annual and perennial C3 grasses and shrubs (e.g. *Altaea*), a higher proportion of annuals and Leguminosae (e.g. *Astragalus*) and single shrubs (*Crataegus*). **C** View of succulent desert in Baja-California, Mexico, with *Pachycereus pringlei* as dominating cactus species. In the undergrowth are shrubs of *Larrea tridentata*, *Encelia* and *Ambrosia*, amongst others. (Photo E.-D. Schulze)

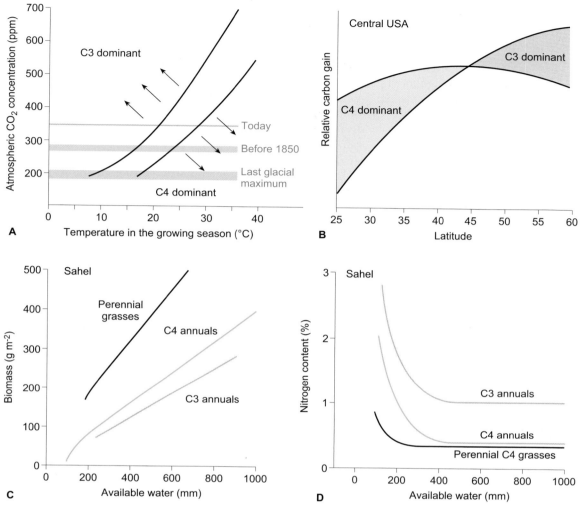

Fig. 2.4.19. A Distribution of C3 and C4 species in relation to temperature in the growing season and atmospheric CO_2 concentration. The *blue lines* indicate the shift of the temperature-CO_2 regime since glaciation. B Relative carbon gain of C3 and C4 species in relation to latitude at present CO_2 concentration (after Ehleringer et al. 1997). Changes in C biomass and D nitrogen concentration of C3 and C4 plants with water availability from rainfall in the Sahel. C4 plants have a lower N concentration than C3 plants and, therefore, are less suitable for grazing. (Penning de Vries and Djitèye 1982)

nitrification in the soil is more drought resistant than the growth of plants. Nitrogen concentration decreases with increasing precipitation and increasing plant production. In subtropical arid climates, annual plants with C4 metabolism are not in any way superior to C3 plants, rather they are inferior, whilst with high precipitation C4 perennial grasses dominate over C3 grasses. This has consequences for the use of land. The **Bedouin** move their herds to grazing sites with annuals which also have high N concentration, whilst with higher precipitation settled people pursue agriculture with C4 grasses which were perennials in their original forms (Penning de Vries and Djitèye 1982; MacFadden and Cerling 1996).

2.4.4
Growth and Storage

2.4.4.1
Introduction to the Carbon Balance

Ultimately, photosynthesis serves the plant to produce biomass and seeds. Assimilate production supplies the material for a continuous increase in the size of the plant body, which is important in competition with other plants and for storage of resources which are required for flowering and production of fruit.

Box 2.4.3   Summary: Reponses of photosynthesis to environmental factors

- Photosynthesis changes reversibly with **weather conditions**: light, temperature and atmospheric humidity. Strong light may lead to irreversible damage (photoinhibition) whereas low light leads to decreased CO_2 assimilation. On average a leaf functions at about 50% of its maximal CO_2 assimilation rate (A_{max}).
- Photosynthesis in the long term is adapted to the **light environment** and the level of **nutrition**.
- Photosynthesis of higher plants responds irreversibly to **water stress**. Lichens in contrast respond reversibly to desiccation.
- Leaves respond to environmental conditions by modifying the **ageing process** which is species-specific.
- There is a tendency towards **optimisation** of CO_2 assimilation and transpiration, although "the optimal" response (water saving) may be disadvantageous in a plant community, as an unused resource in the soil becomes available for neighbouring plants or tillers.
- **C3, CAM and C4 plants** occupy niches which depend on the geological and more recent conditions of atmospheric CO_2 concentration and temperature in the growing season. C4 plants dominate at low CO_2 concentrations under high temperatures whereas in contrast C3 plants dominate at low temperatures. However, with high CO_2 concentrations, C3 plants can also dominate at high temperatures. This trend is strengthened by nutrition. Perennial C4 grasses have smaller N concentration in their leaves than C3 plants and are thus, in subtropical climates and also with limited nutrition, superior to C3 plants.

Table 2.4.1. Estimated annual balances of a beech forest (Schulze 1970; Scarascia et al. 1999), spruce forest (Fuchs et al. 1977; Scarascia-Mugnozza et al. 2000) and a barley crop (Biscoe et al. 1975; Jones 1994) in t C ha^{-1} year^{-1}

	Beech	Spruce	Barley
A_{max} (mg CO_2 g^{-1} h^{-1})	10	5	20
GPP (t C ha^{-1} year $^{-1}$)	8.6 (100%)	14.9 (100%)	8.3 (100%)
Respiration	2.4 (28%)	7.8 (52%)	1.7 (20%)
Leaf	1.3	6.4	1.5
Shoot	0.4	1.0	0.0
Stem and root	0.7	0.4	0.2
Litter	3.2 (37%)	2.9 (20%)	6.6 (80%)
Leaves	1.8	1.2	4.4
Fine roots	1.4	1.7	2.2
Growth	3.0 (35%)	4.2 (28%)	0.0
Large roots	0.4	0.7	0.0
Branches	1.4	1.5	0.0
Trunk	1.3	2.0	0.0

For biomass production additional energy is required for catabolic processes. This is independent of the energy required to maintain the existing biomass. In both cases, this energy is made available by the consumption of carbohydrates. **Net primary production (NPP)** results from the **net photosynthesis (A)** and the **respiration of the autotrophic whole plant (R_a)**; respiration without light; see Chap. 2.4.1). Net photosynthesis (A) is often also called **gross primary production (GPP)**:

$$NPP = A - R_a \qquad (2.4.23)$$

The **material balance** of the plant indicates the magnitude of these processes.

Table 2.4.1 shows that barley with the highest photosynthetic rates (A_{max}) does not have the highest C gain (GPP). Spruce has a C gain which is about 80% higher than that of barley with about 25% of the photosynthetic rate. Reasons for this difference are that spruce has double the leaf mass of barley and the growing season is three times longer than that of barley. The deciduous beech is between these extremes. Costs for evergreen needle cover are paid, in spruce, by a significantly higher respiration. On the other hand, spruce invests less carbon in the growth of branches than beech, therefore the stem growth of spruce is almost a third higher than that of beech. For both tree species the harvested growth in stems is only a smaller fraction of the C gain (beech 15%, spruce 13%). Grain yield for barley would be comparable to the growth of stems and with a harvest index (grain yield/above ground biomass) of 0.4 about 1.8 t C/ha. This is about 20% of net photosynthesis and thus significantly higher than in trees.

The example shows that many factors determine NPP and that the plant kingdom has many ways of regulating biomass production. These are, amongst others:

- C balance over a growing season (mean rate of net photosynthesis*mean leaf area*length of the growing season; Schulze 1982);
- distribution of assimilates to different organs (Stitt and Schulze 1994);
- respiration in existing and growing biomass (Merino et al. 1982);
- storage (Chapin et al. 1990).

2.4.4.2
Respiration

Respiration of mitochondria is obviously an important component in reducing the C gain. The amount of C required for the synthesis of certain products is very different and may differ by two orders of magnitude according to the product (Penning de Vries 1975, 1983; Table 2.4.2).

It is possible to calculate C requirements of growing organs from their synthetic products, but the requirement of existing organs is not quantified by this. McCree (1983; Amthor 1989) suggested the following terms to divide these two functions of respiration:

- **growth respiration, R_g** (respiration serving growth); and

Table 2.4.2. Respiratory requirement for a plant to synthesise substrates required for growth, and for respiration of organs. (After Penning de Vries 1975)

		Respiratory CO_2 requirement mg CO_2 g^{-1}
Substrate	Organic acids	11
	Carbohydrates	170
	Proteins	544
	Lipids	1720
Plant organ	Leaves	333
	Stems	278
	Wood	426
	Rice grain	186
	Beans	420

- **maintenance respiration, R_m** (respiration for maintenance of organs).

Dark respiration (respiration of autotrophic plants), R_d (mg CO_2 plant^{-1} time^{-1}), of a plant with weight W consists of the maintenance respiration (mg CO_2 plant^{-1} time^{-1}) and the growth respiration (mg CO_2 plant^{-1} time^{-1})

$$R_d = R_m + R_g \times dW/dt \qquad (2.4.24)$$

Dividing by the weight yields the respiration rates per unit weight

$$R_d/W = R_m/W + R_g \times dW/dt \times 1/W \quad (2.4.25)$$

where $dW/dt \times 1/W$ is the so-called **relative growth rate (RGR)**. If the dark respiration, R_d is plotted as a function of RGR, for short periods

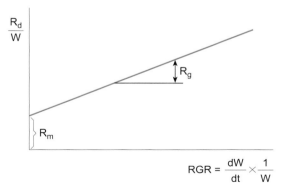

Fig. 2.4.20. Visual presentation of the definitions of growth-induced respiration (R_g) and maintenance respiration (R_m). If dark respiration (R_d per unit weight) is measured in relation to the relative growth rate (RGR=increase in weight per unit total weight of the plant), then the slope of the curve is a measure of growth-induced respiration and the intercept on the y-axis is a measure of maintenance respiration

of time a straight line should emerge, the slope corresponds to the growth respiration and intersection with the *y*-axis, R_m (Fig. 2.4.20). The relation between R_m and R_g depends on the time in which individual organs are photosynthetically active. In herbaceous plants the root respires for 24 h, whilst the shoot shows net respiration only during the night. In woody plants branches and sapwood respire corresponding to the amount of living cells for 24 h.

Research into respiration has been neglected compared with research on photosynthesis, so that there are still many uncertainties about the conditions relating acclimatisation and adaptation to resources (Amthor 1989).

2.4.4.3
Growth

Growth of plants and the processes of accumulation can only be shown as a mathematical model as there is no satisfactory physiological model explaining the regulation of C distribution to various organs and gain in mass (Fig. 2.4.21). CO_2 assimilation depends on the CO_2 gradient, the stomatal conductance and the leaf area. Assimilates formed produce an assimilate pool as intermediary storage from which the distribution to growth of green and other organs takes place. In both cases growth is added to the existing biomass. Particularly in leaves self-shading may occur and old leaves are shed (see Chap. 2.4.5.3: *Urtica*). Turnover in the root region is similar.

Growth of leaves has a positive feed-back on CO_2 assimilation, which produces additional re-

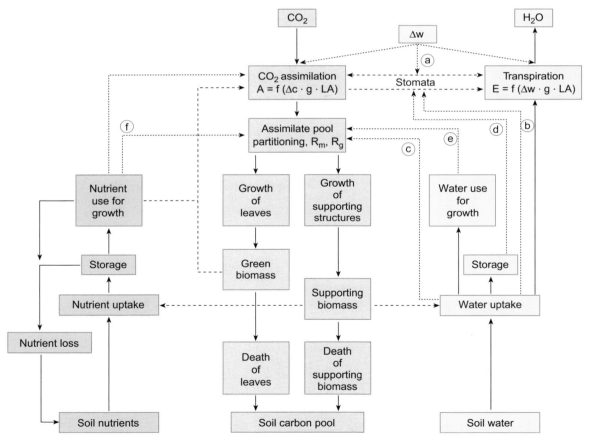

Fig. 2.4.21. Schematic model of internal carbon, water and nutrient pools and fluxes within the plant for shoots and roots (*continuous line*), as well as the important feed-back (*broken line*) and regulation between C, N and water balance. Regulating factors are (*a*) the effects of climatic factors, (*b*), (*c*), (*d*), and (*e*) regulation of stomata and carbon partitioning by the water balance, and (*f*) regulation of assimilation and C partitioning by the nutrient balance. (Schulze and Chapin 1987)

quirements for nutrients and water. Growth of non-green organs has a negative feed-back on CO_2 assimilation, but stimulates the uptake of nutrients and water. Regulation of assimilate distribution and rates of senescence determines the balance between assimilating and respiring organs, where the latter are responsible for the uptake of nutrients and water. A special situation occurs in woody plants, because the biomass which dies remains in the stem (**heartwood**) and only a small ring of vessels (**sapwood**) is metabolically active. Thus the heartwood does not respire, but serves to increase the vegetative structure and is thus very important in competition with other species.

There are several other regulatory mechanisms for the **"communication" of shoot and root**. The carbohydrate supply gives, of course, the decisive signal for the growth of root and stem. Roots regulate, via cytokinin, the shoot with respect to CO_2 assimilation as well as the distribution of assimilates. The supply of nutrients, particularly nitrate (Scheible et al. 1997), and the availability of carbohydrates (W. Schulze et al. 1991) may also act as signals regulating carbon allocation.

Of course, gain of resources and consumption of resources need not always take place synchronously. This applies particularly to the uptake of nutrients and CO_2 assimilation. If plants were only to take up nutrients synchronously with their consumption, neighbouring plants would have the possibility to gain these resources if they are available in the soil (see Chap. 2.4.3.7). At the same time, light must be controlled to maintain the existing photosynthetic apparatus, when little carbohydrate is necessary (e.g. in drought periods) as without the transfer of electrons to carbon, nitrogen or sulfur the chlorophyll is damaged by irradiation. Therefore, the assimilate and nutrient pool is very important as a **"store"** from which various requirements of the plant are covered.

2.4.4.4
Storage and Feed-Back

Plants use resources for **growth, defence** against herbivores and **reserves**, and they **accumulate** these passively if the gain of resources is greater than their consumption. Only part of these resources may be recovered and only this is considered a "store" (Fig. 2.4.22). Subdivision into accumulation and formation of reserves is difficult. **Formation of reserves** is the process in which stored products at the time of their production by metabolism compete with growth processes.

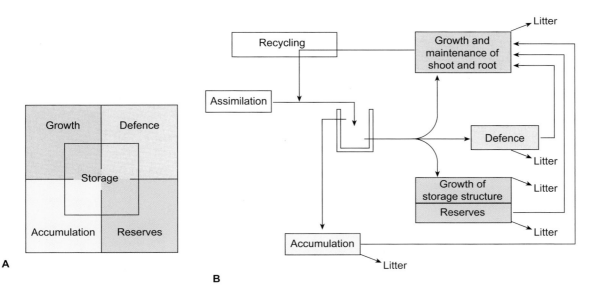

A   **B**

Fig. 2.4.22. A Schematic presentation of the partitioning of carbon in a plant for particular functions: growth, defence, formation and accumulation of reserves. Only part of this C can be reallocated and is thus a "store". B Flux of carbon assimilates from CO_2 assimilation to growth and the reutilisation of C with death of plant parts (e.g. leaf fall). Accumulation occurs when C production (assimilation plus reallocation) exceeds immediate requirements. Formation of reserves occurs when the conditions for formation of storage products (e.g. starch) competes with growth processes. Short-term assimilate pools, which act as physiological control, are shown as a "well". (Chapin et al. 1990)

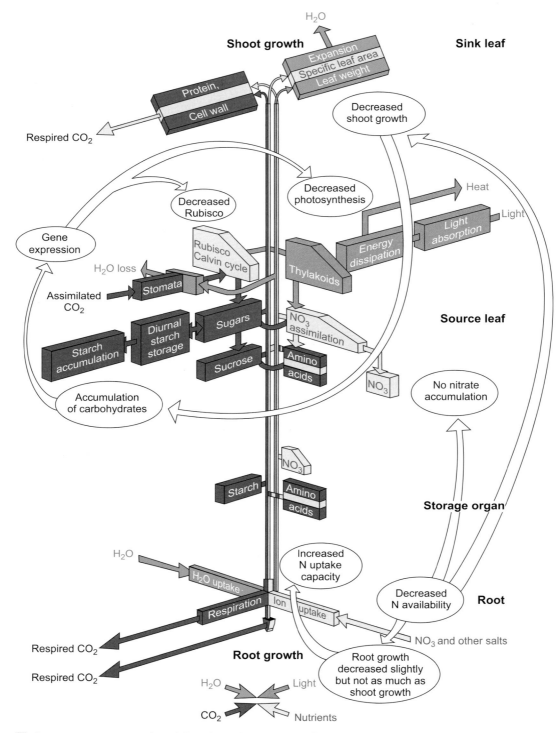

Fig. 2.4.23. A conceptual model to show the sequence of changes in metabolism resulting from changes in resource availability, e.g. nutrient deficiency results in reduction of growth in sink organs. Consequently, carbohydrates accumulate in source leaves. This causes Rubisco and light-harvesting systems to decrease (yellowing of old leaves with N deficiency). Thus nitrogen becomes initially available again for growth. (After Stitt and Schulze 1994)

Box 2.4.4 **Summary: Growth**

- **Carbon balance** of a plant is substantially determined by morphological characteristics and the longevity of the assimilatory organs (e.g. beech, spruce, barley).
- **Respiration** plays an important regulatory role. Distinction is drawn between the function of respiration in "maintenance respiration" and "respiration required for growth".
- **Increased growth (net primary production)** is only possible when the material produced exceeds that required for maintenance of existing organs. In the extreme case plants grow towards the light even at the cost of maintenance of existing organs, which therefore die off. This strategy is

particularly seen in trees with formation of heartwood, an important step towards the reduction of maintenance respiration. Sapwood, which respires, is converted into heartwood, which does not respire, but still supports the plant individual through its woody structure.
- Resource gain and consumption of C and N do not proceed synchronously so **storage** of resources is an important component of all growth processes. Distinction is drawn between passive accumulation of substances (resource acquisition > consumption: nitrate in leaves) and formation of reserves (reserve formation competes with growth: starch in potato).

In contrast, **accumulation** is a process in which the acquisition of resources exceeds consumption by growth at the time of production.

In Fig. 2.4.21 it becomes clear that the C, N, water and energy balances in the plant interact and that the various material fluxes are interconnected. It is not only the distribution of resources to shoot and root, but also distribution between various plant parts in which growth, CO_2 assimilation or storage take place. To understand the interaction between these plant parts and their function, a model with several levels is required (Fig. 2.4.23) allowing feed-back signals between them to be considered. Excess of carbohydrates not only affects stimulation of "sink" activity in shoot and root, but also stimulates nitrate reduction and leads to degradation of photosynthetic activity to produce organic nitrogen. Conversely, lack of nitrogen leads to reduced growth and thus to accumulation of carbohydrates and a reduction in photosynthetic capacity. The ecological consequences of storage in different types of plants are discussed in Chapter 2.4.5 and Chapter 4.3.

2.4.5

C and N Balance in Different Types of Plants

Plant species differ by more than one order of magnitude regarding the relation between green organs for assimilation (leaves, needles, phyllodes, phylloclades) and non-green biomass. In tropical rain forests only 2% of the biomass is leaves, in a meadow more than 50% (Table 2.4.3). Nevertheless, the material gain per year in the tropical forest is not different to that in tropical grasslands and even higher than in temperate grasslands. The average monthly NPP calculated over a year is very similar (Fig. 2.4.24), showing that there are structural elements which not only differentiate the plant kingdom, but which also act compensatorily regarding biomass production.

The analysis of plant structures in botany which is independent from the taxonomic description of a species leads to the term **life-form**. The definition of the life-form has two

---

Box 2.4.5 **Plant life forms**

In plant ecology different forms are distinguished according to:

- **Raunkiaer:** trees, shrubs, perennial herbs, annuals, geophytes;

- **Grime:** r-strategies, k-strategies, stress-tolerant species;
- **Monsi:** annuals vs. perennials, herbaceous vs. woody, evergreen vs. deciduous.

Table 2.4.3. Change in biomass and net primary production in various types of global vegetation and the percentage distribution of biomass in leaves, above-ground organs and roots. (Schulze 1982)

Vegetation types	Biomass (kg m^{-2})	Primary production (kg m^{-2})	Mass of green material (photosynthetically active organs) (%)	Only respiring organs (%)	
				Above-ground woody material	Roots and under-ground shoots
Evergreen trees of tropical and sub-tropical forests	41–65	6–17	ca. 2%	80–90% [a]	10–20% [a]
Deciduous trees of temperate zones	18–60	0.4–2.5	1–2%	ca. 80% [a]	ca. 20% [a]
Evergreen trees in taiga and mountain forests	20–90	0.2–1.5	4–5%	ca. 75% [a]	ca. 20% [a]
Dwarf trees of the forest margins	5–10	0.1–0.5	ca. 25%	ca. 30% [a]	ca. 45% [a]
Ericaceous dwarf shrubs of heaths and tundra	1–6	0.1–0.5	10–20%	ca. 20% [a]	60–70% [a]
Meadow plants	–	0.1–1.3	ca. 50%	–	ca. 50%
Alpine grass lands	0.1–3	0.1–1	ca. 30%	–	ca. 70%
Steppe plants Wet years Dry years	– 0.3–3	0.1–1 –	ca. 30% ca. 10%	– –	ca. 70% ca. 90%
Plants at high altitude	0.1–4	0.1–0.5	10–20%	–	80–90%

[a] A large part of the mass is dead supporting material

goals. Geographers and botanists visiting "foreign" countries wanted to describe a taxonomically foreign vegetation figuratively. They also wanted to analyse those strategies with which plants survived in their environment (Box 2.4.5). The term life-form has been extended by the term **"functional groups"**, which not only comprise structural characteristics, but also physiological characteristics (C3/C4 plants, N$_2$ fixers, deep roots and many others; see Chap. 4.3).

To understand the distribution of resources in plants, the scheme by Monsi (1960) has proved particularly useful. The most important forms will be explained in the following based on their C flux (see Fig. 2.4.21).

2.4.5.1
Annual Species

Annual species are described by the following characteristics:

- They have a short life cycle (2–3 weeks from germination to formation of seeds in *Linaria haelva*, Scrophulariaceae).

- All tissues are physiologically active (lignification is exceptional: *Helianthus annuus*, Compositae).
- The shoot/root relation is shifted towards the shoot (strong feed-back coupling of leaf formation to the production process), hardly any subterranean storage organs (except after breeding for cultivation: radishes = *Raphanus sativus*, Crucifereae).
- High yield of seeds after a very short developmental phase. The harvest index (yield/above-ground biomass) may reach up to 60% (rice: *Oryza sativa*, Gramineae).

Within a very short time, multiplication of individuals in the population occurs as the number of seeds is larger than the number of parents. Thus annuals colonise wastelands very effectively (r-strategy according to Grime). With limited area there is soon intensive competition between individual plants, as the leaf area index (LAI) remains constant.

Crop plants are the most important representatives of annuals. In wheat (Fig. 2.4.25), particularly in older varieties, even the number of shoots increases after germination, as several

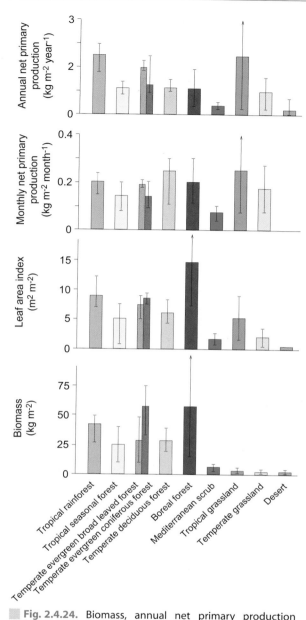

Fig. 2.4.24. Biomass, annual net primary production (NPP$_a$), leaf area index and monthly net primary production of different types of vegetation in different parts of the globe. Despite large differences in biomass and NPP$_a$ the monthly rate of NPP is very similar, i.e. differences in NPP$_a$ are mainly caused by differences in the duration of the growing season. (Schulze 1982)

flowering shoots form from the basal rosette. After about 40 days this leads to competition between shoots, and self-thinning (Chap. 3.2.1), with some of the resources stored in the dying shoots relocated into the remaining plant. One could consider the formation of such shoots as a strategy to occupy space and to store resources

from the soil temporarily. Only after stabilisation of the number of shoots and the development of a closed leaf cover with constant LAI, does the biomass of the remaining shoot increase. Growth of new roots and leaves stops with formation of the ear. At the end of the life cycle, all resources which can be relocated are deposited into the developing grains. Filling of grain with carbohydrates is supported by awns, which do not possess functional stomata and thus can supply carbohydrates for the final ripening of seeds even at the beginning of drought. The physiological achievement of these plants is enormous, if one considers that in a very short time (1–2 weeks) 60% of the above-ground dry weight is relocated from senescing leaves and stalks to grains in a regulated manner. The relation of grain yield/biomass (the so-called **harvest index**) in high-yielding crops is 0.5 (wheat) to 0.6 (rice) and is thus significantly higher than for natural annuals (0.3) on average.

Regarding the distribution of assimilates, annuals are the plant group with a very high relocation in the direction of the leaf from the time of germination. This is possible because these plants have a very effective transport system for water and an effective root system to take up nutrients. Most herbaceous species have VAM mycorrhiza which are very effective in making phosphorus available from the soil (see Chap. 2.3.2.3).

Comparing annuals which are native to soils with different fertility, it may be shown that all species hardly differ regarding the vegetative phase with low N supply (Fig. 2.4.26; Fichtner and Schulze 1992). Growth rates of species adapted to nutrient-rich sites are faster, particularly with greater supply of resources. As shown in Chapter 2.3.2.3, the main difference between species is that only those species which are adapted to the lower N supply flower (*Teesdalia nudicaulis, Filago vulgaris*) at low N supply. Species of nutrient-rich sites lack **flowering induction** at nutrient-poor sites and remain vegetative (*Galeopsis tetrahit, Urtica urens*), and die.

In natural vegetation annuals are particularly successful on sites with a periodically abundant supply of resources (deserts, flooded meadows). Limits of the distribution of annuals are determined by the length of the growing season; therefore, they are missing in boreal climates. There are various adaptations to increase the duration of vegetative growth. This applies particularly to **winter annuals** (e.g. *Gallium apar-*

Fig. 2.4.25. A Changes with time in above-ground biomass and numbers of shoots from germination to harvest in wheat. Figures show the cumulative biomass of individual organs. The *hatched areas* show the biomass per organ. B Relative distribution of growth into roots, leaves, stems, ears, and grain. The figure shows accumulated growth in the individual organs (Schulze 1982). C Flowering of the winter annual *Coriopsis biglowii* in the Mohavi Desert which is dominated in the dry season by the perennial shrub *Larria tridentata*. (Photo E.-D. Schulze)

ine) which germinate in autumn and flower the next year. For these plants, as for all winter plants including winter wheat, there is the danger of dying because of frost drought. A lengthening of the growing period to extend flowering occurs in the facultative biennial species (e.g. *Daucus carota*) and the true **biennials** (e.g. *Arctium tomentosum*).

With annuals, for example, it is possible to use a model to study the structural characteristic of a productive **crop plant**. This is independent of the potential physiological change possible through gene modifications (Miflin 2000). The structural characteristics include:

- **One stalk per rosette:** Formation of fewer stalks, as the distance between seeds when sowing the crop should regulate competition, and the supply of resources should be controlled by fertiliser and herbicides.
- **Length of stem:** Stems with ca. 3 leaves are needed. It has been shown that the uppermost leaf (flag leaf in cereals) is essentially responsible for grain filling. The lower leaves supply stem and root. A tall stem is an advantage in competition with other species. However, this is an unnecessary C sink if weeds are eradicated with herbicides. A short stem also stands better when carrying a large ear.

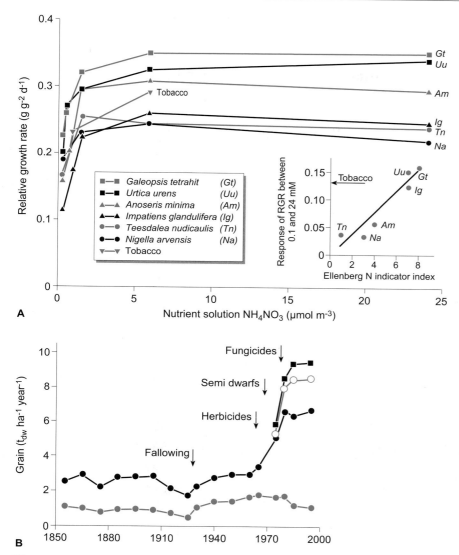

Fig. 2.4.26. A Alterations in biomass of native annuals in relation to the nitrogen concentration of the nutrient solution. As it is a physiological laboratory experiment tobacco is also used as a test plant. Tobacco has a particular function in ecophysiological laboratory studies, as it can be genetically transformed and single parameters which influence growth can be regulated genetically. It is clear that some annuals of the native flora have faster growth rates than tobacco. The insert shows that the relative growth rate correlates with the Ellenberg indicator values for nitrogen (Fichtner and Schulze 1992; for tobacco studies, see Stitt and Schulze 1994). B Influence of particular crop management procedures on grain yield of wheat in the long-term experiment at Rothamsted. (After Miflin 2000)

- **Many seeds per stem:** The yield of grain is proportional to the number of seeds and less to the weight per grain. An additional seed is thus a better C sink than a larger grain, which is important for the relocation of material during seed ripening.
- **Position of the leaf:** Erect leaves determine, at constant irradiation, the maximum leaf area index regulating the C balance.
- **Depth of root:** Deeper reaching, thin roots to increase root volume and exploit resources to

as great a depth as possible. This is important for water relations at the time of seed ripening.
- **Awns:** Awns were bred out of crop plants because of the unpleasant characteristics during threshing. With machine threshing the awn gains new significance as security at the time of seed ripening. *Triticale* [crossing of *Triticum* (wheat) with *Secale* (rye)] is one of the very productive modern cereals with very long awns.

- **Control of diseases and competition:** Yields of cereals increased after regulation of nutrition by (1) use of herbicides, (2) change of crops, (3) introduction of dwarf varieties, and (4) use of fungicides (Miflin 2000; Fig. 2.4.26 B).

2.4.5.2
Biennial Species

Biennial species have a transitional position between annual and perennial herbaceous species. They occur in the succession only for a short period between ruderal plants and the perennial vegetation (Fig. 2.4.27; Heilmeier et al. 1997).

Biennials are characterised by:

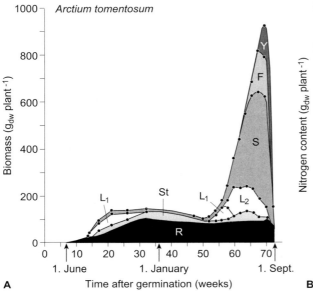

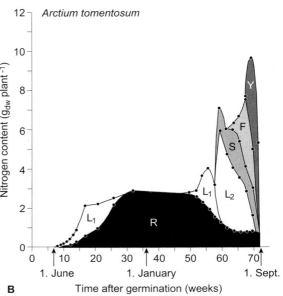

Fig. 2.4.27. Changes with time in A dry mass and B amount of N in different organs of *Arctium tomentosum* during the 2 years of growth from germination until death after seed production. Development of the storage roots (*R*) is particularly noteworthy for it supports early leaf emergence from the rosette in the second year. The large biomass production of *Arctium* in its second year is mainly due to the "exploitation" of the habitat due to its rosette leaves (*L₁*) in its first year and the basal rosette in the second (L₁ and L₂), which makes possible the harvest of nitrogen from an area of about 1 m². This nitrogen gain permits growth of large flowering shoots (*S*) and of the leaves on the shoot (*F*) which assimilate CO₂ after L₁ and L₂ die. All resources are finally transferred to the fruits (*Y*). During flowering, when the rosette and the stem leaves are already dying, the plant receives some 15% of its total N from the root. Exploitation by the basal rosette of the area in which the plant grows is so complete and long-lasting that the seeds of this species can establish themselves in the area without significant competition from other competing species. Thus the biannual *Arctium* occupies an area for many years (Heilmeier et al. 1986). C *Arctium lappa* in a ruderal situation in competition with couch grass and thistles. Campus of the University of Bayreuth. (Photo E.-D. Schulze)

- Behaviour analogous to annuals in the first year, but the formation of a storage organ (often the hypocotyl) occurs very early and is genetically fixed. This storage organ is formed during growth (formation of reserve) or is filled with resources only after the termination of growth (accumulation);
- Storage of amino acids predominantly, sometimes lipids;
- Early emergence in the following year because of the stored N products at a time when the root is not yet active;
- Formation of the basal rosette which reduces competition with other species dependent on the size of leaves, and which also enables exploitation of a larger area and also volume of soil, increasing availability of resources, in particular N and water;
- Formation of a flowering shoot in the second year, supplied with nitrogen by the dying leaves of the basal rosette;
- Relocation of all resources to the seed during a period of 1–2 weeks with an harvest index corresponding to that of annuals.

Biennials are, because of the formation of the basal rosette, often very successful in out-competing other species even in the long term. After flowering many seeds drop at the site where the basal rosette of the mother plants died. Seeds germinate and, because of the enormous interspecies competition, only a few are left at the end of the new growing season and then flower again. Thus large-leaved biennials are able to occupy habitats for decades.

Biennial species occur in a very wide range of sites. At nutrient-poor sites these are often biennial legumes able to fix N_2 (*Melilothus officinalis*), at nutrient-rich sites it is usually species with large leaves. Species from nutrient-poor sites often have many small seeds, those from nutrient-rich sites few large seeds.

Biennials are a suitable object to consider strategies and transitions between storage and accumulation. In *Arctium*, formation of the storage organ and filling occur after the development of the leaf so that the store accumulates excess products. In contrast, for *Dipsacus sylvestris* or *Daucus carota*, the development of the store occurs at the same time as the development of the leaf, so that storage competes with growth (Steinlein et al. 1993).

2.4.5.3
Perennial Herbaceous Species

Perennial herbaceous species behave similarly to annuals after germination, forming storage organs, creeping shoots, tubers and other vegetative organs, which may also serve for vegetative multiplication, but do not enter the reproductive phase. Thus perennial species have the following characteristics:

- Individual plants live for many years.
- Storage of C and N dominates before reproduction.
- Reserve material allows plants to start early and maintain a long period of growth.
- Many species are able to die back to very few vegetative apices and emerge or re-grow.

In contrast to annuals where the increase in the population is most important, in perennial species, it is maintenance and growth of the individual plant. Seed production is delayed to a time with good resources and storage.

In **grasses**, carbohydrate transport occurs in the phloem of a rhizome predominantly in the direction of the vegetative apex which is younger than the producing leaf and thus enhances the sink (see Chap. 2.3.1.3). Transport into older organs is very small. Thus older shoots are more of an "insurance" for situations where the young shoot is damaged. In this case older shoots re-grow.

Different **storage** products may accumulate at different times in the same shoot during the season (Fig. 2.4.28). Thus, in summer, nettles store starch, which is required in autumn to produce new runners after the death of the above-ground shoots. Starch is also used for the reduction of nitrate, which is available in the soil in autumn and taken up. Storage of amino acids thus occurs in autumn and winter and is the basis for early emergence in spring. Young leaves are very quickly self-sufficient with respect to carbon. In herbaceous perennial plants there is, similar to the situation in a wheat field, very early strong competition between shoots. The LAI remains constant and individual shoots compete by the continuous formation of new leaves with the old leaves dying simultaneously. Thus, *Urtica dioica* leaves are exchanged about four times during the growing period (see also Chap. 2.4.4.3). Formation of below-ground rhizomes also shows many forms in nettles. On nutrient-poor sites, rhizomes, which may be up to 3 years old,

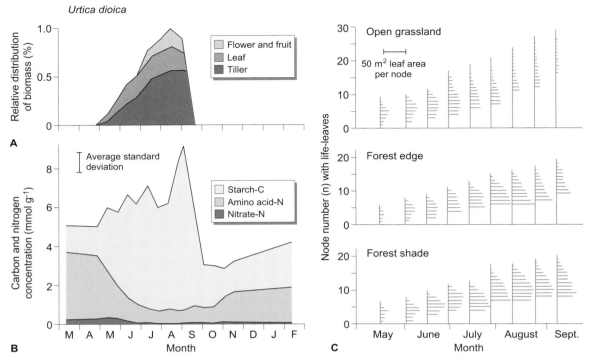

Fig. 2.4.28. Annual progression of A growth in biomass and B changes in storage products starch, amino acids and nitrate in the rhizome of the stinging nettle, *Urtica dioica*. It is interesting that rhizomes of nettles function in summer as a starch store and in winter as an N store for amino acids. C Schematic of leaf development in *Urtica*. Height of stems and size of leaves are shown. With growth of stems, new leaves are formed at their tips, and at the same time leaves at the base of the stem die, so the number of leaves per stem remains constant. In shaded areas fewer but larger leaves are formed. In open areas there are more leaves of smaller area. In this way, more stems per unit area can exist in brightly illuminated locations. (Stitt and Schulze 1994)

meander through the soil and new shoots are formed at their tip; eventually, the end of the rhizome dies off. On nutrient-rich sites, rhizomes (more than 12 years old) are formed which are probably only destroyed by burrowing animals. On dry sites taproots with secondary growth in thickness are formed, supplying a whole cohort of shoots with short rhizomes with water. Therefore, it is not surprising that it is very difficult to eradicate a bed of nettles (*Urtica dioica*) or ground elder (*Aegopodium podagraria*) in a garden. Couch grass (*Agropyron repens*) is an example of a successful perennial rhizomatous weed in crops.

Perennial herbaceous species are successful where there are **continuously poor growing conditions** for growth. They occupy shady forest floors, salty sites, dry sites and cold habitats. It is these plants that occur at greatest elevation in Alpine regions (*Stellaria decumbens* in the Himalayas above 6000 m) and go furthest north in the Arctic (*Saxifrage oppositifolia*, 83′ north). *Allocasia macrocarpa* is the species in which the

lowest light saturation of photosynthesis was measured (80 μmol m^{-2} s^{-1} photons). Some perennial herbaceous species only flower once and require several years to store sufficient resources for flowering. These "monocarpic" species not only include *Agava*, but also bamboo species and tropical alpine giant rosette plants (*Lobelia*, *Senecio*; see Chap. 1.3.6.7).

For herbaceous perennial species there is a **maximum size** of the vegetative body, when respiration in non-photosynthetically active organs consumes the C gained by leaves. Bananas have to be cut back to maintain the development of flowers and fruits. Old shrubs do not develop flower panicles. Some species cope with this limitation of structure by secondary lignification of the shoot (e.g. sunflower). Secondary thickening is rather rare in perennial herbaceous species, but does occur, for example, in the root of nettles. Many herbaceous temperate species have close relatives in the woody flora of tropical regions.

The fact that a balance of resources between respiring and assimilating biomass occurs in perennial herbaceous species becomes particularly obvious in grasses where maximum production is reached with **grazing or mowing**. Grasses are predestined for such a use as they are able to regenerate new leaves quickly after herbivory, because of the intercalar growth of the leaf sheath. Grasses of the "old world" are better adapted to grazing than those of the "new world". The typical cluster grass of the American Prairie, the genus *Bouteloua*, was completely eradicated after introduction of horses, as *Bouteloua* does not root firmly enough in the soils and the clumps were ripped out by horses.

2.4.5.4
Woody Plants

Woody plants, **trees and shrubs**, are always perennial. They often flower and fruit only after decades. They differ from herbaceous species particularly by the fact that the growth of the woody body is balanced by the transition of living **sapwood** into dead **heartwood**. This does not have to occur synchronously, but is influenced by environmental conditions and species-specific characteristics. In the whole plant the capacity of the xylem determines the leaf area, and the leaf area in turn determines growth and area of sapwood. This was shown in the **"pipe model"** (Shinozaki et al. 1964), starting from a balance of growth processes in the stem, branches and leaves which is regulated by the conductive area of the xylem. The ring-porous oak only has three to five functioning annual rings in contrast to spruce which has over 30, as spruce wood consists of tracheids with low hydraulic conductance and little medullary ray parenchyma. It is important for the C balance that the respiring woody body remains constant, independent of growth and changes with the leaf mass (see also Chap. 2.2.2.2). Using dead, that is non-respiring biomass (heartwood), as the supporting apparatus, the functional limitation of the **size of the vegetative body** no longer applies, removing the limitation to growth in plants that do not lignify. However, even in trees there is a functional maximum size. This is achieved in the tallest trees on earth (*Eucalyptus marginata*, South West Australia; 140 m) and probably the thickest trees (*Agatis australis*, New Zealand, 7 m diameter, 50 m height; Fig. 2.4.29 A) or in trees with the greatest volume (*Sequoia gigantea*, California, General Sherman tree, 96 m height, 6 m diameter at the root, volume 5500 m^3). The maximum size at which respiration of non-green parts is in balance with assimilation of green parts is not only achieved in large trees, but also in shrubs. For *Calluna*, for example, flowering depends on grazing which regulates the ratio of green to non-green biomass. For ungrazed plants the non-green biomass increases, the amount of shoots remains constant and the investment in flowers decreases with age. Similar effects have been shown for fruiting trees (apple), which need to be "cut back" in order to increase the yield of fruits.

Storage of carbohydrates and nitrogen-containing substances is also very important in trees. Leaf emergence and early tree ring growth occur from the mobilisation of amino acids and carbohydrates from the woody parenchyma. In spruce, N concentration in the sap water increases to >5 mM in spring. Bottle trees (e.g. *Adansonia digitata*; separating pages to Chap. 1.6) do not store water, but carbohydrates and amino acids for dry periods (Schulze et al. 1998). In vegetation which regenerates by fire (Mediterranean vegetation), there are so-called **seeders**, fruits of which open only with fire allowing seeds to fall into the fresh ash and germinate. These species do not have storage parenchyma in roots and the starch concentration in the root is small (1.9±0.5 mg starch per g dry weight of root). This contrasts to so-called **sprouters** which emerge after the fire from the root (Fig. 2.4.29 B); these have 14.1 g starch per dry weight root (Bell et al. 1996). Obviously, in cold winter climates, most N is stored (as the soil is still cold at the time of emergence), whilst in fire climates predominantly carbohydrates are stored, as the ash contains sufficient nutrients for the new vegetation.

A particularly impressive C economy exists in trees which become very old; *Pinus aristata* is the **longest living** tree species (Fig. 2.4.29 C, D; disregarding species with runners) with more than 4000 years. This species occurs in the high Alpine dry regions of Nevada. In this climate, wood is only slowly degraded and conditions allow only very slow growth. Most of its cambium dies within a 1000 years. Only a small strip of the living bast remains, keeping the ratio of green biomass to respiring biomass almost constant. Trees grow like a board, 1–2 m wide and only 10–15 cm thick. Without external interference (lightning, storms) these trees may potentially live forever (LaMarche et al. 1984; Fritts et al. 1991).

Fig. 2.4.29. **A** Barrel-like trees: *Agatis australis*, Kauri, in the subtropical forest of New Zealand's North Island. The base of the stem is branchless and may achieve 45 m in height with 6–7 m diameter. Dimensions become clear with Waltraud Schulze climbing a liana. **B** *Eucalyptus pauciflora* as an example of sprouting plants, i.e. tree species which re-generate from hypocotyl buds after fire. **C** *Pinus arsitata* in the Snake Mountains of Nevada at 3500 m above sea level; an example of extreme longevity. Trunks may be more than 4000 years old, resulting from death of the cambium which, except for a narrow strip, grows in balance with the resource supply from the shoot. Thus an equilibrium is achieved between assimilation and respiration and between shoot and root. The trunk grows only in width on the side with the living cambium, i.e. the trunk develops in the shape of a plank over a long period. A trunk in broad aspect with E.-D. Schulze and **D** side aspect, with Valmore LaMarche in the picture

E Aerial roots of *Ficus*, growing through the canopy of a rain forest in Costa Rica. F After reaching the ground with its aerial root and thus securing water, *Ficus* enmeshes the host with a root net, Lamington, Queensland, and thus kills the host. G *Ficus superba* with stilt roots which grow from the canopy to the soil, supporting the canopy and supplying it with water and nutrients, Yakushima, Japan. H Central hole in the trunk of a *Ficus*, showing the position of the original host. (Photos E.-D. Schulze)

Amongst the many life-forms termed "tree" (Vareschi 1980) are **figs**, which are masters in carbohydrate economy. They germinate as epiphytes in the canopy of the rain forest and grow with a large aerial root through the canopy (Fig. 2.4.29 C, F). As soon as the roots have reached the soil and thus water, they enclose the host with a mesh of roots. The host dies as its phloem transport is interrupted by strangulation from the fig, which then uses nutrients released from the decomposing wood of the host. In the end only a chimney-like structure remains of the host (Fig. 2.4.29 H). The fig then increases in size by forming new aereal stilt-like supporting roots and conquers a new habitat for the tree. *Ficus benegalensis* (Fig. 2.4.29 G) produces many hundreds of stilt roots covering an area of > 20 ha, under which "an army of 20,000 men could camp in the shade", according to Warburg (1913). Similar areas are covered by *Populus deltoides*, with underground runners, in the southern boreal forests of Canada.

Trees and **shrubs** are distinguished from each other by height (greater or less than 2 m, respectively, according to Ellenberg (1978), or greater or less than 5 m according to the FAO (2000), and are functionally distinguished by the different arrangement of regenerating buds (Fig. 2.4.30). In trees there is an apical dominance, also called **acrotony** (e.g. in spruce) in which the terminal bud remains. The term **amphitony** is used if the terminal bud remains, but only one of the lateral buds develops (*Fagus*). In some trees the terminal bud dies off and the next bud at the upper side of twigs takes the lead, which is called **hypotony**, e.g. in *Acer* or *Thilia*. Some deciduous trees have acrotonic growth in the juvenile period and hypotonous growth when older (*Acer pseudoplatanus*). In contrast, shrubs have renewal buds predominantly in the lower region of branches (hazel, **basitonic dominance**) or on the underside of branches, also called **epitonic growth** (e.g. *Rosa, Rubus*). Obviously, there are many transitions between these extremes, but it is usually possible to determine the tree form from the dominance of bud development along the main axis of the stem and along the branches. Thus, true trees are **monopodial** (one stem) while shrubs and tree-like shrubs are mostly **sympodial** (many stems). These different types of growth determine competition and succession in hedgerows (Küppers 1989).

In woody plants the shoot-root communication depends on the species and is tuned so that shoot and root growth are tightly correlated (Fig. 2.4.31; Heilmeier et al. 1997) – even if, under extreme stress conditions, very different tree sizes are reached. For the almond, *Prunus dulcis*, there is tight correlation between root and shoot biomass as well as between leaf area and length of fine roots. Such regulation is also observed in basitonic shrubs. Evenari et al. (1982) called the phenomenon of a root-shoot regulation **"survival through dieback"** which is common in arid regions. In a dry year part of the shrub dies back and only a few shoots survive which are in balance with the root.

In addition to the regulation of the respiring mass of their woody body, trees have another means of regulation, **the life span of assimilatory organs**. Distinction is made between:

- **deciduous** species (trees of temperate forests and rain-green savannahs) with seasonal changes in leaves;
- **semi-evergreen** species with a life span of assimilatory organs of about 12–14 months, when the old leaves are shed with the emergence of new leaves (*Eucalyptus* and many tropical species);
- **evergreen** species with a life span of their assimilation organs of up to 35 years (*Pinus aristata*, California).

Deciduous and evergreen assimilatory organs show functional differences:

- **Evergreen** species have a larger dry weight per area because they usually are forced to survive very unfavourable conditions (cold, drought).
- A smaller rate of CO_2 assimilation in evergreen species than in deciduous species correlates with the larger dry weight per area. Short-lived leaves have a greater CO_2 gain per time than long-lived leaves, which experience so-called "diminishing returns" (smaller returns per unit of investment with time). This investment should be compared with a possible maximisation of physiological activity with lower investment in protecting cell walls.
- Evergreen species are able to use intermittently favourable weather conditions to assimilate (spruce is able to assimilate CO_2 on warm days during the European winter). Assimilation starts earlier in spring than for deciduous species and lasts longer in autumn. For deciduous species the growing season is often limited by early or late frosts.

A

Longitudinal symmetry ↓	Basitonic	Acrotonic (Sympodial ⟷ Monopodial)		
Growth form ↑	Shrub	Tree-Shrub	Shrub-Tree	Tree
Lateral symmetry		Epitonic Hypotonic Amphitonic ⟷		

B

	Rubus	Rosa	Ribes	Prunus	Crataegus	Cornus	Acer	Fagus
Branching pattern	Sympodial	Sympodial	Sympodial	Sympodial	Sympodial	Monopodial	Monopodial	Monopodial
Longitudinal symmetry	Basitonic	Basitonic	Weakly basitonic	Mesotonic acrotonic	Mesotonic acrotonic	Mesotonic acrotonic	Mesotonic acrotonic	Mesotonic acrotonic
Lateral symmetry	Strongly epitonic	Strongly epitonic	Strongly epitonic	Weakly epitonic	Epitonic and hypotonic	Weakly epitonic	Strongly hypotonic	Amphitonic
				Prunus spinosa	*Crataegus macrocarpa*		*Acer campestre*	*Fagus sylvatica*
Volume gain per dry-matter investment of single twigs (m³ kg⁻¹)				0.038	0.078		0.134	0.549

Fig. 2.4.30. A Definitions of terms in dominance of buds in vertical (main stem) and horizontal (branches) axes of a woody plant. Shoot dominance ultimately determines the growth forms of woody plants. B Schematic of the important features of symmetry in native woody plants in a hedge (Troll 1939; Küppers 1985; Schulze et al. 1987) and quantification of the competitiveness of selective species based on the volume of the living space occupied per unit of dry mass and per unit photosynthetic carbon acquisition of the leaves. Species in the later succession have a greater capacity to exploit the space and also a larger assimilate acquisition per unit of invested twig mass. C Hedge landscape on limestone near Stadtsteinach, Upper Frankonia, Germany. The hedge shows a typical succession from the edge to the centre with *Prunus spinosa* as the woody pioneer plant at the edge followed by *Rubus* and *Rosa* species. Then *Crataegus* and finally *Rhamnus cathartica* and *Acer campestre* follow. (Photo E.-D. Schulze)

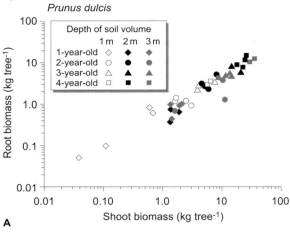

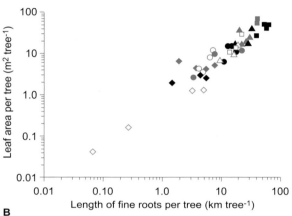

Fig. 2.4.31. Correlation between A root and shoot biomass and B leaf area and length of fine roots in *Prunus dulcis*. Plants were grown at the Avdat research station in the Negev Desert, in containers 3 m in diameter and 1, 2, or 3 m deep. Plants were watered only once in spring and had to regulate shoot and root growth in relation to the water stored in the soil. The strong correlation between shoot and root is independent of the absolute water supply and the size of the plant, the allometry between shoot and root is constant. Environmental factors determine the capacity for growth in this woody plant but not the partitioning of material. The plant is a grafted cultivated plant in which shoot and root have their own genetic programme, so the equilibrium is regulated by resource distribution within the plant (Heilmeier et al. 1997). C View of experiments on almonds at the runoff farm, Avdat. (Evenari et al. 1982)

- **Deciduous species** must form their assimilation organs again each year, which leads to substantial consumption of carbohydrate reserves. Evergreen species in contrast are able to put up with a greater respiration of needles as they do not have the enormous demand for resources required to completely build up the assimilating biomass. The material balance of both leaf types is surprisingly similar (see Table 2.4.1) and the amount of usable wood mass depends again on the distribution to stem and branches which depends on the species. The allocation scheme of C distribution is genetically fixed. Thus material gain is dependent on the environment, but the shoot-root relations remain almost constant (Heilmeier 1997).
- Deciduous growth requires a high nutrient uptake at the time of emergence. Thus deciduous species are more frequently found on nutrient-rich soils than evergreen species.

It becomes obvious that there are several advantages and disadvantages of evergreen and deciduous assimilatory organs and it is, therefore, not surprising that in many plant communities both leaf types (deciduous and evergreen) exist side by side. Analysing advantages and disadvantages of both types shows:

- All factors (**shade, cold**) that reduce the **C gain** of the plant (**assimilation×leaf area**) lead to longer life of the assimilatory organs. Plants with high respiratory rates and low C gain must minimise investment into new assimilatory organs in order to safeguard the supply to the respiring organs. The plant manages this only by prolonging the life span of assimilatory organs. For example, the boreal pine forest succeeds temperate deciduous forest in Alpine regions as well as at higher latitudes where the growing period becomes shorter. With increased supply of nutrients,

Box 2.4.6   Summary: The carbon balance

- **CO_2 assimilation**, also termed **net photosynthesis**, is the balance between photosynthetic CO_2 fixation and respiration of a leaf. It is an important quantity in considering the ecological carbon balance. It depends on climatic factors (light, temperature, atmospheric humidity) and also on factors within the plant (nutrition, water status, age). The physical process of CO_2 diffusion into the leaf is regulated by the stomatal aperture. Linear relationships occur, over a wide range, between the nitrogen content of leaves and specific leaf area and between nitrogen content and net photosynthesis, as well as between CO_2 exchange and conductance of leaves and of canopies.

- **Plant growth** is determined by the CO_2 assimilation balanced against respiration of all non-assimilating parts of the plant. Distinction is drawn between growth respiration (energy from respiration which is required for growth) and maintenance respiration (energy from respiration used for maintenance of the existing living organism). The balance between assimilation and respiration is called net primary production. Plant species are distinguished particularly by the way in which accumulated assimilates are distributed to shoots and roots and how parts of the plant die (i.e. require no further energy from maintenance respiration) or maintain their structure (heartwood formation). The carbon economy is further determined by the turnover of the leaf cover; a functional distinction is drawn between annual species, biannual species, herbaceous perennials, evergreen and deciduous woody forms.

- The **vegetation** of the earth and the invasion of different habitats by species are explicable on the basis of resource use, particularly of water and nutrients (see Chap. 4).

---

e.g. after a fire, these unfavourable climatic conditions are compensated, so that succession may occur at first via deciduous birch or poplar. In the central Asian continental climate, the evergreen boreal forest is replaced by deciduous larch forest where investment in needles is particularly low (Schulze et al. 1995). This species is, therefore, able to utilise the warm continental summer better than evergreen species in oceanic climates. Additionally, in the continental climate with extremely cold winters, the investment in protection of evergreen needles increases and a bud is less endangered than a fully developed assimilatory organ. Obviously, the functional causes of the change from evergreen to deciduous boreal conifers are diverse. Larch is dominant in Asiatic but not in the North American boreal forests. The difference between continents is the reaction to dryer periods in summer in continental Asia and compared to the high temperatures in the Siberian summer that do not limit photosynthesis, i.e. deciduous leaves are an advantage. In the Siberian winter, on the other hand, temperatures are so cold (–50 to –70 °C) that damage

to evergreen needles is possible; this would greatly affect the C balance. In East Siberia the evergreen *Picea obovata* still occurs on riverbanks so that drought and related **fires** are probably also deciding factors responsible for the dominance of larch.

- **Nutrient deficiency** leads to reduced photosynthesis, and higher investment in roots is required. This leads generally to evergreen growth (example: tropical evergreen forests, Australian sclerophyll woodlands).

- **Lack of water** stimulates evergreen growth (Mediterranean sclerophyll woodlands) where in the winter rain regions occasional rains are also possible in summer (thunder storms) and thus the evergreens are able to bridge the short dry periods (deep roots). In Southern California and Mexico there are shrubs, the so-called ombrophytes (genus *Fouqueria*), whose leaves emerge after each precipitation many times per year but are only active for a few days. As these plants are not able to store water, the duration of the drought period determines which species occur. Even in the Mediterranean vegetation there are deciduous species at particularly dry sites. The subtropical savannah is a further example of the change from evergreen tropical to deciduous vegetation. However, drought, together with nutrient deficiency, can again be of advantage for evergreen species which often do not form leaves but phylodes or phyloclades, similarly to, for example, *Acacia* in Australia. Very long drought periods are thus of advantage to evergreen species, often together with reduction of leaves and formation of assimilating shoots (Chenopodiaceae in North Africa).

References

Amthor JS (1989) Respiration and crop productivity. Springer, Berlin Heidelberg New York, 215 pp

Arneth A, Kelliher FM, McSeveny TM, Byers JN (1999) Assessment of annual carbon dioxide exchange in a water-stressed *Pinus radiata* plantation: an analysis based on eddy covariance measurements and an integrated biophysical model. Global Change Biol 5:531–545

Arneth A, Lloyd J, Santrucova H, et al (2002) Response of central Siberian Scots pine to soil water deficit and long-term trends in atmospheric CO_2 concentration. Global Biogeochem Cycles 16:5–13

Bell TL, Pate JS, Dixon KW (1996) Relationship between fire response, morphology, root anatomy and starch distribution in south-west Australian Epacridaceae. Ann Bot 77:357–364

Biscoe PV, Scott RK, Monteith JL (1975) Barley and its environment. III. Carbon budget of the stand. J Appl Ecol 12:269–293

Björkman O (1971) Comparative photosynthetic CO_2 exchange in higher plants. In: Hatch MD, Osmond CB, Slatyer RO (eds) Photosynthesis and photorespiration. Wiley, New York, pp 18–34

Björkman O (1981) Responses to different quantum flux densities. Encycl Plant Physiol 12A:57–108

Björkman O, Demmig-Adams B (1994) Regulation of photosynthetic light energy capture, conversion, and dissipation in leaves of higher plants. Ecological Studies 100. Springer, Berlin Heidelberg New York, pp 17–70

Chapin FS III, Schulze ED, Mooney HA (1990) The ecology and economics of storage in plants. Annu Rev Ecol Syst 21:423–447

Clayton WD (1981) Evolution and distribution of grasses. Ann Mo Bot Gard 68:5–14

Cowan IR, Farquhar GD (1977) Stomatal function in relation to leaf metabolism and environment. In: Jennings JR (eds) Interaction of activity in the higher plant. Cambridge University Press, Cambridge, pp 471–505

dePury DGG, Farquhar GD (1999) A commentary on the use of a sun/shade model to scale from the leaf to a canopy. Agric For Met 95:257–260

Ehleringer JR, Cerling TE (2001) Photosynthetic pathways and climate. In: Schulze E-D, Heimann M, Harrison S, Holland E, Lloyd J, Prentice C, Schimel D (eds) Global biogeochemical cycles in the climate system. Academic Press, San Diego, 350 pp

Ehleringer JR, Cerling TE, Helliker BR (1997) C4 photosynthesis, atmospheric CO_2, and climate. Oecologia 112:385–399

Ellenberg H (1978) Vegetation Mitteleuropas mit den Alpen. Ulmer, Stuttgart, 981 pp

Evans LT (1972) Evolutionary, adaptive and environmental aspects of the photosynthetic pathway. In: Hatch MD, Osmond CB, Slatyer RO (eds) Photosynthesis and photorespiration. Wiley, New York, pp 130–137

Evenari M, Shanan L, Tadmor N (1982) The Negev; the challenge of a desert. Harvard University Press, Cambridge, 437 pp

FAO (2000) Forest resources of Europe, CIS, North America, Australia, Japan and New Zealand. Main report. United Nations, New York, Geneva, 445 pp

Farquahr G, Lloyd J (1993) Carbon and oxygen isotope effects in the exchange of carbon dioxide between terrestrial plants and the atmosphere. In: Ehleringer JR, Hall AE, Farquhar GD (eds) Stable isotopes and plant carbon-water relations. Academic Press, San Diego, pp 47–70

Farquhar GD, von Caemmerer S (1982) Modelling of photosynthetic response to environment. Encycl Plant Physiol 12B:549–587

Farquhar GD, Ehleringer JR, Hubick KT (1989) Carbon isotope discrimination and photosynthesis. Annu Rev Plant Physiol Plant Mol Biol 40:503–537

Farquhar GD, von Caemmerer S, Berry JA (1980) A biochemical model of photosynthetic CO_2 assimilation in leaves of C3 species. Planta 149:78–90

Fichtner K, Schulze E-D (1992) The effect of nitrogen nutrition on growth and biomass partitioning of annual plants originating from habitats of different nitrogen availability. Oecologia 92:236–241

Field C, Mooney HA (1986) The photosynthesis-nitrogen relationship in wild plants. In: Givnish TJ (ed) On the economy of plant form and function. Cambridge University Press, Cambridge, pp 25–56

Fritts HC, Vaganov EA, Sviderskaya IV, Shashkin AV (1991) Climatic variation and tree-ring structure in conifers: empirical and mechanistic models of tree-ring width, number of cells, cell size, cell-wall thickness and wood density. Climate Res 1:97–116

Fuchs M, Schulze E-D, Fuchs MI (1977) Spacial distribution of photosynthetic capacity and performance in a mountain spruce forest of northern Germany. II. Climatic control of carbon dioxide uptake. Oecologia 29:329–340

Gifford RM (1974) A comparison of potential photosynthesis, productivity and yield of plant species with differing photosynthetic metabolism. Aust J Plant Physiol 1:107–117

Gillon J, Yakir D (2001) Influence of carbonic anhydrase activity in terrestrial vegetation on the ^{18}O content of atmospheric CO_2. Science 291:2584–2587

Harley PC, Tenhunen JD, Lange OL (1986) Use of an analytical model to study limitations on net photosynthesis in *Arbutus unedo* under field conditions. Oecologia 70:393–401

Hattersley PW (1992) C4 photosynthetic pathway variation in grasses (Poaceae): its significance for arid and semi-arid lands. In: Chapman G (ed) Desertified grasslands: their biology and management. Academic Press, London, pp 181–212

Heilmeier H, Schulze E-D, Whale DM (1986) Carbon and nitrogen partitioning in the biennial macrocarp *Arctium tomentosum* Mill. Oecologia 70:466–474

Heilmeier H, Erhart M, Schulze E-D (1997) Biomass allocation and water use under arid conditions. In: Bazzaz F, Grace J (eds) Plant resource allocation. Academic Press, San Diego, pp 93–112

Hollinger DY, Kelliher FM, Byers JN, Hunt JE, McSeveny TM, Weir PL (1994) Carbon dioxide exchange between an undisturbed old-growth temperate forest and the atmosphere. Ecology 75:134–150

Jarvis PG (1971) The estimation of resistances to carbon dioxide transfer. In: Sestak Z, Catsky J, Jarvis PG (eds) Plant photosynthetic production: manual of methods. Junk, Den Haag, pp 566–631

Jarvis PG (1976) The interpretation of the variations in leaf water potential and stomatal conductance found in canopies in the field. Philos Trans R Soc Lond B 273:593–610

Jones HG (1994) Plants and microclimate, 2nd edn. Cambridge University Press, Cambridge, 428 pp

Jones HG (1999) Use of thermography for quantitative studies of spacial and temporal variation of stomatal conductance over leaf surfaces. Plant Cell Environ 22:1043–1055

Kaiser WM (1982) Correlation between changes in photosynthetic activity and changes in total protoplast volume in leaf tissue from hygro-, meso- and xerophytes under osmotic stress. Planta 154:538–545

Kappen L, Lange OL, Schulze E-D, Evenari M, Buschbom U (1976) Distributional pattern of water relations of *Hammada scoparia* (Pomel) Iljin in a desert environment. Oecologia 23:323–334

Kappen L, Lange OL, Schulze E-D, Evenari M, Buschbom U (1972) Extreme water stress and photosynthetic activity of the desert plant *Arteminsia herba-alba*, Asso. Oecologia 10:177–182

Kirschbaum MUF, Farquhar GD (1984) Temperature dependence of whole-leaf photosynthesis in *Eucalyptus pauciflora* Sieb. Ex Spreng. Aust J Plant Physiol 11:519–538

Küppers M (1985) Carbon relations and competition between woody species in a central European hedgerow. IV. Growth form and partitioning. Oecologia 66:343–352

Küppers M (1989) Ecological significance of aboveground architectural patterns in woody plants: a question of cost-benefit relationships. Trends Ecol Evol 4:375–379

LaMarche VC Jr, Graybill DA, Fritts HC, Rose MR (1984) Increasing atmospheric carbon dioxide: tree ring evidence for growth enhancement in natural vegetation. Science 252:1019–1021

Lange OL (1959) Untersuchungen über den Wärmehaushalt und die Hitzeresistenz mauretanischer Wüsten- und Savannenpflanzen. Flora 147:595–651

Lange OL (1965) Experimentell-ökologische Untersuchungen an Flechten der Negev-Wüste. I. CO$_2$-Gaswechsel von *Ramalina maciformis* (Del.) Bory unter kontrollierten Bedingungen im Laboratorium. Flora 158:324–359

Lange OL (1988) Ecophysiology of photosynthesis: performance of poikilohydric lichens and homoiohydric Mediterranean sclerophylls. The seventh Tansley lecture. J Ecol 76:914–937

Lange OL, Schulze E-D, Evenari M, Kappen L, Buschbom U (1975a) The temperature-related capacity of plants under desert conditions. II. Possible controlling mechanisms for the seasonal changes of the photosynthetic response to temperature. Oecologia 18:45–53

Lange OL, Schulze E-D, Kappen L, Evenari M, Buschbom U (1975b) CO$_2$-exchange patterns under natural conditions of *Caraluma negevensis*, a CAM plant of the Negev Desert. Photosynthetica 9:318–326

Lange OL, Geiger IL, Schulze E-D (1977) Ecophysiological investigations on lichens of the Negev Desert. V. A model to simulate net photosynthesis and respiration of *Ramnalina maciformis*. Oecologia 28:247–259

Lange OL, Beyschlag W, Tenhunen JD (1987) Control of leaf carbon assimilation – input of chemical energy into ecosystems. Ecological Studies 61. Springer, Berlin Heidelberg New York, pp 148–163

Larcher W (1994) Ökophysiologie der Pflanzen. UTB, Eugen Ulmer, Stuttgart, 394 pp

Leuning R (1995) A critical appraisal of a combined stomatal-photosynthesis model for C3 plants. Plant Cell Environ 18:339–355

Leuning R, Dunin FX, Wang YP (1998) A two-leaf model for canopy conductance, photosynthesis and partitioning of available energy. II. Comparison with measurements. Agric Fort Met 91:113–125

Lloyd J, et al (1995a) A simple calibrated model of Amazon rainforest productivity based on leaf biochemical properties. Plant Cell Environ 18:1129–1145

Lloyd J, et al. (1995b) Measuring and modelling whole-tree gas exchange. Aust J Plant Physiol 22:987–1000

Lloyd J, Kruijt B, Hollinger DY, Grace J, Francey RJ, Wong SC, Kelliher FM, Miranda AC, Fraquhar GD, Gash JHC, Vygodskaya NN, Wright IR, Miranda HS, Schulze ED (1996) Vegetation effects on the isotopic composition of atmospheric CO$_2$ at local and regional scales: theoretical aspects and a comparison between rain forest in Amazonia and a boreal forest in Siberia. Aust J Plant Physiol 23:377–399

Loreto F, Velikova V, Di Marco G (2001) Respiration in the light measured by $^{12}CO_2$ emission in $^{13}CO_2$ atmosphere in maize leaves. Aust J Plant Physiol 28:1103–1108

Lüttge U (1999) One morphotype, three physiotypes: sympatric species of *Clusia* with obligate C3 photosynthesis, obligate CAM and C3-CAM intermediate behaviour. Plant Biol 1:138–148

Lüttge U, Kluge M, Bauer G (1988) Botanik. VCH, Weinheim, 577 pp

MacFadden BJ, Cerling TE (1996) Mammalian herbivore communities, ancient feeding ecology and carboisotopes: a 10-million-year sequence from the Neogene of Florida. J Vertebrate Paleontol 16:103–115

McCree KJ (1983) Carbon balance as a function of plant size in *Sorghum* plants. Crop Sci 20:82–93

Merino J, Field C, Mooney HA (1982) Construction and maintenance costs of Mediterranean-climate evergreen and deciduous leaves. I. Growth and CO$_2$ exchange analysis. Oecologia 53:208–213

Miflin B (2000) Crop improvement in the 21st century. J Exp Bot 51:1–8

Monsi M (1960) Dry-matter reproduction in plants. I. Schemata of dry-matter reproduction. Bot Mag 73:82–90

Morison JIL, Piedade MTF, Müller E, Long SP, Junk WJ, Jones MB (2000) Very high productivity of the C4 aquatic grass *Echinochloa polystachia* in the Amazon floodplain confirmed by net ecosystem flux measurements. Oecologia 125:400–411

Mott KA, Gordon ZG, Berry JA (1993) Asymmetric stomatal closure for the two surfaces of *Xynthium strumarium* L. leaves at low humidity. Plant Cell Environ 16:25–34

Mott KA, Parkhust DF (1991) Stomatal response to humidity in air and helox. Plant Cell Environ 14:509–515

Orians GH, Solbrig OT (1977) A cost-income model of leaves and roots with special reference to arid and semiarid areas. Am Nat 111:677–690

Pearcy RW, Pfitsch WA (1994) The consequences of sunflecks for photosynthesis and growth of forest understory plants. Ecological Studies 100. Springer, Berlin Heidelberg New York, pp 343–357

Penning de Vries FWT (1975) Use of assimilates in higher plants. In: Cooper JP (ed) JGP 3: photosynthesis and productivity in different environments. Cambridge University Press, Cambridge, pp 459–480

Penning de Vries FWT (1983) Modelling of growth and productivity. Encycl Plant Physiol 12D:117–150

Penning de Vries FWT, Djitèye MA (1982) La productivité des pataurages Sahéliens: Une érude des sols, des végetations et de l'expoilation de cette resource naturelle. PUDOC, Wageningen, 52 pp

Penning de Vries FWT, van Laar HH, Chardon MC (1983) Bioenergetics of growth of seeds, fruits, and storage organs. In: Potential productivity of field crops under different environments. International Rice Institute, Los Banos, Philippines, pp 37–59

Raschke K (1979) Movements of stomata. Encycl Plant Physiol 7:383–441

Raven JA (1994) Photosynthesis in aquatic plants. Ecological Studies 100. Springer, Berlin Heidelberg New York, pp 299–318

Roden JS, Ehleringer JR (1999) Observations of hydrogen and oxygen isotopes in leaf water confirm the Craig-Gordon model under wide-ranging conditions. Plant Physiol 12:1165–1173

Scarascia-Mugnozza G, Bauer GA, Persson H, Mateucci G, Marci A (2000) Tree biomass, growth and nitrogen pools. Ecological Studies 142. Springer, Berlin Heidelberg New York, pp 49–62

Schäfer C (1994) Controlling the effects of excessive light energy fluxes: dissipative mechanisms, repair processes, and long-term acclimation. In: Schulze E-D (ed) Flux control in biological systems. Academic Press, San Diego, pp 37–56

Scheible WR, Gonzáles-Fortes A, Lauerer M, Müller-Röber B, Caboche M, Stitt M (1997) Nitrate acts as a signal to induce organic acid metabolism and repress starch metabolism in tobacco. Plant Cell 9:783–798

Schulze E-D (1970) Der CO_2-Gaswechsel der Buche (*Fagus silvatica* L.) in Ahhängigkeit von den Klimafaktoren im Freiland. Flora 159:177–232

Schulze E-D (1982) Plant life forms and their carbon water and nutrient relations. Encycl Plant Physiol 12B:616–676

Schulze E-D, Chapin FS III (1987) Plant specialization to environments of different resource availability. Ecological Studies 61. Springer, Berlin Heidelberg New York, pp 120–148

Schulze E-D, Hall AL (1982) Stomatal responses, water loss and CO_2 assimilation rates of plants in contrasting environments. Encycl Plant Physiol 1213:181–230

Schulze E-D, Küppers M, Matyssek R (1987) The role of carbon balance and branching pattern in the growth of woody species. In: Givnish TJ (ed) On the economy of the plant form and function. Cambridge University Press, Cambridge, pp 585–602

Schulze W, Stitt M, Schulze E-D, Neuhaus HE, Fichtner K (1991) A quantification of the significance of assimilatory starch for growth of *Arabidopsis thaliana* L. Heynh. Plant Physiol 95:890–895

Schulze E-D, Kelliher FM, Körner C, Lloyd J, Lenning P (1994) Relationships among maximum stomatal conductance, ecosystem surface conductance, carbon assimilation and plant nitrogen nutrition: a global ecology scaling exercise. Annu Rev Ecol Syst 25:629–660

Schulze E-D, Schulze W, Kelliher FM, Vygodskaya NN, Ziegler W, Kobak KI, Koch H, Arneth A, Ksnetsova WA, Sogachev A, Issajev A, Bauer G, Hollinger DY (1995) Above ground biomass and nitrogen nutrition in a chronosequence of pristine Dahurian *Larix* stands in eastern Siberia. Can J For Res 25:943–960

Schulze E-D, Ellis R, Schulze W, Trmborn P, Ziegler H (1996) Diversity, metabolic types and $\delta^{13}C$ carbon isotope ratios in the grass flora of Namibia in relation to growth form, precipitation and habitat conditions. Oecologia 106:352–369

Schulze E-D, Williams RJ, Farquhar GD, Schulze W, Langridge J, Miller JM, Walker BH (1998) Carbon and nitrogen isotope discrimination and nitrogen nutrition of trees along a rainfall gradient in northern Australia. Aust J Plant Physiol 25:413–425

Shinozaki K, Yoda K, Hozumi K, Kira T (1964) A quantitative analysis of plant form – the pipe model theory. II. Further evidence of the theory and its application in forest ecology. Jpn J Ecol 14:133–139

Steinlein T, Heilmeier H, Schulze E-D (1993) Nitrogen and carbohydrate storage in biennials originating from habitats of different resource availability. Oecologia 93:374–382

Stitt M, Schulze E-D (1994) Plant growth, storage, and resource allocation: from flux control in a metabolic chain to the whole plant level. In: Schulze E-D (ed) Flux control in biological systems. Academic Press, San Diego, pp 57–118

Strasburger E (1999) Lehrbuch der Botanik. G. Fischer, Stuttgart, 1161 pp

Tjoelker MG, Oleksyn J, Reich PB (2001) Modelling respiration of vegetation: evidence for a general temperature-dependent Q_{10}. Global Change Biol 7:223–230

Troll W (1939) Vergleichende Morphologie der Höheren Pflanzen. Bd. 1: Vegetationsorgane. Verlag Gebrüder Bornträger, Berlin, 2005 pp

Vareschi V (1980) Vegetationsökologie der Tropen. Ulmer, Stuttgart, 293 pp

Volkens G (1887) Die Flora der ägyptisch-arabischen Wüste auf Grundlage anatomisch-physiologischer Forschung. Gebrüder Bornträger, Berlin, 151 pp

Von Caemmerer S, Evans JR, Hudson GS, Andrews TJ (1994) The kinetics of ribulose-1,5-bisphosphate carboxylase/oxygenase in vivo interfered from measurements of photosynthesis in leaves of transgenic tobacco. Planta 195:88–97

Warburg O (1913) Die Pflanzenwelt, Bd 1. Bibliographisches Institut, Leipzig Wien

West NE, Young JA (2000) Intermountain valleys and lower mountain slopes. In: Barbour MG, Billings WD (eds) North American terrestrial vegetation. Cambridge University Press, Cambridge, pp 255–284

Woodward GR (1976) Photosynthesis and expansion of leaves of soybean grown in two environments. Photosynthetica 10:274–279

Chapter 3

Ecology of Ecosystems

Ecosystems are networks between organisms and interactions between organisms and their environment on limited space. The space limitation which determines the intensity of these interactions between organisms and environment is determined by the available area of ground. A cross-section through an ecosystem already shows the levels where these interactions are most intense. At the one end this is the leaf canopy where different plant life forms (trees, shrubs, herbs) compete for light by outshading the neighbors. At the other end intense competition exists in the soil where roots compete for water and nutrients. In the organic layer litter fall, decomposition and nutrient uptake interact chemically in such a way that organic acids are lost. This causes leaching of cations and results eventually in podsolization, which may make the area unhabitable for some species. Only some species can penetrate into the resource rich deeper soil layers.

3.1

The Ecosystem Concept

Experimental stand of beech trees "B1" in Solling. The experimental site was important in the International Biological Program (IBP). It was the first time that all the fluxes in a terrestrial forest ecosystem were investigated. Methods developed in the years 1965–1975 at this site served as a model for the global work of the IBP (Ellenberg 1971; Ellenberg et al. 1986). Photo E.-D. Schulze

Recommended Literature

To understand the processes taking place in the ecosystem the following literature is recommended:

- Brady and Weil: Elements of the nature and properties of soil, 2nd edn. Prentice-Hall, Englewood Cliffs, New Jersey, 2004
- Schlesinger: Biogeochemistry. Academic Press, London, 1997
- Schulze: Flux control in biological systems. Academic Press, San Diego, 1994
- Schulze: Carbon and nitrogen cycling in European forest ecosystems. Ecol Studies vol 142. Springer, Berlin Heidelberg New York, 2000.

In previous chapters the focus was on the responses of cellular processes (Chap. 1: Stress physiology) and the use of resources by individual plants (Chap. 2: Whole plant ecology). In the following, these responses will be related to conditions where plants:

- do not grow on their own but form stands, i.e. they compete with individual plants of the same species (perhaps even of the same rhizome) or with other species,
- are subject to use by other organisms (herbivory, pathogens),

- rely on resources and conditions which arise from the activity of other species. This concerns particularly feedback supply of nutrients by microorganisms from dead organic matter into forms which can be used by plants.

The botanical analysis of these diverse interactions deals with the temporal and spatial dynamics of vegetation (history of vegetation, distribution of plant species, competition and succession). This will be discussed in Chapter 4: Synecology. However, there are also processes dealing with the turnover and the distribution of resources at certain sites. This "ecosystem aspect" will be discussed in this chapter.

By moving from the level of the individual plant to the level of material turnover at a site, the following conditions are changed:

- the reference system, and
- the availability of resources.

Reference system: Turnover no longer depends on the concentration ($g\,g^{-1}$ or $mol\,g^{-1}$) of material in certain organs or individual plants, but on the use of the habitat where the ground surface area is the only constant reference ($g\,m^{-2}_{ground}$ or $mol\,m^{-2}_{ground}$) based on which air and ground surface area may be used by different organisms. The density of individuals and the biodiversity are just as important and variable parameters in considering turnover per ground surface area as is turnover in different partial systems which relate to the ground area and are interconnected. These partial systems range from the living plant cover, via litter, to soil organisms. They may be individually or as a whole connected laterally with neighbouring systems.

Availability of resources: New system characteristics become important with the focus on the ground area of the stand. The plant does not exist on its own and independently in the space, but is incorporated into a complicated structure where the resources are also turned over by neighbours and made available, within limits, by soil organisms. The limitations of space also limit the use of external resources (light, water, CO_2).

3.1.1

What Is an Ecosystem?

The understanding that, at the level of the vegetation, additional higher order parameters were determined by the system itself led to the introduction of the term "ecosystem". Tansley (1935) realised, in his definition of the term, that it is not a description of a symbiosis or parts of a super-organism, but the interaction of plants and animals with the physical-chemical environment. Because of the importance of the basic concepts describing the development of the term "ecosystem", the original text is cited here:

I have already given my reasons for rejecting the term "complex organism" and "biotic community". Clements' earlier term "biome" for the whole complex of organisms inhabiting a given region is unobjectable, and for some purposes convenient. But the more fundamental conception is, as it seems to me, the whole system (in some sense of physics), including not only the organism complex, but also the whole complex of physical factors forming what we call the environment of the biome – the habitat factors in the widest sense. Though the organisms may claim our prime interest, when we are trying to think fundamentally, we cannot separate them from their special environment, with which they form one physical system.

It is the systems so formed which, from the point of view of the ecologist, are the basic units

of nature on the face of the earth. Our natural human prejudices force us to consider organisms (in the sense of biologists) as the most important part of these systems, but certainly the inorganic "factors" are also part – there could be no system without them, and there is constant interchange of the most various kinds within each system, not only between the organisms but between the organic and inorganic. These ecosystems, as we may call them, are of the most various kinds and size. They form one category of the multitudinous physical systems of the universe, which range from the universe as a whole down to the atom.

Ecosystems Are Thus Networks of Interrelations Between Organisms and Their Environment in a Defined Space

In this definition (1) boundaries of ecosystems and (2) their compartmentalisation remain unresolved. It is not resolved (3) whether new system characteristics occur which concern the system as a whole. Occasionally, ecosystems are defined as networks of interrelations without reference to space. In these cases, too, the interaction between organisms becomes only critical within the limitation of space.

3.1.2

Boundaries of Ecosystems

The size of an ecosystem is not pre-defined. The region should be uniform regarding the biogeochemical turnover, and contain all fluxes above and below the ground area under consideration. Likens (1992) considers river catchment areas as basic units for ecosystems within regional spaces, as material balance may only be completely quantified within such region. However, a river catchment area is subdivided into regions near brooks and those away from them and have, per ground area, very different turnover if peaty river valleys and dry woodlands are considered, for example. Considerable turnover occurs also in the flowing water itself, so that the balance of regions away from the flowing water appears almost impossible. River catchment areas integrate very heterogeneous parts of the region and would thus to be too wide a demarcation to be valid as a basic unit of ecosystems. The opposite extreme would be to consider a rotting tree in a forest as an ecosystem.

The limits of an ecosystem must, clearly, extend so far that the essential parts of material turnover per ground area (e.g. carbon assimilation, nitrogen mineralisation, formation of ground water, etc.) are taken into account quantitatively. A rotting tree trunk is, considered from this point of view, only a partial system within a forest. Only the total turnover describes the characteristics and limits of, for example, a forest ecosystem. This is independent of the fact that some organisms (migrating birds) also have influence beyond these limits or that partial areas of the system possess their own dynamics.

3.1.3

Compartmentalisation

The division of ecosystems into different compartments depends on the question posed. The following divisions appear, amongst others, sensible:

- Above-ground and below-ground compartments: This division separates autotrophic and heterotrophic processes. In addition, it is possible to subdivide into soil horizons, and stems, branches and leaves. This classification describes material fluxes and separates the ecosystem regarding atmosphere and ground-water.
- Trophic level: Producers, consumers and decomposers describe energy flux.
- Functional groups: Groups of species which behave similarly regarding certain characteristics are often considered together (e.g. nitrogen-fixing plants, insects sucking phloem, parasites, and many others). They may reflect important interfaces within the trophic level.
- Structural characteristics: The structure of vegetation is particularly important in the coupling of exchanges of vegetation with the atmosphere. The division into trees, shrubs and herbaceous plants is important here.

3.1.4

System Characteristics

The network of interrelations is complex, i.e. it is determined by a multitude of factors and interactions. They are far away from an equilibrium and undetermined, i.e. there is no goal for certain dynamic change. Ecosystems behave linearly only within a short time span. Because there are no closed systems, there are always irregularities. Thus ecosystems may "break down" and make space available for new compositions of species. Open systems may be disturbed externally, particularly by anthropogenic and climatic influences.

In ecosystems, several new system characteristics occur, whereby all transitions to whole plant ecology are transient. This applies particularly to the structure (e.g. roughness of surface, climate of the stand, spatial compartmentalisation) already discussed in Chapters 2.1, 2.2 and 2.3. New characteristics occur regarding the use of resources at the level of the ecosystem, and regarding the interaction of specific functions of many species (**biodiversity**). From the point of view of the individual plant, the most important system characteristic is that there are neighbours, which, in contrast to the very variable physical-chemical environment, possess a multitude of options and thus codetermine the success or failure of an individual or a species. Because of the interaction between organisms the following system characteristics are particularly important:

- **Material balance**: This concerns all organisms of the ecosystem. Compared to whole plant ecology, material pools and material fluxes and the resulting ecosystem balance become increasingly important when studying ecosystems. Even in the future it will hardly be possible to trace and measure all processes. Thus the balance of material fluxes consisting of input and output remains as the most important quantitative characteristic at the scale of a stand. Similarly to whole plant ecology, the following quantities are observed:
  - amount of material (pool size; $g\,m^{-2}$),
  - material flux ($g\,m^{-2}\,time^{-1}$),
  - material balance, and here particularly loss and gain,
  - mechanisms regulating the size of the flux: regulation by substrate = **feed-forward**, regulation by products = **feed-back**, branching, modulation, Co-limitation (see also Chaps. 1 and 2),
  - in addition to material fluxes, there are also "information fluxes", i.e. material fluxes are started (e.g. pollination), without the amount becoming visible in the material fluxes.

- **Differentiation between species and individual plants**: Ultimately, it is individual plants that successfully dominate or die within an ecosystem. Depending on neighbouring individuals, differences occur between the course of growth of different plants in an ecosystem, even in clonal monocultures. In addition, individual species have different direct or indirect effects on the whole system (so-called keystone species). Behaviour under conditions of competition is difficult to predict, as slight differences between species may have far-reaching cumulative consequences.
- **Time scale**: Accumulation and consumption of resources change basic life conditions in the long term. Often seconds are sufficient to assess physiological reactions. Material balance is often determined on a yearly basis. However, if it concerns conditions at a site, then dependent on losses and gains, centuries or millennia are appropriate time scales (Chadwick et al. 1999; see Fig. 3.5.1).
- **Random events and interference**: Survival of individual plants in an ecosystem is not only determined by physiological characteristics of the species, but often also randomly by who the neighbour is (see also Chap. 4.1.4). The chance whether, in a microspatial mosaic of environmental conditions, a plant germinates or grows next to a less competitive neighbour

may determine the success or failure of a species. The constitution of vegetation is decided during the seedling phase. With longer time scales individual processes, so-called interference, also become more important; storm damage, breakage caused by snow, drought, fire or economic measures of human beings may drastically change ecosystems within minutes. Material pools that accumulated over millennia may degrade within a very short time.

References

Chadwick OA, Derry LA, Vitousek PM, Huebert BJ, Hedin LO (1999) Changing resources of nutrients during four million years of ecosystem development. Nature 397:491–497

Ellenberg H (1971) Integrated experimental ecology. Methods and results of ecosystem research in the German Solling project. Ecological Studies, Vol 2. Springer, Berlin Heidelberg New York, 214 pp

Ellenberg H, Mayer R, Schauermann J (1986) Ökosystemforschung; Ergebnisse des Sollingprojektes 1966–1986. Eugen Ulmer Verlag, 597 pp

Likens GE (1992) Some applications of the ecosystem approach to environmental problems and resource management. In: Teller A, Mathy P, Jeffers JNR (eds) Responses of forest ecosystems to environmental changes. Elsevier Applied Science, London, pp 16–30

Tansley AG (1935) The use and abuse of vegetational concepts and terms. Ecology 42:237–245

Processes in Stands and Ecosystems

Self-thinning of a *Pinus contorta* forest in the Canadian Rocky Mountains. *Pinus contorta* has cones that only open after heating in fire, enabling the species to rejuvenate itself after a fire which kills the crowns of older trees. This results in a thick carpet of young trees that compete with each other, the weaker ones die and so the forest is thinned. The picture shows a large amount of dead wood, i.e. a large number of fallen dead trees and also a number of severely bent trees that are too weak to survive the snowfall in winter in this area. Self-thinning of growing trees is clearly visible. Thinning continues also in mature forests, unless other factors such as fires on the forest floor decrease the number of trees per area below a size-dependent maximum density. Alberta, Jaspers National Park, Canada. Photo E.-D. Schulze

3.2.1

Self-Thinning

Light is used in a stand according to Beer's extinction law, so that light in the stand of vegetation decreases exponentially (see Chap. 2.1.2). The upper limit for light capture by a stand is determined by the flux of radiation and the maximum leaf area index (LAI_{max}), which in turn is determined by the inclination and position of the leaf (horizontal, vertical, clumped; see Chap. 2.1.2.3). The consequence of this upper limit is that individual plants, living on a given ground area, must share this maximum possible leaf area. The leaf area may occupy different layers of the vegetation. Based on Reineke (1933), Yoda et al. (1963) further formalised this relation and expressed the biomass per individual plant (W) as a function of density of individual plants (n), where c is a proportionality factor, depending on light and nutrient supply:

$$W = cn^{-3/2} \qquad (3.2.1)$$

The equation states that in a closed, growing stand where the biomass per individual plant increases, the number of individual plants per area must necessarily decrease. Fewer but larger individual plants survive at the cost of smaller individuals, which die. This process is called **self-thinning** of stands, where the factor −3/2 is called the self-thinning constant. The coefficient may be explained by the spatial expansion of mass (exponent 3) and the expansion of the projected area of an individual plant (exponent 2; Osawa and Allen 1993).

As the biomass per area (B) corresponds to the product of (W×n), the self-thinning of stands result, according to Westoby (1984), from the multiplication of Eq. (3.2.1) by the factor n:

$$B = cn^{-1/2} \qquad (3.2.2)$$

Taking the logarithm of this equation yields the linear equation:

$$\log B = \log c - \frac{1}{2}\log n \qquad (3.2.3)$$

The equation shows that the maximum biomass which may be achieved on an area depends, for a particular species, on the number of individual plants. The slope of the line (−0.5) applies to a broad range of growth forms (herbaceous plants, shrubs, trees) in as far as these are kept in comparable conditions, in monoculture, and the maximum leaf area is reached dependent on the available light. The parameter c gives the productivity, which is determined by many factors such as site conditions and growth characteristics of the species. From the equation it follows that in a closed stand some of the individual plants must die when the critical limit of the leaf area is reached and if the biomass of the stand is to increase. The maximum achievable biomass depends essentially on the growth form of the dominant plant species (trees, herbaceous plants, position of the leaf and form of the canopy) and the available radiation.

An example of the process of self-thinning is shown in Fig. 3.2.1 A (Stitt and Schulze 1994). In a growing stand of nettles, the stems belong physiologically to the same organism, because of rhizomes. Initially, many individual plants may coexist, as long as their leaf biomass fills the growth space vertically and horizontally (Fig. 3.2.1 A, arrow 1). After that, the process of self-thinning starts, i.e. the biomass of the stand increases with the simultaneous decrease in the number of individual plants (Fig. 3.2.1 A, arrow

2). With the onset of flowering, the biomass of stems increases further with constant number of individual plants, but the flower stalks do not increase leaf area (Fig. 3.2.1 A, arrow 3). Biomass production is different between sites due to different light availability.

Deviations from the linear trend may occur under natural conditions predominantly in forests:

- **Decline of old growth forests:** Stem density decreases in old growth forest to an extent that it can no longer be compensated by the remaining trees. Individual trees die because of statistical events, e.g. lightning, storms or diseases, and the growth of the remaining stand, depending on species, results in a canopy that is no longer closed. With the opening of the canopy, external influences (e.g. wind) become more important and thus the number of individual plants is then further reduced. Gaps emerge which are used by other species or individuals of the same species and ultimately leads to the rejuvenation of the stand or a change in the vegetation (see Chap. 4.1.5.3). In plant ecology, this phase in the development of a stand is often called "the phase of stand collapse". This term does not describe the causes of the collapse, i.e. that self-thinning and stochastic events reduced the number of individual plants and that the remaining stand is no longer able to close the canopy.
- **Availability of nutrients and water:** The theory of self-thinning is based on the assumption that light is the exclusive limiting factor. However, there are other limiting factors, e.g. nutrients which determine the density of the stand; in this case, competition takes place in the ground and not in the canopy. This may be observed very clearly in forests where a large part of the nutrients available in the ecosystem is bound in the existing biomass. With increasing total biomass of the stand, and because of the limited weathering of primary minerals, increasingly less nutrient is available (Schulze 1995), leading to a change in growth form and composition of participating species.
- **Use of light:** The form of the forest canopy changes with age thus causing self-thinning, which is flatter or steeper than the −0.5 slope discussed earlier. Thus, e.g., the canopy of pines changes from a form of a pointed cone

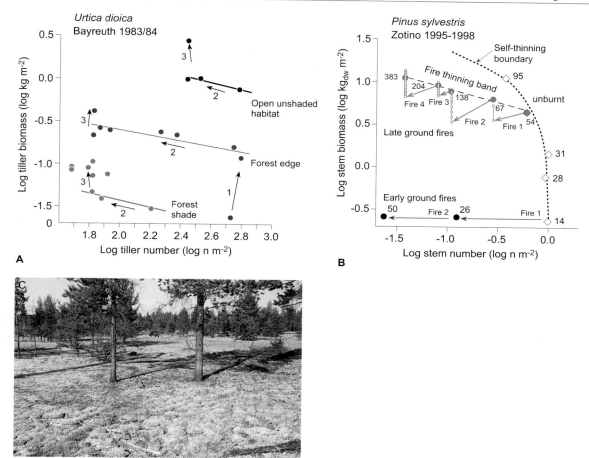

Fig. 3.2.1. A Self-thinning of *Urtica dioica* stands in the shadow of a riverine forest, a forest margin, and at a site with full sunlight. Production differs depending on the available light. *Arrow 1* shows the development when the canopy is not fully closed, *arrow 2* shows self-thinning when the canopy is closed, and *arrow 3* shows flowering, when shoot biomass increases whilst leaf biomass decreases (Stitt and Schulze 1994). B Self-thinning of *Pinus sylvestris* in Siberia after regeneration following a crown fire. Each large symbol represents a different forest stand. The *numbers* give the age of the stand. *Dotted line* Self-thinning without the influence of fire. Self-thinning usually occurs after the canopy closes, when the trees are approximately 54 years old. Late ground fires (i.e. the first fire occurred when the trees were 50 years old) resulted in a reduction in biomass and in the number of trunks. After this first ground fire it takes about 10 years until the same production is reached as pre-fire at higher stand density. However, before reaching the self-thinning line stands usually experience a repeated ground fire that continues to decrease the number of trees and the biomass. With increasing age of trees the regeneration phase takes longer (*small open circles* show the increase in biomass within 10 years). With early ground fires in young stands (< 50 years), the number of trunks may be reduced considerably. Stands may become so open that a compensation of biomass at the stand level by increases from the remaining trees is no longer possible. In these stands the biomass remains low. The smaller number of tree individuals prevents new ground fires, as there is not much burnable biomass (Wirth et al. 1999). C View of a park-like landscape with 60-year-old pines in central Siberia after an early intensive fire. The vegetation on the forest floor is formed by a close cover of *Cladonia* species which suppress germination of pine seeds. Such areas remain in this state over centuries and are marked in maps as "forest free" sites. (Photo E.-D. Schulze)

in the juvenile phase (many individual plants fit into a space), to a wide-spreading, flat crown (fewer individual plants fit into a space than would have done if the juvenile form were kept the same into old age).

- **External disturbances:** There are many external disturbances affecting the number of individual plants in a stand (lightning, wind and

snow breakages) which will be discussed in detail in Chapter 3.2.5. In many ecosystems, fire has a large effect on the number of individual plants in a stand, independent of the supply of nutrients. Self-thinning in Siberian pine (*Pinus sylvestris*) forests depends on the frequency of fires, as well as on the rate of growth (Fig. 3.2.1 B; Wirth et al. 1999). Siberian pine forests are rejuvenated by so-called canopy fires which destroy the stand. Very densely growing, young stands of the same age develop (see also Fig. 3.2.1), which are also selectively very prone to fires. A fire in a juvenile stand causes a reduction in the number of individual plants and the biomass decreases (Fig. 3.2.1 B, fire 1). It takes several decades until the remaining stand accumulates biomass again until a stage is reached where self-thinning starts again. This regeneration would be possible, but, because of the climate, it is more probable that repeated soil fires occur (Fig. 3.2.1 B, fires 2–4), again reducing the number of individual plants and thus reducing the biomass. The result is a thinning line, caused by fire, which probably keeps the biomass per area almost constant. Lacking competitive pressure the pine canopy changes; it no longer grows in height, but in width, thus strengthening the trend that biomass no longer increases despite decreasing number of stems.

Fires in a young stand could also prevent formation of a completely closed canopy. Park-like stands develop with low growing individual stems (Fig. 3.2.1 C). Biomass in the Siberian pine forest is thus determined by fire in juvenile stands and the resulting number of individual trees.

- **Economic use:** In agriculture as well as in forestry, death of individual plants which are not harvested is uneconomic. Additionally, the economic aim, namely to attain a certain size of tree within a reasonable time span, may only be achieved if the individual trees do not compete for light. In cultivated forests the density of the stand is regulated by man through thinning. In agriculture, crop density is similarly regulated by the number of seeds sown. Here, the relation between biomass and number of individual plants (regulated by cultivation) is similar to that in natural, nutrient-poor systems which is below that of potential self-thinning.

Strictly speaking, the law of self-thinning only applies to monocultures of the same age. But the same principles apply (proportionality of canopy area to the volume of the canopy) even in mixed stands of different ages where several vegetative layers share the same habitat. In these cases the thinning curve is steeper, because in biodiverse stands there is a complementary use of niches involving many factors, such as rooting depths, form of canopy, growth of vegetation. Therefore, diverse stands may have a higher productivity than monocultures, often termed over-yielding (Hector et al. 1999).

The asymmetric competition for light, i.e. the fact that taller individual plants harvest a larger proportion of the "light" resource compared with shorter plants, differentiates the stand from juvenile stands with many small and shorter individual plants (distribution shifted to the left or right). With the onset of self-thinning the stand develops normally again, as mainly smaller individual plants die because of competition. If the stand is very uniform in its size distribution (e.g. pine stands after fires), it may happen that growth stops until differentiation starts because of external influences (storm, snow).

3.2.2
Reversible and Irreversible Site Changes Related to Resource Exploitation

3.2.2.1
Material Fluxes Accompanying Plant Growth

Growth of plant stands not only depends on assimilation of CO_2 and the availability of water, but also on the turnover of nutrients (see Chap. 2.4.3.7). Water as well as CO_2 may be regarded in ecosystems as renewable resources from an indefinitely large atmospheric pool. This is different for nutrients. Ecology has the task of establishing the flux balances of carbon, water and nutrient elements. Generally, nutrients are released during decomposition of litter or weathering of primary minerals, and they are then reversibly stored by the soil exchanger or in soil organic substance. The ash content of biomass shows the amount of nutrients taken up by plants from soil. If the organic mass is not harvested, but remains as dead biomass (litter) and is degraded again, then these cations are returned to the soil (see Chap. 3.3: material cycles). Ulrich (1987) has formalised the connection between availability of CO_2, water and ions, and their incorporation into organic substances, in an equation of material balance for organic matter in ecosystems:

$$aCO_2 + xM^+ + yA^- + (y - x)H^+ + zH_2O$$
$$+ \text{energy} \leftrightarrow \left(C_aH_{2z}O_zM_xA_y\right)org \cdot matter$$
$$+ (a + ...)O_2 \qquad (3.2.4)$$

where M^+ and A^- are the consumption of cations and anions and the coefficients a, x, y and z are the amount of molar ratio in the soil solution. To maintain large production in managed systems, according to Eq. (3.2.4) the loss of cations due to harvesting must be replaced by fertilisation.

3.2.2.2
Immobilisation of Nutrients and Nutrient Imbalances

In a balanced system, synthesis of material and mineralisation of material would occur simultaneously and balance. This equilibrium does not occur in the real world, as there are considerable shifts in time between consumption and feedback of resources, described by the mean residence time in the appropriate compartment. Leaves, e.g., are synthesised within 1 year, but the litter is decomposed over many years, i.e. nutrients bound in leaves will, on average, only be available for further growth after 2–8 years (Persson et al. 2000). The mean residence time of these nutrients in the foliage is thus 2–8 years. In wood, nutrient may be bound in the plant body for more than 100 years. The decomposition of a tree trunk takes decades, even centuries, and thus the delay between uptake of resources and making the same resource available again takes a lot longer for wood than for leafy litter.

The accumulation of litter in the form of raw humus is a sign that the shedding of leaves or needles exceeds the capacity of soil organisms to decompose the litter, and that fast decomposition is hindered by substances which are difficult to metabolise or by unfavourable climates. Raw humus is only decomposed when the tree stand becomes lighter (e.g. by tree fall or wind damage) and thus the supply of litter decreases and also the open stand provides better conditions for mineralisation (higher soil temperature and moisture, change of soil organisms). However, the turnover of raw humus into highly decomposed forms of humus (mull, moder) is not continuous but depends on the chemistry of the original substance, as intermediary products are formed which may be decomposed at different speeds or accumulated. A distinction is made between rapidly and slowly decomposed soil carbon although these terms are not well defined [< 30 years: recent soil carbon; 30–100 years: intermediary soil carbon; 100 to > 1000 years: black carbon (charcoal, soot); > 1000 years: "recalcitrant" humus (Townsend et al. 1995; Schlesinger 1997; Schulze et al. 2000)].

The delay between use and feed-back of nutrients leads, even in a year, to imbalances between, e.g., nitrification in autumn and nitrate uptake in summer.

Loss of Resources

Chemical conditions in the soil are primarily dependent on the constitution of the original bed rock (see Chap. 2.3). However, these conditions are changed as a consequence of the mobilisation and consumption of cations by plants and by the inevitable loss of cations through leaching into lower soil layers or into the groundwater. Seasonality of plant growth and formation of new organic compounds in the course of decomposition of inorganic matter (humic acids) lead to relocation of ions and to changes in soil chemistry (Kaiser and Guggenberger 2000). The temporal shift between formation and consumption of nitrate shows, again, that loss of nutrients occurs even in natural ecosystems. As nitrate in the soil is not bound to minerals it may be leached into the groundwater as acid anions, taking along cations. Nitrate is also formed in autumn when most plants stop growing; nitrate and cation losses thus occur particularly during winter. In summer, however, the nitrogen requirement of vegetation exceeds supply from the soil. This asynchronous pattern of supply and demand leads, in the end, to changes in conditions in the habitat with local over-exploitation (loss of cations in the upper mineral layer = podsolisation and acidification of soils, see Chap. 2.3.1) or to accumulation of intermediary products, in as far as degradation is impeded by decreasing pH (e.g. raw humus).

Chemical conditions in the soil are particularly changed by strong acids (SO_4^{2-}, NO_3^-) from anthropogenic emissions and the subsequent relocation of cations. In particular, the deposition of acids (Fig. 3.2.2 A) in the uppermost horizon of mineral soils leads to a large decrease in pH and finally to release of Al ions. An acidification horizon is formed which may affect the complete zone of weathering. In this case, pH in-

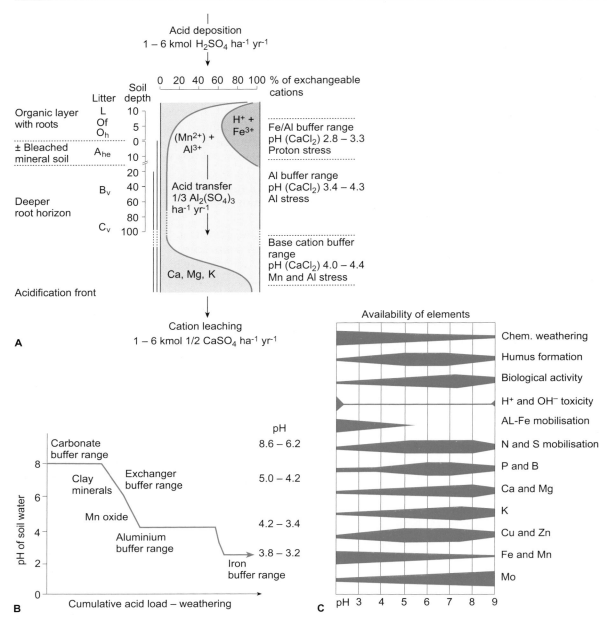

Fig. 3.2.2. A Depth of acidification with acid rain (FBW 1989; Last and Watling 1991) showing that when strong acids are deposited, horizons from A- to the upper C-horizon can be acidified, without becoming visible as soil horizon. The base saturation rises in the lower C-horizons. Due to cation uptake by roots and shedding of needles the organic matter on the forest floor also becomes more alkaline. B Changes in pH of the soil solution with continuing weathering as a consequence of the cumulative proton stress, i.e. acid deposition (after Schulze and Ulrich 1991). C Availability of nutrients dependent on the pH of the soil solution. (Larcher 1994)

creases only near the original bed rock. Stronger alkaline saturation and higher pH also occur in the deposited humus, as cations from roots from lower soil layers are taken up into the plant and reach the organic deposits via the litter.

The rate of soil acidification depends on the mineral constitution of the bed rock and the cu-

mulative acid stress (Fig. 3.2.2 B). On limestone soils with high $CaCO_3$ the imbalance of cations triggered by fixation of cations in organic matter or by relocation of cations is, at first, balanced by weathering of carbonate.

$$CaCO_3 + H_2CO_3 \leftrightarrow Ca^{2+} + 2\,HCO_3^- \quad (3.2.5\,a)$$

where

$$2\,HCO_3^- \leftrightarrow CO_2 + H_2O \qquad (3.2.5\,b)$$

The released Ca ions occupy the charges that become free on the soil exchangers (see Chap. 2.3.1). With the loss of organic matter, e.g. by harvesting and leaching of cations from the clay minerals and humus complexes, $CaCO_3$ is continually consumed. Over a long period, the soil pH decreases and a reversible exchange of cations occurs with clay minerals and humus. With continuing loss of cations and H^+-buffering by metal oxides and hydroxides, a pH-dependent increase in the availability of certain metal ions occurs. Thus Mn becomes mobile at a pH between 5 and 4.2. At a pH of 4.2, the soil reaches another stable buffer system as with the availability of lime, but in this case the pH is buffered by Al hydroxides (see Chap. 1.8); Fe buffers below pH 3.8. The availability of ions is very variable during the course of this process and each element is specifically dependent on the pH of the soil solution (Fig. 3.2.2 C; Larcher 1994).

The chemical changes in the soil are reversible, i.e. by fertilisation or liming, provided that the clay minerals are not restructured. As soon as the crystalline structure of silicates and clay minerals is changed (e.g. by dissolving the Al lattice as a replacement of alkaline cations by protons, Chap. 2.1), a reverse into the original state is no longer possible, not even by supplying cations (liming of forests; see Chap. 3.5.1).

3.2.3

Complexity and Non-linear Behaviour

Ecosystems are by definition complex structures, which are far removed from equilibrium and therefore change dynamically. From the multitude of processes related to this complexity, some processes are listed in the following which, even at the level of the ecosystem, occur non-linearly and irregularly without the sole regulation by the individual plant. It becomes obvious that most ecosystem processes become saturated with increasing intensity of a regulating variable or decreased again. Only very few processes, above all the dependence of respiration on temperature, continue to increase over a broad range.

- **Photosynthesis, respiration:** Photosynthesis follows a saturation function which on the whole is regulated by the availability of light and CO_2. Nutrient supply determines the level at which saturation occurs (see Chap. 2.4.1). In contrast, respiration of non-photosynthetic organs, and soil respiration of heterotrophic soil organisms, increases exponentially with temperature (Lloyd and Taylor 1994). Thus the reaction of ecosystems to the increase in global temperatures is very dependent on respiration.
- **Sensible and latent heat:** The turnover of sensible and latent heat depends most of all on solar radiation and the water supply (see Chap. 3.2.4). Latent and sensible heat fluxes increase initially in proportion. In a climate with high precipitation and moderately high solar radiation (Fichtelgebirge in Germany, Fig. 3.2.3 A), relatively low irradiation limits the transport of sensible heat and advectively transported dry air masses are important which mainly affect evapotranspiration from wet surfaces. The light limitation of turnover becomes obvious in assimilation (Fig. 3.2.3 B) which also reaches an upper limit, although evaporation still increases. A different scenario occurs in the continental climate of Siberia (Fig. 3.2.3 C, D) where evaporation and sensible heat flux are coupled over a wide range and evaporation reaches the upper limit sooner than the sensible heat flux. Assimilation and evaporation are coupled closely to each other at low rates over a very wide range.
- **Formation of biomass:** Formation of biomass in a stand is similar to the saturation function for an individual plant. After exponential growth up to stand closure the phase of self-thinning follows and, with age, biomass of the stand is limited by plant density (Fig. 3.2.4 A; Schulze et al. 1999). The maximum attainable biomass depends on climate, structure of trees and nutrient supply. Climate conditions lead to regional differentiation. The yield of forests in southern Germany is higher than in northern Germany because of the more favourable climatic conditions there. In managed forests, the biomass (and thus the competition between trees) is additionally regulated by thinning (Fig. 3.2.4 B; Kramer 1988).

The saturation function applies to all forms of vegetation (Schulze 1982), even for herbac-

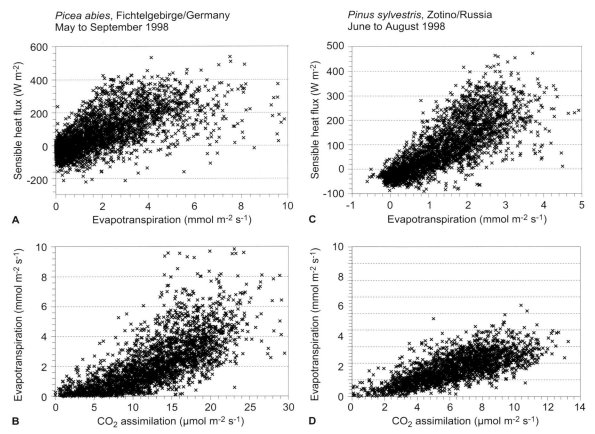

Fig. 3.2.3. A, C Changes in evaporation and latent heat transport and B, D changes in evaporation and assimilation in spruce trees in the Fichtelgebirge, Germany (A, B) and pine forests in Siberia (C, D). It is obvious in temperate climates that there is not a linear relationship, i.e. the evaporation rises with constant sensible heat transport or constant assimilation. In a continental climate the flows are much smaller, with the linear part of the graph representing spruce trees (*Picea abies*: C. Rebmann, unpubl., *Pinus sylvestris*: A. Knohl, unpubl.)

eous plant stands. Mowing of meadows occurs at a time before the biomass reaches the plateau of saturation.

Particular irregularities in biomass accumulation are observed in annual field crops caused by the change from vegetative to reproductive growth (flowering and fruiting). After a certain period (**determinate species**) or after storage or availability of certain resources (**non-determinate species**) flowering occurs, leading to fruiting and finally to death of plants.

- **Harvesting** of field crops leads, in summer, to a substantial change in water, heat and nutrient balances of fields, shown here as an example of the complexity of interactions at the

next higher level, the landscape. Under certain conditions, harvesting may even affect the weather. If the sensible heat flux of the harvested areas increases and evaporation on neighbouring forest areas is high, convective thunderstorms occur. Because of the convective transport of air masses from the ground into the higher atmosphere volatile organic compounds rise into the troposphere and affect the chemical conditions in the atmosphere and the NO-ozone cycle. Thus oxidation of NO to NO_3^- occurs and thus deposition of nitrogenous compounds from the atmosphere.

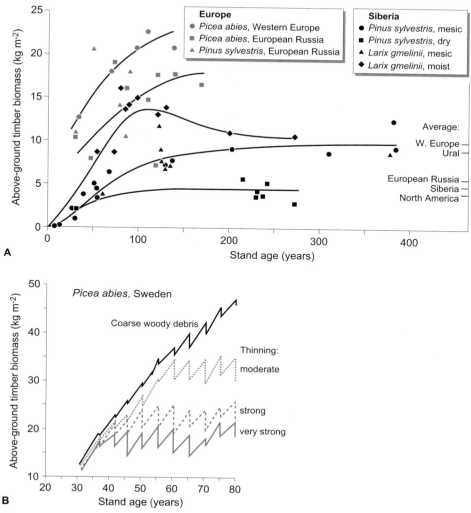

Fig. 3.2.4. A Increase in biomass with age of trees in managed spruce forests in Germany compared with unmanaged forests of spruce, pine and larch in eastern Europe and Siberia (Schulze et al. 1999). It is shown that even unmanaged forests reach a maximum biomass, but that this is not an equilibrium between assimilation and respiration. It is the result of stresses (fire, wind). **B** Influence of forest management showing the effect of thinning on the development of a stand of spruce in southern Sweden. The "zig-zags" in the development of the stand are due to the removal of biomass in forest management and the subsequent recovery of the stand. (After Kramer 1988)

3.2.4

Number of Species and Habitat Partitioning

3.2.4.1
Rank Dominance and Keystone Species

In the so-called rank dominance distribution one parameter, characterising the presence of a species (number of individual plants, biomass, ground cover per species), is plotted with decreasing proportion of that parameter as shown by the different species of that community (Sala et al. 1996). In many vegetation types a few species, often only one species, comprise the largest fraction of individuals, biomass and canopy cover. Other species obtain a lesser fraction.

Increase or decrease of plant species, or the presence of certain functional types, may have very different, usually non-linear effects on ecosystem processes. Generally, productivity increases with biodiversity because of the better temporal and spatial use of the site (Hector et al. 1999). With the loss of plant species different developments are possible (Sala et al. 1996). There are species which achieve the highest biomass in monocultures (Fig. 3.2.5 A). Removing such spe-

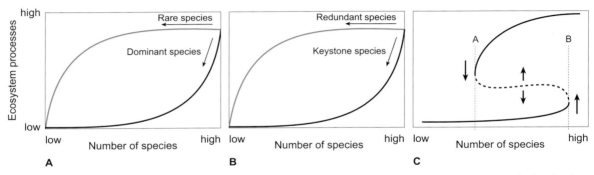

Fig. 3.2.5. The effect of dominance by a single type of organism on ecosystem processes. A Removal of a dominant species by a stress has a greater impact than the loss of a rare species. B If a keystone species dies out then the ecosystem is affected more than expected from the comparatively small proportion of biomass that was removed by extinction of the keystone species. The effect is much greater than for species whose function can be replaced (redundant species). C Depending on the structure (plant life form) of the predominant vegetation, there are various stable states that the ecosystem can develop with increasing or decreasing biodiversity. The *dotted line* shows alternative states that an ecosystem under moderate stress could return to. *Points A and B* are threshold values at which the system changes from one state to another. (Sala et al. 1996; WBGU 1998)

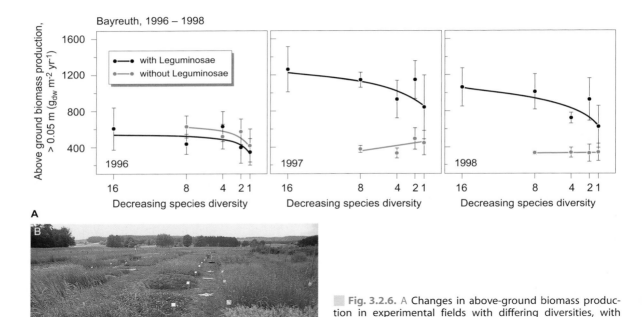

Fig. 3.2.6. A Changes in above-ground biomass production in experimental fields with differing diversities, with and without leguminous plants. The fields were planted in 1996 and mown twice a year. In 1998, productivity of plots containing legumes was significantly higher than those without. In contrast, the productivity of plots without legumes decreased after five mowings (Scherer-Lorenzen 1999). B Plots of the biodiversity experiment in Bayreuth. (Photo E.-D. Schulze)

cies results, even in mixed stands, in massive losses of yield. There are also minor species which appear to be redundant (Fig. 3.2.5 B) with little influence on the immediate ecosystem processes (e.g. orchids in a meadow). The absence of these plants hardly affects the biomass production of the stand. If the loss of biodiversity is associated with a change of life form (see Chap. 2.4.5), very different yield levels may be reached by the same numbers of species according to the presence of a specific life form at the site (Fig. 3.2.5 C). The system may, with a loss of a species, jump from one level to another with consequences for all processes in the ecosystem.

There are deviations from this general observation. It may happen that one of the introduced species has a much greater effect on the ecosystem than would have been assumed based on its fractional share of resources. Such species are called **keystone species** (Bond 1994). An example of such keystone species are nitrogen fixers in a meadow (Fig. 3.2.6 A). In an experiment in which meadow communities of differing diversity were sown (Fig. 3.2.6 B), an increase in above-ground biomass occurred with increasing number of species. This effect was, however, only observed if Leguminoseae (particularly *Trifolium rubrum*) were included in the stand. In the first year after sowing, there were still sufficient nutrients available in the soil and the effects were not seen. With increasing depletion of the soil because of the loss of nutrients through harvesting, the effect of Leguminoseae became stronger in the following years (Scherer-Lorenzen 1999). Keystone species are often animals, which affect vegetation composition although this may not be obvious (see, e.g., Ernest and Brown 2001).

3.2.4.2
Distribution of Above- and Below-Ground Biomass in a Habitat

Exploitation of the habitat between different species and individual plants affects above as well as below-ground parameters (Fig. 3.2.7 A, B). Competition is usually asymmetric, i.e. large individuals use a much larger proportion of available resources. Above ground the inclination of leaves is important. Tall, growing shrubs with horizontal leaves may dominate a stand, because they effectively shade competitors (*Petasites, Urtica*; see Chap. 2.4.5.3). Below-ground competition operates mainly via the formation of root biomass, and particularly via the renewal of root tips (Fig. 3.2.7 B). This is shown clearly in a comparison of fertilised (i.e. nutrient-rich) and unfertilised (nutrient-poor) meadows in central Europe. Forty to 50 species grow in nutrient-poor meadows, both dicotyledenous and monocotyledenous species, but with a greater variety of the former than the latter in the canopy (Fig. 3.2.7 C). Light penetrates through the low vegetation cover and reaches the vegetation layer just above the ground where the largest proportion of leaf area is located, and where low growing rosette plants still find conditions enabling

them to survive. In the unfertilised meadow about 75% of the biomass is in roots. Comparing this with a well-fertilised meadow, then the number of species decreases to 10 or 20 species, with new species invading. The remaining species have higher stems and may form a closed canopy at considerable height above the soil surface (Fig. 3.2.7 D). At first, grasses dominate. With further eutrophication and availability of nutrients, dicotyledonous species which grow even taller become dominant. The large leaf area index (LAI) near the ground in Fig. 3.2.7 A originates from the lower leaves of these tall, growing species during early development of the vegetation, but these lower leaves will die off with further growth of the stand. Because of the dense and high canopy little light penetrates to the ground and thus low growing species are excluded with time. Tall growth is stimulated by only investing 30% of the biomass into roots. The example shows that the reduction of root competition changes the competition for light, regulated predominately by the height of the vegetation.

3.2.4.3
Mycorrhizae

Assessment of ecosystems is made more complicated by the association of plants with mycorrhizae, where only some are species specific. Herbaceous species and grasses are generally associated with vesicular-arbuscular (VA) mycorrhizae, whilst woody plants are associated with ectomycorrhizae. There are several ecologically significant differences between these two types. VA mycorrhizae are able to use nutrients from the soil (particularly P) whilst ectomycorrhizae are able to use organic and inorganic nitrogen (ammonium, nitrate). In the uptake of organic compounds by ectomycorrhizae, the use of amino acids from falling litter is particularly important (Wallenda et al. 2000; Nordin et al. 2001). With a change in the type of external N supply, e.g. from amino acids to ammonium or nitrate, the occurrence of ectomycorrhizal species may change.

3.2.4.3.1
Vesicular-Arbuscular Mycorrhizae

The same VA mycorrhiza (i.e. the same mycelium) connects several plant species. It could almost be assumed that individual plants and species in a

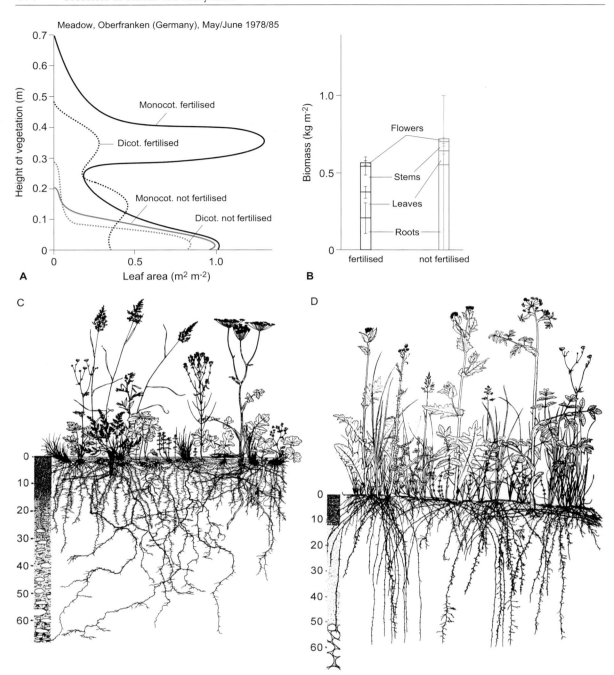

Fig. 3.2.7. A Change in leaf area with height of vegetation and B distribution of flowers, stems, leaves and roots in fertilised and unfertilised meadows. It is clear that only in fertilised meadows is a greater leaf area formed at greater height above the soil surface. In contrast, in unfertilised fields, most leaves are near the soil surface. Unfertilised plants invest up to two to three times the amount of biomass in the growth of the roots compared with their fertilised counterparts. C Nutrient-poor yellow oat meadow has a 70-cm-deep root system. Plants from *left* to *right* are: *Nardus stricta, Ranunculus acris, Meum athamanticum, Trisetum flavescens* (three stalks), *Lathyrus linifolius, Trollius europaeus, Hypericum maculatum, Festuca rubra, Hypericum perforatum, Heracleum sphondyleum, Alchemilla vulgaris.* D Nutrient-rich thistle meadow with roots that go down to 60 cm only. Plants from *left* to *right*: *Cirsium oleraceum, Carex acutiformis, Cirsium palustre, Lotus uliginosus, Holcus lanatus, Galium palustre, Filipendula ulmaria, C.o., H.i., C.a., Geum rivale, Angelica sylvestris, Ranunculus acris, Poa trivialis.* (After Hundt 1958, 1962)

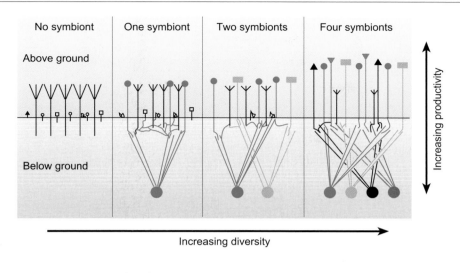

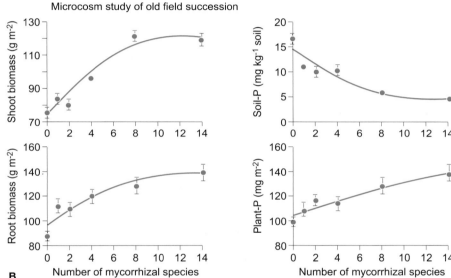

Fig. 3.2.8. A Schematic presentation of the interactions between various plant types in a meadow with one or more types of VA mycorrhizae (Read 1994). B Changes in shoot and root biomass and changes in concentration of available phosphate in the plant related to the number of types of VA mycorrhizal fungi. (After van der Heijden et al. 1998)

Table 3.2.1. Transfer of ^{14}C-labelled assimilates to neighbouring plants by VA mycorrhizae. Donor plant: *Festuca ovina*, not VAM inoculated: *Rumex acetosa*. (Grime et al. 1987; Smith and Read 1997)

	Activity of ^{14}C in the shoots (decays min[-1])
Festuca ovina	9276 (donor)
Briza media	14002
Poa pratensis	6241
Plantago lanceolata	18764
Hieracium pilosella	60716
Centaurea nigra	45081
Leontodon hispidus	15363
Scabiosa columbaria	23912
Centaurium erythraea	4213
Rumex acetosa	494 (not inoculated)

meadow are the assimilatory organs of a large VAM growing under ground (Fig. 3.2.8 A). This has consequences for the assimilate and nutrient supply of individual plants, e.g. because transport between species and individual plants is possible and has, in fact, been demonstrated (Table 3.2.1). If photosynthetically produced assimilates of the grass *Festuca ovina* are labelled with ^{14}C, transfer takes place of labelled sugars from the labelled plant to other plants which did not receive [14]CO_2 (in Table 3.2.1 predominantly *Hieracium pilosella*). It is even possible that ^{14}C accumulates in the receiver plant. Species unconnected to VAM do not show the ^{14}C signal (*Rumex acetosa*).

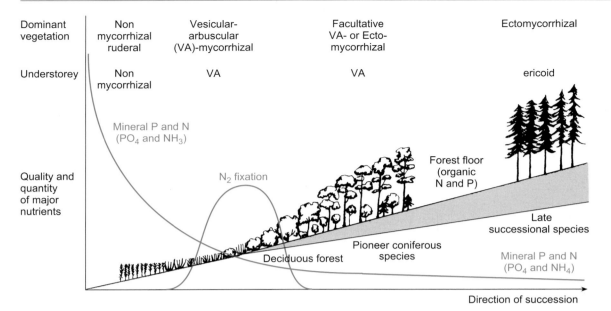

Fig. 3.2.9. Changes in mineralisation and availability of organic forms of N and P, which cause a change in the vegetation and their associated types of mycorrhizae in a succession starting with mineral soil and ending in a late successional species. Early ruderal types are not infected with mycorrhizal fungi. VA mycorrhizae occur mainly in perennial herbaceous plants. With increasing development of the site and reduction in available P supply, nitrogen-fixing plants and woody shrubs invade. With the woody plants a further reduction in P and N availability in the soil follows, resulting in the formation of a litter layer that can be colonised by ectomycorrhizal fungi at this stage. N and P are stored predominantly in the organic layer. (Read 1994)

Ectomycorrhizae

In contrast to herbaceous species, woody plants are not connected with each other via their own ectomycorrhiza and the same root may be occupied by several individuals of different ectomycorrhizal species but ectomycorrhizae do not connect between roots or species. This does not exclude that a species of mycorrhiza is not species-specific regarding the host, and uses different resources (Wallenda et al. 2000).

The number of fruiting mycorrhizal species decreases with external input of ammonium and nitrate. With small N influx about 18 fungal species were found in the spruce forests of northern Sweden, but only 7 species with large N input in the Fichtelgebirge in Germany. At the same time 15 species of northern Sweden have a narrow range of distribution (regional endemic species) but only one species was regional in the Fichtelgebirge. In contrast, the number of ubiquitous species increases from one in northern Sweden to six in the Fichtelgebirge (Taylor et al. 2000).

Distribution of Mycorrhizae

The well-known succession from annual plants which are able to distribute quickly on nutrient-rich mineral soils, to woody plants, is related to a substrate-specific progression in the mycorrhizal occupation (Fig. 3.2.9). The content of mineral N and P in the soil decreases quickly with establishment of vegetation. With increasing N deficiency (at a still large P supply) perennial herbaceous plants and N_2-fixing species follow. The first woody species establish with increasing organic layer. Then, with decreasing nutrient supply, deciduous shrubs are replaced by evergreen conifers. This sequence is accompanied by mycorrhizal succession. Herbaceous plants are settled by VAM, which are particularly able to release P from the soil. With the establishment of woody plants and increasing organic matter on the soil, ectomycorrhizae follow, which are able to remobilise N and P from the increasing organic mass. Finally, with very low N and cation supply, ericoid mycorrhizae follow (Read 1994).

3.2.5

Disturbances

The idea that ecosystems are in equilibrium with their environment (Gleason 1926) has been proven incorrect – short-term variability of climate and the occurrence of small or large spatial "catastrophes" cause continuous change in the biogeochemical conditions and turnover of the participating species. Disturbances affect individuals, species, as populations, ecosystems and aspects of the material balance, up to the existence of the affected organism or system. Disturbances affect processes in:

- Individual plants: transient damage (late frosts), weakening by parasites, failing reproduction because of weather, death by windfall.
- Populations: changes in the structure of populations and gene pools by reduction of the number of individual plants, extinction by events occurring over large areas (volcanic eruption).
- Ecosystems: creeping or spontaneous losses due to fire or leaching, changes in the species composition.

Disturbances are thus events changing the continuous material turnover suddenly and in unexpected directions. At the level of the ecosystem, it is important whether the system loses resources or whether these resources are only moved around within the system and relocated. This is well shown by the carbon balance, where the following conditions are distinguished (Fig. 3.2.10; Schulze et al. 1999):

1. Factors exerting a continuous "stress" (weather, CO_2),
2. Factors interrupting the turnover of C, but the organic matter and resources bound in them remain in the ecosystem (twig and leaf fall due to wind, insect frass),
3. Factors removing organic matter and resources from the system (fire, harvest).

These disturbances may lead to changes in the assembly of species and this may cause new patterns of material turnover in an ecosystem.

3.2.5.1
Continuous Stress and Disturbances Where the Organic Matter Remains in the Ecosystem

Disturbance from continuous changes of the carbon balance are caused by changing **weather**. There are years with large and small carbon gain and rates of material turnover. In the long term, permanent but changing **conditions of growth** (e.g. increase in CO_2 concentration in the atmosphere, N-deposition, global climate change) disturb the balance of resources. Thus, continuously increasing CO_2 concentrations at first affect growth of plants by increasing their resource requirements and only secondarily, with a delay of about 30 years, through enhanced decomposition processes in the soil (Melillo et al. 1996). This delay is caused by the intermediate storage of assimilates in biomass (e.g. wood) and the slow transition of decomposition of organic matter along the chain of organisms participating in the decomposition process (see Chap. 3.3.2). Thus there is accumulation of intermediate products in the ecosystem, which are

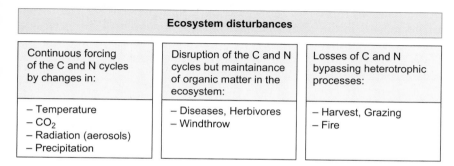

Ecosystem disturbances		
Continuous forcing of the C and N cycles by changes in:	Disruption of the C and N cycles but maintainance of organic matter in the ecosystem:	Losses of C and N bypassing heterotrophic processes:
– Temperature – CO_2 – Radiation (aerosols) – Precipitation	– Diseases, Herbivores – Windthrow	– Harvest, Grazing – Fire

Fig. 3.2.10. Classification of ecosystem disturbances according to their effect on the C and N budgets of ecosystems. With respect to C, it is important to know whether C remains on the site, if carbon is added to the soil, or if the biomass is removed (in the case of fire or harvesting). Removal of biomass also means that nutrients are removed. (Schulze et al. 1999)

not stable (e.g. raw humus), but will probably be decomposed later.

These continuously changing parameters and their influences are thus different from disturbances, which interrupt the synthesis or decomposition of matter. In this category belong "**catastrophes**" such as wind damage, snow damage or being eaten and damaged by insects, and also smaller disturbances such as by moles or wild boar. These disturbances change mainly the aggregate structure of the soil or directly accelerate decomposition of soil organic matter. This type of disturbance may lead to temporary accumulation of organic matter in certain compartments (e.g. raw humus) and re-allocation of resources. However, they generally do not change the ecosystem, only if certain pathogens stop the regeneration of dominating species, as happens in Australia where *Phytophtora* causes the death of Proteaceae and of some eucalypt species.

3.2.5.2
Disturbances by Export of Organic Matter from Ecosystems

Disturbances in which biomass and nutrients have been removed from the ecosystem (**export of resources**) have rather different impacts than disturbances where resources remain in the ecosystem. Loss of organic matter occurs particularly by grazing, harvesting and fire. In all three processes biomass is lost or exported from the ecosystem and degraded somewhere else, e.g. in human-dominated systems, in sewage works or by burning of rubbish. Heterotrophic organisms in the ecosystem in which the organic matter was produced no longer participate in decomposition.

In **harvesting** and **grazing**, organic matter as well as the cations bound in it are removed from the ecosystem. As roots normally remain in the ecosystem heterotrophic organisms are at first stimulated, but later soil C is decomposed. Loss of nutrients by harvesting leads quickly to degradation of the total system, if nutrients are not re-supplied by fertilisation. The influence of two mowings per year in a newly planted meadow is measurable even 3 years later (see Fig. 3.2.6; Scherer-Lorenzen 1999).

Historically, litter raking in forests was an important harvest when the newly fallen leaves were collected and used during the winter as bedding for animals in stables and taken to the fields in spring as fertiliser. As leaves and needles have considerably higher cation contents than wood, this form of forest use drastically decreased soil fertility and led to relocation of cations from forests to fields over large areas of land. The effect of this use is still visible after decades as particularly weakly developed humus layers in the affected forests (see Schulze 2000, site at Aubure in France).

A particular type of disturbance is **fire**, because a large part of the standing biomass over large areas may be destroyed. At sites where fires occur regularly, vegetation has adapted to fires. Of course, the intensity of the fire depends on the available biomass. Therefore, rare fires, in which the biomass accumulated in the long interval between the fires is consumed, have more drastic effects than frequent and thus less intense fires (Fig. 3.2.11 A, B). During savannah fires, temperatures at ground level usually remain below 100 °C and 10 cm deep into the ground 40 °C is rarely reached. The reason for this is the very short duration (only minutes) of the fire at the same site because of the limiting biomass. The renewal buds (of grasses) below ground are not affected and the seeds below ground ("seed bank") are hardly damaged, and these may germinate and produce seedlings very quickly. Luxuriant growth of herbaceous species is often a consequence of surface fires, as many minerals become available in the ash (Fig. 3.2.11 C). Also, seeds of many plants, particularly those that survive frequent fires, receive a germination stimulus from the cold smoke (Dixon et al. 1995; Roche et al. 1998). Even in woody plants with relatively little biomass usually only the outer layer of the shoot turns to charcoal so that a regeneration of the shoot from living tissues at the base of the stem is possible. The Australian grass tree even contains a resin which is difficult to burn and protects the stem from fire. For many plants a sub-lethal fire acts as a stimulus to flowering. In other plants, the so-called **pyrophyte** fruits open only after a fire (Fig. 3.2.11 D).

Besides these positive stimulations of ecosystem processes, **fire** takes carbon and nitrogen from the system in the form of different gaseous oxidation products, although base cations remain in the ash in the ecosystem. Part of the remaining organic bound nitrogen is transformed into ammonium and nitrate. Thus young plants and surviving rhizomes have better conditions for growth initially than before the fire, which

Fig. 3.2.11. A, B Fire vegetation on Mount Kilimanjaro (Shira Plateau). A *Erica arborea* as stunted vegetation that regenerates from charred branches. On average there is a fire every 3–5 years. B Charred *Erica arborea* at a site with less frequent fires. The bifurcated twigs show that the plant had survived at least one fire, between the last and the most recent fire a substantial trunk has developed, and the intensity of the fire was therefore high. Both pictures were taken 2 years after the fire. Rejuvenation of the bushes had occurred with bushy growth on the frequently burnt site where little biomass had accumulated between fires. In contrast, growth from the charred thick trunk was comparatively sparse. In the *foreground, Helichrysum splendidum*, a typical fire indicator (Photo E. Beck). C Vigorous germination of *Festuca obturbans* and *Kniphofia thomsonii* after an intense fire in the alpine zone of Mount Kilimanjaro. In the foreground charred twigs of *Erica arborea* and *E. trimera* (Photo E. Beck). D Fruits of the Australian *Hakea* (Proteaceae) open only after a fire. (Photo E. Beck)

is, therefore, used worldwide as an agricultural measure in grasslands and savannahs to activate new growth. With fires the soil is supplied with carbon that is difficult to degrade (charcoal and soot). In the long term fire leads to a reduction of soil fertility, particularly the N supply.

In boreal coniferous forests, the fire sequence determines the amount of carbon which may be stored in the soil (Fig. 3.2.12). Calculated over a period of 6000 years (since the end of the Ice Age) the frequently burnt *Pinus banksiana* only contains half as much C in the soil than the less frequently burnt *Picea mariana* and these amounts are significantly lower than in very rarely burnt blanket bog where, independent of the fire frequency, the high water table conserves the carbon in the soil; this ecosystem indicates the potential to accumulate litter. In all cases a saturation curve occurs, i.e. there is a balance between the synthesis of organic matter in the soil and the consumption by fire, which is determined not only by respiration or burning, but also by the high frequency of fires and by the reduced productivity of the vegetation (Harden et al. 2000).

3.2.5.3
Effects of Changes in Species Composition

Disturbances not only change the immediate material fluxes, but also affect the composition of species within the system. Areas suitable for growth are opened, which were previously occupied by other species now weakened by the disturbance or killed. The remaining, surviving organisms may spread or new species enter. The greatest number of species is found with average

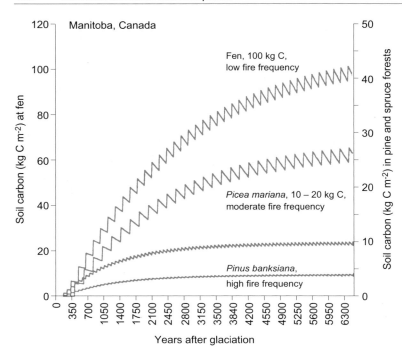

Fig. 3.2.12. Changes in soil carbon in a sedge bog with low frequency of fires and in *Picea mariana* and *Pinus banksiana* stands exhibiting increasing frequency. The zig-zags on the curves show the frequency at which fires occur. The figure illustrates the cumulative amount of C that is removed from these ecosystems directly or indirectly by fires. (Harden et al. 2000)

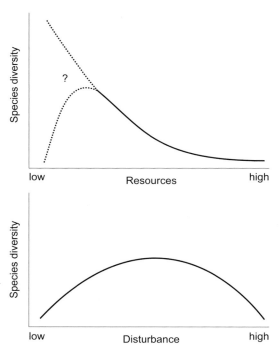

Fig. 3.2.13. Schematic presentation of the relationship between species diversity and resource availability, and between species diversity and habitat disturbance. Species diversity reaches a maximum at average ecosystem disturbance. (Hobbie et al. 1994)

disturbance intensities (*intermediate disturbance hypothesis*; Fig. 3.2.13; Hobbie et al. 1994; see also Chap. 4.2). If the frequency of disturbance increases, only a few specialists remain. The number of species also decreases in the absence of external disturbance. Either only a few very competitive species dominate or there is competition for other resources, and thus biodiversity increases further (see also Fig. 3.2.5).

Two examples demonstrate this effect:

1. **Invasion and water use:** For individual plants the limitation of water use was discussed in the context of adaptation to stress and optimisation of water use (see Chap. 2.4), but at the level of a plant stand the situation is different. If a plant "saves water", this may have the consequence that another species or individual plants of the same species uses this water. Opportunists which do not save water have an advantage, inasfar as they manage to sustain the species, e.g. by early seed production. The "saver of water" could dry out under these conditions. This occurs particularly at sites where new species invade existing vegetation (invasion, Fig. 3.2.14). Invasion of Mediterranean *Bromus* species into the North American *Artemisia tridentata* prairie led to a marked reduction of *Artemisia* (West and Young 2000). *Bromus* species use the water supply without limitation at the beginning of

Fig. 3.2.14. A Spread of invasive species is generally along roads. *Salsola kali* (Chenopodiaceae) can be seen close to roads in semi-deserts of Utah, western North America. *Salsola* is a salt-tolerant species from Asian deserts. Away from the edge of the road the Mediterranean *Bromus* types dominate. B Mediterranean *Bromus* types in the Artemisia steppes of Wyoming. Artemisia cover is already broken. (Photo E.-D. Schulze)

the growing season because they are annual species which form their seeds before the drought starts and then die. The high water use of *Bromus* means that the perennial *Artemesia*, which must survive the dry period, does not have enough water later. *Artemesia* dies, often without forming seeds and without having the ability to regenerate as fast as *Bromus*; also, seedlings of *Artemesia* are not able to compete with *Bromus*. The effect of differential water use is enhanced by fire. Dry stalks of *Bromus* increase the frequency of fire, whereby *Artemesia* is not fire-tolerant. Grazing also plays a role as *Artemesia* is very sensitive to mechanical disturbance from trampling by animals which is not the case for *Bromus*.

2. **Grazing**: Disturbances causing a change in the assembly of the vegetation are particularly caused by **grazing**. Grazing animals have par-

ticular effects because they selectively eat species which may be destroyed if they are not adapted to grazing pressure. *Bouteloua* cluster grasses in North America are not adapted to grazing by horses, as they remove the whole clump and pull the roots out of the soil, so the plant dies off. Similarly, grasses from Australia, with auxiliary buds high on the stem, are adapted to kangaroos but not to grazing by cows or sheep; kangaroos pick individual leaves from shoots, whilst cows and sheep bite the above-ground shoots completely off and thus stop re-sprouting of the plant. In both cases, grazing with European domestic animals caused far-reaching changes in the flora. Additionally, there are indirect disturbances, e.g. trampling by animals compacts the soils and there is relocation of resources with the deposition of faeces, e.g. in cow pats, or places where animals congregate.

Box 3.2.1   Summary: Characteristics of ecosystems

- Ecosystems are complex webs between organisms and their environment on a defined and limited area of ground, whereby the assimilation of material by plants and its degradation by soil microorganisms plays an essential role.
- When considering an ecosystem, flows and balances of material and energy must be considered per unit area. The distribution of material between individuals of a single species or between different species is important. The mass balance quantifies the over-use of substances or their accumulation.
- The partitioning of a habitat by individuals of a species follows the laws of self-thinning. When partitioning of a habitat between different species occurs then host–parasite interactions and mycorrhizae become important. In the case of managed land, man controls the density.
- Availability of resources (especially water and nutrients) determines the turnover rates of an ecosystem. In this case the cycling and the losses of nutrients are a major factor. The uptake of nutrients by plants and their remineralisation usually do not occur simultaneously, hence in natural ecosystems carbon is accumulated and losses of nitrogen and cations may occur.
- Biomass harvesting is an important factor in removing resources from an ecosystem.

These must be replaced by fertiliser or liming to avoid degradation of the site.
- Ecosystems are characterised by non-linear processes. These include saturation of the production of organic matter with increasing biomass, exponential increase of respiration with temperature, exponential demand for resources, threshold values in buffering of soils and changes in turnover with the composition of species.
- Biodiversity decreases with increasing resource availability. It is more difficult to predict what happens to biodiversity when resources are scarce. In this case, either the number of species may increase or only few species gain dominance. This depends on what is limiting (nitrogen, water or cations).
- Disturbances often lead to an initial increase in diversity, but beyond a certain optimum the number of species falls, depending on the strength of the disturbance.
- Ecosystems are generally not at equilibrium with respect to the various processes of accumulation and decomposition. Disturbances constantly change the dynamics. Disturbances can be factors such as the seasonal change in the weather, long-term changes in climate, catastrophic events that result in resources being either added (dust storms) or removed (fire, harvest, grazing) from the system.

References

Bond WJ (1994) Keystone species. Ecol Studies 99:237–254

Dixon KW, Roche S, Pate JS (1995) The promotive effect of smoke derived from burnt native vegetation on seed germination of western Australian plants. Oecologia 101: 185–192

Ernest SKM, Brown JH (2001) Delayed compensation for missing keystone species by colonization. Science 292: 101–103

FBW Forschungsbeirat Waldschäden/Luftverunreinigungen (1989) Dritter Bericht an die Bundesregierung. Forschungszentrum, Karlsruhe, 611 pp

Gleason HA (1926) The individualistic concept of the plant association. Bull Torrey Bot Club 53:7–26

Grime JP, Mackey JML, Hillier SH, Read DJ (1987) Floristic diversity in a model system using experimental microcosms. Nature 328:420–422

Harden JW, Trumbore SE, Stocks BJ, Hirsch A, Cower ST, O'Neill KP, Kasischke ES (2000) The role of fire in the boreal carbon budget. Global Change Biol 6:174–184

Hector A, Schmid B, Beierkuhnlein C, Caldeira MC, Diemer M, Dimitrakopoulos PC, Finn JA, Freitas H, Giller PS, Good J, Harris R, Högberg P, Kuss-Danell K, Joshi J, Jumpponen A, Körner C, Leadley PW, Loreau M, Minns A, Mulder CPH, O'Donovan G, Otway SJ, Pereira JS, Prinz A, Read DJ, Scherer-Lorenzen M, Schulze E-D, Siamantziouras D, Spehn EM, Terry AC, Troumbis AY, Woodward FI, Yachi S, Lawton JH (1999) Plant diversity and productivity experiments in European grasslands. Science 286:1123–1127

Hobbie SE, Jensen DB, Chapin ES III (1994) Resource supply and disturbance as control over present and future plant diversity. Ecological studies, vol 99. Springer, Berlin Heidelberg New York, pp 385–408

Hundt R (1958) Beiträge zur Wiesenvegetation Mitteleuropas. I. Die Auenwiesen an der Elbe, Saale und Mulde. Nova Acta Leopoldina NF 20:135

Hundt R (1962) Die Bergwiesen des Harzes, Thüringer Waldes und Erzgebirges. Habilitationsschrift Halle/Saale, 250 pp

Kaiser K, Guggenberger G (2000) The role of DOM-sorption to mineral surfaces in the preservation of organic matter in soils. Org Geochem 31:711–725

Kramer H (1988) Waldwachstumslehre. Parey, Hamburg, 374 pp

Larcher W (1994) Ökophysiologie der Pflanzen. Ulmer, Stuttgart, 394 pp

Last FT, Watling R (1991) Acid deposition, its nature and impacts. Proc R Soc Edinb, Section B, 97, 343 pp

Lloyd J, Taylor JA (1994) On the temperature dependence of soil respiration. Funct Ecol 8:315–323

Mellilo JM, Prentice IC, Farquhar GD, Schulze E-D, Sala OE (1996) Terrestrial biotic responses to environmental change and feedbacks to climate. Climate Change 1995 – The science of climate change WG I. Cambridge University Press, Cambridge, pp 445–482

Nordin A, Högberg P, Näsholm T (2001) Soil N availability and plant N uptake along a boreal forest productivity gradient. Oecologia 129:125–132

Osawa A, Allen RB (1993) Allometric theory explains self-thinning relationship of mountain beech and red pine. Ecology 74:1020–1032

Persson T, Rudebeck A, Jussy JH, Clin-Belgrand M, Prieme A, Dambrine E, Karlsson PS, Sjöberg M (2000) Soil nitrogen turnover – mineralisation, nitrification and denitrification in European forest stands. Ecological studies, vol 142. Springer, Berlin Heidelberg New York, pp 297–331

Read D (1994) Plant-microbe mutualism and community structure. In: Schulze E-D, Mooney HA (eds) Biodiversity and ecosystem functions. Ecological studies, vol 99. Springer, Berlin Heidelberg New York, pp 181–210

Reineke LH (1933) Perfecting a stand-density index for even-aged forests. I. Agric Res 46:627–638

Roche S, Dixon KW, Pate JS (1998) For everything a season – smoke-induced seed germination and seedling recruitment in a western Australian Banksia woodland. Aust J Ecol 23:111–120

Sala OE, Lauenroth WK, McNaughton SJ, Rusch G, Zhang X (1996) Biodiversity and ecosystem functioning in grasslands. In: Mooney HA, Cushman JH, Medina E, Sala OE, Schulze E-D (eds) Functional role of biodiversity: a global perspective. SCOPE 55:129–150

Scherer-Lorenzen M (1999) Effects of plant diversity on ecosystem processes in experimental grassland communities. Bayreuther Forum Ökol 75:193

Schlesinger WH (1997) Biogeochemistry; an analysis of global change. Academic Press, San Diego, 588 pp

Schulze E-D (1982) Plant life forms and their carbon, water and nutrient relations. Encycl Plant Physiol New Ser 12B:615–676

Schulze E-D (1995) Flux control at the ecosystem level. Trends Ecol Evol 10:40–43

Schulze E-D (2000) Carbon and nutrient cycling in European forest ecosystems. Ecological studies, vol 142. Springer, Berlin Heidelberg New York, 498 pp

Schulze E-D, Ulrich B (1991) Acid rain – a large-scale, unwanted experiment in forest ecosystems. SCOPE 45:89–106

Schulze E-D, Lloyd J, Kelliher FM, Wirth C, Rebmann C, Lühker B, Mund M, Knohl A, Milyokova IM, Schulze W,

Ziegler W, Varlagin A, Sogachev AF, Valentini R, Dore S, Grigoriev S, Kolle O, Panfyorov MI, Tchebakova N, Vygodskaya NN (1999) Productivity of forests in the Eurosiberian boreal region and their potential to act as a carbon sink – a synthesis. Global Change Biol 5:703–722

Schulze E-D, Högberg P, van Oene H, Persson T, Harrison AF, Read D, Kjöller A, Matteucci G (2000) Interactions between the carbon and nitrogen cycle and the role of biodiversity: a synopsis of a study along a north-south transect through Europe. Ecological studies, vol 142. Springer, Berlin Heidelberg New York, pp 468–492

Smith SE, Read DJ (1997) Mycorrhizal symbiosis. Academic Press, London, 605 pp

Stitt M, Schulze E-D (1994) Plant growth, storage, and resource allocation: from flux control in a metabolic chain to the whole plant level. In: Schulze E-D (ed) Flux control in biological systems. Academic Press, San Diego, pp 57–118

Taylor AFS, Martin F, Read DJ (2000) Fungal diversity in ecomycorrhizal communities of Norway spruce (Picea abies) and beech (Fagus sylvatica) along north-south transects in Europe. Ecological studies, vol 142. Springer, Berlin Heidelberg New York, pp 343–365

Townsend AR, Vitousek PM, Trumbore SE (1995) Soil organic matter dynamics along gradients in temperature and land use on the island of Hawaii. Ecology 76:721–733

Ulrich B (1987) Stability, elasticity, and resilience of terrestrial ecosystems with respect to matter balance. Ecological studies, vol 61. Springer, Berlin Heidelberg New York, pp 11–49

van der Heijden MAG, Klironomus JN, Ursic M, Moutoglis P, Streitwolf-Engel R, Boller T, Wiemke A, Sanders IR (1998) Mycorrhizal fungal diversity determines plant biodiversity, ecosystem variability and productivity. Nature 396:69–71

Wallenda T, Stober C, Högbom L, Schinkel H, George E, Högberg P, Read DJ (2000) Nitrogen uptake processes in roots and mycorrhizae. Ecological studies, vol 142. Springer, Berlin Heidelberg New York, pp 122–143

WBGU (1998) Welt im Wandel: Strategien zur Bewältigung globaler Umweltrisiken. Wissenschaftlicher Beirat der Bundesregierung Globale Umweltveränderungen. Jahresgutachten 1998. Springer, Berlin Heidelberg New York, 383 pp

West NE, Young JA (2000) Intermountain valleys and lower mountain slopes. In: Barbour MG, Billings WD (eds) North American terrestrial vegetation. Cambridge University Press, Cambridge, pp 255–284

Westoby M (1984) The self-thinning rule. Adv Biol Res 14:167–225

Wirth C, Schulze E-D, Schulze W, von Stünzner-Karbe D, Ziegler W, Miljukova IM, Sogachev A, Varlagin A, Panvyorov M, Grigoriev S, Kusnetzova W, Siry M, Hardes G, Zimmermann R, Vygodskaya NN (1999) Above-ground biomass and structure of pristine Siberian Scots pine forests as controlled by competition and fire. Oecologia 121:66–80

Yoda K, Kira T, Ogawa H, Hozumi H (1963) Self-thinning in overcrowded pure stands under cultivated and natural conditions. I. Inst Polytech Osaka City Univ Ser D 14:107–129

3.3

The Biogeochemical Cycles

The study of biogeochemical cycles in ecosystems requires not only extensive observations (see introductory page to Chap. 3), but also experiments outside the laboratory (see Mooney et al. 1991). Technical requirements for such sites in the field are demanding. An example is the "Shelter" experiment in a forested watershed conducted by the EU project "Exman". The canopy was separated from the roots by a roof. Rainwater was collected from this cover and pollutants (sulfur and nitrogen deposition) were removed. The purified rainwater was then returned to the soil. Thus it was possible to separate the effects of pollutants on the crown of the trees from the effects of acid deposition on the roots. As it is not possible to derive statistically significant information from one plot, the experiment was repeated at five sites within the EU. Gorsjön, southern Sweden. Photos E.-D. Schulze

The interactions between autotrophic and heterotrophic organisms of an ecosystem have been combined in the biogeochemical cycles, where the coupling between the trophic levels only occurs by making substrates available. In each ecosystem many alternative paths exist for the synthesis and decomposition of materials. Physicochemical conditions and composition of species in the ecosystem often decide which path is used preferentially within the nutrient network. Feedback effects of organisms on the physicochemical boundary conditions occur mainly via weathering and loss of minerals as well as the heat and water balances (for change of optical characteristics and surface roughness, see Chaps. 2.1 and 2.2).

According to the extent of exchange of substances with the environment, i.e. material leaves the ecosystem or is re-cycled into the ecosystem, a distinction is made between open and closed cycles. Transitions are possible and, indeed, under natural conditions, transitions are the rule rather than the exception.

Open cycles occur

- with water: the requirement for water is so large that storage is not possible;
- with carbon: as plants obtain CO_2 from the free atmosphere and CO_2 is released back to the atmosphere through the respiration of autotrophic and heterotrophic organisms; transfer of organic carbon from heterotrophic

to autotrophic species can be neglected (amino acids);

- in managed systems (grazing, agriculture and forestry): Wherever material is taken out of the ecosystem and perhaps other materials (fertilisation) are added, the biogeochemical cycles are open;
- in ecosystems subjected to high input of S and N from the atmosphere; intermediate storage in the system may occur (e.g. for N) which, in the first instance, accelerates turnover within the ecosystem. Release of these elements to the atmosphere or to groundwater may occur later or be started earlier by external disturbances.

Closed cycles are found under favourable conditions

- for nitrogen, e.g. when the external supply of N and denitrification are low compared with the internal turnover in the ecosystem;
- for cations and phosphate, although losses of these elements through leaching cannot be excluded. The balance between weathering of primary minerals and leaching determines the succession of the ecosystem.

The ideal view of closed material cycles has not been achieved, even in ecosystems undisturbed by man (Chadwick et al. 1999; see Fig. 3.5.1). In the following, the turnover of water and the **carbon** and **nitrogen** cycles are discussed in more detail.

3.3.1

Water Turnover

Water flows through ecosystems and it is stored only to a small degree (see Chap. 2.2), i.e. it would be more correct to speak of a hydrological balance rather than of a water cycle. The ecosystem gains water as precipitation (rain, snow, dew = total precipitation). The structure of the vegetation may increase the water input, e.g. by "combing out" of clouds via increased surface area onto which fog droplets settle. An example is the laurel forests in Tenerife which are, to a large extent, dependent on water harvested from clouds. Ecosystems lose water to the atmosphere because of the free evaporation from the wet surfaces, and by transpiration and by seepage into the groundwater. The hydrological

balance is positive if excess water seeps below the root horizon into deeper soil layers and negative if precipitation is completely used by evapotranspiration or if transpiration is fed by supplies which do not originate from immediate precipitation (advective groundwater, melting permafrost, capillary rise of water from deeper horizons). According to the amount of precipitation, the hydrological balances are variable, but, on average, about 50–60% is used by plants. This applies in all climatic regions irrespective of their different conditions (see Fig. 2.2.3 in Chap. 2.2).

As transpiration and CO_2 assimilation are coupled via stomata (see also Fig. 3.2.5), the hydrological balance controls, to a first approximation, vegetation growth, the so-called net primary production (NPP, see Chap. 3.3.2, Fig. 3.3.9). This is particularly important for agriculture in dry areas (DeWitt 1978; Fischer and Turner 1978).

$$NPP = m\Sigma E/\Sigma E_0 \qquad (3.3.1)$$

where ΣE is the sum of transpiration integrated over the period of the NPP measurement and ΣE_0 is the sum of daily evaporation from an area of free water. The equation is analogous to Eq. (2.4.7) in Chapter 2.4, describing the diffusion of CO_2 across the stomata ($A = \Delta c \, g$ and $\Delta c = A/g$, where $g = E/D$), because ΣE is the sum of the water consumption by transpiration and ΣE_0 is proportional to the mean saturation deficit of air (D). The coefficient m is thus a parameter analogous to the mean internal mesophyll CO_2 concentration (Schulze 1982). This coefficient varies for C3 plants between 10 and 14 g dry matter per m^2 and reaches 21–23 g m^2 in C4 plants. Assuming that the transpiration corresponds to the hydrological balance (precipitation minus seepage), it is then possible to use this equation for a rough estimate of yield from precipitation. For particular crops, e.g. for cereal grain, a ratio of grain yield to biomass, i.e. the harvest index, must be considered. Generally, it is 0.5 for high-yielding varieties (Fischer and Turner 1978). If in a sub-arid region 200 mm precipitation is available for the growth of plants, then about 2400 g dry matter harvest m^{-2} biomass production are to be expected. For a harvest index of 0.5, this results in a grain yield of 1.2 t grain ha^{-1}.

Independent of the fact that yields may be calculated from Eq. (3.3.1) as first approximation, there are several restrictions. Particularly the distribution of precipitation is a constraint in arid areas. For example, many light rains may "imply" a large amount of precipitation; however, most of this water would evaporate immediately from the moist ground and thus not be available for the plant. This shows that the hydrological balance is the important parameter and not precipitation. The distribution of precipitation is particularly important in planning sowing and harvesting in short and long rainy seasons.

3.3.2

Carbon Turnover

3.3.2.1
Carbon Turnover in Ecosystems

The term carbon cycle is often used for ecosystems. This is incorrect, as it does not take into account that CO_2 from the free atmosphere used in photosynthesis mainly. Only a small amount originates from respiration at the same site. Atmospheric turbulence leads to a rapid mixing in the atmosphere. Thus the CO_2 which is assimilated enters the ecosystem by advection via the atmospheric transport of air masses and is lost again in the same way (see Chap. 2.1).

The plant cover assimilates CO_2 from the atmosphere by photosynthesis (Fig. 3.3.1). The sugars synthesised are either used immediately for growth, to form or maintain existing structures, or are stored in the form of starch (e.g. see Chap. 2.4). The sum of photosynthetic C bound over a certain period (e.g. 1 year) is called **gross primary production (GPP)** neglecting light-induced respiration (photorespiration, see Loreto et al. 1999).

About 50% of the photosynthetically assimilated carbon is consumed by the plant itself for maintenance and synthesis of biomass. The balance of assimilation and respiration of plants is called **net primary production (NPP)**. A distinction is drawn between the more frequently measured **above-ground primary production (ANPP)** and the **below-ground primary production (BNPP)** because it is easier to measure ANPP. Depending on the organisation of individual plant structures, there are allometric relations between ANPP and BNPP (for trees, on average, BNPP/NPP = 0.3). Quantitative assessments of plant biomass on earth and of NPP were made in the 1960s, within the International Biological Programme (IBP). These data are still the basis for many model calculations, but there are still, according to the subject area, many different interpretations about the "productivity" of plants. For the farmer it is the grain yield, for the forester the increase in stem growth and wood volume, for the biologist the total increase including fruit and fine roots. There is no direct connection between biomass and NPP. Biomass formed by NPP remains for very different periods in the organism or in the stand, thus leading to different values of biomass (see Table 3.3.1). For **annual species** the total biomass, except seeds, dies off at the end of the growing season and is again supplied to the heterotrophic organisms in the soil as litter. Disregarding rhizomes, bulbs or corms which are permanent organs in **perennial herbaceous plants**, almost all the total biomass resulting from the NPP also dies and becomes litter. In woody plants about 50% of the NPP is wood. In the lignified organs, part of the sapwood is changed to dead heartwood, depending on the C assimilated, and this is converted into litter with a long delay, because the heartwood forms the tree's structure (see Chap. 2.4.5.4). Even for trees about 50% of the NPP reaches the soil each year

---

| Box 3.3.1 | **The water cycle** |

- Ecosystems have no water cycle, but a hydrological balance between precipitation (dew, rainfall and snow) and evaporation plus transpiration, deep percolation and runoff. The hydrological balance is controlled, in physiological terms, by responses of stomata, the optical properties determining the absorption of incident radiation and the roughness of the surfaces (see also Chaps. 2.1.2.2 and 2.2.4).
- Net primary production increases in proportion to transpiration and decreases with increasing potential evaporation (NPP = m E/E_0). The proportionality factor m is 10–14 g dry mass in C3 plants and 21–23 g dry mass m^{-2} in C4 plants.

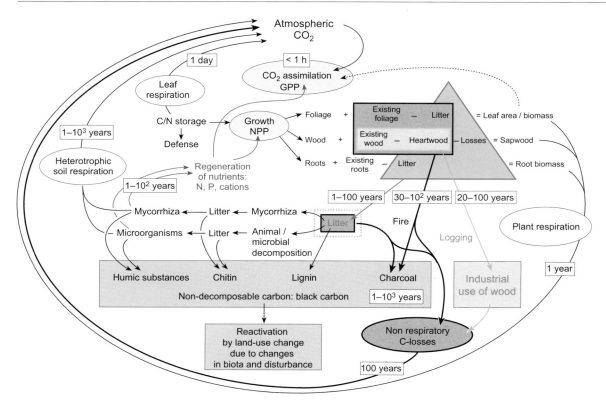

Fig. 3.3.1. Turnover of carbon in ecosystems (Schulze 2000a). Turnover begins with photosynthetic assimilation of CO_2 by the plant. Products are distributed to leaves, shoots and roots and, in the case of trees, to heartwood. Maintenance and growth of biomass require energy that may be measured as respiration. However, a large part of the biomass is wood which no longer respires. The autotrophic vegetation is linked to the soil by leaf litter and mycorrhizae. Additional losses result from harvests and fires. Organic substances that occur in the soil are turned over and are decomposed by various organisms and eventually are released as CO_2 by respiration (in the process of mineralisation). In ecosystems only black carbon remains in the ecosystem for a very long period of time

as leaf, twig and root litter. For herbaceous species this litter production corresponds to the NPP (see also Fig. 2.4.20 in Chap. 2.4).

The problem in determining NPP is mainly the difficulty in assessing the turnover of fine roots (<2 mm diameter) because this part of growth is almost impossible to measure. In the tropics the determination of NPP of epiphytes is

an additional problem. For temperate forests the **mean life span of fine roots** is about 0.5 to 2 years, i.e. fine roots are turned over about once or twice a year, and are continuously replaced by new fine roots (Stober et al. 2000). The turnover in grasses is much greater with sufficient water supply, i.e. the life span of fine roots is shorter. The proportion of fine roots as

Table 3.3.1. Biomass, net primary production (NPP), and litter production in different vegetation types of the earth. (Schulze 1982; Schlesinger 1997; Schachtschabel et al. 1998)

Ecosystem	Biomass (kg C m^{-2})	NPP (kg C m^{-2} a^{-1})	Leaf litter (kg C m^{-2} a^{-1})
Tropical rainforest	20–32	3–10	0.5–1.4
Temperate deciduous forest	5–30	0.2–1.2	0.1–0.6
Temperate coniferous forest	15–75	0.4–1.3	0.1–0.6
Boreal coniferous forest	8–10	0.3–0.4	0.1–0.5
Savannah	1–2	0.4–0.6	0.1–0.4
Grassland	0.2–2.2	0.1–1.0	<0.1–1.0
Agricultural land	0.5	0.3–0.5	0.1–0.2
Desert	0.2–3	<0.1–0.5	<0.1–0.2
Tundra	0.1–2	<0.1–0.2	<0.1

Table 3.3.2. The biomass of fine roots (<2 mm diameter) and leaves in different vegetation types of the earth. (Schulze 1982; Jackson et al. 1997)

Vegetation type	Roots Total (kg m^{-2})	Fine roots Mass (kg m^{-2})	Length (kg m^{-2})	Root surface index (m^2 m^{-2})	Leaves or needles Mass (kg m^{-2})	Leaf surface index (m^2 m^{-2})
Tropical rain forest	4.88	0.57	4.1	7.4	2.5	11
Temperate coniferous forest	4.40	0.82	6.1	11.0	1.3	9
Temperate deciduous forest	4.14	0.78	5.4	9.8	0.4	7
Boreal forest	2.92	0.60	2.6	4.6	1.8	11
Shrub vegetation	4.82	0.52	8.4	11.6	0.4	8
Savannah	1.40	0.99	60.4	42.5	0.9	3
Temperate grassland	1.56	1.51	112.0	79.1	0.6	3
Tundra	1.25	0.96	4.1	7.4	0.4	2
Desert	4.13	0.27	4.0	5.5	0.1	<1
Average	3.28	0.78				

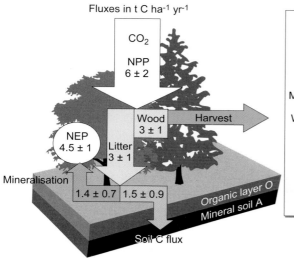

Fluxes in t C ha^{-1} yr^{-1}

CO$_2$

NPP 6 ± 2

NEP 4.5 ± 1

Wood 3 ± 1   Harvest

Litter 3 ± 1

Mineralisation

1.4 ± 0.7   1.5 ± 0.9

Organic layer O

Mineral soil A

Soil C flux

	MRT (years)
Litter	<1 – 3
Wood	1 – 250
Managed forest	Mean: 80
Wood products	15 – 20
Organic layer	14 – 52
A horizon	70 – 170

Fig. 3.3.2. The flow of carbon in a forest ecosystem and the mean residence time (MRT) of litter, wood and wood products in a managed forest. The figure shows that almost half the net primary production is in litter and the other half in accumulated wood. Of the leaf litter, half remains in the soil as organic substances with an MRT of >100 years. (After Schulze 2000 a)

part of biomass is, on average, 28% (Table 3.3.2). Fine roots in forests reach a total length of 2–8 km m^{-2} and a projected area of 4–11 m^2 m^{-2}, corresponding in magnitude to the leaf area index. In grasslands the length of fine roots (>100 km m^{-2}) is a factor of ten greater than in forests. The NPP of fine roots probably corresponds to the turnover of leaves (Schulze 2000b).

Ultimately, in natural ecosystems, all plant parts reach the ground in the form of litter and are decomposed and mineralised. We distinguish between **decomposition**, which describes the breakdown of organic substances into subunits and its re-assembly into new organic molecules, and **mineralisation**, where the organic substances are oxidised to CO$_2$ or to methane. Large differences occur in how long individual organs remain on the plant or in the soil. An example of an European forest ecosystem is given in Fig. 3.3.2, with synthesis and decomposition of fine roots occurring in the same year, but leaves and needles having a life span of 1–10 years (*Pinus aristata* 30 years) and decomposition takes another 1–20 years. Wood remains on the plant >100 years (oldest living trees 4000 years: *Pinus aristata*, Fig. 2.4.29, Chap. 2.4) and the decomposition of wood takes, in general, 50 to >100 years. These periods are comparable to the average life span of woody materials, corresponding to the 15–25 years for the turnover of litter. It is also important that the mean retention of C in the organic layer of soils is of the same magnitude as that in forest biomass.

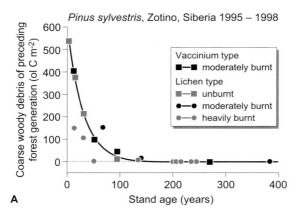

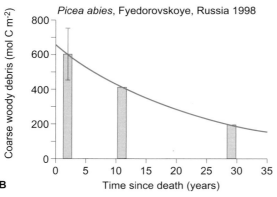

Fig. 3.3.3. A Degradation of dead wood after a fire in a Siberian pine forest. The mean residence time is only about 40 years, despite the cold climate. This is because of the repeated fires at ground level. As these fires only char the outside of the wood (see Fig. 3.3.8 C), single dead trunks can be traced back 400 years (Wirth et al. 2002). **B** Deadwood after wind falls in a natural forest reserve in European Russia. The mean residence time in the east European climate is about 15 years. (Knohl et al. 2002)

Degradation of wood has mainly been studied in boreal coniferous forests (Fig. 3.3.3 A; Wirth et al. 2002). Trunks killed by fire are degraded with a half-life of 25 years. Decomposition is finished after about 120 years with part of the dead wood being burnt because of periodic ground fires. In this case, decomposition becomes accelerated compared to microbial decomposition (Fig. 3.3.3 B). Because of unfavourable mineral composition (< 0.01 mol N g^{-1} dry matter) microbial decomposition of wood is slower than that of litter (leaves and fine roots).

Imbalances between litter fall and decomposition may lead to accumulation of organic matter (raw humus), which may be decomposed at other times in the development of the stand. A balance between supply of organic matter and decomposition can only be expected seldomly because both processes depend on different conditions. Imbalances occur particularly under the following conditions:

- Bogs: C decomposition is limited because of anaerobic conditions and low pH.
- Forests: C decomposition is limited by unfavourable mineral conditions and by acidification of the soil (accumulation of raw humus). The formation of heartwood is also a type of "litter production". In this case decomposition is delayed by decades. Another form of stabilisation of C is the binding of soluble organic carbon to heavy metals. This process is particularly important in tropical soils, where organic substances would otherwise be quickly decomposed and are only immobilised by such reactions.
- Meadows: C decomposition is delayed by binding of organic substance to clay minerals, occurring after passing through the intestines of earth worms (stable clay humus complexes). Despite this, the amount of C in the long-term grassland experiments at Rothamsted did not increase.
- Arable fields: Soil organisms are C limited, as the above-ground organic material is removed during harvesting. After the change from forests or natural grasslands to arable fields, degradation of organic carbon in the soil takes place. Carbon content is additionally affected by mechanical working of soils. This was shown particularly impressively for prairie soils in North America, following agricultural use; during a period of about 50 years, 50% of the carbon in the soil was lost (see Chap. 3.5; Matson et al. 1997). With changing agricultural practices (e.g. shallower ploughing or zero tillage) this carbon started to accumulate again (Post and Kwon 2000; Smith et al. 2000).

3.3.2.2
Heterotrophic Decomposition of Soil Organic Matter

A multitude of organisms (fungi, bacteria), specialised in certain partial processes, degrade organic substances in soil. The activity of heterotrophic soil organisms is C limited, in contrast to plants where production is limited by nutrients. However, several organic substances in the soil "resist" decomposition to different degrees.

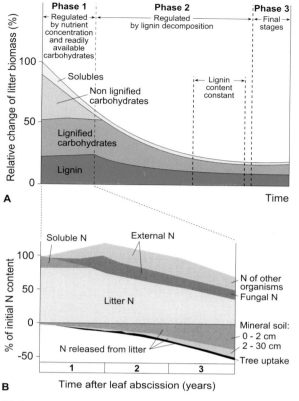

Fig. 3.3.4. A Degradation of leaf litter from beech over time. Initially, the easily available carbohydrates were consumed. Then lignin decomposition started with the breakdown of lignified carbohydrates rather than lignin itself. At the end about 20% of the leaf litter remained (after Berg and Matzner 1996). B Parallel with the decomposition of dry matter, decomposition of the N-containing substances followed. The N content of the leaf litter increased initially with colonisation by microorganisms, but then decomposition of compounds containing organic N occurred with transport to the mineral soil. After 3 years 60% of the N was decomposed. (After Cotrufo et al. 2000)

ner et al. 2001). The temporal course of litter decomposition is the most important basis for modelling carbon turnover in the soil (Gholz et al. 2000).

Figure 3.3.4 shows that models of litter decomposition based on a change of total biomass describe global turnover rates sufficiently well for many purposes, but not well enough to enhance our understanding of long-term storage of C in soils where decomposition rates depend on the substance (Gleixner et al. 2001):

Cellulose forms most of the dry matter of plant biomass (15–40% of dry weight). Cellulose is synthesised from glucose units, whilst hemicellulose (10–43% of dry weight) is formed from hexoses and pentoses. Cellulose and hemicellulose are directly used by microorganisms as energy sources and to form their body substance. In these organisms a resynthesis of carbohydrates and new cell wall material (e.g. chitin) may occur. Particularly the newly formed microbial polysaccharides (bacterial slime) bind to clay and silt fractions in the soil and this stabilises these substances against further decomposition. The large amounts of carbohydrates, which are also found in deeper layers of soils, originate from the microbial biomass and their metabolic products. Thus, carbohydrates circulate in the soil between microbial populations and are thus only relatively slowly mineralised to CO_2.

Lignin forms about 25–40% of the dry matter of plants. These are high molecular mass, three-dimensionally structured compounds of phenylpropane units which enclose cellulose fibrils and stabilise and protect them from decomposition. Conifers form lignin from coniferyl alcohol and deciduous trees use both coniferyl and sinapyl alcohols. Grasses also use coumaryl alcohol. The monomers are linked by C–C- and C–O–bonds. Lignin-degrading organisms are not able to grow on lignin being the only carbon source. Degradation occurs by laccase-forming fungi (white rots), which break bonds in the side chains and the aromatic rings by forming oxygen radicals (Fig. 3.3.5; Zech and Kögel-Knabner 1994). In the first step C–O–bonds (ether bonds) are broken, followed by degradation of C–C–carbohydrate chains. It is unlikely that the OH groups of the cyclic bonds are broken, because it would be difficult in biological decomposition to disrupt the hydrophobic benzene ring. Residual polymers, which are water soluble, remain and are relocated into deeper soil layers (**DOC = dissolved organic carbon**) or the chemically modi-

Decomposition occurs in several steps, with the dynamics for nitrogen (Fig. 3.3.4 B) being different to that of carbon (Fig. 3.3.4 A). In a newly fallen leaf, the N content rises initially as microorganisms and fungi settle on the dead leaf (for beech this takes about 1 year). At the same time the C content of the leaf decreases because of the use of easily decomposed C compounds (sugar, hemicellulose, cellulose). Finally, N-containing substances are decomposed and the N content of the leaf decreases as organisms retreat from the leaf (for beech after about 3 years). At this time the leaf has lost about 60% of its mass. Further decomposition is much slower. Lignin is now decomposed by fungi, but for this process an additional carbon source is required (Gleix-

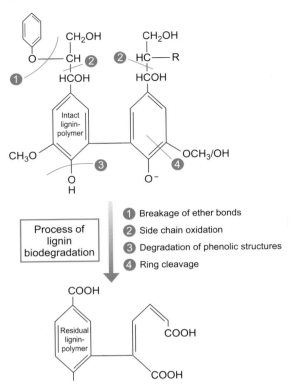

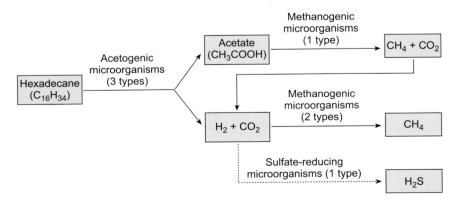

Process of lignin biodegradation

1 Breakage of ether bonds
2 Side chain oxidation
3 Degradation of phenolic structures
4 Ring cleavage

Fig. 3.3.5. Schematic presentation of the decomposition of lignin. The first step is breakage of the ether bonds, then oxidation of the side chains and, finally, opening of the double bond of the benzene ring, as long as the molecule is still hydrophilic. (Zech and Kögel-Knabner 1994)

fied lignin fractions react, forming new polymers, the humic substances.

Waxes and lipids are long-chain hydrocarbons which form only 1–10% of plant dry matter but they are the most difficult material to decompose, as short-chain lipids are formed in the reaction which may be toxic to microbial metabolism. However, long-chain lipids are decomp-

osable, e.g. by methanogenic bacteria living under anaerobic conditions in small spaces in soil aggregates, and convert alkanes into acetate and then into methane (Fig. 3.3.6; Parkes 1999; Krüger et al. 2000).

At the end of this material degradation, substances remain which are either derived from plant metabolism or are newly synthesised by microbial metabolism. This means that degradation of plant substances consists of a series of several cycles (Fig. 3.3.7):

- conversion of polymers into monomers;
- cleavage of heterocyclic compounds via the side chains;
- uptake and incorporation of plant material into microbial biomass (recycling of carbohydrates, amino acids, pyridine);
- degradation of carbohydrates or terminal groups (e.g. R-COOH or R-CH$_2$) to CO$_2$ or CH$_4$;
- binding of polar groups to clay minerals. This last step is the actual stabilisation (protection from further degradation) of the organic substance in soil. Thus the clay content determines the ability of soils to store C (Bird et al. 2001);
- even if plant substances can no longer be produced in the original form (e.g. lignin) it does not mean that the substance has been mineralised to CO$_2$, but rather that some parts of the molecules (e.g. benzene) can remain for a long time in the soil, whilst other molecular parts (pyridine, amino acids) are passed on from generation to generation and from organism to organism;
- binding to clay minerals occurs via an ester or ether bond, hydrogen bridges or in the form of ionic interactions.

Fig. 3.3.6. Schematic representation of the degradation of long-chain carbohydrates

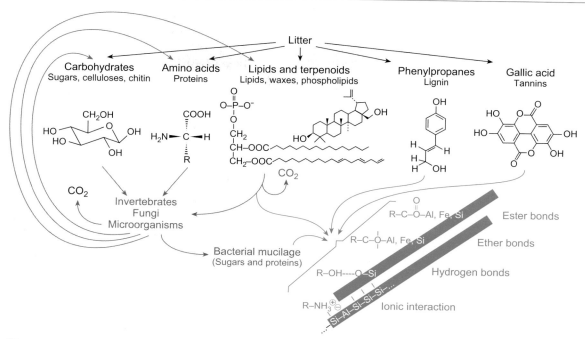

Fig. 3.3.7. Schematic representation of microbial recycling of plant substances from leaf litter and the formation of decomposition products, which bind to clay minerals. The figure shows a number of substances, such as carbohydrates, that remain a long time in the cycle and are passed from one generation of microorganisms to the next. Only a proportion is mineralised to the level of CO_2. Stabilisation of organic carbon is only through binding with clay minerals or heavy metals. (After Schulze 2000a)

In the soil profile, related to the soil C in the respective horizon, a relative accumulation of aromatic structures (e.g. aryl-C from the degradation of lignin) and of long-chain carbohydrates (lipids: alkyl-C) occurs, but there is a relative decrease in polysaccharides (O-alkyl-C), because of the decomposition processes.

Changes in the chemical composition of litter observed with increased atmospheric CO_2 are not sufficient to change the general trend of litter decomposition (Norby et al. 2001).

The remaining organic substances form new polymers which are called **humus**, which not necessarily consist only of recalcitrant organic substances, but may also contain molecules which are easy to decompose (e.g. sugars), but these are protected by clay minerals from further decomposition (Torn et al. 1997). Under changing conditions, when other organisms occur or when mechanical treatment of soils destroys the aggregated structure, these semi-stable compounds are again subjected to further decomposition. In general, decomposition results in a decrease in the O/C and H/C ratios, i.e. the proportion of cyclic aromatics increases (Haumeier and Zech 1995).

Charcoal (black carbon): There is a further path forming the so-called recalcitrant carbon which is difficult to degrade, that is by fire. When charcoal or soot is produced, recrystallisation of carbon takes place, forming polyaromatics with a structure similar to graphite (Fig. 3.3.8 A; Gleixner et al. 2001). These structures are almost inert to microbial decomposition. The residues of the carbonisation process are called **black carbon**. However, in forest fires, only a small proportion of the biomass is burned or changed into charcoal (Fig. 3.3.8 B). The largest proportion of the biomass is dead, unburned wood, where a charcoal cover protects the inner wood from decomposition (Fig. 3.3.8 C). It has been shown that the colour of black soils (chernozem) in steppes is based on soot and charcoal residues and is not just a product of humus formation (Schmidt et al. 1999). However, black carbon is not accumulated in savannahs despite frequent fires because charcoal burns again in the next fire. Also, the life span even of black carbon is not indefinite. It may be oxidised by strong acids and alkalis.

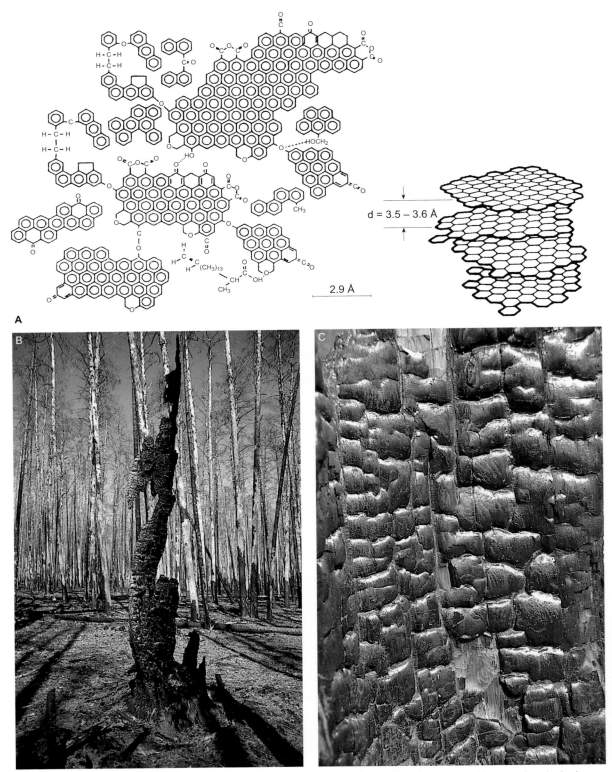

Fig. 3.3.8. A The putative structure of black carbon. In charcoal and soot there is a recrystallisation of cyclic hydrocarbon molecules to a condensed lattice of benzene rings (Gleixner et al. 2001). B Residue of a burnt tree trunk from the previous generation of trees in a pine forest in central Siberia. C Surface of a burnt tree trunk. It is clear that only the surface of the stem is charred, i.e. little charcoal is formed during a fire. The wood structure of a large proportion of the stem remains intact. During death of roots, resins are over-produced, impregnating the core of the trunk and protecting it against microbial decomposition. (Photo E.-D. Schulze)

3.3.2.3
Ecosystem and Biome Productivity

The sum of assimilatory and respiratory processes in carbon balance is called **net ecosystem productivity (NEP)**.

$$NEP = GPP - R_a - R_h = NPP - R_h \qquad (3.3.2)$$

where R_a is the respiration of autotrophic plants and R_h the respiration of heterotrophic organisms (Fig. 3.3.9; Schulze and Heimann 1998; Schulze et al. 2000).

The NEP gives no information where the accumulated C is deposited. This could take place with low R_a in the biomass (increase of stems and heartwood in a forest) and with limited R_h in the soil as humus. Thus, NEP should not be equated with formation of humus only. Whether NEP is accumulated temporarily at the level of the stand, or as undecomposed carbon in soils waiting to be transferred into the chain of heterotrophic organisms at a later date (for trees >100 years), can only be established after observation over longer periods or at a regional scale.

Figure 3.3.10 (Rebmann 2001) shows net ecosystem carbon fluxes as measured by a micro-meteorological approach (eddy covariance method, see Chap. 2.2, Box 2.2.6), as an example. Photosynthetic activity during summer is clearly detectable. It balances and exceeds respiration during the night from mid-March until September. Also in winter there are times when net CO_2 assimilation is greater than respiration of spruce. Respiration of the ecosystem is significantly higher in summer than in winter. Under certain conditions (low irradiation) the forests may also be at the compensation point in summer. This stand assimilated, over the whole year, a total of 13.8 t C ha^{-1} year^{-1} (GPP). Of this, 13 t C ha^{-1} year^{-1} was lost through respiration of biomass and soil. In the end NEP was only 0.8 t C ha^{-1} year^{-1}, which was deposited mainly in wood, as a consequence of growth. The balance may also become negative, i.e. losses exceed the gain from assimilation. As the wood is harvested in managed forests the amount of C is only transiently available in the ecosystem and thus the balance of this stand in the ecosystem is negative.

In addition to heterotrophic degradation, natural and anthropogenic exports of C occur mainly by **harvesting** (of agricultural crops or wood or animals) and **fire**. Including non-respi-

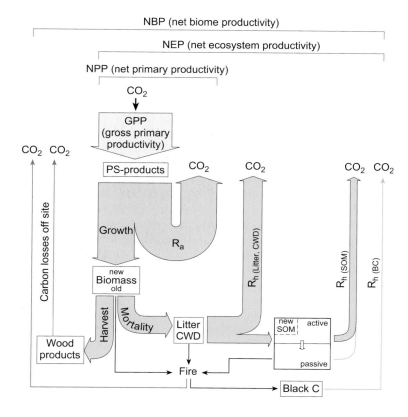

Fig. 3.3.9. Definitions of the term "productivity" in the carbon cycle (Schulze et al. 2000a). The initial process is the gross primary production (GPP), which corresponds to photosynthesis. Growth and maintenance requires about 50% of the assimilates for the energy requirement of the plant. Biomass is formed that appears as growth (net primary production, NPP). A proportion of this annual increase in biomass is returned to the soil as litter (leaves, roots, flowers) and, of this, a proportion returns to the atmosphere due to soil respiration. The "net ecosystem productivity" (NEP) is the balance between assimilation and total respiration. Independent of soil respiration are processes that remove C from the system without appearing in the respiration term. Examples are harvesting by man, grazing and fire. The balance of all these C turnovers is called "net biome productivity" (NBP). *CWD* Coarse woody debris; *SOM* soil organic matter; *BC* black carbon; R_h heterotrophic respiration; R_a respiration of autotrophic plants

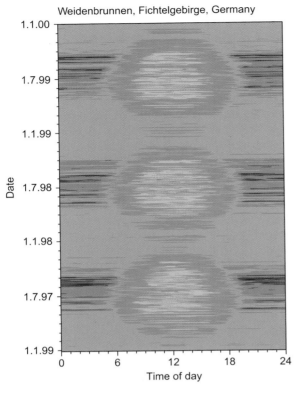

Weidenbrunnen, Fichtelgebirge, Germany

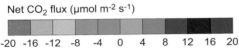

Net CO_2 flux (μmol m^{-2} s^{-1})

-20 -16 -12 -8 -4 0 4 8 12 16 20

Fig. 3.3.10. Annual and daily changes of net ecosystem CO_2 exchange in a spruce forest in the Fichtelgebirge (Germany). In three subsequent years, CO_2 assimilation can be seen during the day in summer, which is higher than respiration at night. In autumn and winter, only respiration is measurable, with the exception of a few days when net CO_2 assimilation occurs also in winter. (Rebmann 2001)

Table 3.3.3. Mean residence time of soil carbon and carbon sequestration and decomposition in the soil of European deciduous and coniferous forests (Schulze et al. 2000a). The mean residence time of carbon in biomass is shown in Fig. 3.3.2

	Deciduous forests	Coniferous forests
Mean residence time (years)		
Litter	7	8
Organic layer	47	51
Mineral soil 0–10 cm	121	126
Mineral soil 10–20 cm	178	195
Net primary production (g C m^{-2} a^{-1})	600	630
Litter production (g C m^{-2} a^{-1})	310	260
Mineralisation (g C m^{-2} a^{-1})	130	150
Net ecosystem productivity (g C m^{-2} a^{-1})	470	480
Increase in soil C (g C m^{-2} a^{-1})	180	110
Proportion of the degradation in		
20 years (%)	54	46
20–100 years (%)	35	39
>100 years (%)	11	15

ratory losses results in the so-called **net biome productivity (NBP;** see Fig. 3.3.9; Schulze and Heimann 1998):

$$NBP = NEP - \text{"non-respiratory" C losses} \quad (3.3.3)$$

Determining NEP by eddy covariance evaluates the net balance without considering from which of the many sources, e.g. from plants or carbon stored in different soil horizons, the respiratory CO_2 is derived. To interpret data from Table 3.3.3 the **mean residence time** (duration) of carbon in the potential source must be known (Harrison et al. 2000; Persson et al. 2000). The mean residence time of carbon in the soil (Fig. 3.3.2) increases from 1 to 8 years in litter to 4 to 50 years in the organic layer and reaches

>100 years in the mineral soil. Thus almost 50% of the carbon supplied to the soil by litter is decomposed in less than 20 years, 30–40% remains less than 100 years and only 10–15% is transformed into substances that are difficult to decompose and which accumulate in the soil where they remain more than 100 years, or these substances are so valuable for heterotrophic organisms (essential amino acids, pyridine, and others) that they are passed on between generations. The maximum age of carbon in the soil is around 3000–6000 years (Schlesinger 1990; Schachtschabel et al. 1998; Schulze et al. 1999). Only if soil horizons are buried, i.e. cut off from microbial decomposition, greater ages are attained in fossilised horizons.

A qualitative understanding of how carbon is transformed in the soil is possible, particularly by using mathematical models. An example is the CENTURY model (Parton et al. 1988), which shows the transformation and its dependence on availability of resources – C, N, P and S (Fig. 3.3.11 A). The model shows that, at all stages in decomposition, carbon is returned to microbial biomass. The proportion of carbon ending up in recalcitrant form is less than 1% of GPP. The turnover of carbon in microbial biomass means

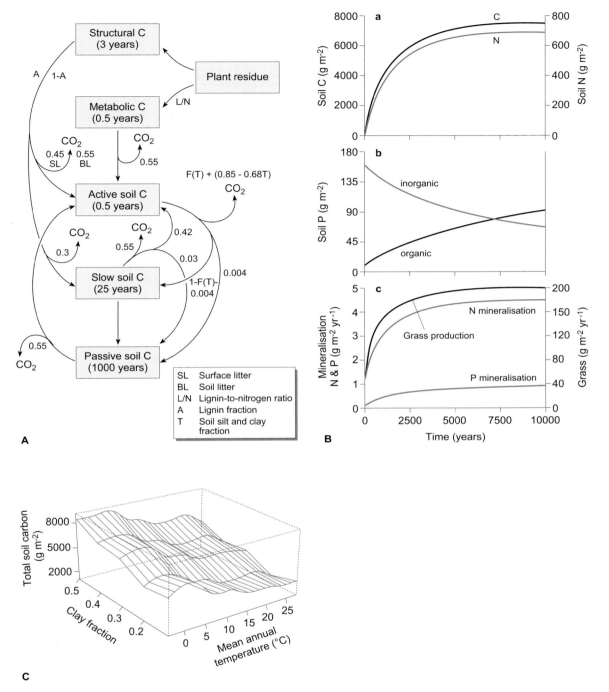

Fig. 3.3.11. A Flow chart of the CENTURY model to calculate the N and C turnover in an ecosystem using a grassland as an example. B Simulated changes in C, N and P content of various compartments. The model shows the magnitude of recycled substances in an ecosystem and also indicates the long-term accumulation of C and N in soil (Parton et al. 1988). C Dependence of soil carbon on ambient temperature and clay content of the soil. Adsorption of organic molecules to clay particles is a significant process that stabilises the soil carbon, thus the accumulation of carbon in a soil rises with increasing clay content. As the activity of soil microorganisms depends on the temperature, C accumulation in soil falls with mean annual temperature. (Schimel et al. 1994)

Box 3.3.2   Carbon turnover

- Carbon turnover in an ecosystem is not a cycle but an open exchange with the atmosphere. Ecosystem balance is determined from assimilation and respiratory processes in plants and soil. Fire and harvesting also determine the C turnover.
- Distinction is made between photosynthetic CO_2 fixation, identified as gross primary production (GPP), the growth of all plant organs, or net primary production (NPP), the net ecosystem productivity (NEP), the balance between assimilation and all respiratory processes, and the net biome productivity (NBP) that also takes into account non-respiratory carbon losses, from processes such as fire, harvesting and grazing.
- Litter couples plant productivity to heterotrophic processes in soil. It is only with great difficulty that the turnover rates of fine roots (<2 mm diameter) can be measured. Fine roots are about 28% of the total root mass and are assumed to turn over in woody plants about once a year, which is comparable to the turnover of leaves. Fine roots may attain $4\,km\,m^{-2}$ of soil surface area in tropical forests and up to $120\,km\,m^{-2}$ in grasslands. The projected area of fine roots is about that of the leaf area index.
- Litter degradation takes about 1–20 years for leaves and needles and up to 100 years for wood. Degradation can be significantly reduced by various local factors such as anaerobic conditions in moors, clay content (which leads to the formation of clay humic complexes) and low pH. Litter degradation is dependent on the chemical composition of the biomass with proteins, amino acids, cellulose and hemicelluloses directly degraded by – and incorporated into – microbes, i.e. they disappear rapidly from litter, whereas lignin and lipids are only slowly degraded and in the case of lignin are degraded without a gain in energy for the organisms (fungi with laccase activity).
- Plant polymers are degraded into monomers, and in part are recycled into microbial biomass (amino acids and pyridine) and are passed from generation to generation and from species to species (recycling).
- During the course of decomposition, organic substances decrease the O/C and H/C ratios, i.e. the proportion of cyclic aromatic substances increases.
- Fire releases CO_2 but also creates charcoal and crystalline carbon which due to the graphite-like structure are difficult to degrade. Black earth soils are enriched with such forms of black carbon.
- In European woodlands, about 46% of the litter is decomposed in 20 years, 39% in 100 years and only 15% remains after 100 years.
- Mathematical models of litter decomposition show the constant recycling of soil carbon, even for substances that are difficult to degrade in the microbial C cycle. This leads to an upper threshold of C storage in the ecosystem, determined by the clay content, duration and environmental temperature. Only about 1% of the assimilated C is held as recalcitrant carbon in the soil.

that the ecosystem reaches, in the long term, a constant value of soil carbon, specific to the system, but dependent mainly on the clay content of the soil (Fig. 3.3.11 B) and the mean annual temperature (Fig. 3.3.11 C; Lloyd and Taylor 1994; Schimel et al. 1994; Bird et al. 2001).

3.3.3

Nitrogen Cycle

Transformation of nitrogen in natural, anthropogenically undisturbed ecosystems (if they still exist) probably corresponds most closely to what is generally called a metabolic cycle (Fig. 3.3.12; Schulze 2000 a). Elemental nitrogen does not occur in nature and most nitrogen is found in the atmosphere as N_2 gas which cannot be directly used by higher plants unless they are in symbiosis with microorganisms. In the ecosystem, nitrogen occurs in inorganic oxidised and in reduced forms (nitrate and ammonium) or with C in organic compounds, particularly as amino ($C-NH_2$) or amide (C-N-C) groups, and so the C and N cycles are tightly coupled. In the following, "N" cycle refers not to N_2, but to mole equivalents of N in different oxidised or reduced forms.

The nitrogen cycle is characterised by continuous change in the oxidation number of N (Fig. 3.3.13 A; Gottschalk 1986; Meyer 1993). Electrons are first derived from degradation of organic substances and used to reduce N_2 to NH_3 (N_2 fixation).

$$N_2 + 18H^+ + 8e^- + 16ATP \rightarrow 2NH_4^+$$
$$+ H_2 + 16ADP + 16P_i \qquad (3.3.4)$$

The change in N_2 gas into organic compounds is achieved by N_2-fixing bacteria which occur either as free-living cyanobacteria, or as bacteria in nodules of Leguminosae or as symbionts with fungi (lichens) or higher plants [alders, cycads plants (Fig. 3.3.13 B–D); *Gunnera*, etc.]. The chemical reaction requires 960 kJ mol^{-1}. At the reduction state of NH_4^+, nitrogen may be transformed in many metabolic processes without changing the reduction state. Only during the transformation of organic substances in the soil are electrons removed from nitrogen via binding to oxygen. A veritable "zoo" of very different soil bacteria is involved to handle the electron. Distinction is made between the following reactions.

Type	Electron donor	Electron acceptor	C source biomass
Chemoorganoheterotrophs	OS	O_2, NO_3^-, SO_4^{2-}, OS, Me(ox)	OS
Chemolithotrophs	H_2, CO, H_2S, Me(red); NH_3, NO_2^-	O_2, NO_3^-, CO_2	CO_2
Photolithoheterotrophs	H_2O, H_2S, S^0, H_2	CO_2	CO_2
Photoorganoheterotrophs	OS	OS	OS

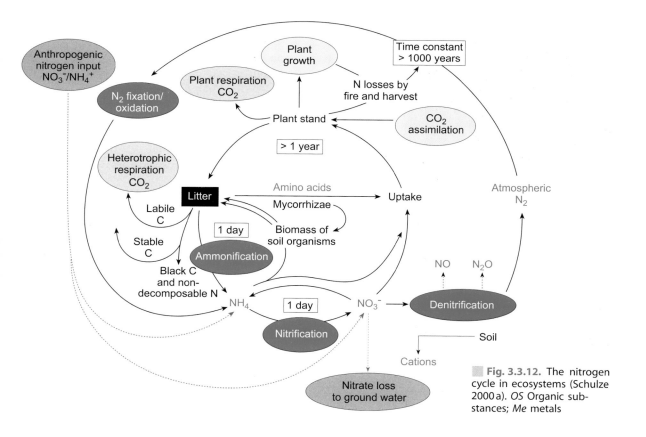

Fig. 3.3.12. The nitrogen cycle in ecosystems (Schulze 2000a). *OS* Organic substances; *Me* metals

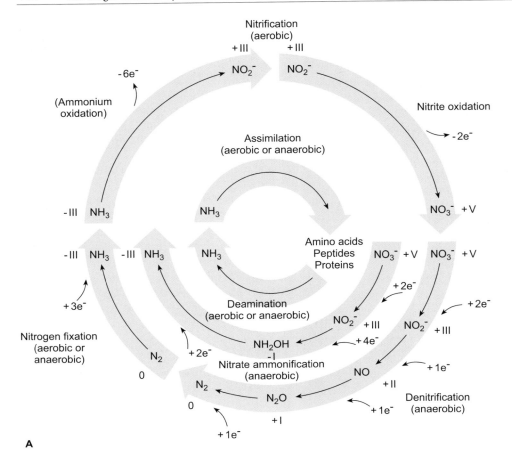

Fig. 3.3.13. A Functional groups of microorganisms in the biogeochemical nitrogen cycle. *Blue arrows* indicate reactions that occur within a single organism. *Small black arrows* are intermediate products. The figure also shows the oxidation state and the uptake or loss of electrons (after Meyer 1993). B Soil acidification as a result of N_2 fixation: During reduction of N_2 protons are released, which leads to acidification in many soil types. In the figure the lowering of pH in the soil close to the pea root is negated by the maize root that raises the pH by absorbing nitrate. A few N_2-fixing species are able to oxidise H^+ to H_2 and thus avoid acidification (Photo: E. George).

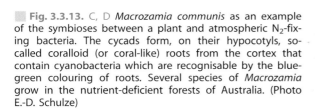

Fig. 3.3.13. C, D *Macrozamia communis* as an example of the symbioses between a plant and atmospheric N_2-fixing bacteria. The cycads form, on their hypocotyls, so-called coralloid (or coral-like) roots from the cortex that contain cyanobacteria which are recognisable by the blue-green colouring of roots. Several species of *Macrozamia* grow in the nutrient-deficient forests of Australia. (Photo E.-D. Schulze)

Transformation of NH_4^+ into oxidised nitrogen occurs by the following reactions:

$$4NH_4^+ + 8O_2 \rightarrow 4NO_2^- + 4H_2O$$
$$+ 8H^+ \left(-352 \text{ kJ mol}_N^{-1}\right) \quad (3.3.5)$$

$$2NO_2^- + O_2^+ \rightarrow 2NO_3^- \left(-73.5 \text{ kJ mol}_N^{-1}\right) \quad (3.3.6)$$

A total of 425.5 kJ mol_N^{-1} is released in the reaction, and is used by the autotrophic soil bacteria of the genus *Nitrosomas* (nitrification) and *Nitrobacter* (formation of nitrate) as an energy source to form ATP. The reaction is complicated, as during the formation of nitrite the oxygen used as electron acceptor comes not from O_2 but from water. Nitrate oxidase, a molybdo-protein at the inner side of the cell membrane, transfers the electron to a cytochrome c at the outer surface of the membrane, which in turn transfers two electrons to a further cytochrome on the inner side of the membrane. This cytochrome transfers the electron to O_2 and thus produces a proton gradient which provides the energy for formation of ATP. In addition, electrons from cytochrome c are transferred to NAD^+ and thus reduction equivalents are formed (Gottschalk 1986).

Chemolithotrophic bacteria are also able to perform the following reactions:

$$NH_4^+ + 2H_2O \rightarrow NO_2^- + 8H^+ + 6e^- \qquad (3.3.7)$$

$$NO_2^- + H_2O \rightarrow NO_3^- + 2H^+ + 2e^- \qquad (3.3.8)$$

where the electrons are used for reduction of NAD^+.

Plants are able to reduce NO_3^- back to NH_3

$$NO_3^- + 9H^+ + 8e^- \rightarrow NH_3 + 3H_2O \qquad (3.3.9)$$

in this case electrons are made available from photosynthesis (see Chap. 2.3).

In another cycle, microorganisms are able to use the oxidised NO_3^- as an electron acceptor, thus gaining the oxygen required for oxidation of other substrates (**anaerobic nitrate ammonification**, also called **nitrate respiration**), where NO_3^- returns to the reduction state of NO_2^- using glucose.

$$C_6H_{12}O_6 + 12NO_3^- \rightarrow 6CO_2 + 6H_2O$$
$$+ 12NO_2^- \left(+1766 \text{ kJ mol}^{-1}\right) \qquad (3.3.10)$$

or NO_3^- is transformed directly into NH_4^+

$$C_6H_{12}O_6 + 3NO_3^- + 6H^+ \rightarrow 6CO_2 + 3NH_4^+$$
$$+ 3H_2O \left(+1766 \text{ kJ mol}^{-1}\right) \qquad (3.3.11)$$

Independent of these reactions, nitrate may be degraded under anaerobic conditions to molecular N_2 (**denitrification**). Nitrate serves as electron acceptor and the oxygen released is used to oxidise organic substrates. The total energy gain by reduction of nitrate to N_2 is 561 kJ per mol electron acceptor, and is thus greater than by anaerobic respiration (475 kJ mol^{-1} O_2). In the conversion of ammonium to nitrate and in denitrification, losses of intermediate products, particularly NO_2, NO and N_2O as gases, are possible: these affect the radiation budget of the earth (see Chap. 2.1). The total balance of denitrification is:

$$10 \text{ glucose} + 48NO_3^- + 48H^+ \rightarrow$$
$$60CO_2 + 24N_2 + 84H_2O\left(+2669 \text{ kJ mol}^{-1}\right)(3.3.12)$$

where this reaction may take place in the same organisms as well as via a chain of organisms.

In ecosystems, nitrogen is not only made available to plants from N_2 by bacteria, but there are additional supplies from the atmosphere, where N_2 is oxidised by lightning or fire, for ex-

Table 3.3.4. The N balance in a spruce forest in Solling, Germany. (Horn et al. 1989)

Net requirement (mmol m^{-2} a^{-1})		Availability (mmol m^{-2} a^{-1})	
Needles	257	Uptake via the shoot	
Branches/twigs	84	$NH_3 + NO_x$	19
Trunks	177	$NH_4 + NO_3$	118
		Uptake via the root	
Roots	609 [a]	$NH_4 + NO_3$	990
Total	1127	Total	1127

[a] Requirement for roots includes turnover for fine roots and therefore is not easily quantifiable.

ample. Anthropogenically produced oxidised nitrogen (NO_x) originates from burning processes, and reduced nitrogen (NH_3) from domestic animals, sewage systems or industrial production of ammonium. The N deposition in ecosystems from such sources is < 5 kg N ha^{-1} a^{-1}. In industrially and agriculturally stressed ecosystems the N deposition is 20 to > 100 kg N ha^{-1} a^{-1} (Schulze and Ulrich 1991).

In ecosystems, N consumption in different plants and their compartments is of interest, but the amount of N available in the ecosystem is particularly important (Table 3.3.4). Part of the requirement is provided by relocation of amino acids prior to leaf shedding. The N content of litter varies between 5 and 10 mg g^{-1} dry matter in needles and leaves and 1 to 5 mg^{-1} dry matter in wood. About 3 t dry matter ha^{-1} of litter reaches the soil in a beech forest and so the total input of reduced N is 15–30 kg N ha^{-1}. This does not cover the measured N requirements for the system. About one-third of the N supply in Germany is obtained via above-ground organs from air pollutants.

The geographic distribution of N supply is variable with respect to both the chemical species as well as the amount. With low supply (N deficiency) and acid soils, fungi are the dominating organisms in the soil (Chap. 3.2.4.3; Smith and Read 1997). They make organic nitrogen available via a protease which is particularly active at low pH, i.e. fungi acidify the substrate by releasing protons and thus directly take up organic nitrogen from litter. Fungi have generally a higher N requirement than plants, as in several species their cell wall is formed from glucosamine (chitin) and thus require a large amount of N to form the structure of their own biomass. Fungi also require carbohydrates which they obtain as mycorrhizae either directly from plants or from saprophytes living on organic substances from the decomposition of dead material in the litter. Mycorrhizal fungi supply amino acids derived from protein degradation to the plant, in counter exchange with carbohydrates. In boreal coniferous forests this "short circuited" cycle of nitrogen, bypassing mineralisation by microbes, is so effective that no free nitrate or ammonium may be found in the soil (Wallenda et al. 2000). Despite the dominance of fungi in the degradation of organic substances and in the uptake of N in boreal forests, there are ammonium-forming and nitrifying bacteria as shown by the presence of spores becoming active after long incubation times (Persson et al. 2000).

With fungal degradation of lignin, DOC (**dissolved organic carbon**) is released and percolates with cations through the soil profile (Chap. 3.2.2.3), and thus advances soil acidification and provides environmental conditions for the acid proteases of fungi. Ammonium and nitrate only occur in soil solutions of boreal climates if the supply of calcium, and thus soil pH, increases (Nordin et al. 2001). Bacteria are more effective than fungi at high pH. Ectomycorrhizal species using amino acids change into ectomycorrhizae which take up inorganic nitrogen. Thus, in boreal climate with low pH, amino acids – and in temperature and warm climes with higher pH nitrate and ammonium – can be detected in the soil solution as the main N products of decomposition (see Fig. 3.3.12; Schulze et al. 2000).

In an ecosystem, oxidation and reduction of nitrogen compounds not only takes place in different horizons but also in the same soil horizon, as inside soil crumbs (aggregates) oxygen-free zones may be formed (Horn 1994).

If there is an excess of ammonium or nitrate, i.e. if external supply or formation in the ecosystem exceeds consumption (e.g. by seasonal variation of growth), this has particular consequences for the ecosystem (Chap. 3.2.2.3). **Ammonium excess** effects release of cations, particularly K and Al from clay minerals (see Chap. 2.3). In contrast to the almost immobile ammonium ion, nitrate is not bound to the soil exchanger and remains mobile in the soil solution. Nitrate excess thus leads to **nitrate leaching** into the groundwater. This loss of anions is coupled to an equimolar loss of cations. Deposition of N from air pollutants generally accelerates N transformation and leads to increased nitrate loss, even without interaction with organisms in the ecosystem (Durka et al. 1994).

Box 3.3.3   The N cycle

The N cycle

- Turnover of N is almost a closed system cycle.
- Nitrogen as organically bound amino N and as inorganic forms ammonia and nitrate undergoes cyclic transformation. Conversion of ammonium into nitrate and from nitrate into ammonium is controlled by microbial processes which are dependent on the redox potential. Soil chemical conditions determine if organic nitrogen, ammonium or nitrate are the dominant forms in the N turnover.
- Ecosystems gain nitrogen through nitrogen fixation by symbiotic, and by free-living N_2-fixing organisms (cyanobacteria, actinomycetes).
- Nitrogen is also gained from the atmosphere through oxidation of N_2 by lightning strikes and from natural and anthropogenic burning processes. Reduced nitrogen comes from sewage works and animal husbandry. The N gained from the atmosphere is mainly from anthropogenic sources and it can be greater than that gained from the natural mineralisation of N from organic substances.
- Anaerobic conditions lead to conversion of nitrate to ammonia, or to denitrification, which releases NO_2, NO and N_2O which are or which can be transformed into greenhouse gases that affect climate.
- Nitrogen losses not only occur via denitrification, but also through leaching of nitrate. Nitrate, in contrast to ammonia, is not bound to soil exchangers. Leaching of nitrate (and other strong acids, i.e. sulfate) also leads to equivalent cation loss.

3.3.4

Cation Turnover

The importance of cation (K, Mg, Ca) supply in ecosystems was apparent already in the N cycle. Cation supply occurs primarily from the chemical weathering of primary minerals (Chap. 2.3.1) or dust particles entering the ecosystem from the atmosphere. Examples of input of dust are the formation of loess in the post-glacial period (Schachtschabel et al. 1998), the supply of dust from the Sahara to the Amazon delta (Lloyd et al. 2001), and buffering of sulfur-containing emissions by industrial dusts in the 1960s which delayed acidification of soils, as the ionic charge of deposited material was neutral.

Cations are taken up by the roots. The return of cations into the soil is not only via litter, but also through leaching from the canopy. Canopy leaching is a consequence of ammonium uptake from air pollution and a consequence of buffering during the input of protons (leaching).

In soils, accumulation of cations in the organic deposits (see Fig. 3.2.4) and a dense root network in the organic layer enable direct re-supply of cations from litter into plants, particularly in nutrient-limited conditions. Cations are also released from the organic matrix and transported together with organic acids (**dissolved organic carbon**, DOC; see Chap. 2.3). Cation uptake by roots and cation losses caused by leaching of DOC decrease the concentration of cations in the soil solution of the upper layers and bleached horizons are formed, especially in nutrient-poor soils (eluvial E horizons) if the losses exceed weathering. Alkaline saturation increases only in deeper soil layers (B and C horizons; see also Chap. 3.2.2.3).

The turnover, i.e. the cycle from the uptake to the release, is very different for individual elements. In a spruce stand on granite (Horn et al. 1989) the calcium turnover is twice that of potassium, and exceeds that of magnesium five-fold. As leaching into the groundwater occurs for all elements at about the same magnitude, different amounts of Ca, K and Mg must be supplied by weathering of primary minerals in the soil profile (Table 3.3.5). Since weathering of granite is slow, this leads to decreased soil pH and to long-term forest damage particularly on acidic rocks (see Chap. 3.5.1).

Leaching of cations from an ecosystem into the groundwater and lateral transport into other ecosystems may have far-reaching consequences for nitrogen cycles of "supplier" and "receiver" systems. Two interactions are possible occur (Fig. 3.3.14): (1) Nitrate (or sulfate) is leached and carries cations down the slope leading to an increased total turnover; this is the "classic" assumption. (2) DOC is leached and cations accumulate in the groundwater. As DOC is microbiologically mineralised during transport there is secondary cation accumulation down the slope. Thus the conditions for nitrification improve along the transport path. Local nitrification and absence of nitrate leaching improve biomass production and thus the material cycles. The transport of DOC appears to dominate in the boreal climate (Högberg 2001) on acid substrates (granite), effecting relocation of cations, e.g. on a slope (Guggenberger and Zech 1993; Kaiser and Guggenberger 2000).

Table 3.3.5. Cation flows in a spruce forest (mmol m^{-2} a^{-1})

	Calcium	Potassium	Magnesium
Soil balance			
Atmospheric input	25	19	10
Leaching from canopy	10	25	1
Weathering	79	52	36
Release from litter	189	54	29
Leaching into groundwater	−45	−21	−33
Available in soil	258	129	43
Plant balance			
Plant uptake	258	129	43
Incorporation into wood	59	50	13
Leaching from canopy	10	25	1
Litter	189	54	29

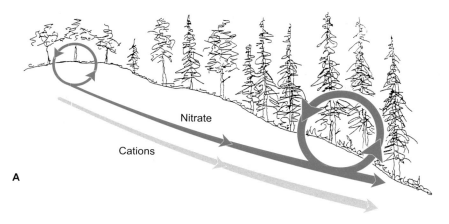

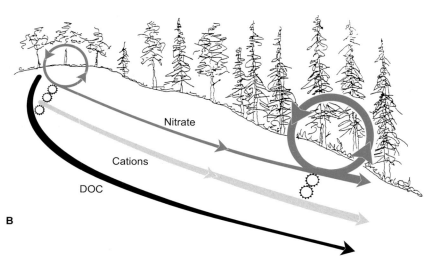

Fig. 3.3.14. Schematic representation of nitrate and cation fluxes down a slope resulting from the groundwater runoff in a boreal forest of Scandinavia. A High nitrate leaching and associated cation loss and B low nitrate loss and large cation loss in association with DOC. It can be shown that cation transport associated with DOC in natural systems contributes significantly to the low availability of cations on slopes. Thus, (B) is the dominant process. (After Högberg 2001)

Box 3.3.4   The cation cycle

The cation cycle

- Cycling of cations is not a completely closed cycle in natural ecosystems. Especially dissolved organic carbon (DOC) and strong acids which are produced anthropogenically displace cations within the soil horizons or this leads to loss of cations to the groundwater.
- Cation losses lead to acidification of soils, when the losses are not compensated by weathering of primary minerals or by import of dust, or by liming operations.

- In an ecosystem, the turnover of Ca is larger than that of K, and both exceed that of Mg.
- Base saturation determines the type and availability of the various N types (amino acids, ammonium, nitrate).
- Lateral transport of cations, together with the transport of DOC, explains the differentiation of soil chemical characteristics and of vegetation even along short hydrological gradients.

References

Berg B, Matzner E (1996) Effect of N deposition on decomposition of Plant litter and soil organic matter in forest systems. Environ Rev 5:1–25

Bird M, Santrůcková H, Lloyd J, Veenendaal E (2001) The global soil organic carbon pool. In: Schulze E-D, Holland E, Harrison S, Lloyd J, Prentice C, Schimel D (eds) Global biogeochemical cycles in the climate system. Academic Press, San Diego, pp 185–199

Chadwick OA, Derry LA, Vitousek PM, Huebert BJ, Hedin LO (1999) Changing resources of nutrients during four million years of ecosystem development. Nature 397:491–497

Cotrufo MF, Miller M, Zeller B (2000) Litter decomposition. Ecological studies, vol 142. Springer, Berlin Heidelberg New York, pp 276–296

DeWitt CT (1978) Simulation of assimilation and transpiration of crops. PUDOC, Wageningen, 141 pp

Durka W, Schulze E-D, Gebauer G, Vorkelius S (1994) Effects of forest decline on uptake and leaching of deposited nitrate determined from ^{15}N and ^{18}O measurements. Nature 372:765–767

Fischer RA, Turner NC (1978) Plant productivity in the arid and semiarid zones. Annu Rev Plant Physiol 29:277–317

Gholz HL, Wedin DA, Smitherman SM, Harmon ME, Parton WJ (2000) Long-term dynamics of pine and hardwood litter in contrasting environments: towards a global model of decomposition. Global Change Biol 6:751–766

Gleixner G, Czimczik CJ, Kramer C, Lühker B, Schmidt MWI (2001) Turnover and stability of soil organic matter. In: Schulze E-D, Holland E, Harrison S, Lloyd J, Prenice C, Schimel D (eds) Global biogeochemical cycles in the climate system. Academic Press, San Diego, pp 201–215

Gottschalk G (1986) Bacterial metabolism. Springer, Berlin Heidelberg New York, 358 pp

Guggenberger G, Zech W (1993) Dissolved organic carbon control in acid forest soils of the Fichtelgebirge (Germany) as revealed by distribution pattern and structural analysis. Geoderma 59:109–129

Harrison AF, Harkeness DD, Rowland AP, Carnett JS, Bacon PJ (2000) Annual carbon and nitrogen fluxes in soils along the European forest transect, determined using ^{14}C-bomb. Ecological studies, vol 142. Springer, Berlin Heidelberg New York, pp 171–188

Haumeier L, Zech W (1995) Black carbon – possible source of highly aromatic components of soil humic acids. Org Geochem 23:191–196

Högberg P (2001) Interactions between hilltops hydrochemistry, nitrogen dynamics and plants in Fennoscannian boreal forest. In: Schulze E-D, Holland E, Harrison S, Lloyd J, Prenice C, Schimel D (eds) Global biogeochemical cycles in the climate system. Academic Press, San Diego, pp 227–233

Horn R (1994) The effect of aggregation of soils on water, gas, and heat transport. In: Schulze E-D (ed) Flux control in biological systems. Academic Press, San Diego, pp 335–364

Horn R, Schulze E-D, Hantschel R (1989) Nutrient balance and element cycling in healthy and declining Norway spruce stands. Ecological studies, vol 77. Springer, Berlin Heidelberg New York, pp 444–458

Jackson RB, Mooney HA, Schulze E-D (1997) A global budget for fine root biomass, surface area and nutrient contents. Proc Natl Acad Sci USA 94:7362–7366

Kaiser K, Guggenberger G (2000) The role of DOM-sorption to mineral surfaces in the preservation of organic matter in soils. Org Geochem 31:711–725

Knohl A, Kolle O, Minajeva T, Milyukova IM, Vygodskaya NN, Foken T, Schulze E-D (2002) Carbon exchange of a Russian boreal forest after disturbance by wind throw. Global Change Biol 8:231–246

Krüger M, Frenzel P, Conrad R (2000) Microbial processes influencing methane emission from rice fields. Global Change Biol 7:49–64

Lloyd J, Taylor JA (1994) On the temperature dependence of soil respiration. Funct Ecol 8:315–323

Lloyd J, Bird MI, Veenendaal E, Kruijt B (2001) Should phosphorous availability be constraining moist tropical forest response to increasing CO_2 concentrations? In: Schulze E-D, Holland E, Harrison S, Lloyd J, Prentice C, Schimel D (eds) Global biogeochemical cycles in the climate system. Academic Press, San Diego, pp 96–114

Matson PA, Parton WJ, Power AG, Swift MJ (1997) Agricultural intensification and ecosystem properties. Science 277:504–509

Meyer O (1993) Functional groups of microorganisms. Ecological studies, vol 99. Springer, Berlin Heidelberg New York, pp 67–96

Mooney HA, Medina E, Schindler DW, Schulze E-D, Walker BH (1991) Ecosystem Experiments. SCOPE 45. Wiley, Chichester, 268 pp

Norby RJ, Cotrufo MF, Ineson P, O'Neill EG, Canadell JG (2001) Elevated CO_2, litter chemistry, and decomposition. Oecologia 127:153–165

Nordin A, Högberg P, Näsholm T (2001) Soil N availability and plant N uptake along a boreal forest productivity gradient. Oecologia 129:125–132

Parkes J (1999) Cracking anaerobic bacteria. Nature 401:217–218

Parton WJ, Stewart JWB, Cole CV (1988) Dynamics of C, N, P and S in grassland soils: a model. Biogeochemistry 5:109–131

Persson T, Rudebeck A, Jussy JH, Clin-Belgrand M, Prieme A, Dambrine E, Karlsson PS, Sjöberg M (2000) Soil nitrogen turnover – mineralisation, nitrification and denitrification in European forest stands. Ecological studies, vol 142. Springer, Berlin Heidelberg New York, pp 297–331

Post WM, Kwon KC (2000) Soil carbon sequestration and land-use change: processes and potential. Global Change Biol 6:317–329

Rebmann C (2001) Carbon dioxide and water exchange of a German *Picea abies* forest. Dissertation, University of Bayreuth, Germany

Schachtschabel P, Blume HP, Brümmer G, Hartge KH, Schwertmann U (1998) Lehrbuch der Bodenkunde. Enke, Stuttgart, 494 pp

Schimel DS, Braswell BH, Holland EA, McKeown R, Ojima DS, Painter TH, Parton WJ, Townsend AR (1994) Climatic, edaphic, and biotic controls over storage and turnover of carbon in soils. Global Biogeochem Cycles 8:279–293

Schlesinger WH (1990) Evidence from chronosequence studies for a low carbon storage potential of soils. Nature 348:232–239

Schlesinger WH (1997) Biogeochemistry; an analysis of global change. Academic Press, San Diego, 588 pp

Schmidt MWI, Skjemstad JO, Gehrt E, Kögel-Knabner I (1999) Charred organic carbon in German chemozemic soils. Eur J Soil Sci 50:351–365

Schulze E-D (1982) Plant life forms and their carbon, water and nutrient relations. Encycl Plant Physiol New Ser 12B:615–676

Schulze E-D (2000a) Carbon and nutrient cycling in European forest ecosystems. Ecological studies, vol 142. Springer, Berlin Heidelberg New York, 498 pp

Schulze E-D (2000b) Der Einfluss des Menschen auf die biogeochemischen Kreisläufe der Erde. MPG Jahrbuch 2000

Schulze E-D, Heimann M (1998) Global carbon and water exchange of terrestrial systems. IGBP Book Ser 3:145–161

Schulze E-D, Ulrich B (1991) Acid rain – a large-scale, unwanted experiment in forest ecosystems. SCOPE 45:89–106

Schulze E-D, Lloyd J, Kelliher FM, Wirth C, Rebmann C, Lühker B, Mund M, Knohl A, Milyokova IM, Schulze W, Ziegler W, Varlagin A, Sogachev AF, Valentini R, Dore S, Grigoriev S, Kolle O, Panfyorov MI, Tchebakova N, Vygodskaya NN (1999) Productivity of forests in the Eurosiberian boreal region and their potential to act as a carbon sink – a synthesis. Global Change Biol 5:703–722

Schulze E-D, Högberg P, van Oene H, Persson T, Harrison AF, Read D, Kjöller A, Matteucci G (2000) Interactions between the carbon- and nitrogen cycle and the role of biodiversity: a synopsis of a study along a north-south transect through Europe. Ecological studies, vol 142. Springer, Berlin Heidelberg New York, pp 468–492

Smith DE, Read DJ (1997) Mycorrhizal symbiosis. Academic Press, London, 605 pp

Smith WN, Desjardins R, Patterey E (2000) The net fluxes of carbon from agricultural soils in Canada 1970–2010. Global Change Biol 6:557–568

Stober C, George E, Persson H (2000) Root growth and response to nitrogen. Ecological studies, vol 142. Springer, Berlin Heidelberg New York, pp 99–121

Torn MS, Trumbore DE, Chadwick OA, Vitousek PM, Hendricks DM (1997) Mineral control of soil carbon storage and turnover. Nature 389:170–173

Wallenda T, Stober C, Högbom L, Schinkel H, George E, Högberg P, Read DJ (2000) Nitrogen uptake processes in roots and mycorrhizae. Ecological studies, vol 142. Springer, Berlin Heidelberg New York, pp 122–143

Wirth C, Schulze E-D, Lühker B, Grigoriev S, Siry M, Hardes G, Ziegler W, Backor M, Bauer G, Vygodskaya NN (2002) Fire and site type effects on the long-term carbon balance in pristine Siberian Scots pine forest. Plant Soil 142:61–63

Zech W, Kögel-Knabner I (1994) Patterns and regulation of organic matter transformation in soils: litter decomposition and humification. In: Schulze E-D (ed) Flux control in biological systems. Academic Press, San Diego, pp 303–334

3.4

Biodiversity and Ecosystem Processes

Temperate rainforest of New Zealand's South Island. This is a highly diverse Tertiary relict forest with *Weinmannia, Metrosideros, Nothofagus, Dacrydium* (Gymnospermae), *Dicksonia* (tree ferns) and a large number of epiphytic mosses, genera common right around the Antarctic. Fjordland, New Zealand. Photo E.-D. Schulze

In the past, ecosystem processes and vegetation dynamics were considered and discussed separately. A relatively new branch of research in ecosystems is trying to find the relationship between biodiversity and processes in ecosystems. This will be considered in the following section, whilst basic considerations of biodiversity will be discussed in Chapter 4.

It is difficult to prove a coupling between biodiversity and ecosystem processes, at the level of the ecosystem, as diversity and historic land use correlate positively as well as negatively. If it is the task to identify the specific influence of di-versity, then it is not sufficient to just compare sites with different diversity (e.g. an orchid-rich hornbeam forest and a species-poor spruce forest). The biogeochemical cycles in natural or managed ecosystems (Chap. 3.2.5.4) are influenced by many uncontrollable factors, such as history, which makes specific experimental investigations necessary.

When dealing with biodiversity and ecosystem processes, it is necessary to distinguish between ecosystem functioning in response to changes in biodiversity, where "functioning" addresses the internal regulation of ecosystems, which ecosystem "goods and services" describes the human needs and expectations to be delivered by ecosystems. This anthropocentric attitude should be assessed critically, as criteria change with time and conditions. For humans, "ecosystem services" include most importantly:

- production of biomass,
- supply of drinking water,
- material degradation, decomposition and mineralisation,
- filtering of air,
- recreation.

Key questions are (GBA 1995; IPCC 1996):

1. Are many species required to achieve certain functions of the ecosystem?
2. If not all species are required, which species are redundant?

The discussion of these difficult questions could perhaps be initiated by asking: How many or how few species are required for a functioning ecosystem? The answer is "5" (Woodward 1994). For millions of years, completely self-sufficient and stable ecosystems consisting of one fungus, one cyanobacterium, one alga, one lichen and one non-photosynthetically active bacterium (material degradation) have existed in the Antarctic. In the Antarctic as a whole, there are about six species of lichens, each forming a stable community. Woodward (1994) also showed that the diversity of microbial forms increased with the diversity of the constituents of the litter, and that the diversity of plant families increased with the minimum temperature. This means that only very few organisms are required under certain (simple or extreme) conditions, but more and more species are required with increasing complexity of living conditions and substrates, in order to balance the requirements for resources with a corresponding supply of resources (for synecological links, see Chap. 4.3).

Functional links cannot be tested with existing ecosystems, as historical development and processes in an ecosystem cannot be distinguished from each other. It is therefore necessary to test these links experimentally and the following examples may demonstrate how difficult it is to establish the link between processes in ecosystems and biodiversity experimentally:

1. In Costa Rica, Ewel et al. (1991) planted stands of different diversity (1–130 species). After 5 years most processes showed a satura-

tion function with fewer than 10 species, i.e. the other 100 species were superfluous for production and soil processes (C storage, availability of nutrients, etc.).

2. Tilman and Downing (1994) designed a biodiversity experiment in the North American prairie to assess the effect of N input. In a dry year experimental areas reacted differently to drought, depending on the diversity. Monocultures were more sensitive than species-rich stands. However, the effect only occurred if the ecosystem reached less than ca. ten species. The interpretation of this experiment was criticised, as the experiment was not designed to test drought, but N tolerance. Monocultures were N-indicator plants which were also very sensitive to drought. If the monocultures had been drought-resistant prairie species, the result would have been different (Huston 1994). In this case, it would be expected that also stands with < 10 species would have been drought-resistant.

3. Tilman et al. (1996) observed in the same experiment in the prairie of North America that nitrate loss from experimental fields decreased linearly with increasing biodiversity and fell to very small values with about eight species. This interpretation was also not conclusive, as the decrease in nitrate loss correlated with the increase in total biomass of the experimental fields and not only with the number of species.

4. Naeem et al. (1994) designed artificial ecosystems with plants, herbivores and destruents in climate chambers and found that species-rich ecosystems had greater productivity than species-poor stands. This experiment can also be questioned, as the species-rich stands contained plants that grew taller than those with fewer species and the result may thus correlate with the dominant growth form.

5. Lawton (1994) designed and carried out a diversity experiment in eight European countries, from northern Sweden to Greece, using experience from the preceding experiments to avoid mistakes in the selection of the experimental design. The mixture of species was therefore randomly selected from an inventory of species occurring in a grassland community around the experiment area. Each diversity level (1, 2, 4, 8 and 16 species) was sown with different combinations of individual species, to be able to distinguish the pure diversity effect from the influence of individual

species. On average, across all experimental fields, productivity increased linearly with diversity up to 16 species (Hector et al. 1999). However, in this experiment, too, there are different possible interpretations. The behaviour was not uniform in all countries. In England, Greece and Ireland there was no difference, whilst in Germany, Switzerland and Sweden the effect was proportionally much larger. In addition, it was shown that some monocultures were just as productive as mixed cultures, but not all species were tested as monocultures. Thus the possibility remains that with increasing number of species some additional, highly productive, species entered the mixture, i.e. the result may not be based on complementarity of different species, but may be the result of a selection effect.

In this experiment, the number of species and also the effects of "functional groups" (N_2 fixers, grasses and dicotyledonous herbaceous plants) were considered. The presence of N_2 fixers is more important for productivity than the influence of biodiversity (see Fig. 3.2.7; Scherer-Lorenzen 1999). In this case it was just a single species, *Trifolium rubrum*, which increased productivity, i.e. it was a **keystone species**. Also changes in further ecosystem processes correlated with change of productivity. Nitrate losses were reduced with diversity, independent of vegetation cover. Also, the rate of litter degradation increased with diversity.

Experience shows that more than one species (genotype) is required to maintain the productivity of a plant community in the long term and regionally. Obviously, maximum production of a plant community is also possible with just one individual species (agriculture) but human care is required (Fig. 3.4.1; Heywood and Watson 1995). However, even in agriculture, it is known that it is risky to only work with one species or genotype (see Chap. 2.4.5.1). In as far as different edaphic conditions apply, several species or crop plants are required to achieve maximum yields. Furthermore, weather conditions vary from year to year, so that in some succession stages different resources are available and thus different species are more suitable for planting, and further diversity is required for future maintenance and breeding. Thus the necessary number of species required to maintain the level of productivity in a region increases far beyond "one".

Considering the links between biomass and biodiversity in different climates (Fig. 3.4.2; Tilman and Pacala 1993), it is striking that biomass increases with biodiversity initially. At a certain point, which appears to be specific to the biome, the curve changes, i.e. highest rates of productivity are measured in stands with few species. This is particularly striking in temperate herbaceous communities whereas, in Mediterranean grasslands, it is less obvious, where about 40 species participate for greatest productivity. It should also be taken into account, considering Fig. 3.4.2, that in a region these stands of different productivity represent also differences in conditions of the site and in the history of the stands. Thus it is not an experimental comparison, but observations in a certain natural region. The figure shows that a repeat of Lawton's experiment on a nutrient-rich substrate might come to a different result.

Spatial and temporal variation of climatic and edaphic conditions requires division of the space amongst several specialised species or genotypes in order to fully use the resources. Evolution did not lead to the formation of "super organisms" (this would be a solution of the optimisation hypothesis), but formed a large spectrum of species differing in the requirements for certain environmental conditions and specialised for par-

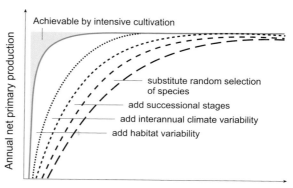

Fig. 3.4.1. Conceptual scheme of the dependence of net primary production (NPP) on the diversity of plant species or genotypes of the dominant forms. With intensive agriculture, monocultures attain the same NPP as mixed cultures. When considering the variability of habitat and climate, the stage in the succession and the substitution of susceptible species that occur not only in a small area but also on the landscape scale, more than one species is necessary (Heywood and Watson 1995). The region between the two curves shows the range of additional types required in order to compensate. The exact value is, naturally, dependent on many factors

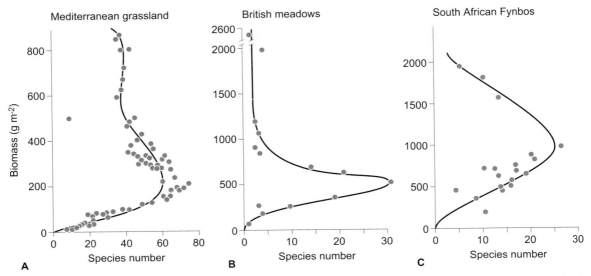

Fig. 3.4.2. Dependence of changes in biomass on diversity of forms of plant growth in A Mediterranean grasslands, B meadows in the British Isles, and C South African scrubland. It is possible to see that in all vegetation types the productivity rises initially with diversity, but then decreases, i.e. the highest biomass production is achieved in species-poor areas. This figure is only partly comparable with Fig. 3.4.1, as this is not an experiment but based on observations of vegetation at different sites that have different uses, fertility and water availability. (Tilman and Pacala 1993)

Box 3.4.1   Biodiversity and ecosystem function

- There are many indicators that diversity of plant types is required in order to maintain the biogeochemical cycles of an ecosystem in the long term. To prove that processes such as productivity rise with increasing diversity (shown for up to 16 species) is extraordinarily difficult, and has not yet been conclusively established. Current knowledge indicates that substantial diversity of the vegetation cover on the landscape scale is required in order to maintain the diversity of a site, and to be able to withstand the long-term risks from climate change.

- In most cases in which diversity had a significant effect on ecosystem processes, effects of specific types have been seen. Integration of species into functional groups to assess an ecosystem is only possible in part.

---

ticular processes. The question whether it is possible to narrow down biodiversity to functional groups thus becomes dubious (Smith et al. 1997), as an increasing functional specialisation will ultimately only be supplied by species. On the basis of certain physiologically regulated processes (assimilation, storage, shoot/root allocation, life span, and many more), Kleidon and Mooney (2000) modelled the most important features of global distribution of biodiversity.

References

Ewel JJ, Mazzarino MJ, Berish CW (1991) Tropical fertility changes under monocultures and successional communities of different structure. Ecol Appl 1:289–302

GBA (1996) Global biodiversity assessment. Cambridge University Press, Cambridge, 1140 pp

Hector A, Schmid B, Beierkuhnlein C, Caldeira MC, Diemer M, Dimitrakopoulos PG, Finn JA, Freitas H, Giller PS, Good J, Harris R, Högberg P, Kuss-Danell K, Joshi J, Jumpponen A, Körner C, Leadley PW, Loreau M, Minns A, Mulder CPH, O'Donovan G, Otway SJ, Pereira JS, Prinz A, Read DJ, Scherer-Lorenzen M, Schulze E-D, Siamantziouras D, Spehn EM, Terry AC, Troumbis AY, Woodward FI, Yachi S, Lawton JH (1999) Plant diversity and productivity experiments in European grasslands. Science 286:1123–1127

Heywood VH, Watson RT (eds) (1995) Global biodiversity assessment. Cambridge University Press, Cambridge, 1140 pp

Huston MA (1994) Hidden treatments in ecological experiments: re-evaluating ecosystem function of biodiversity. Oecologia 110:449–460

IPCC (1996) Climate change 1995. Second assessment report. Cambridge University Press, Cambridge

Kleidon A, Mooney HA (2000) A global distribution of biodiversity inferred from climatic constraints: results from a process-based modelling study. Global Change Biol 6:507–524

Lawton JH (1994) What do species do in ecosystems. Oikos 71:367–374

Naeem S, Thompson LJ, Lawler SP, Lawton JH, Woodfin RM (1994) Declining biodiversity can alter the performance of ecosystems. Nature 368:734–737

Scherer-Lorenzen M (1999) Effects of plant diversity on ecosystem processes in experimental grassland communities. Bayreuther Forum Ökol 75:193

Smith TM, Shuargt HH, Woodward FI (1997) Plant functional types. IGBP Book Series, vol 1. Cambridge University Press, Cambridge, 369 pp

Tilman D, Downing JA (1994) Biodiversity and stability in grasslands. Nature 367:363–365

Tilman U, Wedin D, Knops J (1996) Productivity and sustainability influenced by biodiversity in grassland ecosystems. Nature 379:718–720

Tilman U, Pacala S (1993) The maintenance of species richness in plant communities. In: Ricklefs RE, Schluter D (eds) Species diversity in ecological communities. University of Chicago Press, Chicago, pp 13–25

Woodward FI (1994) How many species are required for a functional ecosystem? Ecological studies, vol 99. Springer, Berlin Heidelberg New York, pp 271–292

3.5

Case Studies at the Scale of Ecosystems

Forest damage at Nusshard, Fichtelgebirge, Germany, in September 1989. In 1983, Zech and Pop diagnosed at this location, for the first time, Mg deficiency in young trees which was previously unknown in this area. During the next 10 years, the visible signs of Mg deficiency developed throughout the Fichtelgebirge. Mg deficiency does not necessarily lead to death of trees, but causes yellowing and early needle loss; combined with frost and drought it causes damage leading to thinning of crowns. With the death of a few individual trees the remaining trees have a better Mg supply. Thus, in the short term, the remaining trees recover but may die later. Thus, slowly, the stand of trees dies from stress, i.e. each year a few trees fall, so that in the end the stand has only a few trees which succumb to external factors. Bark beetles increased the rate of tree death as they attacked the relatively healthy trees rather than those suffering severe Mg stress. At the end of the 1980s, about 10,000 ha was affected in the Fichtelgebirge. Increased tree removal and liming helped to regenerate these forests; this occurred during the time when less SO_2 and SO_4^{2-} was released due to changes in the law regulating combustion of coal. Critics doubted that forest dieback had anything to do with the amount of pollution in the atmosphere or that the trees were dying as a result of SO_2 and SO_4^{2-}. Rather they considered that it was due to complex forest "diseases" primarily related to factors in the soil that weakened the plant. The only way to confirm the cause would be to subject forest areas again to pollution, equivalent to values in the 1970s. The scientific investigations stimulated the "Advisory Council of the Federal Republic of Germany on Forest Decline" (Forschungsbeirat Waldschäden der Bundesregierung) in 1986 to conclude that, in all the different forms of forest dieback that were studied, air pollution played a significant role. Photo E.-D. Schulze

It is possible to demonstrate processes and interactions of organisms at the scale of the ecosystem in various ways (Mooney et al. 1991). These are:

- observation of natural catastrophes (El Niño);
- observation of the consequences of human intervention (clearing of forests, acid rain);
- experiments with radioactive labelled materials (e.g. release of ^{14}C from atomic bomb tests);
- ecosystem experiments (fumigation with CO_2, SO_2 or O_3).

These "experiments" allow observations over areas differing in size (even globally) of the effects of climate change or of interference on ecosystems, or determination of the transport of particular substances in ecosystems. This is particularly important as scientifically planned experiments in ecosystems are not acceptable to the public or they are not practicable.

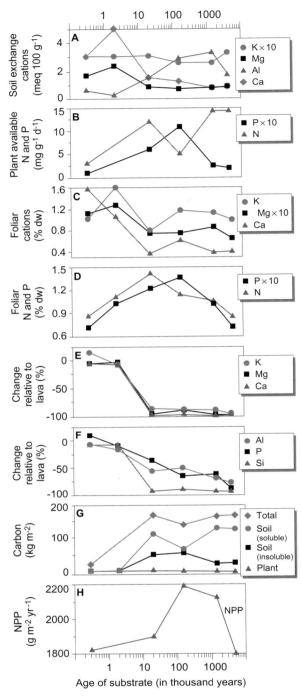

Fig. 3.5.1. Changes in concentrations of Ca, Mg, N and P in lava, the soil derived from the weathered lava and in leaves following weathering of lava over the past 400,000 years on Hawaii. The associated changes in soil acidification and biomass production are also shown. (Chadwick et al. 1999)

From some of these observations and experiments at different scales, conclusions may be drawn about the causes and effects. From the many available case studies, three examples will be used to show how very complex the links are.

3.5.1

Soil Acidification and Forest Damage

Ecosystems do not seem to be able to avoid loss of cations. Even in natural ecosystems, without management and with a high density of roots, organic acids (DOC) are released which causes relocation of cations into deeper layers. In these, microorganisms metabolise the organic substances, leading to secondary accumulation of cations (see Fig. 3.3.14). This process is known from the boreal zone as podsolisation (Schachtschabel et al. 1998; Brady and Weil 2004) and occurred in Scandinavia, for example, during the first settlement after the land rose and was evident even after only 400 years (Starr 1991). It is often assumed that other vegetation, particularly in the tropics, is so well adapted to the poor nutrient conditions that cation losses can be ignored. However, Chadwick et al. (1999) have shown that the same processes occur also in tropical climates. Similar cation losses to those in boreal zones were shown for vegetation on lava flows of different ages (Fig. 3.5.1; Chadwick et al. 1999). As soon as the first critical step of weathering is finished (after 10,000 years), the system stabilises at a smaller mineral concentration. It has not been explained whether this is, in fact, a state of equilibrium or a consequence of disturbances occurring stochastically.

Natural processes causing cation loss may be accelerated by strong acids, particularly if they form acid anions which then enter the groundwater. To these acid anions belong not only sulfate, but also chloride and nitrate, insofar as they are not used in lower soil layers and thus enter the groundwater. Strong acids do not occur in excess under natural, anthropogenically unaffected conditions. Since industrialisation, ecosystems have been increasingly stressed by these acids (Schulze 1989). Deposition of acids in Europe over a period of about 30 years has caused acidification of soils (Fig. 3.5.2) with base saturation in all soil horizons decreasing from 10 to 50% at the start of the period to 5% on average a few decades later (Ulrich 1987).

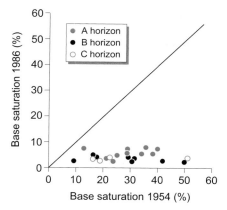

Fig. 3.5.2. Changes in the cation-exchange capacity of beech forests over 30 years on loess covering red sandstone in Niedersachsen, Germany (Hildebrand, pers. comm.; FBW 1989)

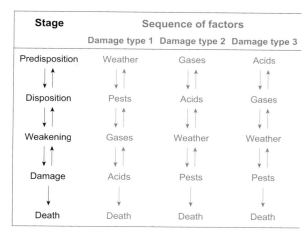

Fig. 3.5.3. Schematic representation of the course of a decease as infection initiated by a combination of factors, using the example of forest decline. (Schulze and Lange 1990)

Forest vegetation should be adapted to soil acidification, as under natural conditions trees occupy sites across a very wide range of soil acidity (Ellenberg 1978). The phenomenon of "new-type forest damage" [Forschungsbeirat Waldschäden 1989 (Advisory Council of the Federal Republic of Germany on Forest Decline)] started a controversy about whether:

- the observed loss of needles and discolouration was natural and would have occurred without the input of acids;
- the damage was triggered by organisms (plant pathogens);
- the damage was a direct response to pollutants;
- or a consequence of acidification of soils.

Schulze and Lange (1990) showed that the different paths leading to damage need not be exclusive, but become effective at different times during the course of the disease (Fig. 3.5.3).

Air pollutants are involved in each of these pathways of decline. The combination of soil acidification, N-dependent growth and ozone together with interaction of insect pests caused damage across Europe (Last and Watling 1991). The photographs at the beginning of Chapter 3.5 give an impression of the situation in forests in high elevations in the Fichtelgebirge, Germany, in 1989. However, after decreased SO$_2$ deposition and additional measures in forest management (liming, substantial clearing), the damaged areas were re-forested. Forest damage to spruce stands is, meanwhile, slightly decreasing but damage to deciduous trees is still increasing [see Waldscha-

denbericht 2003 (Report on Forest Damage 2003)].

It was necessary to initially examine the range of possible factors in order to identify the main causes:

- Primary pathogens could not be demonstrated, but there are several parasites and pathogens (bark beetles, stem rot) which attack weakened trees and, ultimately, cause their death.
- During the last century, high concentrations of pollutant gases in emissions from industries caused damage but the more recent damage symptoms were different. These new damage symptoms were related to tropospheric ozone, but the effect of ozone was shown to be very complicated. Plants react to it with changes in stomatal opening (see Chap. 1.9). Needles fumigated with ozone in one year only show increased sensitivity to ozone in the following year, and, only then, were they finally damaged.
- Acidification of soils causes root damage, particularly with release of Al. However, individual tree species react differently to Al; some of the Al reacts with phosphate in the mycorrhiza and is thus immobilised (Kottke and Oberwinkler 1986). Thus, soil acidification alone could not explain the observed damage.
- One type of forest damage, characterised by yellowing of needles caused by magnesium deficiency, could be explained as a consequence of pollutants at the ecosystem scale

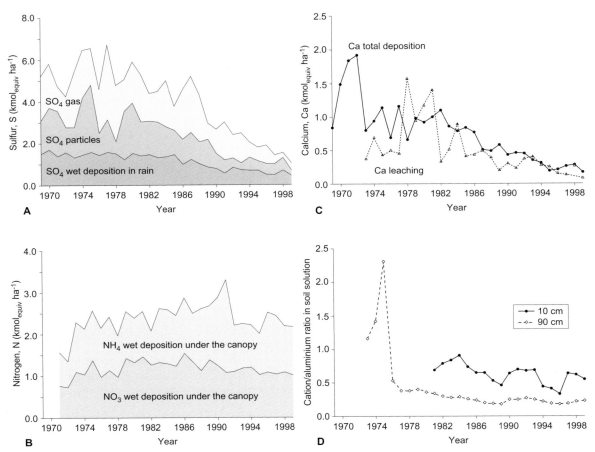

Fig. 3.5.4. Changes with time in deposition of A sulfur, B nitrogen, and C deposition of Ca, and leaching of Ca in the groundwater in a forest ecosystem in Solling, Germany (after Ulrich 1994). Deposition of Ca in dust fell at the beginning of the 1970s; S deposition remained high till the 1980s. Calcium leaching into the groundwater decreased with reduction in S deposition and therefore contributed significantly to the regeneration of forest ecosystems. D Changes with time of the base cations (K, Mg, Ca) to Al ratios in the soil solution. In the 1970s, the cation/Al ratio was >1 due to mobilisation of cations by acid rain. After about 1976, cations were exhausted up to a depth of 90 cm in a soil. The soil was then buffered by Al. Due to cation transport from roots at deeper layers to leaves, followed by leaf fall, the cation/Al ratio increased in the upper surface layer but, despite the small increase, there is still a tendency of a decrease (data: Lower Saxony Forest Institute)

(Schulze 1989). Soil acidification strongly reduced the availability of magnesium (and calcium). This is not only caused by the reduced base saturation of the soil exchanger occurring simultaneously with acidification, but also by competitive inhibition of Mg uptake by ammonium. In addition to ammonification, ammonium in the soil originates from atmospheric deposition, particularly from animal husbandry. Ammonium causes release of Mg from the exchangers in the soil and stimulates release of Al. Finally, Lange et al. (1989) proved, in a very elegant experiment, that the interaction with growth causes the deficiency. Buds were removed from opposite

lateral twigs on some spruce twigs or not removed on opposite twigs along the same branch. Only on that side with twigs of the branch where buds were not removed and where growth occurred was the damage observed (see Chap. 2.3). Obviously, growth of trees is significantly regulated by the N supply (Oren and Schulze 1989). Thus the uptake by the canopy of N from air-borne pollutants (in rain and dew) becomes particularly important, because this additional N supply is not balanced by cation uptake, but leads to increased growth and the observed yellowing. In the case of cation deficiency, growth is not regulated by availability of the limiting nutri-

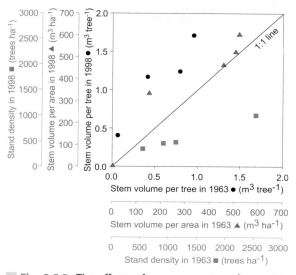

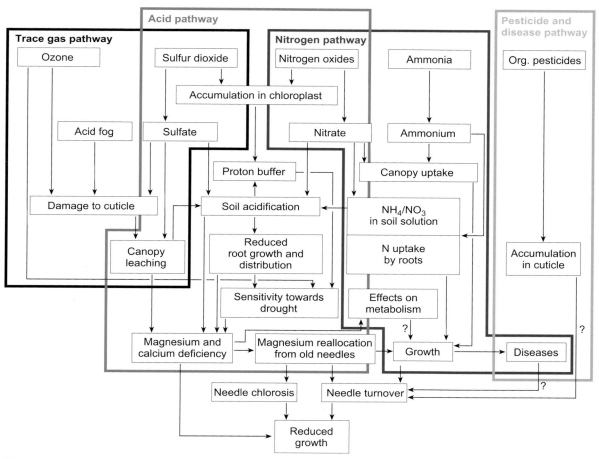

Fig. 3.5.5. The effects of management on forests. The figure shows that logging in the 1980s left free-standing single trees. With less S pollution and greater N the remaining individual trees grew faster. Despite fewer trunks and a smaller leaf area, the volume of growth per stand remained the same. (Mund et al., 2002)

ent (Marschner 1994). Some nutrients (particularly nitrogen) participate more in the growth process than others.

The model of a nitrogen–cation interaction with limited cation supply resulting from soil acidification observed in forest decline could also be related to other observed cation deficiencies, particularly K deficiency on bogs, Mn and Fe deficiency on limestone, and the rarer Ca deficiency.

With the decrease in SO_2 deposition resulting from regulations controlling emissions from large electric power plants, input of sulfur sank and thus the rate of soil acidification also (Fig. 3.5.4; Ulrich 1994). With reduced S and N input, loss of Ca decreased. This together with so-called compensation liming, which was supposed to balance the acid input, has resulted in partial recovery of soils with respect to base saturation.

Fig. 3.5.6. Schematic representation of the processes that lead to forest decline. (After Schulze and Lange 1990)

Heavy clearing reduced the density of trees in declining forests of the Fichtelgebirge (Germany) far below the recommended values of yield tables (Fig. 3.5.5). Thus, the cation supply per tree increased and, together with the high N deposition and with the higher light availability, growth of individual trees improved. Despite the reduced density of stands wood growth per area was eventually maintained.

Reducing the sulfur stress does not solve the problem of forest damage, as there is obviously more than one path of damage and complicated interactions occur between pollutants and organisms (Fig. 3.5.6; Schulze 1989). With the shift from S to N deposition other types of damage occurred, particularly to deciduous trees where insect damage increased. Tropospheric ozone concentrations are still damaging, particularly for herbaceous plants with high stomatal conductance (FBW 1989).

3.5.2

Effect of Deciduous and Coniferous Forests on Processes in Ecosystems

Forest damage started discussions in public and in forest science whether management of stands as monocultures, usually dominated by spruce, is sustainable, i.e. whether or not this management affects the productivity of a site with a turnover time of about 100 years over several generations, and whether the change from deciduous forests to coniferous forests, which was enforced by man, increased the damage observed, and whether reverting from coniferous forests to deciduous forests would avoid such damage in future.

Deciduous and coniferous forests differ with respect to several parameters, including:

- Differences in radiation and heat balance (Chap. 2.1; Schulze 1982);
- Differences in water relations (Chap. 2.2; Schulze 1982);
- Differences in growth (Chap. 2.4; Schulze 1982);
- Differences in the formation of humus (Mitscherlich 1975).

Heat Balance
Seasonal shedding of leaves in deciduous forests results in the energy exchanging surface being near the ground in winter and spring, but high in the canopy in summer (as with spruce; see Chap. 2.1, Fig. 2.1.9). Prior to leaf emergence in spring, temperatures in the litter rise rapidly and reach values far above the freezing point. This leads to activation of the species-rich ground vegetation (spring geophytes), which are important not only regarding the diversity of forests, but also for the storage of nutrients in the ecosystem because these herbaceous plants utilise nitrate that is formed in spring when tree roots are still inactive. In coniferous forests the permanent needle cover prevents light penetrating to the ground. Lack of light prevents the development of the spring flora. The soil remains cold, thus slowing down decomposition of litter. During the summer months, the climate for both types of trees is similar.

Water Relations
The greater needle and branch area of conifers compared with deciduous trees increases interception of precipitation by coniferous forests (Fig. 3.5.7; Schulze 1982). Transpiration for beech and spruce is approximately the same. Obviously, the increased needle area balances decreased stomatal conductance of conifers. It is the lower interception which leads to ca. 20% higher flow of water to the groundwater in deciduous forests than in coniferous forests. This is particularly important for the ecosystem service to supply water for human consumption. Areas acting as sources for water are therefore presently re-forested with deciduous forests or with herbaceous shrubs.

Carbon Balance
Conifers grow faster than deciduous trees in temperate climates because they start to assimilate earlier in the year and continue longer. This difference, however, is counterbalanced by the higher assimilation rates of deciduous trees. Conifers have an important additional advantage because only a fraction of their assimilating organs is exchanged every year, whilst deciduous trees renew the complete leaf mass. Also, in spruce, the ratio of twigs to stem mass is lower than for beech or oak (see Chap. 2.4.5.1). Thus, more assimilates remain for building stem wood. The increase in spruce is on average $10 \text{ m}^3 \text{ a}^{-1}$ compared with $5 \text{ m}^3 \text{ a}^{-1}$ for deciduous trees (Kramer 1988).

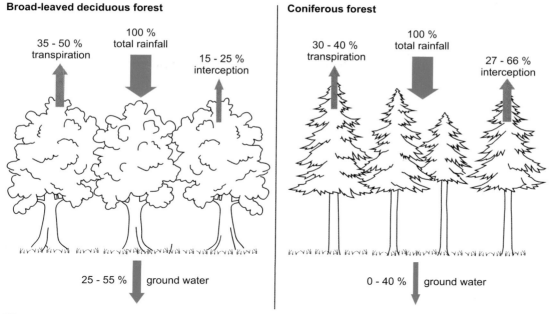

Broad-leaved deciduous forest

35 - 50 %
transpiration

100 %
total rainfall

15 - 25 %
interception

25 - 55 %   ground water

Coniferous forest

30 - 40 %
transpiration

100 %
total rainfall

27 - 66 %
interception

0 - 40 %   ground water

Fig. 3.5.7. Comparison of the hydrological balance of deciduous and coniferous forests (after Schulze 1982). Coniferous forests are drier than deciduous forests because of the increased evaporation from their wetter surfaces which depends on leaf area index

Nutrient Balance

Beech and spruce differ in their ability to utilise nitrate (Bauer et al. 2000). Coniferous trees have only a low nitrate reductase activity and thus take up ammonium predominantly, leading to nitrate leaching and increasing acidification in coniferous forests. Deciduous trees together with the more vigorous ground vegetation take up nitrate predominantly, so nitrate leaching is very low.

Formation of Humus

Underneath deciduous trees, the formation of raw humus is less than under coniferous trees, as the litter is more alkaline and richer in nutrients than in coniferous forests. The community of humus-decomposing organisms in the soil is thus more active and includes more species. The lower proportion of resins and other secondary metabolites makes decomposition easier, although deciduous trees as well as conifers contain specific materials that slow down decomposition (tannins in oaks, terpenes in conifers). Underneath deciduous forests, depending on cation availability, leaf mull or moder is formed with a larger cation-exchange capacity than in raw humus of conifers.

All these differences might be arguments for changing monocultures of spruce back into deciduous forests. However, at the moment (year

2004), deciduous forests are damaged more than coniferous forests by atmospheric pollutants.

Differences between deciduous and coniferous forests were studied on a transect between northern Sweden and central Italy, where conditions of the field sites were kept as constant as possible, i.e. beech and spruce grew on acid substrates in neighbouring stands (Schulze 2000). There were no conclusive differences in mineralisation and other soil parameters between deciduous and coniferous forests (Fig. 3.5.8; Schulze et al. 2000 a, b). Apparently, some of the differences which we have discussed so far were related to the fact that conifers, either planted or in natural stands, grow on sites which are more acid and nutrient poorer than sites on which deciduous trees grow. If conifers and deciduous trees grow on the same site under the same conditions, differences between tree types are lost.

Data from the European Transect show important features of ecosystems, particularly that production of litter increases with the supply of nutrients from mineralisation and deposition. In contrast, mineralisation compared with the supply of litter is too slow, i.e. the decomposition of litter over a larger area is disturbed. The imbalance increases with N deposition. This means that forest ecosystems in Europe accumulate carbon in the soil and this accumulation increases

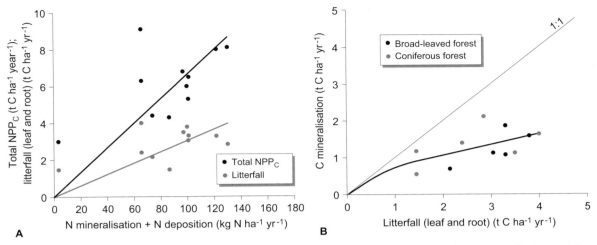

Fig. 3.5.8. The relationship between A growth (total NNP and litter) and N availability and B C mineralisation and litter availability in various deciduous and coniferous forests in Europe (Schulze et al. 2000a). It can be seen that growth is generally related to N availability. Saturation of growth with N availability is not noticeable. In contrast, mineralisation does not follow the availability of litter, i.e. at present there is an accumulation of C in the organic layer over large areas of Europe. It is still unclear which factors are controlling this imbalance between availability and use in soil

with N deposition. There are indications that this type of accumulation could provide easily decomposable carbon, i.e. forests could change into important carbon sources with climate change.

3.5.3
Plants of Limestone and Siliceous Rocks

It has been observed since a long time that the flora on limestone differs from that on siliceous rock. The change in flora is particularly obvious in the Alps, where so-called vicarious species, e.g. *Rhododendron hirsutum*, occurs on limestone, whereas *R. ferrugineum* is found on siliceous rocks. In general terms, differences in geology are related to differences in flora (Fig. 3.5.9). The question as to which factors cause these changes in flora can only be answered at the level of the ecosystem. Similarly to the change in the substrate, the following ecological conditions of the site alter:

- limestone sites are usually drier than siliceous sites, as the water from precipitation seeps rapidly into deep soil layers.
- limestone sites are warmer than siliceous sites because of the lower soil water content.
- limestone sites have a different soil chemistry than siliceous sites (limestone: deficient in Fe,

Fig. 3.5.9. View of a limestone ecosystem with dry meadow and deciduous forest supporting a large biodiversity (in the *foreground*), and a poor diversity of species in a coniferous forest on siliceous rocks (*background*) near the Franconian fault line close to the village of Zeyern (Upper Franconia, Germany). (Photo E.-D. Schulze)

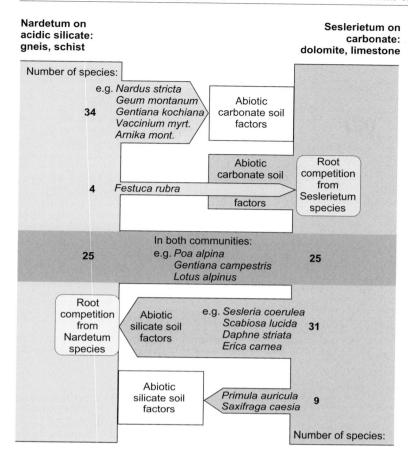

Fig. 3.5.10. Relationship between lime and silica vegetation of two alpine plant ecosystems, mat grass (*Nardus stricta*) and blue Sesleria (*Sesleria caerulea*). The number of species unable to invade the other's root space, either because of root competition or other abiotic factors, is shown. (Gigon 1987)

Box 3.5.1	Study of ecosystems

What can be learned from studies of ecosystems?

- Only at the scale of ecosystems can observations such as "forest decline" or long-term effects of management be understood.
- Forest decline is an excellent example of the interaction between soil and vegetation. Damage indicated by yellowing of foliage is a consequence of the stimulation of growth through N deposition and, at the same time, a decreased availability of cations in the soil due to acidification. Knowing this sequence of causal effects, remediation is possible.
- Deciduous and coniferous forests have different impacts on almost all ecosystem processes. Nevertheless, the turnovers in soils are quite similar and are more controlled by the soil chemical parameters of the base rock rather than by the tree cover.
- Differences between vegetation, such as they occur on chalky or silicate soils, can be seen clearly. They are controlled by a number of complex factors and not by a single parameter. Soil chemical and physical factors (dryness, warmth, availability of ions) and biological factors (such as competition), combined, lead to species that grow on chalk being unable to invade silica sites, and vice versa.

no Al; siliceous: deficient in Mo and alkaline cations but excess of Al).

- on limestone sites litter decomposition leads to mulch (mull) as the dominating form of humus, while siliceous sites are characterised by raw humus or moder.
- N mineralisation on limestone sites leads to nitrate as the dominating N form, whereas on siliceous sites it is ammonium.

The multitude of factors effecting a site show that there is not one single factor which explains the simple observation of a difference in vegetation. According to Gigon (1987), most siliceous plants do not grow on limestone because of the soil chemistry (Fig. 3.5.10). Conversely, competition in the root regions stops migration of limestone species onto siliceous sites, although they could grow there if there is no competition. Whilst 34 species of the mat grass meadows (Nardetum) are not able to colonise blue grass meadows (Seslerietum) because of abiotic factors, it is mainly competition by roots of the mat grass species that stops invasion by bluegrass species. Abiotic factors, on the other hand, only affect nine species.

References

Bauer GA, Persson H, Persson T, Mund M, Hein M, Kummetz E, Matteucci G, van Oene H, Scarascia-Mugnozza G, Schulze E-D (2000) Linking plant nutrition and ecosystem processes. Ecological studies, vol 142. Springer, Berlin Heidelberg New York, pp 63–98

Brady N, Weil R (2004) Elements of the nature and properties of soil, 2nd edn. Prentice-Hall, Englewood Cliffs

Chadwick OA, Derry LA, Vitousek PM, Huehert BJ, Hedin LO (1999) Changing resources of nutrients during four million years of ecosystem development. Nature 397:491–497

Ellenberg H (1978) Vegetation Mitteleuropas mit den Alpen. Ulmer, Stuttgart, 981 pp

Forschungsbeirat Waldschäden/Luftverunreinigungen FBW (1989) Dritter Bericht an die Bundesregierung. Forschungszentrum Karlsruhe, 611 pp

Gigon A (1987) A hierarchic approach in causal ecosystem analysis. The calcifuge-calcicole problem in alpine grasslands. Ecological studies, vol 61. Springer, Berlin Heidelberg New York, pp 228–244

Kottke I, Oberwinkler F (1986) Mycorrhiza of forest trees – structure and function. Trees 1:1–24

Kramer H (1988) Waldwachstumslehre. Parey, Hamburg, 374 pp

Lange OL, Weikert RM, Wedler M, Gebel J, Heber U (1989) Photosynthese und Nährstoffversorgung von Fichten aus einem Waldschadensgebiet auf basenarmem Untergrund. Allg Forstz 3:54–63

Last FT, Watling R (1991) Acid deposition, it's nature and impacts. Proc R Soc Edinb Sect 8, 97:343 pp

Marschner H (1994) Mineral nutrition of higher plants. Academic Press, London, 889 pp

Mitscherlich G (1975) Wald, Wachstum und Umwelt, 3. Bd: Boden, Luft und Produktion. Sauerländers Verlag, Frankfurt, 351 pp

Mooney HA, Medina E, Schindler DW, Schulze E-D, Walker BH (1991) Ecosystem experiments. SCOPE 45:268 pp

Mund M, Kummetz E, Hein M, Bauer GA, Schulze E-D (2002) Growth and carbon stocks of a spruce forest chronosequence in central Europe. Forest Ecology and Management 171:275–296

Oren R, Schulze E-D (1989) Nutritional disharmony and forest decline: a conceptual model. Ecological studies, vol 77. Springer, Berlin Heidelberg New York, pp 425–443

Schachtschabel P, Blume HP, Brümmer G, Hartge KH, Schwertmann U (1998) Lehrbuch der Bodenkunde. Enke, Stuttgart, 494 pp

Schulze E-D (1982) Plant life forms and their carbon, water and nutrient relations. Encycl Plant Physiol New Ser 128:615–676

Schulze E-D (1989) Air pollution and forest decline in a spruce (Picea abies) forest. Science 244:776–783

Schulze E-D (2000) Carbon and nutrient cycling in European forest ecosystems. Ecological studies, vol 142. Springer, Berlin Heidelberg New York, 498 pp

Schulze E-D, Heinmann M, Wirth C (2000a) Managing forests after Kyoto. Science 289:2058–2059

Schulze E-D, Högberg P, van Oene H, Persson T, Harrison AF, Read D, Kjöller A, Matteucci G (2000b) Interactions between the carbon and nitrogen cycle and the role of biodiversity: a synopsis of a study along a north-south transect through Europe. Ecological studies, vol 142. Springer, Berlin Heidelberg New York, pp 468–492

Schulze E-D, Lange OL (1990) Die Wirkungen von Luftverunreinigungen auf Waldökosysteme. Chem Unserer Zeit 24:117–130

Starr MR (1991) Soil formation and fertility along a 5000 year chronosequence. Geol Surv Finland, Spec Pap 9:99–104

Ulrich B (1987) Stability, elasticity, and resilience of terrestrial ecosystems with respect to matter balance. Ecological studies, vol 61. Springer, Berlin Heidelberg New York, pp 11–49

Ulrich B (1994) Nutrient and acid-base budget of central European forest ecosystems. In: Effects of acid rain on forest processes. Wiley-Liss, Chichester, pp 1–50

Waldschadensbericht 2003 Bundesministerium für Verbraucherschutz, Ernährung und Landwirtschaft: "Bericht über den Zustand des Waldes 2003 – Ergebnisse des förstlichen Unweltmonitorings", Bonn

Chapter 4

Syndynamics, Synchorology, Synecology

Small scale vegetation mosaic in the Afro-Alpine region of the Bale mountains (south-east Ethiopia) 3400 m above sea level with shrubby communities (*Erica arborea*), dwarf shrubby vegetation (different species of *Alchemilla* and *Helichrysum*) and individual giant lobelias (*Lobelia rhynchopetalum*) on the dry rocky slopes and also in the grassland communities and marshy depressions at the moist foot of the slopes. Photo K. Müller-Hohenstein

In this chapter a new level of organisation is discussed. Consideration of plant ecology, and thus the many aspects between autecology and research into ecosystems, necessarily requires **progression from the laboratory to natural conditions.** Subsequent to the study of individual plants or plant species under controlled conditions with predominantly experimental treatment, in this chapter, we build on the previous analysis of ecological systems (Chap. 3), which recognise the **spatial distribution and communities of plants,** including the description and understanding of the relative success of the individual plant (or species) in complex communities.

This goal is linked to synecological questions which have been formulated following the laws of Thienemann. Summarising for plants these state that no plant can exist on its own, only in **communities (biogeocenes)** in interactions comprising living plants and animals. These communities develop with a limited number of plant species and individuals in a limited space in certain temporal rhythms. It is assumed that it is possible to distinguish between **plant communities (phytocenoses).**

With the increasing complexity of processes to be considered comes a decreasing ability to make prognoses about development. Synecology is a science of observation, rather than experimentation, mainly because of the spatial as well as the temporal dimensions of the areas of distribution, and of processes to be considered. Synecological experiments are carried out by nature itself, including all anthropogenic influences, which increase the complexity considerably. The task is to recognise patterns in the experimental structure and to describe them, as well as to define the limiting conditions. However, the goal of synecology extends beyond mere description. Comparable to experiments under controlled conditions, explanations are sought; however, quantitative measurements are much more difficult to obtain. Thus, quantitative measurements slip into the background, whilst qualitative assessment gains importance.

In analysing ecosystems (Chap. 3), it became obvious that two aspects are connected with the step into field, conditions which so far have only been marginally addressed. Communities – and of course also plant communities – develop during the course of time and may display directed or cyclic dynamics. Their history and rhythms of development must be known in order to understand their actual structure. Here, the influences of human settlement and management are particularly important. **Historical-genetic aspects** of plant communities are discussed in **Chapter 4.1** as **syndynamics.** During their development over time, plants and plant communities conquered habitats and expanded into available space. The **basis of the spatial distribution** of plant communities is discussed in **Chapter 4.2** as **synchorology.** In **Chapter 4.3, synecology** and **biotic interactions** between plants and animals are considered on the basis of syndynamics and synchorology.

Because of the complexity, it is not possible to comprehensively describe synecology, only a selection of generalised knowledge of temporal dynamics and stability, of spatial expansion and diversity, as well as of competition and coexistence is presented.

As further literature the textbooks by

- Begon M, Harper JL, Townsend C (1999) Ecology, 3rd ed. Blackwell, Oxford
- Begon M, Mortimer M, Thompson D (1996) Population ecology. A unified study of animals and plants, 3rd ed. Blackwell, Oxford
- Chapin SF III, Matson PA, Mooney HA (2002) Principles of terrestrial ecosystem ecology. Springer, New York
- Crawley MJ (1997) Plant ecology, 2nd ed. Blackwell, Oxford
- Krebs JR, Davies NB (1997) Behavioural Ecology. An evolutionary approach, 4th ed. Blackwell, Oxford
- Odum EP (1971) Fundamentals of ecology, 3rd ed. Saunders, Philadelphia
- Remmert H (1980) Ecology: a textbook. Springer, Berlin Heidelberg New York

are recommended.

4.1

Historic-Genetic Development of Phytocenoses and Their Dynamics

The species-rich segetal flora in an annual crop of lentils and in a perennial crop of olive trees demonstrates the typical anthropogenic replacement of communities in an area of the European Mediterranean region which is still little influenced by herbicides. Photo K. Müller-Hohenstein

Recommended Literature

To understand the development of the plant cover on earth and provide detailed explanations on individual temporal periods, as well as on the general basic aspects of vegetation dynamics, the following books are recommended in addition to those mentioned at the beginning of Chapter 4:

- Burrows CJ (1990) Processes of vegetation change. Unwin, London
- Ellenberg H (1988) Vegetation ecology of central Europe, 4th ed. Cambridge Univ Press, Cambridge
- Graham LA (1993) Origin of land plants. Wiley, New York
- Lovett Doust J, Lovett Doust L (eds) (1988) Plant reproductive ecology. Patterns and strategies. Oxford Univ Press, Oxford
- Solomon AM, Shugart HH (eds) (1993) Vegetation dynamics and global change. Chapman & Hall, New York London

- Sukopp H, Hejny S (eds) (1990) Urban ecology. SPB Acad Publ, The Hague
- Thompson JN (1995) The coevolutionary process. Univ of Chicago Press, Chicago

Recent ecological interactions between living organisms and their environment are the basis of the present structure and distribution of vegetation. Thus, present-day conditions can only be understood on the basis of abiotic and biotic interactions, i.e. ecologically. However, the existence of species and communities may only be explained historically on the basis of knowledge of evolution and distribution.

Three important geological events have contributed significantly to the formation of present-day patterns of distribution:

- continuous **migration of the continents in relation to the poles** (Fig. 4.1.1, see also Table 4.1.1). According to measurements of palaeomagnetism, the magnetic North Pole in the Cambrium was in the Pacific, not far from

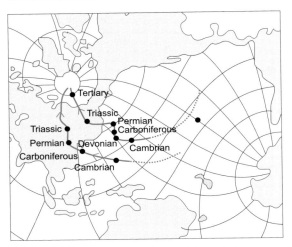

Fig. 4.1.1. Changes in the position of the magnetic North Pole during geological time (determined from palaeomagnetic measurements of North American (upper curve) and British (lower curve) rocks. (Kreeb 1983)

These events are linked to two influences directly affecting plants and their evolution. Firstly, climatic conditions have changed drastically, and secondly the possibility for expansion of plants by the opening or closing of land bridges or by the rise of mountain barriers was limited or enhanced. In this context events related to catastrophic **asteroid impacts** which greatly reduced biodiversity at the end of the Permian (Barbault and Sastrapradja 1995) and the Mesozoic should be mentioned.

In the recent past, the development of vegetation has been changed worldwide to a much greater extent and within a much shorter time span by the continuously growing **influence of human settlement and land use**. This shows clearly that palaeo-ecological links and historical development must be known to understand the present-day vegetation and its structure, composition and spatial distribution.

In the following, older periods of the history of life on earth, including selected aspects of the phylogeny and the coevolution of organisms (eophyticum, palaeophyticum, mesophyticum), will only be briefly outlined. The neophyticum will be discussed in more detail with two of its most important periods:

the Japanese island group, but in the Trias it was in north-east Asia.

- formation of continents arising from the **permanent changes in position of parts of the earth's crust** (Fig. 4.1.2). Despite controversy (plate tectonics) the theory of continental shift formulated by Wegener is valid and confirmed in its basic features.
- **solar effects** (different radiation conditions) arising from the composition of the atmosphere, and from the changing distances between earth and sun.

1. Late and postglacial development of vegetation. The links between climate and vegetation in the most recent geological past will be central.

2. Direct and indirect influence of humans on plant cover. These influences dominate partic-

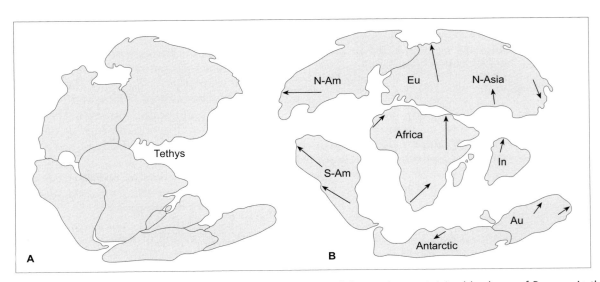

Fig. 4.1.2. Stages in development of the present distribution of the continents. A Joined landmass of Pangaea in the Triassic. B Distribution of continents at the end of the Cretaceous. (After Bick 1993)

Table 4.1.1. The putative evolution of life forms and ecosystems during the history of the earth. (After Kreeb 1983)

	Time in millions of years	Geological formation	Plant	Animal	Ecosystem type
Neophyticum (Angiosperm time)	0	Present	Agricultural techniques	*Homo faber*	Anthropogenic ecosystem disruption
	0.005	Holocene	Cultivated plants	Domestication of animals	Anthropogenic changes in ecosystems
	0.5	Pleistocene		*Homo sapiens*	All land ecosystems, deserts, halophytic communities, cold areas
	30	Tertiary	Deciduous trees	Freshwater fish, humanisation	
	95	Cretaceous	Angiosperms		
Mesophyticum (Gymnosperm time)	150	Jurassic	Pine trees, first flowering and seed plants	Early birds	Plant adaptation to different climate zones
	200	Triassic		Dinosaurs, early mammals	
Palaeophyticum (Pteridophyte time)	230	Permian			Species diversity decreases slightly
	280	Carboniferous	First tree-like ferns: Lycopods Calamites Horsetails Ferns	Reptiles and dinosaurs	Swamp forests (dry land not colonised)
	340	Devonian		Lung fish, amphibians, insects	First highly developed land ecosystems in moist places
	450	Silurian	First land plants: early ferns	First vertebrates	Simple ecosystems without consumers on land near coasts
Eophyticum (algal time)	500	Cambrian	Algae	All animal types except vertebrates	Higher developed aquatic ecosystems
	2000	Algoncium	Photosynthesis, respiration using oxygen		(Oxygen atmosphere) simple aquatic ecosystems
	3000	Archaean	First chemosynthetically active organisms		(Anaerobic aquatic ecosystems?) thermophilic organisms
	4000	Early ocean/early atmosphere	Start of biological evolution: first cells		(Oxygen-free environment) (Salt-free ocean?)

ularly in old, cultural landscapes developed by man and in regions of intensive agriculture and forestry.

The main focus of the following subchapters is Europe. More recent developments in other continents will be mentioned briefly. Problems of global change will be discussed comprehensively in Chapter 5.

4.1.1

History of Vegetation to the End of the Tertiary

In the **Precambrium** two large separate landmasses (first continents) had formed, each near the poles: in the northern hemisphere **Laurasia**, in the southern hemisphere **Gondwana** (Table 4.1.1). These two landmasses merged over time forming one large landmass, the **Pangaea**,

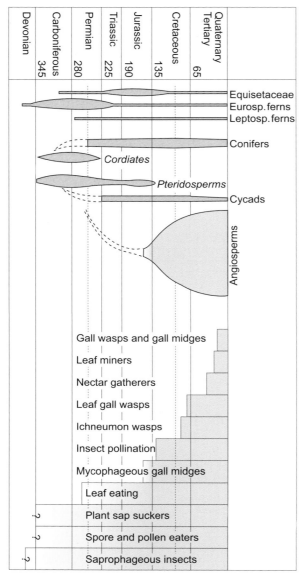

Fig. 4.1.3. Age and development of important groups of vascular plants, and of phyto- and entomophageous insects, as well as evidence of pollination and herbivory. (After Zwölfer 1978)

The most important developmental step occurred with the settling of the land at the change from the eophytic to the **palaeophytic** during the Silurian period. The first land plants possessed cells with large vacuoles, already had stomata and had developed supporting tissues. These autotrophic producers lived together with fungi and bacteria as decomposers and formed the first biocenoses.

Evolution of animal and plant species and communities progressed in parallel (see Table 4.1.1 and Fig. 4.1.3). Psilophytes (archetypal ferns) are regarded as precursors of the Pteridophyta (ferns and their allies), to which Filicinae (ferns proper), Equisitinae (horsetails) and Lycopodiniae (club mosses) belong. At that time Bryophyta (mosses) split off and remained at this developmental stage, but the other groups in the warm and humid climate of the **Carboniferous** formed luxurious forests with tree-like horsetails, club mosses and Cordiates, which later became extinct, on the swampy and boggy sites. Analyses of deposits of bituminous coal allow exact reconstruction of this very structured vegetation, including indications of symbiotic interactions (mycorrhiza) and the animal kingdom linked to it.

At the transition from the Carboniferous to the **Permian** climatic conditions became dryer. Many species did not survive and many land plants were unable to adapt their water relations. Thus the transition from the palaeophytic to the mesophytic is characterised by a decrease in species diversity. At the beginning of the **Triassic**, the Tethys Ocean separated off the eastern part of Pangaea (Fig. 4.1.2). During the **Jurassic**, the North Atlantic developed, and during the Cretaceous period the South Atlantic formed; in the early **Tertiary** the Antarctic and Australia seperated. The continents moved into their present position only in the **Pliocene**.

Up to the **Cretaceous** period the flora was very similar worldwide. The oceans forming between the drifting continents were no obstacles to the exchange of flora. The history of vegetation up to the **mesophytic** is also called the period of the gymnosperms. After the extinction of the larger club mosses and horsetails, gymnosperms gained space, particularly conifers and the Ginkgoaceae. The only present-day representative of the Ginkgoaceae is *Ginkgo biloba*, regarded as a "living fossil". In the northern regions the first representatives of the Pinaceae and the genus *Juniperus* have been found. Cu-

which remained until the Palaeozoic (about 220 million years ago; see Fig. 4.1.1) with changing positions towards poles and equator.

Traces of life and the first single-cell prokaryotes (bacteria, cyanobacteria) existed for about 3 billion years in an oxygen-poor atmosphere. Eukaryotes and multicellular forms could only develop with increasing oxygen content. This period, extending into the **Silurian** (about 400 million years ago), is called the **eophytic** (proterophytic) or the algal period.

pressaceae, as well as the genus *Araucaria*, which today is limited to the tropics of the southern hemisphere, occurred worldwide.

The boundary between the Jurassic and Cretaceous periods also divides the mesophytic from the neophytic and the period of gymnosperms from that of the angiosperms. The first angiosperms occurred at the end of the Jurassic period. In a relatively short period, 25 million years of the Cretaceous period, flowering plants developed very rapidly and suppressed many of the gymnosperms which had dominated until then. Almost at a stroke all main angiosperm groups developed; all available sites which could be occupied were filled with adapted species and the intercontinental flora exchange was still not too difficult. A much stronger floristic separation occurred during the upper Cretaceous period. The so-called **plant kingdoms** developed and – corresponding to the slightly earlier division in the south – distinction is made between the three floristic realms in the southern hemisphere (**Antarctic, Australis and Capensis**), two tropical equatorial floristic realms (**Neotropics and Palaeotropics**) and only one northern hemisphere floristic realm (**Holoarctic**).

Zwölfer (1978) has given an overview of the geological occurrence of vascular plants as well as phytophageous and entomophageous insects, and thus of the development of communities. There is proof that pollen and dead plant material were eaten as early as the Devonian period and in the Permian leaves were consumed. In the Triassic period insect pollination of flowers occurred and there were entomophageous parasites (ichneumon wasps) and plant galls. From the Tertiary period onwards all present-day phytophages are represented: herbivores, nectar collectors, leaf miners, gall flies and gall gnats. Figure 4.1.3 shows that development of phytophageous and entomophageous forms is geologically fairly recent and occurred at the same time as the development of angiosperms.

Mutual adaptations of floristic and faunistic partners is a consequence of the **selection pressure** linked to this development. Plants developed thorns, spines or chemical defence substances, animals responded with adaptive changes to their mouth parts or resistance against plant toxins. Some flowering plants were, however, particularly successful as they were able to protect themselves against herbivory; e.g. gentians (defence by indoalkaloids) or deadly nightshades (defence by tropanalkaloids). During this evolution, some insects used secondary plant metabolites for their own defence, e.g. against entomophagous enemies.

The most important groups of flowering plants were present at the beginning of the Tertiary period and, therefore, the period of the history of vegetation from then to the present day is called the **neophytic** or angiosperm period. Amongst the flowering plants, specialists adjusted to stress environments such as deserts and saline soils developed. Along with the formation of mountain ranges, in the northern hemisphere, including the central Asiatic and European Mediterranean mountains, young mountain floras developed (**oreophytes**, closely related to flora in plains). Often individual altitudinal steps are characterised by vicarious species and genera.

Holoartic flora has been found in Palaeozoic to Eocene lignite deposits in Spitzbergen, where not only remains of plants (e.g. *Acer, Betula, Fagus, Quercus, Salix, Tilia, Pinus* and *Picea*) growing today in central Europe under conditions of a temperate climate were found, but also those which now grow only in humid, subtropical conditions (e.g. *Taxodium, Magnolia, Liriodendron*), as well as species which survived in Ice Age refuges in North America and east Asia. Comparable plants (e.g. *Aesculus, Castanea, Plantanus, Vitis*) found in Greenland represent the so-called **arcto-tertiary flora**, the basis of the Holoarctic flora.

From the Eocene flora from southern England and the "flora from the Geiseltal" near Merseburg, Germany, plant lists were compiled containing families of plants (e.g. species of Annonaceae, Pandanaceae, Sterculiaceae) which now occur in seasonally moist tropical regions. At that time the vegetation in Europe was similar to that in mountain regions of Southeast Asia. Europe only took its current position during the Tertiary, evidenced by fossils from the early Tertiary (Miocene and Pliocene).

In plant remains of **Pliocene** in central Europe, tropical species could no longer be found, but representatives of present-day genera (*Fagus, Quercus, Salix, Fraxinus, Populus, Pinus*), and also species of genera which are at present extinct in this region (*Liriodendron, Sequoia*). Comparable fossils from north-east Asia and North America indicate **worldwide progressive cooling**. In Europe, climate and vegetation zones shifted to the south. The west-east extension of the Alps and the Mediterranean made it difficult for species adapted to a warm climate to survive; some got extinct, others were pushed into limited regions. The relative uniformity of the Pliocene flora in the Holoarctic was lost. Large distribution areas were separated into several spatially limited regions, the so-called **large Tertiary disjunctions** (e.g. *Sequoia* and *Metasequoia*, Magnoliaceae). For some species, e.g. of the genera *Styrax*, *Plantanus*, *Melia* and *Castanea*, the moist warm sites in the eastern Black Sea region (Colchis) became important refuges.

Development of Mediterranean sclerophyllic vegetation and the recent steppe, semi-desert and savannah flora is also often connected to the general cooling of global climate in the Tertiary period. Cooling in the Pliocene may be regarded as a precursor of the multiple quaternary climate changes in the most recent neophytic,

with lasting influence on the central European and American flora.

4.1.2

Change of Climate and Vegetation in the Pleistocene

The change from cold to warm periods is very important in central Europe. Temperatures continued to decrease in the Pleistocene and this decrease lasted about 2 million years, with periodically changing cold and warm periods up to present. Average annual temperatures decreased in central Europe by at least 8 and as much as 12 °C below present-day temperatures. In tropical regions they probably fell only about 6 °C.

Table 4.1.2. Vegetation and climatic elements of late- and postglacial time. Columns for time, pollination zone I–XII (from Overbeck 1975), vegetation period, climate history and prehistory of man. (Walter and Straka 1970)

Time	Zone	Vegetation period	Climate history		Prehistory of man
1000	XII	Forest plantations			
	Beech		Post-interglacial period (sub-Atlanticum) (relatively cool and moist)		Historical period
	XI				Iron Age
0		Beech – oak	Late interglacial period (sub-boreal) (warm and dry)		Bronze Age
–1000	X				
–2000					
–3000	IX	Mixed oak forest (oak, elm, lime, ash)			Late
			Middle interglacial period (Atlanticum) (warm and moist, climate optimum)	Postglacial	Middle Neolithic
–4000	VIII				
–5000					Early
–6000					
	VII	Hazel	Early interglacial (boreal) (warm and dry)		Mesolithic
–7000	VI	Hazel–pine			
–8000	V	Birch–pine	Pre-interglacial (increasing temperatures)		
	IV	Tree-poor tundra	Late sub-arctic period (return of cold)		
–9000	III	Birch–pine	Middle sub-arctic period (Alleröd) (temporarily warmer)	Late Ice Age	
–10000	II	Tree-poor tundra	Early sub-arctic period		Palaeolithic
–11000	I	Treeless tundra	Late arctic period (cold)	Main glaciation	
–12000					

Climatic variations in the Holocene are usually explained by periodic changes of solar radiation caused by alterations in the orbit of the rotational axis of the earth (Milankovitch theory, see also Chap. 5).

Direct and indirect consequences of **Quaternary climate variations** may be summarised as follows: On both hemispheres, starting from the polar regions, enormous inland ice masses up to 3000 m thick developed, reaching e.g. in Germany to some mountain ridges such as the Harz and the Weserbergland. Enormous glaciers also covered higher mountain ranges and during the maximum of the Alpine ice cover only few peaks rose on top of the ice cover (Nunataker). The glaciers extended far north into the foothills of mountainous regions, so that the ice-free space between the Alpine and Polar ice caps was in Europe hardly more than 300 km wide. However, at the same time, sea level sank to about 200 m below the present level (eustatic changes) so that movement of plants in the cold period became easier between landmasses currently separated by shelf oceans.

For Europe six cold periods are recognised with intermittent warm periods and short-term climate changes; the interstadial (e.g. Paudorf-Arcy) or deviations (e.g. Alleröd) are proven, whereby the terms for glacial advances are taken from the appropriate regional ice cap positions (Table 4.1.2). For a long time it was assumed that cold periods at higher latitudes corresponded to pluvial periods in dry regions at lower latitudes, but even here there are different opinions (Pachur 1987). In this context, terms are used for the **cold periods** which apply to the European glaciation of mountainous regions:

- **Biber and Danube ice age** in the early Pleistocene about 1 million years ago;
- **Günz and Mindel ice age** in the middle Pleistocene, about 250,000 years ago;
- **Riss ice age** about 230,000 to 120,000 years before the present;
- **Würm glaciation** (about 90,000 to 10,000 years before the present) in the late Pleistocene.

The increasing extinction of warmth-requiring tropical and subtropical species becomes obvious from Fig. 4.1.4, as well as the alternating dominance of woody species in the warm periods and herbaceous species and grasses in cold periods. Trees in particular disappeared locally or survived unfavourable periods in **refuges** of

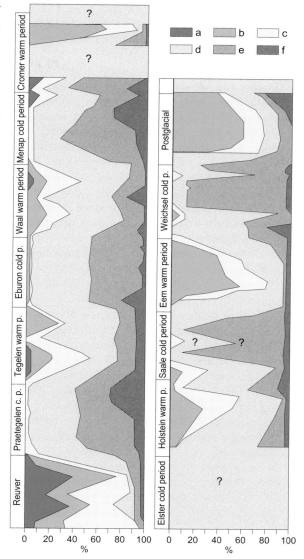

Fig. 4.1.4. Development of the vegetation in ice-free central Europe during the Quaternary. Simplified pollen diagram from the end of the Tertiary to the postglacial period with the percentage of *a* tree species of the Tertiary (e.g. of the genera *Sequoia, Taxodium, Liquidambar*; *b* thermophilic tree species (e.g. of the genera *Quercus, Castanea, Corylus*); *c* woody species of moist to wet sites (e.g. of the genera *Alnus, Carya, Vitus*); *d* conifers of different genera; *e* Ericales; *f* grasses and herbs. (After Frenzel 1968, from Strasburger and Sitte 1998)

southern latitudes. As herbaceous plants, grasses and low-growing dwarf shrubs expand faster because of their shorter time of regeneration, there are far fewer losses of such species than of trees. In North America no mountain barriers blocked the way for warmth-loving plants that wanted to move south. According to Ellenberg (1978), a comparison of North America and Europe shows about the same number of herbaceous species and grasses, but the ratio of herbaceous species and trees is 124 to 53, respectively.

Some thermophilic species were able to occupy refuges and survived to the present, but their original closed area was separated into several **disjunct areas.** A **disjunct distribution** is shown by *Rhododendron ponticum* with present-day occurrence in southwest Spain, in the Pontic region and in the Lebanon, or by cedars, with some species in the North African mountains, in the Taurus and in Lebanon. Present-day growth areas of **arcto-tertiary relics** played an important role as refuges for forests during cold periods.

During cold periods, only very few species successfully remained in mountains, surrounded by glaciers, on the Nunatakers rising out of the ice. These are mainly mosses and lichens but also some high Alpine flowering plants. The area expansion of some species towards the south, beyond the equator, is also attributed to the changed climate during cold periods. There are several migratory paths – the East African rift valley, the American Cordillieras and the bridge southeast Asia – New Guinea – Australia, where these plants found places to grow and even today they occur in **bipolar distribution regions.** Examples are the genera *Carex, Erica, Epilobium* and *Empetrum*.

Frenzel's map (1968) of the vegetation in Europe during the **peak of the Würm glaciation** (Fig. 4.1.5) shows the shift of vegetation zones towards the south, compared to the present day. Island-like remains of oceanic summer green Mediterranean deciduous mixed forests occurred on Mediterranean islands. The Mediterranean sclerophyllic vegetation was limited to the present arid area of North Africa. Large parts of the Iberian and Balkan peninsulas were covered by forest steppes. The regions of central Europe between the edges of the ice sheet were almost tree free.

The vegetation of tundras and cold steppes of that time was reconstructed from plant remains deposited in lakes. The indicator plant of this flora is the arctic alpine *Dryas octopetala* which is now found on the species-rich grassland that occurs on limestone with a very shallow soil. This plant occurs together with species which occupy similar sites, e.g. *Polygonum viviparum, Silene acaulis, Oxyria digyna, Tofieldia calyculata*, as well as numerous mosses and dwarf and espalier shrubs such as *Loiseleuria procumbens,*

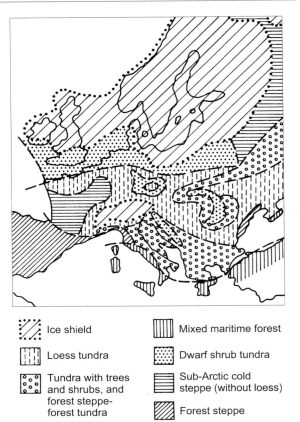

Ice shield

Loess tundra

Tundra with trees and shrubs, and forest steppe-forest tundra

Mixed maritime forest

Dwarf shrub tundra

Sub-Arctic cold steppe (without loess)

Forest steppe

Fig. 4.1.5. Distribution of vegetation types in Europe during the time of maximal glaciation in the Würm glacial period. (After Frenzel 1968, from Kreeb 1983)

Salix herbacea, Empetrum nigrum and *Betula nana*. At locations further away from the edges of the ice sheets in eastern Europe, under continental climatic conditions, the cold steppe expanded with a rich herbaceous flora with *Artemisia, Centaurea, Ephedra* and *Chenopodium* species as well as numerous Cyperaceae and Poaceae of the genera *Stipa, Festuca, Poa* and *Agropyron*.

During the warm periods, separated by cold periods, an **interglacial vegetation** developed, similar to the postglacial vegetation discussed in Chapter 4.1.3. In the interglacial period a mixed forest of lime trees, elms, alder, oak and hornbeam established. This forest developed gradually from a forest in which spruce and birch dominated, and which again dominated before the onset of the Würm glaciation.

4.1.3

Late and Postglacial Climate and Vegetation History

The discussion of the history of vegetation so far has shown two points:

- the enormous development of species taking place dependent on astronomical, tectonic and climatic events as well as on the communities in bioscenoses.
- a distinct spatial separation of the large parts of the earth's crust occurred. The formation of young mountains is almost finished. Now developments over smaller areas are started in which regional floristic, and environmental characteristics of the site play a decisive role.

The history of climate and vegetation during the Holocene in Europe has long been documented in its basic features, particularly because the availability of new methods such as **pollen analysis** and **radiocarbon dating** provided supplementary research tools. Almost all plant species found have survived to the present day.

A noticeable warming of the climate occurred about 20,000 years ago, with the retreat of glaciers into the mountains and to the north allowing warmth-demanding plants, particularly trees, to move back into the area of central Europe occupied by dwarf shrub communities and cold steppes. This did not occur continuously or from the same refuges. Climatic variations also occurred in the late and postglacial periods. They can be easily observed from the position

of the timber line in the last 20,000 years, which was probably about 1200 m or even 1600 m lower in the Apennine in the last cold period compared with the present. The course of the line shows that a rapid increase in the **Alleröd period** in the middle-late glacial was abruptly interrupted before the timber line reached its present position. This happened in the postglacial **boreal**. In the following **Atlantic period** about 6000 years ago the timberline in the Alps was about 400 m higher than today. The situation in the mountains of central Germany was similar and in Scandinavia the timberline was lower. However the forest area extended far into the present-day tundras (Fig. 4.1.6).

The movement of the most important tree species back to the earlier positions was reconstructed by comparison of pollen profiles, so-called **iso-pollen maps**, and occurred in different ways and at different periods, where the requirements of species for the site, the speed of migration and the position of the cold period refuges are important.

Spruce came from an easterly direction, following the "northern path" from the Urals, south of the present-day northern coasts and along northern borders of the central European mountain chain and the northern borders of the Alps. Figure 4.1.7 shows the temporal sequence of the expansion of spruce along the edges of the Alps. Fir trees, and also almost all deciduous trees (beech), originated from the Mediterranean areas and reached central Europe via the Burgundian Gate or the Pannonian Basin.

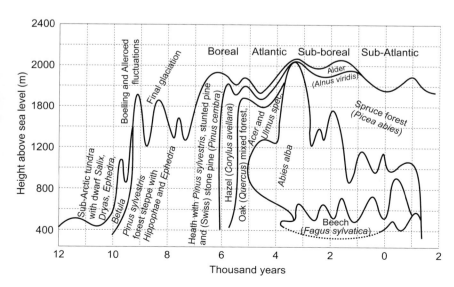

Fig. 4.1.6. Development of altitudinal zones of vegetation in the northern Swiss Alps since the maximum of the Würm glaciation. (Strasburger and Sitte 1998)

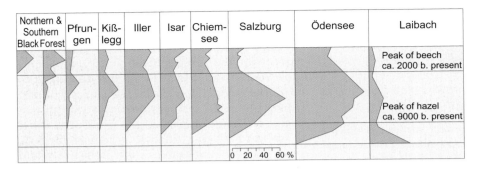

Fig. 4.1.7. Migration of spruce (*Picea abies*) in postglacial times along the margins of the Alps. (After Walter 1986)

Data from pollen analyses, based on the evaluation and comparison of many pollen diagrams, allows the late and postglacial history of vegetation to be divided into several sections (Figs. 4.1.8 and 4.1.9A,B).

In the **oldest tundra period**, also called the Dryas period after the indicator species *Dryas octopetala*, a continental steppe vegetation predominated with scattered tree-free tundra islands. In the following warmer **Alleröd** epoch, sparse spruce and birch forests and willow shrubs were able to exist, but these species receded again about 1000 years later. The steppes advanced from the east under the still extremely continental conditions. Only in the early **warm period** (preboreal and boreal) was the temperate forest able to extend again because conditions were no longer so cold in winter; birch was replaced by hazel and other deciduous trees (first oak and elm, followed by lime and ash). Man in the middle Stone Age about 8000 years ago was surrounded by species rich forest communities dominantly hazel. Residues of tundra occupied the increasingly melting edges of the ice sheet, and steppes were pushed towards the southeast.

The warmest climatic conditions, and the corresponding development of vegetation, were experienced by Neolithic Man in the **middle warm**

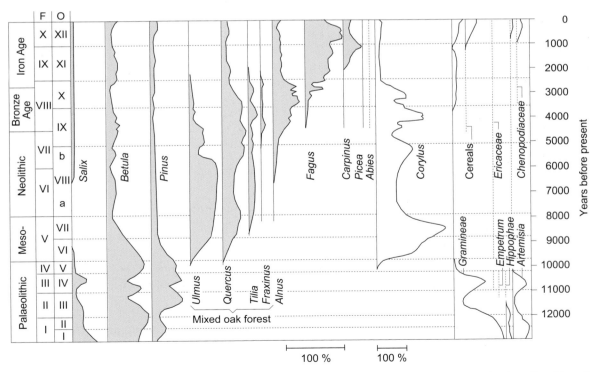

Fig. 4.1.8. Pollen diagram from the Luttersee (Göttingen, northern Germany, 160 m above sea level, a.s.l.), with pollen zones according to Firbas (F) and Overbeck (O) (after Walter 1986). Scale: sum of tree pollen 100%, without hazel (*Corylus*)

Fig. 4.1.9. A Part of the almost natural "Pillermoor" (1600 m a.s.l.) which is a protected area in the lower Pitztal (Tyrol) and B part of the same raised bog where peat was removed more than 30 years before. Pollen analysis from this bog shows the postglacial development of vegetation of the montane region in the Tyrol. (Photos K. Müller-Hohenstein)

period (Atlantic period) about 6000 to 7000 years ago. In northern Europe, mean annual temperatures, with oceanic conditions during this time of the "**climatic optimum**", were 2–3 °C higher than present temperatures. Mixed oak forests with deciduous trees requiring good climatic and edaphic conditions and few beech trees were dominant. In the montane areas, fir dominated in the western Alps, spruce in the eastern Alps and pines in the eastern part of central Europe on nutrient-poor sites. Only on particularly dry sites did steppe vegetation still occur with thermophilic species.

Glacial relics from the cold periods are still maintained in present-day vegetation as islands, e.g. *Betula nana* in the foothills of the Alps or *Aster alpinus* and *Pulsatilla alpina* in the Harz mountains in Germany in tree-free, particularly cold sites (edges of bogs); similarly, species from the warmest periods were also able to hold their own. These **xerotherm relics**, submediterranean species (*Quercus pubescens, Helianthemum nummularium*) or types from the south Siberian and Pontic area (*Stipa div. spec, Adonis vernalis, Linum flavum*) were able to survive after the onset of cooling in the subboreal forest, on sites hostile to growth of trees (extremely shallow sites exposed to the south) and were able to expand again onto anthropogenic tree-free areas (meadows on soils derived from limestone that are

shallow, where the site is dry and comparatively warm, but nevertheless rich in species).

Beech only became dominant in the forests of central Europe in the **late warm period** and took over the role of hornbeam which dominated in the interglacial period and was now predominant further to the east. Beech forms, together with spruce and fir, the montane forests up to the montane belt. Even though beech has only been dominating the forests of central Europe for 30 to 50 tree generations, distinct forest communities were formed everywhere until humans intervened (Ellenberg 1978).

Species which required higher temperatures for their development migrated back into warmer parts and outcompeted the cold period vegetation, except for a few relict species. Their expansion partly followed the edges of the ice sheet and thus many closed areas became divided and **disjunctions** were formed. Some are concentrated on the southern European mountains (e.g. species of the genera *Primula, Saxifraga, Gentiana*), others form the arcto-alpine disjunctions with interspersed occurrence on the highest parts of the mountains of central Germany (e.g. *Nigritella nigra coll., Gnaphalium supinum*). Disjunctly distributed, also including the North American region, are *Betula nana, Salix herbacea, Dryas octopetala* and the circumpolar *Loiseleuria procumbens* and *Eriophorum scheuchzeri*.

Only in recent decades precise dates of the history and climate of the African dry areas have been collected (Pachur 1987). According to these findings, the long-established views of a synchronous sequence of cold and warm periods in moderate latitudes and humid (pluvial) and dry periods in present dry areas must be corrected. During the last cold period (evidence for a period of ca. 20,000 years before the present day), an even shift to the south must be assumed. The Sahara could have been "green" and rain forest regions became narrower, at least from the north (Lauer and Frankenberg 1979). Mountains in the Sahara possessed a strongly Mediterranean vegetation similar to that in the later humid period during the climate optimum. Pachur (1987) speaks of a semiarid climate in the east African region.

During the climate optimum, with semiarid conditions and summer rain in the south and winter rain in the north, the Sahara was reduced to a small region from both sides. Neumann (1988) assumes on the basis of charcoal analyses that the Sahelian vegetation with species such as *Balanites aegyptiaca*, *Acacia albida* and *Cadaba farinosa* established up to 600 km further north in sparse dry woodlands. The southwest shift of Mediterranean influences is regarded as far smaller. After the moister conditions around 8000 years ago, Neolithic Man in the Sahara experienced increasing drought from 5000 years ago until now (Fig. 4.1.10 A–C). The tropical savannah reached its actual position again 3300 years ago. The rock relief of "crying cows" of Terarart in front of a former drinking place near Djanet in southern Algeria is taken as a symbol of this drying. For the Sahara, even today, two relatively stable and interchanging vegetational states are assumed, a "green" Sahara and a "red" Sahara, which is bare of vegetation (Claussen 2001).

Quaternary climate change was also effective in the tropics of South America. In areas near the equator the forest line fell in the high glacial period and rose again in the postglacial optimum. At the edges of the tropics a horizontal shift of vegetation limits occurred (Lauer 1986).

Fig. 4.1.10. A, B and C Rock paintings and engravings indicate that there were once more humid climatic conditions in the central Saharan mountains. Pictures of hunters (A) and large grazing herds (B) near Sefar (Tassili), southern Algeria, are nearly 8000 years old. The "crying cows from Terarart" (C) near Djanet are about 5000 years old and indicate the gradual increase in aridity. (Photos K. Müller-Hohenstein)

In the tropical lowlands of South America the expanded moist forests shrank in the high glacial period and allowed a stronger floral and faunal exchange between the dry area taxa than was previously possible. Moist forest areas became more isolated. After the favourable conditions of the climate optimum the timber line fell again, however very quickly because of human influence. Small *Polylepsis* stands are witness to this; today they are found far above the actual tree limit. In lowlands, moist forests expanded initially. The long uninterrupted period of development assumed in the history of rain forests cannot be confirmed for the Neotropis. Because of increasing drought in the late Holocene and again through human intervention, areas of most forests have decreased considerably.

4.1.4

Changes in Vegetation Because of Human Influence

Present-day global distribution of vegetation can only be understood by considering human influences affecting the plant cover for thousands of years. Nowadays, in central Europe, no plant communities exist which are not influenced by humans. It would potentially be possible to have forests everywhere, except for a few sites above the timberline in high mountains, on coasts or in extremely moist areas. The present vegetation is the result of a long interaction between the requirements of humans in different cultural situations and resources which offered natural landscapes (Deil 1997).

4.1.4.1
Forms of Human Influence on Vegetation

Human activity has always had effects on vegetation, as humans are directly or indirectly dependent on plants for nutrition, energy and raw materials. This influence was fairly small initially and was restricted to the search for food. Over time the influence increased with the increase in population and changing technologies (Ellenberg 1996). The mosaic of anthropogenic plant communities became more colourful, corresponding to the **type, duration, intensity and extent of human influence**. Gathering, hunting,

wood cutting, grazing and clearing led to specific **replacement communities** (Müller-Hohenstein 1973). Soon coppiced forests, managed meadows and other, previously unknown, vegetational units arose (Box 4.1.1).

The human influence on forests was initially fairly small, but extended over large areas. With increasing industrialisation and with the formation of urban settlements, industrial areas, and refuse dumps, human influence on small areas became more intense (Sukopp and Wittig 1998). Since industrialisation not only the influence of supplying resources, but also of management of anthropogenic waste products has become increasingly noticeable. Whilst once the working of the soil or watering and draining changed sites locally, it is now also pollutants and the effects of fertilisation that have increased man's effect on vegetation.

For the vegetation of our arable landscapes not only ecophysiological rules of regulation by temperature, light, water, and nutrients apply, but also effects of pollutants, pesticides and fertilisers must be considered.

4.1.4.2
From the Neolithic to Mass Migration

For a long time the **effect of prehistoric man** on the cover of vegetation was underestimated. Too much trust was put in the reports of Roman writers describing Germania as an impenetrable forest area. Today it is possible to prove human activity for the periods in which, during postglacial times, the edges of the ice sheet retreated and woodland species immigrated. These activities were at first restricted to **hunting** and **gathering of fruits**. The transition to agriculture occurred in Europe only during the Neolithic about 5000 years ago, a transition that is decisive for the dynamics of vegetation.

Wissmann (1957) regards the area around the Gulf of Bengal and the northern savannah landscapes of India as the oldest centres of **agriculture**. At first rural cultures with agriculture and animal husbandry extended slowly, via Iran, into Mesopotamia, for a long time thought to be the cradle of agriculture, where technical progress was made with irrigation. From this region of the "fertile crescent" agriculture and animal husbandry reached central Europe via the Mediterranean region. The important steps in cultural development away from pure gathering to using

| Box 4.1.1 | Typical methods of forest and agricultural management |

Forestry

Coppice (Niederwald): In the Middle Ages, such forests were used to obtain oak bark for tanning and firewood (see Fig. 4.1.12 D). The whole forest was used in 30-year cycles and regenerated from the coppiced trees (coppicing). Thus species that could regenerate were selected for (e.g. hazel, oak, hornbeam). Today, in many developing countries, afforestation (e.g. with *Eucalyptus* species) is used as coppiced forest.

Mittelwald: A form of management in the Middle Ages (Fig. 4.1.12 C) in combination with agriculture. Few tree individuals (mainly oak) were grown to supply timber for construction and more tree individuals being used as coppice for firewood in a 30-year cycle. Valuable oak for veneers comes today often from these forests (still widely distributed in France). Earlier in these forests births and marriages were celebrated by planting 5–10 year old trees grown from seed. Thus an open canopy of unequally aged canopy trees was maintained and a sustainable supply of timber for use in construction was ensured.

Hochwald: This consists of trees which had grown from seed (in contrast to regrowth from coppiced trees in low forest; Fig. 4.1.12 B). The stand of trees was completely managed. Use was by (1) **clear felling:** All trees on an area were felled at the same time, (2) **partial felling (umbrella felling):** Some of the trees remained, as protection and for seed production, distributed uniformly over the area. Regeneration then occurred "under an umbrella". The use of the protective trees then proceeded either after successful regeneration (beech) or after twice the normal cycle of use (pine, oak). Thus some of the trees were twice as old as the average age of the stand. For oak, which becomes most valuable after more than 300 years, the space between the trunks was filled with some tree generations of beech in order to minimise growth of shoots from dormant buds. (3) **Selective thinning and shelter wood selection:** Such thinning resulted in production of stands which were not of uniform age; only some of the trees were removed according to their size

and usefulness and the distribution of the diameters of the trunks left standing remained constant. Regeneration in selectively thinned forests took place where the individual trees were removed. In sheltered woods regeneration occurred on areas where groups of trees had been harvested. Because of the difference in light and size of the regeneration area a species-rich and multi-storey, economically but sustainable exploited forest cover resulted.

ARD: Afforestation, reforestation and deforestation attained particular significance in the Kyoto Protocol (see Chap. 5). **Deforestation** refers to changing forest into other forms of land use (e.g. roads), **reforestation** is establishment of forests on areas which had been forests earlier (e.g. planting of forests on valley meadows), **afforestation** means establishment of forests on land which had not been forested earlier (e.g. forests on moorlands). **Revegetation** is the re-establishment of forests on areas which had been free of vegetation (e.g. slag heaps). **Degradation** is use of wood in excess of growth, that is the number of individual trees clearly falls below the limit set by self-thinning and density of the stand which would have occurred with maximal growth. The current definition of a forest (10–30% cover, 2–4 m high) allows degradation to these limiting values before **conversion** (e.g. from primary to secondary forest or to plantations). **Harvests** are currently classified not as emissions in the calculations, as it is linked to regeneration of stands in normal forest management.

Agriculture

Economically productive grasslands: This term refers to areas of grass, used for production of hay or for grazing. In Germany these grasslands occur mainly on heavier (clay) soils which are difficult to plough in spring, or on areas where the growing period for cereals is too short (mountain meadows). The species richness of such grasslands depends strongly on the intensity with which they are used (number of mowings, fertilisation, etc.; Ellenberg 1996).

Box 4.1.1	Typical methods of forest and agricultural management (continued)

Arable farming: Distinction is made (Swift and Anderson 1993) according to:

- **Type of soil manipulation:** ploughing, disc harrowing. With the latter a breakdown of organic matter in soil is reduced. With low tillage, seed is sown in the furrows made by the disc harrow. This method decreases the compaction of soils and leads to deeper rooting, which may increase yields in semi-arid regions. With zero tillage there is no soil manipulation.
- **Type of crop: root crops** (potatoes, beet) and **cereals.** Earlier agriculture employed intensive soil manipulation ("Hackfrucht" in German = crops that required hoeing, e.g. potatoes) and thinning after sowing as a means of controlling weeds and crop density. Today, hoeing is no longer essential as weeds are controlled chemically with herbicides and the number of plants is regulated by machine. In cereal cultivation distinction is drawn between **winter cereals** which are sown in autumn (e.g. winter wheat) and **spring cereals** (barley, rye, oats and spring wheat) which are sown in spring. Spring cereals have smaller yields but avoid the risk of frost damage in winter. Particular types of crops are those grown for **oil seed** (rape: sown in autumn, sunflower; sown in spring) and **maize**, sown in late spring after frost in May because this C4 plant requires warm temperatures for growth. Cultivation of oil seeds and maize in central Europe has increased in importance considerably in the last decades.

Rain-fed agriculture occurs in dry areas (Fig. 4.1.24 B): In the first year fields are ploughed but not sown (fallow land). Precipitation is stored in the soil after rain and the soil surface is often harrowed in order to decrease evaporation from the soil and the capillary rise of water from deep in the soil to the surface. In the second year the field is sown, so the crop benefits from the 2 years of stored rainfall available.

Shifting cultivation: This type of agriculture is dominant in tropical regions (Fig. 4.1.28 A–C): smaller areas of forest are cleared and burnt in order to make nutrients available for the cultivation, e.g. of rice, manioc, banana, etc., for a number of years.

After a period of time, the nutrient availability is exhausted by the continuous harvesting and the area is abandoned and a new area is cleared for use. Depending on the duration of this cycle, secondary forests can establish on the abandoned areas. With very rapid rotation, degradation occurs because the fallow period is inadequate for the accumulation of nutrients in soils and vegetation. A number of crops (e.g. pepper) require intensive poisoning of the soil in order to control root pests and diseases so that any succession on the fallow areas is prevented. Frequent rotations prevent establishment of forests. Grass species (e.g. *Imperata cylindrica*) invade; these are not eaten by animals because of their large Si content and must be controlled by fire. Consequently, there is a transition from species-rich forest to monotonous grasslands (see also Fig. 4.1.34).

Agroforestry (predominantly in the tropics) describes economic use in which forest regeneration and timber production (for fodder and fire wood, respectively) are linked with field crop production in space and time. There is also another meaning of agroforestry, with mixed cultivation in which the growth of woody plants for firewood and fodder and short-term crops occurs only within the limits of the field or land owned by the farmer.

Multiple cropping (mainly in the moist tropics and oases of the Sahara): in this case (Fig. 4.1.35 B) there is a permanent layer of fruit trees (mango, coconut) above useful shrubs (herbs, banana) which in turn cover herbaceous crops (ginger, taro, manioc).

many techniques to grow crops were taken far away from Europe.

Neolithic agriculture in southern-central Europe started about 7000 years ago, but in the northern region only about 5500 years ago mainly in areas where it was possible because of climatic and edaphic characteristics (dry warm, nutrient-poor sites) as present in sparse mixed oak forests. Areas were cleared without particular tools by fire, particularly in river valleys and on the fertile loess soils bordering the central European mountain regions. These enormous loess deposits also occurred in the Rhine, Moselle and Nahe Valleys and the dry inner Alpine valleys.

Gradmann (1933) was the first to point to the close relation between vegetation, occupation and development of managed landscapes in his **"Steppenheidetheorie"** (**steppe heathland theory**). He assumed that thermophilic, often xerophytic, species of Mediterranean origin indicated the preferred early sites of settlement. Ellenberg (1954) argued against this theory, because the typical "steppe heathland species" were missing in the North. Rather Ellenberg developed the **"Waldweidetheorie"** (**forest grazing theory**) according to which Neolithic man had to win his agricultural land from sparse, easily clearable forest where forest grazing made regeneration difficult and attributes the formation of such xerothermic vegetational units to zoochoric expansion. Today, it is assumed that plant communities limited to these dry warm sites are relics from the postglacial period (Pott 1996). Pontic-Pannonic as well as Mediterranean geoelements were able to penetrate to central and north Europe via the open spaces at that time. With the change from Mesolithic to Neolithic non-tree pollen increased, including pollen of light-demanding species, such as cereals, and of segetal and ruderal species such as *Centaurea cyanus*, *Vicia cracca*, *Plantago lanceolata* and *Artemisia vulgaris*.

The type of land use in the Neolithic is described as „**unregulated forest-field management**"; after clearing, agriculture was practised for a few years then the area was left fallow for a long period. Regulated rotation with sowing, grazing and use of wood in certain restricted periods on an area was only developed in the Bronze and Iron Ages (about 1700 b.c.), when sickles and iron ploughs replaced the old wooden hook plough. In Germany the "Hauberge" in the Siegerland and the "Birkenberge" in the

Bavarian Forest are relics of land use by such a **rotation**.

Crops grown were wheat, emmer, einkorn and spelt. Regionally, buckwheat was important and later barley and rye. Grazing in the forest with cattle and pigs played always a role and the use of wood for building and burning also influenced forests. The first **"Niederwälder"** (**coppiced forests**) were developed in the Bronze Age. Wood was used for charcoal kilns and smelting of iron ore, as well as oak coppicing, long before the birth of Christ. Hedges developed along the rows of collected stones (Reif 1987). Species-rich edges of forests, nutrient-poor meadows and dwarf shrub heathland were to expand while regeneration of grazed forest areas was endangered. Very early forest degradation occurred and scrub with species possessing defensive thorns developed. Many deciduous trees were lopped to provide animal fodder for the winter.

Thus, natural vegetation was not only considerably changed on arable fields and replaced by crop plants and their accompanying vegetation, but also changed in structure and species composition and in large areas around settlements by grazing, trampling, tree felling and other uses of trees and other vegetation for fodder. Major effects, such as soil erosion, cannot be excluded.

4.1.4.3
Medieval Forest Clearing

The period between the end of the period of mass human **migration** (about 600 A.D.) and the beginning of modern times (since 1500) is characterised in central Europe by several **periods of clearing** and may be called the time of pre-industrial extensive management.

The German terms "Niederwälder", "Hochwälder" and "Mittelwälder" are used to describe types of forest management. "Niederwälder" are forests where the trees are harvested (after approx. 30 years in Germany, Eucalpytus in Morocco every 12 years) and then they regrow from the still existing (and producing) roots. This is only possible for broadleaved trees. This special management was widespread in central Europe and in the Mediterranean. Common species for this type were oak, beech, and hornbeam. "Hochwälder" are forests where the trees are planted and harvested as single trees (mainly for timber) after 100 or more years. These trees may be conifers. After harvesting, they must be replanted. "Mittelwälder" are a mixture of both types of management, which can still be found in France today. Here, the "Niederwald" part is used today for firewood and the "Hochwald" for timber.

After forests expanded during the period of mass migration, systematic clearing of forests started in the early Middle Ages (900 A.D.) caused by population pressure. The clearing was by both the secular and religious bodies which owned the land, in southern Germany particularly the Franconian kings and monasteries. The aim was to gain new areas for agriculture, whilst forests were degraded by grazing animals and also by the increased requirement for wood. Wood was the only energy source before the opening of coal deposits, and was used in small smelters and by blacksmithies as well as for salt making and glass production domestically.

In central Europe the first major clearing period was from the sixth to the ninth century. During this time, most forests were cleared, even those not suitable for agriculture and also sometimes the protected forest reserves for hunting. Most forests were used for **forest grazing**. The old settlement areas, with village names ending in -*ingen*, -*heim*, -*hausen*, were founded at that time. In the second clearing period from the eleventh to the thirteenth century the area of the central European mountains was included in the land acquisition. Many village names of this younger settlement period end in -*ried*, -*reuth*, -*rode*, and -*schlag*.

The **relation of forest to open land** at the end of this period was about 70:30, despite Neolithic and Roman settlements, but in the thirteenth century it was reversed and had thus reached a state that applies to many landscapes in central Europe even today. Almost natural forests only existed in locations unfavourable for agriculture. Towards the end of the Middle Ages periods of social breakdown led to a slight increase in forest areas (Ellenberg 1996). The first forest regulations of the sixteenth century introduced protection for and limitation on uses. Regionally, as early as the twelfth century, grazing of goats in forests was forbidden, as they eat woody species.

Forest areas had not only decreased drastically, but the remaining forests were structurally and floristically changed. To safeguard the energy requirements and to consciously save areas of forests for grazing, coppiced forests (which had existed in the Iron Age) were managed. Oak and hornbean were particularly suited to this kind of forest management, as they regenerate easily. Oak, beech and hazel and their fruits were not only important animal fodder, but also part of human nutrition and were cultivated in open forests, so shade-demanding woody species

decreased. Oaks were grown not only for acorns (animal feed), but also for their bark which was used for tanning, and large, emergent trees were retained in "**Mittelwälder**" as the timber, that was required for construction. Such "**Mittelwälder**" and coppices still survive regionally in some parts of central Europe (oak forests in France and Lower Franconia) where they are managed today to produce valuable timber.

Different forms of management of the remaining forests have not contributed to the loss of species; on the contrary, opened up tall forests allowed several light-demanding herbaceous plants and grasses to establish. Losses of species occurred with the heavy grazing and when the surface litter of forests was used. Over centuries the latter caused loss of cations from forests and increased cation supply to the fields via manure from stables. Thus the use of litter substantially contributed to soil acidification and to loss of nutrients from forests, and to the large differences in fertility between forests and arable land which can still be seen (see Chap. 2.3). Excessive use of forests on sandy soils caused the formation of heathland in northern Europe. Erosion by wind and water endangered many areas. In many chronicles scarcity of wood is described, which led to the **use of peat from bogs**. Regulations to protect forests were not always followed. Early attempts were made to reforest land, e.g. in 1368, these attempts were recorded for the forest "Nürnberger Reichswald". This was the beginning of the change from deciduous forests to coniferous forests in modern times (Fig. 4.1.11). Large areas of mixed forests were retained until the nineteenth century because of the many possible uses, but were also degraded. With the industrialisation reforestation started with spruce and pine on the degraded areas and this trend has increased to meet requirements for building wood and commercial timber.

In Fig. 4.1.12 A–D characteristic forms of forest management are shown.

Ellenberg (1996) regards grazing in forests worldwide as the anthropogenic factor which influenced vegetation the most. Individual steps of degradation from a natural forest to wasteland are shown in Fig. 4.1.13. The increasing level of grazing had two consequences. Independent of the original stage, the number and type of grazing animals and the characteristics of the site, many **plant communities dominated by herbs and grasses** developed. Moist meadows, nutrient-deficient meadows, hay meadows and pas-

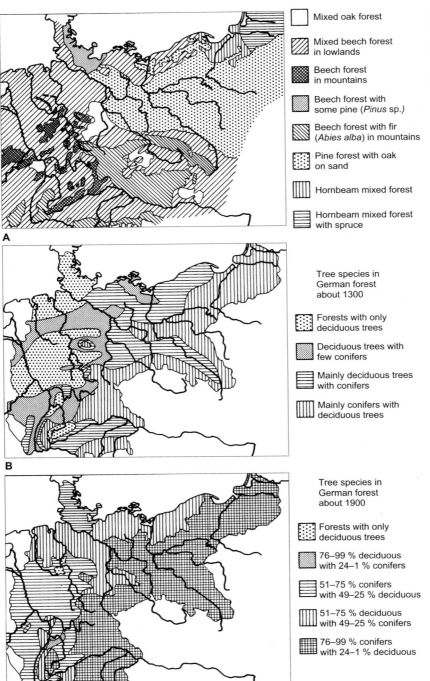

Mixed oak forest

Mixed beech forest
in lowlands

Beech forest
in mountains

Beech forest with
some pine (*Pinus* sp.)

Beech forest with fir
(*Abies alba*) in mountains

Pine forest with oak
on sand

Hornbeam mixed forest

Hornbeam mixed forest
with spruce

Fig. 4.1.11. Development of forests in central Europe from A after the warm period about 2000 b.p. (after Firbas 1949–1952) through B the Middle Ages, until C the nineteenth century. (After Hausrath, from Kreeb 1983)

A

Tree species in
German forest
about 1300

Forests with only
deciduous trees

Deciduous trees with
few conifers

Mainly deciduous trees
with conifers

Mainly conifers with
deciduous trees

B

Tree species in
German forest
about 1900

Forests with only
deciduous trees

76–99 % deciduous
with 24–1 % conifers

51–75 % conifers
with 49–25 % deciduous

51–75 % deciduous
with 49–25 % conifers

76–99 % conifers
with 24–1 % deciduous

C

tures with grasses able to regenerate rapidly expanded and excluded woody species. Fewer animals and occasional burning stimulated some herbaceous species whilst others disappeared. Erosion and continuous nutrient depletion led to degradation of meadows. More animals led to an increase of weeds (e.g. thistles, nettles) in the pastures and those plants sensitive to trampling disappeared. Poisonous species and those protected against being eaten became dominant. Animals contributed to the expansion of shrubs such as *Prunus spinosa*, *Juniperus communis* and *Rubus* species, dwarf shrubs such as *Ononis spinosa* and various broom species, herbaceous spe-

Fig. 4.1.12. Important man-made forest types in central Europe and North Africa. A Almost naturally mixed forests (*Quercus faginea, Q. rotundifolia, Cedrus atlantica*) with trees of all age classes in the central Atlas Mountains (Morocco). B Beech forest close to Bayreuth (Bavaria). Trees are either clear felled or the largest trees selectively removed. C Oak forest (*Quercus robur, Q. pubescens*) in Burgundy. The best stems for timber are only felled after 100 or more years, the rest for firewood every 30 years. D A *Eucalyptus* coppice in northern Morocco, cut 2 years before with new shoots forming which will be harvested after 12–15 years. (Photos K. Müller-Hohenstein)

cies such as *Ranunculus acris, Taraxacum officinale, Salvia pratensis* or *Nardus stricta*, a grass which indicates heavy grazing. Farmers also regulated time and frequency of mowing, and the periods of grazing and the number of animals and thereby the species composition of permanently used grasslands. Meadows for mowing increased as animals were kept in stables and forest litter was substituted by hay. A particular feature of

the vegetation is the large number of nitrophilic species in areas where many animals were kept.

Previously unknown plant communities also developed with agriculture. During the Middle Ages the permanent cultivation of rye without crop rotation led together with the growth of other cereals and buckwheat and with the input of organic material obtained from soils removed from forests and finally the slash and burn man-

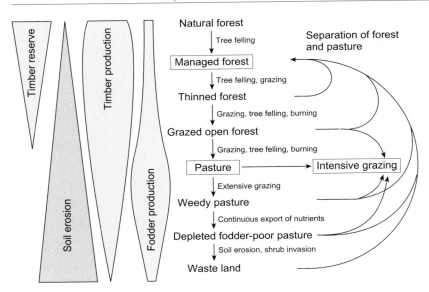

Fig. 4.1.13. Human influences on the vegetation of central Europe, including harvested timber and fodder yields as well as estimates of timber reserves and soil erosion. (Ellenberg 1996)

agement (Hüppe 1989) to the **"three-field" crop rotation.** The succession was winter cereals (sowing in autumn), summer cereals (sowing in spring) and usually a compulsory grazing fallow period which was supposed to balance the nutrient loss by input of manure as fertiliser. Because of this change in cropping, different weeds devel-

oped in pastures and meadows and arable fields (Burrichter et al. 1993). Weeds on arable fields – e.g. *Adonis aestivalis*, *Falcaria vulgaris*, *Caucalis platycarpos* – originated predominantly from the grass steppes of southeastern Europe and were quickly dispersed by grazing animals (epi- and endozoochoric). Others grew naturally in river

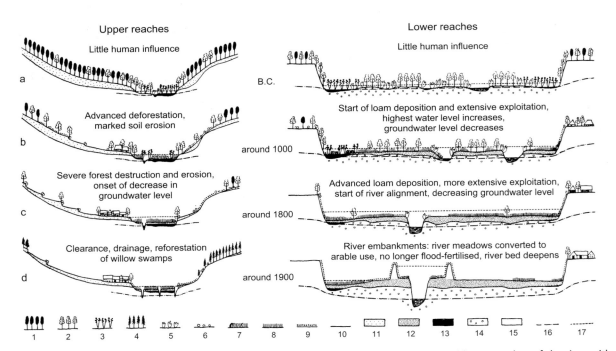

Fig. 4.1.14. Development of a central European river valley landscape in the upper and lower reaches of the river with increasing deforestation, drainage, erosion and deposition of loam in flood meadows (from Ellenberg 1996). *1* Beech forest; *2* oaks and other mixed deciduous forests; *3* alder swamp; *4* conifer reforestation; *5* willow scrub; *6* other scrub; *7* wet grassland; *8* moist grassland; *9* dry grassland; *10* arable fields; *11* loess soils; *12* meadow loam; *13* moorland; *14* gravel; *15* other soil types; *16* mean groundwater level; *17* highest water level

valleys, e.g. *Stellaria media*, *Poa annua*, *Vicia* and *Trifolium* species. The first communities of weeds on arable land still contained many perennial species, because of the fallow period, and the relative rare disruption from ploughing the soil.

Today, it can be assumed that the highest diversity (number of species per region) in central Europe occurred at the end of the Middle Ages because of the activities of man, and this diversity did not only concern plant species but also plant communities and their habitats. Ellenberg (1954) drew characteristic profiles for the valley landscapes in central Europe and thus showed the most important processes and their consequences (Fig. 4.1.14): the valleys were important in their differentiation over small areas and in their significance for the expansion of economic innovation as well as for the dispersal of plants.

The increase in richness of the flora was only possible because of the disturbance of natural sites and the creation of new sites, by the accumulation as well as depletion of nutrient elements, by the microclimatic differences between forest and field, and by watering and drainage (Ellenberg 1996). New, open sites favoured the expansion of short-lived species with broad amplitude in their demands for sites. In the **agricultural landscape of the Middle Ages** an extremely **varied mosaic** of plant communities developed very quickly a diversity, which has been lost again, or is very much endangered with the subsequent mechanisation in agriculture. Species which have become naturalised (**archaeophyts and neophyts**), as well as those that have become extinct, were summarised by Scherer-Lorenzen et al. (2002; Fig. 4.1.15). The **peak of floristic diversity** is confirmed for the middle of the nineteenth century, and the consequent decrease is evident.

4.1.4.4
Development of Vegetation in Modern Times

The beginning of the industrial age is linked with new anthropogenic influences on the plant cover. At the onset of industrialisation most remaining forests in central Europe had already been thinned and degraded: at times soil was very eroded, depleted of nutrients and in the upper layers acidified. However, it was not so much the conditions of forests which led to changes, but rather the new energy source available as coal. The very tight linkage between use of wood and charcoal as well as mining and industry no longer existed, and many traditional minor activities of forestry were no longer practised. However, the population grew and with it the extension of towns and industry and so the demand for wood for construction and commercial timber, as well as for cellulose and paper.

The "new forest management" started with plantations of **conifers** on degraded forest areas and abandoned fields. Experiments with exotic trees such as Douglas fir were successful and larch was planted beyond its natural boundaries. Coppiced and medium-height forests slowly changed to **tall forests**. Various forms of forest management were tried, e.g. clear cutting, shelterwood-compartment systems and shelterwood-selection systems (see Box 4.1.1). The aim was to produce commercial timber as quickly and as frequently, but as sustainably, as possible.

The success of managed forests (e.g. thinning) had many reasons, e.g. forests were no longer used for grazing, pruning, and sod-cutting was no longer practised and less litter was used. New food crops (amongst them potato) were planted and the yield per cropping area increased because of fertiliser applications. The most important change in forests was, however, the change from the once dominant deciduous trees to coniferous trees which triggered its own

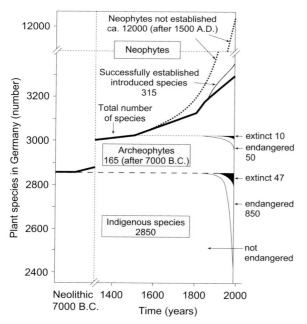

Fig. 4.1.15. Increase and decrease in plant species in central Europe since Neolithic times. (Scherer-Lorenzen et al. 2000)

vegetation dynamics. All coniferous species, particularly pine and spruce, are relatively undemanding and can be sown without problem. Only later they were planted. They grow rapidly, so that very much shorter turnover times may be planned. Conversion particularly affected deciduous trees on good soils and the fast change and the extent of the change from predominantly deciduous forests to coniferous forests are shown for the last centuries by maps from the German forests (Fig. 4.1.11).

Reforestation with only conifers is problematic, for different reasons. Measurements showed soil erosion to be very much higher under spruce forests than under mixed deciduous forests. According to Remmert (1964) reforestation with mixed forests on *Empetrum* heaths of the primarily forest-free island Amrun caused a decline in the wood mouse population and an increase in voles, which disturbed large areas of the island and are thought to have been partly responsible for the failure of dykes during the storm tide of 1962. Such examples show that the change of species may have consequences for the site and the whole biocenose. According to Goudie (1994), twice as many bird species and numbers of birds lived in deciduous forests than in coniferous forests. Research on bird populations in south Chilean deciduous forests and spruce forests gave even more pronounced differences (Finckh 1995).

The **separation of forest and grazing** was very important for the development of vegetation in open spaces. To protect forest and arable land from animals, fences were put around many grazing areas. In early summer with an excess of food, animals picked only the tastiest species. Areas of rank growth – eutrophicated areas because of excrement – developed and gave grazing areas a characteristic pattern. Damage followed from trampling and erosion by too many animals.

Using mineral fertilisers and new varieties of crops, yields increased. Soils of low fertility giving crops of low yield were fertilised and sown with grass ("Vergrünlandung") so the ratio of arable to pasture land shifted. Meadows were mowed, often several times per year, to provide enough fodder for stable animals. Cereal fields were also used for grazing after the harvest (stubble fields) and this influenced the segetal flora. The once characteristic migratory sheep herds disappeared from many regions because wool became uneconomic, due to cheap imports. Many nutrient-poor meadows were invaded by

scrub, and sites for thermophilic and xerophilic species became rarer. This example shows how new trade patterns and inclusion into the global market affected the development of vegetation.

In agriculture, the **improved three-field crop rotation** was increasingly used. The fallow was abandoned and replaced by root crops, particularly potato. Also, since the middle of the nineteenth century, mineral N and P fertiliser had become available and differences in the fertility of fields could be equilibrated. The **diversity of sites was decreased** which also reduced the floristic diversity. Because of fewer fallow fields, and the increasing use of **fertilisers** and **herbicides** and **modern agricultural techniques**, many perennial species of the segetal flora disappeared, e.g. bulbous geophytes like *Tulipa sylvestris*, *Muscari* and *Allium* species. Other perennial species, e.g. *Cirsium arvense* and *Convolvulus arvensis*, with rhizomes which regenerate strongly, expanded. Bogs and wetlands shrank. Bogs and marshes were used for agriculture and grazing, particularly in northern Europe because of the newly developed management of raised bogs (without burning, with sand mixtures). Many marshes, bogs and river forests, e.g. in the southern Upper Rhine Valley, were drained and changed to meadows or pastures.

Currently, intensive land use with fertilisation, ploughing, drainage and the use of herbicides has thus led to drastic losses of diversity in the landscape and plant communities in all regions of Europe. The colourful mosaic of a rural landscape developed for extensive use since the Middle Ages has only been sustained in some remote areas. Even there, it is endangered by increasing eutrophication.

4.1.4.5
Current Trends in the Development of Vegetation

The current influences affecting habitats and the vegetation developed over such a short time span during the last decades have no parallel in the past with respect to intensity and consequences. The goal of intensifying and increasing production in agriculture is continuing. With increasingly fewer small subsistence farms it is no longer necessary to combine arable crops with animal husbandry. The **balance of forest, grazing land and arable land** once required in the rural landscape has been lost. Several special crops are no longer cultivated (flax, linseed or dyer's woad). Areas with marginal yields (site conditions as well as economically) are no longer cropped, so-called **social fallow lands** developed because of changes in working practices and changing job opportunities.

Farming became increasingly intensive with planting of specialised crops. **Highly technical cropping practices on large areas** were promoted after the **redistribution of farmland**; in Europe, fields were traditionally small and these were enlarged in the redistribution (Schreiber 1995). The important aim of this was to provide the best, most economic conditions for use of machinery, so field size had to be increased. Edges of fields, hedges, terraces and marginal biotopes, all with important interconnecting functions, were drastically reduced and differences in sites were equilibrated by drainage and fertilisation. Small biotopes disappeared and wet and moist meadows, mat-grass (*Nadus stricta*) and nutrient-deficient meadows were changed to **uniform, intensively farmed agricultural land.**

Schreiber (1995) demonstrated how various central European grassland communities, which had developed up to the middle of the nine-teenth century, were changed by new agricultural practices into intensive grassland (Fig. 4.1.16). Even in the 1940s only 2% of the meadows in the Allgäu (southern Germany) were cut three times or more; today 95% are cut four times or more. At the same time there was a reduction in species from 75 to 20 per ha (Abt 1990), a consequence that can be seen in all forms of intensive agriculture including animal husbandry and grazing.

Plants associated with cultivated pastures, meadows and fields are now cosmopolitan and persistent "resistant weeds" (e.g. *Galium aparine*). Intensively used pastures and meadows were also sown with a smaller range of highly productive varieties, because of the EU-wide unification of the seed trade, so species and genotypes no longer correspond to the original types of meadows. Ellenberg (1996) describes this type of meadow as the "most boring plant community type" for anyone interested in vegetation.

The redistribution of land was only one precondition for the development of modern agriculture. More important was the policy of permanent subsidies, requiring high application of fertilisers, frequently accompanied by run-off

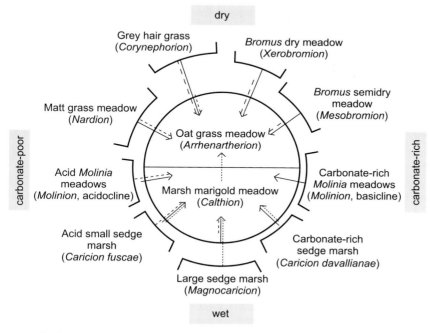

Fig. 4.1.16. Characteristics of habitats of different herbaceous plant communities. (After Schreiber 1995)

——→ Fertilisation, especially with nitrogen
------→ Liming
– – –→ Rain or irrigation
···········→ Drainage

and percolation into surrounding waters and their eutrophication. Application of pesticides accelerated planting of crops without the need for rotation. **Liquid manure** created by **intensive rearing of animals** stimulated **planting of maize**, which tolerates large amounts of liquid manure. The formation of a "liquid manure flora" consisting of meadow chervil, chickweed and several types of daisies is often observed.

Tractors and machines in agriculture become increasingly heavier and cause **soil compaction** and **problems in soil water relations**. Soil organisms suffer, particularly the macrofauna with Lumbricides. However, yields are still increasing, because modern plant-breeding programmes continuously provide new **varieties with increased yield potential**. Varieties have to be continuously improved, as they become resistant towards xenobiotica which also require continuous change. An unwanted "co-evolution" takes place. The WBGU (2000) risk assessment points to the dangers posed by crops modified genetically for herbicide and virus resistance, if such transgenic crop plants become wild or cross with indigenous species.

Intensive agricultural practices result in fewer and fewer species in the associated flora, which are often resistant to pesticides and herbicides. Therefore, **measures for the protection** of the segetal flora are required. Various attempts have been made: mixed cropping, intercropping, management of strips at the edge of fields. Within the framework of the subsidised **field margin programme** emphasis is put on increasing local alpha diversity and the promotion of useful non-cropping species. Heitzmann-Hofmann (1993) shows, using examples from Switzerland, that in the medium term succession in the sense of **biotope management** may be possible so that stable communities can be developed.

These attempts are not always successful. Under present-day climatic conditions it should be possible to regenerate raised bogs. However, atypical plants and animals have to be excluded and those species typical of raised bogs must be reintroduced when the area becomes wet again. Success is questionable, as, with the present annual N influx of between 20 and 100 kg/ha in central Europe, the required oligotrophic conditions may no longer be achieved. It is, therefore, very important to maintain all those raised bog areas that are left, even if degraded.

Thus, the present-day agricultural landscape is characterised not only by mechanisation, spe-

cialisation and high production, but also by homogenisation and contamination. In the agricultural landscape there is, on the one hand, a growing uniformity and depletion of differences within one site, but in other places new sites are created with new vegetation units, e.g. developed by canalisation of rivers, building of new infrastructure, mining and slag heaps. River valleys play an important role in the mosaic of our landscapes, because they are refuges for endangered species and transit spaces for invading species, and, because of the high morpho- and hydrodynamic characteristics of regions near rivers, they become growing sites for many specialists (Müller 1995).

The use of land for settlement and industrial sites has grown enormously. Habitats and communities, which are without parallel in the natural landscape, are investigated in **urban ecology**. Figure 4.1.17 gives an overview of the changes to sites, vegetation and fauna in such areas. Urban areas are basically warm islands where warmth- and light-demanding species find a refuge, but they need to be relatively insensitive to mechanical disturbance and pollutants. Such urbanophilic species are, e.g., *Amaranthus albus*, *Chenopodium botrys*, *Poa compressa* and *Silene vulgaris*. These plants characterise the warm, dry sites in towns polluted by heavy metals.

The **urban flora** is fairly diverse and develops many rather constant plant communities, because of the new non-natural sites and because of the ruderal species settling here. According to Wittig and Diesing (1989), urban plant communities may be associated with various types of structures within towns (e.g. dense block buildings, semidetached or town houses, open spaces, areas around stations, etc.). **Lichen flora** in towns is particularly well known; epiphytic lichens are often taken as the standard for assessment of SO_2 pollution and evaluated regarding their **toxi-tolerance**. Figure 4.1.18 shows an example of the zonation of lichens in the region around Frankfurt at a time of high SO_2 pollution. With the reduction of SO_2 emissions, lichen establishment in urban conurbations has increased again.

New characteristic plant communities are also found in villages. Wittkamp et al. (1995) compared the vegetation of northern Bavarian and southern Thuringian villages on both sides of the former border between western and eastern parts of Germany and found that variation of use is linked to variation in vegetation, e.g. the

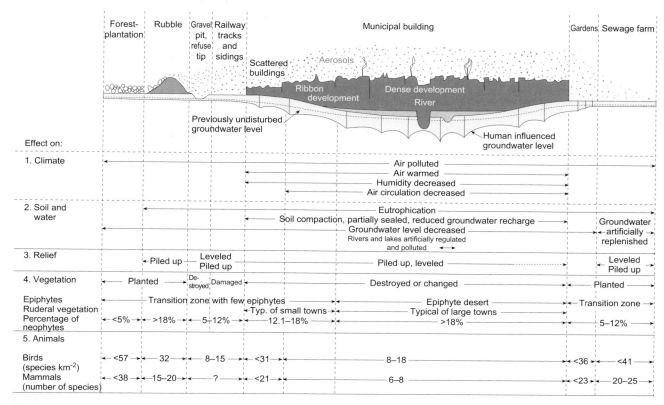

Fig. 4.1.17. Ecological organisation of a large town, stressing interactions between human influences and abiotic and biotic conditions in this ecosystem. (After Sukopp 1990, from Sukopp and Wittig 1998)

species-rich gardens in Thuringia (former East Germany) had almost no parallel to those in northern Franconia (part of Bavaria, former West Germany). The comparison also showed that social structure and economic activity influenced vegetation. Differences in vegetation caused by the site are of secondary importance compared with differences as a consequence of usage. Deil (1995) used the example of landscapes north and south of the Strait of Gibraltar to determine how much agro-political measures, culture-specific characteristics and the economic activity influence the vegetation of large areas, and whether this influence is stronger than the site conditions. With almost identical natural initial conditions, a completely different inventory of communities developed with the intensive, market-orientated land use of Spain compared with the subsistence-orientated land use of Morocco with traditional, almost non-mechanised forms of agriculture.

A particular inventory of species also occurs at the edges of roads. Schmidt (1989) gives an overview of the **ruderal vegetation** of the motor-

way network in North Rhine-Westphalia. Direct (exhaust fumes) and indirect (gritting with salt) effects of traffic influence the differentiation of these sites. Basic composition of vegetation on road verges is relatively unspecialised as specialists in the fauna and flora have hardly any chance of survival. The refuge and interconnected effects of road verges should not be overrated. The negative effects of separating and fragmenting areas of distribution are ecologically more significant.

Recent influence of man on vegetation in central Europe is well documented by the **new type of forest decline** (see Chap. 3.5.1). Damage to trees and complete forest areas by smoke and other pollutants from industry has been reported since the beginning of the industrial age. It was also known that rejuvenation of forests in central Europe had become more difficult for several reasons, amongst them occupation of soils of old forest stands by grasses from grazing by animals, damage by pests, attacks by fungi or other pathogens, climatic abnormalities (breakage because of storms or snow, fire, frost peri-

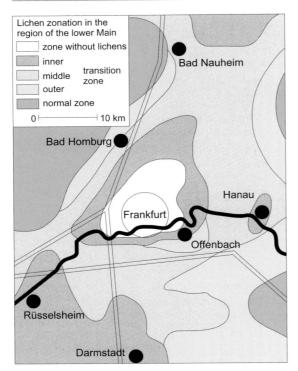

Fig. 4.1.18. Zonation of lichens in and around Frankfurt. (After Steubing 1978, from Sukopp and Wittig 1998)

ods, dry years) and most of all from acidification of the upper soil layer. It is now reasonably certain that the soils of many semi-natural woodlands and managed forests were depleted because of litter removal, erosion and monoculture practices over centuries. Therefore, forests are particularly susceptible to stresses mentioned.

The "new forest decline" affecting complete forest ecosystems has only been observed since about 30 years. Since the 1970s, damage over large areas in fir and spruce forests have become obvious, but these areas were far away from heavy industry. Damage was attributed to the influx of strong acid from the atmosphere via long-distance transport in the form of **acid rain**. The discussion in Chapter 3.5.1 shows that, ultimately, nutrient deficiencies and imbalances in ion compositions cause the decline of forests. Nevertheless research into forest damage also showed that forests are able, to a large extent, to recover.

Altering nitrogen influx causes changes in the flora which are thus an indicator for increased N (Fig. 4.1.19). With repeated evaluation of forest vegetation, a shift in the mean nitrogen indicator values (mN) in the direction of higher N-

indicators took place. This was independent of the closed canopy of stands, as the indicator values for light (mL) showed. Thus, the change in vegetation is caused by alteration of the conditions of the site related to N deposition independent of management.

Stress by pollutants is associated with a CO_2 increase in the atmosphere as discussed in the context of climate change. Carbon dioxide is a plant nutrient and an increase in it may lead to higher rates and greater total production. Plants are able to compensate for part of the emission of fossil fuels (see Chap. 5). Globally, one could also envisage a shift of biomes (Melillo et al. 1996).

From the analysis of the recent history of vegetation it has become clear that if the present-day vegetation is to be understood "it is not sufficient to know the current management methods in forests and fields. At least with respect to

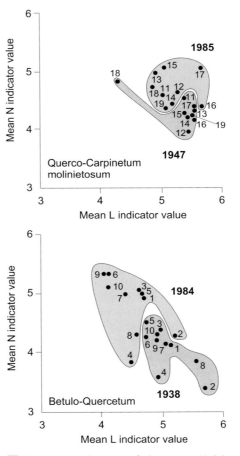

Fig. 4.1.19. Changes of the mean N (nitrogen) and L (light) values in mixed deciduous forests in Switzerland during the course of 38 or 46 years. (After Kuhn 1993, from Ellenberg 1996)

forests and heathlands, but also to many green grassland areas and bogs, it is necessary to always keep in mind earlier management methods and their effects" (Ellenberg 1996).

4.1.4.6
Attempts to Classify and Evaluate Anthropogenic Influences and Their Consequences for Vegetation

Processes and results of human influence on the plant cover, its expansion and retreat, increase and decrease of plant species and vegetation units have also been considered with the view to objectively report, **classify** and **evaluate** the changes.

Jäger (1977) made the initial attempt to classify anthropogenic effects on vegetation, and made three categories:

- **original** (natural) **vegetation** (in the sub-Atlantic period, as perhaps shown on the map by Firbas in Fig. 4.1.11);
- **actual** (recent) **vegetation** under present-day conditions of site and use;
- **potential natural vegetation** (pnV), a term introduced by Tüxen (1956), describing the vegetation which would occur under the present conditions of the site (without further changes).

Natural vegetation no longer exists in central Europe, so pnV is very important in considering the protection of nature and in spatial planning, but the actual vegetation and its sites are at the centre of discussions.

Evaluating anthropogenic influences is essentially a balance between gain (introduction, immigration, naturalisation) and losses (extinction, exclusion) of species. Compared with natural vegetation, **gains** as well as **losses** mean damage to the "natural" state. An approach is to characterise and typify anthropogenic vegetation by defining the **"level of naturalness"**. Several proposals have been made to scale naturalness. **Synanthropic successors** are the "winners". They are subdivided in many ways (Schröder 1969) and consist of apophytes (indigenous species on anthropogenic sites) and anthropochors (non-indigenous species with expansion dependent on man). The term **hemerochors** is also used for those species whose expansion is dependent on man. Plants may be hemerophilic, requiring cul-

tivation, or hemerophobic. Human influence on ecosystems is called hemeroby.

Another subdivision of **anthropochors** was given by Sukopp (1972), based on Schröder, but occasionally using slightly different terminology. Sukopp used three criteria:

1. **Based on the time of immigration** (see Fig. 4.1.15): Archaeophytes (old adventives) immigrating in prehistoric times are divided from neophytes (new adventives) which only came in historical times.
2. **According to the method of immigration**, i.e. the type of human interaction in immigration. These are **ergasiophytes** (intentionally introduced species, e.g. crop plants and their forms that grow wild, ornamental plants and also examples from botanical gardens) as well as **xenophytes** (unintentionally introduced species, e.g. weeds accompanying imported seeds, plants from bird food). Occasionally, an added difference is drawn between these and akulotophytes, plants only able to invade after humans provide suitable sites.
3. **According to the degree of naturalisation**, how well they establish permanently at the new site.

The latter group is subdivided into five additional groups, in some cases based on several causes:

- **idiochorophytes** (indigenous species which existed prior to anthropogenic influences);
- **agriophytes** (new indigenous species, nowadays competitive without human activity);
- **epecophytes** (species dependent on cultivation which disappear as soon as the crop is no longer planted);
- **ephemerophytes** (unpersistent, ephemeral species, which disappear quickly);
- **ergasiophytes** (cultivated species which must be protected from competition).

This division is not always adhered to by different authors (Jäger 1988). Ultimately, only three criteria are important: the time of naturalisation, the type of naturalisation and the length of naturalisation.

The term **neophyte** will be discussed in more detail here. These new indigenous species with a firm place in the present day pnV are also called agriophytes by Sukopp (1972). A plant must be introduced or imported, establish after reaching its new sites and be naturalised and establish permanently without direct help by humans, and finally expand. The hypothetical number of

Table 4.1.3. Characteristics of successful neophytes. (After Sukopp 1987; Jaeger 1988; Di Castri 1990; Roy 1990, from Sukopp and Wittig 1998)

1. Related to reproduction and biology of distribution
Early capacity to reproduce (rapid flowering after the vegetative phase = short juvenile period)
Single parent reproduction
Self-compatibility; probable, although not obligatory self-pollination or apomictic
If cross-pollinated then unspecific pollinator or wind
Seed production under a wide range of environmental conditions and continuous high reproductive capacity (production of many propagules)
Particularly large seed production under favourable conditions
Very resistant and long-lived seed [capacity to build up seed (diaspore) bank]
Fruit and seed morphology suitable for extensive distribution by wind and animals including man
Unspecialised seedling and developmental processes; therefore, wide ecological potential
Discontinuous germination by induced dormancy
Rapid seedling growth

2. Related to vegetative growth and phenology
Rapid growth as a consequence of fast exploitation of resources (large photosynthesis and respiration capacity)
Often able to exploit large N supply
Very flexible distribution of assimilates
If perennial, marked vegetative reproduction, able to regenerate from lower nodes and roots
Generally short and simple growth cycle
Frequently photoperiodic: day length neutral
Dormancy

3. Genetic characteristics
Large genetic variability
Polyploidy; hybrids
Very flexible genetic system; thus alterations of recombination rates possible
Frequently phylogenetically young group

4. Population dynamics and ecological characteristics
Generalists: broad climatic and edaphic range
Large acclimation potential; often phenotypically plastic = increases ecological potential
Rapid population increase due to high growth rates and early, as well as large, reproductive capacity
r Strategy
Very competitive through particular features such as rosette form, parasitic growth, allelopathy or fast and vigorous growth

Table 4.1.4. Classification of vegetation dependent on the degree of human influence. (After Dierschke 1984)

Bernátzky (1905)	Tüxen (1958)	Falinski (1969)	Ellenberg (1963)	Seibert (1980)	Dierschke (1984)	Sukopp (1969, 1972)
Not influenced Original structure	Mature community	Autogenic — Original	Determined by nature — Undisturbed	Natural	Natural to almost natural	Ahemerob
			Natural			
Influenced		Natural	Almost natural		Almost natural	Oligohemerob
			Relatively natural			
Modified structure	1. stage	Anthropogenic — Half-natural	Determined by cultivation — Relatively unnatural	Relatively unnatural	Half-natural	Mesohemerob Beta-Euhemerob
	2. stage	Pro-synanthropic	Distant from nature	Distant from nature	unnatural	Alpha-
Plantations	3. stage	Eu-synanthropic	Unnatural			
	4. stage		Artificial	Artificial	Artificial	Polyhemerob

(Replacement community — vertical label over Tüxen stages 1–4)

species that are successful in this sequence decreases with each new step. Plants must possess the characteristics listed in Table 4.1.3 in order to be successful.

The classification of vegetation according to the "degree of naturalness" has also differed. The most important differences are compared by Dierschke (1984; Table 4.1.4). It is now assumed that the proportion of agriophytes in vegetational units correlates with the degree of human influence. Therefore, it is possible to determine, quantitatively, the degree of human influence (**degree of hemeroby**) in a unit of vegetation by the proportion of agriophytes and neophytes and the loss of indigenous species (Table 4.1.5).

Bornkamm (1980) uses the classification by Sukopp (1972) for planning of land use. The proportion of neophytes increases with the loss of indigenous species (Fig. 4.1.20). He also reconstructed the distribution of land with the same degree of hemeroby for two Bavarian villages during the course of historical development and was able to demonstrate the increasing human influence (Fig. 4.1.21).

Recently, the consequences of gain and loss of species on the indigenous vegetation have been discussed. The loss of barriers to distribution leads to **mixing of the flora** and fauna from various bioareas. Elton (1958) regards this as a decisive, recent change in the biosphere. Two marked historical epochs must be distinguished: the time after the discovery of America up to the sixteenth century with increasing possibilities for travel between continents, and the time from the nineteenth century when new anthro-

Table 4.1.5. Proportion of neophytes and loss of native species related to the degree of human interference (hemeroby). (After Sukopp 1972)

	Proportion of neophytes	Loss of native vascular plant species (per 1000 km^2)
Ahemerob	0%	0%
Oligohemerob	<5%	<1%
Mesohemerob	5–12%	1–5%
Euhemerob	13–20%	>6%
Polyhemerob	21–(80)%	?
Metahemerob	>80%	?

pogenic sites opened up for the establishment of plants.

Lohmeier and Sukopp (1992) analysed the consequences of introduced foreign plants on the actual vegetation and present ecosystems in Europe, and Jäger (1988) gave percentage and absolute figures of synanthropic species worldwide (Fig. 4.1.22). In industrial countries about 100 species per 100,000 km^2 are naturalised, but there are exceptions such as the 800 species in Japan, where three floral regions meet. Lövei (1997) has shown (Table 4.1.6) that the proportion of **synanthropic species** has increased since the research by Jäger. Sukopp (1972) assumed fewer than 1% of introduced plants, but, according to Lövei (1997), this has increased to 6%. Sukopp (1972) considered that 54% of naturalised species in Germany originate from Europe itself and west Asia, 30% from areas with moderate climates in North America, 9% from central and east Asia. From these values of distribu-

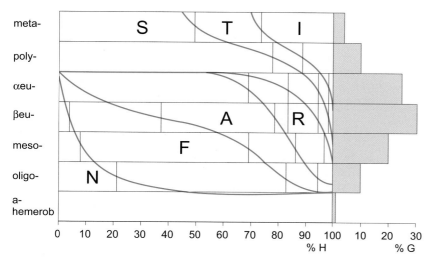

Fig. 4.1.20. Schematic relationship between type of land use and classification of human influence, also called hemeroby (after Bornkamm 1980). % *H* Proportion of total land surface under particular types of human influence (hemeroby); % *G* proportion of a particular hemeroby class in the total landscape area. Surface use: *I* industry; *V* transport; *S* settlement; *E* recreation; *L* agriculture and gardens; *F* forestry; *N* nature reserves (see also Table 4.1.5)

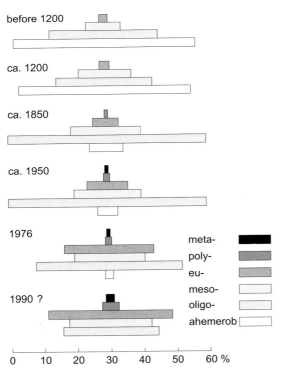

Fig. 4.1.21. Distribution of areas with the same type of human influence (hemeroby value) during the historical development of two villages, Kochel am See and Schlehdorf, in Bavaria, Germany (see also Table 4.1.5)

Table 4.1.6. The contribution of non-indigenous species to the flora of different regions. After Lövei (1997)

Region	Number of species		Percent of non-indigenous species
	Indigenous	Non-indigenous	
Russian Arctic	1403	104	6.9
Europe	11820	721	5.7
USA	17300	2100	10.8
South Africa	20573	824	3.9
Australia	15638	1952	11.1
Ontario	2056	805	28.1
New York State	1940	1083	35.8
Perth region (Australia)	1510	547	26.6
British Isles	1255	945	43.0
Hawaii	1143	891	43.8
New Zealand	2449	1623	39.9

trend to include areas nearer the poles and/or oceans. As a cultivated landscape possesses a varied site mosaic, the probability of species meeting and hybridising is larger. Particularly crossing with sympatric families is eased. Thus several families developed quickly and became species-rich, e.g. the *Oenothera* species, after their introduction into central Europe.

Agriophytes are plants introduced for economic reasons which established in natural habitats (*Robinia pseudoacacia*, *Junglans regia*, *Prunus serotina*, *Castanea sativa*, *Helianthus tuberosus*, *Isatis tinctoria*), ornamental plants (*Centranthus ruber*, *Cymbalaria muralis*, *Heracleum mantegazzianum*, *Impatiens glandulifera*, *Tulipa sylvestris*, *Reynoutria japonica*, *Laburnum anagyroides*), species originating from botanical gardens (*Impatiens parviflora*, *Galinsoga parviflora*, *Elodea canadensis*), and also species which were consciously planted in natural areas (*Lupinus div. spec.*). Merkel and Walter (1982) listed more than 70 such species for Upper Franconia alone.

Agriophytes were not able to establish everywhere. They are particularly numerous on sites disturbed by man, in towns and industrial areas. Only few species established in woodland regions. Examples in forests are the wild cherry (*Prunus serotina*) which was originally introduced to accelerate the accumulation of humus, but impedes natural rejuvenation. The aggressive robinea (*Robinia pseudoacacia*) which fixes nitrogen and as a consequence of the nitrogen accumulation leads to an increase of nitrophilic species. The tree of heaven (*Ailanthus altissima*) which invades in warmth-demanding forest communities; and the small balsam (*Impatiens parviflora*) which is becoming more frequent in the undergrowth of beech forests are additional examples.

Along the coasts the cord-grass (*Spartina anglica*), planted at one time to gain land, has widely replaced glasswort (*Salicornia europaea*) and Sea Poa (*Puccinellia maritima*), and has thus become an unwanted invader. This applies also to the Canadian pond weed (*Elodea canadensis*), but in many waters it has been decreased again due to increasing eutrophication of waterways.

Areas around river banks provide particularly favourable conditions for **immigration and expansion** of agriophytes (see Chap. 4.1.4.3), as new open spaces always develop, due to the natural dynamics of water flow, and because there

tion, it may be considered that these species behaved in their naturalisation in central Europe according to the **"law of relative constant sites"** (Walter 1960): "If the climate changes in a certain direction within the area of a species, this species will change its biotope in order to compensate the climatic change". There is also a

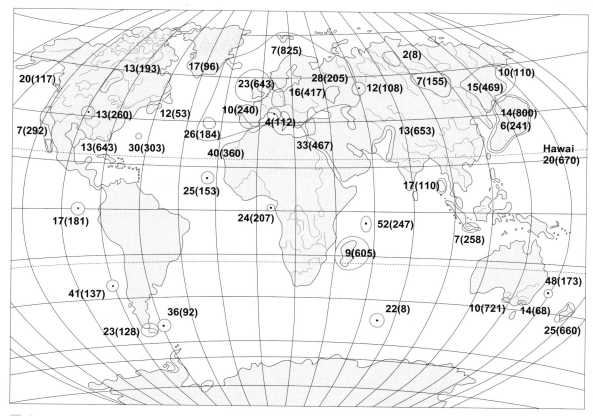

Fig. 4.1.22. The proportion, in percent, and absolute numbers (in parentheses) of vascular plant species which are always associated with human activity (synanthropic agrio- and epecophytes). (After Jäger 1988)

are few competitors for immigrants. Schwabe and Kratochwil (1991) described nicheing of some species and the associated consequences. They distinguish between five "functional types":

1. Species with relatively low cover and good adaptation with respect to existing vegetation as well as enrichment of the nectar supply for insects, e.g. *Mimulus guttatus*, *Aster lanceolatus* and *A. tradescantii*.
2. Species with a tendency for further expansion and suppression of other species, e.g. the golden-rod (*Solidaga canadensis* and *S. gigantea*), which flower late and thus provide good food for many diptera and butterflies.
3. Species covering large areas of the site and exclude competitors by shading: *Impatiens glandulifera* belongs to this type.
4. The giant hogweed (*Heracleum mantegazzianum*) is put into its own, fourth group as it may act as biologically enriching, but brings danger for human health (eczema follow skin contact).

5. Species which dominate quickly and vigorously exclude indigenous species. Amongst those are the rhizome-forming knot grass species (*Reynoutria japonica* = *Polygonum cuspidatum* and *R. sacchalinense* = *P. sacchalinense*).

The "gain" of agriophytes may be linked to considerable disadvantages for indigenous species, perhaps even extinction. Plant communities change their floristic compositions and structure, uniform stands or stands with only a few species arise, instead of the diversity and multitude of structures of the original plant communities. Managed forests, intensive greenland, persistent ruderal fields and nitrophilic riverbank communities are part of this. The replacement of near-natural communities by those distinct from the original vegetation is linked with a change in site conditions, such as nutrients, moisture and humus in the soil and/or microclimatic conditions.

Most agriophytes are not grazed, or are accepted only by a few polyphagous indigenous insects as a source of food. In Great Britain fewer than 10 species of insects were counted on introduced trees, e.g. robinia, whilst on indigenous oak trees more than 300 species occurred (Lohmeier and Sukopp 1992). On the other hand, robinia may be regarded as important for foraging bees. More mono- and oligophageous insect species were found on indigenous *Impatiens* species than on introduced species. By excluding indigenous flowering plants, species relying on specific food sources, so-called stenophageous animals, are lost.

Are neophytes a danger to nature? The number of alien species in central Europe exceeds the extinct species, according to Böcker et al. (1995; see Fig. 4.1.15). At present, about 5–25% of the flora in central Europe may be anthropochor, in towns about 50% is reached. There is evidence for the decrease in indigenous species because of the advance of neophytes. Two species with a particularly high invasion potential, *Solidago canadensis* in Berlin and *Tribulus terrestris* in the east African savannahs, were analysed in 1991 by Cornelius using a key-lock model to explain their invasion of niches. Particularly if – as in these cases – demands on resources, tolerance to climate stress and strategies of adaptation to competition and regeneration (key traits) agree with the climatic conditions and the adaptation to disturbance and succession (lock), then settling in is easy and this endangers the existing mosaic of species and communities.

At present, neophytes are not regarded as a danger in Europe, apart from a few special cases. They are hardly responsible for the present loss of species. However, these losses have only been documented since the beginning of the twentieth century. According to Jäger (1988), in Europe, in areas of up to 1000 km^2, a loss of between 6 and 27% (maximum) of the original species was estimated. Within the urban area of Frankfurt/Main with a size of 195 km^2 about 17% of the original species disappeared. For areas of 30,000 km^2 a loss of about 5% is assumed. In the USA with 7.8 million km^2 a loss of 0.5% is estimated. Comparing data before and after 1950 in the flora of the Netherlands, species such as *Salvinia natans*, *Verbena officinalis*, *Eriophorum latifolium*, *Hammarbya paludosa*, *Narthecium ossifragum* and *Pinguicula vulgaris* have disappeared in more than 80% of locations where they were previously established. Particularly species with limited competitive ability are affected.

4.1.4.7
Anthropogenic Influences on Vegetation Outside Central Europe

Human influences have changed the natural vegetation in all climatic regions and biomes. There are specific developments connected to the natural basis of plant growth as well as specific human influences. Examples have been chosen from three biomes showing the spectrum of possible consequences: the **Mediterranean region**, the **dry regions of Africa** (keyword "desertification") and the **humid tropics of Africa** (keyword "destruction of tropical forest").

Mediterranean Region

Plants in the Mediterranean region are particularly stressed because of the **dry periods in summer**, which may be of different length, but are always significant. The **influence of fire** must also be considered, an influence which has increased by human intervention. Tree species of Mediterranean forests in the lower and upper mountain zones, listed in the scheme of altitudinal zones in Fig. 4.1.23, are thus almost all drought resistant and stimulated rather than damaged by fire.

Land use affecting large areas started in the western Mediterranean region (bays of Alicante and Catalonia) in the early Neolithic about 7000 years ago (Badal et al. 1994; Riera-Mora and Esteban-Amat 1994). The evergreen oak forests (*Quercus rotundifolia*) near the coast was intermixed with deciduous oaks (*Quercus faginea*, *Q. pubescens*) was thinned and shrubs which demanded more light (heliophilic shrubs) occupied the area. Typical Mediterranean shrub communities, the **macchie**, developed. Inland areas remained untouched for a long time, disregarding the first transhumance, e.g. shepherds moving in the hot, dry summers from the plain into the mountains near the coast, and establishing a "vertical" migratory pattern of grazing management. The farms on the coastal plain, with favourable soils and availability of water, e.g. the Spanish "huertas", were the first areas with intensive agricultural crops. Evidence of crop plants introduced from the Mediterranean into North Africa demonstrates the development of an increasingly richer flora in the agriculturally managed landscapes (Le Floch et al. 1990). In the Palaeolithic period barley (*Hordeum vulgare*) was evident, in the Neolithic period wheat (*Triticum* spp.) emerged as well as fruit trees (*Phoe-*

semihumid-humid zonation sequence		**Altitudinal zone**	semiarid-arid zonation sequence	
Reforestation with	Natural vegetation		Natural vegetation	Reforestation with
	Mountain grassland and dwarf shrub communities	subalpine/alpine (oro-mediterranean)	Mountain steppes, dwarf shrub communities and thorny cushion plants	
Pinus silvestris	Mountain forests with *Fagus silvatica* *Abies alba* *Pinus silvestris* *Pinus uncinata*	montane (montane-mediterranean)	Mountain forests with *Cedrus atlantica* *Cedrus libani* *Abies pinsapo* *Abies cilicica, Pinus nigra*	*Pinus nigra* *Populus* div. spp.
Pinus radiata *Pinus pinaster* *Eucalyptus* div. spp. *Populus* div. spp.	Deciduous forests with *Quercus cerris* *Quercus pubescens* *Quercus faginea* *Carpinus orientalis*	submontane (sub-mediterranean, supra-mediterranean)	Evergreen and deciduous forests with *Quercus boissieri* *Quercus pubescens* *Quercus coccifera* *Quercus ilex, Pinus brutia*	*Pinus pinaster* *Eucalyptus* div. spp.
Pinus radiata *Pinus halepensis* *Eucalyptus* div. spp.	Evergreen forests with *Quercus ilex* *Quercus suber* *Pinus pinea* *Pinus pinaster*	basal/foothills (eu-mediterranean)	Evergreen forests with *Tetraclinis articulata* *Juniperus phoenicea* *Pinus halepensis*	*Pinus halepensis* *Eucalyptus* div. spp. *Tamarix* div. spp.

Fig. 4.1.23. The altitudinal zones of dominant tree species of natural vegetation and the most important exotic tree species used in reforestation in the Mediterranean region. (After Müller-Hohenstein 1991)

nix dactylifera, Ziziphus spp., *Lawsonia inermis*), and Fabaceae (*Lens culinaris, Pisum sativum, Vicia faba*).

The Phoenecians brought olives, vine, pomegranates and figs and the Romans introduced garlic, onions, apples and pears. During the Arab period the number of species from central and east Asia increased, e.g. citrus, mulberry and carob trees, hemp and sugar cane. Species from the New World followed after the discovery of America. During that time those plants now regarded as characteristic of the region reached the Mediterranean basin: agave, opuntia as well as maize, tobacco and tomato. In the nineteenth century many ornamental plants were added. Economic reasons resulted in the successful introduction of acacia and eucalyptus. About 200 exotic species are today naturalised in North Africa, corresponding to 4% of the total flora (Le Floch et al. 1990). Many species were introduced unintentionally, along with the crop plants, and became established. The number of those species originating from the New World is considerable, amongst them so-called aggressive invaders which established particularly on ruderal sites (species of the genera *Amaranthus, Cuscuta* and *Conyza*, as well as *Heliotropium curassavicum, Solanum eleagnifolium, Xanthium spinosum*). The three last mentioned, as well as

some shrubs (*Ricinus communis* and *Nicotiana glauca*), are expanding rapidly in North Africa at the moment.

In the **segetal flora**, on the other hand, indigenous species found new niches. The ca. 50 species on fields and fallow land include *Ammi majus*, and *A. visnaga, Anagallis arvensis* and *A. foemina, Echium italicum, Ridolfia segetum, Sinapis arvensis, Calendula arvensis, Cirsium arvense*, as well as *Carduncellus, Convolvulus, Cyperus* and *Diplotaxis* species. The number of sometimes thorny weeds on pastures is just as high (*Astragalus armatus, Atractylis serratuloides, Calycotome villosa, Scolymus hispanicus* and *S. grandiflorum*), and also partly poisonous or at least non-edible species (*Asphodelus fistulosus, A. macrocarpus, A. tenuifolius, Haloxylon scoparium, Hertia cheirifolia, Peganum harmala, Solanum nigrum, Stipagrostis pungens* and *S. capensis*). Among the nutrient indicators (nitrophils) are, e.g., *Aizoon* and *Mesembryanthemum* species, *Calendula arvensis, Chenopodium murale, Hyoscyamus albus* and *H. niger, Malva parviflora* and *Withania somnifera* (Le Floch et al. 1990).

For the Mediterranean regions the same applies as for central Europe: Naturalisation, expansion and disappearance of individual species is closely connected to agricultural practices.

Deil (1997) showed for the areas bordering the Strait of Gibraltar, how, to a high degree of certainty, vegetational landscapes may be read as history books, and how historic and actual forms of use show religious regulation, as well as subsistence-orientated management of the indigenous population, or the market-oriented management of colonial times. Thus, even today, it is possible to demonstrate, from the spectrum of different species, an Islamic cemetery from the time before the reconquista, just as it is possible to show the different use of herbicides and mechanical control of weeds in the fields of southern Spain or northern Morocco.

The recent **history of forests in the Mediterranean regions** is determined by man and will be discussed in more detail, particularly as it is possible to explain essential problems of site conditions. During the Greek colonisation of Dalmatia from the eighth century B.C., forests were cleared. The Italian peninsula was predominantly deforested during Roman times, the Iberian peninsula mostly from the 6th century B.C. onwards. Consequences for vegetation and site have often been shown (Müller-Hohenstein 1973; Finckh and Deil 1989). Forest degradation often starts with structural changes (age structure, density of stand and closure of canopy); the grazing in forests leads to invasion of ruderal species, decline of rejuvenation and therefore to thinner stands.

At first forests on more favourable sites were **cleared**. Arable fields extended with not very productive dry land agriculture. Clearing occurred also, often supported by fires, to gain grazing areas. Le Houerou (1992) showed how and for what reasons Mediterranean dwarf shrub communities (**macchie** with various regionally different terms such as **garrigue, tomillares, phrygana, matorral**) and pastures differing in their floristic compositions are anthropogenically determined (see Box 4.1.2).

Clearing was not only an intervention with irreversible consequences for vegetation, but particularly because of soil erosion down to the bed rock and resulted in sedimentation in valleys. At present, floods signal the considerable changes in water relations. The view that degradation has had negative economic consequences, and also the acute lack of wood for the last 50 years, has led to increased reforestation, at first in southern European regions and later in north African countries. Any trend to establish nearly natural economic forests is, however, hardly recognisable. **Exotic, fast-growing types of trees** are chosen for reforestation, in part pine species, but predominantly eucalyptus species. Figure 4.1.23 shows the most important forest spe-

---

| **Box 4.1.2** | **Fire and grazing influenced types of forest degradation in the Mediterranean region (after Le Houerou 1992)** |

Many studies have been made of the sequence of woodland degradation by regular burning and/or grazing in the Mediterranean region. Braun-Blanquet (1928) developed the first scheme. Le Houerou has distinguished between two series, one in the semihumid southern European Mediterranean, called the "*Quercus ilex* series", and another for the semi-arid north African Mediterranean region called the "*Pinus halepensis* series".

Quercus rotundifolia (= *Qu. ilex*) oak forest when burnt is transformed into cork oak (*Quercus suber*) dominated forest, but only on silicate soils. With further burning numerous, mainly evergreen shrubs form the vegetation (e.g. *Erica arborea, Calycotome villosa, Myrtus communis*) followed by rock roses (*Cistus crispus, C. ladaniferus, C. monspeliensis*). The final stage of this fire-determined development is a scrub vegetation with dwarf shrubs and geophytes (e.g. *Helianthemum guttatum, H. tuberaria, Urginea marittima*).

The sequence in dryer and more heavily grazed regions of the north African Mediterranean starts with Aleppo pine forest (with *Pinus halepensis, Juniperus phoenicea*) which is degraded by fire and grazing initially into a "garrigue" with rock roses and dwarf shrubs (*Rosmarinus officinalis, Lavandula stoechas, Cistus libanotis*). Finally, grasses of the dry steppes (*Stipa tenacissima, Lygeum spartum*) become dominant. The final stage of the degradation is pasture with weeds (e.g. *Peganum harmala, Noaea mucronata*).

cies for individual altitudinal zones used presently for reforestation.

Where the reforestation was successful, "forest" areas were increased, but also caused uniformity. The hoped-for economic yields have not always materialised, and no positive effects on water relations and formation of soil have so far been found. The negative side effects on the fauna and organic substances in the soil, attacks by pests and fires, etc., known from monocultures, are deplorable. With the rich Mediterranean variety of different woody species, the preferential use of exotic species would not have been required. One could have limited those for protective reforestation, e.g. on areas where a rapid protection from further erosion was required. In the long term economic success could have been sought in indigenous species (production reforestation).

Fig. 4.1.24. Typical types of agricultural land use in countries around the Mediterranean. A Subsistence farming on a small area with mixed crops and many cultivated plant species (Central Atlas, Morocco). B Grain crops and fodder plants for the national market on large-scale farms with high input of agrochemicals and machinery (Tuscan Hills, Italy). C Mixed agroforestry with grain crops for the growers consumption, and cork (*Quercus suber*) for the national market (Extremadura, Spain). D Unregulated, excessive grazing with severely degraded forests and soil erosion (Central Atlas, Morocco). (Photos K. Müller-Hohenstein)

In south European countries, the pressure on using wood from forests is also declining and recovery in the sclerophyllic and deciduous species can be observed. In north African countries, however, the pressure on the last near-natural remnants of forests is growing. It is feared that shortly the last cedar will be cut, and only sparse woods with particularly drought-resistant species, such as *Pinus halepensis* and *Tetraclinis articulata*, will remain locally.

Also, in the European/North African-Mediterranean region, it is obvious that subsistence-oriented land management in small family units coincides with a greater diversity of landscape and vegetation. Modern market-oriented management is always linked with a loss of diversity at all levels. In the recent past an agro-sylvo-pastoral balance was recommended; however, without developing precise ideas of it. Typical forms of the Mediterranean land use are shown in Fig. 4.1.24 A–D.

Desertification on the Edges of the Sahara

The term **desertification**, coined by Aubréville (1949), has been used at least since the many years of drought in the Sahel at the end of the 1970s to describe environmental problems in dry areas. However, it is not always used with the same meaning. Today it is obvious that this term **not only** describes **climatic stress** in long-lasting drought periods, but also complex interactions **which include particularly human interventions** on vegetation and landscape. In the context of ecosystems in dry areas, and of the often-quoted **man-made deserts**, it should be stressed that, although often described as unusual, extended dry periods are a characteristic feature of dry (desert) areas. It is not only the small amount of available water after precipitation together with high temperatures, but also the temporal, episodic and spatial distribution of this precipitation which cannot be anticipated.

In the Saharan region dry periods lasting several years have always occurred, as shown by reports in historical sources, and the interpretation of old lake sediments (Nicholson 1978). The recent dry period in the Sahel had such catastrophic consequences because it was preceded by a relatively moist period, and the population (which had meanwhile grown considerably) was not prepared for this in its land use. Better medical supplies and technical innovations (deep wells to tap fossil water) improved grazing conditions and the

number of animals increased continuously (Müller-Hohenstein 1993). Recent meteorological data indicate large regional differences in the amount of precipitation, but a general trend of increasing drought is hardly visible.

It is incorrect to regard, in this context, ecosystems of dry areas as particularly labile systems. These ecosystems are adapted to extreme climatic variability. Autochthonous plants and animals are able to adapt in many ways, and thus are able to survive under such conditions. The human population in dry areas also knows how to maintain supplies and is prepared for variations in yield (Ibrahim 1988).

Figure 4.1.25 shows a **"schematic of desertification"** with the most important causes and the consequent land degradation, in dry regions. It is important to consider the discrepancy between growth of population and – despite all technological progress – the limited availability of renewable resources as well as the substitution of traditional forms of management (nomadic life style) by modern forms of grazing and agriculture on dry fields. In the last 100 years, the human population around the Sahara has grown fivefold (Goudie 1994). Today examples of poorly adapted agriculture can be found in all areas near deserts, e.g. agriculture in northeastern Syria or eastern Jordan, with precipitation below 200 mm/year, or growing animal fodder using fossil water from more than 1000 m deep in Algerian oases, or supplying drinking water for animals in the Sahelian Ferlo, where vegetation thus degrades even further.

Human influence on the vegetation in dry areas is not so much linked to the introduction of species foreign to the flora of the region, more to the disturbance of sites and the original plant cover. Thus woody plants have disappeared in many regions because of the increased requirement for energy. The naturally sparse, so-called **contracted vegetation** (Walter 1973) is damaged by overgrazing, shown by the decrease in cover and primary production, and a shift of the floristic constitution. Good fodder plants become locally extinct in dry areas and toxic or thorny species invade. Ultimately, loss of species is to be expected. Local changes resulting from the increased loss of vegetation are seen in **remobilisation of dunes** and increased number of **dust storms**. Also water relations of areas are affected by modern irrigation installations which result in **salinisation of soils** and an increase in halophytes (Fig. 4.1.26).

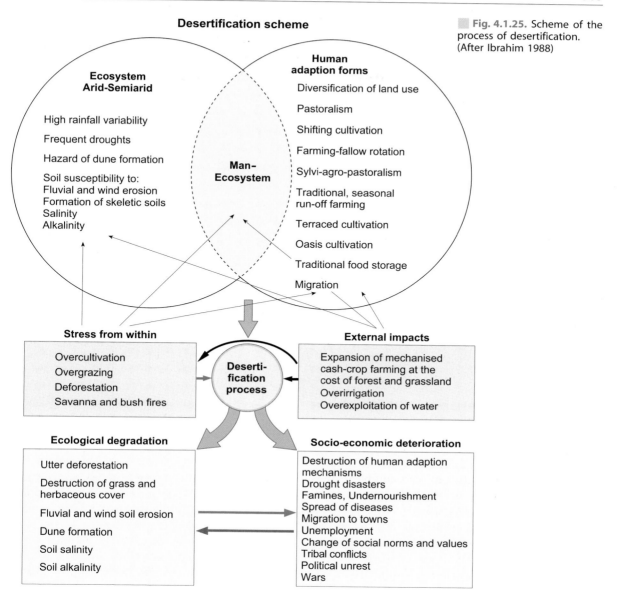

Desertification scheme

Fig. 4.1.25. Scheme of the process of desertification. (After Ibrahim 1988)

Without doubt, the recent deficiency of precipitation has worsened degradation, locally and regionally. The desert area has probably grown by 15% in the last 100 years; between 1958 and 1975 the Sahara is believed to have extended 100 km to the north and to the south (Lamprey 1975). However, such growth of the desert is also questioned; Hellden (1991) interpreted satellite pictures and was able to show a close relationship between precipitation and the vegetation, but could not find evidence for expansion of desert areas. Questions remain: are the observed changes permanent degradation and do the processes shown lead to irreversible condi-

tions, or is regeneration possible? The latter is understood as the sum of processes in an ecosystem, by which lost elements may be regained and thus re-establish themselves equivalent to their original situation. This question cannot be answered yet, as there are many positive and negative interactions between climatic events, the development of vegetation and sites, all of which are inadequately known. However, in all dry areas of the Old World, there are examples of a rapid recovery of vegetation after precipitation. Obviously, **the ability to regenerate in dry regions** depends on the variability of precipitation and the linked natural stresses, and has

Fig. 4.1.26. Desertification is obvious in areas where people apply inappropriate forms of exploitation. A A single tree (*Commiphora africana*) in the southern Sahel of Mauretania is witness to former removal of dry forests, which disappeared because of excessive grazing and movement of sand dunes. B Incorrect irrigation with water of high salt content and in-adequate drainage has caused salinisation in oases which had functioned for centuries with traditional cultivation (Dakhla Oasis, New Valley, Egypt). (Photos K. Müller-Hohenstein)

probably been underestimated. However, despite this, man may be causing the changes in dry areas, via global climate changes resulting from alterations to the albedo and the increasing dust load in the atmosphere, as well as to changes in soil moisture.

Destruction of Tropical Forests

Destruction of tropical forests has been discussed in public even more than the problem of desertification. Not the climatic but the edaphic preconditions, particularly the availability of nutrients, are the limiting factor. It has long been known that soils weather intensively and **nutrients are leached out** in uniformly high temperatures and with continuous moisture. Although litter production as well as decomposition is rapid reserves, e.g. in the form of humus, are available. Even fertilisation in the two-layered clay mineral soils is not sustainable, because they are weak exchangers. Weischet spoke as early as 1977 of a "disadvantaged tropics". The system can only remain functional if the **short-circuited nutrient cycle** is maintained, perhaps with the help of mycorrhizae or fine roots. The export of organic substances by harvesting results in far-reaching consequences. Exceptions exist only where primary cations are released because of the geological-mineralogical condi-

tions, e.g. in some regions on Java and Sulawesi (east Asia) where, with young, relatively nutrient-rich volcanic soils, permanent rice crops can be grown.

Clearing and land use have taken place in tropical rain forests for thousands of years, in India more than 9000 years ago, in Africa only 3000 years ago. The consequences of these early influences are considered to be small. Intervention over large areas began with colonial times. Of the ca. 1.5 million described animal and plant species of the permanently moist tropics – in total about 30–50 million (Furley 1993) – many thousands had probably become extinct before they could be scientifically classified. In contrast to temperate forests, "modern" forestry methods have very negative effects in the tropics, as perhaps only one single tree trunk is used per hectare and many neighbouring trees are destroyed. Even the mangrove stands in tropical coastlands are not protected for **wood management**. Sites of these unique plant communities are used in east Asia, as well as Equador, for **breeding and cultivation of prawns**.

Not only the management of forests leads to loss of species. Settlers followed the woodcutters and limited the development of secondary forests. Governments of several rain forest states saw the forests as a "valve" for the growing pop-

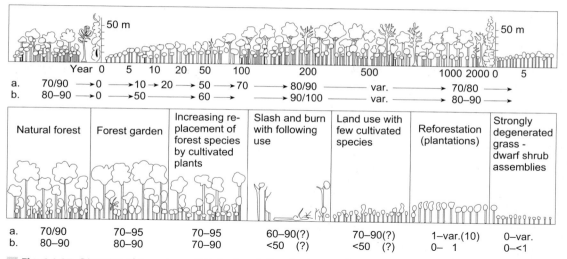

Fig. 4.1.27. Diversity of trees in undisturbed and disturbed tropical rainforests (*top* natural succession, *bottom* following increasing intensity of land use): *a* species richness as % of the maximum attainable species number and *b* evenness as % of the maximum attainable species number. (After Bruenig 1991)

ulation pressure. Thus, state subsidies were used to clear enormous areas for "ranching" establishments during the inland colonisation of Brazil (Kohlhepp 1991). At that time grass seed was sown from planes, but subsequent grazing was mostly given up after a few years as **replacement communities with hard grasses** (sclerophyllic grasses, e.g. *Imperata cylindrica*, and others) developed which were not suitable species for animal fodder. The practice of **shifting cultivation with slash and burn** used commonly in all moist, tropical areas was previously regarded as damaging. Today this form of land use is regarded as less damaging, particularly if fallow periods last long enough. However, almost all-over the tropical regions the fallow periods were shortened because of pressure from fast-growing populations. Regeneration, particularly of mycorrhizae, is no longer guaranteed. Bruenig (1991) compared the consequences of mild intervention with "modern" intervention and assessed the consequences with the help of two profiles (Fig. 4.1.27). In Fig. 4.1.28 A–C typical phases of the development of land use from the natural forest to unproductive fallow areas are shown.

Worrying numbers showing the loss of tropical moist forests have been published. The FAO documents a faster rate of decrease in rain forests from the 1980s onwards and estimates for the year 1991 alone indicate a loss of 2% of tropical forest area. Klötzli (1993) quotes 0.3 million ha/year, Bruenig (1991) calculated

more than 7 million ha/year. Even if starting from the assumption of a relatively low β-diversity (differences of diversity between different sites), these area losses affect complete plant communities with highly endemic species, and particularly the specialists amongst plants and animals. Genetic material for breeding, species for medical use, food and various commodeties are lost (WBGU 2000). Erosion on the cleared areas increases manifold, **changes in water relations** occur. There are local climatic changes at the micro- and mesoscale range. Because of the increased atmospheric CO_2 content global **climate change** is expected, with increased greenhouse effect with rising temperature and changed precipitation (IPCC-WGI 2001).

Linked to the destruction of tropical rain forests, the establishment of more protected areas than so far established has been demanded. However, many millions of people live in these areas, so concepts for sustainable management must be developed. It is often overlooked that such concepts already exist, and that there are examples of sustainable land use. The earlier hunters and gatherers, and the first settled agriculturists, independent of each other, developed well-adapted forms of land use in most tropical regions. Low population density allowed long fallow periods. The population was less mobile, stimulating a closed cover of several "storeys" from different crop plants. The original land use simulated (intuitively?) the structure and biodiversity of a natural rainforest with useful plants.

Figure 4.1.29 A–C shows forms of sustainable land use in the permanent rain forest, and in the seasonally moist rain forests of the tropics.

Wood extraction by foresters cannot be sustainable in the continuously moist tropical rain forests because of the imbalanced nutrient supply. Integrated forms of use, with crop plants adapted to – and supplementing – the conditions (e.g. supply with nutrients and water) and affecting the site (e.g. creation of particular microclimatic conditions) must be developed or taken over from indigenous populations. However, in doing this, the expectations of high yields often linked to land use in the tropics must be revised. Sustainability must be considered more than mere technologies and rates of production; the ultimate aim is maintenance of the cultural heritage in particular environments. Some elements of sustainable use are generally valid. These are **agroforestry, mixed cropping, mulching, biological pest control**, etc. (Furley 1993).

Examples of recent attempts to protect the environment exist but almost everywhere a creeping loss of protected areas can be observed. Many questions are also open about the scientific basis for nature protection in the tropics. It is, for example, assumed that a suitable number of individual plants, able to reproduce, must be available to maintain a species. Assuming this number to be 500, this would require, in the rain forest ecosystem, probably several 100 ha per species. This does not (only) concern the protection of species, but the protection of plant communities in an area. Little is known about the protection of communities in environments, about the minimum size of such spaces required and the bordering buffer zones. The borders of national parks and biosphere reserves were

Fig. 4.1.28. The three photographs show the typical processes and sequences in exploitation of tropical rainforest (example from central Sulawesi, Indonesia). A Uncontrolled clearing (slash and burn) of primary forest, done often by groups of people without knowledge of methods appropriate for the environment. B Agricultural use of the cleared forests for only a few years (without fertiliser application) until the fertility of the land is exhausted by the cultivated plants grown to fulfil the people's needs. C The unproductive area is abandoned and quickly invaded by alang-alang grass (*Imperata cylindrica*) and bracken (*Pteridium aquilinum*). (Photos K. Müller-Hohenstein)

usually roughly estimated, even if not determined according to political and economic criteria. These are important tasks for ecology which
is concerned with the protection of tropical ecosystems.

4.1.5

Basis of General Vegetation Dynamics

Vegetational units are permanently subjected to
changes in space and time. Each recording of
vegetation is only a momentary event in a complex dynamic process. The temporal dynamics
in the structure of species in space, and the corresponding changing patterns, are closely linked
to the different demands of species, to their life
cycle, mechanisms for reproduction and response to competitive pressures, and to the
available resources, in the community of species.
To understand the dynamics of vegetation, a
knowledge of stress situations and responses to
stress is important.

Vegetation dynamics aims to record and to
explain similarities of vegetation patterns and
processes with time and then to derive characteristics or typical responses and models. The
causes of processes taking place may be found
in disturbances of very different kinds and they
are particularly important.

Discussions of vegetation dynamics are made
difficult by a confusing multitude of terms,
which is caused by insufficient consideration **of
spatial and temporal scales.** Vegetation dynamics on a few square centimetres of bare rock
must be described differently to that of square
kilometres of large forests. For boreal coniferous
forests a different terminology should probably

Fig. 4.1.29. In the humid as well as in seasonally moist
tropical regions, types of sustainable agricultural land use
have been developed on all continents. A "Continuous"
rice cultivation in south-east Asia, often combined with cultivation of different palm trees (Sulawesi, Indonesia). B In
almost all tropical regions, small home gardens are multi-
storied with different layers of cultivated plants, which 'copies' the species-rich tropical forests, e.g. trees such as oil
palm (*Elaeis guineensis*), cashew nut (*Anacardium occiden-
tale*) and banana (*Musa paradisiaca*) and annual vegetables
below (Guinea-Bissau). C Sophisticated irrigation schemes
on widespread terrace complexes have been in use for
many centuries for cultivation of annual crops such as sorghum (*Sorghum bicolor*) and perennial shrubs such as coffee (*Coffea arabica*) and qat (*Catha edulis*) in the Yemen
Arab Republic. (Photos K. Müller-Hohenstein)

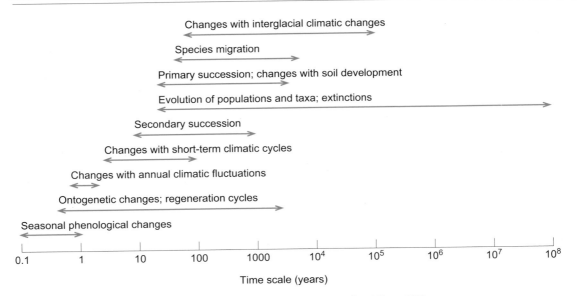

Fig. 4.1.30. Time scales for the dynamic changes in vegetation. (After Miles 1987)

be used to that for tropical rain forests. Temporal differences are probably even more important, reaching from the course of a day to centuries (Fig. 4.1.30). Ecology of vegetation must deal with extreme complexity, in the temporal sequence and the close spatial arrangement of species, populations and vegetation units.

4.1.5.1
Aspects of Daily and Seasonal Vegetation Dynamics

Plants need to adapt to changing daily and seasonal conditions in their habitat, particularly periodic changes of radiation, day length and temperatures, as well as the amount and distribution of precipitation (see Chap. 2.1). The **short-term dynamics** of plants and vegetational units is considered by the discipline of **phenology**, defined as the science of seasonal sequences of life cycles of plants and plant communities. Visible changes in the life cycle of plants are recorded and stages of development defined, and attempts made to explain these by changes with time and biotic and abiotic factors in the habitat. Not only typical sequences are of interest, but also differences in weather conditions from year to year which affect the time of flowering, conditions for germination, the amount of material production and its distribution and formation of fruit and seeds, as well as the start and duration of individual phenological stages.

Phenological characteristics have been known for a long time, because they are easy to observe. In the **daily rhythm** leaves and petals move, e.g. to protect against excessive radiation, or to capture the highest possible amount of radiation. The production of odorous substances, the secretion of nectar or the supply of pollen by flowers may be coupled with the active phases of animal partners and change during the day. This is regulated by population processes in the vegetation at a microscale as well as by the daily change of light and dark periods.

Different aspects of flowering, harvesting or colouration of leaves are basic observations in phenology. The regulation of these processes is by **photoperiodic responses** and light quality. Further important factors are temperature extremes and temperature sums or even human intervention. Examples for the spatial heterogeneity are the mosaic of vegetation on snow patches or the use of light by spring geophytes in nemoral deciduous forests (Fig. 4.1.31), or the **flowering aspects** of economically exploited meadows and pastures. Particularly important for economically useful plants, and thus of interest to many researchers, are the factors delaying growth of species at temperature limits during the course of the year. Plants may require particular temperatures in order to germinate (**stratification**) or for flower induction (**vernalisation**). Annual, biannual and perennial species behave differently, making the derivation of general rules difficult.

Box 4.1.3   Methods in phenology

Phenological studies focus on the appearance of plants during their development throughout the year and describe them quantitatively and qualitatively. The characteristics include floral development (reproduction) and leaves (vegetative growth). In spring observations are made weekly, and later at two or more week intervals. The number of flowers and the frequency of flowering (the proportion of flowering individuals in the total population of the species), number of shoots, leaves and fruits as well as the degree of cover are counted or measured.

Dierschke (1994) provides an example of such analysis in deciduous trees in nemoral forests, and reproductive stages in phenology.

- Vegetative phenological stages
  0. buds completely closed
  1. buds with green tips
  2. green leaf emergence
  3. leaves 25% unfolded
  4. leaves 50% unfolded
  5. leaves 75% unfolded
  6. leaves fully expanded
  7. first leaves yellowing
  8. leaves 50% turned colour
  9. leaves 75% turned colour
  10. leaves <75% turned colour
  11. bare
Reproductive phenological stages
  0. without flower buds
  1. flower buds recognisable
  2. flower buds swollen
  3. shortly before flowering
  4. start of flowering
  5. up to 25% flowers mature
  6. up to 50% flowers mature
  7. full flowering
  8. flowering decreasing
  9. flowering ceased
  10. fruiting
  11. fruit dispersal

Comparable scales have been developed for herbs, grasses and cryptogams. For general phenological examination, in which the whole plant stand or vegetation unit is considered, permanent areas are marked and regularly observed. This may include all, or only selected, species in vegetative and reproductive

stages of development (phenophases). In addition, environmental data are recorded, particularly those related to weather conditions as in other analysis of plant communities. The data is categorised by the start of flowering or the length of flowering period.

Subdivisions of the different phases in the development during the year into phenophases are based on phenological plant types. They have the same developmental rhythm, which appears in comparable leaf characteristics, time of flowering and duration of the growing season. Applicability of these types is limited to particular regions because individual species behave differently in different communities. Phenophases are initiated by, for example, initiation of flowering of particular plant species. Examples are flowering of *Taraxacum officinale* or seed production of *Stipa* sp. Leaf unfolding, leaf colouration and leaf fall are also important.

In phenophase diagrams, representatives of important phenological plant types are used to present phenology during the course of the year (Fig. 4.1.33). Dierschke (1989) has shown that quantitative-synthetic phenological spectra provide a precise understanding of the floristic structural features of vegetation and also allow floral and distribution aspects of biology to be understood in their interactions, thus providing the basis for the study of biocenotic relationships. **Phenological maps** are widely used to show spatial differentiation, e.g. of the start of spring (e.g. based on the initiation of flowering of apple or lilac). The selected plant species used for this must fulfil two conditions. First, they must be frequent, and widely distributed; second, they must be clearly distinguishable and have easily assessable phenological characteristics. In mesoclimatic regions trees are generally selected. Herbs represent the climate near the ground. Phenological maps, which now are made from aerial photographs, show differences within small areas such as towns and their suburbs. In agriculture, phenological characteristics are used to establish maps of growth climates and temperature ranges to assess the potential use or the probability of damage to particular types of crops.

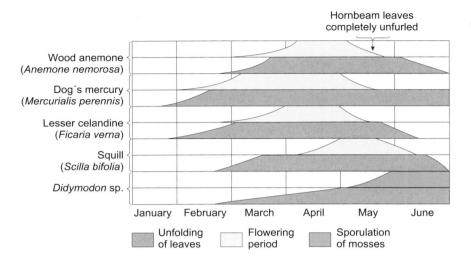

Fig. 4.1.31. Period of flowering for geophytes during spring in a hornbeam (*Carpinus betulus*) forest. (After Schmidt 1969)

Hornbeam leaves completely unfurled

Wood anemone (*Anemone nemorosa*)

Dog's mercury (*Mercurialis perennis*)

Lesser celandine (*Ficaria verna*)

Squill (*Scilla bifolia*)

Didymodon sp.

January   February   March   April   May   June

Unfolding of leaves   Flowering period   Sporulation of mosses

Fig. 4.1.32. Zonation of plant communities on the sides of large wadis in North Yemen (Yemen Arab Republic), determined by runoff. A Wadi Mawr in the Tihama mountains with highly variable water discharge during the year (Photo K. Müller-Hohenstein). B Exaggerated and schematic profile from the bed of the wadi to the lower terraces to the top of the wadi bank. Only therophytes such as *Bacopa monnieri* and *Phyla nodiflora* are able to colonise the frequently moving gravel banks. In the more strongly consolidated regions of the banks, grasses with particular root systems (rhizomes) such as *Desmostachya bipinnata* and very elastic woody species, such as *Tamarix nilotica*, are able to survive episodic flooding. The resulting changes in vegetation are relatively rapid and aperiodic.
(After Deil and Müller-Hohenstein 1985)

1 m

0

1 m

0   Exaggerated and schematic profile

Cadaba rotundifolia
Acacia oerfota
Acacia ehrenbergiana,
Aloe vera
Euphorbia inarticulata
Acacia tortilis s.str.
Commiphora div. spec.
Anisotes trisulcus
Adenium obesum
Salvadora persica
Acacia ehrenbergiana
Cassia senna, Jatropha villosa
C. rotundifolia and other lianas
Cissus quadrangularis
Aristolochia arborea
Tamarix nilotica
Jatropha curcas
Desmostachya bipinnata
Young plants
Tamarix nilotica
Phyla nodiflora
Bacopa monnieri
Actual course of river

B

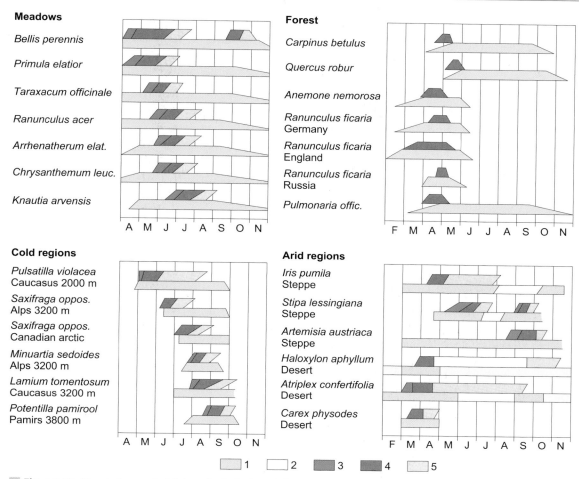

Fig. 4.1.33. Vegetative period (phenological phases) for meadow plants (oat grass – *Arrhenatherum* – in Poland), for trees and herbs in a mixed oak forest in northern Germany (with comparison of *Ranunculus ficaria* to those in Russia and England), and also for plant species from cold regions (high mountains, arctic regions) and from semiarid and arid regions (steppe, deserts). After Larcher (1994). *1* Time required for complete leaf cover; *2* death due to drought; *3* flower buds visible; *4* flowering period; *5* fruit ripening and seed dispersal

There are also short-term periodic or episodic events which cannot be explained by the usual phenological characteristics, but determine the dynamics of these communities decisively. These include regularly occurring floods in river basins, requiring particular adaptations to the extreme water supply, and problems of root respiration and perhaps mechanical disturbance (Fig. 4.1.32 A, B). Another example is the stress caused by avalanches, with the subsequent characteristic vegetation patterns in the Alpine belt. Regularly repeated human influences are important, e.g. mowing once or twice a year and grazing with different numbers or species of animals.

Other growth processes also occur in phases, e.g. of shoots or roots, but this may not always be visible (Fig. 4.1.34).

Phases of activity and dormancy are characteristic for all regions with a seasonal climate. A distinction is made between phases or periods of stronger activity of vegetative and reproductive growth. Occasionally, several vegetative **pulses of growth** occur; for example, in late summer some tree species rapidly form very distinct new shoots. Seasons may be determined by temperature or from water supply. In the latter case, seasonally changing water supply is the most important regulatory factor for short-term dynamics of vegetation. Even under Mediterranean conditions, for example, summer annuals of temperate zones are replaced by winter annuals, flowering periods shift into autumn. In the tropics with seasonal precipitation the flowering phase is induced by the onset of the rains.

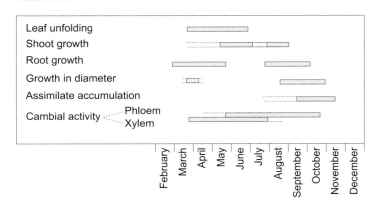

Leaf unfolding	
Shoot growth	
Root growth	
Growth in diameter	
Assimilate accumulation	
Cambial activity ···· Phloem / Xylem	

February March April May June July August September October November December

Fig. 4.1.34. Growth periods and storage of assimilates by trees in temperate zones during the year. (After Larcher 1994)

In woody species, two types have evolved. "Late flowering" plants flower only after the development of leaves or after shedding of leaves at the end of the rainy season, whilst "early flowering" plants start to flower before the emergence of leaves, i.e. before the rainy season begins. For both types biological processes ensure pollination and distribution, i.e. the simultaneous occurrence of pollinators or seasonal periods with regular winds. In extremely dry regions, where therophytes dominate, definite flowering periods no longer occur, because of the high variability of precipitation in time and space. But after rain the **"flowering desert"** quickly develops. Many annuals of dry areas may finish their life cycle within a few weeks (Fig. 4.1.35).

Because of the usually favourable conditions of temperature and moisture in the moist tropics, plants often grow continuously. Nevertheless, irregular bursts of growth may be observed, with differences in the trunks even for an individual plant. However, definite flower periods or other phenological phases can hardly be established. Some individuals flower and carry ripe fruits at the same time. Occasionally, slight periodicity may be observed, which is triggered by very slight changes in temperature or endogenously. It is remarkable that several species of plants only flower very episodically, sometimes only after several decades.

Timing and duration of individual phenological phases within the year is very closely correlated with the sequence of weather during the year. These short-term dynamics, occurring year by year, but not necessarily cyclic, are often termed **fluctuation**. Changes are registered at the level of individual plants. The most important expression of fluctuation is the change of dominance of the participating species. They

may deviate from the hypothetical average sequence, mostly determined by environmental stress. A return to the previous state is possible and thus this differs from succession. In open fields it is not easy to distinguish between fluctuation and succession, as both overlap and influence each other.

Fluctuations in dry regions with fairly high variations in precipitation are particularly striking. **Annuals in deserts** may fail for many years, but after precipitation, they determine the aspect. The biblical seven fat and seven lean years

Fig. 4.1.35. After one of the rare rainfall events in extreme deserts, the "flowering desert" (Arabic, acheb) quickly develops. Such an unpredictable change in vegetation is called a fluctuation and is a plant community composed only of therophytes. This example is from the Arabian Desert (United Arab Emirates) and contains *Silene villosa, Senecio glaucus* and *Plantago amplexicaulis*. (Photo K. Müller-Hohenstein)

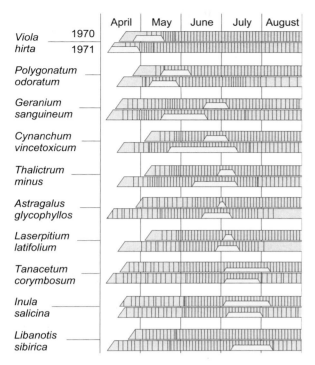

	April	May	June	July	August

Viola hirta 1970 / 1971

Polygonatum odoratum

Geranium sanguineum

Cynanchum vincetoxicum

Thalictrum minus

Astragalus glycophyllos

Laserpitium latifolium

Tanacetum corymbosum

Inula salicina

Libanotis sibirica

Fig. 4.1.36. A 2-year phenological spectrum for some species bordering a forest. After Dierschke (1994). The small trapezoidal area shows the flowering period

point towards fluctuations and their significance in dryland agriculture. In mountains of moderate latitude, simple or complex snow patch communities are formed depending on the time scale and thus document fluctuations. Figure 4.1.36 shows the phenological spectrum of species of woodland edges for two different annual sequences, documenting the extent of such fluctuations.

Fluctuations may also occur because of a massive attack by herbivores. Genetically determined fluctuations are, for example, the so-called mast years with production of many fruits. Ultimately, fluctuations are often the result of human intervention, e.g. changing the rotation in grazing management or changing crops in agriculture. Rabotnov (1974) gives a classification of fluctuations according to their cause and progression.

Evaluations of synecological and biocenological links are only emerging, e.g. of the temporal niches of flowering species in plant communities, of the synchronisation of insects and animals which eat and distribute pollen, fruits and seeds. This would not only make pollen calendars available for those with allergies, but also

help those protecting nature, i.e. by providing dates for mowing, for extensive maintenance, or as a control for the success of different types of land use.

4.1.5.2
Aspects of Long-Term Vegetation Dynamics

Medium- and long-term changes of the plant cover over several decades and up to millennia are analysed as **research of successions**. Until a few decades ago, the empirical data were easy to grasp and from them principles and models were derived. However, from the beginning, there was controversy in the scientific discussions between those with holistic and those with reductionist approaches. There were those who always wanted to consider the complete ecosystem, and those who did not believe that this was possible and therefore concentrated on individual functions and processes in those systems. Both approaches had the same aim in trying to recognise the causes of vegetation dynamics, to explain the resulting effects and, if possible, to predict them. Recently, new theories have been added, not always based on broad empirical information. There is still belief that there are **basic rules of dynamic sequences**, but many processes are now seen as stochastic. It is generally accepted that it is necessary to consider spatial and temporal scales in greater detail.

Beginnings of Succession Research
Systematic scientific research into vegetation dynamics started relatively recently and is connected with the names of the geographer Cowles, the ecologists Clements and Gleason and the botanist Gams. Clements (1916) is regarded as the founder of the discipline of succession, starting from the idea that only undemanding species grow first on bare substrates. With time they influence each other and also the conditions at the site. The latter leads to a succession by different communities which are adapted to the changing conditions. Clear temporal periods are recognisable until the development of a uniform, final community, the so-called **climax community**, representing a relative equilibrium. Small fluctuations are possible but not a reversal of the clearly directed processes leading to this climax community.

In his later work, Clements assumed three succession sequences. One of these sequences has its origin in a fresh water basin. During the processes of receding water and emerging land in temperate latitudes, deciduous forests develop as a climax via a boggy and pre-forest stage (**hydroseries**). Another sequence starts from saline substrate (**haloseries**), a third on bare rock (**xeroseries**), but all end in the same deciduous forest climax. Changes in the site always originate from plants themselves, they cause changes. Also, in a large area with the same climatic conditions, the same final community will always emerge (**monoclimax**).

This concept was well received, because of the belief that all vegetation units fitted into this concept, but there were critics who could not empirically confirm this theory. The reason for the discrepancy was that Clements concentrated on the dynamics of undisturbed vegetation (**primary succession**) and interferences of any kind, and developments arising from them (**secondary succession**), were disregarded.

Clement's theory, which regarded plant communities as organisms, was soon challenged and rejected by Gleason (1926), who stressed that there was also an individualistic type of vegetation dynamics without clear steps and without formation of the different vegetation units. Gleason started from the assumption that changes of species at a site depended on the species composition and the influx of diaspores to that site.

Following this controversy two important movements become clear, which set the tone of succession research to this day:

- relatively general interpretation of the broad spectrum of dynamic events in ecosystems; and
- recognition of the enormous complexity of conditions and attempts to clarify individual aspects.

Even if the concepts of Clements and Gleason are no longer accepted in their pure form, it is still to the credit of the first researchers of succession that they introduced the principle of dynamics into an ecological analysis which had been rather static before.

Definition of Successions

Vegetation dynamics is the **change of structure and species constitution** in vegetation units **in space and time**. Short-term, daily and seasonal changes are included. All forms may be described by the term **"patch dynamics"** (Pickett and White 1985).

Successions are medium- to long-term dynamic processes in a **directed, temporal sequence** of species communities in an ecosystem. It is often stressed that these sequences are irreversible and – within limits – predictable. This sequence may be triggered by endogenous or exogenous processes, e.g. an explosion in the propagation of individual species or anomalous weather conditions. During succession, self-organisation in the ecosystem (on the precondition that there is no disturbance) increases and a balance between primary production and mineralisation develops. Odum (1980) lists a total of 24 different ecosystem characteristics able to change during the succession sequence. He regarded the development as a well-ordered process, resulting from changes caused by the vegetation and ultimately leading to a stable ecosystem, where maximum functional interconnections are achieved. The hypothetical final state is understood as a complex community of organisms with complex links and interactions, in which the equilibrium once achieved may, of course, change again.

However, successions are often also understood as stochastic processes, basically because the seed input in a biocenose at a site is random; the same applies also to the germination rates or the availability of necessary safe sites and, of course, the occurrence of disturbance – their type, intensity and degree – which are generally not predictable.

Based on Dierschke (1994), here succession is understood as a long-term, directed change in the composition of vegetation and its structure at a site. Main features are the changes in quantitative and qualitative characteristics of a stand (abundance and combinations of species). The result is a more or less controlled sequence of different plant communities, depending on the conditions of sites and how they change.

Succession Types

Succession may be considered over large or small areas, or as fast or slow changes. It may be directed or cyclic, and may be affected by endogenous or exogenous processes which many differ in type, intensity, duration or extent. It is important to consider the geographic location within different climatic zones of the region, whether development occurs on newly formed soils, or on those previously colonised and still established. Finally, participating plant species differ in their ability to win space and, in their

Box 4.1.4 Methods for studying succession

Research into succession has followed two complementary paths. In one the development of the vegetation with time is studied on a particular site with experimental treatments. The other is an older approach in which the composition of vegetation is related to changes over time (false time series, **location for time**). An example which is often given is the littoral zone of a lake which in its spatial development may be seen as an ecological series but in its temporal processes on the same site may be interpreted as succession.

Indicator plants, age structure and diversity of stands or analysis of seed banks often help to establish the temporal sequence of particular developmental stages. Indicators from outside the vegetation being studied are often used, such as analysis of the differences in soil profiles or historical records from archives on land-use registries and account books of farms which often have data about fertilisation or use of herbicides at particular times. An example of a derived succession is that of different types of plants in abandoned vineyards (Fig. 4.1.37). There are numerous important studies from areas covered with volcanic lava flows of different ages which can be dated accurately (see Chap. 3.5.1).

There are problems in drawing conclusions from spatial associations about temporal succession. Therefore, more direct methods of understanding succession have been established and are increasingly used. Spatially limited units of vegetation are established and in regular sequence evaluated individually (**biomonitoring**). This long-term observation on **permanent plots** provides detailed analysis about population dynamics as the vegetation changes. Evaluation of aerial photographs and repeated satellite data promise much, although current technical methods still allow speculation. Only a few parameters can be measured. The scale is not sufficient for observation of individuals, although it is suitable for comparison of the average state of stands, and structural aspects of the plant cover are most obvious whilst inventories of species are not comparable. Experimental studies of succession, for example of economic use, are carried out on comparable areas using a range of treatments (e.g. different fertiliser applications, mowing regimes, single or multiple soil tillage, fencing and exclusion of grazing or other sorts of herbivory) and the effects on the vegetation during the following period are measured. Particular attention is paid to experiments relating to the problems of biodiversity and to competition within and between species. Also these questions are linked to succession in stands (EU project *Biodepth*; Hector et al. 1999). Biomonitoring is used in analysis of succession for regulation and manipulation of measures in nature conservation in order to show trends in development of the vegetation.

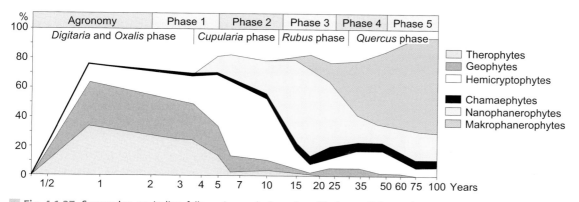

Fig. 4.1.37. Succession on Italian fallow vineyards, based on life forms. (After Richter 1989, from Dierschke 1994)

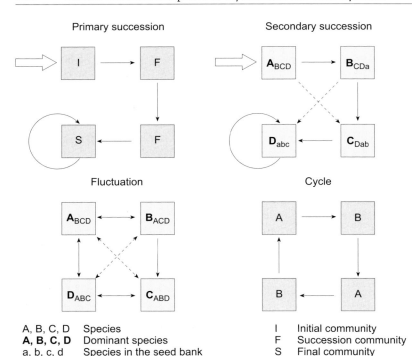

Fig. 4.1.38. Types of directed and cyclic vegetation dynamics. (After Jochimsen 1993)

A, B, C, D   Species
A, B, C, D   Dominant species
a, b, c, d   Species in the seed bank

I   Initial community
F   Succession community
S   Final community

life cycles, their demands on the site, the qualities for competition and strategies. Dynamic processes are triggered if net production and mineralisation in an ecosystem are not balanced. In this case it is possible, for example, to accumulate organic matter (formation of bogs, **autotrophic succession**) or the organic matter is consumed (use of humus by agricultural systems, **heterotrophic succession**).

Considering these aspects, many succession types on different spatial and temporal scales have been described. Van der Maarel (1996) attempted to show the spatial and temporal relations and how they are related and differ (Table 4.1.7).

Succession dynamics are visible by the loss of species and life forms possibly replaced by others. Often only short-term changes in abundance or dominance of species within a vegetation unit are noticeable. On this basis, it is hardly possible to determine a certain type of succession.

Figure 4.1.38 shows successional types schematically. These are the most important examples of progressive and regressive, directed as well as cyclic vegetation dynamics.

Table 4.1.7. Relationships between spatial and temporal dimensions in the changes in vegetation. (After van der Maarel 1996)

	Individual	Patch	Population	Community	Landscape	Region
Fluctuation	×	××	××			
Gap dynamics	×	××	××			
Patch dynamics	×	×	×			
Cyclic succession		×	××	×		
Regeneration succession		××	××	××		
Secondary succession		×	××	××	××	
Primary succession			××	××	××	
Secular succession				×	×	×

The terms in the table header refer to spatial dimensions. A patch is a small homogeneous area (ecotope), a gap a small open space in the forest

Primary Successions

Primary successions are very important for understanding processes of vegetation dynamics, but in reality they are rarely observed. There are two reasons for this: they only occur slowly over decades and centuries, and one of the main prerequisites for this type of succession is missing – a completely bare abiotic substrate where such a directed development may start. Knowledge of individual stages of the sequence of primary succession is mainly from newly formed sites, for example, after volcanic eruptions (island of Surtsey near Iceland, in 1963), or in newly developed coastal regions or at the feet of melting glaciers (Fig. 4.1.39 A–C). Anthropogenic sites, such as rubble heaps, quarries, etc., may be regarded as starting points of primary succession. Despite the differences in sites, uniform trends and basic patterns may be derived from such situations (see also Chap. 3, Fig. 3.2.14).

Only very few plants are able to cope with the extreme conditions of a site during the initial phases. On rocks, cryptogamic communities develop first, perhaps lithophilic lichens, then fruticose lichens, mosses and ferns. In unfavourable exposed positions, e.g. on steep rock walls or on mobile debris, the development does not go beyond this phase (permanent pioneer communities). Usually, the pioneer communities, which themselves depend on the input of propagules from the surrounding areas, change the site over the course of time because of soil formation. Herbaceous pioneers occurring in such a site are many Leguminosae, leading to accumulation of nitrogen. Later pioneer plants change the microclimate of their habitat. If flowering plants have not established during the first phase of succession, they will now follow. These are predominantly heliophilic, epigaeic germinating therophytes or, where the climatic conditions do not allow such establishment, undemanding herbaceous hemicryptophytes and chamaephytes, e.g. on the moraine of the Aletsch glacier (Fig. 4.1.40).

Fig. 4.1.39. Three photographs showing stages of primary succession. A On fresh volcanic lava dense moss and lichen communities have developed after 8 years. B Only specialists among the vascular plants (e.g. *Pozoa volcanica*, Apiaceae) establish quickly on the almost unweathered rocks almost without soil. C Only after several decades do the first trees (*Nothofagus obliqua*, *N. dombeyi*) form an open woody vegetation. Photos were taken on sites of different ages on the volcano Llaima in southern Chile. (Photos K. Müller-Hohenstein)

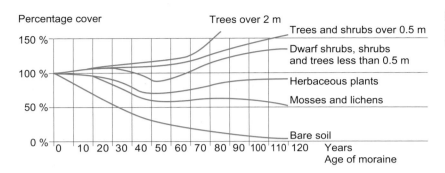

Fig. 4.1.40. Succession on moraines of the Aletsch glacier (Switzerland). (After Klötzli 1993)

Pioneers are slowly excluded. More demanding species gain space. If this change takes place solely because of the changes in the vegetation itself it is called **autogenic succession**. If other causes are more important – e.g. natural climate change or lower groundwater table caused by human extraction of water – this is called **allogenic succession**. If successions proceed under steady external conditions, there are further stages, after the pioneer stage, where competing species occur, which are superior to the pioneer species in vegetative and reproductive growth. These species grow taller, despite lower rates of growth, because of their longer life span (occurrence and increase of phanerophytes), they are more shade tolerant but often have less effective mechanisms for distribution, despite their more effective occupation of space in the long term. Trees are superior to shrubs, **forming polycormones** (see Chap. 2.4, Fig. 2.4.30), which enable them to dominate for a certain time. In the final phase of such development, trees dominate (see Chap. 3; Fig. 3.2.14). This type of primary succession is understood to be progressive, as the diversity increases at the level of the species as well as with regard to their structure.

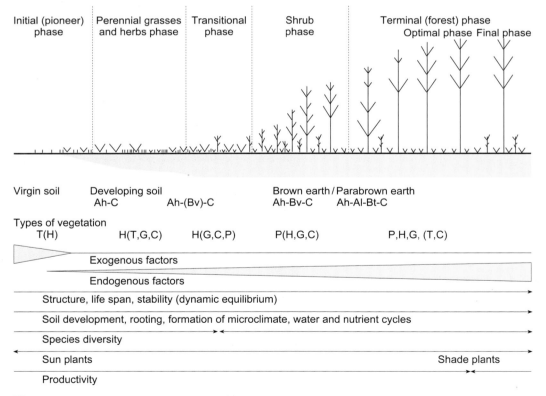

Fig. 4.1.41. Main characteristics of the progress of primary succession (on silicate rock and under subatlantic climatic conditions). (Dierschke 1994)

Dierschke (1994) tried to summarise common themes and dynamic trends, despite the apparent individuality of responses (Fig. 4.1.41). At the beginning of primary succession, chaotic interactions dominate, which cannot be predicted, as input and establishment of propagules are, to a high degree, stochastic. Widely distributed therophytes dominate. Between the development of vegetation and changes in the site feed-back mechanisms occur (Table 4.1.8). This means that plants themselves contribute, to a considerable degree, to creating environmental conditions for their species. The dominance of exogenous factors is only slowly substituted by endogenous factors, and is accompanied by a change of species and life forms. In the labile pioneer stages, intra- and interspecific competition is not very important, but in the later stages competition plays a decisive role in the development of communities (see Chap. 3.2.1) which are more and more resistant to external disturbance, and, from the point of view of the plant community, is termed an increasingly saturated community.

Primary succession occurs faster under warm, humid climate conditions than under cold or dry conditions; deep soils are more favourable than bare rock. However, it is most important that development is not affected by disturbance, which can now only be very rarely excluded. Thus primary successions are particularly important for understanding of secondary successions which determine the actual vegetation dynamics in our environment.

Table 4.1.8. Environmental changes during succession. After Klötzli (1993)

1. Species structure

Species composition	First rapid, then stepwise change
Number of autotrophic species (autotrophic diversity)	Increasing, often early in secondary succession
Number of heterotrophic species (heterotrophic diversity)	Increasing, until late in secondary succession
Species diversity	Initially increasing, then stable or again decreasing
Niche specialists	Initially broad then narrow
Size of organism	Initially small then large
Life cycle	Initially brief and simple, then long and complex
Selection pressure	Initially r-selection then K-selective
Type of production	Initially quantitative then qualitative

2. Nutrient cycles

Cycles	Initially open then closed
Nutrient exchange	Initially rapid then slow
Role of organic debris (detritus)	Initially unimportant then very important

3. Organic structure

Total biomass	Initially small then large
Stratification	Initially one layer then multiple
Inorganic nutrients	Initially in soil then in biomass
Recalcitrant organic material (e.g. humus)	Initially little then much
Biochemical diversity (e.g. pigments)	Initially low then high (increasing accumulation of toxins!)
Chlorophyll amount	Initially small then large (in secondary succession little difference!)

4. Energy flow

Relation to the food chain	Initially simple (food chain) then complex (food web)
Gross primary production	During early phase of primary succession increasing (only limited or no increase in secondary succession)
Net primary production	Continuously decreasing
Total respiration	Continuously increasing
Primary production per unit respiration	Initially primary production greater than equal to respiration (steady-state condition)
Primary production per unit biomass	Initially large then small
Biomass per unit of energy	Initially small then large; therefore, minimal use of energy per unit of biomass

5. Homeostasis (ecological steady state, result of irreversible processes)

Internal symbiosis	Initially not developed then developed
Nutrient storage	Initially small then large
Stability (resistance to disturbance)	Initially small then large
Entropy (increasing entropy)	Initially large (small) then small (constant)
Information	Initially small then large

Secondary Successions

Primary successions may develop into secondary successions because of disturbance (see also Chap. 3.2.5). There is a multitude of different types of **disturbance** which affect the sequence of vegetation so various secondary successions occur (Fig. 4.1.42 A, B).

Succession sequence may be classified into three types, according to the responses to disturbance (regarding the material balance of the ecosystem, see Chap. 3.2.5):

- Disturbance may interrupt the dynamics and the vegetation may thus remain at a certain stage (permanent communities).
- Changes occurring without clear direction within vegetation, e.g. because of long-term fluctuations in the water level.
- Influences mentioned can lead to faster or slower, and also irreversible, alterations. Such processes result in a reverse response of the direction of changes which is termed as regressive succession or also regression or retrogression. These include successions which occur as a consequence of over-exploitation or selective use of forests and pastures.

The most important secondary successions are those which aim to achieve the previous state after disturbance. These progressive secondary successions hardly differ in their development from primary successions. Here, too, the changes in direction lead to a more complex form of organisation in the plant community. However, secondary successions have a different initial stage. Their dynamic changes start from an already settled substrate and may build on an existing seed bank. This means that secondary successions progress faster than primary successions; right from the start there is competition for space and resources and only species able to compete are able to invade.

In central Europe numerous studies were made on secondary succession on fallow land and meadows. Schmidt (1993) describes succession over 25 years on (previously sterilised) fallow fields. After only 2 years occupation by therophytes, persistent herbaceous plants established until the eighth year, after which hemicryptophytes and shrubs occurred up to the twentieth year. Finally, successions continued with pioneer forest, or a pre-forest stage. These phases were initially limited by nutrients and light. Even if individual phases develop relatively regularly it is difficult to analyse this development and to determine the decisive factors determining the succession because of the many factors influencing and feeding back into the process (Fig. 4.1.43).

Fig. 4.1.42. Secondary successions develop after disturbances, which may be natural, e.g. in A when accumulated dead wood results from volcanic activity and subsequent fire in a forest community (in lower mountain forests on the Lanin volcano in southern Chile). However, B the disturbances can also be man-made, e.g. forests cleared by fire for range lands, not for timber, in southern Chile near Aisen. (Photos K. Müller-Hohenstein)

Box 4.1.5   The importance and differentiation of disturbances in the dynamics of vegetation

Disturbances which cause deviation from the normal developmental processes and may have unexpected consequences in removing some species and forming space for new may be endogenous. They result from the community itself and cause stress situations to which the community cannot adapt rapidly. An example is the explosive increase of herbivorous insects causing denudation of the vegetation. Inherent disturbances are separated from endogenous disturbances (Richter 1997). The former occur regularly; they are a feature of the system and therefore organisms in the community adapt. This is the case for seasonal changes and for changes such as frequent, regular flooding of meadows. Most disturbances which then lead to secondary succession are exogenous. They may be natural, e.g. catastrophic storms or landslides and avalanches. However, in our managed landscapes, anthropogenic disturbance dominates, starting with clearance or mowing or other processes which immediately affect individual plants or which alter the environment and affect the whole community, e.g. use of fertilisers and herbicides, or are slower in effect, such as lowering of the groundwater. There are spatial and temporal patterns in disturbance which help to understand the patterns of succession. Richter (1997) attempted in the following table to characterise disturbances in different climate zones:

Type of disturbance	1. Polar and subpolar regions	2. Boreal region	3. Moist temperate region	4.1 Grass steppes	4.2 Deserts/semi-deserts	5.1 Deserts/semi-deserts dry regions	5.2 Thorn steppe/thorn savannah	6. Mediterranean subtropical	7. Monsoon subtropical	8. Seasonally moist tropics	9. Permanently moist tropics	10a) extra-tropical	10b) high deserts	10c) high tropical
Solifluction	●	◔	○	○	○	○	○	○	○	○	○	◑	◑	◑
Ice/snow breakage	○	◑	◔	○	○	◔	○	○	○	○	○	○	○	○
Burrowers	◕	◔	◔	●	◑	◑	◔	○	◔	◔	◔	◕	◕	◑
Soil leaching	○	◔	◑	○	○	◔	◔	○	◑	○	◔	○	○	○
Animal damage	◔	◔	◑	○	○	○	◔	◔	◕	○	◔	◔	◔	◔
Phytophages	◔	◔	◑	◔	○	◑	○	◑	◕	○	◔	◔	◑	◔
Rain inudation incl. splashing	◑	○	○	◕	●	●	●	◑	○	◔	◑	◔	●	◔
Salinisation	○	○	○	●	●	●	◑	○	○	○	○	◔	○	○
Fire	◔	●	○	◑	○	◕	◑	●	○	◔	◔	◔	○	◕
Drought	○	◔	◔	◕	◔²	○	○²	○	◑	●	○	◔	○²	◔
Floods	○²	◔²	◔²	◑	◑³	◑³	◔	◔²	◔²	◔²	○	○	○	○
Frosts		◔²	◔²	○	○²	◑	○	◑	○	○	○	◔²	○²	○²
Strong winds/hurricanes	○	◔	◔¹	○	◔	◑	◔	◑	○	◑	◔¹	◔	○	○
Rapid large-scale movements	○	○	○	○	○	◑	○	○	○	○	●	◔	◑	

1 = in places catastrophic: e.g. hurricanes in the Carribean, tornadoes in west Patagonia
2 = frequent, but (mainly) ineffective   3 = seldom, but effective
Disturb. eff. seldom, never: ○   Weak, seldom: ◔   Mild, occasional: ◑   Clear, frequent: ◕   Strong, often: ●

Compl. clearance - effect on repro.	◔	◑	◔¹	◕	◕	◕	◕	◕	○¹	◑	○¹	◔	◔	◔
Clearings - effect on repro.	○	○	◔	○	○	○	○	◔	◑	○	◔	○	○	○
Patches - effect on repro.	◑	○	○	●	◔	○	○	○	○	○	○	◔	◔	◔
Effect of self reproduction	◔	◑	◑	◕	◕	◕	◕	◔	◑	◕	◑	◑	◑	◑

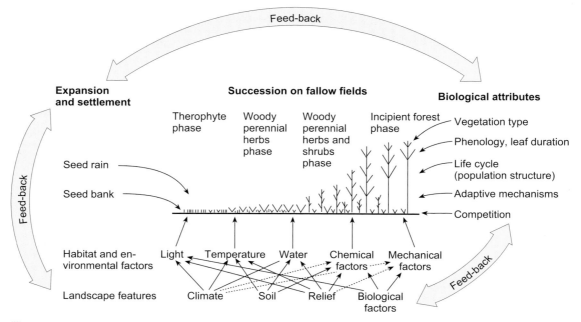

Fig. 4.1.43. Successions on fallowed agricultural fields: influencing factors and interrelations. (Schmidt 1993)

Secondary succession on fallow pasture is difficult because of the existing dense grassland community. Schreiber (1995) shows, from observations over 20 years, that establishment of woody plants occurs in several ways. Occasionally, well-known basic processes in the succession of different types of plants from annuals to woody species occur. However, pastures, initially relatively homogeneous, often show formation of dominance patterns with few species that cover the area well after just a few years. With good nutrient supply herbaceous plants dominate because biomass is not removed (auteutrophication), but with poor nutrient supply grasses dominate. The temporal sequence of individual stages differs considerably. On some areas, 10–15 m high pre-forest vegetation occurs; on other potential forest sites neither trees nor shrubs grow. The difference in appearance and establishment of woody plants does not fit any succession model so far described; a prediction on changes of life forms and species is not yet possible, even if occasionally such phases in vegetation dynamics may be clearly seen.

Secondary successions not only develop on fallow or abandoned land, but also in plant communities affected by disturbance such as from fire or avalanches. Here processes directed towards a re-establishment of the original status occur and fit into a **cyclic regeneration scheme**. Examples originate from managed forests where man is the driving force of such cycles. Pignatti and Pignatti (1984) analysed such regeneration cycles for Mediterranean forests (Fig. 4.1.44) and showed two variants – one for regeneration after clearing, and one, more regressive, succession after several fires. After clearing various weeds appear which are excluded by oaks. Repeated fires lead to a permanent stage, with regeneration occurring – if at all – only after a long period.

A special case of secondary succession is the polycormophyte succession. Vegetative side shoots of plants form shoot colonies, able to expand in closely covered herbaceous plant communities faster than via seeds. This type of succession usually starts with a pioneer woody species with defence against herbivores, e.g. *Prunus spinosa*. Such plants are able to survive over large areas for decades. Finally, higher growing unprotected shrubs and trees establish in the centres of such areas, so that forest islands and, ultimately, closed forest areas may form (Hard 1975). This development may be interpreted as an autogeneous type of succession, regulated by the vegetation itself. Study of this form of succession allows strategies of competition in woody species to be recognised (Fig. 4.1.45).

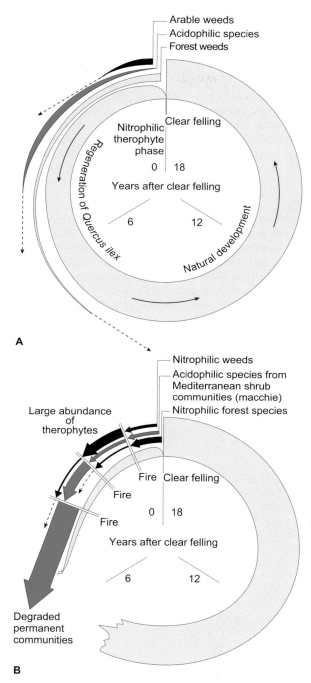

These changes over time are very complex, there are many variables influencing development, e.g. site, biological reproduction, space and time. Particularly important is the type, intensity and duration of disturbance. All these factors make it difficult to regulate and predict successions.

Cyclic Vegetation Dynamics

Cyclic processes in the development of vegetation are also important, in addition to the directed – progressive or regressive – dynamic processes. Glavac (1996) interprets the final phase of secondary succession as a sort of self-preservation cycle. In a cyclic succession, different ages of plants enter and replace each other in the same vegetational community. Structural changes with the same or different species at one site are important. Remmert (1985) in particular – stimulated by ideas on cyclic successions from Aubréville (1949) – built on this interpretation and confirmed it theoretically, as well as practically. Further concepts about **cyclic vegetation dynamics** originated from Watt (1947) who introduced the term **"gaps"** into the discussion, i.e. sites where these processes take place. In each case an important observation was that the climax stage (mature stage) does not extend over enormous areas in natural forests, but that various phases of development are spread like a mosaic over the whole area. Displaced phases occur side by side, in small areas at all stages. For central European forest areas three phases are distinguished:

- an optimal phase corresponding to a forest of uniform age with few species; a closed stand with little undergrowth;
- ageing and decaying phases when the tree layer is disrupted over large areas and species requiring light and nutrient are able to invade;
- a rejuvenating and juvenile phase, with young plants of the same or different tree species, with the previous phases occurring again. Often light-demanding trees invade first, followed by shade-tolerant trees.

As explained in Chapter 3.2.1 these phases may be regarded as a continuous process of **self-thinning**.

Figure 4.1.46 shows schematically the cyclic dynamics for a tropical rain forest. The size of the pieces of the mosaic differs, depending on the diversity of species. In nemoral deciduous forests an average size of 1–2 ha is assumed, in

Fig. 4.1.44. Succession in a Mediterranean oak forest. A Cycles following clear felling. B Regression after multiple fires. (After Pignatti and Pignatti 1984, from Dierschke 1994)

The concept of successions as a directed, more or less deterministic process, and therefore also predictable, must be corrected according to empirical results obtained in recent decades.

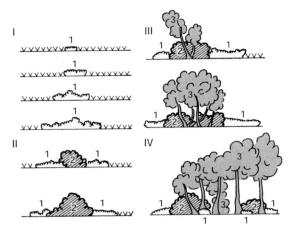

Fig. 4.1.45. Polycormophyte succession of woody species in grassland: *1* with establishment of low-growing woody species; *2* followed by tall-growing woody species; *3* with woody, tall trees. (After Hard 1975, from Dierschke 1994)

cycles last several thousands of years. Processes of vegetation dynamics similar to **mosaic cycles** have also been described for North Atlantic heath and bog complexes. For tropical communities (rain forests, savannahs, mangroves, coral reefs) this type of change occurs over time. This does not mean that the cycles must always be uniform. Certain phases may be left out.

Disturbance is again seen as the driving force for cyclic vegetation dynamics. The life span of "key organisms" is important, and competition following the death of key organisms for light and nutrients. Mechanical influences (wind breakage, fire) play an important role. Changed conditions in the site result from disturbance. Species which are able to obtain the necessary resources from the site after the disturbances can establish and their regeneration strategy enables them to start a new cycle.

Constant conditions are not to be expected in an **pristine forest**, it is a **mosaic of asynchronous phases of cyclic vegetation dynamics**. During the individual phases, structural characteristics of forests as well as the diversity change. This means that large sections of a forest contain all phases and possess normal population distribution of the dominant species. As a consequence, all phases in such vegetation dynamics

boreal forests the pieces of the mosaic are several square kilometres because of fires; in contrast, in tropical rain forests they are hardly ever larger than 100 m² (**treefall gaps**). The duration of cycles also differs. For the well-analysed forests of the boreal zone several centuries are assumed, in the North American sequoia forests

Phases:
1. Destruction 2. Regrowth 3. Competition 4. Death of pioneer species 5. Homeostasis

Fig. 4.1.46. Mosaic cycle in a tropical rainforest. From Richter (1997). *Open tree crown* Pioneer species; *thick tree crown* canopy species; *medium tree crown* shade-tolerant species

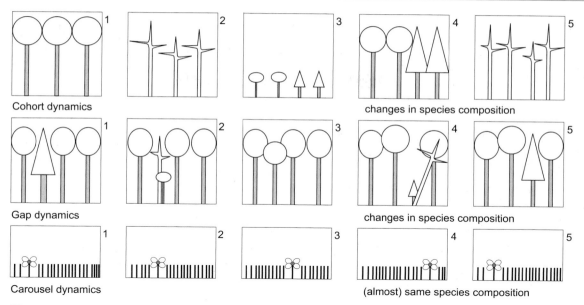

Fig. 4.1.47. Developmental phases of different types of plants during the changes in vegetation. (After Richter 1997)

must be regarded as a (dynamic) ecosystem with all biotic partners and the also changing abiotic conditions, as occurs in **sigma sociology** (Schwabe 1991). The term climax is also regarded in this mosaic concept as the sum of different stages of the affected system over a large area (Jax 1994).

Today, further types of cyclic vegetation dynamics are distinguished, based on questions of scale and preferential occurrence in different biomes. Formation of mosaics over large areas in Hawaii as a consequence of **"death of cohorts"** is described by Müller-Dombois (1995). Demographically unfavourable situations caused and maintained by fire and storm damage are the driving force. In this context, the endogenous mass-dying of bamboo-like grasses in all tropical regions should also be included; so far this has not been convincingly explained.

In **"cohort dynamics"**, as in the mosaic cycle, the species composition may change. However, in the **"carousel dynamics"**, the pattern formation in grasslands, occurring over small areas, is not included according to Van der Maarel and Sykes (1993). The basic idea of this change over time is that species are able to recycle in the short term and on smallest areas. A **"regeneration gap"** is sufficient free space for seeds and establishment of germinating plants. These spaces become available through endogenous death of individual plants, and are conquered in

a sort of "guerrilla strategy" or even according to the lottery principle of species in the community in which all have occupied the same regeneration niche. As these species are short lived, the carousel model describes vegetation dynamics at the smallest space and of the shortest duration. Populations of a species are always available, but are very mobile. The species composition remains constant. Figure 4.1.47 compares different spatial and temporal scales of cohort, gap and carousel dynamics schematically.

Aspects of Applied Succession Research

The dynamic nature of plant communities has often been recognised via bio-indicators. It is assumed that the response of a plant community to disturbance is specific, and perhaps quantifiable. The vitality of species of the plant community and shifts in the species spectrum are measured. Knowledge about the formation of plant communities and their regulation is gained by empirical findings of many succession studies. For instance pioneer plants with uniform seeds are selected for greening of open spaces, or to stabilise open slopes after road building (Fig. 4.1.48 A, B). It was believed, in many cases, that vegetation dynamics could be predicted.

Today, we know about asynchronous vegetation cycles and have doubts about the term "ecological equilibrium" and therefore realise the limits to practical application of current knowl-

Fig. 4.1.48. Pioneer plant species are able to start the succession on areas which require protection, such as those subject to erosion. *Pennisetum setaceum* (A) is a tussock grass with extensive roots which is suitable for stabilisation of steep slopes (mountains in Yemen Arab Republic). B As part of a project to protect against severe degradation of vegetation and soils in the Central Atlas Mountains (Morocco), a mixture of suitable plant species, such as dwarf and brushwood scrubs, dwarf palms and *Opuntia* cactus, was used to achieve the initial stages in regeneration of the area. (Photos K. Müller-Hohenstein)

edge of vegetation dynamics. Measures for maintenance also need to be rethought, as well as minimum spatial dimensions of protected areas or the concepts of a biotope (Baierlein 1991). Without question, current knowledge of vegetation dynamics helps in the selection of replacement areas, where neighbouring areas have been lost because of disturbance and new communities are to develop (Beierkuhnlein 1998).

Biomonitoring was developed in order to understand syndynamic processes, to indicate damaging influences so that they could be quickly counteracted. Examples are air pollution, as well as eutrophication of water. Vegetation changes resulting from interventions at certain sites have also been recorded with biomonitoring. Knowledge of vegetation dynamics is important for cultivation and maintenance of plant communities, formed during the development of our landscape, which might get lost without traditional forms of management. Grasslands without any fertilisation on not very fertile soils and grasslands on very shallow dry soils are examples of this.

Human influences may also degrade the vegetation and this can also be monitored. Multiple scales on hemeroby of spaces for vegetation have been devised (see Chap. 4.1.4.6). Red List species, loss of species, proportion of therophytes and neophytes are important values for structuring vegetation units according to the degree of human intervention. Ultimately, knowledge about vegetation dynamics is applied in attempts to improve areas to be used for agriculture or forestry and to control such attempts. Thus, for example, application of Ca-containing fertilisers in order to combat acidification of soils in forests and the effects of herbicide application in vineyards were assessed in this way.

4.1.5.3
Vegetation Dynamics and Strategy Models

Plants grow faster or slower, are able to tolerate more or less shade or are distributed near or far away from the mother plant. Such characteristics, acquired during the course of evolution, enable the plant to gain ground from competitors and to become established, and are often summarised by the term "strategy". It is defined as the sum of genetically fixed physiological and morphological adaptations required to conquer a habitat and to persist with optimal use of resources (Dierschke 1994). Individual plants and populations are also classified using strategic aspects as plant functional types.

McCook (1994) showed, with five examples, how two different plant species with different characteristics may behave in competition (Fig. 4.1.49). The following basic variants are possible: One species loses out to the other at different rates, both species achieve a similar distribution, or both species become dominant at different times.

All strategy models are based on such assumed forms of behaviour, and differ only in the way they are interpreted. External influences are not considered (e.g. climate change, herbivory, mechanisms of distribution). As overlapping anthropogenic interference is also excluded, the knowledge gained is relatively limited. Other models originate from functional characteristics of the whole ecosystem and ask which of these have changed over time and how. These models usually generalise too much and the results are only roughly valid. Some models are only descriptive, others try to make predictions or attempt to explain current dynamic processes. However, no model provides a comprehensive explanation for the empirical findings from the field.

Initial Floristic Composition

The model based on Egler (1954) of initial floristic composition (IFC) is still used to describe the sequence of successions, because it represents sequences which are physiognomically recognisable. According to this model the complete set of species is present from the beginning and a sequence of succession takes place with only a few of these species – according to their special characteristics – becoming dominant. Figure 4.1.50 shows the course of growth for six species from germination via establishment of seedlings, through the vegetative and finally to reproductive growth phases. Species 1 to 4 are relatively short-lived therophytes to short-lived woody species, and species 5 and 6 are long-lived and shade tolerant. When the latter species are fully developed, the short-lived species are no longer able to maintain themselves and die off.

IFC is accepted as a **descriptive model** of primary as well as of secondary successions. As Egler stressed, there are no generally valid succession sequences because of external disturbance and the stress situations caused by them. Egler introduced the concept of **gradual change** as the centre point and prefers the term development of vegetation to that of succession. The great limitation of such a model is the exclusion of the propagule influx.

K and r Strategies

MacArthur and Wilson (1967) developed a model of r and K selection, within the framework of their work on island biogeography (see Chap. 4.2.3.1) which is used by botanists and zoologists to stress particularly contrasted behaviour of species. K means here "maximum population size" and r is the "rate of reproduction". When classifying species in one or other group the type of reproduction is critical.

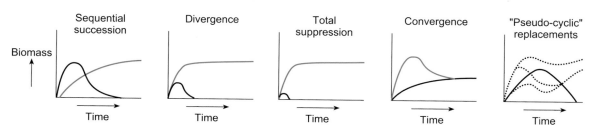

Fig. 4.1.49. Possible behaviour of two species during the course of succession. (After Huston and Smith 1987, from McCook 1994)

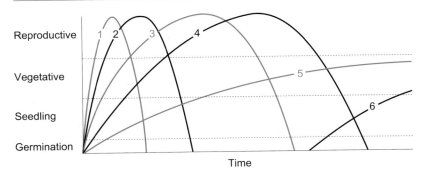

Fig. 4.1.50. Schematic of the initial floristic composition model of succession (the curves show the behaviour of six species). (After Finegan 1984)

r strategists form many, very small seeds representing a high proportion of their phytomass, have an efficient mechanism for distribution, grow fast without high rates of biomass accumulation, tolerate long periods of seed dormancy and can be activated very quickly. They are **short-lived opportunists**, able to establish faster in their environment than shade-tolerant species, but they are inferior to K strategists in their biotic environment.

K strategists are **long-lived,** slow growing and accumulate large amounts of biomass over time. For this reason, and because they are shade tolerant, they are able to gain ground in competition with the r strategists. They need to invest less in their reproduction and have only a few, large seeds which are not necessarily formed in each growing season (mast years). However, they need to form metabolites for defense to protect long-lived leaves and other organs from herbivory. It therefore follows that r strategists

determine the early and early K strategists the late stages of succession. On fallow land, for example, annual and biennial species are replaced over time by shrubs and finally trees.

The classification of species into only two groups has often been criticised. The characteristics mentioned above are accepted as decisive, but a continuum is seen between the extreme positions of r and K strategists. Figure 4.1.51 shows this continuum and also indicates that not only habitats are modified by r strategists which are disturbed in the short term, but also that they do not allow stress-free growth of the long-term established K strategists. With the requirement for **stress tolerance**, a **further strategy type** is indicated.

Strategy Types of Grime (C-S-R Model)

Grime (1974, 1979) and Grime et al. (1988) worked out one of the most well-known models of vegetation dynamics: The **triangle model of ecological primary strategies.** Stress tolerance, adaptation to unfavourable conditions and reaction to disturbance missing in the r/K strategy model were regarded as particularly important and therefore expanded. Three strategy types were introduced:

- **Competitor strategist** (C): Long-lived, competitive species on favourable sites without limitation of resources and almost stress free. They use resources particularly well, often possess storage organs and show considerable plasticity in root and shoot formation, continuously produce leaves which only live for a short time, and have low seed production. These are perennial herbs, shrubs and trees, hardly adapted to negative environmental influences as this is not required. They form medium to late succession stages.

- **Stress-tolerant strategist** (S): Species adapted to unfavourable sites with poor availability of

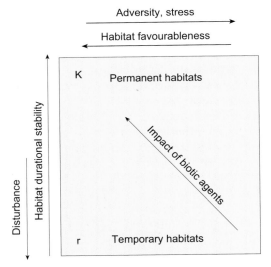

Fig. 4.1.51. Model of K- and r-selection considering the effects of stress. (After Southwood 1977, from Brown 1985)

resources (inadequate light, drought, nutrient deficiency, frequent frosts, etc.). They are long-lived, but with low productive and reproductive rates and switch to sites with little competition (e.g. nutrient-poor grassland, saline sites). Extremely stress-tolerant species are lichens on cold and dry sites.

- **Ruderal strategists (R):** Short-lived, usually herbaceous species with fast growth rates and high seed production, usually self-pollinated with rapid seed ripening and distribution, disturbance-tolerant opportunists and pioneers but weak competitors. Therefore, they grow on sites with frequent, natural disturbance, such as rubble heaps and mechanically disturbed river banks.

However, it is difficult to classify many plant types in only one of these three extremes. Transitions can be observed frequently – plants with characteristics of several strategy types in different combinations. Thus, for example, on favourable sites where competitor strategists should dominate, C-R transition forms are found, if the favourable conditions are temporarily disturbed, for example, by mowing on agricultural meadows. Stress-tolerant competitor strategists (C-S) are long-lived species, e.g. many tree species of nemoral forests, adapted to non-optimum sites. Stress-tolerant ruderal strategists (S-R) grow on unfavourable sites which are often disturbed. Excluded is also an intermediary type (C-S-R) species combining several strategies, and often also in temporal sequence (e.g. many grasses).

Grime (1988) attributed life forms to some of his strategy types, and included them in areas of his **"strategic triangle"**; he also indicated these strategy types as succession sequences (Fig. 4.1.52) and suggested different possible rates of production. On productive sites development proceeded from ruderals via competitively strong types to those plants with competitive stress strategies. This applies in central Europe, e.g. to beech forests on limestone. On less productive sites, the final stage is determined by stress-tolerant species. The more productive the interactions at the site, the higher the proportion of competitively strong species in the middle succession period. The intensity of competition increases with increasing productivity at the site; however, Tilman (1990) contradicts this conclusion.

The universally valid system of classification which Grime tried to establish with his C-S-R

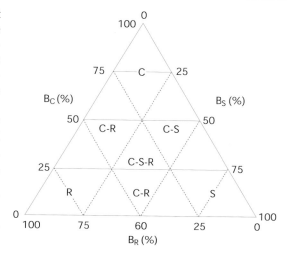

Fig. 4.1.52. C-S-R diagram of the different types of strategy according to Grime. *C* competitor species; *S* stress-tolerant species; *R* ruderal and intermediate types with the relative importance of competition (B_C), stress (B_S) and disturbance (B_R). (After Grime et al. 1988)

system was immediately criticised, because such a classification into individual types of strategy is not random, but is also not possible unequivocally. This makes quantitative evaluation difficult. Stress tolerance and ability to compete are often seen as two aspects of the same mechanism. Ultimately, in addition to genetically fixed characteristics of plants, those acquired are also important. They are not considered in this concept. Nevertheless, it cannot be left out of the discussion on vegetation dynamics because it started a controversy and provoked further models.

Resource Ratio Model of Tilman

All plant species are limited in their distribution by resources, which are difficult to acquire, but required for survival. If one species is successful in competition for such a **limiting resource**, it usually loses out in competition for another. This is the basic premise of Tilman (1990). He assumes further that the most important limiting resources in terrestrial habitats are either in the soil (and there usually nitrogen supply), or light. If these resources are limited they stress plants. These resources often behave inversely, i.e. with low nitrogen supply there are usually favourable light conditions, and commonly at sites with favourable conditions for plant nutrition, light is not easily available. Gradients between those two extremes lead to succession stages where plants replace each other according

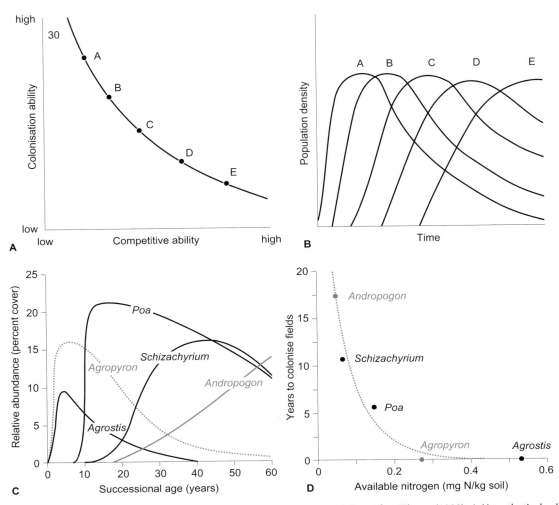

Fig. 4.1.53. Relationship between competition and colonisation ability. After Tilman (1990). A Hypothetical relation for five species (*A–E*). B Changes in the species *A–E* over time, based on their characteristics. C Observed changes in succession of five grass species (Tilman 1988). D Observed relationship between the time required for colonisation and competitive ability (expressed as available N) for the five grasses. (Tilman and Wedin 1991)

to their demands and their specific competitiveness. Each species grows fastest and reproduces best with the resources to which it is best adapted and where it, therefore, wins in competition. Sufficient root biomass is very important for obtaining sufficient nutrients, but also sufficient above-ground biomass is essential for light capture.

This explains not only the early and late stages of primary succession, but also secondary succession on nutrient-poor substrates. In primary succession, species able to cope with a poor nitrogen demand exclude those that require nitrogen. With time the nutrient situation improves because of mineralisation and nitrogen influx. Now species able to cope with less light are competitively

stronger. This hypothesis is the basis of the **resource ratio model** or the **nutrient-light relation model**. Simpler than this model are the ideas of the nutrient colonisation and light colonisation models. The former again applies to nutrient-limited habitats. Colonisers producing many seeds which they are able to distribute quickly are initially successful. However, they are weak in the competition for nutrients. Species that invest quickly in their root system are successful and therefore win the competition for nutrients. The corresponding situation applies to nutrient-rich habitats for light as the limiting factor. In Fig. 4.1.53, Tilman shows these interactions for five grass species demonstrating their ability for competition and colonisation.

From these models, consequences for biodiversity within areas may be derived. The more heterogeneous a space to be colonised – particularly regarding its natural features (nutrients, light, water etc.) and the natural and anthropogenic interference – the more species are able to grow there. It follows that with increasing heterogeneity not only biodiversity increases but, in the habitat, average required resources are available. Questions of dynamics and diversity are most closely linked according to Tilman's interpretation.

Tilman's ideas were not without controversy. He argued, for example at the species level, that in nature it is individual plants which compete with each other. It is suggested that he neglected dynamic processes in favour of assuming states of equilibrium. It is also difficult to imagine that species able to minimise their requirements would ultimately push out all other species. Despite this, the ideas of Tilman have led to the most widely accepted models of vegetation dynamics.

Facilitation – Tolerance – Inhibition – Models by Connell and Slatyer

Competition for resources at the site which may change in type and amount over time and disturbance of all kinds are also regarded by Connell and Slatyer (1977) as the driving forces of vegetation dynamics. They also stress the question of scale and thus suggest that certain forms of vegetation dynamics are only relevant at certain scales.

Three models, **succession pathways**, are considered by Connell and Slatyer to be at the centre (see Box 4.1.6):

- **Facilitation model:** Facilitation is understood as promotion or enabling, starting from the assumption that the first colonisers change the site conditions over the course of time autogeneously in such a way (change in substrate, formation of humus, etc.) that colonisation of more demanding species is stimulated. This is usually linked to displacement of the first colonisers as they are unable to cope with the competition of the newcomers.
- **Tolerance model:** Late succession species are neither stimulated nor inhibited. However, they are only able to establish if previously established individuals "make room". The species now present compete and behave similarly to the resource ratio model of Tilman.

Species able to use resources most efficiently succeed.
- **Inhibition model:** Earlier colonists suppress or inhibit subsequent invaders. These are only able to establish if the stand is disturbed or short-term space becomes available because of death of individuals, but not because of their competitive strength.

All three models have been tested in field experiments. The facilitation model may be observed in primary successions, where pioneer species prepare the substrate, as well as after disturbance, because the succession is thrown back into an earlier phase. Both other model versions were tested in later, species-rich succession stages. The final steady-state stage is regarded as relatively stable, but cyclic dynamics are not excluded.

Connell and Slatyer also consider the question of stability (see Chap. 4.1.6) and regard succession as a balancing reaction of a "stable" system, which has been badly disturbed. Spatial and temporal extent of the disturbance as well as their type and intensity are decisive for the initial stage of following new successions. Connell and Slatyer conceded that their models, too, did not explain vegetation dynamics sufficiently. Exogenous influences, heterogeneity in small spaces as well as influences by faunistic partners are not included. There is a need to further differentiate between the three pathways formulated here because there are differences between facultative and obligate stimulation, between partial and exclusive inhibition, etc. Ultimately, species of early succession may stimulate as well as inhibit for subsequent colonisers (McCook 1994).

4.1.5.4
Vegetation Dynamics and Influence of Animals

At any time of a succession two important influences by animals must be taken into account. The spectrum of species may be changed by herbivory, or at least the conditions for competition are changed. This is rarely fully taken into account, as **herbivores** often eat seeds and seedlings and the extent of such disturbance is very difficult to evaluate. Often it is a matter of speculation, how the vegetation would have developed without herbivores. However, **animals** are also **vectors for propagules** and thus for the dis-

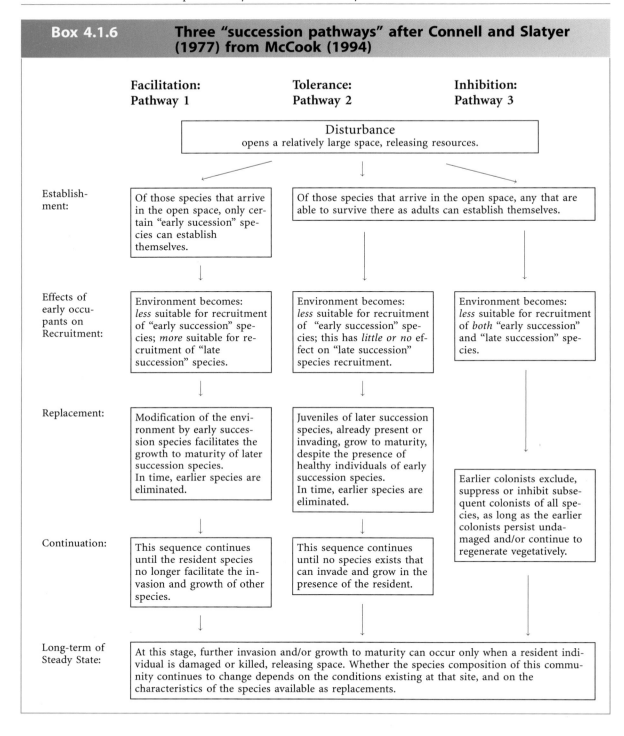

Box 4.1.6   **Three "succession pathways" after Connell and Slatyer (1977) from McCook (1994)**

Facilitation:
Pathway 1

Tolerance:
Pathway 2

Inhibition:
Pathway 3

Disturbance
opens a relatively large space, releasing resources.

Establishment:

Of those species that arrive in the open space, only certain "early sucession" species can establish themselves.

Of those species that arrive in the open space, any that are able to survive there as adults can establish themselves.

Effects of early occupants on Recruitment:

Environment becomes: *less* suitable for recruitment of "early succession" species; *more* suitable for recruitment of "late succession" species.

Environment becomes: *less* suitable for recruitment of "early succession" species; this has *little or no* effect on "late succession" species recruitment.

Environment becomes: *less* suitable for recruitment of *both* "early succession" and "late succession" species.

Replacement:

Modification of the environment by early succession species facilitates the growth to maturity of later succession species.
In time, earlier species are eliminated.

Juveniles of later succession species, already present or invading, grow to maturity, despite the presence of healthy individuals of early succession species.
In time, earlier species are eliminated.

Continuation:

This sequence continues until the resident species no longer facilitate the invasion and growth of other species.

This sequence continues until no species exists that can invade and grow in the presence of the resident.

Earlier colonists exclude, suppress or inhibit subsequent colonists of all species, as long as the earlier colonists persist undamaged and/or continue to regenerate vegetatively.

Long-term of Steady State:

At this stage, further invasion and/or growth to maturity can occur only when a resident individual is damaged or killed, releasing space. Whether the species composition of this community continues to change depends on the conditions existing at that site, and on the characteristics of the species available as replacements.

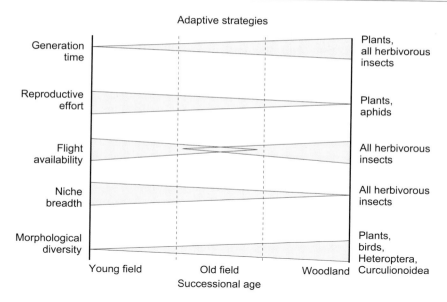

Fig. 4.1.54. Adaptive strategies of plants and animals during secondary succession. (After various sources from Brown and Southwood 1987)

tribution of species, and they participate decisively in the formation of spatial patterns and the composition of vegetation units. In addition, animals change the site by their excrement (e.g. resting sites) and by their mechanical activities and soil disturbance.

There is much evidence that animals, too, exhibit a distinct dynamics. In the initial stages of succession, herbivores dominate with 93% of all insect species during older stages this proportion decreases to 51%, and in forests it is only 44%. During the initial stages, sap-sucking phytophages make up half of that population, later only a quarter. Macroinvertebrates and predators associated with them increase with the age of the succession. Brown and Southwood (1987) tried to derive from these observations basic adaptation strategies for plants and animals during succession (Fig. 4.1.54). They concluded that faunistic partners in the early stages of succession usually are opportunists (r strategists) investing in their reproduction. Many insects are able to fly, promising fast colonisation. Phytophages are generalists with only simple nutrition chains. In the middle stage, secondary consumers are also represented amongst the animals, particularly insectivores. Nutrient chains and the complete structural organisation of the habitat become more complex. Litter may be colonised. Many insects no longer have wings, invertebrates are uniformly distributed. The enormous structural diversity of vegetation in the mature phase means a large number of niches for specialists. Morphological (and trophical) di-

versity in invertebrates (particularly insects) and vertebrates (particularly birds) is high and K strategists dominate even for animals.

Some models formulated for vegetation dynamics may also be transferred to animals or were originally developed for them (K and r strategists), an important aspect for understanding dynamics and biocenoses.

4.1.5.5
Future Aspects for the Understanding of Vegetation Dynamics

Concepts of vegetation dynamics incorporated into the enormous complexity of ecosystems should be supplemented, e.g. those concerning **convergence and divergence** in the development of successions (Leps and Rejmanek 1991), the **continuum concept** by Austin (1985) or the discussion of **chaos theory and non-linear systems** (Stone and Ezrati 1996). These models, as well as those with partially overlapping concepts covered previously, show that it is not possible to describe vegetation dynamics (and even less so dynamics of communities or ecosystems) with "one simple formula". Complex processes and pattern of such a dynamics may only be generalised or modelled to a certain extent. Descriptive models of the sequence of individual species are accepted, but explain little. There is also little emphasis of the fact that a species behaves differently in its juvenile stage than in its older stages. As summarised by Bazzaz (1990): "Despite much progress in modelling succession, the tension between simplicity of models for prediction and complexity to include all relevant parameters remains unsolved."

A path towards better understanding of processes and mechanisms of vegetation dynamics could be the integration of previous information from experimental concepts. Note should be taken of different spatial and temporal scales and integration and organisational levels of plants – individual, species, population, community. Empirical results of long-term studies should be used for verification. The results by Schreiber (1995) on very detailed succession studies over more than 20 years (on fallow land) do not fit into any succession model. This means that succession can hardly be predicted, and planning based on such predictions is risky.

4.1.6

Stability of Plant Communities

The topics of succession and cyclic vegetation dynamics touch questions of "stability" of plant communities and whole ecosystems as well as the concept of **ecological balance**. There is still much controversy surrounding this complex topic, particularly the broad spectrum of the understanding of what stability is and of the characteristics required for stability (Grimm et al. 1992). Temporal and spatial scales are not considered sufficiently, stability is related to momentary conditions, years extended to centuries, the phytocenoses considered extrapolate from only a few square centimetres up to many square kilometres. In all cases the stability-instability is linked to disturbance and stress.

Stability is often discussed together with **diversity** and **complexity** (Pimm 1984; see also Chap. 4.2.4). For a long time it was believed that high diversity would bring high stability, and should be regarded as the basic precondition for stability. Meanwhile, results have been obtained for the other extreme, namely high stability with low diversity. It appears plausible that species-rich and niche-rich biocenes are particularly stable, because they are able to better balance the loss of a species, because their functions may be taken over by another species. However, it is very difficult to recreate very disturbed cycles.

4.1.6.1
Breadth of the Terms "Ecological Stability" and "Ecological Equilibrium"

The many definitions of ecological stability point to special, as well as many common, aspects. Generally, these definitions are linked to the idea of a system able to maintain its structures and functions in the long term. Sizes of populations of species may fluctuate around a mean value and the range is understood as ecological equilibrium. Changes of species are possible to a limited extent, but not that of life forms or functional groups. However, it is actually the latter that provide functional relations, the many different niches and feed-back mechanisms in a system. Theoretically, **stability** may be defined as the **sum of all system connections**.

Stability is a dynamic concept, despite all continuity in the face of changing environmental conditions, as the stability of processes is included. Stable systems react to disturbance and return to the initial stage by (self) regulation. Ecological stability includes cyclic changes, but not successions. A labile system is not able to balance changing external influences. Ultimately, stability may not be equated with constancy, as the latter excludes any change.

According to Schaefer (1992), four **basic types of stability** may be distinguished which could be applied to phytocenoses:

- **constancy** (the system is not disturbed and does not change from within);
- **cyclicity** (the system changes from within, but returns to the initial stage);
- **resistance** (the system is disturbed, but does not change);
- **resilience** (the system changes with disturbance, but returns to the initial stage).

These interpretations of stability consider the stress concept and were developed again by Pimm (1984) and Gigon (1984). Whilst stability is often taken as the basic precondition for the functioning of systems, occasionally stability is considered irrelevant (as not existing in any form), because no such order is recognisable in ecosystems (chaos theory).

Closely linked to ecological stability is **ecological balance,** which does not describe constant relations, but a dynamic system. According to Bick (1993) this implies two aspects. One of these is the export and import of nutrients and water, and the formation and degradation of organic substances in an ecosystem (**equilibrium**). In agriculture the attempt is made to recreate this balance after harvesting by fertilisation. The others are biocenotic equilibria, species-to-species relations, and those of plants to herbivores or of partners in symbiosis. The (self) regulation of ecosystems is regarded as the most important factor for the maintenance of such dynamic equilibria.

4.1.6.2
Stress, Disturbance and Ecological Stability

Disturbance is not necessarily negative for the stability of ecosystems or communities and it can be essential for the maintenance of a dynamic balance. Thus a boreal larch forest would develop into quite a different system without the regular influence of fires. Influences which only transiently cause deviations from the system are called "strain", those that actually change are "stress". The same interfering factors may thus have different consequences for a system. Ultimately, disturbances have different spatial dimensions (Fig. 4.1.55).

Disturbance and strain are generally seen as influences which indicate a "situation deviating from the norm" and which lead to stress situations (Guderian and Braun 1993). To what extent the system can cope with the strain depends on the type, the intensity of the disturbance, the duration and the extent (see Fig. 4.1.55). However, the stability of a system is based on its sensitivity towards disturbance and its characteristics for regeneration after a disturbance. It may be particularly resistant or able to quickly re-

turn to the initial state (i.e. before the disturbance). If a system is able to cope with disturbance it is called **resilient**.

Disturbance may be inherent in the system, come randomly from outside, or may happen endogenously or exogenously, the latter caused naturally or anthropogenically. The failure for several years of precipitation in desert regions is an internal disturbance to the system, as is the regulation of population density based on predator-prey relationships, or on the dynamics of avalanches or earth flow of montane ecosystems. It is often difficult to distinguish which disturbance is caused by endogenous biological disturbances and which are caused by environmental influences.

Walker (1989) summarised natural disturbance in an hierarchical order. Different spatial as well as temporal scales are taken into account. The scale extends from disturbances by continental drift with a scale of millions of square kilometres and years, to climate change and fluctuations which may only affect one climatic subzone and for a few thousand years, to damage by spring tides, late frosts or extreme herbivory effecting a few hectares over a very short time span.

4.1.6.3
Pimm and Gigon's Concepts of Ecological Stability

Pimm (1984) attempted to provide a common basis for further understanding of ecological processes by clear differentiation of complexity and stability contrasted with interpretation of ecological stability. For the complexity in a system he regards **the number of species, connectance and interaction strength** and the **evenness of species distribution** as the most important characteristics. This leads to five different terms currently used in discussion on stability.

- Stability, in its narrower definition, implies that all system elements affected by a disturbance return to the original balanced state (an ecological balance).
- Stability is related to the period required until the original state is re-established. This shows the resilience of the system.
- Persistence is the third term, also connected to time. The deviation of the period which passes before individual elements of the sys-

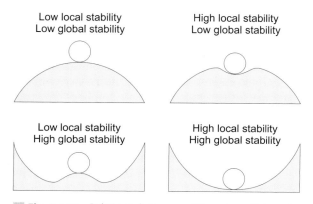

Fig. 4.1.55. Relations between different spatial scales (local, global) and stability. (Begon et al. 1999)

Low local stability
Low global stability

High local stability
Low global stability

Low local stability
High global stability

High local stability
High global stability

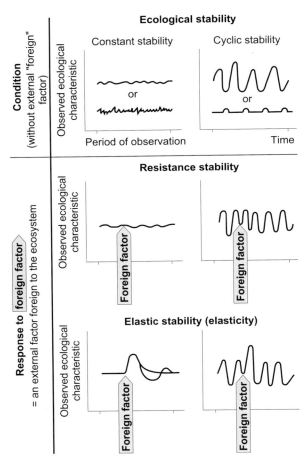

Fig. 4.1.56. Basic types of ecological stability, according to the dynamics of chosen characteristics and to the presence or absence of external factors. (Gigon 1984)

the basic dynamic behaviour of ecosystems and the availability (or lack) of disturbance. He also states much more clearly than before that imbalances and instabilities in nature are just as decisive for evolution as balance and stability.

Gigon thus differentiates:

- **ecological stability,** which includes the immutability of a system or its ability to achieve the initial position again after a disturbance;
- **ecological instability,** where changes after a disturbance cannot be reversed;
- **ecological lability** which is a transient phase with a strong disposition to change by disturbance.

Forms of ecological stability may be described as constancy, if no actual changes take place (except the change of individual plants) or as resistance, if disturbance is buffered (Fig. 4.1.56). In these cases, the affected systems remain almost unchanged. Other forms where a major dynamic is apparent, but still the initial position is reached, may be called cyclic with regular fluctuations and regeneration cycles, or as resilient, if regeneration takes place after irregularly occurring disturbance.

Forms of instability (Fig. 4.1.57) lead to changes: these may be triggered endogenously (e.g. in autogenic successions) or exogenously (because of the effects of disturbance) or on the other hand cause either endogenous or exogenous fluctuations (e.g. mass reproduction of insects or fluctuations of yield in agriculture because of pathogen attack).

Forms of stability and instability sketched here may occur in the same system. An individual tree behaves differently to a complete forest; a locally destructive fire may be necessary for the maintenance of the system over a large area. With this interpretation a clear, practically oriented concept is provided, which may, in many cases, serve as an ordering scheme. Only few cases do not fit into this concept because of insufficient observations or insufficient knowledge of the interfering factors. It must be stressed that no value judgement is implied by this scheme. A stable system will possibly be judged differently by a farmer than by an environmentalist, by a skier differently to a hunter. **Evaluation of stability,** oriented on standards and models, must include a **practice oriented synecology.**

tem are permanently changed by the disturbance is measured.

- Resistance, as the fourth term, expresses the extent of change of a system element after disturbance.
- Variability of the system must be considered. This includes the variance of population density and abundance over time, measured as deviation of mean densities.

Pimm (1984) explains that it is very important to include temporal and spatial scales in all discussion of ecological stability.

Gigon (1984) also starts from this basis and suggests from this that ecological stability should not only be related to considerations of balance. Other stabilising mechanisms have more influence, such as inertia, buffer effects, the replacement principle and risk distribution in an ecosystem. Important characteristics are

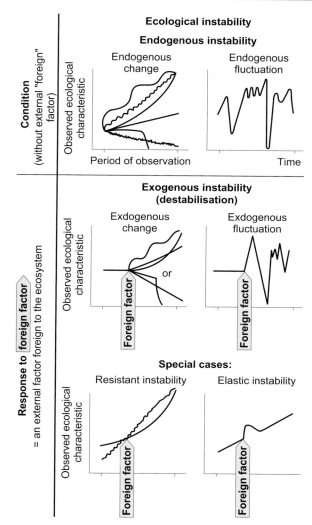

Fig. 4.1.57. Basic types of ecological instability, according to the dynamic of chosen characteristics and to the presence or absence of external foreign factors. (Gigon 1984)

References

Abt K (1990) Auswirkungen des Agrarstrukturwandels auf Streuwiesen und zweischürige Futterwiesen im württembergischen Allgäu. Verh Ges Ökol 19/2:434–441

Aubréville A (1949) Climats, fôrets et désertification de l'Afrique tropicale. Soc Ed maritimes et coloniales, Paris

Austin MP (1985) Continuum concept, ordination methods and niche theory. Ann Rev Ecol Syst 16:39–61

Badal E, Bernabeu J, Vernet JL (1994) Vegetation changes and human action from the Neolithic to the Bronze Age (7000–4000 bp) in Alicante, Spain, based on charcoal analysis. Veget Hist Archeobot 3:155–166

Baierlein F (1991) Biotopverbundsysteme und das Mosaik-Zyklus-Konzept. Laufener Seminarbeiten 5/91:45–51

Barbault R, Sastrapradja SD (1995) Generation, maintenance and loss of biodiversity. In: Heywood VH, Watson RI (eds) Global biodiversity assessment. Cambridge University Press, Cambridge, pp 193–274

Bazzaz FA (1990) Plant-plant interactions in successional environment. In: Grace JB, Tilman D (eds) Perspectives on plant competition. Academic Press, San Diego, pp 239–263

Beierkuhnlein C (1998) Biodiversität und Raum. Die Erde 128:81–101

Begon M, Harper JL, Townsend C (1999) Ecology, 3rd edn. Blackwell, Oxford

Bick H (1993) Ökologie. Fischer, Stuttgart

Böcker R, Gebhardt H, Konold W, Schmidt-Fischer S (1995) Neophyten – Gefahr für die Natur? Zusammenfassende Betrachtung und Ausblick. In: Böcker R, Gebhardt H, Konold W, Schmidt-Fischer S (Hrsg) Gebietsfremde Pflanzenarten. Auswirkungen auf einheimische Arten, Lebensgemeinschaften und Biotope. Kontrollmöglichkeiten und Management. Ecomed, Landsberg, pp 209–215

Bornkamm R (1980) Hemerobie und Landschaftsplanung. Landschaft und Stadt 12:49–55

Braun-Blanquet J (1928) Pflanzensoziologie, Grundzüge der Vegetationskunde. Springer, Berlin Heidelberg New York

Brown VK (1985) Insect herbivores and plant succession. Oikos 44/1:17–22

Brown VK, Southwood TRE (1987) Secondary succession: patterns and strategies. In: Gray AJ, Crawley MJ, Edwards PJ (eds) Colonisation, succession and stability. Blackwell, Oxford, pp 315–337

Bruenig EF (1991) Functions of the tropical rainforest in the local and global context. Gießener Beitr Entwicklungsforsch Reihe 1(19):1–13

Burrichter E, Hüppe J, Pott R (1993) Agrarwirtschaftlich bedingte Vegetationsbereicherung und -verarmung in historischer Sicht. Phytocoenologia 23:427–447

Claussen M (2001) Biogeographical feedbacks and the dynamics of climate. In: Schulze ED (ed) Global biogeochemical cycles in the climate system. Academic Press, San Diego

Clements FE (1916) Plant succession: an analysis of the development of vegetation. Carnegie Institute, Washington

Connell JH, Slatyer RO (1977) Mechanisms of succession in natural communities and their role in community stability and organisation. Am Nat 111:1119–1144

Cornelius R (1991) Populationsbiologische Grundlagen des speziellen Artenschutzes. Verh Ges Ökol 20:905–916

Deil U (1995) Vegetation und rezenter Landschaftswandel im Campo de Gibraltar (Südwestspanien) und im Tangerois (Nordwestmarokko). Geoökodynamik 16:109–136

Deil U (1997) Zur geobotanischen Kennzeichnung von Kulturlandschaften – Vergleichende Untersuchungen in Südspanien und Nordmarokko. Erdwissenschaftliche Forschung 36, Wiesbaden Stuttgart

Deil U, Müller-Hohenstein K (1986) Beiträge zur Vegetation des Jemen. I. Pflanzengesellschaften und Ökotopgefüge der Gebirgstihamah am Beispiel des Beckens von At Tur (J.A.R.). Phytocoenologia 13:1–102

Di Castri F (1990) Biological invasions in Europe and the Mediterranean basin. Kluwer, Dordrecht

Dierschke H (1984) Natürlichkeitsgrade von Pflanzengesellschaften unter besonderer Berücksichtigung der Vegetation Mitteleuropas. Phytocoenologia 12:173–184

Dierschke H (1989) Kleinräumige Vegetationsstruktur und phänologischer Rhythmus eines Kalk-Buchenwaldes. Verh Ges Ökol 17:131–144

Dierschke H (1994) Pflanzensoziologie. Grundlagen und Methoden. Ulmer, Stuttgart

Egler FE (1954) Vegetation science concepts I. Initial floristic composition, a factor in old-field vegetation development. Vegetatio 4:412–417

Ellenberg H (1954) Zur Entwicklung der Vegetationssystematik in Mitteleuropa. Angew Pflanzensoziol 1:133–143

Ellenberg H (1978) Wege der Geobotanik zum Verständnis der Pflanzendecke. In: Lauer W, Klink HJ (Hrsg) Pflanzengeographie. Wege der Forschung Bd 130, Wissenschaftliche Buchgesellschaft, Darmstadt, pp 40–65

Ellenberg H (1996) Die Vegetation Mitteleuropas mit den Alpen. Ulmer, Stuttgart

Elton CS (1958) The ecology of invasion by animals and plants. Methuen, London

Finckh M (1995) Die Wälder des Villarrica-Nationalparks (Südchile) – Lebensgemeinschaften als Grundlage für ein Schutzkonzept. Diss Bot 259:1–181 Berlin Stuttgart

Finckh M, Deil U (1989) Approches de létude de la degradation des forets du Jebel Bougriy (Moyen Atlas Central). RGM 13/1:55–69

Finegan B (1984) Forest succession. Nature 312:109–114

Firbas F (1949–1952) Waldgeschichte Mitteleuropas. 3 Bd. Fischer, Jena

Frenzel B (1968) Grundzüge der pleistozänen Vegetationsgeschichte Nord-Eurasiens. Erdwissenschaftliche Forsch 1:1–326

Furley PA (1993) Tropical moist forests: transformation or conservation. In: Roberts N (ed) The changing global environment. Blackwell, Oxford, pp 309–331

Gigon A (1984) Typologie und Erfassung der ökologischen Stabilität und Instabilität mit Beispielen aus Gebirgsökosystemen. Verh Ges Ökol 12:13–30

Glavac V (1996) Vegetationsökologie. Grundfragen, Aufgaben, Methoden. Fischer, Jena

Gleason HA (1926) The individualistic concept of the plant association. Bull Torrey Bot Club 53:7–26

Goudie A (1994) Mensch und Umwelt. Spektrum, Heidelberg

Gradmann R (1933) Die Steppenheide Stuttgart. Dtsch Lehrerver Naturkd 98–128

Grime JP (1974) Vegetation classification by reference to strategies. Nature 250:26–31

Grime JP (1979) Plant strategies and vegetation processes. Wiley, Chichester

Grime JP, Hodgson JP, Hunt R (1988) Comparative plant ecology. Unwin, London

Grimm V, Schmidt E, Wissel C (1992) On the application of stability concepts in ecology. Ecol Modell 63:143–161

Guderian R, Braun H (1993) Belastbarkeit von Ökosystemen. In: Kuttler W (Hrsg) Handbuch zur Ökologie. Analytica, Berlin, pp 55–60

Hard G (1975) Vegetationsdynamik und Verwaldungsprozesse auf den Brachflächen Mitteleuropas. Die Erde 4:243–276

Hector A, Schmid B, Beierkuhnlein C, Caldeira MC, Diemer M, Dimitrakopoulos PG, Finn J, Freitas H, Giller PS, Good J, Harris R, Högberg P, Huss-Danell K, Joshi J, Jumpponen A, Körner C, Leadley PW, Loreau M, Minns A, Mulder CPU, O'Donovan G, Otway SJ, Pereira JS, Prinz A, Read DJ, Scherer-Lorenzen M, Schulze ED, Siamantziouras ASD, Spehn E, Terry AC, Troumbis AY, Woodward FI, Yachi S, Lawton JH (1999) Plant diversity and productivity experiments in European grasslands. Science 286:1123–1127

Heitzmann-Hofmann A (1993) Einsaat und Sukzession ausgewählter, nützlingsfördernder Pflanzenarten in Ackerrandstreifen. Verh Ges Ökol 22:66–72

Hellden U (1991) Desertification – time for an assessment? Ambio 20:372–383

Hüppe J (1989) Die Genese moderner Agrarlandschaften in vegetationsgeschichtlicher Sicht. Verh Ges Ökol 19:424–432

Ibrahim FN (1988) Ecological imbalance in the Republic of the Sudan – with reference to desertification in Darfur. Bayreuther Geowissenschaftliche Arbeiten 6

IPCC-WGI (2001) Climate change 2001, the science of climate change. Contribution of working group I to the 3rd assessment report of the intergovernmental panel on climate change. Cambridge University Press, Cambridge

Jäger EJ (1977) Veränderungen des Artenbestandes von Floren unter dem Einfluß des Menschen. Biol Rundsch 15/5:287–300

Jäger EJ (1988) Möglichkeiten der Prognose synanthroper Pflanzenausbreitung. Flora 180:101–131

Jax K (1994) Mosaik-Zyklus und patch-dynamics: Synonyme oder verschiedene Konzepte? Eine Einladung zur Diskussion. Z Ökol Natursch 3:107–112

Jochimsen ME (1993) Sukzession. In: Kuttler W (Hrsg) Handbuch für Ökologie. Analytica, Berlin, pp 418–424

Klötzli F (1993) Ökosysteme, 3. Aufl. Fischer, Stuttgart

Kohlhepp G (1991) Ursachen und aktuelle Situation der Vernichtung tropischer Regenwälder im brasilianischen Amazonien. Kieler Geogr Schr 73:87–110

Kreeb KH (1983) Vegetationskunde. Ulmer, Stuttgart

Lamprey HF (1975) Report on the desert encroachment reconnaissance in northern Sudan. 21 October to 10 November 1975, UNESCO/UNEP

Larcher W (1994) Ökologie der Pflanzen. Ulmer, Stuttgart

Lauer W (1986) Die Vegetationszonierung der Neotropis und ihr Wandel seit der Eiszeit. Ber Dtsch Bot Ges 99:211–235

Lauer W, Frankenberg P (1979) Der Jahresgang der Trockengrenzen in Afrika. Erdkunde 33/4:249–257

Le Floch E, Le Houerou HN, Mathez J (1990) History and patterns of plant invasion in northern Africa. In: Di Castri F, Hansen AJ, Debussche M (eds) Biological invasion and the Mediterranean basin. Kluwer, Dordrecht, pp 105–133

Le Houerou HN (1992) Climatic change and desertization. Impact Sci Soc 42:183–201

Leps J, Rejmanek M (1991) Convergence or divergence: what should we expect from vegetation succession? Oikos 62/2:261–264

Lohmeier W, Sukopp H (1992) Agriophyten in der Vegetation Mitteleuropas. Schriftenr Vegetationskde 25, 185 pp

Lövei GL (1997) Global change through invasion. Nature 388:627–628

MacArthur RH, Wilson EO (1967) Biogeographie von Inseln. Wissenschaftliche Taschenbücher, Goldmann, München

McCook LJ (1994) Understanding ecological community succession. Vegetatio 110:115–147

Melillo JM, Prentice IC, Farquahr GD, Schulze ED, Sala OE (1996) Terrestrial biotic responses to environmental change and feedbacks to climate. In: JPCC-WGI, 2nd Assessment report. Cambridge University Press, Cambridge, pp 445–482

Merkel J, Walter E (1982) Rote Liste seltener und bedrohter Farn- und Blütenpflanzen in Oberfranken. Regierung von Oberfranken, Bayreuth

Miles J (1987) Vegetation succession: past and present perceptions. In: Gray AJ, Crawley MJ (eds) Colonisation, succession and stability. Blackwell Scientific, Oxford

Müller N (1995) Zum Einfluß des Menschen auf Flora und Vegetation von Flußauen. Schriftenr Vegetationskde 27:289–298

Müller-Dombois D (1995) Biological diversity and disturbance regimes in island ecosystems. In: Vitousek PM, Loope LL, Andersen H (eds) Islands. Springer, Berlin Heidelberg New York, pp 163–175

Müller-Hohenstein K (1973) Die anthropogene Beeinflussung der Wälder im westlichen Mittelmeerraum unter besonderer Berücksichtigung der Aufforstungen. Erdkunde 27:55–68

Müller-Hohenstein K (1991) Der Mittelmeerraum. Ein vegetationsgeographischer Überblick. Geogr Rundsch 43/7–8: 409–411

Müller-Hohenstein K (1993) Auf dem Weg zu einem neuen Verständnis von Desertifikation – Überlegungen aus der Sicht einer praxisorientierten Geobotanik. Phytocoenologia 23:499–518

Neumann K (1988) Die Bedeutung der Holzkohleuntersuchungen für die Vegetationsgeschichte der Sahara – das Beispiel Fachi/Niger. Würzb Geogr Arb 69:71–85

Nicholson SE (1978) Climatic variations in the Sahel and other African regions during the past five centuries. J Arid Environ 1:3–24

Odum EP (1980) Grundlagen der Ökologie. Bd 1. Thieme, Stuttgart

Pachur HJ (1987) Gerinnenetze, Seen und Ergs der östlichen Sahara als Indikatoren quartärer Formungsdynamik. Verh Dtsch Geographentages 45:167–173

Overbeck F (1975) Botanisch-geologische Moorkunde unter besonderer Berücksichtigung der Moore Nordwestdeutschlands als Quellen zur Vegetations-, Klima- und Siedlungsgeschichte. Wacholtz, Neumünster

Pickett STA, White PS (1985) The ecology of natural disturbance and patch dynamics. Academic Press, New York

Pignatti E, Pignatti S (1984) Sekundäre Vegetation und floristische Vielfalt im Mittelmeerraum. Phytocoenologia 12:351–358

Pimm SL (1984) The complexity and stability of ecosystems. Nature 307:321–326

Pott R (1996) Die Entwicklungsgeschichte und Verbreitung xerothermer Vegetationseinheiten in Mitteleuropa unter dem Einfluß des Menschen. Tuexenia 16:337–369

Rabotnov TA (1974) Differences between fluctuations and successions. In: Knapp R (ed) Vegetation dynamics. Handbook of vegetation science 8. Junk, The Hague, pp 19–24

Reif A (1987) Vegetation der Heckensäume des hinteren und südlichen Bayerischen Waldes. Hoppea, Denkschriften der Regensburger Bot Ges 45:277–343

Remmert H (1964) Änderungen der Landschaft und ihre ökologischen Folgen, dargestellt am Beispiel der Insel Amrum. Veröffentl Inst Meeresforsch Bremerhaven 9:100–108

Remmert H (1985) Was geschieht im Klimax-Stadium? Ökologisches Gleichgewicht aus desynchronen Cyclen. Naturwissenschaft 10:505–511

Remmert H (ed) (1991) The mosaic-cycle concept of ecosystems. Springer, Berlin Heidelberg New York

Remmert H (1992) Ökologie, 5. Aufl. Springer, Berlin Heidelberg New York

Richter M (1997) Allgemeine Pflanzengeographie. Teubner, Stuttgart

Riera-Mora S, Esteban-Amat A (1994) Vegetation history and human activity during the last 6000 years on the central Catalan coast (northeastern Iberian peninsula). Veget Hist Archeobot 3:7–23

Schaefer M (1992) Ökologie. Fischer, Jena

Scherer-Lorenzen M, Elend A, Nöllert S, Schulze E-D (2000) Plant invasions in Germany – general aspects and impact of nitrogen deposition. In: Mooney HA, Hobbs RJ (eds) Invasive species in a changing world. Island Press, Washington, pp 351–368

Schmidt G (1969) Vegetationsgeographie auf ökologisch-soziologischer Grundlage. Teubner, Leipzig

Schmidt W (1989) Struktur und Funktion von Straßenrändern in der Agrarlandschaft. Verh Ges Ökol 19:566–591

Schmidt W (1993) Sukzession und Sukzessionslenkung auf Brachäckern – neue Ergebnisse aus einem Dauerflächenversuch. Scripta Geobot 20:65–104

Schreiber KF (1995) Renaturierung von Grünland – Erfahrungen aus langjährigen Untersuchungen und Managementmaßnahmen. Ber Tüxen-Ges 7:111–139

Schröder FG (1969) Zur Klassifizierung der Anthropochoren. Vegetatio 16:225–238

Schwabe A (1991) Perspectives of vegetation complex research and bibliographic review of vegetation complexes in vegetation science and landscape ecology. Exzerpta Bot 28:223–243

Schwabe A, Kratochwil A (1991) Gewässer-begleitende Neophyten und ihre Beurteilung aus Naturschutz-Sicht unter besonderer Berücksichtigung Südwestdeutschlands. NNA-Berichte 411:14–27

Stone L, Ezrati I (1996) Chaos, cycles and spatio-temporal dynamics in plant ecology. J Ecol 84:279–291

Strasburger E, Sitte P (1998) Lehrbuch der Botanik für Hochschulen. Fischer, Stuttgart

Sukopp H (1972) Wandel von Flora und Vegetation in Mitteleuropa unter dem Einfluß des Menschen. Ber Landwirtsch 50:112–139

Sukopp H, Wittig R (eds) (1998) Stadtökologie, 2nd edn. Gustav Fischer, Stuttgart

Swift MJ, Anderson JM (1993) Biodiversity and ecosystem function in agricultural systems. Ecological studies, vol 99. Springer, Berlin Heidelberg New York, pp 15–41

Tilman D (1988) Plant strategies and the dynamic and structure of plant communities. Princeton University Press, Princeton

Tilman D (1990) Constraints and tradeoffs: towards a predictive theory of competition and succession. Oikos 58:3–15

Tilman D, Wedin D (1991) Oscillation and chaos in the dynamics of a perennial grass. Nature 353:653–655

Tüxen R (1956) Die heutige potentielle natürliche Vegetation als Gegenstand der Vegetationskartierung. Angew Pflanzensoziol 13:5–42

van der Maarel E (1996) Pattern and process in the plant community: fifty years after AS Watt. J Veg Sci 7

van der Maarel E, Sykes MT (1993) Small scale species turnover in a limestone grassland: the carousel model and some comments on the niche concept. J Veg Sci 4:179–188

Walker D (1989) Diversity and stability. In: Chervett JH (ed) Ecological concepts. University Press, Oxford, pp 115–145

Walter H (1960) Grundlagen der Pflanzenverbreitung. I. Teil: Standortslehre, 2. Aufl. Stuttgart

Walter H (1973) Die Vegetation der Erde. I. Die tropischen und subtropischen Zonen, 3. Aufl. Fischer, Jena

Walter H (1986) Allgemeine Geobotanik. Ulmer, Stuttgart

Walter H, Straka H (1970) Arealkunde (Floristisch-historische Geobotanik), 2. Aufl. Ulmer, Stuttgart

Watt AS (1947) Pattern and process in the plant community. J Ecol 35:1–22

Weischet W (1977) Das ökologische Handicap der Tropen in der Wirtschafts- und Kulturentwicklung. In: 41. Deutscher Geographentag Mainz. Tagungsbericht und wissenschaftliche Abhandlung, pp 25–41

Wissenschaftlicher Beirat der Bundesregierung Globale Umweltveränderungen (WBGU) (2000) Welt im Wandel: Erhaltung und nachhaltige Nutzung der Biosphäre. Springer, Berlin Heidelberg New York

Wissmann H von (1957) Ursprungsherde und Ausbreitungswege von Pflanzen- und Tierzucht und ihre Abhängigkeit von der Klimageschichte. Erdkunde 11:175–193

Wittig R, Diesing D (1989) Beziehungen zwischen Stadtstruktur und Stadtvegetation in Düsseldorf. Braun-Blanquetia 3:99–105

Wittkamp J, Deil U, Beierkuhnlein C (1995) Sozialstruktur und Dorfvegetation – im Vergleich von Dörfern beiderseits der ehemaligen innerdeutschen Grenze. Die Erde 126:107–126

Zwölfer H (1978) Mechanismen und Ergebnisse der Co-Evolution von phytophagen und entomophagen Insekten und höheren Pflanzen. Sonderb Naturwiss Ver Hamburg 2:7–50

4.2

Synchorology: Basis of Spatial Distribution of Plants

Vegetation mosaic of evergreen gallery riverine forest and dry woodlands of deciduous species in higher elevations in seasonally moist, tropical, western Ethiopia.
Photo K. Müller-Hohenstein.

Recommended Literature

In addition to the literature listed in Chapter 4.1 the following literature on the spatial context is recommended:

- Brown JH, Lomolin MV (1998) Biogeography. Sinauer Associates, Sunderland
- Brown GB, Gibson AC (1983) Biogeography. Mosby, St. Louis
- Forman RTT (1995) Land mosaics. The ecology of landscapes and regions. Cambridge Univ Press, Cambridge
- Hengeveld R (1990) Dynamic Biogeography. Cambridge Univ Press, Cambridge
- Hubbell SP (2001) The unified neutral theory of diversity and biogeography. Princeton Univ Press, Princeton
- Remmert H (ed) (1991) The mosaic-cycle concept of ecosystems. Ecol Stud 85, Springer, Berlin

- Rosenzweig ML (1995) Species diversity in space and time. Cambridge Univ Press, Cambridge

For literature in English with all the terms concerning introduced plant species (invasive plants, aliens, neophytes):

- Richardson D. M., Pysek P., Rejmanek M., Barbour M. G., Panetta F. D., West C. J. (2000) Naturalisation and invasion of alien plants: concepts and definitions. Divers Distrib 6:93–107
- Williamson M., Fitter A. (1996) The characteristics of successful invaders. Biol Conserv 78:163–170

The previous chapter showed how plants and plant communities develop over time and their dynamics in the short and long term. These dynamics lead to patterns of distribution at the landscape level. It is the task of **synchorology** to recognise such distribution patterns, describe them and explain their actual spatial distribu-

tion. After the temporal aspects of synchorology, it is now the spatial aspects that are of central focus. Both aspects are prerequisites for understanding synecological connections, which will be discussed in Chapter 4.3.

The following chapter deals first with the basis for distribution ecology ("Arealkunde", part of plant geography), later questions of species-area relations are discussed with particular emphasis on island biogeography. The synchorological part of Chapter 4 closes with the topic of biodiversity which cannot be discussed meaningfully without reference to space.

4.2.1

Dispersal of Plants

The life cycle of usually sessile plants also includes a mobile phase. In this phase generative **propagules** (spores, seeds, fruits, syncarps or even complete plants carrying seeds) as well as vegetative propagules (bulbs, shoots, runners, adventitious buds, parts of rhizomes, clonal growth, etc.; Fig. 4.2.1 A) are transported over different distances, on their own or with the help of abiotic or biotic factors. The aim of this process is to find a site for the establishment of the propagule, a so-called **safe site**. Germination and further survival should be guaranteed there.

One of the limits of dispersal are physical barriers. Too great a difference in the relief, or extended oceans, cannot be bridged. Other limits are the demands of species on their environment (**ecological demands**) and the supply of resources at the site. However, man has taken away some of the barriers and is, at the moment, a particularly important **vector** for plant distribution by deliberately and knowingly or unknowingly transporting propagules beyond

Fig. 4.2.1. Plants have developed many different methods of effective dispersal. A *Aeloropus littoralis* is a salt-tolerant coastal grass which spreads by vegetative runners (blastochory) as here in south-western Arabia. B Self-dispersal (autochory) in *Trifolium stellatum* takes a special form (herpochory) with awns on the fruit having hygroscopic characteristics which enable the seed to move over short distances. C A special form of secondary animal dispersal (zoochory) is provided by coprochory. Dung beetles (many types of scarabs) collect the droppings of animals (e.g. cattle) and form it into balls. The dung contains seeds that are then buried just below the soil surface, where they may have a chance to germinate.
(Photos K. Müller-Hohenstein)

natural distribution barriers, and ensuring suitable growing sites.

Propagules are also **functional units** adapted to transport by wind, water and animals, or with their own means of distribution. Such adaptation includes, e.g., morphological structures on seeds, such as barbs which cling to coats or feathers. Seeds with tissues containing air may float and those with wings are carried by the wind. Nutritious, fleshy fruits entice animals.

4.2.1.1
Vectors of Propagule Transport

The great number of different means of transport for propagules requires a structured overview of the vectors and mechanisms. Three large groups are distinguished:

- **autochory**, where the plant itself carries out the dispersal of its propagules,
- **allochory**, where the plant exploits different means of transport (**vectors**),
- **atelochory**, where dispersal is inhibited (Table 4.2.1).

Autochory

Plants have evolved many mechanisms which ensure distribution in different ways. In the simplest form of autochory, **barochory**, propagules are transported via gravity without special aids, a method that may only result in distribution over a wider area on steep slopes. Usually, the highest density of seeds is reached near the mother plant (seed shade). In contrast, with **blastochory**, propagules only find suitable growing sites by growth processes, e.g. via scions (vegetative shoots) or pedicels as in *Cymbalaria muralis*. In **herpochory** propagules move themselves short distances, e.g. the awns of *Trifolium stellatum* have hygroscopic characteristics, and twist with changes in humidity, dispersing the propagules (Fig. 4.2.1 B).

Special forms of autochory are summarised under the term **ballochory**, where propagules are propelled by a single impulse from the

Table 4.2.1. Distribution syndrome. Collected from Müller-Schneider (1977), Lindacher (1995), Frey and Lösch (1998)

Autochory (self dispersal)	Barochory (transport via gravity)
	Blastochory (dispersal via runners)
	Herpochory (transport via active creeping)
	Ballochory (self seeder)
	– Zooballochory (impetus provided by animals)
	– Anemoballochory (impetus provided by wind)
	– Hydroballochory (impetus provided by water)
	– Autoballochory (propulsion mechanisms based on sap pressure or drying)
Allochory (dispersal via a vector)	Anemochory (transport via wind)
	– Chamaechory (transport close to the soil because of large size and soil adherence to animals, etc.)
	– Meteochory (transport in air for small seeds)
	– Boleochory (transport started by wind, further dispersal assured by other mechanisms)
	Hydrochory (transport in water)
	– Nautochory (transport by movement in the sea)
	– Bythisochory (drifting in flowing water)
	– Ombrochory (transport via rain drops)
	Zoochory (dispersal via animals), further differentiation by animal types, e.g.:
	– Ornithochory, myrmecochory, etc.
	– Epichory (transport by attachment of propagules to animals)
	– Endochory (transport of propagules during passage through the gut)
	– Stomatochory (transport in the mouth)
	– Dysochory (transport of accidentally ingested propagules)
	Hemerochory (dispersal by man)
	– Ethelochory (deliberate dispersal)
	– Speirochory (dispersal due to accidental dispersal with seeds)
	– Agochory (unintentional dispersal)
Atelochory (transport and dispersal are not impeded)	

mother plant. This may be triggered by animals, wind or even a raindrop. In **autoballochory** even such impulses are not required and the pressure is produced via differences in turgour (*Ecballium elaterium*) or drying fruits or seed cases (*Bauhinia purpurea*, broom species). Seeds can be thrown over considerable distances, often several metres.

Allochory

Anemochory

Wind is a very important vector for allochoric seed transport. Even propagules blown by wind across the ground surface possess morphological adaptations. Such **chamaechory** is frequent in dry regions where there are rarely impediments to such transport. More important, however, is transport by air currents (**meteochory**). Small, light propagules which do not settle easily are transported in vertical – as well as horizontal – air streams across large distances, e.g. seeds of orchids or spores of cryptograms (so-called dust-fliers). **Balloon fliers** (*Astragalus spinosus*) possess special morphological adaptations, as do **seeds or fruits with parachutes** (*Taraxacum officinale*) and **wings** (*Acer* and *Fraxinus* species). Wind also triggers seed transport in plants which scatter seeds, e.g. the scatter mechanisms of *Papaver* species (**boleochory**).

Hydrochory

Transport in, and with the help of, water is important for many plant species. Some propagules are able to float because of special tissues or large intercellular spaces, have a low specific weight and an external cover which is difficult to wet (*Nymphea* and *Nuphar* species). Coconuts, as well as seeds and seedlings of mangrove species, are even able to stay in salt water for long periods without damage. Seed dispersion in salt water and stagnant water is called **nautochory**; that in flowing water is called **bythisochory**. In flowing water seeds are transported by floating, and often drift over large distances. Small distances are often achieved by the impact of raindrops (**ombrochory**, e.g. *Anastatica hierochuntica* in dry regions). It is important that seeds in water do not germinate prematurely because of continuously moist conditions.

Zoochory

The most important and ecologically most complex forms of allochoric distribution have devel-

oped in **zoochory**. Close interrelations between some plant and animal species point towards a long co-evolutionary development. This applies particularly to **endochory**, where propagules are taken up by the animal and pass through the intestines. During this time (retention time) they are transported by the animal. Most such seeds have a relatively hard shell and do not get damaged during passage through the gut, nor is it necessary for germination. However, after excretion, seeds are provided with very good starting conditions for germination in the nutrient-rich excrement. Some of the propagules are taken up randomly, particularly by large herbivorous mammals.

In addition to endochory, there are many other ways in which seeds are distributed by animals: Birds and bats, as well as ants, are specifically attracted; plants invest in nutrient-rich fruits and attract attention by striking colours or strong smells. Ants are particularly well known for their distribution processes (**myrmecochory**, however, this is a form of epichory, see below) and so are birds (**ornithochory**). The former carry seeds possessing lipid-rich elaiosomes (e.g. *Corydalis cava*) but the seeds remain untouched. This form of distribution is also called **synchory**. Birds react first and foremost to colours and are able to distinguish ripe seeds from unripe seeds.

In **dysochory** propagules are eaten and sometimes damaged. Such propagules, which are often starch-rich, are collected and accumulated as reserves (e.g. seeds of *Pinus cembra* collected by a bird, *Nucifraga caryocatactes*), but some propagules still have a chance of surviving because not all hiding places are found again and some seeds are lost during transport. Some propagules are taken, together with the fruit pulp, into the mouth and spit out again (**stomatochory**) by many species of monkeys.

Propagules and their fruit pulp or endosperm are not always used as food. These means of attraction are often not developed at all, but still seeds or whole fruiting bodies are transported by animals. Propagules often possess glue-like excretions, glandular hair, barbs with awns and other outgrowths formed from the pericarp. Therefore, they are easily attached to fur and feathers and are transported until they fall off or are stripped off by animals during grooming and preening. In this form of transport, **epichory**, animals distributing the seeds are not rewarded by food or energy and the plant invests less. In endochory close interaction exists be-

Table 4.2.2. Relationship between propagules and dispersal by vertebrates. (Howe and Westley 1986, with additions)

Animal/animal group	Propagule colour	Propagule smell	Propagule form	Use to animals
Mammals in herds	Brown	Little smell	Thick husked nuts, do not burst open	Seeds
Birds in flocks	Green, brown	Without	Seeds without wings and small nuts	Seeds
Frugivor mammals in trees	Yellow, green, white, orange, brown	Aromatic	Seeds often with arils, whole fruits, burst open	Arils, pulp rich in proteins and sugars
Bats	Green, white, light yellow	Aromatic, musty	Diverse, often pendent fruit	Lipid- and starch-rich fruits
Ground living and frugivorous mammals	Green, brown	Without	Hard, over 50 mm long fruits, do not burst open	Lipid-rich fruits
Frugivorous birds (obligate)	Black, blue, red, green	Without	Big seeds with arils, whole seeds often burst open	Lipid- and protein-rich fruit flesh
Frugivorous birds (facultative)	Black, blue, red, white	Without	Small seeds with arils, berries and stone fruits	Mostly carbohydrate-rich fruit
Furry or feathery	Insignificant	Without	Sticky and barbed hooks	None

tween plant and animals and distribution is regulated, sometimes even targeted. Epichory, in contrast, is often random. Some of the close links between characteristics of propagules and the animals distributing them are summarised in Table 4.2.2 (Howe and Westley 1986).

Hemerochory

Man plays an increasingly important role in the recent history of plant distribution. In this particular allochoric form, **hemerochory** or **anthropochory**, any distances may be covered and all geographical and ecological barriers overcome. In **ethelochory**, plants are purposefully moved to different regions, e.g. to provide food or ornament. If distribution occurs unintentionally along with other propagules (e.g. weed seeds in seeds of cereal crops), this is called **speirochory** or in the case of random distribution **agochory**.

Atelochory

The most important methods of distribution, **autochory and allochory**, are contrasted with **atelochory** (also called **achory**). This is a special form of distribution, as it is prevented. The consequence of this evolutionary development is that reproduction takes place at the site where the mother plant grows, which is favourable to the species. Examples are *Arachis hypogaea* or *Trifolium subterraneum*. After pollination pedicel and ovary penetrate into the ground.

Heterospory is widely used by therophytes in arid regions as the chance for survival are particularly good at sites where the mother plant is able to form fruits. Only some of the propagules are distributed to "conquer" new growing sites (Evenari et al. 1982).

4.2.1.2
Effectiveness of Mechanisms for Seed Dispersal

The dispersal of propagules is successful if they reach a site which allows germination and growth of a new plant. It is also important for survival of a species to exploit suitable growing sites further from the mother plant and to establish there, thus increasing the area of distribution, and the population's chances of survival. To a large degree this depends on the available mechanisms for dispersal and their effectiveness regarding a targeted (suitable site for growth) and broad (gain space) transport of propagules. However, such "targets" are not achieved by any of the forms of dispersal and therefore different vectors have proved particularly useful in certain regions. With the "choice" of vector, different strategies are developed during evolution in which safe sites and territorial expansion are balanced.

Howe and Smallwood (1982) studied seed dispersal in temperate forests in North America, as well as in neo- and palaeotropic forests. The data show that most trees are morphologically adapted to zoochory in the humid tropics as well as in the tropics with rainy and dry seasons. In temperate forests this also applies to

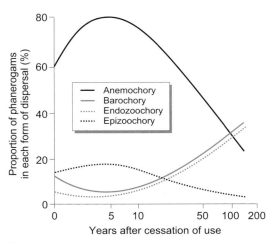

Fig. 4.2.2. Relative frequency of four dispersal mechanisms in phanerogamic flora of fallow fields close to Montpellier (France) at different times after their abandonment. (After Lepart and Escarre 1983)

shrubs, but trees are predominantly anemochoric. This change in the form of dispersal is explained by regular winds occurring in temperate latitudes, but many attempts to explain linkage of certain species with certain vectors have so far not been successful. In dry areas, where obstacles hardly limit distribution by wind, anemochory predominates, but there are no recognisable trends that would indicate that autochoric forms are linked to particular biomes. In these forms, in addition to "primary" dispersal, "secondary" dispersal by a particular vector becomes important (Chambers 1994). Propagules reaching the ground by gravity (barochoric) or excreted by animals (endochoric) may drift in the wind or water, or be taken up by other animals. Engel (2000) reports this for dung beetles which take seeds from elephants' dung and transport them over short distances before burying them and thus acting as a secondary vector; he called this **coprochory** (Fig. 4.2.1 C). The importance of "secondary" distribution is often underestimated. The example of dung beetles shows that the most favourable micro-growth sites are often only found in the second transport phase. The spatial and temporal component is also important. A major vector in one year need not be so important in another when conditions have changed. Lepart and Escarre (1983; Fig. 4.2.2) showed how the proportion of the four mechanisms for seed dispersal changes in a fallow field. During the first years, anemochoric species establish predominantly via long-dis-

tance transport, but barochoric and endozoochoric species become more important after the first two decades and finally, after a century, replace anemochoric species as the most important species.

Plants species often do not use one form of seed dispersal only. Different forms may supplement each other to better safeguard dispersal. Particularly under unfavourable external conditions, e.g. a short vegetation period in high mountains or long dry periods, reproductive dispersal is combined with vegetative propagation. Some plant species form different forms of propagules (**heterospory**) increasing their chances of dispersal.

Several hypotheses and models have been developed to explain the link between certain plant species and their chosen vector. The **low investment model**, for example, is based on the view that plants that produce many small seeds are linked to vectors for long-distance dispersal (anemochory, epichory). Thus they are able to disperse over large areas in a very short time; however, the fate of seeds distributed in such a way is fairly uncertain. According to the **high investment model**, some plants only form very few seeds but these are large and well equipped with energy and nutrients and are thus very attractive to birds and bats. They are only distributed over short distances, but usually find relatively safe conditions for germination. In zoochory both strategies are used, epichory (with low investment) and endochory (with high investment). The **directed dispersal hypothesis** of Howe and Smallwood (1982), of targeted, relatively safe dispersal, also corresponds to the high investment model. This contrasts with the **colonisation hypothesis** where opportunists exploit opportunities for rapid dispersal over large areas. The premise for the **escape hypothesis** is that the chances for establishment and germination depend on low density and therefore the proximity of the mother plant must be avoided.

There are very few empirical results confirming particular hypotheses. It is certain that many plants do not use only one vector, but possess morphological and other adaptations to exploit several vectors. Such **polychory** improves the chances of dispersal considerably.

The efficiency of seed dispersal has qualitative and quantitative aspects. The quality of a seed may decide whether or not a bird accepts it, how the seed is treated by the bird so that it is transported, and if what remains is able to ger-

Table 4.2.3. Factors affecting efficiency of dispersal. (After Schupp 1993)

I. Quantity of seed dispersal
A. *Number of visitors*
   1. Density of dispersal agent
   2. Type of nutrition
   3. Reliability of the visit
B. *Number of seeds dispersed per visit*
   1. Number of seeds touched per visit
   2. Probability of dispersal of a seed touched

II. Quality of seed dispersal
A. *Quality of treatment*
   1. Seeds are transported intact or broken
   2. Change in germination rate
B. *Quality of seed deposition*
   1. Transport type
      a. Targeted choice of habitat
      b. Targeted transport
   2. Deposition type
      a. Proportion of deposited seeds
      b. Mixing of different seeds

minate. Of quantitative importance are the number of seeds and the number of visits of the distributor to the plant. Schupp (1993) tried to develop a hierarchical classification of the most important components for efficient seed dispersal (Table 4.2.3). The density of dispersal, as well as the type of seed treatment (intact or damaged), and patterns of dispersal (targeted or random dispersal) are particularly important (see also Box 4.2.1).

4.2.1.3
Propagule Bank and Establishment of Germination

Seed dispersal is only successful if the transported propagules germinate at a potential site or are in the propagule bank (**seed bank**) in the ground.

Many propagules have a rest period before germination. This may have several reasons. Germination-inhibiting substances may prevent further development at first: sometimes temperatures must fall below a certain minimum value (**vernalisation**) before the seedling can develop. Such rest periods are called **dormancy** and may be determined genetically or by external conditions, e.g. if the position of seed is too deep in the soil and can only germinate after disturbance when it gets enough light as with many segetal species.

The period of **dormancy** is different for individual types of propagules even under the same conditions. In tropical rainforests, shade trees germinate immediately if they are in a suitable

---

| Box 4.2.1 | Hypotheses on the effectiveness of dispersal mechanisms |

In their mobile phase, plants move themselves (self-dispersal or autochory) by means of propagules (diaspores, e.g. spores, seeds, fruits, corms and runners); the most important form of autochory is barochory with the propagules falling under gravity and therefore not moving very far laterally. Alternatively, propagules are moved by various vectors (allochory), the most important of which are wind, water and animals and – particularly more recently – man. The propagules reach a location with favourable conditions allowing survival and establishment (safe site), and leading to further growth: this depends on the environment and specific requirements of the species and the physical parameters that hinder or aid dispersal.

Various hypotheses describe how effective the dispersal mechanisms are. The directed dispersal hypothesis – considers a mechanism where the propagules are specifically targeted, taken and dispersed (i.e. by animals). The colonisation hypothesis, in contrast, considers that opportunists use wind and water primarily as vectors. The first hypothesis is a high-investment model, suggesting that many resources are invested in the propagule as "rewards" for the dispersal vector (i.e. nectar for humming birds, fruits for bats). In low-investment models which apply to many opportunists, little is invested in the individual seeds. Here, dispersal and chance colonisation are based on the large number of seeds produced.

Distribution of propagules is successful when germination and growth of young plants are successful that finally produce seeds of their own. This does not have to happen directly after dispersal. Many propagules remain dormant in the soil for long periods and then are able to germinate under favourable growth conditions.

growing site. Seeds of light-requiring trees remain dormant until favourable conditions occur and then germinate, e.g. after a fallen tree opens a gap in the canopy, a so-called **tree fall gap**. In dry regions with very variable wet periods, species differ considerably in dormancy, even within one species. Generally, it may be assumed that dormancy of propagules serves to tune germination to growth conditions, in order to bridge a cold winter or a dry season.

The stock of all dispersal units in the soil is called the **propagule bank (seed bank or seed potential)**. Seeds may remain viable for several years, in some cases even centuries, until more favourable conditions for development occur. This propagule bank is usually in the uppermost 10 cm of soil. Temporary propagule banks with accumulation of seeds which will germinate in the short term (next year) are distinguished from permanent banks. The latter are particularly important for the regeneration of plant communities. With propagules in temporary banks having only limited ability to germinate – as for the tropical shade trees mentioned above – regeneration of forests after severe interference is unlikely. This also applies, for example, to rainforests in southern Chile outside the tropics. A few years after clearing of the almost natural stands and reforestations of the area with *Pinus radiata* the local seed banks contained hardly any propagules of indigenous species (Scherer, unpubl. data). This underlines the importance of propagule banks for the protection of species and biotopes.

The phase of **seedling establishment** is particularly sensitive in the life cycle of plants. Pathogens, herbivores and competitors, but also climatic abnormalities, may lead to large losses. Ryser (1993) found in germination experiments that some seedlings require the protection of neighbouring species (e.g. *Arabis hirsuta*, *Primula verde*), but for others germination is reduced by neighbouring species (*Platago lanceolata*, *Sanguisorba minor*). A third group of species was able to germinate under all experimental conditions (e.g. *Medicago lupulina*). Large, time-dependent fluctuations were also observed. Espigares and Peco (1993) found close relations between rates of germination and interannual fluctuations of climatic conditions, particularly of temperatures. Most species germinated more successfully at higher temperatures, others germinated better at lower temperatures (e.g. different species of *Trifolium*).

It is still not possible to satisfactorily explain dormancy and germination in detail. Even if edaphic and climatic conditions at the growing site satisfy the demands of the dispersed species, if pollinators are present, and if the species is able to stand its ground against competitors and protect itself against pathogens, its permanent establishment is only safeguarded by a permanent input of propagules in addition to its own propagule production.

4.2.2

Basis of Spatial Distribution (Phytogeography, "Arealkunde")

A consequence of dispersal of propagules across short distances is that as many potential growing sites as possible are occupied near the mother plant, whereas long-distance dispersal leads to spatial gain. The result of **dispersal of propagules (active process)** is permanent establishment in a site, the **distribution (passive state)** of plant species into new sites. A growing site which can be limited geographically is called an **area**, i.e. spatial distribution.

It is the aim of the science of **spatial distribution** of plants to describe the pattern of forms of areas as they are today, and in the past, and to explain them. The two main goals are: to recognise types and characteristic patterns of distribution (dispersal) and to describe their organisation (Meusel et al. 1965, 1978; Merxmüller 1952, 1953, 1954) and to attempt to explain the development of patterns of distribution (Walter and Straka 1970). A comparative assessment of geographical areas leads to characterisation of **floristic elements** and **area types** and to a hierarchical and spatial classification based on scientific understanding. Thus studies of areas are the basis of any further understanding of vegetation distribution.

4.2.2.1
Interpretation of Area of Distribution

There are various ways to map areas. Frequently, only the borders of areas in which the species occur are drawn, however, providing no information on the distribution and abundance of species within the area. This is avoided by **dot** maps which contain each sighting, however often, of the expected distribution rather than the real, observed distribution. Information on geographical areas is usually presented in **grid maps**. However, these maps only show a section of the area, with the distribution of the species (without, however, the frequency). Such maps were provided by Haeupler and Schönfelder (1988) for the Federal Republic of Germany (following the indispensable classical presentation by Meusel et al. in outline maps). These distribution maps show, for example, the mesoclimatic differentiation of areas often better than those based on meteorological data. Such maps are indispensable for formulating basic questions on taxonomy and vegetation, as well as for applied tasks, e.g. nature protection.

The expansion and form of areas depend on historical as well as ecological factors, that is the ecological demands of species and their competitiveness, as well as the potential supply of resources at the growing site, plus the competitiveness of other species. Attempts have been frequently been made to explain limits of distribution by limiting conditions at the site using isotherms. However, these attempts should be viewed critically. Plants hardly react to average climatic values; furthermore, conditions at a site are so complex that it is not possible to assess individual factors and then identify the decisive one. Limiting conditions for plants in large areas are very different. Beech (see Chap. 2.1), at its eastern limits, suffers from low precipitation during the year, but is particularly damaged by cold winters (limit of resistance of buds −30 °C). In the south, beech is limited by summer droughts and in the north by prolonged winters and late frosts. However, in the north west of the British Isles, beech has probably not reached all potential growing sites since the end of glaciation. The complexity of limiting factors at a site may also be shown by the course of the **tree limit** for **olive trees** in the Mediterranean region (Fig. 4.2.3). In higher mountainous regions longer-lasting frosts occur and limit the short growing season, in southern Europe the early summer is too moist, making pollination and fruit setting difficult, but, in North Africa, towards the south, increasing drought limits its distribution. **Walter's law of the relative constancy of habitat** (see Chap. 4.1.6) should be applied to understand the occurrence of plants. *Quercus pubescens*, for example, indicates in its southern distribution moist, early outposts of Mediterranean habitats, but in the north, in the upper Rhine valley, it is found only on the warmest and driest, south-facing slopes.

It is often forgotten that the expansion of areas is subject to change, which may be climatic. The postglacial, warmer climate caused large-scale **shifts in areas**, making it possible to gain information on the rate of species migration. These species came from their refugia to occupy their present areas. For the most important central European tree species, expansion at a rate of some 100 m/year is calculated, rather a large rate, considering that many tree species only form fruits after several years. Climatic change and growing competition, particularly human influences, may also lead to **areas shrinking**. Thus, dynamics of areas can mean them contracting, expanding or shifting, with the consequence that making an inventory of species for a region is never finished. In addition, neophytes and synanthropic species

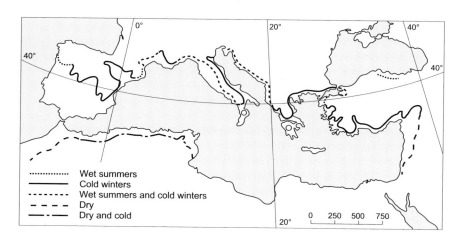

.... Wet summers
———— Cold winters
- - - - - Wet summers and cold winters
– – – – Dry
—·—·— Dry and cold

0   250   500   750

Fig. 4.2.3. Limit of the distribution of olive trees (*Olea europaea*) in the Mediterranean area and the most important climatic factors determining it. (After Birot 1964, modified from Müller-Hohenstein 1981)

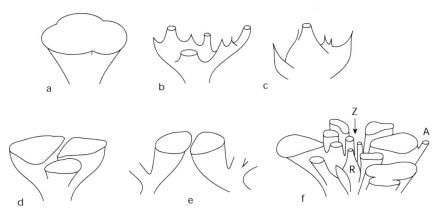

Fig. 4.2.4. Possible means by which plants exploit space over a period of time (time axis vertical, space axis horizontal, cut surfaces show the current situation) (Strasburger 1998). a Area expansion; b death of populations and shrinkage to disjunct areas; c as in b with development of relict palaeoendemic areas; d allopatric differentiation of three vicarious related groups; e pseudovicarious species, living in ecologically or geographically similar conditions; f a distribution of closely related species with a centre of diversity (Z), relict endemics (R) and neoendemic species (A). There are no fixed relationships between the age of the species, diversity of the group or size of the area

make this task even more difficult and, strictly speaking, **potential and actual areas** should be considered separately. The potential area comprises all suitable growing sites, whereas actual real area is usually much smaller and is determined by limits of the site and geographical barriers, conditions of competition and migrational behaviour of species. Figure 4.2.4 shows schematically how differently the space-time formation of areas may occur. Areas may grow or shrink; they can also divide (**disjunction**) or form species by allopatric differentiation.

4.2.2.2
Characterisation of Areas

Areas are divided according to (1) their size, (2) form and (3) geographical location. Differentiation into mainly **cosmopolitan** and **endemic** species is based on the size of areas. The former occur in large areas, extending beyond continents, over large climate regions. Cosmopolitans have very effective dispersal mechanisms, are strongly competitive and are old species, phylogenetically speaking. Bracken (*Pteridium aquilinum*) and the annual meadow grass (*Poa annua*) are the most quoted examples. Cosmopolitans are differentiated from **ubiquists** in that they are not able to grow on all sites.

Endemics are, in contrast to cosmopolitans, only found in small areas, e.g. in isolated mountain regions or on islands, strictly speaking also on 'inland islands'. Two variants exist.

Phylogenetically old species, which once were widely distributed, were pushed back to smaller areas by increasing competition. These species are called **palaeo-endemics** or **relict-endemics**. Giant redwood trees (*Sequoia gigantea* and *Metasequoia*) or the southwest African gymnosperm *Welwitschia mirabilis*, as well as the eastern Asian *Ginkgo biloba*, are examples. In contrast to palaeoendemics are **neoendemics**, phylogenetically younger species which have not been able to establish in potential areas because of time limitation, or which are restricted to smaller areas because of insurmountable barriers to their expansion. Data from Frey and Lösch (1998) for selected island groups show that the distance of the island to the mainland and the

Table 4.2.4. Proportion of endemics in the flora of different islands and island groups. (After Frey and Lösch 1998)

Island/island group	Endemics in %	Distance to the nearest mainland (in km)
Fernando Po	12.0	100
Canary Islands	53.5	170
Sao Tomé	19.4	250
Cape Verde Islands	15.0	500
Juan Fernandez	66.7	750
Madeira	10.5	970
Galapagos	40.9	1120
Azoren	36.0	1460
St. Helena	88.9	1920
Hawaii	94.4	4400
Marquesas	52.3	6000

duration of isolation are reflected in the proportion of endemics in the flora (Table 4.2.4).

Areas are also differentiated by their form, particularly whether they are closed areas, i.e. the species is established in a single, clearly delimited space, or whether the area consists of several partial areas and is thus **disjunct** (see Chap. 4.1.2). In closed areas, gaps between individual growing sites are so small that they may be bridged easily and quickly by transport of propagules or pollen. In disjunct areas this is no longer possible. It may be assumed that polyphyletic origin of the same species does not occur and therefore other explanations for the genesis of disjunctive areas must be found. One explanation might be an extremely rare distribution event, e.g. by migrating birds, or atmospheric anomalies. In many cases, however, it is known that present disjunct areas were once closed and were either separated by tectonic events (e.g. continental drift), formation of mountains, or climatic changes (e.g. change in cold and warm periods). For the latter there are many examples with Arcto-Alpine species (e.g. *Draba aizoides*).

With the separation of once closed areas, socalled **vicarious areas** may develop. In the partial areas, the populations of once uniform species developed further in different ways. This would be called **geographical vicariance** with examples of the genera *Kleinia* and *Aeonium* (Fig. 4.2.5). The **centres of diversity** of these species in southern and eastern tropical Africa as well as in Macronesia and Cap Verde were separated by the north African dry regions. If subspecies or other species of a genus are established in the same space at different sites, this is called **ecological vicariance**; examples are the two alpine rhododendrons, *Rhododendron hirsutum* and *R. ferrugineum*, respectively, on limestone and silicate rocks.

If many related species are distributed closely together, it may be concluded that they have developed within the same space and that the area is a **centre of diversity** (**genetic centre**, central zone of related groups) or at least a **maintenance centre** of this genus. Plant breeders aim to find such centres for economically important plants, as they hope to find important gene reserves.

4.2.2.3
Area Types – Floristic Elements – Geoelements

Areas of similar basic structures, size and geographical positions are called **area types**, which are somewhat abstract units. Various species do not occupy absolutely identical areas, but all species of the same area type are considered to be **geoelements** if spatial aspects are more important, and **floristic elements** if floristic aspects are considered. Nevertheless, these terms may be regarded as synonyms. At times **genoelements** (the same phylogenetic origin of a species group) and **chronoelements** (the same period of development of a species group) are used (Frey and Lösch 1998).

The spatial distribution of area types is clearly seen in climatic characteristics: (1) zonal temperature dependence with latitude, (2) distribution shown in the duration of the growing season with height above sea level, (3) distribution according to the influence of oceanic or continental climates which affect temperature ranges. Floristic types of Europe are included in this three-dimensional presentation of area types (Meusel et al. 1965). Groups of geoelement for Europe are shown on a map designed by Walter (1986; Fig. 4.2.6). The following abbreviations are generally used for the zonal sequence from north to south:

- arct = arctic
- bor = boreal
- cen = central European, also temp for temperate or nem for nemoral
- med = Mediterranean

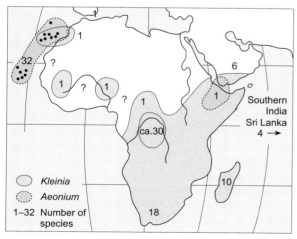

Fig. 4.2.5. Vicariance of the two genera *Kleinia* and *Aeonium*. (After Deil and Müller-Hohenstein 1984, from Richter 1997)

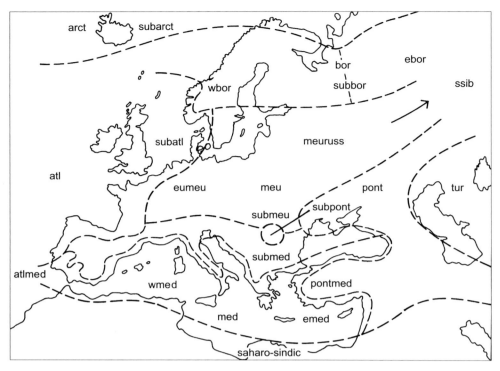

Fig. 4.2.6. Classification of geoelements (similar area types) of central Europe. (From Kreeb 1983)

These can be subdivided, e.g. arctic into sub-arctic, mediterranean to sub-mediterranean, etc. It is important for further subdivision that clearly defined floristic contrasts exist between the observed areas.

For changes in altitude the following terms are used:

- plan (planar belt of lowlands)
- coll (colline belt)
- mont (montane belt)
- subalp (subalpine belt to the timberline)
- alp (alpine belt)
- niv (nival belt)

For the west–east change the following terms are used:

- atl (atlantic)
- cen (central European)
- ssib (southern Siberian)

Here, too, intermediate steps are often used. Meusel et al. (1965) suggested that the terms continental and oceanic be used as classifications. Examples for geoelements influencing central Europe are shown in Table 4.2.5.

Vegetation may also be regarded as the combination of species for a certain area distribution or type. Causes of boundaries between area types are only poorly understood but the evaluation and interpretation of regional floras using **area type spectra** are based on the ecological characteristics of species. Filzer (1963) provided

Table 4.2.5. Examples of types of central European geoelements and neighbouring geoelements

Central European (eu-mi):	*Fabus sylvatica, Quercus petraea, Hedera helix*
Sub-arctic (subarct):	*Betula nana, Salix herbacea, Rubus chamaemorus*
Boreal (bor):	*Picea abies, Larix decidua, Ledum palustre*
Atlantic (atl):	*Erica tetralix, E. cinerea, Sarothamnus scoparius, Ilex aquifolium*
Central Russian (mi-ru):	*Carpinus betulus, Quercus robur, Alnus glutinosa, Melampyrum nemorosum*
Sub-Mediterranean (submed):	*Acer monspessulanum, Quercus pubescens, Sorbus terminalia, Bromus erectus*
Mediterranean (med):	*Quercus rotundifolia, Arbutus unedo, A. andrachne*
Pontic (pont):	*Adonis vernalis, Anemone sylvestris, Stipa pennata, St. capillata*
South-Siberian (ssib):	*Daphne mezereum, Betula verrucosa, Astragalus danicus*
Arctic-alpine (arct-alp):	*Loiseleuria procumbens, Poa alpina, Arctostaphylos alpinus*

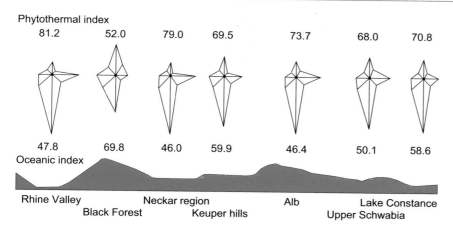

Phytothermal index

| 81.2 | 52.0 | 79.0 | 69.5 | 73.7 | 68.0 | 70.8 |

| 47.8 | 69.8 | 46.0 | 59.9 | 46.4 | 50.1 | 58.6 |

Oceanic index

Rhine Valley   Neckar region   Alb   Lake Constance
Black Forest   Keuper hills   Upper Schwabia

Fig. 4.2.7. Spectrum of area types in landscapes on a transect from the upper Rhine valley to Lake Constance. (After Filzer 1963, from Reichelt and Wilmanns 1973)

such an evaluation for a region of southern Germany and thus differentiated oceanic and continental influences, as well as thermally favoured areas (Fig. 4.2.7). Similarly, Frankenberg (1978) analysed floristic gradients in North Africa. Müller-Hohenstein (1988) characterised vegetation units on the Arabian peninsula using an area typological approach, which was used to interpret the views of climatologists and plant geographers concerning the boundaries between tropics and subtropics, and the palaeotropics and holoarctic (Fig. 4.2.8). The figure shows these different interpretations. The area analysis showed that the north-eastern Arabian coastal regions may not be classified as tropical.

4.2.2.4
Plant Kingdoms

Area types and the corresponding geoelements are the basis of a hierarchical division of the earth according to floral relationships. At the highest level of this hierarchy are the six **plant kingdoms**. This division is made on the best possible homogeneity of such plant kingdoms and the greatest contrast between neighbouring units. The differentiation is mainly based on the geographical positions in which these species have developed for different periods in isolation. The early separation of the southern continents with the corresponding formation of three plant

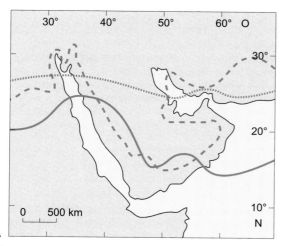

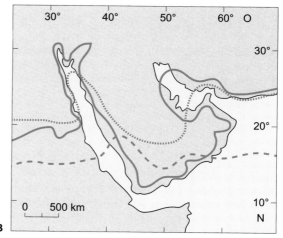

Fig. 4.2.8. A Position of the boundaries between the Holarctic and the Palaeotropic plant kingdoms on the Arabian Peninsula according to Diels (1908, *dotted line*), Al Hubaishi and Müller-Hohenstein (1984, *continuous line*) and Kürschner (1986, *broken line*). B Boundaries between the subtropics and tropics on the Arabian Peninsula according to Troll and Paffen (1964, *dotted line*), von Wissmann (1962, *continuous line*), from Blüthgen (1964), and Creutzburg and Habbe (1964, *broken line*), from Blüthgen (1964)

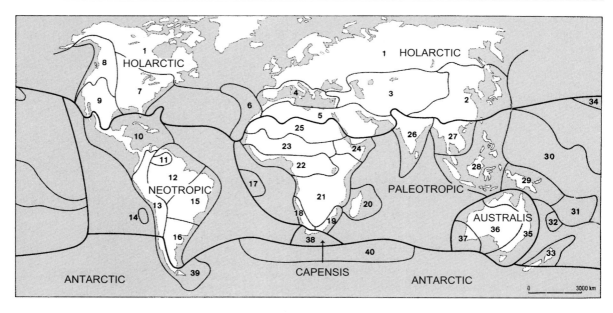

Plant kingdom: Holarctic *(can be divided into Paleoarctic and Nearctic)*
Floral regions:

1 Circumboreal	*4 Mediterranean*	*7 North American-Atlantic*
2 East Asian	*5 North Saharan-Arabian*	*8 Rocky Mountains region*
3 Irano-Turanic	*6 Macaronesian*	*9 Madric*

Plant kingdom: Neotropic
Floral regions:

10 Caribbean	*13 Andean region*	*16 Argentinian-East Patagonian*
11 Guyanese	*14 Juan-Fernandez islands*	
12 Amazonian	*15 Brazilian*	

Plant kingdom: Paleotropic *(can be divided into African, Indomalaysian and Polynesian regions)*
Floral regions:

17 Acenscion Island and St. Helena	*23 Sudano-Sahelian*	*29 Papua-New Guinean*
18 Karoo-Namibian	*24 Eritreo-Jemenitic*	*30 Polynesian*
19 Zulu region	*25 South Saharan*	*31 Fijian*
20 Madagascan	*26 Indian*	*32 New Caledonian*
21 Angolo-Zambesian	*27 Indochinese*	*33 New Zealand*
22 Guinean-Congolesian	*28 Malaysian*	*34 Hawaiian*

Plant kingdom: Australis	**Plant kingdom: Capensis**	**Plant kingdom: Antarctic**
Floral regions:	*Floral regions:*	*Floral regions:*
35 Northeast Australian	*38 Capensic*	*39 South Chilenian-Magellanic*
36 Central Australian		*40 Subantarctic*
37 West Australian		

Fig. 4.2.9. Plant kingdoms and floral regions. (After Mattick 1964; Takhtajan 1986, from Richter 1997)

kingdoms, **Antarctic, Capensis** and **Australis,** is particularly important. The northern continents, which are still together, consist of the plant kingdom of middle and higher latitudes of the northern hemisphere, the **Holarctic** (see also Chaps. 4.1.1 and 4.1.2). In the lower latitudes of the tropics, the **Palaeotropics** and **Neotropics** are differentiated. Figure 4.2.9 illustrates the division of the earth's vegetation according to phytogeographical principles (areas). To define the plant kingdoms higher taxonomic units (families) are used. This definition is not just a matter of their exclusive distribution in individual plant kingdoms, but also of their spatial centres of distribution.

The **Holarctic** is the largest plant kingdom with distribution centres of many plant families (Apiaceae, Betulaceae, Brassicaceae, Caryophyllaceae,

Fagaceae, Primulaceae, Ranunculaceae, Rosaceae, Salicaceae). Current differences, e.g. between Holarctic spaces in North America and Eurasia, are caused by recent geological events (ice ages). However, in more recent geological periods, there have been no insurmountable barriers.

This does not apply to the southern, tropical regions. The separation of the African continent from South America led to the subdivision of these two tropical plant kingdoms; this subdivision is justified, despite existing parallels (pantropical species and families, e.g. Annonaceae). Particularly characteristic families in the Palaeotropics, including the African continent and the Southeast Asian archipelagoes, are Combretaceae, Dipterocarpaceae, Euphorbiaceae, Moraceae (with over 1000 species of the genus *Ficus*), Nepenthaceae, Pandanaceae and Zingiberaceae.

For the **Neotropics**, including most parts of Central and South America, species of Araceae, Bromeliaceae, Cactaceae and Solanaceae are particularly characteristic. Tropaeolaceae are entirely limited to this plant kingdom.

The **Capensis** in the southwest of the African continent is the smallest plant kingdom in area, but is a particularly autonomous realm, where some families have developed into many species. This applies particularly to Ericaceae and Mesembryanthemaceae. In these two families relations to the Holarctic and Antarctic become obvious. The Bruniaceae is an endemic family of the Cape, and representatives of the Proteaceae and Restionaceae are dominant. The southern hemisphere plant kingdom of **Australis** comprises only the Australian continent and Tasmania; at the level of genera and species it is particularly rich in endemic species. *Eucalyptus* species (Myrtaceae) are particularly important and are now distributed worldwide. The neighbouring New Zealand belongs in part to the Palaeotropics, but in the south partly to the third plant kingdom of the southern hemisphere, the **Antarctic**, which has its largest area inhabited by plants in the southern tip of South America. In this region southern beeches (genus *Nothofagus*) developed. The floristic characteristics of the Andean mountain ranges in the south are relatively close to those of the neotropical high mountain areas in the north.

Plant kingdoms are subdivided into **floral regions** and **floral provinces**; divisions are not possible in the same detail for all plant kingdoms and boundaries differ at times. The subdivisions according to Takhtajan (1986; see Fig. 4.2.9) provide a good basis for discussion.

4.2.3

Relationship Between Area and Species

The type of distribution of plants living together in a space is called **sociability**. Developing patterns depend on the dispersal mechanisms of

---

Box 4.2.2	**Characterisation of areas**

The study of areas considers the results of plant dispersal, the plant species distribution. Distribution maps (mainly individual point distributions or grid maps) show the areas occupied by the species; these areas are characterised according to size. Plants distributed across climatic zones, over very large areas, are called cosmopolitans. They are often phylogenetically old species with particularly effective dispersal mechanisms having no specific environmental requirements. Species occurring in microspaces, e.g. only on an island or in an isolated mountain area, are called endemics. Areas are also characterised by their form with particular distinction drawn between closed and disjunct distribution areas. In the latter, the area of distribution consists of several partial areas. Disjunct areas may be explained by climate changes and tectonic events. Disjunct areas also show that they are subject to changes over time (dynamic); they can grow if the local conditions change in their favour, or shrink if the opposite occurs.

Species occupying similar areas are characterised as area types (floristic elements or geoelements; e.g. Atlantic or boreal types). Area types are the basis for the organisation of large floristic provinces and regions, and finally of the six plant kingdoms of the earth, the northern hemisphere Holarctic, the Palaeotropics and Neotropics, as well as the southern hemisphere Australis, Capensis and Antarctic (see Fig. 4.2.11).

participating species, rates of reproduction, competitiveness, etc. In nature, clumped distribution is particularly frequent, i.e. distribution is not uniform, rather an "island-like" distribution exists, where larger or smaller spaces are covered more densely, so that there are differences in **abundance**. Ecologists seeking the origin of such developing patterns need to know how many species (and individuals) are able to live in a certain space, and whether – and if yes, which – interactions exist between number of species and size of area, the so-called **species area interaction**.

Interactions of the process of biological distribution, establishment of organisms and the size of areas have been particularly analysed for **islands**. Islands have fewer species than mainland areas of the same size, as in the latter plants are able to quickly establish from the surrounding area. Due to their spatial isolation, islands are rich in endemic species and are therefore special cases. They are clearly delimited, easy to comprehend, with a limited number of different habitats under relatively uniform climatic conditions. They occur in various sizes and are situated at different distances from the mainland and therefore serve as examples to clarify the following basic relations between number of species and size of area:

* How do plants establish on islands?
* What limits the number of species on islands?

The first question is relatively easily answered. Vectors for dispersal on islands situated far from the mainland, and thus from the closest source of propagules, can only be by **long-distance dispersal**; various types of autochory are not applicable. Transport by sea birds on various established routes may be a method of dispersal (particularly epichoric dispersal), but also abiotic vectors are possible, such as air and sea currents, or exceptional events, e.g. tropical cyclones. For the Pacific islands and groups of islands the proportion of participating vectors was estimated with morphological characteristics of propagules. On islands near the mainland birds are very important, for larger distances movement by wind and seas are dominating. Propagules are carried to islands from all directions. Almost half of all species on Hawaii originate from the Indo-Pacific region, more than a quarter from the Holarctic and 17% originate from cold temperate southern hemisphere areas (Fenner 1985).

It can also be shown how plants establish on islands; Arrhenius (1921) expressed the relation between the size of an island and number of species by the following equation:

$$S = CA^z \qquad (4.2\,a)$$

i.e.

$$\log S = \log C + z \log A \qquad (4.2\,b)$$

where S is the number of species of a taxon on the island, A the area, z a parameter without dimension (constant), which changes little worldwide (slope of the linear regression, when log S is plotted against log A, values between 0.17 and 0.4). C is the gradient dependent on the dimensions in which A was measured, the biogeographical area and the taxonomic group.

The relationship between species and area shown in equation 4.2 results in the fact that the number of species of the group considered is halved if the area is reduced by a factor of 10. This attempt to provide a mathematically comprehensible theoretical expression relating the number of species to the size of island is one of the important bases of the **island biogeography steady-state theory**. Darlington (1957) proved this empirically for reptiles on West Indian islands, and Johnson and Simberloff (1974) confirmed this for plant species of the Scottish Islands (Fig. 4.2.10). These relationships are explained by two hypotheses. The **habitat diversity hypothesis** (Gorman 1979), suggesting that on larger islands there is a greater number of diverse habitats, and the **area alone hypothesis** (Kohn and Walsh 1994) assuming a direct relationship between island size and number of species.

4.2.3.1
Island Biogeography Steady-State Theory According to Preston, MacArthur and Wilson

Preston (1962), but mainly MacArthur and Wilson (1963, 1967), built on previous knowledge of establishment and number of species on islands. They started from the premises that:

* Fewer species occurred on islands than on the same area on the mainland;
* The number of species on islands increased exponentially with the size of the island;
* The pools of species on the mainland supply propagules;

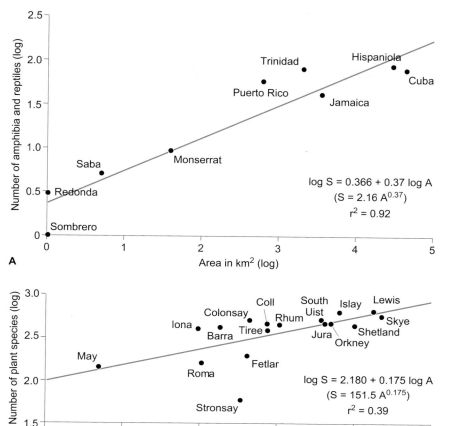

Fig. 4.2.10. Species-area relationships. A Reptile (herpeto-) fauna from selected West Indian islands (after Darlington 1957). B Plant species from selected Scottish islands. (After Johnson and Simberloff 1974)

- That the distance from the mainland is a very important determinant of the number of species on islands.

In addition, they assumed that the number of species on islands depends on the diversity of habitat and that other islands between the island and the mainland may play an important role as **stepping stones for island hopping**. It was also assumed that islands possess a limited capacity for taking in new species and that, therefore, an equilibrium between **colonisation** and **extinction** is established. It should be noted that some islands may be "oceanic" islands (e.g. formed by volcanic eruptions) and so never had direct contact to the mainland, or "continental" islands, where contact existed and where, therefore, a proportion of established species originated from that period of contact.

In summary, these observations and considerations lead to formulation of a general theory attempting to explain the different distributions of organisms. The most important parameters for such an explanation were, as previously, the size of the area and the distance to the mainland. Three statements were made:

- increased size of islands means increased number of species;
- increased distance from the mainland (supplier of propagules) means decreased number of species;
- with a constant number of species a continuous shift of species results because of colonisation and extinction.

The course of **colonisation and extinction** is shown schematically in Fig. 4.2.11 A where the intersection of both curves, **number of species** and **turnover**, shows the steady state (balanced state). The **rate of establishment** is dependent on the distance from the mainland. The larger the distance, the more difficult is the establishment. The quality of the "source" as well as the type and number of propagules that might settle

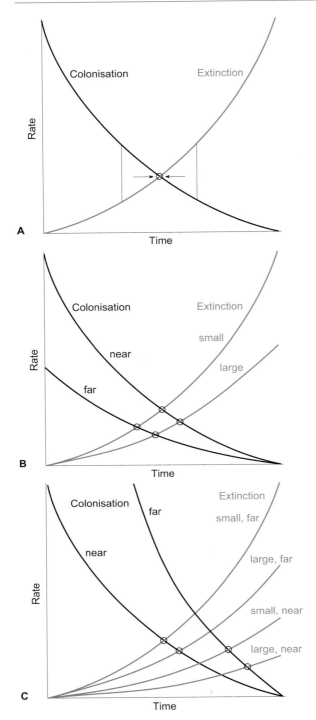

Fig. 4.2.11. Basic concepts in the theory of island biogeography. A Processes of colonisation and extinction. B Equilibrium model after MacArthur and Wilson (1967). C Survival effect according to the equilibrium theory. (After Brown and Gibson 1983)

on the island must also be noted. **Rate of extinction**, however, is determined by the size of the island and is higher on small islands than on large islands. This leads to an additional modification (Fig. 4.2.11 B) from which the following may be deduced:

- small islands have smaller numbers of species than large islands as well as higher turnover rates;
- islands near to the mainland have more species than those further away and also a faster turnover rate;
- an island near the mainland returns faster to the steady state after interference than one further away.

The steady-state theory was not generally accepted. Some of the predictions of the model were verified empirically, e.g. by Simberloff and Wilson (1969), who observed four islands off Florida after complete sterilisation and found reestablishment with the expected number of species and turnover rates in relation to size and position of the islands. Bush and Whittaker (1991) reconstructed rates of colonisation and extinction for spermatophytes on the volcano Rakata on the basis of expedition reports, and confirmed the theory (Fig. 4.2.12). On the other hand, different developments were observed, suggesting that extinction rate was not only dependent on the size of island, but also on the position of the island relative to the pool of propagules. The turnover of species on islands near the pool of propagules is rather low, because of the continuous supply of propagules which is of greater significance than the size of the island. This **"salvation effect"** is shown in Fig. 4.2.11 C.

Criticism of the models of MacArthur and Wilson (1963, 1967) is directed at the type of predictive mathematical models used. Barkman (1990), for example, believes that to describe complex functional relations in ecosystems only descriptive models with limited validity are possible. The main criticism of the theory of steady state of island biogeography is directed towards the characteristics of individual plant species and their behaviour towards each other (e.g. competitive relations) not considered at all in these models. It is also assumed that the increased number of species is exclusive due to colonisation; genetic evolution is not considered and neither are the **problems of saturation of species**. Climatic changes and geological tectonic events question the steady-state model as well.

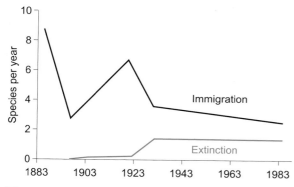

Fig. 4.2.12. Immigration and extinction of vascular plants on Rakata between 1883 and 1989. (After Bush and Whittaker 1991)

The role of stepping-stone biotopes is recognised but not considered further. The possibly important diversity of the habitat is not considered sufficiently, a factor which is very important, particularly in large habitats.

It is now difficult to find empirical proof for basically very simple assumptions of the theory of island geography, as experimental and model areas of islands which appeared ideal have been changed drastically by human influences. However, this theory has been and will be discussed because of its undisputed empirical significance and will be applied to contexts far beyond oceanic islands.

4.2.3.2
"Oceanic" and "Mainland" Islands

The results of island biogeography were formulated for islands and island groups in the sea and thus need not be applicable for all island-like habitats. Nevertheless, attempts have been made to transfer this knowledge to the mainland and island-like habitats there. These habitats are islands in lakes, mountain peaks in mountainous areas, "Inselberge" in the tropics and very small, well-isolated systems such as individual deciduous trees in a coniferous forest, caves or flower heads. Nowadays, all **anthropogenic forests** or **biotope fragments** in our managed landscapes could be interpreted as islands.

There certainly are a number of common aspects which appear to justify the application of island biogeography models to mainland islands. They have defined areas, relatively sharp borders to neighbouring habitats, are smaller than the

surrounding area, and are often situated in an hostile surrounding area, at least for the taxa within them. However, differences should not be overlooked and terms such as **isolates** (genetic separation) and **separates** (spatial separation) have been suggested (Kratochwil 1999). Usually, the distance to neighbouring islands (e.g. other forest fragments) is not very large, the surrounding area may be hostile, but allows short-term bridging. Most of all, the turnover is certainly increased as immigration rates are higher (e.g. by species avoiding intensive agriculture and fleeing into residual forests) as well as emigration rates (e.g. because of the relative proximity of comparable neighbouring islands or also sudden external interference).

The disappearance of a species in a habitat need not be connected to the extinction of the species at all. If the tree line in mountains is lower because of a deterioration of the climate, species probably find refuge in the valley. The risk of extinction is low. With subsequent warming these species will establish again in higher locations. The same principle can be applied to the diversity of species in regions which became mainland in cold periods and then became islands again in warm periods. In this case the steady state was contrasted with the **relict theory**, i.e. the present-day occurrence of species is explained by historical events.

For intensively used, managed landscapes with many small area habitats a **"mosaic concept"** was developed (Duelli 1993). The number of species is explained as individual stones in a mosaic; within the habitat the number of species increases with the number of habitat types (even those created by man). In a mosaic landscape there are several transitional stages (**ecotones**) which may be settled by specialists. Amongst animals the **diversity of the habitat** favours those which are dependent on a seasonal change of habitat. This concept touches on the importance of transitions and edges of regions.

For small forest islands, species-rich **marginal zones** can be observed where light-demanding species occur, but not actual forest species. In near-natural spaces, marginal zones are often **buffer zones** and provide a gradual transition to the inside of the island, forming an area of minimum size which provides the habitat for obligate forest species. In intensively used agricultural landscapes such buffer zones are often lacking and the gradient to the island edges is steeper.

The connection between number of species and area may also differ according to the proportion of the marginal and the core zone. In small spaces the spectrum of species is expressed by the species of the marginal zone. With increasing area, the relative diversity of species decreases and species typical of forests appear. The highest diversity is achieved in the transition from the marginal zone to the core zone. In special cases this apparently simple relation is complicated by the different influences of the marginal zone because of differences in the quality of the influences and the distance of these influences between the marginal and the core zone. A distinction must also be drawn between natural influences (radiation, wind) and anthropogenic influences (emissions, fertilisation, mechanical disturbance).

The function of **habitat fragmentation** in providing **stepping stones** between larger mainland islands should also be noted as they may stimulate exchange processes between habitats by allowing a transient residence of taxa without being the permanent habitat. At the same time they may act as **refuges**. It is assumed that species expand more via stepping stones than without. This appears logical and intuitively correct, but empirical verification is still missing.

There are examples showing that mainland islands are a good proof of the validity of area and species relationships according to the theory of island biogeography, if the influences of man on the island are not too great (Fig. 4.2.13 A). These were confirmed, for example, by Porembski et al. (1995) for island mountains on the Ivory Coast, where the number of species increases steadily with increasing area. However, May and Stumpf (2000) report from a tropical rain forest in Malaysia that with increasing areas a significant saturation of species is found (in the reported case with an area of 50 ha; Fig. 4.2.13 B). This contradiction has far-reaching consequences, particularly as nowadays **extinction rates** of plant and animal species, for example for the increasing losses of tropical rain forests, are calculated on the basis of species area curves. The course of the curve shown here allows a (too) broad spread of extinction rates.

The saturation rate in tropical rainforests for an area of about 50 ha shown here also indicates that plant sociological research examining minimum areas in such forests is theoretically possible, but not practically.

4.2.3.3
Application of Steady-State Theory to Island Biogeography in Protected Areas

Today we live in managed landscapes with a high degree of fragmentation and therefore it appears obvious to apply island biogeography to the actual problems of **protected areas**. The relation of core to marginal zones in small habitats is important here. With a decrease in such habitats the diversity of conditions at the site increases linearly, but the quality of these conditions decreases exponentially (Mader 1983). Species with special demands – including demands for space – migrate, but broadly distributed species, well adapted to the site (euryoecic species), may remain established for a long time in the marginal zones, unless they lose their habitat by frequent interference. Therefore, application of the theory of island biogeography is, at the moment, only limited.

However, valid relations of size of area and distance (for mainland islands the degree of iso-

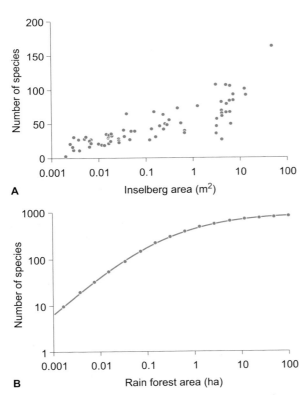

Fig. 4.2.13. Relationship between the number of species and surface area A on "Inselbergs" on the Ivory Coast (after Porembski et al. 1993); B in a tropical rainforest in Malaysia. (After May and Stumpf 2000)

lation) have stimulated discussions on the **minimum size of areas which should be sustained.** Of course, the size of protected areas should not be calculated according the rules of island biogeography only, as strictly forest species would not be protected, because of the large demand for space. Habitats of the same or similar quality should be maintained not too far away as balancing spaces and (perhaps only intermittently required) refuge areas, pointing to the previously mentioned **stepping stones** by MacArthur and Wilson (1967). These stepping stones are an important component of the concept of **interconnecting biotopes** for protected areas. In our agriculturally managed landscape, such stepping stones could be small forest islands, as well as hedges, edges of fields, long-term fallow land, disused stone quarries or railway lines, etc. Concepts of nature protection must incorporate buffer zones and smaller areas of habitat fragments around the protected area, in addition to the closed protected areas which should be as large as possible. Number of species should not be the sole aim for protection. Large areas of **mosaics of optimal and suboptimal habitats** should be considered. There cannot be a generally applicable size for protected areas and stepping stones, nor for the spatial pattern of interconnected biotopes (particularly the distances between stepping stones and the protected area). These values depend on the communities to be protected. There are very few examples in which minimum areas and distances were established empirically for individual groups of organisms. Current, urgent attempts to create protected areas are decided on local conditions and considerations of plausibility. Increasingly, the more dynamic **metapopulation concept** by Gilpin and Hanski (1991) is becoming important.

4.2.3.4
Further Models of Island Biogeography Related to Number of Species and Area

The theory of island biogeography was taken as a paradigm. Results that did not fit into these models did not result in their rejection, rather the critical experiments and their results were questioned. Since the 1970s and 1980s various interpretations have been advanced and discussed. Those who emphasise stochastic processes explain establishment of plant species on islands differently to those who favour determin-

ism. All theoretical considerations are based on the same factors which are decisive for the establishment of plants; however, they are weighted differently. Particularly important are the pool of propagules on the mainland, mechanisms for dispersal, the distance to the island as well as its size, characteristics of the habitat, phases of succession and the conditions of competition on the island.

Connor and Simberloff (1979) assume in their simulation model that establishment of plants occurs **stochastically** without competition. They tested this model with actual data and concluded that competition does not play a role. In their interpretation, it was the parameters of dispersal that determined the success of a coloniser.

Gilpin and Diamond (1980, 1982) particularly criticised this interpretation, regarding **competition** as the decisive factor. They mentioned that closely neighbouring islands possess different spectra of species, so an exchange of species would be possible. However, it does not take place because the appropriate niches are already occupied and immigrants are not able to succeed in the face of already established competitors. In their more empirical model the explanation of diversity on islands is not possible without considering competition.

These and other models use only those parameters that are considered as important. The dimension of time is often not considered. However, time could – as shown by the models of Grime (1979) or Tilman (1988; see Chap. 4.1.1.1) – be the most important factor in the course of establishment of different strategies of species. One could – in order to build a bridge between the stochastic and deterministic interpretations – regard the former as early establishment phases and the latter as late phases.

The models by Whittaker and Jones (1994), which criticise purely stochastic models, show how much the immigration of species depends on the dispersing vector and on the stage of succession on the island of Rakata (Krakatau; Fig. 4.2.14) during the course of colonisation over 100 years. In the first phase, those species that reached the island across the sea established on almost undeveloped substrates. In the second phase, anemochoric species became more important. Only in the third phase, when substrates and first succession stages of vegetation had developed, did zoochory play an increasingly important role. These results also suggest

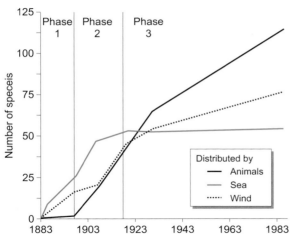

Fig. 4.2.14. Pioneer spermatophytes on Rakata from 1883 to 1989 (after Whittaker and Jones 1994). The calculation is based on a minimum turnover. On the *y*-axis the data for number of species from expeditions are shown. Species introduced by man are not considered

an initial stochastic but later deterministic establishment of species. It is overlooked in many interpretations that the change of species is not an inherent feature of the system, but is considerably regulated by changes in the environment. In the analysis and calculations by Whittaker and Jones a minimum turnover rate is considered, but actual numbers of species are not available.

More recent models clarifying species-area relations (e.g. Wissel and Maier 1992) have a decreasing empirical basis but increasing mathematical structure and so do not increase knowledge. Species-area relations, which appeared rather simple at first sight, are so complex that reductionism may lead to incorrect conclusions; holistic attempts, however, are often limited to superficial descriptions.

4.2.4

Biodiversity

Biodiversity has been, for a long time, an important subject of study in ecology. Beyond science, however, biodiversity gained interest with the general public after the Biodiversity Summit in Rio in 1992 where the ownership of **national genetic resources** was regulated (WBGU 2000). People from all walks of life, including politicians, became aware of the loss of species, a loss caused by human influences being a thousand-fold greater than natural rates of extinction. Scientists recognised that knowledge of biodiversity and topics linked to it was rather modest and feared that numerous organisms would become extinct without ever having been even scientifically recorded (Mooney et al. 1996).

| **Box 4.2.3** | **Steady-state theory in island biogeography** |

In vegetation ecology relationships between the size of an area and the number of living plant species are sought. Initially, islands were chosen for study with investigation of how they were colonised and how the number of species was determined. Understanding that developed from characterisation of an area and the species on it developed into the steady-state theory of island biogeography. This underlines the importance of stepping stones for the colonisation and is based on the idea that, over long periods of time, colonisation and extinction rates are in equilibrium. The number of species is determined by the size of the island and the distance from sources of diaspores of potential colonists, as well as the diversity of habitats which determines survival.

The theory of island biogeography was criticised mostly because the competitive relationships between species were not taken into account. Despite this, this theory is used in mainland "island" biogeography. It is the basis of biotope organisation and is used in determination of the minimum size for maintenance of habitats in nature conservation. Anthropogenic influences are present in almost all habitats, and the consequent disturbance of the environment, make it increasingly difficult to determine rules characterising areas. Currently, it is considered that the processes are less and less deterministic and are becoming increasingly stochastic.

Mere numbers of species were not regarded sufficient to understand communities in their habitats. Plants and animals were not only to be regarded as resources, but as decisive influences on processes in ecosystems (see Chap. 3). Clearly **biodiversity** developed through **evolutionary processes** by adaptation to abiotic conditions in areas with already established competitors. Why some plants form communities with few species and other with many species, what regulates the composition of species and how this influences ecosystem processes was – and still is – unknown.

At the moment ecosystems are increasingly disturbed by man and habitats are lost, whilst new sites are developed by human interference; man is responsible for the previously unknown diversity in traditional agricultural landscapes of central Europe and, therefore, it is very urgent to clarify important questions on development, loss and function of biodiversity.

A short examination of the present knowledge of the status of species will be followed by an examination of the origins of research on biodiversity based on the work of Whittaker. Questions about the hierarchy, and temporal and spatial dimensions of biodiversity will be central. Finally, functional aspects of biodiversity of biocenoses and ecosystems will be discussed (see Chap. 3) and questions related to loss of biodiversity discussed in relation to problems of environmental protection.

4.2.4.1
Species Diversity and Other Forms of Biotic Diversity

Numbers of species are only one out of several definitions of biodiversity. Without numbers and knowledge of these species – at least in their systematic structure – it would be impossible to understand the complicated topic of biodiversity. Thus recording **diversity of species** was the first aim of all inventories.

Records of numbers of species in the literature are wide-ranging. It is thought that almost 2 million plants have been described, of these about 270,000 are vascular plants. However, individual groups of species – according to their attractiveness, accessibility and ease of determination – have been recorded to different degrees. Probably a considerable proportion of flowering plants is known – the estimated total number is

320,000 – but it is assumed that less than 5% of microorganisms are described. Vertebrates are better researched than invertebrates, even though almost 1 million insect species have been recorded.

Estimates of the **total number of all species** on earth vary greatly. A realistic estimate is 10 million but the figure may be by a factor of ten greater (Groombridge 1992; Heywood and Watson 1995). On the basis of this incomplete knowledge and with particular assumptions, calculation of the total number has been attempted. One assumption is that the growth in number of species (for individual groups of organisms) described over time can be extrapolated. Numbers of endemic species or certain **keystone species** may be projected. Species occupying very large areas and therefore acting as a protection for others, so-called **umbrella species**, were chosen as well as those that are particularly favoured, so-called **flagship species**, e.g. orchids. From the number of primary consumers that of destruents is estimated, the absolute size of species is considered, as well as how common or rare they are (May 1988). Numbers calculated on such bases are contradictory and very questionable, as the importance of the selected species and parameters for diversity are not or only poorly known.

Not only the absolute number of species, but also their **spatial distribution** is of interest. Known species are not distributed evenly across the earth. There are hostile regions, e.g. permanent ice or extreme deserts, but also favourable regions such as coral reefs and tropical rain forests. The latter occupies only 6% of the surface of the earth, but more than 50% of all species live there. On a square kilometre of primary forest on the eastern slopes of the Andes in Ecuador, probably one of the regions with most flowering species, 1200 different plant species were found. The high diversity in the tropics is explained by the favourable climatic conditions enabling long and undisturbed **evolution and specialisation** as well as substantial **niche differentiation** which is an important precondition for evolution of species. Geologically, old crustal regions of the earth are generally particularly rich in species because of the long history, in addition regions where there are many small-scale structures (habitats) in a given space. Climatic regions requiring much adaptation by organisms, such as boreal forest biomes or tundras, are often relatively poor in species. According to Körner (1995), alpine mountain regions, in gen-

Table 4.2.6. The twenty-five hot spots of biodiversity currently known. (After Myers et al. 2000)

Hot spots	Original extent of natural vegetation (km²)	Remnants of the natural vegetation (km²)[a]	Protected areas (km²)[b]	Plant species	Number of endemic plant species[c]
Tropical Andes	1 258 000	314 500 (25.0)	79 687 (25.3)	45 000	20 000 (6.7%)
Central America	1 155 000	231 000 (20.0)	138 437 (59.9)	24 000	5 000 (1.7%)
Caribbean	263 500	29 840 (11.3)	29 840 (100.0)	12 000	7 000 (2.3%)
Atlantic forests of Brazil	1 227 600	91 930 (7.5)	33 084 (35.9)	20 000	8 000 (2.7%)
West Ecuador	260 600	63 000 (24.2)	16 471 (26.1)	9 000	2 250 (0.8%)
Cerrado of Brazil	1 783 200	356 630 (20.0)	22 000 (6.2)	10 000	4 400 (1.5%)
Central Chile	300 000	90 000 (30.0)	9 167 (10.2)	3 429	1 605 (0.5%)
California	324 000	80 000 (24.7)	31 443 (39.3)	4 426	2 125 (0.7%)
Madagascar[d]	594 150	59 038 (9.9)	11 548 (19.6)	12 000	9 704 (3.2%)
Forests in Kenya and Tanzania	30 000	2 000 (6.7)	2 000 (100.0)	4 000	1 500 (0.5%)
Forests of West Africa	1 265 000	126 500 (10.0)	20 324 (16.1)	9 000	2 250 (0.8%)
Cape Province	74 000	18 000 (24.3)	14 060 (78.1)	8 200	5 682 (1.9%)
Succulent-rich Karoo	112 000	30 000 (26.8)	2 352 (7.8)	4 849	1 940 (0.6%)
Mediterranean area	2 362 000	110 000 (4.7)	42 123 (38.3)	25 000	13 000 (4.3%)
Caucasus	500 000	50 000 (10.0)	14 050 (28.1)	6 300	1 600 (0.5%)
Sunda Islands	1 600 000	125 000 (7.8)	90 000 (72.0)	25 000	15 000 (5.0%)
Wallacea	347 000	52 020 (15.0)	20 415 (39.2)	10 000	1 500 (0.5%)
Philippines	300 800	9 023 (3.0)	3 910 (43.3)	7 620	5 832 (1.9%)
Indo-Burmese border region	2 060 000	100 000 (4.9)	100 000 (100.0)	13 500	7 000 (2.3%)
Southern-central China	800 000	64 000 (8.0)	16 562 (25.9)	12 000	3 500 (1.2%)
Western Ghats and Sri Lanka	182 500	12 450 (6.8)	12 450 (100.0)	4 780	2 180 (0.7%)
South-western Australia	309 850	33 336 (10.8)	33 336 (100.0)	5 469	4 331 (1.4%)
New Caledonia	18 600	5 200 (28.0)	5 267 (10.1)	3 332	2 551 (0.9%)
New Zealand	270 500	59 400 (22.0)	52 068 (87.7)	2 300	1 865 (0.6%)
Polynesia and Micronesia	46 000	10 024 (21.8)	4 913 (49.0)	6 557	3 334 (1.1%)
Total	17 444 300	2 122 891 (12.2)	800 767 (37.7)	[e]	133 149 (44%)

[a] In parentheses, as % of the original area
[b] In parentheses, as % of the hot-spot area
[c] In parentheses, as % of the globally estimated endemic plant species (300,000)
[d] Madagascar includes the neighbouring island groups
[e] As some hot spots overlap, it is not possible to give a sum

eral, have only between 200 and 300 species. Generally, there is a global north–south gradient with increasing numbers of species. This has been often described, however, without giving conclusive explanations. Interactions between temperature and number of species are also assumed. Woodward (1987) found a linear relation between the number of plant families and the absolute minimum temperature (for land surfaces along 15 °N latitude). In absolutely frost-free areas, the number of plant families exceeded 250; below a minimum of 10 °C, the number was less than 100.

So-called **hot spots, centres of high diversity,** are of particular scientific (and economic) importance; these have been determined from knowledge of the number of species and their distribution. For individual hot spots, information about the area of occurrence, protected areas, areas with almost natural vegetation, as well as number of species and endemics, has been established (Table 4.2.6). The high fre-

quency of centres of diversity in equatorial regions of South America and Oceania is very striking. Values are also relatively high for the European Mediterranean region. However, it cannot be excluded that regional differences are partly caused by more or less intensive knowledge about these regions.

Barthlott et al. (1996) presented a detailed world map of **phytodiversity** (of exclusively vascular plants) in which values from available floras were re-calculated to a 10,000-km² grid. Ten **diversity zones** are graded according to the number of species, from fewer than 100 to more than 5000. Despite the rough resolution, based only on vascular plants, such hot spots are recognisable: The centres are Costa Rica, tropical East Andes, Atlantic-Brazil, East Himalayas, North Borneo and New Guinea. Kleidon and Mooney (2000) compared the map by Barthlott et al. (1996) with a map in which the global diversity of vascular plants was constructed on the basis of a climate model. Despite the different

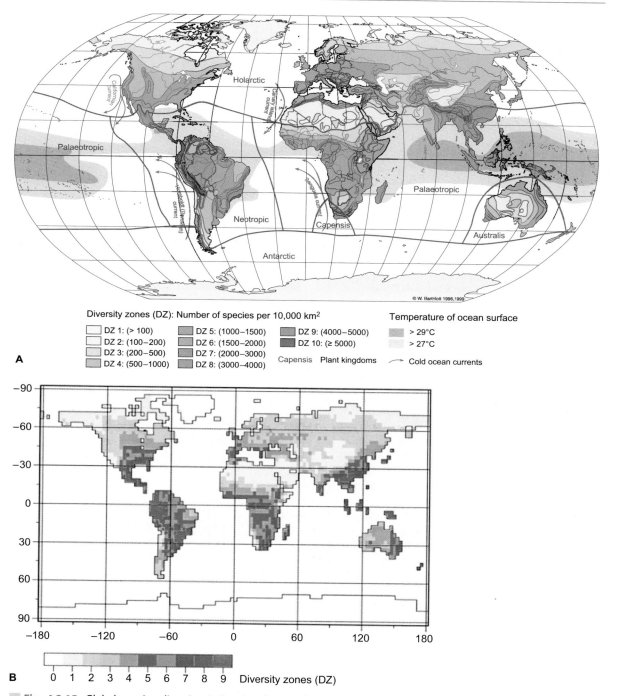

Fig. 4.2.15. Global species diversity. A Species diversity based on empirical data; map (above) from Barthlott et al. (1996, 1999). B Map from a simulation based on growth-limiting climatic scenarios by Kleidon and Mooney (2000)

resolutions, both maps agree to a large extent (Fig. 4.2.15). The authors concluded that climatic conditions explain biodiversity to a large extent. Precipitation at the time of germination and development of young plants appear decisive factors. The smaller the number of days with fa-

vourable conditions for plant growth, the larger the stress for growth and the lower the diversity of species.

Biodiversity not only comprises the number of species. Nowadays it is also assumed that **structures and functions** at the different integrational

Fig. 4.2.16. Species richness can be easily seen in a comparison of plant communities. A A species-rich natural, moist tropical forest in the Shimba Hills (Kenya) compared with B a coniferous forest in the Mediterranean region which has only one tree species (*Pinus halepensis*). In both cases, there has been little human interference in the forests. (Photos K. Müller-Hohenstein)

and organisational levels need to be considered and put into a spatial and temporal context. This complex topic area will be discussed after considering classical interpretations of biodiversity.

4.2.4.2
Classical Interpretations of Biodiversity

Research into biodiversity first considered the dimensionless number of species per unit of area (richness of species). Later, abundance and/ or dominance values were added and distribution in the space (clumped, individual, etc.) was noted. Figure 4.2.16 A, B shows two forests, hardly influenced by man, which have very different numbers of species per unit area. The tropical humid forest from the Shimba Hills (Kenya) has many more species than the Mediterranean Aleppo pine forests in the central Atlas (Morocco).

Relations between the number of species per unit area were soon expressed in rules and indices. Two **"biocenotic basic laws"** that were advanced by Thienemann (1920) and modified by Remmert (1998) state:

• The more diverse the environmental conditions, and the closer they correspond to the biological optimum, the larger the number of species;

• The more extreme the environmental conditions and the further away from the basic biological optimum, the fewer species occur and the more dominant individual species become.

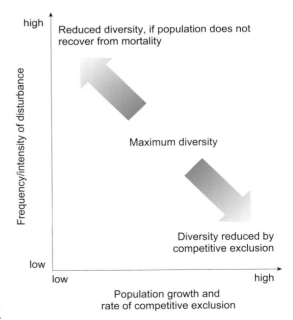

Fig. 4.2.17. Intermediate disturbance hypothesis. (After Huston 1997, from Refisch 2001)

Box 4.2.4   Quantification of biodiversity

The best-known and most frequently used index is that of Shannon and Weaver (1949):

$$H_s = -\sum_{i=1}^{s} (p_i \times \ln p_i)$$

H_s diversity index
S number of species present in the group
p_i relative frequency per area (abundance) of the ith species measured from 0–1

(e.g. the second most frequent species is given the value $i=2$, so if 10% of all individuals belong to this group, $p_i=0.10$)

$\ln p_i$ natural logarithm of p_i

With the help of this index the **abundance** and the **dominance** characteristics of plant communities can be described. The H_s value is a diversity index. It rises with increasing number of species and increasing uniformity of distribution of relative abundance (cover) of individual species. In habitats with single species the value is zero. A maximum H_s value indicates that all species in a habitat are evenly distributed although there could be a large number of species if the area is structurally homogeneous. This value says nothing about the characteristics of the individual species: all are treated equally. A value was introduced by Pielou (1966) to describe **evenness**, the uniformity of species distribution in a habitat. Haeupler (1982) used this value to develop comparative diagrams of habitats by taking into account the number of species.

Use of these indices and statistical processes provided research into biodiversity with quantitative and descriptive methods of analysis.

An initial inclusive concept to analyse diversity was provided by Whittaker (1962, 1972, 1977). He attempted to take account of all previous discussions on species diversity and particularly the spatial aspects. Distinction was drawn between:

- **alpha diversity** (discrete number of species within habitats);
- **beta diversity** (dimensionless comparative number of species in different units of vegetation or between habitats);
- **gamma diversity** (a discrete number of species in a limited space);
- **delta diversity** (dimensionless comparative number of species applied to changes over large scales, the functional equivalent of beta diversity at the higher organisational level of the landscape).

Alpha and gamma diversity are thus related and measured on particular areas, the former on those which are occupied by a community, the latter on larger spatial units; ecosystems, landscapes. Beta diversity, in contrast, describes alterations in the number of species in comparison of habitats on particular areas and must be calculated and may also be used for comparisons of number of species in the same habitat over time, and is then a measure of **species turnover**. Whittaker's measures of diversity are still used to describe spatial distribution of vegetation.

It should be stressed here that environmental conditions may also become more diverse because of disturbance (intermediate disturbance hypothesis) and the biological optimum also must consider all biological interactions (see Fig. 4.2.17).

4.2.4.3
Present Understanding of Biodiversity

It has long been thought that diversity is limited only to species diversity and is correlated to long-term development in undisturbed areas or ecosystems. During the last two decades, the scope of the term biodiversity has been extended and, at the same time, used more frequently in public. The resulting complexity in the science, contrasting with simplification in general use, requires fundamental clarification.

The term, initially only used to refer to organisms (species), was transferred to other topics and levels of organisation. To fully understand biodiversity, other levels of integration of organs and cells, but most of all plant communities (and the difficulty to define biocenoses) and ecosystems, must be included (Fig. 4.2.18 and Chap. 3). Consideration of species not only concerns genetic di-

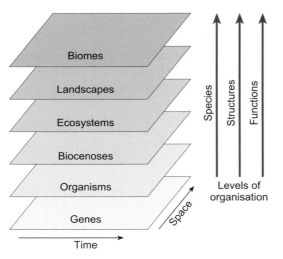

Fig. 4.2.18. Levels of organisation of biodiversity based on characteristics in space and time. (Beierkuhnlein 1999)

versity, but also structural diversity, related to composition or form of growth (Lamont 1995). Ultimately, the diversity of functions, of relations between species, and interactions between species and abiotic factors need to be considered.

This extended approach to describe biodiversity would not be complete without considering the required temporal and spatial dimensions which are partly contained in Whittaker's con-

cept, and are regarded as particularly important. In Fig. 4.2.18 the elements mentioned, levels of organisations, and temporal and spatial scales of biodiversity are related. In the following, more detailed, discussion the temporal and spatial aspects of species and structures will be outlined. More detailed functional descriptions about biodiversity are given in Chapter 3.1.

Biodiversity cannot be described reasonably without considering **spatial** and **temporal scales**. Spatial characteristics of biodiversity are **patterns of distribution** of **individuals, species, genera, communities** and **ecosystems**. Recognition of these patterns depends on the scope of the research. Of course, to identify species diversity in a cushion of epiphytic living mosses on a tree trunk in the rain forest involves different spatial scales rather than recording communities in a landscape where spatial patterns depend on the **naturally determined diversity of the site**, as well as on **diversity due to human influences** (Fig. 4.2.19 A, B). The latter resulted in maximum species diversity in the traditionally managed landscapes of central Europe up to the middle of the last century, but thereafter it decreased due to intensification of land use (see also Chap. 4.1). For populations and plant communities, intra- and interspecific competition are the factors determining diversity.

Fig. 4.2.19. Anthropogenic species diversity is to be found in all climatic zones in traditionally cultivated landscapes. This is shown by A the large number of cultivated rice varieties in a rural Indonesian market (Palu, Sulawesi) and B a home garden in southern Chile (Puerto Montt). In both cultivated areas agrochemicals and modern agronomic techniques have little impact. On such small-holdings, practicing subsistence agriculture, evidence of species diversity with intermediate disturbance (medium disturbance hypothesis) can be found. (Photos K. Müller-Hohenstein)

Table 4.2.7. Categories of plants by life form. From various authors. (After Schulze 1982)

Humboldt (1806)	Drude (1887)	Raunkiaer (1904)	Monsi (1960) and Walter (1973)	Schmithüsen (1968)
Palms	Woody plants with leaves	Phanerophytes	Herbaceous plants	Trees with crowns
Banana form	Trees	Chamaephytes	Annuals	Trees with apical bunched leaves
Mallow form	Bushes	Hemicryptophytes	Biennials	Giant grasses
Mimosa form	Lianas	Cryptophytes	Deciduous	Strangler figs
Heathers	Mangroves	Therophytes	Persistent	Lianas
Cactus form	Parasites on woody plants		Evergreen	Shrubs
Orchids	Leafless woody plants	Subdivided after	Persistent	Dwarf trees
Casuarinas	Stem succulents	Leaf size	Woody plants	Stem succulents
Pines	Leafless bushes	Leaf duration	Deciduous	Herbaceous plants
Arum form	Small bushes	Vegetative reproduction	Lignified	Epiphytes
Lianas	Perennial herbs		Evergreen	Dwarf bushes
Aloes	Rosette plants		Lignified	Small bushes
Grass form	Leaf succulents			Dwarf succulents
Ferns	Epiphytes			Chamaephytic perennial herbs
Lilies	Hapaxanthic plants			Hemicryptophytic woody plants
Willow form	Land plants			Hemicryptophytic perennial herbs
Myrtle form	Water plants			Winter annuals
Melastoma form	Lichens			Geophytic perennial herbs
Laurel form	Saprophytes/parasites			Therophytic herbs
				Floating leaf plants
				Submerged herbs

Similar considerations apply to **diversity of structures**. Important structural characteristics of a plant are leaf form and branching. Several attempts were made by plant geographers, as well as by ecologically orientated botanists, to differentiate between life forms based on structural features predominantly. These attempts show that it is very difficult to cope with the great diversity of structural features in the plant kingdom (Table 4.2.7). In closed stands, structures such as layering caused by the life form, type of canopy or intertwining with lianas increase structural diversity (Fig. 4.2.20). In a landscape, structures created by man must also be considered, e.g. fragments of almost natural stands or linear elements such as hedges and windbreaks. At this level it is clear that the natural heterogeneity contributes to high diversity, and that in transitional areas diversity changes greatly, for species as well as for structures (ecotone).

In landscape ecology, where the **importance of scale** is underlined, biodiversity is regarded as equal to geodiversity and summarised as **landscape diversity** (Leser and Nagel 1998). **Geodiversity** is defined here as the diversity of non-biotic systems. There is no doubt that abiotic features of landscapes are very important for biodiversity. It is also understood that landscapes show diversity and that these may be described. However, it is difficult to measure – a problem which also exists for structures and functions. Species or genes can be counted and used for calculations. For communities and ecosystems – provided their existence is accepted – this is difficult because of defining limits. The same applies to attributes of geodiversity, such as classification of slopes and measuring water supply or salt content of soils. Such variables may be subdivided in many ways.

The evaluation of species as **endemic, dominant and keystone** is attempted in order to improve results. However, the biggest problem is insufficient and uneven knowledge of the spatial distributions of many groups of organisms. Despite this difficulty the three-dimensional, spatial diversity of species and structures at all organisational levels is an essential aspect when considering biodiversity.

This applies just as much to **temporal diversity**. Biodiversity is a mirror image of temporal processes and developments. The composition of species and their number change during the

Fig. 4.2.20. Biodiversity is not only species-richness but also structural diversity. The photographs show clearly the association between the two aspects of diversity. A Combination of both characteristics in a tropical rain forest in Indonesia, rich in species and in structures. B An extra-tropical rain forest, poor in species but rich in structure. The number of higher plant species differs ten-fold. Cultivated cereal fields are single layered and poorer in structure than forests, although they can have more species. C A species-rich, but structure-poor fallow and D a species- and structure-poor cereal field, both influenced by the Mediterranean conditions in Morocco but on very differently cultivated areas. (Photos K. Müller-Hohenstein)

course of successions (see Chap. 4.1). Type, intensity and frequency of disturbance, e.g. landslides, fires, grazing, etc., influence species and structures, as well as the many functional interactions in biocenoses and ecosystems. It may be assumed that long periods with similar exogenous conditions and without disturbances are required for great diversity of species and ecosystems, particularly because it was possible to

develop a large diversity of habitats during such long periods.

The different scales of the **"time" dimension** must also be considered. Local and regional diversity is determined, to a large extent, by abiotic conditions and evolution. The time scale for the latter should also be applied to climate change (cold and warm periods) and to the diversity dynamics linked to it. In addition to this

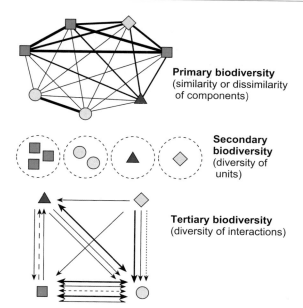

Primary biodiversity
(similarity or dissimilarity
of components)

Secondary
biodiversity
(diversity of
units)

Tertiary biodiversity
(diversity of interactions)

Fig. 4.2.21. Schematic of the three basic types of biodiversity: primary diversity (variability, beta diversity, turnover), secondary diversity (number, alpha and gamma diversity) and tertiary diversity (functional diversity, ecological complexity). (After Beierkuhnlein 1999)

"phylogenetic" time scale, other, shorter time scales – perhaps that of human influence or only a section of this, e.g. the industrial age – and their influence on biodiversity must be considered. **Regeneration phases** after disturbance, growing seasons and **phenophases** are further scales for research on biodiversity dynamics. Without considering temporal developments – the change from traditional to agro-industrial intensive agriculture with international markets and the resulting uniformity – changes of diversity at the level of species, structures and functions cannot be understood. The consideration of such changes in a relatively short time span contributed to the formulation of the **intermediate disturbance hypothesis** according to Huston (1997; see Fig. 4.2.17) which assumes that with average disturbance, e.g. in traditional agricultural landscapes, the highest diversity of species is achieved.

Beierkuhnlein (1999) formulated a new comprehensive **definition of biodiversity** considering spatial and temporal relations at various organisational levels (see Fig. 4.2.18) and their differentiation into actual things and abstract concepts (e.g. on one side individual, plant stand, landscape and on the other species, association, type of landscape). The definition states: "Biodi-

versity is an expression of the primary, secondary or tertiary diversity of organisms at all organisational levels in a factual or abstract, spatial or temporal sphere of relations."

In this definition **primary diversity** is the similarity or (its reciprocal) difference between biotic units (Fig. 4.2.21) and corresponds to beta diversity or is now interpreted as turnover. The determination of the number of such units, which would correspond to the alpha and gamma diversity, is called here **secondary diversity**. **Tertiary diversity** is the diversity of relations between units and is very difficult to record as it relates to the complete ecological complexity, and concerns all functional connections and interactions which exist between qualitatively and quantitatively determined units.

4.2.4.4
Biodiversity and Stability

Pimm (1993), Tilman and Downing (1994) and Rejmanek (1996) regard higher diversity as greater complexity of function and deduce that this represents more resistance (e.g. immigration of neophytes) and resilience towards external influences. Loss of diversity thus leads to decreased ecological integrity and to more susceptible, labile systems (Chapin et al. 2000; Fig. 4.2.22).

Experiments have shown that ecosystems possess a surprising **buffer capacity** against **loss of species**. However, if a so-called **keystone species** (Bond 1993) is lost, which affects the complete system, they may change in the long term.

It is now known that species richness does not guarantee ecological stability, but this does not mean that species-poor systems are particularly labile. The nemoral forests of North America and Europe differ considerably in the number of species, but both forest ecosystems obviously "function" similarly. Facts applying to temperate zones need not apply to tropical habitats. Here, too, spatial and temporal aspect and scales need to be considered.

Recently, "rating" of species and thus identification of keystone species have been the focus of attention. Obviously, not all species have the same function in an ecosystem and even if this were the case, their abundance or even dominance should be weighted as much as their temporal occurrence (e.g. annuals in niches). Terms such as **"functional groups"** and **"plant func-**

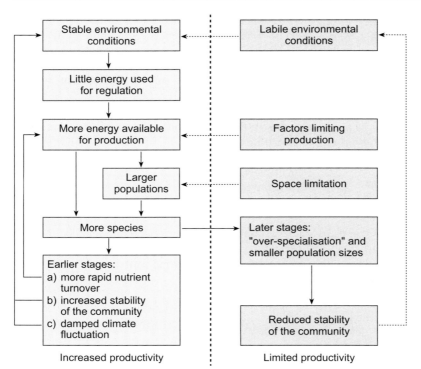

Fig. 4.2.22. Model of the relationships between diversity and stability (production and regulation of species diversity in ecosytems). (After Connell and Orias 1964, from Beierkuhnlein 1999)

tional types" (Smith et al. 1997) were created. These are species with **comparable physiological behaviour** (e.g. C_3 and C_4 plants), **similar morphology** (e.g. stem succulent bottle trees, lianas), **temporal niches** (e.g. spring geophytes, pluviotherophytes), **similar distribution syndromes** (e.g. anemochory, zoochory) and form **similar spatial patterns of distribution** (e.g. dominant species, marginal species). Plants were also grouped according to their demands on resources (water, light) or their effect in the system (shade). Subdivisions are easier according to morphological criteria and are much more detailed, as Denslow (1996) showed for tropical forests. Körner (1999) grouped plants of alpine ecosystems according to growth forms (dwarf shrubs, rosette-forming herbaceous plants, cluster grasses, cushion plants). A generally applicable classification, however, does not appear to be possible. The division depends on the question asked (Hector et al. 1999).

This approach, aimed directly at **functional diversity**, despite important historical approaches, duplicated a step which in animal ecology is already standard (Schulze 1982). In animal ecology, corresponding faunistic groups are called **"guilds"**. Predators, parasites, herbivores and carnivores, etc., can be regarded as such. It appears easier to order the fauna into such guilds than plant organisms into plant functional types. Many plants may belong to several functional groups; at the same time they may be "evergreen", "zoochoric", "deep rooting", "nitrate storing", etc., to name just a few. According to the questions posed, the same species may be classified in different groups (Beierkuhnlein and Schulte 2000). No binding proposals have yet been made and a problem is that work with functional groups is undertaken without fully understanding the function. For the group Leguminosae it is easy to understand the function because of their ability to fix nitrogen and thus to classify them accordingly. However, for groups such as "grasses" or "herbaceous plants", this applies only partially (position of leaves, capacity to form fine roots, etc.). It is thus questionable whether such a subdivision for plants would be justified in order to understand the ecological behaviour of a species within the plant community. Classification of species in a plant community according to functional groups is very difficult with our present knowledge of groups and their role in ecosystems (Schulze and Mooney 1993).

There is a further difficulty. As **plant functional types** are not only **abstract types** but also **concrete species**, and as they are seen as functionally equivalent in systems in which they live, they are also classified as redundant. If a species with this function in the system is lost, it is replaced by one from the same functional group and, because of this compensation, the system is not affected. As plant types belong to different functional groups, it is generally only possible to classify some of their functions within ecosystems. Therefore, the term **redundancy** should be used very carefully. Structural redundancy is not necessarily ecological redundancy. The latter can only occur if two species in one system compete for the same limiting resource in the same way, which is unlikely. Redundancy suggests that it is possible to do without one of these species. As long as we do not know all the functions of individual species within the ecosystem and do not know how environmental conditions will change, so that each species will have in future a potential new, special functional meaning in the ecosystem or will be able to achieve it, so there is no redundancy. This shows clearly that biodiversity per se is important (Schmid 1996; Grime 1997).

As the role of biodiversity in ecosystems is only known approximately from a few experimental studies, and may be regarded as uncertain, and actual (empirical) data are lacking, it is important to return to hypotheses formulated during the last two decades.

A generally accepted **hypothesis** is the intermediate disturbance hypothesis of Connell and Slatyer (1977) and Huston (1994), in which **medium interference** to ecosystems leads to **high diversity of species**. The traditional central European agricultural landscapes support this. Similarly, the resource availability hypothesis by Tilman and Pacala (1993), according to which the diversity of species cannot be larger than the spatial and temporal availability of resources, is accepted.

Whilst these hypotheses describe diversity in ecosystems generally, the following are primarily targeted at the importance of diversity for ecosystem functions.

Theoretically, one could think of several connections between ecosystem functions and biodiversity (Vitousek and Hooper 1993; Tilman et al. 1997):

- The process observed increases linearly with the number of species;
- The process observed reaches saturation with a certain number of species;
- One species is sufficient to maintain the process.

Conversely, various consequences of a loss of species may be hypothesised:

- With decreasing number of species a threshold is reached at which the system collapses (rivet popper hypothesis; Ehrlich 1994). The hypothesis was formulated by analogy to an aeroplane from which more and more screws and rivets are removed: At first nothing happens, but after a certain number of missing connections the construction breaks down; the aeroplane crashes.
- With decreasing number of species there is an increasing probability that a keystone species is missing with disproportionate consequences (Bond 1993). This hypothesis assumes that some species are more important for the ecosystem than others, even though they only amount to a small proportion of the biomass or the turnover rate. The effect on the ecosystem is similar to that of the rivet popper hypothesis, only the reaction occurs in several steps with the disappearance of keystone species.
- Each loss of species contributes to decreased function of the ecosystem (diversity stability hypothesis; Johnson et al. 1996).
- Some species are important; however, most species are unimportant for the maintenance of processes. As long as all-important functional groups (e.g. N fixers, primary producers, destruents) are represented, the ecosystem may be depleted to a minimum diversity (redundant species hypothesis; Walker 1992).
- Under normal or average conditions only a few species are required to make the system function. With sudden changes, however, previously unimportant species may "jump in" and continue the system under changed conditions. These species function as "insurance" (the insurance hypothesis; Schulze 1995).
- There is a relationship between biodiversity and function of the ecosystem, but the direction and effect as well as the intensity cannot be predicted, because it depends on conditions and participating species (idiosyncratic response hypothesis; Lawton 1994).
- The **zero hypothesis** (Vitousek and Hooper 1993) states that diversity has no influence on the functions of ecosystems.
- With increasing number of species saturation is reached.

These hypotheses contradict each other in important aspects, and the authors provide proof

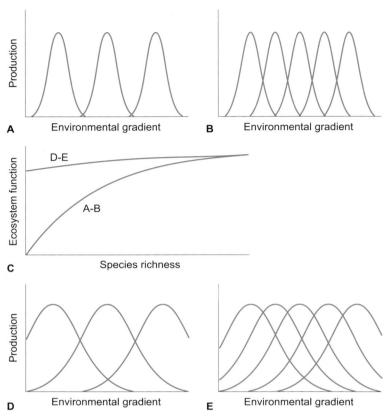

Fig. 4.2.23. Comparison of two models of the importance of the relationship between species-richness and ecosystem functions. C Species-poor and species-rich communities with relatively stenoecic species which have requirements (and functions) which hardly overlap (A, B) as well as species-poor and species-rich communities with relative euryoecic species which have requirements (and functions) which substantially overlap (D, E). In the two last cases functional redundancy occurs. (After Wright 1989)

and counter-proof. According to Schläpfer et al. (1999), most ecologists regard the redundant species hypothesis as the most important one. However, the problem of redundancy of species must, once again, be clarified. The model according to Wright (1989) shows the different effect of redundancy on the functions of species-rich ecosystems and therefore species cannot be regarded as superfluous (Fig. 4.2.23).

4.2.4.5
Endangering and Protecting Biodiversity

During the course of global history, there has always been turnover of species. This means that species that did not find their niche died out or were eliminated by natural catastrophes. However, evolution and speciation balanced this loss of species. At present, vastly more species are lost than are formed during the same period. According to May (1988), about half of the species developed in the last 50–100 million years will be eradicated in the next 10–50 years, if the current scale of forest destruction in the tropics is maintained. This dramatic relationship be-

tween the rate at which new species form to the rate of species loss is possibly too optimistic according to Nepstadt et al. (1999), as the loss of species in the remaining tropical forests by fires and extensive use is not included in the loss calculations for tropical forests.

There is no linear relationship between number of species and area. Pimm and Raven (2000) predict that with loss of half of all humid forests "only" 15% of species living there would be lost. However, if only 5% of forests remain undisturbed, only half of the forest species will be able to survive. For hot spots of species distribution much higher losses are predicted. However, exact figures are hard to obtain and those available are unreliable. It is impossible to transfer loss of species from one group (e.g. butterflies) to another (e.g. birds) along a linear gradient of exploitation, as the loss in the same area differs considerably for different groups of organisms (Lawton et al. 1998).

At present, **direct** and **indirect human intervention** are the most important causes of the **increasing loss of species**. In the early years of growing environmental consciousness, pollution of the biosphere with pesticides and other toxic substances was regarded as the main cause for the loss of species and Rachel Carson (1962) described this impressively in her book *The Silent Spring*. Today, increasing intensive agriculture and industrialisation are seen as causes. These are linked to fragmentation of the remaining almost natural areas, with drainage, eutrophication, loss of traditional rotation methods in agriculture and grazing, and replacement by monocultures, developments which are described by Krebs et al. (1999) as the "Second Silent Spring". The consequence is not only the direct loss of species, but also the loss of rare habitats. Changes resulting from this **global change** (see Chap. 5) cannot yet be estimated.

Man is breaking all existing biogeographical barriers. In addition to **species extinction**, there is a noticeable invasion (**neophytisation**), particularly a trend to global floristic uniformity with euryoecic species dominating. Lövei (1997) speaks of a 'MacDonaldisation' of the biosphere.

Maintaining and protecting biological diversity at all organisational levels require no special reasons other than the numerous arguments from ethics, religion, economy and ecology. Because we expect the decrease in species not only to affect the stability and function of our ecosystems, but also to limit future developments, we must apply controls and protective measures. Spatial and environmental planning requires instructions, to protect species, communities and their habitats, which are understandable and can be rapidly and practically applied. Simple **biomonitoring**, with individual species accurately registered and regularly traced during certain periods in controlled areas, would be a first step in underpinning assumptions and estimates with real data. Reduction in pollution of the environment and attempts to maintain the remnants of natural habitats in all biomes are obviously necessary.

Scientists have developed several instruments for the protection of the environment and some have already been successfully used in practice. It is clear that:

- protection of species alone does not suffice; the **habitat** and the natural processes occurring there must also be **protected**;
- increasing fragmentation must be counteracted by **integration of habitats** (biotope network);

Box 4.2.5	**Biodiversity and stability**

Biodiversity is mainly understood to be the number of species (richness). These developed, via evolutionary processes, over time and with spatial differentiation of specific niches in habitats. In the first inclusive concepts of biodiversity, particular attention was placed on the number of species in a specific area (i.e. plant communities) and between selected areas (within and between habitat diversity; Whittaker 1977). Later, it was shown that diversity could be described in another way. Thus, concepts such as keystone species were used to express the fact that not all species have the same function in an ecosystem. Discussion is now mainly on plant functional types, particularly those that have an important place in ecosystems and their interactions and functions.

Later, it was appreciated that biodiversity is not only the number of species. Of equal importance is the diversity of structures and the functional interactions between them. More importantly the increased numbers of aspects that can be investigated – from molecular diversity, via species to communities of species to the ecosystem – in various types of habitat and at various times.

Current thinking is that the interactions between diversity and stability need to be clarified, since it has been shown that the species-richness does not guarantee stability of communities. Of the current hypotheses, particular attention is paid to the redundant species hypothesis, stating that in a community redundant species occur, i.e. their loss does not affect the stability of the community. However, it is difficult to establish redundancy in all aspects of the community (physiological, structural, ecological, etc.). The protection of a community has to reach beyond the maintenance of species and must take into account the protection of communities and habitats. Nevertheless, there are centres of high diversity, so-called hot spots, predominantly in the tropics and subtropics, which need particular attention.

- in managed landscapes **protection of traditional processes of sustainable management** must not be forgotten;
- **hot spots** require particular protection.

Decision-makers in politics and industry responsible for the implementation of protective measures and concepts always ask for data and numbers. Therefore, steps must be taken to establish the data on biodiversity. It is relatively easy to do this at the level of the species, even if in many habitats (tropics) and for taxonomic groups (e.g. mosses, lichens) there are still enormous difficulties. However, even if these difficulties have been solved, the indices designed by scientists must be tested for practical application. Knowledge is only useful if functions can be linked to the number of species. An enormous challenge for ecologists is to **quantify functions of ecosystems dependent on diversity**, as well as working out the connection between species and structures influencing the functioning of ecosystems. For obvious reasons this would mean in the first instance working with species and communities of the macroflora and macrofauna. However, the interactions at the microbial level should not be overlooked. There are important tasks for ecologists in the future.

It will become problematic at higher levels of aggregation. Is it possible to count communities or ecosystems? If yes, how can we count the rarity, the economic significance, or the aesthetic impression? Ecology must not shy away from normative approaches and must take a position in the problems of evaluation. This must happen soon, because the scientific protection of natural habitats puts plant ecology, as no other scientific discipline, under an enormous time pressure.

References

Al Hubaishi A, Müller-Hohenstein K (1984) An introduction to the vegetation of Yemen. Ecological basis, floristic composition, human influence. GTZ, Eschborn

Arrhenius O (1921) Species and area. J Ecol 9:95–99

Barkman JJ (1990) Controversies and perspectives in plant ecology and vegetation science. Phytocoenologia 18:565–590

Barthlott W, Lauer W, Placke A (1996) Global distribution of species diversity in vascular plants: towards a world map of phytodiversity. Erdkunde 50:317–327

Barthlott W, Biedinger N, Braun G, Kier G, Mutke J (1999) Terminological and methodological aspects of the mapping and analysis of global diversity. Acta Bot Fenn 162:103–110

Beierkuhnlein C (1999) Biodiversitätsuntersuchungen in nordbayerischen Landschaften. In: Beierkuhnlein C (Hrsg) Rasterbasierte Biodiversitätsuntersuchungen in nordbayerischen Landschaftsräumen. Bayreuther Forum Ökol 69:1–9

Beierkuhnlein C, Schulte A (2000) Plant functional types – Einschränkungen und Möglichkeiten funktionaler Klassifikationsansätze in der Vegetationsökologie. In: Jax K, Breckling B (Hrsg) Funktionsbegriff und Unsicherheit in der Ökologie. Lang, Frankfurt

Blüthgen J (1964) Allgemeine Klimageographie. Lehrbuch der allgemeinen Geographie, Band 2. De Gruyter, Berlin

Bond WJ (1993) Keystone species. Ecol Stud 99:237–253

Brown JH, Gibson AC (1983) Biogeography. Mosby, St. Louis

Bush MB, Whittaker RJ (1991) Krakatau: colonisation patterns and hierarchies. J Biogeogr 18:341–356

Carson R (1962) Silent spring. Houghton Mifflin, Boston

Chambers JC (1994) A day in the life of a seed: movements and fates of seeds and their implications for natural and managed systems. Annu Rev Ecol Sys 25:263–292

Chapin FS III, Zavaleta ES, Eviner VT, Naylor RL, Vitousek PM, Reynolds HL, Hooper DU, Lavorel S, Sala OE, Hobbie SE, Mack MC, Diaz S (2000) Consequences of changing biodiversity. Nature 405:234–242

Connell JH, Orias E (1964) The ecological regulation of species diversity. Am Nat 98:399–414

Connell JH, Slatyer RO (1977) Mechanisms of succession in natural communities and their role in community stability and organisation. Am Nat 111:1119–1144

Connor EF, Simberloff D (1979) The assembly of species communities: change or competition? Ecology 60:1132–1140

Darlington PJ (1957) Zoogeographie: the geographical distribution of animals. Wiley, New York

Denslow JS (1996) Functional group diversity and responses to disturbance. In: Orians GH, Dirzo R, Cushman JH (eds) Biodiversity and ecosystem processes in tropical forests. Ecological Studies 122, Springer, Berlin

Diels L (1908) Pflanzengeographie. GJ Göschen, Leipzig

Duelli P (1993) Ökologischer Ausgleich in der Kulturlandschaft: Eine Herausforderung für Politik, Naturschutz und ökologische Forschung. Verh Ökol 22:3–8

Ehrlich PR (1994) Energy use and biodiversity loss. Philos Trans R Soc Lond 344:99–104

Engel TR (2000) Seed dispersal and forest regeneration in a tropical lowland biocoenosis (Shimba Hills, Kenya). PhD Thesis, University of Bayreuth, Germany

Espigares T, Peco B (1993) Mediterranean pasture dynamics: the role of germination. J Veg Sci 4:189–194

Evenari M, Shanan L, Tadmor N (1982) The challenge of a desert. Harvard University Press, Cambridge

Fenner M (1985) Seed ecology. Chapman and Hall, London

Filzer P (1963) Ein botanischer Beitrag zur Charakterisierung natürlicher Landschaften Süddeutschlands. Ber Dtsch Landeskd 31:69–83

Frankenberg P (1978) Methodische Überlegungen zur floristischen Pflanzengeographie. Erdkunde 32:251–258

Frey W, Lösch R (1998) Lehrbuch der Geobotanik. Pflanze und Vegetation in Raum und Zeit. Fischer, Stuttgart

Gilpin ME, Diamond JM (1980) Subdivision of nature reserves and the maintenance of species diversity. Nature 285:567–568

Gilpin ME, Diamond JM (1982) Factors contributing to non-randomness in species co-occurrences on islands. Oecologia 52:75–84

Gilpin ME, Hanski I (1991) Metapopulation dynamic: empirical and theoretical investigations. Academic Press, London

Grime JP (1979) Plant strategies and vegetation processes. Wiley, Chichester

Grime JP (1997) Biodiversity and ecosystem function: the debate deepens. Science 277:1260–1261

Gorman ML (1979) Island ecology. Chapman and Hall, London

Groombridge B (ed) (1992) Global biodiversity. Status of the earth's living resources. A report compiled by the World Conservation Monitoring Centre. Chapman and Hall, London

Haeupler H (1982) Evenness – als Ausdruck der Vielfalt in der Vegetation. Dissertationes Botanicae 65. Cramer, Vaduz

Haeupler H, Schönfelder P (1988) Atlas der Farn- und Blütenpflanzen der Bundesrepublik Deutschland. Ulmer, Stuttgart

Hector A, Schmid B, Beierkuhnlein C, Caldeira MC, Diemer M, Dimitrakopoulos PG, Finn J, Freitas H, Giller PS, Good J, Harris R, Högberg P, Huss-Danell K, Joshi J, Jumpponen A, Körner C, Leadley PW, Loreau M, Minns A, Mulder CPH, O'Donovan G, Otway SJ, Pereira JS, Prinz A, Read DJ, Scherer-Lorenzen M, Schulze ED, Siamantziouras ASD, Spehn E, Terry AC, Troumbis AY, Woodward FI, Yachi S, Lawton JH (1999) Plant diversity and productivity experiments in European grasslands. Science 286:1123–1127

Heywood VH, Watson RT (1995) Global biodiversity assessment. Cambridge University Press, Cambridge

Howe HF, Smallwood J (1982) Ecology of seed dispersal. Annu Rev Ecol Syst 13:201–228

Howe HF, Westley LC (1986) Ecology of pollination and seed dispersal. In: Crawley MG (ed) Plant ecology. Blackwell, Oxford, pp 185–215

Huston MA (1997) Hidden treatments in ecological experiments: re-evaluating the ecosystem function of biodiversity. Oecologia 110:449–460

Johnson MP, Simberloff DS (1974) Environmental determinants of island species in the British Isles. J Biogeogr 1:149–154

Johnson KH, Vogt KA, Clark HJ, Schmitz OJ, Vogt DJ (1996) Biodiversity and the productivity and stability of ecosystems. Trends Ecol Evol 11:372–377

Kleidon A, Mooney HA (2000) A global distribution of biodiversity inferred from climatic constraints: results from a process-based modelling study. Global Change Biol 6:507–523

Körner C (1995) Alpine plant diversity: a global survey and functional interpretations. Ecol Studies 113:45–62

Körner C (1999) Alpine plant life. Functional plant ecology of high mountain ecosystems. Springer, Berlin Heidelberg New York

Kohn DD, Walsh DM (1994) Plant species richness – the effect of island size and habitat diversity. J Ecol 82:367–377

Kratochwil A (1999) Biodiversity in ecosystems. Academic Press, Kluwer, New York, Dordrecht

Krebs JR, Wilson JD, Bradbury RB, Siriwardena GM (1999) The second silent spring? Nature 400:611

Kreeb KH (1983) Vegetationskunde. Ulmer, Stuttgart

Kürschner H (1986) Omanisch-makranische Disjunktion. Ein Beitrag zur pflanzengeographischen Stellung und zu den florengenetischen Beziehungen Omans. Bot Jahrb Syst 106:541–562

Lamont BB (1995) Testing the effect of ecosystem composition/structure on its functioning. Oikos 74:283–295

Lawton JH (1994) What do species do in ecosystems? Oikos 71:367–374

Lawton JH, Bignell DE, Bolton B, Bloemers GF, Eggleton B, Hammond PM, Hodda M, Holt RD, Larsen TB, Mawdsley NA, Stork NE, Srivastava DS, Watt AD (1998) Biodi-versity inventories, indicator taxa and effects of habitat modification in tropical forests. Nature 391:72–73

Lepart J, Escarre J (1983) La succession végétale, mécanismes et modèles: analyse bibliographique. Bull Ecol 14:133–178

Leser H, Nagel P (1998) Landscape diversity – a holistic approach. In: Barthlott W, Winiger M (eds) Biodiversity. A challenge for development research and policy. Springer, Berlin Heidelberg New York

Lindacher H (1995) Phanart. Datenbank der Gefäßpflanzen Mitteleuropas. Veröff Geobot Inst ETH, Stiftung Rübel, Zürich 125:1–436

Lövei GL (1997) Global change through invasion. Nature 388:627–628

MacArthur RH, Wilson EO (1963) An equilibrium theory of insular zoogeography. Evolution J 7:373–387

MacArthur RH, Wilson EO (1967) Biogeographie von Inseln. Wissenschaftliche Taschenbücher, Goldmann, München

Mader HJ (1983) Warum haben kleine Inselbiotope hohe Artenzahlen? Nat Landschaft 58:367–370

May RM (1988) How many species are there on earth? Science 241:1441–1449

May RM, Stumpf PH (2000) Species area relations in tropical forests. Science 290:2084–2086

Merxmüller H (1952) Untersuchung zur Sippengliederung und Arealbildung in den Alpen. I. Jahrbuch des Vereins zum Schutz der Alpenpflanzen und -Tiere 17:96–133

Merxmüller H (1953) Untersuchung zur Sippengliederung und Arealbildung in den Alpen. II. Jahrbuch des Vereins zum Schutz der Alpenpflanzen und -Tiere 18:135–158

Merxmüller H (1954) Untersuchung zur Sippengliederung und Arealbildung in den Alpen. III. Jahrbuch des Vereins zum Schutz der Alpenpflanzen und -Tiere 19:97–139

Meusel H, Jäger EJ, Weinert E (1965) Vergleichende Chorologie der zentraleuropäischen Floren, Bd. 1. Fischer, Jena

Meusel H, Jäger EJ, Weinert E, Rauschert S (1978) Vergleichende Chorologie der zentraleuropäischen Floren, Bd. 2. Fischer, Jena

Mooney HA, Cushman JH, Medina E, Sala OE, Schulze ED (1996) Functional roles of biodiversity. Wiley, Chichester

Müller-Hohenstein K (1981) Die Landschaftsgürtel der Erde, 2. Aufl. Teubner, Stuttgart

Müller-Hohenstein K (1988) Zur Arealkunde der arabischen Halbinsel. Die Erde 119:65–74

Müller-Schneider P (1977) Verbreitungsbiologie (Diasporologie) der Blütenpflanzen, 2. Aufl. Veröff Geobot Inst ETH, Stiftung Rübel, Zürich

Myers N, Mittermeier RA, Mittermeier CG, da Fonseca GAB, Kent J (2000) Biodiversity hot-spots for conservation priorities. Nature 403:853–858

Nepstadt DC, Verissimo A, Alencart A, Nobre C, Lima E, Lefebre P, Schlesinger P, Potter C, Moutinho P, Mendoza E, Cochrane M, Brooks V (1999) Large-scale empoverishment of Amazonian forests by logging and fire. Nature 398:505–508

Pielou EC (1966) Species-diversity and pattern-diversity in the study of biological collections. J Theor Biol 10:370–383

Pimm SL (1993) Biodiversity and the balance of nature. Ecol studies, vol 99. Springer, Berlin Heidelberg New York, pp 347–359

Pimm SL, Raven P (2000) Extinction by numbers. Nature 403:843–845

Porembski S, Brown G, Barthlott W (1995) An inverted latitudinal gradient of plant diversity in shallow depressions on Ivorian inselbergs. Vegetatio 117:151–163

Preston FW (1962) The canonical distribution of common-ess and rarity. Ecology 43:185–215, 410–432

Refisch (2001) Einfluss der Wilderei auf Affen und die sekundären Effekte auf die Vegetation im Tai-Nationalpark, Elfenbeinküste. Dissertation, University of Bayreuth, Germany

Reichelt G, Wilmanns O (1973) Vegetationsgeographie. Das geographische Seminar. Westermann, Braunschweig

Rejmanek M (1996) Species richness and resistance to invasions. Ecol studies, vol 122. Springer, Berlin Heidelberg New York, pp 153–172

Remmert H (1998) Terrestrische Systeme. Spezielle Ökologie Bd 3. Springer, Berlin Heidelberg New York

Richter M (1997) Allgemeine Pflanzengeographie. Teubner, Stuttgart

Ryser P (1993) Influences of neighbouring plants on seedling establishment in limestone grassland. J Veg Sci 4:195–202

Schläpfer F, Schmid B, Seidl I (1999) Expert estimates about effects of biodiversity on ecosystem processes and services. Oikos 84:346–352

Schmid B (1996) Wieviel Natur brauchen wir? GAIA 5:225–235

Schönfelder P, Bresinsky A (Hrsg) (1990) Verbreitungsatlas der Farn- und Blütenpflanzen Bayerns. Ulmer, Stuttgart

Schulze ED (1982) Plant life forms related to plant carbon, water and nutrient relations. Encycl Plant Physiol 12B:615–676

Schulze ED (1995) Flux control at the ecosystem level. Trends Ecol Evol 10:40–43

Schulze ED, Mooney HA (1993) Biodiversity and ecosystem function. Ecological studies, vol 99. Springer, Berlin Heidelberg New York

Schupp EW (1993) Quantity, quality and the effectiveness of seed dispersal by animals. Vegetatio 107:15–29

Shannon CE, Weaver W (1949) The mathematical theory of communication. University of Illinois Press, Urbana

Simberloff DS, Wilson EO (1969) Experimental zoogeography of islands: the colonisation of empty islands. Ecology 50:278–298

Smith TM, Shugart HH, Woodward FI (1997) Plant functional types. Their relevance to ecosystem properties and global change. Cambridge University Press, Cambridge

Strasburger E, Sitte P (1998) Lehrbuch der Botanik für Hochschulen. Fischer, Stuttgart

Takhtajan A (1986) Floristic regions of the world. University of California Press, Berkeley

Thienemann A (1920) Biologische Seentypen. Arch Hydrobiol

Tilman D (1988) Plant strategies and the dynamic and structure of plant communities. Princeton University Press, Princeton

Tilman D, Downing JA (1994) Biodiversity and stability in grasslands. Nature 367:363–365

Tilman D, Pacala S (1993) The maintenance of species richness in plant communities. In: Ricklefs RE, Schluter D (eds) Species diversity in ecological communities. University of Chicago Press, Chicago, pp 13–25

Tilman D, Knops J, Wedin D, Reich P, Ritchie M, Siemann E (1997) The influence of functional diversity and composition on ecosystem processes. Science 277:1300–1302

Vitousek PM, Hooper DM (1993) Biological diversity and terrestrial ecosystem biogeochemistry. Ecological studies, vol 99. Springer, Berlin Heidelberg New York, pp 3–14

Walker BH (1992) Biodiversity and ecological redundancy. Conserv Biol 6:18–23

Walter H (1986) Allgemeine Geobotanik. Ulmer, Stuttgart

Walter H, Straka H (1970) Arealkunde (Floristisch-historische Geobotanik), 2. Aufl. Ulmer, Stuttgart

Whittaker RH (1962) Classification of natural communities. Ber Rev 28:1–239

Whittaker RH (1972) Convergences of ordination and classification. In: Tüxen H (Hrsg) Grundfragen und Methoden in der Pflanzensoziologie. Junk, Den Haag, pp 39–58

Whittaker RH (1977) Evolution of species diversity in land communities. Evol Biol 10:1–67

Whittaker RJ, Jones SH (1994) Structure in rebuilding insular ecosystems: an empirically derived model. Oikos 69:524–529

Wissel C, Maier B (1992) A stochastic model for the species-area relationship. J Biogeography 19:355–362

Wissenschaftlicher Beirat der Bundesregierung Globale Umweltveränderungen (WBGU) (2000) Welt im Wandel: Erhaltung und nachhaltige Nutzung der Biosphäre. Springer, Berlin Heidelberg New York

Woodward FI (1987) Climate and plant distribution. Cambridge University Press, Cambridge

Wright DH (1989) A simple, stable model of mutualism handling time. Am Nat 134:664–667

4.3

Interactions Between Vegetation and Abiotic and Biotic Environments – Synecology

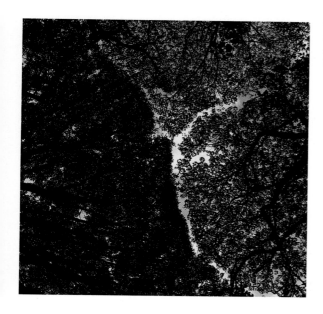

Competition or coexistence? View of the almost completely closed canopy of a mountain rainforest on Kilimanjaro (Machame, 2400 m above sea level). Photo K. Müller-Hohenstein

Previous chapters discussed aspects of plants and development of plant communities in the course of time, and their distribution in space. This knowledge is indispensable for understanding plants and their spatial dynamics. The most important relations between plants and their environment are the requirements of individual species and the supply of abiotic factors – light, temperature, water, nutrients – which have been well studied (see Chap. 2).

Plants and plant communities also affect their environment, changing the climatic conditions and soils and thus contribute to temporal dynamics and spatial changes (see Chap. 4.1). How this change takes place and its intensity will be discussed here (Chap. 4.3.1) and illustrated with examples.

For the formation of plant communities, interactions between plant species, plant populations and within communities are just as important as the interactions between plants and their abiotic environment. Their niches in communities (**biocenoses**) are determined by **competition**

and **coexistence**, mutual relations are just as important as parasites and pathogens (Chap. 4.3.2).

Plant communities (**phytocenoses**) are only part of the whole community. Animals also influence the coexistence of organisms and affect plant communities discussed here; they work as pollinators and dispersers (see Chap. 4.2) and are also herbivores and consume seeds. Thus, the basis of **biocenotics** is the **interaction between plants and animals**, and this is the topic considered in Chapter 4.3.3.

For the synecological section, the following literature is recommended in addition to that previously mentioned in Chapters 4.1 and 4.2:

- Crawley MJ (1983) Herbivory: the dynamics of animal-plant interactions. Blackwell, Oxford
- Douglas AE (1994) Symbiotic interactions. Oxford Univ Press, Oxford
- Heywood VH, Watson RT (eds) (1995) Global diversity assessment. UNEP, Cambridge

- Huston MA (1994) Biological diversity. The coexistence of species on changing land-scapes. Cambridge Univ Press, Cambridge
- Pielou EC (1974) Population and community ecology. Principles and methods. Gordon and Breach, New York
- Putman RJ (1994) Community ecology. Chapman & Hall, London
- Schulze ED, Mooney HA (eds) (1993) Biodiversity and ecosystem function. Ecol Stud 99, Springer, Berlin
- Tilman D (1982) Resource competition and community structure. Princeton Univ Press, Princeton

4.3.1

Influences of Vegetation on the Site

The extent to which vegetation influence the growing conditions at the site becomes clear when the vegetation is disturbed or completely removed. According to Lovelock (1992), there would be drastic changes on earth if there were no life, particularly the composition of the atmosphere, which would become oxygen-free, and the current surface temperatures of about 300 °C would be affected.

Plant cover not only influences the whole biological community, but also the abiotic environment. Already the **micro-climatic conditions** change over small distances. Increased **soil erosion** at an intermediate scale is witness to the change in runoff of water and to the protective effect of vegetation cover (Fig. 4.3.1). Over large areas the importance of climate for soils and water relations is discussed within the scope of the problems of global change (see Chap. 5).

Plants and plant communities not only obtain their requirements for light, water and nutrients from the supply in the area where they grow, but also affect it. This may improve the conditions at the site to the plant's advantage – by increasing the humus content of the soil which provides a better water supply due to the increased water storage capacity – or they make conditions worse because they create conditions for species which out-compete them (see the facilitation model according to Connel and Slatyer 1977; see also Chap. 4.1.5.3.5). Undemanding pioneers (e.g. lichens on bare rock) must make way for more demanding species, e.g. mosses

Fig. 4.3.1. Vegetation has a marked effect on the environment in this photograph of a lower hill slope, with advanced degradation of vegetation, in the central Atlas Mountains (Morocco). The roots of the few remaining bushes (*Quercus rotundifolia, Pistacia lentiscus*) protect the soil in which they are growing from being eroded. It looks as if the plants are growing on a pedestal. (Photo K. Müller-Hohenstein)

and flowering plants on the substrates prepared by **biogenic weathering**.

Wilson and Agnew (1992) distinguish various feedback switches, almost like electrical control systems, which are triggered by vegetation in relation to changes at the site. Thus a plant community not only changes its environment, but in addition also affects neighbouring plant communities (e.g. by shading, wind protection). In each of these cases such effects must be regarded as dynamic processes. They concern mostly the climatic and edaphic relations, but also aspects of relief formation and water and nutrient relations at several spatial and temporal scales. In the following, these connections will be explained with examples at the level of a stand of vegetation (community).

4.3.1.1

Effect of Vegetation on Climatic Conditions at Sites

Conditions at a site are related to the vegetation and include the **climate of the stand** (also **eco-climate**) and thus the areas occupied by the vegetation and directly influenced by it (see Chap.

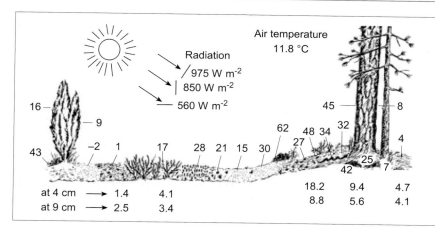

Fig. 4.3.2. Surface temperatures along a transect from a forest edge to a juniper heath in Holland (soil temperatures were measured at 4 and 9 cm depth, air temperature 1 m above the ground and was 11.8 °C, the input radiation to surfaces at different inclinations was 560, 850 or 975 W m⁻²). (After Stoutjesdijk 1977, from Stoutjesdijk and Barkman 1992)

2.1). In the case of forests this may be beyond the micro-climatic space (between soil surface and 2 m height). Within the space occupied by the vegetation, horizontal and vertical patterns and gradients of climatic parameters must be measured, in order to be able to recognise the interactions between vegetation and climate. Figure 4.3.2 shows the degree of difference between stands, particularly at transitional sites, and the dependence on exposure of sites. Surface temperatures measured only a few metres apart at the edge of a forest in the Netherlands at noon on a clear day in March correspond, in their extremes, to those in boreal forests (north side) and temperate deserts (south side). However, these differences apply only under solar radia-

tion and disappear completely under cloudy skies. It is obvious that characterisation of the climate in a stand requires the temporal course of a climatic variable which is as important as spatial differentiation.

For the climate of a stand the **albedo** (see Chap. 2.1) is just as important as the layers of the vegetation, the type of branching of trees and shrubs, as well as the density and position of leaves. These structural characteristics of plant communities determine, ultimately, the amount of light reaching the assimilating organs of individual plants. A dense tree canopy may severely decrease the light available for light-requiring species, whilst also providing shade for shade-demanding plants. Oasis cultures occur all over the world: Their mul-

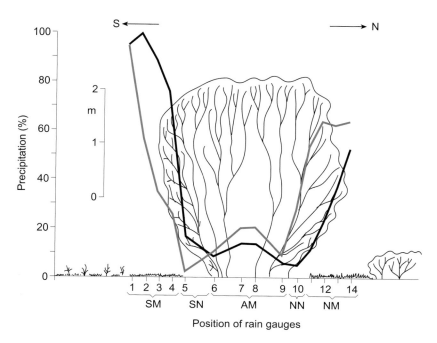

Fig. 4.3.3. Distribution of rainfall on a transect through a juniper bush measured with 14 rain gauges with a northerly wind (*black line*) and southerly wind (*blue line*). Maximum rainfall is equal to 100%. *SM* South, mossy; *SN* south, needle litter; *AM* without moss; *NN* north, needle litter; *NM* north mossy. (After Stoutjesdijk and Barkman 1992)

tiple layers of annual and permanent crops – cereals and vegetables, fruit-bearing shrubs and small trees, closed palm canopies – would not be possible without the shade provided by the date palms in the strong radiation conditions and with the dry air in arid regions.

In low, one-layered stands, e.g. in lichen communities and on moss carpets during the day, higher temperatures are reached than on neighbouring open areas. However, because of the high re-radiation during the night, temperatures may fall much more than in multi-layered stands. In the latter, **temperature layers** may be observed (see Chap. 2.1). The first maximum, higher than the temperature in open spaces, is reached in the canopy at higher day temperatures; a second occurs at the ground surface especially in more open areas. In the space between the canopy and soil surface temperatures are more balanced. Temperatures on the ground may even be further affected by the consistency of litter. According to Stoutjesdijk and Barkman (1992) on a clear winter night −4 °C was measured under Douglas fir, under pine −9 °C, but under larch and oaks −14 °C. Thus, in near-natural, species-rich forests considerable differences occur over small spaces. For the development of spring geophytes, the favourable light and temperature conditions in deciduous forests are important; conditions under oak are more favourable than under beech and hornbeam.

Vegetation also influences precipitation over small distances (see Chap. 2.2). This was measured at different wind speeds by Barkman et al. in 1977 (in Stoutjesdijk and Barkman 1992) for isolated juniper bushes with dense needles on the southern side, standing in a shrub-bush and grass community (Fig. 4.3.3). **Interception** is very important in multi-layered stands. The path of a raindrop is determined primarily by the structural characteristics of plant cover. Some plant species are able, because of the form of their leaves or needles, to comb out precipitation (*Pinus patula*, *P. canariense*). Runoff paths on branches and stems and the distribution of water at the base of the stem are also important. In total, the measured interception by conifers is about twice that of deciduous trees, but also depends on the abundance and intensity of the precipitation. Gaps in the stand, development of greening (summer and winter) and layering of the stand are important determinants of the amount of water actually reaching the ground. Furthermore, relative humidity inside the stand

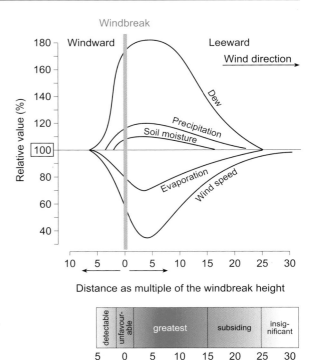

Fig. 4.3.4. Influence of a shelter belt on the microclimate. (After Reichelt and Wilmanns 1973)

is higher and more balanced than on open spaces.

Various forms of **wind shear** show impressively the influence of wind on vegetation. It may be concluded that plant stands also weaken wind, for hedges provide **protective wind barriers** (Fig. 4.3.4). There is a dependence on height, width and permeability of the vegetation and the reduction in wind speed and the development of turbulence, in turn, cause large differences in conditions within small patches of vegetation. Also the transport of energy and materials and how they are affected and absorbed by vegetation must be evaluated.

Dune systems along coastlines worldwide characterise the littoral zones. The sequence of different sites along the coast into the hinterland is shown in Fig. 4.3.5. Plants are able to stabilise the mobile sand, which is transported by **wind**, and influences transitions from the coast to the hinterland enormously. These plants are able to withstand the mechanical effects of wind and the salt carried by it. Following from the sea towards the land, communities are sea rocket (*Cakile maritima*), lyme grass (*Elymus arenarius*) and marram grass (*Ammophila arenaria*). The latter is the most important primary dune spe-

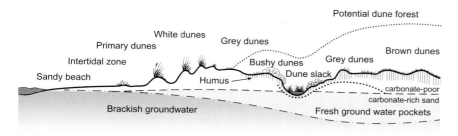

Fig. 4.3.5. Sequence of habitats in coastal regions with dune formation. (After Ellenberg 1996)

cies and is not only able to stabilise dunes, but also to tolerate being covered by sand because it forms layers of rhizomes and survives the cover of **primary dunes (white dunes)** which are often metres high. If the marram grass is not covered by sand, **secondary** and **tertiary dunes (grey and brown dunes)** develop from the gradual accumulation of humus from the decaying plant material. Tertiary dunes are recognised by an increasingly closed cover of dune grasses and shrub communities. Without plant species adapted in such a way, this formation of relief and zonation would not be possible. At the moment, dune complexes disturbed by tourism are successfully protected by planting with the salt-tolerant sand dune couch grass (*Agropyron junceum*) and marram grass (*Ammophila arenaria*) which are tolerant to being covered by sand.

Plants also play a role in triggering formation of inland dunes. Long (1954) traced the origin of the **Nebket** (Arabian term for dune systems) in North Africa to single, particularly resistant, dwarf shrubs. Sand blown in by the wind is deposited on the leeward and windward sides of these shrubs. With time the accumulation of sand improves nutrient and water supply of the 'initial shrub' which is able to grow better and thus offers possibilities for other plants to establish and finally for animals to settle. Thus, particularly at the edges of deserts, island-like dune systems develop with communities surprisingly rich in species in an otherwise hostile environment.

This shows that vegetation, with its floristic composition and most of all with its structural characteristics, greatly influences the variability of environmental conditions in the stand. Many vegetation patterns in small spaces can only be understood if the influences of vegetation which cause the differences in the local climate are known.

4.3.1.2
Influences of Vegetation on Weathering and Formation of Relief

Even though climatic and tectonic factors are most important for geomorphological processes, influences of organisms on the formation of relief and thus for changing areas must not be overlooked. Viles (1988) distinguishes, in his volume on biogeomorphology, between active and passive relations between organisms and the site factors which depend on relief. The former are biogenic weathering, formation of **biogenic sediments** (e.g. lime deposits), **bioturbation** (e.g. burrowing animals) and also **bioerosion** (e.g. from grazing animals). Passive relations, from interrelations between components of the vegetation, can be seen in dune formation and in accumulation of organic matter (e.g. in bogs or as a consequence of damming rivers). These interactions will be explained with some examples (see also Chap. 2.3).

Weathering or **formation of soils** was generally interpreted as an exogenous, climatic and physicochemically regulated process. Today, organisms are regarded as playing an important role in weathering in all climatic zones of the earth. For example, cyanobacteria participate in the formation of **desert varnish**, a covering of iron and manganese compounds – thus securing their own habitat with a protective crust. The metabolic processes of lichens, blue-green algae and fungi result in release of acids and chelating compounds which, under humid conditions, dissolve some components in rocks either completely (as with limestone) or selectively dissolve and remove the mineral components. Lichens, in particular those living within rocks (endolithic: types such as chasmoendoliths, euendoliths and cryptoendoliths) and also those living on the surface (epilithic), influence weathering in all climatic conditions (Belnap and Lange 2001). Under moist conditions, crusted rocky surfaces are conserved by lichen cover, but in arid regions lichens can be very destructive. Danin (1986) recognised in the weathering forms observed in the Negev a dynamic equilibrium between surface destruction and crust formation. Formation of particular types of crusts and patterns of dissolution caused by different moisture conditions allow conclusions to be drawn about palaeoclimatic conditions.

Bioturbation and its various forms (e.g. by earthworms in temperate habitats, ground-living small mammals in tropical high mountains) and consequences for habitats are only mentioned here, as is **bioerosion** with its often catastrophic consequences in overgrazed mountain regions (see Fig. 4.1.30 D and Chap. 4.1). An example of the passive role of vegetation in forming the relief is the living submerged macrophytic vegetation. **Dynamics of river beds** and **river valleys** is particularly regulated by vegetation. Plants occupying river banks, or submerged, influence water flow and thus affect erosion and deposition of materials transported in the river. In non-canalised rivers in Europe, for example the lower Loire, islands covered with canary grass (*Phalaris canariensis*) develop in the river bed. The German tamarisk (*Myricaria germanica*), now very endangered, not only withstands the mechanical strain of floods, but also contributes considerably to the stabilisation of river banks in Alpine low lands.

In other climatic zones there are similar, typical influences of vegetation on the formation of areas along rivers and their banks. For example, in the low land tropics, vegetation near river banks acts as zones trapping sediments and floating materials, thus slowing the flow of the river and providing protection from erosion by damming the river. In near-natural river valleys small mosaics of different plant communities frequently occur. These communities provide information on the water supply and the mechanical strain caused by water, as well as about the modifying influences of plants. Such mosaics can only be understood if the interactions between vegetation and site are considered (see also Fig. 4.1.38 and Chap. 4.1).

4.3.1.3
Influences of Vegetation on Soils

Influence of vegetation on the fertility and water relations of soils is considered by Van Breemen (1991) to be a prime example of biotic–abiotic interactions in ecosystems. Earlier discussion of primary successions emphasised the contribution of pioneer plants in providing the first **organic litter** in formation of soils, and thus in preparing conditions at the site for more demanding plants (see also Chap. 2.3). For higher plants, **Leguminosae** play an important role in the accumulation of **nitrogen**. Quality and amount of organic litter are very important for pedogenic processes and the characteristics of soils. This litter determines the C/N ratio of soils as well as possibly starting or increasing soil acidification. Not only the content of certain nutrients, but particularly their availability, are closely linked to the organic material in soil. However, accumulation of **allelochemicals** and organic substances that are difficult to degrade may render a site unsuitable for a particular plant species.

Vegetation not only affects the chemistry of soils, but also their physical characteristics. Dependent on the rooting systems of plant species growing at a site and on the type of litter, soil structures are formed which allow aeration of the soil and contribute to the transformation of an abiotic substrate into a habitat for a very wide range of organisms in the soil. There are very close interactions between the organisms, and all trophic levels are represented in the smallest space. The organisms living in the soil (**edaphon**) may span from microbes to mammals.

Structural characteristics of soils and their content of organic substances brought about by vegetation are ultimately closely linked to the water relations of the soil. A close plant cover not only protects against erosion, but may also increase water retention, contributing to more balanced runoff and may limit flooding over large areas.

Vegetation also influences the **input of N** and other nutrients (as well as pollutants). Rode et al. (1996) showed, in northern Germany, how different these inputs are depending on the species of trees and shrubs. Input is particularly high in birch-pine forests, caused mainly by the roughness of these stands and the presence of needles on pines in winter. Interception is three to ten times higher than for oak and beech forests. That individual tree species and individuals are able to determine the chemical characteristics of soils was shown by Koch and Matzner (1993) for beech (*Fagus sylvatica*). The content of exchangeable nutrients (K, Mg, Ca, Al) in the

Box 4.3.1   Interactions between plants and their environment

Plants and their communities not only make demands on the habitat, but also change it. Through qualitative and quantitative changes in nutrient availability, and modification of the meso- and micro-climate, species alter conditions, in some cases making them more favourable to themselves, but in others making them less favourable, and providing the environment required for other species to establish.

The climate within the community is particularly important (eco-climate). In well-structured communities, i.e. forests, the environment within the crown, between the tree trunks, and close to the soil surface can be very different. Even amounts of precipitation are modified via the surface roughness and interception in comparison with the conditions outside the forest. Also, the influence of the wind can be reduced, or it creates adapted plant types in small-scale vegetation patterns that can be seen in dune complexes, for example (see Fig. 4.3.5). Even the variations in river valleys and river beds are not caused just by the physical runoff, the vegetation plays a part. Plants assist in biological weathering as well as in weathering of stony material, aiding soil formation, and are responsible for the formation of surface crusts especially in dry areas. Furthermore, some plant species are able to influence the site by producing organic substances which are difficult to degrade and allelochemicals; others (e.g. Leguminosae) influence soil conditions, just as nitrogen fixation changes habitats by enrichment with nitrogen.

upper soil decreased, as did the soil pH, with increasing distance from the base of the stem. Detailed explanations of the effects of vegetation on soils, outlined here with a few examples, are given in Chapter 2.3.

4.3.2

Interactions Between Plants and Animals

Synecology is the science of relations between different organisms and their environment and includes interactions between plants and animals. For Tischler (1993), synecology is the ecology of communities, **biocenoses**. Kühnelt recognised as early as 1943 that the composition of **communities of organisms** is the best expression of all conditions in habitats. For a long time, abiotic conditions and the competition between plants were seen as decisive for their abundance and distribution. The influence of animals – pollination, dispersal, herbivory – was basically known, but not discussed further. Only in the science of ecosystems (see Chap. 3) were the far-reaching and complicated relations between plants and animals and their significance recognised.

Causal-analytical and functional interpretations are sought to develop general rules describing the relations between plants and animals. The question is what is the importance of an animal for functioning of the community. Plants are not only regulated by competition, nor are herbivores only affected by their natural enemies. Certain stress symptoms in a community may be explained by different causes such as competition and nutrient deficiency, but also depend on herbivory. What would happen to the stands of Siberian cedars (*Pinus cembra*) in the Central Alps if the bird nutcracker (*Nucifraga caryocatactes*) that disperses the seeds were to disappear. Or what would happen to the nutcracker if there were no seeds of Siberian cedars in its breeding areas. What sort of changes in dynamics would one expect? Answers to such questions are not only interesting from an ecological point of view, but are also very topical, practical questions.

Ecologists from botany and zoology should whenever possible work comparatively. This is difficult, because **animal communities** and **plant communities** differ for several reasons. Animal communities are species richer; complete recording of this diversity is very time consuming and can only be carried out by many specialists. Animals use spatially and temporally different resources, which allows them to move between sites. Consumers of the higher order are only indirectly bound to plants as resources. Animals differ in mobility and have different spheres of

action. This makes an assessment of animal communities difficult; for example, the seasonal migrations of many animal species relate to their ontogenetic development and the necessity to change abiotic and biotic conditions.

Therefore, animal ecologists have only recorded part of the **zoocenoses**, considering primarily groups (**guilds, taxonomic units, life forms**) which are easy to work with and have a high indicator value for their habitat. Grids selected for zoocenological research are usually well established, e.g. floristic-sociological, physiognomic-structural **phytocenoses** or phytocenose complexes, because they are relatively easy to interpret. Biocenology attempts to develop approaches that will lead to new methods (Kratochwil and Schwabe 2001).

Initial research on plant–animal relations was at the level of individual organisms. Various types of relations were found, e.g. **mutualistic relations**, where both partners profit, such as animals visiting flowers for nectar or pollen leading to pollination and fruit set. Also there are **parasitic relations** as well as interactions of advantage to one partner and disadvantage to the other such as **herbivory** or **carnivory**. Various forms are distinguished: **Neutralism** where no partner suffers loss of fitness (e.g. chance, random visit to flowers); **amensalism** where one partner suffers (e.g. visit to rob flowers of seeds); **commensalism** where one partner is advantaged without negative influences on the other (e.g. visits to flowers as meeting places). Figure 4.3.6 shows three examples of the diversity of relations between plants and animals.

In the following, some important relations between plants and animals at the level of species are listed. Of the important topics of plant–animal interactions, aspects of flower biology (**pollination**) and **herbivory** are considered (dispersal of propagules by animals; see Chap. 4.2.1.1). This chapter ends by presenting the basis for the emerging scientific discipline of biocenology. Results gained so far, particularly in the bioce-

Fig. 4.3.6. The three pictures show examples of the multiplicity of interactions which may occur between plants and animals in all habitats. *Drosophyllum lusitanicum* is a Mediterranean sundew that "catches" insects and thus derives additional nutrients (A). In wet mountainous areas of Ecuador, cicadas have a "meeting place" for mating on Solanaceae (B). "Termite savannahs" are a widespread vegetation type in the alternate wet and dry tropical African areas (C). (Photos K. Müller-Hohenstein)

notic research on functional interactions and relationships within communities, have shown that this discipline is particularly suited to uncover complex processes in ecosystems research.

4.3.2.1
Relations Between Plants and Animals as Organisms

Influence of Vegetation on Animals

Many characteristics of individual plants and of plant communities have considerable influence on animals. These are:

- **nutrient supply** (leaf mass, fruits, wood, nectar, pollen, etc.);
- **structure** (horizontal branches, closed canopy, dead wood, etc.);
- **information** (searching for partner, food and protection).

Food Supply

Food webs should be particularly noted, not only the direct consequences of eating and being eaten, but also the indirect and diverse feedback. Specialised food supplies may contribute to particular dispersal patterns and to succession and regeneration of plants, and so the diversity of plant and animal communities is affected. The example of interaction between the snow shoe rabbit and the Canadian lynx demonstrates that the long-discussed hypothesis of predation should be counteracted by a nutrient deficiency hypothesis, to provide the classical predator–prey relationship with a new aspect of interpretation, initially overlooked.

The **predation hypothesis** states that the rabbit population only increases if there is limited predation (Fig. 4.3.7). Because of the favourable

conditions for the prey, the number of lynx increases. However, the number of rabbits then decreases because of predation, the lynx population collapses because of insufficient food and the rabbit population is able to recover. The same events are also explained by the **nutrient deficiency hypothesis** but in a different way. Because of the large rabbit population and the consequent pressure on amount of grazing, the nutrient content of the fodder decreases (Holtmeier 1999). In the shoots which regenerate after herbivory, toxic substances and resins accumulate protecting the shoots from being eaten. The number of rabbits decreases because of starvation, and as a consequence the number of lynx also decreases. This example shows that the relations between plants and animals can be very complex and are not completely understood, in many cases.

Structure

Animals, except monophagous species, are not so much affected by the available plant species, but much more by the structure of plants and vegetation. Plants and vegetation are, in the broadest sense, sites where animals rest, but animals are very selective with respect to their resting site. Numerous invertebrates lay their eggs and find shelter from hostile weather conditions in leaves, under bark and in **dead wood**. Height and layering of plant stands are more important than their floristic composition. It is not the formation of a mesobrometum (dry *Bromus* grassland) which is the important aspect, but that it is a **dry** grassland. The meadow pipit (*Anthus pratensis*) makes its mating flight from green vegetation, whereas the tree pipit (*Anthus trivialis*) flies from tall trees at forest margins. Structural, and not floristic, characteristics of the vegetation are important, in both cases.

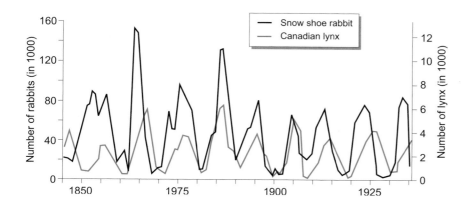

Fig. 4.3.7. Population cycles of Canadian lynx and snow shoe rabbit. (After Holtmeier 1999)

Fig. 4.3.8. Schematic of a capercaillie biotope. (After Von Hessberg, unpubl. results); 1. beech buds as spring fodder for hens; 2. protected nesting site; 3. courtship display area (tree display); 4. grit removal from root holes of up-rooted trees; 5. high and vital blueberry bushes; 6. dead wood for wood-living insects; 7. ant heap; 8. courtship display area (ground display); 9. pine needles for winter food; 10. grazing area; 11. sheltered roost

Complex structured plants and types of vegetation offer numerous microhabitats for a species-rich fauna: similarly, **stand mosaics** are particularly important in satisfying demands of many birds. Birds require, in addition to food from plants and animals, nesting and breeding sites such as holes in trees, singing and hunting platforms, and mating and pairing sites, and they also require roosting sites and protection from enemies. For many species such a diverse environment is only available in a structure-rich landscape, where small vegetation units join up to form vegetation complexes. Kratochwil (1987) analysed habitats of the rock bunting (*Emberiza cia*) in the southern Black Forest and in Graubünden and showed that a very similar type of vegetation, particularly in its structure, was required. The demands of the capercaillie (*Tetrao urogallus*) demonstrate the great extent to which the floristic and structural characteristics of vegetation need to be interlinked to fulfil the bird's demands on the habitat (Fig. 4.3.8). Of the 11 habitat characteristics mentioned only three are linked to food and thus to particular plant species. The other characteristics refer to structural features of the vegetation required in the biotope for capercaillie.

Information

Plants can also inform animals about the state of available resources, the possible presence of a partner or enemy, and the suitability of the habitat for certain stages in the life cycle, for example. Form, colour, smell and stage of development of plants are information carriers. Plants not only signal the current stage, but possibly also future development. Migratory birds breeding in meadows must know the future development of the vegetation when they arrive in spring, in order to be protected as much as possible during the breeding season. Many insect imagos are able to find the required type of vegetation early, to provide the habitat and food required for the later developmental stages of the larvae. Another example is the migratory locust in many dry regions of the Old World.

Effects of Animals on Vegetation

The effects of animals on individual plants and vegetation units may be interpreted, in many cases, as a response to the resources provided by plants. Animals need particular species and amounts of plants for their food supply, thus affecting plants directly, perhaps decreasing the photosynthetically active surface and influencing reproduction via pollination and thus propagation. Ultimately, many animals are the only, or most important, vector for the dispersal of numerous plant species in all biomes (see Chap. 4.2.1.1).

The far-reaching influences of animals on the formation of vegetation becomes obvious from terms such as termite savannah or beaver meadow. In tropical mountains and in the Andes, **animals** which **burrow** and live below ground cause partial or even complete destruction of vegetation (Werner 1977). **Bioturbation** is only a side effect. Large mammals may contribute to soil compaction and, of course, to total destruction of vegetation.

In addition, organic substances are, in many cases, more easily degraded and the plant nutrition improved because of excretion by animals which changes the mineral status of soils. Research showed that 90% of the litter in tropical rain forests would not be degraded without invertebrates. Dung beetles are very important for such turnover. The widely occurring "fly pest" in Australia was only curtailed after introduction of dung beetles (species of *Scarabaeus* and *Ontophagus*). Birds are responsible for considerable transport of material: Sea birds transport large amounts of nutrients from the sea to the mainland and greatly affect sites. Guano deposits in the North Chilean coastal regions are witness to this.

Animals are also important as 'switches' and 'amplifiers' in the ecosystem (Remmert 1992). If deer in deciduous forests eat buds, and small mammals destroy seeds and seedlings but also disperse fruiting bodies of mycorrhizae, and birds pollinate flowers, the consequences for ecosystems are decisive, even though the energy turnover is only small. Animals often only use 10% of the material available in the ecosystem in which they live, but regulate the most important system processes (e.g. pollination, dispersal of propagules) and thus contribute substantially to the ecological stability of these systems. This shows that ecosystems cannot be described and understood by energy and material fluxes alone.

Pollination by Animals

An important field for interactions between plants and animals is **pollination biology**. Most flowering plants are not able to propagate without visitors to the flowers. Trees of nemoral forests are, to a large extent, wind pollinated, but in the shrub and herbaceous layers entomogamous species dominate. Richards (1991) classified plant communities in western Ireland according to the plant succession and the occurrence of wind and insect pollination. Figure 4.3.9 shows that in almost all plant communities insect pollination dominates and that special pollination mechanisms have developed, particularly in "old" species-rich communities (e.g. Festuco-Brometea and Sedo-Scleranthetea communities).

Teleologically expressed, many animals 'expect' to obtain 'payment' from flowering plants

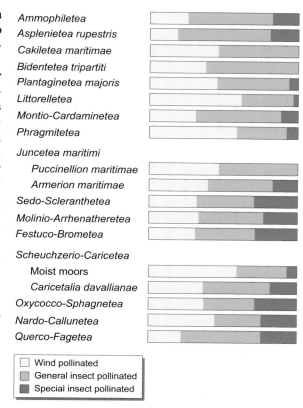

Fig. 4.3.9. Plant communities (classes) from western Ireland and the proportions of different methods of pollination. (After Richards 1991)

for their contribution to pollination and plants 'expect' to obtain 'payment' for the supply of 'rewards'. Thus predominantly mutual relationships develop. Only in rare case are the 'expectations' of plants frustrated by pollen or nectar robbers or those of animals frustrated because flowers of plants mimic potential sexual partners (e.g. insect flowers such as various *Ophrys* species) or even flowers which keep visitors captive until the flower is pollinated (e.g. flowers that are insect traps such as *Arum* species).

In **pollination symbiosis**, pollen of a flower must stick to animals and should be transported to the stigma of the next flower. To enable this process to take place, plants must possess certain characteristics and provide 'payments' or 'services' (to use teleological expressions again). Animals are mainly attracted by various foods, but in arid regions a supply of water may also be important. The most important nutrients are energy-rich proteins and lipids in pollen, and nectar containing sugars, as well as oils and resins. The supply is often directed to particular

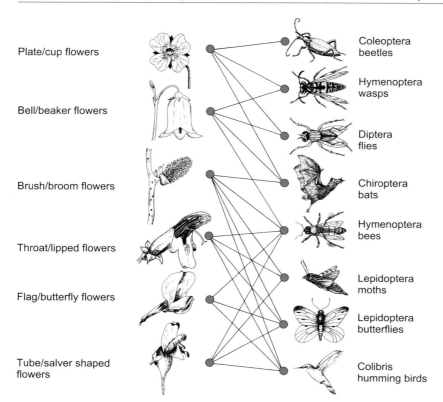

Plate/cup flowers

Bell/beaker flowers

Brush/broom flowers

Throat/lipped flowers

Flag/butterfly flowers

Tube/salver shaped flowers

Coleoptera beetles

Hymenoptera wasps

Diptera flies

Chiroptera bats

Hymenoptera bees

Lepidoptera moths

Lepidoptera butterflies

Colibris humming birds

Fig. 4.3.10. Interaction of flower types and pollinators. (After Hess 1990)

visitors, where the flowers of plants attract by colours, shapes and smells. Thus, bats and bees do not profit from the same species. Usually, the supply of individual flowers is so limited that animals need to visit other flowers and thus pollination is more likely to become successful.

Birds and insects are usually enticed by the colour of flowers whereas bats, which play an important role as pollinators in tropical communities, are attracted by smell. The structure of some flowers is such that many pollinators gain access, and guarantee success. In many cases, however, there is a special combination which is particularly reliable for considerably less pollen. In anemophilic species the relation of pollen grains to pollinated ovules is between 10:1 to 6:1, but the ratio may be 1:1 for highly specialised entomogamous species (e.g. orchids).

Special plant animal combinations can be recognised from the forms of the flowers. Hess (1990) grouped the proportions of different types of flowers in particular groups. They are shown, together with their faunistic partners, in Fig. 4.3.10. Amongst insects, beetles (Coleoptera) are regarded as the original, oldest groups of pollinators, followed by the Hymenoptera, which are the most important group now, then the

Diptera. Only relatively recently did Lepidoptera, and finally vertebrates, particularly humming birds and nectar birds as well as bats and flying foxes, develop as pollinators.

The many possible specialisations were seen as a solution to restrict the great **competition for pollinators**. This is also indicated by the fact that plants using the same pollinators flower at different times. In species-rich plant communities the number of species pollinated by insects increases, however, the number of pollinators also increases. As Boucher (1985) recognised, there is a relation between the density of plant species (and individual plants) and the available pollinators which plants attract (Fig. 4.3.11). With few flowers in an area, only few pollinators are attracted, with increasing numbers there are more, leading to mutualistic interactions. If the number of flowers increases further, a point is reached when the reservoir of pollinators is exhausted. There is, therefore, competition for pollinators.

Pollinators (and also herbivores) visit at a certain time and place flowers or plants which may be irregularly distributed. Such temporal and spatial scales have very rarely been considered in research into such plant–animal interactions.

Bronstein (1994) pointed out that the spatial relations between plants and their pollinators should be regarded quite differently from those between plants and herbivores. Plants need to attract pollinators, but at the same time need to avoid herbivores as much as possible, so time and space are important variables.

Many examples show that **flowering periods** of sympatric species competing for the same pollinators are shifted, particularly in regions without clearly differentiated seasons. Some species have very short flowering periods, others considerably longer. Flowering dates of individual flowers are not well synchronised. In regions without natural differences between seasons, temperature and photoperiod do not play an important role; species can flower once a year, as in temperate climates, or other flowering rhythms may occur. Bronstein (1994) distinguishes four different types: annual flowering, those that flower several times a year, those flowering at longer intervals, and those flowering continuously (Fig. 4.3.12 a–d).

Spatial aspects are linked to the number and distribution of potential food plants and pollinators. Theoretically, it might be assumed that animals gather food using the least possible energy. This is confirmed by systematic grazing and gathering, and limited maximum distances travelled, for example, by bees visiting sites of food and the nest (about 6 km). Tropical bats and flying foxes may cover many kilometres. Amongst birds there are real 'nomad' species that follow the regional gradient of flowering species, moving to different altitudes as required as their food species flower considerably later there. Others are aggressively "territorial"; e.g. some

a) Frequently in the year at different times

b) Once per year at different times

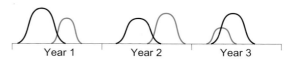

c) At more than yearly intervals

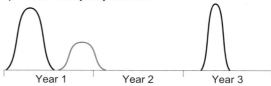

d) Continuous with varying intensity

Fig. 4.3.12. Patterns of flowering relating to species from a tropical rainforest in Costa Rica. (After Newstrom et al. 1991, from Bronstein 1994)

humming birds in Ecuador occupy a region and defend it. These show the importance of assessing temporal and spatial aspects of interactions between pollinators and flowering plants.

Temporal and **spatial synchronisation**, particularly the very different forms of flowers and the corresponding mouth parts of insects or bills of birds, show the very close interdependence of plant and animal partners, and has often been interpreted as a result of co-evolutionary processes. The obligate linkage of many insect imagos with flowers providing nectar as their only food source supports such an interpretation.

Figures are often quoted as a remarkable example of a particularly specialised **pollination system** which cannot be interpreted as random. Bertin (1989) described the cycle for *Ficus sycomorus* (Fig. 4.3.13). The syconium, the large, almost closed inflorescence of *Ficus sycomorus*, has a small distal opening, the ostiulum. Females of one wasp genus, *Agaonides*, are attracted by the smell of the flowers and carry pollen through this opening into the inner space (only in one direction). They distribute pollen

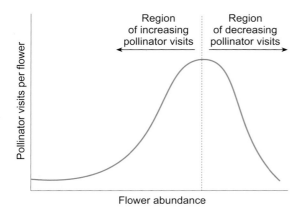

Fig. 4.3.11. Relationship between pollinator visits and flower density. (After Boucher 1985)

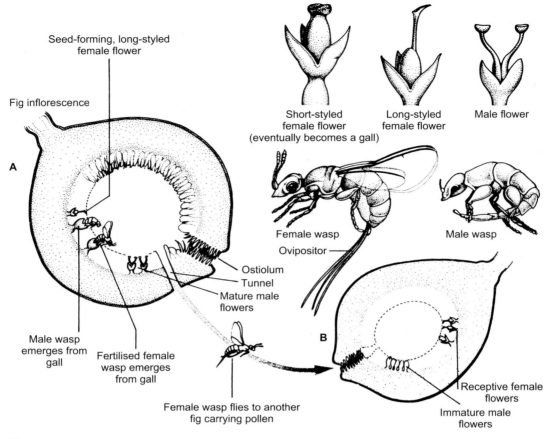

Fig. 4.3.13. *Ficus sycomorus* and its wasp pollinators. (After Meeuse and Morris 1984, from Bertin 1989)

to the numerous individual female flowers in the inner space. In some of them, particularly those with shorter stems, they lay eggs before they die. At the same time the individual figs develop and the larvae of the fig wasp feed on the gall-like growing fig tissue. First the male wasps hatch and find galls with females and fertilise them. The males die, or dig tunnels and reach the outside. The females pass through these tunnels to the outside, taking up pollen near the tunnel opening in the process, so the cycle starts again.

For such co-evolution, a common floristic and faunal history must be assumed. This also applies to herbivory, which is discussed next.

Basis of Herbivory

Herbivory is a very complex field of interaction between plants and animals. Plant are not just eaten. Herbivores influence plants in many ways, affecting their fitness and growth, including expansion of the area in which they grow and the distribution within it, as well as the composi-

tion, diversity, structure and dynamics of plant communities. They change the terms of competition and usually cause stress, tolerated by plants or not, but which they may counteract successfully.

For herbivory to occur, sufficient plants must be available so that animals may find them, for which they require suitable sensors. Animals will eat plants which provide them with suitable food and that are not able to protect themselves against being eaten. Sometimes whole plants are destroyed, sometimes only parts are lost which they may be able to compensate for and survive. These processes, which are simple to describe, not only occur for individual plants, but also for whole communities, where the interactions are much more complicated, particularly if the numerous feedback effects are incorporated together with the poorly understood synecological relations (Fig. 4.3.14 A, B).

The most important interactions between the supply of food from plants and the food requirements of animals are outlined in Box 4.3.2, in-

Fig. 4.3.14. A specific and well-known example of "indirect" herbivory between different types of trees and the leaf cutter ants (*Atta* of diverse species), often considered as symbiosis. The insects provide their symbiont fungus (e.g. *Rhozites* of diverse spp.) with chewed leaf material cut from leaves, as substrate (A), and often carried considerable distances to their nests (B). (Photo K. Müller-Hohenstein)

cluding effects beyond phytophagy. Consumption of phytomass (e.g. leaves, but also seeds) is a direct effect of herbivores and is important, but also the indirect effect, e.g. on the site and also on competition and vegetation dynamics, etc., must be considered.

In the following, various forms of herbivory are explained together with the possible responses of plants as well as the most important consequences.

Herbivores which only take pollen have little influence on plants and communities, but the influence of herbivores eating seed and seedlings is much greater. The particular demands of animals need to be known before their influence can be assessed.

The most important herbivores, because they are also the most well known, are the large vertebrates, for example in savannahs of semiarid tropical Africa and man-made vegetation in temperate climates. There are also many invertebrate species using vegetation and their herbivory need not only relate to eating leaves. Particularly invertebrates have found ways of using plant resources, and suck sap, eat pollen or seeds, or target other organs, such as buds or young shoots. It therefore seems useful to make a distinction between vertebrates and invertebrates.

In all vertebrate groups there are phytophagous species. Most important are, without doubt, mammals, followed by frugivorous birds. Insects are the most important phytophagous group within the invertebrates, with molluscs and nematodes of lesser importance. They affect leaves, flowers, seeds and roots by eating, mining, boring and burrowing, sap-sucking, and forming galls. Reichelt and Wilmanns (1973) showed the different effects of guilds of phytophages on nemoral forest ecosystems and the different extent to which they are able to use resources from plants (Table 4.3.1).

Vertebrates and invertebrates are able to disturb growth of plants in very similar ways, affecting their regeneration and contributing to early death. However, there are differences; different types of metabolism and mobility, and thus access to the required resources. Vertebrates are mostly polyphagous, with the exception of such specialists as the panda and koala which consume bamboo and eucalyptus species, respectively. Invertebrates are oligo- to monophage, thus their effects are much more selective than those of vertebrates. Vertebrates consume much more biomass because they are usually larger, sometimes consuming whole plants in one go. However, their populations are much smaller than those of invertebrates.

Tscharntke (1998) describes three possible interactions between plants and herbivores: (1) there is no damage to the plants as they are re-

Box 4.3.2 Relationship between nutrient availability and requirements and the effects of herbivores

The relationship between nutrient availability from the vegetation and the nutrient requirement of herbivores living in the same biocenose depends not only on the floral composition of the vegetation, but also on the types of herbivores and their numbers and on many other factors. This already complex interaction is further complicated as herbivores have other influences on plants and their environment in addition to consuming (phyto)biomass and the input of dung. Interactions are shown in a table, amended from Holtmeier (1999).

Nutrient availability (vegetation) amount and quantity depends on:
- composition
- structure (age distribution, layering)
- phase of succession
- time of year (phenological development)
- productivity
- regeneration (seeds, reproduction, vegetative)
- nutrient content
- digestibility (digestion of raw protein, raw fibre, protein, cellulose, hemi-cellulose, lignin, cutin, silicic acid)
- mechanical protection

Nutrient availability depends on:
- number of individuals
- demographic structure
- fitness
- time of year
- type of nutrition (generalists, specialists)
- rearing young

Effect of herbivores, due to grazing, trampling and excretion (dung):
- use of biomass (possible stimulatory effects)
- selection, competition
- seed distribution (epizoochory, endozoochory and synzoochory)
- pollination
- mycorrhizal infection
- alteration to soils (biodisturbance, nutrients, mineralisation)
- inhibition of regeneration, regrowth, dynamic changes in vegetation

sistant; (2) if plants are not resistant predation takes place, i.e. the plant is eaten; and (3) parts of plants are eaten and damage is compensated by changes in growth or accelerated growth. Individual species show a wide range of resistance, predation or compensation responses.

Resistance means that the plant has defence mechanisms towards herbivory. Permanent and induced resistance are distinguished. Permanent (and at least partial) protection is achieved by characteristics which are independent of the influence of herbivores, e.g. tannins in many trees or high content of silicic acid in some grasses. Induced defence (partially as well as permanent), for example by chemicals (**antixenosis**), which stops or limits damage, is possible. Long-

Table 4.3.1. Phytophagous insects in forest and woodland ecosystems in Germany. (After Reichelt and Wilmanns 1973)

Life style	Examples
Leaf chewers	Gypsy moth (*Lymantria dispar*), black arches (*L. monacha*), pine looper moth (*Bupalus pinarius*), European saw fly (*Neodiprion sertifer*), little spruce sawfly (*Pristiphora abietma*), cock chafer (*Melolontha vulgaris*)
Excavators	White satin moth (*Leucoma salicis*), poplar leaf-beetle (*Chrysomela populi*)
Leaf miners	Larch case bearer moth (*Coleophora laricella*), horse chestnut leaf miner (*Cameraria ohridella*)
Bark borers	Large pine weevil (*Hylobius abietis*), European fir engraver beetle (*Pityokteines vorontzovi*), European spruce bark beetle (*Ips typographus*), pine shoot bark beetle (*Tomicus piniperda*), lesser pine shoot beetle (*T. minor*), large elm bark beetle (*Scolytus scolytus*), and smaller European elm bark beetle (*S. multistiatus*), carriers of Dutch elm disease
Wood borers	Various bark beetles, e.g. spruce bark beetle (*Dendroctonus micans*)
Sap suckers	Sitka spruce aphid (*Liosomaphis abietinum*), fir shoot aphid (*Chermes abietis*), fir aphid (*Dreyfusia nordmanniana*)
Bud and shoot eaters	Pine beetle (*Myelophilus* spp.), European oak leafroller (*Tortrix viridana*)
Root eaters	Larvae of click beetles (Elateridae) and cock chafer (*Melolontha vulgaris*)
Seedling eaters	Click beetle larvae (Elateridae), pine beauty (*Panolis flammea*)

lived plants contain substances such as lignified cell walls or tissues which are particularly rich in crude fibre and inhibit digestion. Short-lived species accumulate bitter substances and poisons (phenols, alkaloids, terpenes). The methods of plant defence need to be looked at from a cost-benefit aspect which suggests that plants should accumulate substances in such concentrations that eating occurs but digestion is affected so that they are avoided (**antibiosis**). Another mechanism of avoiding herbivores is to attract antagonists (e.g. parasitoides) and thus subject phytophages themselves to increased predation (**promotion of antagonists**). Kessler and Baldwin (2001) showed this experimentally and achieved over 90% reduction of herbivores on *Nicotiana attenuata* (Solanaceae).

Polyphages live in a different environment to monophages and deal with many plant toxins and defence mechanisms. Their food uptake is particularly limited by lignified and silicified tissues and they tolerate specific poisons because of the 'dilution effect' which occurs as a result of **polyphagy**. Monophages, amongst them many insects, need to find their food plant first. Their choice may be limited but competition from other potential herbivores is decreased by the plant's toxic materials which they are able to detoxify. Thus the same plant community may become the habitat for a monophagous insect and a polyphagous mammal.

If plants are not resistant to herbivores, they may be eaten (**predation**). Many species if they are only partially eaten with loss of leaves re-

spond with **compensatory growth**. This growth differs according to the type of plant. If grasses are eaten, formation of runners and tillers may be stimulated, for example. Trees and shrubs form thorns or significantly more resistant tissues. With little pressure from herbivores there may be over-compensation in growth. The theoretical effects of herbivory on growth and thus fitness of plants are outlined by Tscharntke (1998; Fig. 4.3.15). Cases A and B assume that there is a linear relation between the intensity with which a plant is eaten and fitness (e.g. seed yield per plant). In case C herbivore pressure without visible effects is initially tolerated, only

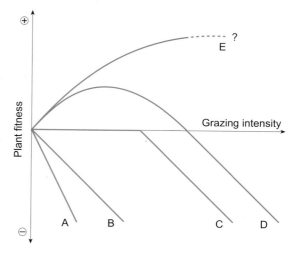

Fig. 4.3.15. Hypothesis considering the consequences of herbivory for plant fitness. (After McNaughton 1983, from Tscharntke 1998)

Fig. 4.3.16. Grazing may have very different consequences for the vegetation. In the Rif Mountains in northern Morocco, branches of summer green oaks (*Quercus faginea*) are cut when animal fodder is in short supply and the trees appear stunted (A). Extreme grazing pressure on *Quercus coccifera* in Jordan leads to stronger and sharper thorns on the small oak trees (B). Strong grazing pressure can also lead to increased frequency of toxic species, e.g. several Lilaceae, shown here in the pastures of the Plateau Central in Morocco (C). If herbs and grasses and other low-growing plants have already fallen victim to excessive grazing the remaining trees, e.g. *Argania spinosa*, are grazed by goats in the Sousse, south Morocco (D). (Photos K. Müller-Hohenstein)

later do significant losses occur. In cases D and E grazing stimulates at first, but this stimulation need not necessarily lead to increased fitness (E); after the initial transient increase there may also be a decrease (D). Increased phytomass production has often been shown following herbivory, but there are doubts that the compensatory growth is actually reflected in greater fitness of plants (Belsky 1986).

These rather theoretical considerations are supported by only qualitative information with very few measured, quantitative data for herbivore–plant relations. The data originate mainly from practical grazing management, fencing and rotation experiments, as well as from experiments with different types and numbers of animals. For many invertebrate phytophages there is controversy whether their number is limited

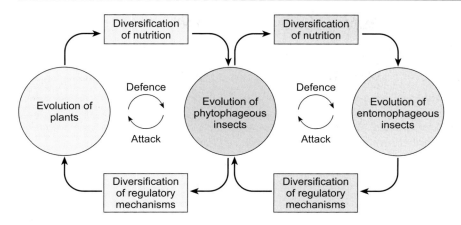

Fig. 4.3.17. Feedback processes in co-evolution of fodder plants, phytophages, and entomophages. (After Zwölfer 1978)

by the available food or by enemies. Figures published by Brunold et al. (1996) show to what different extents young plants in forests are eaten and how this regulates selection and succession. Aspen, elm and fir trees were less than 10% intact, for heather, blueberry and mountain ash about a quarter, but half of the viburnums and willows survived, whilst beech was almost undamaged. From grazing practice it is known that the age of grazed plants is a factor regulating the removal of biomass because of the changing nutrient and crude fibre contents. Spatial patterns of grazing in areas with few animals and plenty of available fodder look different to those where the grazing pressure is particularly high. Walter and Volk (1954) showed that with different grazing pressure concentric circles (including trampling damage) develop around water holes in otherwise homogeneous vegetation, with plant communities reacting specifically to different grazing pressure and the preferred grazing species become rarer and 'grazing weeds' (toxic, thorny species) increase. In Fig. 4.3.16 A–D various consequences of grazing for vegetation are shown.

Ultimately, herbivory leads to changes in the site and therefore indirectly influences plant cover. An extreme example is of areas where many animals congregate, such as resting places frequently visited by large, ruminating mammals, excreta of which significantly change the nutrient situation. Changes in the site may also occur by erosion or soil compaction caused by trampling and also by herbivorous burrowing animals.

Plants are protected by poisonous secondary materials or by mechanical barriers such as thorns and barbs. In parallel, herbivorous animals have developed morphological and physiological adaptations to overcome these impediments. Some insects also accumulate plant poisons, to which they themselves are resistant, as protection against their enemies.

These evolutionary processes – similar to those for pollinators and their partners – are often interpreted as co-evolutionary. Even though there are some warnings not to overestimate the role of evolution (Howe and Smallwood 1982; Dirzo 1984), it is difficult to interpret some of these findings otherwise. Zwölfer (1978) sees the relations between flowering plants and insects (phytophagous and entomophagous species) as a process causing insects to store information about the plant (poisonous, difficult to digest, etc.); these processes may quickly lead to evolutionary processes starting the development of new species or races (Fig. 4.3.17). He considers this as explaining the extraordinarily fast, parallel phylogenetic development of insects and angiosperms during geological development (see Chap. 4.1.1).

Temporal and spatial **intensity of grazing** and the composition of the grazing animal population are important influences on vegetation and need to be known if grazing management is to be successful: grazers preferring grasses and herbaceous species and browsers which also eat lignified species. Feasibility studies for sustainable grazing management and acceptable numbers of animals are difficult to evaluate (Müller-Hohenstein 1999). Overgrazing is particularly apparent in the semi-arid subtropical and tropical regions, because the human populations involved in grazing management have not yet adopted suitable forms of management, and because of the generally rapid growth of populations. It is questionable whether information from northern European grazing management could be transferred to near-natural ecosystems such as the savannahs of Africa, with their large herbivores. The visible effects of overgrazing are rare, even though herbivores take out between 20–60% of the phytomass for fodder. Corresponding losses in beech forests are below 10%. Similarly, these estimates should not be accepted uncritically. Not only is it difficult to measure such values, but also the consequences for the plant communities depend not only on how much is damaged or removed, but also what was eaten. Consumption of seeds and buds may have more far-reaching consequences for the whole ecosystem than consumption of the same amount of leaves.

The influence of grazing on plant diversity may be very large and reaches a maximum with medium grazing pressure. Medium to high grazing pressure has a strong influence on the composition of species and through selection has a noticeable effect on the structure of the vegetation. Poisonous and thorny species expand because of competitive advantages. Competitive conditions are changed anyway, leading to alterations in temporal dynamics and succession. In the early stages of succession herbivores are rare, but in the middle stages their numbers increase with generalists dominating. In later stages specialists dominate. Spatial patterns are thus changed and temporal patterns shifted. Ultimately, stress conditions also change. Herbivore stress is added to water stress, but light stress may decrease because of grazing.

4.3.2.2
Relations Between Plants and Animals in Communities – Basis of Biocenology

In the previous section relations between plants and animals as organisms could not always be separated from the relations between plant and animal communities. These are at the centre of considerations in **biocenology**. Plants and animals affect each other in many ways and, in doing so, are at least partially dependent on each other. This applies also to communities, i.e. biocenoses. Here, the results of phytocenology and zoocenology are combined, syntheses are aimed at a better understanding of ecosystems.

Kratochwil (1987) indicated that achieving advances in biocenology would be very difficult. **Phytocenology**, particularly in the form of plant sociology, is established as a discipline in biology and ecology in central Europe, whilst **zoocenology** is not equally established. The required synthesis is difficult not only because of the different methods used, but also because of the difficulty in counting animal communities with the same completeness as plant communities. Nevertheless biocenological information is very important, particularly for basic research on ecosystems and also for practical environmental protection.

Historical Approach:
Basic Principles in Biocenotics
Möbius (1877) introduced the term **biocenose** and applied it to a marine community of plants and animals in a limited space (**biotope**), where they undergo all stages of their development, and where species may promote or impede each other. The capacity for self-regulation in a **biocenotic equilibrium** is regarded as particularly important.

Other work followed much later. Thienemann (1920, 1939), working on limnic communities, formulated the first **biocenotic principles** (see Chap. 4.1):

- particularly diverse living conditions, with many species living in a biocenose, but usually with few individuals of a species, are difficult to record, because of the complexity;
- extreme (monocultural) living conditions, with species-poor biocenoses, often have many individuals of a species, and are easy to record because of their simple structure and interactions.

Krogerus (1932) added a third basic principle starting from the premise that:

- in diverse ecosystems euryoecic species are most abundant, in extreme systems stenoecic species.

Franz (1952) introduced another basic principle, taking into account historical aspects. However, the considerations on stability contained in this principle have been contradicted. This 'rule' states:

- The longer the period during which conditions at a site develop and the longer the same conditions have existed, the more species-rich, the more balanced and the more stable is the community.

Schwabe (1991) added important concepts to the basic principles of biocenotics and explained their validity not only for individual sites (biotopes) for which they were formulated, but also for higher and more varied complexes of sites and vegetation. This solved a difficult methodical problem in biocenotic research, namely that phytocenoses and zoocenoses have not (always) developed simultaneously in space and time. Schwabe also stressed human influences which have not been sufficiently considered: they may have positive effects (in the sense of variety of species and communities) if moderate, but if great then can cause monotonous and uniform stands.

Tüxen (1965) added further 'laws' to these basic principles. The first is the **law of social order of living organisms** and states that no organism, be it plant or animal, can live alone. The second law, the **law of exogenous order of communities**, is that only a few species can live in a biocenose, depending on conditions of the site. The third **law of temporal order** and the fourth **law of spatial order** stress that communities order themselves in a certain spatial coexistence (with contact communities) and a certain temporal dynamics. Ultimately, a fifth law becomes important, the **law of endogenous functional order**, implying that there are functional inter-linkages in metabolism, growth, expansion, ageing, decay and renewal of communities. These "laws" should not always be interpreted literally, but, together with the rules and principles mentioned, they provided a very early theoretical framework which was accepted only recently in biocenotic research.

Present Biocenology: Definitions, Tasks and Aims

Research into biocenology aims to describe, record, examine and explain, by observation and experiments, characteristics of communities primarily in the field, and considering as many organisms as possible. The research also provides functional analyses: these can only be achieved with the close cooperation of plant, animal and landscape ecologists as well as of biogeographers and landscape scientists.

The central feature is the biocenose, defined by Kratochwil and Schwabe (1999) as follows:

A **biocenose** is a community with a composition of species which have similar requirements for abiotic and biotic conditions at a site. Mutual interactions (nutritional chains, mutualistic relations, and others) are available, at least for some of the species. Typical characteristics in relation to structural-functional interactions may be established. Existing nutritional networks are not exclusively restricted to the biocenose, but are concentrated there in one or several places. Biocenoses are usually compartmented. Partial biocenoses, however, are dependent on the structure of the biocenose which is often determined by plants.

This precise definition differs from the original version by Möbius, particularly in not assuming that all species need to be in a biocenose during their complete ontogenesis. Influence by man is considered. There are also secondary biocenoses, for example there are often very young pioneer communities on sites affected by man with (still) very low numbers of species, in contrast to very old tropical biocenoses. Development can lead, albeit with large fluctuations, to species-rich systems for which a biocenotic equilibrium is assumed. The assembly of species is interpreted as occurring stochastically as well as deterministically.

The linkage of species to a biocenose is also seen very differently. According to Wittig (1993), species specific to a biocenose may spend their complete life cycle there (**homotope**), or at least spend a characteristic phase of the life cycle in it (**heterotope**), but a distinction is drawn between visitors with a short, targeted stay (**hospites**) and neighbours (**vicini**) entering for a short, random stay, or those passing through (**permigrants**), some perhaps arriving in certain seasons and some arriving by accident (**aliens**) and found episodically. A distinction is also drawn between species which are **euceonic** (including **stenoecic**, those using a special supply of a resource), **cenophilic** (with a preference), **tychozeonic** (**euryoecic**, using a broad spectrum of plants), **acoenic** (**ubiquists**) and **xenozoenic** (connection to another biocenose).

Because of the enormous complexity of biocenoses and, particularly, the almost impossible task of completely recording all groups of organisms, partial biocenoses and partial habitats have been analysed. In this, a subdivision similar to the **concept of synusiae** in geobotany proved useful in considering particular groups of organisms (guilds, life forms, functional groups) in certain parts of a biotope. Examples are a **stratocenose** in a **stratotope** (e.g. organisms in a layer, such as in the canopy or the herbaceous layer), **choriocenes** in a **choriotope** (e.g. inhabitants of a dead, woody stem or a moss cushion), and **merocenes** in a **merotope** (e.g. organisms on an inflorescence).

Methodical Approaches and Disciplines in Biocenology

At the beginning biocenology was purely descriptive. Later inductive-typological approaches became more important (Kratochwil 1999). The main problem is to decide at which level a phyto- and zoo-cenological synthesis (i.e. the bringing together of plants and animals) should take place to describe the biocenose. A system with two species may be characterised by biocenotic relations, whilst relations in communities can be shown much more comprehensively. Plant sociologists have provided a detailed reference system and offer a matrix into which animal communities may be added. A plant community does not always correspond to an animal community and this level is not always sufficient to recognise the coincidence of plant and animal communities. The **level of association** (provided by **plant sociology**) does not necessarily guarantee the required synthesis, but the level of **vegetation complexes** (provided by **sigma sociology**) and perhaps also the **science of communities of life forms** (provided on the bases of **structural characteristics** of plants and plant communities, e.g. of life forms) does. Only in this way is it possible to consider the multiple conditions, and the demands made on the habitat, during the life cycles of some animals. Particularly for bird communities, numerous relations to plant and vegetation structures have been shown (Blab 1979; Bezzel et al. 1980). Phyto- and zoo-cenolo-

gists need to be aware of the different levels and refer to actual examples in the same system.

In addition to the biocenological-symbiological approach of Wilmanns (1987), Kratochwil (1999) and Schwabe (1990), there are other approaches. Passarge (1981) proposed a typological approach. Animal communities should be recorded independent of plant communities, but characterised according to plant sociological patterns and called 'zoo-associations', and perhaps be incorporated into a plant sociological system later. Mühlenberg (1989) took a quantitative approach and sought connections between density of leaves, number of species and density of individual plants, for example. All approaches consider the functional relations and dynamics. Theoretically, listing all species is required but in practice this may only be accomplished partially by zoo-cenologists because of the many different groups of organisms. Different groups of insects are suitable invertebrate, and often birds have been chosen to represent vertebrates.

Kratochwil (1999) listed various research disciplines in biocenology, together with the most important methodical approaches, aims and problems. In Box 4.3.3 the most important partial disciplines and research topics are listed (they may overlap of course). Thus **cenomorphology** provides an inventory of species and structure, **cenoecology** the exogenous effects of and on biocenoses, **cenochorology** and **cenodynamics** assess the spatial distribution and tem-

---

Box 4.3.3	**The biological disciplines involved in biocenology and their research tools. (After Kratochwil 1999)**

A number of subsidiary disciplines have developed during the study of biocenoses, with their own research subjects and themes: the following are distinguished:

Biocenological subsidiary discipline	**Research tools**
Cenomorphology	Structure of the biocenose (structural organisation)
	– species inventories, dominance of individuals
	– attachment to the biocenose
	– dispersal of species and individuals
Research on functional interactions	Interactions of organisms (functional organisation)
Cenoecology	External biotic and abiotic factors
Cenochorology	Spatial distribution
Cenodynamics	Short-term developments with time
Cenophylogeny/cenoevolution	Formation of biocenoses during the course of evolution
Cenosystematics/cenotaxonomy	Systematic grouping and naming of biocenoses
Experimental biocenology	Agricultural and forestry aspects, environmental protection

poral development. In **cenosystematics** the aim is to achieve a systematic order of biocenoses. Currently, applied **biocenology** is regarded as important as it is closely connected to environmental protection, where the protection of communities and habitats, in addition to the protection of species, is increasingly discussed.

Research into Functional Interactions

A particularly important field of biocenology is **research into functional interactions** between organisms. **Biocenotic interactions** describe the relations between organisms in a habitat or a smaller spatial unit (microhabitat). It is particularly characterised by nutritional requirements and dependencies, but also other (inter)actions (Schaefer 1992). The total direct and indirect linking between an organism and other plants (e.g. spruce in a coniferous forest and the herbaceous layer or epiphytic mosses), as well as all animals (nesting and seed-eating birds or damaging insects), is described by functional interactions which may also be at the level of the (obligate) cooperation of a plant and an animal, but usually a complete or partial biocenose is considered.

At the beginning of such research an inventory is always required. Rabeler (1967) discovered close relationships for various faunistic guilds in forest communities of northwest Germany. The list in Table 4.3.2 may be interpreted as a plant community table. Besides those insects that occur frequently are several ubiquists and also a range of characteristics and different species, which ultimately are closely linked with

Table 4.3.2. Distribution of specific animal groups in particular plant communities in northwest Germany. (Shortened and simplified from Rabeler 1967, in Wilmanns 1998)

Animal groups	Plant communities	Lithospermo-Quercetum	Carici-Fagetum		Melico-Fagetum						Querco-Carpinetum				Luzulo-Fagetum
			seslerietosum	typicum	typicum	elymetosum	elymetosum	typcium	typicum	allietosum	dryopteridetosum	asperuletosum	asperuletosum	athyrietosum	athyrietosum
Limonia modesta	S	+	+	+	+	+	+	+	+	+	+	+	+	+	+	−
Stenodema laevigata	W	+	+	+	+	+	+	+	+	+	+	+	+	+	+	−
Lygus pratensis	W	+	+	+	+	−	+	+	+	+	+	+	−		+	−
Abax ater	L	+		+	−		+	−	+	+	−		−		+	+
Phyllobius argentatus	R		−	+	+	−	+	+	+	+	+	+	+	+	+	+
Abax ovalis	L	+	+		+	+	+	+	−		+	+	+		−	+
Athous haemorrhoidalis	E	−		+	+	+	+			−	+		−			
Limonia maculata	S		+	+		+	+				+					
Molops elatus	L			−	+		+		−							
Athous vittatus	E					−	+	−	+	+	+	+	+	+	+	
Tipula scripta	S					−	+	+			−	+	+	−	+	+
Allolobophora caliginosa	A					+	+		+	+	+	+	+	+	−	
Philonothus decorus	S						+	−	+	+		+	+	+	+	
Lumbricus rubellus	A						+	+	−		+	+	+	+	+	+
Pterostichus oblongopunctatus	L							+	−	−	−		+	−	+	+
Leptothorax nylanderi	S	+	+	+	+											
Limonius parvulus	E	+	+	−	−											
Ectobius sylvestris	S	+			+											
Agriotes acuminatus	E					+	−		−		+	−				
Pterostichus metallicus	L						−		+	+			−			−
Nebria brevicollis	L											+	+	+	−	
Phytocoris longipennis	W											−	−	+	+	
Coeliodes erythroleucus	R											+	−	−		
Ceutorrhynchus rugulosus	R											+		−	−	

A = Earth worms (Lumbricidae); E = Click beetles (Elateridae); L = Ground beetles (Carabidae); W = Bugs (Hemiptera); R = Weevils (Curculionidae); S = Other: midges, ants
+, Several individuals caught; −, One individual caught

the selected forest communities. Similar relations were also found by Müller-Hohenstein (1978) for plant communities and beetle biocenoses in dry regions of North Africa. This example shows that the relations are subject to considerable temporal dynamics and therefore the time of sampling is particularly important (Table 4.3.3).

Such listings of data do not provide information on causes and effects of biocenotic interactions, but are a necessary precondition. The concepts of guilds according to life forms or ecological demands or functional groups may lead to explanations. Thus biocenotic research into functional interactions is very closely related to functionally orientated ecosystem research.

4.3.3

Interactions Between Plants

Plants do not live with each other or next to each other at random. This becomes particularly obvious in vegetation units which abut, even if these units are not affected by man. A form of mutual relations is neutralism, where plants are able to live next to each other without influencing each other (recognisably), but this is a special case. The order observed in plant communities and ecosystems arises by interactions.

Interactions take place between individual plants of the same species (**intraspecific**) or also between individuals of different species (**interspecific**) and ultimately also at the level of plant

Table 4.3.3. Dynamics of species of beetles in a *Stipa tenacissima* community on the high plateau of eastern Morocco. (After Müller-Hohenstein 1978)

Date caught	26. X	14. XI	17. I	25. II	20. III	25. IV	24. V	15. VI
Pachychila lesnei	1	1						
Scaurus tristis	•	2						
Pachyscleodes semiasperula	•	•						
Trox barbarus	1		1					
Geotrupes puncticollis	•		1					
Paracelia simplex	1	1		•			•	
Ontophagus taurus	•	•			1	•		
Gonocephalum prolixum	2	2	2	1	2	2	1	
Cymindis setifensis	2	1	1	1	1	1		1
Micipsa instriata	1	1	2	1		•	•	1
Timarcha latipes	1	1	1	2	•	1	•	1
Pimelia boyeri	1	1	•	•	1	1	1	1
Hoplarion tumidum		2	1		•			
Gonocephalum rusticum		1		1		•		
Adelostema sulcatum		•		•			1	
Hoplarion latissimus			1	1		2		
Rhytirrhinus compressipennis		•				•	•	
Chrysomela hyperici			1			•	1	
Adesmia metallica ssp. faremonti			1		1	1	•	•
Entemocelis rumicis				1	•			
Chrysomela sanguinolenta				1	1		•	
Scarabaeus puncticollis					1	•		
Scarabaeus laticollis					1	•	2	
Onitis ion					2	•		
Scarabaeus variolosus					1	1		•
Pimelia gibba						•	1	
Graphopterus exclamationis						•	1	
Chrysomela bicolor						•	1	
Scaurus dubius						2		1
Julodis manipularis						•	1	•
Mylabris brevicollis							1	1
Mylabris baulnyi							1	2
Acinopus sabulosus							•	•
Aethiessa floralis							•	1
Zophosis ghilianii							1	1

Beetles were caught in the same area at approximately monthly intervals between October 1973 and June 1974 (•=only one, 1=several, 2=many)

communities (see Chap. 3). There is a certain selection and patterns become visible as a result of conditions at the site (**exogenic**) or by competition (**endogenic**). They are interlinked by coexistence as is clearly visible.

Competition and **coexistence** are two important forms of interaction between plants. There are, of course, other forms of interaction (also with animals, see Chap. 4.3.2) contributing to the formation of patterns of plant communities in space and time. However, the long-established idea that the phenomenon of competition alone is the decisive interaction between plants must be corrected.

It became obvious in the discussion of temporal vegetation dynamics (Chap. 4.1.1.1) that interactions may stimulate succession: They may be neutral or without influence, or they may be inhibitory (Connell and Slatyer 1977). Neutral coexistence of two species (in different ecological niches) may occur after competition over time.

According to Wilson (1969), there is an early pioneer stage in primary succession where there are no contacts between individual plants, the so-called non-interactive species equilibrium. Then the spaces fill in and there are interactions, the so-called interactive species equilibrium. After competition and occupation of space, and formation of niches, the assortative

species equilibrium follows with relatively stable self-renewal and maintenance of the community until the next disturbance, the so-called evolutionary species equilibrium. The word "equilibrium" is used here to mean balance of species.

Plants may have very different functions in the biocenose from the point of view of their plant or animal partners. Mistletoes are parasites for trees on which they grow, hosts for some plant-eaters and have mutualistic relations with birds. Some species live during their early development in symbioses with others, but later behave antagonistically. For herbaceous species shade trees are not competitors for light, but partners providing protection against climatic extremes and allowing coexistence.

Interactions become even more complicated when not two but several partners participate, with different effects on each other, or if the interactions at the level of plant communities and vegetation mosaics are studied. They are subjected to temporal dynamics and thus cause changes in the spectrum of interactions.

Possibilities outlined here show that it is difficult, because of the temporal change of interactions, to find a comprehensive typology of interactions. However, to gain an overview of minimum order, the attempts of Glavac (1996) and Schubert (1991) are discussed. Table 4.3.4 summarises current concepts.

Box 4.3.4 **Interactions between plants and animals**

Plants live together with animals in communities (biocenoses) and influence each other. Plants offer animals nutrition and they offer certain structures (e.g. nesting sites and mating areas) and are a framework for information (e.g. meeting places and nutrient availability). Animals influence plant life not only by herbivory and by modifying the site (e.g. soil burrowers and termites), but particularly in their roles as pollinators and dispersers. Here, there are countless mutual interactions. Birds and butterflies are pollinators during the day as they are attracted via the colours of flowers or availability of nectar and pollen, where as bats are active at night and are attracted by smell, e.g. of ripe fruit. Synchronised interactions are often very specialised in time and location, and are considered to result from co-evolution.

A large influence is herbivory: distinction is drawn between grazers which mainly eat herbs and grasses in pastures, and browsers which also eat woody species, often including roots. In natural ecosystems generally only a small proportion of the available standing biomass is used. Plants have developed chemical and physical defence mechanisms and respond with compensatory growth, overcoming excessive herbivory.

The relationship between plants and animals at the level of communities is considered in the biocenology. Here the principle of a biocenotic equilibrium is recognised, and countless rules describing community organisation in biocenoses have been formulated. A particularly rich area is research into functional interactions between single organisms and their environment.

Table 4.3.4. Potential interactions between two organisms

Type of interaction	Organism 1	Organism 2	Type of interaction
Symbiosis (mutalism and protocooperation)	+	+	Interaction beneficial to both organisms
Commensalism (parabiosis, epecology, e.g. epiphytes, epizoics, metabiosis)	+	o	Interaction beneficial to one organism, without disadvantaging the other
Parasitism (antibiosis, allelopathy and antagonism)	+	–	Interaction benefits one organism to the detriment of the other
Neutralism	o	o	Interaction without a beneficial or detrimental effect
Amensalism	–	o	Interaction leads to a detrimental influence on one organism without aiding the other
Competition	–	–	Interaction leads to mutual disadvantage

o, neutral influence; +, positive, advantageous influence; –, negative, disadvantageous influence

4.3.3.1
Symbiosis and Other Mutualistic Relations

Symbiosis is understood as the interaction between two organisms, with advantages for both. If this interaction is obligate, it is a **eu-symbiosis (mutualism)**, if it is advantageous, but not required, it is called **proto-cooperation**. Thus the relations between plants and their pollinators and dispersers (Chap. 4.3.2) are in many cases to be regarded as proto-cooperative.

A number of obligate interactions such as lichens, nitrogen fixers and mycorrhizae are classified as eu-symbiosis; they are both scientifically interesting and economically important, particularly nitrogen fixers and mycorrhizae.

Lichens

Symbiosis between **autotrophic algae** [green and blue-green algae (cyanobacteria), photobionts] and **heterotrophic fungi** (ascomycetes, mycobionts) has long been known and investigated. Participating fungi receive from their algal partners carbohydrates and nitrogen compounds in particular. Fungi, in turn, offer algae enclosed in their thalli protection from external stress (excessive radiation, rapid drying, etc.). In addition, algae receive mineral substances from their fungal partners. It appears that algae are stimulated by fungi at certain times to produce more assimilates, at other times the fungal hyphae penetrate the algal cells and remove nutrients and live saprophytically on the dead algae. Lichen symbiosis is obligate, as the algae have lost their ability for reproductive propagation. Lichens are able to occupy the most extreme sites because of their close symbiosis and resistance against drying and thus can avoid competition

Fig. 4.3.18. In the Afro-Alpine region of Ethiopia at more than 4000 m above sea level, lichen communities live on rocks, which are subjected to frost and strong winds almost daily and receive most of their nutrition from bird droppings (ornithocoprophily). (Photo K. Müller-Hohenstein)

from more demanding species (Fig. 4.3.18), but they grow very slowly. For *Rhizocarpon geographicum*, used in **lichenometry** to date recent geological deposits (e.g. moraines left after glacier movement), growth rates of a square centimetre in 60 years are recorded. Lichens play a considerable role in biological weathering of rocks in moist as well as in arid climates.

N$_2$-Fixing Microorganisms

Blue-green algae (cyanobacteria) are not only important partners in lichen communities; those of the genus *Anabaena* form symbiosis with the water fern *Azolla* resulting in nitrogen fixation of up to 1000 kg N ha^{-1} a^{-1} in tropical rice fields and thus allows continuous rice cultivation in tropical regions.

Bacteria of the genus *Rhizobium* also fix N$_2$ in symbiosis with several genera of the Fabaceae which occur worldwide (see Chap. 3, N cycle). These bacteria live in nodules on the roots and are extremely effective, with N$_2$ fixation rates of 45–670 kg N ha^{-1} a^{-1}, and are very important for the global nitrogen budget. In agriculture, many Fabaceae are used as green manures, being ploughed into the soil. Bacteria living saprophytically in the soil enter the roots of host plants and induce development of nodules. They receive water, minerals and assimilates; in turn, they supply the host with nitrogen. Young plants of Fabaceae need to be inoculated and acidify the soil because of proton release.

Comparable symbiosis exist in alder where roots are occupied by bacteria of the genus *Frankia,* and in some Poaceae which form symbiosis with bacteria of the genus *Azosporillum.* There are also 'above-ground' forms, e.g. some epiphytic blue-green algae supply their hosts with N. Also there are associations between particular *Rhizobium* species and Fabaceae (e.g. *Sesbania* spp.), with formation of shoot nodules which fix N$_2$.

Mycorrhizae

Probably the most important and widest distributed form of symbiosis is characterised by the keyword **mycorrhizae** (see also Chap. 2.3). The most important studies were summarised by Smith and Read (1997). Almost all plants interact with mycorrhizal fungi, and in most cases real symbiosis occurs. Now it is assumed that all terrestrial plant communities (and ecosystems) are greatly influenced by mycorrhizae, amongst other factors (see Chap. 3). However, mycorrhizae are not so important in cold habitats, such as the polar regions and high mountains, or in most arid areas.

Mycorrhizae are a symbiosis between fungi (ascomycetes and basidiomycetes, but also zygomycetes) and roots or rhizoids of higher plants. The type of contact between the fungal hyphae and roots of the host plant, as well as the participating fungal species, leads to classification of mycorrhizae into several types (Allen 1991). Only the most important ones will be mentioned here. If fungi (e.g. basidiomycetes) form

a network (Hartig net) around the root tips of higher plants, e.g. coniferous trees, and only penetrate between the cells of the root cortex, then they are called **ectomycorrhizae.**

Forms of **endomycorrhizae** occur mainly with ascomycetes. Hyphae penetrate the root cortex but remain connected to the fungal mycelium in the external soil. **Ectendomycorrhizae** occur when an endomycorrhiza is linked to the intracellular fungal hyphae. Special forms of endomycorrhizae occur in the families of Ericaceae and Orchidaceae.

A frequent form of endomycorrhizae in herbaceous plants is the **vesicular-arbuscular mycorrhiza (VAM)**. Fungi (often zygomycetes) form finely intertwined, tree-like hyphae with haustoria (arbuscles). Forms of VAM are known which not only transfer material between fungus and higher plant, but also act almost as a bridge between different individual higher plants (see Chap. 3).

Fungi are often associated with a certain host plant, but host plants may associate with several mycorrhizae. Usually, host plants increase their phosphorus and nitrogen supply via mycorrhizae, and sometimes also their water supply, because the root surface is increased 100- to 1000-fold. It is also assumed that mycorrhizae protect against pathogenic organisms. In turn, higher plants provide carbon compounds to the fungus. Because of this exchange, plants are able to occupy nutrient-poor sites, where they would otherwise be unable to grow. Today, it is thought that forest damage might be a consequence of increased nitrogen input which damages mycorrhizae and thus disturbs the symbiosis.

4.3.3.2
Forms of One-Sided Benefit (Commensalism, etc.)

Interactions between organisms are not always of benefit to all participants. If only one partner is advantaged, and the other one is not disadvantaged, it is a form of **commensalism (parabiosis)**. Such forms exist predominantly in animals, but the terms commensals and hosts are also applied to plants. Individuals of some plants live mainly or exclusively under the protection of other species (e.g. guests on cushion plants in dry areas or in high mountain habitats). In extreme cases they survive only because they cannot be eaten or are not exposed to excessive solar or very strong winds. Dwarf shrub communities in Afro-Alpine regions are many such examples. In temperate zones herbaceous species are probably only able to survive in forests because of shade. The basis of all those relations is the variability over small areas caused by the plants themselves (climate of the stand, water relations, availability of nutrients).

Also, the so-called **paroecy** ('tolerated neighbourhood'), e.g. individuals of species living epiphytically on other species, could be interpreted as a form of commensalism. There are, however, transitions to forms of **amensalism**. Here, one partner is disadvantaged, without the other being significantly advantaged. This could be applied to epiphytes, as old trees with epiphytes growing on them may break because of the enormous mechanical stress. **Neutralism** should also be mentioned. It is assumed that regularly associated organisms neither suffer advantages nor disadvantages because of the coexistence. No partner influences the other visibly or in other ways so far identified. It is difficult to assess indirect interactions, in which one partner changes the site so that conditions previously unavailable are created for other species, but under which they can no longer exist. This form of **metabiosis** is the basis of the **facilitation theory** of Connell and Slatyer (1977); see Chap. 4.1.5.3.

4.3.3.3
Parasitism

An antagonistic relationship, so-called parasitism, exists if a partner (**parasite**) inhibits or damages the other (**host**) and thus gains advantages. Most widespread examples are of one partner (the parasite) taking nutrients from the other (host) and thus increasing its growth and inhibiting growth of the host without, however, damaging the host severely. Parasitic plants are either **heterotrophic** (without chlorophyll, holoparasites or complete parasites), or they are able to produce assimilates themselves but use var-

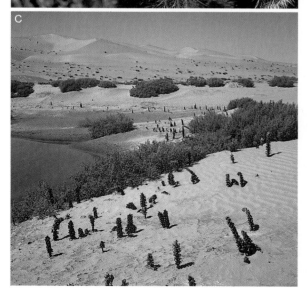

Fig. 4.3.19. Parasitic plants have developed in all biomes. A In cool temperate southern Chile *Misodendron punctatum* on southern beech (*Nothofagus antarctica*). B In semi-arid northern Chile a completely leafless Loranthaceae (*Tristerix aphyllus*) grows on many cacti (*Trichocereus* spp.). C In the completely arid Arabian desert *Cistanche violacea* is parasitic on various host plants, e.g. even on halophytes (*Suaeda fruticosa*). (Photos K. Müller-Hohenstein)

ious inorganic compounds and water from the host (hemiparasites). The former are species tapping the host via haustoria, below ground (*Orobanche* spp.) or above ground (*Cuscuta* spp.). The latter include Scrophulariaceae (species of *Bartsia*, *Melampyrum* and *Rhinanthus*) and Loranthaceae (species of *Viscum*) living epiphytically. Interaction forms similar to parasitism are classified as allelopathy. Examples of parasitism from different habitats are given in Fig. 4.3.19 A–C.

Allelopathy (also **antibiosis**) is a specific form of interaction. One partner excretes metabolites which inhibit the other. The partner excreting these materials is thus, indirectly, advantaged. Materials such as alkaloids, phenols, glucosides and terpenes can be formed in bark, leaves or roots, and inhibit germination and growth; they are actively released into the soil as root exudates. Occasionally, they are formed and released only during decay of dead organic material. Excreted substances not only inhibit growth, but may also prevent seeds from rotting. Comparable substances excreted by microorganisms are called **antibiotics**. Allelopathic substances often only affect certain types of organisms or certain stages of development of these species (perhaps seedlings).

One of the best-known examples of allelopathy is the walnut tree (*Juglans regia*). From the glucoside-rich litter, a toxic substance (juglon) is formed by hydrolysis and oxidation and inhibits development of many species. Other often-quoted examples are from vegetation of regions which are dry in summer, e.g. Mediterranean macchies (*Rosmarinus officinalis*) or the Californian chaparral (*Larrea* spp.).

4.3.3.4
Competition and Coexistence

Since Darwin (1859) identified "The struggle for survival", it has been regarded as the mechanism and driving force of evolution. In subsequent decades unequivocal proof of the phenomenon of competition has been sought, but only been partly achieved. In addition to experimental studies to clarify the effect of competition, many models were developed to explain the coexistence of plants in, or their mutual exclusion from, communities.

Various approaches to understanding competition will be explained in the following, based on experiments from which the basic rules of coexistence of plants will be derived and the characteristics underlying the competitive strength of individual species explained. As examples of application of practical evidence and experimental knowledge, indicator values and ecogrammes will be shown. Discussion of competition models with particular emphasis on niche concepts will address what is the basis of coexistence, at present stressed more than competition (Tokeshi 1998).

Concepts and Definitions of Competition

It is generally assumed that two living organisms with identical or very similar ecological demands can only coexist if there are few individual plants distributed in a large space so that the resources can be shared and are not fully used. It follows that **competition** starts when one or several of the required factors, essential for life, are only available in limited supply so that there is a shortage of these resources, resulting in adverse effects on (or even cessation of) survival, growth and propagation. Such a competitive situation not only necessarily leads to total elimination of the weaker, less competitive, species, but also to regulation of the density of participating populations. Regarding the type and amount of resources, several different forms of competition may be distinguished. Above ground there is, first and foremost, competition for light, carbon dioxide and favourable temperatures, as well as for pollinators and dispersers of propagules. Below ground there is competition for nutrients and water. The former often regulate composition of stands, the latter, so-called **root competition**, is additional to competition for light (as stated in the theory of self-thinning, see Chap. 3) and is responsible for the density of the stand.

However, competition for essential but limited requirements for life is only one of the several possible ways of understanding competition. There are direct, negative influences of one plant on another. Many species are able, for example, to suppress other species by excretion of special toxins or simply by shading shoots and leaves. There is, therefore, competition by interference in addition to competition for resources.

A further important difference between forms of competition is shown in the competition between individual plants (of one species), called **intraspecific**, and between species, called **interspecific**. The intraspecific form was regarded as stimulating evolution. Selection results in the strongest, best-adapted individual surviving and thus contributing to maintenance of the species and its competitive strength. In interspecific competition, closely related species exclude each other completely in the extreme case, so possibilities for coexistence are restricted.

Intraspecific competition occurs particularly in crop plants. It has been shown, for example, that increasing sowing densities do not increase yields to the same extent, but increase mortality and self-thinning (see Chap. 3). Theoretically, more phytomass per unit area can only be achieved by taller growing individual plants. This is prevented by competition. Intraspecific competition is avoided if the habitat offers ways of avoidance (see later discussion of ecological niches) or by evolutionary processes (e.g. formation of ecotypes or new species in the course of adaptive radiation). **Interspecific competition** largely determines the actual distribution of representatives of different species in space. It is assumed that present distribution patterns may be a consequence of intensive competition a long time ago and that at present competition no longer exists.

Features and Characteristics of Competitive Strength

Following from the observations concerning intra- and interspecific competition, explanation of **competitive advantages** were sought, particularly genetically determined physiological and morphological characteristics which would improve success of species in competition with other species. It is assumed that such attributes of individual developmental phases of plants may be considered separately and that there are no linear relations between individual traits and competitive strength.

The **seed and germination stages** are the first important stages subject to competition. Early release of seed (in the vegetative period), an effective mechanism of dispersal, large content of reserves, a short period of dormancy, long duration of ability to germinate and high germination rates, as well as fast growth of seedlings, are all advantageous. Inhibitors, excreted by seedlings and impeding growth of competitors, are also beneficial (**allelopathy**, see Chap. 4.3.3.3).

The **growth stage** is the second important phase. Physiological characteristics such as high photosynthetic rates, and thus correspondingly rapid growth of shoots and roots, are the most important. Adaptation of the life cycle to seasonal changes in conditions and, most of all, duration of the life span (annual/perennial) is important. Equally important is tolerance towards unfavourable environmental conditions (shade, water, nutrient deficiency, mowing and grazing). Competitive advantages are also achieved by symbiosis. The strength of competition is visible morphologically in the form of growth (e.g. tall plants, large leaves and a large, shading, crown) with a far-reaching root system, and adaptations to unfavourable environmental conditions (e.g. xeromorphic traits, succulence, formation of light and shade leaves, etc.).

The third stage is the **reproductive phase**. Species with many attractive flowers and quickly ripening pollen have considerable advantage, as do those with sexual reproduction as well as vegetative reproduction; further characteristics that bring advantages include self-fertilisation, formation of ecotypes, and capacity to adapt to changing conditions within the community.

Aarssen (1989) listed the most important attributes contributing to strength of competition. He assumed that these characteristics are linked to each other and may be ordered hierarchically (Box 4.3.5).

Experimental Approaches to Clarify Phenomena of Competition

The role of competition in nature is difficult to understand and competition is an ecological factor which is difficult to determine experimentally. There have been several attempts to clarify the role of competition experimentally, particularly as practical agriculture is looking for answers, e.g. for problems of competition between crops and segetal species. However, frequently only two (or a few) species were studied under the influence of a few, controlled, environmental factors, in an attempt to limit complexity.

Different approaches may be used. Species or layers are removed from existing stands (or added) and the effects observed. Sometimes the same or different seeds or seedlings of only two or a few species were sown on bare areas of land or in enclosures, and partially regulated external conditions (e.g. supply of water or fertilisers) applied: the success of the individual species was recorded. Occasionally, experiments were performed with functional groups of plants or with phytometers, target species from which much information is available.

Box 4.3.5 — Increasing competitive strength of plants. (After Aarssen 1989)

Primary attribute	Secondary attribute	Tertiary attribute
Better water use rate	← Higher root density	← Faster dispersal
	Greater lateral distribution of roots	← Earlier germination
Better use of nutrients (N, P, K)	← Faster uptake by root hairs	← Larger seed diameter
	Greater root density	← Higher photosynthesis rates
	Taller growth forms	← Better use of surplus assimilates
Better use of light	← Larger leaf area index	← More effective association with mycorrhizae
	Greater expansion of the plant	← Production of more toxic substances
	More effective leaf arrangement	← Greater resistance to pathogens or robbers
More attractive to pollinators	← More flowers, high density of flowers	← Increased tolerance to lower temperatures
	More attractive flowers	← Ability to attract pathogens or robbers or pass them to neighbours
More attractive to distributing organisms	← More fruits/seeds, high density of fruits/seeds	← Higher resistance to physical disturbance
	More attractive fruits/seeds	← Greater use of other resources
Increased inhibition of competition	← More leaf shading	Greater tolerance in use of resources by others
Increased inhibition of competition through pollination	← More effective pollen allelopathy	Greater longevity (via clones)
Release of toxic substances in the soil		
Increased tolerance to water use by neighbouring plants		
Greater tolerance to use of nutrients by neighbouring plants		
Increased tolerance to light use by neighbouring plants		
Greater resistance to allelopathic substances		
Maximising fertility by use of resources not used by neighbours		

Observations under natural conditions, as well as from experiments in the field and under controlled conditions, have provided insight into the numerous mechanisms and features by which plants are able to compete effectively. Those listed here show the hierarchy of primary attributes, secondary attributes dependent on them, and the tertiary attributes that depend on the secondary ones.

Attempts to quantify competitive strength are not lacking. Groves and Williams (1975) showed that when *Trifolium subterraneum* and *Chondrilla juncea* were sown together, root competition reduced yield by 65%, but shoot competition by only 47%, compared with the pure crop. Measuring characteristics of competition under controlled conditions is very difficult. Grime (1973) tried, therefore, to determine the strength of competition by developing competition indices, in which height of plants, growth form and duration of life span of participating species were recorded (see Chap. 4.1.5.3).

The relative rate of growth is also seen as an approximation of competitiveness. The dry matter production of individual species in relation to that of all other species involved was used to assess their competitiveness. Bornkamm (1961) regarded the relative growth rate and the competitive pressure, which is given by the ratio of the dominant species to the total number of species, as suitable measures to describe success in competition. Further measurable indicators are the number of viable seeds or, depending on the question to be asked, phytomass production of particular parts, e.g. shoot-to-root dry matter ratio.

The "Hohenheimer groundwater experiment" in Stuttgart Hohenheim is a classical experiment for determination of interspecific competition, as it incorporates competitive exclusion, nicheing to avoid competition and the resulting divergent development in the direction of so-called site equivalence, namely relative site constancy. It shows that plants in nature do not necessarily grow where their demands are completely satisfied (**physiological area**) but that they compete with other species and usually exist in a smaller area (**ecological area**). Here, the relations to the so-called fundamental (corresponding to the physiological) and the actual niche are shown clearly (Howe and Westley 1993).

The experiment was conducted in a basin with a sloping surface so that with the same water supply different groundwater levels occurred. The area was subdivided into four plots, three with pure cultures of grasses – one with a dry-land grass species (*Bromus erectus*), another with a species from moist meadows (*Alopecurus pratensis*), and the third with oat grass (*Arrhenatherum elatius*) with intermediate characteris-

Stuttgart Hohenheim is an agricultural university in Germany.

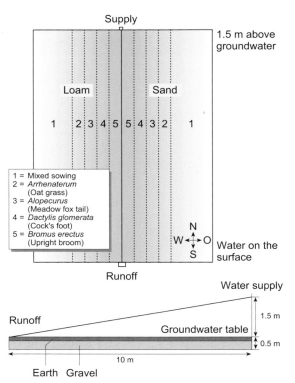

Fig. 4.3.20. Scheme of the "Hohenheimer groundwater experiment" in plan and section. (After Ellenberg 1953)

tics; another plot was sown with a mixture of all three grasses (Fig. 4.3.20). A fourth grass species, *Dactylis glomerata* was not included in the evaluation. The most important result was that all three grass species grew best at average to high moisture, but the ranges for optimum growth in the mixed sowing were significantly shifted. *Arrhenatherum* achieved greatest rates of production under average conditions, with relatively narrow physiological requirements. *Alopecurus* was most widely distributed in moist conditions, with *Bromus* in the dry zones. The latter two attained their ecological optimum under physiologically suboptimal conditions (Fig. 4.3.21).

Ellenberg (1953) concludes from this that a species which is particularly weak in competition and needs to evade it to survive has ecological and physiological optima which deviate considerably. He distinguishes between a **physiological potential** with an optimum, and a potential amplitude determined by the genetically determined range of responses to exogenous influences, as well as an **ecological potential** [which corresponds to the ecological optimum and according to Walter (1960) is the actual range in

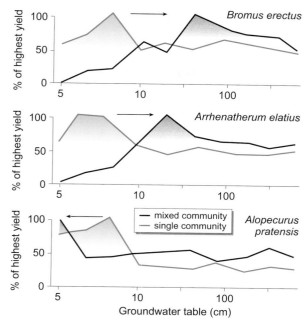

Fig. 4.3.21. Yields of the three meadow grasses *Arrhenatherum elatius*, *Alopecurus pratensis* and *Bromus erectus* in pure and mixed stands with differing soil moisture. (After Ellenberg 1953)

which the plant exists in nature], again with an optimal range.

Dierschke (1994) followed that there are several types of **ecological potential** and **ecological occurrence** (in the sense of the physiological and ecological optimum) based on the results by Ellenberg from these experiments; these are shown in Fig. 4.3.22. In the first two cases (top), the optimum lies in the average range but with broad and narrow amplitude, respectively. However, in the next two cases, the optimum is in suboptimal, marginal ranges. The strength of competition of one species, shown in the outline in the bottom row, at the same ecological potential becomes clear by the position of the existence optima. Cases 5 and 6 indicate similar competitive strength from the position of the

optima, but the other cases express weak competition, as the fields for potential and existence deviate strongly.

The Hohenheimer groundwater experiment, and the results shown here, were criticised as the effects of only one environmental factor – water supply – was considered in isolation. Compared with natural conditions the experiment was very simple and thus does not allow far-reaching conclusions about the physiological behaviour of plants. However, the opposite view is that the effects of environmental conditions may only be analysed by considering single factors. In any case, the experiment shows that conclusions about the physiological demands of plants should not be drawn from their occurrence in natural communities. The important difference between ecological and physiological potential and amplitude seen by Ellenberg is the basis of the ecogrammes discussed in the following.

Indicator Plants, Indicator Values and Ecogrammes

Results of experimental competition experiments and empirical results from plant ecology and land use led to the development of simple methods with practical applications.

Plants have long been used as **indicators** for site conditions in agriculture and forestry. Species tolerating alkaline or acid soils, standing water or drought are examples of this (see Chaps. 2.3.8 and 3.4). Such indicator plants were first identified by Ellenberg in 1965 (see Ellenberg 1974, 1992) for central Europe and later developed for other areas (Landolt 1977).

Plants are now assigned to indicator values which reflect important climatic and edaphic variables. In listing **indicator values** on relative scales (one-dimensional ordination), experience from many years is used for. They are not supported by measurements and are not experimen-

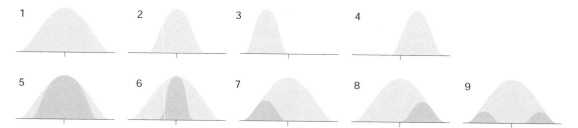

Fig. 4.3.22. Scheme of the theoretical position of ecological potential (*1–4*) and occurrence (*5–9*) of plant species related to an ecological gradient (average value shown). (After Dierschke 1994)

tally verified. Wetness indicators do not necessarily indicate that plants require moist conditions, but their tolerance. This reservation applies to other indicator characteristics as well. However, most importantly, indicator values for plants relate to their ecological behaviour, i.e. under conditions in the open field and in competition. They do not give the physiological requirements of plants, nor do they allow conclusions to be drawn about the amount of the resource, although they provide an indication. Stenoecic plants (those with very narrow qualitative and quantitative requirements for resources) are best suited as indicator plants because they show the qualitative and quantitative limitations of a range of appropriate resources. Ellenberg et al. (1992) distinguished the following indicator values:

- L = light (radiation) from 1 (deep shade) to 9 (full sun) for plants in full leaf during the vegetative period.
- T = temperature, from 1 (cold indicator) to 9 (extreme heat indicator) at all altitudes from the nival belt to lowlands.
- K = continentality, from 1 (in oceanic regions) to 9 (the most continental sites in eastern central Europe) on an continentality gradient.
- F = moisture, from 1 (indicator for very dry sites) to 11 (water plant) and 12 (submerged plant) in a range of sites from dry rocks to free water.
- R = response, from 1 (strongly acid) to 9 (alkaline and limestone) following the soil pH.
- N = nitrogen, from 1 (nitrogen-poorest site) to 9 (nitrogen-richest sites) following the gradient of nitrogen available to plants.
- S = salinity, from 0 (not salt-tolerant) via 1 (salt-tolerant on salt-poor substrates) to 9 (hypersaline, on extremely saline substrates).

Using B or b for some species indicates the relative resistance to heavy metals. Over time, further characteristics were introduced, e.g. by Landolt (1977), for the humus content and aeration of soils. Other characteristics might be added with particular practical applications, such as fodder value and tolerance to mowing in grasslands.

Such indicator values and indicator plants have been criticised, particularly as many important features of the site were not considered (additional nutrients, tolerance to trampling, frost resistance, etc.). Also, the ecological amplitude of species was not described, nor were complex interactions shown reliably. Yet indicator values are an attempt to quantify ecological behaviour. It is often forgotten that these values are cardinal numbers, so that values should not be averaged and that all mathematical calculations need to be interpreted very carefully. These indicator values do not indicate the demands of species, only their ecological behaviour within the range of a specific plant community.

Indicator plants and indicator values should not be used as ways of providing measured values. They only indicate type and magnitude of important environmental variables and have proved to be simple and easy to use values for comparison of sites and their conditions in space and time, and even dynamic changes. It is helpful to recognise, as early as possible, practical problems in many areas such as **land use** and **soil protection**, passive **bioindication, nature protection, environmental monitoring** and **early recognition of environmental damage.** Potential of sites may be shown, approximately, by indicator values of plants growing there.

Ecogrammes are also indications based on empirical results, and attempt to show the "spatial" neighbourhood of species in relation to selected site variables. Usually two variables are selected and expressed two-dimensionally. In the space between these variables the competitive interactions between these species (or communities) become clear in relation to the selected variables. A distinction is made between the physiologically determined possibilities (ecological potential) and the actual success in competition (ecological existence).

In the ecogrammes developed by Ellenberg (taken from Glavac 1996), soil moisture supply and acidity are used as variables in the submontane regions of central Europe. Temperature was regarded as less important in determining vegetation at this altitude. The ecogrammes for individual species (Ellenberg et al. 1992) show that some species actually occupy the physiologically optimal site (ecological potential; e.g. beech), so that ecological potential and ecological occurrence are almost the same. Other species are pushed out, into physiologically extreme regions. This applies, for example, to pine which requires light for germination and so is out-competed by shade trees (Box 4.3.6).

The pattern of distribution of central European forest trees must be understood as a consequence of the ecophysiological constitution of the trees as well as of the competitive behaviour

Box 4.3.6	Single ecogrammes for selected central European tree species. (After Ellenberg et al. 1992)

Ellenberg developed ecogrammes for the most important central European tree species, comparing similar site requirements (very similar potential ecological ranges). Individual species have different success rates, in part due to being pushed to the extremes of their distribution (their existence area) by more successful competitors. Note that these ecogrammes consider only soil moisture and soil pH (as a measure of nutrient availability). Also, only submontane regions of central Europe have been considered; in these areas there are locations that are too dry or wet for trees to grow and these have been taken into account.

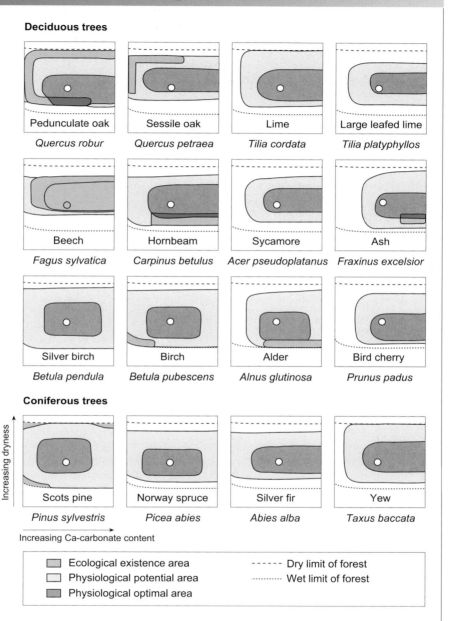

Deciduous trees

Pedunculate oak — *Quercus robur*
Sessile oak — *Quercus petraea*
Lime — *Tilia cordata*
Large leafed lime — *Tilia platyphyllos*

Beech — *Fagus sylvatica*
Hornbeam — *Carpinus betulus*
Sycamore — *Acer pseudoplatanus*
Ash — *Fraxinus excelsior*

Silver birch — *Betula pendula*
Birch — *Betula pubescens*
Alder — *Alnus glutinosa*
Bird cherry — *Prunus padus*

Coniferous trees

Scots pine — *Pinus sylvestris*
Norway spruce — *Picea abies*
Silver fir — *Abies alba*
Yew — *Taxus baccata*

Increasing dryness ↑

Increasing Ca-carbonate content →

■ Ecological existence area
□ Physiological potential area
▨ Physiological optimal area
----- Dry limit of forest
········· Wet limit of forest

towards sympatric species occurring in the same space, and of management by man. Competitive conditions between central European, forest tree species (submontane belt) are shown in Fig. 4.3.23. Ultimately, ecogrammes may also be constructed from field data, as shown by Böcker et al. (1983) for southern German forest communities using data from Oberdorfer (1957). Numerical values for moisture and reaction numbers (Ellenberg et al. 1992) were used (Fig. 4.3.24). This constructed ecogramme confirms the one of Ellenberg (Fig. 4.3.23).

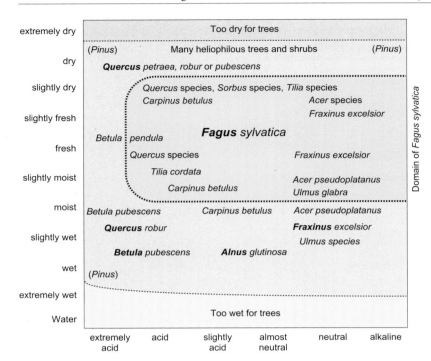

extremely dry

dry

slightly dry

slightly fresh

fresh

slightly moist

moist

slightly wet

wet

extremely wet

Water

Too dry for trees

(*Pinus*)   Many heliophilous trees and shrubs   (*Pinus*)

Quercus petraea, robur or pubescens

Quercus species, *Sorbus* species, *Tilia* species
Carpinus betulus   *Acer* species
Fraxinus excelsior

***Fagus* sylvatica**

Betula pendula

Quercus species   *Fraxinus excelsior*

Tilia cordata

Carpinus betulus   *Acer pseudoplatanus*
Ulmus glabra

Betula pubescens   *Carpinus betulus*   *Acer pseudoplatanus*

Quercus robur   ***Fraxinus*** excelsior
Ulmus species

Betula pubescens   ***Alnus*** glutinosa

(*Pinus*)

Too wet for trees

Domain of *Fagus sylvatica*

extremely   acid   slightly   almost   neutral   alkaline
acid   acid   neutral

Fig. 4.3.23. Ecogramme of the most important submontane forest trees in central Europe. (After Ellenberg 1978, from Glavac 1996)

Models of Intra- and Interspecific Competition

Models were developed to explain and understand mechanisms of competition in addition to specific observations, empirical results and identification of single characteristics conferring and improving competitiveness. Two models, those of Grime (1979) and Tilman (1977, 1982), will be mentioned again; they were previously applied to vegetation dynamics (see Chap. 4.1.5.3).

It becomes clear in Grime's **three-strategy model** that **competitors** succeed at low interference rates and low stress. They are competitively strong, because they use the available resources particularly well. They are persistent, but not able to compete under stress, either excess or deficiency (e.g. of light and water). Many sites with different high stresses exist, and only **stress-tolerant** species are able to compete. **Ruderals** are best adapted as they are able to quickly occupy sites without competition.

According to Grime (1979) and Grime et al. (1988), competition occurs when plants species or individuals in close proximity use the same limited amounts of light, water, ions, etc. Grime assumes that productivity of a plant community increases in favourable conditions and the site is occupied by many productive plants; therefore, competition is intense. Between species growing slowly and with little demands, competition is weak. The intensity of competition grows with increasing productivity. This applies particularly to sites with predominantly above-ground competition. On unproductive sites, below-ground competition increases (root competition).

Tilman considers that for each site there is one essential resource in limited supply so species compete. If it is nutrients, plants may form a larger root mass, and thus compete more in the soil. If it is light, more is invested in shoot and leaf growth. Species competing in such a way may also occur in successions (Fig. 4.3.25). Tilman developed from this evidence, which is experimentally supported, the **resource ratio model** with five types of competition-dependent occupation (see Chap. 4.1.5.3).

Grime considers the effect of total competition and assumes that it is stronger on productive sites; however, Tilman regards competition more specifically. He stressed bottlenecks for plant production and improvements for allocation used by plant species and individual plants to respond to them. Species able to lower their demands furthest will ultimately win the competition.

The contrasts outlined here are, in reality, not as large as is often expressed. It depends very much on what is considered: the total effect of competition or particular processes and mechanisms, or the complete stand of species or individual plant species. In 1994, Tilman developed

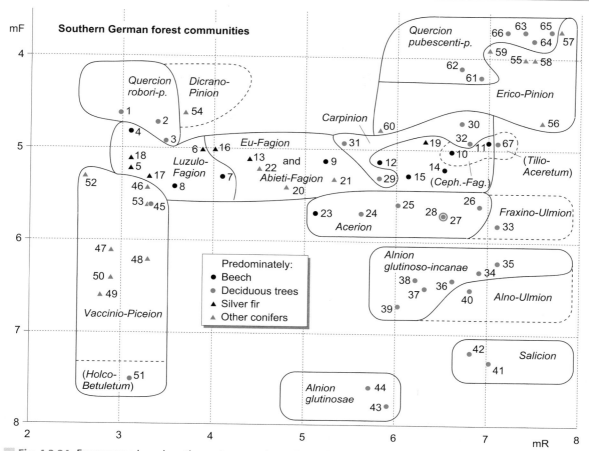

Fig. 4.3.24. Ecogramme based on the moisture and reaction indicator values (mF, mR) for forest communities in southern Germany described by Oberdorfer 1957. (After Böcker et al. 1983, from Glavac 1996)

a mathematical model to describe the effects of neighbours on plants and patterns of distribution in competitive situations, showing that coexistence of many species and individuals is not only possible, but actually the rule (see the following paragraphs concerning coexistence).

Concept of Ecological Niches

The term "ecological niche" brings together the concepts of competition and coexistence. The **concept of niches** was developed in connection with questions of **coexistence** of organisms, and modified several times over the years. Niches refer to a synecological phenomenon, namely the coexistence of individuals and species in communities. They are regarded as important as they provide links between various areas of ecology.

A niche was first understood to be the habitat, but even then the question was asked whether all habitats in the observed communities are occupied, and whether several species

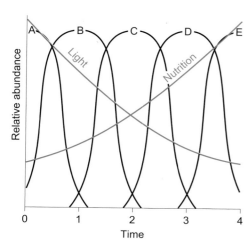

Fig. 4.3.25. Diagram of the relative abundance of light or nutritional limitation of species (*A–E*) in succession. (After Tilman 1994)

are able to occupy the same habitat. Relations between ecological potential of species and the resource potential of their habitat were considered. Spatial dimensions are just as important as nutrition.

In Elton's (1927) niche concept the coexistence of species in a niche is possible as soon as these species differ significantly in their demands, but are otherwise linked, e.g. via a nutrition chain. Niches are a micro-habitat linked to functional aspects; there are similar niches in every ecosystem which may be occupied by different species with the same function. Elton speaks of the "profession" of individual species, now called **site equivalence**. Finally, he not only considers the environmental demands of organisms in a niche, but the influence they have on their environment, particularly regarding the use of resources.

Hutchinson (1978) introduced another niche concept, separate from the ambiguous connections with spatial dimensions, defining a niche as the sum of all environmental factors influencing an organism. In an n-dimensional coordinate system where each axis represents an environmental factor, a virtual habitat may be defined in which an organism is able to exist and function in relation to its requirements (Cody 1991). This **ecological niche** offers the required abiotic and biotic factors. A niche is thus a system in which the organism occupies a permanent position ('job', role, status, address) and should not be confused with an actual space (e.g. ecotope) nor with the conditions in a site. The term niche shows that each organism has its place in an ecosystem and plays a certain role there with particular functions. In such a system new species may only settle when the niche is empty.

Competition arises in such an ecological niche when several organisms occur in the same niche at the same time, making demands on the same resources. It is thus important to differentiate between **fundamental** and **attained niches**. The former characterises a niche where an organism has unrestricted access to all available resources which are used to achieve particular functions. The attained niche is the area actually occupied by the organism, with sharing of resources and achieving certain functions in supplementing ways. This is shown in Fig. 4.3.26 where the niche of a plant is outlined three-dimensionally, corresponding to three selected resources. Each point in the space, resulting from

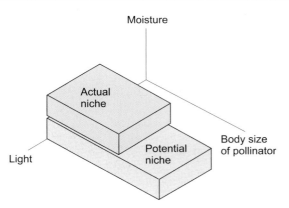

Fig. 4.3.26. Schematic representation of the niche of a plant species in relation to the resources of moisture, light and size of the pollinator. (After Howe and Westley 1993)

the variables light, moisture and size of pollinating bees, is shown in the virtual space and represents the conditions under which the plant is able to survive and propagate. In reality this space is reduced as bees also pollinate other plants so this resource has to be shared.

In interspecific competition several species have the potential to use the same niche, but are restricted to an attainable niche; consequently, with several competing species, the attainable niche becomes smaller for each. In contrast, intraspecific competition, and the resulting strengthening of the affected species, causes consolidation of the dominant species or expansion of the attainable niche. It is, however, also assumed that niches may overlap. According to Schoener (1985), this overlap is only slight if the competing species have 'arranged' themselves previously. If, however, there is a strong competition in small habitats (e.g. for nutrients), then niche overlap is possible. In large areas of resource-rich habitats, overlap will be small even if competition is strong. The actual niche is the product of intraspecific and interspecific competition. The niche structure of a plant community is the result of a long evolutionary adaptation in the sense of **synevolution** (Dierschke 1994). Competition may have been important in the past, even without **differentiation of niches**, which decreases interspecific competition but increases intraspecific competition.

To make the multidimensional, theoretical term 'niche' more practical, Grubb (1977) modified the concept distinguishing habitat niches, life form niches, regeneration niches and phenological niches. **Habitat niches** are characterised physically and chemically, **life form niches** have close relations to production, the **regeneration niche** comprises all conditions for propagation, and the **phenological niche** is determined by temporal development. **Temporal niches** occur for species flowering at different times but at the same site and having the same pollinator; this also applies to spring geophytes in nemoral forests regarding the use of light.

Terms such as **spatial niche** (e.g. stones in a forest occupied by lichens and mosses) or **structural niches** (e.g. the habitat in dead wood) are also used, and there are nutritional niches and breeding site niches, together with niches for species and individual plants. This inflation of terms contributed to criticism of the niche concept. However, it should be remembered that, even though the concept of the ecological niche was questioned, it enriched discussions on basic questions of competition and coexistence, in connection with invaders (neophytes) and the question of 'open positions'. In this context, the principle of competitive exclusion (Gause 1934) is very important; this states that two species with identical demands cannot coexist in the same living space. The counter argument is, however, provided by **niche overlap** of species. Similar to the question of niches, the key phrase 'competitive exclusion' also leads to basic concepts of coexistence.

Competitive Exclusion or Coexistence?

The consequence of the **principle of competitive exclusion** enunciated by Gause (1934) is that species with identical ecological demands are not able to exist side by side. Thus, sympatric species are ecologically distinguished and do not compete.

Lotka (1932) and Volterra (1926) developed models supporting this principle mathematically. They assumed that each further individual arriving in an existing population (or community) worsens the existence and growth conditions as a whole. In this model of competition, growth rates of two species are related to each other in an equation. Gause established his ideas with *Paramecium*, but they are also applicable to plants arriving in an existing plant community (Law and Watkinson 1989).

Aarssen (1983), in particular, considered this principle of competitive exclusion postulating that one condition required for competition exclusion was a long period with constant conditions. However, these do not exist, because of continuous environmental changes. Endogenous

developments and exogenous interference lead continuously to the formation of new niches, enabling competing species to coexist and avoiding competitive exclusion. Permanent niche differentiation is an important process. Positive interactions which exceed the negative influences of competition lead to a (dynamic) contact between individuals and species, and to **coexistence.**

Aarssen (1983, 1989) developed three hypotheses which would lead to avoidance of competition and thus guarantee coexistence. In the first, the balance between supply and demand is decisive for the occurrence of species. Exclusion is only possible when supply is smaller than demand. The second relates to the limited demands of several species for the same resource: If the demands of species are focused on a particular resource, exclusion is the consequence, but not if the resources are different. The third hypothesis relates to the strength of competition: If this is the same or similar, coexistence is possible. These three hypotheses are the building blocks of Aarssen's **general evolution theory** of coexistence. His idea of **ecological combining ability** (niche differentiation) and **competitive combining ability** (competitive strength) aims at the evolutionary aspects of conditions at the site and the general conditions important for the coexistence of organisms. The classical theory of competitive exclusion is contrasted against a modern theory in which spatial and temporal scales of coexistence are incorporated with the same characteristics of competition. Differences in demographic processes have been little noted, nor the distribution of niches under aspects of patch dynamics, or succession and regeneration.

Hulme (1996) listed other theoretical approaches to explain coexistence (Table 4.3.5). They may be grouped into those where competition is regulated by resources, and those where competition is linked to the concept of ecological niches and niche differentiation ("peaceful niche sharing"). These results from the 1970s and 1980s are still discussed and show that there is still no unanimous theory or final clarification of the interconnections between competition and coexistence.

Growth of plants in close proximity cannot occur without mutual interference. Competition alone is not the decisive factor, as many species obviously do not compete with each other, but coexist. Competition and coexistence should not be regarded as opposites. Coexistence may be

Table 4.3.5. Summary of mechanisms often advanced for the coexistence of plants in natural communities. (After Hulme 1996)

Shorthand term for theory	General description	Most important assumptions	Author
(a) Competition for resources			
Resource sharing	Species differ in their ability to use resources	Trade-offs in ability to compete for two or more restricted resources	Tilman (1982)
Spatial heterogeneity	In one of many microhabitats one species is able to exclude all other species	There are as many species as there are habitats	Pacala and Rough-garden (1982)
Neighbour effect	Intraspecific and spatial aggregation increases intraspecific competition and aids coexistence	Clumped distribution of plant species involved	Pacala (1986)
Heterogeneity with time	Important species compete at different times	Communities consist of pioneers and long-lived species	Warner and Chesson (1986)
(b) Competition in niche differentiation			
Regeneration niches	No competition, as species differ in requirements for regeneration	Many different micro-habitats	Grubb (1977)
Disturbance	Species diversity is maximal at intermediate disturbance	Habitat productivity and disturbance are inversely proportional	Grime (1973)
Lottery model	Seeds colonise available microhabitats randomly and are strong enough to ensure further colonisation	Long-living, fertile species; colonisation is a function of seed production	Sale (1977)

reached by avoiding competition and thus by tolerating stress.

Experiments and Observations Showing Coexistence

Gigon (1994) and Gigon and Ryser (1996) listed experimental evidence of positive interactions between plants, and also provided important examples of proven and assumed positive influences. Facultative or obligate relationships between two partners are termed positive if one benefits and the other is not inhibited. It should be noted that these are relations between individuals, populations or species. Only the present, and sometimes subsequent, generations are considered if favourable conditions are indirectly created. The space is defined as a community and its site (ecosystem), as well as by directly neighbouring systems.

For a dry grassland in Switzerland, the question was asked how up to 40 different plants species manage to live together on 1 m² without negative effects, i.e. competition, reducing the number of species (Fig. 4.3.27). This is explained by the numerous positive interactions which prove that these plant species are mutually dependent. In a simplified scheme of the system, the interactions are outlined for only seven plant species, for the field mouse (*Microtus arvalis*), and the clover canker fungus (*Sclerotina trifo-*

lium) as well as *Rhizobium*, mycorrhizae, pollinators and dispersers. This system is a close web of predominantly positive (direct or indirect) interactions between the participating partners.

A direct positive effect is provided, for example, by **nurse plants**, adult individuals which protect seedlings of their own species, or of a different species, by providing shade or because of protective thorns (Fig. 4.3.28). A positive influence is provided indirectly when a competing species is eliminated by pathogens or herbivores. Such indirect advantage occurs with *Trifolium pratense* in mixed cultures with *Dactylis glomerata*, where the grass provides a barrier for spread of the clover canker fungus, for example. Furthermore, *Dactylis* has the advantage of a better nitrogen supply. In principle a short-term negative 'nutritional relationship' may be positive in the long term for pasture plants.

Direct positive influences between two plant species (from grassland communities in central Europe) without participation of other organisms are:

- physical support from neighbouring plants (e.g. for epiphytes, vines or as protection from wind damage);
- stabilisation of mobile substrates (e.g. plants which stabilise rock and scree slopes);

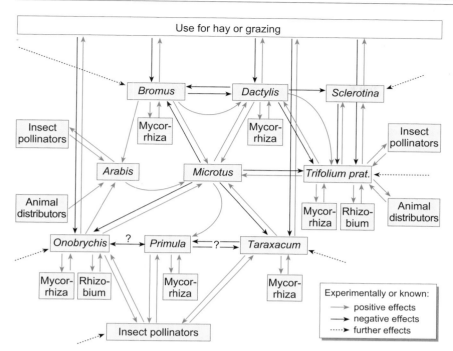

Fig. 4.3.27. Scheme of interactions between seven species of plants, a field mouse (*Microtis arvalis*), the fungus *Sclerotina trifolium*, *Rhizobium*, mycorrhizae, pollinators and dispersers in a semi-dry grassland. (After Gigon 1994)

- protection from extreme temperatures (e.g. frost protection for herbaceous species in dense clusters of lignified dwarf shrubs);
- advantage because of the reduction of salt content in soil solutions (e.g. salt-exporting halophytes);

Fig. 4.3.28. A relatively robust cushion plant (*Plantago rigida*) in the paramo community in Equador protects a much more sensitive species (*Castilleja pumila*) with red flowers. The former species may be termed a "nurse plant", the latter as a "cushion guest". (Photo K. Müller-Hohenstein)

- chemical advantage because of neighbouring plants (e.g. the previous example of *Trifolium* and *Dactylis*).

Indirect positive influences between two species with the participation of microorganisms or animals (multiple relations):

- advantage through Leguminosae (via nitrogen-fixing nodule bacteria);
- reduction of fungal infections (grasses are able to protect each other against infection with *Fusarium* spp.);
- reduction of insect damage (in mixed crops monophagous insects are more easily controlled by parasites);
- reduction of grazing (by toxic species protecting their non-toxic neighbours);
- promotion of pollination (by neighbouring species with attractive flowers).

It is deduced from these results that competition plays an important role for vegetation dynamics and thus for the development of ecosystems. However, in established, ecologically stable stages, coexistence of species and thus positive interactions are the determining characteristics.

Epiphytes are a very impressive example of coexistence in "old" communities. Epiphytes and lianas are examples of two types of plants able to exploit special resources. They are most diverse and frequent in canopies of mountainous forests under very high rainfall. Exploitation of their niche may be interpreted as avoidance of competition, or as a special form of commensalism, but also as coexistence. They need to be physiologically and morphologically particularly adapted.

Lianas form special supporting tissues and vascular bundles situated next to each other in the cambium. Wide pores and efficient root pressure provide sufficient water and nutrients along the very long transport paths. Epiphytes secure their water and nutrient supplies by particular morphological structures (leaf rosettes and funnels) and special organs allow some orchids and bromeliads to take up water directly from fog and rain. Epiphyllic plants (a special case of epiphytes) have particular symbiotic relations, e.g. with Cyanophyceae.

Competition and Coexistence, Diversity and Dynamics

Both theoretical considerations and experimental results have shown that synecological relationships may be both positive and negative from the point of view of the participating partners. It must be possible to share a niche or the latter needs to be further differentiated. There must be spatial and temporal refuges safeguarding survival for competitively weak species. Important mechanisms in plant communities are only then understandable if both, competition and coexistence are recognised as basic principles.

Many interactions are still not well understood. Better explanations of many functions of characteristics and processes are required. Experiments in the laboratory and open field, as well as the use of mathematical models, have brought enormous advances in recent years. Better consideration of spatial and temporal scales has been identified as important as has working in the field. Descriptive work is often (unjustifiably) regarded as a pre-scientific stage and not regarded as valuable. It is forgotten that precise observation may be the basis for formulating good hypotheses to advance understanding.

Mathematical-statistical treatment of synecological questions has not always brought the required gain in knowledge. Even in developing models the complexity of ecosystem interactions is not fully understood, as each simplification means an increasing distance from reality. However, simulation and modelling should not be neglected as they also show gaps in knowledge and provide the basis for new questions. In vegetation ecology, the statement by Tischler in the

first edition of his Introduction to Ecology (1976) is confirmed: "Nature at the highest level of development of life does not allow itself to be forced into a few rules".

References

Aarssen LW (1983) Ecological combining ability and competitive combining ability in plants: towards a general evolutionary theory of coexistence in systems of competition. Am Nat 122:707–731

Aarssen LW (1989) Competitive ability and species coexistence: a "plants eye" view. Oikos 56:386–401

Allen MF (1991) The ecology of mycorrhizae. University Press, Cambridge

Belnap J, Lange OL (eds) (2001) Biological soil crusts. Structure, function and management. Ecological studies, vol 150. Springer, Berlin Heidelberg New York

Belsky AJ (1986) Does herbivory benefit plants? A review of the evidence. Am Nat 127:870–892

Bertin RI (1989) Pollination biology. In: Abrahamson WG (ed) Plant-animal interactions. McGraw-Hill, New York

Bezzel E, Lechner F, Ranftl H (1980) Arbeitsatlas der Brutvögel Bayerns. Kilda, Greven

Blab J (1979) Schutzwürdige Natur im Bonner Raum. Rheinische Landschaften 16. Ges für Buchdruck, Neuss

Böcker R, Kowarik I, Bornkamm R (1983) Untersuchungen zur Anwendung der Zeigerwerte nach Ellenberg. Verh Ges Ökol 11:35–56

Bornkamm R (1961) Zur quantitativen Bestimmung von Konkurrenzkraft und Wettbewerbsspannung. Ber Dtsch Bot Ges 74:75–83

Boucher DH (1985) The biology of mutualism. Croom Helm, London

Bronstein JL (1994) Our current understanding of mutualism. Q Rev Biol 69:31–51

Brunold C, Rüegsegger A, Brändle R (Hrsg) (1996) Stress bei Pflanzen: Ökologie, Physiologie, Biochemie, Molekularbiologie. Haupt, Bern

Cody ML (1991) Niche theory and plant growth form. Vegetatio 97:39–55

Connell JH, Slatyer RO (1977) Mechanisms of succession in natural communities and their role in community stability and organisation. Am Nat 111:1119–1144

Danin A (1986) Patterns of biogenic weathering as indicators of palaeoclimates in Israel. Proc R Soc Edinb Sect B (Biol) 89b:243–253

Darwin CR (1859) The origin of species by means of natural selection, or the preservation of favoured races in the struggle for life. Murray, London

Dierschke H (1994) Pflanzensoziologie. Grundlagen und Methoden. Ulmer, Stuttgart

Dirzo R (1984) Herbivory: a phytocentric overview. In: Dirzo R (ed) Perspectives on plant population ecology. Sinauer Assoc, Sunderland, pp 141–165

Ellenberg H (1953) Physiologisches und ökologisches Verhalten derselben Arten. Ber Dtsch Bot Ges 65:350–361

Ellenberg H (1996) Die Vegetation Mitteleuropas mit den Alpen. Ulmer, Stuttgart

Ellenberg H, Weber HE, Düll R, Wirth V, Werner W, Paulißen D (1992) Zeigerwerte von Pflanzen in Mitteleuropa, 2. Aufl. Ser Geobot 18:1–258

Elton C (1927) Animal ecology. Sidgewick and Jackson, London

Franz H (1952/53) Dauer und Wandel der Lebensgemeinschaften. Schr Ver Naturwiss Kenntnisse 93:27–45

Gause GF (1934) The struggle for existence. Williams and Wilkins, Baltimore (reprinted 1964 by Hafner, New York)

Gigon A (1994) Positive Interaktionen bei Pflanzen in Trespen-Halbtrockenpflanzen. Verh Ges Ökol 23:1–7

Gigon A, Ryser P (1986) Positive Interaktionen zwischen Pflanzenarten Teil I. Veröff Geobot Inst ETH Stiftung, Rübel 87:372–387

Glavac V (1996) Vegetationsökologie. Grundfragen, Aufgaben, Methoden. Fischer, Jena

Grime JP (1973) Competitive exclusion in herbaceous vegetation. Nature 242:344–347

Grime JP (1979) Plant strategies and vegetation processes. Wiley, Chichester

Grime JP, Hodgson JG, Hunt R (1988) Comparative plant ecology. Allen and Unwin, London

Groves RH, Williams JD (1975) Growth of skeleton weed (Chondrilla juncea L.) as affected by growth of subterranean clover (Trifolium, subterraneum L.) and infection by Puccinia chondrilla, Bubak and Syd. Aust J Agric Res 26:975–983

Grubb P (1977) The maintenance of species richness in plant communities: the importance of the regeneration niche. Biol Rev Camb Pholos Soc 52:107–145

Hess D (1990) Die Blüte. Ulmer, Stuttgart

Holtmeier FK (1999) Tiere als ökologische Faktoren in der Landschaft. IfL, Westfälische Wilhelms-Universität, Münster

Howe HF, Smallwood J (1982) Ecology of seed dispersal. Ann Rev Ecol Sys 13:201–228

Howe HF, Westley LC (1993) Anpassung und Ausbeutung: Wechselbeziehungen zwischen Pflanzen und Tieren. Spektrum, Heidelberg

Hulme PE (1996) Herbivory, plant regeneration and species coexistence. Ecology 84:609–613

Hutchinson GE (1978) An introduction to population ecology. Yale University Press, New Haven

Kessler A, Baldwin IT (2001) Defensive function of herbivore-induced plant volatile emissions in nature. Science 291:2141–2144

Koch AS, Matzner E (1993) Heterogeneity of soil solution chemistry under Norway Spruce (Picea abies L.) as influenced by distance from the stem basis. Plant Soil 151:227–237

Kratochwil A (1987) Zoologische Untersuchungen auf pflanzensoziologischem Raster – Methoden, Probleme und Beispiele biozönologischer Forschung. Tüxenia 7:15–51

Kratochwil A (1999) Biodiversity in ecosystems. Academic Press/Kluwer, New York/Dordrecht

Kratochwil A, Schwabe A (1999) Interaktion von Pflanzen- und Tierarten in Lebensgemeinschaften: ausgewählte Aspekte biozönologischer Forschung. Ber Tüxen-Ges 11:201–221

Kratochwil A, Schwabe A (2001) Ökologie der Lebensgemeinschaften. Ulmer, Stuttgart

Krogerus R (1932) Ökologie und Verbreitung der Arthropoden der Treibsandgebiete an den Küsten Finnlands. Acta Zool Fenn 12:1–308

Kühnelt W (1942–1962) Handbuch der Biologie. Akad Verl-Ges Athenaion, Wiesbaden

Landolt E (1977) Ökologische Zeigerwerte zur Schweizer Flora. Veröff Geobot Inst ETH Stiftung Rübel 64, Zürich

Law R, Watkinson AR (1989) Competition. In: Cherrett JM (ed) Ecological concepts. Blackwell, Oxford, pp 243–284

Long G (1954) Contribution a l'étude de la végétation de la Tunisie centrale. Ann Serv Bot et Agric Tunisie 27:1–38

Lotka AJ (1932) The growth of mixed populations: two species competing for a common food supply. J Wash Acad Sci 22:461–469

Lovelock J (1992) Gaia – Die Erde ist ein Lebewesen. Scherz, Munich

Möbius K (1877) Die Auster und die Austernwirtschaft. Wiegand, Hempel und Parey, Berlin

Mühlenberg M (1989) Freilandökologie, 2. Aufl. Quelle und Meyer, Heidelberg

Müller-Hohenstein K (1978) Die ostmarokkanischen Hochplateaus. Erlanger geographische Arbeiten 7, Erlangen

Müller-Hohenstein K (1999) Weideökologisches Management. Erfahrungen in der dritten Welt. Geogr Rundsch 51/5:275–279

Oberdorfer E (1937) Süddeutsche Pflanzengesellschaften. Fischer, Jena

Passarge H (1981) Gedanken zur Biozönoseforschung. Tüxenia 1:243–247

Rabeler W (1967) Die Pflanzengesellschaften als Grundlage für landbiozönologische Forschung. In: Tüxen R (Hrsg) Biosoziologie. Junk, Den Haag

Reichelt G, Wilmanns O (1973) Vegetationsgeographie. Das geographische Seminar. Westermann, Braunschweig

Remmert W (1992) Ökologie, 5. Aufl. Springer Berlin Heidelberg New York

Richards AJ (1991) The pollination of flowers by insects. Academic Press, London

Rode MW, Dageförde A, Görlitz G (1996) Einfluss der Baumart auf den Nährstoffeintrag und seine Bedeutung für die natürliche Waldentwicklung auf nährstoffarmen Böden Norddeutschlands. Verh Ges Ökol 26:139–145

Schaefer M (1992) Ökologie. Fischer, Jena

Schoener TW (1985) Some comments on Connells and my reviews of field experiments on inter-specific competition. Ann Nat 125:730–740

Schwabe A (1990) Stand und Perspektiven der Vegetations-Komplex-Forschung. In: Pott R (Hrsg). Ber Tüxen-Ges 2:45–60

Schwabe A (1991) Perspectives of vegetation complex research and bibliographic review of vegetation complexes in vegetation science and landscape ecology. Exzerpta Bot 28:223–243

Smith SE, Read DJ (1997) Mycorrhizal symbiosis, 2nd edn. Academic Press, San Diego

Stoudtjesdijk PH, Barkman JJ (1992) Microclimate, vegetation and fauna. Opulus Press, Knivsta

Thienemann A (1920) Biologische Seentypen. Arch Hydrobiol

Thienemann A (1939) Grundzüge einer allgemeinen Ökologie. Arch Hydrobiol 35:267–285

Tilman D (1977) Resource competition between planctonic algae: an experimental and theoretical approach. Ecology 58:338–348

Tilman D (1982) Resource competition and community structure. Princeton University Press, Princeton

Tilman D (1994) Competition and biodiversity in spatially structured habitats. Ecology 75:2–16

Tischler W (1993) Einführung in die Ökologie, 4. Aufl. Fischer, Stuttgart

Tokeshi M (1998) Species coexistence and diversity. Ecological and evolutionary perspectives. Blackwell, Oxford

Tscharntke T (1998) Populationsdynamik in der Agrarlandschaft: Wechselwirkungen zwischen Lebensraum-Inseln. Schriftenr Landschaftspl Natursch 56:121–146

Tüxen R (1965) Wesenszüge der Biozönose. Gesetze des Zusammenlebens von Pflanzen und Tieren. In: Tüxen R (Hrsg) Biosoziologie. Junk, Den Haag, pp 10–13

van Breemen N (1991) Decomposition and accumulation of organic matter in terrestrial ecosystems: research priorities and approaches. Commission of the European Communities, Brussels

Viles HA (1988) Biogeomorphology. Blackwell, Oxford

Volterra V (1926) Variations and fluctuations of the numbers of individuals in animal species living together. Reprinted 1931. In: Chapman (ed) Animal ecology. McGraw Hill, New York

Walter H (1960) Grundlagen der Pflanzenverbreitung. I. Teil: Standortslehre, 2. Aufl. Stuttgart

Walter H, Volk O (1954) Die Grundlagen der Farmwirtschaft in Südwestafrika. Ulmer, Stuttgart

Werner DJ (1977) Vegetationsveränderungen in der argentinischen Puna unter dem Einfluss von Bodenwühlern der Gattung Ctenomys Blainville. In: Tüxen R (ed) Vegetation und Fauna. Ber Int Symp Ver Vegetationsk, Rinteln, pp 433–449

Wilmanns O (1987) Zur Verbindung von Pflanzensoziologie und Zoologie in der Biozönologie. Tüxenia 7:3–12

Wilmanns O (1998) Ökologische Pflanzensoziologie, 6. Aufl. Quelle und Meyer, Heidelberg Wiesbaden

Wilson EO (1969) The species equilibrium. In: Diversity and stability in ecological systems. Brookhaven Symposia in Biology 22, Brookhaven National Laboratory. Upton, New York, pp 38–47

Wilson JB, Agnew DQ (1992) Positive-feedback switches in plant communities. In: Begon M, Fitter AH (eds) Advances in ecological research 23. Academic Press, London, pp 263–336

Wittig R (1993) Biozönose. In: Kuttler W (Hrsg) Handbuch zur Ökologie. Analytica, Berlin, pp 89–91

Zwölfer H (1978) Mechanismen und Ergebnisse der Co-Evolution von phytophagen und entomophagen Insekten und Höheren Pflanzen. Sonderb Naturwiss Verh Hamburg 2:7–50

Chapter 5

Global Aspects
of Plant Ecology

Opening page of chapter top left: Vapour trails from aeroplanes in the sky above Bayreuth, Upper Franconia, Germany. The vapour trails have an impact on the radiation balance of the earth and on the atmospheric chemical processes. Bottom left: Agricultural uses in the American mid-west, an area that was originally an open oak "woodland" and grassland. Top right: Thunderstorms caused by convection from forest fires which are used to clear land in Malaysia. Bottom right: Fish farms, used to rear crabs, on the north coast of Java, were originally mangrove swamps; due to the spread of diseases only a small proportion of this area is still useable. Photos E.-D. Schulze

Global Change and Global Institutions

The study of global change is primarily concerned with the question: In what way has man interfered with the structure and functioning of natural ecosystems? How many people can the earth sustain, i.e. what resources can man use? The figure shows a stream of people leaving Beijing for the surrounding hills on a public holiday. A tight snake of patient, happily conversing people make their way up a narrow path to the top of the "Fragrant Hill" to admire the view. They return to the bottom on a parallel path and the surrounding vegetation remains largely undisturbed. Many people carry a single, autumnal, coloured leaf back to Beijing as a memento of their trip. In the background, barely visible in the photochemical smog, is Beijing with 10 million inhabitants. Photo E.-D. Schulze

Recommended Literature

For a summary of problems of global change, see *World in transition: conservation and sustainable use of the biosphere* (WBGU 2001a) and *The terrestrial biosphere and global change* (Walker et al. 1999). Current knowledge on climate change is summarised in the third report of the IPCC-WG I (IPCC-WG I 2001).

Global change includes changes in land use and climate of the planet caused naturally and by man (anthropogenic; definition from IGBP: Walker et al. 1999):

global change =
  change in climate + changes in land use

Land use and changes in land use may have many direct and indirect consequences, for example, destruction of soil, erosion, and desertification. During geological time, changes in the earth's climate and vegetation have always occurred independently of these human influences. However, the rate and extent of the changes caused by human activity have increased dramatically since the beginning of industrialisation, so that, within a very short period of about 50 years, the conditions required for human life are in jeopardy. The plant ecological aspect of global change may be formulated as:

- Questions about the interaction between climate and land ecosystems (IPCC-WG I, Chap. 9; Melillo et al. 1996)

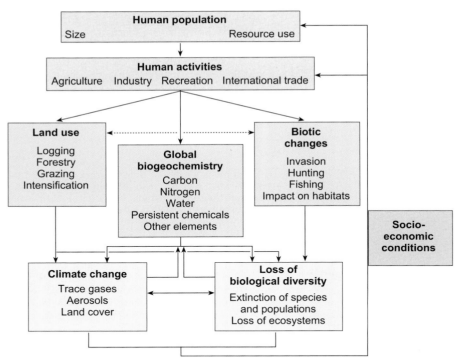

Fig. 5.1.1. Schematic illustration of the interaction between human activity and global change. Human population size and use of resources via specific activities (agriculture, industry, leisure and trade) have effects on land use, the global biogeochemical cycles and biodiversity. These influences initiate changes in climate and in biodiversity and both, in turn, influence populations and resources used by people. How this feedback occurs, and how strong it is, depends on socio-economic parameters. Thus it is difficult to predict scientifically how climate change will affect the situation in developed and in developing countries. After Vitousek et al. (1997)

– What are the effects on terrestrial ecosystems of changes in climate and land use?
– What are the effects on the climate of feedback reactions resulting from changes in terrestrial ecosystems?
• Questions about the importance of species for ecosystem function (GBA 1996, Chap. 7; Mooney et al. 1996)
– Does the presence of many or few species have any effects on the "functioning" of ecosystems?
– Are species with similar functions in ecosystems exchangeable, or are there effects on the material turnover in these ecosystems?

"Functions" of ecosystems are understood to be the many processes that are important to man, for example, biological productivity, filtration and purification of air and water, replacement of ground water, storage of carbon dioxide, etc.

The questions mentioned above are discussed at different levels elsewhere this volume (ecosystems: Chap. 3; synecology: Chap. 4). Some of

these questions will be discussed in the following at a global level with particular emphasis on the interactions between emissions, climate and global material cycles. Considering these aspects, plant ecology is part of other scientific subject areas particularly geo-ecology which considers anthropogenic pollutants, in addition to natural material changes. Also biogeochemistry examines material cycles between atmosphere, ocean and land. These global material cycles are regulated by organisms particularly with respect to changes at the boundary layer between atmosphere and land.

The influence of man on natural material cycles is determined by the population size and consumption of resources (Fig. 5.1.1; Vitousek et al. 1997) shown by "activities" in agriculture and forestry, industrial production, world trade and tourism. These activities are expressed as:

• land use,
• changes of the biological conditions in natural ecosystems,
• changes in global material cycles.

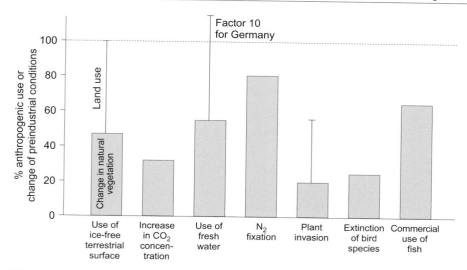

Fig. 5.1.2. An example of the influence of man on global processes in comparison to the period before industrialisation (conditions in 1880 = 100%). Here, the use of land area, the rise in CO_2 concentration, the extent of freshwater usage (in Germany one water molecule that falls as rain is used ten times, including as cooling water, before it reaches the sea), biological and industrial N_2 fixation, changes in natural flora by invasion of foreign species, loss of bird species and the use of natural fish stocks are shown. (After Vitousek et al. 1997)

These changes influence global climate and biodiversity and, by feedback reactions, may affect humanity. How these feedback reactions operate essentially depends on socio-economic parameters in the future (see below).

The extent of man's use of natural resources can no longer be neglected (Fig. 5.1.2, after Vitousek et al. 1997). At present, there is no spot on the ice-free surface of the earth that is not used by man for food production, raw material extraction and processing, settlements, infrastructure or tourism. Natural vegetation has been entirely displaced by man from about 50% of the earth's surface, and the other half is used for grazing, hunting, gathering and for tourism. This massive exploitation of the globe, together with industrialisation, is the cause of the CO_2 concentration of the earth's atmosphere to have increased by a third since industrialisation. Globally, about 50% of fresh water is used by humans. In Germany, the same litre of water is used two to three times before it reaches the sea (Lehn et al. 1996). On a global scale, industrial nitrogen fixation at present is similar in magnitude to natural N_2 fixation. Invading plants replace 20% of natural plants in ecosystems (up to 50% in some types of vegetation). About 20% of bird species are extinct, 60% of fish stocks is overused by man for food or to provide fish meal as food for farmed fish (Naylor et al. 2000). Thus, globally, man has intervened in all

aspects of life without evaluating the natural resources, let alone any consideration of planned management on a global scale.

Yet man's influence is not restricted to the present time (see also Chap. 4.2). Man's war of conquest against nature started at the transition from Pliocene to Pleistocene and reached Europe approximately 1.7 million years ago (China 1.9 million years ago and Java 1.8 million years ago; Fig. 5.1.3 A; Balter and Gibbons 2000). These are not individual immigration waves, but different immigrations by different subspecies of man (Balter 2001). Intensive settlement in the Mediterranean region occurred 30,000 years ago, when *Homo sapiens* lived together with *Homo neanderthalensis* in southern Europe (Gibbons 2001); probably at that time the first settlements occurred. North America was reached by man about 19,000 years ago.

The terms "environment" and "environmental change" have several meanings in the context of global change. Biological aspects need not necessarily be the most important. The following aspects should be distinguished:

- Conditions under which the individual lives and works (job security, social security, indoor climate, etc.). These social environmental conditions can be improved, independently of global ecological environmental problems. Social well-being does not mean a "healthy"

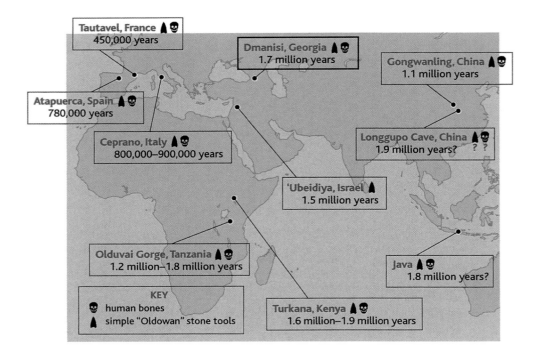

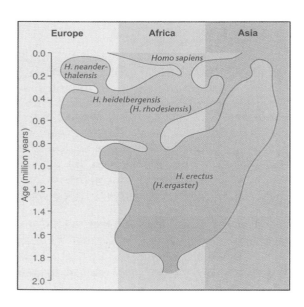

Fig. 5.1.3. A The oldest human fossils and tools in southern Europe and Asia (Balter and Gibbons 2000). B Development of the human species and subspecies in the last 2 million years and their distribution in Africa, Europe and Asia (Balter 2001). C The migration of modern man into southern Europe via the Middle East. (Gibbons 2001)

environment. Prosperous nations contribute substantially to global ecological and climatological problems even though the individual may live in a secure environment.

- Conditions of the economy at the national level. This includes exhaustion of resources, e.g. by clearing forests, use of mineral resources and increasing industrial production,

where economic growth and intervention in the biological environment are closely linked.

- Effects of certain measures on global cycles, particularly on emissions. This aspect is closely coupled with the points mentioned before but it is dealt with separately here, because of the effects of most emissions on climate.

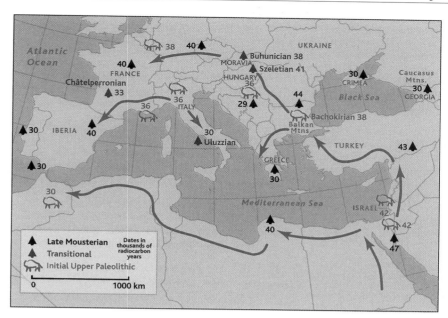

Fig. 5.1.3 C

Box 5.1.1   International organisations and analyses of global change

Global change is initiated by

1. Decisions made at national and international level
2. The sum of many small individual decisions: This ranges from individuals to the world society (see Fig. 5.4.3). Within this range are a number of organisations that have particular interest in global change (WBGU 2001 b), those that have direct influence on land use, e.g. FAO (Food and Agriculture Organisation), or indirectly through the decisions it makes, e.g. the WTO (World Trade Organisation). Between these types of organisation are the financial organisations that have no direct contact with agriculture and forestry, but that distribute resources and so have a more direct impact on nations than the WTO. A few examples are the World Bank, IMF (International Monetary Fund) and the GEF (Global Environmental Facility, which finances projects in the area of biodiversity and energy saving), as well as the UNDP (United Nations Development Programme).

Parallel to these are organisations that scientifically study and analyse global change. These include:

- organisations of the UN (UN Environment Programme, UNEP), the World Meteorological Organisation (WMO) and the UN Educational, Scientific and Cultural Organisation (UNESCO);
- organisations that are financially involved also in the global environmental audits (e.g. World Bank);
- scientific organisations: ICSU (International Committee of Scientific Unions) and the ISSC (International Social Science Committee).

There are various organisations supporting worldwide studies of global change:

- WCRP (World Climate Research Programme), initiated by the WMO and supported directly by nations within WMO;
- IGBP (International Geosphere Biosphere Programme), a branch of the ICSU;

- Diversitas (International Programme on the Documentation of Diversity) that was started by the International Union of Biological Sciences (IUBS);
- IHDP (International Human Dimension Programme) initiated by ISSC;
- SCOPE (Scientific Committee on Problems of the Environment), a UNESCO programme.

Also there are two large projects that study and analyse climate change and biodiversity, and report to the UN. These are:

- IPCC (Intergovernmental Panel on Climate Change) started in 1988 by the WMO and UNEP. In 2000 the IPCC was funded by the World Bank under the auspices of "Conference of the Parties" (COP), i.e. the 182 nations that signed the convention on climate change. The IPCC is subdivided into "Working group 1" (WG1) that studies the scientific fundamentals of climate change (IPCC-WG 1 1996, 2001) and WG II that studies the consequences, adaptive and mitigating strategies (IPCC-WG II 1996, 2001). WG III considers economic and social effects of global change (IPCC-WG III 1996, 2001). In 2001 the IPCC published the third report on climate (IPCC-WG I–III 2001), and additional "special" reports, such as the "Special Report on Land Use, Land Use Change and Forestry" which is important for ecology as it looks at the interactions of climate change and land use (IPCC LULUCF 2000). COP appoints the authors of the IPCC report, which is then being reviewed by independent scientists and by the nations belonging to COP. The final report is published by COP; the executive summary is discussed word for word by the signatory states who agree to the final version. The salient point of the executive summary in the IPCC report of 1996 was: "The balance of evidence suggests a discernible human influence on global climate". This statement led to the discussion and finalisation of the Kyoto Protocol as part of the Framework Convention on Climate Change.

- The GBA (Global Biodiversity Assessment) report of 1140 pages, published in 1996 by the UNEP and financed by the World Bank (GBA 1996), is the first attempt to catalogue the earth's biodiversity. In contrast to the IPCC, GBA is not part of the COP initiative on biological diversity. The report was evaluated by governments of countries that have signed the convention of biodiversity. So far the GBA process has not been repeated; instead UNEP plans a millennium assessment of global ecosystems.

For the second IPCC report about 4000 scientists were involved in writing and reviewing processes, for the GBA this meant about 1100 scientists. Hence, in both cases, an all-encompassing, well-balanced (i.e. minimum consensus) report was produced that describes the state of the world.

Environmental policy is organised in different ways, depending on nations. In Germany, for example, analysis and scientific recommendations to government occur via the following organisations:

- Council for Sustainable Development, whose remit is to make decisions concerning environmental policy accessible to the general public;
- Scientific Advisory Committee on Global Change (WBGU). This is an interdisciplinary group which advises the Federal Government on all matters relating to the environment, e.g. soil, drinking water, biodiversity and environmental risks (WBGU 1994, 1998, 1999, 2000a);
- German Council of Environmental Experts (SRU). This advises the Environment Minister on questions of National and EU importance;
- National Committee of Global Changes (NKGC) of the German Research Council (DFG). This advises the DFG and the Federal Minister for Biological Research about scientific research programmes.

References

Balter M, Gibbons A (2000) A glimpse of human's first journey out of Africa. Science 288:948–950

Balter M (2001) In search of the first Europeans. Science 291:1722–1725

EAO (2000) World Forest Resource Assessment, FAO

GBA (1996) Global biodiversity assessment. Cambridge University Press, 1140 pp

Gibbons A (2001) The riddle of coexistence. Science 291: 1725–1729

IPCC-LULUCF (2000) Special report on land use, land use change and forestry (IPCC-XVI/Doc. 2). IPCC-Sekretariat der WMO, Genf

IPCC-WG I (1996) Climate change 1995. The science of climate change. Contribution of Working Group I to the second assessment report of the Intergovernmental Panel on Climate Change. Cambridge University Press, 572 pp

IPCC-WG II (1996) Climate change 1995. Impacts, adaptations and mitigation of climate change: scientific-technical analysis; Contribution of Working Group II to the second assessment report of the Intergovernmental Panel on Climate Change. Cambridge University Press, 878 pp

IPCC-WG III (1996) Climate change 1995; economic and social dimensions of climate change; contribution of Working Group III to the second assessment report of the Intergovernmental Panel on Climate Change. Cambridge University Press

IPCC-WG I (2001) Climate Change 2000. Third assessment report. Cambridge University Press, Cambridge

IPCC-WG II (2001) Climate Change 2000. Third assessment report. Cambridge University Press, Cambridge

IPCC-WG III (2001) Climate Change 2000. Third assessment report. Cambridge University Press, Cambridge

Lehn H, Steiner M, Mohr H (1996) Wasser – die elementare Ressource. Leitlinien einer nachhaltigen Nutzung. Springer, Berlin Heidelberg New York, 368 pp

Melillo JM, Prentice IC, Farquhar GD, Schulze E-D, Sala OE (1996) Terrestrial biotic responses to environmental change and feedbacks to climate. In: Climate change 1995, the science of climate change. Cambridge University Press, Cambridge, pp 445–482

Naylor RL, Goldburg RJ, Primavera JH, Kautsky N, Beveridge MCM, Clay J, Folke C, Lubchenko J, Mooney H, Troell M (2000) Effect of aquaculture on world fish supply. Nature 405:1017–1025

Vitousek PM, Mooney HA, Lubchenco J, Melillo JM (1997) Human domination of earth's ecosystems. Science 277:494–499

Walker B, Steffen W, Canadell J, Ingram J (1999) The terrestrial biosphere and global change. IGBP book series 4. Cambridge University Press, Cambridge, 439 pp

WBGU (1995) World in transition: the thread to soils. German Advisory Council on Global Change (WBGU), Economia, Bonn, 263 pp

WBGU (1999) World in transition: ways towards sustainable management of freshwater resources. German Advisory Council on Global Change (WBGU). Springer, Berlin Heidelberg New York, 392 pp

WBGU (2000) World in transition: strategies for managing global environmental risks. German Advisory Council on Global Change (WBGU). Springer, Berlin Heidelberg New York, 359 pp

WBGU (2001a) World in transition: conservation and sustainable use of the biosphere. German Advisory Council on Global Change (WBGU). Earthscan, London, 451 pp

WBGU (2001b) World in transition: new structures for global environmental policy. German Advisory Council on Global Change (WBGU). Earthscan, London, 211 pp

5.2

Global Element Cycles

Most element cycles are not closed entities in ecosystems. This is particularly true for water, carbon and the nutrients nitrogen and sulphur. At the scale of landscapes resources are often imported and exported from one ecosystem to another. The figure shows the export of soluble organic carbon in humic and fulvic acids, which co-transport heavy metals, from boreal pine forests of Siberia. The dissolved organic carbon reaches the ocean via streams and rivers. The river is the Dubces, a tributary of the Yenisei. Photo E.-D. Schulze

Element cycles (Fig. 5.2.1; Schulze 2000) of water, carbon, nitrogen and sulphur are characterised (1) by the degree of storage in the atmosphere, sea and on continents; (2) by the turnover between these compartments, the so-called fluxes; and (3) the turnover within the compartments, the so-called internal cycles of ecosystems. The turnover between the earth's surface and the atmosphere is essentially controlled by organisms, whilst the turnover in the atmosphere is predominantly dependent on energy from solar radiation. Global fluxes between continents, oceans and the atmosphere will be considered later. For comparison, it is important to know that the surface of the earth is about 505 million km^2 of which about 353 million km^2 are oceans, i.e. 70% of the earth's surface is covered by oceans. The area of continents is about 152 million km^2, but only 135 million km^2 (88% of continents) are ice-free. Europe (the 15 countries of the European Union, EU_{15}) has an area of 3.2 million km^2.

5.2.1

Water Cycle

The **water cycle** (Fig. 5.2.2; Schlesinger 1997; see also Chaps. 2.1.1 and 2.2.4) is characterised by the large reservoir in the oceans. An H_2O molecule has a mean residence time (MRT) in the ocean of about 37,000 years calculated as reservoir/flux. The MTR in groundwater of the continents is 300 years and water bound in ice 16,000 years; the MRT in the atmosphere is three orders of magnitude smaller (MRT: 9 days), the MRT for water in soil is 280 days.

Transport of water vapour from the ocean to land is smaller than the turnover across the oceans or land masses. This means that precipitation in coastal regions evaporates and this evaporated water is then precipitated over the interior of the land masses again (see Fig. 3.2.5). A "wave" of rain, evaporation and rain again "rolls" across the continent. In the case of the Eurosiberian regions, the same water molecule is calculated to undergo five to seven evapora-

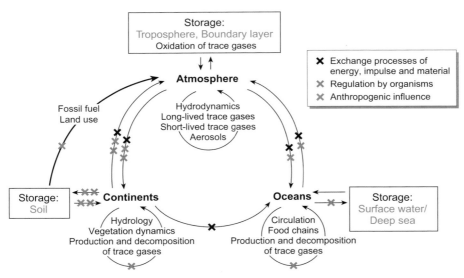

Fig. 5.2.1. Schematic presentation of the global cycling of material between land, sea and air. The *arrows* show the mass flows (mass per unit area per time). *Crosses* identify the places where the flow rates are controlled by organisms

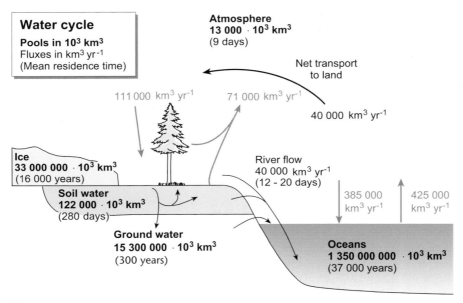

Fig. 5.2.2. Schematic presentation of the global water cycle. Shown are the reservoirs (pool sizes), the flows, and the average retention time of a molecule in each compartment. (After Schlesinger 1997; Reeburgh 1996)

tions and precipitation cycles before it reaches the Pacific. In this process losses by surface run-off and seepage occur, so that precipitation of about 1000 mm in montane regions of Germany is reduced to 300 mm in central Siberia and 150 mm in eastern Siberia (Schulze et al. 1999). Related to area, the average turnover of water on land is lower than the turnover of oceans.

With the large amounts of water vapour and precipitation which are converted globally it is not surprising that humans do not have much influence, particularly as they use surface water predominantly, i.e. the excess of the hydrological balance (see Chap. 2.2.1). Despite the large amounts converted, there are human influences on the global water balance (see WBGU 1999), particularly:

• Changes in runoff because of changes in land use. These start with change from forest to

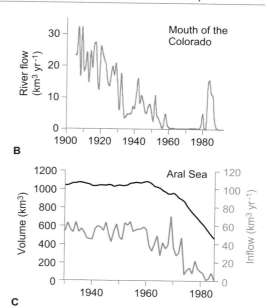

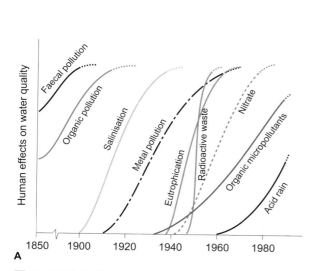

Fig. 5.2.3. A Changing water quality in the industrialised world from 1850 to the present; B change with time in the flow of the Colorado River below the dams; and C change in the volume of water reaching the Aral Sea since 1930. (WBGU 1999)

agriculture and continue with intensive mechanical working practices, fertilisation, use of pesticides and erosion on agricultural land, and last not least by construction. Changes in land use influence not only the amount, but also the quality of water (Fig. 5.2.3 A; WBGU 1999).

- Changes in runoff caused by dam building and irrigation (partially from fossil ground water storage). Well-known examples of the effects of irrigation and dam building on surface runoff are the drastically reduced flow of the Colorado in Arizona and the drying out of the Aral Sea (Fig. 5.2.3 B, C; WBGU 1999). Changes in water levels of the lake caused by the Aswan Dam (Egypt) and Lake Chad (Chad) are further impressive examples of global changes in the water cycle (Evans 1996).

- Changes in the distribution of precipitation (Fig. 5.2.4 A; Toon 2000; Fig. 5.2.4 B; Cerveny and Balling 1998). Because of production of aerosols, more nucleation bodies reach the atmosphere so delaying precipitation (Toon 2000). This explains the statistically established periodicity in weekly precipitation (Cerveny and Balling 1998) in the eastern USA where aerosol concentration increases rapidly at the beginning of the week and reaches a maximum on Wednesday/Thursday.

This delays rainfall from the atmosphere. Precipitation in the first half of the week is low, increases only in the second half of the week, and reaches its statistical maximum on Saturday. Statistically, least precipitation falls on Monday.

5.2.2

Carbon Cycle

The **carbon cycle** (Fig. 5.2.5; Schlesinger 1997) has, as with the water cycle, a large reservoir in the ocean and additional large storage in sedimentary rocks. The CO_2 in the atmosphere is 2‰ of the amount in oceans, only slightly higher than the amount of C bound in the biomass of plants and only half that stored in the soil. The mean residence time of a CO_2 molecule in the atmosphere is three years. As CO_2 concentration is not only determined by re-assimilation but also by respiration during litter decomposition (see Fig. 3.3.1) it would take about 750 years to halve the present increase of CO_2, even if present emissions were stopped immediately. At present CO_2 increases in the atmosphere by 5% per year, i.e. 3×10^9 t carbon.

The biological carbon cycle is characterised by very high rates of carbon uptake and release.

Anthropogenic impact on atmosphere

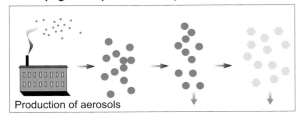

Production of aerosols

Natural atmosphere

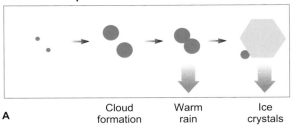

A
Cloud formation   Warm rain   Ice crystals

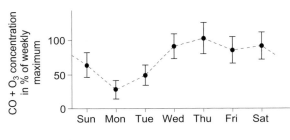

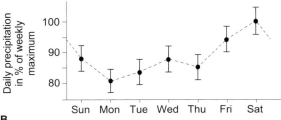

B

Fig. 5.2.4. A Schematic presentation of droplet formation in the atmosphere, with or without aerosols. In the presence of aerosols the number of nuclei for condensation seed molecules rises. At constant water vapour concentration the size of the droplets and the amount of precipitation therefore decrease. In the atmosphere vapour remains as haze that does not develop into rain (after Toon 2000). B Statistical distribution of anthropogenic gases as an indicator of aerosols and of rainfall during a week in northeastern USA. (After Cerveny and Balling 1998)

Uptake is by CO_2 assimilation in photosynthesis, release by respiration of plants and heterotrophic organisms, as well as from burning vegetation (see Fig. 3.3.9). These fluxes are almost balanced under natural conditions. In addition there are two anthropogenic fluxes which are larger than the natural C balance from photo-synthesis and respiration, namely emissions from consumption of fossil fuels and release of CO_2 by changes in land use. The human signal thus interferes significantly in the natural carbon cycle; the effects are analysed in Chapter 5.3.

The CO_2 cycle does not consider the turnover of further C-containing trace gases which can have an even greater effect on climate change than CO_2. In particular methane, produced mainly in wet areas of the globe, including rice cultivation, and also from rubbish heaps, termites, animal husbandry and burning of biomass (Reeburgh 1996).

5.2.3

Nitrogen Cycle

The largest amount of nitrogen (Fig. 5.2.6; Reeburgh 1996; Schlesinger 1997) is stored in gaseous form in the atmosphere (4×10^{15} t with a MRT of 10^7 years). Storage in other compartments is negligible compared with this, even though turnover rates are high. Biological N_2 fixation is the starting point of biological N turnover on continents and in oceans (see Fig. 3.3.12); it is significantly higher on land than in oceans. In contrast, denitrification on land and in the oceans is almost identical. The N cycle is particularly affected by industrial N_2 assimilation resulting in NH_3 production, and by NO_x production in combustion. The present rate of industrial N_2 fixation corresponds to biological N_2 fixation which is also influenced by growing Leguminosae in agriculture. Internal turnover of organically and inorganically bound nitrogen in ecosystems exceeds the net fluxes by about a factor of 10.

It is difficult to determine the global N balance because of uncertainties in estimating denitrification. Changes in the atmosphere are also difficult to measure directly, because of the large amount and high concentration of N_2. Estimates point to an eutrophication process in which N_2 fixation exceeds denitrification by a third (Table 5.2.1). It is possible, therefore, that denitrification in the stratosphere and in oceans is underestimated (Tabazadeh et al. 2001).

In Germany, the nitrate content in groundwater correlated linearly with N deposits from the atmosphere and fertilisation in agriculture (Lehn et al. 1996). In Baden-Württemberg, Ger-

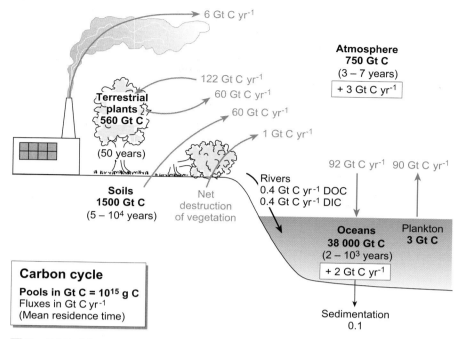

Fig. 5.2.5. Schematic presentation of the global carbon cycle. Shown are the reservoirs (pool sizes), the fluxes, and the mean residence time of a molecule in each compartment. *DOC* Dissolved organic carbon; *DIC* dissolved inorganic carbon. (After Schlesinger 1997; Reeburgh 1996)

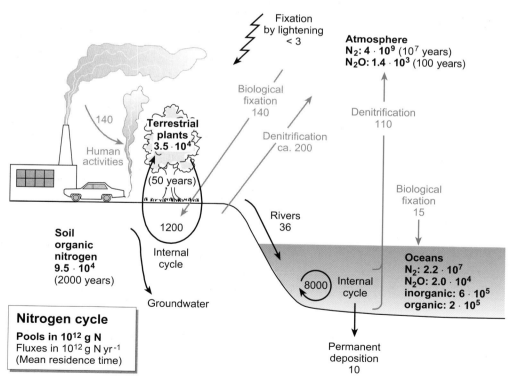

Fig. 5.2.6. Schematic presentation of the global nitrogen cycle. The reservoirs (pool sizes), the fluxes, and the mean residence time of a molecule in each compartment are shown. (After Schlesinger 1997; Reeburgh 1996)

Table 5.2.1. The global N_2 balance. All values are subject to considerable uncertainty. (After Reeburgh 1996; Schlesinger 1997; Vitousek et al. 1997)

Process	N_2 fixation $(10^{12}$ g N $a^{-1})$	Denitrification $(10^{12}$ g N year$^{-1})$
Natural terrestrial	190	147
Natural oceanic	40	110
Planting Leguminosae	40	0
Fertilisers and industry	90	0
Industrial burning	20	20
Biomass burning		12
Sum	380	289

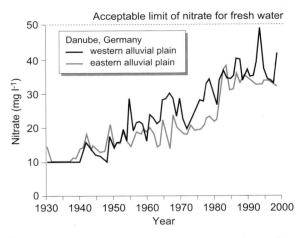

Fig. 5.2.7. The change in nitrate concentration in Donauried since 1930. (After Lehn et al. 1996)

many, a total of 550 water sources (more than 20% of the total number) were taken out of the water supply network between 1980 and 1992 because of anthropogenic pollution. Thus, dependence on long-distance water supply was increased. In 1993 there were only three, large-volume, long-distance water supply systems left, the area called Donauried, Lake Constance, and the drinking water reservoirs in the Black Forest. The Donauried supplies the metropolitan region of Stuttgart. In this important region for water supply, nitrate concentration rose continuously from 10 mg l^{-1} in 1930 to 40 mg l^{-1} in 1993 (Fig. 5.2.7; Lehn et al. 1996). In 1990, it was predicted that this source region would have to be taken out of the supply network in 10–20 years (because the EU limit for nitrate in drinking water of 50 mg l^{-1} would be exceeded). However, there are indications that nitrate pollution has stabilised, possibly as a consequence of environmental measures (reduced input of liquid fertiliser in the source region and nature protection). This shows that environmental problems can be managed if it is politically desired.

5.2.4

Sulphur Cycle

The **sulphur cycle** (Fig. 5.2.8; Reeburgh 1996; Schlesinger 1997) is characterised by high turnover across the oceans caused by the release of dimethyl sulphide (DMS), a gas produced by metabolism of several genera of marine algae which possess chlorophyll a and c. These are:

- all dinoflagellates
- green algal families in the Prasinophyceae
- almost all macro green algae
- a few Diatomeae
- a few Rhodophyceae
- no brown algae
- no cyanobacteria

The turnover rate of DMS in the atmosphere is very high (MRT: 1 day), as it is oxidised to sulphate, a large proportion of which usually returns to the oceans in rain. Natural turnover is two orders of magnitude lower on land than on oceans. Thus anthropogenic S emissions become the largest S sources on land, exceeding natural S emissions by approximately a factor of 10, and contributing significantly to acidification of soils (see Fig. 3.2.2). In Germany, SO_2 emissions were significantly reduced by regulation in 1983 of power plants and other large SO_2 sources (see Fig. 3.5.4), and presently reach a pre-industrial level.

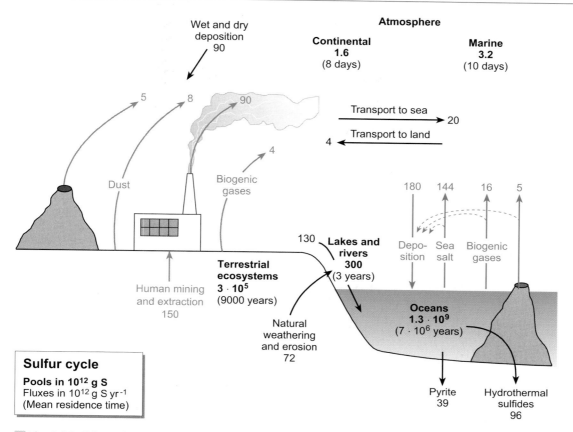

Fig. 5.2.8. Schematic presentation of the global sulphur cycle. Reservoirs (pool sizes), fluxes, and mean residence time of a molecule in each compartment are shown. (After Schlesinger 1997; Reeburgh 1996)

References

Cereny RS, Balling RC (1998) Weekly cycles of air pollutants, precipitation and tropical cyclones in the coastal NW Atlantic region. Nature 394:561–563

Evans TE (1996) The effect of changes in the world hydrological cycle on availability of water resources. In: Bazzaz F, Sombroek W (eds) Global climate change and agricultural production. Wiley, Chichester, pp 15–48

Lehn H, Steiner M, Mohr J (1996) Wasser – die elementare Ressource. Leitlinien einer nachhaltigen Nutzung. Springer, Berlin Heidelberg New York, 368 pp

Reeburgh WS (1996) "Soft spots" in the global methane budget. In: Lidstrom ME, Tabita FR (eds) Microbial growth on C1-compounds. Kluwer, Amsterdam, pp 334–342

Schlesinger WH (1997) Biogeochemistry; an analysis of global change. Academic Press, San Diego, 588 pp

Schulze E-D (2000) Der Einfluß des Menschen auf die biogeochemischen Kreisläufe der Erde. Max-Planck-Gesellschaft Jahrbuch 2000, pp 39–58

Schulze E-D, Lloyd J, Kelliher FM, Wirth C, Rebmann C, Lühker B, Mund M, Knohl A, Milyukova IM, Schulze W, Ziegler W, Varlagin AB, Sogachev AE, Valentini R, Dore S, Grigoriev S, Kolle O, Panfyorov MI, Tchebakova N, Vygodskaya NN (1999) Productivity of forests in the Eurosiberian boreal region and their potential to act as a carbon sink – a synthesis. Global Change Biol 5:703–722

Tabazadeh A, Jensen EJ, Toon OB, Drdla K, Schoeberl MR (2001) Role of the stratospheric polar freezing belt in denitrification. Science 291:2591–2593

Toon OB (2000) How pollution suppresses rain. Science 287:1763–1765

Vitousek PM, Mooney HA, Lubchenco J, Melillo JM (1997) Human domination of earth's ecosystems. Science 277:494–499

WBGU (1999) World in transition: ways towards sustainable management of freshwater resources. German Advisory Council on Global Change (WBGU). Springer, Berlin Heidelberg New York, 392 pp

Human Impacts on the Carbon Budget and Its Significance for the Global Climate

A particularly important form of human intervention in the carbon cycle is deforestation of primary forests (to obtain fibre and timber and to create usable land). In the tropics this is usually associated with land use change (slash and burn agriculture). In boreal forests deforestation is usually followed by regeneration. Even so, this initial harvest of trees is associated with a significant increase in carbon emissions, as primary forests have a higher biomass than secondary forests, and as a consequence of harvest there is a destruction of the organic layer which accumulated in primary forests over thousands of years. The top figure shows the fully mechanised harvest of a boreal forest in Russia, and the lower figure the boundary between primary forest and clear-cut areas in the Pacific northwest of Canada. Photo E.-D. Schulze

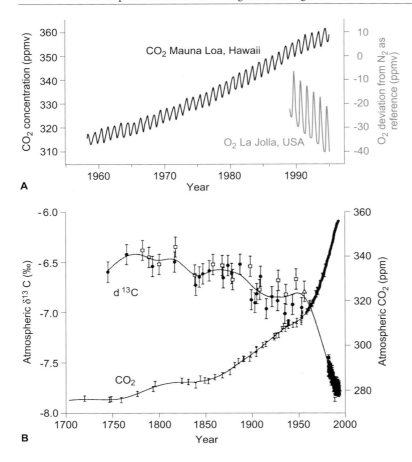

Fig. 5.3.1. A CO_2 concentration in the atmosphere measured on Mauna Loa. Here, continuous measurements have demonstrated the increasing trend of CO_2 concentration, and also the annual cycle with a minimum during the growing period in summer and a maximum during the dormant phase in winter of the northern hemisphere. The simultaneous reduction in O_2 concentration measured at La Jolla, California, is also shown. The O_2 concentration shows annual oscillations that are opposite to CO_2 (after Heimann 1997). B Changes in atmospheric CO_2 concentration and the $\delta^{13}C$ value since 1700. Since 1960 the $\delta^{13}C$ value has decreased with increasing CO_2

The CO_2 concentration in the atmosphere is currently increasing by 0.5% per year. To fully understand the implications, the long-term trend of CO_2 in the atmosphere needs to be considered. Also, it is important to know where the anthropogenic CO_2 originates from (Fig. 5.3.1 A; Heimann 1997). Since 1959 a continuous rise in CO_2 concentration has been measured on Mauna Loa on Hawaii with minima corresponding to the growing season in the northern hemisphere summer and maxima corresponding to the dormant phase in winter, when CO_2 production is also very high. A decrease in the oxygen concentration was observed in parallel to this increase in CO_2. It is proof that the rise in CO_2 is caused by combustion and is not the consequence of simple CO_2 release, for example, from the oceans. At the current rate of consumption, oxygen will be depleted in 50,000 years, but the potential use of oxygen also depends on the availability of fossil fuels. Estimates of reserves of fossil fuels are uncertain and depend on the costs of extraction. Extractable reserves of 600–1200 Gt (100–200 years supply at current rates

of use) are calculated. Including reserves that are difficult to extract, the figure is around 4000–7000 Gt, calculated as a mixture of sources, with 13.6 g C/MJ gas, 21.8 g C/MJ oil and 27.3 g C/KJ coal (1 kg oil = 1.44 mineral coal units).

The stable isotope ^{13}C (Fig. 5.3.1 B) is another indicator showing that gases from fossil fuels enter the earth's atmosphere. In pre-industrial times, the so-called $\delta^{13}C$ value (atmospheric $^{13}C/^{12}C$ ratio compared with a standard) was –6.5‰. Adding CO_2, depleted in ^{13}C, from fossil C-sources has decreased the $\delta^{13}C$ by ca. 1‰ in the last 40 years.

Parallel to the increase in CO_2 concentration the concentration of methane has also changed, rising with the increase in population as a consequence, to a large extent, of growing rice in wet areas and keeping ruminants (Krüger et al. 2001; see also Chap. 3).

Thus it has become clear from oxygen and isotope measurements that the increased CO_2 concentration in the atmosphere is a consequence of combustion. It is now necessary to explain how anthropogenic CO_2 enters into the

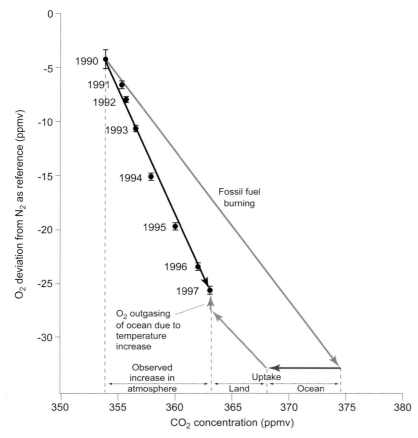

Fig. 5.3.2. Changes in the O_2 concentration and its dependence on CO_2. When fossil fuels are burnt O_2 consumption is proportional to the CO_2 released. However, CO_2 is absorbed by the oceans (without releasing an equivalent amount of O_2) and by photosynthesis (where O_2 is simultaneously produced). These three processes result in the changes in measured O_2 and CO_2. (After Keeling et al. 1996)

carbon cycle (Fig. 5.3.2; Keeling et al. 1996). During burning, a fixed amount of oxygen is consumed in relation to carbon. If the recent consumption of fossil fuels is known, it is possible to calculate the corresponding requirements for oxygen and the CO_2 produced and the concentration to be expected if the CO_2 formed remains in the atmosphere. Observations in the atmosphere show a significantly lower CO_2 concentration than expected from the use of fossil fuels. This difference is caused by photosynthesis of land plants in which oxygen proportional to CO_2 consumption is released into the air. At the surface of oceans more CO_2 is consumed than O_2, as the solubility of CO_2 in water at $20\,^{\circ}C$ (0.878 ml $CO_2\,l^{-1}$ H_2O) is much greater than that of O_2 (0.0311 l $O_2\,l^{-1}$ H_2O; Sestak et al. 1971). Calculated from these turnover rates ca. 50% of CO_2 from fossil fuels remains in the atmosphere, 30% is taken up by the oceans, and 20% is assimilated by plants (Keeling et al. 1996).

It is to be expected that the increased concentrations of CO_2, methane, N_2O and other anthro-

pogenic trace gases will affect climate because of their specific energy absorption characteristics (see Fig. 2.1.2). This is confirmed by geological events, in which a sudden release of marine methane hydrate caused a 5–7 K warming of the lower atmosphere (Norris and Röhl 1999). At the transition from the Palaeocene to the Eocene (55 million years ago), 1200–2000 Gt CH_4 was released at the continental shelf in the north Atlantic. This corresponds to the release of CO_2 expected from fossil fuels. In this process stable methane hydrates, formed under cooler conditions and buried under sediments, were released as gases as the water warmed, such as might occur in an interglacial period. At the foot of the continental shelf sediments slipped and the methane gas was released in a chain reaction (Kennet et al. 2000). Methane concentration in the atmosphere was high for 120,000 years until the gas was re-assimilated and the atmosphere cooled again. There are indications that the evolutionary separation of man from other apes occurred during this time of enormous warming at the transition from the Palaeocene to the Eo-

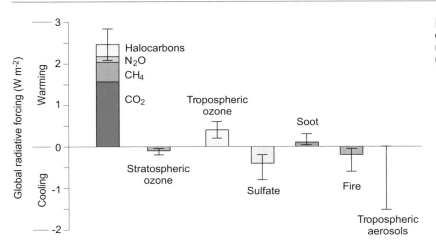

Fig. 5.3.3. Influence of trace gases and aerosols on the solar radiation balance of the earth. (Schimel et al. 1997)

cene (Dickens 1999). During the warming after the last ice age no such methane release occurred.

Independent of the indications of warming of the lower atmosphere with increasing CO_2 concentration, there are several uncertainties making predictions very difficult (see also Veizer et al. 2000). These uncertainties are in meteorology as well as in oceanography:

- Meteorological uncertainties
  Aerosols: Radiation balance not only depends on outgoing radiation, but also on incoming radiation. Incoming radiation is reduced by the increased reflection of clouds and aerosols. This compensates for the effect of reduced re-radiation of long-wave heat radiation and therefore cooling caused by increased CO_2. The influence of gases and aerosols (Fig. 5.3.3) was assessed by IPCC-WG I (1996): Despite all uncertainties the conclusion remains that the predominant effect of trace gases is to cause global warming. The influence of incoming radiation had also been seriously discussed in a different connection, namely the atomic winter (Ehrlich et al. 1983; Turco et al. 1983). According to calculations, an atomic war would lead to an enormous development of soot and aerosols from fires in large cities, and this would decrease the incoming radiation to such an extent that within 1–2 weeks the earth's mean temperature would decrease to –15 to –25 °C for >1 year and thus survival of life on earth would be unlikely. This applies particularly to a start of such a war during the growing season in the northern hemisphere. This knowledge led to the realisation that an atomic war would jeopardise the sur-

vival of both sides, and it thus influenced negotiations on nuclear disarmament.

- Oceanographic uncertainties about **global marine currents**
  Conveyor belt: One ocean current is particularly important for Europe, the oceanic conveyor belt, which connects the oceans (Fig. 5.3.4 A; Commission of Inquiry of Global Climate Change, Federal Parliament of Germany 1992). Warm surface water flows from the south Atlantic to the north Atlantic as the Gulf Stream. Because of evaporation, and the stream of salt-rich water from the Mediterranean, this water becomes increasingly more saline and therefore does not freeze when it meets the cold Arctic water and the front of sea ice off Greenland. The salt-rich water cools and sinks into the depth of the north Atlantic and flows back as a cold, salt-containing deep sea current. It has long been known that the heat released during the cooling and sinking of the surface stream causes the mild, moderate climate in Europe (Driscoll and Haug 1998). This oceanic conveyor belt reacts sensitively to the salt content of water in the north Atlantic. Salt-depleted water would not sink to the depth of the oceans. Thus heat would not be produced in the north Atlantic and Europe would cool down. This occurred during the post-glacial period when the large inland lake of North America, Agassiz, which formed from the melting ice in the region of Alberta, Saskatchewan and Montana, flowed into the north Atlantic. Consequently, the Younger Dryas ice age occurred in Europe. Melting ice in the Arctic or a decrease of water flow from the

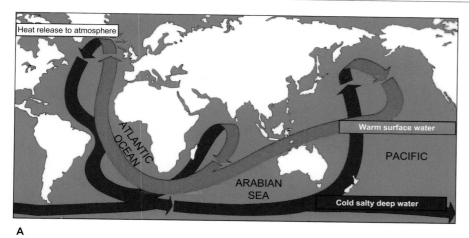

A

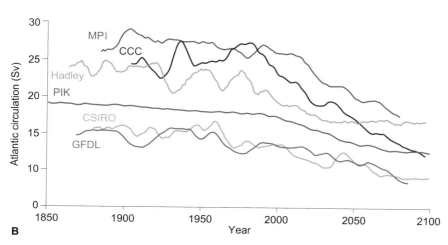

B

Fig. 5.3.4. A Schematic presentation of the oceanic "conveyer belt". The warm upper currents spread from the Pacific to the Atlantic. This water becomes saltier and does not freeze when it meets the cold water and ice front of the Arctic. The surface water sinks near the coast of Norway and north of Iceland and forms deep, salty water that flows back to the Pacific (after the Commission of Enquiry of Global Climate Change of the Federal Republic of Germany; Ramstorf et al. 1999). B Comparison of models of deep-water formation in the north Atlantic. All models agree in predicting that, with further global warming, the strength of the Gulf Stream will be reduced. This has potentially serious consequences for the European climate. (After Ramstorf et al. 1999)

Siberian rivers could have a similar effect to a cooling of the Gulf Stream, as the Arctic ice masses are derived from the fresh water of the Siberian rivers. Redirection of the Siberian rivers for irrigation of Asiatic steppes, planned in the 1960s, would have had enormous climatic consequences for Europe. Even a weakened Gulf Stream could cause a cooling of western Europe and this would result in an enormous increase of atmospheric CO_2, as the CO_2-rich water would no longer sink into the deep sea and would produce a significant gradient of precipitation. A comparison of coupled ocean-atmosphere models shows a weakening of the Gulf Stream with continuing warming (Fig. 5.3.4 B; Broeker 1997; Rahmstorf 1999).

El Niño: There is another marine stream which affects climate, the so-called El Niño. Periodically, the surface water in the eastern Pacific becomes significantly warmer, so that the regular currents transporting water from east to west no longer occur. This has enormous effects on the weather conditions in such a year (Fig. 5.3.5; Bengtsson 1997). Catastrophic rainfall occurs in South America, and drought in Australia and parts of Indonesia. The harvest in South Africa is affected. In addition to changes in the distribution of precipitation, the warming of the Pacific leads to

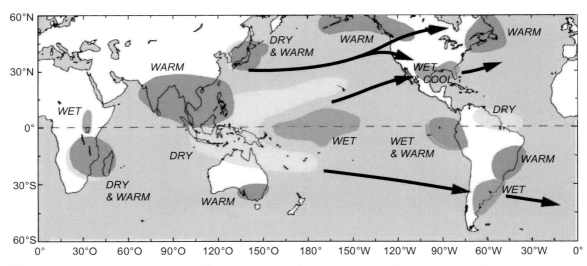

Fig. 5.3.5. Influence of the El Niño effect on the regional climates in Asia, Africa and America. (After Bengtsson 1997)

release of large amounts of CO_2 in the nearby continents. About 1 year later Europe notices the effects of El Niño, i.e. Europe's climate depends on events occurring in the Pacific (Taylor et al. 1998; Rodwell et al. 1999).

North Atlantic oscillation (NAO): This is a current in the north Atlantic corresponding to El Niño which determines the position of a high-pressure area in the Azores and thus the air pressure gradient between the Azores and the low-pressure areas over Iceland. The position of the Azores high pressure decides whether rain falls over the Mediterranean region in summer or over Scandinavia. NAO is positive, with a strong pressure gradient between Iceland and the Azores, a sign of a strong thermo-haline circulation (THC) and thus for a warm winter in northern Europe. Despite the prediction that the THC would decrease with global warming, at the moment an increased THC (possibly transient) is observed (Hurrell et al. 2001).

The *Intergovernmental Panel on Climate Change* (IPCC) discussed the effects that various scenarios of future increased CO_2 concentration would have on climate. The conclusion drawn, in 1996, from a wide scientific forum (Fig. 5.3.6 A; Azar and Rodhe 1997), was that a short-term increase in CO_2 concentration to about 400 ppm, but a decrease to 350 ppm within the next 100 years, would increase global temperature by 0.5 K compared to the last 1000 years. A temperature increase of 1 K is regarded as a critical

limit. This limit is exceeded at 450 ppm. In the year 2000 the global CO_2 concentration was ca. 375 ppm and thus 95 ppm above the pre-industrial CO_2 concentration of 280 ppm. In 1998 the temperature increase was 0.75 K, near the critical limit of 1 K. At the moment, a doubling or tripling of the pre-industrial CO_2 concentration is predicted, leading to a calculated temperature increase of 3–4 K. This is confirmed in the third report of the IPCC.

Because of the complicated interaction between oceans and atmosphere, and because weather determines irregularities in marine currents, the validity of the prediction by the IPCC, that man was able to affect global climate, were regarded sceptically for a long time. However, the predictions of the IPCC have been confirmed over time. In 1998 the average global temperature differed significantly from the trend of the last 1000 years (Fig. 5.3.6 B; Kerr 2000). The temperature increased by 0.75 K, exceeding the temperature maxima of the last 1000 years. The delay between the increase in CO_2 and temperature is caused by the heat capacity of oceans (they act as a heat sink; Levitus et al. 2000) and the melting of the polar ice caps (energy required to supply the latent heat required for melting; Robock et al. 1999). The observed global increase in temperature since 1960 is confirmed by worldwide analysis of the annual growth rings of trees (see, e.g., LaMarche et al. 1984; Vaganov et al. 1999). It has been shown that the warming of oceans since 1950 was caused by trace gases produced by human activity (Barnett et al. 2001).

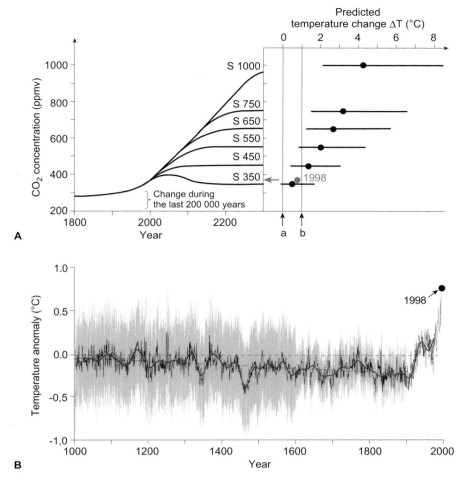

Fig. 5.3.6. A Model predicting the influence of future scenarios of higher CO_2 concentration on the average earth temperature. Shown are the scenarios used (*S 350* to *S 1000*) and on the *right* the expected changes in the average global temperature. The *vertical lines* are the average pre-industrial temperature and the critical boundary at which significant effects are expected (1 K temperature rise). Average values are shown with the uncertainties in the predictions (*vertical error bars*) as well as measured values in 1998. B Global changes in temperature since the year 1000. Long-term trends from 1000 to 1900 (*dotted line*), the running averages for 30 years (*bold line*) and 5 years (*thin black line*), and the yearly extremes (*thin red line*) and 2-sigma uncertainty in the past (yellow thin line) are given. (After Kerr 2000)

The temperature trend of the last 1000 years shows a slight but continuous decrease up to 1900. The question is whether slight, but natural, fluctuations are noticed at all by man. There are several historic events that correlate with the temperature minima. Around 1200 the last major period of forest clearance started in Europe. In the second half of the nineteenth century large numbers of people emigrated to America after the catastrophic failure of harvests. The minimum at the turn of the century followed the eruption of Krakatau in 1883. The year 1880 is often regarded as the base year of pre-industrial times.

There are indications that anthropogenic sources are no longer the sole cause, but that there is a positive feedback of the temperature increase on respiration (degradation of organic matter; Stott et al. 2000). Schimel et al. (1994) calculated from the Century Model that the global C pool in soils decreases by 11 Gt per K temperature increase (this corresponds to a decrease of soil C by about 0.5%).

The evidence that anthropogenic trace-gas emissions may lead to climate change was the basis for the Framework Convention on Climate Change (FCCC) (Benedick 2001) and the commitment to reduce CO_2 emissions in the Kyoto Protocol (WBGU 1998); see also Chapter 5.4.2.

References

Azar C, Rohde H (1997) Targets for stabilization of atmospheric CO_2. Science 276:1818–1819

Barnett TP, Pierce DW, Schnur R (2001) Detecting of anthropogenic climate change in the world's oceans. Science 292:267–279

Benedick RE (2001) Contrasting approaches: the ozone layer, climate change and resolving the Kyoto dilemma. In: Schulze E-D (ed) Global biogeochemical cycles in the climate system. Academic Press, San Diego, pp 317–331

Bengtsson L (1997) Modelling and prediction of the climate system. Alexander von Humboldt Magazine 69:3–14

Broeker WS (1997) Thermohaline circulation, the Achilles heel of our climate system: Will manmade CO_2 upset the current balance? Science 278:1582–1588

Commission of Inquiry, Federal Parliament of Germany (1992) Enquete-Kommission "Vorsorge zum Schutz der Erdatmosphäre" des Deutschen Bundestages, Müller CF (ed). Economica Verlag, Heidelberg

Dickens GR (1999) The blast in the past. Nature 401:752–753

Driscoll NW, Haug GH (1998) A short circuit in the thermohaline circulation: A cause for northern hemisphere glaciation? Science 282:436–438

Ehrlich PR, Harte J, Harwell MA, Raven PH, Sagan C, Woodwell GM, Berry J, Ayensu ES, Ehrlich AH, Eisner T, Gould JS, Grover HD, Herrera R, May RM, Mayr E, McKay CP, Mooney HA, Myers N, Pimentel D, Teal JM (1983) Long-term biological consequences of nuclear war. Science 222:1293–1300

Heimann H (1997) A review of the contemporary global carbon cycle and as sees a century ago by Arrhenius and Högbom. Ambio 26:17–24

Hurrell JW, Kushnir Y, Visbeck M (2001) The North Atlantic oscillation. Science 291:603–604

IPCC-WG I (1996) Climate change 1995; the science of climate change; contribution of Working Group I to the second assessment report of the Intergovernmental Panel on Climate Change. Cambridge University Press, Cambridge, 572 pp

Keeling RF, Piper SC, Heimann M (1996) Global and hemispheric CO_2 sinks deduced from changes in atmospheric O_2 concentration. Nature 381:218–221

Kennett JP, Cannariato KG, Hendy IL, Behl BJ (2000) Carbon isotope evidence for methane hydrate instability during Quaternary intertidals. Science 288:128–133

Kerr RA (2000) Draft report affirms human influence. Science 288:589–590

Krüger M, Frenzel P, Conrad R (2001) Microbial processes influencing methane emission from rice fields. Global Change Biol 7:49–64

LaMarche VC, Graybill DA, Fritts HC, Rose MR (1984) Increasing atmospheric carbon dioxide: tree ring evidence for growth enhancement in natural vegetation. Science 225:1019–1021

Levitus S, Antonov JI, Boyer TP, Stephens C (2000) Warming of the world's oceans. Science 287:225–229

Norris RD, Röhl U (1999) Carbon cycling and chronology of climate warming during the Palaeocene/Eocene transition. Nature 401:775–778

Rahmstorf S (1999) Shifting seas in the greenhouse. Nature 399:523–524

Robock A, Stouffer RJ, Walsh JE, Parkinson CL, Cavalier DJ, Mitchell JFB, Garrett D, Zakharov VF (1999) Global warming and northern hemisphere sea ice extent. Science 286:1934–1937

Rodwell MJ, Rowell DP, Folland CR (1999) Oceanic forcing of the wintertime North Atlantic oscillation and European climate. Nature 398:320–322

Schimel DS, Braswell BH, Holland E, McKowen R, Ojima DS, Painter TH, Parton WJ, Townsend AR (1994) Climatic, edaphic, and biotic controls over storage and turnover of carbon on soils. Global Biogeochem Cycles 8:279–293

Sestak Z, Catsky J, Jarvis PG (1971) Plant photosynthetic production. Manual of methods. Junk, The Hague, 818 pp

Stott PA, Tett SFB, Jons GS, Allen MR, Mitchell JEB, Jenkins GJ (2000) External control of 20th century temperature by natural and anthropogenic forcing. Science 290:2133–2137

Taylor AM, Jordon MB, Stephens JA (1998) Gulf stream shifts following ENSO events. Nature 393:638–639

Turco RP, Toon OB, Ackermann TP, Pollack JB, Sagan C (1983) Nuclear winter: global consequences of multiple nuclear explosion. Science 222:1283–1292

Vaganov EA, Hughes MK, Kirdyanov AV, Schweingruber FH, Silkin PP (1999) Influence of snowfall and melting time on tree growth in subarctic Eurasia. Nature 400:149–151

Veizer J, Godderis Y, Francois LM (2000) Evidence for decoupling of atmospheric CO_2 and global climate during the Phanerozoic eon. Nature 408:698–700

WBGU (1998) The accounting of biological sinks and sources under the Kyoto protocol: a step forwards or backwards for global environmental protection? German Advisory Council on Global Change (WBGU) Special Report 1998. WBGU, Bremerhaven, 75 pp

5.4

Significance of Changes in Land Use for the Global Carbon Cycle

The Middle East is considered to be the oldest farmed area on earth. Deforestation and agricultural usage over the centuries have led to the erosion of soil from slopes and to secondary deposition of fine material in valley floors. The figure shows an agricultural area near Hebron, currently in Israel. From traces of worn paths it can be seen that the slopes were grazed. Small areas on the lower slopes were used for cereal crops. Fruit trees and cereal crops could only be grown in the floor of the valley where dry stone walls separated the fields and thus prevented loss of topsoil. Barley and wheat were the predominant cereals and almonds, apricots, pomegranates and peaches the main fruit trees. Photo E.-D. Schulze

5.4.1

Land Use and CO_2 Emissions

The influence of CO_2 emissions from burning of fossil fuels on the global climate is intensified by the release of CO_2 from changes in land use (see Fig. 5.2.6). Changes in land use amount to about 20% of global CO_2 emissions – the trend is increasing. Man influences the global C balance by:

- changing forests into agricultural and grazing systems. The biomass of the forest is used as firewood or it is destroyed in slash-and-burn clearing;
- mechanical working of soils of natural grasslands and of converted forest ecosystems. Mechanical working of prairie soils leads over a period of about 50 years to a loss of about

50% of the original natural C contents (Fig. 5.4.1; Matson et al. 1997) due to decomposition of easily mineralisable C compounds. It is unclear why decomposition of soil carbon stops at 50%, despite further working. It has been shown that the black soils of steppes and prairies were formed, to a large extent, from charcoal and soot particles as a result of vegetation burning about 5000 years ago (Schmidt et al. 1999). This black carbon (BC) is resistant to decomposition, even with mechanical working. Less intensive ploughing, the so-called low tillage cultivation, leads to renewed accumulation of soil C. This is caused by accumulation of an easily decomposable humus fraction which, however, can be easily mineralised again after a change of management (deep ploughing following low tillage).

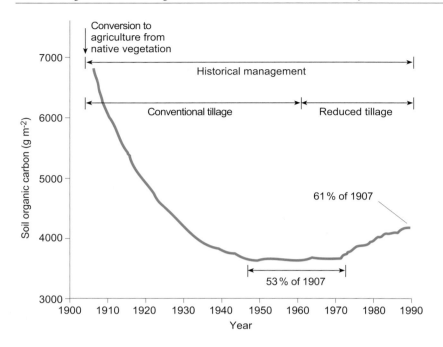

Fig. 5.4.1. Change in the carbon content of agricultural soils after the natural prairie soils were ploughed in 1900. Within 50 years the carbon content decreased to about half of the original value, then remained constant (until 1972) and then increased slightly. Recovery is related to the introduction of changes in ploughing technique, from conventional deep furrows to "reduced furrows" with a plate harrow (low-till). (After Matson et al. 1997)

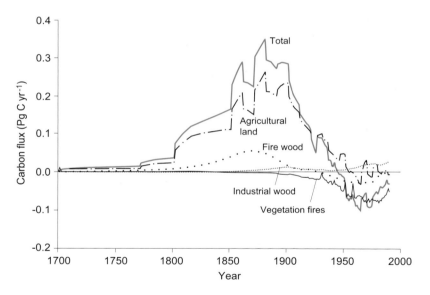

Fig. 5.4.2. Annual emission (source: positive values) and sequestration (sinks: negative values) of CO_2 in the USA from agriculture, forests and through fire. Total emissions from land use reached a maximum in 1900, subsequently they fell, and since 1950 the USA is a sink, due in great part to growth of young forests. The capacity to take up CO_2 has fallen more recently. (After Houghton et al. 1999)

The effects of changes in land use (clearing and mechanical working) on the C balance of a country was analysed, particularly in the USA, as the historical changes since the acquisition of land by European immigrants can still be reconstructed (Houghton et al. 1999). Since the acquisition of land in 1770, up to 1945, about 27×10^9 t C were released by changing grassland into agricultural land, by the use of wood for fuel and industry, as well as fire (Fig. 5.4.2; positive values characterise the flux from the land surface to the atmosphere), which was the domi-

nant factor. The highest annual loss to the atmosphere was 0.3×10^9 t C year^{-1} in 1880. Release of C decreased after the turn of the century, as most of the large-scale changes had happened by then. Since 1945 the trend is reversed. Because of fire fighting and forest successions on open, marginal agricultural areas, the USA has become a C sink (Fig. 5.4.2; negative values indicate the flow from the atmosphere to the land). The sink capacity has decreased since 1970 and was almost balanced in 1990 (compensation point for C fluxes). The maximum C fixation by

Table 5.4.1. Carbon balance between 1980 and 1989 and from 1990 until 1999 (Gt C). Negative values show a flow from the atmosphere to the land or ocean. Numbers in brackets indicate predicted values. (After Schimel et al. 2001)

	1980–1989	1990–1999
Emissions (fossil fuels and cement)	5.4 ± 0.3	6.3 ± 0.4
Increase in the atmosphere	3.3 ± 0.1	3.2 ± 0.1
Atmosphere-ocean flow	-1.9 ± 0.5	-1.7 ± 0.5
Atmosphere-land flow	-0.2 ± 0.7	-1.4 ± 0.7
Changes in emission due to land use	1.7 (0.6–2.5)	1.6 ± 0.8
Gross terrestrial sink	-1.9 (-3.8–0.3)	-3.0 (uncertain)
Net flow atmosphere-land		
North America		-0.8 (-2.1–0.1)
Eurasia		-1.7 (-2.5–0.2)
Northern hemisphere (non-tropical)		-2.4 (-4.3–1.5)
Tropical and southern hemisphere		-0.4 (-1.2–0.8)
Global		-2.8 (-4.3–1.7)

the biological sink corresponded to about 10–30% of the US oil consumption. In 2000 a net sink of -0.8 Gt year^{-1} ($+0.1$ to -2.1 Gt year^{-1} as flux from the atmosphere into vegetation) was expected for North America (USA and Canada).

Conditions in the tropics are different. Research on the effects of clearing in Brazil shows that this region is at present a C source (0.2 Gt year^{-1}). This development corresponds to the situation in the USA in the year 1850 (Houghton et al. 2000). The tropical region is, despite clearing, a sink of -0.4 Gt year^{-1} (-1.2 to 0.8; see Table 5.4.1).

5.4.2

The Kyoto Protocol: Attempts to Manage the Global Carbon Cycle

It is clear from the global processes and from their effects on climate as discussed above that it is beyond the scope of a single nation to solve the problems of climate change, loss of biodiversity, destruction of soil, etc. These questions, therefore, were presented at the United Nations Summit Meeting for Climate, Environment and Development (UNCED) in 1992 in Rio de Janeiro. Various proposals were discussed for international conventions to address these prob-

lem areas, and three important conventions were signed (Fig. 5.4.3; WBGU 2001):

- the **Framework Convention on Climate Change (FCCC)**,
- the **convention on biodiversity (CBD)**,
- the **convention to combat formation of deserts (CCD,** literally: Agreement of the United Nations to combat formation of deserts in countries heavily affected by drought and/or formation of deserts, particularly in Africa).

An international agreement to protect forests was not passed because of conflicting interests. The statement of the IPCC (1996) that "a recognisable influence of man on global climate" exists, resulted in the negotiations of the so-called **Kyoto Protocol** (1997) as part of FCCC. This protocol anticipated a legally binding obligation to reduce the emission of six greenhouse gases (CO_2, CH_4, N_2O, CFCs, PFCs, SF_6) on average by 5.2% below the level of 1990 within the period from 2008–2012. The European Union (EU) as a whole promised a reduction of 8%, Germany a reduction of 21%. This obligation to reduce emissions was carried by the 30 so-called Annex I states, i.e. industrial nations and states in transition to a market economy. The other 159 nations of the UN did not agree to such obligations. The ratification is still in progress. The United States decided not to sign the protocol.

Those areas causing global CO_2 emissions are not equally distributed across the globe (Fig. 5.4.4 A; Vitousek et al. 1997). The main sources are concentrated in the eastern USA, central Europe and eastern Asia. The anthropogenic contributions to the carbon cycle thus originate in particular groups of the 189 member states of the UN, that is the Annex I states. The same applies to N depositions (Fig. 5.4.4 B,C; WBGU 2000).

In order to achieve the reduction commitment not only by industrial activities, the Kyoto Protocol, for the first time, considers also an enhancement of biological sinks. The idea was to incorporate biological processes into the calculations, based on the fact that the obligation for a 5.2% reduction is only a fraction of the natural carbon fluxes of assimilation and respiration, and that a slight change in these fluxes would compensate, to a large extent, the obligations for reduction (see Fig. 5.2.5).

The following measures were considered in the Kyoto Protocol (Fig. 5.4.5):

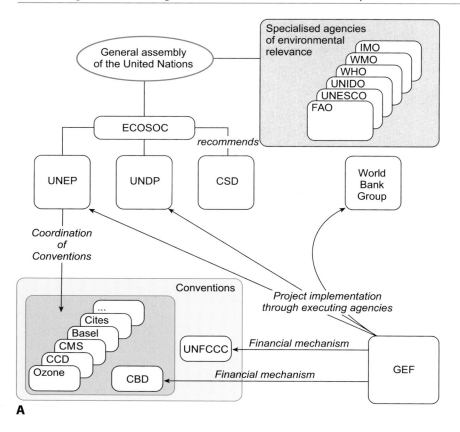

A

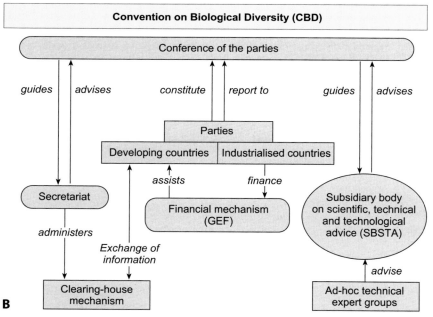

B

Fig. 5.4.3. A The environment as seen by the UN. The responsible organisations and conventions, as well as the methods of financing, are shown. *ECOSOC* United Nations Economic and Social Council; *UNEP* UN Environment Programme; *UNDP* UN Development Programme; *CSD* Commission for Sustainable Development; *IMO* International Maritime Organisation; *WMO* World Meteorological Organisation; *WHO* World Health Organisation; *UNIDO* UN Industrial Development Organisation; *UNESCO* UN Educational, Scientific and Cultural Organisation; *FAO* Food and Agricultural Organisation; *CITES* Convention on the International Trade in Endangered Species of Wild Flora and Fauna = Washington Agreement on the Protection of Species; *CMS* Convention on Migratory Species; *Basel* Basel agreement on the control of dangerous substances and their disposal across borders; *CCD* Convention on Commencement of Deserts; *UNFCCC* UN Framework Convention on Climate Change; *CBD* Convention on Biological Diversity; *GEF* Global Environment Facility. B Institutional structure of the Biodiversity Convention.

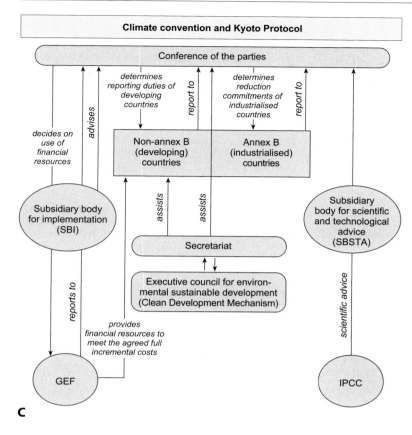

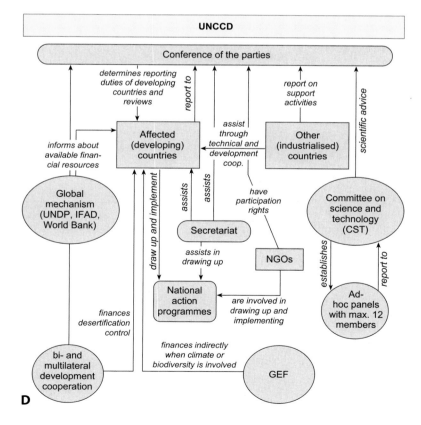

Fig. 5.4.3. C Institutional structure of the Climate Convention. D Institutional structure of the Desert Convention. (After WBGU 2001)

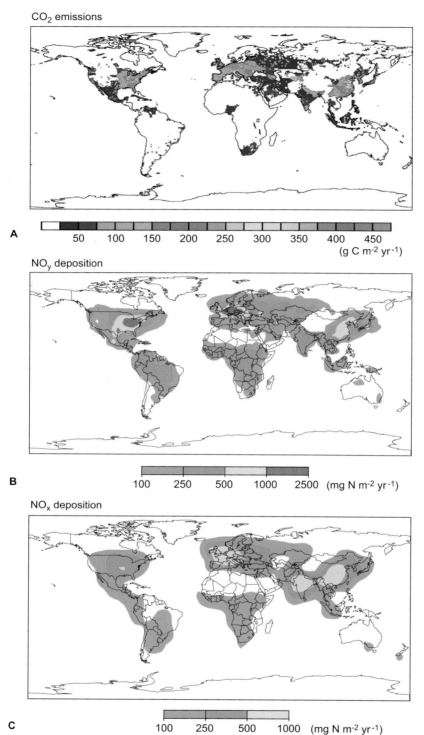

CO₂ emissions

A

50   100   150   200   250   300   350   400   450

(g C m⁻² yr⁻¹)

NO$_y$ deposition

B

100   250   500   1000   2500   (mg N m⁻² yr⁻¹)

NO$_x$ deposition

C

100   250   500   1000   (mg N m⁻² yr⁻¹)

Fig. 5.4.4. A Global distribution of CO_2 emissions. From Vitousek et al. (1997). B Global distribution of oxidised nitrogen. From WBGU (2000). C Global distribution of reduced nitrogen emissions. (After WBGU 2000)

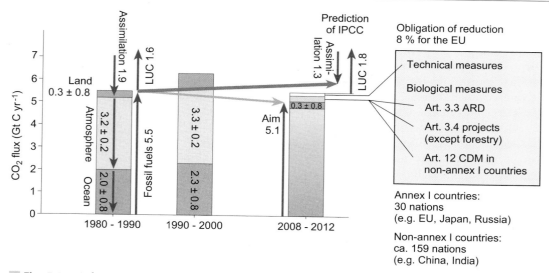

Fig. 5.4.5. *Left* Schematic representation of the global carbon sources and sinks considered important on the time scales of the Kyoto Protocol. *Right* Obligations and legal requirements of the Kyoto Protocol and nations participating in the Kyoto Protocol. *Art* Article; *ARD* afforestation, reforestation, deforestation; *CDM* clean development mechanism. The bars (*left*) show the CO_2 emissions in the years 1980–1990 and 1990–2000, as well as the planned emissions for the years 2008–2012 according to the Kyoto Protocol. The emissions are compensated via CO_2 uptake by the oceans and the land related to change in atmospheric CO_2 concentration. Net assimilation of the land is the consequence of emissions caused by land use changes (clearing, LUC) and net photosynthesis (the balance between photosynthesis and respiration at ecosystem level). The balance between net photosynthesis and emissions from land use was higher from 1990 to 2000 than between 1980 to 1990, possibly because of lower temperatures due to the eruption of Mt. Pinatubo and the effect of this on respiration. (Schulze 2000)

1. **Technical measures** to reduce emissions in the energy sector (including traffic), industry, agriculture and waste treatment;
2. **Increase biological sinks in forests** by promoting afforestation and avoiding clearing (article 3.3);
3. Introduction of **emission reducing measures (article 3.4), e.g. in agriculture.** A conference of the nations bound by the protocol decides which additional measures will be credited and the criteria and guidelines for the obligation to reduce emission. Credit for forest management has been heatedly discussed, as the Annex I nations that are rich in primary forests (Canada and Russia) do not want to be impeded in their use of boreal natural forests, and transformation of primary forests into "sustainable" plantations which are not credited. Points 1 to 3 may be introduced by one nation, either on its own or together with another Annex I state.
4. **Trade with emission certificates** between industrial nations is of particular interest to countries not able to reduce emissions in their own country compared to 1990. The trade with emission certificates is also sensible in those cases where a large decrease of

emissions may be realised with relatively simple measures (threshold countries).
5. **Projects in developing countries** to increase sinks and to reduce emission (e.g. by increasing the efficiency of energy use), the so-called **Clean Development Mechanism** (CDM, article 12), where an industrial nation finances measures for CO_2 reduction in the area of agriculture and forestry in a developing country. The resulting CO_2 reduction is credited to the industrial nation. The industrial country is awarded rights of possession in the developing nation with forestry CDM projects.

The measures proposed in the Kyoto Protocol were critically evaluated in WBGU (1998) and Schulze et al. (2002). The ecological effects were (partially) evaluated and discussed in the IPCC report on changes in land use and forestry (IPCC-LULUCF 2000). The main problems are

- The absence of protection of primary, natural forests which are not an "anthropogenic" sink and thus cannot be credited.
- The "non-credit" of forestry. Problems occur, for example, because **harvest** is not credited as emission, as in sustainable forestry management the harvest corresponds to the in-

crease of biomass in younger stands. Only changing forests into other forms of use (**deforestation**) is calculated as emission, but harvesting prior to land-use change is also not considered as source. In the same way the **change** from primary forest into a forest plantation is not a land-use change and it is thus not calculated as emission. Thus, the Kyoto Protocol contributes to the expressed promotion of anthropogenic increased forest plantations and substantially contributes to the destruction of primary forests as they have assimilation of carbon that is not anthropogenic.

- The **forest** definition (forests are stands with trees greater than 0.5 ha, 2 m in height and with 10% cover) does not protect against degradation (over-use) of forests. Emissions resulting from degradation are not accounted.
- **Support for forest plantations** with fast-growing tree species, which very often are alien to the natural flora (*Eucalyptus* plantations in Portugal, *Pinus radiata* plantations in Chile and New Zealand, etc.). In plantations only the increase in stemwood (NPP) is counted, but not the C balance of the ecosystem (NEP), which contains soil respiration, and soil C may be lost under intensive forest cultivation.
- The transfer of food and wood production to developing nations with simultaneous afforestation (which is credited) in the industrial nations (**leakage**). As areas required in developing countries are made available by clearing primary forests, this process is an emission and not a sink in the global carbon balance. A process is started which begins with the harvesting of forests, which is not credited as emission, continues to degradation (not accounted) and deforestation (e.g. by slash and burn; not accounted in developing countries) and finally degradation to *Imperata* grasslands (see Chap. 4.1), which then are reforested as plantations (credited as sink).

By not incorporating forestry and relocation of production into the developing nations, there are many possibilities for crediting additional anthropogenic sinks, but without taking emissions into account. Only with a complete global and national C balance (**full carbon accounting**, in contrast to the above-mentioned partial processes which may be credited) will it be possible to monitor the goals of protection of the climate

in the Kyoto Protocol (Steffen 1998; Schulze et al. 2002).

In the period from 1980–1990, emissions of 5.5 Gt C year^{-1} contributed to a large extent to the increased atmospheric CO_2 (Fig. 5.4.5). Net uptake by the land surface was very low in 1990, and was the result of two considerably larger partial fluxes. The CO_2 assimilation of the land surface was almost 2 Gt C year^{-1}, that is 36% of anthropogenic emissions. However, this sink capacity was compensated by forest clearing which released 1.6 Gt C year^{-1}. Basically, afforestation could be attempted or clearing could be stopped; this anthropogenic part of the reduction in emissions can be credited against the industrial emissions in the year 2010.

The reality in 1999 was quite different. Total emissions increased in 2000 to 6.3 Gt C year^{-1}. Surprisingly, the capacity of the biological sink on land doubled. However, this was not because of special human achievements in response to the Kyoto Protocol, but because of reduced respiration as a consequence of transient global cooling resulting from the eruption of Mt. Pinatubo. The increase of global sinks was a consequence of an increase in the ocean sink and not because of a change of the C uptake on the continents.

The predictions of the IPCC for 2010 are very different to those in the Kyoto Protocol (Kaisar 2000). Because developing nations are not obliged to reduce emissions, they will increasingly clear forests, in order to make available areas for the CDM measure of industrial countries. Thus Brazil plans to change 18 million ha of rainforest into agricultural areas for growing soya (Avanca-Brazil project; Bonnie et al. 2000), a goal which is strengthened by the predicted requirements for animal food in Europe as a consequence of the prohibition on use of animal meal because of BSE. This could result in C emissions of about 4.5×10^9 t C, doubling the annual increase of CO_2 in the atmosphere. This emission is not included in the calculations, as Brazil did not agree to the obligation to reduce emissions. In addition there are clearings around newly planned infrastructure and "hidden" (not recognisable on satellite pictures) changes (Nepstad et al. 1999), and the breakdown of fragmented jungle remnants (Laurance et al. 1997). The predicted fragmentation of the Amazon basin is shown in Fig. 5.4.6 A under favourable conditions (little expansion or degradation along the main infrastructure routes) and

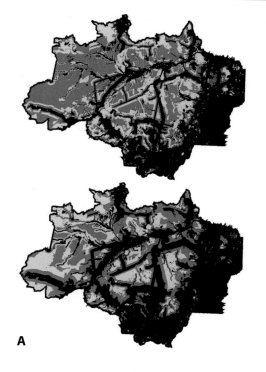

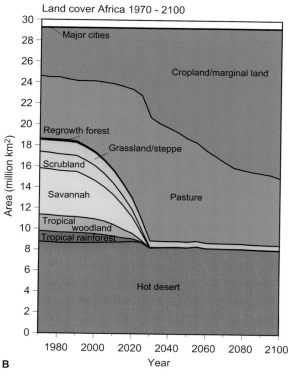

Fig. 5.4.6. A Expected changes in land use in Brazil up to 2020, calculated with optimistic (low rates of degradation along main roads) and pessimistic assumptions (increased land use along main roads). *Black* Deforested or strongly degraded; *red* degraded; *yellow* slightly degraded; *green* virgin primary forest (Laurance et al. 2001). B Changes in the land coverage of Africa from 1970 to 2100. (Leemanns, pers. comm.)

unfavourable conditions (with expansion of degradation along the routes). In any case, up to the year 2010, extensive fragmentation of the Brazilian primary forest is to be expected; in the worst scenario only a few remnants in the northeastern region of the country will remain. Similar predictions are made for Africa (Fig. 5.4.6 B), where it is predicted that the primary forest will have to make way for an extension of agricultural areas and grazing land until the year 2020 (Leemanns, pers. comm.).

It is known that agricultural areas in tropical regions cannot be managed sustainably, thus these areas will degrade (Goldammer 1999) and be offered to industrial nations, within the framework of CDM measures for afforestation, at a later date. It will take centuries for the burned and mismanaged areas until forests form a biomass corresponding to that currently seen in primary forests. However, this is not to be expected, as afforestations will be required to yield building materials, fibres and fuels as soon as possible. Therefore, there is no intention to aim at a natural succession, but to establish planta-

tions with fast-growing tree species, fertilised (turnover time for *Pinus* in Brazil is ca. 8 years) without taking into account the effects of forest fertilisation and liming on the atmosphere. The effect of N_2O emissions on climate is a factor of 310 (g g^{-1}) greater than that of CO_2; the conversion factor for CH_4 is 21. It is predicted that in 2010 the biological balance will be shifted further in the direction of CO_2 emission, i.e. the acquisition of land will exceed assimilation by about 0.5 Gt C year^{-1} (Kaisar 2000). This shows that the crediting of biological sinks within the framework of CDM measures leads to desertification of primary forests and to release of corresponding amounts of CO_2, with subsequent afforestation being very unlikely as long as the developing countries are not obliged to make any reductions in CO_2. Fertilisation of plantations and the N_2O emissions shift the CO_2 equivalent balance further in the direction of increased emissions. Effects on biological diversity are not even considered. Obviously, the implementation of the Kyoto Protocol is difficult because there are so many possible interpretations of what

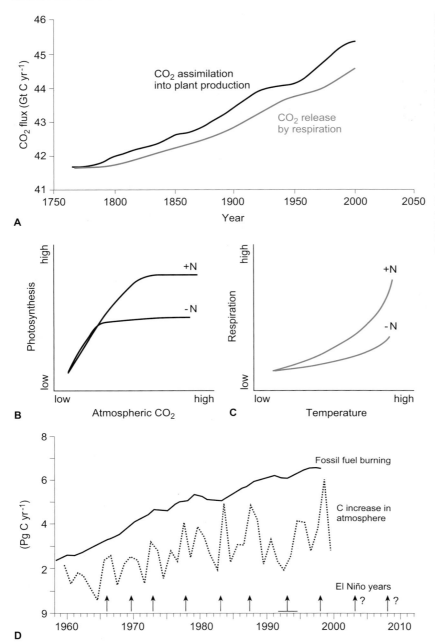

Fig. 5.4.7. A Large-scale change in CO_2 assimilation and respiration since 1750 (from Melillo et al. 1996). Schematic representations of B photosynthetic dependence on CO_2 concentration, C respiration and temperature, D trend in fossil fuel use since 1958 and annual increase in atmospheric CO_2 concentration. Annual changes in the atmosphere are controlled by the equilibrium between photosynthesis and ecosystem respiration (IPCC-WG 1 2001). The *arrow* on the *x*-axis shows the El-Niño event. The *horizontal line* over the *x*-axis shows when Mt. Pinatubo erupted. The area between the two lines represents the global carbon sink

constitutes a sink that might be taken into account, that emissions are covered (see Chap. 3, Fig. 3.3.9). This became obvious during negotiations in Den Haag (Töpfer 2001) and Bonn (Schulze et al. 2002).

Carbon emissions in the EU_{15} were 0.905 Gt in 1990. With Norway, Switzerland and the new countries entering the EU the rates of emission will increase in the year 1990 to 1.325 Gt (Germany 0.275 Gt = 30% of the emission of EU_{15}). In 1999, C emissions in the EU_{15} were 0.892 Gt

(−1.5%). The C emissions in Germany decreased in 1998 to 0.239 Gt (−13%).

As the turnover of carbon in the different soil layers requires time, and a large number of soil organisms are involved in humus formation, carbon assimilation precedes decomposition (Fig. 5.4.7 A; Melillo et al. 1996). At the moment, plant production increases because of increased CO_2 concentration but decomposition is delayed by about 30 years. This could change in the future, as photosynthesis may reach saturation with increasing CO_2 concentration (Fig. 5.4.7 B). In contrast, decomposition of material by respiration will be stimulated by increasing temperatures and litter fall (Fig. 5.4.7 C; see also Chap. 3.2.3). This means that plant production not only fluctuates considerably from year to year (Knapp and Smith 2001), but also that terrestrial ecosystems which are still a C sink at present CO_2 concentration and temperature may become a C source in the future. These differential responses of assimilation and respiration may lead to a self-perpetuating increase in temperature in the predictions by Stott et al. (2000).

The importance of respiration for the global CO_2 balance becomes obvious when the increase of atmospheric CO_2 concentration is considered (Fig. 5.4.7 D). There are years with considerable increase in CO_2, followed closely by years with smaller increases. These fluctuations are apparently caused by changes in the ratio of respiration plus fire to assimilation. Years of El Niño events stand out, with very high CO_2 emissions. In 1998 the increase in CO_2 concentration in the atmosphere corresponded to the total consumption of fossil fuels, i.e. in the net balance, continents and oceans did not take up CO_2. The year 1990 is interesting regarding the Kyoto Protocol, as there was no El Niño and the increase in CO_2 concentration was low, i.e. the earth surface was a significant sink.

The Kyoto Protocol is obviously interested in a balance of environmental interests (reduction of emissions) and economic interests (use of primary forests and conversion in plantations). Therefore, the interests of the participating nations in this agreement are important. If the countries are subdivided according to their per head income and the per head forest area (Maini 2000; Schulze 2000), then there is no conflict between Annex I and non-Annex I countries, but there is conflict between forest-rich and forest-poor countries. In countries with high income and large forest area, the concern is sustainable development of the economy, independent of protection of the atmosphere. In countries with low income and large forest area, the use of the primary forest is directly for economic development. Forest-poor countries with low income are dependent on wood imports from forest-rich countries and thus are against protection of forests. There are other countries with high incomes and moderate forest areas that support protection of forests almost in isolation.

From 1989–1998, emissions from burning fossil fuels were on average 6.3×10^9 t year^{-1} and the net sink provided by the continents (considering the emissions from changes of land use) was -1.7×10^9 t year^{-1}. If the intention was to balance the total obligations for reduction (5.2% of emissions) by increasing the biological sink then the existing net sink of 0.7 Gt year^{-1} would have to be increased by 0.33 Gt year^{-1} by 2010, an increase of 47%. This appears impossible at present. Furthermore, the third IPCC report (Prentice et al. 2001) shows that with afforestation of all areas which have been cleared by man until now, the CO_2 concentrations in the atmosphere would only be decreased in 2010 by 40 ppm, whilst clearing the existing primary forests would increase the CO_2 concentration by about 200–400 ppm.

Independent of attempts to manage the carbon balance, there are also "futuristic" concepts for the technical removal of CO_2 (Keith 2001; Schneider 2001). These include placement of aerosols and reflectors in the stratosphere, so decreasing the net energy load on the earth, or sequestration of CO_2 by storage in deep layers of the ocean or in rocks.

5.4.3

Importance of Climate Change for Europe

A prediction of the effects of an increase in climate-effective trace gases (CO_2, N_2O, CH_4 and others) is only possible using model calculations based on certain "scenarios" of their increase (see Fig. 5.3.6 A) and by coupling land, ocean and atmosphere processes to develop understanding of how the climate develops and changes. For Europe, such a model calculation (Parry 2000) has been made with the lower limit of CO_2 increase assumed to be 490 ppm and the upper limit to be 570 ppm in 2100. Since 1970 Europe has warmed up between 0.1 and 0.4 K per decade. It has been shown that the probability of a cold winter (one in 10 years) in northern Scandinavia would decrease to 0% by 2080. At the same time, the probability of a warm summer in northern and central Europe will decrease. However, the probability of a hot summer will increase in southern Europe. These temperature predictions show an increased effect of the Gulf Stream on Europe, with a change in precipitation as an immediate consequence. According to these predictions the Atlantic coast and northeast of Europe will become more humid, but central and southern Europe will become drier.

The predictions may be summarised as follows:

- warming will be greatest across north-eastern and southern Europe. Warming particularly affects winter temperatures (European Russia +0.15 to 0.6 K per decade). The warming in summer is less (0.08 to 0.3 K per decade for central Europe, 0.2 to 0.6 K for southern Europe). The probability that this warming will be a "natural trend" is 5%.
- precipitation is predicted to increase by 1–2% per decade in northern Europe and by 1% per decade in southern Europe. These changes are, to a large extent, within the range of natural variability. Winters will become moister and summers will show a steeper gradient between northern and southern Europe.

For land use in Europe the consequences will be:

- current differences in the water supply between northern und southern Europe will increase. This applies to extreme droughts as well as to an increased tendency of flooding in southern Europe.
- warming of northern Europe will have significant effects on soils (decomposition of humus), with the tree limit of conifers and deciduous species expanding northwards. The frequency of fires in southern Europe will increase.
- the NPP of managed forests in northern Europe will increase but decrease in southern Europe. Yields of agricultural crops are predicted to increase in northern Europe, in southern Europe the increasing drought will limit yields.
- several socio-economic consequences will occur because of the predicted increased gradient between northern and southern Europe. These include changes in the energy sector, changes in tourism (it will be too hot in southern Europe) and changes in the distribution of diseases.

References

Bonnie R, Schwartzmann S, Oppenheimer M, Bloomfield J (2000) Counting the cost of deforestation. Science 288:1763–1764

Goldammer G (1999) Forests on fire. Science 284:1782–1783

Houghton RA, Hackler JL, Lawrence KT (1999) The US carbon budget: contributions from land use change. Science 285:574–578

Houghton RA, Skole DL, Nohre CA, Hackler IL, Lawrence KT, Chomentowski WH (2000) Annual fluxes of carbon from deforestation and regrowth in the Brazilian Amazon. Nature 403:301–304

IPCC-LULUCF (2000) Special report on land use, land use change and forestry (IPCC-XVI/Doc. 2). IPCC-Sekretariat der WMO, Genf

IPCC (1996) Climate change 1995. Second assessment report. Cambridge University Press, Cambridge

Kaisar J (2000) Panel estimates possible carbon 'sinks'. Science 288:942–943

Keith DW (2001) Geoengineering. Nature 409:420

Knapp AK, Smith MD (2001) Variation among biomes in temporal dynamics of aboveground production. Science 291:481–484

Kyoto Protocol (1997) Kyoto Protocol to the United Nations Framework Convention on Climate Change FCCC/CP/1997/Add. 1. Decision 1/CP 3, Annex 7

Laurance WF, Laurance SG, Ferreira LV, Rankin-de Merona JM, Gascon C, Lovejoy TE (1997) Biomass collapse in Amazonian forest fragments. Science 278:1117–1118

Laurance WF, Cochrane MA, Bergen S, Fearnside PM, Dalamonica P, Barber C, D'Angelo S, Fernandes T (2001) The future of the Brazilian Amazon. Science 291:438–439

Maini JS (2000) Boreal forests: social, economic and environmental considerations. In: The role of boreal forests and forestry in the global carbon budget. Edmonton, May 8 to 12, 2000, Abstracts

Matson PA, Parton WJ, Power WJ, Swift MJ (1997) Agricultural intensification and ecosystem properties. Science 277:504–508

Melillo JM, Prentice IC, Farquhar GD, Schulze E-D, Sala OE (1996) Terrestrial biotic responses to environmental change and feedbacks to climate. In: IPCC, Climate change 1995. The science of climate change. Cambridge University Press, Cambridge, pp 445–482

Nepstad DC, Verissimo A, Alencar A, Nobre C, Lima E, Lefebvre P, Schlesinger P, Potter C, Moutinho P, Mendoza E, Cochrane M, Brooks V (1999) Large-scale impoverishment of Amazonian forests by logging and fire. Nature 398:505–508

Parry M (2000) Assessment of potential effects and adaptations for climate change in Europe. The Europe ACACIA Report. Jackson Environment Institute, University of East Anglia, Norwich, UK, 320 pp

Prentice IC, Farquhar GD, Fasham MJR, Goulden ML, Heimann M, Jaramillo VJ, Kheshi HS, Le Quéré C, Scholes RJ, Wallace DWR (2001) The carbon cycle and atmospheric CO_2. In: IPCC-WG I third assessment report. Cambridge University Press, Cambridge

Schimel DS, House JI, Hibbard KA, Bousquet P, Ciais P, Peylin P, Braswell BH, Apps MJ, Baker D, Bondeau A, Canadell J, Chukina G, Cramer W, Denning AS, Field CB, Friedlingstein P, Goodale C, Heimann M, Houghton RA, Melillo JM, Moore B III, Murdiyarso D, Noble I, Pacala SW, Prentice IC, Raupach MR, Rayner JP, Scholes RJ, Steffen WL, Wirth C (2001) Recent patterns and mechanisms of carbon exchange by terrestrial ecosystems. Nature 414:169–172

Schmidt MWI, Skjemstad JO, Gehrt E, Kögel-Knabner I (1999) Charred organic carbon in German chernozemic soils. Eur J Soil Sci 50:351–365

Schneider SH (2001) Earth systems: engineering and management. Nature 409:417–421

Schulze E-D (2000) Der Einfluß des Menschen auf die biogeochemischen Kreisläufe der Erde. Max-Planck-Gesellschaft. Jahrbuch 2000, pp 39–58

Schulze E-D, Valentini R, Sanz M-J (2002) The long way from Kyoto to Marrakesh: implications of the Kyoto protocol negotiations for global ecology. Global Change Biol 8:505–518

Steffen W (1998) The terrestrial carbon cycle: implications for the Kyoto protocol. The IGBP Terrestrial Carbon Working Group. Science 280:1393–1394

Stott PA, Tett SFB, Jons GS, Allen MR, Mitchell JFB, Jenkins GJ (2000) External control of 20th century temperature by natural and anthropogenic forcing. Science 290:2133–2137

Töpfer K (2001) Climate change: whither after The Hague? Science 291:2095–2097

Vitousek PM, Mooney HA, Lubchenco J, Melillo JM (1997) Human domination of earth's ecosystems. Science 277:494–499

WBGU (1998) The accounting of biological sinks and sources under the Kyoto Protocol: a step forward or backwards for global environmental protection? German Advisory Council on Global Change (WBGU). Special Report 1998. WBGU, Bremerhaven, 76 pp

WBGU (2000) World in transition: strategies for managing global environmental risks. German Advisory Council on Global Change (WBGU). Springer, Berlin Heidelberg New York, 359 pp

WBGU (2001) World in transition: new structures for global environmental policy. German Advisory Council on Global Change (WBGU). Earthscan, London, 211 pp

Influence of Human Activities on Biodiversity

Deserts are by no means places of low biological diversity; however, the majority of the plants occur as seeds in the soil (soil seed bank). After periodic, or often very occasional, rain a proportion of the seeds germinate. Germination is species-specific and variable, depending on temperature, intensity of rain and light conditions, etc. Hence the flora changes every time it rains. The photograph shows sand dunes in Harsi Fehl in southern Algeria. Photo E.-D. Schulze

5.5.1

Decrease in Biodiversity

Managing C sinks brings a conflict between the Climate Convention and the Biodiversity Convention, as the Kyoto Protocol explicitly avoids the protection of existing C storage in primary forests and aims at the establishment of plantations with low biomass, but high productivity (NPP), on cleared areas.

In Chapter 4 a detailed case is made that biodiversity means more than diversity of species. Despite this, diversity of species is the only parameter available for an assessment of the situation at global scale. Considering the world map of plant distribution (see also Chap. 4.1), there are 25 so-called **hot spots** (Fig. 5.5.1) – regions with very high diversity and **genetic centres** of crop plants, and they only partially overlap. Originally, these hot spots covered about 12% of the earth's surface. Including the genetic centres, both cover about 20% of the earth's surface. Currently, about 1.1 billion people live on the original

area of the hot spots (Cincotta et al. 2000); together with forestry industries and changes in land use they have decreased these areas to about 1.4% of the earth's surface. If it were possible to protect these residual spaces at present, it would be possible to protect 44% of all plant species, as well as 35% of birds, mammals, reptiles and amphibians. Whether this will succeed depends essentially on ecologists and their ability to bring together diversity and ecosystem research (Schulze and Mooney 1993), i.e. to create a bond between the Kyoto Protocol and the Biodiversity Convention.

The decline in species has several causes (Fig. 5.5.2 A; Schulze and Gerstberger 1993). For Germany, the changes in management of agriculture and forestry are responsible for 50% of the decline in species. The remaining 50% is due to changes in land use (tourism, mining, industry, infrastructure). Some species are also endangered because of scientific research, and from collectors.

In the German flora, orchids are particularly protected, but despite this the distribution of all

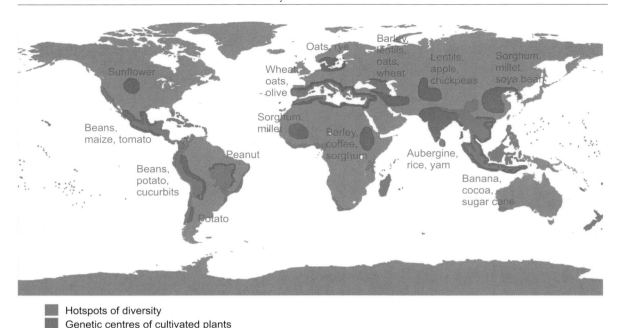

Hotspots of diversity
Genetic centres of cultivated plants

Fig. 5.5.1. Global distribution of the so-called diversity hot spots (Meyers et al. 2000) and the genetic origins of economically important plants (Reid and Miller 1989), with an indication of the most important crop plants

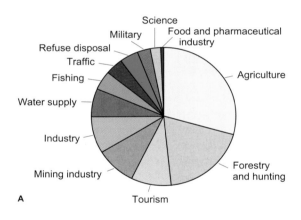

A

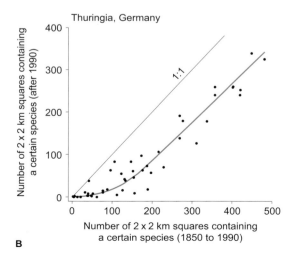

B

orchid species has significantly decreased (Fig. 5.5.2B). Species covering less than 100 grid cells (2×2 km) at the beginning of the last century are now almost extinct (2000 A.D.), showing the limitations of methods of protection, and also how relatively rare species assume a particular and important indicator function, to illustrate the effects of global change.

The effect of intensified and extended agriculture on the diversity of species can be seen worldwide. It is a direct consequence of increasing populations as well as of changes in food habits, including increased meat consumption which requires more animal feed (only 5% of N eaten by animals is converted into meat). Despite all attempts to increase agricultural production, cereal production per head of the world population (Fig. 5.5.3 A; WBGU 1999) is decreasing at present. With increasing scarcity of food, the scope for reduction of agricultural expansion is very limited, as is the scope for the stabilisation and protection of climate, and also for the

Fig. 5.5.2. A Anthropogenic factors that led to extinction of species in Germany (from Schulze and Gerstberger 1993). B Distribution of species of orchids in Thuringia, Germany, before 1990 (observed since 1900) compared to the period after 1990. All species showed a decline in distribution in about 150 grid cells (2×2 km). Each *dot* represents a species of orchid

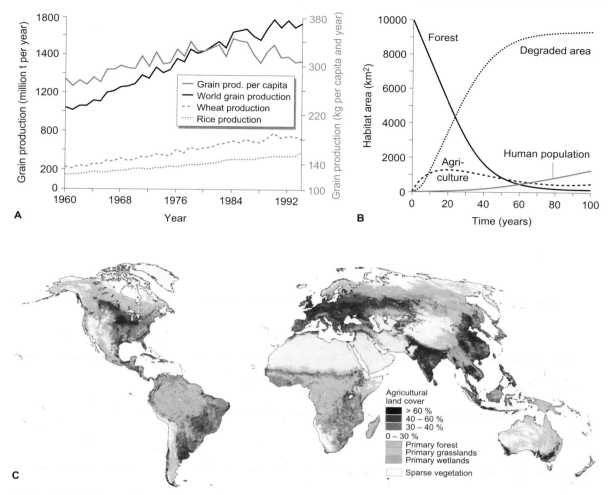

Fig. 5.5.3. A Changes in cereal production since 1960 (WBGU 1999). B A model of dynamic land use and human population on an area of 10,000 km² with an initial population of 50 people. The significant decrease in forest corresponds to the increase in degraded land and a slight decrease in the land available for agriculture is important (after Dobson et al. 1997). C Global distribution of agricultural land, both farmed and grazed. (World Resource Institute 2001)

protection of species. The estimated area of land suitable for agricultural use on earth is between 1.5×10^9 ha (used in 1990) and 4×10^9 ha (WBGU 2001). In 2001 a total of about 3.6×10^9 ha were used for agriculture (1.5×10^9) and for managed grazing (about 27% of the global land surface excluding Greenland and the Antarctic). Agricultural areas (Fig. 5.5.3 B) are concentrated in the temperate zones in the northern and southern hemisphere, India, southeast Asia and southeast Brazil. Large, extensively used regions are the Congo Basin and the Amazon. With steady yields and increasing population the potential agriculturally usable land may not be sufficient to feed humanity in the future. If the agricultural area were to remain constant, yield per area would have to increase by the year

2050 by a factor of 4. The increasing requirement for agriculturally usable land becomes clear from the changes in land use in Africa and South America (see Fig. 5.4.6).

According to model calculations, it is improbable that the estimated maximum agricultural area of 4×10^9 ha will ever be usable at any one time, as erosion, salination, acidification of soils and other factors will result in a degradation of parts of the area (Fig. 5.5.3 B; Dobson et al. 1997). Obviously, long-term sustainability is not achieved in agriculture. Man continuously wastes land for food production. With degradation, agricultural production has to be relocated to other land and permanently new arable land will be required in order to keep the existing useable agricultural land area constant. Expansion and compensation for degradation by agriculture occur primarily at the cost of forests, with the fully degraded areas having the potential to be reforested. This would be good for biodiversity if reforestation is not with fast-growing forest plantations (*Eucalyptus, Pinus* spp.), which are generally monocultures. By implementing the Kyoto Protocol, the probability increases that these degraded areas will never return to a "semi-natural" condition of high biodiversity.

| **Box 5.5.1** | **Convention on Biological Diversity, CBD** |

The Convention on Biological Diversity was signed in 1992 in Rio de Janeiro, and was implemented in 1993; 160 of the 189 countries of the UN are signatories. This is an interdisciplinary convention (see Fig. 5.4.3; WBGU 1999) the goal of which was not only to maintain biological diversity, but also to sustain development and the equity of uses and advantages (Fig. 5.5.4). From this diverse focus and from the all-encompassing starting position stem the conflicts of the dual goals of protection and use, especially at the margins of agriculture and forestry. The convention also clarified the legal principles related to the use of genetic resources; these are no longer a collective property that all have access to but are property of nations. Thus the interests of industries, the rights of local and indigenous peoples with their traditional knowledge, and the sovereignty of the nations have been brought together. The use of biotechnology (Biosafety) was added as an appendix in 1999. After terrestrial genetic resources belong to sovereign nations, only the sea remains as a collective resource. It is still unclear whether the transfer of the ownership of genetic resources also carries with it the responsibility of nations to maintain them for humanity.

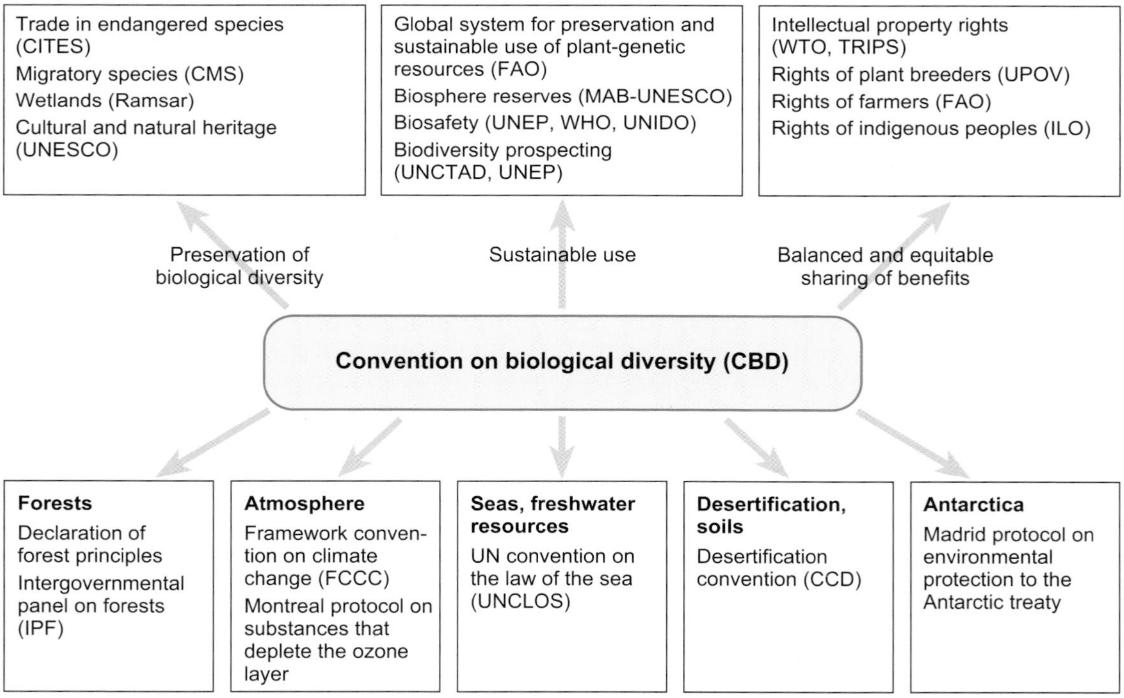

Trade in endangered species (CITES) Migratory species (CMS) Wetlands (Ramsar) Cultural and natural heritage (UNESCO)	Global system for preservation and sustainable use of plant-genetic resources (FAO) Biosphere reserves (MAB-UNESCO) Biosafety (UNEP, WHO, UNIDO) Biodiversity prospecting (UNCTAD, UNEP)	Intellectual property rights (WTO, TRIPS) Rights of plant breeders (UPOV) Rights of farmers (FAO) Rights of indigenous peoples (ILO)
Preservation of biological diversity	Sustainable use	Balanced and equitable sharing of benefits

Convention on biological diversity (CBD)

Forests Declaration of forest principles Intergovernmental panel on forests (IPF)	**Atmosphere** Framework convention on climate change (FCCC) Montreal protocol on substances that deplete the ozone layer	**Seas, freshwater resources** UN convention on the law of the sea (UNCLOS)	**Desertification, soils** Desertification convention (CCD)	**Antarctica** Madrid protocol on environmental protection to the Antarctic treaty

Fig. 5.5.4. Integration of the Biodiversity Convention into environmental politics. (WBGU 1999)

References

Cincotta RP, Wisnewski J, Engelmann R (2000) Human populations in the biodiversity hotspots. Nature 404:990–992

Dobson AP, Bradshaw AD, Baker AJM (1997) Hopes for the future: restoration ecology and conservation biology. Science 277:515–522

Reid WV, Miller KR (1989) Keeping options alive: the scientific basis for conserving biodiversity. World Resource Institute, Washington, 128 pp

Schulze E-D, Gerstberger P (1993) Functional aspects of landscape diversity: a Bavarian example. Ecological studies, vol 99. Springer, Berlin Heidelberg New York, pp 453–466

Schulze E-D, Mooney HA (1993) Biodiversity and ecosystem function. Ecological studies, vol 99. Springer, Berlin Heidelberg New York, 525 pp

WBGU (1999) World in transition: Ways towards sustainable management of fresh water. German Advisory Council on Global Change (WBGU). Springer, Berlin Heidelberg New York, 392 pp

WBGU (2001) World in transition: conservation and sustainable use of the biosphere. German Advisory Council on Global Change (WBGU). Earthscan, London, 451 pp

World Resource Institute (2001) World Resources 2000–2001. People and ecosystems; the fraying web of life. World Resource Institute, Washington, 389 pp

5.6

Socio-economic Interactions

Increased agricultural production was only possible by breeding high-yielding crops. Despite concentration on a few, especially productive, crops it is necessary to maintain diversity, in order to maintain resistance to plant diseases in the high-yielding crops. This resistance is the result of cross-breeding with wild varieties. Genetic material for the maintenance of crop plants is held by international breeding institutes which collect and keep them. So the International Crop Research Institute for the Semi-arid Tropics, ICRISAT, Patancheru, near Hyderabad, India, is responsible for maintenance and breeding of pulses and has played an important part in the "green revolution". The picture shows (*above*) the experimental fields of chickpea (*Cicer arietinum*). Breeding high-yielding types does not necessarily lead to sustainable agriculture. More often exploitation and "dust bowls" are observed, indicating over-use of natural resources. The photograph shows (*below*) a dust storm in the wheat area near Adelaide, south-western Australia. The original grass-eucalyptus vegetation has been completely destroyed and the soil is bare of vegetation for almost half a year, when summer wheat is sown. Photo E.-D. Schulze

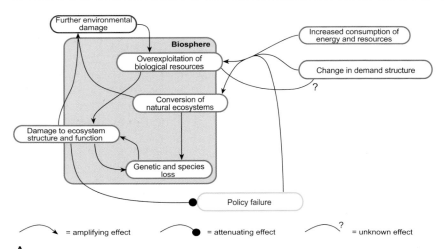

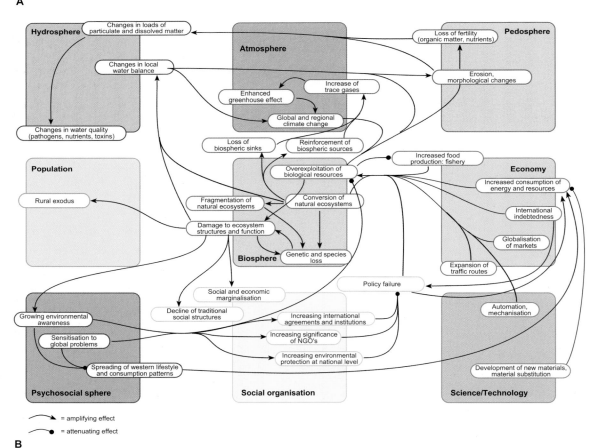

Fig. 5.6.1. A Global trends affecting bio-geochemical events in the hydro-, atmo-, pedo- and biospheres. Also, socio-economic factors such as population size, economic, psycho-social spheres and scientific/technical effects which change the global trends are indicated (WBGU 2001). B Example of a systems analysis of the exploitation syndrome. (WBGU 2001)

5.6.1

Syndromes

Previous considerations of C balance show that it is no longer possible to explain and predict global changes on a natural science basis only

(see Fig. 5.1.1, socio-economic feedback; see also Chapin et al. 2000).

To show the interactions with human activities more clearly, the so-called **syndrome concept** was developed. It is based on the view that there are global trends (WBGU 2000), arising from socio-economic as well as edaphic-climatic

Box 5.6.1	List of the syndrome groups as symptoms of global change (for further information, see WBGU 1993)

1. Syndrome group "use"

- agricultural over-production in marginal areas: Sahel Syndrome;
- exploitation of natural ecosystems: Exploitation Syndrome;
- environmental degradation due to abandonment of traditional land use: Flight from the Land Syndrome;
- non-sustainable management of soil and water: Dust Bowl Syndrome;
- environmental degradation from use of non-renewable resources: Katanga Syndrome;
- containment and damage of natural spaces for recreation activities: Mass Tourism Syndrome;
- environmental damage due to military use: Burnt Earth Syndrome.

2. Syndrome group "development"

- environmental damage through mismanaged or unfinished, central government large-scale "projects": Aral Sea Syndrome;
- environmental and development problems through adoption of agricultural management regimes inappropriate to that situation. Green Revolution Syndrome;
- neglect of ecological standards during high economic growth: Small Tiger Syndrome;
- environmental degradation by unregulated urbanisation: Favela Syndrome;
- environmental degradation by planned expansion of towns and industries: *Suburbia* Syndrome;
- individual or localised anthropogenic environmental catastrophes from towns and infrastructure: Havarie Syndrome.

3. Syndrome group "sinks"

- environmental degradation due to large-scale, diffuse distribution of mostly long-lived active substances: High Chimney Syndrome;
- environmental use of controlled and uncontrolled dumping of refuse: Rubbish Dump Syndrome;
- local contamination of environments particularly by industrial sites: Brown Field Syndrome.

factors, which interact in various ways, i.e. they are not independent, but strengthen or weaken each other, and both influence land surface, land use and vegetation. Resulting from this are the so-called **interaction links** (Fig. 5.6.1 A, B; WBGU 2000), changing to "symptoms" or even **syndromes**, in certain circumstances. The syndrome concept thus considers the highly complicated dynamics of man–environment interaction between biosphere, atmosphere, pedosphere and hydrosphere, on the one hand, and economy, population, organisation of societies and psycho-social spheres, as well as science and technology, on the other.

In the following, the distribution of some global syndromes will be described to show that ecology alone will no longer be able to protect natural ecosystems, but that ecology is confronted with land use and over-use of biological resources everywhere on the globe. The essential element of anthropogenic changes in the biosphere is rooted in the socio-economic sphere.

The **Green Revolution** is an example of a syndrome occurring on large areas with direct effects on the ecological situation of a country (Fig. 5.6.2 A; WBGU 1998). The Green Revolution Syndrome describes the rapid modernisation of agriculture with imported, non-adapted agricultural technology over large areas, planned by the nation. Any negative side effects on the natural conditions of production or social structure over large areas are tolerated. In the first stage (1965–1975), the green revolution was effective in combating hunger and achieved the independence of nations from food imports by intensifying agriculture on their own territory. Growing crop plants twice a year led to new employment opportunities; however, these were lost again, because of increasing mechanisation. The decline in traditional agriculture was welcomed as a sign of progress. The high energy consumption linked to the green revolution played no major role at first because of low energy prices. The "oil crises" of the 1970s marked the end of

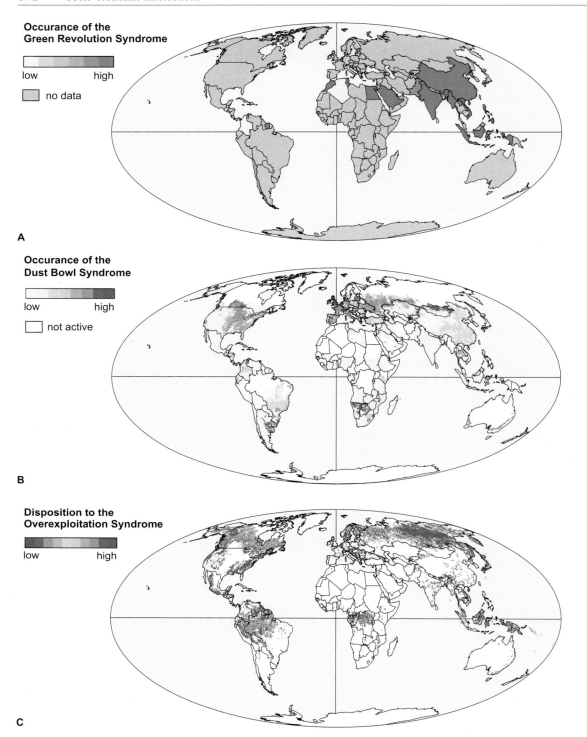

Occurance of the Green Revolution Syndrome

low   high

no data

A

Occurance of the Dust Bowl Syndrome

low   high

not active

B

Disposition to the Overexploitation Syndrome

low   high

C

Fig. 5.6.2. Global distribution of A the Green Revolution (WBGU 1999), B the Dust Bowl Syndrome (WBGU 2000), and C the Exploitation Syndrome. (WBGU 2001)

the first phase. In the second stage (1975–1985), negative feedbacks came to the fore. Cultivation of cereals was expanded to climatically and edaphically unfavourable sites, and thus the expected yields were no longer achieved or maintained. The sensitivity of high-yielding varieties to pests and climatic extremes required additional intensification of pest control and irrigation. With decreasing water resources soils became increasingly saline and erosion was an additional consequence. Increasing mechanisation made manual workers increasingly redundant. Feudal power and land holdings resulted in production aimed at export of agricultural products and not at feeding the local population, and increased the trend. This led to the third phase (since the mid-1980s) characterised by food production stagnating or declining. Continued intensification of production (fertilisation, irrigation, pesticides) caused over-exploitation of soils. Resulting from the Green Revolution the Sahel Syndrome developed over time (agricultural over-use); the Fevala Syndrome (uncontrolled urbanisation), the Dust Bowl Syndrome (unsustainable land use) and the Aral Sea Syndrome (mismanaged large projects) followed.

The **Dust Bowl Syndrome** (Fig. 5.6.2 B; WBGU 2000) relates to consequences in the natural environment resulting from industrialised, non-sustainable agriculture. The breadth of damage ranges from a change in hydrological conditions, to eutrophication and contamination of surface and groundwater reservoirs, and to losses of biodiversity, as well as to accumulation of pesticides in the food chain (with subsequent health damage), and emission of greenhouse gases (e.g. N_2O). The Dust Bowl Syndrome occurs in industrialised as well as developing countries. Typical for the Dust Bowl Syndrome are intensified agriculture with high-yielding varieties, fertilisation, irrigation and use of pesticides, and increased emission of methane from animal husbandry, as well as increased degradation of soils.

The **Exploitation Syndrome** takes a similar direction to the Dust Bowl Syndrome and the Green Revolution, but this syndrome is not only related to agriculture, but also to forestry (Fig. 5.6.2 C; WBGU 2000). The essential characteristic is a discrepancy between the use of natural resources and their natural regeneration. Overuse leads to damage of managed systems, e.g. by soil compaction, erosion, acidification and salination. The exploited region is not regenerated,

rather the next region is exploited. This applies particularly to the use of primary forests. Exploitation is one of the most widespread syndromes covering the largest area. In the tropics it is the conversion of pristine ecosystems into agriculture, whilst in temperate and boreal climates degradation of ecosystems predominates (Fig. 5.6.3; WBGU 2000).

5.6.2

Evaluation of Risks to Biodiversity in Ecosystems

The declining number of species, the necessity to grow agricultural crops and the future aim to use the entire biosphere to compensate for human activities (protection of climate C sinks) requires careful differentiation between divergent aims. From an economic point of view, the problem of sustainable land use is often seen as a conflict between the economic interest for use (particularly of biomass production) and the required protection of the biosphere. The conflict may be solved despite the conflict with economy, as in many cases it is possible to develop protective measures and gradual differences exist. Different types of use exist:

- **protection from use:** This refers to landscape with particular value regarding environmental aspects. These are unique ecosystems (e.g. World Heritage Sites) or regionally important ecosystems needing protection from unlimited economic use (protected forests). Thus, the interest of environmental protection outweighs the economic value. The WBGU (2001) recommends that 10–20% of the earth's surface should be in this category. In 2004, 11% of the land surface was protected.

- **protection despite use:** In this case, exploitation (agriculture, mass tourism) outweighs other considerations. The introduction of environmental protective measures would bring great economic costs from not using the important economic development potential. Nevertheless, even in these intensively used areas, basic principles of environmentally friendly use need to be applied. Winter sport in the Alps and tourism in the Mediterranean region demonstrate that this does not always succeed and it is often too late when long-term consequences are recognised. Observa-

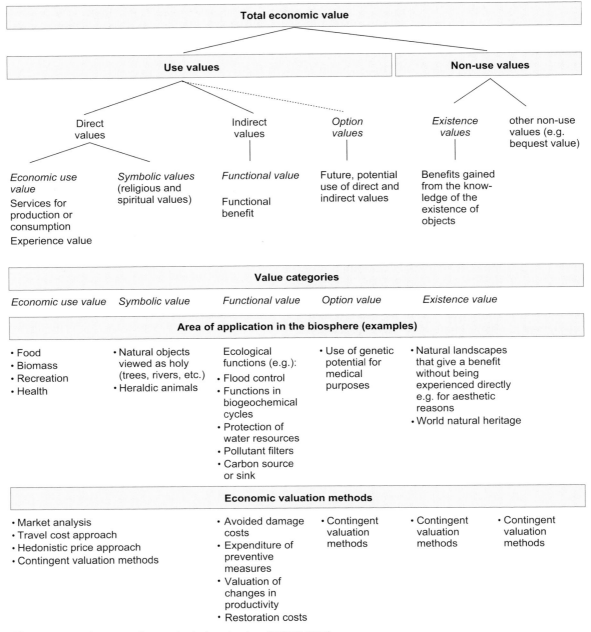

Fig. 5.6.3. Schematic of an ecological evaluation. (WBGU 2001)

tions in national parks in developing countries show an increasing degradation of these protected areas by illegal use (Liu et al. 2001).

- **protection by use:** This type of landscape is characterised by acceptance of a degree of human intervention, but the economic exploitation is limited (e.g. to maintain soils of medium fertility). Thus it is possible to satisfy both needs by natural and infrastructural measures (e.g. targeted tourism in national parks). With regard to protection of species, protection by use may lead to better sustainability than protection from use.

In the final evaluation of which economic and ecological aims to pursue, it is necessary to also estimate the value of the biosphere (Fig. 5.6.3). The economic evaluation is as follows:

1. Identification of output and services from the biosphere, i.e. economic relevant functions.

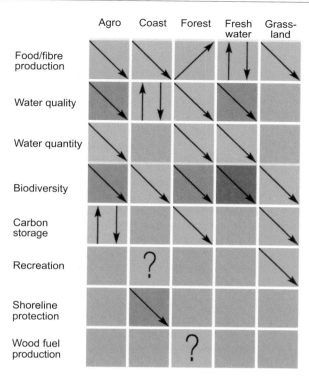

Fig. 5.6.4. Trends in the last 20–30 years in the situation of particular ecosystem "functions" in different biomes. (World Resources Institute 2001)

Condition

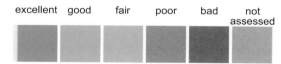

excellent   good   fair   poor   bad   not assessed

Changing capacity

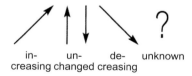

in-   un-   de-   unknown
creasing changed creasing

This step shows that in higher plants, for example, only 70,000 of the total 270,000 species are directly used:
- 3000 species of food plants
- 25,000 species of medicinal plants
- 10,000 species of wood-producing plants
- 5000 species of fibre-producing plants
- 10,000 species which improve sustainability, e.g. plants in the herb layer under an oak forest which help prevent production of sappy shoots by oak and so enable production of good quality veneer

- 15,000 species of ornamental plants
- 2000 species used scientifically

Of the 200,000 species which are not used, 25,000 are protected, and 30,000 are interesting for bioprospecting for future technological development. Thus about 145,000 species remain that are not directly of use to human beings, but fulfil very important ecological roles in the ecosystem, thus contributing to the stability or succession in ecosystems.

| Box 5.6.2 | **Summary: global change** |

- The Kyoto Protocol was the start of a new economic age, in which man actively determines the global element cycles through agriculture and forestry, but is not able to recognise the ecological issues appropriately.
- Global collective goods require special protection against economic pressures. Collective goods include the atmosphere, oceans and those parts of the genetic resources not belonging to nations (perhaps the ownership of genetic resources by nations is a step too far). To protect these global goods against the economic interests, organisational structures will be required. Exploitation of the element cycles of the earth is associated with high risks that occur because it is not currently possible to determine the point beyond which the resultant changes cannot be controlled technically.
- Predictions are uncertain as the socio-economic feedbacks have not yet been taken fully into account. The question whether

policies such as the Kyoto Protocol's reduction of CO_2 emissions are effective will depend on the globalisation of world trade in developing countries which have no obligations to reduce emissions and which may develop industries with large CO_2 production. In this case the Kyoto Protocol would be met by the industrial nations but CO_2 concentrations would still rise.
- The projections for the biochemical cycles to take in the future require a strong environmental consciousness in all layers of society. People can live and work at much higher or lower temperatures, but agricultural plants and ecosystems are not able to withstand such changes. Beyond this, the carbon cycle is involved in our daily lives via our energy requirements. Therefore, without a deeper understanding of the long-term environmental risks for all human societies, the management of the carbon cycle will not be effective.

2. Monitoring the suitability of a cost benefit analysis for the biosphere. Criteria of limited substitution and irreversibility of damage are in the foreground, restricting the application of economic calculations.
3. Determining the monetary value (monetarisation) according to various economic procedures.
4. Calculation of the present monetary value of use of resources; future use and damage need to be discounted at the present value. In this calculation, the determination of discounting factors presents enormous problems.

These considerations of protective categories and economic evaluation result in an **economic total value** (WBGU 2001). There have been very few attempts to work out the total economic value of the biosphere. Costanza et al. (1997) analysed a total of 17 ecosystem outputs (gas regulation, climate regulation, interference regulation, water regulation, water supply, degradation of pollutants, pollination, biological pest control, regulation of habitat, production of food, raw material production, genetic resources, recreation, cultural values) in a total of 12 types of

landscape, and found that the output of the biosphere exceeds economic output (measured as global gross national product) by a factor of 2. Valuation of coastal areas is large, based particularly on their effects on the food cycle.

The enormous speed at which global change is progressing justifies a risk analysis for the changes in material cycles and in climate (WBGU 2000). Analysing the probability of occurrence (P) and the extent of damage (D) (WBGU 2000), a range (P high, D low) of normal everyday risks with which mankind has to live, e.g. domestic refuse dumps, is obtained. There are further limiting areas requiring particular attention which should still be technically solvable, e.g. special refuse such as atomic waste, refuse dumps with P low, D very high, and those which should be avoided under all circumstances and without consideration of cost. In this category, for example, is the danger of reversal of the thermohaline circulation in the north Atlantic. On the path leading to this totally unacceptable range are various uncertain processes which cannot be fully evaluated (P high, D low), but which may reach a point where they can no longer be managed technically. These are the creeping climate changes, an increasing greenhouse effect and the loss of bio-diversity.

Evaluation and risk assessment do not give an analysis of the effects of particular functions that are important to humans caused by changes in global ecosystems. The World Resource Institute (2001) has suggested a simple form of evaluation and indicated the development of "outputs" from five important biomes in the last 20–30 years as shown in Fig. 5.6.4 with arrows. Of the 24 areas analysed, there is only one arrow showing a tendency to increase, and that is the demand and supply for wood which is essentially covered by plantations in the northern hemisphere. All other "ecosystem functions" have decreased in intensity.

References

Chapin FS III, Zavaleta ES, Eviner VT, Naylor RL, Vitousek PM, Reynolds HL, Hooper DU, Lavorel S, Sala OE, Hobbie SE, Mack MC, Diaz S (2000) Consequences of changing biodiversity. Nature 405:234–242

Costanza R, Darge R, de Groot R, Farber S, Grasso M, Hannon B, Limburg K, Naeem S, O'Neill RV, Paruelo J, Raskin RG, Sutton P, van den Belt M (1997) The value of the world's ecosystem services and natural capital. Nature 387:253–260

Liu J, Linerman M, Ouyang Z, An L, Yang J, Zhang H (2001) Ecological degradation in protected areas: The case of Wolong Nature Reserve for Giant Pandas. Science 292:98–100

WBGU (1993) World in transition: Basic structure of global human-environment interactions. German Advisory Council on Global Change (WBGU). Economica, Bonn, 224 pp

WBGU (1999) World in transition: Ways towards sustainable management of freshwater resources. German Advisory Council on Global Change (WBGU). Springer, Berlin Heidelberg New York, 392 pp

WBGU (2000) World in transition: Strategies for management of global environmental risks. German Advisory Council on Global Change (WBGU). Springer, Berlin Heidelberg New York, 359 pp

WBGU (2001) World in transition: Conservation and sustainable use of the biosphere. German Advisory Council on Global Change (WBGU). Earthscan, London, 451 pp

World Resource Institute (2001) World Resources 2000–2001. People and ecosystems; the fraying web of life. World Resource Institute, Washington, 389 pp

Subject Index